Advanced Accounting
Consolidations, Partnerships, and Government Accounting

11e

Paul Marcus Fischer, PhD, CPA
Jerry Leer Professor of Accounting
University of Wisconsin, Milwaukee

William James Taylor, PhD, CPA, CVA
Professor Emeritus of Accounting
University of Wisconsin, Milwaukee

Rita Hartung Cheng, PhD, CPA
Professor of Accounting
Southern Illinois University, Carbondale

SOUTH-WESTERN
CENGAGE Learning

Australia • Brazil • Japan • Korea • Mexico • Singapore • Spain • United Kingdom • United States

SOUTH-WESTERN
CENGAGE Learning™

Advanced Accounting: Consolidations, Partnerships, and Government Accounting, 11th International Edition

Paul M. Fischer, William J. Taylor, and Rita H. Cheng

Vice President of Editorial, Business: Jack W. Calhoun

Editor-in-Chief: Rob Dewey

Executive Editor: Sharon Oblinger

Developmental Editor: Lauren Athmer, LEAP Publishing Services, Inc.

Associate Content Project Manager: Jana Lewis

Marketing Manager: Natalie Livingston

Media Editor: Bryan England

Manufacturing Planner: Doug Wilke

Production Service: Cenveo Publisher Services

Compositor: Cenveo Publisher Services

Art Director: Stacy Jenkins Shirley

Internal Designer: Mike Stratton

Cover Designer: Patti Hudepohl

Cover Photo Credits:
  B/W Image: Getty Images/Rubberball
  Color Image: Shutterstock Images/Ken Schulze

ExamView® is a registered trademark of eInstruction Corp. Windows is a registered trademark of the Microsoft Corporation used herein under license.

Excel®, 2010™. Used with permission from Microsoft.

Library of Congress Control Number: 2011930047
International Edition: ISBN 13: 978-0-538-48029-1
International Edition: ISBN 10: 0-538-48029-7

Cengage Learning International Offices

Asia
www.cengageasia.com
tel: (65) 6410 1200

Australia/New Zealand
www.cengage.com.au
tel: (61) 3 9685 4111

Brazil
www.cengage.com.br
tel: (55) 11 3665 9900

India
www.cengage.co.in
tel: (91) 11 4364 1111

Latin America
www.cengage.com.mx
tel: (52) 55 1500 6000

UK/Europe/Middle East/Africa
www.cengage.co.uk
tel: (44) 0 1264 332 424

Represented in Canada by Nelson Education, Ltd.
www.nelson.com
tel: (416) 752 9100/(800) 668 0671

Cengage Learning is a leading provider of customized learning solutions with office locations around the globe, including Singapore, the United Kingdom, Australia, Mexico, Brazil, and Japan. Locate your local office at: **www.cengage.com/global**

For product information: **www.cengage.com/international**
Visit your local office: **www.cengage.com/global**
Visit our corporate website: **www.cengage.com**

Portions of various GASB and FASB documents, copyright by the Financial Accounting Foundation, 401 Merritt 7, PO Box 5116, Norwalk, CT 06856-5116, USA, are reproduced with permission. Complete copies of those documents are available from the GASB and FASB.

Material from the Uniform CPA Examination Questions and Unofficial Answers: Copyright American Institute of Certified Public Accountants, Inc. All rights reserved. Used with permission.

Except where otherwise noted, all content is property of Cengage Learning.

Printed in Canada
1 2 3 4 5 6 7 17 16 15 14 13 12 11

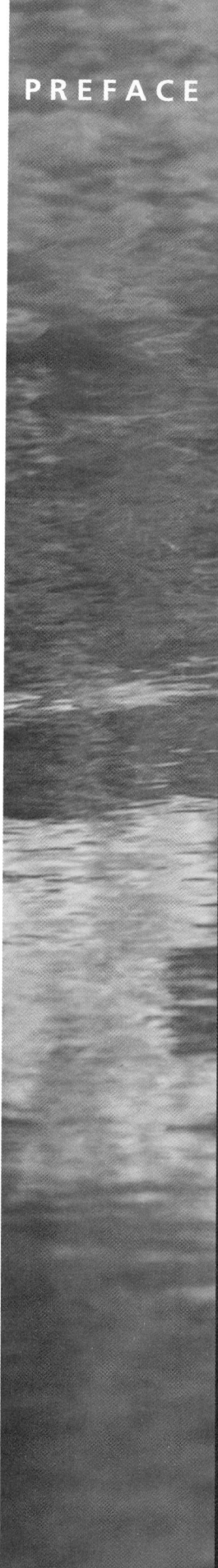

Advanced Leadership

INNOVATION

The eleventh edition of *Advanced Accounting: Consolidations, Partnerships, and Government Accounting* raises the standard in accounting education. Providing the most innovative, up-to-date, and comprehensive coverage of advanced financial accounting topics on the market today, this edition incorporates pedagogically strong elements throughout. The end result is a valuable and useful resource for both the present and the future. Fischer/Taylor/Cheng's *Advanced Accounting: Consolidations, Partnerships, and Government Accounting* offers the learner the ability to understand, and then to apply, new knowledge like no other advanced accounting text available. Leading the way are these unique, innovative, and helpful features:

- **Understanding and applying the new Financial Accounting Standards Board codification terms:**

  - Coverage of International Financial Reporting Standards (IFRS).
  - References throughout have been updated to reflect codification terms.
  - All subsidiary accounts are adjusted to full fair value whenever control is achieved. The noncontrolling interest is adjusted to fair value.
  - Instead of allocating the available amount to fixed assets in a bargain purchase, all accounts are recorded at full fair value and the bargain results in a gain.
  - Changes in the parent's ownership interest are treated as equity transactions with no impact on income.
  - Changes in the subsidiary's equity are treated as equity transactions with no impact on income.

- **Excelling with ease—easy-to-follow Excel® tutorials and convenient electronic working papers available on the text's Web site (www.cengagebrain.com):**

  - This unique tutorial teaches a step-by-step process for completing consolidations worksheets in an Excel-based environment. The tutorial makes it possible to master consolidations worksheets more quickly.
  - The tutorial guides the student through the creation of Excel worksheets. Each chapter of the tutorial adds the consolidations processes to parallel those presented in Chapters 1–6 of the text.

  - The electronic working papers in Excel format provide students with the basic worksheet structure for selected assignments throughout the text. These assignments are identified in the text by the icon shown here.

- **Comprehending through consistency—common coding for the worksheets:**

  - All consolidations worksheets use a common coding for the eliminations and adjustments. A complete listing of the codes is presented on the inside of the front cover. Students are now able to quickly recall worksheet adjustments as they move from one chapter to the next.
  - Within the chapter narrative, the worksheet eliminations and adjustments are shown in journal entry form and are referenced using the same coding. This provides consistent

reinforcement of the consolidations process and aids students in their understanding of the worksheet procedures. An example follows:

(CY1)	Eliminate current-year equity income:		
	Subsidiary Income	60,000	
	Investment in Company S.		60,000
(EL)	Eliminate 80% of subsidiary equity against investment in subsidiary account:		
	Common Stock ($10 par)—Company S	80,000	
	Retained Earnings, January 1, 2011—Company S	56,000	
	Investment in Company S.		136,000
(IS)	Eliminate intercompany merchandise sales:		
	Sales	100,000	
	Cost of Goods Sold		100,000

- ◆ The same codes are continued in the Excel tutorial and the worksheet solutions.

- ◆ **Taming a tough topic—coverage of derivatives and related accounting issues in a module:**

  - ◆ A comprehensive module deals with derivative instruments and related accounting issues. This module, located just before Chapter 10, sets forth the basic characteristics of derivative financial instruments and explains the features of common types of derivatives. Accounting for derivatives held as an investment and as a part of a hedging strategy is discussed. Although covering the derivatives module prior to Chapter 10 is recommended, Chapter 10 can be taught without coverage of the derivatives module.
  - ◆ Fair value and cash flow hedges are clearly defined, and the special accounting given such hedges is set forth in a clear and concise manner. Options, futures, and interest rate swaps are used to demonstrate accounting for fair value hedges and cash flow hedges.
  - ◆ New explanations, examples, and end-of-chapter problems have been added to help simplify this complex topic.
  - ◆ The more complex issues that are associated with the use of forward contracts are introduced in the module and then fully addressed in Chapter 10. Thus, Chapter 10's discussion of hedging foreign currency transactions is more streamlined and less cumbersome.
  - ◆ Most of the chapter's discussion of hedging foreign currency transactions involves the use of forward contracts. The focus is on the use of such contracts to hedge foreign currency transactions, commitments, and forecasted transactions.

- ◆ **Accounting for change—coverage of new government reporting model and estate tax planning:**

  - ◆ Comprehensive coverage of governmental standards through GASB Statement No. 59, including the historic changes to the reporting model.
  - ◆ Government and not-for-profit chapters include material for CPA Exam preparation.
  - ◆ Chapters are designed for use in advanced accounting courses or in standalone governmental and not-for-profit courses.

- ◆ **Measuring student mastery—Learning Objectives:**

  - ◆ Each chapter begins with a list of measurable learning objectives, which are repeated in the margin near the related coverage.
  - ◆ The exercises and problems at the end of the chapter indicate the specific learning objectives that they reinforce. This helpful indicator, along with the assignment titles, provides a quick reference for both student and instructor.

- ◆ **Staying up to date—IASB Perspectives**

  - ◆ Within relevant chapters, a new box feature provides information and commentary regarding how standards differ between U.S. GAAP and IFRS.
  - ◆ This feature provides students with a clear understanding as to how IASB proposals may differ and what questions to consider moving forward with their studies.

1

OBJECTIVE

Explain why transactions between members of a consolidated firm should not be reflected in the consolidated financial statements

IASB PERSPECTIVES

IASB *standards*

- IFRS considers potential voting rights if they are currently exercisable, in measuring control, while GAAP does not.

- IFRS also allows consolidation when there is "de facto" control. This is a situation in which there is only one large stockholder that owns less than 50% of the shares, but other share holdings are disbursed and the owners do not generally exercise their voting rights. This is similar to the SEC position indicated above.

◆ **Communicating the core content—Reflection:**

◆ Concluding every main section is a reflection on the core information contained in that section.
◆ These reflections provide students with a clear picture of the key points they should grasp and give them a helpful tool for quick review.

REFLECTION

- The combining of the statements of a parent and its subsidiaries into consolidated statements is required when parent ownership exceeds 50% of the controlled firm's shares.

- Consolidation is required for any company that is controlled, even in cases where less than 51% of the company's shares is owned by the parent.

◆ **Thinking it through—Understanding the Issues:**

◆ These questions at the end of the chapter emphasize and reinforce the core issues of the chapter.

UNDERSTANDING THE ISSUES

1. A parent company paid $500,000 for a 100% interest in a subsidiary. At the end of the first year, the subsidiary reported net income of $40,000 and paid $5,000 in dividends. The price paid reflected understated equipment of $70,000, which will be amortized over 10 years. What would be the subsidiary income reported on the parent's unconsolidated income statement, and what would the parent's investment balance be at the end of the first year under each of these methods?

   a. The simple equity method
   b. The sophisticated equity method
   c. The cost method

2. What is meant by date alignment? Does it exist on the consolidated worksheet under the following methods, and if not, how is it created prior to elimination of the investment account under each of these methods?

   a. The simple equity method
   b. The sophisticated equity method
   c. The cost method

◆ They encourage students to think in greater depth about the topics and expand their reasoning skills. Discussion skills are also developed through use of the questions as springboards for class interaction.

THEORY BLENDED WITH APPLICATION

With a strong tradition of combining sound theoretical foundations with a hands-on, learn-by-example approach, the eleventh edition continues its prominent leadership position in advanced accounting classrooms across the country. The authors build upon *Advanced Accounting: Consolidations, Partnerships, and Government Accounting's* clear writing style, comprehensive coverage, and focus on conceptual understanding.

Realizing that students reap the greatest benefits when they can visualize the application of theories, *Advanced Accounting: Consolidations, Partnerships, and Government Accounting* closely links theory and practice by providing examples through relevant exhibits and tables that are common to real-world accounting. When students can visualize the concept being discussed and apply it directly to an example, their understanding greatly improves. This focus on conceptual understanding makes even the most complex topics approachable.

Assignments are clearly defined. End-of-chapter questions are used to reinforce theory, and exercises are short, focused applications of specific topics in the chapter. These exercises are very helpful when students use them as preparation for possible class presentations. The book's problems, which are designed to be more comprehensive than the exercises, often combine topics and are designed to work well as after-class assignments. For group projects, the cases found at the end of the text provide an innovative way to blend theoretical and numerical analysis.

ENHANCED COVERAGE

Advanced Accounting: Consolidations, Partnerships, and Government Accounting reflects changes in accounting procedures and standards while improving on those features that aid in student comprehension.

◆ **Chapter 1**
  ◆ Updated statistics on merger activity.
  ◆ Detailed discussion of the six U.S. Federal Trade Commission merger types (backward vertical integration, forward vertical integration, horizontal merger, product extension merger, market extension merger, conglomerate merger).
  ◆ Revised discussion of fair value of a contingent asset or liability.
  ◆ New Learning Objective 8: Understanding that some non-publicly traded companies may use special rules that differ from the methods in this chapter.
  ◆ Added coverage of the great recession and its consequences.

◆ **Chapter 2**
  ◆ IFRS position on the valuation of goodwill.
  ◆ New coverage of alternative valuations of the noncontrolling interest.

◆ **Chapter 3**
  ◆ New information on disclosure for an intraperiod purchase.

◆ **Chapter 4**
  ◆ Updated end-of-chapter material.

◆ **Chapter 5**
  ◆ Updated end-of-chapter material.

◆ **Chapter 6**
  ◆ Improved coverage of amortizations of excess cost as they impact cash flow statement.
  ◆ Section on nonconsolidated investments has been moved to an appendix.
  ◆ Updated consolidated statement of cash flows example.

◆ Revised coverage of consolidated earnings per share.

◆ Revised coverage of taxation of consolidated companies including foreign subsidiaries.

◆ **Chapter 7**
  ◆ Updated coverage on sale of parent interest in a subsidiary.

◆ **Chapter 8**
  ◆ Revised discussion of subsidiary stock dividends.
  ◆ New section called "Parent Company Shares Purchased by Subsidiary.
  ◆ Section on stick swap has been removed.
  ◆ The reciprocal method of consolidating ownership of parent shares by the subsidiary has been eliminated.

◆ **Special Appendix: Accounting for Influential Investments**
  ◆ Revised content to reflect current FASB Codification updates.
  ◆ Updated section called "Fair Value Option."
  ◆ Updated end-of-appendix material.

◆ **Chapter 9**
  ◆ Updated discussion of the scale of international activity and how it relates to foreign currency transactions, foreign currency translation, and international standard setting.
  ◆ Added coverage of the current positions of the Financial Accounting Standards Board (FASB), the International Accounting Standards Board (IASB), and the Securities and Exchange Commission (SEC) regarding convergence to IFRS.

◆ **Chapter 10**
  ◆ Simplified entries necessary to account for derivatives.
  ◆ Revised end-of-chapter materials place a greater focus on the impact of hedging on both financial position and operating results.
  ◆ Updated coverage of highlights of the IASB's proposed standard on hedging are set forth in the "IASB Perspectives" feature.

◆ **Chapter 11**
  ◆ New illustration of the consolidation of a U.S. parent and a foreign subsidiary.
  ◆ Incorporated new standards as they relate to consolidations.

◆ **Chapter 12**
  ◆ End-of-chapter materials have been updated and revised.
  ◆ All footnotes have been changed to reference relevant sections of the Accounting Standards Codification (ASC).

◆ **Chapter 13**
  ◆ End-of-chapter materials have been updated and revised.
  ◆ All footnotes have been changed to reference relevant sections of the Accounting Standards Codification.

◆ **Chapter 14**
  ◆ End-of-chapter materials have been updated and revised.
  ◆ All footnotes have been changed to reference relevant sections of the Accounting Standards Codification.

◆ **Chapter 15**
  ◆ Updated section on "Accounting for the General Fund—An Expanded Example" with new material on the five classifications of fund balances (nonspendable, restricted, committed, assigned, and unassigned).
  ◆ New section called "Investments in Derivatives."
  ◆ Updates throughout the chapter reflect FASB Codification revisions.
  ◆ Updated end-of-chapter material.

- **Chapter 16**
  - Updated entries for examples.
  - Updated end-of-chapter material.

- **Chapter 17**
  - Updated entries for examples.
  - Updated end-of-chapter material.

- **Chapter 18**
  - Updated entries for examples.
  - Updated end-of-chapter material.

- **Chapter 19**
  - Updated entries for examples.
  - Updated end-of-chapter material.

- **Chapter 20**
  - Revised exclusions and rates are employed and an explanation for this logic is set forth at the beginning of the chapter.
  - Updated pedagogical aspects of accounting for estates and trusts are firmly set forth.
  - Updated Web site material is conveyed regarding Congressional actions concerning estate taxation (www.cengagebrain.com).

- **Chapter 21**
  - End-of-chapter materials have been updated and revised.
  - All footnotes have been changed to reference relevant sections of the Accounting Standards Codification.

- **Appendix**
  - Applies the equity method to nonconsolidated (influential) investments.
  - Updated coverage includes the fair value option.

FLEXIBILITY

The book's flexible coverage of topics allows for professors to teach the course at their own pace and in their preferred order. There are no dependencies between major sections of the text except that coverage of consolidations should precede multinational accounting if one is to understand accounting for foreign subsidiaries. It is also advisable that students master the module on derivatives before advancing to the chapter on foreign currency transactions. The book contains enough coverage to fill two advanced courses, but when only one semester is available, many professors find it ideal to cover the first four to six chapters in business combinations.

The text is divided into the following major topics:

Business Combinations—Basic Topics (Chapters 1–6)

Chapter 1 demonstrates the FASB rules for assigning the cost of an acquired company to its assets and liabilities. Goodwill impairment replaces amortization and is fully explained.

Chapters 2 through 5 cover the basics of preparing a consolidated income statement and balance sheet. In 1977, we introduced two schedules that have been much appreciated by students and faculty alike—the determination and distribution of excess schedule and income distribution schedule. The determination and distribution schedule (quickly termed the D&D schedule by students) analyzes the difference between the fair value of the acquired company and the underlying equity of the subsidiary. The D&D schedule has been reconfigured to revalue the entire company, including the noncontrolling interest. It provides a check figure for all subsequent years' worksheets, details all information for the distribution of differences between book and fair values, and reveals all data for the amortization of the differences. The schedule provides rules for all types of acquisition situations. The income distribution schedule (known as the IDS) is a set of T accounts that distributes income between the noncontrolling and controlling interests. It also provides a useful check function to ensure that all intercompany eliminations are properly accounted for. These chapters give the student all topics needed for the CPA Exam. (For easy reference, the text contains a callout in the margin, as shown here, that ties the narrative to the worksheets. In addition, the related narrative pages are indicated in the upper right side of each worksheet. This allows the reader to quickly locate important explanations.)

Worksheet 3-1: page 146

With regard to the alternative worksheet methods and why we follow the approaches we do, consider the method used to record the investment in the subsidiary's and the parent's books. There are two key points of general agreement. The first is that it doesn't really matter which method is used, since the investment account is eliminated. Second, when the course is over, a student should know how to handle each method: simple equity, full (we call it sophisticated) equity, and cost. The real issue is which method is the easiest one to learn first. We believe the winner is simple equity, since it is totally symmetric with the equity accounts of the subsidiary. It simplifies elimination of subsidiary equity against the investment account. Every change in subsidiary equity is reflected, on a pro rata basis, in the parent's investment account. Thus, the simple equity method becomes the mainline method of the text. We teach the student to convert investments maintained under the cost method to the simple equity method. In practice, most firms and the majority of the problems in the text use the cost method. This means that the simple equity method is employed to solve problems that begin as either simple equity or cost method problems.

We also cover the sophisticated equity method, which amortizes the excess of cost or book value through the investment account. This method should also adjust for intercompany profits through the investment account. The method is cumbersome because it requires the student to deal with amortizations of excess and intercompany profits in the investment account before getting to the consolidated worksheet, which is designed to handle these topics. This means teaching consolidating procedures without the benefit of a worksheet. We cover the method after the student is proficient with a worksheet and the other methods. Thorough understanding of the sophisticated method is important so that it can be applied to influential investments that are not consolidated. (This is covered in the Appendix.)

Another major concern among advanced accounting professors has to do with the worksheet style used. There are three choices: the horizontal (trial balance) format, the vertical (stacked) method, and the balance sheet only. Again, we do cover all three, but the horizontal format is our main method. Horizontal is by far the most appealing to students. They have used it in both introductory and intermediate accounting. It is also the most likely method to be found in practice. On this basis, we use it initially to develop all topics. We cover the vertical format but not until the student is proficient with the horizontal format. There is no difference in the elimination procedures; only the worksheet logistics differ. It takes only one problem assignment to teach the students this approach so they are prepared for its possible appearance on the CPA Exam. The balance-sheet-only format has no reason to exist other than its use as a CPA Exam testing shortcut. We cover it in the Appendix.

Chapter 6 may be more essential for those entering practice than it is for the CPA Exam. It contains cash flow for consolidated firms, consolidated earnings per share, and taxation issues. Support schedules guide the worksheet procedures for consolidated companies, which are taxed as separate entities. Taxation is the most difficult application of consolidation procedures. Every intercompany transaction is a tax allocation issue. Teaching the tax allocation issues with every topic as it is introduced is very confusing to students. We prefer to have the students fully understand worksheet procedures without taxes and then introduce taxes.

Business Combinations—Specialized Topics (Chapters 7 and 8)

These chapters deal with topics that occasionally surface in practice and have seldom appeared on the CPA Exam. Studying these chapters perfects the students' understanding of consolidations and stockholders' equity accounting, thus affording a valuable experience. Chapter 7 deals with piecemeal acquisitions of an investment in a subsidiary, sale of the parent's investment, and the impact of preferred stock in the subsidiary's equity structure. Chapter 8 deals with the impact of subsidiary equity transactions including stock dividends, sale of common stock shares, and subsidiary reacquisitions of shares. The chapter also considers indirect or three-tier ownership structures and reciprocal holdings where the subsidiary owns parent shares.

Accounting for equity method investments is located in the Appendix that follows Chapter 8. The methods used for consolidations are adapted to influential investments. The IDS schedule used to distribute consolidated net income is used to calculate investment income.

Multinational Accounting and Other Reporting Concerns (Chapters 9–11 and Module)

As business has developed beyond national boundaries, the discipline of accounting also has evolved internationally. As our global economy develops, so, too, does the demand for reliable and comparable financial information. Chapter 9 discusses the international accounting environment and current efforts to converge U.S. generally accepted accounting principles with international standards.

The use of derivative financial instruments and the related accounting is a very complex subject that is discussed in a separate module. The principles set forth in FASB Codification are set forth in a clear manner. The module may be used to support a standalone topic dealing with derivatives or as a preface to the multinational chapter dealing with foreign currency transactions. Regardless of how one chooses to use the module, students will benefit from an understanding of this important topic. The nature of derivatives is discussed along with a more in-depth look at the common types of derivative instruments. The basic accounting for derivatives held as an investment is illustrated. Options, futures, and interest rate swaps are used for illustrative purposes. The accounting for derivatives that are designated as a hedge is illustrated for both fair value and cash flow hedges. More specifically, the use of a derivative to hedge a recognized transaction (asset or liability), an unrecognized firm commitment, or a forecasted transaction is discussed and illustrated. Throughout the module, illustrative entries and graphics are used to improve the students' understanding of this topic.

Chapter 10 discusses the accounting for transactions that are denominated or settled in a foreign currency. Following this discussion, the hedging of such transactions with the use of forward contracts is introduced. Hedging foreign currency recognized transactions, unrecognized firm commitments, and forecasted transactions is discussed in order to illustrate the business purpose and special accounting associated with such hedging strategies in an international setting. The chapter is not overly complicated, given the fact that the concept of hedging and the special accounting given hedges have already been discussed in a separate module on derivatives and related accounting issues.

Chapter 11 demonstrates the remeasurement and/or translation of a foreign entity's financial statements into a U.S. investor's currency. Wherever possible, examples of footnote disclosure relating to international accounting issues are presented.

The usefulness of financial information naturally increases if it is communicated on a timely basis. Therefore, interim financial statements and reporting requirements are now widely accepted. In Chapter 12, the concept of an interim period as an integral part of a larger annual accounting period is set forth as a basis for explaining the specialized accounting principles of interim reporting. Particular attention is paid to the determination of the interim income tax provision including the tax implications of net operating losses. Chapter 12 also examines segmental reporting and the various disclosure requirements. A worksheet format for developing segmental data is used, and students are able to review the segmental footnote disclosure for a large public company.

Accounting for Partnerships (Chapters 13 and 14)

Chapters 13 and 14 take students through the entire life cycle of a partnership, beginning with formation and ending in liquidation. Although new forms of organization such as the limited liability corporation are available, partnerships continue to be a common form of organization. Practicing accountants must be aware of the characteristics of this form of organization and the unique accounting principles. The accounting aspects of profit and loss agreements, changes in the composition of partners (admissions and withdrawals), and partnership liquidations are fully illustrated. The end-of-chapter material in this area focuses on evaluating various alternative strategies available to partners, for example, deciding whether it would be better to liquidate a partnership or admit a new partner.

Governmental and Not-for-Profit Accounting (Chapters 15–19)

Chapters 15–19 provide comprehensive coverage of accounting and financial reporting of state and local governments, colleges and universities, health care entities, and not-for-profit organizations. Since the tenth edition of this text was released, standards-setting bodies have issued several accounting, auditing, and financial reporting standards that impact topics covered in these chapters. This edition discusses recent developments in state and local government accounting and financial reporting.

Chapter 15 covers the unique accounting and financial reporting issues of state and local governments. It describes the basics of accounting and financial reporting of the general fund and account groups. The chapter incorporates GASB guidance on accounting for revenues and expenditures using a financial resources measurement focus and a modified accrual basis of accounting. The unique ways of accounting for capital assets and long-term debt are detailed.

Chapter 16 details accounting for the specialized funds of government, e.g., those established to account for restricted operating resources, long-term construction projects or acquisition of major fixed assets, and servicing of principal and interest on long-term debt. The chapter also covers the unique accounting for various trust funds, including permanent funds and proprietary (business-type) funds. Illustrated examples include accounting for pensions, postretirement benefits other than pensions, recognition of assets and liabilities and related disclosures arising from securities lending transactions, accounting for certain investments at fair value, and accounting for landfill operations.

Chapter 17 presents the required governmental basic financial statements. The unique features of the *funds-based statements,* which maintain the traditional measurement focus and basis of accounting for both governmental and proprietary funds, and the *government-wide statements,* which use the flow of economic resources measurement focus and full accrual basis of accounting for both the government and proprietary activities, are detailed. The chapter includes a discussion of the requirement for governments to report all capital assets, including retroactive reporting of infrastructure assets. Detailed illustrations help to clarify the requirements to report depreciation or use the modified approach. The chapter contains a sample government-wide statement of net assets that reports governmental and proprietary activities in separate columns and a program- or function-oriented statement of activities. The requirements for the *management's discussion and analysis* (MD&A) are highlighted. End-of-chapter problems are designed to link theory to practice through the use of electronic working papers and supporting schedules. Additional coverage surrounds key issues in governmental audit, including the single audit requirements, from AICPA, OMB, and GAO authoritative sources.

Chapter 18 begins with an overall summary of the accounting and financial reporting standards as they apply to all not-for-profit organizations. Coverage of ASC 958 is included. Expanded illustrations enable the student to better grasp the unique requirements for revenue and expense recognition of not-for-profit organizations. External financial statements are illustrated without a funds structure. Since the FASB standards have shifted financial reporting away from fund accounting, funds are viewed as internal control and management tools throughout this chapter. The appendix to the chapter includes a discussion of the fund structure traditionally used in not-for-profit organizations and illustrates financial statements incorporating the funds.

Chapter 19 offers a complete description of accounting for private and governmental universities and private and governmental health care organizations. The concepts from Chapters 15–18 are applied to college and university accounting. A comparison of the governmental and nongovernmental reporting requirements and/or practices is highlighted to enable the student to gain a better understanding of differences between them. Updated illustrations and end-of-chapter materials are also designed to compare and contrast the government and private-sector requirements.

Fiduciary Accounting (Chapters 20 and 21)

The role of estate planning and the use of trusts are important to many individuals and present some unique accounting principles. The tax implications of estate planning are discussed so that the student has a basic understanding of this area. Various accounting reports necessary for the administration of an estate or trust are illustrated in Chapter 20. Current estate tax rates and unified credit amounts are set forth in the chapter.

No business is immune from financial difficulty. Chapter 21 discusses various responses to such difficulties, including troubled debt restructuring, quasi-reorganizations, corporate liquidations, and corporate reorganizations.

UNPARALLELED SUPPORT

Supplementary Materials for the Instructor (cengage.com/international)

Solutions Manual. This manual provides answers to all end-of-chapter "Understanding the Issues" questions and solutions to all exercises, problems, and cases. The electronic files for this ancillary can be found on the companion Web site, www.cengage.com/international.

Test Bank. Consisting of a variety of multiple-choice questions and short problems and the related solutions, this test bank had been newly updated and revised by Maria Mitchell of Thomas More College. The content includes testing questions for the text chapters and the derivatives module. The test bank is available electronically in Word and *ExamView*® on the companion Web site, www.cengage.com/international.

PowerPoint® *Slides.* Instructor PowerPoint presentations, revised by Anne M. Oppegard of Augustana College, are available on the companion Web site, www.cengage.com/international.

Valuable Supplementary Materials for the Student

Excel® *Tutorial and Working Papers.* Provided on the text's Web site (www.cengagebrain .com), this step-by-step tutorial carefully guides students as they learn how to set up worksheets in Excel and apply their consolidations knowledge learned in Chapters 1–6 of the text. In addition, Excel working papers for selected text problems are provided to assist students in completing homework. These selected end-of-chapter assignments are identified in the text by the icon shown here.

Dedicated Product Web Site (www.cengagebrain.com). The Student Resources section of the text Web site contains:

- ◆ **Excel**® **Tutorial and Electronic Working Papers.**
- ◆ **Learning Objectives.** These are repeated from the text to serve as a study aid.
- ◆ **Chapter Quizzes.**
- ◆ **Glossary.**
- ◆ **Flashcards.**
- ◆ **Crossword Puzzles.**

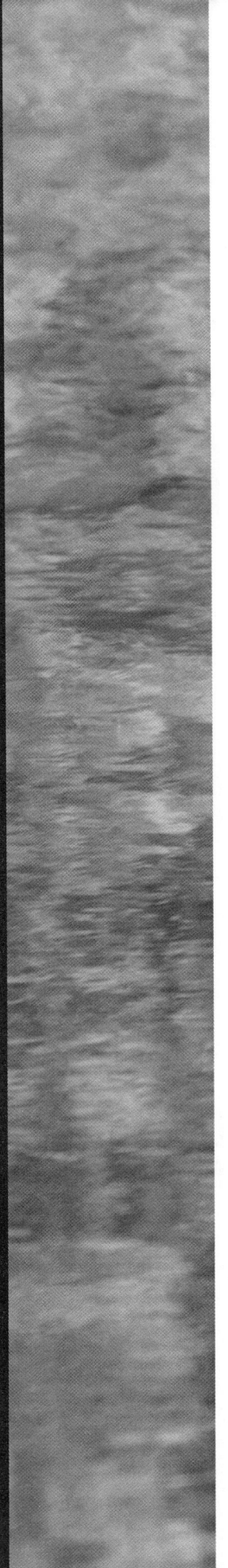

Acknowledgments

In preparation for the new edition, the following individuals shared detailed ideas and suggestions for changes and improvements, of which many have been implemented in this eleventh edition text and supplements. We thank them all for their timely information.

Marie Archambault, Marshall University
Philip Kintzele, Central Michigan University
Terry Unruh, Oral Roberts University
Douglas Asbury, University of Findlay

We thank the following ancillary writers and verifiers for their conscientious effort to make sure the support materials are accurate and tie closely to the text's up-to-date content.

Writers:
Test Bank: Maria Mitchell (Thomas More College)

PowerPoint: Anne M. Oppegard (Augustana College)

Web Quizzes: Sheila Ammons (Austin Community College)

Verifiers:
Text and Solutions Manual: Sara Wilson and Jim Emig (Villanova)

Test Bank: Gary Bower

PowerPoint: Jim Emig (Villanova)

Their patience in the revision process is greatly appreciated.

We are particularly grateful to Daniel Neely (University of Wisconsin-Milwaukee) for his significant contributions to this revision. Finally, a special thank you goes to Carol Fischer (University of Wisconsin—Waukesha) for her many hours of extensive, creative work on developing the Excel tutorial and working papers materials. These products provide easy-to-follow assistance to students as they learn the worksheet process.

Paul Fischer
William Taylor
Rita Cheng

About the Authors

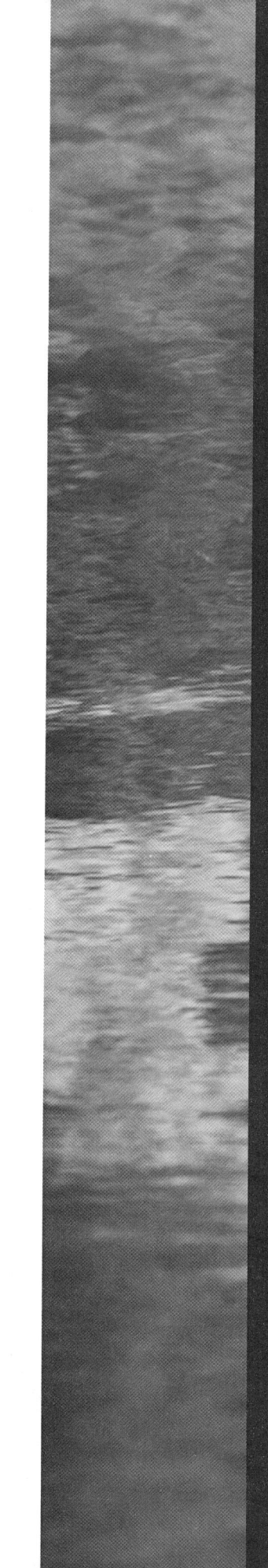

Paul M. Fischer is the Jerry Leer Professor of Accounting and Accounting Area Chair at the University of Wisconsin, Milwaukee. He teaches intermediate and advanced financial accounting and has received both the AMOCO Outstanding Professor Award and the School of Business Administration Advisory Council Teaching Award. He also teaches continuing education classes and provides executive training courses for several large corporations. He earned his undergraduate accounting degree at Milwaukee and earned an MBA and Ph.D. at the University of Wisconsin, Madison. Dr. Fischer is a CPA and is a member of the American Institute of CPAs, the Wisconsin Institute of CPAs, and the American Accounting Association. He is a past president of the Midwest Region of the American Accounting Association. Dr. Fischer has previously authored *Cost Accounting: Theory and Applications* (with Frank), *Financial Dimensions of Marketing Management* (with Crissy and Mossman), journal articles, and computer software. He actively pursues research and consulting interests in the areas of leasing, pension accounting, and business combinations.

William J. Taylor has primarily taught financial accounting and auditing at both the undergraduate and graduate levels. In addition, he was involved in providing executive training courses for several large corporations and through an executive MBA program. He has been recognized for his teaching excellence and has received both the AMOCO Outstanding Professor Award and the School of Business Administration Advisory Council Teaching Award. He earned his Ph.D. from Georgia State University and is a CPA and a CVA (Certified Valuation Analyst). His professional experience includes working for Deloitte and Touche and Arthur Andersen & Co. in their audit practices. His private consulting activities include business valuations, litigation services, and issues affecting closely held businesses. Dr. Taylor is a member of the American Institute of CPAs and the National Association of Certified Valuation Analysts. He serves as a director and officer for a number of organizations.

Rita H. Cheng currently serves as Chancellor of Southern Illinois University and holds the academic rank of Professor of Accounting at Southern Illinois. Dr. Cheng has primarily taught government, not-for-profit accounting and advanced financial accounting. She has published numerous journal articles and technical reports and is often asked to speak on government and not-for-profit accounting topics. She has been recognized for her teaching excellence and is a recipient of the University of Wisconsin-Milwaukee School of Business Administration Advisory Council Outstanding Teaching Award and the Sheldon B. Lubar School of Business Executive MBA Teacher of the Year Award. She earned her Ph.D. from Temple University, an MBA from University of Rhode Island, and an undergraduate degree in accounting from Bishop's University. Dr Cheng is a CPA and a Certified Government Financial Manager. Her research focuses on the quality of accounting and financial reporting by state and local governments and the influence of accounting regulation on corporate business competitiveness. She is a member of the Government and Nonprofit Section of the American Accounting Association and has served as the GNP Section's president. Dr. Cheng has coordinated the academic response to several GASB proposed standards and also testified before the Governmental Accounting Standards Board.

Brief Contents

Contents

Combined Corporate Entities and Consolidations

The acquisition of one company by another is a commonplace business activity. Frequently, a company is groomed for sale. Also, the recent proliferation of new technology businesses and financial services firms that merge into larger companies is an expected, and often planned for, occurrence. For three decades, prior to 2001, accounting standards for business combinations had remained stable. Two models of recording combinations had coexisted. The pooling-of-interests method brought over the assets and liabilities of the acquired company at existing book values. The purchase method brought the acquired company's assets and liabilities to the acquiring firm's books at fair market value. FASB Statement No. 141, issued in July 2001, ended the use of the pooling method and gave new guidance for recording business combinations under purchase accounting principles.

Two new FASB Statements issued in 2007 brought major changes to accounting for business combinations. FASB Statement 14lr required that all accounts of an acquired company be recorded at fair value, no matter the percentage of interest acquired or the price paid. FASB Statement 160 required new rules for accounting for the interest not acquired by the acquiring firm. This interest is known as the noncontrolling interest. It is now recorded at fair value on the acquisition date and is considered a part of the stockholder's equity of the consolidated firm.

The contents of FASB Statements 14lr and 160 are now incorporated into FASB ASC 805 and 810, respectively. ASC stands for Accounting Standards Codification. These statements are unique in that they were produced in a joint effort with the International Accounting Standards Board (IASB). Some minor differences still exist between U.S. GAAP and international rules. They are described in Chapter 2. Throughout this book, a new feature called "IASB Perspectives" will address the ever-changing relationship between U.S. GAAP and International Financial Reporting Standards (IFRS). This feature is not found in all chapters, but has been included where applicable.

There are two types of accounting transactions to accomplish a combination. The first is to acquire the assets and liabilities of a company directly from the company itself by paying cash or by issuing bonds or stock. This is called a *direct asset acquisition* and is studied in Chapter 1. The assets and liabilities of the new company are directly recorded on the parent company's books. All of the theory involving acquisitions is first explained in this context.

The more common way to achieve control is to acquire a controlling interest, usually over 50%, in the voting common stock of another company. The acquiring company simply records an investment account for its interest in the new company. Both companies maintain their own accounting records. However, when two companies are under common control, a single set of *consolidated statements* must be prepared to meet external reporting requirements. The investment account is eliminated and the individual assets and liabilities of the acquired company are merged with those of the parent company. Chapters 2 through 8 provide the methods for consolidating the separate statements of the affiliated firms into a consolidated set of financial statements. The consolidation process becomes a continuous activity, which is further complicated by continuing transactions between the affiliated companies.

Business Combinations: New Rules for a Long-Standing Business Practice

CHAPTER 1

Learning Objectives

When you have completed this chapter, you should be able to

1. Describe the major economic advantages of business combinations.

2. Differentiate between accounting for an acquisition of assets and accounting for an acquisition of a controlling interest in the common stock of a company.

3. Explain the basics of the acquisition model.

4. Allocate the acquisition price to the assets and liabilities of the acquired company.

5. Demonstrate an understanding of the tax issues that arise in an acquisition.

6. Explain the disclosure that is required in the period in which an acquisition occurs.

7. Apply the impairment test to goodwill and adjust goodwill when needed.

8. Explain special and different rules that apply to acquisitions by companies that are not publicly traded

9. Estimate the value of goodwill. (Appendix)

Business combinations have been a common business transaction since the start of commercial activity. The concept is simple: A business combination is the acquisition of all of a company's assets at a single price. *Business combinations* is a comprehensive term covering all acquisitions of one firm by another. Such combinations can be further categorized as either mergers or consolidations. The term *merger* applies when an existing company acquires another company and combines that company's operations with its own. The term *consolidation* applies when two or more previously separate firms join and become one new, continuing company. Business combinations make headlines not only in the business press but also in the local newspapers of the communities where the participating companies are located. While investors may delight in the price received for their interest, employees become concerned about continued employment, and local citizens worry about a possible relocation of the business.

The popularity of business combinations grew steadily during the 1990s and peaked in 1998. From then until 2003, activity slowed considerably, with the dollar amount of deals falling even more than the number of deals. From 2003 to 2007, there was a steady rise in deals and the dollar amount of acquisitions. By 2009, the number of deals and their value fell to roughly half of their 2007 levels. Exhibit 1-1 includes the Merger Completion Record covering 1999 through 2009. The data include all acquisitions in which a U.S. company was involved as either a buyer or seller. The drastic change in business combinations can be attributed to several possible causes, such as the following:

♦ The growth period prior to 2002 reflects, in part, the boom economy of that period, especially in high-tech industries. There was also a motivation to complete acquisitions prior to July 1, 2001, when FASB Statement No. 141, *Business Combinations,* became effective. FASB Statement No. 141 eliminated the pooling-of-interests method. Pooling allowed companies to record the acquired assets at existing book value. This meant less depreciation

Exhibit 1-1
10-Year Merger Completion Record: 1999–2009

	10-Year Merger Completion Record: 1999 to 2009			
Year	No. of Deals	% Change	Value ($bil)	% Change
1999	9,248	—	1,423.1	—
2000	8,974	–3.0	1,786.3	25.5
2001	6,423	28.4	1,155.4	–35.3
2002	5,685	–11.5	626.7	–45.8
2003	6,269	10.3	526.9	15.9
2004	7,350	17.2	866.4	64.4
2005	8,249	12.2	1,012.2	16.8
2006	9,141	10.8	1,431.3	41.4
2007	9,575	4.7	1,808.1	26.3
2008	7,917	–17.3	999.2	–44.7
2009	5,514	–30.4	703.1	–29.6

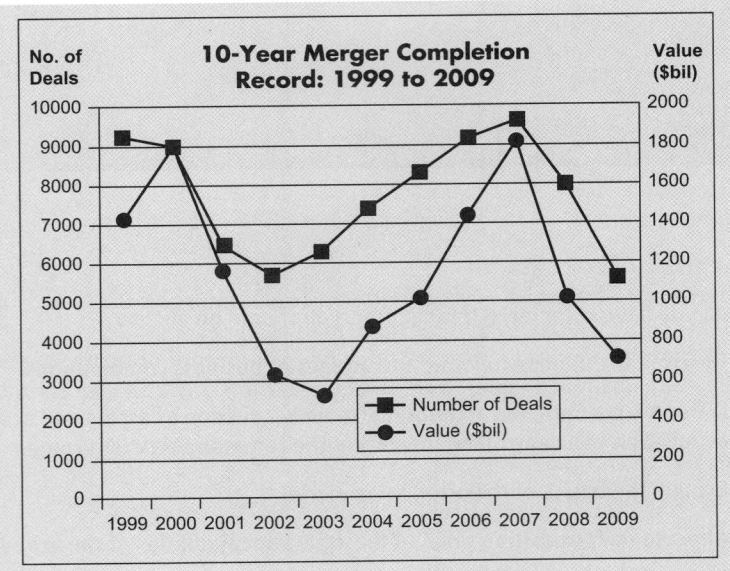

Source: Mergers and Acquisitions Almanac, February 2010, p. 31.

and amortization charges in later periods. When the alternative purchase method was used prior to 2001, any goodwill that was recorded could be amortized over 40 years. After 2001, FASB Statement No. 141 required goodwill impairment testing, which meant there was a risk of a major goodwill impairment loss in a future period.

◆ The decline in acquisition activity could also be attributed to the soft economy during the post-2001 period. The high-tech sector of the economy, which had been a hotbed of combinations, was especially weak. Add to it the increased scrutiny of companies being acquired, as caused by the accounting and business scandals of the period, and the motivation to acquire was lessened.

◆ Aside from broad-based accounting infractions, specific allegations of precombination beautification arose. It became clear that adjustments were made to the books of the company being acquired to make it look more valuable as a takeover candidate. This included arranging in advance to meet the pooling-of-interests criteria and making substantial write-offs to enhance post-acquisition income. In the fall of 1999, it was alleged that Tyco International arranged to have targeted companies take major write-downs before being acquired by Tyco. This concern caused a major decline in the value of Tyco shares and led to stockholder suits against the company.

◆ The steady increase in acquisition activity after 2002 could be attributed to a growing economy and stabilization in the accounting method used.

◆ The steep decline in activity since 2007 is likely a result of the deep recession during that time period. With improvements in the economy during 2010, business acquisitions have accelerated.

1

OBJECTIVE

Describe the major economic advantages of business combinations.

ECONOMIC ADVANTAGES OF COMBINATIONS

Business combinations are typically viewed as a way to jump-start economies of scale. Savings may result from the elimination of duplicative assets. Perhaps both companies will utilize common facilities and share fixed costs. There may be further economies as one management team replaces two separate sets of managers. It may be possible to better coordinate production, marketing, and administrative actions. The U.S. Federal Trade Commission defines six types of mergers. They are:

Backward Vertical Integration. This is a deal where a company moves down the production–marketing cycle by acquiring a supplier of products or services it provides.

Example: The 2010 acquisition of Smith International by Slumberger. Smith International is a provider of drilling bits and fluids to the oil industry. Slumberger is an oil field service company providing a range of services to oil companies including drilling of oil wells. The transaction was stock for stock and will likely be a tax-free exchange for investors (to be explained in a following section).

Forward Vertical Integration. This is a merger where a company moves up the production–marketing cycle by acquiring a company that uses its products.

Example: The 2010 acquisition of Healthvision Solutions, Inc., by Lawson Software. Lawson is a provider of software solutions including healthcare applications. Healthvision provides integrated healthcare technologies directly to healthcare organizations. This was an acquisition for cash.

Horizontal Merger. This is a 2010 merger of companies that offer similar products or services and are likely competitors in the same market space.

Example: The huge drug store chain, Walgreen Company, acquired the New-York-based drug store chain of Duane Reade Holdings, Inc. This cash acquisition quadrupled the number of stores Walgreen has in the metro New York area.

Product Extension Merger. This is a merger where the acquiring company is expanding its product offerings in the marketplace in which it already sells products and/or services.

Example: In early 2010, R. R. Donnelley & Sons Company acquired, for cash, Browne & Company. Donnelley provides integrated communication services for a wide range of customers. Browne provides critical capital markets communications.

Market Extension Merger. This merger increases the geographic market coverage of the same products or services already offered by the acquiring company.

Example: In 2010, First Energy acquired Allegheny Energy. Both companies are power companies. The acquisition expands First Energy's market in Pennsylvania and extends its market to include portions of West Virginia, Maryland, and Virginia.

Conglomerate Merger. Example: This is an acquisition of a firm in an unrelated line of business. In effect, the acquiring firm has a portfolio of investments. Some have said that a conglomerate is similar to a mutual fund in its purpose to maximize returns over a range of companies.

In early 2010, Thomas H. Lee Partners acquired for cash CKE Restaurants, Inc. CKE owns the Carl's Jr. and Hardee's quick service restaurant chains. Thomas H. Lee Partners businesses include information services, lending, publishing, music, and consumer products, including Snapple.

Tax Advantages of Combinations

Perhaps the most universal economic benefit in business combinations is a possible tax advantage. The owners of a business, whether sole proprietors, partners, or shareholders, may wish to retire from active management of the company. If they were to sell their interest for cash or accept debt instruments, they would have an immediate taxable gain. If, however, they accept the common stock of another corporation in exchange for their interest and carefully craft the transaction as a "tax-free reorganization," they may account for the transaction as a tax-free exchange. No taxes are paid until the shareholders sell the shares received in the business combination. The shareholder records the new shares received (for tax purposes) at the book value of the exchanged shares.

In early 2005, SBC proposed to acquire AT&T. The following information was proposed to shareholders:

AT&T shareholders will receive .7792 shares of SBC common stock for each share of AT&T. Based on SBC's closing stock price on January 28, 2005, this exchange ratio equals $18.41 per share. In addition, at the time of closing AT&T will pay its shareholders a special dividend of $ 1.30 per share. The stock consideration in the transaction is expected to be tax free to AT&T shareholders.[1]

---

1 AT&T News Release, 2005-02-22, AT&T Formally Begins Merger Approval Process, http://www.corp.att.com/news/2005/02/22.

Further tax advantages exist when the target company has reported losses on its tax returns in prior periods. Section 172 of the Internal Revenue Code provides that operating losses can generally be carried back two years to obtain a refund of taxes paid in previous years. In an effort to stimulate the economy, Congress enacted a special 5-year carryback for 2008 and 2009 operating losses. Should the loss not be offset by income in the allowed prior years, the loss may be carried forward up to 20 years to offset future taxable income, thus eliminating or reducing income taxes that would otherwise be payable. These loss maneuvers have little or no value to a target company that has not had income in the two prior years and does not expect profitable operations in the near future. However, tax losses are transferable in a business combination. To an acquiring company that has a profit in the current year and/or expects profitable periods in the future, the tax losses of a target company may have real value. That value, viewed as an asset by the acquiring company, will be reflected in the price paid. However, the acquiring company must exercise caution in anticipating the benefits of tax loss carryovers. The realization of the tax benefits may be denied if it can be shown that the primary motivation for the combination was the transfer of the tax loss benefit.

A tax benefit may also be available in a subsequent period as a consolidated tax return is filed by the single remaining corporation. The losses of one of the affiliated companies can be used to offset the net income of another affiliated company to lessen the taxes that would otherwise be paid by the profitable company.

REFLECTION

- Business combinations may have a wide range of economic advantages to a firm including vertical and horizontal integration, market and product expansion and diversification as a conglomerate company.

- Potential sellers may be motivated by the tax advantages available to them in a business combination.

ACQUISITION OF CONTROL

Control of another company may be achieved by either acquiring the assets of the target company or acquiring a controlling interest (typically over 50%) in the target company's voting common stock. In an *acquisition of assets,* all of the company's assets are acquired *directly* from the company. In most cases, existing liabilities of the acquired company also are assumed. When assets are acquired and liabilities are assumed, we refer to the transaction as an acquisition of "net assets." Payment could be made in cash, exchanged property, or issuance of either debt or equity securities. It is common to issue securities since this avoids depleting cash or other assets that may be needed in future operations. Legally, a *statutory consolidation* refers to the combining of two or more previously independent legal entities into one new legal entity. The previous companies are dissolved and are then replaced by a single continuing company. A *statutory merger* refers to the absorption of one or more former legal entities by another company that continues as the sole surviving legal entity. The absorbed company ceases to exist as a legal entity but may continue as a division of the surviving company.

In a *stock acquisition,* a controlling interest (typically, more than 50%) of another company's voting common stock is acquired. The company making the acquisition is termed the *parent* (also the acquirer), and the company acquired is termed a *subsidiary* (also the acquiree). Both the parent and the subsidiary remain separate legal entities and maintain their own financial records and statements. However, for external financial reporting purposes, the companies usually will combine their individual financial statements into a single set of consolidated statements. Thus, the term "consolidation" may refer to a statutory combination or, more commonly, to the consolidated statements of a parent and its subsidiary.

There may be several advantages to obtaining control by acquiring a controlling interest in stock. The most obvious one is that the total cost is lower, since only a controlling interest in the assets, and not the total assets, must be acquired. In addition, control through stock ownership may be simpler to achieve since no formal negotiations or transactions with the acquiree's management are necessary. Further advantages may result from maintaining the separate legal identity of the acquiree company. First of all, risk is lowered because the legal liability of each corporation is limited to its own assets. Secondly, separate legal entities may be desirable when only one of the companies, such as a utility company, is subject to government control. Lastly, tax advantages may result from the preservation of the legal entities.

Stock acquisitions are said to be "friendly" when the stockholders of the acquiree corporation, as a group, decide to sell or exchange their shares. In such a case, an offer may be made to the board of directors by the acquiring company. If the directors approve, they will recommend acceptance of the offer to the shareholders, who are likely to approve the transaction. Often, a two-thirds vote is required. Once approval is gained, the exchange of shares will be made with the individual shareholders. If the officers decline the offer, or if no offer is made, the acquirer may deal directly with individual shareholders in an attempt to secure a controlling interest. Frequently, the acquirer may make a formal *tender offer*. The tender offer typically will be published in newspapers and will offer a greater-than-market price for shares made available by a stated date. The acquirer may reserve the right to withdraw the offer if an insufficient number of shares is made available to it. Where management and/or a significant number of shareholders oppose the acquisition of the company by the intended buyer, the acquisition is viewed as hostile. Unfriendly offers are so common that several standard defensive mechanisms have evolved. Following are the common terms used to describe these defensive moves.

Greenmail. The target company may pay a premium price ("greenmail") to buy back its own shares. It may either buy shares already owned by a potential acquiring company or purchase shares from a current owner who, it is feared, would sell to the acquiring company. The price paid for these shares in excess of their market price may not be deducted from stockholders' equity; instead, it is expensed.[2]

White Knight. The target company locates a different company to acquire a controlling interest. This could occur when the original acquiring company is in a similar industry and it is feared that current management of the target company would be displaced. The replacement acquiring company, the "white knight," might be in a different industry and could be expected to keep current management intact.

Poison Pill. The "poison pill" involves the issuance of stock rights to existing shareholders to purchase additional shares at a price far below fair value. However, the rights are exercisable only when an acquiring company purchases or makes a bid to purchase a stated number of shares. The effect of the options is to substantially raise the cost to the acquiring company. If the attempt fails, there is at least a greater gain for the original shareholders.

Selling the Crown Jewels. This approach has the management of the target company selling vital assets (the "crown jewels") of the target company to others to make the company less attractive to the acquiring company.

Leveraged Buyouts. The management of the existing target company attempts to purchase a controlling interest in that company. Often, substantial debt will be incurred to raise the funds needed to purchase the stock; hence the term "leveraged buyout." When bonds are sold to provide this financing, the bonds may be referred to as "junk bonds," since they are often high-interest and high-risk due to the high debt-to-equity ratio of the resulting corporation.

Further protection against takeovers is offered by federal and state law. The Clayton Act of 1914 (Section 7) is a federal law that prohibits business combinations in which "the effect of such acquisition may be substantially to lessen competition or to tend to create a monopoly."

---

2 FASB ASC 505-30-25-4, *Equity-Treasury Stock—Recognition* (Norwalk, CT , 2010).

The Williams Act of 1968 is a federal law that regulates tender offers; it is enforced by the Securities and Exchange Commission (SEC). Several states also have enacted laws to discourage hostile takeovers. These laws are motivated, in part, by the fear of losing employment and taxes.

Accounting Ramifications of Control

When control is achieved through an asset acquisition, the acquiring company records on its books the assets and assumed liabilities of the acquired company. From the acquisition date on, all transactions of both the acquiring and acquired company are recorded in one combined set of accounts. The only new skill one needs to master is the proper recording of the acquisition when it occurs. **Once the initial acquisition is properly recorded, subsequent accounting procedures are the same as for any single accounting entity.** Combined statements of the new, larger company for periods following the combination are automatic.

Accounting procedures are more involved when control is achieved through a stock acquisition. The controlling company, the parent, will record only an investment account to reflect its interest in the controlled company, the subsidiary. Both the parent and the subsidiary remain separate legal entities with their own separate sets of accounts and separate financial statements. Accounting theory holds that where one company has effective control over another, there is only one economic entity and there should be only one set of financial statements that combines the activities of the entities under common control. The accountant will prepare a worksheet, referred to as the *consolidated worksheet,* that starts with the separate accounts of the parent and the subsidiary. Various adjustments and eliminations will be made on this worksheet to merge the separate accounts of the two companies into a single set of financial statements, which are called *consolidated statements.*

This chapter discusses business combinations resulting from asset acquisitions, since the accounting principles are more easily understood in this context. The principles developed are applied directly to stock acquisitions that are presented in the chapters that follow.

REFLECTION

- Control of another company is gained by either acquiring all of that firm's assets (and usually its liabilities) or by acquiring a controlling interest in that company's voting common stock.

- Control through an acquisition of assets requires the correct initial recording of the purchase. Combined statements for future periods are automatically produced.

3

OBJECTIVE

Explain the basics of the acquisition model.

EVOLUTION OF ACCOUNTING METHODS

Prior to the issuance of FASB Statement No. 141 in 2001, two methods were used to account for business combinations. These were the purchase method and the pooling-of-interests method. The *purchase method* usually recorded all assets and liabilities of the company acquired at fair value. The purchase method was the primary method in use. However, under some circumstances, the pooling-of-interests method was allowed. The *pooling-of-interests method* recorded the assets and liabilities of the acquired firm at their existing book values. This method was intended to be applied to business combinations that were a "merger of equals." Specific criteria existed as to combinations that would qualify. Ninety percent of the stock of the firm acquired had to be received in exchange for the shares of the acquiring firm. All shareholders of the acquired firm had to be treated equally. Numerous other criteria also attempted to guarantee a fusion of existing owners rather than a takeover of one company by another. In the end, some companies engaged in a series of equity transactions prior to the combination so that they would be able to meet the pooling criteria. Pooling allowed the carry over of book values to the acquiring firm. That resulted in greater future income because of typically lower depreciation and amortization charges on assets. Pooling did not result in new goodwill being recorded. At that time goodwill was amortized. Thus, pooling also led to greater income in the future since there would be no goodwill amortization.

FASB Statement No. 141 eliminated the pooling method. Assets and liabilities acquired in a pooling of interests, that began prior to the effective date of FASB Statement No. 141, were allowed to continue as originally recorded. This means that current-era financial statements still include assets and liabilities of a firm acquired in a pooling that were initially recorded at their book values on the acquisition date.

The purchase method required under FASB Statement No. 141 focused only on recording fair values for the portion of the assets and liabilities acquired in the purchase. The accounts of the acquired company would only be adjusted to full fair value if the parent company acquired a 100% interest in the acquired firm. If, for example, the purchasing company bought only an 80% interest in the acquired firm, accounts would be adjusted by only 80% of the difference between book and fair value. Thus, in an 80% purchase, an asset with a book value of $6,000 and a fair value of $10,000 would be recorded at $9,200 ($6,000 book value plus 80% × $4,000 excess of fair value over book value).

The new *acquisition method* included in FASB Statement No. 14lr (now included in FASB ASC 805), issued in 2007, requires that all assets and liabilities be recorded at fair value regardless of the percentage interest purchased by the acquiring company (provided that the interest purchased is large enough to constitute a controlling interest). In the above example, the asset illustrated would be recorded at the full $10,000 fair value even though the acquiring company only purchased an 80% interest in the company that owns the asset. The acquisition method also eliminated the prior practice of discounting of fixed and intangible assets to a value less than fair value. This would happen under the purchase method when, in a rare case, the acquiring firm made a "bargain purchase." A *bargain purchase* occurs when the price paid for a company is less than the sum of the fair value of its net assets (sum of all assets minus all liabilities).

Applying the Acquisition Method

The four steps in the acquisition method are as follows:

1. Identify the acquirer.
2. Determine the acquisition date.
3. Measure the fair value of the acquiree (the company being acquired).
4. Record the acquiree's assets and liabilities that are assumed.

Identify the Acquirer. In an asset acquisition, the company transferring cash or other assets and/or assuming liabilities is the acquiring company. In a stock acquisition, the acquirer is, in most cases, the company transferring cash or other assets for a controlling interest in the voting common stock of the acquiree (company being acquired). Some stock acquisitions may be accomplished by exchanging voting common stock. Most often, the company issuing the voting common stock is the acquirer. In some cases, the acquiree may issue the stock in the acquisition. This "reverse acquisition" may occur when a publicly traded company is acquired by a privately traded company. The appendix at the end of Chapter 2 considers this situation and provides the applicable accounting methods.

When an acquisition is accomplished through an exchange of equity interests, the factors considered in determining the acquirer firm include the following:

1. Voting rights—The entity with the largest share of voting rights is typically the acquirer.
2. Large minority interest—Where the company purchases only a large minority interest (under 50%) and no other owner or group has a significant voting interest, the company acquiring the large minority interest is likely the acquirer. Determination of control could be based on domination of the decision-making process to obtain the related economic benefits.
3. Governing body of combined entity—The entity that has the ability to elect or appoint a majority of the combined entity is likely the acquirer.
4. Terms of exchange—Typically, the acquirer pays a premium over the precombination market value of the shares acquired.

Determine the Acquisition Date. This is the date that the acquiring firm makes payment by transferring assets, issuing stock, and assuming the liabilities of the acquired company. Normally, this is also the legal closing date. The closing can, however, occur after the acquisition date if there is a written agreement that the acquirer obtains control of the acquiree.

The acquisition date is critical because it is the date used to establish the total fair value of the company acquired, and it is usually the date that fair values are established for the assets and liabilities of the acquired company.

Measure the Fair Value of the Acquiree. Unless there is evidence to the contrary, the fair value of the acquiree as an entity is assumed to be the price paid by the acquirer. The price paid is based on the sum of the fair values of the assets transferred, liabilities assumed, and the stock issued by the acquirer. If the information to establish the fair value of the acquiree is not available on the acquisition date, a *measurement period* is available to ascertain the value. This period ends when either the needed information is available or is judged to not be obtainable. In no case can the measurement period exceed one year after the acquisition date.

Specific guidance as to what may be included in the price calculation is as follows:

a. The price includes the estimated value of contingent consideration. Contingent consideration is an agreement to issue additional consideration (assets or stock) at a later date if specified events occur. The most common agreements focus on a targeted sales or income performance by the acquiree company. An estimate must be made of the probable settlement cost and that amount is included in the price paid. The measurement period is available to refine the estimated value. Contingent agreements that result in the issue of stock are not remeasured. Subsequent to the measurement period, agreements that create a liability are remeasured and the changes are included in the income of the subsequent period.

b. The costs of accomplishing the acquisition, such as accounting costs and legal fees, are not included in the price of the company acquired and are expensed. In the period of the acquisition, the notes to the financial statements must disclose the amount of the acquisition costs and state the line item expense on the income statement that includes these costs. Where the consideration used is the stock of the acquirer, the issue costs may also be expensed or they can be deducted from the value assigned to paid-in capital in excess of par, but they are not included in the price paid. This text will deduct issue costs form paid-in capital in excess of par in examples, exercises and problems.

Record the Acquiree's Assets and Liabilities That Are Assumed. The fair values of all identifiable assets and liabilities of the acquiree are determined and recorded. *Fair value* is the amount that the asset or liability would be bought or sold for in a current, normal (nonforced) sale between willing parties. Fair values are determined following the guidance of FASB ASC 820, *Fair Value Measurement and Disclosure.* FASB ASC 820-10-35-39 provides a hierarchy of values, where the highest level measurement possible should be used. The hierarchy is as follows:

◆ Level 1—Unadjusted quoted market value in an actively traded market. This method would apply to actively traded investments and to inventory.

◆ Level 2—Adjusted market value based on prices of similar assets or on observable other inputs such as interest rates. This approach might apply to work-in-process inventory and plant and equipment that sells in an organized market.

◆ Level 3—Fair value based on unobservable inputs, such as the entities' best estimate of an exit (sale) value. The value of plant and equipment, not normally sold in an active market, would likely be calculated under this approach.

There are a few exceptions to the fair value rule that will be discussed. The sum of all identifiable assets, less liabilities recorded, is referred to as the fair value of the net assets. The identifiable assets never include goodwill that may exist on the acquiree's books. The only goodwill recorded in an acquisition is "new" goodwill based on the price paid by the acquirer. The fair value recorded for the net assets is not likely to be equal to the fair value of the acquiree as an entire entity (which is normally equal to the price paid).

Goodwill. Goodwill results when the price paid exceeds the fair value of the acquiree's net identifiable assets. The excess of the fair value of the acquiree over the values assigned to net identifiable assets is "new" goodwill. The goodwill recorded is not amortized but is impairment tested in future accounting periods.

Bargain Purchase. A bargain purchase occurs when the fair value assigned to the net identifiable assets exceeds the price paid. When this occurs, every effort should be made to revalue the amounts assigned to net identifiable assets to eliminate the difference. If, after reconsideration of the fair values, an excess of fair value of the net identifiable assets over the price paid still exists, the excess is recorded as a "gain" on the acquisition by the acquirer. Disclosure for the period of the acquisition must show the gain as a separate line item on the income statement or identify the line item that includes the gain. Exhibit 1-2, The Combined Income Statement and related note for Sapphire Wines LLC— Emerald Wines LLC, shows a "Gain on bargain purchase of a business" among "Other income (expense) items" in the income statement. Note 3 explains the calculation of the gain.

Exhibit 1-2
Combined Statements of Operation

	Six Months Ended June 30, 2009 (unaudited)	Six Month Ended June 30, 2008 (unaudited)	Year Ended December 31, 2008	Period from March 20, 2007 (inception) to December 31, 2007
Net sales	$ 8,319,703	$5,685,506	$13,611,015	$5,289,614
Cost of sales	5,085,652	2,776,101	7,340,035	3,689,376
Gross Profit	3,234,051	2,909,405	6,270,980	1,600,238
Selling, general and administrative expenses	2,314,524	1,553,422	3,506,517	662,008
Income from operations	919,527	1,355,983	2,764,463	938,230
Other (income) and expense				
Gain on bargain purchase of business	(1,835,928)	—	—	—
Income from solar power agreement	(128,758)	—	—	—
Interest income	—	—	(906)	(3,474)
Interest expense	1,465,564	1,231,686	2,529,766	778,159
Other (income) expense	(64,198)	—	2,598	17,486
Other (income) and expense-net	(563,320)	1,231,686	2,531,458	792,171
Net income	$ 1,482,847	$ 124,297	$ 233,005	$ 146,059

Sapphire Wines, LLC
Emerald Wines, LLC
Notes to Combined Financial Statements

Note 3—Business combinations

Acquisition of Briarcliff Wine Group, LLC (unaudited). As part of the purchase agreement, the sellers may also receive up to approximately $1,524,000 should all of the purchased wine inventory be sold within a ten-year period. The approximate pay out schedule based on the Company's projected case sales are as follows: 2009 – $47,000: 2010 – $1,440,000 and 2011 – $37,000. These contingent payment are recorded at their approximate fair value of $1,447,000 on the balance sheet as a current obligation.

(continued)

The aggregate purchase price was approximately $3,447,000. The following summarizes the estimated fair values, using level 3 inputs, of the assets acquired at the date of acquisition. The estimated fair values are subject to change pending a final analysis of the total purchase price and the fair value of the assets acquired, a gain of approximately $1,835,928 reflecting the bargain purchase of Briarcliff was reflected in the results of operations for the six months ended June 30, 2009.

Inventories	$3,957,696
Intangible assets-brand	$1,325,000

Proforma effect of acquisition (unaudited). The purchase of Briarcliff has been included in the financial statement of the company since March 9, 2009.

The unaudited proforma information below presents the results of operations as if the acquisitions of Briarcliff had occurred on the first day of the preceding year. The unaudited proforma information is presented for informational purposes only and is not intended to represent or be indicative of the results of operations of the combined companies had these events occurred at the beginning of the year presented nor is it indicative of future results:

	Six Months June 30 2009	Six Months Ended June 30, 2008	Year Ended December 31, 2008	Period from March 20, 2007 (inception) to December 31, 2007
Total revenue	$8,789,718	$7,307,722	$16,846,791	$7,879,330
Net income (loss)	$1,515,561	$ (335,145)	$ (683,878)	$ 62,637

Note 4—Inventories

A summary of inventories by entity consists of the following:

	June 30, 2009 (unaudited)	December 31, 2008	December 31, 2007
Raw maicrials	$ 447,292	$ 485,133	$ 496,677
Bulk wine	8,720,773	9,007,186	6,006,823
Finished goods	4,874,385	1,988,595	1,880,389
Tasting room	120,529	114,294	87,060
	$14,162,979	$11,595,210	$8,470,949

Note 5—Property, plant and equipment

A summary of property, plant and equipment by entity consists of the following

	June 30, 2009 (unaudited)	December 31, 2008	December 31, 2007
Land	$ 1,447,051	$ 1,447,051	$ 638,660
Building	16,570,639	16,446,530	15,844,828
Computers and equipment	42,000	15,122	15,122
Furniture and fixtures	96,234	93,811	59,412
Winery equipment and fixtures	3,313,660	3,310,942	3,010,215
Vehicles	32,500	32,500	32,500
Barrels	707,427	707,427	502,495
Leasehold improvements	1,709,132	1,697,625	23,575
Construction in progress	35,358	35,358	61,643
	23,954,091	23,786,366	20,188,450
Loss accumulated depreciation	(3,152,510)	(2,214,380)	(598,323)
	$20,801,581	$21,571,986	$19,590,127

(continued)

Included in property, plant and equipment is certain equipment which is leased under capital lease agreements. The combined balance sheets include the following capital leases:

	June 30, 2009 (unaudited)	December 31, 2008	December 31, 2007
Equipment under capital leases	$ 412,444	$ 412,441	$412,441
Accumulated amortization	(245,372)	(180,032)	(49,351)
Net equipment under capital leases	$ 167,069	$ 232,409	$363,090

Prior to FASB 141r, there was an extraordinary gain when the price paid exceeded the total of only current assets minus all liabilities. Under current rules, there is an "ordinary" gain when fair value of the net identifiable assets exceeds the price paid.

REFLECTION

- The acquisition method records all accounts of the acquiree at fair value. Any goodwill on the acquiree's books is ignored.

- An acquisition cost in excess of the fair value of the acquiree's net identifiable assets results in goodwill.

- An acquisition cost less than the fair values of the acquiree's net identifiable assets results in an ordinary gain being recorded by the acquirer.

VALUATION OF IDENTIFIABLE ASSETS AND LIABILITIES

4

OBJECTIVE

Allocate the acquisition price to the assets and liabilities of the acquired company.

The first step in recording an acquisition is to record the existing asset and liability accounts (except goodwill). As a general rule, assets and liabilities are to be recorded at their individually determined fair values. The preferred method is quoted market value when an active market for the item exists. Where there is not an active market, independent appraisals, discounted cash flow analysis, and other types of analysis are used to estimate fair values. There are some exceptions to the use of fair value that apply to accounts such as assets for resale and deferred taxes.

The acquiring firm is not required to establish values immediately on the acquisition date. A measurement period of up to one year is allowed for measurement. Temporary values would be used in financial statements prepared prior to the end of the measurement period. A note to the statements would explain the use of temporary values. Any change in the recorded values is adjusted retroactively to the date of the acquisition. Prior-period statements are revised to reflect the final values and any related amortizations.

The procedures for recording the assets and liabilities of the acquired firm are as follows:

1. **Current assets**—These are recorded at estimated fair values. This would include recording accounts and notes receivable at the estimated amounts to be collected. Accounts and notes receivable are to be recorded in a net account that represents the probable cash flows; a separate valuation account for uncollectible accounts is not allowed. All accounts share the rule that only the net fair value is recorded, and valuation accounts are not used.

2. **Existing liabilities**—These are also recorded at fair value. For current contractual liabilities, that is likely to be the existing recorded value. For estimated liabilities, a new fair value may be used in place of recorded values. Long-term liabilities will be adjusted to a value different from recorded value if there has been a material change in interest rates.

3. **Property, plant, and equipment**—Operating assets will require an estimate of fair value and will be recorded at that net amount with no separate accumulated depreciation account.

4. **Existing intangible assets, other than goodwill**—These will also be recorded at estimated fair value. The valuation of these items, such as patents and copyrights, will typically require the use of discounted cash flow analysis.

5. **Assets that are going to be sold rather than used in operations**—Such assets are *not* recorded at fair value. They are recorded at net realizable value and are listed as current assets.

6. **When the acquiree is a lessee with respect to assets in use**—The original classification of a lease as operating or capital is not changed by the acquisition unless the terms of the lease are modified as part of the acquisition. The acquiree has no recorded asset for assets under operating leases. If, however, the terms of the lease are favorable as compared to current market rent rates, an intangible asset would be recorded equal to the discounted present value of the savings. If the lease terms are unfavorable, an estimated liability would be recorded equal to the discounted present value of the rent in excess of fair rental rates.

EXAMPLE

The acquiree is a party to a 5-year remaining term operating lease requiring payments of $1,000 per month at the start of each month. The current rental rate for such an asset on a new 5-year lease would be $1,300 per month. Assuming an annual interest rate for this type of transaction of 8%, the calculation would be as follows:

Payment	$ 300 (excess of fair rent value over contractual amount)
n	60
Rate	8/12%
Present Value	$14,894 (beginning mode)

An intangible asset, Favorable Operating Lease Terms, would be recorded and amortized over five years. The effective interest method of amortization should be applied.

If the acquiree is a party to a capital lease, the asset would be recorded at fair value as would the liability under the capital lease.

7. **When the acquiree may have acted as a lessor**—Again, the classification of the lease is not changed unless the terms are changed. For operating leases, the acquiree has the asset recorded on its balance sheet. The asset is recorded at fair value, and it is not impacted by the terms of any lease applicable to that asset. If the terms of the operating lease include rental rates that are different than current rental rates, an intangible asset or estimated liability is recorded. An intangible asset would be recorded for favorable lease terms, and an estimated liability would be recorded for unfavorable terms. Note that the lessor terms are favorable when the contract rental rate exceeds fair rental value, and terms are unfavorable when the fair rental value exceeds the contract rate. The value of the intangible asset or estimated liability uses the same procedure as illustrated for the lessee above.

If the lease is a capital lease, the acquiree has no asset recorded other than the minimum lease payments receivable account. This account would be remeasured at the discounted present value of the payments at the current market interest rate for such a transaction.

EXAMPLE

The acquiree/lessor has a minimum lease payment receivable on its books at $178,024 (96 beginning-of-the-month payments of $2,500 at 8% annual interest rate). If the current market rate of interest for this transaction is 12% annual, the fair value of the minimum lease payment receivable would be calculated and recorded as follows:

Payment	$ 2,500, beginning of the month
n	96 months
Rate	12%/12 = 1%
Present Value	$155,357 (This is the amount of the minimum lease payment receivable that would be recorded.)

8. **Intangible assets not currently recorded by the acquiree**—Identifiable intangible assets must be separately recorded; their value cannot be swept into the "goodwill" classification. An intangible asset is identifiable if it arises from contractual or other legal rights (even if it is not separable) or is separable. For example, the acquiree may have a customer list that could be sold separately and has a determinable value. The acquiree cannot record the value of this self-developed intangible asset. However, this value must be estimated and recorded as one of the assets acquired in the acquisition.

FASB ASC 805-20-55 provides the following list of possible intangible assets and classifies them as contractual/legal versus only separable.[3]

Contractual/Legal	Separable
Trademarks, copyrights, trade names, service marks, collective marks, certification marks	Customer lists
Trade dress (unique color shape or package design)	Noncontractual customer relationships
Newspaper mastheads	Unpatented technology
Internet domain names	
Noncompetition agreements	
Order or production backlog	Databases
Customer contracts and related customer relationships	
Plays, operas, ballets	
Books, magazines, newspapers, and other literary works	
Musical works such as compositions, song lyrics, advertising jingles	
Pictures, photographs	
Video and audiovisual material, including motion pictures or films, music videos, television programs	
Licensing, royalty, standstill agreements	
Advertising, construction, management services, or supply contracts	
Lease agreements (applicable to lessees and lessor)	
Construction permits	
Franchise agreements	
Operating and broadcast rights	
Servicing contracts	
Employment contracts	
Use rights, such as for water, timber, air, minerals, or routes	
Patented technology	
Computer software	
Trade secrets	

Note that an assembled workforce is specifically stated in ASC 805-20-55-6 as not qualifying as an identifiable intangible asset. Whatever value it has would be included in the value recorded for goodwill.

---

3 FASB ASC 805-20-55, *Business Combinations—Identifiable Assets and Liabilities and any Noncontrolling Interest—Implementation and Guidance* (Norwalk, CT , 2010).

9. **Research and development assets**—The fair values of both tangible and intangible research and development assets are recorded even where the assets do not have alternative future uses (the usual criteria for capitalization of R&D assets). Where the assets included in the acquisition have value only for a given project, the assets are considered to have an "indefinite" life and are not amortized until the project is completed. Upon completion, the useful life is to be estimated and used as the amortization period. The assets are to be expensed at the completion or abandonment of an unsuccessful project.

     Tangible and intangible R&D assets that are used for multiple R&D projects are separately recorded and are amortized based on the projects served by the assets.

10. **Contingent assets and liabilities**—This refers to contingent assets and liabilities possessed by the acquiree on the acquisition date and must not be confused with contingent consideration that is part of the acquisition agreement. The fair value of a contingent asset or liability is recorded at its fair value on the acquisition date, if such a value exists. The measurement period allows added time to estimate these values.

     If a fair value does not exist on the acquisition date, guidance for estimating the value comes from FASB ASC 805-25-20. Two criteria must be met for an estimate of the contingent asset or liability to be recorded:

     ◆ Information available by the end of the measurement date indicates that it is probable that an asset existed or a liability had been incurred as of the acquisition date. It is implicit in this condition that it must be probable at the acquisition date that one or more future events confirming the existence of the asset or liability will occur.

     ◆ The amount of the asset or liability can be reasonable estimated.

     Examples of contingent assets would include possible bonuses, refunds stemming from tax disputes, and possible favorable outcomes of lawsuits. Contingent assets can not be recorded except as a part of a business acquisition. Contingent liabilities include pending claims such as unfavorable lawsuits, warranty costs, premiums and coupons, and environmental liabilities.

11. **Liabilities associated with restructuring or exit activities**—The fair value of an existing restructuring or exit activity for which the acquiree is obligated is recorded as a separate liability. To record a liability, there must be an existing obligation to other entities.[4] The possible future costs connected with restructuring or exit activities that may be planned by the acquirer are not part of the cost of the acquisition and are expensed in future periods.

12. **Employee benefit plans**—The asset or liability under employee benefit plans is not recorded at fair value. Instead, a liability is recorded if the projected benefit obligation exceeds the plan assets. An asset is recorded when the plan assets exceed the projected benefit obligation. The same procedure is applicable to other employee benefit plans.

13. **Deferred taxes**—Some acquisitions will be structured as nontaxable exchanges as to the acquiree. In such cases, the acquirer must continue to base deductions for amortization or depreciation of acquired accounts on their existing tax basis. A deferred tax liability is recorded for added estimated taxes caused by the excess of fair value depreciation over book value depreciation. A deferred tax asset is recorded for estimated future tax savings.

     The acquirer would also record deferred tax assets or liabilities for temporary tax differences, such as using straight-line depreciation for financial reporting and an accelerated depreciation method for tax purposes.

     The acquirer will also record a deferred tax asset for any operating tax losses or investment credit carryovers acquired from the acquiree.

     Taxation issues are considered in the "Tax Issues" section of this chapter.

Applying the Acquisition Model

Let us assume that the Johnson Company to be acquired by Acquisitions, Inc., has the following balance sheet on the October 1, 2017, acquisition date:

---

4 FASB ASC 420-10-25-2, *Exist or Disposal Cost Obligations—Overall—Recognition* (Norwalk, CT , 2010).

Johnson Company
Balance Sheet
October 1, 2017

Cash	$ 40,000	Current liabilities	$ 25,000
Marketable investments..........	60,000	8%, 5-year bond payable	100,000
Inventory	100,000	Total liabilities	$125,000
Land..........................	30,000	Common stock ($1 par).............	$ 10,000
Buildings (net)	150,000	Paid-in capital in excess of par	140,000
Equipment (net)	80,000	Retained earnings	185,000
		Total equity	$335,000
Total assets..................	$460,000	Liabilities plus equity	$460,000

Note 1: A customer list with significant value exists.
Note 2: There is an unrecorded warranty liability on prior-product sales.

Fair values for all accounts have been established as of October 1, 2017 as follows:[5]

Account	Method of Estimation	Fair Value	
Cash	Book value	$ 40,000	
Marketable investment	Level 1—Market value	66,000	
Inventory	Level 1—Market value	110,000	
Land	Level 2—Adjusted market value	72,000	
Buildings	Level 2—Adjusted market value	288,000	
Equipment	Level 1—Market value	145,000	
Customer list	Level 3—Other estimate, discounted cash flow based on estimated future cash flows	125,000	
Total assets			$ 846,000
Current liabilities	Book value	$ (25,000)	
Bonds payable	Face value (adjusted with premium/discount)	(100,000)	
Premium on bonds payable	Level 2—adjusted market value, using market-based interest rate applied to contractual cash flows	(4,000)	
Warranty liability	Level 3—other estimate, discounted cash flow based on estimated future cash flows	(12,000)	
Total liabilities			(141,000)
Fair value of net identifiable assets			$ 705,000

Recording the Acquisition. The price paid for the company being acquired is normally measured as the sum of the consideration (total assets) exchanged for the business. This would be the sum of the cash, other assets, debt securities issued, and any stock issued by the acquiring company. In a rare case, the fair value of the company being purchased may be more determinable than the consideration given. This could be the case where stock is issued that is not publicly traded and the fair value of the business acquired is more measurable. The basic procedures to record the purchase are as follows:

◆ All accounts identified are measured at estimated fair value as demonstrated above. This is true even if the consideration given for a company is less than the sum of the fair values of the net assets (assets minus liabilities assumed, $705,000 in the above example).

---

5 FASB ASC 820, *Fair Value Measurement and Disclosure* (Norwalk, CT, 2010)

◆ If the total consideration given for a company exceeds the fair value of its net identifiable assets ($705,000), the excess price paid is recorded as goodwill.

◆ In a rare case where total consideration given for a company is less than the fair value of its net identifiable assets ($705,000), the excess of the net assets over the price paid is recorded as an ordinary gain in the period of the purchase.

◆ All acquisition costs are expensed in the period of the purchase. These costs could include the fees of accountants and lawyers that were necessary to negotiate and consummate the purchase. In the past, these costs were included as part of the price paid for the company purchased.

Examples of Recording an Acquisition Using Value Analysis. Prior to attempting to record a purchase, an analysis should be made comparing the price paid for the company with the fair value of the net assets acquired.

◆ If the price exceeds the sum of the fair value of the net identifiable assets acquired, the excess price is goodwill.

◆ If the price is less than the sum of the fair value of the net identifiable assets acquired, the price deficiency is a gain.

1. Price paid exceeds fair value of net identifiable assets acquired.
   Acquisitions, Inc., issues 40,000 shares of its $1 par value common stock shares with a market value of $20 each for Johnson Company, illustrated above. Acquisitions, Inc., pays related acquisition costs of $35,000.

Value Analysis:

Total price paid (consideration given), 40,000 shares × $20 market value	$ 800,000
Total fair value of net assets acquired from Johnson Company	(705,000)
Goodwill (excess of total cost over fair value of net assets)	$ 95,000
Expense acquisition costs	$ 35,000

	Dr.	Cr.
To record purchase of net assets:		
Cash	40,000	
Marketable Investments	66,000	
Inventory	110,000	
Land	72,000	
Buildings	288,000	
Equipment	145,000	
Customer List	125,000	
Goodwill	**95,000**	
Current Liabilities		25,000
Bonds Payable		100,000
Premium on Bonds Payable		4,000
Warranty Liability		12,000
Common Stock ($1 par, 40,000 shares issued)		40,000
Paid-In Capital in Excess of Par ($20 per share × 40,000 shares less $40,000 assigned to par)		760,000
Dr. = Cr. Check Totals	*941,000*	*941,000*
To record acquisition costs:		
Acquisition Expense	35,000	
Cash		35,000

2. Price paid is less than fair value of net identifiable assets acquired.

Acquisitions, Inc., issues 25,000 shares of its $1 par value common stock with a market value of $20 each for Johnson Company, illustrated above. Acquisitions, Inc., pays related acquisition costs of $35,000.

Value Analysis:

Total price paid (consideration given), 25,000 shares × $20 market value	$ 500,000
Total fair value of net assets acquired from Johnson Company	(705,000)
Gain on purchase of business (excess of fair value of net assets over total cost)	$(205,000)
Expense acquisition costs	$ 35,000

Entries to record the purchase and related costs are as follows:

	Dr.	Cr.
To record purchase of net assets:		
Cash	40,000	
Marketable Investments...................................	66,000	
Inventory	110,000	
Land...	72,000	
Buildings	288,000	
Equipment	145,000	
Customer List	125,000	
Current Liabilities.....................................		25,000
Bonds Payable..		100,000
Premium on Bonds Payable		4,000
Warranty Liability		12,000
Common Stock ($1 par, 25,000 shares issued)		25,000
Paid-In Capital in Excess of Par ($20 per share × 25,000 shares less $25,000 assigned to par)		475,000
Gain on Acquisition of Business........................		**205,000**
Dr. = Cr. Check Totals	*846,000*	*846,000*
To record acquisition costs:		
Acquisition Expense	35,000	
Cash		35,000

The gain must be reported as a separate line item in the income statement of the acquirer in the period of the acquisition. Notes must include an explanation of the reasons that allowed the gain to exist.

Recording Changes in Value During Measurement Period

During the measurement period, values assigned to accounts recorded as a part of the acquisition may be adjusted to better reflect the value of the accounts as of the acquisition date. It is possible that new assets and liabilities that existed on the acquisition date may become known during the measurement period; they must also be recorded as part of the adjustment. Changes in value caused by events that occur after the acquisition date are not part of this adjustment. They would usually be adjusted to income in the period in which they occur.

The values recorded on the acquisition date are considered "provisional." They must be used in financial statements with dates prior to the end of the measurement period. The measurement period ends when the improved information is available or it is obvious that no better information is available. In no case can the measurement period exceed one year from the acquisition date.

Let us return to the earlier example of the acquisition of Johnson Company in exchange for stock with a total value of $800,000. Assume now that the values assigned to the buildings, customer list, and warranty liability are provisional. The 2017 financial year will include the income statement accounts for the acquired, Johnson Company, starting as of the October 1 acquisition date. The values and resulting adjustments to income for 2017 and projected for 2018 are as follows:

Account	Provisional Value	Depreciation/Amortization Method	Recorded in 2017 (3 months)	Projected for 2018 (full year)
Buildings	$288,000	20-year straight-line with $48,000 residual value. $240,000/ 20 years = $12,000 per year, $1,000 per month	$3,000	$12,000
Customer List	125,000	5-year amortization, calculated monthly. $125,000/5 years = $25,000 per year, ¼ annual amount for 2017	6,250	25,000
Warranty Liability	(12,000)	Debited as repairs are made	3,500	7,000

Better estimates of values for these accounts become available in early 2018. The new values and revised depreciation/amortization are as follows:

Account	Revised Value	Depreciation/Amortization Method	Adjusted Amount for 2017	Amount to Be Recorded in 2018
Buildings	$320,000	20-year straight-line with $50,000 residual value. $270,000/ 20 years = $13,500 per year, $1,125 per month	$3,375	$13,500
Customer List	150,000	5-year amortization, calculated monthly. $150,000/5 years = $30,000 per year, $2,500 per month	7,500	30,000
Warranty Liability	(18,000)	Debited as repairs are made	3,500	10,000

The recorded values are adjusted during 2018 as follows:

	Dr.	Cr.
Buildings ($320,000 new estimate – $288,000 provisional value)	32,000	
Customer List ($150,000 new estimate – $125,000 provisional value)	25,000	
Warranty Liability ($18,000 new estimate – $12,000 provisional value)		6,000
Goodwill (sum of above adjustments)		51,000

Goodwill would normally absorb the impact of the adjustments to all other accounts since it is the difference between the price paid and the values assigned to identifiable net assets. Had there been a gain on the original acquisition date, the gain would be adjusted at the end of the measurement period. Since the gain was recorded in the prior period, the entry to adjust the amount of the gain would be made to retained earnings. If there is goodwill but the increase in net assets is greater than the amount of goodwill, a gain would be recorded for the balance of the adjustment.

The depreciation/amortizations for the prior period must also be adjusted retroactively. The entry made in 2018 would be as follows:

	Dr.	Cr.
Retained Earnings (net adjustment of $375 + $1,250)	1,625	
Accumulated Depreciation—Buildings		375
Customer List		1,250

The comparative statements, which include 2017, would include the revised amounts. The revised depreciation and amortization amounts ($13,500 and $30,000, respectively, for 2018) would be recorded in 2018.

Recording Contingent Consideration

Let us again revisit the acquisition of Johnson Company. This time, we will assume that the acquirer issued 40,000 shares of stock with a market value of $800,000. In addition to the stock issue, the acquirer agreed to pay an additional $100,000 on January 1, 2020, if the average income during the 2-year period of 2018–2019 exceeds $80,000 per year. The expected value is calculated as $40,000 based on the 40% probability of exceeding an average income of $80,000 and having to pay the added $100,000. The revised value analysis and recording of the acquisition would be as follows:

Value Analysis:

Total price paid:		
Stock issued, 40,000 shares × $20 market value	$800,000	
Estimated value of contingent payment	40,000	$ 840,000
Total fair value of net assets acquired from Johnson Company		(705,000)
Goodwill		$ 135,000
Expense acquisition costs		$ 35,000

Entries to record acquisition and related costs are as follows:

	Dr.	Cr.
To record purchase of net assets:		
Cash	40,000	
Marketable Investments	66,000	
Inventory	110,000	
Land	72,000	
Buildings	288,000	
Equipment	145,000	
Customer List	125,000	
Goodwill	**135,000**	
Current Liabilities		25,000
Bonds Payable		100,000
Premium on Bonds Payable		4,000
Warranty Liability		12,000
Estimated Liability for Contingent Consideration		40,000
Common Stock ($1 par, 40,000 shares issued)		40,000
Paid-In Capital in Excess of Par ($20 per share × 40,000 shares less		
$40,000 assigned to par)		760,000
Dr. = Cr. Check Totals	*981,000*	*981,000*
To record acquisition costs:		
Acquisition Expense	35,000	
Cash		35,000

If during the measurement period, the contingent consideration was revalued based on improved information, the estimated liability and the goodwill (or gain in a bargain acquisition) would be adjusted. For example, assume that within the measurement period the estimate was revised to $50,000, the adjustment would then be as follows:

Goodwill ($50,000 new estimate − $40,000 provisional value)	10,000	
Estimated Liability for Contingent Consideration		10,000

If the estimate is again revised after the measurement period, the adjustment is included in the income of the later period. If the estimate was revised to $65,000 after the measurement period, the following adjustment would be recorded:

Expense, Increase in Estimated Contingent Consideration Payment	15,000	
Estimated Liability for Contingent Consideration		15,000

The above procedure applies to any contingent payment payable in a form other than issuing additional shares of stock. An agreement to issue added stock upon the occurrence of a future event is considered to be a change in the estimate of the value of the shares issued. No liability is recorded at the acquisition date. The only entry made is at the date of the added stock issue. The procedure on that date is to reassign the original consideration assigned to the stock to a greater number of shares.

Returning to the example of the acquisition of Johnson Company for $800,000 in stock, assume that there was an agreement to issue 5,000 additional shares if the average income during the 2-year period of 2018–2019 exceeded $80,000 per year. There would be no change in the entry made at the top of page 17 to record the acquisition on October 1, 2017. Prior to the termination of the contingency, it would be described in a footnote.

Assuming the contingent event occurs, the following entry would be made after December 31, 2019, to reassign the $800,000 original consideration to 45,000 total shares:

Paid-In Capital in Excess of Par (5,000 shares × $1)	5,000	
Common Stock ($1 par, 5,000 shares issued)		5,000

Accounting for the Acquisition by the Acquiree

The goodwill recorded by the acquirer is not tied to the gain (or loss) recorded by the acquiree. The acquiree records the removal of net assets at their book values. Recall the initial example of the acquisition of Johnson Company for $800,000 (on page 18). The excess of the price received by the seller ($800,000) over the sum of the net asset book value of $335,000 ($460,000 assets − $125,000 liabilities) is recorded as a gain on the sale. In this case, the gain is $465,000. The entry on Johnson's books would be as follows:

	Dr.	Cr.
Investment in Acquisitions, Inc., Stock	800,000	
Current Liabilities	25,000	
8% 5-Year Bonds Payable	100,000	
Cash		40,000
Marketable Investments		60,000
Inventory		100,000
Land		30,000
Buildings (net)		150,000
Equipment (net)		80,000
Gain on Sale of Business		465,000
Dr. = Cr. Check Totals	*925,000*	*925,000*

The only remaining asset of Johnson Company is the stock of Acquisitions, Inc. Johnson would typically distribute the stock received to its shareholders and cease operations.

REFLECTION

- The acquirer records all accounts of the acquiree company at fair value on the acquisition date, but adjustments are allowed during the measurement period.

- The acquisition cost includes the estimated expected value of contingent consideration (except for the issuance of additional acquirer shares).

- The acquiree removes the book values of the accounts transferred and records a gain or loss on the sale.

TAX ISSUES

5

OBJECTIVE

Demonstrate an understanding of the tax issues that arise in an acquisition.

In some acquisitions, the acquiree may have operating losses in periods prior to the acquisition. The acquirer may be able to carry these losses forward to offset its income taxes payable periods after the acquisition. This is a "deferred tax asset" to which value will be assigned. The sale of a business may be structured as either a taxable or nontaxable event, which means the seller pays taxes on any gain in a taxable exchange but defers the taxes on a gain in a nontaxable exchange. If the exchange is taxable, the acquirer records all accounts at fair value for tax purposes and gets depreciation and amortization deductions based on the fair value of the assets on the acquisition date. There may be some differences in the tax basis and recorded financial accounting amounts. If the exchange is nontaxable, the acquirer will base future amortization and depreciation on the book value of the acquiree's accounts on the acquisition date. This leads to deferred tax assets or liabilities that need to be recorded on the acquisition date.

Tax Loss Carryovers

Tax law provides that an existing company with a tax loss may first carry the loss back to the previous two years to offset income and thus receive a refund of taxes paid in the preceding years. If the loss exceeds income available in the prior 2-year period, the loss can be carried forward up to 20 years to offset future income and, therefore, reduce the taxes that otherwise would be paid. As mentioned earlier, Congress has extended the carryback period to five years for losses incurred in 2008–2009. Our examples will use a 2-year carryback period. The acquired company may have unused tax loss carryovers that it has not been able to utilize due to an absence of sufficient income in prior years. This becomes a potential benefit for the purchasing company. Tax provisions limit the amount of the net operating loss (NOL) available to the acquiring company to discourage business combinations that are motivated primarily by tax loss carryovers. The purchaser is allowed to use the acquired company's tax loss carryovers to offset its own income in the current and future periods (but not prior periods) subject to limitations contained in Internal Revenue Code Section 382.

The value of the expected future tax loss carryovers is recorded as a deferred tax asset (DTA) on the date of the acquisition. It is, however, necessary to attempt to determine whether there will be adequate future tax liabilities to support the value of the deferred tax asset. The accountant would have to consider existing evidence to make this determination. If it is likely that some or all of the deferred tax asset will not be realized, the contra account Allowance for Unrealizable Tax Assets would be used to reduce the deferred tax asset to an estimated amount to be realized.[6] This may have the practical effect of the contra account totally offsetting the deferred tax asset. The inability to record a net deferred tax asset often will result in the consideration paid for the NOL carryover being assigned to goodwill. This occurs because the price paid will exceed the value of the net assets that are allowed to be recorded.

EXAMPLE

Bergen Company had the following book and fair values on the date it was acquired by Panther Company:

Account	Book Value	Fair Value
Cash	$ 30,000	$ 30,000
Accounts Receivable	80,000	80,000
Inventory	100,000	120,000
Land	140,000	200,000
Building (net)	250,000	465,000
Equipment (net)	50,000	75,000
Patent	0	50,000
Accounts Payable	(90,000)	(90,000)
Bonds Payable	(100,000)	(100,000)
Net Assets	$ 460,000	$ 830,000

---

6 FASB ASC 740-10-30-5, *Income Tax—Overall—Initial Measurement* (Norwalk, CT , 2010).

Assume that the price paid for Bergen Company is $1,000,000. Bergen Company has tax loss carryforwards of $200,000.

The value of the tax loss carryforward is calculated as follows:

Losses that may be carried forward	$200,000
Applicable tax rate	× 40%
Potential tax savings	$ 80,000
Adjustment for amount not likely to be usable	(30,000)
Net value of tax loss carryforward	$ 50,000

Value Analysis:

Total price paid:	
Stock issued, 50,000 shares × $20 market value	$1,000,000
Fair value of net assets acquired	(830,000)
Net value of tax loss carryforward	(50,000)
Goodwill	$ 120,000

The entry to record the acquisition is as follows:

	Dr.	Cr.
To record purchase of net assets:		
Cash	30,000	
Accounts Receivable	80,000	
Inventory	120,000	
Land	200,000	
Buildings	465,000	
Equipment	75,000	
Patent	50,000	
Deferred Tax Asset	**80,000**	
Goodwill	**120,000**	
Valuation Allowance for Deferred Tax Asset		**30,000**
Accounts Payable		90,000
Bonds Payable		100,000
Common Stock ($1 par, 50,000 shares issued)		50,000
Paid-In Capital in Excess of Par ($20 per share × 50,000 shares less $50,000 assigned to par)		950,000
Dr. = Cr. Check Totals	*1,220,000*	*1,220,000*

If there is a decrease in estimate for the valuation account within one year of the acquisition date, goodwill is reduced for the same amount. Thus, if within one year, the valuation account were lowered by $20,000 (from $30,000 to $10,000), Goodwill would be credited for $20,000 as follows:

Valuation Allowance for Deferred Tax Asset	20,000	
Goodwill		20,000

However, if the adjustment is caused by events that occur after the acquisition, the credit would be to the current provision for taxes.[7] Changes in the valuation account after the 1-year period result in an adjustment to the tax provision for the period in which the new estimate is made.

---

7 FASB ASC 805-740-45-4, *Business Combinations—Income Taxes—Other Presentation Matters* (Norwalk, CT , 2010).

Tax Values in an Acquisition

There may be limitations on amounts that can be assigned to certain accounts even in a taxable exchange. For example, a fixed asset may have the following values:

Book value on the books of acquiree	$75,000
Estimated fair value for financial accounting	90,000
Basis required at acquisition for tax purposes	50,000

This would occur when the company used straight-line depreciation for financial reporting, but used accelerated depreciation for its tax returns. The asset would still be recorded at the fair value of $90,000, but a deferred tax liability (DTL) would be recorded for the lost tax deductibility equal to the tax rate (40%) times the excess of the fair value over tax value calculated as follows:

Fair value	$90,000
Tax value	50,000
Excess not deductible	40,000
Tax rate	× 40%
Deferred tax liability	$16,000

The DTL would be amortized over the depreciable life of the asset. Assuming a 5-year asset life and straight-line depreciation, the annual tax impact using a 40% tax rate would be $3,200 ($16,000/5 years), which would be recorded as follows:

Deferred Tax Liability	3,200	
Current Tax Liability		3,200

Goodwill, while not amortized for financial reporting purposes, is amortized straight-line over 15 years for tax purposes.

Nontaxable Exchange

In a nontaxable exchange, the acquirer is limited to deductions for amortization and depreciation based on the book values of the acquiree on the acquisition date. Despite this, all accounts are still recorded at full fair value, and deferred tax liability or asset accounts are recorded as follows:

Difference	Results in:
Fair value of identifiable asset exceeds book value	DTL
Book value of identifiable asset exceeds fair value	DTA
Fair value of liability exceeds book value	DTA
Book value of liability exceeds fair value	DTL

EXAMPLE

To understand the impact of a nontaxable exchange, consider an example of the acquisition of Book Company for $1,500,000. The consideration was 50,000 shares of $1 par value shares of the acquirer company. The market value of an acquirer share was $30. The tax rate is 40%. Fair values are compared to the tax basis of Book Company as shown on page 26.

Column	1	2	3	4
Account	Fair Value	Tax Basis	Fair Value in Excess of Tax Basis (Col. 1. – Col. 2)	DTA (DTL) (–40% × Col. 3)
Cash	$ 100,000	$ 100,000	$ 0	$ 0
Accounts Receivable	150,000	180,000	(30,000)	12,000
Inventory	200,000	160,000	40,000	(16,000)
Land	200,000	150,000	50,000	(20,000)
Building	600,000	450,000	150,000	(60,000)
Equipment	300,000	200,000	100,000	(40,000)
Copyrights	100,000	2,000	98,000	(39,200)
Accounts Payable	(250,000)	(250,000)	0	0
Bonds Payable	(315,000)	(300,000)	(15,000)	6,000
Net Identifiable Assets	$1,085,000	$ 692,000	$393,000	$(157,200)

Value Analysis:

Total price paid:		
Stock issued, 50,000 shares × $30 market value		$1,500,000
Fair value of net assets acquired	$1,085,000	
DTL.	157,200	
Net identifiable assets less net DTL.		927,800
Goodwill		$ 572,200

The entry to record the acquisition is as follows:

	Dr.	Cr.
To record purchase of net assets:		
Cash	100,000	
Accounts Receivable	150,000	
Inventory	200,000	
Land.	200,000	
Buildings	600,000	
Equipment	300,000	
Copyright	100,000	
Goodwill.	**572,200**	
DTL		**157,200**
Accounts Payable		250,000
Bonds Payable.		300,000
Premium on Bonds Payable		15,000
Common Stock ($1 par, 50,000 shares issued)		50,000
Paid-In Capital in Excess of Par ($30 per share × 50,000 shares less		1,450,000
$50,000 assigned to par)		
Dr. = Cr. Check Totals	*2,222,200*	*2,222,200*

While the DTL is recorded as a single amount, each component would be realized separately. The amount applicable to accounts payable would be realized as the accounts are collected; the amount applicable to inventory would be realized when the inventory is sold. The amounts applicable to the land would be deferred until the land is sold. All other amounts are amortized over the life of the accounts to which the DTA/DTL pertains.

- The acquisition may include a tax loss carryover from the acquiree which results in the recording a deferred tax asset (DTA).

- In a taxable exchange, the values used for taxation may differ from those assigned in the acquisition. Typically, lower book values will be used for depreciation in future years. This results in a deferred tax liability (DTL).

- The acquisition may be a nontaxable exchange, which means the book values will be used for taxation and fair values will be used for financial reporting. Because book values are usually lower than fair value, this also results in a DTL.

REQUIRED DISCLOSURE

Substantial disclosure requirements for an acquisition occur during the reporting period. These requirements are detailed in FASB ASC 805-10-50-2[8] and can be summarized as follows:

a. The name and description of the acquiree.
b. The acquisition date.
c. The percentage of voting equity interest acquired.
d. The primary reasons for the acquisition and the factors that contributed to the recording of goodwill (if any).
e. A qualitative description of factors that make up the goodwill recognized.
f. The acquisition date fair value of all types of consideration, including cash, other assets, contingent consideration, and debt and equity instruments issued.
g. Detailed information concerning contingent consideration, including a description of the arrangements and the range of outcomes.
h. Details concerning acquired receivables, including gross amount, fair value and the expected collections.
i. Disclosure showing amounts recorded for each major class of assets and liabilities. For the acquisition of Johnson Company for $800,000 in stock on page 18, the disclosure information would appear as follows:

Current assets	$216,000
Property, plant, and equipment	505,000
Intangible assets subject to amortization	125,000
Intangible assets not subject to amortization	0
Goodwill	95,000
Total assets acquired	$941,000
Current liabilities	$ 37,000
Long-term debt	104,000
Total liabilities assumed	$141,000
Net assets acquired	$800,000

Exhibit 1-3 is an example of an actual disclosure for the acquisition of Metavante, a Milwaukee data processing company, by Fidelity National Information Services, Inc. The allocation of the price paid included intangible assets and a large amount of goodwill.

6

O B J E C T I V E

Explain the disclosure that is required in the period in which an acquisition occurs.

---

8 IFRS for SMEs, International Accounting Standards Board, 2009, London, Section 19.

Exhibit 1-3
Fidelity National Information Services, Inc. and Subsidiaries
Notes to Consolidated Financial Statements

(6) Acquisitions and Dispositions

The results of operations and financial position of the entities acquired during the years ended December 31, 2009, 2008, and 2007 are included in the Consolidated Financial Statement from and after the date of acquisition. There were no significant acquisitions in 2008.

2009 Significant Acquisition

Metavante. On October 1, 2009, we completed the acquisition of Metavante (the "Metavante Acquisition") Metavante expands the soale of FIS core processing and payment capabilities, adds trust and wealth management services and includes the NYCE Network, a leading national EFT network, In addition, Metavante adds significant scale to treasury and cash management offerings and provides an entry into the emerging markets of healthcare and government payments. Pursuant to the Agreement and Plan of Merger (the "Metavante Merger Agreement") dated as of March 31, 2009, Metavante became a wholly-owned subsidiary of FIS, Each issued and outstanding share of Metavante common stock, par value $0.01 per share, was converted into 1.35 shares of FIS common stock. In addition, outstanding Metavanto stock options and other stock-based awards converted into comparable FIS stock options and other stock-based awards at the same conversion ratio.

The total purchase price was as following (in millions):

Value of Metavante common stook	$4,066.4
Value of Metavante stock awards	121.4
Total purchase price	$4,187.8

We have recorded a preliminary allocation of the purchase price to Metavante tangible and identifiable intangible assets acquired and liabilities assumed based on their fair values as of October 1, 2009. Goodwill has been recorded based on the amount by which the purchase price exceeds the fair value of the net assets acquired. The preliminary purchase price allocation is as follows (in millions):

Cash	$ 439.7
Trade and other receivables	237.9
Land, buildings, and equipment	119.8
Other assets	144.4
Computer software	287.7
Intangible assets	1,572.0
Goodwill	4,083.1
Liabilities assumed	(2,673.4)
Noncontroling interest	(23.4)
Total purchase price	$ 4,187.8

The preliminary allocation of the purchase price to intangible assets, including computer software and customer relationships, is based on valuations performed to determine the fair value of such assets as of the merger date. The Company is still assessing the economic characteristics of certain software projects and customer relationships. The Company expects to substantially complete this assessment during the first quarter of 2010 and may adjust the amounts recorded as of December 31, 2009 to reflect any revised evaluations. Land and building valuations are based upon appraisals performed by certified property appraisers.

j. Information on assets and liabilities arising from contingencies.
k. The goodwill that will be deductible for tax purposes.
l. Goodwill assigned to reportable segments (if any).
m. Information concerning transactions between the companies that are not recorded as part of the acquisition.
n. Disclosure of acquisition costs and issue costs associated with the transaction. This includes identifying the line item of the income statement that includes the acquisition costs.
o. Any gain resulting from the acquisition. The gain is to be disclosed as a separate line item on the income statement. The reasons for the gain must also be disclosed.
p. The fair value of the noncontrolling interest and the method used to value it.
q. The gain or loss on prior investments in a step acquisition. A step acquisition is where a controlling interest is purchased in stages (explained in Chapter 7).
r. Publicly traded firms must disclose the following performance measures:

1. Revenue and earnings of the acquiree since the acquisition date
2. Pro forma revenue and earnings had the acquisition occurred at the start of the reporting period
3. If comparative statements are issued, pro forma revenue and earnings for all prior periods for which comparative statements are issued

Exhibit 1-4 is an example of a pro forma disclosure from Merck & Co., Inc.

Exhibit 1-4
Supplemental Pro Forma Data

Schering-Plough's results of operations have been included in New Merck's financial statement for periods subsequent to the completion of the Merger. Schering-Plough contributed revenues of $3.4 billion and estimated losses of $2.2 billion to New Merck for the period from the consummation of the Merger through December 31, 2009. The following unaudited supplemental pro forma data presents consolidated information as if the Merger had been completed on January 1, 2008:

Years Ended December 31	2009	2008
Sales	$45,970.7	$46,749.6
Earnings attributable to Merck & Co., Inc.	6,069.7	3,020.4
Earnings available to Merck & Co., Inc. common shareholders	5,934.7	2,883.2
Basic earnings per common share available to common shareholders	1.91	0.92
Earning per common share assuming dilution available to common shareholders	1.90	0.92

The information included in Exhibit 1-4 is also to be included in the notes for an acquisition that occurs after the balance sheet date but prior to the issuance date of the financial statement. If the initial accounting for the acquisition is incomplete, those disclosures that could not be made and why they could not be made must be stated.

REFLECTION

• There are detailed disclosure requirements for the period in which an acquisition occurs.

• Disclosure includes pro forma amounts for revenue and earnings for the entire period and for prior periods shown in comparative statements.

GOODWILL IMPAIRMENT

Goodwill is no longer amortized for financial reporting purposes. It was amortized for up to 40 years for financial reporting prior to the issuance of FASB Statement No. 142, *Goodwill and Other Intangible Assets,* in 2001, and it still is amortized over 15 years for tax purposes. Since the issuance of FASB Statement No. 142, goodwill is now subject to *impairment testing*. Impairment testing is a procedure for testing and estimating goodwill at the end of each financial reporting period.

Five specific concerns need to be addressed to apply impairment testing:

1. Goodwill must be allocated to reporting units if the acquired company contains more than one reporting unit.
2. Methods for valuing the reporting unit must be established.
3. Impairment testing is normally done on an annual basis. There are, however, exceptions to annual testing and some cases where testing may be required between annual testing dates.
4. The procedure for determining if impairment has occurred must be established.
5. The procedure for determining the amount of the impairment loss, which is also the decrease in the goodwill amount recorded, must be established.

Allocating Goodwill to Reporting Units

In most cases, the company acquired will be made up of more than one reporting unit. For purposes of segment reporting, under FASB ASC 280-10-50-1,[9] a reporting unit is either the same level or one level lower than an operating segment. To be a reporting unit that is one level below an operating unit, both of the following criteria must be met:

◆ Segment managers measure and review performance at this level.

◆ The unit has separate financial information available and has economic characteristics that distinguish it from other units of the operating segment.

All assets and liabilities are to be allocated to the underlying reporting units. Goodwill is allocated to the reporting segments by subtracting the identifiable net assets of the unit from the estimated fair value of the entire reporting unit. The method of estimating the fair value of the reporting unit should be documented. In essence, an estimate must be made of the price that would have been paid for only the specific reporting unit.

Reporting Unit Valuation Procedures

The steps in the reporting unit measurement process will be illustrated with the following example of the acquisition of Lakeland Company, which is a purchase of a single operating unit.

    A. Determine the valuation method and estimated fair value of the identifiable assets, goodwill, and all liabilities of the reporting unit.

        At the time of acquisition, the valuations of Lakeland Company's identifiable assets, liabilities, and goodwill were as shown on page 31. [The asterisk (*) indicates numbers have been rounded for presentation purposes.]

---

9 FASB ASC 280-10-50-1, *Segment Reporting—Overall—Disclosure* (Norwalk, CT , 2010).

Assets	Comments	Valuation Method	Fair Value
Inventory available	Replacement cost	Market replacement cost for similar items	$ 45,000
Accounts receivable	Recorded amount is adjusted for estimated bad debts	Aging schedule used for valuation	28,000
Land	Per-acre value well established	Five acres at $10,000 per acre	50,000
Building	Most reliable measure is rent potential	Rent estimated at $20,000 per year for 20 years, discounted at 14% return for similar properties; present value of $132,463 reduced for $50,000 land value	80,000*
Equipment	Cost of replacement capacity can be estimated	Estimated purchase cost of equipment with similar capacity	50,000
Patent	Recorded by seller at only legal cost; has significant future value	Added profit made possible by patent is $11,600 per year for four years; discounted at risk adjusted rate for similar investments of 20% per year; PV equals $30,029	30,000*
Brand-name copyright	Not recorded by seller	Estimated sales value	40,000
Current liabilities	Recorded amounts are accurate	Recorded value	(5,000)
Bonds payable	Specified interest rate is above market rate	Discount at market interest rate	(21,000)
Net identifiable assets at fair value			$297,000
Price paid for reporting unit			360,000
Goodwill	Believed to exist based on projected future cash flows	Implied by price paid	$ 63,000

*Rounded to nearest thousands to reflect nature of estimate.

B. Measure the fair value of the reporting unit and document assumptions and models used to make the measurement. This measurement is made to:

◆ Serve as a test for the amount of goodwill recorded for the reporting unit.

◆ Establish the procedure to be used to value the reporting unit in later periods.

If the stock of the reporting unit is publicly traded, the market capitalization of the reporting unit may be indicative of its fair value, but it need not be the only measure considered. The price paid to acquire all of the shares or a controlling interest could exceed the product of the fair value per share times the number of shares outstanding. A common method used to estimate fair value is to determine the present value of the unit's future cash flows. The following is an example of that approach.

Assumptions:

1. The reporting unit will provide operating cash flows, net of tax, of $40,000 during the next reporting period.
2. Operating cash flows will increase at the rate of 10% per year for the next four reporting periods and then will remain steady for 15 more years.
3. Forecast cash flows will be adjusted for capital expenditures needed to maintain market position and productive capacity.
4. Cash flows defined as net of cash from operations less capital expenditures will be discounted at an after-tax discount rate of 12%. An annual rate of 12% is a reasonable risk-adjusted rate of return for investments of this type.
5. An estimate of salvage value (net of tax effect of gains or losses) of the assets at the end of 20 years will be used to approximate salvage value. This is a conservative assumption, since the unit may be operated after that period.

Schedule of net tax cash flows:

Year	Net of Tax Operating Flow*	Capital Expenditure	Salvage Value	Net Cash Flow
1	$40,000			$ 40,000
2	44,000			44,000
3	48,400			48,400
4	53,240			53,240
5	58,564	$(25,000)		33,564
6	58,564			58,564
7	58,564			58,564
8	58,564			58,564
9	58,564			58,564
10	58,564	(30,000)		28,564
11	58,564			58,564
12	58,564			58,564
13	58,564			58,564
14	58,564			58,564
15	58,564	(35,000)		23,564
16	58,564			58,564
17	58,564			58,564
18	58,564			58,564
19	58,564			58,564
20	58,564		$75,000	133,564

Net present value at 12% annual rate				$376,173

*Reflects assumed 10% annual increase in years 2–5.

C. Compare fair value of reporting unit with amounts assigned to identifiable net assets plus goodwill.

Estimated fair value of reporting unit	$376,173
Price paid for reporting unit	360,000
Excess of fair value of reporting unit over net assets	**$16,173**

An excess of the fair value of the reporting unit over the value of the net assets indicated that the price paid was reasonable and below a theoretical maximum purchase price. It requires no adjustment of assigned values. If, however, the fair value of the net assets, including goodwill, exceeds the fair value of the reporting unit, the model used to determine the fair value of the reporting unit should be reassessed. If the re-estimation of the values assigned to the net assets, including goodwill, and the reporting unit still indicates an excess of the value of the net assets, including goodwill, over the value of the reporting unit, goodwill is to be tested for impairment. This would likely result in an impairment loss being recorded on the goodwill at the time of the acquisition.

Frequency of Impairment Testing

The normal procedure is to perform impairment testing of goodwill on an annual basis. Testing need not be done at period-end; it can be done on a consistent, scheduled, annual basis during the reporting period.

The annual impairment test is not needed if *all* the following criteria are met:

◆ The assets and liabilities of the unit have not significantly changed since the last valuation;

◆ The last calculation of the unit's fair value far exceeded book value, thus making it unlikely that the unit's fair value could now be less than book value; and

◆ No adverse events indicating that the fair value of the unit has fallen below book value have occurred since the last valuation.

There may also be instances when goodwill must be impairment tested sooner than the normal annual measurement date. These situations include the occurrence of an adverse event that could diminish the unit's fair value, the likelihood that the unit will be disposed of, the impairment of a group of the unit's assets (under FASB Statement No. 121), or a goodwill impairment loss that is recorded in a higher-level organization of which the unit is a part.

Impairment Testing in Later Periods

Goodwill is considered to be impaired if the implied fair value of the reporting unit is less than the *carrying value* of the reporting unit's net assets (*including* goodwill). Remember, since the acquired net assets were recorded at their fair values as of the acquisition date, it is the subsequent carrying (book) value based on those amounts that is used for later periods of impairment testing.

Let us revisit the Lakeland Company example. Assume that the following new estimates were made at the end of the first year:

Estimated implied fair value of the reporting unit, based on analysis of projected cash flow (discounted at 12% annual rate)	$320,000
Existing net book value (including values assigned on acquisition date) of the reporting unit (including goodwill)	345,000

Since the recorded net book value of the reporting unit exceeds its implied fair value, goodwill is considered to be impaired. If the estimated fair value exceeds the existing book value, there is no impairment, and there is no need to proceed to calculate a goodwill impairment loss.

Goodwill Impairment Loss in Later Periods

If the above test indicates impairment, the impairment loss must be estimated. **The impairment loss for goodwill is the excess of the *implied fair value* of the reporting unit over the fair value of the reporting unit's identifiable net assets (*excluding* goodwill) on the impairment date.** These are the values that would be assigned to those accounts if the reporting unit were purchased on the date of impairment measurement.

For our example, the following calculation was made for the impairment loss:

Estimated implied fair value of reporting unit, based on cash flow analysis (discounted at a 12% annual rate)	$320,000
Less: Fair value of net assets on the date of measurement, exclusive of goodwill	285,000
Implied fair value of goodwill	$ 35,000
Existing recorded goodwill	63,000
Estimated impairment loss	$ (28,000)

The following journal entry would be made:

Goodwill Impairment Loss	28,000	
Goodwill		28,000

The impairment loss will be shown as a separate line item within the operating section unless it is identified with a discontinued operation, in which case, it is part of the gain or loss on disposal. **Once goodwill is written down, it cannot be adjusted to a higher amount.**

Two important issues must be understood at this point.

1. The **impairment test** compares the implied fair value of the reporting unit, $320,000, to the unit's **book value (including goodwill), $345,000.** The **impairment loss calculation** compares the implied fair value of the reporting unit, $320,000, to the unit's **estimated fair values (excluding goodwill), $285,000,** on the impairment date.

2. While fair values of net assets are used to measure the impairment loss, they are not recorded. The existing book values on the impairment date remain in place (unless they are adjusted for their own impairment loss).

Significant disclosure requirements for goodwill exist in any period in which goodwill changes. A note must accompany the balance sheet in any period that has a change in goodwill. The note would explain the goodwill acquired, the goodwill impairment losses, and the goodwill written off as part of a disposal of a reporting unit. It is further required that information be included that provides the details of any impairment loss recorded during the period. The information would include the reporting unit involved, the circumstances leading to the impairment, and the possibility of further adjustments.

REFLECTION

- Procedures must be established for estimating goodwill.

- Goodwill is subject to impairment testing.

- When impaired, the goodwill is reduced to a lower estimated value.

8

OBJECTIVE

Explain special and different rules that apply to acquisitions by companies that are not publicly traded.

SPECIAL METHODS FOR SMALLER COMPANIES

In July 2009, the International Accounting Standards Board (IASB) issued special standards designed for use by small and medium-sized entities (SMEs).[10] The AICPA Governing Board recognizes the IASB as an accounting standards-setting body. This allows CPAs to report using financial accounting standards in conformity with International Financial Reporting Standards, which includes IFRS for SMEs. The use of these standards is really not based on size; rather, it is based on the source of the company's equity and debt financing. The standards are available for companies that issue financial statements to external users but do not have publicly traded bonds or stock. External users would include bank regulatory agencies.

Acquisition Costs and Assigning Value

SMEs do not expense acquisition-related costs. Instead, SMEs include these costs in the purchase cost for the entity acquired. There is no difference in accounting for the costs of issuing securities used as consideration. They are deducted from the value assigned to the securities issued.

There are some differences concerning contingent liabilities, employee benefit plans, and deferred taxes. The major difference is that **goodwill is amortized** instead of being subject to impairment adjustment. If the company cannot make a reliable estimate of the amortization period, the life is presumed to be 10 years.

REFLECTION

- SMEs may use special standards available to them under IFRS. The major difference in this chapter is that acquisition costs are expensed and goodwill is amortized.

---

10 IFRS for SMEs, International Accounting Standards Board, 2009, London, Section 19.

APPENDIX: ESTIMATING THE VALUE OF GOODWILL

9
OBJECTIVE

Estimate the value of goodwill.

An acquirer may attempt to forecast the future income of a target company in order to arrive at a logical purchase price. Goodwill is often, at least in part, a payment for above-normal expected future earnings. A forecast of future income may start by projecting recent years' incomes into the future. When this is done, it is important to factor out "one-time" occurrences that will not likely recur in the near future. Examples would include extraordinary items, discontinued operations, or any other unusual event. Expected future income is compared to "normal" income. Normal income is the product of the appropriate industry rate of return on assets times the fair value of the gross assets (no deduction for liabilities) of the acquired company. Gross assets include specifically identifiable intangible assets such as patents and copyrights but do not include existing goodwill. The following calculation of earnings in excess of normal might be made for the Johnson Company example on page 16:

Expected average future income		$100,000
Less normal return on assets:		
Fair value of total identifiable assets	$846,000	
Industry normal rate of return	× 10%	
Normal return on assets		84,600
Expected annual earnings in excess of normal		$ 15,400

Several methods use the expected annual earnings in excess of normal to estimate goodwill. A common approach is to pay for a given number of years of excess earnings. For instance, Acquisitions, Inc., might offer to pay for four years of excess earnings, which would total $61,600 ($15,400 × 4 years). Alternatively, the excess earnings could be viewed as an annuity. The most optimistic purchaser might expect the excess earnings to continue forever. If so, the buyer might capitalize the excess earnings as a perpetuity at the normal industry rate of return according to the following formula:

$$\text{Goodwill} = \frac{\text{Annual Excess Earnings}}{\text{Industry Normal Rate of Return}}$$
$$= \frac{\$15,400}{0.10}$$
$$= \$154,000$$

Another estimation method views the factors that produce excess earnings to be of limited duration, such as 10 years, for example. This purchaser would calculate goodwill as follows:

Goodwill = Discounted present value of a $15,400-per-year annuity for 10 years at 10%

      = $15,400 × 10-year, 10% present value of annuity factor

      = $15,400 × 6.1446

      = $94,627

Other analysts view the normal industry earning rate to be appropriate only for identifiable assets and not goodwill. Thus, they might capitalize excess earnings at a higher rate of return to reflect the higher risk inherent in goodwill.

All calculations of goodwill are only estimates used to assist in the determination of the price to be paid for a company. For example, Acquisitions might add the $94,627 estimate of goodwill to the $705,000 fair value of Johnson's other net assets to arrive at a tentative maximum price of $799,627. However, estimates of goodwill may differ from actual negotiated goodwill. If the final agreed-upon price for Johnson's net assets was $790,000, the actual negotiated goodwill would be $85,000, which is the price paid less the fair value of the net assets acquired.

REFLECTION

- Goodwill estimates are based on an estimate of predicted income in excess of normal.

- Predicted excess income is typically discounted either as perpetuity or as a limited term annuity.

UNDERSTANDING THE ISSUES

1. Identify each of the following business combinations as being vertical-backward, vertical-forward, horizontal, product extension, market extension, or conglomerate:

   a. An inboard marine engine manufacturer is acquired by an outboard engine manufacturer.
   b. A cosmetics manufacturer acquires a drug store chain.
   c. A financial holding company acquires a mail order movie rental company.
   d. A computer manufacturer acquires a chip manufacturer.
   e. The Walt Disney Company acquires a broadcasting company.
   f. A California-based electric utility acquires a Colorado electric utility company.

2. Abrams Company is a sole proprietorship. The book value of its identifiable net assets is $400,000, and the fair value of the same net assets is $600,000. It is agreed that the business is worth $850,000. What advantage might there be for the seller if the company is exchanged for the common stock of another corporation as opposed to receiving cash? Consider both the immediate and future impact.

3. Major Corporation is acquiring Abrams Company by issuing its common stock in a nontaxable exchange. Major is issuing common stock with a fair value of $850,000 for net identifiable assets with book and fair values of $400,000 and $600,000, respectively. What values will Major assign to the identifiable assets, to goodwill, and to the deferred tax liability? Assume a 40% tax rate.

4. Panther Company is about to acquire a 100% interest in Snake Company. Snake has identifiable net assets with book and fair values of $300,000 and $500,000, respectively. As payment, Panther will issue common stock with a fair value of $750,000. How would the transaction be recorded if the acquisition is:

   a. An acquisition of net assets?
   b. An acquisition of Snake's common stock and Snake remains a separate legal entity?

5. Puncho Company is acquiring the net assets of Semos Company in exchange for common stock valued at $900,000. The Semos identifiable net assets have book and fair values of $400,000 and $800,000, respectively. Compare accounting for the acquisition (including assignment of the price paid) by Puncho with accounting for the sale by Semos.

6. Panther Company is acquiring the net assets of Sharon Company. The book and fair values of Sharon's accounts are as follows:

Accounts	Book	Fair
Current Assets	$100,000	$120,000
Land	50,000	80,000
Building and Equipment	300,000	400,000
Customer List	0	20,000
Liabilities	100,000	100,000

What values will be assigned to current assets, land, building and equipment, the customer list, liabilities, goodwill, and gain under each of the following acquisition price scenarios?

a. $800,000
b. $450,000

7. Pam Company acquires the net assets of Jam Company for an agreed-upon price of $900,000 on July 1, 2011. The value is tentatively assigned as follows:

Current assets	$ 100,000
Land	50,000
Equipment	200,000 (5-year life)
Building	500,000 (20-year life)
Current liabilities	(150,000)
Goodwill	200,000

Values are subject to change during the measurement period. Depreciation is taken to the nearest month. The measurement period expires on July 1, 2012, at which time the fair values of the equipment and building as of the acquisition date are revised to $180,000 and $550,000, respectively.

At the end of 2012, what adjustments are needed for the financial statements for the period ending December 31, 2011 and 2012?

8. Harms acquires Blake on January 1, 2011, for $1,000,000. The amount of $800,000 is assigned to identifiable net assets. Goodwill is being impairment tested on December 31, 2015. There have not been any prior impairment adjustments. The following values apply on that date:

Estimated fair value of the Blake operating unit	$1,200,000
Fair value of net identifiable assets (excluding goodwill)	1,120,000
Book value of net identifiable assets (including goodwill)	1,250,000

The book values include those resulting from assignment of fair value to accounts included in the January 1, 2011, acquisition.

Is goodwill impaired? If it is, what is the amount of the impairment adjustment?

9. What are the accounting ramifications of each of the three following situations involving the payment of contingent consideration in an acquisition?

a. P Company issues 100,000 shares of its $50 fair value ($1 par) common stock as payment to buy S Company on January 1, 2011. P agrees to pay $100,000 cash two years later if S income exceeds an income target. The target is exceeded.
b. P Company issues 100,000 shares of its $50 fair value ($1 par) common stock as payment to buy S Company on January 1, 2011. P agrees to issue 10,000 additional shares of its stock two years later if S income exceeds an income target. The target is exceeded.
c. P Company issues 100,000 shares of its $50 fair value ($1 par) common stock as payment to buy S Company on January 1, 2011. P agrees to issue 5,000 additional shares two years later if the fair value of P shares falls below $50 per share. Two years later, the stock has a fair value below $50, and added shares are issued to S.

10. P Company acquired the S Company for an agreed value of $900,000 and issues its common stock to make the deal. The fair value of the Company S net identifiable assets is $800,000. The issue costs of the stock used for payment is $50,000. If P Company was eligible to use IFRS for SME's and decided to do so, how would the recording of the transaction differ from U.S. GAAP?

EXERCISES

Exercise 1 *(LO 2, 3, 4)* **Asset versus stock acquisition.** Barton Company is contemplating the acquisition of the net assets of Crowley Company for $850,000 cash. To complete the transaction, acquisition costs are $15,000. The balance sheet of Crowley Company on the purchase date is as follows:

Crowley Company
Balance Sheet
December 31, 2011

Assets		Liabilities and Equity	
Current assets	$ 80,000	Liabilities	$100,000
Land.	50,000	Common stock ($10 par). . . .	100,000
Building	450,000	Paid-in capital in excess of par	150,000
Accumulated depreciation—building . . .	(200,000)	Retained earnings	230,000
Equipment	300,000		
Accumulated depreciation—equipment .	(100,000)		
Total assets.	$ 580,000	Total liabilities and equity .	$580,000

The following fair values have been obtained for Crowley's identifiable assets and liabilities:

Current assets	$100,000
Land.	90,000
Building	300,000
Equipment	275,000
Liabilities	102,000

1. Record the acquisition of the net assets of Crowley Company on Barton Company's books.
2. Record the sale of the net assets on the books of Crowley Company.
3. Record the acquisition of 100% of the common stock of Crowley Company on Barton's books. Crowley Company will remain a separate legal entity.

Exercise 2 *(LO 3, 4)* **Bargain acquisition.** Norton Corporation agrees to acquire the net assets of Payco Corporation. Just prior to the acquisition, Payco's balance sheet is as follows:

Payco Corporation
Balance Sheet
January 1, 2011

Assets		Liabilities and Equity		
Accounts receivable	$200,000	Current liabilities	$ 80,000	
Inventory	270,000	Mortgage payable	250,000	$330,000
Equipment (net)	100,000	Stockholders' equity:		
		Common stock ($10 par).	$100,000	
		Retained earnings	140,000	240,000
Total assets.	$570,000	Total liabilities and equity		$570,000

Fair values agree with book values except for the equipment, which has an estimated fair value of $40,000. Also, it has been determined that brand-name copyrights have an estimated value of $15,000. Norton Corporation pays $25,000 in acquisition costs to consummate the transaction.

Record the acquisition on the books of Norton Corporation assuming the cash paid to Payco Corporation is $160,000.

Suggestion: Use value analysis to guide your calculations and entries.

Exercise 3 *(LO 3, 4)* **Acquisition with goodwill.** Smyth Company is acquired by Radar Corporation on July 1, 2011. Radar exchanges 60,000 shares of its $5 par stock, with a fair value of $20 per share, for the net assets of Smyth Company.

Radar incurs the following costs as a result of this transaction:

Acquisition costs	$25,000
Stock registration and issuance costs.	10,000
Total costs	$35,000

The balance sheet of Smyth Company, on the day of the acquisition, is as follows:

Smyth Company
Balance Sheet
July 1, 2011

Assets			Liabilities and Equity		
Cash		$ 100,000	Current liabilities	$ 80,000	
Inventory		300,000	Bonds payable	550,000	$ 630,000
Property, plant, and equipment:			Stockholders' equity:		
Land	$200,000		Common stock	$200,000	
Buildings (net)	250,000		Paid-in capital in excess of par . . .	100,000	
Equipment (net)	200,000	650,000	Retained earnings	120,000	420,000
Total assets		$1,050,000	Total liabilities and equity		$1,050,000

The appraised fair values as of July 1, 2011, is as follows:

Inventory	$250,000
Equipment	220,000
Land	180,000
Buildings	300,000
Current liabilities	80,000
Bonds payable	410,000

Record the acquisition of Smyth Company on the books of Radar Corporation.

Exercise 4 *(LO 3, 4)* **Acquisition with special valuations.** Pederson Company acquires the net assets of Shelby Company by issuing 100,000 of its $1 par value shares of common stock. The shares have a fair value of $20 each. Just prior to the acquisition, Shelby's balance sheet is as follows:

Shelby Company
Balance Sheet
January 1, 2011

Assets		Liabilities and Equity		
Accounts receivable	$100,000	Current liabilities	$ 80,000	
Inventory	210,000	Bonds payable	200,000	$280,000
Equipment (net)	100,000	Stockholders' equity:		
Land	200,000	Common stock ($1 par)	$ 10,000	
Building (net)	300,000	Retained earnings	620,000	630,000
Total assets.	$910,000	Total liabilities and equity		$910,000

Fair values agree with book values except for the building, which is appraised at $450,000. The following additional information is available:

◆ The equipment will be sold for an estimated price of $200,000. A 10% commission will be paid to a broker.

◆ A major R&D project is underway. The accumulated costs are $56,000, and the estimated value of the work is $90,000.

◆ A warranty attaches to products sold in the past. The estimated future repair costs under the warranty are $40,000.

◆ Shelby has a customer list that has value. It is estimated that the list will provide additional income of $100,000 for three years. An intangible asset such as this is valued at a 20% rate of return.

Record the acquisition of Shelby Company on the books of Pederson Company. Provide calculations where needed.

Exercise 5 *(LO 4)* **Contingent consideration.** Gull Company purchased the net assets of Hart Company on January 1, 2011, and made the following entry to record the purchase:

Current Assets	100,000	
Equipment	150,000	
Land	50,000	
Buildings	300,000	
Goodwill	100,000	
Liabilities		80,000
Common Stock ($1 par)		100,000
Paid-In Capital in Excess of Par		520,000

Make the required entry on January 1, 2013, for each of the following independent contingency agreements:

1. An additional cash payment will be made on January 1, 2013, equal to twice the amount by which average annual earnings of the Hart Division exceed $25,000 per year, prior to January 1, 2013. Net income was $50,000 in 2011 and $60,000 in 2012. Assume that the liabilities recorded on January 1, 2011, included an estimated contingent liability recorded at an estimated amount of $40,000.
2. Added shares will be issued on January 1, 2013, equal in value to twice the amount by which average annual earnings of the Hart Division exceed $25,000 per year, prior to January 1, 2013. Net income was $50,000 in 2011 and $60,000 in 2012. The market price of the shares on January 1, 2013, will be $5.
3. Added shares will be issued on January 1, 2013, to compensate for any fall in the value of Gull common stock below $6 per share. The settlement will cure the deficiency by issuing added shares based on their fair value on January 1, 2013. The market price of the shares on January 1, 2013, will be $4.

Exercise 6 *(LO 4)* **Measurement period.** Avery Company acquires the net assets of Iowa Company on July 1, 2011. The net assets acquired include plant assets that are provisionally estimated to have a fair value of $600,000 with a 10-year usable life and no salvage value. Depreciation is recorded based on months in service. The remaining unallocated amount of the price paid is $300,000, which is recorded as goodwill.

At the end of 2011, Avery prepares the following statements (includes Iowa Company for the last six months):

Balance Sheet			
Current assets	$ 300,000	Current liabilities	$ 300,000
Equipment (net)	600,000	Bonds payable	500,000
Plant assets (net)	1,600,000	Common stock ($1 par)	50,000
Goodwill	300,000	Paid-in capital in excess of par	1,300,000
		Retained earnings	650,000
Total assets	$2,800,000	Total liabilities and equity	$2,800,000

Summary Income Statement

Sales revenue		$800,000
Cost of goods sold		520,000
Gross profit		$280,000
Operating expenses	$150,000	
Depreciation expense	80,000	230,000
Net income		$ 50,000

In March 2012, the final estimated fair value of the acquired plant assets is $700,000 with no change in the estimate of useful life or salvage value.

1. Prepare any journal entries required in March 2012.
2. Prepare the revised balance sheet and income statement for 2011 that will be included in the 2012 comparative statements.

Exercise 7 *(LO 5)* **Deferred tax liability.** Your client, Lewison International, has informed you that it has reached an agreement with Herro Company to acquire all of Herro's assets. This transaction will be accomplished through the issue of Lewison's common stock.

After your examination of the financial statements and the acquisition agreement, you have discovered the following important facts.

The Lewison common stock issued has a fair value of $800,000. The fair value of Herro's assets, net of all liabilities, is $700,000. All asset book values equal their fair values except for one machine valued at $200,000. This machine was originally purchased two years ago by Herro for $180,000. This machine has been depreciated using the straight-line method with an assumed useful life of 10 years and no salvage value. The acquisition is to be considered a tax-free exchange for tax purposes.

Assuming a 30% tax rate, what amounts will be recorded for the machine, deferred tax liability, and goodwill?

Exercise 8 *(LO 5)* **Tax loss carryover.** Lakecraft Company has the following balance sheet on December 31, 2011, when it is acquired for $950,000 in cash by Argo Corporation:

Lakecraft Company
Balance Sheet
December 31, 2011

Assets		Liabilities and Equity		
Current assets	$100,000	Current liabilities		$ 60,000
Equipment (net)	200,000	Stockholders' equity:		
Building (net)	270,000	Common stock ($5 par)	$100,000	
		Retained earnings	410,000	510,000
Total assets	$570,000	Total liabilities and equity		$570,000

All assets have fair values equal to their book values. The combination is structured as a tax-free exchange. Lakecraft Company has a tax loss carryforward of $300,000, which it has not recorded. The balance of the $300,000 tax loss carryover is considered fully realizable. Argo is taxed at a rate of 30%.

Record the acquisition of Lakecraft Company by Argo Corporation.

Exercise 9 *(LO 7)* **Goodwill impairment.** Anton Company acquired the net assets of Hair Company on January 1, 2011, for $600,000. Using a business valuation model, the estimated value of Anton Company was $650,000 immediately after the acquisition. The fair value of Anton's net assets was $400,000.

1. What amount of goodwill was recorded by Anton Company when it acquired Hair Company?

2. Using the information on page 41, answer the questions posed in the following two independent situations:

   a. On December 31, 2012, there were indications that goodwill might have been impaired. At that time, the existing recorded book value of Anton Company's net assets, including goodwill, was $500,000. The fair value of the net assets, exclusive of goodwill, was estimated to be $340,000. The value of the business was estimated to be $520,000. Is goodwill impaired? If so, what adjustment is needed?

   b. On December 31, 2014, there were indications that goodwill might have been impaired. At that time, the existing recorded book value of Anton Company's net assets, including goodwill, was $450,000. The fair value of the net assets, exclusive of goodwill, was estimated to be $340,000. The value of the business was estimated to be $400,000. Is goodwill impaired? If so, what adjustment is needed?

APPENDIX EXERCISE

Exercise 1A-1 *(LO 9)* **Estimating goodwill.** Green Company is considering acquiring the assets of Gold Corporation by assuming Gold's liabilities and by making a cash payment. Gold Corporation has the following balance sheet on the date negotiations occur:

Gold Corporation
Balance Sheet
January 1, 2016

Assets		Liabilities and Equity	
Accounts receivable	$100,000	Total liabilities	$200,000
Inventory	100,000	Capital stock ($10 par)	100,000
Land	100,000	Paid-in capital in excess of par	200,000
Building (net)	220,000	Retained earnings	300,000
Equipment (net)	280,000		
Total assets	$800,000	Total liabilities and equity	$800,000

Appraisals indicate that the inventory is undervalued by $25,000, the building is undervalued by $80,000, and the equipment is overstated by $30,000. Past earnings have been considered above average and were as follows:

Year	Net Income
2011	$ 90,000
2012	110,000
2013	120,000
2014	140,000*
2015	130,000

*Includes a nonrecurring gain of $40,000.

It is assumed that the average operating income of the past five years will continue. In this industry, the average return on assets is 12% on the fair value of the total identifiable assets.

1. Prepare an estimate of goodwill based on each of the following assumptions:

   a. The purchasing company paid for five years of excess earnings.
   b. Excess earnings will continue indefinitely and are to be capitalized at the industry normal return.
   c. Excess earnings will continue for only five years and should be capitalized at a higher rate of 16%, which reflects the risk applicable to goodwill.

2. Determine the actual goodwill recorded if Green pays $690,000 cash for the net assets of Gold Corporation and assumes all existing liabilities.

PROBLEMS

Problem 1-1 *(LO 3)* **Purchase of two companies with goodwill.** Bar Corporation has been looking to expand its operations and has decided to acquire the assets of Vicker Company and Kendal Company. Bar will issue 30,000 shares of its $10 par common stock to acquire the net assets of Vicker Company and will issue 15,000 shares to acquire the net assets of Kendal Company.

Vicker and Kendal have the following balance sheets as of December 31, 2011:

Assets	Vicker	Kendal
Accounts receivable	$ 200,000	$ 80,000
Inventory	150,000	85,000
Property, plant, and equipment:		
Land	150,000	50,000
Buildings	500,000	300,000
Accumulated depreciation	(150,000)	(110,000)
Total assets	$ 850,000	$ 405,000

Liabilities and Equity	Vicker	Kendal
Current liabilities	$160,000	$ 55,000
Bonds payable	100,000	100,000
Stockholders' equity:		
Common stock ($10 par)	300,000	100,000
Retained earnings	290,000	150,000
Total liabilities and equity	$850,000	$405,000

The following fair values are agreed upon by the firms:

Assets	Vicker	Kendal
Inventory	$190,000	$100,000
Land	300,000	80,000
Buildings	450,000	400,000
Bonds payable	90,000	95,000

Bar's stock is currently trading at $40 per share. Bar will incur $5,000 of acquisition costs in acquiring Vicker and $4,000 of acquisition costs in acquiring Kendal. Bar will also incur $15,000 of registration and issuance costs for the shares issued in both acquisitions.

Bar's stockholders' equity is as follows:

Common stock ($10 par)	$1,200,000
Paid-in capital in excess of par	800,000
Retained earnings	750,000

Record the acquisitions on the books of Bar Corporation. Value analysis is suggested to guide your work. ◄ ◄ ◄ ◄ ◄ **Required**

Problem 1-2 *(LO 3, 4)* **Value analysis, alternative prices.** Brass Corporation agrees to acquire the net assets of Warn Corporation on January 1, 2011. Warn has the following balance sheet on the date of acquisition:

Warn Corporation
Balance Sheet
January 1, 2011

Assets		Liabilities and Equity	
Accounts receivable	$ 79,000	Current liabilities	$145,000
Inventory	112,000	Bonds payable	100,000
Other current assets	55,000	Common stock	200,000
Equipment (net)	294,000	Paid-in capital in excess of par . . .	50,000
Trademark	30,000	Retained earnings	75,000
Total assets	$570,000	Total liabilities and equity	$570,000

An appraiser determines that in-process R&D exists and has an estimated value of $14,000. The appraisal indicates that the following assets have fair values that differ from their book values:

	Fair Value
Inventory	$120,000
Equipment	340,000
Trademark	30,000

Required ▶ ▶ ▶ ▶ ▶   Use value analysis to prepare the entry on the books of Brass Corporation to acquire the net assets of Warn Corporation under each of the following purchase price scenarios:

1. Purchase price is $550,000.
2. Purchase price is $350,000.

Problem 1-3 *(LO 3, 4)* **Alternate consideration, bargain.** Kiln Corporation is considering the acquisition of Williams Incorporated. Kiln has asked you, its accountant, to evaluate the various offers it might make to Williams Incorporated. The December 31, 2011, balance sheet of Williams is as follows:

Williams Incorporated
Balance Sheet
December 31, 2011

Assets			Liabilities and Equity		
Current assets:			Accounts payable		$ 40,000
Accounts receivable	$ 50,000				
Inventory	300,000				
		$350,000	Stockholders' equity:		
Noncurrent assets:			Common stock	$ 40,000	
Land	$ 20,000		Paid-in capital in excess of par . . .	110,000	
Building (net)	70,000	90,000	Retained earnings	250,000	400,000
Total assets		$440,000	Total liabilities and equity		$440,000

The following fair values differ from existing book values:

Inventory	$250,000
Land	40,000
Building	120,000

Record the acquisition entry for Kiln Corporation that would result under each of the alternative offers. Value analysis is suggested. ◄ ◄ ◄ ◄ ◄ **Required**

1. Kiln Corporation issues 20,000 of its $10 par common stock with a fair value of $25 per share for the net assets of Williams Incorporated.
2. Kiln Corporation pays $385,000 in cash.

Problem 1-4 *(LO 3, 4)* **Revaluation of assets.** Jack Company is a corporation that was organized on July 1, 2011. The June 30, 2016, balance sheet for Jack is as follows:

Assets

Investments		$ 400,500
Accounts receivable	$1,250,000	
Allowance for doubtful accounts	(300,000)	950,000
Inventory		1,500,000
Prepaid insurance		18,000
Land.....................................		58,000
Machinery and equipment (net)		1,473,500
Goodwill		100,000
Total assets...........................		$4,500,000

Liabilities and Equity

Current liabilities	$1,475,000
Common stock ($10 par)....................	1,200,000
Retained earnings	1,825,000
Total liabilities and equity	$4,500,000

The experience of other companies over the last several years indicates that the machinery and equipment can be sold at 130% of its book value.

An analysis of the accounts receivable indicates that the realizable value is $925,000. An independent appraisal made in June 2016 values the land at $70,000. Using the lower-of-cost-or-market rule, inventory is to be restated at $1,200,000.

Calway Corporation plans to exchange 18,000 of its shares for the 120,000 Jack shares. During June 2016, the fair value of a share of Calway Corporation is $270. Acquisition costs are $12,000.

The stockholders' equity account balances of Calway Corporation as of June 30, 2011, are as follows:

Common stock ($10 par)..	$2,000,000
Paid-in capital in excess of par	580,000
Retained earnings	2,496,400
Total stockholders' equity	$5,076,400

Record the acquisition of Jack Company by Calway on July 1, 2016. Use value analysis to support the acquisition entries. ◄ ◄ ◄ ◄ ◄ **Required**

Problem 1-5 *(LO 3, 4)* **Cash purchase with goodwill.** Tweeden Corporation is contemplating the acquisition of the net assets of Sylvester Corporation in anticipation of expanding its operations. The balance sheet of Sylvester Corporation on December 31, 2011, is as follows:

Sylvester Corporation
Balance Sheet
December 31, 2011

Current assets:			**Current liabilities:**		
Notes receivable	$ 24,000		Accounts payable	$ 45,000	
Accounts receivable	56,000		Payroll and benefit-related liabilities	12,500	
Inventory	31,000				
Other current assets.	18,000		Debt maturing in one year	10,000	
Total current assets.		$129,000	Total current liabilities		$ 67,500
Investments		65,000			
Fixed assets:			**Other liabilities:**		
Land.	$ 32,000		Long-term debt.	$248,000	
Building	245,000		Payroll and benefit-related liabilities	156,000	
Equipment	387,000				
Total fixed assets		664,000	Total other liabilities.		404,000
Intangibles:			**Stockholders' equity:**		
Goodwill	$ 45,000		Common stock.	$100,000	
Patents	23,000		Paid-in capital in excess of par	250,000	
Trade names	10,000		Retained earnings	114,500	
Total intangibles		78,000	Total equity		464,500
Total assets		$936,000	Total liabilities and equity		$936,000

An appraiser for Tweeden determined the fair values of Sylvester's assets and liabilities to be as shown below.

Assets		Liabilities	
Notes receivable	$ 24,000	Accounts payable	$ 45,000
Accounts receivable	56,000	Payroll and benefit-related liabilities—current.	12,500
Inventory	30,000		
Other current assets.	15,000	Debt maturing in one year	10,000
Investments	63,000		
Land.	55,000	Long-term debt.	248,000
Building	275,000	Payroll and benefit-related liabilities—long-term. . .	156,000
Equipment	426,000		
Goodwill	—		
Patents	20,000		
Trade names	15,000		

The agreed-upon purchase price is $580,000 in cash. Acquisition costs paid in cash total $20,000.

Required ▶ ▶ ▶ ▶ ▶   Using the above information, do value analysis and prepare the entry on the books of Tweeden Corporation to acquire the net assets of Sylvester Corporation on December 31, 2011.

Problem 1-6 *(LO 3, 4)* **Acquisition with contingent consideration.** Hite Corporation is contemplating the acquisition of Smith Company's net assets on December 31, 2011. It is considering making an offer, which would include a cash payout of $200,000 along with giving 15,000 shares of its $2 par value common stock that is currently selling for $20 per share. Hite also agrees that it will pay an additional $50,000 on January 1, 2014, if the average net income of Smith's business unit exceeds $80,000 for 2012 and 2013. The likelihood of reaching that target is estimated to be 75%. The balance sheet of Smith Company is given below, along with estimated fair values of the net assets to be acquired.

Smith Company
Balance Sheet
December 31, 2011

	Book Value	Fair Value		Book Value	Fair Value
Current assets:			**Current liabilities:**		
Notes receivable	$ 33,000	$ 33,000	Accounts payable	$ 63,000	$ 63,000
Inventory	89,000	80,000	Taxes payable	15,000	15,000
Prepaid expenses	15,000	15,000	Interest payable	3,000	3,000
Total current assets	$137,000	$128,000	Total current liabilities	$ 81,000	$ 81,000
Investments	$ 36,000	$ 55,000			
Fixed assets:			**Other liabilities:**		
Land	$ 15,000	$ 90,000	Bonds payable	$250,000	$250,000
Buildings	115,000	170,000	Discount on bonds payable	(18,000)	(30,000)
Equipment	256,000	250,000			
Vehicles	32,000	25,000			
Total fixed assets	$418,000	$535,000	Total other liabilities	$232,000	$220,000
Intangibles:			**Stockholders' equity:**		
Franchise	$ 56,000	$ 70,000	Common stock	$ 50,000	
			Paid-in capital in excess of par . . .	200,000	
			Retained earnings	84,000	
			Total equity	$334,000	
Total assets	$647,000	$788,000	Total liabilities and equity	$647,000	

1. Do value analysis and prepare the entry on the books of Hite Corporation to record the acquisition of Smith Company.   ◄ ◄ ◄ ◄ ◄ **Required**
2. Assume that the net income of the Smith business unit is $120,000 for 2012. As a result, the likelihood of paying the contingent consideration is believed to be 90%. What, if any, adjusting entry is required as of December 31, 2012?

Problem 1-7 *(LO 3, 4)* **Cash acquisition with a gain.** Heinrich Company, owned by Elennor and Al Heinrich, has been experiencing financial difficulty for the past several years. Both Elennor and Al have not been in good health and have decided to find a buyer. P&F International, after reviewing the financial statements for the previous three years, has decided to make an offer of $150,000 for the net assets of Heinrich Company on January 1, 2012. The balance sheet as of this date is as follows:

Heinrich Company
Balance Sheet
January 1, 2012

Current assets:			**Current liabilities:**	
Accounts receivable	$ 87,000		Accounts payable	$ 56,000
Inventory	36,000		Accrued liabilities	14,000
Other current assets	14,000			
Total current assets	$137,000		Total current liabilities	$ 70,000
Fixed assets:			**Other liabilities:**	
Equipment	$105,000		Notes payable	$ 30,000
Vehicles	69,000			
Total fixed assets	$174,000		Total liabilities	$100,000

Intangibles:		Stockholders' equity:	
Mailing lists	$ 4,000	Common stock	$ 60,000
		Paid-in capital in excess of par	100,000
		Retained earnings	55,000
		Total equity	$215,000
Total assets	$315,000	Total liabilities and equity	$315,000

In reviewing the above balance sheet, P&F's appraiser felt the liabilities were stated at their fair values. He placed the following fair values on the assets of the company.

Heinrich Company
Fair Values
January 1, 2012

Current assets:	
Accounts receivable	$ 90,000
Inventory	30,000
Other current assets	8,000
Total current assets	$128,000
Fixed assets:	
Equipment	$ 80,000
Vehicles	50,000
Total fixed assets	$130,000
Intangibles:	
Mailing list	$ 10,000
Total assets	$268,000

Required ▶ ▶ ▶ ▶ ▶ Using this information, do value analysis, and prepare the entry to record the acquisition of the net assets of Heinrich Company on the books of P&F International.

Problem 1-8 *(LO 3, 4, 6)* **Pro forma income after an acquisition.** Moon Company is contemplating the acquisition of Yount, Inc., on January 1, 2011. If Moon acquires Yount, it will pay $730,000 in cash to Yount and acquisition costs of $20,000.

The January 1, 2011, balance sheet of Yount, Inc., is anticipated to be as follows:

Yount, Inc.
Pro Forma Balance Sheet
January 1, 2011

Assets		Liabilities and Equity	
Cash equivalents	$100,000	Current liabilities	$ 30,000
Accounts receivable	120,000	Long-term liabilities	165,000
Inventory	50,000	Common stock ($10 par)	80,000
Depreciable fixed assets	200,000	Retained earnings	115,000
Accumulated depreciation	(80,000)		
Total assets	$390,000	Total liabilities and equity	$390,000

Fair values agree with book values except for the inventory and the depreciable fixed assets, which have fair values of $70,000 and $400,000, respectively.

Your projections of the combined operations for 2011 are as follows:

Combined sales.	$200,000
Combined cost of goods sold, including Yount's beginning inventory, at book value, which will be sold in 2011	120,000
Other expenses not including depreciation of Yount assets	25,000

Depreciation on Yount fixed assets is straight-line using a 20-year life with no salvage value.

1. Prepare a value analysis for the acquisition and record the acquisition.   ◄ ◄ ◄ ◄ ◄ **Required**
2. Prepare a pro forma income statement for the combined firm for 2011. Show supporting calculations for consolidated income. Ignore tax issues.

Problem 1-9 *(LO 3, 4, 6)* Issue stock, goodwill, pro forma disclosure.

Part A. Garman International wants to expand its operations and decides to acquire the net assets of Iris Company as of January 1, 2012. Garman issues 10,000 shares of its $5 par value common stock for the net assets of Iris. Garman's stock is selling for $27 per share. In addition, Garman pays $10,000 in acquisition costs. A balance sheet for Iris Company as of December 31, 2011, is as follows:

Current assets:			**Current liabilities:**		
Accounts receivable		$ 15,000	Accounts payable		$ 22,000
Inventory		38,000	Interest payable.		2,000
Prepaid expenses		12,000			
Total current assets.		$ 65,000	Total current liabilities		$ 24,000
Investments		19,000			
Fixed assets:			**Other liabilities:**		
Land.	$30,000		Long-term notes payable		40,000
Building	70,000				
Equipment	56,000				
Total fixed assets		156,000	Total liabilities		$ 64,000
Intangibles:			**Stockholders' equity:**		
Patent.	$17,000		Common stock.	$ 40,000	
Copyrights.	22,000		Paid-in capital in excess of par	120,000	
Goodwill	8,000		Retained earnings	63,000	
Total intangibles		47,000	Total equity		223,000
Total assets		$287,000	Total liabilities and equity		$287,000

In reviewing Iris's balance sheet and in consulting with various appraisers, Garman has determined that the inventory is understated by $2,000, the land is understated by $10,000, the building is understated by $15,000, and the copyrights are understated by $4,000. Garman has also determined that the equipment is overstated by $6,000, and the patent is overstated by $5,000.

The investments have a fair value of $33,000 on December 31, 2011, and the amount of goodwill (if any) must be determined.

Part A. Using the information above, do value analysis, and record the acquisition of Iris Company on Garman International's books on January 1, 2012.   ◄ ◄ ◄ ◄ ◄ **Required**

Part B. Garman International wishes to estimate its pro forma disclosure of operations for 2012 resulting from acquisition of Iris. Pro forma disclosure includes revenue and net income. Projected income statements for 2012 are as follows:

Income Statement Accounts	Garman International	Iris Company
Sales Revenue	$(350,000)	$(125,000)
Cost of Goods Sold	147,000	55,000
Gross Profit	$(203,000)	$ (70,000)
Selling Expenses*	$ 100,000	$ 20,000
Administrative Expenses*	50,000	30,000
Depreciation Expense	12,500	8,600
Amortization Expense	1,000	3,900
Total Operating Expenses	$ 163,500	$ 62,500
Operating Income	$ (39,500)	$ (7,500)
Nonoperating Revenues and Expenses:		
Interest Expense		3,000
Investment Income	(12,000)	(4,500)
Income Before Taxes	$ (51,500)	$ (9,000)
Provision for Income Taxes (40% rate).	20,600	3,600
Net Income	$ (30,900)	$ (5,400)

*Does not include depreciation or amortization expense.

Garman International estimates that the following amount of depreciation and amortization should be taken on the revalued assets of Iris Company:

Building depreciation	$4,000
Equipment depreciation	5,000
Patent amortization	1,200
Copyright amortization	2,600

Required ▶ ▶ ▶ ▶ ▶   **Part B.** Using the above information, prepare a pro forma income statement for Garman International combined with Iris Company for the year ended December 31, 2012. Schedule your calculations for revenue and net income.

Problem 1-10 *(LO 3, 4)* **Revaluation of leases** Sentry, Inc., acquires for $2,300,000 in cash, the net assets of New Equipment Company. The acquisition is made on December 31, 2011, at which time New Equipment has prepared the following balance sheet:

New Equipment Company
Balance Sheet
December 31, 2011

Assets		Liabilities and Equity	
Current assets	$ 100,000	Current liabilities	$ 150,000
Assets under operating leases	520,000	Obligation under capital lease of equipment	35,000
Net investment in direct financing (capital leases).	730,000	Common stock ($5 par)	100,000
		Paid-in capital in excess of par	400,000
Leased equipment under capital lease (net)	40,000	Retained earnings	955,000
Buildings (net)	200,000		
Land	50,000		
Total assets	$1,640,000	Total liabilities and equity	$1,640,000

The following information is available concerning the assets and liabilities of New Equipment:

a. Current assets and liabilities are stated fairly. No payments resulting from leases are included in current accounts, since all payments are due each December 31 and payment for 2011 has been made.

b. Assets under operating leases have an estimated value of $580,000. This figure includes consideration of remaining rents and the value of the assets at the end of the lease terms.

c. The net investment in direct financing leases represents receivables at their discounted present values. All leases except one are based on the current market interest rate of 12%. One equipment lease is included at an amount of $199,636. This lease includes five and of the year payments of $50,000 present valued at an 8% interest rate. This lease should be adjusted to its real fair value using a 12% annual interest rate.

d. The buildings and land have appraised fair values of $400,000 and $100,000, respectively.

e. The leased equipment under the capital lease pertains to a computer used by New Equipment. The obligation under the capital lease of equipment includes the present value of five remaining payments of $9,233 due at the end of each year and discounted at 10%. Title transfers to the lessee at the end of the lease term. The current interest rate for this type of transaction is 12%. The fair value of the equipment under the lease is $60,000.

f. New Equipment has expended $100,000 on R&D leading to new equipment applications. Sentry estimates the value of this work to be $200,000.

g. New Equipment has been named in a $200,000 lawsuit involving an accident by a lessee using its equipment. It is likely that New Equipment will be found liable in the amount of $50,000.

Record the acquisition of New Equipment Company by Sentry, Inc. Carefully support your entry. You may assume that the price will allow goodwill to be recorded. ◄ ◄ ◄ ◄ ◄ **Required**

Problem 1-11 *(LO 5)* **Tax-free exchange, tax loss carryover.** Hanson Company issues 10,000 shares of $10 par common stock for the net assets of Marcus Incorporated on December 31, 2012. The stock has a fair value of $65 per share. Acquisition costs are $10,000, and the cost of issuing the stock is $3,000. At the time of the purchase, Marcus had the following summarized balance sheet:

Assets		Liabilities and Equity	
Current assets	$150,000	Bonds payable	$200,000
Equipment (net)	200,000	Common stock ($10 par).	100,000
Land and buildings (net)	250,000	Retained earnings	300,000
Total assets.	$600,000	Total liabilities and equity . . .	$600,000

The only fair value differing from book value is equipment, which is worth $350,000. Marcus has $180,000 in operating losses in prior years. The previous asset values are also the tax basis of the assets, which will be the tax basis for Hanson, since the acquisition is a tax-free exchange. Hanson is confident that it will recover the entire tax loss carryforward applicable to the past losses of Marcus. The applicable tax rate is 30%.

Record the acquisition of the net assets of Marcus Incorporated by Hanson Company. You may assume the price paid will allow goodwill to be recorded. Use value analysis to support your solution. ◄ ◄ ◄ ◄ ◄ **Required**

Problem 1-12 *(LO 6)* **Income statements after acquisition.** On July 1, 2011, Faber Enterprises acquired Ann's Tool Company. Prior to the merger of the two companies, each company calculated its income for the entire year ended December 31, 2011. (It may be assumed that all Ann amounts occurred evenly over the year.) These estimates are as follows:

Income Statement Accounts	Faber Enterprises		Ann's Tool Company	
Sales Revenue		$550,000		$140,000
Cost of Goods Sold		200,000		50,000
Gross Profit		$350,000		$ 90,000
Selling Expenses	$125,000		$30,000	
Administrative Expenses	150,000		45,000	
Depreciation Expense	13,800		7,500	
Amortization Expense	5,600		2,000	
Total Operating Expenses		294,400		84,500

Operating Income	$ 55,600	$ 5,500
Nonoperating Revenues and Expenses:		
Interest Expense		4,000
Interest Income	7,000	
Dividend Income	4,000	
Income Before Taxes	$ 66,600	$ 1,500
Provision for Income Taxes (30% rate). . . .	19,980	450
Net Income	$ 46,620	$ 1,050

An analysis of the merger agreement revealed that the purchase price exceeded the fair value of all assets by $40,000. The book and fair values of Ann's Tool Company on July 1, 2011, are given in the table below along with an estimate of the useful lives of each of these asset categories.

Asset Account	Book Value	Fair Value	Useful Life
Inventory	$30,000	$ 28,000	Sold August 2011
Land.	50,000	80,000	Unlimited
Buildings	75,000	125,000	25 years
Equipment	32,000	56,000	8 years
Truck	1,000	3,000	2 years
Patent.	12,000	18,000	6 years
Computer Software	0	10,000	2 years
Copyright	0	20,000	10 years

Management believes the company will be in a combined tax bracket of 30%. The company uses the straight-line method of computing depreciation and amortization and assigns a zero salvage value.

Required ▶ ▶ ▶ ▶ ▶

1. Using the above information, prepare the Faber Enterprises income statement for the year ending December 31, 2011. Provide supporting calculations.
2. Prepare the required summarized disclosure of 2011 results if the acquisition occurs at the start of the year.

Problem 1-13 *(LO 4, 6)* **Contingent consideration.** Door Corporation acquires the net assets, exclusive of cash, of Walsh Company on January 1, 2011, at which time Walsh Company's balance sheet is as follows:

Assets		
Current assets:		
Cash	$ 30,000	
Accounts receivable.	50,000	$ 80,000
Noncurrent assets:		
Investments in marketable securities	$120,000	
Land.	600,000	
Buildings (net)	450,000	
Equipment (net)	800,000	
Goodwill	100,000	2,070,000
Total assets		$2,150,000

Liabilities and Stockholders' Equity		
Current liabilities:		
Accounts payable	$ 150,000	
Income tax payable	190,000	$ 340,000
Equity:		
Common stock ($5 par)	$1,200,000	
Retained earnings	610,000	1,810,000
Total liabilities and equity		$2,150,000

Door Corporation feels that the following fair values should be used for Walsh's book values:

Cash (no change)	$ 30,000
Accounts receivable	60,000
Investment in marketable securities	150,000
Land	450,000
Buildings (no change)	450,000
Equipment	600,000
Accounts payable	120,000
Income tax payable (no change)	190,000

Door issues 20,000 shares of its common stock with a $2 par value and a quoted fair value of $60 per share on January 1, 2011, to Walsh Company to acquire the net assets. Door also agrees that two years from now it will issue additional securities to compensate Walsh shareholders for any decline in value below that on the date of issue.

1. Record the acquisition on the books of Door Corporation on January 1, 2011. Include support for calculations used to arrive at the values assigned to the assets and liabilities. Use value analysis to aid your solution.
2. Record payment (if any) of contingent consideration on January 1, 2013, assuming that the quoted value of the stock is $57.50. (Round shares to nearest whole share.)

APPENDIX PROBLEM

Problem 1A-1 *(LO 9)* **Estimate goodwill, record acquisition.** Caswell Company is contemplating the purchase of LaBelle Company as of January 1, 2016. LaBelle Company has provided the following current balance sheet:

Assets		Liabilities and Equity	
Cash and receivables	$ 150,000	Current liabilities	$120,000
Inventory	180,000	9% Bonds payable	300,000
Land	50,000	Common stock ($5 par)	100,000
Building	600,000	Paid-in capital in excess of par	200,000
Accumulated depreciation	(150,000)	Retained earnings	150,000
Goodwill	40,000		
Total assets	$ 870,000	Total liabilities and equity	$870,000

The following information exists relative to balance sheet accounts:

a. The inventory has a fair value of $200,000.
b. The land is appraised at $100,000 and the building at $600,000.
c. The 9% bonds payable have five years to maturity and pay annual interest each December 31. The current interest rate for similar bonds is 8% per year.
d. It is likely that there will be a payment for goodwill based on projected income in excess of the industry average, which is 10% on total assets. Caswell will project the average past five years' operating income and will pay for excess income based on an assumption of a 5-year life and a risk rate of return of 16%. The past five years' net incomes for LaBelle are as follows:

2011	$120,000
2012	140,000
2013	150,000
2014	200,000 (includes $40,000 extraordinary gain)
2015	180,000

1. Provide an estimate of fair value for the bonds and for goodwill.
2. Using the values derived in part (1), record the acquisition on the Caswell books.

Consolidated Statements: Date of Acquisition

CHAPTER

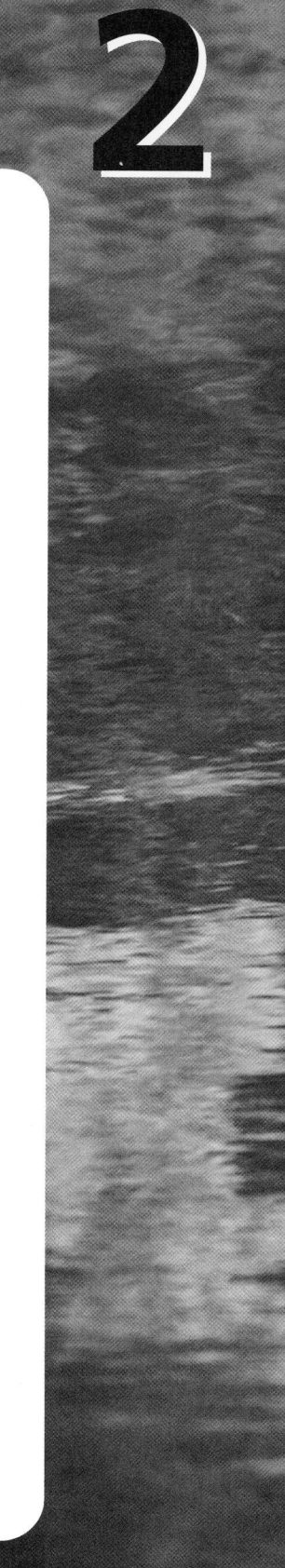

2

Learning Objectives

When you have completed this chapter, you should be able to

1. Differentiate among the accounting methods used for investments, based on the level of common stock ownership in another company.

2. State the criteria for presenting consolidated statements, and explain why disclosure of separate subsidiary financial information might be important.

3. Demonstrate the worksheet procedures needed to eliminate the investment account.

4. Demonstrate the worksheet procedures needed to consolidate parent and subsidiary accounts.

5. Apply value analysis to guide the adjustment process to reflect the price paid for the controlling interest.

6. Develop a determination and distribution of excess (D&D) schedule that will guide the worksheet procedures needed to consolidate a subsidiary.

7. Explain the impact of a noncontrolling interest on worksheet procedures and financial statement preparation.

8. Show the impact of preexisting goodwill on the consolidation process, and be able to include prior investments in the acquisition price.

9. Define push-down accounting, and explain when it may be used and its impact.

10. Demonstrate worksheet procedures for reverse acquisitions. (Appendix)

The preceding chapter dealt with business combinations that are accomplished as asset acquisitions. The net assets of an entire company are acquired and recorded directly on the books of the acquiring company. Consolidation of the two companies is automatic because all subsequent transactions are recorded on a single set of books.

A company will commonly acquire a large enough interest in another company's voting common stock to obtain control of operations. The company owning the controlling interest is termed the *parent*, while the controlled company is termed the *subsidiary*. Legally, the parent company has only an investment in the stock of the subsidiary and will only record an investment account in its accounting records. The subsidiary will continue to prepare its own financial statements. However, accounting principles require that when one company has effective control over another, a single set of *consolidated statements* must be prepared for the companies under common control. The consolidated statements present the financial statements of the parent and its subsidiaries as those of a single economic entity. Worksheets are prepared to merge the separate statements of the parent and its subsidiary(s) into a single set of consolidated statements.

This chapter is the first of several that will show how to combine the separate statements of a parent and its subsidiaries. The theory of *acquisition accounting*, developed in Chapter 1, is applied in the consolidation process. In fact, the consolidated statements of a parent and its 100%

owned subsidiary look exactly like they would have had the net assets been acquired. **This chapter contains only the procedures necessary to prepare consolidated statements on the day that the controlling investment is acquired.** The procedures for consolidating controlling investments in periods subsequent to the acquisition date will be developed in Chapter 3. The effect of operating activities between the parent and its subsidiaries, such as intercompany loans, merchandise sales, fixed asset sales, bonds, and leases, will be discussed in Chapters 4 and 5. Later chapters will deal with taxation issues and changes in the level of ownership.

LEVELS OF INVESTMENT

1

OBJECTIVE

Differentiate among the accounting methods used for investments, based on the level of common stock ownership in another company.

The purchase of the voting common stock of another company receives different accounting treatments depending on the level of ownership and the amount of influence or control caused by the stock ownership. The ownership levels and accounting methods can be summarized as follows:

Level of Ownership	Initial Recording	Recording of Income
Passive—generally under 20% ownership.	At cost including brokers' fees.	Dividends as declared (except stock dividends).
Influential—generally 20% to 50% ownership.	At cost including brokers' fees.	Ownership share of income (or loss) is reported. Shown as investment income on financial statements. (Dividends declared are distributions of income already recorded; they reduce the investment account.)
Controlling—generally over 50% ownership.	At cost.	Ownership share of income (or loss). (Some adjustments are explained in later chapters.) Accomplished by consolidating the subsidiary income statement accounts with those of the parent in the consolidation process.

To illustrate the differences in reporting the income applicable to the common stock shares owned, consider the following example based on the reported income of the investor and investee (the company whose shares are owned by investor):

Account	Investor*	Investee
Sales	$500,000	$300,000
Less: Cost of goods sold	250,000	180,000
Gross profit	$250,000	$120,000
Less: Selling and administrative expenses	100,000	80,000
Net income	$150,000	$ 40,000

*Does not include any income from investee.

Assume that the investee company paid $10,000 in cash dividends. The investor would prepare the following income statements, depending on the level of ownership:

Level of Ownership	10% Passive	30% Influential	80% Controlling
Sales	$ 500,000	$ 500,000	$ 800,000
Less: Cost of goods sold	250,000	250,000	430,000
Gross profit	$ 250,000	$ 250,000	$ 370,000
Less: Selling and administrative expenses	100,000	100,000	180,000

(continued)

Level of Ownership	10% Passive	30% Influential	80% Controlling
Operating income.	$ 150,000	$ 150,000	
Dividend income (10% × $10,000 dividends).	1,000		
Investment income (30% × $40,000 reported income)		12,000	
Net income	**$151,000**	**$162,000**	$ 190,000
Distribution of income:			
Noncontrolling interest (20% × $40,000 reported income)			$ 8,000
Controlling interest (100% of investor's $150,000 + 80% of investee's $40,000).			**$182,000**

With a 10% passive interest, the investor included only its share of the dividends declared by the investee as its income. With a 30% influential ownership interest, the investor reported 30% of the investee income as a separate source of income. With an 80% controlling interest, the investor (now termed the parent) merges the investee's (now a subsidiary) nominal accounts with its own amounts. Dividend and investment income no longer exist. A single set of financial statements replaces the separate statement of the entities. If the parent owned a 100% interest, net income would simply be reported as $190,000. Since this is only an 80% interest, the net income must be shown as distributed between the noncontrolling and controlling interests. The noncontrolling interest is the 20% of the subsidiary that is not owned by the parent. The controlling interest is the parent income plus 80% of the subsidiary income.

REFLECTION

- An influential investment (generally over 20% ownership) requires recording, as a single line-item amount, the investor's share of the investee's income as it is earned.

- A controlling investment (generally over 50% ownership) requires that subsidiary income statement accounts be combined with those of the parent company.

- The essence of consolidated reporting is the portrayal of the separate legal entities as a single economic entity.

FUNCTION OF CONSOLIDATED STATEMENTS

Consolidated financial statements are designed to present the results of operations, cash flow, and the balance sheet of both the parent and its subsidiaries as if they were a single company. Generally, consolidated statements are the most informative to the stockholders of the controlling company. Yet, consolidated statements do have their shortcomings. The rights of the noncontrolling shareholders are limited to only the company they own, and, therefore, they get little value from consolidated statements. They really need the separate statements of the subsidiary. Similarly, creditors of the subsidiary need its separate statements because they may look only to the legal entity that is indebted to them for satisfaction of their claims. The parent's creditors should be content with the consolidated statements, since the investment in the subsidiary will produce cash flows that can be used to satisfy their claims.

Consolidated statements have been criticized for being too aggregated. Unprofitable subsidiaries may not be very obvious because, when consolidated, their performance is combined with that of other affiliates. However, this shortcoming is easily overcome. One option is to prepare separate statements of the subsidiary as supplements to the consolidated statements. The second option, which may be required, is to provide disclosure for major business segments. When subsidiaries are in businesses distinct from the parent, the definition of a segment may parallel that of a subsidiary.

Criteria for Consolidated Statements

Generally, statements are to be consolidated when a parent firm owns over 50% of the voting common stock of another company. There may be instances where consolidation is appropriate

2

OBJECTIVE

State the criteria for presenting consolidated statements, and explain why disclosure of separate subsidiary financial information might be important.

even though less than 51% of the voting common stock is owned by the parent. SEC Regulation S-X defines control in terms of power to direct or cause the direction of management and policies of a person, whether through the ownership of voting securities, by contract, or otherwise. Thus, control has been said to exist when a less than 51% ownership interest exists but where there is no other large ownership interest that can exert influence on management.

IASB PERSPECTIVES

IASB *standards*

- IFRS considers potential voting rights if they are currently exercisable, in measuring control, while GAAP does not.

- IFRS also allows consolidation when there is "de facto" control. This is a situation in which there is only one large stockholder that owns less than 50% of the shares, but other share holdings are disbursed and the owners do not generally exercise their voting rights. This is similar to the SEC position indicated above.

The FASB and IASB were working on a joint definition of *control* and were scheduled to issue an exposure draft in 2011. The reader should check FASB Codification Section 810 for developments on this definition. The exception to consolidating when control exists is if control is only temporary or does not rest with the majority owner. For example, control would be presumed not to reside with the majority owner when the subsidiary is in bankruptcy, in legal reorganization, or when foreign exchange restrictions or foreign government controls cast doubt on the ability of the parent to exercise control over the subsidiary.

Prior to 1988, it was acceptable to exclude subsidiaries from consolidation when their operations were not homogeneous with those of the parent. It was common for a manufacturing-based parent to exclude from consolidations those subsidiaries involved in banking, financing, real estate, or leasing activities, but this exception for "nonhomogeneity" came under criticism and was eliminated.

Nonconsolidated subsidiaries now have become a rarity. When they do exist, they are accounted for as an investment under the equity method. The accounting methods for such an investment are discussed in the Appendix.

REFLECTION

- The combining of the statements of a parent and its subsidiaries into consolidated statements is required when parent ownership exceeds 50% of the controlled firm's shares.

- Consolidation is required for any company that is controlled, even in cases where less than 51% of the company's shares is owned by the parent.

3

OBJECTIVE

Demonstrate the worksheet procedures needed to eliminate the investment account.

TECHNIQUES OF CONSOLIDATION

This chapter builds an understanding of the techniques used to consolidate the separate balance sheets of a parent and its subsidiary immediately subsequent to the acquisition. The consolidated balance sheet as of the acquisition date is discussed first. The impact of consolidations on operations after the acquisition date is discussed in Chapters 3 through 8.

Chapter 1 emphasized that there are two means of achieving control over the assets of another company. A company may directly acquire the assets of another company, or it may acquire a controlling interest in the other company's voting common stock. In an *asset acquisition*, the company whose assets were acquired is dissolved. The assets acquired are recorded directly on the books of the acquirer, and consolidation of balance sheet amounts is automatic. Where control is achieved through a *stock acquisition,* the acquired company (the subsidiary) remains as a separate legal entity with its own financial statements. While the initial accounting for the two types of acquisitions differs significantly, a 100% stock acquisition and an asset acquisition have the same effect of creating one larger single reporting entity and should produce the same consolidated balance sheet. There is, however, a difference if the stock acquisition is less than 100%. Then, there will be a noncontrolling interest in the consolidated balance sheet. This is not possible when the assets are purchased directly.

In the following discussion, the recording of an asset acquisition and a 100% stock acquisition are compared, and the balance sheets that result from each type of acquisition are studied. Then, the chapter deals with the accounting procedures needed when there is less than a 100% stock ownership and a noncontrolling equity interest exists.

Reviewing an Asset Acquisition

Illustration 2-1 demonstrates an asset acquisition of Company S by Company P for cash. Part A of the exhibit presents the balance sheets of the two companies just prior to the acquisition. Part B shows the entry to record Company P's payment of $500,000 in cash for the net assets of Company S. The book values of the assets and liabilities acquired are assumed to be representative of their fair values, and no goodwill is acknowledged. The assets and liabilities of Company S are added to those of Company P to produce the balance sheet for the combined company, shown in Part C. Since account balances are combined in recording the acquisition, **statements for the single combined reporting entity are produced automatically, and no consolidation process is needed.**

Illustration 2-1
Asset Acquisition

Part A. Balance sheets of Companies P and S prior to acquisition:

Company P Balance Sheet

Assets		Liabilities and Equity	
Cash	$ 800,000	Current liabilities	$ 150,000
Accounts receivable	300,000	Bonds payable	500,000
Inventory	100,000	Common stock	100,000
Equipment (net)	150,000	Retained earnings	600,000
Total	$1,350,000	Total	$1,350,000

Company S Balance Sheet

Assets		Liabilities and Equity	
Accounts receivable	$200,000	Current liabilities	$100,000
Inventory	100,000	Common stock	200,000
Equipment (net)	300,000	Retained earnings	300,000
Total	$600,000	Total	$600,000

Part B. Entry on Company P's books to record acquisition of the net assets of Company S by Company P:

Accounts Receivable	200,000	
Inventory	100,000	
Equipment	300,000	
Current Liabilities		100,000
Cash		500,000

(continued)

Part C. Balance sheet of Company P (the combined company) subsequent to asset acquisition:

Company P Balance Sheet

Assets		Liabilities and Equity	
Cash	$ 300,000	Current liabilities	$ 250,000
Accounts receivable	500,000	Bonds payable	500,000
Inventory	200,000	Common stock	100,000
Equipment (net)	450,000	Retained earnings	600,000
Total	$1,450,000	Total	$1,450,000

Consolidating a Stock Acquisition

In a stock acquisition, the acquiring company deals only with existing shareholders, not the company itself. Assuming the same facts as those used in Illustration 2-1, except that Company P will acquire all the outstanding stock of Company S from its shareholders for $500,000, Company P would make the following entry:

Investment in Subsidiary S	500,000	
Cash		500,000

This entry does not record the individual underlying assets and liabilities over which control is achieved. Instead, the acquisition is recorded in an investment account that represents the controlling interest in the net assets of the subsidiary. If no further action was taken, the investment in the subsidiary account would appear as a long-term investment on Company P's balance sheet. However, such a presentation is permitted only if consolidation were not required (i.e., when control does not exist).

Assuming consolidated statements are required (i.e., when control does exist), the balance sheet of the two companies must be combined into a single consolidated balance sheet. The consolidation process is separate from the existing accounting records of the companies and requires completion of a worksheet. No journal entries are actually made to the parent's or subsidiary's books, so the elimination process starts anew each year.

Worksheet 2-1: page 88

The first example of a consolidated worksheet, Worksheet 2-1, appears later in the chapter on page 88. (The icon in the margin indicates the location of the worksheet at the end of the chapter.) The first two columns of the worksheet include the trial balances (balance sheet only for this chapter) for Companies P and S. The trial balances and the consolidated balance sheet are presented in single columns to save space. Credit balances are shown in parentheses. Obviously, since there are no nominal accounts listed, the income statement accounts have already been closed to Retained Earnings.

The consolidated worksheet requires elimination of the investment account balance because the two companies will be treated as one. (How can a company have an investment in itself?) Similarly, the subsidiary's stockholders' equity accounts are eliminated because its assets and liabilities belong to the parent, not to outside equity owners. In general journal form, the elimination entry is as follows:

(EL)	Common Stock, Company S	200,000	
	Retained Earnings, Company S	300,000	
	Investment in Company		500,000

Note that the key (EL) will be used in all future worksheets. Keys, once introduced, will be assigned to all similar items throughout the text. For quick reference, a listing of these keys is provided on the inside front cover of this text. The balances in the Consolidated Balance Sheet column (the last column) are exactly the same as in the balance sheet prepared for the preceding asset acquisition example—as they should be for a 100% stock acquisition.

R E F L E C T I O N					

- Consolidation when a parent owns 100% of the subsidiary's voting common stock produces the same balance sheet that would result in an asset acquisition.

- Consolidated statements are derived from the individual statements of the parent and its subsidiaries.

ADJUSTMENT OF SUBSIDIARY ACCOUNTS

In the last example, the price paid for the investment in the subsidiary was equal to the net book value of the subsidiary (which means the price was also equal to the subsidiary's stockholders' equity). In most acquisitions, the price will exceed the book value of the subsidiary's net assets. Typically, fair values will exceed the recorded book values of assets. The price may also reflect unrecorded intangible assets, including goodwill. Let us revisit the last example and assume that instead of paying $500,000 cash, Company P paid $700,000 cash for all the common stock shares of Company S and made the following entry for the purchase:

4

OBJECTIVE

Demonstrate the worksheet procedures needed to consolidate parent and subsidiary accounts.

Investment in Subsidiary S.	700,000	
Cash		700,000

Use the same Company S balance sheet as in Illustration 2-1, with the following additional information on fair values:

Company S Book and Estimated Fair Values					
December 31, 2011					
Assets	Book Value	Fair Value	Liabilities and Equity	Book Value	Fair Value
Accounts receivable	$ 200,000	$ 200,000	Current liabilities	$100,000	$ 100,000
Inventory	100,000	120,000			
Equipment (net)	300,000	400,000	**Market value of net assets**		
			(assets − liabilities).		**$620,000**
Total assets	**$600,000**	**$720,000**			

If this were an asset acquisition, the identifiable assets and liabilities would be recorded at fair value and goodwill at $80,000. This is the price paid of $700,000 minus the $620,000 ($720,000 total assets − $100,000 total liabilities) fair value of net assets. Adding fair values to Company P's accounts, the new balance sheet would appear as follows:

Company P				
Consolidated Balance Sheet				
December 31, 2011				
Assets		Liabilities and Equity		
Current assets:		Current liabilities	$250,000	
Cash	$100,000	Bonds payable	500,000	
Accounts receivable.	500,000	Total liabilities		$ 750,000
Inventory	220,000			
Total current assets		$ 820,000		

(continued)

Assets			Liabilities and Equity		
Long-term assets:			Stockholders' equity:		
Equipment (net)	$550,000		Common stock	$100,000	
Goodwill	80,000		Retained earnings	600,000	
Total long-term assets . . .		630,000	Total equity		700,000
Total assets		$1,450,000	Total liabilities and equity . . .		$1,450,000

Worksheet 2-2: page 89

As before, the consolidated worksheet should produce a consolidated balance sheet that looks exactly the same as the preceding balance sheet for an asset acquisition. Worksheet 2-2, on page 89, shows how this is accomplished.

◆ The (EL) entry is the same as before: $500,000 of subsidiary equity is eliminated against the investment account.

◆ Entry **(D)** distributes the remaining cost of $200,000 to the acquired assets to bring them from book to fair value and to record goodwill of $80,000.

In general journal entry form, the elimination entries are as follows:

(EL)	Common Stock, Company S	200,000		
	Retained Earnings, Company S.	300,000		
	Investment in Company S.		500,000	
(D1)	Inventory (to increase from $100,000 to $120,000)	20,000		
(D2)	Equipment (to increase from $300,000 to $400,000)	100,000		
(D3)	Goodwill ($700,000 price minus $620,000 fair value			
	assets).	80,000		
(D)	Investment in Company S ($700,000 price minus			
	$500,000 book value eliminated above)		200,000	

The Consolidated Balance Sheet column of Worksheet 2-2 includes the subsidiary accounts at full fair value and reflects the $80,000 of goodwill included in the purchase price. The formal balance sheet for Company P, based on the worksheet, would be exactly the same as shown above for the asset acquisition.

Acquisition of a subsidiary at a price in excess of the fair values of the subsidiary equity is as simple as the case just presented, especially where there are a limited number of assets to adjust to fair value. For more involved acquisitions, where there are many accounts to adjust and/or the price paid is less than the fair value of the net assets, a more complete analysis is needed. We will now proceed to develop these tools.

5

OBJECTIVE

Apply value analysis to guide the adjustment process to reflect the price paid for the controlling interest.

Analysis of Complicated Purchases—100% Interest

The previous examples assumed the purchase of the subsidiary for cash. However, most acquisitions are accomplished by the parent issuing common stock (or, less often, preferred stock) in exchange for the subsidiary common shares being acquired. This avoids the depletion of cash and, if other criteria are met, allows the subsidiary shareholders to have a tax-free exchange. In most cases, the shares are issued by a publicly traded parent company that provides a readily determinable market price for the shares issued. The investment in the subsidiary is then recorded at the fair value of the shares issued. Less frequently, a nonpublicly traded parent may issue shares to subsidiary shareholders. In these cases, the fair values are determined for the net assets of the subsidiary company, and the total estimated fair value of the subsidiary company is recorded as the cost of the investment.

In order to illustrate the complete procedures used to record the investment in and the consolidation of a subsidiary, we will consider the acquisition of a 100% interest in Sample Company. The book and fair values of the net assets of Sample Company on December 31, 2011, when Parental, Inc., acquired 100% of its shares, were as follows:

Assets	Book Value	Market Value	Liabilities and Equity	Book Value	Market Value
Accounts receivable	$ 20,000	$ 20,000	Current liabilities	$ 40,000	$ 40,000
Inventory	50,000	55,000	Bonds payable	100,000	100,000
Land....................	40,000	70,000	**Total liabilities**...............	**$140,000**	**$140,000**
Buildings	200,000	250,000			
Accumulated depreciation ..	(50,000)		Stockholders' equity:		
Equipment	60,000	60,000	Common stock ($1 par).............	$ 10,000	
Accumulated depreciation ..	(20,000)		Paid-in capital in excess of par	90,000	
Copyright		50,000	Retained earnings	60,000	
			Total equity	**$160,000**	
Total assets	$300,000	$505,000	**Net assets**....................	**$160,000**	**$365,000**

Assume that Parental, Inc., issued 20,000 shares of its $1 par value common stock for 100% (10,000 shares) of the outstanding shares of Sample Company. The fair value of a share of Parental, Inc., stock is $25. Parental also pays $25,000 in accounting and legal fees to accomplish the purchase. Parental would make the following entry to record the purchase:

Investment in Sample Company (20,000 shares issued × $25 fair value) ... 500,000
    Common Stock ($1 par value) (20,000 shares × $1 par)............   20,000
    Paid-In Capital in Excess of Par ($500,000 − $20,000 par value)   480,000

Parental would record the costs of the acquisition as follows:

Acquisition Expense (closed to Retained Earnings since only balance sheets
    are being examined).. 25,000
    Cash...   25,000

A value analysis schedule has been designed to compare the fair value of the company acquired with the fair value of the net assets. In this case, the fair value of the company is based on the value of the shares exchanged by Parental, Inc. The schedule includes a column for a noncontrolling interest (NCI) for later cases when the parent does not acquire a 100% interest.

Value Analysis Schedule	Company Implied Fair Value	Parent Price (100%)	NCI Value (0%)
Company fair value..................................	$ 500,000	$ 500,000	N/A
Fair value of net assets excluding goodwill	365,000	365,000	
Goodwill......................................	**$135,000**	**$135,000**	
Gain on acquisition	N/A	N/A	

Notice the following features of the value analysis:

◆ In this case, the company fair value exceeds the fair value of the net assets. This means that all subsidiary accounts will be adjusted to fair value, and goodwill of $135,000 will be shown on the consolidated balance sheet.

◆ If the company fair value was less than the fair value of the net assets, all of the subsidiary accounts would still be adjusted to fair value and a gain on the acquisition would be recorded.

REFLECTION

• The value analysis schedule determines if there will be goodwill or a gain as a result of consolidating the subsidiary with the parent.

6

Develop a determination and distribution of excess (D&D) schedule that will guide the worksheet procedures needed to consolidate a subsidiary.

DETERMINATION AND DISTRIBUTION OF EXCESS SCHEDULE

The *determination and distribution of excess (D&D) schedule* is used to compare the company fair value with the recorded book value of the subsidiary. It also schedules the adjustments that will be made to all subsidiary accounts in the consolidated worksheet process. The D&D schedule below is for a 100% interest, but is built to accommodate an NCI in later examples.

Determination and Distribution of Excess Schedule

	Company Implied Fair Value	Parent Price (100%)	NCI Value (0%)
Fair value of subsidiary	$ 500,000	$500,000	N/A
Less book value of interest acquired:			
Common stock ($1 par)	$ 10,000		
Paid-in capital in excess of par	90,000		
Retained earnings	60,000		
Total stockholders' equity	$ 160,000	$160,000	
Interest acquired		100%	
Book value		$160,000	
Excess of fair value over book value	**$340,000** ←	$340,000	

Adjustment of identifiable accounts:

	Adjustment		Worksheet Key
Inventory ($55,000 fair − $50,000 book value)	$ 5,000		**debit D1**
Land ($70,000 fair − $40,000 book value).	30,000		**debit D2**
Buildings ($250,000 fair − $150,000 net book value)	100,000		**debit D3**
Equipment ($60,000 fair − $40,000 net book value) .	20,000		**debit D4**
Copyright ($50,000 fair − $0 book value).	50,000		**debit D5**
Goodwill.	**135,000**		**debit D6**
Total	**$340,000** ←		

Note the following features of the above D&D schedule:

◆ Since this is a 100% interest, the parent price and the implied value of the subsidiary are equal.

◆ The total adjustment that will have to be made to subsidiary net assets on the worksheet is $340,000.

◆ The schedule shows the adjustments to each subsidiary account. Recall that in Chapter 1, we recorded the entire value of the subsidiary accounts in the acquisition entry. Now the subsidiary assets are already listed on the worksheet at book value, and they only need to be adjusted to fair value.

The D&D schedule provides complete guidance for the worksheet eliminations. Study Worksheet 2-3 on page 90 and note the following:

Worksheet 2-3: page 90

◆ Elimination (EL) eliminated the subsidiary equity purchased (100% in this example) against the investment account as follows:

(EL)	Common Stock ($1 par)—Sample	10,000	
	Paid-In Capital in Excess of Par—Sample	90,000	
	Retained Earnings—Sample	60,000	
	Investment in Sample Company.		160,000

◆ The (D) series eliminations distribute the $340,000 excess to the appropriate accounts, as indicated by the D&D schedule. A valuable check is to be sure that the investment account is now eliminated. If it has not been eliminated, there has been an error in the balances entered into the Balance Sheet columns of the worksheet. Worksheet eliminations are as follows:

(D1)	Inventory	5,000	
(D2)	Land	30,000	
(D3)	Buildings	100,000	
(D4)	Equipment	20,000	
(D5)	Copyright	50,000	
(D6)	Goodwill	135,000	
(D)	Investment in Sample Company [remaining excess after (EL)]		340,000
Dr. = Cr.	*Check Totals*	*340,000*	*340,000*

The amounts that will appear on the consolidated balance sheet are shown in the final column of Worksheet 2-3. Notice that we have consolidated 100% of the fair values of subsidiary accounts with the existing book values of parent company accounts.

Formal Balance Sheet

The formal consolidated balance sheet resulting from the 100% purchase of Sample Company, in exchange for 20,000 Parental shares, has been taken from the Consolidated Balance Sheet column of Worksheet 2-3.

Parental, Inc.
Consolidated Balance Sheet
December 31, 2011

Assets			Liabilities and Equity		
Current assets:			Current liabilities	$120,000	
Cash	$ 84,000		Bonds payable	300,000	
Accounts receivable	92,000		Total liabilities		$ 420,000
Inventory	135,000				
Total current assets		$ 311,000			
Long-term assets:			Stockholders' equity:		
Land	$ 170,000		Common stock ($1 par)	$ 40,000	
Buildings	800,000		Paid-in capital in excess of par	680,000	
Accumulated			Retained earnings	456,000	
depreciation	(130,000)				
Equipment	320,000		Total controlling equity		1,176,000
Accumulated					
depreciation	(60,000)				
Copyright (net)	50,000				
Goodwill (net)	135,000				
Total long-term assets		1,285,000			
Total assets		$1,596,000	Total liabilities and equity		$1,596,000

Bargain Purchase

A bargain purchase refers to an acquisition at a price that is less than the fair value of the subsidiary net identifiable assets. Let us change the prior example to assume that Parental, Inc., issued only 12,000 shares of its stock. The entry to record the purchase would be as shown on page 66.

Investment in Sample Company (12,000 shares issued × $25 fair value)	300,000	
Common Stock ($1 par value) (12,000 shares × $1 par)...........		12,000
Paid-In Capital in Excess of Par ($300,000 − $12,000 par value) ..		288,000

The entry to record the costs of the acquisition would be as follows:

| Acquisition Expense (closed to Retained Earnings since only balance sheets are being examined) .... | 25,000 | |
| Cash .... | | 25,000 |

The value analysis schedule would compare the price paid with the fair value of the subsidiary net identifiable assets as follows:

Value Analysis Schedule	Company Implied Fair Value	Parent Price (100%)	NCI Value (0%)
Company fair value....................	$ 300,000	$ 300,000	N/A
Fair value of net assets excluding goodwill ..	365,000	365,000	
Goodwill	N/A	N/A	
Gain on acquisition	**$(65,000)**	**$(65,000)**	

The D&D schedule would be as follows for the $300,000 price:

Determination and Distribution of Excess Schedule

	Company Implied Fair Value	Parent Price (100%)	NCI Value (0%)
Fair value of subsidiary	$ 300,000	$300,000	N/A
Less book value of interest acquired:			
Common stock ($1 par).....................	$ 10,000		
Paid-in capital in excess of par	90,000		
Retained earnings	60,000		
Total equity	$ 160,000	$160,000	
Interest acquired		100%	
Book value.....................................		$160,000	
Excess of fair value over book value	**$140,000**	$140,000	

Adjustment of identifiable accounts:

	Adjustment		Worksheet Key
Inventory ($55,000 fair − $50,000 book value)	$ 5,000		**debit D1**
Land ($70,000 fair − $40,000 book value).....	30,000		**debit D2**
Buildings ($250,000 fair − $150,000 net book value)	100,000		**debit D3**
Equipment ($60,000 fair − $40,000 net book value)	20,000		**debit D4**
Copyright ($50,000 fair − $0 book value)......	50,000		**debit D5**
Gain on acquisition	**(65,000)**		**credit D7**
Total	**$140,000**		

Note the following features of the above D&D schedule:

♦ All identifiable net assets are still adjusted to full fair value even though it was a bargain purchase.

♦ A gain will be distributed to the parent on the worksheet.

The D&D schedule provides complete guidance for the worksheet eliminations. Study Worksheet 2-4 on page 91 and note the following:

Worksheet 2-4: page 91

♦ Elimination (EL) eliminated the subsidiary equity purchased (100% in this example) against the investment account as follows:

(EL)	Common Stock ($1 par)—Sample	10,000	
	Paid-In Capital in Excess of Par—Sample	90,000	
	Retained Earnings—Sample	60,000	
	Investment in Sample Company		160,000

♦ The (D) series eliminations distribute the $100,000 excess to the appropriate accounts, as indicated by the D&D schedule. Worksheet eliminations are as follows:

(D1)	Inventory	5,000	
(D2)	Land	30,000	
(D3)	Buildings	100,000	
(D4)	Equipment	20,000	
(D5)	Copyright	50,000	
(D7)	**Retained Earnings—Parental***		**65,000**
(D)	Investment in Sample Company [remaining excess after (EL)]		140,000
Dr. = Cr.	*Check Totals*	*205,000*	*205,000*

*Since only a balance sheet is being prepared, the gain on the acquisition is closed directly to Parental Retained Earnings.

The amounts that will appear on the consolidated balance sheet are shown in the final column of Worksheet 2-4. Notice that 100% of the fair values of subsidiary accounts has been consolidated with the existing book values of parent company accounts.

There could be an unusual situation where the price paid by the parent is less than the book value of the subsidiary net assets. For example, if the price paid by the parent was only $150,000, the value analysis schedule would be as follows:

Value Analysis Schedule	Company Implied Fair Value	Parent Price (100%)	NCI Value (0%)
Company fair value....................	$ 150,000	$ 150,000	N/A
Fair value of net assets excluding goodwill ..	365,000	365,000	
Goodwill	N/A	N/A	
Gain on acquisition	**$(215,000)**	**$(215,000)**	

The D&D schedule would be as follows for the $150,000 price:

Determination and Distribution of Excess Schedule

	Company Implied Fair Value	Parent Price (100%)	NCI Value (0%)
Fair value of subsidiary	$ 150,000	$150,000	N/A
Less book value of interest acquired:			
Common stock ($1 par)	$ 10,000		
Paid-in capital in excess of par	90,000		
Retained earnings	60,000		
Total equity.........................	$ 160,000	$160,000	
Interest acquired		100%	
Book value............................		$160,000	
Excess of fair value over book value	$ (10,000)	$ (10,000)	

Adjustment of identifiable accounts:

	Adjustment	Worksheet Key
Inventory ($55,000 fair − $50,000 book value)	$ 5,000	**debit D1**
Land ($70,000 fair − $40,000 book value)...	30,000	**debit D2**
Buildings ($250,000 fair − $150,000 book value)	100,000	**debit D3**
Equipment ($60,000 fair − $40,000 book value)	20,000	**debit D4**
Copyright ($50,000 fair − $0 book value)....	50,000	**debit D5**
Gain on acquisition*	**(215,000)**	**credit D7**
Total	**$ (10,000)**	

*Agrees with total (company) gain in the value analysis schedule.

The eliminations on the worksheet would be as follows:

♦ Elimination (EL) eliminated the subsidiary equity purchased (100% in this example) against the investment account as follows:

(EL)	Common Stock ($1 par)—Sample	10,000	
	Paid-In Capital in Excess of Par—Sample	90,000	
	Retained Earnings—Sample	60,000	
	Investment in Sample Company.....................		160,000

♦ The (D) series eliminations distribute the $10,000 negative excess to the appropriate accounts, as indicated by the D&D schedule. Worksheet eliminations are as follows:

(D1)	Inventory	5,000	
(D2)	Land.	30,000	
(D3)	Buildings	100,000	
(D4)	Equipment	20,000	
(D5)	Copyright	50,000	
(D7)	Retained Earnings—Parental*.		215,000
(D)	Investment in Sample Company [remaining excess after		
	(EL)]	10,000	
Dr. = Cr.	*Check Totals*	*215,000*	*215,000*

*Since only a balance sheet is being prepared, the gain on the acquisition is closed directly to Parental Retained Earnings.

A worksheet, in this case, would debit the investment account $10,000 to cure the distribution of adjustments to subsidiary accounts that exceed the amount available for distribution.

REFLECTION

- The D&D schedule compares the price paid for the investment in the subsidiary with subsidiary book values and schedules the adjustments to be made on the worksheet.

- The worksheet adjusts the subsidiary accounts to fair values and adds them to the parent accounts to arrive at a consolidated balance sheet.

CONSOLIDATING WITH A NONCONTROLLING INTEREST

7

OBJECTIVE

Explain the impact of a noncontrolling interest on worksheet procedures and financial statement preparation.

Consolidation of financial statements is required whenever the parent company controls a subsidiary. In other words, a parent company could consolidate far less than a 100% ownership interest. If a parent company owns 80% of the common stock of a company, the remaining 20% interest is noncontrolling interest. Several important ramifications may arise when less than 100% interest is consolidated.

◆ The parent's investment account is eliminated against only its ownership percentage of the underlying subsidiary equity accounts.[1] The NCI is shown on the consolidated balance sheet in total and is not broken into par, paid-in capital in excess of par, and retained earnings. The NCI must be shown as a component of stockholders' equity. In the past, the NCI has also been displayed on the consolidated balance sheet as a liability, or in some cases has appeared between the liability and equity sections of the balance sheet. These alternatives are no longer allowed.

◆ The entire amount of every subsidiary nominal (income statement) account is merged with the nominal accounts of the parent to calculate consolidated income. *The noncontrolling interest is allocated its percentage ownership times the reported income of the subsidiary only.* The precise methods and display of this interest are discussed in Chapter 3. In the past, this share of income has often been treated as an other expense in the consolidated income statement. FASB ASC 810-10-65-1 requires that it not be shown as an expense but, rather, as a distribution of consolidated income.

◆ Subsidiary accounts are adjusted to full fair value regardless of the controlling interest percentage. Prior to 2009, subsidiary accounts would only be adjusted to the controlling interest percentage ownership interest. For example, assume that the parent owns an 80% interest in the subsidiary. Further assume that the book value of equipment is $100,000 and that its fair value is $150,000. Past practice would have been to adjust the asset by $40,000

1 FASB ASC 810-10-65-1.

(80% ownership interest × $50,000 fair value-book value difference). The new requirement is that the asset will be adjusted for the full $50,000 difference no matter what size the controlling interest is.

Analysis of Complicated Purchase with a Noncontrolling Interest

We will illustrate consolidation procedures using the 80% acquisition of Sample Company by Parental, Inc. Presented below are the balance sheet amounts and the fair values of the assets and liabilities of Sample Company as of December 31, 2011 (same as prior example on page 63).

Assets	Book Value	Market Value	Liabilities and Equity	Book Value	Market Value
Accounts receivable	$ 20,000	$ 20,000	Current liabilities	$ 40,000	$ 40,000
Inventory	50,000	55,000	Bonds payable	100,000	100,000
Land.................	40,000	70,000	**Total liabilities**...............	**$140,000**	**$140,000**
Buildings	200,000	250,000			
Accumulated depreciation	(50,000)		Stockholders' equity:		
Equipment	60,000	60,000	Common stock ($1 par).............	$ 10,000	
Accumulated depreciation	(20,000)		Paid-in capital in excess of par	90,000	
Copyright		50,000	Retained earnings	60,000	
			Total equity	$ 160,000	
Total assets	**$300,000**	**$505,000**	**Net assets**.....................	**$160,000**	**$365,000**

Assume that Parental, Inc., issued 16,000 shares of its $1 par value common stock for 80% (8,000 shares) of the outstanding shares of Sample Company. The fair value of a share of Parental, Inc., stock is $25. Parental also pays $25,000 in accounting and legal fees to accomplish the purchase. Parental would make the following entry to record the purchase:

Investment in Sample Company (16,000 shares issued × $25 fair value)	400,000	
Common Stock ($1 par value) (16,000 shares × $1 par)......		16,000
Paid-in Capital in Excess of Par ($400,000 − $16,000 par value)		384,000

Parental would record the costs of the acquisition as follows:

Acquisition Expense (closed to Retained Earnings since only balance sheets are being examined)	25,000	
Cash		25,000

The following value analysis would be prepared for the 80% interest:

Value Analysis Schedule	Company Implied Fair Value	Parent Price (80%)	NCI Value (20%)
Company fair value....................	$ 500,000	$ 400,000	$100,000
Fair value of net assets excluding goodwill ..	365,000	292,000	73,000
Goodwill........................	**$135,000**	**$108,000**	**$ 27,000**
Gain on acquisition....................	N/A	N/A	

Several assumptions went into the above calculation.

♦ Company fair value—It is assumed that if the parent would pay $400,000 for an 80% interest, then the entire subsidiary company is worth $500,000 ($400,000/80%). We will refer to this as the "implied value" of the subsidiary company. Assuming this to be true, the NCI is worth 20% of the total subsidiary company value (20% × $500,000 = $100,000).

This approach assumes that the price the parent would pay is directly proportional to the size of the interest purchased. We will later study the situation where this presumption is defeated. **Unless otherwise stated, exercises and problems in this text will assume the value of the NCI is "implied" by the price the parent pays for the controlling interest.**

◆ Fair value of net assets excluding goodwill ($365,000)—The fair values of the subsidiary accounts are from the comparison of book and fair values. All identifiable assets and all liabilities will be adjusted to 100% of fair value regardless of the size of the controlling interest purchased.

◆ Goodwill—The total goodwill is the excess of the "company fair value" over the fair value of the subsidiary net assets. It is proportionately allocated to the controlling interest and NCI.

Determination and Distribution of Excess Schedule

The D&D schedule that follows revalues the entire entity, including the NCI.

Determination and Distribution of Excess Schedule

	Company Implied Fair Value	Parent Price (80%)	NCI Value (20%)	
Fair value of subsidiary	$ 500,000	$400,000	$100,000	
Less book value of interest acquired:				
Common stock ($1 par)	$ 10,000			
Paid-in capital in excess of par	90,000			
Retained earnings	60,000			
Total equity.	$ 160,000	$160,000	$160,000	
Interest acquired		80%	20%	
Book value.		$128,000	$ 32,000	
Excess of fair value over book value	**$340,000**	$272,000	$ 68,000	

Adjustment of identifiable accounts:

	Adjustment		Worksheet Key
Inventory ($55,000 fair – $50,000 book value)	$ 5,000		**debit D1**
Land ($70,000 fair – $40,000 book value).	30,000		**debit D2**
Buildings ($250,000 fair – $150,000 net book value)	100,000		**debit D3**
Equipment ($60,000 fair – $40,000 net book value) .	20,000		**debit D4**
Copyright ($50,000 fair – $0 book value).	50,000		**debit D5**
Goodwill ($500,000 fair – $365,000 book value) .	**135,000***		**debit D6**
Total	**$340,000**		

*Agrees with total (company) goodwill in the value analysis schedule.

Note the following features of a D&D schedule for a less than 100% parent ownership interest:

◆ The "fair value of subsidiary" line contains the implied value of the entire company, the parent price paid, and the implied value of the NCI from the above value analysis schedule.

◆ The total stockholders' equity of the subsidiary (equal to the net assets of the subsidiary at book value) is allocated 80/20 to the controlling interest and the NCI.

◆ The excess of fair value over book value is shown for the company, the controlling interest, and the NCI. This line means that the entire adjustment of subsidiary net assets will be $340,000. The controlling interest paid $272,000 more than the underlying book value of subsidiary net assets. This is the excess that will appear on the worksheet when the parent's 80% share of subsidiary stockholders' equity is eliminated against the investment account.

Finally, the NCI share of the increase to fair value is $68,000.

◆ All subsidiary assets and liabilities will be increased to 100% of fair value, just as would be the case for a 100% purchase.

Worksheet 2-5: page 92

The D&D schedule provides complete guidance for the worksheet eliminations. Study Worksheet 2-5 on page 92 and note the following:

◆ Elimination (EL) eliminated the subsidiary equity purchased (80% in this example) against the investment account as follows:

(EL)	Common Stock ($1 par)—Sample	8,000	
	Paid-In Capital in Excess of Par—Sample	72,000	
	Retained Earnings—Sample	48,000	
	Investment in Sample Company....................		128,000

◆ The (D) series eliminations distribute the excess applicable to the controlling interest plus the increase in the NCI [labeled (NCI)] to the appropriate accounts, as indicated by the D&D schedule. The adjustment of the NCI is carried to subsidiary retained earnings. Recall, however, that only the total NCI will appear on the consolidated balance sheet. Worksheet eliminations are as follows:

(D1)	Inventory	5,000	
(D2)	Land...	30,000	
(D3)	Buildings	100,000	
(D4)	Equipment	20,000	
(D5)	Copyright	50,000	
(D6)	Goodwill	135,000	
(D)	Investment in Sample Company [remaining excess after (EL)].....................................		272,000
(NCI)	Retained Earnings Sample (NCI share of fair market adjustment).....................................		68,000
Dr. = Cr.	*Check Totals*	*340,000*	*340,000*

Worksheet 2-5 has an additional column, the NCI column. The components of the NCI are summed and presented as a single amount in this balance sheet column. Notice that 100% of the fair values of subsidiary accounts has been consolidated with the existing book values of parent company accounts. The amounts that will appear on the consolidated balance sheet are shown in the final column of Worksheet 2-5. The Balance Sheet columns of the worksheet will show the components of controlling equity (par, paid-in capital in excess of par, and retained earnings) and the total NCI.

Formal Balance Sheet

The formal consolidated balance sheet resulting from the 80% purchase of Sample Company, in exchange for 16,000 Parental shares, has been taken from the Consolidated Balance Sheet column of Worksheet 2-5. Recall, this is the date of acquisition. Chapter 3 will explain the impact of subsequent period activities on the consolidated financial statements.

Parental, Inc. Consolidated Balance Sheet December 31, 2011			
Assets		**Liabilities and Equity**	
Current assets:		Current liabilities	$120,000
Cash	$ 84,000	Bonds payable	300,000
Accounts receivable........	92,000	Total liabilities	$ 420,000
			(continued)

Assets			Liabilities and Equity		
Inventory	135,000				
Total current assets		$ 311,000			
Long-term assets:			Stockholders' equity:		
Land	$ 170,000		Common stock ($1 par)	$ 36,000	
Buildings	800,000		Paid-in capital in excess of par . .	584,000	
Accumulated depreciation . . .	(130,000)		Retained earnings	456,000	
Equipment	320,000		Total controlling equity		1,076,000
Accumulated depreciation . . .	(60,000)		**Noncontrolling interest** .		**100,000**
Copyright	50,000		Total equity		$1,176,000
Goodwill	135,000				
Total long-term assets		1,285,000			
Total assets		$1,596,000	Total liabilities and equity		$ 1,596,000

Adjustment of Goodwill Applicable to NCI

The NCI goodwill value can be reduced below its implied value if there is evidence that the implied value exceeds the real fair value of the NCI's share of goodwill. This could occur when a parent pays a premium to achieve control, which is not dependent on the size of the ownership interest.

The NCI share of goodwill could be reduced to zero, but the NCI share of the fair value of net tangible assets is never reduced. **The total NCI can never be less than the NCI percentage of the fair value of the net assets** (in this case, it cannot be less than 20% × $365,000 = $73,000).

If the fair value of the NCI was estimated to be $90,000 ($10,000 less than the value implied by parent purchase price), the value analysis would be modified as follows (changes are boldfaced):

Value Analysis Schedule	Company Implied Fair Value	Parent Price (80%)	NCI Value (20%)
Company fair value	**$490,000**	$400,000	**$90,000**
Fair value of net assets excluding goodwill	365,000	292,000	73,000
Goodwill	**$125,000**	$108,000	**$17,000**
Gain on acquisition	N/A	N/A	

Several assumptions went into the above calculation.

♦ Company fair value—This is now the sum of the price paid by the parent plus the newly estimated fair value of the NCI.

♦ Fair value of net assets excluding goodwill—The fair values of the subsidiary accounts are from the comparison of book and fair values. These values are never less than fair value.

♦ Goodwill—The total goodwill is the excess of the "company fair value" over the fair value of the subsidiary net assets.

The revised D&D schedule with changes (from the previous example) in boldfaced type would be as shown on page 74.

Determination and Distribution of Excess Schedule

	Company Implied Fair Value	Parent Price (80%)	NCI Value (20%)
Fair value of subsidiary	$ 490,000	$400,000	**$ 90,000**
Less book value of interest acquired:			
Common stock ($1 par)	$ 10,000		
Paid-in capital in excess of par	90,000		
Retained earnings	60,000		
Total equity	$ 160,000	$160,000	$160,000
Interest acquired		80%	20%
Book value		$128,000	$ 32,000
Excess of fair value over book value	**$330,000**	$272,000	**$ 58,000**

Adjustment of identifiable accounts:

	Adjustment		Worksheet Key
Inventory ($55,000 fair − $50,000 book value)	$ 5,000		**debit D1**
Land ($70,000 fair − $40,000 book value)	30,000		**debit D2**
Buildings ($250,000 fair − $150,000 book value) . . .	100,000		**debit D3**
Equipment ($60,000 fair − $40,000 book value)	20,000		**debit D4**
Copyright ($50,000 fair − $0 book value)	50,000		**debit D5**
Goodwill ($490,000 fair − $365,000 book value) .	**125,000***		**debit D6**
Total	**$330,000**		

*Agrees with total (company) goodwill in the value analysis schedule.

  If goodwill becomes impaired in a future period, the impairment charge would be allocated to the controlling interest and the NCI based on the percentage of total goodwill each equity interest received on the D&D schedule. In the original example, where goodwill on the NCI was assumed to be proportional to that recorded on the controlling interest, the impairment charge would be allocated 80/20 to the controlling interest and NCI. In the above example, where goodwill was not proportional, a new percentage would be developed as follows:

	Value	Percentage of Total
Goodwill applicable to parent from value analysis schedule	$108,000	86.4%
Goodwill applicable to NCI from value analysis schedule	17,000	13.6%
Total goodwill	$125,000	

No Goodwill on the Noncontrolling Interest

Currently, International Accounting Standards provide a choice in accounting for the noncontrolling interest. The NCI can be recorded at fair value, which would result in goodwill applicable to the NCI, as demonstrated above. The other choice is to record the NCI at the NCI percentage of the fair value of the net identifiable assets only, with no goodwill on the NCI. Under the non-NCI goodwill model, the preceding example would be modified to appear as shown below.[2]

  If the fair value of the NCI is estimated to be $73,000 (20% × $365,000 fair value of subsidiary company net identifiable assets), the value analysis would be modified as follows (changes are boldfaced):

Value Analysis Schedule	Company Implied Fair Value	Parent Price (80%)	NCI Value (20%)
Company fair value	**$473,000**	$400,000	**$73,000**
Fair value of net assets excluding goodwill . .	365,000	292,000	73,000
Goodwill	**$108,000**	$108,000	**$ 0**
Gain on acquisition	N/A	N/A	

2 IFRS 3, *Business Combinations* (International Accounting Standards Board, January 2008), para. 19.

Several assumptions went into the calculation on page 74.

◆ Company fair value—This is now the sum of the price paid by the parent plus the NCI share of net identifiable assets.

◆ Fair value of net assets excluding goodwill—The fair values of the subsidiary accounts are from the comparison of book and fair values. These values are never less than fair value.

◆ Goodwill—The only goodwill recorded is that applicable to the controlling interest.

The revised D&D schedule with changes (from the previous example) in boldfaced type would be as follows:

Determination and Distribution of Excess Schedule

	Company Implied Fair Value	Parent Price (80%)	NCI Value (20%)
Fair value of subsidiary	$ 473,000	$400,000	**$ 73,000**
Less book value of interest acquired:			
Common stock ($1 par)	$ 10,000		
Paid-in capital in excess of par	90,000		
Retained earnings	60,000		
Total equity.	$ 160,000	$160,000	$160,000
Interest acquired		80%	20%
Book value.		$128,000	$ 32,000
Excess of fair value over book value	**$313,000**	$272,000	**$ 41,000**

Adjustment of identifiable accounts:

	Adjustment		Worksheet Key
Inventory ($55,000 fair − $50,000 book value)	$ 5,000		**debit D1**
Land ($70,000 fair − $40,000 book value).	30,000		**debit D2**
Buildings ($250,000 fair − $150,000 book value) . .	100,000		**debit D3**
Equipment ($60,000 fair − $40,000 book value) . . .	20,000		**debit D4**
Copyright ($50,000 fair − $0 book value).	50,000		**debit D5**
Goodwill ($473,000 fair − $365,000 book value)	**108,000***		**debit D6**
Total	**$313,000**		

*Agrees with total (company) goodwill in the value analysis schedule.

If goodwill becomes impaired in a future period, the impairment charge would apply only to the controlling interest.

Gain on Purchase of Subsidiary

Let us now study the same example, except that the price paid by the parent will be low enough to result in a gain. Assume that Parental, Inc., issued 10,000 shares of its $1 par value common stock for 80% of the outstanding shares of Sample Company. The fair value of a share of Parental, Inc., stock is $25. Parental also pays $25,000 in accounting and legal fees to complete the purchase. Parental would make the following journal entry to record the purchase:

Investment in Sample Company (10,000 shares issued × $25 fair value) . .	250,000	
Common Stock ($1 par value) (10,000 shares × $1 par).		10,000
Paid-In Capital in Excess of Par ($250,000 − $10,000 par value) . . .		240,000

Parental would record the costs of the acquisition as follows:

Acquisition Expense (closed to Retained Earnings since only balance sheets are being examined)	25,000	
Cash.		25,000

Refer back to the prior comparison of book and fair values for the subsidiary. The following value analysis would be prepared for the 80% interest:

Value Analysis Schedule	Company Implied Fair Value	Parent Price (80%)	NCI Value (20%)
Company fair value.....................	$ 323,000	$ 250,000	$73,000
Fair value of net assets excluding goodwill . .	365,000	292,000	73,000
Goodwill	N/A	N/A	
Gain on acquisition	**$(42,000)**	**$(42,000)**	

Several assumptions went into the above calculation.

◆ Company fair value—It is assumed that if the parent would pay $250,000 for an 80% interest, then the entire subsidiary company is worth $312,500 ($250,000/80%). We will refer to this as the "implied value" of the subsidiary company. Assuming this to be true, the NCI is worth 20% of the total subsidiary company value (20% × $312,500 = $62,500). The NCI value, however, can never be less than its share of net identifiable assets ($73,000). Thus, the NCI share of company value is raised to $73,000 (replacing the $62,500).

◆ Fair value of net assets excluding goodwill—The fair values of the subsidiary accounts are from the comparison of book and fair values.

◆ Goodwill—There can be no goodwill when the price paid is less than the fair value of the parent's share of the fair value of net identifiable assets.

◆ Gain on acquisition—The only gain recognized is that applicable to the controlling interest.

The following D&D would be prepared:

Determination and Distribution of Excess Schedule

	Company Implied Fair Value	Parent Price (80%)	NCI Value (20%)	
Fair value of subsidiary	$ 323,000	$250,000	$ 73,000	
Less book value of interest acquired:				
Common stock ($1 par)......................	$ 10,000			
Paid-in capital in excess of par	90,000			
Retained earnings	60,000			
Total equity...............................	$ 160,000	$160,000	$160,000	
Interest acquired		80%	20%	
Book value..................................		$128,000	$ 32,000	
Excess of fair value over book value	**$163,000**	$122,000	$ 41,000	

Adjustment of identifiable accounts:

	Adjustment	Worksheet Key
Inventory ($55,000 fair — $50,000 book value)	$ 5,000	**debit D1**
Land ($70,000 fair — $40,000 book value).........	30,000	**debit D2**
Buildings ($250,000 fair — $150,000 book value) . .	100,000	**debit D3**
Equipment ($60,000 fair — $40,000 book value) . . .	20,000	**debit D4**
Copyright ($50,000 fair — $0 book value).........	50,000	**debit D5**
Gain (only applies to controlling interest). . . .	**(42,000)**	**credit D7**
Total	**$163,000**	

Worksheet 2-6: page 93   Worksheet 2-6 on page 93 is the consolidated worksheet for the $250,000 price. The D&D schedule provides complete guidance for the worksheet eliminations.

◆ Elimination (EL) eliminated the subsidiary equity purchased (80% in this example) against the investment account as follows:

(EL)	Common Stock ($1 par)	8,000	
	Paid-In Capital in Excess of Par	72,000	
	Retained Earnings	48,000	
	Investment in Sample Company.....................		128,000

◆ The (D) series eliminations distribute the excess applicable to the controlling interest plus the increase in the NCI [labeled (NCI)] to the appropriate accounts as indicated by the D&D schedule. Worksheet eliminations are as follows:

(D1)	Inventory	5,000	
(D2)	Land..	30,000	
(D3)	Buildings	100,000	
(D4)	Equipment	20,000	
(D5)	Copyright	50,000	
(D7)	Gain on Purchase of Subsidiary (since we are dealing only with a balance sheet, this would be credited to Controlling Retained Earnings)		42,000
(D)	Investment in Sample Company [remaining excess after (EL)]		122,000
(NCI)	Retained Earnings—Sample (NCI share of fair market adjustment)		41,000
Dr. = Cr.	*Check Totals*	*205,000*	*205,000*

Valuation Schedule Strategy

Here are steps to valuation that will always work if prepared in the order shown below.

Step 1: Enter value for cell A2 (sum of fair values of company's net identifiable assets). Then, enter appropriate percentage of that value into cells B2 and C2. These amounts are fixed regardless of the price paid by the parent. They will never change.

Value Analysis Schedule	A: Company Implied Fair Value	B: Parent Price (80%)	C: NCI Value (20%)
1. Company fair value			
2. Fair value of net assets excluding goodwill.....	**365,000**	**292,000**	**73,000**
3. Goodwill			
4. Gain on acquisition			

Step 2: Enter price paid for controlling interest by the parent in cell B1.

Value Analysis Schedule	A: Company Implied Fair Value	B: Parent Price (80%)	C: NCI Value (20%)
1. Company fair value........................		**$420,000**	
2. Fair value of net assets excluding goodwill.....	365,000	292,000	73,000
3. Goodwill			
4. Gain on acquisition			

Step 3: Compare B1, the price paid by the parent, and B2, the parent's share of the fair value of the company's net identifiable assets.

Step 3(a): If B1>B2, enter B3, which is the goodwill applicable to the parent. If B2>B1, go to Step 3(b) in the "Analysis with a Gain" section. Then, complete cell C1. Normally, this amount will be proportional to B1. It can be a different amount (based on estimated fair value) but never less than cell C2. In this case, it is estimated to be $90,000. The proportionate value would be $105,000 for this example. Calculate the value for C3.

Value Analysis Schedule	A: Company Implied Fair Value	B: Parent Price (80%)	C: NCI Value (20%)
1. Company fair value........................		$ 420,000	**$90,000***
2. Fair value of net assets excluding goodwill.....	365,000	292,000	73,000
3. **Goodwill**		**$128,000**	**$17,000**
4. Gain on acquisition			

*Must be greater than $73,000; can be different than proportionate value, 20%/80% × $420,000 = $105,000. Recall the earlier example where the fair value of the NCI was estimated to be $90,000 ($15,000 less than the value implied by parent purchase price).

Step 4: Complete remaining cells:

Value Analysis Schedule	A: Company Implied Fair Value	B: Parent Price (80%)	C: NCI Value (20%)
Company fair value........................	**$510,000**	$420,000	$90,000
Fair value of net assets excluding goodwill.......	365,000	292,000	73,000
Goodwill................................	**$145,000**	**$128,000**	**$17,000**
Gain on acquisition			

Analysis with a Gain

Let us redo the analysis with a parent price paid of $250,000:

Step 1: Enter and allocate fair values.

Value Analysis Schedule	A: Company Implied Fair Value	B: Parent Price (80%)	C: NCI Value (20%)
Company fair value			
Fair value of net assets excluding goodwill......	**365,000**	**292,000**	**73,000**
Goodwill			
Gain on acquisition			

Step 2: Enter the price paid by the parent.

Value Analysis Schedule	A: Company Implied Fair Value	B: Parent Price (80%)	C: NCI Value (20%)
Company fair value........................		**$250,000**	
Fair value of net assets excluding goodwill.......	365,000	292,000	73,000
Goodwill			
Gain on acquisition			

Step 3(b)1: Where B2>B1: Calculate the gain applicable to the parent.

Value Analysis Schedule	A: Company Implied Fair Value	B: Parent Price (80%)	C: NCI Value (20%)
Company fair value........................		$250,000	
Fair value of net assets excluding goodwill.......	365,000	292,000	73,000
Goodwill			
Gain on acquisition.........................		**$ 42,000**	

Step 3(b)2: Complete remaining cells:

Value Analysis Schedule	A: Company Implied Fair Value	B: Parent Price (80%)	C: NCI Value (20%)
Company fair value.	**$323,000**	$ 250,000	**$73,000**
Fair value of net assets excluding goodwill	365,000	292,000	73,000
Goodwill			
Gain on acquisition	**$ (42,000)**	**$(42,000)**	$ (0)

Cell C1 cannot be less than Cell C2.

If the fair value of the NCI exceeded $73,000, the excess of the cost over fair value would be an offset to the gain on the controlling interest. Consider the following analysis when the NCI has a fair value of $90,000:

Value Analysis Schedule	A: Company Implied Fair Value	B: Parent Price (80%)	C: NCI Value (20%)
Company fair value.	**$340,000**	$250,000	**$90,000**
Fair value of net assets excluding goodwill	365,000	292,000	73,000
Goodwill			
Gain on acquisition	**$ (25,000)**	$ (42,000)	**$17,000**

The elimination to distribute the excess on the worksheet would be as follows:

Investment in Subsidiary	42,000	
NCI		17,000
Gain on Acquisition of Subsidiary		25,000

Parent Exchanges Noncash Assets for Controlling Interest

The parent must bring to fair value any assets, other than cash, that it exchanges for the controlling interest. If those assets are retained and used by the subsidiary company, the gain must be eliminated in the consolidation process.

Assets transferred would be retained by the subsidiary when either:

1. The assets are transferred to the former shareholders of the subsidiary company and the shareholders sell the assets to the subsidiary company, or
2. The assets are transferred directly to the subsidiary company in exchange for newly issued shares or treasury shares.

The gain would be deferred using the procedures demonstrated in Chapter 4 for the parent sale of a fixed asset to the subsidiary.

REFLECTION

- A less than 100% interest requires that value analysis be applied to the entire subsidiary.
- Subsidiary accounts are adjusted to full fair value regardless of the controlling percentage ownership.
- The noncontrolling interest shares in all asset and liability fair value adjustments.

- The noncontrolling interest does not share a gain on the acquisition (when applicable).
- The noncontrolling share of subsidiary equity appears as a single line-item amount within the equity section of the balance sheet.

8

OBJECTIVE

Show the impact of preexisting goodwill on the consolidation process, and be able to include prior investments in the acquisition price.

PREEXISTING GOODWILL

If a subsidiary is purchased and it has goodwill on its books, that goodwill is ignored in the value analysis. The only complication caused by existing goodwill is that the D&D schedule will adjust existing goodwill, rather than only recording new goodwill. Let us return to the example involving the 80% acquisition of Sample Company on page 63 and change only two facts: assume Sample has goodwill of $40,000 and its retained earnings is $40,000 greater. The revised book and fair values would be as follows:

Assets	Book Value	Market Value	Liabilities and Equity	Book Value	Market Value
Accounts receivable	$ 20,000	$ 20,000	Current liabilities	$ 40,000	$ 40,000
Inventory	50,000	55,000	Bonds payable	100,000	100,000
Land......................	40,000	70,000	**Total liabilities**...........	**$140,000**	**$140,000**
Buildings	200,000	250,000	**Stockholders' equity:**		
Accumulated depreciation	(50,000)		Common stock ($1 par)........	$ 10,000	
Equipment	60,000	60,000	Paid-in capital in excess of par...	90,000	
Accumulated depreciation	(20,000)		Retained earnings	100,000	
Copyright		50,000	Total equity	$ 200,000	
Goodwill	40,000		Total liabilities and equity	**$340,000**	
Total assets	**$340,000**	**$505,000**	**Net assets**.................		**$365,000**

Assume that Parental, Inc., issued 16,000 shares of its $1 par value common stock for 80% (8,000 shares) of the outstanding shares of Sample Company. The fair value of a share of Parental, Inc., stock is $25. Parental also pays $25,000 in accounting and legal fees to accomplish the purchase. Parental would make the following entry to record the purchase:

Investment in Sample Company (16,000 shares issued × $25 fair value)	400,000	
Common Stock ($1 par value) (16,000 shares × $1 par)...............		16,000
Paid-In Capital in Excess of Par ($400,000 − $16,000 par value)		384,000

Parental would record the costs of the acquisition as follows:

Acquisition Expense (closed to Retained Earnings since only balance sheets are being examined)..	25,000	
Cash		25,000

The value analysis schedule is unchanged. The fair value of the Sample Company net assets does not include goodwill.

Value Analysis Schedule	Company Implied Fair Value	Parent Price (80%)	NCI Value (20%)
Company fair value.........................	$ 500,000	$ 400,000	$100,000
Fair value of net assets excluding goodwill	365,000	292,000	73,000
Goodwill...............................	**$135,000**	**$108,000**	**$ 27,000**
Gain on acquisition			

The D&D schedule differs from the earlier one only to the extent that:

◆ The Sample Company retained earnings is $40,000 greater.

◆ The implied goodwill of $135,000 is compared to existing goodwill of $40,000.

Determination and Distribution of Excess Schedule

	Company Implied Fair Value	Parent Price (80%)	NCI Value (20%)	
Fair value of subsidiary	$ 500,000	$400,000	$100,000	
Less book value of interest acquired:				
Common stock ($1 par)	$ 10,000			
Paid-in capital in excess of par	90,000			
Retained earnings	**100,000**			
Total equity.	$ 200,000	$200,000	$200,000	
Interest acquired		80%	20%	
Book value.		$160,000	$ 40,000	
Excess of fair value over book value	**$300,000**	$240,000	$ 60,000	

Adjustment of identifiable accounts:

	Adjustment	Worksheet Key
Inventory ($55,000 fair − $50,000 book value)	$ 5,000	**debit D1**
Land ($70,000 fair − $40,000 book value).	30,000	**debit D2**
Buildings ($250,000 fair − $150,000 net book value)	100,000	**debit D3**
Equipment ($60,000 fair − $40,000 net book value) .	20,000	**debit D4**
Copyright ($50,000 fair − $0 book value).	50,000	**debit D5**
Goodwill ($135,000 fair − $40,000 book value) . .	**95,000**	**debit D6**
Total	**$300,000**	

The D&D schedule provides complete guidance for the worksheet eliminations. Changes from Worksheet 2-5 are in boldface. Study Worksheet 2-7 on page 94 and note the following: Worksheet 2-7: page 94

◆ Elimination (EL) eliminated the subsidiary equity purchased (80% in this example) against the investment account as follows:

(EL)	Common Stock ($1 par)—Sample	8,000	
	Paid-In Capital in Excess of Par—Sample	72,000	
	Retained Earnings—Sample	**80,000**	
	Investment in Sample Company.		**160,000**

◆ The (D) series eliminations distribute the excess applicable to the controlling interest plus the increase in the NCI [labeled (NCI)] to the appropriate accounts, as indicated by the D&D schedule. The adjustment of the NCI is carried to subsidiary retained earnings.

(D1)	Inventory	5,000	
(D2)	Land.	30,000	
(D3)	Buildings	100,000	
(D4)	Equipment	20,000	
(D5)	Copyright	50,000	
(D6)	Goodwill **($135,000 − $40,000 book value)**	**95,000**	
(D)	Investment in Sample Company [remaining excess after (EL)] . . .		**240,000**
(NCI)	Retained Earnings Sample (NCI share of fair market adjustment)		**60,000**
Dr. = Cr.	*Check Totals*	*300,000*	*300,000*

The Consolidated Balance Sheet column of Worksheet 2-7 is the same as those for Worksheet 2-5 and the resulting balance sheet (as shown on page 73 is unchanged).

REFLECTION

- Where the acquired firm already has goodwill on its books, the D&D adjusts from the recorded goodwill to the goodwill calculated in the valuation schedule.

OWNERSHIP OF A PRIOR NONCONTROLLING INTEREST

The acquirer may already own a noncontrolling investment (less than 50%) interest in a company. It may then decide to buy additional shares of common stock to achieve a controlling interest. The previously owned shares are adjusted to fair value and a gain or loss is recorded on the investment. The fair value of the shares is then added to the price paid for the new shares. The prior plus new interest is treated as one price paid for a controlling interest. Normally, the fair value of the previously owned shares is based on the price paid for the controlling interest.

For example, assume Company P owns a 10% interest (10,000 shares) in Company S that Company P purchased at a prior date for $20 per share. At a later date, Company P purchases another 50,000 shares (50% interest) for $30 per share.

The 10,000 previously purchased shares would be adjusted to fair value as follows:

Investment in Company S shares (10,000 shares × $10 increase)	100,000	
Unrealized Gain on Revaluation of Investments		100,000

This entry would increase the carrying value of the 10,000 previously owned shares to $300,000. The acquisition price for the controlling 60% interest would be calculated as follows:

Fair value of previously owned 10% interest	$ 300,000
Acquisition of 50,000 shares at $30	1,500,000
Total acquisition cost	$1,800,000

Assuming cash is paid for the 50,000 shares, the acquisition entry would be as follows:

Investment in Subsidiary Company S	1,800,000	
Cash (50,000 shares at $30)		1,500,000
Investment in Company S (10,000 shares × $30)		300,000

Value analysis and the D&D schedule would be constructed for a single 60% interest with an acquisition price of $1,800,000.

Two observations that should be made about the prior investment that is rolled into the total acquisition cost are as follows:

1. The above investment was a passive investment that is held at the original purchase cost. Such an investment is a part of the year-end market value adjustments that are made for passive investments. The portfolio of investments would no longer include the investment that has been rolled into a controlling investment. Any adjustment applicable to those shares would be reversed out of the portfolio at the next period-end.

2. The previously owned interest may be large enough to be accounted for under the equity method (typically greater than a 20% interest). If that is the case, the investment will be carried at equity-adjusted cost. It will be adjusted to fair value on the date of the later acquisition that creates control.

- Any previously owned interest in the acquiree is adjusted to fair value based on the price paid for the later interest that creates control.

PUSH-DOWN ACCOUNTING

Thus far, it has been assumed that the subsidiary's statements are unaffected by the parent's purchase of a controlling interest in the subsidiary. None of the subsidiary's accounts is adjusted on the subsidiary's books. In all preceding examples, adjustments to reflect fair value are made only on the consolidated worksheet. This is the most common but not the only accepted method.

Some accountants object to the inconsistency of using book values in the subsidiary's separate statements while using fair value-adjusted values when the same accounts are included in the consolidated statements. They would advocate *push-down accounting*, whereby the subsidiary's accounts are adjusted to reflect the fair value adjustments. In accordance with the new basis of accounting, retained earnings are eliminated, and the balance (as adjusted for fair value adjustments) is added to paid-in capital. It is argued that the purchase of a controlling interest gives rise to a new basis of accountability for the interest traded, and the subsidiary accounts should reflect those values.

If the push-down method were applied to the example of a 100% purchase for $500,000 on page 63, the following entry would be made by the subsidiary on its books:

Inventory	5,000	
Land	30,000	
Buildings	100,000	
Equipment	20,000	
Copyright	50,000	
Goodwill	135,000	
Paid-In Capital in Excess of Par		340,000

This entry would raise the subsidiary equity to $500,000. The $500,000 investment account would be eliminated against the $500,000 subsidiary equity with no excess remaining. All accounts are adjusted to full fair value, even if there is a noncontrolling interest. The SEC staff has adopted a policy of requiring push-down accounting, in some cases, for the separately published statements of a subsidiary. The existence of any significant noncontrolling interests (usually above 5%) and/or significant publicly held debt or preferred stock generally eliminates the need to use push-down accounting. **Note that the consolidated statements are unaffected by this issue.** The only difference is in the placement of the adjustments from the determination and distribution of excess schedule. The conventional approach, which is used in this text, makes the adjustments on the consolidated worksheet. The push-down method makes the same adjustments directly on the books of the subsidiary. Under the push-down method, the adjustments are already made when consolidation procedures are applied. Since all accounts are adjusted to reflect fair values, the investment account is eliminated against subsidiary equity with no excess. The difference in methods affects only the presentation on the subsidiary's separate statements.

- IFRS does not allow "push-down" accounting to be used.

IASB *standards*

REFLECTION

- Push-down accounting revalues subsidiary accounts directly on the books of the subsidiary based on adjustments indicated in the D&D schedule.

- Since assets are revalued before the consolidation process starts, no distribution of excess (to adjust accounts) is required on the consolidated worksheet.

10
OBJECTIVE

Demonstrate worksheet procedures for reverse acquisitions.

APPENDIX: REVERSE ACQUISITION

A reverse acquisition occurs when a publicly traded firm issues its shares to acquire an interest in a larger privately owned company. The number of shares issued to the privately owned firm is so large that the owners of the private firm then own more shares than the original owners of the public firm. Thus, the new owners own a controlling interest in the public company. The end result is a role reversal because the acquiring firm is really the private firm since its owners are the ones in control. The example that follows is based directly on the example used in FASB ASC 840-40-55-4 to allow the reader further understanding. Assume the following balance sheets pertain to Private Company and Public Company prior to the acquisition:

Private Company (the acquirer, but the company receiving public shares)
Balance Sheet
December 31, 2011

Assets		Liabilities and Equity	
Current assets	$ 700	Long-term liabilities	$1,700
Fixed assets	3,000	Common stock (60 shares) ($1 par) . .	60
		Paid-in capital in excess of par	540
		Retained earnings	1,400
Total assets.	$3,700	Total liabilities and equity	$3,700

Public Company (the acquiree, but the company issuing public shares)
Balance Sheet
December 31, 2011

Assets	Book Value	Fair Value	Liabilities and Equity	Book Value	Fair Value
Current assets	$ 500	$ 500	Long-term liabilities	$ 700	$700
Fixed assets	1,300	1,500	Common stock (100 shares) ($1 par)	100	
			Paid-in capital in excess of par.	200	
			Retained earnings	800	
Total assets.	$1,800	$2,000	Total liabilities and equity	$1,800	

The shareholders of Private Company request 150 Public Company shares in exchange for all of their 60 Private Company shares. This is an exchange ratio of 2.5 to 1. While alternative fair values may be used, the most likely value would be that of the current fair value ($16 each) of the Public shares prior to the acquisition. The value of the interest acquired by Private Company is calculated as follows:

Fair value of existing Public Company equity (100 shares × $16)	$1,600
Private Company interest in Public Company	× 60%*
	$ 960

*150 new Public Company shares issued to Private Company/(150 new +100 existing shares) = 60% (Private Company's ownership share of Public Company).

Upon issuing the 150 new shares, Public Company would make the following investment entry:

Investment in Private Company	960	
Common Stock ($1 par value) (150 shares × $1 par)		150
Paid-In Capital in Excess of Par ($960 − $150 par value)		810

Despite the fact that Public Company is the legal parent, the shareholders of Private Company now hold the controlling interest in Public Company. They own 60% (150 of 250 shares) of the combined company.

The following diagram depicts the change in ownership:

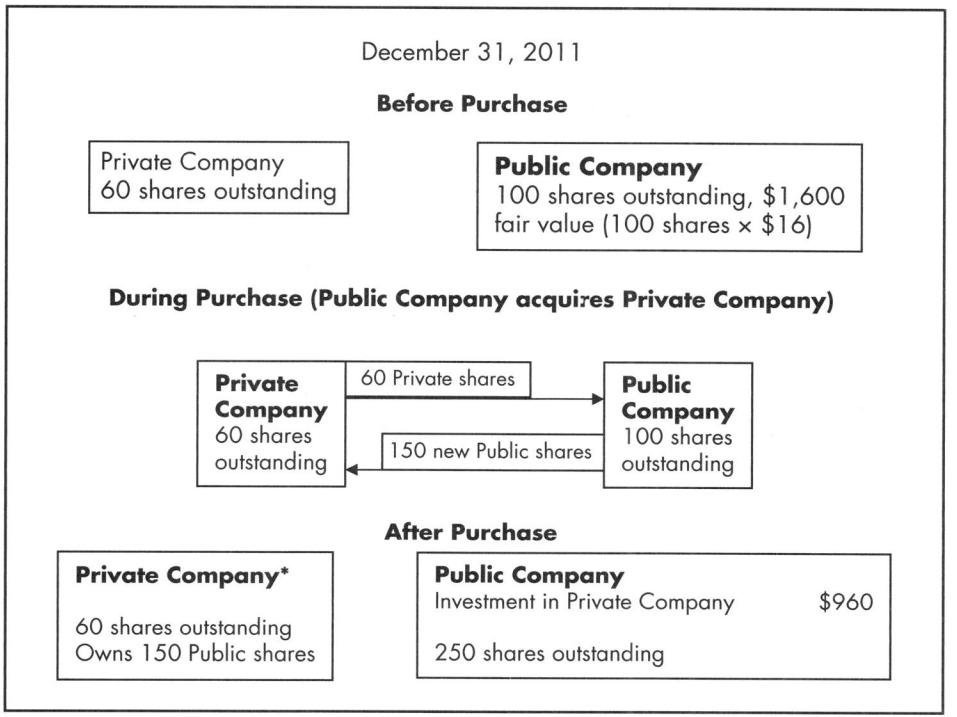

Because the shareholders of Private Company are the controlling interest, Private Company cannot revalue its assets to fair value. The controlled company is Public Company; thus, it is the company that must have its net assets adjusted to fair value. This means that value analysis is only applied to Public Company.

The following value analysis would be prepared for Public Company. The fair value analysis would apply to only those assets present just prior to the acquisition. The fair value of Public Company at the time of the acquisition can be calculated as $1,600 (100 shares × $16 market value).

Value Analysis Schedule	Company Implied Fair Value	Parent Price[b] (60%)	NCI Value[c] (40%)
Company fair value[a]	$1,600	$ 960	$ 640
Fair value of net assets excluding goodwill	1,300	780	520
Goodwill	**$ 300**	**$180**	**$120**
Gain on acquisition	N/A	N/A	

[a]Values are prior to acquisition (100 shares × $16 market value).
[b]Subsequent to acquisition, Private Company is the "parent" with 60% ownership; prior to acquisition, Private Company has 0% ownership of Public Company.
[c]Prior to acquisition, this represents 100% ownership of Public Company; subsequent to acquisition, these holders of 100 of the 250 shares of Public Company become the 40% NCI.

Determination and Distribution of Excess Schedule

	Company Implied Fair Value	Parent Price* (60%)	NCI Value (40%)
Fair value of subsidiary	$1,600	$ 960	$ 640
Less book value interest acquired:			
Common stock ($1 par)	$ 100		
Paid-in capital in excess of par	200		
Retained earnings	800		
Total equity	$1,100	$1,100	$1,100
Interest acquired		60%	40%
Book value		$ 660	$ 440
Excess of fair value over book value	**$ 500**	$ 300	$ 200

Adjustment of identifiable accounts:

	Adjustment		Worksheet Key
Fixed assets ($1,500 fair − $1,300 book value)	$ 200		**debit D1**
Goodwill	**300**		**debit D2**
Total	**$ 500**		

Worksheet 2A-1: page 95

Worksheet 2A-1 on page 95 contains the consolidation procedures used for this acquisition. The first step is to eliminate Investment in Public Company and Investment in Private Company against 60% of the equity of Public Company *at the time of the acquisition* as follows:

(EL)	Common stock ($1 par)—Public Company (60% × $100)	60	
	Paid-In Capital in Excess of Par—Public Company (60% × $200)	120	
	Retained Earnings—Public Company (60% × $800)	480	
	Investment in Private Company		660

Then, the $500 adjustment of Public Company assets to fair value is made. The Private Company retained earnings (as of the acquisition date) receives the increase.

(D1)	Fixed Assets	200	
(D2)	Goodwill	300	
(D)	Investment in Private Company		300
(NCI)	Retained Earnings—Public Company		200

Finally, the following amounts are reassigned to the outstanding, new Public Company shares:

(adj)	**Common Stock ($1 par)—Private Company**	**60**	
	Paid-In Capital in Excess of Par—Private Company . .	**540**	
	Common Stock ($1 par)—Public Company		**150**
	Paid-In Capital in Excess of Par—Public Company		
	($600 − $150 par)		**450**

Private Company shares no longer exist outside the consolidated company. Any equity applicable to them must be reassigned to Public Company shares.

The resulting balance sheet shows the remaining shares of the original Public Company equity as the NCI.

Public Company and Subsidiary Private Company
Balance Sheet
December 31, 2011

Assets		Liabilities and Equity	
Current assets	$1,200	Long-term liabilities	$2,400
Fixed assets	4,500	Equity	
Goodwill	300	NCI	$1,600
		Common stock, (150 shares) ($1 par) . .	150
		Paid-in capital in excess of par	450
Total assets	$6,000	Retained earnings	1,400
		Total equity	$3,600
		Total liabilities and equity	$6,000

Worksheet 2-1

100% Interest; Price Equals Book Value
Company P and Subsidiary Company S
Worksheet for Consolidated Balance Sheet
December 31, 2011

Worksheet 2-1 (see page 60)

		Trial Balance		Eliminations & Adjustments		Consolidated Balance Sheet	
		Company P	Company S	Dr.	Cr.		
1	Cash	300,000				300,000	1
2	Accounts Receivable	300,000	200,000			500,000	2
3	Inventory	100,000	100,000			200,000	3
4	Investment in Company S	500,000			(EL) 500,000		4
5							5
6	Equipment (net)	150,000	300,000			450,000	6
7	Goodwill						7
8	Current Liabilities	(150,000)	(100,000)			(250,000)	8
9	Bonds Payable	(500,000)				(500,000)	9
10	Common Stock—Company S		(200,000)	(EL) 200,000			10
11	Retained Earnings—Company S		(300,000)	(EL) 300,000			11
12	Common Stock—Company P	(100,000)				(100,000)	12
13	Retained Earnings—Company P	(600,000)				(600,000)	13
14	Totals	0	0	500,000	500,000	0	14

Eliminations and Adjustments:

(EL)　Eliminate the investment in the subsidiary against the subsidiary equity accounts.

Worksheet 2-2

100% Interest; Price Exceeds Book Value
Company P and Subsidiary Company S
Worksheet for Consolidated Balance Sheet
December 31, 2011

Worksheet 2-2 (see page 62)

		Trial Balance		Eliminations & Adjustments		Consolidated Balance Sheet	
		Company P	Company S	Dr.	Cr.		
1	Cash	100,000				100,000	1
2	Accounts Receivable	300,000	200,000			500,000	2
3	Inventory	100,000	100,000	(D1) 20,000		220,000	3
4	Investment in Company S	700,000			(EL) 500,000		4
5					(D) 200,000		5
6	Equipment (net)	150,000	300,000	(D2) 100,000		550,000	6
7	Goodwill			(D3) 80,000		80,000	7
8	Current Liabilities	(150,000)	(100,000)			(250,000)	8
9	Bonds Payable	(500,000)				(500,000)	9
10	Common Stock—Company S		(200,000)	(EL) 200,000			10
11	Retained Earnings—Company S		(300,000)	(EL) 300,000			11
12	Common Stock—Company P	(100,000)				(100,000)	12
13	Retained Earnings—Company P	(600,000)				(600,000)	13
14	Totals	0	0	700,000	700,000	0	14

Eliminations and Adjustments:

(EL) Eliminate the investment in the subsidiary against the subsidiary equity accounts.
(D)   Distribute $200,000 excess of cost over book value as follows:
(D1) Inventory, $20,000.
(D2) Equipment, $100,000.
(D3) Goodwill, $80,000.

Worksheet 2-3

100% Interest; Price Exceeds Market Value of Identifiable Net Assets

Parental, Inc. and Subsidiary Sample Company
Worksheet for Consolidated Balance Sheet
December 31, 2011

Worksheet 2-3 (see page 64)

(Credit balance amounts are in parentheses.)	Balance Sheet Parental	Sample	Eliminations & Adjustments Dr.	Cr.	Consolidated Balance Sheet	
Cash	84,000				84,000	1
Accounts Receivable	72,000	20,000			92,000	2
Inventory	80,000	50,000	(D1) 5,000		135,000	3
Land	100,000	40,000	(D2) 30,000		170,000	4
Investment in Sample Company	500,000			(EL) 160,000		5
				(D) 340,000		6
Buildings	500,000	200,000	(D3) 100,000		800,000	7
Accumulated Depreciation	(80,000)	(50,000)			(130,000)	8
Equipment	240,000	60,000	(D4) 20,000		320,000	9
Accumulated Depreciation	(40,000)	(20,000)			(60,000)	10
Copyright			(D5) 50,000		50,000	11
Goodwill			(D6) 135,000		135,000	12
Current Liabilities	(80,000)	(40,000)			(120,000)	14
Bonds Payable	(200,000)	(100,000)			(300,000)	13
Common Stock—Sample		(10,000)	(EL) 10,000			14
Paid-In Capital in Excess of Par—Sample		(90,000)	(EL) 90,000			15
Retained Earnings—Sample		(60,000)	(EL) 60,000			16
Common Stock—Parental	(40,000)				(40,000)	17
Paid-In Capital in Excess of Par—Parental	(680,000)				(680,000)	18
Retained Earnings—Parental	(456,000)				(456,000)	19
Totals	0	0	500,000	500,000	0	20

Eliminations and Adjustments:

(EL) Eliminate 100% subsidiary equity against investment account.
(D) Distribute remaining excess in investment account plus NCI adjustment to:
(D1) Inventory.
(D2) Land.
(D3) Buildings (recorded cost is increased without removing accumulated depreciation). The alternative is to debit Accumulated Depreciation for $50,000 and Buildings for $50,000. This would also restate the net asset at fair value.
(D4) Equipment (recorded cost is increased without removing accumulated depreciation). The alternative is to debit Accumulated Depreciation for $20,000. This would also restate the net asset at fair value.
(D5) Copyright.
(D6) Goodwill.

Worksheet 2-4

100% Interest; Price Exceeds Fair Value of Net Identifiable Assets

Parental, Inc. and Subsidiary Sample Company
Worksheet for Consolidated Balance Sheet
December 31, 2011

Worksheet 2-4 (see page 67)

(Credit balance amounts are in parentheses.)	Balance Sheet		Eliminations & Adjustments		Consolidated Balance Sheet	
	Parental	Sample	Dr.	Cr.		
Cash	84,000				84,000	1
Accounts Receivable	72,000	20,000			92,000	2
Inventory	80,000	50,000	(D1) 5,000		135,000	3
Land	100,000	40,000	(D2) 30,000		170,000	4
Investment in Sample Company	300,000			(EL) 160,000		5
				(D) 140,000		6
Buildings	500,000	200,000	(D3) 100,000		800,000	7
Accumulated Depreciation	(80,000)	(50,000)			(130,000)	8
Equipment	240,000	60,000	(D4) 20,000		320,000	9
Accumulated Depreciation	(40,000)	(20,000)			(60,000)	10
Copyright			(D5) 50,000		50,000	11
Goodwill						12
Current Liabilities	(80,000)	(40,000)			(120,000)	13
Bonds Payable	(200,000)	(100,000)			(300,000)	14
Common Stock—Sample		(10,000)	(EL) 10,000			15
Paid-In Capital in Excess of Par—Sample		(90,000)	(EL) 90,000			16
Retained Earnings—Sample		(60,000)	(EL) 60,000			17
Common Stock—Parental	(32,000)				(32,000)	18
Paid-In Capital in Excess of Par—Parental	(488,000)				(488,000)	19
Retained Earnings—Parental	(456,000)			(D7) 65,000	(521,000)	20
Totals	0	0	365,000	365,000	0	21

Eliminations and Adjustments:

(EL) Eliminate 100% subsidiary equity against investment account.
(D) Distribute remaining excess in investment account plus NCI adjustment to:
(D1) Inventory.
(D2) Land.
(D3) Buildings (recorded cost is increased without removing accumulated depreciation).
The alternative is to debit Accumulated Depreciation for $50,000 and
Buildings for $50,000. This would also restate the net asset at fair value.

(D4) Equipment (recorded cost is increased without removing accumulated depreciation).
The alternative is to debit Accumulated Depreciation for $20,000.
This would also restate the net asset at fair value.
(D5) Copyright.
(D7) Gain on acquisition (close to Parental's Retained Earnings since balance sheet only worksheet)

Worksheet 2-5

80% Interest; Price Exceeds Fair Value of Net Identifiable Assets

Parental, Inc. and Subsidiary Sample Company
Worksheet for Consolidated Balance Sheet
December 31, 2011

Worksheet 2-5 (see page 72)

	(Credit balance amounts are in parentheses.)	Balance Sheet Parental	Balance Sheet Sample	Eliminations & Adjustments Dr.		Eliminations & Adjustments Cr.		NCI	Consolidated Balance Sheet	
1	Cash	84,000							84,000	1
2	Accounts Receivable	72,000	20,000						92,000	2
3	Inventory	80,000	50,000	(D1)	5,000				135,000	3
4	Land	100,000	40,000	(D2)	30,000				170,000	4
5	Investment in Sample Company	400,000				(EL)	128,000			5
6						(D)	272,000			6
7	Buildings	500,000	200,000	(D3)	100,000				800,000	7
8	Accumulated Depreciation	(80,000)	(50,000)						(130,000)	8
9	Equipment	240,000	60,000	(D4)	20,000				320,000	9
10	Accumulated Depreciation	(40,000)	(20,000)						(60,000)	10
11	Copyright			(D5)	50,000				50,000	11
12	Goodwill			(D6)	135,000				135,000	12
13	Current Liabilities	(80,000)	(40,000)						(120,000)	13
14	Bonds Payable	(200,000)	(100,000)						(300,000)	14
15	Common Stock—Sample		(10,000)	(EL)	8,000			(2,000)		15
16	Paid-In Capital in Excess of Par—Sample		(90,000)	(EL)	72,000			(18,000)		16
17	Retained Earnings—Sample		(60,000)	(EL)	48,000	(NCI)	68,000	(80,000)		17
18	Common Stock—Parental	(36,000)							(36,000)	18
19	Paid-In Capital in Excess of Par—Parental	(584,000)							(584,000)	19
20	Retained Earnings—Parental	(456,000)							(456,000)	20
21	Totals	0	0		468,000		468,000			21
22	NCI							(100,000)	(100,000)	22
23	Totals							0	0	23

Eliminations and Adjustments:

(EL)   Eliminate **80%** subsidiary equity against investment account.
(NCI)   **Adjust NCI to fair value (credit to Sample's Retained Earnings).**
(D)   **Distribute remaining excess in investment account plus NCI adjustment to:**
(D1)   Inventory.
(D2)   Land.
(D3)   Buildings (recorded cost is increased without removing accumulated depreciation).
The alternative is to debit Accumulated Depreciation for $50,000 and Buildings for $50,000. This would also restate the net asset at fair value.

(D4)   Equipment (recorded cost is increased without removing accumulated depreciation).
The alternative is to debit Accumulated Depreciation for $20,000.
This would also restate the net asset at fair value.
(D5)   Copyright.
(D6)   Goodwill.

Worksheet 2-6

80% Interest; Price Is Less Than Fair Value of Net Identifiable Assets

Parental, Inc. and Subsidiary Sample Company
Worksheet for Consolidated Balance Sheet
December 31, 2011

Worksheet 2-6 (see page 76)

(Credit balance amounts are in parentheses.)	Balance Sheet Parental	Balance Sheet Sample	Eliminations & Adjustments Dr.		Eliminations & Adjustments Cr.		NCI	Consolidated Balance Sheet	
Cash	254,000							254,000	1
Accounts Receivable	72,000	20,000						92,000	2
Inventory	80,000	50,000	(D1)	5,000				135,000	3
Land	100,000	40,000	(D2)	30,000				170,000	4
Investment in Sample Company	250,000				(EL)	128,000			5
					(D)	122,000			6
Buildings	500,000	200,000	(D3)	100,000				800,000	7
Accumulated Depreciation	(80,000)	(50,000)						(130,000)	8
Equipment	240,000	60,000	(D4)	20,000				320,000	9
Accumulated Depreciation	(40,000)	(20,000)						(60,000)	10
Copyright			(D5)	50,000				50,000	11
Goodwill									12
Current Liabilities	(80,000)	(40,000)						(120,000)	13
Bonds Payable	(200,000)	(100,000)						(300,000)	14
Common Stock—Sample		(10,000)	(EL)	8,000			(2,000)		15
Paid-In Capital in Excess of Par—Sample		(90,000)	(EL)	72,000			(18,000)		16
Retained Earnings—Sample		(60,000)	(EL)	48,000	(NCI)	41,000	(53,000)		17
Common Stock—Parental	(36,800)							(36,800)	18
Paid-In Capital in Excess of Par—Parental	(603,200)							(603,200)	19
Retained Earnings—Parental	(456,000)				(D7)	42,000		(498,000)	20
Totals	0	0		333,000		333,000			21
NCI							(73,000)	(73,000)	22
Totals								0	23

Eliminations and Adjustments:

(EL) Eliminate 80% subsidiary equity against investment account.
(NCI) Adjust NCI to fair value (credit to Sample's Retained Earnings).
(D) Distribute remaining excess in investment account plus NCI adjustment to:
(D1) Inventory.
(D2) Land.
(D3) Buildings (recorded cost is increased without removing accumulated depreciation). The alternative is to debit Accumulated Depreciation for $50,000 and Buildings for $50,000. This would also restate the net asset at fair value.

(D4) Equipment (recorded cost is increased without removing accumulated depreciation). The alternative is to debit Accumulated Depreciation for $20,000. This would also restate the net asset at fair value.
(D5) Copyright.
(D7) Gain on acquisition (close to Parental's Retained Earnings since balance-sheet-only worksheet).

Worksheet 2-7

80% Interest; Price Exceeds Fair Value of Net Identifiable Assets
Preexisting Goodwill

Parental, Inc. and Subsidiary Sample Company
Worksheet for Consolidated Balance Sheet
December 31, 2011

Worksheet 2-7 (see page 81)

	(Credit balance amounts are in parentheses.)	Balance Sheet — Parental	Balance Sheet — Sample	Eliminations & Adjustments Dr.	Eliminations & Adjustments Cr.	NCI	Consolidated Balance Sheet	
1	Cash	84,000	20,000				84,000	1
2	Accounts Receivable	72,000	20,000				92,000	2
3	Inventory	80,000	50,000	(D1) 5,000			135,000	3
4	Land	100,000	40,000	(D2) 30,000			170,000	4
5	Investment in Sample Company	400,000			(EL) 160,000			5
6					(D) 240,000			6
7	Buildings	500,000	200,000	(D3) 100,000			800,000	7
8	Accumulated Depreciation	(80,000)	(50,000)				(130,000)	8
9	Equipment	240,000	60,000	(D4) 20,000			320,000	9
10	Accumulated Depreciation	(40,000)	(20,000)				(60,000)	10
11	Copyright			(D5) 50,000			50,000	11
12	Goodwill		**40,000**	**(D6) 95,000**			135,000	12
13	Current Liabilities	(80,000)	(40,000)				(120,000)	13
14	Bonds Payable	(200,000)	(100,000)				(300,000)	14
15	Common Stock—Sample		(10,000)	(EL) 8,000		(2,000)		15
16	Paid-In Capital in Excess of Par—Sample		(90,000)	(EL) 72,000		(18,000)		16
17	Retained Earnings—Sample		(100,000)	(EL) 80,000	NCI 60,000	(80,000)		17
18	Common Stock—Parental	(36,000)					(36,000)	18
19	Paid-In Capital in Excess of Par—Parental	(584,000)					(584,000)	19
20	Retained Earnings—Parental	(456,000)					(456,000)	20
21	Totals	0	0	460,000	460,000			21
22	NCI					(100,000)	(100,000)	22
23	Totals					0	0	23

Eliminations and Adjustments:

(EL)   Eliminate 80% subsidiary equity against investment account.

(NCI)   Adjust NCI to fair value (credit to Sample's Retained Earnings).

(D)   Distribute remaining excess in investment account plus NCI adjustment to:

(D1)   Inventory.

(D2)   Land.

(D3)   Building (recorded cost is increased without removing accumulated depreciation). The alternative is to debit Accumulated Depreciation for $50,000 and Buildings for $50,000. This would also restate the net asset at fair value.

(D4)   Equipment (recorded cost is increased without removing accumulated depreciation). The alternative is to debit Accumulated Depreciation for $20,000. This would also restate the net asset at fair value.

(D5)   Copyright.

(D6)   **Goodwill.**

Copyright.

Worksheet 2A-1

Reverse Acquisition
Public Company and Subsidiary Private Company
Worksheet for Consolidated Balance Sheet
December 31, 2011

Worksheet 2A-1 (see page 86)

	(Credit balance amounts are in parentheses.)	Balance Sheet Private	Balance Sheet Public	Eliminations & Adjustments Dr.	Eliminations & Adjustments Cr.	NCI	Consolidated Balance Sheet	
1	Current Assets	700	500				1,200	1
2	Investment in Private Company		960		(EL) 660			2
3					(D) 300			3
4	Fixed Assets	3,000	1,300	(D1) 200			4,500	4
5	Goodwill			(D2) 300			300	5
6	Long-Term Liabilities	(1,700)	(700)				(2,400)	6
7	Common Stock—Private	(60)		(adj) 60				7
8	Paid-In Capital in Excess of Par—Private	(540)		(adj) 540				8
9	Retained Earnings—Private	(1,400)					(1,400)	9
10	Common Stock—Public (100 + 150)		(250)	(EL) 60		(190)		10
11	*Continuing Equity of Public Company*				(adj) 150		(150)	11
12	Paid-In Capital in Excess of Par—Public (200 + 810)		(1,010)	(EL) 120		(890)		12
13	*Continuing Equity of Public Company*				(adj) 450		(450)	13
14	Retained Earnings—Public		(800)	(EL) 480	(NCI) 200	(520)		14
15	Totals	0	0	1,760	1,760			15
16	NCI					(1,600)	(1,600)	16
17	Totals						0	17

Eliminations and Adjustments:

(EL) Eliminate investment account and 60% of original Public Company equity at the time of the acquisition.

(D)/(NCI) Distribute the excess applicable to the investment and the adjustment to fair value for the NCI as follows:

(D1) Increase fixed assets from $1,300 to $1,500.

(D2) Record goodwill.

(adj) Convert Private Company equity to that of Public Company. Assign $600 total paid-in capital as follows:
Common Stock, Public—150 shares at $1 par = $150.
Paid-in Capital in Excess of Par, $600 − $150 par = $450.

UNDERSTANDING THE ISSUES

1. Jacobson Company is considering an investment in the common stock of Biltrite Company. What are the accounting issues surrounding the recording of income in future periods if Jacobson purchases:

   a. 15% of Biltrite's outstanding shares.
   b. 40% of Biltrite's outstanding shares.
   c. 100% of Biltrite's outstanding shares.
   d. 80% of Biltrite's outstanding shares.

2. What does the elimination process accomplish?

3. Paulos Company purchases a controlling interest in Sanjoy Company. Sanjoy had identifiable net assets with a book value of $500,000 and a fair value of $800,000. It was agreed that the total fair value of Sanjoy's common stock was $1,200,000. Use value analysis schedules to determine what adjustments will be made to Sanjoy's accounts and what new accounts and amounts will be recorded if:

   a. Paulos purchases 100% of Sanjoy's common stock for $1,200,000.
   b. Paulos purchases 80% of Sanjoy's common stock for $960,000.

4. Pillow Company is purchasing a 100% interest in the common stock of Sleep Company. Sleep's balance sheet amounts at book and fair values are as follows:

Account	Book Value	Fair Value
Current Assets	$ 200,000	$ 250,000
Fixed Assets.....................	350,000	800,000
Liabilities	(200,000)	(200,000)

   Use valuation analysis schedules to determine what adjustments to recorded values of Sleep Company's accounts will be made in the consolidation process (including the creation of new accounts), if the price paid for the 100% is:
   a. $1,000,000.
   b. $500,000.

5. Pillow Company is purchasing an 80% interest in the common stock of Sleep Company. Sleep's balance sheet amounts at book and fair values are as follows:

Account	Book Value	Fair Value
Current Assets	$ 200,000	$ 250,000
Fixed Assets.....................	350,000	800,000
Liabilities	(200,000)	(200,000)

   Use valuation analysis schedules to determine what adjustments to recorded values of Sleep Company's accounts will be made in the consolidation process (including the creation of new accounts), if the price paid for the 80% is:

   a. $800,000.
   b. $600,000.

6. Pillow Company is purchasing an 80% interest in the common stock of Sleep Company for $800,000. Sleep's balance sheet amounts at book and fair value are as follows:

Account	Book Value	Fair Value
Current Assets	$ 200,000	$ 250,000
Fixed Assets.....................	350,000	800,000
Liabilities	(200,000)	(200,000)

Use a valuation analysis schedule to determine what will be the amount of the non-controlling interest in the consolidated balance sheet and how will it be displayed in the consolidated balance sheet.

EXERCISES

Exercise 1 *(LO 1)* **Investment recording methods.** Salvania Corporation is considering investing in Farnorth Corporation, but is unsure about what level of ownership should be undertaken. Salvania and Farnorth have the following reported incomes:

	Salvania	Farnorth
Sales	$700,000	$400,000
Cost of goods sold.	300,000	230,000
Gross profit	$400,000	$170,000
Selling and administrative expenses . . .	120,000	75,000
Net income	$280,000	$ 95,000

Farnorth paid $15,000 in cash dividends to its investors. Prepare a pro forma income statement for Salvania Corporation that compares income under 10%, 30%, and 80% ownership levels.

Exercise 2 *(LO 1, 5, 6, 7, 8)* **Prior investment, control with later acquisition.** Boon Corporation purchased a 10% interest in Doyle Company on January 1, 2011, as an available-for-sale investment for a price of $40,000.

On January 1, 2016, Boon Corporation purchased 7,000 additional shares of Doyle Company from existing shareholders for $315,000. This purchase raised Boon's interest to 80%. Doyle Company had the following balance sheet just prior to Boon's second purchase:

Assets		Liabilities and Equity	
Current assets	$165,000	Liabilities	$ 65,000
Buildings (net)	140,000	Common stock ($10 par).	100,000
Equipment (net)	100,000	Retained earnings	240,000
Total assets.	$405,000	Total liabilities and equity	$405,000

At the time of the second purchase, Boon determined that Doyle's equipment was understated by $50,000 and had a 5-year remaining life. All other book values approximated fair values. Any remaining excess was attributed to goodwill.

1. Prepare the value analysis and the determination and distribution of excess schedule for the 2016 purchase.
2. Record the investment made by Boon on January 1, 2016, and any required adjustment of the prior 10% interest.

Exercise 3 *(LO 3)* **Asset compared to stock purchase.** Glass Company is thinking about acquiring Plastic Company. Glass Company is considering two methods of accomplishing control and is wondering how the accounting treatment will differ under each method. Glass Company has estimated that the fair values of Plastic's net assets are equal to their book values, except for the equipment, which is understated by $20,000.

The following balance sheets have been prepared on the date of acquisition:

Assets	Glass	Plastic
Cash	$540,000	$ 20,000
Accounts receivable	50,000	70,000
Inventory	50,000	100,000
Property, plant, and equipment (net) . . .	230,000	270,000
Total assets.	$870,000	$460,000

Liabilities and Equity		
Current liabilities	$140,000	$ 80,000
Bonds payable	250,000	100,000
Stockholders' equity:		
Common stock ($100 par).	200,000	150,000
Retained earnings	280,000	130,000
Total liabilities and equity	$870,000	$460,000

1. Assume Glass Company purchased the net assets directly from Plastic Company for $530,000.

   a. Prepare the entry that Glass Company would make to record the purchase.
   b. Prepare the balance sheet for Glass Company immediately following the purchase.

2. Assume that 100% of the outstanding stock of Plastic Company is purchased from the former stockholders for a total of $530,000.

   a. Prepare the entry that Glass Company would make to record the purchase.
   b. State how the investment would appear on Glass's unconsolidated balance sheet prepared immediately after the purchase.
   c. Indicate how the consolidated balance sheet would appear.

Exercise 4 *(LO 5)* **Simple value analysis.** Flom Company is considering the cash purchase of 100% of the outstanding stock of Vargas Company. The terms are not set, and alternative prices are being considered for negotiation. The balance sheet of Vargas Company shows the following values:

Assets		Liabilities and Equity	
Cash equivalents	$ 60,000	Current liabilities	$ 60,000
Inventory	120,000	Common stock ($5 par).	100,000
Land.	100,000	Paid-in capital in excess of par . . .	150,000
Building (net)	200,000	Retained earnings	170,000
Total assets.	$480,000	Total liabilities and equity	$480,000

Appraisals reveal that the inventory has a fair value of $160,000 and that the land and building have fair values of $120,000 and $300,000, respectively.

1. Above what price will goodwill be recorded?
2. Below what price will a gain be recorded?

Exercise 5 *(LO 5, 6)* **Recording purchase with goodwill.** Wood'n Wares, Inc., purchased all the outstanding stock of Pail, Inc., for $950,000. Wood'n Wares also paid $10,000 in direct acquisition costs. Just before the investment, the two companies had the following balance sheets:

Assets	Wood'n Wares, Inc.	Pail, Inc.
Accounts receivable	$ 900,000	$ 500,000
Inventory	600,000	200,000
Depreciable fixed assets (net)	1,500,000	600,000
Total assets.	$3,000,000	$1,300,000

Liabilities and Equity		
Current liabilities	$ 950,000	$ 400,000
Bonds payable	500,000	200,000
Common stock ($10 par).	400,000	300,000
Paid-in capital in excess of par	500,000	380,000
Retained earnings	650,000	20,000
Total liabilities and equity	$3,000,000	$1,300,000

Appraisals for the assets of Pail, Inc., indicate that fair values differ from recorded book values for the inventory and for the depreciable fixed assets, which have fair values of $250,000 and $700,000, respectively.

1. Prepare the entries to record the purchase of the Pail, Inc., common stock and payment of acquisition costs.
2. Prepare the value analysis and the determination and distribution of excess schedule for the investment in Pail, Inc.
3. Prepare the elimination entries that would be made on a consolidated worksheet.

Exercise 6 *(LO 5, 6)* **Purchase with a gain.** Libra Company is purchasing 100% of the outstanding stock of Genall Company for $700,000. Genall has the following balance sheet on the date of acquisition:

Assets		Liabilities and Equity	
Accounts receivable	$ 300,000	Current liabilities	$ 250,000
Inventory	200,000	Bonds payable	200,000
Property, plant, and equipment		Common stock ($5 par).	200,000
(net)	500,000		
		Paid-in capital in excess of par . . .	300,000
Computer software	125,000	Retained earnings	175,000
Total assets.	$1,125,000	Total liabilities and equity	$1,125,000

Appraisals indicate that the following fair values for the assets and liabilities should be acknowledged:

Accounts receivable	$300,000
Inventory	215,000
Property, plant, and equipment.	700,000
Computer software	130,000
Current liabilities	250,000
Bonds payable	210,000

1. Prepare the value analysis schedule and the determination and distribution of excess schedule.
2. Prepare the elimination entries that would be made on a consolidated worksheet prepared on the date of purchase.

Exercise 7 *(LO 5, 6, 7)* **80% purchase, alternative values for goodwill.** Quail Company purchases 80% of the common stock of Commo Company for $800,000. At the time of the purchase, Commo has the following balance sheet:

Assets		Liabilities and Equity	
Cash equivalents	$ 120,000	Current liabilities	$ 200,000
Inventory	200,000	Bonds payable	400,000
Land.	100,000	Common stock ($5 par).	100,000
Building (net)	450,000	Paid-in capital in excess of par . . .	150,000
Equipment (net)	230,000	Retained earnings	250,000
Total assets.	$1,100,000	Total liabilities and equity	$1,100,000

The fair values of assets are as follows:

Cash equivalents	$120,000
Inventory	250,000
Land	200,000
Building	650,000
Equipment	200,000

1. Prepare the value analysis schedule and the determination and distribution of excess schedule under three alternatives for valuing the NCI:

   a. The value of the NCI is implied by the price paid by the parent for the controlling interest.
   b. The market value of the shares held by the NCI is $45 per share.
   c. The international accounting option, which does not allow goodwill to be recorded as part of the NCI, is used.

2. Prepare the elimination entries that would be made on a consolidated worksheet prepared on the date of purchase under the three alternatives for valuing the NCI:

   a. The value of the NCI is implied by the price paid by the parent for the controlling interest.
   b. The market value of the shares held by the NCI is $45 per share.
   c. The international accounting option, which does not allow goodwill to be recorded as part of the NCI, is used.

Exercise 8 *(LO 5, 6, 7, 8)* **80% purchase with a gain and preexisting goodwill.** Venus Company purchases 8,000 shares of Sundown Company for $64 per share. Just prior to the purchase, Sundown Company has the following balance sheet:

Assets		Liabilities and Equity	
Cash	$ 20,000	Current liabilities	$250,000
Inventory	280,000	Common stock ($5 par)	50,000
Property, plant, and equipment (net) .	400,000	Paid-in capital in excess of par	130,000
Goodwill	100,000	Retained earnings	370,000
Total assets	$800,000	Total liabilities and equity	$800,000

Venus Company believes that the inventory has a fair value of $400,000 and that the property plant, and equipment is worth $500,000.

1. Prepare the value analysis schedule and the determination and distribution of excess schedule.
2. Prepare the elimination entries that would be made on a consolidated worksheet prepared on the date of acquisition.

Exercise 9 *(LO 9)* **Push-down accounting.** On January 1, 2017, Knight Corporation purchases all the outstanding shares of Craig Company for $950,000. It has been decided that Craig Company will use push-down accounting principles to account for this transaction. The current balance sheet is stated at historical cost.

The following balance sheet is prepared for Craig Company on January 1, 2017:

Assets			Liabilities and Equity		
Current assets:			Current liabilities		$ 90,000
Cash	$ 80,000		Long-term liabilities:		
Accounts receivable	260,000		Bonds payable	$300,000	
			Deferred taxes	50,000	350,000
Prepaid expenses	20,000	$ 360,000	Stockholders' equity:		
Property, plant, and equipment:			Common stock ($10 par)	$300,000	
Land	$200,000		Retained earnings	420,000	720,000
Building (net)	600,000	800,000			
Total assets		$1,160,000	Total liabilities and equity		$1,160,000

Knight Corporation receives the following appraisals for Craig Company's assets and liabilities:

Cash	$ 80,000
Accounts receivable	260,000
Prepaid expenses	20,000
Land.......................	250,000
Building (net)	700,000
Current liabilities	90,000
Bonds payable	280,000
Deferred tax liability	40,000

1. Record the investment.
2. Prepare the value analysis schedule and the determination and distribution of excess schedule.
3. Record the adjustments on the books of Craig Company.
4. Prepare the entries that would be made on the consolidated worksheet to eliminate the investment.

APPENDIX EXERCISE

Exercise 2A-1 *(LO 10)* **Reverse acquisition.** Private Company acquired a controlling interest in Public Company. Private Company had the following balance sheet on the acquisition date:

Private Company (the acquirer)
Balance Sheet
December 31, 2011

Assets		Liabilities and Equity	
Current assets	$1,000	Long-term liabilities	$2,000
Fixed assets	5,000	Common stock ($1 par) (100 shares)	100
		Paid-in capital in excess of par	900
		Retained earnings	3,000
Total assets..................	$6,000	Total liabilities and equity	$6,000

Public Company had the following book and fair values on the acquisition date:

Assets	Book Value	Fair Value	Liabilities and Equity	Book Value	Fair Value
Current assets	$1,000	$1,000	Long-term liabilities	$1,000	$1,000
Fixed assets	2,000	3,000	Common stock ($1 par) (200 shares)	200	
			Paid-in capital in excess of par.............	800	
			Retained earnings	1,000	
			Total liabilities and		
Total assets.........	$3,000	$4,000	equity...........	$3,000	

The shareholders of Private Company requested 300 Public Company shares in exchange for all of their 100 shares. This was an exchange ratio of 3 to 1. The fair value of a share of Public Company was $25.

Prepare an appropriate value analysis and a determination and distribution of excess schedule.

PROBLEMS

Problem 2-1 *(LO 3, 4, 5, 6)* **100% purchase, goodwill, worksheet.** On December 31, 2011, Adam Company purchases 100% of the common stock of Sampson Company for $475,000 cash. On this date, any excess of cost over book value is attributed to accounts with fair values that differ from book values. These accounts of Sampson Company have the following fair values:

Cash	$ 40,000
Accounts receivable	30,000
Inventory	140,000
Land.	45,000
Buildings and equipment.	225,000
Copyrights.	25,000
Current liabilities	65,000
Bonds payable	105,000

The following comparative balance sheets are prepared for the two companies immediately after the purchase:

	Adam	Sampson
Cash	$ 160,000	$ 40,000
Accounts receivable	70,000	30,000
Inventory	130,000	120,000
Investment in Sampson Company	475,000	
Land.	50,000	35,000
Buildings and equipment.	350,000	230,000
Accumulated depreciation	(100,000)	(50,000)
Copyrights.	40,000	10,000
Total assets.	$1,175,000	$415,000
Current liabilities	$ 192,000	$ 65,000
Bonds payable		100,000
Common stock ($10 par)—Adam	100,000	
Common stock ($5 par)—Sampson . . .		50,000
Paid-in capital in excess of par	250,000	70,000
Retained earnings	633,000	130,000
Total liabilities and equity	$1,175,000	$415,000

Required ▶ ▶ ▶ ▶ ▶

1. Prepare the value analysis schedule and the determination and distribution of excess schedule for the investment in Sampson Company.
2. Complete a consolidated worksheet for Adam Company and its subsidiary Sampson Company as of December 31, 2011.

Problem 2-2 *(LO 3, 4, 5, 6, 7)* **80% purchase, goodwill, worksheet.** Using the data given in Problem 2-1, assume that Adam Company purchases 80% of the common stock of Sampson Company for $380,000 cash.

The following comparative balance sheets are prepared for the two companies immediately after the purchase:

(continued)

	Adam	Sampson
Cash	$ 255,000	$ 40,000
Accounts receivable	70,000	30,000
Inventory	130,000	120,000
Investment in Sampson Company	380,000	
Land.	50,000	35,000
Buildings and equipment.	350,000	230,000
Accumulated depreciation	(100,000)	(50,000)
Copyrights.	40,000	10,000
Total assets.	$1,175,000	$415,000
Current liabilities	$ 192,000	$ 65,000
Bonds payable		100,000
Common stock ($10 par)—Adam	100,000	
Common stock ($5 par)—Sampson . . .		50,000
Paid-in capital in excess of par	250,000	70,000
Retained earnings	633,000	130,000
Total liabilities and equity	$1,175,000	$415,000

1. Prepare the value analysis and the determination and distribution of excess schedule for the investment in Sampson Company.   ◄ ◄ ◄ ◄ ◄ **Required**
2. Complete a consolidated worksheet for Adam Company and its subsidiary Sampson Company as of December 31, 2011.

Use the following information for Problems 2-8 through 2-11:

In an attempt to expand its operations, Palto Company acquires Saleen Company on January 1, 2011. Palto pays cash in exchange for the common stock of Saleen. On the date of acquisition, Saleen has the following balance sheet:

Saleen Company
Balance Sheet
January 1, 2011

Assets		Liabilities and Equity	
Accounts receivable	$ 20,000	Current liabilities	$ 40,000
Inventory	50,000	Bonds payable	100,000
Land.	40,000	Common stock ($1 par).	10,000
Buildings	200,000	Paid-in capital in excess of par	90,000
Accumulated depreciation	(50,000)	Retained earnings	60,000
Equipment	60,000		
Accumulated depreciation	(20,000)		
Total assets.	$300,000	Total liabilities and equity	$300,000

An appraisal provides the following fair values for assets:

Accounts receivable	$ 20,000
Inventory	60,000
Land.	80,000
Buildings	320,000
Equipment	60,000
Copyright	50,000

Problem 2-3 *(LO 3, 4, 5, 6)* **100% purchase, goodwill, consolidated balance sheet.** On July 1, 2016, Raabe Company exchanged 18,000 of its $40 fair value ($1 par value) shares for all the outstanding shares of Dalke Company. Raabe paid acquisition costs of $40,000. The two companies had the following balance sheets on July 1, 2016:

Assets	Raabe	Dalke
Other current assets...............	$ 50,000	$ 70,000
Inventory	120,000	60,000
Land...........................	100,000	40,000
Building (net).....................	300,000	120,000
Equipment (net)	430,000	110,000
Total assets....................	$1,000,000	$400,000

Liabilities and Equity		
Current liabilities	$ 180,000	$ 60,000
Common stock ($1 par).............	40,000	20,000
Paid-in capital in excess of par	360,000	180,000
Retained earnings	420,000	140,000
Total liabilities and equity	$1,000,000	$400,000

The following fair values applied to Dalke's assets:

Other current assets...........	$ 70,000
Inventory	80,000
Land.........................	90,000
Building	150,000
Equipment	75,000

Required ▶ ▶ ▶ ▶ ▶
1. Record the investment in Dalke Company and any other entry necessitated by the purchase.
2. Prepare the value analysis and the determination and distribution of excess schedule.
3. Prepare a consolidated balance sheet for July 1, 2016, immediately subsequent to the purchase.

Problem 2-4 *(LO 3, 4, 5, 6, 7)* **80% purchase, goodwill, consolidated balance sheet.** Using the data given in Problem 2-3, assume that Raabe Company exchanged 14,000 of its $40 fair value ($1 par value) shares for 16,000 of the outstanding shares of Dalke Company.

Required ▶ ▶ ▶ ▶ ▶
1. Record the investment in Dalke Company and any other purchase-related entry.
2. Prepare the value analysis schedule and the determination and distribution of excess schedule.
3. Prepare a consolidated balance sheet for July 1, 2016, immediately subsequent to the purchase.

Problem 2-5 *(LO 3, 4, 5, 6, 7)* **80% purchase, bargain, elimination entries only.** On March 1, 2015, Penson Enterprises purchases an 80% interest in Express Corporation for $320,000 cash. Express Corporation has the following balance sheet on February 28, 2015:

Express Corporation
Balance Sheet
February 28, 2015

Assets		Liabilities and Equity	
Accounts receivable	$ 60,000	Current liabilities	$ 50,000
Inventory	80,000	Bonds payable	100,000
Land...........................	40,000	Common stock ($10 par)............	50,000
Buildings	300,000	Paid-in capital in excess of par	250,000

Assets		Liabilities and Equity	
Accumulated depreciation—buildings	$(120,000)	Retained earnings	$ 70,000
Equipment	220,000		
Accumulated depreciation—equipment	(60,000)		
Total assets	$ 520,000	Total liabilities and equity	$520,000

Penson Enterprises receives an independent appraisal on the fair values of Express Corporation's assets and liabilities. The controller has reviewed the following figures and accepts them as reasonable:

Accounts receivable	$ 60,000
Inventory	100,000
Land	50,000
Buildings	200,000
Equipment	162,000
Current liabilities	50,000
Bonds payable	95,000

1. Record the investment in Express Corporation.
2. Prepare the value analysis schedule and the determination and distribution of excess schedule.
3. Prepare the elimination entries that would be made on a consolidated worksheet prepared on the date of acquisition.

 **Required**

Problem 2-6 *(LO 5, 6, 9)* **100% purchase, goodwill, push-down accounting.** On March 1, 2015, Collier Enterprises purchases a 100% interest in Robby Corporation for $480,000 cash. Robby Corporation applies push-down accounting principles to account for this acquisition.

Robby Corporation has the following balance sheet on February 28, 2015:

Robby Corporation
Balance Sheet
February 28, 2015

Assets		Liabilities and Equity	
Accounts receivable	$ 60,000	Current liabilities	$ 50,000
Inventory	80,000	Bonds payable	100,000
Land	40,000	Common stock ($5)	50,000
Buildings	300,000	Paid-in capital in excess of par	250,000
Accumulated depreciation—buildings	(120,000)	Retained earnings	70,000
Equipment	220,000		
Accumulated depreciation—equipment	(60,000)		
Total assets	$ 520,000	Total liabilities and equity	$520,000

Collier Enterprises receives an independent appraisal on the fair values of Robby Corporation's assets and liabilities. The controller has reviewed the following figures and accepts them as reasonable:

Accounts receivable	$ 60,000
Inventory	100,000
Land	55,000
Buildings	200,000
Equipment	150,000
Current liabilities	50,000
Bonds payable	98,000

Required ▶ ▶ ▶ ▶ ▶
1. Record the investment in Robby Corporation.
2. Prepare the value analysis schedule and the determination and distribution of excess schedule.
3. Give Robby Corporation's adjusting entry.

Problem 2-7 *(LO 3, 4, 5, 6)* **100% purchase, bargain, elimination entries only.** On March 1, 2016, Carlson Enterprises purchases a 100% interest in Entro Corporation for $400,000. Entro Corporation has the following balance sheet on February 28, 2015:

Entro Corporation
Balance Sheet
February 28, 2015

Assets		Liabilities and Equity	
Accounts receivable	$ 60,000	Current liabilities	$ 50,000
Inventory	80,000	Bonds payable	100,000
Land	40,000	Common stock ($5 par)	50,000
Buildings	300,000	Paid-in capital in excess of par	250,000
Accumulated depreciation—building	(120,000)	Retained earnings	70,000
Equipment	220,000		
Accumulated depreciation—equipment	(60,000)		
Total assets	$ 520,000	Total liabilities and equity	$520,000

Carlson Enterprises receives an independent appraisal on the fair values of Entro Corporation's assets and liabilities. The controller has reviewed the following figures and accepts them as reasonable:

Accounts receivable	$ 60,000
Inventory	100,000
Land	40,500
Building	202,500
Equipment	162,000
Current liabilities	50,000
Bonds payable	95,000

Required ▶ ▶ ▶ ▶ ▶
1. Record the investment in Entro Corporation.
2. Prepare the value analysis and the determination and distribution of excess schedule.
3. Prepare the elimination entries that would be made on a consolidated worksheet prepared on the date of acquisition.

Problem 2-8 *(LO 3, 4, 5, 6)* **100% purchase, goodwill, worksheet.** Use the preceding information for Palto's purchase of Saleen common stock. Assume Palto purchases 100% of the Saleen common stock for $500,000 cash. Palto has the following balance sheet immediately after the purchase:

Palto Company
Balance Sheet
January 1, 2011

Assets		Liabilities and Equity	
Cash	$ 61,000	Current liabilities	$ 80,000
Accounts receivable	65,000	Bonds payable	200,000
Inventory	80,000	Common stock ($1 par)	20,000
Investment in Saleen	500,000	Paid-in capital in excess of par	180,000
Land	100,000	Retained earnings	546,000

Assets		Liabilities and Equity	
Buildings	$ 250,000		
Accumulated depreciation	(80,000)		
Equipment	90,000		
Accumulated depreciation	(40,000)		
Total assets	**$1,026,00**	**Total liabilities and equity** . .	**$1,026,00**

1. Prepare the value analysis schedule and the determination and distribution of excess schedule for the investment in Saleen. ◄ ◄ ◄ ◄ ◄ **Required**
2. Complete a consolidated worksheet for Palto Company and its subsidiary Saleen Company as of January 1, 2011.

Problem 2-9 *(LO 3, 4, 5, 6, 7)* **80% purchase, goodwill, worksheet.** Use the preceding information for Palto's purchase of Saleen common stock. Assume Palto purchases 80% of the Saleen common stock for $400,000 cash. The shares of the noncontrolling interest have a fair value of $46 each. Palto has the following balance sheet immediately after the purchase:

Palto Company
Balance Sheet
January 1, 2011

Assets		Liabilities and Equity	
Cash	$ 161,000	Current liabilities	$ 80,000
Accounts receivable	65,000	Bonds payable	200,000
Inventory	80,000	Common stock ($1 par)	20,000
Investment in Saleen	400,000	Paid-in capital in excess of par . . .	180,000
Land	100,000	Retained earnings	546,000
Buildings	250,000		
Accumulated depreciation	(80,000)		
Equipment	90,000		
Accumulated depreciation	(40,000)		
Total assets	$1,026,000	Total liabilities and equity	$1,026,000

1. Prepare the value analysis schedule and the determination and distribution of excess schedule for the investment in Saleen. ◄ ◄ ◄ ◄ ◄ **Required**
2. Complete a consolidated worksheet for Palto Company and its subsidiary Saleen Company as of January 1, 2011.

Problem 2-10 *(LO 3, 4, 5, 6, 7)* **80% purchase, bargain, purchase, worksheet.** Use the preceding information for Palto's purchase of Saleen common stock. Assume Palto purchases 80% of the Saleen common stock for $300,000 cash. Palto has the following balance sheet immediately after the purchase:

Palto Company
Balance Sheet
January 1, 2011

Assets		Liabilities and Equity	
Cash	$ 261,000	Current liabilities	$ 80,000
Accounts receivable	65,000	Bonds payable	200,000
Inventory	80,000	Common stock ($1 par)	20,000

Assets		Liabilities and Equity	
Investment in Saleen	$ 300,000	Paid-in capital in excess of par ..	$ 180,000
Land......................	100,000	Retained earnings	546,000
Buildings	250,000		
Accumulated depreciation	(80,000)		
Equipment	90,000		
Accumulated depreciation	(40,000)		
Total assets...............	$1,026,000	Total liabilities and equity	$1,026,000

Required ▶ ▶ ▶ ▶ ▶

1. Prepare the value analysis and the determination and distribution of excess schedule for the investment in Saleen.
2. Complete a consolidated worksheet for Palto Company and its subsidiary Saleen Company as of January 1, 2011.

Use the following information for Problems 2-12 through 2-15:

Purnell Corporation acquires Sentinel Corporation on December 31, 2011. Sentinel has the following balance sheet on the date of acquisition:

Sentinel Corporation
Balance Sheet
December 31, 2011

Assets		Liabilities and Equity	
Accounts receivable	$ 50,000	Current liabilities	$ 90,000
Inventory	120,000	Bonds payable	200,000
Land......................	100,000	Common stock ($1 par)........	10,000
Buildings	300,000	Paid-in capital in excess of par ..	190,000
Accumulated depreciation	(100,000)	Retained earnings	140,000
Equipment	140,000		
Accumulated depreciation	(50,000)		
Patent.....................	10,000		
Goodwill	60,000		
Total assets...............	$ 630,000	Total liabilities and equity	$630,000

An appraisal is performed to determine whether the book values of Sentinel's net assets reflect their fair values. The appraiser also determines that intangible assets exist, although they are not recorded. The following fair values for assets and liabilities are agreed upon:

Accounts receivable	$ 50,000
Inventory	100,000
Land......................	200,000
Buildings	400,000
Equipment	200,000
Patent.....................	150,000
Computer software	50,000
Current liabilities	90,000
Bonds payable	210,000

Problem 2-11 *(LO 3, 4, 5, 6, 7)* **100% purchase, bargain, worksheet.** Use the preceding information for Palto's purchase of Saleen common stock. Assume Palto purchases 100% of the Saleen common stock for $400,000 cash. Palto has the following balance sheet immediately after the purchase:

Palto Company
Balance Sheet
January 1, 2011

Assets			Liabilities and Equity		
Cash	$	161,000	Current liabilities	$	80,000
Accounts receivable		65,000	Bonds payable ($1 par)		200,000
Inventory		80,000	Common stock................		20,000
Investment in Saleen		400,000	Paid-in capital in excess of par ..		180,000
Land.......................		100,000	Retained earnings		546,000
Buildings		250,000			
Accumulated depreciation		(80,000)			
Equipment		90,000			
Accumulated depreciation		(40,000)			
Total assets...............		$1,026,000	Total liabilities and equity		$1,026,000

1. Prepare the value analysis schedule and the determination and distribution of excess schedule for the investment in Saleen. ◄ ◄ ◄ ◄ ◄ **Required**
2. Complete a consolidated worksheet for Palto Company and its subsidiary Saleen Company as of January 1, 2011.

Problem 2-12 *(LO 3, 4, 5, 6, 8)* **100% purchase, bargain, several adjustments, worksheet.** Use the preceding information for Purnell's purchase of Sentinel common stock. Assume Purnell exchanges 16,000 shares of its own stock for 100% of the common stock of Sentinel. The stock has a market value of $50 per share and a par value of $1. Purnell has the following trial balance immediately after the purchase, as shown on page 110.

Purnell Corporation
Trial Balance
December 31, 2011

Cash	20,000
Accounts Receivable	300,000
Inventory	410,000
Investment in Sentinel	800,000
Land...	800,000
Buildings	2,800,000
Accumulated Depreciation	(500,000)
Equipment	600,000
Accumulated Depreciation	(230,000)
Current Liabilities..	(150,000)
Bonds Payable...	(300,000)
Common Stock ($1 par)	(89,000)
Paid-In Capital in Excess of Par	(3,361,000)
Retained Earnings	(1,100,000)
Total...	0

1. Prepare the value analysis schedule and the determination and distribution of excess schedule for the investment in Sentinel. ◄ ◄ ◄ ◄ ◄ **Required**
2. Complete a consolidated worksheet for Purnell Corporation and its subsidiary Sentinel Corporation as of December 31, 2011.

Problem 2-13 *(LO 3, 4, 5, 6, 8)* **100% purchase, goodwill, several adjustments, worksheet.** Use the preceding information for Purnell's purchase of Sentinel common stock. Assume Purnell exchanges 22,000 shares of its own stock for 100% of the common stock of Sentinel. The stock has a market value of $50 per share and a par value of $1. Purnell has the following trial balance immediately after the purchase:

Purnell Corporation
Trial Balance
December 31, 2011

Cash	20,000
Accounts Receivable	300,000
Inventory	410,000
Investment in Sentinel	1,100,000
Land	800,000
Buildings	2,800,000
Accumulated Depreciation	(500,000)
Equipment	600,000
Accumulated Depreciation	(230,000)
Current Liabilities	(150,000)
Bonds Payable	(300,000)
Common Stock ($1 par)	(95,000)
Paid-In Capital in Excess of Par	(3,655,000)
Retained Earnings	(1,100,000)
Total	0

Required ▶ ▶ ▶ ▶ ▶

1. Prepare the value analysis schedule and the determination and distribution of excess schedule for the investment in Sentinel.
2. Complete a consolidated worksheet for Purnell Corporation and its subsidiary Sentinel Corporation as of December 31, 2011.

Problem 2-14 *(LO 3, 4, 5, 6, 7, 8)* **80% purchase, bargain, several adjustments, worksheet.** Use the preceding information for Purnell's purchase of Sentinel common stock. Assume Purnell exchanges 10,000 shares of its own stock for 80% of the common stock of Sentinel. The stock has a market value of $50 per share and a par value of $1. Purnell has the following trial balance immediately after the purchase:

Purnell Corporation
Trial Balance
December 31, 2011

Cash	20,000
Accounts Receivable	300,000
Inventory	410,000
Investment in Sentinel	500,000
Land	800,000
Buildings	2,800,000
Accumulated Depreciation	(500,000)
Equipment	600,000
Accumulated Depreciation	(230,000)
Current Liabilities	(150,000)
Bonds Payable	(300,000)
Common Stock ($1 par)	(83,000)
Paid-In Capital in Excess of Par	(3,067,000)
Retained Earnings	(1,100,000)
Total	0

1. Prepare the value analysis schedule and the determination and distribution of excess schedule ◄ ◄ ◄ ◄ ◄ **Required**
   for the investment in Sentinel.
2. Complete a consolidated worksheet for Purnell Corporation and its subsidiary Sentinel Corporation as of December 31, 2011.

Problem 2-15 *(LO 3, 4, 5, 6, 7, 8)* **80% purchase, goodwill, several adjustments, worksheet.** Use the preceding information for Purnell's purchase of Sentinel common stock. Assume Purnell exchanges 19,000 shares of its own stock for 80% of the common stock of Sentinel. The stock has a market value of $50 per share and a par value of $1. Purnell has the following trial balance immediately after the purchase:

Purnell Corporation
Trial Balance
December 31, 2011

Cash	20,000
Accounts Receivable	300,000
Inventory	410,000
Investment in Sentinel	950,000
Land.	800,000
Buildings	2,800,000
Accumulated Depreciation	(500,000)
Equipment	600,000
Accumulated Depreciation	(230,000)
Current Liabilities.	(150,000)
Bonds Payable.	(300,000)
Common Stock ($1 par)	(92,000)
Paid-In Capital in Excess of Par	(3,508,000)
Retained Earnings	(1,100,000)
Total.	0

1. Prepare the value analysis schedule and the determination and distribution of excess schedule ◄ ◄ ◄ ◄ ◄ **Required**
   for the investment in Sentinel.
2. Complete a consolidated worksheet for Purnell Corporation and its subsidiary Sentinel Corporation as of December 31, 2011.

APPENDIX PROBLEM

Problem 2A-1 *(LO 10)* **Reverse acquisition** On January 1, 2012, the shareholders of Untraded Company request 6,000 Traded shares in exchange for all of their 5,000 shares. This is an exchange ratio of 1.2 to 1. The fair value of a share of Traded Company is $60. The acquisition occurs when the two companies have the following balance sheets:

Untraded Company (the acquirer)
Balance Sheet
December 31, 2011

Assets		Liabilities and Equity	
Current assets	$ 10,000	Long-term liabilities	$ 5,000
Building (net)	150,000	Common stock ($1 par) (5,000	
		shares).	5,000
Equipment (net)	100,000	Paid-in capital in excess of par . . .	115,000
		Retained earnings	135,000
Total assets.	$260,000	Total liabilities and equity	$260,000

Traded Company (the acquiree)
Balance Sheet
December 31, 2011

Assets	Book Value	Fair Value	Liabilities and Equity	Book Value	Fair Value
Current assets	$ 5,000	$ 5,000	Long-term liabilities	$ 10,000	$10,000
Building (net)	100,000	200,000	Common stock ($1 par)		
			(4,000 shares)	4,000	
Equipment (net)	20,000	40,000	Paid-in capital in excess of par	96,000	
			Retained earnings	15,000	
Total assets.	$125,000	$245,000	Total liabilities and equity . . .	$125,000	

Required ▶ ▶ ▶ ▶ ▶ 1. Prepare an appropriate value analysis and a determination and distribution of excess schedule.
2. Complete a consolidated worksheet for Untraded Company and its subsidiary, Traded Company, as of January 1, 2012.

Consolidated Statements: Subsequent to Acquisition

Learning Objectives

When you have completed this chapter, you should be able to

1. Show how an investment in a subsidiary account is maintained under the simple equity, sophisticated equity, and cost methods.

2. Complete a consolidated worksheet using the simple equity method for the parent's investment account.

3. Complete a consolidated worksheet using the cost method for the parent's investment account.

4. Describe the special worksheet procedures that are used for an investment maintained under the sophisticated equity method.

5. Distribute and amortize multiple adjustments resulting from the difference between the price paid for an investment in a subsidiary and the subsidiary equity eliminated.

6. Demonstrate the worksheet procedures used for investments purchased during the financial reporting period.

7. Demonstrate an understanding of when goodwill impairment loss exists and how it is calculated.

8. Consolidate a subsidiary using vertical worksheet format. (Appendix A)

9. Explain the impact of tax-related complications arising on the purchase date. (Appendix B)

This chapter's mission is to teach the procedures needed to prepare consolidated income statements, retained earnings statements, and balance sheets in periods subsequent to the acquisition of a subsidiary. There are several worksheet models to master. This variety is caused primarily by the alternative methods available to a parent for maintaining its investment in a subsidiary account. **Accounting principles do not address the method used by a parent to record its investment in a subsidiary that is to be consolidated. The method used is of no concern to standard setters since the investment account is always eliminated when consolidating.** Thus, the method chosen to record the investment usually is based on convenience.

In the preceding chapter, worksheet procedures included asset and liability adjustments to reflect fair values on the date of the purchase. This chapter discusses the subsequent depreciation and amortization of these asset and liability revaluations in conjunction with its analysis of worksheet procedures for preparing consolidated financial statements. Appendix A, page 141, explains the vertical worksheet as an alternative approach to the horizontal worksheet, which is primarily used in this text chapter for developing consolidated statements.

This chapter does not deal with the income tax issues of the consolidated company except to the extent that they are reflected in the original acquisition price. Appendix B, page 141, considers tax issues that arise as part of the original purchase. These include recording procedures for deferred tax liabilities arising in a tax-free exchange and tax loss carryovers. A full discussion of tax issues in consolidations is included in Chapter 6.

1

OBJECTIVE

Show how an investment in a subsidiary account is maintained under the simple equity, sophisticated equity, and cost methods.

ACCOUNTING FOR THE INVESTMENT IN A SUBSIDIARY

A parent may choose one of two basic methods when accounting for its investment in a subsidiary: the equity method or the cost method. The equity method records as income an ownership percentage of the reported income of the subsidiary, whether or not it was received by the parent. The cost method treats the investment in the subsidiary like a passive investment by recording income only when dividends are declared by the subsidiary.

Equity Method

The equity method records as income the parent's ownership interest percentage multiplied by the subsidiary reported net income. The income is added to the parent's investment account. In a like manner, the parent records its share of a subsidiary loss and lowers its investment account for its share of the loss. Dividends received from the subsidiary are viewed as a conversion of a portion of the investment account into cash; thus, dividends reduce the investment account balance. The investment account at any point in time can be summarized as follows:

Investment in Subsidiary (equity method)

Original cost	less: Ownership interest × Reported losses of
plus: Ownership interest × Reported income of subsidiary since acquisition	subsidiary since acquisition
	less: Ownership interest × Dividends declared by subsidiary since acquisition
equals: Equity-adjusted balance	

The real advantage of using the *simple equity method* when consolidating is that every dollar of change in the stockholders' equity of the subsidiary is recorded on a pro rata basis in the investment account. This method expedites the elimination of the investment account in the consolidated worksheets in future periods. It is favored in this text because of its simplicity.

For some unconsolidated investments, the *sophisticated equity method* is required. Under this method, a company's investment is adjusted for amortizations of excess shown on the determination and distribution of excess schedule. For example, assume that the price paid for an investment in a subsidiary exceeded underlying book value and that the determination and distribution of excess schedule attributed the entire excess to a building. Just as a building will decrease in value and should be depreciated, so should that portion of the price paid for the investment attributed to the building also be amortized. If the estimated life of the building is 10 years, then the portion of the investment price attributed to the building should be amortized over 10 years. This would be accomplished by reducing the investment income each year by the amortization, which means that the income posted to the investment account each year is also less by the amount of the amortization.

The sophisticated equity method is required for influential investments (normally 20% to 50% interests) and for those rare subsidiaries that are not consolidated. Its use for these types of investments is fully discussed in the Special Appendix. The sophisticated equity method also is used by some parent companies to maintain the investment in a subsidiary that is to be consolidated. This better reflects the investment account in the parent-only statements, but such statements may not be used as the primary statements for external reporting purposes. Parent-only statements may be used as supplemental statements only when the criteria for consolidated statements are met. The use of this method for investments to be consolidated makes recording the investment income and the elimination of the investment account more difficult than under the simple equity method.

Cost Method

When the *cost method* is used, the investment in subsidiary account is retained at its original cost-of-acquisition balance. No adjustments are made to the account for income as it is earned by the subsidiary. Income on the investment is limited to dividends received from the subsidiary. The cost method is acceptable for subsidiaries that are to be consolidated because, in the consolidation process, the investment account is eliminated entirely.

The cost method is the most common method used in practice by parent companies. It is simple to use during the accounting period and avoids the risk of incorrect adjustments. Typically, the correct income of the subsidiary is not known until after the end of the accounting period. Awaiting its determination would delay the parent company's closing procedures. Companies that use the cost method may convert to the simple equity method as part of the consolidation process.

Example of the Equity and Cost Methods

The simple equity, sophisticated equity, and cost methods will be illustrated by an example covering two years. This example, which will become the foundation for several consolidated worksheets in this chapter, is based on the following facts:

1. The following D&D schedule was prepared on the January 1, 2011, date of purchase. It is assumed that the value of the NCI is proportionate to the price paid by Company P for the controlling interest. This schedule is similar to that of the preceding chapter but is modified to indicate the period over which adjustments to the subsidiary book values will be amortized. This expanded format will be used in preparing all future worksheets.
2. Income during 2011 was $25,000 for Company S; dividends declared by Company S at the end of 2011 totaled $10,000.
3. During 2012, Company S had a loss of $12,000 and declared dividends of $5,000.
4. The balance in Company S's retained earnings account on December 31, 2012, is $73,000.

Company P and Subsidiary Company S
Determination and Distribution of Excess Schedule

	Company Implied Fair Value	Parent Price (90%)	NCI Value (10%)
Fair value of subsidiary	$150,000	$135,000	$ 15,000
Less book value of interest acquired:			
Common stock ($10 par).	$ 50,000		
Retained earnings	70,000		
Total stockholders' equity.	$120,000	$120,000	$120,000
Interest acquired		90%	10%
Book value.		$108,000	$ 12,000
Excess of fair value over book value	**$ 30,000**	$ 27,000	$ 3,000

Adjustment of identifiable accounts:

	Adjustment	Amortization per Year	Life	Worksheet Key
Patent ($150,000 fair – $120,000 book value)	**$ 30,000**	$ 3,000	10	**debit D**

Event	Entries on Parent Company's Books—Simple Equity Method		
2011			
Jan. 1 Purchase of stock	Investment in Company S	135,000	
	Cash................................		135,000
Dec. 31 Subsidiary income of $25,000 reported to parent	Investment in Company S	22,500	
	Subsidiary Income		22,500
31 Dividends of $10,000 declared by subsidiary	Dividends Receivable	9,000	
	Investment in Company S................		9,000
	Investment Balance, Dec. 31, 2011		**$148,500**
2012			
Dec. 31 Subsidiary loss of $12,000 reported to parent	Loss on Subsidiary Operations	10,800	
	Investment in Company S................		10,800
31 Dividends of $5,000 declared by subsidiary	Dividends Receivable	4,500	
	Investment in Company S................		4,500
	Investment Balance, Dec. 31, 2012		**$133,200**

The journal entries and resulting investment account balances shown above and on page 117 record this information on the books of Company P using the simple equity, cost, and sophisticated equity methods. Note that the only difference between the sophisticated and simple equity methods is that the former records 90% of the subsidiary's reported income of $25,000. The sophisticated equity method records 90% of the subsidiary's income of $25,000 less the amortization adjustment of $3,000. Thus, the sophisticated equity share of income the first year is 90% of $22,000, or $19,800.

REFLECTION

- The simple equity method records investment income (loss) equal to the parent ownership interest multiplied by the reported subsidiary income (loss).

- The sophisticated equity method records investment income (loss) equal to the parent ownership interest multiplied by the reported subsidiary income (loss) and deducts amortizations of excess allocable to the controlling interest.

- The cost method records only dividends as received.

2
OBJECTIVE

Complete a consolidated worksheet using the simple equity method for the parent's investment account.

ELIMINATION PROCEDURES

Worksheet procedures necessary to prepare consolidated income statements, retained earnings statements, and balance sheets are examined in the following section. **Recall that the consolidation process is performed independently each year since the worksheet eliminations of previous years are never recorded by the parent or subsidiary.**

Entries on Parent Company's Books—Cost Method		Entries on Parent Company's Books—Sophisticated Equity Method	
Investment in Company S 135,000		Investment in Company S 135,000	
Cash.......................	135,000	Cash.......................	135,000
No entry.		Investment in Company S^a........ 19,800	
		Subsidiary Income	19,800
Dividends Receivable 9,000		Dividends Receivable 9,000	
Subsidiary (Dividend) Income	9,000	Investment in Company S.......	9,000
Investment Balance, Dec. 31,2011	**$135,000**	**Investment Balance, Dec. 31, 2011**	**$145,800**
No entry.		Loss on Subsidiary Operations 13,500	
		Investment in Company S^b......	13,500
Dividends Receivable 4,500		Dividends Receivable 4,500	
Subsidiary (Dividend) Income	4,500	Investment in Company S.......	4,500
Investment Balance, Dec. 31, 2012.............	**$135,000**	**Investment Balance, Dec. 31, 2012**.............	**$127,800**

^aParent's share of subsidiary income = 90% × ($25,000 – $3,000 amortization adjustment).
^bParent's share of subsidiary loss = 90% × (–$12,000 – $3,000 amortization adjustment).

The illustrations that follow are based on the facts concerning the investment in Company S, as detailed in the previous example. The procedures for consolidating an investment maintained under the simple equity method will be discussed first, followed by an explanation of how procedures would differ under the cost and sophisticated equity methods. (See the inside front cover for a complete listing of the elimination codes used in this text.)

Effect of Simple Equity Method on Consolidation

Examine Worksheet 3-1 on pages 146 and 147, noting that the worksheet trial balances for Company P and Company S are preclosing trial balances and, thus, include the income statement accounts of both companies. Look at Company P's trial balance and note that Investment in Company S is now at the equity-adjusted cost at the end of the year. The balance reflects the following information:

Worksheet 3-1: page 146

Cost...	$135,000
Plus equity income (90% × $25,000 Company S income).....................	22,500
Less dividends received (90% × $10,000 dividends paid by Company S)	(9,000)
Balance......................................	$148,500

If we are going to eliminate the subsidiary equity against the investment account and get the correct excess, **the investment account and subsidiary equity must be at the same point in time**. Right now, the investment account is adjusted through the end of the year, and the subsidiary retained earnings is still at its January 1 balance. Eliminating (reversing) the entries that affected the investment balance during the current year creates date alignment. First, the entry for (CY1) [for Current Year entry #1] eliminates the subsidiary income recorded against the investment account as follows:

Eliminate current-year investment income for **date alignment**:

| **(CY1)** | Subsidiary Income (Company P account) .... | 22,500 | |
| | Investment in Company S............................... | | 22,500 |

This elimination also removes the subsidiary income account. This is appropriate because we will, instead, be including the income statement accounts of the subsidiary. The intercompany dividends paid by the subsidiary to the parent will be eliminated next as follows with entry (CY2):

	Eliminate intercompany dividends:		
(CY2)	Investment in Company S	9,000	
	Dividends Declared (Company S account)		9,000

After this entry, only subsidiary dividends paid to the noncontrolling shareholders will remain. These are dividends paid to the "outside world" and, as such, belong in the consolidated statements.

Once you have created date alignment, it is appropriate to eliminate 90% of the subsidiary equity against the investment account with entry (EL) [for Elimination entry]. This entry is the same as described in Chapter 2.

	Eliminate 90% subsidiary equity against investment account:		
(EL)	Common Stock ($10 par)—Company S (90% eliminated)	45,000	
	Retained Earnings, January 1, 2011—Company S (90% eliminated)	63,000	
	Investment in Company S.		108,000

The excess ($135,000 balance after eliminating current-year entries − $108,000 = $27,000) should always agree with that indicated by the D&D schedule. The next procedure is to distribute the excess and adjust the NCI with entry (D) [for Distribute entry] and (NCI) [to adjust the NCI] as indicated by the D&D schedule as follows:

	Distribute excess investment account balance to accounts to be adjusted:		
(D)/(NCI)	Patent.	30,000	
	Investment in Company S (remaining balance)		27,000
	NCI (use the subsidiary's retained earnings account) . .		3,000

The D&D schedule indicates that the life of the patent was 10 years. It must now be amortized for the first year with entry (A) [for Amortization entry]:

	Amortize excess for current year:		
(A)	Patent Amortization Expense ($30,000/10 years)	3,000	
	Patent.		3,000

Patent amortization expense should be maintained in a separate account, so that it will be available for the income statement as a separate item.

The Consolidated Income Statement column follows the Eliminations & Adjustments columns. The adjusted income statement accounts of the constituent companies are used to calculate the *consolidated net income* of $62,000. This income is distributed to the controlling interest and NCI. Note that the NCI receives 10% of the $22,000 adjusted net income of the subsidiary, or $2,200. The controlling interest receives the balance of the consolidated net income, or $59,800.

The distribution of income is handled best by using *income distribution schedules (IDS)*, which appear at the end of Worksheet 3-1. The subsidiary IDS is a "T account" that begins with the reported net income of the subsidiary. This income is termed *internally generated net income,* which connotes the income of only the company being analyzed without consideration of income derived from other members of the affiliated group. **All amortizations of excess resulting from the consolidations process are adjusted to the subsidiary's IDS.** Since the NCI shares in the original asset adjustments, it is also adjusted for the amortizations. Subsidiary adjusted net income is calculated after adjustment for the amortizations of excess. In Worksheet 3-1, the subsidiary adjusted net income is multiplied by the noncontrolling ownership percentage to calculate the NCI share of income. A similar T account is used for the parent IDS. The parent's share of subsidiary net income is added to the internally generated net income of the parent. The balance in the parent T account is the controlling share of the consolidated net income. **The IDS is a valuable self-check procedure since the sum of the income distributions should equal the consolidated net income on the worksheet.**

The NCI column of the worksheet summarizes the total ownership interest of noncontrolling stockholders on the balance sheet date. The noneliminated portion of subsidiary common stock at par, additional paid-in capital in excess of par, retained earnings (including the NCI adjustment), the NCI share of income, and dividends declared are extended to this column. The total of this column is then extended to the Consolidated Balance Sheet column as the noncontrolling interest. The formal balance sheet will show only the total NCI and will not provide information on the components of this balance.

The Controlling Retained Earnings column produces the controlling retained earnings balance on the balance sheet date. The beginning parent retained earnings balance, as adjusted by eliminations and adjustments (in later worksheets), is extended to this column. Dividends declared by the parent are also extended to this column. The controlling share of consolidated income is extended to this column to produce the ending balance. The balance is extended to the balance sheet column as the retained earnings of the consolidated company.

The Consolidated Balance Sheet column includes the consolidated asset and liability balances. The capital accounts balances of the parent are extended as the consolidated capital accounts balances. As mentioned above, the aggregate balances of the NCI and the Controlling Retained Earnings columns are also extended to the Consolidated Balance Sheet column.

Separate debit and credit columns may be used for the consolidated balance sheet. This arrangement may minimize errors and aid analysis. Single columns are not advocated but are used to facilitate the inclusion of lengthy worksheets in a summarized fashion.

The information for the following formal statements is taken directly from Worksheet 3-1:

Company P
Consolidated Income Statement
For Year Ended December 31, 2011

Revenue	$ 175,000
Expenses	(110,000)
Patent amortization expense	(3,000)
Consolidated net income	$ 62,000
Distributed to:	
Noncontrolling interest	$ 2,200
Controlling interest	$ 59,800

Company P
Consolidated Retained Earnings Statement
For Year Ended December 31, 2011

	Noncontrolling	Controlling
Retained earnings, January 1, 2011	$10,000	$123,000
Consolidated net income	2,200	59,800
Dividends declared	(1,000)	
Retained earnings, December 31, 2011	$11,200*	$182,800

*This does not appear as a separate item on the worksheet.

(continued)

Company P
Consolidated Balance Sheet
December 31, 2011

Assets		Stockholders' Equity		
Net tangible assets	$372,000	Controlling interest:		
Patent.................	27,000	Common stock	$200,000	
		Retained earnings	182,800	$382,800
		Noncontrolling interest		16,200
Total assets	$399,000	Total stockholders' equity ...		$399,000

You should notice several features of the consolidated statements.

◆ Consolidated net income is the total income earned by the consolidated entity. The consolidated net income is then distributed to the noncontrolling interest (NCI) and the controlling interest.

◆ The retained earnings statement includes Noncontrolling and Controlling Interest columns. The Noncontrolling Interest column includes the dividends declared to noncontrolling shareholders.

◆ The consolidated balance sheet shows the NCI as a subdivision of stockholders' equity as discussed in Chapter 2. The NCI is shown only as a total and is not itemized.

Exhibit 3-1 is taken from the 2009 financial statements of Pfizer Inc. for a real-world example of disclosure for the NCI. Look at the lower portion of the consolidated income statement, and you will see the highlighted allocation of income to the noncontrolling interest. Look at the lower area of the equity section of the consolidated balance sheet, and you will see the highlighted noncontrolling interest in equity.

Exhibit 3-1
Pfizer, Inc. and Subsidiaries
Consolidated Statements of Income and Balance Sheets

Consolidated Statements of Income
Pfizer Inc, and Subsidiary Companies

	Year Ended December 31,		
(Millions, Except per Common Share Data)	2009	2008	2007
Revenues	**$50,009**	$48,296	$48,418
Costs and expenses:			
Cost of sales[a]	**8,888**	8,112	11,239
Selling, informational and administrative expenses[a]........................	**14,875**	14,537	15,626
Research and development expenses[a] ...	**7,845**	7,945	8,089
Amortization of intangible assets........	**2,877**	2,668	3,128
Acquisition-related in-process research and development charges	**68**	633	283
Restructuring charges and certain acquisition-related costs	**4,337**	2,675	2,534
Other (income)/deductions—net	**292**	2,032	(1,759)
Income from continuing operations before provision for taxes on income.........	**10,827**	9,694	9,278
Provision for taxes on income	**2,197**	1,645	1,023
Income from continuing operations	**8,630**	8,049	8,255
Discontinued operations—net of tax	**14**	78	(69)

| (Millions, Except per Common Share Data) | Year Ended December 31, | | |
	2009	2008	2007
Net income before allocation to noncontrolling interests	8,644	8,127	8,186
Less: Net income attributable to noncontrolling interests	9	23	42
Net income attributable to Pfizer, Inc.	**$ 8,635**	**$ 8,104**	**$ 8,144**
Earnings per common share—basic			
Income from continuing operations attributable to Pfizer Inc. common shareholders	**$ 1.23**	$ 1.19	$ 1.19
Discontinued operations—net of tax	—	0.01	(0.01)
Net income attributable to Pfizer Inc. common shareholders	**$ 1.23**	$ 1.20	$ 1.18
Earnings per common share—diluted			
Income from continuing operations attributable to Pfizer Inc. common shareholders	**$ 1.23**	$ 1.19	$ 1.18
Discontinued operations—net of tax	—	0.01	(0.01)
Net income attributable to Pfizer Inc. common shareholders	**$ 1.23**	**$ 1.20**	$ 1.17
Weighted-average shares—basic.........	**7,007**	6,727	6,917
Weighted-average shares—diluted	**7,045**	6,750	6,939

[a] Exclusive of amortization of intangible assets except as disclosed in *Note 1L Significant Accounting Policies: Amortization of Intangible Assets, Deprecistion and Certain Long-Lived Assets.*

See Notes to Consolidated Financial Statements, which are an integral part of these statements.

Consolidated Balance Sheets
Pfizer Inc. and Subsidiary Companies

| (Millions, Except Preferred Stock Issued and Per Common Share Data) | As of December 31, | |
	2009	2008
Assets		
Cash and cash equivalents	**$ 1,978**	$ 2,122
Short-term investments	**23,991**	21,609
Accounts receivable, less allowance for doubtful accounts: 2009—$176; 2008—$190....................	**14,645**	8,958
Short-term loans.......................................	**1,195**	824
Inventories...	**12,403**	4,381
Current deferred tax assets and other current assets	**6,962**	5,034
Assets held for sale	**496**	148
Total current assets..............................	**61,679**	43,076
Long-term investments and loans	**13,122**	11,478
Property, plant and equipment, less accumulated depreciation............................	**22,780**	13,287
Goodwill	**42,376**	21,464
Identifiable intangible assets, less accumulated amortization........................	**68,015**	17,721
Noncurrent deferred tax assets and other noncurrent assets	**4,986**	4,122
Total assets...	**$212,949**	$111,148
Liabilities and Shareholders' Equity		
Short-term borrowings, including current portion of long-term debt 2009—$27; 2008—$937	**$ 5,469**	$ 9,320
Accounts payable	**4,370**	1,751
Dividends payable	**1,454**	2,159

(continued)

	As of December 31,	
(Millions, Except Preferred Stock Issued and Per Common Share Data)	2009	2008
Income taxes payable	**10,107**	656
Accrued compensation and related items	**2,242**	1,667
Current deferred tax liabilities and other current liabilities	**13,583**	11,456
Total current liabilities	**37,225**	27,009
Long-term debt	**43,193**	7,963
Pension benefit obligations	**6,392**	4,235
Noncurrent deferred tax liabilities	**17,839**	2,959
Postretirement benefit obligations	**3,243**	1,604
Other taxes payable	**9,000**	6,568
Other noncurrent liabilities	**5,611**	3,070
Total liabilities	**122,503**	53,408
Preferred stock, without par value, at stated value; 27 shares authorized; issued: 2009—1,511; 2008—1,804	**61**	73
Common stock, $0.05 par value; 12,000 shares authorized; issued: 2009—8,869; 2008—8,863	**443**	443
Additional paid-in capital	**70,497**	70,283
Employee benefit trusts	**(333)**	(425)
Treasury stock, shares at cost; 2009—799; 2008—2,117	**(21,632)**	(57,391)
Retained earnings	**40,426**	49,142
Accumulated other comprehensive income/(expense)	**552**	(4,569)
Total Pfizer Inc. shareholders' equity	**90,014**	57,556
Equity attributable to noncontrolling interests	**432**	184
Total shareholders' equity	**90,446**	57,740
Total liabilities and shareholders' equity	**$212,949**	$111,148

See Notes to Consolidated Financial Statements, which are an integral part of these statements.

Now consider consolidation procedures for 2012 as they would apply to Companies P and S under the simple equity method. This will provide added practice in preparing worksheets and will emphasize that, at the end of each year, consolidation procedures are applied to the separate statements of the constituent firms. In essence, **each year's consolidation procedures begin as if there had never been a previous consolidation.** However, reference to past worksheets is commonly used to save time.

Worksheet 3-2: page 148

The separate trial balances of Companies P and S are displayed in the first two columns of Worksheet 3-2, pages 148 and 149. The investment in subsidiary account includes the simple equity-adjusted investment balance as calculated on page 116. Note that the balances in the retained earnings accounts of Companies P and S are for January 1, 2012, because these are the pre-closing trial balances. The beginning retained earnings amounts are calculated as follows:

Company P:	January 1, 2011, balance	$123,000
	Net income, 2011 (including Company P's share of subsidiary income under simple equity method)	62,500*
	Balance, January 1, 2012	$185,500

*Company P's own 2011 net income ($100,000 revenue – $60,000 expenses) + Company P's share of Company S 2011, $25,000 net income ($25,000 × 90%) = $40,000 + $22,500 = $62,500.

Company S:	January 1, 2011, balance	$ 70,000
	Net income, 2011	25,000
	Dividends declared	(10,000)
	Balance, January 1, 2012	$ 85,000

As before, entry (CY1) eliminates the subsidiary income recorded by the parent, and entry (CY2) eliminates the intercompany dividends. Neither subsidiary income nor dividends declared by the subsidiary to the parent should remain in the consolidated statements. In journal form, the entries are as follows:

Create date alignment and eliminate current-year subsidiary income:

(CY1)	Investment in Company S	10,800	
	Subsidiary Loss		10,800
(CY2)	Investment in Company S	4,500	
	Dividends Declared (Company S account)		4,500

At this point, the investment account balance is returned to $148,500 ($133,200 on the trial balance + $10,800 loss + $4,500 dividends), which is the balance on January 1, 2012. Date alignment now exists, and elimination of the investment account may proceed. Entry (EL) eliminates 90% of the subsidiary equity accounts against the investment account. Entry (EL) differs in amount from the prior year's (2011) entry only because Company S's retained earnings balance has changed. Always eliminate the subsidiary's equity balances as they appear on the worksheet, not in the original D&D schedule. In journal form, entry (EL) is as follows:

Eliminate investment account at beginning-of-year balance:

(EL)	Common Stock—Company S (90%)	45,000	
	Retained Earnings, January 1, 2012—Company S (90%) ..	76,500	
	Investment in Company S.		121,500

Entries (D) and (NCI) are exactly the same as they were on the 2011 worksheet. We are always adjusting the subsidiary accounts as of the acquisition date. It will be necessary to make this same entry every year until the markup caused by the purchase is fully amortized or the asset is sold. In entry form, entry (D)/(NCI) is as follows:

Distribute excess of cost (patent):

(D)/(NCI)	Patent.	30,000	
	Investment in Company S.		27,000
	NCI (Retained Earnings—Company S)		3,000

Finally, entry (A) includes $3,000 per year amortization of the patent for 2011 and 2012. The expense for 2011 is charged to Company P retained earnings and the NCI in the 90%/10% ratio. The charge is made to both interests because the asset adjustment was made to both interests. In journal form, the entry is as follows:

Amortize patent for current and prior year:

(A)	Retained Earnings, January 1, 2012—Company P	2,700	
	NCI (Retained Earnings—Company S)	300	
	Patent Amortization Expense (for current year)	3,000	
	Patent.		6,000

Note that the 2013 worksheet will include three total years of amortization, since **the entries made in prior periods' worksheets have not been recorded in either the parent's or subsidiary's books.** Even in later years, when the patent is past its 10-year life, it will be necessary to use a revised entry (D), which would adjust all prior years' amortizations to the patent as follows:

Retained Earnings—Company P (10 years × $2,700).	27,000	
NCI	3,000	
Investment in Company S (the excess)		30,000

Note that the original D&D schedule prepared on the date of acquisition becomes the foundation for all subsequent worksheets. Once prepared, the schedule is used without modification.

REFLECTION

- Date alignment is needed before an investment can be eliminated.

- For an equity method investment, date alignment means removing current-year entries to return to the beginning-of-year investment balance.

- All amortizations of excess resulting from the consolidations process are adjusted to the subsidiary's IDS.

- Many distributions of excess must be followed by amortizations that cover the current and prior years.

- The consolidated net income derived on a worksheet is allocated to the controlling and noncontrolling interests using an income distribution schedule.

- Each year's consolidation procedures begin as if there had never been a previous consolidation.

3

OBJECTIVE

Complete a consolidated worksheet using the cost method for the parent's investment account.

Worksheet 3-3: page 150

Effect of Cost Method on Consolidation

Recall that parent companies often may choose to record their investments in a subsidiary under the cost method, whereby the investments are maintained at their original costs. Income from the investments is recorded only when dividends are declared by the subsidiary. The use of the cost method means that the investment account does not reflect changes in subsidiary equity. Rather than develop a new set of procedures for the elimination of an investment under the cost method, **the cost method investment will be converted to its simple equity balance at the beginning of the period** to create date alignment. Then, the elimination procedures developed earlier can be applied.

Worksheet 3-3, pages 150 and 151, is a consolidated financial statements worksheet for Companies P and S for the first year of combined operations. The worksheet is based on the entries made under the cost method, as shown on page 117. Company P's Trial Balance column in Worksheet 3-3 reveals that the investment in the subsidiary account at year-end is still stated at the original $135,000 cost, and the income recorded by the parent as a result of subsidiary ownership is limited to $9,000, or 90% of the dividends declared by the subsidiary. **When the cost method is used, the account title *Dividend Income* may be used in place of *Subsidiary Income*.**

There is no need for an equity conversion at the end of the first year. Date alignment is automatic; the investment in Company S account and the subsidiary retained earnings are both as of January 1, 2011. There is no entry (CY1) under the cost method; only entry (CY2) is needed to eliminate intercompany dividends. All remaining eliminations are the same as for 2011 under the equity method. In journal form, the complete set of entries for 2011 is as follows:

	Eliminate current-year dividends:		
(CY2)	Subsidiary (or Dividend) Income	9,000	
	Dividends Declared (Company S account)		9,000
	Eliminate investment account at beginning-of-year balance:		
(EL)	Common Stock—Company S	45,000	
	Retained Earnings, January 1, 2011—Company S	63,000	
	Investment in Company S.		108,000
	Distribute excess of cost (patent):		
(D)/(NCI)	Patent.	30,000	
	Investment in Company S.		27,000
	NCI (use Retained Earnings—Company S)		3,000

Amortize patent for current year:

(A)   Patent Amortization Expense............................ 3,000
          Patent...   3,000

The last four columns of Worksheet 3-3 are exactly the same as those for Worksheet 3-1, resulting in the same consolidated statements.

For periods after 2011 (first year of consolidation), date alignment will not exist, and an equity conversion entry will be needed. Worksheet 3-4 on pages 152 and 153, is such an example. The worksheet is for 2012 and parallels Worksheet 3-2 except that the cost method is in use. The balance in the investment account is still the original cost of $135,000. The retained earnings of the subsidiary is, however, at its January 1, 2012, balance of $85,000. Note that the parent's January 1, 2012, retained earnings balance is $172,000, which is $13,500 less than in Worksheet 3-2 because it does not include the 2011 undistributed subsidiary income of $13,500 ($22,500 income less $9,000 dividends received). In order to get date alignment, an equity conversion entry, (CV), is made to convert the investment account to its January 1, 2012, simple equity balance. This conversion entry is always calculated as follows:

Worksheet 3-4: page 152

Parent's % × (Subsidiary retained earnings at the beginning of the current year
  −Subsidiary retained earnings on the date of purchase) = Equity conversion adjustment

For example:

	Date	Amount
Retained earnings—Company S (start of current year)..........	Jan. 1, 2012	$85,000
Retained earnings (date of purchase)......................	Jan. 1, 2011	70,000
Change in subsidiary retained earnings....................		$15,000
Parent ownership interest................................		× 90%
Equity conversion adjustment (parent share of change).........		$13,500

Based on this calculation, the conversion entry on Worksheet 3-4 is as follows in journal entry form:

Convert investment to simple equity method as of
    January 1, 2012:

(CV)   Investment in Company S 13,500
          Retained Earnings, January 1, 2012—Company P..........   13,500

With date alignment created, remaining eliminations parallel Worksheet 3-2 except that there is no entry (CY1) for current-year equity income. Entry (CY2) is still used to eliminate intercompany dividends. In journal form, the remaining entries for Worksheet 3-4 are as follows:

Eliminate current-year dividends:

(CY2)   Subsidiary (or Dividend) Income.......................... 4,500
          Dividends Declared (Company S account)   4,500

Eliminate investment account at beginning-of-year balance:

(EL)   Common Stock—Company S 45,000
        Retained Earnings, January 1, 2012—Company S 76,500
          Investment in Company S.............................   121,500

Distribute excess of cost (patent):

(D)/(NCI)   Patent.. 30,000
          Investment in Company S.............................   27,000
          NCI (Retained Earnings—Company S)   3,000

Amortize patent for current and prior years:

(A)		
Retained Earnings, January 1, 2012—Company P	2,700	
NCI (Retained Earnings—Company S)	300	
Patent Amortization Expense	3,000	
Patent		6,000

The last four columns of Worksheet 3-4 are exactly the same as those for Worksheet 3-2, as are the consolidated financial statements for 2012.

The simplicity of this technique of converting from the cost to the simple equity method should be appreciated. At any future date, in order to convert to the simple equity method, it is necessary only to compare the balance of the subsidiary retained earnings account on the worksheet trial balance with the balance of that account on the original date of acquisition (included in the D&D schedule). Specific reference to income earned and dividends paid by the subsidiary in each intervening year is unnecessary. The only complications occur when stock dividends have been issued by the subsidiary or when the subsidiary has issued or retired stock. These complications are examined in Chapter 8.

REFLECTION

- For a cost method investment, date alignment means converting the investment account to its equity-adjusted balance at the start of the year. (No adjustment is needed the first year.)

- Once converted, all other investment eliminations are the same as for the equity method.

<table>
<tr><td>

4

OBJECTIVE

Describe the special worksheet procedures that are used for an investment maintained under the sophisticated equity method.

</td><td>

EFFECT OF SOPHISTICATED EQUITY METHOD ON CONSOLIDATION

In some cases, a parent may desire to prepare its own separate statements as a supplement to the consolidated statements. In this situation, the investment in the subsidiary must be shown on the parent's separate statements at the sophisticated equity balance. This requirement may lead the parent to maintain its subsidiary investment account under the sophisticated equity method. Two ramifications occur when such an investment is consolidated. **First, the current year's equity adjustment is net of excess amortizations; second, the investment account contains only the remaining unamortized excess applicable to the investment.**

The use of the sophisticated equity method complicates the elimination of the investment account in that the worksheet distribution and amortization of the excess procedures are altered. However, there is no impact on the other consolidation procedures. To illustrate, the information given in Worksheet 3-2 will be used as the basis for an example covering 2012. The trial balance of Company P will show the following changes as a result of using the sophisticated equity method:

</td></tr>
</table>

1. The Investment in Company S will be carried at $132,300 ($137,700 simple equity balance less parent's share of two years' amortization of excess at $2,700 per year).

2. The January 1, 2012, balance for Company P Retained Earnings will be $187,300 ($190,000 under simple equity less parent's share of one year's amortization of excess of $2,700).

3. The subsidiary loss account of the parent will have a balance of $13,500 ($10,800 share of the subsidiary loss plus $2,700 amortization of excess).

Based on these changes, a partial worksheet under the sophisticated equity method follows:

Company P and Subsidiary Company S
Partial Worksheet for Consolidated Financial Statements
For Year Ended December 31, 2012

(Credit balance amounts are in parentheses.)	Trial Balance		Eliminations & Adjustments			
	Company P	Company S	Dr.		Cr.	
Investment in Company S	132,300		(CY1)	13,500	(EL)	126,000
			(CY2)	4,500	(D)	24,300
Patent			(D)	27,000	(A)	3,000
Retained Earnings, January 1, 2012—Company P	(187,300)					
Common Stock ($10 par)—Company S		(50,000)	(EL)	45,000		
Retained Earnings, January 1, 2012—Company S		(90,000)	(EL)	81,000	(NCI)	2,700
Revenue	(100,000)	(50,000)				
Expenses	80,000	62,000				
Patent Amortization			(A)	3,000		
Subsidiary Loss	13,500				(CY1)	13,500
Dividends Declared		5,000			(CY2)	4,500

Eliminations and Adjustments:

(CY1) Eliminate the current-year entries made in the investment account to record the subsidiary loss. The loss account now includes the $2,700 excess amortization.
(CY2) Eliminate intercompany dividends.
(EL) Using the balances at the beginning of the year, eliminate 90% of the Company S equity balance against the remaining investment account.
(D)/(NCI) Distribute the remaining unamortized excess applicable to the controlling interest on January 1, 2011 ($27,000 on purchase date less $2,700 amortization), to the patent account. Adjust the NCI for the remaining excess attributable to its 10% share ($3,000 – $300 amortization for 2011). The total adjustment to the patent account is $27,000 (the remaining balance at the start of the year).
(A) Amortize the patent for the current year only; prior-year amortization has been recorded in the parent's investment account and has been reflected in the NCI adjustment.

The sophisticated equity method essentially is a modification of simple equity procedures. The major difference in the consolidation procedures under the two methods is that, subsequent to the acquisition, the original excess calculated on the determination and distribution of excess schedule does not appear when the sophisticated equity method is used. Only the remaining unamortized excess appears. Since the investment account is eliminated in the consolidation process, the added complexities of the sophisticated method are not justified for most companies and seldom are applied to consolidated subsidiaries.

REFLECTION

- The investment account is already adjusted for amortizations of excess resulting from the D&D schedule.

- Only the remaining unamortized excess remains in the investment account, and only the unamortized balance is distributed to appropriate accounts.

- Comparison of worksheet methods (shown on page 128):

	Simple Equity	Cost	Sophisticated Equity
Investment balance	Cost + parent % of sub (income – dividends)	Cost	Cost + parent % of sub (income – dividends – amortization of excess)
Adjustment needed to eliminate	None	Convert to simple equity as of start of year (first year not needed)	None
Elimination entry	Eliminate beginning-of-year balance	Eliminate beginning-of-year balance	Eliminate beginning-of-year balance
Excess distribution	Original amount from D&D	Original amount from D&D	Remaining **unamortized** balance from D&D
Amortizations of excess	Prior years to retained earnings; current year to nominal accounts	Prior years to retained earnings; current year to nominal accounts	**Only** current year to nominal accounts

5

OBJECTIVE

Distribute and amortize multiple adjustments resulting from the difference between the price paid for an investment in a subsidiary and the subsidiary equity eliminated.

DETERMINATION OF THE METHOD BEING USED

Before you attempt to prepare a consolidated worksheet, you need to know which of the three methods is being used by the parent to record its investment in the subsidiary. You cannot begin to eliminate the intercompany investment until that is determined. The most efficient approach is as follows:

1. Test for the use of the cost method. If the cost method is used:
   a. The investment account will be at the *original cost* shown on the determination and distribution of excess schedule.
   b. The parent will have recorded as its share of subsidiary income its *ownership interest times the dividends declared* by the subsidiary. In most cases, this income will be called "subsidiary dividend income," but some may call it "subsidiary income" or "dividend income." Therefore, do not rely on the title of the account.

2. If the method used is not cost, check for the use of simple equity as follows:
   a. The investment account will *not be at the original cost.*
   b. The parent will have recorded as subsidiary income its *ownership percentage times the reported net income of the subsidiary.*

3. If the method used is neither cost nor simple equity, it must be the sophisticated equity method. Confirm that it is by noting that:
   a. The investment account will *not be at the original cost.*
   b. The parent will have recorded as subsidiary income its ownership percentage times the reported net income of the subsidiary *minus the amortizations of excess for the current period.*

COMPLICATED PURCHASE, SEVERAL DISTRIBUTIONS OF EXCESS

In Worksheets 3-1 through 3-4, it was assumed that the entire excess of cost over book value was attributable to a patent. In reality, the excess will seldom apply to a single asset. The following example illustrates a more complicated purchase.

Worksheet 3-5: page 154

Worksheet 3-5 on pages 154 to 155 is an example of the first year of an 80% purchase with goodwill. The following table shows book and fair values of Carlos Company on the date of purchase:

Carlos Company Book and Estimated Fair Values
December 31, 2011

	Book Value	Market Value	Life		Book Value	Market Value	Life
Assets				**Liabilities**			
Inventory	$ 75,000	$ 80,000	1	Current liabilities	$ 50,000	$ 50,000	1
Land.	150,000	200,000	—	Bonds payable	200,000	186,760	4
Buildings	600,000	500,000	20	Total liabilities	$250,000	$236,760	
Accumulated depreciation	(300,000)			Stockholders' equity:			
Equipment	150,000	80,000	5	Common stock.	$100,000		
Accumulated depreciation	(50,000)			Paid-in capital in excess of par . .	150,000		
Patent.	125,000	150,000	10	Retained earnings	250,000		
				Total equity	$500,000		
Total assets.	$ 750,000	$1,010,000		Net assets	$500,000	$773,240	

The parent company, Paulos, paid $720,000 for an 80% interest in Carlos Company on January 1, 2011. It is assumed that the fair value of the NCI is proportionate to the price paid by Paulos for the controlling interest. The following value analysis schedule was prepared:

Value Analysis Schedule	Company Implied Fair Value	Parent Price (80%)	NCI Value (20%)
Company implied fair value	$ 900,000	$ 720,000	$180,000
Fair value of net assets excluding goodwill	773,240	618,592	154,648
Goodwill	**$126,760**	**$101,408**	**$ 25,352**

Based on the above information, the following D&D schedule is prepared:

Determination and Distribution of Excess Schedule

	Company Implied Fair Value	Parent Price (80%)	NCI Value (20%)
Fair value of subsidiary	$ 900,000	$720,000	$180,000
Less book value of interest acquired:			
Common stock ($10 par).	$ 100,000		
Paid-in capital in excess of par	150,000		
Retained earnings	250,000		
Total equity.	$ 500,000	$500,000	$500,000
Interest acquired		80%	20%
Book value.		$400,000	$100,000
Excess of fair value over book value	**$400,000**	$320,000	$ 80,000

(continued)

Adjustment of identifiable accounts:

	Adjustment	Amortization per Year	Life	Worksheet Key
Inventory ($80,000 – $75,000)	$ 5,000		1	**debit D1**
Land ($200,000 – $150,000)	50,000			**debit D2**
Buildings ($500,000 – $300,000 net book value). . . .	200,000	$ 10,000	20	**debit D3**
Equipment ($80,000 – $100,000 net book value). . . .	(20,000)	(4,000)	5	**credit D4**
Patent ($150,000 – $125,000)	25,000	2,500	10	**debit D5**
Discount on bonds payable ($200,000 – $186,760) .	13,240	3,310	4	**debit D6**
Goodwill.	**126,760**			**debit D7**
Total	**$400,000**			

Eliminations for 2011, in journal entry form, are as follows:

Eliminate subsidiary income recorded by the parent company:

(CY1)	Subsidiary Income	48,000	
	Investment in Carlos		48,000

Eliminate dividends paid by Carlos to Paulos:

(CY2)	Investment in Carlos	16,000	
	Dividends Declared by Carlos		16,000

Eliminate 80% of Carlos equity against investment in Carlos:

(EL)	Common Stock—Carlos	80,000	
	Paid-In Capital in Excess of Par—Carlos	120,000	
	Retained Earnings, January 1, 2011—Carlos	200,000	
	Investment in Carlos		400,000

Distribute excess of cost over book value:

(D1)	Cost of Goods Sold (inventory)	5,000	
(D2)	Land.	50,000	
(D3)	Buildings	200,000	
(D4)	Equipment		20,000
(D5)	Patent.	25,000	
(D6)	Discount on Bonds Payable	13,240	
(D7)	Goodwill	126,760	
(D)	Investment in Carlos (noneliminated excess)		320,000
(NCI)	Retained Earnings—Carlos (to adjust NCI to fair value)		80,000

Amortize excess for current year as shown on schedule with following entry:

(A3)	Depreciation Expense—Buildings.	10,000	
(A3)	Accumulated Depreciation—Buildings		10,000
(A4)	Accumulated Depreciation—Equipment	4,000	
(A4)	Depreciation Expense—Equipment.		4,000
(A5)	Other Expenses (patent amortization)	2,500	
(A5)	Patent.		2,500
(A6)	Interest Expense.	3,310	
(A6)	Discount on Bonds Payable		3,310

A summary of depreciation and amortization adjustments is as follows:

Account Adjustments to Be Amortized	Life	Annual Amount	Current Year	Prior Years	Total	Key
Inventory	1	$ 5,000	$ 5,000	—	$ 5,000	(D1)
Subject to annual amortization:						
Buildings	20	$10,000	$10,000	—	$10,000	(A3)
Equipment	5	(4,000)	(4,000)	—	(4,000)	(A4)
Patent.	10	2,500	2,500	—	2,500	(A5)
Bonds payable	4	3,310	3,310	—	3,310	(A6)
Total amortizations		$11,810	$11,810	—	$11,810	
Controlling retained earnings adjustment.					—	
NCI retained earnings adjustment.					—	

Note also in Worksheet 3-5 that the subsidiary IDS schedule picks up the entire adjustment of the cost of goods sold and all current-year amortizations. This means in the end that the NCI will absorb 20% of all adjustments, and the remaining 80% will go to the controlling interest. This is automatic because the adjusted subsidiary income is distributed 20%/80%.

Worksheet 3-6 on pages 158 and 159 is based on the same example, but is prepared as of December 31, 2012, the end of the second year.   **Worksheet 3-6**: page 158

Eliminations in journal entry form are as follows:

	Eliminate subsidiary income recorded by the parent company:		
(CY1)	Subsidiary Income.	80,000	
	Investment in Carlos.		80,000
	Eliminate dividends paid by Carlos to Paulos:		
(CY2)	Investment in Carlos.	16,000	
	Dividends Declared by Carlos.		16,000
	Eliminate 80% of Carlos equity against investment in Carlos:		
(EL)	Common Stock—Carlos	80,000	
	Paid-In Capital in Excess of Par—Carlos	120,000	
	Retained Earnings, January 1, 2012—Carlos	232,000	
	Investment in Carlos.		432,000
	Distribute excess of cost over book value:		
(D1)	Retained Earnings, January 1, 2012—Paulos (80% of $5,000 prior-year inventory amount)	4,000	
(D1)	Retained Earnings, January 1, 2012—Carlos (20% of $5,000 prior-year inventory amount)	1,000	
(D2)	Land.	50,000	
(D3)	Buildings	200,000	
(D4)	Equipment		20,000
(D5)	Patent.	25,000	
(D6)	Discount on Bonds Payable	13,240	
(D7)	Goodwill	126,760	
(D)	Investment in Carlos (noneliminated excess)		320,000
(NCI)	Retained Earnings—Carlos (to adjust NCI to fair value)		80,000

(continued)

Amortize excess for current year as shown on schedule with
following entry:

(A3)	Depreciation Expense—Buildings......................	10,000	
(A3)	Accumulated Depreciation—Buildings		20,000
(A4)	Accumulated Depreciation—Equipment...................	8,000	
(A4)	Depreciation Expense—Equipment.....................		4,000
(A5)	Other Expenses (patent amortization)	2,500	
(A5)	Patent..		5,000
(A6)	Interest Expense......................................	3,310	
(A6)	Discount on Bonds Payable		6,620
(A3–A6)	Retained Earnings, January 1, 2012—Paulos	9,448	
(A3–A6)	Retained Earnings, January 1, 2012—Carlos	2,362	

A summary of depreciation and amortization adjustments is as follows:

Account Adjustments to Be Amortized	Life	Annual Amount	Current Year	Prior Years	Total	Key
Inventory	1	$ 5,000	$ —	$ 5,000	$ 5,000	(D1)
Subject to annual amortization:						
Buildings	20	$10,000	$10,000	$10,000	$20,000	(A3)
Equipment	5	(4,000)	(4,000)	(4,000)	(8,000)	(A4)
Patent.....................	10	2,500	2,500	2,500	5,000	(A5)
Bonds payable	4	3,310	3,310	3,310	6,620	(A6)
Total amortizations		$11,810	$11,810	$11,810	$23,620	
Controlling retained earnings adjustment...............				$ 9,448*		(A3–A6)
NCI retained earnings adjustment...............				2,362**		(A3–A6)

*$11,810 × 80% = $9,448
**$11,810 × 20% = $2,362

Take note of the following issues in Worksheet 3-6:

♦ The adjustment of the inventory, at the time of the purchase on January 1, 2011, now goes to parent and NCI retained earnings, since it is a correction of the 2011 cost of goods sold.

♦ The amortizations of excess for prior periods and the inventory adjustment are carried to controlling (80%) and NCI (20%) retained earnings. Since the NCI shared in the fair value adjustments as of the purchase date, it must share in current- and prior-year amortizations.

♦ The controlling and NCI retained earnings balances are adjusted for the above amortizations of excess before they are extended to the Controlling Retained Earnings and NCI columns.

If a worksheet were prepared for December 31, 2013, the prior years' amortizations of excess would cover two prior years as follows:

Account Adjustments to Be Amortized	Life	Annual Amount	Current Year	Prior Years	Total	Key
Inventory	1	$ 5,000	$ —	$ 5,000	$ 5,000	(D1)
Subject to amortization:						
Buildings	20	$10,000	$10,000	$20,000	$ 30,000	(A3)
Equipment	5	(4,000)	(4,000)	(8,000)	(12,000)	(A4)

Account Adjustments to Be Amortized	Life	Annual Amount	Current Year	Prior Years	Total	Key
Patent..................	10	2,500	2,500	5,000	7,500	(A5)
Bonds payable	4	3,310	3,310	6,620	9,930	(A6)
Total amortizations		$11,810	$11,810	$23,620	$ 35,430	
Controlling retained earnings adjustment ...				$18,896*		(A3–A6)
NCI RE adjustment.......				4,724**		(A3–A6)

*$23,620 × 80% = $18,896
**$23,620 × 20% = $4,724

Worksheet 3-6 would be the source document for the formal consolidated statements included in Exhibit 3-2.

Exhibit 3-2
Consolidated Financial Statements for Paulos Company

Paulos Company
Consolidated Income Statement
Period Ending December 31, 2012

Sales revenue		$700,000
Less cost of goods sold................................		320,000
Gross profit		$380,000
Less operating expenses:		
Depreciation expense (building $65,000 + equipment $36,000)	$101,000	
Other operating expenses (with patent amortization $2,500)..	125,500	226,500
Operating income......................................		$153,500
Interest expense		15,310*
Consolidated net income................................		$138,190
Distributed to noncontrolling interest		$ 17,638
Distributed to controlling interest		$120,552

*Rounded down from $15,313 to tie to worksheet income

Paulos Company
Consolidated Retained Earnings Statement
Period Ending December 31, 2012

	Controlling Retained Earnings	Noncontrolling Interest
Balance, January 1, 2012.........................	$714,552	$134,638
Net income	120,552	17,638
Dividends paid		(4,000)
Balance, December 31, 2012	$835,104	$148,276

(continued)

Paulos Company
Consolidated Balance Sheet
December 31, 2012

Assets			Liabilities and Equity		
Current assets:			Current liabilities	$ 190,000	
Cash	$ 452,000		Bonds payable		
			(6%, due December 31, 2014) .	200,000	
Inventory	330,000		Discount on bonds payable	(6,620)	
Total current assets.		$ 782,000	Total liabilities		$ 383,380
Long-term assets:					
Land.	$ 400,000				
Buildings	1,600,000				
Accumulated depreciation.	(470,000)		Stockholders' equity:		
Equipment	530,000		Common stock.	$1,500,000	
			Retained earnings	835,104	
Accumulated depreciation.	(172,000)		Controlling interest.	$2,335,104	
Patent (net)	120,000		Noncontrolling interest		198,276
Goodwill	126,760				
Total long-term assets		2,134,760	Total equity.		$2,533,380
Total assets		$2,916,760	Total liabilities and equity		$2,916,760

REFLECTION

- There may be many asset (and possibly liability) adjustments resulting from the D&D schedule. Each adjustment is distributed as a part of the elimination procedure.

- Most distribution adjustments will require amortization, each over the appropriate life. The amortizations should be keyed to the distribution entry.

6
OBJECTIVE

Demonstrate the worksheet procedures used for investments purchased during the financial reporting period.

INTRAPERIOD PURCHASE UNDER THE SIMPLE EQUITY METHOD

The accountant will be required to apply special procedures when consolidating a controlling investment in common stock that is acquired during the fiscal year. The D&D schedule must be based on the subsidiary stockholders' equity on the interim purchase date, including the subsidiary retained earnings balance on that date. Also, the consolidated income of the consolidated company, as derived on the worksheet, is to include only subsidiary income earned subsequent to the acquisition date.

Assume that Company S has the following trial balance on July 1, 2011, the date of an 80% acquisition by Company P:

Current Assets	68,000	
Equipment	80,000	
Accumulated Depreciation		30,000
Liabilities		10,000

Common Stock ($10 par)		50,000
Retained Earnings, January 1, 2011		45,000
Dividends Declared	5,000	
Sales		90,000
Cost of Goods Sold	60,000	
Expenses	12,000	
Total	225,000	225,000

If Company P requires Company S to close its nominal accounts as of July 1, Company S would increase its retained earnings account by $13,000 with the following entries:

Sales	90,000	
Cost of Goods Sold		60,000
Expenses		12,000
Retained Earnings		18,000
Retained Earnings	5,000	
Dividends Declared		5,000

Assume Company P pays $106,400 for its 80% interest in Company S. Assume also that all assets have fair values equal to book value and that any excess is attributed to goodwill. It is assumed that the value of the NCI is proportional to the price paid by the parent for the controlling interest. The value analysis would be as follows:

Value Analysis Schedule	Company Implied Fair Value	Parent Price (80%)	NCI Value (20%)
Company fair value	$133,000	$106,400	$26,600
Fair value of net assets excluding goodwill	108,000*	86,400	21,600
Goodwill	**$ 25,000**	$ 20,000	$ 5,000

*Common stock $50,000 + retained earnings ($45,000 + $18,000 − $5,000) = $108,000

Based on the above information, the following D&D schedule is prepared:

Determination and Distribution of Excess Schedule			
	Company Implied Fair Value	Parent Price (80%)	NCI Value (20%)
Fair value of subsidiary	$133,000	$106,400	$ 26,600
Less book value of interest acquired:			
Common stock ($10 par)	$ 50,000		
Retained earnings	58,000		
Total equity	$108,000	$108,000	$108,000
Interest acquired		80%	20%
Book value		$ 86,400	$ 21,600
Excess of fair value over book value	**$ 25,000**	$ 20,000	$ 5,000

Adjustment of identifiable accounts:

	Adjustment		Worksheet Key
Goodwill	**$ 25,000**		**debit D1**

Worksheet 3-7: page 162

Proceeding to the end of the year, assume that the operations of Company S for the last six months result in a net income of $20,000 and dividends of $5,000 are declared by Company S on December 31. Worksheet 3-7, pages 162 to 163, includes Company S nominal accounts for only the second 6-month period since the nominal accounts were closed on July 1. Company S Retained Earnings shows the July 1, 2011, balance. The trial balance of Company P includes operations for the entire year. The subsidiary income listed by Company P includes 80% of the subsidiary's $20,000 second six months' income. Company P's investment account balance shows the following:

Original cost	$106,400
80% of subsidiary's second six months' income of $20,000	16,000
80% of $5,000 dividends declared by subsidiary on December 31	(4,000)
Investment balance, December 31, 2011	$118,400

In conformance with acquisition theory, the Consolidated Income Statement column of Worksheet 3-7 includes only subsidiary income earned after the acquisition date. Likewise, only subsidiary income earned after the purchase date is distributed to the NCI and controlling interest. Income earned and dividends declared prior to the purchase date by Company S are reflected in its July 1, 2011, retained earnings balance, of which the NCI is granted its share. The notes to the statements would have to disclose what the income of the consolidated company would have been had the purchase occurred at the start of the year.

INTRAPERIOD PURCHASE UNDER THE COST METHOD

There are only two variations of the procedures discussed in the preceding section if the cost method is used by the parent company to record its investment in the subsidiary:

1. During the year of acquisition, the parent would record as income only its share of dividends declared by the subsidiary. Thus, eliminating entries would be confined to the intercompany dividends.
2. For years after the purchase, the cost-to-equity conversion adjustment would be based on the change in the subsidiary retained earnings balance from the intraperiod purchase date to the beginning of the year for which the worksheet is being prepared.

DISCLOSURE FOR AN INTRAPERIOD PURCHASE

The consolidated income statement will include the subsidiary income starting on the acquisition date. That was the case for the Pfizer consolidated income statement included in Exhibit 3-1. The largest acquisition of 2009 was the acquisition of Wyeth Pharmaceutical Company by Pfizer on October 15, 2009. The 2009 consolidated income statement includes Wyeth's accounts only as of October 15. It is required that the notes to the consolidated financial statements show the amount of the acquired firm's revenue and income or loss included in the consolidated income statement. Exhibit 3-3 includes Pfizer's disclosure Note D, Actual and Pro Forma Impact of Acquisition, which follows behind the financial statements included in Exhibit 3-1. The note must also include a pro forma display of what income would have been had the acquired firm (Wyeth) been consolidated with the parent firm (Pfizer) for all of 2009 and for any prior periods included in the financial statements (2008).

Exhibit 3-3
Pfizer Inc. and Subsidiaries Note D to Consolidated Financial Statements

Notes to Consolidated Financial Statements
Pfizer Inc. and Subsidiary Companies

D. Actual and Pro Forma Impact of Acquisition

The following table presents information for Wyeth that is included in Pfizer's consolidated statements of income from the acquisition date, October 15, 2009, through Pfizer's domestic and international year-ends in 2009:

(Millions of Dollars)	Wyetw's Operations included in Pfizer's 2009 Results
Revenues	$ 3,303
Loss from continuing operations attributable to Pfizer Inc. common shareholders[a]	(2,191)

[a] Includes purchase accounting charges related to the fair value adjustments for acquisition-date inventory that has been sold ($904 million pre-tax), amortization of identifiable intangible assets acquired from Wyeth ($512 million pre-tax), and restructuring charges and additional depreciation—asset restructuring ($2.1 billion pre-tax).

The following table presents supplemental pro forma information as if the acquisition of Wyeth had occurred on January 1, 2009 for the year ended December 31, 2009 and January 1, 2008 for the year ended December 31, 2008.

	Unaudited Pro Forma Consolidated Results	
	Year Ended December 31.	
(Millions of Dollars. Except Per Share Data)	2009	2008
Revenues	$68,599	$71,130
Income from continuing operations attributable to Pfizer Inc. common shareholders	11,537	8,917
Diluted earnings per common share attributable to Pfizer inc. common shareholders	1.43	1.11

The unaudited pro forma consolidated results were prepared using the acquisition method of accounting and are based on the historical financial information of Pfizer and Wyeth, reflecting both in 2009 and 2008 Pfizer and Wyeth results of operations for a 12-month period. The historical financial information has been adjusted to give effect to the pro forma events that are: (i) directly attributable to the acquisition, (ii) factually supportable and (iii) expected to have a continuing impact on the combined results. The unaudited pro forma consolidated results are not necessarily indicative of what our consolidated results of operations actually would have been had we completed the acquisition on January 1, 2009 and on January 1, 2008. In addition, the unaudited pro forma consolidated results do not purport to project the future results of operations of the combined company nor do they reflect the expected realization of any cost savings associated with the acquisition. The unaudited pro forma consolidated results reflect primarily the following pro forma pre-tax adjustments:

◆ Elimination of Wyeth's historical intangible asset amortization expense (approximately $88 million in the pre-acquisition period in 2009 and $79 million in 2008).
◆ Additional amortization expense (approximately $2.4 billion in 2009 and $2.9 billion in 2008) related to the fair value of identifiable intangible assets acquired.
◆ Additional depreciation expense (approximately $200 million in 2009 and $266 million in 2008) related to the fair value adjustment to property, plant and equipment acquired.

(continued)

◆ Additional interest expense (approximately $316 million in 2009 and $1.2 billion in 2008) associated with the incremental debt we issued in 2009 to partially finance the acquisition and a reduction of interest income (approximately $320 million in 2009 and $857 million in 2008) associated with short-term investments under the assumption that a portion of these investments would have been used to partially fund the acquisition. In addition, a reduction in interest expense (approximately $129 million in 2009 and $163 million in 2008) related to the fair value adjustment of Wyeth debt.

◆ Elimination of $904 million incurred in 2009 related to the fair value adjustments to acquisition-date inventory that has been sold, which is considered non-recurring. There is no long-term continuing impact of the fair value adjustments to acquisition-date inventory, and, as such, the impact of those adjustments is not reflected in the unaudited pro forma operating results for 2009 and 2008.

◆ Elimination of $834 million of costs incurred in 2009. which are directly attributable to the acquisition, and which do not have a continuing impact on the combined company's operating results. Included in these costs are advisory, legal and regulatory costs incurred by both legacy Pfizer and legacy Wyeth and costs related to a bridge term loan credit agreement with certain financial institutions that has been terminated.

In addition, all of the above adjustments were adjusted for the applicable tax impact. The taxes associated with the fair value adjustments for acquired intangible assets, property, plant and equipment and legacy Wyeth debt, as well as the elimination of the impact of the fair value step-up of acquired inventory reflect the statutory tax rates in the various jurisdictions where the fair value adjustments occurred. The taxes associated with incremental debt to partially finance the acquisition reflect a 38.3% tax rate since the debt is an obligation of a U.S. entity and is taxed at the combined effective U.S. federal statutory and state rate. The taxes associated with the elimination of the costs directly attributable to the acquisition reflect a 28.4% effective tax rate since the costs were incurred in the U.S. and were either taxed at the combined effective U.S. federal statutory and state rate or not deductible for tax purposes depending on the type of expenditure.

REFLECTION

- Purchases during the year require the D&D schedule to be based on the subsidiary equity on the "during the year" purchase date.

- The parent's share of subsidiary income that was earned prior to the purchase date was earned by stockholders that are not members of the consolidated company. The accounts of the acquired company are included in the consolidated income statement starting on the date of the acquisition.

- There must be disclosure as to what amount of the acquired firm's revenue and income is included in the consolidated income statement. Disclosure is also required as to what income would have been had the acquisition occurred on the first day of the earliest year included in the comparative income statements.

SUMMARY: WORKSHEET TECHNIQUE

At this point, it is wise to review the overall mechanical procedures used to prepare a consolidated worksheet. It will help you to have this set of procedures at your side for the first few worksheets you do. Later, the process will become automatic. The following procedures are designed to provide for both efficiency and correctness:

1. When recopying the trial balances, always sum them and make sure they balance before proceeding with the eliminations. At this point, you want to be sure that there are no errors in

transporting figures to the worksheet. An amazing number of students' consolidated balance sheets are out of balance because their trial balances did not balance from the start.

2. Carefully key all eliminations to aid future reference. You may want to insert a symbol, a little "p" for parent or a little "s" for subsidiary, to identify each worksheet adjustment entry that affects consolidated net income. Such an identification will make it easier to locate the adjustments that must be posted later to the income distribution schedules. Recall that any adjustment to income must be assigned to one of the company's income distribution schedules. (In this chapter, all adjustments are to the subsidiary IDS schedule.) This second step will become particularly important in the next two chapters where there will be many adjustments to income that will go to either the controlling or the NCI IDS schedule.

3. Sum the eliminations to be sure that they balance before you begin to extend the account totals.

4. Now that the eliminations are completed, cross foot account totals and then extend them to the appropriate worksheet column. Extend each account in the order that it appears on the trial balance. Do not select just the accounts needed for a particular statement. For example, do not work only on the income statement. This can lead to errors. There may be some accounts that you will forget to extend, and you may not be aware of the errors until your Consolidated Balance Sheet column total fails to equal zero. Extending each account in order assures that none will be overlooked and allows careful consideration of the appropriate destination of each account balance.

5. Calculate consolidated net income.

6. Prepare income distribution schedules. Verify that the sum of the distributions equals the consolidated net income on the worksheet. Distribute the NCI in income to the NCI column and distribute the controlling interest in income to the Controlling Retained Earnings column.

7. Sum the NCI column and extend that total to the Consolidated Balance Sheet column. Sum the Controlling Retained Earnings column and extend that total to the Consolidated Balance Sheet column as well.

8. Verify that the Consolidated Balance Sheet column total equals zero (or that the totals are equal if two columns are used).

GOODWILL IMPAIRMENT LOSSES

7

OBJECTIVE

Demonstrate an understanding of when goodwill impairment loss exists and how it is calculated.

When circumstances indicate that the goodwill may have become impaired (see Chapter 1), the remaining goodwill will be estimated. If the resulting estimate is less than the book value of the goodwill, a *goodwill impairment loss* is recorded. The impairment loss is reported in the consolidated income statement for the period in which it occurs. It is presented on a before-tax basis as part of continuing operations and may appear under the caption "other gains and losses."

The parent company could handle the impairment loss in using one of two methods:

1. The parent could record its share of the impairment loss on its books and credit the investment in subsidiary account. This would automatically reduce the excess available for distribution, including the amount available for goodwill. This would mean that the impairment loss on the controlling interest would already exist before consolidation procedures start. The NCI share of the loss would be recorded on the worksheet. The summed loss would automatically be extended to the Consolidated Income Statement column. Since the parent already recorded its share of the loss, the NCI share would be a debit to the IDS schedule of the subsidiary.

2. The impairment loss could be recorded only on the consolidated worksheet. This would adjust consolidated net income and produce a correct balance sheet. The only complication affects consolidated worksheets in periods subsequent to the impairment. The investment account, resulting goodwill, and the controlling retained earnings would be overstated. Thus, on the worksheet, an adjustment reducing the goodwill account, the controlling retained earnings, and the NCI would be needed.

Recall from Chapter 1, that small and medium-sized entities (SMEs) may elect to use IASB accounting standards for SMEs. Under these standards, goodwill is amortized rather than being subject to impairment procedures. Unless the company can defend a different life, the presumed life is 10 years.

The procedure used in this text will be to follow the first method (shown on page 139) and directly adjust the investment account on the parent's books. This approach would mean the price used in the D&D schedule would be reduced by the amount of the impairment.

The impairment test is based on adjusted subsidiary balance sheet amounts. The impairment procedures are based on the subsidiary values as adjusted for distributions of excess. The impairment test must use the sophisticated equity investment balance (simple equity balance less amortizations of excess to date). For example, suppose Company P purchased an 80% interest in Company S in 2012 and the price resulted in total subsidiary goodwill of $165,000. On a future balance sheet date, say December 31, 2014, the following information would apply to Company S:

Subsidiary book value based on acquisition date, amortized balances on December 31, 2014	$1,000,000
Estimated fair value of Company S	900,000
Estimated fair value of net identifiable assets	850,000

Determining if goodwill has been impaired would be calculated as shown here.

Subsidiary (adjusted for acquisition values) book value on December 31, 2014	$1,000,000
Estimated fair value of subsidiary	900,000

Because the investment amount exceeds the fair value, goodwill is impaired, and a loss must be calculated.

The impairment loss would be calculated as follows:

Estimated fair value of Company S	$ 900,000
Estimated fair value of net identifiable assets	850,000
Estimated goodwill	$ 50,000
Existing goodwill	165,000
Goodwill impairment loss	$(115,000)

The impairment entry on Company P's books would be as follows:

Goodwill Impairment Loss (80% × $115,000)	92,000	
Investment in Company S		92,000

The remaining $23,000 impairment loss applicable to the NCI would be entered on the consolidated worksheet. The above example assumes that original goodwill was allocated 80%/20% on the acquisition date based on the assumption that the value of the NCI was proportionate to the price paid for the controlling interest. If that were not the case and the NCI share was less than 20% of the total goodwill, the allocation percentage used in the above example would be adjusted.

IASB *standards*

I A S B   P E R S P E C T I V E S

- Recall that including goodwill on the noncontrolling interest is optional under IFRS. If no goodwill was recorded applicable to the noncontrolling interest, then impairment testing and adjustment would only apply to the controlling interest share of goodwill.

R E F L E C T I O N

- When the fair value of a subsidiary is less than its consolidated balance sheet equity, any goodwill arising from the acquisition is impaired, and a related loss must be recognized.

APPENDIX A: THE VERTICAL WORKSHEET

This chapter has used the horizontal format for its worksheet examples. Columns for eliminations and adjustments, consolidated income, NCI, controlling retained earnings, and the balance sheet are arranged horizontally in adjacent columns. This format makes it convenient to extend account balances from one column to the next. This is the format that you used for trial balance working papers in introductory and intermediate accounting. It is also the most common worksheet format used in practice. The horizontal format will be used in all nonappendix worksheets in subsequent chapters and in all worksheet problems unless otherwise stated.

The alternative format is the vertical format. Rather than beginning the worksheet with the trial balances of the parent and the subsidiary, this format begins with the completed income statements, statements of retained earnings, and the balance sheets of the parent and subsidiary. This method, which is seldom used in practice and harder to master, commonly has been used on the CPA Exam.

The vertical format is used in Worksheet 3-8 on pages 164 and 165. This worksheet is based on the same facts used for Worksheet 3-6 (an equity method example for the second year of a purchase with a complicated distribution of excess cost). Worksheet 3-8 is based on the determination and distribution of excess schedule shown on page 129.

Note that the original separate statements are stacked vertically upon each other. Be sure to follow the carrydown procedure as it is applied to the separate statements. The net income from the income statement is carried down to the retained earnings statement. Then, the ending retained earnings balance is carried down to the balance sheet. Later, this same carrydown procedure is applied to the consolidated statements.

Understand that there are no differences in the elimination and adjustment procedures as a result of this alternative format. Compare the elimination entries to those in Worksheet 3-6. Even though there is no change in the eliminations, there are two areas of caution. First, the order in which the accounts appear is reversed; that is, nominal accounts precede balance sheet accounts. This difference in order will require care in making eliminations. Second, the eliminations to retained earnings must be made against the January 1 beginning balances, not the December 31 ending balances. The ending retained earnings balances are never adjusted but are derived after all eliminations have been made.

The complicated aspect of the vertical worksheet is the carrydown procedure used to create the retained earnings statement and the balance sheet. Arrows are used in Worksheet 3-8 to emphasize the carrydown procedure. Note that the net income line in the retained earnings statement and the retained earnings lines on the balance sheet are never available to receive eliminations. These balances are always carried down. The net income balances are derived from the same income distribution schedules used in Worksheet 3-6.

8

OBJECTIVE

Consolidate a subsidiary using vertical worksheet format.

Worksheet 3-8: page 164

REFLECTION

- On vertical worksheets for consolidations subsequent to acquisition, the income statement accounts appear at the top, followed by the retained earnings statement accounts, and then the balance sheet accounts appear in the bottom section.

- Net income is carried down to the retained earnings section.

- Ending retained earnings is then carried down to the balance sheet section.

APPENDIX B: TAX-RELATED ADJUSTMENTS

Recall from Chapter 1 that a deferred tax liability results when the fair value of an asset may not be used in future depreciation calculations for tax purposes. (This occurs when the acquisition is a *tax-free exchange* to the seller.) In this situation, future depreciation charges for tax purposes must be based on the book value of the asset, and a liability should be acknowledged in the determination and distribution of excess schedule by creating a deferred tax liability account. Consider the following determination and distribution of excess schedule for a subsidiary that has a building with a

9

OBJECTIVE

Explain the impact of tax-related complications arising on the purchase date.

book value for tax purposes of $120,000 and a fair value of $200,000. Assuming a tax rate of 30%, there is a deferred tax liability of $24,000 ($80,000 excess of fair value over tax basis × 30%).

As is true in all determination and distribution of excess schedules, any remaining unallocated value becomes goodwill. In the following example, the remaining unallocated value on the determination and distribution of excess schedule is $44,000.

Determination and Distribution of Excess Schedule

	Company Implied Fair Value	Parent Price (100%)	NCI Value
Fair value of subsidiary	$ 600,000	$600,000	N/A
Less book value of interest acquired:			
Common stock ($10 par).	$ 100,000		
Retained earnings	400,000		
Total equity.	$ 500,000	$500,000	
Interest acquired		100%	
Book value.		$500,000	
Excess of fair value over book value	**$100,000**	$100,000	

Adjustment of identifiable accounts:

	Adjustment	Amortization per Year	Life	Worksheet Key
Building ($200,000 − $120,000).	$ 80,000	$4,000	20	**debit D1**
Deferred tax liability (building), 30% × $80,000.	(24,000)	(1,200)	20	**credit D2**
Goodwill (balance)	**44,000**			**debit D3**
Total	**$100,000**			

The worksheet entry to distribute the excess of cost over book value would be as follows:

Building (to fair value)	80,000	
Goodwill (balance of excess)	44,000	
Deferred Tax Liability.		24,000
Investment in Subsidiary S (excess cost after elimination of subsidiary equity).		100,000

Worksheet eliminations will be simpler if each deferred tax liability is recorded below the asset to which it relates. It is possible that inventory could have a fair value in excess of its book value used for tax purposes. This, too, would require the recognition of a deferred tax liability.

A second tax complication arises when the subsidiary has tax loss carryovers. To the extent that the tax loss carryovers are not recorded or are reduced by a valuation allowance by the subsidiary on its balance sheet, the carryovers may be an asset to be considered in the determination and distribution of excess schedule. When a tax-free exchange occurs during the accounting period, a portion of the tax loss carryover may be used during that period.[1] The amount that may be used is the acquiring company's tax liability for the year times the percentage of the year that the companies were under common control. If, for example, the acquiring company's tax liability was $100,000 and the acquisition occurred on April 1, 3/4 of $100,000, or $75,000, of the tax loss carryover could be utilized. The current portion of the tax loss carryover is recorded as *Current Deferred Tax Asset.* Any remaining carryover is carried forward and recorded as a noncurrent asset using the account, *Noncurrent Deferred Tax Asset.* If it is probable that the deferred tax expense will not be fully realized, a contra-valuation allowance is provided.

Let us consider the example of a subsidiary that has the following tax loss carryovers on the date of purchase:

Tax loss carryover to be used in current period	$100,000
Tax loss carryover to be used in future periods	200,000

---

1 Section 381(c)(1)(B) of the Federal Tax Code.

Assume that the parent has anticipated future tax liabilities against which the tax loss carryovers may be offset and has a 30% tax rate. The value analysis would be prepared as follows:

Value Analysis Schedule	Company Implied Fair Value	Parent Price (80%)	NCI Value (20%)
Company fair value...........................	$1,118,750	$895,000	$223,750
Fair value of net assets excluding goodwill	987,500	790,000	197,500
Goodwill...................................	**$ 131,250**	$105,000	$ 26,250

Based on the above information, the following D&D schedule is prepared:

Determination and Distribution of Excess Schedule

	Company Implied Fair Value	Parent Price (80%)	NCI Value (20%)
Fair value of subsidiary	$1,118,750	$895,000	$223,750
Less book value of interest acquired:			
Common stock ($10 par)......................	$ 300,000		
Retained earnings	597,500		
Total equity................................	$ 897,500	$897,500	$897,500
Interest acquired		80%	20%
Book value..................................		$718,000	$179,500
Excess of fair value over book value	$ 221,250	$177,000	$ 44,250

Adjustment of identifiable accounts:

	Adjustment	Amortization per Year	Life	Worksheet Key
Current deferred tax asset ($100,000 × 30%).......	$ 30,000		1	**debit D1**
Noncurrent deferred tax asset ($200,000 × 30%)....	60,000			**debit D2**
Goodwill ($1,118,750 fair − $987,500 book value).....................................	131,250			**debit D3**
Total.....................................	**$221,250**			

Comprehensive Example.. Both of the preceding tax issues will complicate the consolidated worksheet. Our example will consider the distribution of the tax adjustments on the worksheet and the resulting amortization adjustments needed to calculate consolidated net income. We will consider a nontaxable exchange with fixed asset and goodwill adjustments in addition to a tax loss carryover.

Assume that Paro Company acquired an 80% interest in Sunstran Corporation on January 1, 2011. Paro expects to utilize $100,000 of tax loss carryovers in the current period and $250,000 in future periods.[2] A building, which has a 20-year remaining life, is understated by $200,000. The following value analysis was prepared:

Value Analysis Schedule	Company Implied Fair Value	Parent Price (80%)	NCI Value (20%)
Company fair value...........................	$1,237,500	$990,000	$247,500
Fair value of net assets excluding goodwill	1,045,000	836,000	209,000
Goodwill...................................	**$ 192,500**	$154,000	$ 38,500

---

2 Considers tax limitations and assumes full realizability of tax loss carryovers.

Based on the information shown on page 143, the following D&D schedule is prepared:

Determination and Distribution of Excess Schedule

	Company Implied Fair Value	Parent Price (80%)	NCI Value (20%)
Fair value of subsidiary	$1,237,500	$ 990,000	$247,500
Less book value of interest acquired:			
Common stock ($10 par).	$ 100,000		
Paid-in capital in excess of par	300,000		
Retained earnings	400,000		
Total equity.	$ 800,000	$ 800,000	$800,000
Interest acquired		80%	20%
Book value.		$ 640,000	$160,000
Excess of fair value over book value	**$ 437,500**	$ 350,000	$ 87,500

Adjustment of identifiable accounts:

	Adjustment	Amortization per Year	Life	Worksheet Key
Current deferred tax asset ($100,000 × 30% tax rate)	$ 30,000		1	**debit D1**
Noncurrent deferred tax asset ($250,000 × 30%). . . .	75,000			**debit D2**
Building	200,000	$ 10,000	20	**debit D3**
Deferred tax liability ($200,000 × 30% tax rate).	(60,000)	(3,000)	20	**credit D3t**
Goodwill.	**192,500**			**debit D4**
Total.	**$ 437,500**			

Worksheet 3-9, pages 166 to 167, is the consolidated worksheet for Paro Company and its subsidiary, Sunstran Corporation, at the end of 2011. Unlike previous worksheets, the nominal accounts of both firms include a 30% provision for tax on internally generated net income. (Paro does not include a tax on subsidiary income recorded.). The calculation of the tax liabilities for affiliated firms is discussed further in Chapter 6. Paro's internally generated income before tax is $800,000. The 30% tax provision would be $240,000. Only $210,000 is currently payable. The parent company is aware of the $30,000 reduction of the tax liability made possible by the current portion of the DTA included in the IDS schedule. On its separate statements, the parent company records the $30,000 as a temporary deferred tax liability (DTL). The parent's tax entry was:

Worksheet 3-9: page 166

Provision for Tax ($800,000 × 30%)	240,000	
Current Tax Liability.		210,000
Deferred Tax Liability.		30,000

The procedures to eliminate the investment account are the same as for previous examples using the equity method. In journal entry form, the eliminations are as follows:

(CY1) Eliminate subsidiary income recorded by parent company:

Subsidiary Income.	84,000	
Investment in Sunstran		84,000

(CY2) Eliminate dividends paid by Sunstran to Paro:

Investment in Sunstran	16,000	
Dividends Declared (by Sunstran)		16,000

(EL) Eliminate 80% of Sunstran equity against Investment in Sunstran:

Common Stock—Sunstran 80,000

Paid-In Capital in Excess of Par—Sunstran 240,000

Retained Earnings—Sunstran 320,000

    Investment in Sunstran 640,000

Distribute excess of cost over book value and adjustment to NCI:

(D1) Deferred Tax Liability (consumption of current DTA) 30,000

(D2) Noncurrent Deferred Tax Asset 75,000

(D3) Building 200,000

(D3t)   Deferred Tax Liability (applicable to building) 60,000

(D4) Goodwill 192,500

(D)   Investment in Sunstran (noneliminated excess) 350,000

(NCI)   Retained Earnings—Sunstran 87,500

Amortize excess for current year as shown on the following schedule:

(A3) Expenses (for depreciation) 10,000

    Accumulated Depreciation—Building 10,000

(A3t) Deferred Tax Liability 3,000

    Provision for Tax 3,000

Amortizations of excess are made for the current year using the following schedule:

Account Adjustments to Be Amortized	Life	Amount Annual	Current Year	Prior Years	Total	Key
Building	20	$10,000	$10,000		$10,000	(A3)
Deferred tax liability (building)	20	(3,000)	(3,000)		(3,000)	(A3t)
Total (excluding inventory)		$ 7,000	$ 7,000		$ 7,000	

Notice that entry (D1) distributes $30,000 to the parent's deferred tax liability account and eliminates the temporary tax liability recorded by the parent. Entry (D2) records the noncurrent portion of the tax loss carryforward as a deferred tax asset. Entry (D3) increases the building by $200,000, and entry (D3t) records the deferred tax liability applicable to the building adjustment. Entry (D4) records goodwill of $192,500.

As a result of the increase in the value of the building, entry (A3) increases the depreciation for the building by $10,000. Given the 30% tax rate, entry (A3t) reduces the provision for tax account by $3,000 as a result of the depreciation adjustment. *This entry is not a reduction in the current taxes payable.* Instead, it is a reduction in the deferred tax liability recorded as part of the distribution of excess [entry (D3)]. Remember that the deferred tax liability reflects the loss of future tax deductions caused by the difference between the building's higher fair value and its lower book value on the date of the purchase. Thus, the net result of the entry is to record the tax provision as if the deductions were allowable (for tax purposes) without changing the tax payable for the current period. There is no amortization of the noncurrent deferred tax asset since it is not used in the current period. **All amortizations of excess and all tax adjustments are carried to the subsidiary's income distribution schedule.** This is again the case since both interests share in the allocation of the excess and, thus, share in its amortization.

REFLECTION

- One of the assets that may be included in the purchase is a tax loss carryover. It should be separated into its current and noncurrent components.

- When assets are part of a tax-free exchange, they must be accompanied by a deferred tax liability equal to the value of the forfeited tax deduction.

Worksheet 3-1

Simple Equity Method
Company P and Subsidiary Company S
Worksheet for Consolidated Financial Statements
For Year Ended December 31, 2011

	(Credit balance amounts are in parentheses.)	Trial Balance	
		Company P	Company S
1	Investment in Company S	148,500	
2			
3			
4	**Patent**		
5	Other Assets (net of liabilities)	237,000	135,000
6	Common Stock ($10 par)—Company P	(200,000)	
7	Retained Earnings, January 1, 2011—Company P	(123,000)	
8	Common Stock ($10 par)—Company S		(50,000)
9	Retained Earnings, January 1, 2011—Company S		(70,000)
10	Revenue	(100,000)	(75,000)
11	**Expenses**	60,000	50,000
12	**Patent Amortization Expense**		
13	**Subsidiary Income**	(22,500)	
14	**Dividends Declared**		10,000
15		0	0
16	**Consolidated Net Income**		
17	**To NCI (see distribution schedule)**		
18	**Balance to Controlling Interest (see distribution schedule)**		
19	Total NCI		
20	Retained Earnings, Controlling Interest, December 31, 2011		
21			

Eliminations and Adjustments:

(CY1)   Eliminate subsidiary income against the investment account.
(CY2)   Eliminate dividends paid by subsidiary to parent. After (CY1) and (CY2), the investment account and subsidiary retained earnings are at a common point in time. Then, elimination of the investment account can proceed.
(EL)   Eliminate the pro rata share of Company S equity balances *at the beginning of the year* against the investment account. The elimination of the parent's share of subsidiary stockholders' equity leaves only the noncontrolling interest in each element of the equity.
(D)/(NCI)   Distribute the $27,000 excess cost and $3,000 NCI adjustment as required by the D&D schedule on page 115. In this example, Patent is recorded for $30,000.
(A)   Amortize the resulting patents over the 10-year period. The current portion is $3,000 per year ($30,000/10 years).

Worksheet 3-1 (see page 117)

Eliminations & Adjustments		Consolidated Income Statement	NCI	Controlling Retained Earnings	Consolidated Balance Sheet	
Dr.	Cr.					
(CY2) 9,000	(CY1) 22,500					1
	(EL) 108,000					2
	(D) 27,000					3
(D) 30,000	(A) 3,000				27,000	4
					372,000	5
					(200,000)	6
				(123,000)		7
(EL) 45,000			(5,000)			8
(EL) 63,000	(NCI) 3,000		(10,000)			9
		(175,000)				10
		110,000				11
(A) 3,000		3,000				12
(CY1) 22,500						13
	(CY2) 9,000		1,000			14
172,500	172,500					15
		(62,000)				16
		2,200	(2,200)			17
		59,800		(59,800)		18
			(16,200)		(16,200)	19
				(182,800)	(182,800)	20
					0	21

Subsidiary Company S Income Distribution

Patent amortization . . . .**(A)**	**$3,000**	Internally generated net income $25,000
		Adjusted net income $22,000
		NCI share . . . . × 10%
		NCI . . . . $ 2,200

Parent Company P Income Distribution

Internally generated net income	$40,000
90% × Company S adjusted income of $22,000.	19,800
Controlling interest	$59,800

Worksheet 3-2

Simple Equity Method, Second Year
Company P and Subsidiary Company S
Worksheet for Consolidated Financial Statements
For Year Ended December 31, 2012

	(Credit balance amounts are in parentheses.)	Trial Balance	
		Company P	Company S
1	**Investment in Company S**	133,200	
2			
3	**Patent**		
4	Other Assets (net of liabilities)	261,500	118,000
5	Common Stock ($10 par)—Company P	(200,000)	
6	**Retained Earnings, January 1, 2012—Company P**	(185,500)	
7	Common Stock ($10 par)—Company S		(50,000)
8	Retained Earnings, January 1, 2012—Company S		(85,000)
9			
10	Revenue	(100,000)	(50,000)
11	Expenses	80,000	62,000
12	**Patent Amortization**		
13	**Subsidiary Loss**	10,800	
14	**Dividends Declared**		5,000
15		0	0
16	**Consolidated Net Income**		
17	**To NCI (see distribution schedule)**		
18	**Balance to Controlling Interest (see distribution schedule)**		
19	Total NCI		
20	Retained Earnings, Controlling Interest, December 31, 2012		
21			

Eliminations and Adjustments:

(CY1) Eliminate controlling share of subsidiary loss.

(CY2) Eliminate dividends paid by subsidiary to parent. The investment account is now returned to its January 1, 2012 balance so that elimination may proceed.

(EL) Using balances at the beginning of the year, eliminate 90% of the Company S equity balances against the remaining investment account.

(D)/(NCI) Distribute the $30,000 excess cost as indicated by the D&D schedule that was prepared on the date of acquisition. The amount is the $27,000 investment excess and the $3,000 NCI adjustment.

(A) Amortize the patent over the selected 10-year period. It is necessary to record the amortization for current and past periods, because asset adjustments resulting from the consolidation process do not appear on the separate statements of the constituent companies. Thus, entry (A) reduces Patent by $6,000 for the 2011 and 2012 amortizations. The amount for the current year is expensed, while the cumulative amortization for prior years ($3,000) is deducted from the beginning controlling ($2,700) and noncontrolling ($300) retained earnings accounts. The NCI shares in the adjustments because the NCI was adjusted for the original asset adjustment.

Worksheet 3-2 (see page 122)

| Eliminations & Adjustments | | Consolidated | NCI | Controlling | Consolidated | |
Dr.	Cr.	Income Statement		Retained Earnings	Balance Sheet	
(CY1) 10,800	(EL) 121,500					1
(CY2) 4,500	(D) 27,000					2
(D) 30,000	(A) 6,000				24,000	3
					379,500	4
					(200,000)	5
(A) 2,700				(182,800)		6
(EL) 45,000			(5,000)			7
(EL) 76,500	(NCI) 3,000		(11,200)			8
(A) 300						9
		(150,000)				10
		142,000				11
(A) 3,000		3,000				12
	(CY1) 10,800					13
	(CY2) 4,500		500			14
172,800	172,800					15
		(5,000)				16
		(1,500)	1,500			17
		6,500		(6,500)		18
			(14,200)		(14,200)	19
				(189,300)	(189,300)	20
					0	21

Subsidiary Company S Income Distribution

Internally generated **loss**	$12,000
Patent amortization . . . . **(A)**	**3,000**
Adjusted loss	$15,000
NCI share	× 10%
NCI	$ 1,500

Parent Company P Income Distribution

90% × Company S adjusted loss of $15,000	$13,500	Internally generated net income	$20,000
		Controlling interest	$ 6,500

Worksheet 3-3

Cost Method
Company P and Subsidiary Company S
Worksheet for Consolidated Financial Statements
For Year Ended December 31, 2011

	(Credit balance amounts are in parentheses.)	Trial Balance	
		Company P	Company S
1	**Investment in Company S**	135,000	
2			
3	**Patent**		
4	Other Assets (net of liabilities)	237,000	135,000
5	Common Stock ($10 par)—Company P	(200,000)	
6	Retained Earnings, January 1, 2011—Company P	(123,000)	
7	Common Stock ($10 par)—Company S		(50,000)
8	Retained Earnings, January 1, 2011—Company S		(70,000)
9	Revenue	(100,000)	(75,000)
10	Expenses	60,000	50,000
11	**Patent Amortization**		
12	**Subsidiary (Dividend) Income**	(9,000)	
13	**Dividends Declared**		10,000
14		0	0
15	Consolidated Net Income		
16	To NCI (see distribution schedule)		
17	Balance to Controlling Interest (see distribution schedule)		
18	Total NCI		
19	Retained Earnings, Controlling Interest, December 31, 2011		
20			

Eliminations and Adjustments:

(CY2) Eliminate intercompany dividends.
(EL)   Eliminate 90% of the Company S equity balances at the beginning of the year against the investment account.
(D)/(NCI) Distribute the $27,000 excess cost and the $3,000 NCI adjustment as indicated by the D&D schedule on page 115.
(A)   Amortize the patent for the current year.

Worksheet 3-3 (see page 124)

Eliminations & Adjustments		Consolidated Income Statement	NCI	Controlling Retained Earnings	Consolidated Balance Sheet	
Dr.	Cr.					
	(EL) 108,000					1
	(D) 27,000					2
(D) 30,000	(A) 3,000				27,000	3
					372,000	4
					(200,000)	5
				(123,000)		6
(EL) 45,000			(5,000)			7
(EL) 63,000	NCI 3,000		(10,000)			8
		(175,000)				9
		110,000				10
(A) 3,000		3,000				11
(CY2) 9,000						12
	(CY2) 9,000		**1,000**			13
150,000	150,000					14
		(62,000)				15
		2,200	(2,200)			16
		59,800		(59,800)		17
			(16,200)		(16,200)	18
				(182,800)	(182,800)	19
					0	20

Subsidiary Company S Income Distribution

Patent amortization . . . . (A) $3,000	Internally generated net income	$ 25,000
	Adjusted net income	$ 22,000
	NCI share	× 10%
	NCI	**$ 2,200**

Parent Company P Income Distribution

Internally generated net income	$ 40,000
90% × Company S adjusted income of $22,000	19,800
Controlling interest	**$59,800**

Worksheet 3-4

Cost Method, Second Year
Company P and Subsidiary Company S
Worksheet for Consolidated Financial Statements
For Year Ended December 31, 2012

	(Credit balance amounts are in parentheses.)	Trial Balance	
		Company P	Company S
1	**Investment in Company S**	135,000	
2			
3	Patent		
4	Other Assets (net of liabilities)	261,500	118,000
5	Common Stock ($10 par)—Company P	(200,000)	
6	**Retained Earnings, January 1, 2012—Company P**	(172,000)	
7	Common Stock ($10 par)—Company S		(50,000)
8	Retained Earnings, January 1, 2012, Company S		(85,000)
9			
10	Revenue	(100,000)	(50,000)
11	Expenses	80,000	62,000
12	Patent Amortization		
13	**Subsidiary (Dividend) Income**	(4,500)	
14	**Dividends Declared**		5,000
15		0	0
16	Consolidated Net Income		
17	To NCI (see distribution schedule)		
18	Balance to Controlling Interest (see distribution schedule)		
19	Total NCI		
20	Retained Earnings, Controlling Interest, December 31, 2012		
21			

Eliminations and Adjustments:

(CV)   Convert to simple equity method as of January 1, 2012.
(CY2)   Eliminate the current-year intercompany dividends.
(EL)   Eliminate 90% of the Company S equity balances at the beginning of the year against the investment account.
(D)/(NCI)   Distribute the $30,000 excess cost as indicated by the D&D schedule that was prepared on the date of acquisition.
            This includes the $27,000 excess and the $3,000 NCI adjustment.
(A)   Amortize the patent for the current year and one previous year.

Worksheet 3-4 (see page 125)

Eliminations & Adjustments				Consolidated Income Statement	NCI	Controlling Retained Earnings	Consolidated Balance Sheet	
Dr.		Cr.						
(CV)	**13,500**	(EL)	121,500					1
		(D)	27,000					2
(D)	30,000	(A)	6,000				24,000	3
							379,500	4
							(200,000)	5
(A)	2,700	**(CV)**	**13,500**			(182,800)		6
(EL)	45,000				(5,000)			7
(EL)	76,500	(NCI)	3,000		(11,200)			8
(A)	**300**							9
				(150,000)				10
				142,000				11
(A)	3,000			3,000				12
(CY2)	**4,500**							13
		(CY2)	4,500		**500**			14
	175,500		175,500					15
				(5,000)				16
				(1,500)	1,500			17
				6,500		(6,500)		18
					(14,200)		(14,200)	19
						(189,300)	(189,300)	20
							0	21

Subsidiary Company S Income Distribution

Internally generated loss		$ 12,000
Patent amortization	(A)	3,000
Adjusted loss		$ 15,000
NCI share	×	10%
NCI		**$ 1,500**

Parent Company P Income Distribution

90% × Company S adjusted loss of $15,000	$13,500	Internally generated net income $20,000
		Controlling interest . . . . $ 6,500

Worksheet 3-5

Simple Equity Method, First Year

Paulos Company and Subsidiary Carlos Company
Worksheet for Consolidated Financial Statements
For the Year Ended December 31, 2011

	(Credit balance amounts are in parentheses.)	Trial Balance	
		Paulos	Carlos
1	Cash	80,000	50,000
2	Inventory	226,000	62,500
3	Land	200,000	150,000
4	Investment in Carlos	752,000	
5			
6			
7			
8	Buildings	800,000	600,000
9	Accumulated Depreciation	(80,000)	(315,000)
10	Equipment	400,000	150,000
11	Accumulated Depreciation	(50,000)	(70,000)
12	Patent (net)		112,500
13			
14	Goodwill		
15	Current Liabilities	(100,000)	
16	Bonds Payable		(200,000)
17	Discount (Premium)		
18			
19	Common Stock—Carlos		(100,000)
20	Paid-In Capital in Excess of Par—Carlos		(150,000)
21	Retained Earnings, January 1, 2011—Carlos		(250,000)
22			
23	Common Stock—Paulos	(1,500,000)	
24	Retained Earnings, January 1, 2011—Paulos	(600,000)	
25			
26	Sales	(350,000)	(200,000)
27	Cost of Goods Sold	150,000	80,000
28	Depreciation Expense—Buildings	40,000	15,000
29	Depreciation Expense—Equipment	20,000	20,000
30	Other Expenses	60,000	13,000
31	Interest Expense		12,000
32	Subsidiary Income	(48,000)	
33	Dividends Declared—Carlos		20,000
34	Totals	0	0
35	Consolidated Net Income		
36	NCI Share		
37	Controlling Share		
38	Total NCI		
39	Retained Earnings, Controlling Interest, December 31, 2011		
40	Totals		

Worksheet 3-5 (see page 128)

Eliminations & Adjustments				Consolidated Income Statement	NCI	Controlling Retained Earnings	Consolidated Balance Sheet	
Dr.		Cr.						
							130,000	1
							288,500	2
(D2)	50,000						400,000	3
		(CY1)	48,000					4
(CY2)	16,000							5
		(EL)	400,000					6
		(D)	320,000					7
(D3)	200,000						1,600,000	8
		(A3)	10,000				(405,000)	9
		(D4)	20,000				530,000	10
(A4)	4,000						(116,000)	11
(D5)	25,000						135,000	12
		(A5)	2,500					13
(D7)	126,760						126,760	14
							(100,000)	15
							(200,000)	16
(D6)	13,240							17
		(A6)	3,310				9,930	18
(EL)	80,000				(20,000)			19
(EL)	120,000				(30,000)			20
(EL)	200,000				(130,000)			21
		(NCI)	80,000					22
							(1,500,000)	23
								24
						(600,000)		25
				(550,000)				26
(D1)	5,000			235,000				27
(A3)	10,000			65,000				28
		(A4)	4,000	36,000				29
(A5)	2,500			75,500				30
(A6)	3,310			15,310				31
(CY1)	48,000							32
		(CY2)	16,000		4,000			33
	903,810		903,810					34
				(123,190)				35
				8,638	(8,638)			36
				114,552		(114,552)		37
					(184,638)		(184,638)	38
						(714,552)	(714,552)	39
							0	40

Eliminations and Adjustments:

(CY1)   Eliminate subsidiary income against the investment account
(CY2)   Eliminate dividends paid by subsidiary to parent. After (CY1) and (CY2), the investment
          account and the subsidiary retained earnings are at the January 1 balances. Then, the
          investment account can be eliminated.
(EL)   Eliminate the controlling share of subsidiary equity balance (as of January 1) against the
          investment account.
          The elimination of the controlling share of subsidiary equity leaves only the NCI portion of each
          subsidiary equity account.
(D)/(NCI) Distribute the $400,000 fair value excess (Paulos share = $320,000; NCI share = $80,000)
          as follows:
(D1)   Inventory is assumed to have been sold, adjust cost of goods sold.
(D2)   Land.
(D3)   Buildings
(D4)   Equipment.
(D5)   Patent.
(D6)   Discount on Bonds Payable.
(D7)   Goodwill.
(A)   Amortize distributions as follows:

Account Adjustments to Be Amortized	Life	Annual Amount	Current Year	Prior Years	Total	Key
Inventory	1	$ 5,000	$ 5,000	—	$ 5,000	(D1)
Subject to amortization:						
Buildings	20	$10,000	$10,000	—	$10,000	(A3)
Equipment	5	(4,000)	(4,000)	—	(4,000)	(A4)
Patent.	10	2,500	2,500	—	2,500	(A5)
Bonds payable	4	3,310	3,310	—	3,310	(A6)
Total amortizations		$11,810	$11,810	—	$11,810	
Controlling retained earnings adjustment .			N/A*			
NCI retained earnings adjustment.			N/A*			

*There is no retained earnings adjustment for the parent or for the NCI because this is the first year of the amortization of
  excess.

Subsidiary Carlos Company Income Distribution

Adjustment to cost of goods sold . . . . (D1)	$ 5,000	Internally generated net income	$ 60,000
Current-year amortizations of excess . . . . (A3–A6)	11,810		
		Adjusted income	$ 43,190
		NCI share	× 20%
		NCI	$ 8,638

Parent Paulos Company Income Distribution

		Internally generated net income	$ 80,000
		Controlling share of subsidiary (80% × $43,190)	34,552
		Controlling interest	$114,552

Worksheet 3-6

Simple Equity Method, Second Year
Paulos Company and Subsidiary Carlos Company
Worksheet for Consolidated Financial Statements
For Year Ended December 31, 2012

	(Credit balance amounts are in parentheses.)	Trial Balance	
		Paulos	Carlos
1	Cash	292,000	160,000
2	Inventory	210,000	120,000
3	Land	200,000	150,000
4	Investment in Carlos	816,000	
5			
6			
7			
8	Buildings	800,000	600,000
9	Accumulated Depreciation	(120,000)	(330,000)
10	Equipment	400,000	150,000
11	Accumulated Depreciation	(90,000)	(90,000)
12	Patent (net)		100,000
13			
14	Goodwill		
15	Current Liabilities	(150,000)	(40,000)
16	Bonds Payable		(200,000)
17	Discount (Premium)		
18			
19	Common Stock—Carlos		(100,000)
20	Paid-In Capital in Excess of Par—Carlos		(150,000)
21	Retained Earnings, January 1, 2012—Carlos		(290,000)
22			
23			
24			
25	Common Stock—Paulos	(1,500,000)	
26	Retained Earnings, January 1, 2012—Paulos	(728,000)	
27			
28			
29			
30	Sales	(400,000)	(300,000)
31	Cost of Goods Sold	200,000	120,000
32	Depreciation Expense—Buildings	40,000	15,000
33	Depreciation Expense—Equipment	20,000	20,000
34	Other Expenses	90,000	33,000
35	Interest Expense		12,000
36	Subsidiary Income	(80,000)	
37	Dividends Declared—Carlos		20,000
38	Totals	0	0
39	Consolidated Net Income		
40	NCI Share		
41	Controlling Share		
42	Total NCI		
43	Retained Earnings, Controlling Interest, December 31, 2012		
44	Totals		

Worksheet 3-6 (see page 131)

Eliminations & Adjustments Dr.		Eliminations & Adjustments Cr.		Consolidated Income Statement	NCI	Controlling Retained Earnings	Consolidated Balance Sheet	
							452,000	1
							330,000	2
(D2)	50,000						400,000	3
		(CY1)	80,000					4
(CY2)	16,000							5
		(EL)	432,000					6
		(D)	320,000					7
(D3)	200,000						1,600,000	8
		(A3)	20,000				(470,000)	9
		(D4)	20,000				530,000	10
(A4)	8,000						(172,000)	11
(D5)	25,000						120,000	12
		(A5)	5,000					13
(D7)	126,760						126,760	14
							(190,000)	15
							(200,000)	16
(D6)	13,240							17
		(A6)	6,620				6,620	18
(EL)	80,000				(20,000)			19
(EL)	120,000				(30,000)			20
(EL)	232,000				(134,638)			21
		(NCI)	80,000					22
(D1)	1,000							23
(A3–A6)	2,362							24
							(1,500,000)	25
								26
(D1)	4,000							27
(A3–A6)	9,448							28
						(714,552)		29
				(700,000)				30
				320,000				31
(A3)	10,000			65,000				32
		(A4)	4,000	36,000				33
(A5)	2,500			125,500				34
(A6)	3,310			15,310				35
(CY1)	80,000							36
		(CY2)	16,000		4,000			37
	983,620		983,620					38
				(138,190)				39
				17,638	(17,638)			40
				120,552		(120,552)		41
					(198,276)		(198,276)	42
						(835,104)	(835,104)	43
							0	44

Eliminations and Adjustments:

(CY1)	Eliminate subsidiary income against the investment account.
(CY2)	Eliminate dividends paid by subsidiary to parent. After (CY1) and (CY2), the investment account and the subsidiary retained earnings are at the January 1 balances. Then, the investment account can be eliminated.
(EL)	Eliminate the controlling share of subsidiary equity balance (as of January 1) against the investment account. The elimination of the controlling share of subsidiary equity leaves only the NCI portion of each subsidiary equity account.
(D)	Distribute the $400,000 fair value excess as follows:

	(D1)	Prior-year inventory is sold, distribute 80%/20% to controlling interest and NCI (subsidiary) retained earnings.
	(D2)	Land.
	(D3)	Buildings.
	(D4)	Equipment.
	(D5)	Patent.
	(D6)	Discount on Bonds Payable.
	(D7)	Goodwill.

(A)	Amortize distributions as follows:

Account Adjustments to Be Amortized	Life	Annual Amount	Current Year	Prior Years	Total	Key
Inventory	1	$ 5,000	$ —	$ 5,000	$ 5,000	(D1)
Subject to amortization:						
Buildings	20	$10,000	$10,000	$10,000	$20,000	(A3)
Equipment	5	(4,000)	(4,000)	(4,000)	(8,000)	(A4)
Patent	10	2,500	2,500	2,500	5,000	(A5)
Bonds payable	4	3,310	3,310	3,310	6,620	(A6)
Total amortizations		$11,810	$11,810	$11,810	$23,620	
Controlling retained earnings adjustment (80% × $11,810)				$ 9,448		(A3–A6)
NCI retained earnings adjustment (20% × $11,810)				2,362		(A3–A6)

Subsidiary Carlos Company Income Distribution

Current-year amortizations of excess .... (A3–A6)	$11,810	Internally generated net income...............	$ 100,000
		Adjusted income	$ 88,190
		NCI share................................	× 20%
		NCI	$ 17,638

Parent Paulos Company Income Distribution

Internally generated net income...............	$ 50,000
Controlling share of subsidiary (80% × $88,190)	70,552
Controlling interest........................	$120,552

Worksheet 3-7

Intraperiod Purchase; Subsidiary Books Closed on Purchase Date
Company P and Subsidiary Company S
Worksheet for Consolidated Financial Statements
For Year Ended December 31, 2011

	(Credit balance amounts are in parentheses.)	Trial Balance	
		Company P	Company S
1	Current Assets	187,600	87,500
2	**Investment in Company S**	**118,400**	
3			
4			
5	Goodwill		
6	Equipment	400,000	80,000
7	Accumulated Depreciation	(200,000)	(32,500)
8	Liabilities	(60,000)	(12,000)
9	Common Stock—Company P	(250,000)	
10	Retained Earnings, **January 1, 2011—Company P**	(100,000)	
11	Common Stock—Company S		(50,000)
12	Retained Earnings, **July 1, 2011—Company S**		(58,000)
13	Sales	(500,000)	(92,000)
14	Cost of Goods Sold	350,000	60,000
15	Expenses	70,000	12,000
16	**Subsidiary Income**	**(16,000)**	
17	Dividends Declared		5,000
18			
19		0	0
20			
21	Consolidated Net Income		
22	To NCI (see distribution schedule)		
23	Balance to Controlling Interest (see distribution schedule)		
24	Total NCI		
25	Retained Earnings, Controlling Interest, December 31, 2011		
26			

Eliminations and Adjustments:

(CY1)   Eliminate the entries made in the investment in Company S account and in the subsidiary income account to record the parent's 80% controlling interest in the subsidiary's second *six months' income.*

(CY2)   Eliminate intercompany dividends. This restores the investment account to its balance as of the **July 1, 2011** investment date.

(EL)   Eliminate 80% of the subsidiary's **July 1, 2011**, equity balances against the *balance* of the investment account.

(D)   Distribute the excess of cost over book value of $20,000 to Goodwill in accordance with the D&D schedule.

Worksheet 3-7 (see page 136)

Eliminations & Adjustments				Consolidated Income Statement	NCI	Controlling Retained Earnings	Consolidated Balance Sheet	
Dr.		Cr.						
							275,100	1
(CY2)	4,000	(CY1)	16,000					2
		(EL)	86,400					3
		(D)	20,000					4
(D)	25,000						25,000	5
							480,000	6
							(232,500)	7
							(72,000)	8
							(250,000)	9
						(100,000)		10
(EL)	40,000				(10,000)			11
(EL)	46,400	(NCI)	5,000		(16,600)			12
				(592,000)				13
				410,000				14
				82,000				15
(CY1)	16,000							16
		(CY2)	4,000		1,000			17
								18
	131,400		131,400					19
								20
				(100,000)				21
				4,000	(4,000)			22
				96,000		(96,000)		23
					(29,600)		(29,600)	24
						(196,000)	(196,000)	25
							0	26

Subsidiary Company S Income Distribution

Internally generated net income **(last six months)**	**$20,000**
Adjusted income	$ 20,000
NCI share	× 20%
NCI	$ 4,000

Parent Company P Income Distribution

Internally generated net income	$ 80,000
80% × Company S adjusted income of $20,000 **(last six months)**.	**16,000**
Controlling interest	$ 96,000

Worksheet 3-8

Vertical Format, Simple Equity Method
Paulos Company and Subsidiary Carlos Company
Worksheet for Consolidated Financial Statements
For Year Ended December 31, 2012

Worksheet 3-8 (see page 141)

	Financial Statements		Eliminations & Adjustments		NCI	Nonconsolidated Balance Sheet	
	Paulos	Carlos	Dr.	Cr.			
Income Statement							1
Sales	(400,000)	(300,000)				(700,000)	2
Cost of Goods Sold	200,000	120,000				320,000	3
Depreciation Expense—Buildings	40,000	15,000	(A3) 10,000			65,000	4
Depreciation Expense—Equipment	20,000	20,000		(A4) 4,000		36,000	5
Other Expenses	90,000	33,000	(A5) 2,500			125,500	6
Interest Expense		12,000	(A6) 3,310			15,310	7
Subsidiary Income	(80,000)		(CY1) 80,000				8
Net Income	(130,000)	(100,000)					9
Consolidated Net Income						(138,190)	10
Noncontrolling Interest (see distribution schedule)					(17,638)		11
Controlling Interest (see distribution schedule WS 3-6)						(120,552)	12
Retained Earnings Statement							13
Retained Earnings, January 1, 2012—Paulos	(728,000)		(D1) 4,000				14
			(A3–A6) 9,448				15
Retained Earnings, January 1, 2012—Carlos		(290,000)				(714,552)	16
			(EL) 232,000	(NCI) 80,000	(134,638)		17
			(D1) 1,000				18
			(A3–A6) 2,362				19
Net Income (carrydown)	(130,000)	(100,000)			(17,638)	(120,552)	20
Dividends Declared		20,000		(CY2) 16,000	4,000		21
Retained Earnings, December 31, 2012	(858,000)	(370,000)					22
Noncontrolling Interest in Retained Earnings, December 31, 2012					(148,276)		23
Controlling Interest in Retained Earnings, December 31, 2012						(835,104)	24

	Account	Paulos	Carlos	Elim. Dr.	Elim. Cr.	Consolidated / Controlling	NCI
25	**Balance Sheet**						
26	Cash	292,000	160,000			452,000	
27	Inventory	210,000	120,000			330,000	
28	Land	200,000	150,000	(D2) 50,000		400,000	
29	Buildings	800,000	600,000	(D3) 200,000		1,600,000	
30	Accumulated Depreciation—Buildings	(120,000)	(330,000)		(A3) 20,000	(470,000)	
31	Equipment	400,000	150,000		(D4) 20,000	530,000	
32	Accumulated Depreciation—Equipment	(90,000)	(90,000)	(A4) 8,000		(172,000)	
33	Investment in Carlos Company	816,000		(CY2) 16,000	(CY1) 80,000		
34					(EL) 432,000		
35					(D) 320,000		
36	Patent		100,000	(D5) 25,000	(A5) 5,000	120,000	
37	Goodwill			(D7) 126,760		126,760	
38	Current Liabilities	(150,000)	(40,000)			(190,000)	
39	Bonds Payable	(200,000)				(200,000)	
40	Discount (Premium)			(D6) 13,240	(A6) 6,620	6,620	
41	Common Stock—Paulos	(1,500,000)				(1,500,000)	
42	Common Stock—Carlos		(100,000)	(EL) 80,000			(20,000)
43	Paid-In Capital in Excess of Par—Carlos		(150,000)	(EL) 120,000			(30,000)
44	Retained Earnings (carrydown)	(858,000)	(370,000)				
45	Retained Earnings, Controlling Interest, December 31, 2012					(835,104)	
46	Retained Earnings, NCI, December 31, 2012						(148,276)
47	Total NCI					(198,276)	(198,276)
48	Total	0	0	983,620	983,620	0	

Worksheet 3-9

Equity Method, Tax Issues
Paro Company and Subsidiary Sunstran Corporation
Worksheet for Consolidated Financial Statements
For Year Ended December 31, 2011

| | (Credit balance amounts are in parentheses.) | Trial Balance | |
		Paro	Sunstran
1	Cash	330,000	30,000
2	Accounts Receivable (net)	354,000	95,000
3	Inventory	540,000	100,000
4	Land	100,000	30,000
5	Building	1,300,000	950,000
6	Accumulated Depreciation—Building	(400,000)	(300,000)
7	**Noncurrent Deferred Tax Asset**		
8	Investment in Sunstran Corporation	1,058,000	
9			
10			
11	Goodwill		
12	Current Liabilities	(248,000)	(20,000)
13	**Deferred Tax Liability**	(30,000)	
14			
15	Common Stock—Paro	(510,000)	
16	Retained Earnings, January 1, 2011, Paro	(1,950,000)	
17			
18	Common Stock—Sunstran		(100,000)
19	Paid-In Capital in Excess of Par—Sunstran		(300,000)
20	Retained Earnings, January 1, 2011—Sunstran		(400,000)
21			
22	Sales	(3,400,000)	(900,000)
23	Cost of Goods Sold	2,070,000	600,000
24	Expenses	530,000	150,000
25			
26	Subsidiary Income	(84,000)	
27	Provision for Tax	240,000	45,000
28			
29	Dividends Declared	100,000	20,000
30		0	0
31	Consolidated Net Income		
32	To NCI (see distribution schedule)		
33	Balance to Controlling Interest (see distribution schedule)		
34	Total NCI		
35	Retained Earnings, Controlling Interest, December 31, 2011		
36			

Worksheet 3-9 (see page 144)

Eliminations & Adjustments				Consolidated Income Statement	NCI	Controlling Retained Earnings	Consolidated Balance Sheet	
Dr.		Cr.						
							360,000	1
							449,000	2
							640,000	3
							130,000	4
(D3)	200,000						2,450,000	5
		(A3)	10,000				(710,000)	6
(D2)	**75,000**						75,000	7
(CY2)	16,000	(CY1)	84,000					8
		(EL)	640,000					9
		(D)	350,000					10
(D4)	192,500						192,500	11
							(268,000)	12
(D1)							(57,000)	13
(A3t)	**3,000**	**(D3t)**	**60,000**					14
							(510,000)	15
						(1,950,000)		16
								17
(EL)	80,000				(20,000)			18
(EL)	240,000				(60,000)			19
(EL)	320,000	(NCI)	87,500		(167,500)			20
								21
				(4,300,000)				22
				2,670,000				23
(A3)	10,000			690,000				24
								25
(CY1)	84,000							26
		(A3t)	**3,000**	282,000				27
								28
		(CY2)	16,000		4,000	100,000		29
	1,250,500		1,250,500					30
				(658,000)				31
				13,600	(13,600)			32
				644,400		(644,400)		33
					(257,100)		(257,100)	34
						(2,494,400)	(2,494,400)	35
							0	36

Eliminations and Adjustments:

(CY1)	Eliminate the parent's share of subsidiary income.
(CY2)	Eliminate the current-year intercompany dividends. The investment account is adjusted now to its January 1, 2011, balance so that it may be eliminated.
(EL)	Eliminate the 80% ownership portion of the subsidiary equity accounts against the investment. A $350,000 excess cost remains.
(D)/(NCI)	Distribute the $350,000 excess cost and $87,500 NCI adjustment as follows, in accordance with the determination and distribution of excess schedule:
(D1)	Record the current portion of tax loss carryover used this period.
(D2)	Record the noncurrent portion of the tax loss carryover.
(D3)	Increase the building by $200,000.
(D3t)	Record the deferred tax liability related to the building increase.
(D4)	Record the goodwill.
(A3)	Record the annual increase in building depreciation; $200,000 net increase in the building divided by its 20-year life equals $10,000.
(A3t)	Reduce the provision for tax account by 30% of the increase in depreciation expense ($3,000).

Subsidiary Sunstran Corporation Income Distribution

Building depreciation .... (A3)	$10,000	Internally generated net income	$ 105,000
Current tax carryover............. (D1)	**30,000**	**Decrease in tax provision (A3t)**...........	**3,000**
		Adjusted income	$ 68,000
		NCI share	× 20%
		NCI	**$ 13,600**

Parent Paro Company Income Distribution

Internally generated net income	$ 590,000
80% × Sunstran Corporation adjusted income of $68,000.......................	54,400
Controlling interest	**$644,400**

UNDERSTANDING THE ISSUES

1. A parent company paid $500,000 for a 100% interest in a subsidiary. At the end of the first year, the subsidiary reported net income of $40,000 and paid $5,000 in dividends. The price paid reflected understated equipment of $70,000, which will be amortized over 10 years. What would be the subsidiary income reported on the parent's unconsolidated income statement, and what would the parent's investment balance be at the end of the first year under each of these methods?

    a. The simple equity method
    b. The sophisticated equity method
    c. The cost method

2. What is meant by date alignment? Does it exist on the consolidated worksheet under the following methods, and if not, how is it created prior to elimination of the investment account under each of these methods?

    a. The simple equity method
    b. The sophisticated equity method
    c. The cost method

3. What is the noncontrolling share of consolidated net income? Does it reflect adjustments based on fair values at the purchase date? How has it been displayed in income statements in the past, and how should it be displayed?

4. A parent company acquired an 80% interest in a subsidiary on July 1, 2011. The subsidiary closed its books on that date. The subsidiary reported net income of $60,000 for 2011, earned evenly during the year. The parent's net income, exclusive of any income of the subsidiary, was $140,000. The fair value of the subsidiary exceeded book value by $100,000. The entire difference was attributed to a patent with a 10-year life.

    a. What is consolidated net income for 2011?
    b. What is the noncontrolling share of net income for 2011?

5. A parent company acquired an 80% interest in a subsidiary on January 1, 2011, at a price high enough to result in goodwill. Included in the assets of the subsidiary are inventory with a book value of $50,000 and a fair value of $55,000 and equipment with a book value of $100,000 and a fair value of $160,000. The equipment has a 5-year remaining life. What impact would the inventory and equipment, acquired in the acquisition, have on consolidated net income in 2011 and 2012?

6. You are working on a consolidated trial balance of a parent and an 80% owned subsidiary. What components will enter into the total noncontrolling interest, and how will it be displayed in the consolidated balance sheet?

7. It seems as if consolidated net income is always less than the sum of the parent's and subsidiary's separately calculated net incomes. Is it possible that the consolidated net income of the two affiliated companies could actually exceed the sum of their individual net incomes?

EXERCISES

Exercise 1 *(LO 2)* **Equity method, first year, eliminations, statements.** Panther Company acquires an 80% interest in Sargo Company for $272,000 in cash on January 1, 2011, when Sargo Company has the following balance sheet:

Assets		Liabilities and Equity	
Current assets	$100,000	Current liabilities	$ 50,000
Depreciable fixed assets (net) ..	200,000	Common stock ($10 par).........	100,000
		Retained earnings	150,000
Total assets...............	$300,000	Total liabilities and equity	$300,000

The excess of the price paid over book value is attributable to the fixed assets, which have a fair value of $260,000, and to goodwill. The fixed assets have a 10-year remaining life. Panther Company uses the simple equity method to record its investment in Sargo Company.

The following trial balances of the two companies are prepared on December 31, 2011:

	Panther	Sargo
Current Assets	38,000	130,000
Depreciable Fixed Assets	400,000	200,000
Accumulated Depreciation	(106,000)	(20,000)
Investment in Sargo Company..................................	288,000	
Current Liabilities..	(60,000)	(40,000)
Common Stock ($10 par)	(300,000)	(100,000)
Retained Earnings, January 1, 2011.............................	(200,000)	(150,000)
Sales	(150,000)	(100,000)
Expenses	110,000	75,000
Subsidiary Income......................................	(20,000)	
Dividends Declared.......................................		5,000
Totals	0	0

1. Prepare a determination and distribution of excess schedule (a value analysis is not needed) for the investment.
2. Prepare all the eliminations and adjustments that would be made on the 2011 consolidated worksheet.
3. Prepare the 2011 consolidated income statement and its related income distribution schedules.
4. Prepare the 2011 statement of retained earnings.
5. Prepare the 2011 consolidated balance sheet.

Exercise 2 *(LO 2)* **Equity method, second year, eliminations, income statement.** The trial balances of Panther and Sargo companies of Exercise 1 for December 31, 2012, are presented as follows:

	Panther	Sargo
Current Assets	130,000	115,000
Depreciable Fixed Assets	400,000	200,000
Accumulated Depreciation	(130,000)	(40,000)
Investment in Sargo Company..................................	292,000	
Current Liabilities..	(80,000)	
Common Stock ($10 par)	(300,000)	(100,000)
Retained Earnings, January 1, 2012.............................	(260,000)	(170,000)
Sales	(200,000)	(100,000)
Expenses	160,000	85,000
Subsidiary Income......................................	(12,000)	
Dividends Declared.......................................		10,000
Totals	0	0

Panther Company continues to use the simple equity method.

1. Prepare all the eliminations and adjustments that would be made on the 2012 consolidated worksheet.
2. Prepare the 2012 consolidated income statement and its related income distribution schedules.

Exercise 3 *(LO 1)* **Compare alternative methods for recording income.** Clark Company acquires an 80% interest in Hebron Company common stock for $400,000 cash on January 1, 2011. At that time, Hebron Company has the following balance sheet:

Assets		Liabilities and Equity	
Current assets	$ 60,000	Accounts payable	$ 60,000
Land.	100,000	Common stock ($5 par).	50,000
Equipment	350,000	Paid-in capital in excess of par	100,000
Accumulated depreciation	(150,000)	Retained earnings	150,000
Total assets.	$ 360,000	Total liabilities and equity	$360,000

Appraisals indicate that accounts are fairly stated except for the equipment, which has a fair value of $250,000 and a remaining life of five years. Any remaining excess is goodwill.

Hebron Company experiences the following changes in retained earnings during 2011 and 2012:

Retained earnings, January 1, 2011.		$150,000
Net income, 2011.	$ 60,000	
Dividends paid in 2011.	(10,000)	50,000
Balance, December 31, 2011		$200,000
Net income, 2012.	$ 45,000	
Dividends paid in 2012.	(10,000)	35,000
Balance, December 31, 2012		$235,000

Prepare a determination and distribution of excess schedule for the investment in Hebron Company (a value analysis is not needed). Prepare journal entries that Clark Company would make on its books to record income earned and/or dividends received on its investment in Hebron Company during 2011 and 2012 under the following methods: simple equity, sophisticated equity, and cost.

Exercise 4 *(LO 1)* **Alternative investment models, more complex D&D.** Mast Corporation acquires a 75% interest in the common stock of Shaw Company on January 1, 2014, for $462,500 cash. Shaw has the following balance sheet on that date:

Assets		Liabilities and Equity	
Current assets	$ 80,000	Current liabilities	$ 50,000
Inventory	40,000	Common stock ($5 par).	50,000
Land.	100,000	Paid-in capital in excess of par	150,000
Buildings and equipment (net) . .	200,000	Retained earnings	200,000
Patent.	30,000		
Total assets.	$450,000	Total liabilities and equity	$450,000

Appraisals indicate that the book values for inventory, buildings and equipment, and patent are below fair values. The inventory has a fair value of $50,000 and is sold during 2014. The buildings and equipment have an appraised fair value of $300,000 and a remaining life of 20 years. The patent, which has a 10-year life, has an estimated fair value of $50,000. Any remaining excess is goodwill.

Shaw Company reports the following income earned and dividends paid during 2014 and 2015:

Retained earnings, January 1, 2014..........................		$200,000
Net income, 2014.......................................	$ 70,000	
Dividends paid in 2014..................................	(20,000)	50,000
Balance, December 31, 2014		$250,000
Net income, 2015.......................................	$ 48,000	
Dividends paid in 2015..................................	(20,000)	28,000
Balance, December 31, 2015		$278,000

Prepare a determination and distribution of excess schedule (a value analysis is not needed) for the investment in Shaw Company and determine the balance in Investment in Shaw Company on Mast Corporation's books as of December 31, 2015, under the following methods that could be used by the parent, Mast Corporation: simple equity, sophisticated equity, and cost.

Exercise 5 *(LO 4)* **Sophisticated equity method, first year, eliminations, statements.** *(Note: Read carefully, as this is not the same as Exercise 1.)* Panther Company acquires an 80% interest in Sargo Company for $272,000 on January 1, 2011, when Sargo Company has the following balance sheet:

Assets		Liabilities and Equity	
Current assets	$100,000	Current liabilities	$ 50,000
Depreciable fixed assets	200,000	Common stock ($10 par).........	100,000
		Retained earnings	150,000
Total assets..............	$300,000	Total liabilities and equity	$300,000

The excess of the price paid over book value is attributable to the fixed assets, which have a fair value of $260,000, and to goodwill. The fixed assets have a 10-year remaining life. Panther uses the sophisticated equity method to record the investment in Sargo Company.

The following trial balances of the two companies are prepared on December 31, 2011:

	Panther	Sargo
Current Assets	38,000	130,000
Depreciable Fixed Assets	400,000	200,000
Accumulated Depreciation	(106,000)	(20,000)
Investment in Sargo Company.............................	283,200	
Current Liabilities..	(60,000)	(40,000)
Common Stock ($10 par)	(300,000)	(100,000)
Retained Earnings, January 1, 2011........................	(200,000)	(150,000)
Sales	(150,000)	(100,000)
Expenses	110,000	75,000
Subsidiary Income (from Sargo Company)	(15,200)	
Dividends Declared.......................................		5,000
Totals	0	0

1. If you did not solve Exercise 1, prepare a determination and distribution of excess schedule for the investment (a value analysis is not needed).
2. Prepare all the eliminations and adjustments that would be made on the 2011 consolidated worksheet.
3. If you did not solve Exercise 1, prepare the 2011 consolidated income statement and its related income distribution schedule.

4. If you did not solve Exercise 1, prepare the 2011 statement of retained earnings.
5. If you did not solve Exercise 1, prepare the 2011 consolidated balance sheet.

Exercise 6 *(LO 3)* **Cost method, first year, eliminations, statements.** *(Note: Read carefully, as this is not the same as Exercise 1 or 5.)* Panther Company acquires an 80% interest in Sargo Company for $272,000 in cash on January 1, 2011, when Sargo Company has the following balance sheet:

Assets		Liabilities and Equity	
Current assets	$100,000	Current liabilities	$ 50,000
Depreciable fixed assets	200,000	Common stock ($10 par).	100,000
		Retained earnings	150,000
Total assets.	$300,000	Total liabilities and equity	$300,000

The excess of the price paid over book value is attributable to the fixed assets, which have a fair value of $260,000, and to goodwill. The fixed assets have a 10-year remaining life. Panther Company uses the cost method to record its investment in Sargo Company.

The following trial balances of the two companies are prepared on December 31, 2011:

	Panther	Sargo
Current Assets	38,000	130,000
Depreciable Fixed Assets	400,000	200,000
Accumulated Depreciation	(106,000)	(20,000)
Investment in Sargo Company.	272,000	
Current Liabilities.	(60,000)	(40,000)
Common Stock ($10 par)	(300,000)	(100,000)
Retained Earnings, January 1, 2012.	(200,000)	(150,000)
Sales	(150,000)	(100,000)
Expenses	110,000	75,000
Dividend Income (from Sargo Company)	(4,000)	
Dividends Declared.		5,000
Totals	0	0

1. If you did not solve Exercise 1 or 5, prepare a determination and distribution of excess schedule for the investment (a value analysis is not needed).
2. Prepare all the eliminations and adjustments that would be made on the 2011 consolidated worksheet.
3. If you did not solve Exercise 1 or 5, prepare the 2011 consolidated income statement and its related income distribution schedules.
4. If you did not solve Exercise 1 or 5, prepare the 2011 statement of retained earnings.
5. If you did not solve Exercise 1 or 5, prepare the 2011 consolidated balance sheet.

Exercise 7 *(LO 4)* **Sophisticated equity method, second year, eliminations, income statement.** The trial balances of Panther and Sargo companies of Exercise 5 for December 31, 2012, are presented as follows:

	Panther	Sargo
Current Assets	130,000	115,000
Depreciable Fixed Assets	400,000	200,000
Accumulated Depreciation	(130,000)	(40,000)

(continued)

	Panther	Sargo
Investment in Sargo Company	282,400	
Current Liabilities	(80,000)	
Common Stock ($10 par)	(300,000)	(100,000)
Retained Earnings, January 1, 2012	(255,200)	(170,000)
Sales	(200,000)	(100,000)
Expenses	160,000	85,000
Subsidiary Income (from Sargo Company)	(7,200)	
Dividends Declared		10,000
Totals	0	0

Panther Company continues to use the sophisticated equity method.

1. Prepare all the eliminations and adjustments that would be made on the 2012 consolidated worksheet.
2. If you did not solve Exercise 2, prepare the 2012 consolidated income statement and its related income distribution schedules.

Exercise 8 *(LO 3)* **Cost method, second year, eliminations, income statement.** The trial balances of Panther and Sargo companies of Exercise 6 for December 31, 2012, are presented as follows:

	Panther	Sargo
Current Assets	130,000	115,000
Depreciable Fixed Assets	400,000	200,000
Accumulated Depreciation	(130,000)	(40,000)
Investment in Sargo Company	272,000	
Current Liabilities	(80,000)	
Common Stock ($10 par)	(300,000)	(100,000)
Retained Earnings, January 1, 2012	(244,000)	(170,000)
Sales	(200,000)	(100,000)
Expenses	160,000	85,000
Dividend Income (from Sargo Company)	(8,000)	
Dividends Declared		10,000
Totals	0	0

Panther Company continues to use the cost method.

1. Prepare all the eliminations and adjustments that would be made on the 2012 consolidated worksheet.
2. If you did not solve Exercise 2 or 7, prepare the 2012 consolidated income statement and its related income distribution schedules.

Exercise 9 *(LO 5)* **Amortization procedures, several years.** Whitney Company acquires an 80% interest in Masters Company common stock on January 1, 2011. Appraisals of Masters' assets and liabilities are performed, and Whitney ends up paying an amount that is greater than the fair value of Masters' net assets and reflects a premium to achieve control. The fair value of the NCI is $235,000. The following partial determination and distribution of excess schedule is created on January 1, 2011, to assist in putting together the consolidated financial statements:

Determination and Distribution of Excess Schedule

	Company Implied Fair Value	Parent Price (80%)	NCI Value (20%)
Fair value of subsidiary	$1,335,000	$1,100,000	$235,000
Less book value of interest acquired:			
Common stock	$ 100,000		
Paid-in capital in excess of par	150,000		
Retained earnings	350,000		
Total equity	$ 600,000	$ 600,000	$600,000
Interest acquired		80%	20%
Book value		$ 480,000	$120,000
Excess of fair value over book value	**$ 735,000**	$ 620,000	$115,000

Adjustment of identifiable accounts:

	Adjustment	Amortization per Year	Life	Worksheet Key
Inventory	$ 6,250			
Investments	15,000		3	
Land	50,000			
Buildings	250,000		20	
Equipment	172,500		5	
Patent	22,500		10	
Trademark	20,000		10	
Discount on bonds payable	12,500		5	
Goodwill	**186,250**			
Total	**$ 735,000**			

Prepare amortization schedules for the years 2011, 2012, 2013, and 2014.

Exercise 10 *(LO 6)* **Acquisition during the year, elimination entries, income statement.** Kraus Company has the following balance sheet on July 1, 2012:

Assets		Liabilities and Equity	
Current assets	$200,000	Current liabilities	$100,000
Equipment (net)	300,000	Common stock ($10 par)	100,000
		Retained earnings	300,000
Total assets	$500,000	Total liabilities and equity	$500,000

On July 1, 2012, Neiman Company purchases 80% of the outstanding common stock of Kraus Company for $310,000. Any excess of book value over cost is attributed to the equipment, which has an estimated 5-year life. Kraus Company closes its books before the acquisition on July 1.

On December 31, 2012, Neiman Company and Kraus Company prepare the following trial balances:

	Neiman	Kraus (July 1–Dec. 31)
Current Assets	220,000	220,000
Equipment	500,000	300,000
Accumulated Depreciation—Equipment	(140,000)	(20,000)
Investment in Kraus Company	310,000	

(continued)

	Neiman	Kraus (July 1–Dec. 31)
Current Liabilities.	(200,000)	(70,000)
Common Stock ($10 par)	(200,000)	(100,000)
Retained Earnings, July 1, 2012	(430,000)	(300,000)
Sales	(300,000)	(100,000)
Cost of Goods Sold	180,000	45,000
General Expenses	60,000	25,000
Totals	0	0

1. Prepare a determination and distribution of excess schedule for the investment (a value analysis is not needed).
2. Prepare all the eliminations and adjustments that would be made on the December 31, 2012, consolidated worksheet.
3. Prepare the 2012 consolidated income statement and its related income distribution schedules.

Exercise 11 *(LO 7)* **Impairment loss.** Albers Company acquires an 80% interest in Barker Company on January 1, 2011, for $850,000. The following determination and distribution of excess schedule is prepared at the time of purchase:

Determination and Distribution of Excess Schedule

	Company Implied Fair Value	Parent Price (80%)	NCI Value (20%)
Fair value of subsidiary	$1,062,500	$850,000	$212,500
Less book value of interest acquired:			
Total equity.	$ 600,000	$600,000	$600,000
Interest acquired		80%	20%
Book value.		$480,000	$120,000
Excess of fair value over book value	$ 462,500	$370,000	$ 92,500

Adjustment of identifiable accounts:

	Adjustment	Amortization per Year	Life	Worksheet Key
Buildings	$ 200,000	$ 10,000	20	**debit D1**
Goodwill.	262,500			**debit D2**
Total	$ 462,500			

Albers uses the simple equity method for its investment in Barker. As of December 31, 2015, Barker has earned $200,000 since it was purchased by Albers. Barker pays no dividends during 2011–2015.

On December 31, 2015, the following values are available:

Fair value of Barker's identifiable net assets (100%)	$ 900,000
Estimated fair value of Barker Company (net of liabilities)	1,000,000

Determine if goodwill is impaired. If not, explain your reasoning. If so, calculate the loss on impairment.

APPENDIX EXERCISES

Exercise 3B-1 *(LO 9)* **D&D for nontaxable exchange.** Rainman Corporation is considering the acquisition of Largo Company through the acquisition of Largo's common stock. Rainman Corporation will issue 20,000 shares of its $5 par common stock, with a fair value of $25 per share, in exchange for all 10,000 outstanding shares of Largo Company's voting common stock.

The acquisition meets the criteria for a tax-free exchange as to the seller. Because of this, Rainman Corporation will be limited for future tax returns to the book value of the depreciable assets. Rainman Corporation falls into the 30% tax bracket.

The appraisal of the assets of Largo Company shows that the inventory has a fair value of $120,000, and the depreciable fixed assets have a fair value of $270,000 and a 10-year life. Any remaining excess is attributed to goodwill. Largo Company has the following balance sheet just before the acquisition:

Largo Company
Balance Sheet
December 31, 2015

Assets		Liabilities and Equity		
Cash	$ 40,000	Current liabilities		$ 70,000
Accounts receivable	150,000	Bonds payable		100,000
Inventory	100,000	Stockholders' equity:		
Depreciable fixed assets (net)	210,000	Common stock ($10 par) . . .	$100,000	
		Retained earnings	230,000	330,000
Total assets	$500,000	Total liabilities and equity		$500,000

1. Record the acquisition of Largo Company by Rainman Corporation.
2. Prepare a value analysis and a determination and distribution of excess schedule.
3. Prepare the elimination entries that would be made on the consolidated worksheet on the date of acquisition.

Exercise 3B-2 *(LO 9)* **D&D and income statement for nontaxable exchange.** Lucy Company issues securities with a fair value of $468,000 for a 90% interest in Diamond Company on January 1, 2011, at which time Diamond Company has the following balance sheet:

Assets		Liabilities and Equity	
Accounts receivable	$ 50,000	Current liabilities	$ 70,000
Inventory	80,000	Common stock ($5 par)	100,000
Land	20,000	Paid-in capital in excess of par	130,000
Building (net)	200,000	Retained earnings	50,000
Total assets	$350,000	Total liabilities and equity	$350,000

It is believed that the inventory and the building are undervalued by $20,000 and $50,000, respectively. The building has a 10-year remaining life; the inventory on hand on January 1, 2011, is sold during the year. The deferred tax liability associated with the asset revaluations is to be reflected in the consolidated statements. Each company has an income tax rate of 30%. Any remaining excess is goodwill.

The separate income statements of the two companies prepared for 2011 are as follows:

	Lucy	Diamond
Sales	$ 400,000	$150,000
Cost of goods sold	(200,000)	(90,000)
Gross profit	$ 200,000	$ 60,000

(continued)

	Lucy	Diamond
General expenses	(50,000)	(25,000)
Depreciation expense	(60,000)	(15,000)
Operating income	$ 90,000	$ 20,000
Subsidiary income (90% × $14,000 subsidiary net income)	12,600	
Net income before income tax	$ 102,600	$ 20,000
Provision for tax (does not include tax on subsidiary income)	(27,000)	(6,000)
Net income	$ 75,600	$ 14,000

1. Prepare a value analysis and a determination and distribution of excess schedule for the investment.
2. Prepare the 2011 consolidated income statement and its related income distribution schedules.

Exercise 3B-3 *(LO 9)* **D&D for nontaxable exchange with tax loss carryforward.** Palto issues 20,000 of its $5 par value common stock shares, with a fair value of $35 each, for a 100% interest in Sword Company on January 1, 2011. The balance sheet of Sword Company on that date is as follows:

Assets		Liabilities and Equity	
Current assets	$100,000	Current liabilities	$ 50,000
Buildings and equipment (net) . .	300,000	Common stock ($5 par)	250,000
		Retained earnings	100,000
Total assets	$400,000	Total liabilities and equity	$400,000

On the purchase date, the buildings and equipment are understated $50,000 and have a remaining life of 10 years. Sword has tax loss carryovers of $200,000. They are believed to be fully realizable at a tax rate of 30%. $40,000 of the tax loss carryovers will be utilized in 2011. The purchase is a tax-free exchange. The tax rate applicable to all transactions is 30%. Any remaining excess is attributed to goodwill.

Prepare a value analysis and a determination and distribution of excess schedule for this investment.

PROBLEMS

Problem 3-1 *(LO 1)* **Alternative investment account methods, effect on eliminations.** On January 1, 2011, Portico Company acquires 8,000 shares of Sauder Company by issuing 10,000 of its common stock shares with a par value of $10 per share and a fair value of $70 per share. The price paid reflects a control premium. The market value of the shares owned by the NCI is $75 per share. At the time of the purchase, Sauder has the following balance sheet:

Assets		Liabilities and Equity	
Current assets	$100,000	Current liabilities	$ 80,000
Investments	150,000	Bonds payable	250,000
Land	120,000	Common stock ($10 par)	100,000
Building (net)	350,000	Paid-in capital in excess of par	200,000
Equipment (net)	160,000	Retained earnings	250,000
Total assets	$880,000	Total liabilities and equity	$880,000

Appraisals indicate that book values are representative of fair values with the exception of the land and building. The land has a fair value of $180,000, and the building is appraised at

$470,000. The building has an estimated remaining life of 20 years. Any remaining excess is goodwill.

The following summary of Sauder's retained earnings applies to 2011 and 2012:

Balance, January 1, 2011.....................	$250,000
Net income for 2011......................	60,000
Dividends paid in 2011...................	(10,000)
Balance, December 31, 2011	$300,000
Net income for 2012......................	50,000
Dividends paid in 2012...................	(10,000)
Balance, December 31, 2012	$340,000

1. Prepare a value analysis and a determination and distribution of excess schedule for the investment in Sauder Company. As a part of the schedule, indicate annual amortization of excess adjustments. ◀ ◀ ◀ ◀ ◀ **Required**
2. For 2011 and 2012, prepare the entries that Portico would make concerning its investment in Sauder under the simple equity, sophisticated equity, and cost methods You may want to set up a worksheet with side-by-side columns for each method so that you can easily compare the entries.
3. For 2011 and 2012, prepare the worksheet elimination that would be made on a consolidated worksheet under the simple equity, sophisticated equity, and cost methods. You may want to set up a worksheet with side-by-side columns for each method so that you can easily compare the entries.

Problem 3-2 *(LO 2)* **Equity method, 80% interest, worksheet, statements.** Sandin Company prepares the following balance sheet on January 1, 2011:

Assets		Liabilities and Equity	
Current assets	$ 50,000	Liabilities	$140,000
Land......................	75,000	Common stock ($10 par).........	100,000
Buildings	350,000	Paid-in capital in excess of par	120,000
Accumulated depreciation—		Retained earnings (deficit)........	(25,000)
buildings	(140,000)		
Total assets..............	$ 335,000	Total liabilities and equity	$335,000

On this date, Prescott Company purchases 8,000 shares of Sandin Company's outstanding stock for a total price of $270,000. Also on this date, the buildings are understated by $40,000 and have a 10-year remaining life. Any remaining discrepancy between the price paid and book value is attributed to goodwill. Since the purchase, Prescott Company has used the simple equity method to record the investment and its related income.

Prescott Company and Sandin Company prepare the following separate trial balances on December 31, 2012:

	Prescott	Sandin
Current Assets	180,000	115,000
Land..	150,000	75,000
Buildings	590,000	350,000
Accumulated Depreciation—Buildings	(265,000)	(182,000)
Investment in Sandin Company.................................	294,000	
Liabilities	(175,000)	(133,000)
Common Stock ($10 par)	(200,000)	(100,000)
Paid-In Capital in Excess of Par		(120,000)
Retained Earnings, January 1, 2012...........................	(503,000)	15,000

(continued)

	Prescott	Sandin
Sales	(360,000)	(120,000)
Cost of Goods Sold	179,000	50,000
Expenses	120,000	45,000
Subsidiary Income	(20,000)	
Dividends Declared	10,000	5,000
Totals	0	0

Required ▶ ▶ ▶ ▶ ▶

1. Prepare a value analysis and a determination and distribution of excess schedule for the investment.
2. Prepare the 2012 consolidated worksheet. Include columns for the eliminations and adjustments, the consolidated income statement, the NCI, the controlling retained earnings, and the consolidated balance sheet. Prepare supporting income distribution schedules.
3. Prepare the 2012 consolidated statements including the income statement, retained earnings statement, and the balance sheet.

Problem 3-3 *(LO 2)* **Simple equity method adjustments, consolidated worksheet.** On January 1, 2011, Peres Company purchases 80% of the common stock of Soap Company for $308,000. Soap has common stock, other paid-in capital in excess of par, and retained earnings of $50,000, $100,000, and $150,000, respectively. Net income and dividends for two years for Soap are as follows:

	2011	2012
Net income	$60,000	$90,000
Dividends.	20,000	30,000

On January 1, 2011, the only undervalued tangible assets of Soap are inventory and the building. Inventory, for which FIFO is used, is worth $10,000 more than cost. The inventory is sold in 2011. The building, which is worth $25,000 more than book value, has a remaining life of 10 years, and straight-line depreciation is used. The remaining excess of cost over book value is attributed to goodwill.

Required ▶ ▶ ▶ ▶ ▶

1. Using this information and the information in the following trial balances on December 31, 2012, prepare a value analysis and a determination and distribution of excess schedule:

	Peres Company	Soap Company
Inventory, December 31	100,000	50,000
Other Current Assets	148,000	180,000
Investment in Soap Company	388,000	
Land.	50,000	50,000
Buildings and Equipment.	350,000	320,000
Accumulated Depreciation	(100,000)	(60,000)
Goodwill		
Other Intangibles.	20,000	
Current Liabilities.	(120,000)	(40,000)
Bonds Payable.		(100,000)
Other Long-Term Liabilities	(200,000)	
Common Stock—Peres Company	(200,000)	
Other Paid-In Capital in Excess of Par—Peres Company	(100,000)	
Retained Earnings—Peres Company.	(214,000)	
Common Stock—Soap Company		(50,000)
Other Paid-In Capital in Excess of Par—Soap Company		(100,000)

	Peres Company	Soap Company
Retained Earnings—Soap Company.		(190,000)
Net Sales.	(520,000)	(450,000)
Cost of Goods Sold	300,000	260,000
Operating Expenses	120,000	100,000
Subsidiary Income.	(72,000)	
Dividends Declared—Peres Company	50,000	
Dividends Declared—Soap Company		30,000
Totals	0	0

2. Complete a worksheet for consolidated financial statements for 2012. Include columns for eliminations and adjustments, consolidated income, NCI, controlling retained earnings, and consolidated balance sheet.

Problem 3-4 *(LO 3)* **Cost method, worksheet, statements.** Bell Corporation purchases all of the outstanding stock of Stockdon Corporation for $220,000 in cash on January 1, 2017. On the purchase date, Stockdon Corporation has the following condensed balance sheet:

Assets		Liabilities and Equity	
Cash	$ 60,000	Liabilities	$150,000
Inventory	40,000	Common stock ($10 par).	100,000
Land.	120,000	Paid-in capital in excess of par	50,000
Building (net)	180,000	Retained earnings	100,000
Total assets.	$400,000	Total liabilities and equity	$400,000

Any excess of book value over cost is attributable to the building, which is currently overstated on Stockdon's books. All other assets and liabilities have book values equal to fair values. The building has an estimated 10-year life with no salvage value.

The trial balances of the two companies on December 31, 2017, appear as follows:

	Bell	Stockdon
Cash	180,000	143,000
Inventory	60,000	30,000
Land.	120,000	120,000
Building (net)	600,000	162,000
Investment in Stockdon Corporation	220,000	
Accounts Payable	(405,000)	(210,000)
Common Stock ($3 par)	(300,000)	
Common Stock ($10 par)		(100,000)
Paid-In Capital in Excess of Par	(180,000)	(50,000)
Retained Earnings, January 1, 2017.	(255,000)	(100,000)
Sales	(210,000)	(40,000)
Cost of Goods Sold	120,000	35,000
Other Expenses	45,000	10,000
Dividends Declared.	5,000	
Totals	0	0

1. Prepare a determination and distribution of excess schedule for the investment. (A value   ◄ ◄ ◄ ◄ ◄ **Required**
   analysis is not needed.)
2. Prepare the 2017 consolidated worksheet. Include columns for the eliminations and adjustments, the consolidated income statement, the controlling retained earnings, and the consolidated balance sheet.
3. Prepare the 2017 consolidated statements, including the income statement, retained earnings statement, and balance sheet.

Problem 3-5 *(LO 3)* **Cost method, consolidated statements.** The trial balances of Charles Company and its subsidiary, Lehto, Inc., are as follows on December 31, 2013:

	Charles	Lehto
Current Assets	590,000	130,000
Depreciable Fixed Assets	1,805,000	440,000
Accumulated Depreciation	(405,000)	(70,000)
Investment in Lehto, Inc..................................	400,000	
Liabilities	(900,000)	(225,000)
Common Stock ($1 par)	(220,000)	
Common Stock ($5 par)		(50,000)
Paid-In Capital in Excess of Par	(1,040,000)	(15,000)
Retained Earnings, January 1, 2013......................	(230,000)	(170,000)
Revenues	(460,000)	(210,000)
Expenses	450,000	170,000
Dividends Declared......................................	10,000	
Totals	0	0

On January 1, 2011, Charles Company exchanges 20,000 shares of its common stock, with a fair value of $20 per share, for all the outstanding stock of Lehto, Inc. Fixed assets with a 10-year life are understated by $50,000. Any excess of cost over book value is attributed to goodwill. The stockholders' equity of Lehto, Inc., on the purchase date is as follows:

Common stock ($5 par).......................	$ 50,000
Paid-in capital in excess of par	15,000
Retained earnings	135,000
Total equity	$200,000

Required ▶ ▶ ▶ ▶ ▶

1. Prepare a determination and distribution of excess schedule for the investment. (A value analysis schedule is not needed.)
2. Prepare the 2013 consolidated statements, including the income statement, retained earnings statement, and balance sheet. (A worksheet is not required.)

Problem 3-6 *(LO 4)* **Sophisticated equity method adjustments, consolidated worksheet.** (This is the same as Problem 3-3, except that the sophisticated equity method is used.) On January 1, 2011, Peres Company purchases 80% of the common stock of Soap Company for $308,000. On this date, Soap has common stock, other paid-in capital in excess of par, and retained earnings of $50,000, $100,000, and $150,000, respectively. Net income and dividends for two years for Soap Company are as follows:

	2011	2012
Net income	$60,000	$90,000
Dividends........................	20,000	30,000

On January 1, 2011, the only undervalued tangible assets of Soap are inventory and the building. Inventory, for which FIFO is used, is worth $10,000 more than cost. The inventory is sold in 2011. The building, which is worth $25,000 more than book value, has a remaining life of 10 years, and straight-line depreciation is used. The remaining excess of cost over book value is attributable to goodwill.

The trial balances for Peres and Soap are as follows:

	Peres Company	Soap Company
Inventory, December 31	100,000	50,000
Other Current Assets	148,000	180,000
Investment in Soap Company	Note 1	
Land	50,000	50,000
Buildings and Equipment	350,000	320,000
Accumulated Depreciation	(100,000)	(60,000)
Goodwill		
Other Intangibles	20,000	
Current Liabilities	(120,000)	(40,000)
Bonds Payable		(100,000)
Other Long-Term Liabilities	(200,000)	
Common Stock—Peres Company	(200,000)	
Other Paid-In Capital in Excess of Par—Peres Company	(100,000)	
Retained Earnings—Peres Company	(204,000)	
Common Stock—Soap Company		(50,000)
Other Paid-In Capital in Excess of Par—Soap Company		(100,000)
Retained Earnings—Soap Company		(190,000)
Net Sales	(520,000)	(450,000)
Cost of Goods Sold	300,000	260,000
Operating Expenses	120,000	100,000
Subsidiary Income	Note 1	
Dividends Declared—Peres Company	50,000	
Dividends Declared—Soap Company		30,000

Note 1: To be calculated.

 ◄ ◄ ◄ ◄ ◄ **Required**

1. Prepare a value analysis and a determination and distribution of excess schedule.
2. Peres Company carries the investment in Soap Company under the sophisticated equity method. In general journal form, record the entries that would be made to apply the equity method in 2011 and 2012.
3. Compute the balance that should appear in Investment in Soap Company and in Subsidiary Income on December 31, 2012 (the second year). Fill in these amounts on Peres Company's trial balance for 2012.
4. Complete a worksheet for consolidated financial statements for 2012. Include columns for eliminations and adjustments, consolidated income, NCI, controlling retained earnings, and consolidated balance sheet.

Problem 3-7 *(LO 3, 5)* **Cost method, 80% interest, worksheet, several adjustments.** Detner International purchases 80% of the outstanding stock of Hardy Company for $1,600,000 on January 1, 2015. At the purchase date, the inventory, equipment, and patents of Hardy Company have fair values of $10,000, $50,000, and $100,000, respectively, in excess of their book values. The other assets and liabilities of Hardy Company have book values equal to their fair values. The inventory is sold during the month following the purchase. The two companies agree that the equipment has a remaining life of eight years and the patents 10 years. On the purchase date, the owners' equity of Hardy Company is as follows:

Common stock ($10 stated value)	$1,000,000
Additional paid-in capital in excess of par	300,000
Retained earnings	400,000
Total equity	$1,700,000

During 2015 and 2016, Hardy Company has income and pays dividends as follows:

	Income	Dividends
2015...................	$ 90,000	$30,000
2016...................	150,000	30,000

The trial balances of the two companies as of December 31, 2017, are as follows:

	Detner International	Hardy Company
Current Assets	632,000	505,000
Equipment (net)	1,320,000	940,000
Patents	100,000	35,000
Other Assets	1,620,000	730,000
Investment in Hardy.	1,600,000	
Accounts Payable	(658,000)	(205,000)
Common Stock ($5 par)	(2,000,000)	
Common Stock ($10 par)		(1,000,000)
Additional Paid-In Capital in Excess of Par	(1,200,000)	(300,000)
Retained Earnings, January 1, 2017.	(1,255,000)	(580,000)
Sales	(905,000)	(425,000)
Cost of Goods Sold	470,000	170,000
Other Expenses	250,000	100,000
Dividend Income	(24,000)	
Dividends Declared.	50,000	30,000
Totals	0	0

The remaining excess of cost over book value is attributable to goodwill.

Required ▶ ▶ ▶ ▶ ▶

1. Prepare the original value analysis and a determination and distribution of excess schedule for the investment.
2. Prepare the consolidated worksheet for December 31, 2017. Include columns for the eliminations and adjustments, the consolidated income statement, the controlling retained earnings, and the consolidated balance sheet.

Problem 3-8 *(LO 6)* **Intraperiod purchase, 80% interest, worksheet, statements.**
Jeter Corporation purchases 80% of the outstanding stock of Super Company for $275,000 on July 1, 2011. Super Company has the following stockholders' equity on July 1, 2011:

Common stock ($5 par).	$150,000
Retained earnings, July 1, 2011	50,000
Total equity	$200,000

The fair values of Super's assets and liabilities agree with the book values, except for the equipment and the building. The equipment is undervalued by $10,000 and is thought to have a 5-year life; the building is undervalued by $50,000 and is thought to have a 20-year life. The remaining excess of cost over book value is attributable to goodwill. Jeter Corporation uses the simple equity method to record its investments.

Since the purchase date, both firms have operated separately, and no intercompany transactions have occurred. Super Company closes its books on the date of acquisition.

The separate trial balances of the firms on December 31, 2011, are as follows:

	Jeter Corporation	Super Company
Cash	296,600	91,000
Land	160,000	90,000
Building	225,000	135,000
Accumulated Depreciation—Building	(100,000)	(50,000)
Equipment	450,000	150,000
Accumulated Depreciation—Equipment	(115,000)	(60,000)
Investment in Super Company	284,600	
Liabilities	(480,000)	(150,000)
Common Stock ($100 par)	(400,000)	
Common Stock ($5 par)		(150,000)
Paid-In Capital in Excess of Par	(40,000)	
Retained Earnings, January 1, 2011	(251,600)	
Retained Earnings, July 1, 2011		(50,000)
Sales	(460,000)	(60,000)
Cost of Goods Sold	220,000	30,000
Other Expenses	210,000	24,000
Subsidiary Income	(9,600)	
Dividends Declared	10,000	
Totals	0	0

1. Prepare a value analysis and a determination and distribution of excess schedule for the investment.   ◄ ◄ ◄ ◄ ◄ **Required**
2. Prepare the 2011 consolidated worksheet. Include columns for the eliminations and adjustments, the consolidated income statement, the NCI, the controlling retained earnings, and the consolidated balance sheet. Prepare supporting income distribution schedules as well.
3. Prepare the 2011 consolidated statements, including the income statement, retained earnings statement, and balance sheet.

Use the following information for Problems 3-9 through 3-13:
Fast Cool Company and Fast Air Company are both manufacturers of air conditioning equipment. On January 1, 2011, Fast Cool acquires the common stock of Fast Air by exchanging its own $1 par, $20 fair value common stock. On the date of acquisition, Fast Air has the following balance sheet:

Fast Air Company
Balance Sheet
January 1, 2011

Assets		Liabilities and Equity	
Accounts receivable	$ 40,000	Current liabilities	$ 30,000
Inventory	60,000	Mortgage payable	200,000
Land	50,000	Common stock ($1 par)	100,000
Buildings	400,000	Paid-in capital in excess of par	200,000
Accumulated depreciation	(50,000)	Retained earnings	180,000
Equipment	150,000		
Accumulated depreciation	(30,000)		
Patent (net)	40,000		
Goodwill	50,000		
Total assets	$710,000	Total liabilities and equity	$710,000

Fast Cool requests that an appraisal be done to determine whether the book value of Fast Air's net assets reflect their fair values. The appraiser determines that several intangible assets exist, although they are unrecorded. If the intangible assets do not have an observable market, the appraiser estimates their value. The appraiser determines the following fair values and estimates:

Accounts receivable	$ 40,000
Inventory (sold during 2011)	65,000
Land	100,000
Buildings (20-year life)	500,000
Equipment (5-year life)	100,000
Patent (5-year life)	50,000
Current liabilities	30,000
Mortgage payable (5-year life)	205,000
Favorable purchase contract (2-year life)	10,000

Any remaining excess is attributed to goodwill.

Problem 3-9 *(LO 2, 5)* **100%, complicated excess, equity method, first year.** Refer to the preceding information for Fast Cool's acquisition of Fast Air's common stock. Assume Fast Cool issues 40,000 shares of its $20 fair value common stock for 100% of Fast Air's common stock. Fast Cool uses the simple equity method to account for its investment in Fast Air. Fast Cool and Fast Air have the following trial balances on December 31, 2011:

	Fast Cool	Fast Air
Cash	147,000	37,000
Accounts Receivable	70,000	100,000
Inventory	150,000	60,000
Land	60,000	50,000
Investment in Fast Air	837,500	
Buildings	1,200,000	400,000
Accumulated Depreciation	(176,000)	(67,500)
Equipment	140,000	150,000
Accumulated Depreciation	(68,000)	(54,000)
Patent (net)		32,000
Goodwill		50,000
Current Liabilities	(80,000)	(40,000)
Mortgage Payable		(200,000)
Common Stock	(100,000)	(100,000)
Paid-In Capital in Excess of Par	(1,500,000)	(200,000)
Retained Earnings, January 1, 2011	(400,000)	(180,000)
Sales	(700,000)	(400,000)
Cost of Goods Sold	380,000	210,000
Depreciation Expense—Buildings	10,000	17,500
Depreciation Expense—Equipment	7,000	24,000
Other Expenses	50,000	85,000
Interest Expense		16,000
Subsidiary Income	(47,500)	
Dividends Declared	20,000	10,000
Totals	0	0

Required ▶ ▶ ▶ ▶ ▶ 1. Prepare a value analysis and a determination and distribution of excess schedule for the investment in Fast Air.

2. Complete a consolidated worksheet for Fast Cool Company and its subsidiary Fast Air Company as of December 31, 2011. Prepare supporting amortization and income distribution schedules.

Problem 3-10 *(LO 2, 5)* **100%, complicated excess, equity method, second year.** Refer to the preceding information for Fast Cool's acquisition of Fast Air's common stock. Assume Fast Cool issues 40,000 shares of its $20 fair value common stock for 100% of Fast Air's common stock. Fast Cool uses the simple equity method to account for its investment in Fast Air. Fast Cool and Fast Air have the following trial balances on December 31, 2012:

	Fast Cool	Fast Air
Cash	396,000	99,000
Accounts Receivable	200,000	120,000
Inventory	120,000	95,000
Land	60,000	50,000
Investment in Fast Air	895,000	
Buildings	1,200,000	400,000
Accumulated Depreciation	(200,000)	(85,000)
Equipment	140,000	150,000
Accumulated Depreciation	(80,000)	(78,000)
Patent (net)		24,000
Goodwill		50,000
Current Liabilities	(150,000)	(50,000)
Mortgage Payable		(200,000)
Common Stock	(100,000)	(100,000)
Paid-In Capital in Excess of Par	(1,500,000)	(200,000)
Retained Earnings, January 1, 2012	(680,500)	(217,500)
Sales	(700,000)	(500,000)
Cost of Goods Sold	380,000	260,000
Depreciation Expense—Buildings	10,000	17,500
Depreciation Expense—Equipment	7,000	24,000
Other Expenses	50,000	115,000
Interest Expense		16,000
Subsidiary Income	(67,500)	
Dividends Declared	20,000	10,000
Totals	0	0

1. Prepare a value analysis and a determination and distribution of excess schedule for the investment in Fast Air. ◄ ◄ ◄ ◄ ◄ **Required**
2. Complete a consolidated worksheet for Fast Cool Company and its subsidiary Fast Air Company as of December 31, 2012. Prepare supporting amortization and income distribution schedules.

Problem 3-11 *(LO 2, 5)* **100% bargain, complicated equity method, second year.** Refer to the preceding information for Fast Cool's acquisition of Fast Air's common stock. Assume Fast Cool issues 25,000 shares of its $20 fair value common stock for 100% of Fast Air's common stock. Fast Cool uses the simple equity method to account for its investment in Fast Air. Fast Cool and Fast Air have the following trial balances on December 31, 2012, are as follows:

	Fast Cool	Fast Air
Cash	396,000	99,000
Accounts Receivable	200,000	120,000
Inventory	120,000	95,000
Land	60,000	50,000
Investment in Fast Air	595,000	
Buildings	1,200,000	400,000
Accumulated Depreciation	(200,000)	(85,000)
Equipment	140,000	150,000
Accumulated Depreciation	(80,000)	(78,000)
Patent (net)		24,000
Goodwill		50,000
Current Liabilities	(150,000)	(50,000)
Mortgage Payable		(200,000)
Common Stock	(85,000)	(100,000)
Paid-In Capital in Excess of Par	(1,215,000)	(200,000)
Retained Earnings, January 1, 2012	(680,500)	(217,500)
Sales	(700,000)	(500,000)
Cost of Goods Sold	380,000	260,000
Depreciation Expense—Buildings	10,000	17,500
Depreciation Expense—Equipment	7,000	24,000
Other Expenses	50,000	115,000
Interest Expense		16,000
Subsidiary Income	(67,500)	
Dividends Declared	20,000	10,000
Totals	0	0

Required ▶ ▶ ▶ ▶ ▶

1. Prepare a value analysis and a determination and distribution of excess schedule for the investment in Fast Air.
2. Complete a consolidated worksheet for Fast Cool Company and its subsidiary Fast Air Company as of December 31, 2012. Prepare supporting amortization and income distribution schedules.

Problem 3-12 *(LO 2, 5)* **80%, first year, equity method, complicated excess.** Refer to the preceding information for Fast Cool's acquisition of Fast Air's common stock. Assume Fast Cool issues 35,000 shares of its $20 fair value common stock for 80% of Fast Air's common stock. Fast Cool uses the simple equity method to account for its investment in Fast Air. Fast Cool and Fast Air have the following trial balances on December 31, 2011:

	Fast Cool	Fast Air
Cash	145,000	37,000
Accounts Receivable	70,000	100,000
Inventory	150,000	60,000
Land	60,000	50,000
Investment in Fast Air	730,000	
Buildings	1,200,000	400,000
Accumulated Depreciation	(176,000)	(67,500)
Equipment	140,000	150,000
Accumulated Depreciation	(68,000)	(54,000)
Patent (net)		32,000
Goodwill		50,000
Current Liabilities	(80,000)	(40,000)
Mortgage Payable		(200,000)
Common Stock	(95,000)	(100,000)
Paid-In Capital in Excess of Par	(1,405,000)	(200,000)
Retained Earnings, January 1, 2011	(400,000)	(180,000)

	Fast Cool	Fast Air
Sales	(700,000)	(400,000)
Cost of Goods Sold	380,000	210,000
Depreciation Expense—Buildings	10,000	17,500
Depreciation Expense—Equipment	7,000	24,000
Other Expenses	50,000	85,000
Interest Expense		16,000
Subsidiary Income	(38,000)	
Dividends Declared	20,000	10,000
Totals	0	0

1. Prepare a value analysis and a determination and distribution of excess schedule for the investment in Fast Air.
2. Complete a consolidated worksheet for Fast Cool Company and its subsidiary Fast Air Company as of December 31, 2011. Prepare supporting amortization and income distribution schedules.

◄ ◄ ◄ ◄ ◄ **Required**

Problem 3-13 *(LO 2, 5)* **80%, second year, equity method, complicated excess.**
Refer to the preceding information for Fast Cool's acquisition of Fast Air's common stock. Assume Fast Cool issues 35,000 shares of its $20 fair value common stock for 80% of Fast Air's common stock. Fast Cool uses the simple equity method to account for its investment in Fast Air. Fast Cool and Fast Air have the following trial balances on December 31, 2012:

	Fast Cool	Fast Air
Cash	392,000	99,000
Accounts Receivable	200,000	120,000
Inventory	120,000	95,000
Land	60,000	50,000
Investment in Fast Air	776,000	
Buildings	1,200,000	400,000
Accumulated Depreciation	(200,000)	(85,000)
Equipment	140,000	150,000
Accumulated Depreciation	(80,000)	(78,000)
Patent (net)		24,000
Goodwill		50,000
Current Liabilities	(150,000)	(50,000)
Mortgage Payable		(200,000)
Common Stock	(95,000)	(100,000)
Paid-In Capital in Excess of Par	(1,405,000)	(200,000)
Retained Earnings, January 1, 2012	(671,000)	(217,500)
Sales	(700,000)	(500,000)
Cost of Goods Sold	380,000	260,000
Depreciation Expense—Buildings	10,000	17,500
Depreciation Expense—Equipment	7,000	24,000
Other Expenses	50,000	115,000
Interest Expense		16,000
Subsidiary Income	(54,000)	
Dividends Declared	20,000	10,000
Totals	0	0

1. Prepare a value analysis and a determination and distribution of excess schedule for the investment in Fast Air.
2. Complete a consolidated worksheet for Fast Cool Company and its subsidiary Fast Air Company as of December 31, 2012. Prepare supporting amortization and income distribution schedules.

◄ ◄ ◄ ◄ ◄ **Required**

Use the following information for Problems 3-14 through 3-18:

Paulcraft Corporation builds large powerboats. On January 1, 2011, Paulcraft acquires Switzer Corporation, a company that manufactures smaller power boats. Paulcraft pays cash in exchange for Switzer common stock. Switzer has the following balance sheet on January 1, 2011:

Switzer Corporation
Balance Sheet
January 1, 2011

Assets		Liabilities and Equity	
Accounts receivable	$ 82,000	Current liabilities	$ 90,000
Inventory	40,000	Bonds payable	100,000
Land.	60,000	Common stock ($1 par).	10,000
Buildings	200,000	Paid-in capital in excess of par . . .	90,000
Accumulated depreciation . . .	(50,000)	Retained earnings	112,000
Equipment	100,000		
Accumulated depreciation . . .	(30,000)		
Total assets.	$402,000	Total liabilities and equity	$402,000

Appraisal values for identifiable assets and liabilities are as follows:

Accounts receivable	$ 82,000
Inventory (sold during 2011).	38,000
Land.	150,000
Buildings (20-year life)	280,000
Equipment (5-year life).	100,000
Current liabilities	90,000
Bonds payable (5-year life)	96,000

Any remaining excess is attributed to goodwill.

Problem 3-14 *(LO 2, 5)* **100%, equity method worksheet, several adjustments, third year, bargain.** Refer to the preceding information for Paulcraft's acquisition of Switzer's common stock. Assume that Paulcraft pays $420,000 for 100% of Switzer common stock. Paulcraft uses the simple equity method to account for its investment in Switzer. Paulcraft and Switzer have the following trial balances on December 31, 2013:

	Paulcraft	Switzer
Cash	160,000	110,000
Accounts Receivable	90,000	55,000
Inventory	120,000	86,000
Land.	100,000	60,000
Investment in Switzer	515,000	
Buildings	800,000	250,000
Accumulated Depreciation	(220,000)	(80,000)
Equipment	150,000	100,000
Accumulated Depreciation	(90,000)	(72,000)
Current Liabilities.	(60,000)	(102,000)
Bonds Payable.		(100,000)
Common Stock	(100,000)	(10,000)
Paid-In Capital in Excess of Par	(900,000)	(90,000)
Retained Earnings, January 1, 2013.	(385,000)	(182,000)

	Paulcraft	Switzer
Sales	(800,000)	(350,000)
Cost of Goods Sold	450,000	210,000
Depreciation Expense—Buildings	30,000	15,000
Depreciation Expense—Equipment	15,000	14,000
Other Expenses	140,000	68,000
Interest Expense		8,000
Subsidiary Income	(35,000)	
Dividends Declared	20,000	10,000
Totals	0	0

1. Prepare a value analysis and a determination and distribution of excess schedule for the investment in Switzer. ◄ ◄ ◄ ◄ ◄ **Required**
2. Complete a consolidated worksheet for Paulcraft Corporation and its subsidiary Switzer Corporation as of December 31, 2013. Prepare supporting amortization and income distribution schedules.

Problem 3-15 *(LO 3, 5)* **100%, cost method worksheet, several adjustments, third year.** Refer to the preceding information for Paulcraft's acquisition of Switzer's common stock. Assume that Paulcraft pays $480,000 for 100% of Switzer common stock. Paulcraft uses the cost method to account for its investment in Switzer. Paulcraft and Switzer have the following trial balances on December 31, 2013 are as follows:

	Paulcraft	Switzer
Cash	100,000	110,000
Accounts Receivable	90,000	55,000
Inventory	120,000	86,000
Land	100,000	60,000
Investment in Switzer	480,000	
Buildings	800,000	250,000
Accumulated Depreciation	(220,000)	(80,000)
Equipment	150,000	100,000
Accumulated Depreciation	(90,000)	(72,000)
Current Liabilities	(60,000)	(102,000)
Bonds Payable		(100,000)
Common Stock	(100,000)	(10,000)
Paid-In Capital in Excess of Par	(900,000)	(90,000)
Retained Earnings, January 1, 2013	(315,000)	(182,000)
Sales	(800,000)	(350,000)
Cost of Goods Sold	450,000	210,000
Depreciation Expense—Buildings	30,000	15,000
Depreciation Expense—Equipment	15,000	14,000
Other Expenses	140,000	68,000
Interest Expense		8,000
Dividend Income	(10,000)	
Dividends Declared	20,000	10,000
Totals	0	0

1. Prepare a value analysis and a determination and distribution of excess schedule for the investment in Switzer. ◄ ◄ ◄ ◄ ◄ **Required**
2. Complete a consolidated worksheet for Paulcraft Corporation and its subsidiary Switzer Corporation as of December 31, 2013. Prepare supporting amortization and income distribution schedules.

Problem 3-16 *(LO 3, 5)* **80%, equity method worksheet, several adjustments, third year.** Refer to the preceding common information for Paulcraft's acquisition of Switzer's common stock. Assume that Paulcraft pays $440,000 for 80% of Switzer common stock. Paulcraft uses the simple equity method to account for its investment in Switzer. Paulcraft and Switzer have the following trial balances on December 31, 2013:

	Paulcraft	Switzer
Cash	138,000	110,000
Accounts Receivable	90,000	55,000
Inventory	120,000	86,000
Land	100,000	60,000
Investment in Switzer	516,000	
Buildings	800,000	250,000
Accumulated Depreciation	(220,000)	(80,000)
Equipment	150,000	100,000
Accumulated Depreciation	(90,000)	(72,000)
Current Liabilities	(60,000)	(102,000)
Bonds Payable		(100,000)
Common Stock	(100,000)	(10,000)
Paid-In Capital in Excess of Par	(900,000)	(90,000)
Retained Earnings, January 1, 2013	(371,000)	(182,000)
Sales	(800,000)	(350,000)
Cost of Goods Sold	450,000	210,000
Depreciation Expense—Buildings	30,000	15,000
Depreciation Expense—Equipment	15,000	14,000
Other Expenses	140,000	68,000
Interest Expense		8,000
Subsidiary Income	(28,000)	
Dividends Declared	20,000	10,000
Totals	0	0

Required ▶ ▶ ▶ ▶ ▶

1. Prepare a value analysis and a determination and distribution of excess schedule for the investment in Switzer.
2. Complete a consolidated worksheet for Paulcraft Corporation and its subsidiary Switzer Corporation as of December 31, 2013. Prepare supporting amortization and income distribution schedules.

Problem 3-17 *(LO 3, 5)* **80%, cost method worksheet, several adjustments, first year.** Refer to the preceding information for Paulcraft's acquisition of Switzer's common stock. Assume that Paulcraft pays $400,000 for 80% of Switzer common stock. Paulcraft uses the cost method to account for its investment in Switzer. Paulcraft and Switzer have the following trial balances on December 31, 2011:

	Paulcraft	Switzer
Cash	178,000	81,000
Accounts Receivable	80,000	35,000
Inventory	90,000	52,000
Land	100,000	60,000
Investment in Switzer	400,000	
Buildings	800,000	200,000
Accumulated Depreciation	(200,000)	(60,000)
Equipment	150,000	100,000
Accumulated Depreciation	(75,000)	(44,000)
Current Liabilities	(50,000)	(88,000)

	Paulcraft	Switzer
Bonds Payable...		(100,000)
Common Stock	(100,000)	(10,000)
Paid-In Capital in Excess of Par	(900,000)	(90,000)
Retained Earnings, January 1, 2011.....................	(300,000)	(112,000)
Sales	(750,000)	(300,000)
Cost of Goods Sold	400,000	180,000
Depreciation Expense—Buildings.......................	30,000	10,000
Depreciation Expense—Equipment......................	15,000	14,000
Other Expenses	120,000	54,000
Interest Expense.......................................		8,000
Dividend Income	(8,000)	
Dividends Declared....................................	20,000	10,000
Totals	0	0

1. Prepare a value analysis and a determination and distribution of excess schedule for the investment in Switzer.   ◄ ◄ ◄ ◄ ◄ **Required**
2. Complete a consolidated worksheet for Paulcraft Corporation and its subsidiary Switzer Corporation as of December 31, 2011. Prepare supporting amortization and income distribution schedules.

Problem 3-18 *(LO 3, 5)* **70%, cost method worksheet, several adjustments, third year.** Refer to the preceding information for Paulcraft's acquisition of Switzer's common stock. Assume that Paulcraft pays $420,000 for 70% of Switzer common stock. Paulcraft uses the cost method to account for its investment in Switzer. Paulcraft and Switzer have the following trial balances on December 31, 2013:

	Paulcraft	Switzer
Cash	157,000	110,000
Accounts Receivable	90,000	55,000
Inventory	120,000	86,000
Land...	100,000	60,000
Investment in Switzer	420,000	
Buildings	800,000	250,000
Accumulated Depreciation	(220,000)	(80,000)
Equipment	150,000	100,000
Accumulated Depreciation	(90,000)	(72,000)
Current Liabilities.....................................	(60,000)	(102,000)
Bonds Payable...		(100,000)
Common Stock	(100,000)	(10,000)
Paid-In Capital in Excess of Par	(900,000)	(90,000)
Retained Earnings, January 1, 2013.....................	(315,000)	(182,000)
Sales	(800,000)	(350,000)
Cost of Goods Sold	450,000	210,000
Depreciation Expense—Buildings.......................	30,000	15,000
Depreciation Expense—Equipment......................	15,000	14,000
Other Expenses	140,000	68,000
Interest Expense.......................................		8,000
Dividend Income	(7,000)	
Dividends Declared....................................	20,000	10,000
Totals	0	0

1. Prepare a value analysis and a determination and distribution of excess schedule for the investment in Switzer.   ◄ ◄ ◄ ◄ ◄ **Required**
2. Complete a consolidated worksheet for Paulcraft Corporation and its subsidiary Switzer Corporation as of December 31, 2013. Prepare supporting amortization and income distribution schedules.

APPENDIX PROBLEMS

Problem 3A-1 *(LO 2, 8)* **Simple equity method adjustments, vertical consolidated worksheet.** (Same as Problem 3-2 except vertical format worksheet is used.) On January 1, 2011, Peres Company purchases 80% of the common stock of Soap Company for $308,000. On this date, Soap has common stock, other paid-in capital in excess of par, and retained earnings of $50,000, $100,000, and $150,000, respectively. Net income and dividends for two years for Soap Company are as follows:

	2011	2012
Net income	$60,000	$90,000
Dividends......................	20,000	30,000

On January 1, 2011, the only undervalued tangible assets of Soap are inventory and the building. Inventory, for which FIFO is used, is worth $10,000 more than cost. The inventory is sold in 2011. The building, which is worth $25,000 more than book value, has a remaining life of 10 years, and straight-line depreciation is used. The remaining excess of cost over book value is attributable to goodwill.

Required ▶ ▶ ▶ ▶ ▶

1. Using this information or the information in the following statements for the year ended December 31, 2012, prepare a determination and distribution of excess schedule.
2. Complete the vertical worksheet for consolidated financial statements for 2012.

Statement—Accounts	Peres Company	Soap Company
Income Statement:		
Net Sales	(520,000)	(450,000)
Cost of Goods Sold	300,000	260,000
Operating Expenses	120,000	100,000
Subsidiary Income................................	(72,000)	
Noncontrolling Interest in Income		
Net Income......................................	(172,000)	(90,000)
Retained Earnings Statement:		
Balance, January 1, 2012—Peres Company	(214,000)	
Balance, January 1, 2012—Soap Company		(190,000)
Net Income (from above).............................	(172,000)	(90,000)
Dividends Declared—Peres Company	50,000	
Dividends Declared—Soap Company		30,000
Balance, December 31, 2012.........................	(336,000)	(250,000)
Consolidated Balance Sheet:		
Inventory, December 31, 2012.........................	100,000	50,000
Other Current Assets	148,000	180,000
Investment in Soap Company	388,000	
Land...	50,000	50,000
Building and Equipment.............................	350,000	320,000
Accumulated Depreciation	(100,000)	(60,000)
Goodwill		
Other Intangibles..................................	20,000	
Current Liabilities..................................	(120,000)	(40,000)
Bonds Payable....................................		(100,000)
Other Long-Term Liabilities..........................	(200,000)	

Statement—Accounts	Peres Company	Soap Company
Common Stock—Peres Company	(200,000)	
Other Paid-In Capital in Excess of Par—Peres Company.........	(100,000)	
Common Stock—Soap Company		(50,000)
Other Paid-In Capital in Excess of Par—Soap Company.........		(100,000)
Retained Earnings, December 31, 2012 (from above)	(336,000)	(250,000)
Totals	0	0

Problem 3A-2 *(LO 2, 6, 8)* **Equity method, later period, vertical worksheet, several excess adjustments.** Baker Enterprises purchases an 80% interest in Kohlenberg International for $850,000 on January 1, 2015. The estimated fair value of the NCI is $190,000. On the purchase date, Kohlenberg International has the following stockholders' equity:

Common stock ($10 par).....................	$150,000
Paid-in capital in excess of par	200,000
Retained earnings	400,000
	$750,000

Also on the purchase date, it is determined that Kohlenberg International's assets are understated as follows:

Equipment, 10-year remaining life	$80,000
Land.......................................	20,000
Building, 20-year remaining life	60,000

The remaining excess of cost over book value is attributed to goodwill. The following summarized statements of Baker Enterprises and Kohlenberg International are for the year ended December 31, 2017:

	Baker Enterprises	Kohlenberg International
Income Statements:		
Sales	(650,000)	(320,000)
Cost of Goods Sold	260,000	240,000
Operating Expenses	170,000	70,000
Depreciation Expense	65,000	30,000
Subsidiary (Income)/Loss	16,000	
Net (Income)/Loss	(139,000)	20,000
Retained Earnings:		
Retained Earnings, January 1, 2017—Baker	(625,000)	
Retained Earnings, January 1, 2017—Kohlenberg		(460,000)
Net (Income)/Loss	(139,000)	20,000
Dividends Declared		10,000
Retained Earnings, December 31, 2017..........	(764,000)	(430,000)
Balance Sheets:		
Cash	288,000	170,000
Inventory	135,000	400,000

(continued)

	Baker Enterprises	Kohlenberg International
Land.	145,000	150,000
Building	900,000	500,000
Accumulated Depreciation—Building	(345,000)	(360,000)
Equipment	350,000	250,000
Accumulated Depreciation—Equipment	(135,000)	(90,000)
Investment in Kohlenberg International	874,000	
Liabilities	(248,000)	(40,000)
Bonds Payable.		(200,000)
Common Stock—Baker	(1,200,000)	
Common Stock—Kohlenberg		(150,000)
Paid-In Capital in Excess of Par		(200,000)
Retained Earnings, December 31, 2017.	(764,000)	(430,000)
Balance	0	0

Required ▶ ▶ ▶ ▶ ▶   Using the vertical format, prepare a consolidated worksheet for December 31, 2017. Precede the worksheet with a value analysis and a determination and distribution of excess schedule. Include income distribution schedules to allocate the consolidated net income to the noncontrolling and controlling interests.

Suggestion: Remember that all adjustments to retained earnings are to beginning retained earnings, and it is the beginning balance of the subsidiary retained earnings account that is subject to elimination. Carefully follow the "carrydown" procedure to calculate the ending retained earnings balances.

Problem 3A-3 *(LO 5, 8)* **Cost method, later period, vertical worksheets.** Harvard Company purchases a 90% interest in Bart Company for $720,000 on January 1, 2011. The investment is accounted for under the cost method. At the time of the purchase, a building owned by Bart is understated by $180,000; it has a 20-year remaining life on the purchase date. The remaining excess is attributed to goodwill. The stockholders' equity of Bart Company on the purchase date is as follows:

Common stock ($10 par).	$350,000
Retained earnings	200,000
Total equity	$550,000

The following summarized statements are for the year ended December 31, 2012. (Credit balance amounts are in parentheses.)

	Harvard	Bart
Income Statements:		
Sales	(580,000)	(280,000)
Cost of Goods Sold	285,000	155,000
Operating Expenses	140,000	55,000
Depreciation Expense	72,000	30,000
Dividend Income	(9,000)	
Net Income.	(92,000)	(40,000)
Retained Earnings Statements:		
Retained Earnings, January 1, 2012—Harvard	(484,000)	
Retained Earnings, January 1, 2012—Bart.		(320,000)
Net Income	(92,000)	(40,000)
Dividends Declared	20,000	10,000
Retained Earnings, December 31, 2012.	(556,000)	(350,000)

	Harvard	Bart
Balance Sheets:		
Cash	330,000	170,000
Inventory	260,000	340,000
Land	99,000	150,000
Building	800,000	500,000
Accumulated Depreciation—Building	(380,000)	(360,000)
Equipment	340,000	250,000
Accumulated Depreciation—Equipment	(190,000)	(90,000)
Investment in Bart Company	720,000	
Current Liabilities	(123,000)	(60,000)
Bonds Payable		(200,000)
Common Stock—Harvard	(800,000)	
Paid-In Capital in Excess of Par—Harvard	(500,000)	
Common Stock—Bart		(350,000)
Retained Earnings, December 31, 2012	(556,000)	(350,000)
Balance	0	0

Using the vertical format, prepare a consolidated worksheet for December 31, 2012. Precede **◄ ◄ ◄ ◄ ◄ Required** the worksheet with a value analysis and a determination and distribution of excess schedule. Include income distribution schedules to allocate the consolidated net income to the noncontrolling and controlling interests.

Suggestion: Remember that all adjustments to retained earnings are to beginning retained earnings, and it is the beginning balance of the subsidiary retained earnings account that is subject to elimination. One of the adjustments to the parent retained earnings account is the cost-to-equity conversion entry. Be sure to follow the carrydown procedure to calculate the ending retained earnings balances.

Problem 3B-1 *(LO 9)* **D&D only, nontaxable exchange, tax loss carryover.** On December 31, 2015, Bryant Company exchanges 10,000 of its $10 par value shares for a 90% interest in Jones Company. The purchase is recorded at the $72 per-share fair value of Bryant shares. Jones Company has the following balance sheet on the date of the purchase:

Assets		Liabilities and Equity	
Cash	$ 100,000	Current liabilities	$ 130,000
Accounts receivable	200,000	Deferred rental income	120,000
Inventory	150,000	Bonds payable	250,000
Investment in marketable		Common stock ($10 par)	100,000
securities	150,000		
Depreciable fixed assets	400,000	Paid-in capital in excess of par	150,000
		Retained earnings	250,000
Total assets	$1,000,000	Total liabilities and equity	$1,000,000

It is determined that the following fair values differ from book values for the assets of Jones Company:

Inventory	$200,000
Depreciable fixed assets (net)	500,000 (20-year life)
Investment in marketable securities	170,000

The purchase is a tax-free exchange to the seller, which means Bryant Company will use the book value of Jones's assets for tax purposes. Jones Company has $200,000 of tax loss carry-overs. Bryant will be able to utilize $40,000 of the losses to offset taxes to be paid in 2016. The balance of the tax loss carryover will not be used within a year but is considered fully realizable in the future. The tax rate for both firms is 30%.

Required ▶ ▶ ▶ ▶ ▶   Record the investment and prepare a value analysis schedule and a determination and distribution of excess schedule.

Suggestion: Asset adjustments should be accompanied by the appropriate deferred tax liability.

Problem 3B-2 *(LO 2, 9)* **Worksheet for nontaxable exchange.** On December 31, 2016, immediately after Todd Company's acquisition of 80% of Keller Company, their balance sheets are as follows:

	Todd	Keller
Cash	$ 1,200,000	$ 50,000
Accounts receivable	2,400,000	300,000
Inventory	11,200,000	1,500,000
Prepayments	422,000	47,000
Depreciable fixed assets	18,978,000	2,100,000
Investment in Keller Company	2,240,000	
Total assets.........................	$36,440,000	$3,997,000
Payables	$ 7,200,000	$1,750,000
Accruals.............................	1,615,000	400,000
Common stock ($100 par)	1,000,000	1,000,000
Paid-in capital in excess of par	8,900,000	
Retained earnings	17,725,000	847,000
Total liabilities and equity	$36,440,000	$3,997,000

An appraisal on December 31, 2016, which is considered carefully and approved by the boards of directors of both companies, places a total replacement value, less depreciation, of $2,800,000 on Keller's depreciable fixed assets. The remaining depreciable life is 20 years.

Todd Company offers to purchase all the assets of Keller Company, subject to its liabilities, as of December 31, 2016, for $2,500,000. Some of the stockholders of Keller Company object to the price because it does not include enough consideration for goodwill. 20% of the share-holders elect not to sell their shares. A counterproposal is made to 80% of the shareholders and an agreement is reached. In exchange for its own shares, Todd acquires 8,000 shares of the com-mon stock of Keller at the agreed-upon $280 per share. The price includes a control premium. The shares held by the NCI are estimated to have a fair value of $250 each. The purchase is structured as a tax-free exchange to the seller; thus, Todd will use the book value of the assets for future tax purposes. The tax rate for both companies is 30%.

Required ▶ ▶ ▶ ▶ ▶   Prepare a consolidated worksheet and a consolidated balance sheet as of December 31, 2016. Include a value analysis and a determination and distribution schedule.

(AICPA adapted)

Problem 3B-3 *(LO 2, 9)* **Worksheet for nontaxable exchange with tax loss carry-over.** The trial balances of Campton Corporation and Dorn Corporation as of December 31, 2011, are as shown on page 199.

	Campton Corporation	Dorn Corporation
Current Assets	150,000	100,000
Land.	400,000	100,000
Building and Equipment (net).	900,000	240,000
Investment in Dorn Corporation.	642,600	
Current Tax Liability.	(3,000)	(12,000)
Other Current Liabilities.	(130,000)	(100,000)
Common Stock ($5 par)	(500,000)	
Common Stock ($50 par)		(200,000)
Paid-In Capital in Excess of Par	(750,000)	
Retained Earnings, January 1, 2011.	(650,000)	(100,000)
Sales	(309,000)	(170,000)
Subsidiary Income.	(12,600)	
Cost of Goods Sold	170,000	80,000
Expenses	89,000	50,000
Provision for Tax	3,000*	12,000
Totals	0	0

*$15,000 tax liability ($50,000 income × 30%) – $12,000 tax loss carryover ($40,000 × 30%)

On January 1, 2011, Campton purchases 90% of the outstanding stock of Dorn Corporation for $630,000. The acquisition is a tax-free exchange for the seller. At the purchase date, Dorn's equipment is undervalued by $100,000 and has a remaining life of 10 years. All other assets have book values that approximate their fair values. Dorn Corporation has a tax loss carryover of $200,000, of which $50,000 is utilizable in 2011 and the balance in future periods. The tax loss carryover is expected to be fully utilized. Any remaining excess is considered to be goodwill. A tax rate of 30% applies to both companies.

1. Prepare a value analysis and a determination and distribution of excess schedule for the investment. ◄ ◄ ◄ ◄ ◄ **Required**
2. Prepare the 2011 consolidated worksheet. Include columns for the eliminations and adjustments, the consolidated income statement, the NCI, the controlling retained earnings, and the consolidated balance sheet. Prepare supporting income distribution schedules as well.
3. Prepare the 2011 consolidated statements, including the income statement, retained earnings statement, and balance sheet.

Suggestion: A deferred tax liability results from the increase in the fair value of the equipment. As the added depreciation is recognized on the equipment, the deferred tax liability becomes payable. Note that income distribution schedules record net-of-tax income. Therefore, be sure that any adjustments to the income distribution schedules consider tax where appropriate.

Intercompany Transactions: Merchandise, Plant Assets, and Notes

Learning Objectives

When you have completed this chapter, you should be able to

1. Explain why transactions between members of a consolidated firm should not be reflected in the consolidated financial statements.

2. Defer intercompany profits on merchandise sales when appropriate and eliminate the double counting of sales between affiliates.

3. Defer profits on intercompany sales of long-term assets and realize the profits over the period of use and/or at the time of sale to a firm outside the consolidated group.

4. Demonstrate an understanding of the profit deferral issues for intercompany sales of assets under long-term construction contracts.

5. Eliminate intercompany loans and notes.

6. Discuss the complications intercompany profits create for the use of the sophisticated equity method.

7. Apply intercompany profit eliminations on a vertical worksheet. (Appendix)

The elimination of the parent's investment in a subsidiary is only the start of the procedures that are necessary to consolidate a parent and a subsidiary. It is common for affiliated companies to transact business with one another. The more integrated the affiliates are with respect to operations, the more common intercompany transactions become. This chapter considers the most often encountered types of intercompany transactions. These include intercompany sales of merchandise and fixed assets as well as loans between members of the consolidated group.

Transactions between the separate legal and accounting entities must be recorded on each affiliate's books. The consolidation process starts with the assumption that these transactions are recorded properly on the separate books of the parent and the subsidiary. However, consolidated statements are those that portray the parent and its subsidiary as a single economic entity. There should not be any intercompany transactions found in these consolidated statements. Only the effect of those transactions between the consolidated company and the companies outside the consolidated company should appear in the consolidated statements. Intercompany transactions must be eliminated as part of the consolidation process. For each type of intercompany transaction, sound reasoning will be developed to support the worksheet procedures. The guiding principle shall come from answering this question: **From the standpoint of a single consolidated company, what accounts and amounts should remain in the financial statements?**

The worksheet eliminations for intercompany transactions are the same no matter what method is used by the parent to maintain its investment in the subsidiary account. The examples in this chapter assume the use of the simple equity method. This is done because any investment that is maintained under the cost method is converted to the simple equity method on the consolidation worksheet. The impact of intercompany transactions on the investment account under the sophisticated equity method is considered later in this chapter. Note, however, that even where the sophisticated equity method is used, there is no change in the procedures for the individual intercompany transactions.

INTERCOMPANY MERCHANDISE SALES

1

OBJECTIVE

Explain why transactions between members of a consolidated firm should not be reflected in the consolidated financial statements.

It is common to find that the goods sold by one member of an affiliated group have been purchased from another member of the group. One company may produce component parts that are assembled by its affiliate that sells the final product. In other cases, the product may be produced entirely by one member company and sold on a wholesale basis to another member company that is responsible for selling and servicing the product to the final users. Merchandise sales represent the most common type of intercompany transaction and must be understood as a basic feature of consolidated reporting.

Sales between affiliated companies will be recorded in the normal manner on the books of the separate companies. Remember that each company is a separate legal entity maintaining its own accounting records. Thus, sales to and purchases from an affiliated company are recorded as if they were transactions made with a company outside the consolidated group, and the separate financial statements of the affiliated companies will include these purchase and sale transactions. However, when the statements of the affiliates are consolidated, such sales become transfers of goods within the consolidated entity. Since these sales do not involve parties outside the consolidated group, they cannot be acknowledged in consolidated statements.

Following are the procedures for consolidating affiliated companies engaged in intercompany merchandise sales:

1. The intercompany sale must be eliminated to avoid double counting. To understand this requirement, assume that Company P sells merchandise costing $1,000 to a subsidiary Company S, for $1,200. Company S, in turn, sells the merchandise to an outside party for $1,500. If no elimination is made, the consolidated income statement would show the following with respect to the two transactions:

Sales	$2,700	($1,500 outside sale + $1,200 sale to Company S)
Less cost of goods sold.	2,200	($1,000 cost to Company P + $1,200 purchase by Company S)
Gross profit	$ 500	(18.5% gross profit rate)

While the gross profit is correct, sales and the cost of goods sold are inflated because they are included twice. As a result, the gross profit percentage is understated, since the $500 gross profit appears to relate to $2,700 of sales rather than to the outside sale of $1,500. The intercompany sale must be eliminated from the consolidated statements. All that should remain on the consolidated income statement with respect to the two transactions is as follows:

Sales	$1,500	(only the final sale to the outside party)
Less cost of goods sold.	1,000	(only the purchase from the outside party)
Gross profit	$ 500	(33.3% gross profit rate)

When the goods sold between the affiliated companies are manufactured by the selling affiliate, the consolidated cost of goods sold includes only those costs that can be inventoried, such as labor, materials, and overhead, and may not include any profit.

The intercompany sale, though eliminated, does have an effect on the distribution of consolidated net income to the controlling interest and NCI. This is true because the reported net income of the subsidiary reflects the intercompany sales price, and the subsidiary's separate income statement becomes the base from which the noncontrolling share of income is calculated. In effect, the intercompany transfer price becomes an agreement as to how a portion of consolidated net income will be divided. For example, if Company S is an 80%-owned subsidiary, the NCI will receive 20% of the $300 ($1,500 − $1,200) profit made on the final sale by Company S, or $60. If the intercompany transfer price is increased from $1,200 to $1,300 and the final sales price remains at $1,500, Company S would earn only $200, and the NCI would receive 20% of $200, or $40.

2. Often, intercompany sales will be made on credit. Thus, intercompany trade balances will appear in the separate accounts of the affiliated companies. From a consolidated viewpoint, intercompany receivables and payables represent internal agreements to transfer funds. As such, **this internal debt should not appear on consolidated statements and must be eliminated.** Only debt transactions with entities *outside* the consolidated group should appear on the consolidated balance sheet.

3. **No profit on intercompany sales may be recognized until the profit is realized by a sale to an *outside* party.** This means that any profit contained in the ending inventory of intercompany goods must be eliminated and its recognition deferred until the period in which the goods are sold to outsiders. In the first example above, assume that the sale by Company P to Company S was made on December 30, 2011, and that Company S did not sell the goods until March 2012. From a consolidated viewpoint, there can be no profit recognized until the outside sale occurs in March of 2012. At that time, consolidation theory will acknowledge a $500 profit, of which $200 will be distributed to Company P and $300 will be distributed to Company S as part of the 2012 consolidated net income. However, until that time, the $200 profit on the intercompany sale recorded by Company P must be deferred. In addition, not only must the $1,200 intercompany sale be eliminated, but the inventory on December 31, 2011, must be reduced by $200 (the amount of the intercompany profit) to its $1,000 cost to the consolidated companies.

Care must be taken in calculating the profit applicable to intercompany inventory. It is most convenient when the gross profit rate is provided so that it can be multiplied by the inventory value to arrive at the intercompany profit. In some instances, however, the profit on sales may be stated as a percentage of cost. For example, one might be told that the cost of units is "marked up" 25% to arrive at the intercompany sales price. If the inventory sales price is $1,000, it cannot be multiplied by 25% to calculate the intercompany profit because the 25% applies to the *cost* and not the sales price at which the inventory is stated. Instead, the gross profit rate, which is a percentage of sales price, should be calculated. The easiest method of accomplishing this is to pick the theoretical cost of $1 and mark it up by 25% (the given percentage of cost) to $1.25 and ask: "What is the gross profit percentage?" In this example, it is $0.25 ÷ $1.25, or 20%. From this point, the $1,000 inventory value can be multiplied by 20% to arrive at the intercompany profit of $200.

The worksheet procedures to eliminate the effects of intercompany inventory sales are discussed in the next four sections as follows:

1. There are no intercompany goods in the beginning or ending inventories.
2. Intercompany goods remain in the ending inventory.
3. There are intercompany goods in the ending inventory, and there were intercompany goods in the beginning inventory. This is the most common situation.
4. Instead of the perpetual inventory method assumed in sections 1-3 above, the companies use the periodic inventory method. There are intercompany goods in the ending inventory, and there were intercompany goods in the beginning inventory.

No Intercompany Goods in Purchasing Company's Inventories

In the simplest case, which is illustrated in Worksheet 4-1, pages 224 and 225, all goods sold between the affiliates have been sold, in turn, to outside parties by the end of the accounting period. Worksheet 4-1 is based on the following assumptions:

Worksheet 4-1: page 224

1. Company S is an 80%-owned subsidiary of Company P. On January 1, 2011, Company P purchased its interest in Company S at a price equal to its pro rata share of Company S's book value. Company P uses the equity method to record the investment.

2. Companies P and S had the following separate income statements for 2011:

	Company P	Company S
Sales	$700,000	$500,000
Less cost of goods sold	510,000	350,000
Gross profit	$190,000	$150,000
Other expenses	(90,000)	(75,000)
Subsidiary income	60,000	
Net income	$160,000	$ 75,000

Note that under the equity method, Company P's income includes 80% of the reported income of Company S.

3. During the year, Company S sold goods that cost $80,000 to Company P for $100,000 (a 20% gross profit). Company P then sold all of the goods purchased from Company S to outside parties for $150,000. Company P had not paid $25,000 of the invoices received from Company S for the goods. (Note that it is assumed in this and Worksheets 4-2 and 4-3 that a **perpetual** inventory system is used.) Consider the journal entries made by each affiliate:

Company S

Accounts Receivable (from Company P)	100,000	
Sales (to Company P)		100,000
Cost of Goods Sold (to Company P)	80,000	
Inventory		80,000
Cash	75,000	
Accounts Receivable (from Company P)		75,000

Company P

Inventory	100,000	
Accounts Payable (to Company S)		100,000
Accounts Receivable (from outside parties)	150,000	
Sales (to outside parties)		150,000
Cost of Goods Sold (to outside parties)	100,000	
Inventory		100,000
Accounts Payable (to Company S)	75,000	
Cash		75,000

The elimination entries for Worksheet 4-1 in journal entry form are as follows:

(CY1)	Eliminate current-year equity income:		
	Subsidiary Income	60,000	
	Investment in Company S		60,000
(EL)	Eliminate 80% of subsidiary equity against investment in subsidiary account:		
	Common Stock ($10 par)—Company S	80,000	
	Retained Earnings, January 1, 2011—Company S	56,000	
	Investment in Company S		136,000
(IS)	Eliminate intercompany merchandise sales:		
	Sales	100,000	
	Cost of Goods Sold		100,000

(IA)   Eliminate intercompany unpaid trade balances at year-end:

Accounts Payable	25,000	
Accounts Receivable		25,000

Entry (IS) is a simplified summary entry that can be further analyzed with the following entry:

Sales (to Company P)	100,000	
Cost of Goods Sold (by Company S to Company P— the intercompany sale)		80,000
Cost of Goods Sold (by Company P to outside parties— the profit recorded by Company S)		20,000

The preceding expanded entry removes the cost of goods sold with respect to the intercompany sale and removes the intercompany profit from the sales made by the parent to outside parties. Note that the parent recorded the cost of the goods sold to outside parties at $100,000, which contains $20,000 of Company S's profit. As shown in the expanded (IS) entry above, the true cost of the goods to the consolidated company is $80,000 ($100,000 less the 20% internal gross profit).

Entry (IA) eliminates the intercompany receivables/payables still remaining unpaid at the end of the year. Income distribution schedules are used in Worksheet 4-1 to distribute the $175,000 of consolidated net income to the noncontrolling and controlling interests. It should be noted that all of the above procedures remain unchanged if the parent is the seller of the intercompany goods.

Intercompany Goods in Purchasing Company's Ending Inventory

Let us now change the example in Worksheet 4-1 to assume that Company P did not resell $40,000 of the total of $100,000 of goods it purchased from Company S. This means that $40,000 of goods purchased from Company S remain in Company P's ending inventory. As shown below, Company S (the intercompany seller) will have the same entries as presented on page 204, and Company P will have the following revised entries:

2

OBJECTIVE

Defer intercompany profits on merchandise sales when appropriate and eliminate the double counting of sales between affiliates.

Company S

Accounts Receivable (from Company P)	100,000	
Sales (to Company P)		100,000
Cost of Goods Sold (to Company P)	80,000	
Inventory		80,000
Cash	75,000	
Accounts Receivable (from Company P)		75,000

Company P

Inventory	100,000	
Accounts Payable (to Company S)		100,000
Accounts Receivable (from outside parties)	90,000	
Sales (to outside parties)		90,000
Cost of Goods Sold (to outside parties)	60,000	
Inventory		60,000
Accounts Payable (to Company S)	75,000	
Cash		75,000

Let us now consider what has happened to the $100,000 of goods sold to Company P by Company S, shown on page 206.

$80,000 is the original cost of the goods sold by Company S that should be removed from the consolidated cost of goods sold since it is derived from the intercompany sale and not the outside sale.

$12,000 is the intercompany profit included in the goods sold by Company P to outside parties. The cost of these sales should be reduced by $12,000 (20% × $60,000) to arrive at the true cost of the goods to the consolidated company.

$8,000 is the intercompany profit remaining in the Company P ending inventory. This inventory, now at $40,000, should be reduced by $8,000 (20% × $40,000) to $32,000. Another way to view this is that 60% of the original intercompany goods (60% × $100,000 = $60,000) has been sold to outside parties. Thus, only the profit on these sales (20% × $60,000 = $12,000) has been realized.

If we follow the above analysis to the letter, we would make the following elimination in entry form:

Sales (by Company S to Company P)	100,000	
Cost of Goods Sold (by Company S)		80,000
Cost of Goods Sold (by Company P)		12,000
Inventory, December 31, 2011 (held by Company P)		8,000

Worksheet 4-2: page 226

In practice, this entry is cumbersome in that it requires an analysis of the destiny of all intercompany sales. The approach used in Worksheet 4-2, pages 226 and 227, is simplified first to eliminate the intercompany sales under the assumption that all goods have been resold, and then to adjust for those goods still remaining in the inventory. This method simplifies worksheet procedures, including the distribution of combined net income. In journal form, the simplified entries are:

(CY1)	Eliminate current-year equity income:		
	Subsidiary Income	60,000	
	Investment in Company S		60,000
(EL)	Eliminate 80% of subsidiary equity against investment in subsidiary account:		
	Common Stock ($10 par)—Company S	80,000	
	Retained Earnings, January 1, 2011—Company S	56,000	
	Investment in Company S		136,000
(IS)	Eliminate intercompany merchandise sales:		
	Sales	100,000	
	Cost of Goods Sold		100,000
(EI)	Eliminate intercompany profit in ending inventory:		
	Cost of Goods Sold	8,000	
	Inventory, December 31, 2011		8,000
(IA)	Eliminate intercompany unpaid trade balance at year-end:		
	Accounts Payable	25,000	
	Accounts Receivable		25,000

The $8,000 adjustment is viewed as the unrealized intercompany inventory profit that may not be realized until a later period when the goods are sold to outside parties.

The unrealized intercompany profit is subtracted from the *seller's* income distribution schedule. In the income distribution schedules for Worksheet 4-2, the unrealized profit of $8,000 is deducted from the subsidiary's internally generated net income of $75,000. The adjusted net income of $67,000 is apportioned, with $13,400 (20%) distributed to the noncontrolling interest and $53,600 (80%) distributed to the controlling interest.

There is no change in worksheet elimination procedures if the parent is the seller and the subsidiary has intercompany goods in its ending inventory. Only the distribution of combined net income changes. To illustrate, assume the parent, Company P, is the seller of the intercompany goods. The income distribution schedules would be prepared as shown on page 207.

Subsidiary Company S Income Distribution		
	Internally generated net income	$ 75,000
	Adjusted income	$ 75,000
	NCI share	× 20%
	NCI	$ 15,000

Parent Company P Income Distribution		
Unrealized profit in ending **inventory** . . . . **(EI) $8,000**	Internally generated net income	$100,000
	80% × Company S adjusted income of $75,000	60,000
	Controlling interest	$152,000

Intercompany Goods in Purchasing Company's Beginning and Ending Inventories

When intercompany goods are included in the purchaser's beginning inventory, the inventory value includes the profit made by the seller. The intercompany seller of the goods has included in the prior period such sales in its separate income statement as though the transactions were consummated. Thus, the beginning retained earnings balance of the seller also includes the profit on these goods. While this profit is reflected on the separate books of the affiliates, it should not be recognized when a consolidated view is taken. Remember: **Profit must not be recognized on a consolidated statement until it is realized in the subsequent period through the sale of goods to an outside party.** Therefore, in the consolidating process, the beginning inventory of intercompany goods must be reduced to its cost to the consolidated company. Likewise, the retained earnings of the consolidated entity must be reduced by deleting the profit that was recorded in prior periods on intercompany goods contained in the buyer's beginning inventory.

To illustrate, using the example of Company P and Company S from Worksheet 4-3 on pages 228 and 229, assume the two companies have the following individual income data for **2012**:

Worksheet 4-3: page 228

	Company P	Company S
Sales	$ 800,000	$ 600,000
Less cost of goods sold.	610,000	440,000
Gross profit	$ 190,000	$ 160,000
Other expenses	(120,000)	(100,000)
Subsidiary income.	48,000	
Net income	$ 118,000	$ 60,000

Assume the following additional facts:

1. Company P's 2012 beginning inventory includes $40,000 of the goods purchased from Company S in **2011**. The gross profit rate on the internal sale was 20%.
2. Company S sold $120,000 of goods to Company P during **2012**.
3. Company S recorded a 20% gross profit on these sales.
4. At the end of **2012**, Company P still owed $60,000 to Company S for the purchases.
5. Company P also had $30,000 of the intercompany purchases in its **2012** ending inventory.

Worksheet 4-3 contains the **2012** year-end trial balances of Company P and Company S. The elimination entries in journal entry form are as follows:

(CY1)	Eliminate current-year equity income:		
	Subsidiary Income.	48,000	
	Investment in Company S.		48,000

(continued)

(EL)	Eliminate subsidiary equity against investment in subsidiary account:		
	Common Stock ($10 par)—Company S	80,000	
	Retained Earnings, January 1, 2012—Company S	116,000	
	Investment in Company S.		196,000
(BI)	Eliminate intercompany profit in beginning inventory and reduce current-year cost of goods sold:		
	Retained Earnings, January 1, 2012—Company P	6,400	
	Retained Earnings, January 1, 2012—Company S	1,600	
	Cost of Goods Sold		8,000
(IS)	Eliminate intercompany merchandise sales:		
	Sales	120,000	
	Cost of Goods Sold		120,000
(EI)	Eliminate intercompany profit in ending inventory:		
	Cost of Goods Sold	6,000	
	Inventory, December 31, 2012.		6,000
(IA)	Eliminate intercompany unpaid trade balance at year-end:		
	Accounts Payable	60,000	
	Accounts Receivable		60,000

Entry (BI) adjusts for the intercompany profit contained in the beginning inventory. At the start of 2012, Company P included $40,000 of goods purchased from Company S in its beginning inventory. During 2012, the inventory was debited to Cost of Goods Sold at $40,000. The cost of goods sold must now be reduced to cost by removing the $8,000 intercompany profit. The intercompany profit also was included in last year's income by the subsidiary. That income was closed to Retained Earnings. Thus, the beginning retained earnings of Company S are overstated by $8,000. That $8,000 is divided between the noncontrolling and controlling interests in retained earnings. Subsidiary retained earnings have been 80% eliminated, and only the 20% noncontrolling interest remains. The other 80% of beginning retained earnings is included in Company P's retained earnings through the use of the equity method.

Note that once the controlling share of subsidiary retained earnings is eliminated, there is a transformation of what was **subsidiary** retained earnings into what now is **NCI** in retained earnings. Entries (IS), (EI), and (IA) eliminate the intercompany sales, ending inventory, and trade accounts in the same manner as was done in Worksheet 4-2. After all eliminations and adjustments are made, the consolidated net income of $132,000 is distributed as shown in the income distribution schedules. **The adjustments for intercompany inventory profits are reflected in the *selling company's schedule*.**

It might appear that the intercompany goods in the beginning inventory are always assumed to be sold in the current period, since the deferred profit of the previous period is realized during the current period as reflected by the seller's income distribution schedule. That assumption need not be made, however. Even if part of the beginning inventory is unsold at year-end, it still would be a part of the $30,000 ending inventory, on which $6,000 of profit is deferred. Note that the use of the LIFO method for inventories could cause a given period's inventory profit to be deferred indefinitely. Unless otherwise stated, the examples and problems of this text will assume a FIFO flow.

Worksheet 4-3 assumed the intercompany merchandise sales were made by the subsidiary. Procedures would differ as follows if the sales were made by the parent:

1. The beginning inventory profit would be subtracted entirely from the beginning controlling retained earnings since only the parent recorded the profit.
2. The adjustments for the beginning and ending inventory profits would be included in the parent income distribution schedule and not in the subsidiary schedule.

Eliminations for Periodic Inventories

In Worksheets 4-1 through 4-3, the cost of goods sold was included in the trial balances, since both the parent and the subsidiary used a perpetual inventory system. However, in Worksheet 4-4 on pages 230 and 231, a periodic inventory system is used. In this illustration, which is based on the same facts as Worksheet 4-3, the following differences in worksheet procedures result from the use of a periodic inventory system:

Worksheet 4-4: page 230

1. The 2012 beginning inventories of $70,000 and $40,000, rather than the ending inventories, appear as assets in the trial balances. The beginning inventories less the intercompany profit in Company P's beginning inventory are extended to the Consolidated Income Statement column as a debit.

2. The purchases accounts, rather than the cost of goods sold, appear in the trial balances and, after adjustment, are extended to the Consolidated Income Statement column.

3. Entry (BI) credits the January 1 inventory to eliminate the intercompany profit.

4. Entry (IS) credits the purchases account, which is still open under the periodic method, and makes the usual debit to the sales account.

5. The ending inventories of both Company P and Company S are entered in each company's trial balances as both a debit (the ending inventory balance sheet amount) and a credit (the adjustment to the cost of goods sold). These inventories are recorded at the price paid for them, which, for intercompany goods, includes the intercompany sales profit. Entry (EI) removes the $6,000 intercompany profit applicable to the ending inventory. The balance sheet inventory is reduced to $104,000. The $104,000 credit balance is extended to the Consolidated Income Statement column.

The elimination entries in journal entry form are as follows:

(CY1)	Eliminate current-year equity income:		
	Subsidiary Income.	48,000	
	Investment in Company S.		48,000
(EL)	Eliminate subsidiary equity against investment in		
	subsidiary account:		
	Common Stock ($10 par), Company S.	80,000	
	Retained Earnings, January 1, 2012—Company S	116,000	
	Investment in Company S.		196,000
(BI)	Eliminate intercompany profit in beginning inventory and		
	reduce current-year cost of goods sold:		
	Retained Earnings, January 1, 2012—Company P	6,400	
	Retained Earnings, January 1, 2012—Company S	1,600	
	Inventory, January 1, 2012.		8,000
(IS)	Eliminate intercompany merchandise sales:		
	Sales	120,000	
	Purchases.		120,000
(EI)	Eliminate intercompany profit in ending inventory:		
	Cost of Goods Sold	6,000	
	Inventory, December 31, 2012.		6,000
(IA)	Eliminate intercompany unpaid trade balance at year-end:		
	Accounts Payable	60,000	
	Accounts Receivable		60,000

Effect of Lower-of-Cost-or-Market Method on Inventory Profit

Intercompany inventory in the hands of the purchaser may have been written down by the purchaser to a market value below its intercompany transfer cost. Assume that, for $50,000, Company S purchased goods that cost its parent company $40,000. Assume further that Company S has all the goods in its ending inventory but has written them down to $42,000, the lower market value at the end of the period. As a result of this markdown, the inventory needs to be reduced by only another $2,000 to reflect its cost to the consolidated company ($40,000). The only remaining issue is how to defer the $2,000 inventory profit in the income distribution schedules. As before, such profit is deferred by entering it as a debit on the intercompany seller's schedule. In the subsequent period, the profit will be realized by the seller.

It may seem strange that the $8,000 of profit written off is realized, in effect, by the seller, since it is not deducted in the seller's distribution schedule. This procedure is proper, however, since the loss recognized by the buyer is offset. Had the inventory been written down to $40,000 or less, there would be no need to defer the offsetting profit in the consolidated worksheet or in the income distribution schedules.

Losses on Intercompany Sales

Assume a parent sells goods to a subsidiary for $5,000 and the goods cost the parent $6,000. If the market value of the goods is $5,000 or less, the loss may be recognized in the consolidated income statement, even if the goods remain in the subsidiary's ending inventory. Such a loss can be recognized under the lower-of-cost-or-market principle that applies to inventory. However, if the intercompany sales price is below market value, the part of the loss that results from the price being below market value cannot be recognized until the subsidiary sells the goods to an outside party. Elimination procedures would be similar, but opposite in direction, to those used for unrealized gains.

REFLECTION

- Merchandise sales between affiliated companies are eliminated; only the purchase and sale to the "outside world" should remain in the statements.

- The profit must be removed from beginning inventory by reducing cost of goods sold and retained earnings.

- The profit must be removed from ending inventory both by reducing inventory and by increasing cost of goods sold. The deduction of inventory from the goods available for sale is too great prior to this adjustment.

- Unpaid intercompany trade payables/receivables resulting from intercompany merchandise sales are eliminated.

3

OBJECTIVE

Defer profits on intercompany sales of long-term assets and realize the profits over the period of use and/or at the time of sale to a firm outside the consolidated group.

INTERCOMPANY PLANT ASSET SALES

Any plant asset may be sold between members of an affiliated group, and such a sale may result in a gain for the seller. The buyer will record the asset at a price that includes the gain, and when the sale involves a depreciable asset, the buyer will base future depreciation charges on the price paid. While these recordings are proper for the companies as separate entities, they must not be reflected in the consolidated statements. Consolidation theory views the sale as an *internal transfer of assets*. There is no basis for recognizing a gain at the time of the internal transfer. A gain on the sale of a nondepreciable asset cannot be reflected in the consolidated statements until the asset is resold to the outside world. However, the recognition of a gain on the sale of a depreciable asset does not have to wait until resale occurs. Instead, the intercompany gain is amortized over the depreciable life of the asset. The buyer's normal intent is to use the asset, not to resell it. Since the asset is overstated by the amount of the intercompany gain, subsequent depreciation is overstated as well. The consolidation process reduces depreciation in future years so that depreciation charges in the consolidated statements reflect the book value of the asset to the consolidated company on the date of the sale. While the gain is deferred in the year of sale, it is realized later through the increased combined net income resulting from the reduction in depreciation expense in subsequent periods. The decrease in depreciation expense for each and every period is equal to the difference between the depreciation based on the intercompany sales price and the depreciation based on the book value of the asset on the sale date.

Intercompany Sale of a Nondepreciable Asset

One member of an affiliated group may sell land to another affiliate and record a gain. For consolidating purposes, there has been no sale; thus, there is no cause to recognize a gain. Since the asset is not depreciable, the entire gain must be deferred until the land is sold to an outside party. This deferment may become permanent if there is no intent to sell at a later date. For example, assume that in 2011, Company S (80% owned) sells land to its parent company, Company P. The sale price is $30,000, and the original cost of the land to Company S was $20,000. Consolidation theory would rule that, until Company P sells the land to an outside party, recognition of the $10,000 profit must be deferred. Elimination (LA) eliminates the intercompany gain in the year of sale.

	Partial Trial Balance		Eliminations & Adjustments	
	Company P	Company S	Dr.	Cr.
Land	30,000			(LA) 10,000
Gain on Sale of Land		(10,000)	(LA) 10,000	

As usual, the selling company's income distribution schedule would reflect the deferment of the gain.

In subsequent years, assuming the land is not sold by Company P, the gain must be removed from the consolidated retained earnings. Since the sale was made by Company S, which is an 80%-owned subsidiary of Company P, the controlling interest must absorb 80% of the deferment, while the noncontrolling interest must absorb 20%. For example, the adjustments in 2012 would be as follows:

	Partial Trial Balance		Eliminations & Adjustments	
	Company P	Company S	Dr.	Cr.
Land	30,000			(LA) 10,000
Retained Earnings, January 1, 2012—Company P	(100,000)*		(LA) 8,000	
Retained Earnings, January 1, 2012—Company S		(20,000)*	(LA) 2,000	

*Arbitrary balance.

Now, assume Company P sells the land in 2013 to an outside party for $45,000, recording a gain of $15,000. When this sale occurs, the $10,000 intercompany gain also is realized. The following elimination would remove the previously unrealized gain from the consolidated retained earnings and would add it to the gain already recorded by Company P. The retained earnings adjustment is allocated 80% to the controlling interest and 20% to the noncontrolling interest, since the original sale was made by the subsidiary.

	Partial Trial Balance		Eliminations & Adjustments	
	Company P	Company S	Dr.	Cr.
Gain on Sale of Land	(15,000)			(LA) 10,000
Retained Earnings, January 1, 2013—Company P	(120,000)*		(LA) 8,000	
Retained Earnings, January 1, 2013—Company S		(17,000)*	(LA) 2,000	

*Arbitrary balance.

The income distribution schedule would add the $10,000 gain to the 2013 internally generated net income of Company S. At this point, it should be clear that the gain on the intercompany sale was deferred, not eliminated. The original gain of $10,000 eventually is credited to the subsidiary. Thus, the gain does affect the noncontrolling share of consolidated net income at a future date. Any sale of a nondepreciable asset should be viewed as an agreement between the controlling and noncontrolling interests regarding the future distribution of consolidated net income.

When a parent sells a nondepreciable asset to a subsidiary, the worksheet procedures are the same, except for these areas:

1. The deferment of the gain in the year of the intercompany sale and the recognition of the gain in the year of the sale of the asset to an outside party flow through only the parent company income distribution schedule.
2. In the years subsequent to the intercompany sale through the year the land is sold to an external company, the related adjustment is made exclusively through the controlling retained earnings.

Intercompany Sale of a Depreciable Asset

Turning to the case where a depreciable plant asset is sold between affiliates, the following example illustrates the worksheet procedures necessary for the **deferment of a gain on the sale *over the asset's useful life.*** Assume that the parent, Company P, sells a machine to a subsidiary, Company S, for $30,000 on January 1, 2011. Originally, the machine cost $32,000. Accumulated depreciation as of January 1, 2011, is $12,000. Therefore, the book value of the machine is $20,000, and the reported gain on the sale is $10,000. Further assume that Company S (*the buyer*) believes the asset has a 5-year remaining life; thus, it records straight-line depreciation of $6,000 ($30,000 cost ÷ 5 years) annually.

The eliminations defer the gain over the 5-year life of the asset by reducing annual depreciation charges. For consolidated reporting purposes, depreciation is based on the asset's $20,000 book value to the consolidated company. Worksheet 4-5 on pages 232 and 233, is based on the following additional facts:

Worksheet 4-5: page 232

1. Company P owns an 80% investment in Company S. The amount paid for the investment was equal to the book value of Company S's underlying equity. The simple equity method is used by Company P to record its investment.
2. There were no beginning or ending inventories, and the companies had the following separate income statements for 2011:

	Company P	Company S
Sales	$ 200,000	$100,000
Cost of goods sold	(150,000)	(59,000)
Gross profit	$ 50,000	$ 41,000
Depreciation expense	(30,000)	(16,000)
Gain on sale of machine	10,000	
Subsidiary income (80%)	20,000	
Net income	$ 50,000	$ 25,000

The elimination entries in journal entry form are:

(CY1)   Eliminate current-year equity income:

Subsidiary Income   20,000

Investment in Company S   20,000

(EL)   Eliminate subsidiary equity against investment in
subsidiary account:

Common Stock ($10 par)—Company S   40,000

Retained Earnings, January 1, 2011—Company S   60,000

Investment in Company S   100,000

(F1)   Eliminate intercompany gain on machine sale and reduce
machine to cost:

Gain on Sale of Machinery   10,000

Machinery   10,000

(F2)   Reduce machinery depreciation to amount based on book value:

Accumulated Depreciation—Machinery   2,000

Depreciation Expense   2,000

Entry (F1) eliminates the $10,000 intercompany gain and restates the asset at its book value of $20,000 on the date of the intercompany sale.

Entry (F2) reduces the depreciation expense for the year by the difference between depreciation based on:

1. The book value [($32,000 − $12,000 = $20,000 depreciable base) ÷ 5 years = $4,000] and
2. The intercompany sales price ($30,000 depreciable base ÷ 5 years = $6,000).

The allocation of consolidated net income of $47,000 is shown in the income distribution schedules. Note that Company S (the buyer in this example) must absorb depreciation based on the agreed-upon sales price, and it is the controlling interest that realizes the benefit of the reduced depreciation as the asset is used. Also, note that the realizable profit for Company P (the seller) in any year is the depreciation absorbed by the buyer minus the depreciation for consolidated purposes ($6,000 − $4,000). If the sale had been made by Company S, the profit deferment and recognition entries would flow through the Company S income distribution schedule.

Worksheets for periods subsequent to the sale of the machine must correct the current-year nominal accounts and remove the unrealized profit in the beginning consolidated retained earnings. Worksheet 4-6 on pages 234 and 235, portrays a consolidated worksheet for 2012, based on the following separate income statements of Company P and Company S: **Worksheet 4-6**: page 234

	Company P	Company S
Sales	$ 250,000	$120,000
Cost of goods sold	(180,000)	(80,000)
Gross profit	$ 70,000	$ 40,000
Depreciation expense	(20,000)	(16,000)
Subsidiary income (80%)	19,200	
Net income	$ 69,200	$ 24,000

The elimination entries in journal entry form are as follows:

(CY1)   Eliminate current-year equity income:

Subsidiary Income   19,200

Investment in Company S   19,200

(EL)   Eliminate subsidiary equity against investment in
subsidiary account:

Common Stock ($10 par)—Company S   40,000

Retained Earnings, January 1, 2012—Company S   80,000

Investment in Company S   120,000

(continued)

(F1)   Eliminate remaining intercompany gain on machine sale, reduce
machine to cost, and adjust accumulated depreciation as
of January 1, 2012:
Retained Earnings, January 1, 2012—Company P   8,000
Accumulated Depreciation—Machinery.   2,000
        Machinery   10,000

(F2)   Reduce current-year machinery depreciation to amount based on
book value:
Accumulated Depreciation—Machinery.   2,000
        Depreciation Expense   2,000

Entry (F1) in this worksheet corrects the asset's net book value, accumulated depreciation, and retained earnings as of the beginning of the year. Since the sale was by the parent, only the controlling interest in beginning retained earnings is adjusted. Had the sale been by the subsidiary, the adjustment would have been split 20%/80% to the noncontrolling and controlling interests, respectively, in beginning retained earnings.

Entry (F2) corrects the depreciation expense, and the accumulated depreciation accounts for the current year. The resulting consolidated net income of $76,000 is distributed as shown in the income distribution schedules that follow Worksheet 4-6. During each year, Company S must absorb the larger depreciation expense that resulted from its purchase of the asset. Company P has the right to realize $2,000 more of the original deferred profit.

It may occur that an asset purchased from an affiliate is sold before it is fully depreciated. To illustrate this possibility, assume that Company S of the previous example sells the asset to a third party for $14,000 at the end of the second year. Since Company S's asset cost is $30,000, with $12,000 of accumulated depreciation, the loss recorded by Company S is $4,000 ($14,000 − $18,000 net book value). However, on a consolidated basis, the $4,000 loss becomes a $2,000 gain, determined as follows:

	On Books of Company S		For Consolidated Entity	
Selling price of machine sold by Company S		$14,000		$14,000
Less book value at end of second year following sale to Company S:				
Cost of machine	$ 30,000		$20,000*	
Accumulated depreciation	(12,000)	18,000	(8,000)	12,000
Gain (loss)		$ (4,000)		$ 2,000

*($32,000 − $12,000) = the net book value on January 1, 2011, the date of intercompany sale.

Worksheet 4-7: page 236   Worksheet 4-7 on pages 236 and 237, is a revision of the previous worksheet so that Company S's subsequent sale of the depreciable asset at the end of the second year is included.

The elimination entries in journal entry form are as follows:

(CY1)   Eliminate current-year equity income:
Subsidiary Income.   16,000
        Investment in Company S.   16,000

(EL)   Eliminate subsidiary equity against investment in
subsidiary account:
Common Stock ($10 par)—Company S   40,000
Retained Earnings, January 1, 2012—Company S   80,000
        Investment in Company S.   120,000

(F3)   Eliminate remaining machinery gain on January 1, 2012,
           and adjust recorded loss on sale to reflect book value at
           the time of sale:

Retained Earnings, January 1, 2012—Company P	8,000	
Depreciation Expense		2,000
Loss on Sale of Machine (as recorded by Company S)		4,000
Gain on Sale of Machine (on consolidated basis)		2,000

Entry (F3) removes the $8,000 remaining intercompany profit ($10,000 original gain − $2,000 realized in 2011) on the asset sale from controlling retained earnings, adjusts current depreciation by $2,000, and converts the $4,000 loss on the sale recorded by the subsidiary into a $2,000 gain on the consolidated statements.

However, a loss on an intercompany sale of plant assets does not have to be deferred if the loss could have been recorded in the absence of a sale. Where there has been an impairment in the value of a fixed asset, it may be written down to a lower market value. Where, however, the asset is sold to an affiliated company at a price below fair market value, the loss is to be deferred in the same manner as an intercompany gain. The loss would be deferred over the depreciation life of the asset. If the asset were sold to a nonaffiliated company, the remaining deferred loss would be recognized at the time of the sale.

Intercompany Long-Term Construction Contracts

One member of an affiliated group of companies may construct a plant asset for another affiliate over an extended period of time. The company constructing the asset will record progress under the completed-contract method or the percentage-of-completion method. During construction, special adjustments may be necessary when consolidating, depending on which of the two methods is used to record the contract by the constructing affiliate. From a consolidated viewpoint, such activity amounts to the self-construction of an asset to be used by the consolidated entity. Once the asset has been sold to an affiliate, consolidation procedures are similar to those used for a normal intercompany sale of a plant asset.

Completed-Contract Method. The constructing affiliate using the completed-contract method records no profit on the asset until it is completed and transferred to the purchasing affiliate. However, costs incurred to date on the contract are capitalized in a special account, such as *Cost of Construction in Progress*. This account will appear on the trial balance of the constructing affiliate. This account should be eliminated and re-recorded as *Assets Under Construction*, which is the usual account for the cost of an asset being constructed for a company's own use.

The constructing affiliate may bill the purchasing affiliate for work done prior to the completion of the asset. When this occurs, the constructing affiliate will record billed amounts by debiting *Contracts Receivable* and crediting *Billings on Long-Term Contracts*. The billings account acts as a contra account to Cost of Construction in Progress. The purchasing affiliate would debit *Assets Under Construction* and credit *Contracts Payable* for billings received. Consolidation procedures require that the constructing affiliate's account Billings on Long-Term Contracts be eliminated against Cost of Construction in Progress. Any excess of cost incurred over the amount of billings is closed to the purchaser's account, Assets Under Construction. In addition, it is necessary to eliminate any remaining intercompany receivable and payable amounts recorded on the long-term contract.

Percentage-of-Completion Method. This method allows the constructing company to recognize a portion of the total estimated profit on the contract as construction progresses. During the construction period, the contracting company debits an account usually entitled *Construction in Progress* for costs that are acquired by outside companies. The contractor also debits Construction in Progress and credits *Earned Income on Long-Term Contracts* for the estimated profit earned during each accounting period. Thus, the construction in progress account includes accumulated costs and estimated earnings. When the purchaser is billed, the contractor will debit the amount billed to Contracts Receivable and credit Billings on Construction in Progress, while the purchaser will debit Assets Under Construction and credit Contracts Payable.

4

OBJECTIVE

Demonstrate an understanding of the profit deferral issues for intercompany sales of assets under long-term construction contracts.

To illustrate the elimination procedures when the percentage-of-completion method is used, assume a subsidiary, Company S, enters into a contract to construct a building for its parent company, Company P, for $500,000 and Company S estimates the cost of the building to be $400,000. During 2011, the building is 50% completed and $200,000 of cost has been incurred as of December 31, 2011, but only $150,000 has been billed. The contract is completed in 2012 at an additional cost of $200,000. The entries on the books of the separate affiliates during 2011 are as follows:

Company S

Construction in Progress	200,000	
Payables (to outsiders)		200,000
To record costs incurred for the long-term contract		
under the percentage-of-completion method.		
Construction in Progress	50,000	
Earned Income on Long-Term Contracts.		50,000
To record pro rata share of estimated profit		
[50% × ($500,000 − $400,000)].		
Contracts Receivable.	150,000	
Billings on Construction in Progress		150,000
To record billing to parent for the portion of amount		
due under the contract.		

Company P

Assets Under Construction.	150,000	
Contracts Payable		150,000
To record billing from subsidiary for amount due.		

The subsidiary's balance sheet prepared at the end of 2011 would list a net current asset of $100,000, as the $150,000 balance in Billings on Construction in Progress would be offset against the $250,000 balance in Construction in Progress. If billings exceed the amount recorded for construction in progress, a net current liability would be shown on the balance sheet.

The following partial consolidated worksheet for 2011 shows the relevant accounts and the eliminations that would appear for this example. The elimination procedures are complex and involve answering this question: What should remain on the consolidated statements? From a consolidated viewpoint, a self-constructed asset is in progress and $200,000 has been spent to date. *All that should remain on the consolidated statements is a $200,000 asset under construction and a $200,000 payable to outside interests.* The income distribution schedule of the constructing affiliate would reflect the profit deferral through a debit for $50,000.

Company P and Subsidiary Company S
Partial Worksheet for Consolidated Financial Statements
For Year Ended December 31, 2011

(Credit balance amounts are in parentheses.)	Partial Trial Balance		Eliminations & Adjustments	
	Company P	Company S	Dr.	Cr.
Assets Under Construction	150,000		**(LT3)** 50,000	
Contracts Receivable		150,000		(LT1) 150,000
Billings on Construction in Progress		(150,000)	**(LT3)** 150,000	
Construction in Progress		250,000		**(LT2)** 50,000
				(LT3) 200,000
Earned Income on Long-Term Contracts		(50,000)	**(LT2)** 50,000	
Contracts Payable	(150,000)			(LT1) 150,000
Payables (to outsiders)		(200,000)		

Eliminations and Adjustments:

(LT1)   Eliminate the intercompany debt and receivable resulting from the long-term contract.
(LT2)   Eliminate the income recorded on the long-term intercompany contract and remove the profit from Construction in Progress.
(LT3)   Eliminate the balances of Construction in Progress and Billings on Construction in Progress and increase Assets Under Construction for the unbilled costs on the long-term intercompany contract.

As is true with all intercompany sales of plant assets, any intercompany profit is deferred until realized through the subsequent sale or use of the asset. Thus, the intercompany profit resulting from a long-term construction contract should be realized as the asset is depreciated. The unrealized profit will result in an adjustment to retained earnings in subsequent years.

REFLECTION

- The gain on an intercompany sale of land cannot be recognized until (if ever) the land is sold to the "outside world." The gain is deducted from the land account. In the year of intercompany sale, the gain is eliminated; in later periods, retained earnings is reduced for the amount of the gain.

- A gain on the intercompany sale of a fixed asset is eliminated in the period of sale. The gain is recognized over the depreciable life of the asset as a reduction in each period's depreciation expense.

- Any fixed asset gain, not amortized through depreciation adjustments, is recognized if the asset is later sold to the "outside world."

- Under the percentage-of-completion method for long-term projects, gains may be recorded prior to completion. Any such gains on an intercompany construction project must also be eliminated and later recognized through depreciation adjustments.

INTERCOMPANY DEBT

Typically, a parent company is larger than any one of its subsidiaries and can secure funds under more favorable terms. Because of this, a parent company often will advance cash to a subsidiary. The parent may accept a note from the subsidiary as security for the loan, or the parent may discount a note that the subsidiary received from a customer. In most cases, the parent will charge a competitive interest rate for the funds advanced to the subsidiary.

5

OBJECTIVE

Eliminate intercompany loans and notes.

In the examples that follow, the more common situation in which the parent is the lender is assumed. If the subsidiary were the lender, the theory and practice would be identical, with the only differences being the books on which the applicable accounts appear and the procedure for the distribution of combined net income.

Assume that on July 1, 2011, an 80%-owned subsidiary, Company S, borrows $10,000 from its parent, Company P, signing a 1-year, 8% note, with interest payable on the due date. This intercompany loan will cause the following accounts and their balances to appear on the December 31, 2011, trial balances of the separate affiliated companies:

Parent Company P		Subsidiary Company S	
Notes Receivable................	10,000	Notes Payable.................	(10,000)
Interest Income..................	(400)	Interest Expense.................	400
Interest Receivable...............	400	Interest Payable................	(400)

While this information is required on the books of the separate companies, it should not appear on the consolidated statements. The procedures needed to eliminate this intercompany note and its related interest amounts are demonstrated in Worksheet 4-8, pages 238 and 239.

Worksheet 4-8: page 238

The elimination entries in journal entry form are as follows:

(CY1)	Eliminate current-year equity income:			
	Subsidiary Income...................................		8,000	
	Investment in Company S...........................			8,000
(EL)	Eliminate subsidiary equity against investment in			
	subsidiary account:			
	Common Stock ($10 par)—Company S..................		40,000	
	Retained Earnings, January 1, 2011—Company S		80,000	
	Investment in Company S...........................			120,000
(LN1)	Eliminate intercompany note and accrued interest:			
	Note Payable to Company P.........................		10,000	
	Accrued Interest Payable............................		400	
	Note Receivable from Company S....................			10,000
	Accrued Interest Receivable........................			400
(LN2)	Eliminate intercompany interest income and expense:			
	Interest Income....................................		400	
	Interest Expense.................................			400

Entry (LN1) eliminates the intercompany receivable and payable for the note and the accrued interest on the note. Entry (LN2) eliminates the intercompany interest income and expense amounts. In this worksheet, it is assumed that the intercompany note is the only note recorded. However, sometimes an intercompany note and its related interest expense, revenue, and accruals are commingled with notes to outside parties. Before the trial balances are entered on the worksheet and before consolidation is attempted, intercompany interest expense and revenue must be accrued properly on the books of the parent and subsidiary.

There might be a temptation to increase the noncontrolling share of consolidated net income by $400 as a result of eliminating the interest expense on the intercompany note, but it is not correct to do so. Even though the interest does not appear on the consolidated income statement, it is a legitimate expense for Company S as a separate entity and a legitimate revenue for Company P as a separate entity. In essence, Company S has agreed to transfer $400 to Company P for interest during 2011, and the NCI must respect this agreement when calculating its share of consolidated net income. Thus, the basis for calculating the noncontrolling share is the net income of Company S as a separate entity. The NCI receives 20% of this $10,000 net income, which is net of the $400 of intercompany interest expense.

A parent receiving a note from a subsidiary subsequently may discount the note at a nonaffiliated financial institution in order to receive immediate cash. This results in a note receivable discounted being recorded by the parent. From a consolidated viewpoint, there is a note payable to outside parties. Consolidation procedures should eliminate the internal note receivable against the note receivable discounted. This elimination will result in the note, now payable to an outside party, being extended to the consolidated balance sheet. Intercompany interest accrued prior to the discounting is eliminated. Interest paid by the subsidiary subsequent to the discounting is paid to the outside party and is not eliminated. The net interest expense or revenue on the discounting of the note is a transaction between the parent and the outside party and, thus, is not eliminated. When consolidated statements are prepared, however, it is desirable to net the interest expense on the note recorded by the maker subsequent to the discounting of the note against the net interest expense or revenue on the discounting transaction.

REFLECTION

- Intercompany debt balances, including accrued interest receivable/payable, are eliminated.

- Intercompany interest expense/revenue is also eliminated. These amounts are equal; thus, there is no effect on consolidated net income.

SOPHISTICATED EQUITY METHOD: INTERCOMPANY TRANSACTIONS

6

OBJECTIVE

Discuss the complications intercompany profits create for the use of the sophisticated equity method.

Chapter 3 demonstrated the use of the sophisticated equity method for the parent's recording of its investment in a subsidiary. Recall that one major difference between the simple and sophisticated equity methods was that the latter records subsidiary income net of amortizations of excess. In contrast, the simple equity method ignores amortizations and records as income for the parent the subsidiary reported income multiplied by the parent's percentage of ownership. Some companies using the sophisticated equity method will proceed to the next level of complexity. Instead of adjusting for their share of the income reported by the subsidiary (as under the simple equity method), they will adjust for their share of subsidiary income after it is adjusted for intercompany profits. This means that, before the parent can make an equity adjustment for income of the subsidiary, it must prepare an income distribution schedule for the subsidiary company. **The adjusted net income derived in the income distribution schedule will become the income to which the parent ownership percentage is applied to arrive at equity income.**

The added complexity of the sophisticated equity method is unwarranted when statements are to be consolidated, since the subsidiary income and the investment in subsidiary accounts are eliminated entirely. However, this procedure must be used in the rare case when a subsidiary is not to be consolidated or when parent-only statements are to be prepared as a supplement to the consolidated statements.

Unrealized Profits of the Current Period

The case of intercompany profits generated only during the current period will be considered first. Although the same procedure applies to all types of subsidiary-generated unrealized intercompany profits and losses of the current period, the impact of the sophisticated equity method will be demonstrated assuming only the existence of inventory profits.

The following example is based on the information presented in Worksheet 4-2, but this time the parent is using the sophisticated equity method. Because of this fact, the parent has to prepare a subsidiary income distribution schedule before it can record its share of subsidiary income. This schedule is shown on the following page. Note that, instead of recording **on its books** a subsidiary income of $60,000, the parent would have recorded $53,600.

Equity Income: Subsidiary Company S		
Unrealized profit in ending inventory	$8,000	Internally generated net income . . . . $ 75,000
		Adjusted income . . . . $ 67,000
		Controlling share . . . . × **80%**
		Controlling interest . . . . **$ 53,600***

*This is the same amount that is shown in the parent's income distribution schedule for Worksheet 4-2.

The only elimination procedure in this example that differs from Worksheet 4-2 is entry (CY1), which eliminates the entry made by the parent to record its share of the subsidiary current-period income. There is no impact on the other worksheet procedures, and the balance of Worksheet 4-2 would be unchanged. A portion of the revised worksheet is shown on page 221.

Unrealized Profits of Current and Prior Periods

The effect of the sophisticated equity method when there are intercompany profits from current and prior periods is demonstrated in the following example, which is based on the information given in Worksheet 4-3. The subsidiary income reported by the parent in 2012 under the sophisticated equity method is calculated as follows:

Equity Income: Parent Company P		
Unrealized profit in ending inventory	$6,000	Internally generated net income . . . . $ 60,000
		Realized profit in beginning inventory. 8,000
		Adjusted income . . . . $ 62,000
		Controlling share . . . . × **80%**
		Controlling interest . . . . **$ 49,600**

The elimination procedures illustrated in the following partial worksheets are applicable to all types of subsidiary-generated intercompany profits and losses of prior and current periods. The differences in the parent's trial balance are explained in the notes that follow the partial worksheet on page 222.

Company P and Subsidiary Company S
Partial Worksheet
For Year Ended December 31, **2011**

(Credit balance amounts are in parentheses.)		Partial Trial Balance		Eliminations & Adjustments			
		Company P	Company S	Dr.		Cr.	
Accounts Receivable		110,000	150,000			(IA)	25,000
Inventory, December 31, 2011		70,000	40,000			(EI)	8,000
Investment in Company S	(b)	**189,600**				**(CY1)**	**53,600**
						(EL)	136,000
Other Assets		314,000	155,000				
Accounts Payable		(80,000)	(100,000)	(IA)	25,000		
Common Stock ($10 par)—Company P		(200,000)					
Retained Earnings, January 1, 2011—Company P		(250,000)					
Common Stock ($10 par)—Company S			(100,000)	(EL)	80,000		
Retained Earnings, January 1, 2011—Company S			(70,000)	(EL)	56,000		
Sales		(700,000)	(500,000)	(IS)	100,000		
Cost of Goods Sold		510,000	350,000	(EI)	8,000	(IS)	100,000
Expenses		90,000	75,000				
Subsidiary Income	(a)	**(53,600)**		**(CY1)**	**53,600**		
		0	0		322,600		322,600

Notes to Trial Balance:

(a) See the previously prepared income distribution schedule.
(b) $136,000 beginning-of-year balance + $53,600 sophisticated equity method income.

Eliminations and Adjustments:

(CY1) Eliminate the entry recording the parent's share (80%) of the subsidiary net income under the sophisticated equity method.
(EL, IS, EI, and IA) Same as Worksheet 4-2.

Company P and Subsidiary Company S
Partial Worksheet
For Year Ended December 31, **2012**

(Credit balance amounts are in parentheses.)	Partial Trial Balance		Eliminations & Adjustments	
	Company P	Company S	Dr.	Cr.
Accounts Receivable	160,000	170,000		(IA) 60,000
Inventory, December 31, 2012	60,000	50,000		(EI) 6,000
Investment in Company S	(c) 239,200			(CY1) 49,600
				(EL) 189,600
Other Assets	354,000	165,000		
Accounts Payable	(90,000)	(80,000)	(IA) 60,000	
Common Stock ($10 par)—Company P	(200,000)			
Retained Earnings, January 1, 2012—Company P	(b) **(403,600)**			
Common Stock ($10 par)—Company S		(100,000)	(EL) 80,000	
Retained Earnings, January 1, 2012—Company S		(145,000)	(Adj) 8,000	
			(EL) 109,600	
Sales	(800,000)	(600,000)	(IS) 120,000	
Cost of Goods Sold	610,000	440,000	(EI) 6,000	(Adj) 8,000
				(IS) 120,000
Expenses	120,000	100,000		
Subsidiary Income	(a) **(49,600)**		(CY1) 49,600	
	0	0	433,200	433,200

Notes to Trial Balance:

(a) See the previously prepared income distribution schedule.
(b) $410,000 simple equity balance − (80% × $8,000 subsidiary beginning inventory profit).
(c) $136,000 original balance + $53,600 sophisticated equity method income for 2011 + $49,600 sophisticated equity method income for 2012.

Eliminations and Adjustments:

(Adj) Eliminate the $8,000 beginning inventory profit from the cost of goods sold and the subsidiary beginning retained earnings accounts. This entry replaces entry (BI) of Worksheet 4-3.
(CY1) Eliminate the entry recording the parent's share (80%) of the subsidiary net income under the sophisticated equity method.
(EL) Eliminate 80% of the subsidiary equity balances against the investment account. The elimination of retained earnings is 80% of the adjusted balance of $137,000 ($145,000 − $8,000).

(IS, EI, and IA) Same as Worksheet 4-3.

When the sophisticated equity method is used, the worksheet elimination of the parent's investment account against the stockholders' equity of the subsidiary is more complicated because there is an inconsistency between the parent's accounts and those of the subsidiary. In the 2012 partial worksheet illustrated, the parent's investment and retained earnings accounts do not reflect the $8,000 beginning inventory profit recorded by the subsidiary. The intercompany profit was removed in the prior period before the parent's share of the subsidiary's net income was recorded. The subsidiary's trial balance does include the $8,000 beginning inventory profit in the January 1 retained earnings balance, and the parent's beginning inventory, now in the cost of goods sold, does include the profit. The inconsistency is removed on the worksheet by making an adjustment, coded "Adj," that removes the intercompany profit from the subsidiary's beginning retained earnings and the parent's beginning inventory. This entry replaces entry (BI) in Worksheet 4-3.

Entry (CY1) of the partial worksheet removes the subsidiary income as recorded by the parent. Entry (EL) reflects the adjustment of the subsidiary's retained earnings. The remaining entries and worksheet procedures are identical to those in Worksheet 4-3.

REFLECTION

- When used properly, the sophisticated equity method should record annual subsidiary income net of all intercompany profits.

- The parent's beginning retained earnings will not include prior periods' intercompany profits, but the subsidiary's beginning retained earnings does when the subsidiary is the seller. The subsidiary's beginning retained earnings must be adjusted for these profits prior to its elimination.

APPENDIX: INTERCOMPANY PROFIT ELIMINATIONS ON THE VERTICAL WORKSHEET

7

OBJECTIVE

Apply intercompany profit eliminations on a vertical worksheet.

In keeping with the overall worksheet format approach of this text, all previous examples in this chapter have been presented using the horizontal worksheet style. Worksheet 4-9, page 240 and 241, provides the reader an opportunity to study the vertical worksheet when intercompany merchandise and plant asset transactions are involved. This worksheet is based on the following facts:

1. Company P acquired an 80% interest in Company S on January 1, 2011. At that time, the following determination and distribution of excess schedule was prepared:

Determination and Distribution of Excess Schedule

	Company Implied Fair Value	Parent Price (80%)	NCI Value (20%)
Fair value of subsidiary	$625,000	$500,000	$125,000
Less book value interest acquired:			
Common stock ($5 par)	$200,000		
Retained Earnings	350,000		
Total equity.	$550,000	$550,000	$550,000
Interest acquired		80%	20%
Book value.		$440,000	$110,000
Excess of fair value over book value	**$ 75,000**	$ 60,000	$ 15,000

Adjustment of identifiable accounts:

	Adjustment	**Worksheet Key**
Goodwill	$ 75,000	debit D1

2. Company P accounts for the investment under the simple equity method.

3. Company S sells merchandise to Company P to yield a gross profit of 20%. Sales totaled $150,000 during 2012. There were $40,000 of such goods in Company P's beginning inventory and $50,000 of such goods in Company P's ending inventory. As of December 31, 2012, Company P had not paid the $20,000 owed for the purchases.

4. On July 1, 2011, Company P sold a new machine that cost $20,000 to Company S for $25,000. At that time, both companies believed that the machine had a 5-year remaining life; both companies use straight-line depreciation.

5. Company S declared and paid $20,000 in dividends during 2012.

Notice that the eliminations in Worksheet 4-9 are identical to those required for the horizontal format. Also, when working with the vertical format, keep in mind the cautions that are stated in Chapter 3: (a) the nominal accounts are presented above the balance sheet accounts, and (b) the eliminations are made only to the beginning retained earnings accounts. The carrydown procedures for the vertical worksheet are the same as those presented in Chapter 3.

REFLECTION

- On a vertical worksheet, the eliminating and adjusting entries are the same as those on a trial balance worksheet.

Worksheet 4-1

Intercompany Sales; No Intercompany Goods in Inventories
Company P and Subsidiary Company S
Worksheet for Consolidated Financial Statements
For Year Ended December 31, **2011**

	(Credit balance amounts are in parentheses.)	Trial Balance	
		Company P	Company S
1	**Accounts Receivable**	110,000	150,000
2	Inventory, December 31, 2011	70,000	40,000
3	Investment in Company S	196,000	
4			
5	Other Assets	314,000	155,000
6	**Accounts Payable**	(80,000)	(100,000)
7	Common Stock ($10 par)—Company P	(200,000)	
8	Retained Earnings, January 1, 2011—Company P	(250,000)	
9	Common Stock ($10 par)—Company S		(100,000)
10	Retained Earnings, January 1, 2011—Company S		(70,000)
11	**Sales**	(700,000)	(500,000)
12	**Cost of Goods Sold**	510,000	350,000
13	Expenses	90,000	75,000
14	Subsidiary Income	(60,000)	
15		0	0
16	Consolidated Net Income		
17	To NCI (see distribution schedule)		
18	Balance to Controlling Interest (see distribution schedule)		
19	Total NCI		
20	Retained Earnings, Controlling Interest, December 31, 2011		
21			

Eliminations and Adjustments:

(CY1)   Eliminate the entry recording the parent's share of subsidiary net income.

(EL)   Eliminate against the investment in Company S account the pro rata portion of the subsidiary equity balances (80%) owned by the parent. To simplify the elimination, there is no discrepancy between the cost and book values of the investment in this example. Also, note that the worksheet process is expedited by always eliminating the intercompany investment first.

(IS)   Eliminate $100,000 intercompany sales to avoid double counting. Now only Company S's original purchase from third parties and Company P's final sale to third parties remain in the consolidated income statement.

(IA)   Eliminate the $25,000 intercompany trade balances resulting from the intercompany sale.

Worksheet 4-1 (see page 203)

Eliminations & Adjustments				Consolidated Income Statement	NCI	Controlling Retained Earnings	Consolidated Balance Sheet	
Dr.		**Cr.**						
		(IA)	**25,000**				235,000	1
							110,000	2
		(CY1)	60,000					3
		(EL)	136,000					4
							469,000	5
(IA)	**25,000**						(155,000)	6
							(200,000)	7
						(250,000)		8
(EL)	80,000				(20,000)			9
(EL)	56,000				(14,000)			10
(IS)	**100,000**			(1,100,000)				11
		(IS)	**100,000**	760,000				12
				165,000				13
(CY1)	60,000							14
	321,000		321,000					15
				(175,000)				16
				15,000	(15,000)			17
				160,000		(160,000)		18
					(49,000)		(49,000)	19
						(410,000)	(410,000)	20
							0	21

Subsidiary Company S Income Distribution

Internally generated net income	$ 75,000
Adjusted income	$ 75,000
NCI share	× 20%
NCI	$ 15,000

Parent Company P Income Distribution

Internally generated net income	$100,000
80% × Company S adjusted income of $75,000. . . .	60,000
Controlling interest	$160,000

Worksheet 4-2

Intercompany Goods in Ending Inventory
Company P and Subsidiary Company S
Worksheet for Consolidated Financial Statements
For Year Ended December 31, **2011**

	(Credit balance amounts are in parentheses.)	Trial Balance	
		Company P	Company S
1	Accounts Receivable	110,000	150,000
2	**Inventory, December 31, 2011**	**70,000**	**40,000**
3	Investment in Company S	196,000	
4			
5	Other Assets	314,000	155,000
6	Accounts Payable	(80,000)	(100,000)
7	Common Stock ($10 par)—Company P	(200,000)	
8	Retained Earnings, January 1, 2011—Company P	(250,000)	
9	Common Stock ($10 par)—Company S		(100,000)
10	Retained Earnings, January 1, 2011—Company S		(70,000)
11	Sales	(700,000)	(500,000)
12	**Cost of Goods Sold**	**510,000**	**350,000**
13	Expenses	90,000	75,000
14	Subsidiary Income	(60,000)	
15		0	0
16	Consolidated Net Income		
17	To NCI (see distribution schedule)		
18	Balance to Controlling Interest (see distribution schedule)		
19	Total NCI		
20	Retained Earnings, Controlling Interest, December 31, 2011		
21			

Eliminations and Adjustments:

(CY1)   Eliminate the entry recording the parent's share of subsidiary net income.
(EL)   Eliminate 80% of the subsidiary equity balances against the investment in Company S account. There is no excess of cost or book value in this example.
(IS)   Eliminate the intercompany sale of $100,000.
(EI)   Eliminate intercompany profit in ending inventory, 20% × $40,000.
(IA)   Eliminate the intercompany trade balances.

Worksheet 4-2 (see page 206)

Eliminations & Adjustments			Consolidated Income Statement	NCI	Controlling Retained Earnings	Consolidated Balance Sheet	
Dr.	Cr.						
	(IA)	25,000				235,000	1
	(EI)	**8,000**				102,000	2
	(CY1)	60,000					3
	(EL)	136,000					4
						469,000	5
(IA)	25,000					(155,000)	6
						(200,000)	7
					(250,000)		8
(EL)	80,000			(20,000)			9
(EL)	56,000			(14,000)			10
(IS)	100,000		(1,100,000)				11
(EI)	**8,000**	(IS) 100,000	768,000				12
			165,000				13
(CY1)	60,000						14
	329,000	329,000					15
			(167,000)				16
			13,400	(13,400)			17
			153,600		(153,600)		18
				(47,400)		(47,400)	19
					(403,600)	(403,600)	20
						0	21

Subsidiary Company S Income Distribution

Unrealized profit in ending inventory .... **(EI)** **$8,000**	Internally generated net income	$ 75,000
	Adjusted income	$ 67,000
	NCI share .... ×	20%
	NCI	$ 13,400

Parent Company P Income Distribution

	Internally generated net income	$ 100,000
	80% × Company S adjusted income of $67,000.....	53,600
	Controlling interest	$ 153,600

Worksheet 4-3

Intercompany Goods in Beginning and Ending Inventories
Company P and Subsidiary Company S
Worksheet for Consolidated Financial Statements
For Year Ended December 31, **2012**

	(Credit balance amounts are in parentheses.)	Trial Balance	
		Company P	Company S
1	Accounts Receivable	160,000	170,000
2	**Inventory, December 31, 2012**	**60,000**	**50,000**
3	Investment in Company S	244,000	
4			
5	Other Assets	354,000	165,000
6	Accounts Payable	(90,000)	(80,000)
7	Common Stock ($10 par)—Company P	(200,000)	
8	**Retained Earnings, January 1, 2012—Company P**	**(410,000)**	
9	Common Stock ($10 par)—Company S		(100,000)
10	**Retained Earnings, January 1, 2012—Company S**		**(145,000)**
11			
12	Sales	(800,000)	(600,000)
13	**Cost of Goods Sold**	**610,000**	**440,000**
14			
15	Expenses	120,000	100,000
16	Subsidiary Income	(48,000)	
17		0	0
18	Consolidated Net Income		
19	To NCI (see distribution schedule)		
20	Balance to Controlling Interest (see distribution schedule)		
21	Total NCI		
22	Retained Earnings, Controlling Interest, December 31, 2012		
23			

Eliminations and Adjustments:

(CY1) Eliminate the entry recording the parent's share of subsidiary net income.

(EL) Eliminate 80% of the subsidiary equity balances against the investment in Company S account. There is no excess of cost or book value in this example.

(BI) Eliminate the intercompany profit of $8,000 (20% × $40,000) in the beginning inventory by reducing both the cost of goods sold and the beginning retained earnings accounts. 20% of the decrease in retained earnings is shared by the noncontrolling interest, since, in this case, the *selling company was the subsidiary*. If the parent had been the seller, only the controlling interest in retained earnings would be decreased. It should be noted that the $8,000 profit is shifted from 2011 to 2012, since, as a result of the entry, the 2012 consolidated cost of goods sold balance is reduced by $8,000. This procedure emphasizes the concept that intercompany inventory profit is not eliminated but only deferred until inventory is sold to an outsider.

(IS) Eliminate $120,000 intercompany sales to avoid double counting.

(EI) Eliminate the intercompany profit of $6,000 (20% × $30,000) recorded by Company S for the intercompany goods contained in Company P's ending inventory, and increase the cost of goods sold balance by this same amount.

(IA) Eliminate the intercompany trade balances.

Worksheet 4-3 (see page 207)

Eliminations & Adjustments Dr.		Eliminations & Adjustments Cr.		Consolidated Income Statement	NCI	Controlling Retained Earnings	Consolidated Balance Sheet	
		(IA)	60,000				270,000	1
		(EI)	**6,000**				104,000	2
		(CY1)	48,000					3
		(EL)	196,000					4
							519,000	5
(IA)	60,000						(110,000)	6
							(200,000)	7
(BI)	**6,400**					(403,600)		8
(EL)	80,000				(20,000)			9
(EL)	116,000							10
(BI)	**1,600**				(27,400)			11
(IS)	120,000			(1,280,000)				12
(EI)	**6,000**	**(BI)**	**8,000**					13
		(IS)	120,000	928,000				14
				220,000				15
(CY1)	48,000							16
	438,000		438,000					17
				(132,000)				18
				12,400	(12,400)			19
				119,600		(119,600)		20
					(59,800)		(59,800)	21
						(523,200)	(523,200)	22
							0	23

Subsidiary Company S Income Distribution

Unrealized profit in ending inventory, 20% × $30,000 . . . . **(EI)** **$6,000**	Internally generated net income . . . . $ 60,000
	Realized profit in beginning inventory,
	20% × $40,000 . . . . **(BI)** **8,000**
	Adjusted income . . . . $ 62,000
	NCI share . . . . × 20%
	NCI . . . . $ 12,400

Parent Company P Income Distribution

	Internally generated net income . . . . $ 70,000
	80% × Company S adjusted income of $62,000 49,600
	Controlling interest $119,600

Worksheet 4-4

Intercompany Goods in Beginning and Ending Inventories; Periodic Inventory
Company P and Subsidiary Company S
Worksheet for Consolidated Financial Statements
For Year Ended December 31, **2012**

	(Credit balance amounts are in parentheses.)	Trial Balance	
		Company P	Company S
1	Accounts Receivable	160,000	170,000
2	**Inventory, January 1, 2012**	**70,000**	**40,000**
3	Investment in Company S	244,000	
4			
5	Other Assets	354,000	165,000
6	Accounts Payable	(90,000)	(80,000)
7	Common Stock ($10 par)—Company P	(200,000)	
8	**Retained Earnings, January 1, 2012—Company P**	**(410,000)**	
9	Common Stock ($10 par)—Company S		(100,000)
10	**Retained Earnings, January 1, 2012—Company S**		**(145,000)**
11			
12	Sales	(800,000)	(600,000)
13	**Purchases**	**600,000**	**450,000**
14	**Inventory, December 31, 2012**	**60,000**	**50,000**
15	**Cost of Goods Sold**	**(60,000)**	**(50,000)**
16	Expenses	120,000	100,000
17	Subsidiary Income	(48,000)	
18		0	0
19	Consolidated Net Income		
20	To NCI (see distribution schedule)		
21	Balance to Controlling Interest (see distribution schedule)		
22	Total NCI		
23	Retained Earnings, Controlling Interest, December 31, 2012		
24			

Eliminations and Adjustments:

(CY1)   Eliminate the entry recording the parent's share of subsidiary net income.

(EL)   Eliminate 80% of the subsidiary equity balances against the investment in Company S account. There is no excess of cost or book value in this example.

(BI)   Eliminate the intercompany profit of $8,000 (20% × $40,000) in the beginning inventory by reducing both the cost of goods sold and the beginning retained earnings accounts. 20% of the decrease in retained earnings is shared by the noncontrolling interest, since, in this case, the *selling company was the subsidiary*. If the parent had been the seller, only the controlling interest in retained earnings would be decreased. It should be noted that the $8,000 profit is shifted from 2011 to 2012, since, as a result of the entry, the 2012 consolidated cost of goods sold balance is reduced by $8,000. This procedure emphasizes the concept that intercompany inventory profit is not eliminated but only deferred until inventory is sold to an outsider.

(IS)   Eliminate $120,000 intercompany sales to avoid double counting.

(EI)   Enter the combined ending inventories of Company P and Company S, $60,000 and $50,000, respectively, less the intercompany profit of $6,000 (20% × $30,000) recorded by Company S for the intercompany goods contained in Company P's ending inventory.

(IA)   Eliminate the intercompany trade balances.

Worksheet 4-4 (see page 209)

Eliminations & Adjustments				Consolidated Income Statement	NCI	Controlling Retained Earnings	Consolidated Balance Sheet	
Dr.		Cr.						
		(IA)	60,000				270,000	1
		(BI)	**8,000**	102,000				2
		(CY1)	48,000					3
		(EL)	196,000					4
							519,000	5
(IA)	60,000						(110,000)	6
							(200,000)	7
(BI)	**6,400**					(403,600)		8
(EL)	80,000				(20,000)			9
(EL)	116,000							10
(BI)	**1,600**				(27,400)			11
(IS)	120,000			(1,280,000)				12
		(IS)	120,000	930,000				13
		(EI)	6,000				104,000	14
(EI)	6,000			(104,000)				15
				220,000				16
(CY1)	48,000							17
	438,000		438,000					18
				(132,000)				19
				12,400	(12,400)			20
				119,600		(119,600)		21
					(59,800)		(59,800)	22
						(523,200)	(523,200)	23
							0	24

Subsidiary Company S Income Distribution

Unrealized profit in ending inventory, 20% × $30,000 . . . . **(EI)** **$6,000**	Internally generated net income	$ 60,000
	Realized profit in beginning inventory, 20% × $40,000 . . . . **(BI)**	**8,000**
	Adjusted income	$ 62,000
	NCI share	× 20%
	NCI	$ 12,400

Parent Company P Income Distribution

	Internally generated net income	$ 70,000
	80% × Company S adjusted income of $62,000	49,600
	Controlling interest	$119,600

Worksheet 4-5

Intercompany Sale of Depreciable Asset
Company P and Subsidiary Company S
Worksheet for Consolidated Financial Statements
For Year Ended December 31, **2011**

	(Credit balance amounts are in parentheses.)	Trial Balance	
		Company P	Company S
1	Current Assets	15,000	20,000
2	**Machinery**	50,000	(a) 230,000
3	**Accumulated Depreciation—Machinery**	(25,000)	(b) (100,000)
4	Investment in Company S	120,000	
5			
6	Common Stock ($10 par)—Company P	(100,000)	
7	Retained Earnings, January 1, 2011—Company P	(10,000)	
8	Common Stock ($10 par)—Company S		(50,000)
9	Retained Earnings, January 1, 2011—Company S		(75,000)
10	Sales	(200,000)	(100,000)
11	Cost of Goods Sold	150,000	59,000
12	**Depreciation Expense**	30,000	(b) 16,000
13	**Gain on Sale of Machine**	(10,000)	
14	Subsidiary Income	(20,000)	
15		0	0
16	Consolidated Net Income		
17	To NCI (see distribution schedule)		
18	Balance to Controlling Interest (see distribution schedule)		
19	Total NCI		
20	Retained Earnings, Controlling Interest, December 31, 2011		
21			

Notes to Trial Balance:

(a)   Includes machine purchased for $30,000 from Company P on January 1, 2011.
(b)   Includes $6,000 depreciation on machine purchased from Company P on January 1, 2011.

Eliminations and Adjustments:

(CY1)   Eliminate the entry recording the parent's share of subsidiary net income for the current year.
(EL)   Eliminate 80% of the subsidiary equity balances against the investment account. There is no excess to be distributed.
(F1)   Eliminate the $10,000 gain on the intercompany sale of the machine, and reduce machine to book value.
(F2)   Reduce the depreciation expense and accumulated depreciation accounts to reflect the depreciation ($4,000 per year) based on the consolidated book value of the machine, rather than the depreciation ($6,000 per year) based on the sales price.

Worksheet 4-5 (see page 212)

Eliminations & Adjustments		Consolidated Income Statement	NCI	Controlling Retained Earnings	Consolidated Balance Sheet	
Dr.	Cr.					
					35,000	1
	(F1) 10,000				270,000	2
(F2) 2,000					(123,000)	3
	(CY1) 20,000					4
	(EL) 100,000					5
					(100,000)	6
				(10,000)		7
(EL) 40,000			(10,000)			8
(EL) 60,000			(15,000)			9
		(300,000)				10
		209,000				11
	(F2) 2,000	44,000				12
(F1) 10,000						13
(CY1) 20,000						14
132,000	132,000					15
		(47,000)				16
		5,000	(5,000)			17
		42,000		(42,000)		18
			(30,000)		(30,000)	19
				(52,000)	(52,000)	20
					0	21

Subsidiary Company S Income Distribution

Internally generated net income	$ 25,000
Adjusted income	$ 25,000
NCI share	× 20%
NCI	$ 5,000

Parent Company P Income Distribution

Unrealized gain on sale of machine .... (F1) **$10,000**	Internally generated net income (including sale of machine)	$30,000
	80% × Company S adjusted income of $25,000........	20,000
	Gain realized through use of machine sold to subsidiary .... (F2)	**2,000**
	Controlling interest	$42,000

Worksheet 4-6

Intercompany Sale of Depreciable Asset
Company P and Subsidiary Company S
Worksheet for Consolidated Financial Statements
For Year Ended December 31, **2012**

	(Credit balance amounts are in parentheses.)	Trial Balance	
		Company P	Company S
1	Current Assets	85,000	60,000
2	**Machinery**	50,000	(a) **230,000**
3	**Accumulated Depreciation—Machinery**	(45,000)	(b) **(116,000)**
4			
5	Investment in Company S	139,200	
6			
7	Common Stock ($10 par)—Company P	(100,000)	
8	**Retained Earnings, January 1, 2012—Company P**	**(60,000)**	
9	Common Stock ($10 par)—Company S		(50,000)
10	Retained Earnings, January 1, 2012—Company S		(100,000)
11	Sales	(250,000)	(120,000)
12	**Cost of Goods Sold**	180,000	80,000
13	**Depreciation Expense**	20,000	(c) **16,000**
14	Subsidiary Income	(19,200)	
15		0	0
16	Consolidated Net Income		
17	To NCI (see distribution schedule)		
18	Balance to Controlling Interest (see distribution schedule)		
19	Total NCI		
20	Retained Earnings, Controlling Interest, December 31, 2012		
21			

Notes to Trial Balance:

(a)   Includes machine purchased for $30,000 from Company P on January 1, 2011.
(b)   Includes $12,000 accumulated depreciation ($6,000 per year) on machine purchased from Company P on January 1, 2011.
(c)   Includes $6,000 depreciation on machine purchased from Company P on January 1, 2011.

Eliminations and Adjustments:

(CY1)   Eliminate the entry recording the parent's share of subsidiary net income for the current year.
(EL)   Eliminate 80% of the subsidiary equity balances against the investment account. There is no excess to be distributed.
(F1)   Eliminate the gain on the intercompany sale as it is reflected in beginning retained earnings on the parent's trial balance. Since the sale was made by the *parent*, Company P, the entire unrealized gain at the beginning of the year (now $8,000) is removed from the controlling retained earnings beginning balance. If the sale had been made by the subsidiary, the adjustment of beginning retained earnings would be split 80% to the controlling interest and 20% to the noncontrolling interest.
(F2)   Reduce the depreciation expense and accumulated depreciation accounts by $2,000 to reflect the depreciation based on the consolidated book value of the asset on the date of sale. This entry will bring the accumulated depreciation account to its correct consolidated year-end balance.

Worksheet 4-6 (see page 213)

Eliminations & Adjustments				Consolidated Income Statement	NCI	Controlling Retained Earnings	Consolidated Balance Sheet	
Dr.		Cr.						
							145,000	1
		(F1)	10,000				270,000	2
(F1)	2,000						(157,000)	3
(F2)	2,000							4
		(CY1)	19,200					5
		(EL)	120,000					6
							(100,000)	7
(F1)	8,000					(52,000)		8
(EL)	40,000				(10,000)			9
(EL)	80,000				(20,000)			10
				(370,000)				11
				260,000				12
		(F2)	2,000	34,000				13
(CY1)	19,200							14
	151,200		151,200					15
				(76,000)				16
				4,800	(4,800)			17
				71,200		(71,200)		18
					(34,800)		(34,800)	19
						(123,200)	(123,200)	20
							0	21

Subsidiary Company S Income Distribution

Internally generated net income		$ 24,000
Adjusted income		$ 24,000
NCI share	×	20%
NCI		$ 4,800

Parent Company P Income Distribution

Internally generated net income		$50,000
80% of Company S adjusted income of $24,000		19,200
Gain realized through use of machine sold to subsidiary	**(F2)**	**2,000**
Controlling interest		$71,200

Worksheet 4-7

Intercompany Sale of a Depreciable Asset; Subsequent Sale of Asset to an Outside Party
Company P and Subsidiary Company S
Worksheet for Consolidated Financial Statements
For Year Ended December 31, **2012**

	(Credit balance amounts are in parentheses.)	Trial Balance	
		Company P	Company S
1	Current Assets	85,000	74,000
2	Machinery	50,000	200,000
3	Accumulated Depreciation—Machinery	(45,000)	(104,000)
4	Investment in Company S	136,000	
5			
6	Common Stock ($10 par)—Company P	(100,000)	
7	**Retained Earnings, January 1, 2012—Company P**	**(60,000)**	
8	Common Stock ($10 par)—Company S		(50,000)
9	Retained Earnings, January 1, 2012—Company S		(100,000)
10	Sales	(250,000)	(120,000)
11	Cost of Goods Sold	180,000	80,000
12	**Depreciation Expense**	20,000	**16,000**
13	**Loss on Sale of Machine**		**4,000**
14	Subsidiary Income	(16,000)	
15	**Gain on Sale of Machine**		
16		0	0
17	Consolidated Net Income		
18	To NCI (see distribution schedule)		
19	Balance to Controlling Interest (see distribution schedule)		
20	Total NCI		
21	Retained Earnings, Controlling Interest, December 31, 2012		
22			

Eliminations and Adjustments:

(CY1)   Eliminate the entry recording the parent's share of subsidiary net income for the current year.
(EL)   Eliminate 80% of the subsidiary equity balances against the investment account. There is no excess to be distributed.
(F3)   Eliminate the gain on the intercompany sale as it is reflected in the parent's beginning retained earnings account, adjust the current year's depreciation expense, and revise the recording of the sale of the equipment to an outside party to reflect the net book value of the asset to the consolidated company.

Worksheet 4-7 (see page 214)

Eliminations & Adjustments				Consolidated Income Statement	NCI	Controlling Retained Earnings	Consolidated Balance Sheet	
Dr.		Cr.						
							159,000	1
							250,000	2
							(149,000)	3
		(CY1)	16,000					4
		(EL)	120,000					5
							(100,000)	6
(F3)	8,000					(52,000)		7
(EL)	40,000				(10,000)			8
(EL)	80,000				(20,000)			9
				(370,000)				10
				260,000				11
		(F3)	2,000	34,000				12
		(F3)	4,000					13
(CY1)	16,000							14
		(F3)	2,000	(2,000)				15
	144,000		144,000					16
				(78,000)				17
				4,000	(4,000)			18
				74,000		(74,000)		19
					(34,000)		(34,000)	20
						(126,000)	(126,000)	21
							0	22

Subsidiary Company S Income Distribution

Internally generated net income	$ 20,000
Adjusted income	$ 20,000
NCI share	× 20%
NCI	$ 4,000

Parent Company P Income Distribution

Internally generated net income	$ 50,000
80% × Company S adjusted income of $20,000	16,000
Gain realized on sale of machine . . . . **(F3)**	**8,000***
Controlling interest	$ 74,000

*$10,000 original gain − $2,000 realized in 2011

Worksheet 4-8

Intercompany Notes
Company P and Subsidiary Company S
Worksheet for Consolidated Financial Statements
For Year Ended December 31, **2011**

	(Credit balance amounts are in parentheses.)	Trial Balance	
		Company P	Company S
1	Cash	35,000	20,400
2	**Note Receivable from Company S**	**10,000**	
3	**Interest Receivable**	**400**	
4	Property, Plant, and Equipment (net)	140,000	150,000
5	Investment in Company S	128,000	
6			
7	**Note Payable to Company P**		**(10,000)**
8	**Interest Payable**		**(400)**
9	Common Stock—Company P	(100,000)	
10	Retained Earnings, January 1, 2011—Company P	(200,000)	
11	Common Stock—Company S		(50,000)
12	Retained Earnings, January 1, 2011—Company S		(100,000)
13	Sales	(120,000)	(50,000)
14	**Interest Income**	**(400)**	
15	Subsidiary Income	(8,000)	
16	Cost of Goods Sold	75,000	20,000
17	Other Expenses	40,000	19,600
18	**Interest Expense**		**400**
19		0	0
20	Consolidated Net Income		
21	To NCI (see distribution schedule)		
22	Balance to Controlling Interest (see distribution schedule)		
23	Total NCI		
24	Retained Earnings, Controlling Interest, December 31, 2011		
25			

Eliminations and Adjustments:

(CY1)   Eliminate the parent's share (80%) of subsidiary net income.

(EL)   Eliminate the controlling portion (80%) of the Company S January 1, 2011, stockholders' equity against the investment in Company S account. No excess results.

(LN1)   Eliminate the intercompany note and accrued interest applicable to the note. This entry removes the *internal note* from the consolidated balance sheet.

(LN2)   Eliminate the intercompany interest expense and revenue. Since an equal amount of expense and revenue is eliminated, there is no change in the combined net income as a result of this entry.

Worksheet 4-8 (see page 218)

Eliminations & Adjustments		Consolidated Income Statement	NCI	Controlling Retained Earnings	Consolidated Balance Sheet	
Dr.	Cr.					
					55,400	1
	(LN1) 10,000					2
	(LN1) 400					3
					290,000	4
	(CY1) 8,000					5
	(EL) 120,000					6
(LN1) 10,000						7
(LN1) 400						8
					(100,000)	9
				(200,000)		10
(EL) 40,000			(10,000)			11
(EL) 80,000			(20,000)			12
		(170,000)				13
(LN2) 400						14
(CY1) 8,000						15
		95,000				16
		59,600				17
	(LN2) 400					18
138,800	138,800					19
		(15,400)				20
		2,000	(2,000)			21
		13,400		(13,400)		22
			(32,000)		(32,000)	23
				(213,400)	(213,400)	24
					0	25

Subsidiary Company S Income Distribution

Internally generated net income	$ 10,000
Adjusted income	$ 10,000
NCI share	× 20%
NCI	$ 2,000

Parent Company P Income Distribution

Internally generated net income	$ 5,400
80% × Company S adjusted income of $10,000	8,000
Controlling interest	$ 13,400

Worksheet 4-9

Vertical Worksheet Alternative
Company P and Subsidiary Company S
Worksheet for Consolidated Financial Statements
For Year Ended December 31, **2012**

Worksheet 4-9 (see page 223)

(Credit balance amounts are in parentheses.)

#	Account	Trial Balance — Company P	Trial Balance — Company S	Eliminations & Adjustments — Dr.	Eliminations & Adjustments — Cr.	NCI	Consolidated
1	**Income Statement**						
2	Sales	(600,000)	(530,000)	(IS) 150,000			(980,000)
3	Cost of Goods Sold	400,000	280,000	(EI) 10,000	(IS) 150,000 (BI) 8,000		532,000
4	Depreciation Expense	40,000	50,000		(F2) 1,000		89,000
5	Other Expenses	60,000	70,000				130,000
6	Subsidiary Income	(104,000)		(CY1) 104,000			
7	**Net Income**	(204,000)	(130,000)				(229,000)
8	NCI (see distribution schedule)					(25,600)	
9	Controlling Interest (see distribution schedule)						(203,400)
10							
11							
12	**Retained Earnings Statement**						
13	Retained Earnings, January 1, 2012—Company P	(600,000)		(BI) 6,400 (F1) 4,500			(589,100)
14							
15	Retained Earnings, January 1, 2012—Company S		(400,000)	(EL) 320,000 (BI) 1,600	(NCI) 15,000	(93,400)	
16							
17	**Net Income (carrydown)**	(204,000)	(130,000)			(25,600)	(203,400)
18							
19	Dividends Declared		20,000		(CY2) 16,000	4,000	
20	**Retained Earnings, December 31, 2012**	(804,000)	(510,000)				
21						115,000	
22	NCI, Retained Earnings, December 31, 2012						
23	Controlling Interest, Retained Earnings, December 31, 2012						(792,500)
24	**Balance Sheet**						
25	Inventory	300,000	250,000	(F1) 500	(EI) 10,000		540,000
26	Accounts Receivable	120,000	180,000	(F2) 1,000	(IA) 20,000		280,000
27	Plant Assets	236,000	400,000		(F1) 5,000		631,000
28	Accumulated Depreciation	(100,000)	(60,000)				(158,500)
29	Investment in Company S	628,000		(CY2) 16,000	(CY1) 104,000 (EL) 480,000 (D1) 60,000		
30							
31							
32							
33	Goodwill			(D1) 75,000			75,000
34	Current Liabilities	(80,000)	(60,000)	(IA) 20,000			(120,000)
35	Common Stock ($5 par)—Company S		(200,000)	(EL) 160,000		(40,000)	
36	Common Stock ($10 par)—Company P	(300,000)					(300,000)
37	**Retained Earnings (carrydown)**	(804,000)	(510,000)				
38	Retained Earnings, Controlling Interest, December 31, 2012						(792,500)
39	Retained Earnings, NCI, December 31, 2012					(115,000)	
40	Total NCI					(155,000)	(155,000)
41	Totals	0	0	869,000	869,000		0

Eliminations and Adjustments:

(CY1)	Eliminate the current-year entries recording the parent's share (80%) of subsidiary net income.
(CY2)	Eliminate intercompany dividends.
(EL)	Eliminate the pro rata portion of the subsidiary equity balances owned by the parent (80%) against the balance of the investment account.
(D1)/(NCI)	Distribute the excess to the goodwill account according to the determination and distribution of excess schedule.
(IS)	Eliminate the intercompany sales made during 2012.
(BI)	Eliminate the intercompany profit in the beginning inventory, 20% multiplied by $40,000. Since it was a subsidiary sale, the profit is shared 20% by the NCI.
(EI)	Eliminate the intercompany profit (20%) applicable to the $50,000 of intercompany goods in the ending inventory.
(IA)	Eliminate the intercompany trade balances.
(F1)	Eliminate the intercompany gain remaining on January 1, 2012, applicable to the sale of the machine by Company P ($5,000 original gain less one-half-year's gain of $500).
(F2)	Reduce the depreciation expense and accumulated depreciation accounts ($1,000 for the current year) in order to reflect depreciation based on the original cost.

Subsidiary Company S Income Distribution

Unrealized profit in ending inventory (20% × $50,000) .... (EI)	$10,000	Internally generated net income	$ 130,000
		Realized profit in beginning inventory (20% × $40,000) .... (BI)	8,000
		Adjusted income	$ 128,000
		NCI share	× 20%
		NCI	**$ 25,600**

Parent Company P Income Distribution

	Internally generated net income	$ 100,000
	Gain realized on sale of machine ...... (F2)	1,000
	80% × Company S adjusted income of $128,000	102,400
	Controlling interest	**$203,400**

UNDERSTANDING THE ISSUES

1. During 2011, Company P sold $50,000 of goods to subsidiary Company S at a profit of $12,000. One-fourth of the goods remain unsold at year-end. If no adjustments were made on the consolidated worksheet, what errors would there be on the consolidated income statement and balance sheet?

2. During 2011, Company P sold $50,000 of goods to subsidiary Company S at a profit of $12,000. One-fourth of the goods remain unsold at year-end. What specific adjustments are needed on the consolidated worksheet to deal with these issues?

3. Company S is 80% owned by Company P. Near the end of 2011, Company S sold merchandise with a cost of $6,000 to Company P for $7,000. Company P sold the merchandise to a nonaffiliated firm in 2012 for $10,000. How much total profit should be recorded on the consolidated income statements in 2011 and 2012? How much profit should be awarded to the controlling and noncontrolling interests in 2011 and 2012?

4. Subsidiary Company S is 80% owned by Company P. Company S sold a machine with a book value of $100,000 to Company P for $150,000. The asset has a 5-year life and is depreciated under the straight-line method. The president of Company S thinks it has scored a $50,000 immediate profit for the noncontrolling interest. Explain how much profit the noncontrolling interest will realize and when it will be awarded.

5. On January 1, 2011, Company P sold a machine to its 70%-owned subsidiary, Company S, for $60,000. The book value of the machine was $50,000. The machine was depreciated using the straight-line method over five years. On December 31, 2013, Company S sold the machine to a nonaffiliated firm for $35,000. On the consolidated statements, how much gain or loss on the intercompany machine sale should be recognized in 2011, 2012, and 2013?

6. Company S is a 70%-owned subsidiary of Company P. Company S is building a ship to be used by Company P. The ship was 40% completed in 2011 and 100% completed in 2012. The actual and budgeted profit on the ship was $100,000. Company S uses the percentage-of-completion method for its long-term construction projects. The ship went into service for Company P on January 1, 2013, and is depreciated straight-line over 20 years. How much profit was recorded by Company S in 2011, 2012, and 2013? How much profit will appear in the consolidated statements for the ship in 2011, 2012, and 2013?

7. Company S is an 80%-owned subsidiary of Company P. Company S needed to borrow $500,000 on January 1, 2011. The best interest rate it could secure was 10% annual. Company P has a better credit rating and decided to borrow the funds needed from a bank at 8% annual and then loaned the money to Company S at 9.5% annual.

   a. Is Company S better off as a result of borrowing the funds from Company P?
   b. What are the interest revenue and expense amounts recorded by Company P and Company S during 2012?
   c. How much interest expense and/or interest revenue should appear on the 2011 consolidated income statement?

EXERCISES

Exercise 1 *(LO 1, 2)* **Gross profit: separate firms versus consolidated.** Sogern is an 80%-owned subsidiary of Partplus Company. The two affiliates had the following separate income statements for 2011 and 2012 shown on page 243).

	Sogern Company		Partplus Company	
	2011	2012	2011	2012
Sales revenue	$250,000	$300,000	$500,000	$540,000
Cost of goods sold..................	150,000	180,000	310,000	360,000
Gross profit	$100,000	$120,000	$190,000	$180,000
Expenses	45,000	56,000	120,000	125,000
Net income	$ 55,000	$ 64,000	$ 70,000	$ 55,000

Sogern sells at the same gross profit percentage to all customers. During 2011, Sogern sold goods to Partplus for the first time in the amount of $120,000. $30,000 of these sales remained in Partplus's ending inventory. During 2012, sales to Partplus by Sogern were $110,000, of which $2$0,000 sales were still in Partplus's December 31, 2012, inventory.

Prepare consolidated income statements including the distribution of income to the controlling and noncontrolling interests for 2011 and 2012.

Exercise 2 *(LO 2)* **Distribution of income with inventory profits.** Norge Company is an 80%-owned subsidiary of Victor Corporation. The separate income statements of the two companies for 2012 are as follows:

	Victor Corporation	Norge Company
Sales	$ 220,000	$120,000
Cost of goods sold...............................	(150,000)	(90,000)
Gross profit	$ 70,000	$ 30,000
Other expenses	(40,000)	(12,000)
Other income....................................	5,000	
Operating income................................	$ 35,000	$ 18,000
Subsidiary income................................	14,400	
Net income	$ 49,400	$ 18,000

The following facts apply to 2012:

a. Norge Company sold $80,000 of goods to Victor Corporation. The gross profits on sales to Victor and to unrelated companies are equal and have not changed from the previous years.
b. Victor Corporation held $20,000 of the goods purchased from Norge Company in its beginning inventory and $30,000 of such goods in ending inventory.
c. Victor Corporation billed Norge Company $5,000 for computer services. The charge was expensed by Norge Company and treated as other income by Victor Corporation.

Prepare the consolidated income statement for 2012, including the distribution of the consolidated net income to the controlling and noncontrolling interests. The supporting income distribution schedules should be prepared as well.

Exercise 3 *(LO 2)* **Inventory profits with lower-of-cost-or-market adjustment.** Hide Corporation is a wholly owned subsidiary of Seek Company. During 2011, Hide sold all of its production to Seek Company for $400,000, a price that includes a 25% gross profit. 2011 was the first year that such intercompany sales were made. By year-end, Seek sold, for $416,000, 80% of the goods it had purchased. The balance of the intercompany goods, $80,000, remained in the ending inventory and was adjusted to a lower fair value of $70,000. The adjustment was a charge to the cost of goods sold.

1. Determine the gross profit on sales recorded by both companies.
2. Determine the gross profit to be shown on the consolidated income statement.

Exercise 4 *(LO 3)* **Land and building profit.** Wavemasters Inc., owns an 80% interest in Sayner Development Company. In a prior period, Sayner Development purchased a parcel of land for $50,000. During 2011, it constructed a building on the land at a cost of $500,000. The land and building were sold to Wavemasters at the very end of 2011 for $750,000, of which $100,000 was for the land. It is estimated that the building has a 20-year life with no salvage value.

1. Prepare all worksheet eliminations that would be made on the 2011 consolidated worksheet as a result of the real estate sale.
2. Prepare all worksheet eliminations that would be made on the 2013 consolidated worksheet as a result of the 2011 real estate sale.

Exercise 5 *(LO 3)* **Resale of intercompany asset.** Hilton Corporation sold a press to its 80%-owned subsidiary, Agri Fab Inc., for $5,000 on January 1, 2012. The press originally was purchased by Hilton on January 1, 2011, for $20,000, and $6,000 of depreciation for 2011 had been recorded. The fair value of the press on January 1, 2012, was $10,000. Agri Fab proceeded to depreciate the press on a straight-line basis, using a 5-year life and no salvage value. On December 31, 2013, Agri Fab, having no further need for the machine, sold it for $2,000 and recorded a loss on the sale.

Explain the adjustments that would have to be made to the separate income statements of the two companies to arrive at the consolidated income statements for 2012 and 2013.

Exercise 6 *(LO 3)* **Machinery sale.** On January 1, 2012, Jungle Company sold a machine to Safari Company for $30,000. The machine had an original cost of $24,000, and accumulated depreciation on the asset was $9,000 at the time of the sale. The machine has a 5-year remaining life and will be depreciated on a straight-line basis with no salvage value. Safari Company is an 80%-owned subsidiary of Jungle Company.

1. Explain the adjustments that would have to be made to arrive at consolidated net income for the years 2012 through 2016 as a result of this sale.
2. Prepare the elimination that would be required on the December 31, 2012, consolidated worksheet as a result of this sale.
3. Prepare the entry for the December 31, 2013, worksheet as a result of this sale.

Exercise 7 *(LO 3)* **Fixed asset sales by parent and subsidiary.** The separate income statements of Danner Company and its 90%-owned subsidiary, Link Company, for the year ended December 31, 2012, are as follows:

	Danner Company	Link Company
Sales	$ 650,000	$ 280,000
Cost of goods sold	(400,000)	(190,000)
Gross profit	$ 250,000	$ 90,000
Other expenses	(180,000)	(70,000)
Other income	20,000	
Operating income	$ 90,000	$ 20,000
Subsidiary income	18,000	
Net income	$ 108,000	$ 20,000

The following additional facts apply:

a. On January 1, 2011, Link Company purchased a building, with a book value of $100,000 and an estimated 20-year life, from Danner Company for $150,000. The building was being depreciated on a straight-line basis with no salvage value.
b. On January 1, 2012, Link Company sold a machine with a cost of $40,000 to Danner Company for $60,000. The machine had an expected life of five years and is being depreciated on a straight-line basis with no salvage value. Link Company is a dealer for the machine.

Prepare a worksheet that shows income statements of Danner and Link with a column for eliminations. Be sure to include the distribution of income to the controlling and non-controlling interest.

Exercise 8 *(LO 4)* **Completed-contract method.** Janis Company contracted with its 80%-owned subsidiary, Essuman Equipment Company, for the construction of two stamping machines. The first machine was completed and put into operation on July 1, 2011. It cost Essuman $60,000 and has a 5-year estimated life with no salvage value. The contract price was $75,000. The machine is being depreciated on a straight-line basis. The second machine, with an estimated total cost of $90,000 and a contract price of $120,000, was 80% complete on December 31, 2011. To date, costs on the second contract total $72,000. By the statement date, Janis had completely paid for the first machine and still owed $3,000 of the $60,000 billed to date on the second machine. Essuman uses the completed-contract method to account for its long-term construction contracts.

1. Prepare the necessary eliminations for the consolidated worksheet on December 31, 2011.
2. What are the effects of these contracts on the income distribution schedules?

Exercise 9 *(LO 4)* **Percentage-of-completion method.** Apple Contractors, an 80%-owned subsidiary, is constructing a warehouse for its parent, Plum Corporation. The following information is available on December 31, 2011:

Percent of completion	60%
Costs incurred to date	$120,000
Estimated costs to complete	80,000
Contract price	250,000
Amount billed to date (no amounts collected)	150,000

Apple uses the percentage-of-completion method to account for its long-term contracts.

Record the journal entries that each of the two companies would have made relative to the construction. Prepare a partial trial balance using the data from your entries, and show the eliminations relating to the contract for the December 31, 2011, consolidated worksheet.

Exercise 10 *(LO 5)* **Intercompany note.** Saratoga Company owns 80% of the outstanding common stock of Windsor Company. On May 1, 2013, Windsor Company arranges a 1-year, $50,000 loan from Saratoga Company. The loan agreement specifies that interest will accrue at the rate of 6% per annum and that all interest will be paid on the maturity date of the loan. The financial reporting period ends on December 31, 2013, and the note originating from the loan remains outstanding.

1. Prepare the entries that both companies would have made on their separate books, including the accrual of interest.
2. Prepare the eliminations, in entry form, that will be made on a consolidated worksheet prepared as of December 31, 2013.

Exercise 11 *(LO 5)* **Intercompany note discounted.** Assume the same facts as in Exercise 10, but in addition, assume that Saratoga is itself in need of cash. It discounts the note received from Windsor at First Bank on July 1, 2013, at a discount rate of 8% per annum.

1. Prepare the entries that both companies would have made on their separate books, including interest accruals.
2. Prepare the eliminations, in entry form, that will be made on a consolidated worksheet prepared as of December 31, 2013.

Exercise 12 *(LO 2, 3)* **Merchandise and fixed asset sale.** Peninsula Company owns an 80% controlling interest in Sandbar Company. Sandbar regularly sells merchandise to Peninsula, which then sells to outside parties. The gross profit on all such sales is 40%. On January 1, 2011,

Peninsula sells land and a building to Sandbar. Tax assessments divide the value of the parcel 20% to land and 75% to structures. Pertinent information for the companies is summarized as follows:

	Peninsula	Sandbar
Internally generated net income, 2011	$520,000	$250,000
Internally generated net income, 2012	340,000	235,000
Intercompany merchandise sales, 2011		100,000
Intercompany merchandise sales, 2012		120,000
Intercompany inventory, December 31, 2011	15,000	
Intercompany inventory, December 31, 2012	20,000	
Cost of real estate sold on January 1, 2011	600,000	
Sale price for real estate on January 1, 2011	800,000	
Depreciable life of building		20 years

Prepare income distribution schedules for 2011 and 2012 for Peninsula and Sandbar as they would be prepared to distribute income to the noncontrolling and controlling interests in support of consolidated worksheets.

PROBLEMS

Problem 4-1 *(LO 2)* **80%, cost, beginning and ending inventory.** On April 1, 2011, Baxter Corporation purchased 80% of the outstanding stock of Crayon Company for $425,000. A condensed balance sheet of Crayon Company at the purchase date is shown below.

Assets		Liabilities and Equity	
Current assets	$180,000	Liabilities	$100,000
Long-lived assets (net)	320,000	Common stock	200,000
		Paid-in capital in excess of par	100,000
		Retained earnings	100,000
Total assets	$500,000	Total liabilities and equity	$500,000

All book values approximated fair values on the purchase date. Any excess cost was attributed to goodwill.

The following information was gathered pertaining to the first two years of operation since Baxter's purchase of Crayon Company stock:

a. Intercompany merchandise sales were summarized as follows:

Date	Transaction	Sales	Gross Profit	Merchandise Remaining in Purchaser's Ending Inventory
April 1, 2011 to	Baxter to Crayon	$35,000	15%	$9,000
March 31, 2012	Crayon to Baxter	20,000	20	3,500
April 1, 2012 to	Baxter to Crayon	32,000	22	6,000
March 31, 2013	Crayon to Baxter	30,000	25	3,000

b. On March 31, 2013, Baxter owed Crayon $10,000, and Crayon owed Baxter $5,000 as a result of the intercompany sales.

c. Baxter paid $25,000 in cash dividends on March 20, 2012 and 2013. Crayon paid its first cash dividend on March 10, 2013, giving each share of outstanding common stock a $0.15 cash dividend.

d. The trial balances of the two companies as of March 31, 2013, follow:

	Baxter Corporation	Crayon Company
Cash	216,200	44,300
Accounts Receivable (net)	290,000	97,000
Inventory	310,000	80,000
Investment in Crayon Company	425,000	
Land	1,081,000	150,000
Building and Equipment	1,850,000	400,000
Accumulated Depreciation	(940,000)	(210,000)
Goodwill.......................................	60,000	
Accounts Payable	(242,200)	(106,300)
Bonds Payable....................................	(400,000)	
Common Stock ($0.50 par).........................	(250,000)	
Common Stock ($1 par)		(200,000)
Paid-In Capital in Excess of Par	(1,250,000)	(100,000)
Retained Earnings, April 1, 2012.....................	(1,105,000)	(140,000)
Sales..	(880,000)	(630,000)
Dividend Income (from Crayon Company)	(24,000)	
Cost of Goods Sold	704,000	504,000
Other Expenses...................................	130,000	81,000
Dividends Declared	25,000	30,000
Totals	0	0

1. Prepare the worksheet necessary to produce the consolidated financial statements of Baxter Corporation and its subsidiary for the year ended March 31, 2013. Include the value analysis and a determination and distribution of excess schedule and the income distribution schedules.
2. Prepare the formal consolidated income statement for the fiscal year ending March 31, 2013.

 ◄ ◄ ◄ ◄ ◄ **Required**

Problem 4-2 *(LO 2)* **80%, equity, beginning and ending inventory, write-down, note.** On January 1, 2011, Silvio Corporation exchanged on a 1-for-3 basis common stock it held in its treasury for 80% of the outstanding stock of Jenko Company. Silvio Corporation common stock had a market price of $40 per share on the exchange date. On the date of the acquisition, the stockholders' equity section of Jenko Company was as follows:

Common stock ($5 par).........................	$ 450,000
Paid-in capital in excess of par	180,000
Retained earnings	370,000
Total......................................	$1,000,000

Also on that date, Jenko Company's book values approximated fair values, except for the land, which was undervalued by $75,000. The remaining excess was attributable to goodwill. Information regarding intercompany transactions for 2013 follows:

a. Silvio Corporation sold merchandise to Jenko Company, realizing a 30% gross profit. Sales during 2013 were $140,000. Jenko had $25,000 of the 2012 purchases in its beginning inventory for 2013 and $35,000 of the 2013 purchases in its ending inventory for 2013. Jenko wrote down to $28,000 the merchandise purchased from Silvio Corporation and remaining in its 2013 ending inventory.
b. Jenko signed a 12%, 4-month, $10,000 note to Silvio in order to cover the remaining balance of its payables on November 1, 2013. No new merchandise was purchased after this date.

The trial balances of Silvio Corporation and Jenko Company as of December 31, 2013, were as follows

	Silvio Corporation	Jenko Company
Cash	140,000	205,200
Accounts Receivable	285,000	110,000
Interest Receivable.	1,500	
Notes Receivable.	50,000	
Inventory	470,000	160,000
Land.	350,000	300,000
Depreciable Fixed Assets	1,110,000	810,000
Accumulated Depreciation	(500,000)	(200,000)
Intangibles.	60,000	
Investment in Jenko Company	1,128,000	
Accounts Payable	(611,500)	(165,000)
Note Payable.		(10,000)
Interest Payable		(200)
Common Stock ($1 par)	(400,000)	
Common Stock ($5 par)		(450,000)
Paid-In Capital in Excess of Par	(1,235,000)	(180,000)
Retained Earnings, January 1, 2013.	(958,500)	(470,000)
Treasury Stock (at cost)	315,000	
Sales	(1,020,000)	(500,000)
Interest Income.	(1,500)	
Subsidiary Income.	(88,000)	
Cost of Goods Sold	705,000	300,000
Other Expenses	200,000	90,000
Totals	0	0

Required ▶ ▶ ▶ ▶ ▶   Prepare the worksheet necessary to produce the consolidated financial statements of Silvio Corporation and its subsidiary for the year ended December 31, 2013. Include the value analysis and determination and distribution of excess schedule and the income distribution schedules.

Problem 4-3 *(LO 2, 3, 4)* **100%, cost, merchandise sales, percentage-of-completion contracts.** Pardon, Inc., purchased 100% of the common stock of Slarno Corporation for $150,000 in cash on June 30, 2011. At that date, Slarno's stockholders' equity was as follows:

Common stock ($1 par)	$100,000
Retained earnings	50,000
Total.	$150,000

The fair values of the assets and liabilities did not differ materially from their book values. Slarno made no adjustments on its books to reflect the purchase by Pardon. On December 31, 2011, Pardon and Slarno prepared consolidated financial statements.

The transactions that occurred between Pardon and Slarno during the next year included the following:

a. On January 3, 2012, land with a $10,000 book value was sold by Pardon to Slarno for $15,000. Slarno made a $3,000 down payment and signed an 8% mortgage note, payable in 12 equal quarterly payments of $1,135, including interest, beginning March 31, 2012.

b. Slarno produced equipment for Pardon under two separate contracts. The first contract, which was for office equipment, was begun and completed during the year at a cost to Slarno of $17,500. Pardon paid $22,000 in cash for the equipment on April 17, 2012. The second contract was begun on February 15, 2012, but will not be completed until May 2013. Slarno incurred $45,000 of costs as of December 31, 2012, and anticipated an additional $30,000 of costs to complete the $95,000 contract. Slarno accounts for all contracts under the percentage-of-completion method. Pardon has made no account on its books for this uncompleted contract as of December 31, 2012.

c. Pardon depreciates all of its equipment over a 10-year estimated economic life, with no salvage value. Pardon takes one-half-year's depreciation in the year of purchase.

d. Pardon sold merchandise to Slarno at an average markup of 12% on cost. During the year, Pardon charged Slarno $238,000 for merchandise purchased, of which Slarno paid $211,000. Slarno had $11,200 of this merchandise on hand on December 31, 2012.

Trial balances of Pardon Inc. and its subsidiary as of December 31, 2012, were as follows:

	Pardon Inc.	Slarno Corporation
Cash	45,000	31,211
Accounts Receivable	119,000	73,500
Billings on Construction in Progress.		(1,201,900)
Mortgage Receivable	8,311	
Unsecured Notes Receivable.	18,000	
Inventories	217,000	117,500
Land.	34,000	42,000
Building and Equipment (net).	717,000	408,000
Investment in Slarno Corporation	150,000	
Accounts Payable	(203,000)	(147,000)
Mortgages Payable.	(592,000)	(397,311)
Common Stock	(250,000)	(100,000)
Retained Earnings, January 1, 2012.	(139,311)	(70,000)
Sales	(1,800,000)	
Earned Income on Long-Term Contracts		(437,000)
Cost of Goods Sold	1,155,000	
Construction in Progress		1,289,000
Selling, General, and Administrative Expenses	497,000	360,000
Interest Income.	(20,000)	
Interest Expense.	49,000	32,000
Gain on Sale of Land.	(5,000)	
Totals	0	0

Prepare the worksheet necessary to produce the consolidated financial statements of Pardon ◄ ◄ ◄ ◄ ◄ **Required** Inc., and its subsidiary for the year ended December 31, 2012. Assume both companies have made all the adjusting entries required for separate financial statements unless an obvious discrepancy exists. Include the determination and distribution of excess schedule.

(AICPA adapted)

Use the following information for Problems 4-4 and 4-5:

On January 1, 2011, Panther Company acquired Sandin Company. Panther paid $60 per share for 80% of Sandin's common stock. The price paid by Panther reflected a control premium. The NCI shares were estimated to have a market value of $55 per share. On the date of acquisition, Sandin had the following balance sheet:

Sandin Company
Balance Sheet
January 1, 2011

Assets		Liabilities and Equity	
Accounts receivable	$ 60,000	Accounts payable	$ 40,000
Inventory	40,000	Bonds payable	100,000
Land.	60,000	Common stock ($1 par).	10,000
Buildings	200,000	Paid-in capital in excess of par . . .	90,000
Accumulated depreciation	(50,000)	Retained earnings	112,000
Equipment	72,000		
Accumulated depreciation	(30,000)		
Total assets.	$352,000	Total liabilities and equity	$352,000

Buildings, which have a 20-year life, were understated by $120,000. Equipment, which has a 5-year life, was understated by $40,000. Any remaining excess was considered goodwill. Panther used the simple equity method to account for its investment in Sandin.

Panther and Sandin had the following trial balances on December 31, 2012:

	Panther Company	Sandin Company
Cash	24,000	132,000
Accounts Receivable	90,000	45,000
Inventory	120,000	56,000
Land	100,000	60,000
Investment in Sandin	512,000	
Buildings	800,000	200,000
Accumulated Depreciation	(220,000)	(65,000)
Equipment	150,000	72,000
Accumulated Depreciation	(90,000)	(46,000)
Accounts Payable	(60,000)	(102,000)
Bonds Payable		(100,000)
Common Stock	(100,000)	(10,000)
Paid-In Capital in Excess of Par	(800,000)	(90,000)
Retained Earnings, January 1, 2012	(365,000)	(142,000)
Sales	(800,000)	(350,000)
Cost of Goods Sold	450,000	208,500
Depreciation Expense—Buildings	30,000	7,500
Depreciation Expense—Equipment	15,000	8,000
Other Expenses	160,000	98,000
Interest Expense		8,000
Gain on Sale of Fixed Assets	(20,000)	
Subsidiary Income	(16,000)	
Dividends Declared	20,000	10,000
Totals	0	0

Problem 4-4 *(LO 3)* **80%, equity, several excess distributions, fixed asset sale.** Refer to the preceding facts for Panther's acquisition of Sandin common stock. On January 1, 2012, Panther held merchandise sold to it from Sandin for $12,000. This beginning inventory had an applicable gross profit of 25%. During 2012, Sandin sold merchandise to Panther for $75,000. On December 31, 2012, Panther held $18,000 of this merchandise in its inventory. This ending inventory had an applicable gross profit of 30%. Panther owed Sandin $20,000 on December 31 as a result of this intercompany sale.

On January 1, 2012, Panther sold equipment with a book value of $35,000 to Sandin for $50,000. Panther also sold some fixed assets to nonaffiliates. During 2012, the equipment was used by Sandin. Depreciation is computed over a 5-year life, using the straight-line method.

Required ▶ ▶ ▶ ▶ ▶

1. Prepare a value analysis and a determination and distribution of excess schedule for the investment in Sandin.
2. Complete a consolidated worksheet for Panther Company and its subsidiary Sandin Company as of December 31, 2012. Prepare supporting amortization and income distribution schedules.

Problem 4-5 *(LO 3)* **80%, equity, several excess distributions, fixed asset sale by parent and subsidiary.** Refer to the preceding facts for Panther's acquisition of Sandin common stock. On January 1, 2012, Sandin held merchandise sold to it from Panther for $20,000. During 2012, Panther sold merchandise to Sandin for $100,000. On December 31, 2012, Sandin held $25,000 of this merchandise in its inventory. Panther has a gross profit of 30%. Sandin owed Panther $15,000 on December 31 as a result of this intercompany sale.

On January 1, 2011, Sandin sold equipment to Panther at a profit of $24,000. Panther also sold some fixed assets to nonaffiliates. Depreciation is computed over a 6-year life, using the straight-line method.

1. Prepare a value analysis and a determination and distribution of excess schedule for the investment in Sandin.
2. Complete a consolidated worksheet for Panther Company and its subsidiary Sandin Company as of December 31, 2012. Prepare supporting amortization and income distribution schedules.

◄ ◄ ◄ ◄ ◄ **Required**

Problem 4-6 *(LO 2)* **100%, equity, ending inventory.** On January 1, 2011, 100% of the outstanding stock of Sand Company was purchased by Plant Corporation for $3,200,000. At that time, the book value of Sand's net assets equaled $3,000,000. The excess was attributable to equipment with a 10-year life.

The following trial balances of Plant Corporation and Sand Company were prepared on December 31, 2011:

	Plant Corporation	Sand Company
Cash	835,000	370,000
Accounts Receivable	400,000	365,000
Inventory	600,000	275,000
Property, Plant, and Equipment (net)	4,000,000	2,300,000
Investment in Sand Company	3,410,000	
Accounts Payable	(35,000)	(100,000)
Common Stock ($10 par)	(1,000,000)	(400,000)
Paid-In Capital in Excess of Par	(1,500,000)	(200,000)
Retained Earnings, January 1, 2011	(5,500,000)	(2,400,000)
Sales	(12,000,000)	(1,000,000)
Cost of Goods Sold	7,000,000	750,000
Other Expenses	4,000,000	40,000
Subsidiary Income	(210,000)	
Totals	0	0

Throughout 2011, sales to Plant Corporation made up 40% of Sand's revenue and produced a 25% gross profit rate. At year-end, Plant Corporation had sold $250,000 of the goods purchased from Sand Company and still owed Sand $30,000. None of the Sand products were in Plant's January 1, 2011, beginning inventory.

Prepare the worksheet necessary to produce the consolidated income statement and balance sheet of Plant Corporation and its subsidiary for the year ended December 31, 2011. Include the determination and distribution of excess schedule.

◄ ◄ ◄ ◄ ◄ **Required**

Use the following information for Problems 4-7 and 4-8:

On January 1, 2011, Packard Corporation acquired 70% of the common stock of Stude Corporation for $400,000. On this date, Stude had the following balance sheet:

Stude Corporation
Balance Sheet
January 1, 2011

Assets		Liabilities and Equity	
Accounts receivable	$ 60,000	Accounts payable	$ 40,000
Inventory	40,000	Bonds payable	100,000
Land.	60,000	Common stock ($1 par).	10,000
Buildings	200,000	Paid-in capital in excess of par. .	90,000
Accumulated depreciation .	(50,000)	Retained earnings	112,000
Equipment	72,000		
Accumulated depreciation .	(30,000)		
Total assets.	$352,000	Total liabilities and equity . . .	$352,000

Buildings, which have a 20-year life, were understated by $150,000. Equipment, which has a 5-year life, was understated by $60,000. The 3,000 NCI shares had a fair value of $50 each. Any remaining excess was considered to be goodwill. Packard used the simple equity method to account for its investment in Stude.

Packard and Stude had the following trial balances on December 31, 2012:

	Packard Corporation	Stude Corporation
Cash	66,000	132,000
Accounts Receivable	90,000	45,000
Inventory	120,000	56,000
Land.	100,000	60,000
Investment in Stude	428,000	
Buildings	800,000	200,000
Accumulated Depreciation	(220,000)	(65,000)
Equipment	150,000	72,000
Accumulated Depreciation	(90,000)	(46,000)
Accounts Payable	(60,000)	(102,000)
Bonds Payable.		(100,000)
Common Stock	(100,000)	(10,000)
Paid-In Capital in Excess of Par	(800,000)	(90,000)
Retained Earnings, January 1, 2012.	(325,000)	(142,000)
Sales	(800,000)	(350,000)
Cost of Goods Sold	450,000	208,500
Depreciation Expense—Buildings.	30,000	7,500
Depreciation Expense—Equipment.	15,000	8,000
Other Expenses	140,000	98,000
Interest Expense.		8,000
Subsidiary Income.	(14,000)	
Dividends Declared.	20,000	10,000
Totals	0	0

Problem 4-7 *(LO 2)* **70%, equity, beginning and ending inventory, subsidiary seller.** Refer to the preceding facts for Packard's acquisition of Stude common stock. On January 1, 2012, Packard held merchandise acquired from Stude for $10,000. This beginning inventory had an applicable gross profit of 25%. During 2012, Stude sold $40,000 worth of merchandise to Packard. Packard held $6,000 of this merchandise at December 31, 2012. This ending inventory had an applicable gross profit of 30%. Packard owed Stude $11,000 on December 31 as a result of these intercompany sales.

1. Prepare a value analysis and a determination and distribution of excess schedule for the ◀ ◀ ◀ ◀ ◀ **Required** investment in Stude.
2. Complete a consolidated worksheet for Packard Corporation and its subsidiary Stude Corporation as of December 31, 2012. Prepare supporting amortization and income distribution schedules.

Problem 4-8 *(LO 2)* **70%, equity, beginning and ending inventory, parent and subsidiary seller.** Refer to the preceding facts for Packard's acquisition of Stude common stock. On January 1, 2012, Packard held merchandise acquired from Stude for $10,000. This beginning inventory had an applicable gross profit of 25%. During 2012, Stude sold $40,000 worth of merchandise to Packard. Packard held $6,000 of this merchandise at December 31, 2012. This ending inventory had an applicable gross profit of 30%. Packard owed Stude $11,000 on December 31 as a result of this intercompany sale.

On January 1, 2012, Stude held merchandise acquired from Packard for $20,000. This beginning inventory had an applicable gross profit of 40%. During 2012, Packard sold $60,000 worth of merchandise to Stude. Stude held $30,000 of this merchandise at December 31, 2012. This ending inventory had an applicable gross profit of 35%. Stude owed Packard $23,000 on December 31 as a result of this intercompany sale.

1. Prepare a value analysis and a determination and distribution of excess schedule for the ◀ ◀ ◀ ◀ ◀ **Required** investment in Stude.
2. Complete a consolidated worksheet for Packard Corporation and its subsidiary Stude Corporation as of December 31, 2012. Prepare supporting amortization and income distribution schedules.

Problem 4-9 *(LO 3)* **80%, equity, fixed asset sales by subsidiary and parent.** On September 1, 2011, Parcel Corporation purchased 80% of the outstanding common stock of Sack Corporation for $152,000. On that date, Sack's net book values equaled fair values, and there was no excess of cost or book value resulting from the purchase. Parcel has been maintaining its investment under the simple equity method.

Over the next three years, the intercompany transactions between the companies were as follows:

a. On September 1, 2011, Sack sold its 4-year-old delivery truck to Parcel for $14,000 in cash. At that time, Sack had depreciated the truck, which had cost $15,000, to its $5,000 salvage value. Parcel estimated on the date of the sale that the asset had a remaining useful life of three years and no salvage value.
b. On September 1, 2012, Parcel sold equipment to Sack for $103,000. Parcel originally paid $80,000 for the equipment and planned to depreciate it over 20 years, assuming no salvage value. However, Parcel had the property for only 10 years and carried it at a net book value of $40,000 on the sale date. Sack will use the equipment for 10 years, at which time Sack expects no salvage value.

Both companies use straight-line depreciation for all assets.

Trial balances of Parcel Corporation and Sack Corporation as of the August 31, 2013, year-end were as shown below:

	Parcel Corporation	Sack Corporation
Cash	120,000	50,000
Accounts Receivable (net)	115,000	18,000
Notes Receivable.............................		10,000
Inventory, August 31, 2013	175,000	34,000
Investment in Sack Corporation..................	217,440	
Plant and Equipment	990,700	295,000
Accumulated Depreciation	(170,000)	(85,000)
Other Assets	28,000	
Accounts Payable	(80,000)	(50,200)
Notes Payable...............................	(25,000)	
Bonds Payable (12%)	(300,000)	
Common Stock ($10 par)	(290,000)	(70,000)
Paid-In Capital in Excess of Par	(110,000)	(62,000)

	Parcel Corporation	Sack Corporation
Retained Earnings, September 1, 2012	(498,850)	(118,000)
Sales	(920,000)	(240,000)
Cost of Goods Sold	598,000	132,000
Selling and General Expenses	108,000	80,000
Subsidiary Income	(23,040)	
Interest Income		(800)
Interest Expense	37,750	
Gain on Sale of Equipment	(63,000)	
Dividends Declared	90,000	7,000
Totals	0	0

Required ▶ ▶ ▶ ▶ ▶   Prepare the worksheet necessary to produce the consolidated financial statements of Parcel Corporation and its subsidiary for the year ended August 31, 2013. Include the income distribution schedules.

Problem 4-10 *(LO 2, 3)* **80%, equity, excess distributions, merchandise, equipment sales.** On January 1, 2011, Peanut Company acquired 80% of the common stock of Salt Company for $200,000. On this date, Salt had total owners' equity of $200,000 (including retained earnings of $100,000). During 2011 and 2012, Peanut appropriately accounted for its investment in Salt using the simple equity method.

Any excess of cost over book value is attributable to inventory (worth $12,500 more than cost), to equipment (worth $25,000 more than book value), and to goodwill. FIFO is used for inventories. The equipment has a remaining life of four years, and straight-line depreciation is used. On January 1, 2012, Peanut held merchandise acquired from Salt for $20,000. During 2012, Salt sold merchandise to Peanut for $40,000, $10,000 of which was still held by Peanut on December 31, 2012. Salt's usual gross profit is 50%.

On January 1, 2011, Peanut sold equipment to Salt at a gain of $15,000. Depreciation is being computed using the straight-line method, a 5-year life, and no salvage value.

The following trial balances were prepared for the Peanut and Salt companies for December 31, 2012:

	Peanut Company	Salt Company
Inventory, December 31	130,000	50,000
Other Current Assets	241,000	235,000
Investment in Salt Company	308,000	
Other Long-Term Investments	20,000	
Land	140,000	80,000
Buildings and Equipment	375,000	200,000
Accumulated Depreciation	(120,000)	(30,000)
Other Intangible Assets		20,000
Current Liabilities	(150,000)	(70,000)
Bonds Payable		(100,000)
Other Long-Term Liabilities	(200,000)	(50,000)
Common Stock	(200,000)	(50,000)
Paid-In Capital in Excess of Par	(100,000)	(50,000)
Retained Earnings, January 1, 2012	(320,000)	(150,000)
Sales	(600,000)	(315,000)
Cost of Goods Sold	350,000	150,000
Operating Expenses	150,000	60,000
Subsidiary Income	(84,000)	
Dividends Declared	60,000	20,000
Totals	0	0

Complete the worksheet for consolidated financial statements for the year ended ◄ ◄ ◄ ◄ ◄ **Required**
December 31, 2012. Include the necessary determination and distribution of excess schedule and income distribution schedules.

Problem 4-11 *(LO 2, 3)* **80%, cost, excess distributions, merchandise, equipment
sales.** (This is the same as Problem 4-10 except for use of the cost method.) On January 1,
2011, Peanut Company acquired 80% of the common stock of Salt Company for $200,000. On
this date, Salt had total owners' equity of $200,000 (including retained earnings of $100,000).
During 2011 and 2012, Peanut accounted for its investment in Salt using the cost method.

Any excess of cost over book value is attributable to inventory (worth $12,500 more
than cost), to equipment (worth $25,000 more than book value), and to goodwill. FIFO is used
for inventories. The equipment has a remaining life of four years, and straight-line depreciation
is used.

On January 1, 2012, Peanut held merchandise acquired from Salt for $20,000. During
2012, Salt sold merchandise to Peanut for $40,000, $10,000 of which was still held by Peanut
on December 31, 2012. Salt's usual gross profit is 50%.

On January 1, 2011, Peanut sold equipment to Salt at a gain of $15,000. Depreciation is
being computed using the straight-line method, a 5-year life, and no salvage value.

The following trial balances were prepared for the Peanut and Salt companies for December
31, 2012:

	Peanut Company	Salt Company
Inventory, December 31	130,000	50,000
Other Current Assets	241,000	235,000
Investment in Salt Company	200,000	
Other Long-Term Investments	20,000	
Land	140,000	80,000
Buildings and Equipment	375,000	200,000
Accumulated Depreciation	(120,000)	(30,000)
Other Intangible Assets		20,000
Current Liabilities	(150,000)	(70,000)
Bonds Payable		(100,000)
Other Long-Term Liabilities	(200,000)	(50,000)
Common Stock	(200,000)	(50,000)
Paid-In Capital in Excess of Par	(100,000)	(50,000)
Retained Earnings, January 1, 2012	(280,000)	(150,000)
Sales	(600,000)	(315,000)
Cost of Goods Sold	350,000	150,000
Operating Expenses	150,000	60,000
Dividend Income	(16,000)	
Dividends Declared	60,000	20,000
Totals	0	0

Complete the worksheet for consolidated financial statements for the year ended ◄ ◄ ◄ ◄ ◄ **Required**
December 31, 2012. Include any necessary determination and distribution of excess schedule and income distribution schedules.

Problem 4-12 *(LO 2, 3, 6)* **80%, sophisticated equity, several excess distributions,
merchandise, equipment sales.** (This is the same as Problem 4-10 except for use of the
sophisticated equity method.) On January 1, 2011, Peanut Company acquired 80% of the
common stock of Salt Company for $200,000. On this date, Salt had total owners' equity of
$200,000. During 2011 and 2012, Peanut appropriately accounted for its investment in Salt
using the sophisticated equity method.

Any excess of cost over book value is attributable to inventory (worth $12,500 more than cost), to equipment (worth $25,000 more than book value), and to goodwill. FIFO is used for inventories. The equipment has a remaining life of four years, and straight-line depreciation is used.

On January 1, 2012, Peanut held merchandise acquired from Salt for $20,000. During 2012, Salt sold merchandise to Peanut for $40,000, $10,000 of which was still held by Peanut on December 31, 2012. Salt's usual gross profit is 50%.

On January 1, 2011, Peanut sold equipment to Salt at a gain of $15,000. Depreciation is being computed using the straight-line method, a 5-year life, and no salvage value.

The following trial balances were prepared for the Peanut and Salt companies for December 31, 2012:

	Peanut Company	Salt Company
Inventory, December 31	130,000	50,000
Other Current Assets	241,000	235,000
Investment in Salt Company	284,000	
Other Long-Term Investments	20,000	
Land	140,000	80,000
Buildings and Equipment	375,000	200,000
Accumulated Depreciation	(120,000)	(30,000)
Other Intangible Assets		20,000
Current Liabilities	(150,000)	(70,000)
Bonds Payable		(100,000)
Other Long-Term Liabilities	(200,000)	(50,000)
Common Stock	(200,000)	(50,000)
Paid-In Capital in Excess of Par	(100,000)	(50,000)
Retained Earnings, January 1, 2012	(297,000)	(150,000)
Sales	(600,000)	(315,000)
Cost of Goods Sold	350,000	150,000
Operating Expenses	150,000	60,000
Subsidiary Income	(83,000)	
Dividends Declared	60,000	20,000
Totals	0	0

Required ▶ ▶ ▶ ▶ ▶   Complete the worksheet for consolidated financial statements for the year ended December 31, 2012. Include any necessary determination and distribution of excess schedule and income distribution schedules.

Problem 4-13 *(LO 2, 5)* **90%, cost, merchandise, note payable.** The December 31, 2012, trial balances of Pettie Corporation and its 90%-owned subsidiary Sunco Corporation are as follows:

	Pettie Corporation	Sunco Corporation
Cash	15,000	45,500
Accounts and Other Current Receivables	410,900	170,000
Inventory	920,000	739,400
Property, Plant, and Equipment (net)	1,000,000	400,000
Investment in Sunco Corporation	1,260,000	
Accounts Payable and Other Current Liabilities	(140,000)	(305,900)
Common Stock ($10 par)	(500,000)	
Common Stock ($10 par)		(200,000)
Retained Earnings, January 1, 2012	(2,800,000)	(650,000)
Dividends Declared		1,000
Sales	(2,000,000)	(650,000)
Dividend Income	(900)	

	Pettie Corporation	Sunco Corporation
Interest Expense...		5,000
Interest Income..	(5,000)	
Cost of Goods Sold	1,500,000	400,000
Other Expenses	340,000	45,000
Totals	0	0

Pettie's investment in Sunco was purchased for $1,260,000 in cash on January 1, 2011, and was accounted for by the cost method. On January 1, 2011, Sunco had the following equity balances:

Common stock.............	$200,000
Retained earnings	600,000
Total equity	$800,000

Pettie's excess of cost over book value on Sunco's investment has been identified as goodwill.

Sunco borrowed $100,000 from Pettie on June 30, 2012, with the note maturing on June 30, 2013, at 10% interest. Correct accruals have been recorded by both companies.

During 2012, Pettie sold merchandise to Sunco at an aggregate invoice price of $300,000, which included a profit of $75,000. As of December 31, 2012, Sunco had not paid Pettie for $90,000 of these purchases, and 10% of the total merchandise purchased from Pettie still remained in Sunco's inventory.

Sunco declared a $1,000 cash dividend in December 2012 payable in January 2013.

Prepare the worksheet required to produce the consolidated statements of Pettie Corporation and its subsidiary, Sunco Corporation, for the year ended December 31, 2012. Include the valuation analysis, the determination and distribution of excess schedule, and the income distribution schedules.   ◄ ◄ ◄ ◄ ◄ **Required**

(AICPA adapted)

Use the following information for Problems 4-14 and 4-15:

On January 1, 2011, Purple Company acquired Salmon Company. Purple paid $300,000 for 80% of Salmon's common stock. On the date of acquisition, Salmon had the following balance sheet:

Salmon Company
Balance Sheet
January 1, 2011

Assets		Liabilities and Equity	
Accounts receivable	$ 50,000	Accounts payable	$ 60,000
Inventory	60,000	Bonds payable	200,000
Land......................	100,000	Common stock ($1 par)........	10,000
Buildings	150,000	Paid-in capital in excess of par ...	90,000
Accumulated depreciation	(50,000)	Retained earnings	60,000
Equipment	100,000		
Accumulated depreciation	(30,000)		
Goodwill	40,000		
Total assets..............	$420,000	Total liabilities and equity	$420,000

Buildings, which have a 20-year life, are understated by $100,000. Equipment, which has a 5-year life, is understated by $50,000. Any remaining excess is goodwill. Purple uses the simple equity method to account for its investment in Salmon.

Problem 4-14 *(LO 2, 3)* **80%, equity, several excess distributions, inventory, fixed assets, parent and subsidiary sales.**   Refer to the preceding facts for Purple's acquisition of Salmon common stock. On January 1, 2012, Salmon held merchandise sold to it by Purple for $14,000. This beginning inventory had an applicable gross profit of 40%. During 2012, Purple sold merchandise to Salmon for $60,000. On December 31, 2012, Salmon held $12,000 of this merchandise in its inventory. This ending inventory had an applicable gross profit of 35%. Salmon owed Purple $8,000 on December 31 as a result of this intercompany sale.

Purple held $12,000 worth of merchandise in its beginning inventory from sales from Salmon. This beginning inventory had an applicable gross profit of 25%. During 2012, Salmon sold merchandise to Purple for $30,000. Purple held $16,000 of this inventory at the end of the year. This ending inventory had an applicable gross profit of 30%. Purple owed Salmon $6,000 on December 31 as a result of this intercompany sale.

On January 1, 2011, Purple sold equipment to Salmon at a profit of $40,000. Depreciation on this equipment is computed over an 8-year life using the straight-line method.

On January 1, 2012, Salmon sold equipment with a book value of $30,000 to Purple for $54,000. This equipment has a 6-year life and is depreciated using the straight-line method.

Purple and Salmon had the following trial balances on December 31, 2012:

	Purple Company	Salmon Company
Cash	92,400	57,500
Accounts Receivable	130,000	36,000
Inventory	105,000	76,000
Land	100,000	100,000
Investment in Salmon Company	381,200	
Buildings	800,000	150,000
Accumulated Depreciation	(250,000)	(60,000)
Equipment	210,000	220,000
Accumulated Depreciation	(115,000)	(80,000)
Goodwill		40,000
Accounts Payable	(70,000)	(78,000)
Bonds Payable		(200,000)
Common Stock	(100,000)	(10,000)
Paid-In Capital in Excess of Par	(800,000)	(90,000)
Retained Earnings, January 1, 2012	(325,000)	(142,000)
Sales	(800,000)	(350,000)
Cost of Goods Sold	450,000	208,500
Depreciation Expense—Buildings	30,000	5,000
Depreciation Expense—Equipment	25,000	23,000
Other Expenses	140,000	92,000
Interest Expense		16,000
Gain on Sale of Fixed Asset		(24,000)
Subsidiary Income	(23,600)	
Dividends Declared	20,000	10,000
Totals	0	0

Required ▶ ▶ ▶ ▶ ▶

1. Prepare a value analysis and a determination and distribution of excess schedule for the investment in Salmon.
2. Complete a consolidated worksheet for Purple Company and its subsidiary Salmon Company as of December 31, 2012. Prepare supporting amortization and income distribution schedules.

Problem 4-15 *(LO 2, 3)* **80%, equity, several excess distributions, inventory, fixed assets, parent and subsidiary sales.** Refer to the preceding facts for Purple's acquisition of Salmon common stock. On January 1, 2013, Salmon held merchandise sold to it from Purple for $12,000. This beginning inventory had an applicable gross profit of 35%. During 2013, Purple sold merchandise to Salmon for $55,000. On December 31, 2013, Salmon held $10,000 of this merchandise in its inventory. This ending inventory had an applicable gross profit of 40%. Salmon owed Purple $7,500 on December 31 as a result of this intercompany sale.

Purple held $16,000 worth of merchandise in its January 1, 2013, inventory from sales from Salmon. This beginning inventory had an applicable gross profit of 30%. During 2013, Salmon sold merchandise to Purple for $35,000. Purple held $20,000 of this inventory at the end of the year. This ending inventory had an applicable gross profit of 35%. Purple owed Salmon $5,000 on December 31 as a result of this intercompany sale.

On January 1, 2011, Purple sold equipment to Salmon at a profit of $40,000. Depreciation on this equipment is computed over an 8-year life using the straight-line method.

On January 1, 2012, Salmon sold equipment with a book value of $30,000 to Purple for $54,000. This equipment has a 6-year life and is depreciated using the straight-line method. Purple and Salmon had the following trial balances on December 31, 2013:

	Purple Company	Salmon Company
Cash	195,400	53,500
Accounts Receivable	140,000	53,000
Inventory	140,000	81,000
Land	100,000	60,000
Investment in Salmon Company	443,600	
Buildings	800,000	150,000
Accumulated Depreciation	(280,000)	(65,000)
Equipment	150,000	220,000
Accumulated Depreciation	(115,000)	(103,000)
Goodwill		40,000
Accounts Payable	(25,000)	(50,000)
Bonds Payable		(100,000)
Common Stock	(100,000)	(10,000)
Paid-In Capital in Excess of Par	(800,000)	(90,000)
Retained Earnings, January 1, 2013	(510,000)	(169,500)
Sales	(850,000)	(500,000)
Cost of Goods Sold	480,000	290,000
Depreciation Expense—Buildings	30,000	5,000
Depreciation Expense—Equipment	15,000	23,000
Other Expenses	210,000	94,000
Interest Expense		8,000
Subsidiary Income	(64,000)	
Dividends Declared	40,000	10,000
Totals	0	0

1. Prepare a value analysis and a determination and distribution of excess schedule for the ◀ ◀ ◀ ◀ ◀ **Required** investment in Salmon.
2. Complete a consolidated worksheet for Purple Company and its subsidiary Salmon Company as of December 31, 2013. Prepare supporting amortization and income distribution schedules.

APPENDIX PROBLEMS

Problem 4A-1 *(LO 2, 3, 7)* **Vertical worksheet, 100%, cost, fixed asset and merchandise sales.** Arther Corporation acquired all of the outstanding $10 par voting common stock of Trent Inc., on January 1, 2012, in exchange for 50,000 shares of its $10 par voting common stock. On December 31, 2011, the common stock of Arther had a closing market price of $15 per share on a national stock exchange. The retained earnings balance of Trent Inc., was $156,000 on the date of the acquisition. Both companies continued to operate as separate business entities maintaining separate accounting records with years ending December 31.

On December 31, 2014, after year-end adjustments but before the nominal accounts were closed, the companies had the following condensed statements:

	Arther Corporation	Trent, Inc.
Income Statement:		
Sales	$(1,900,000)	$(1,500,000)
Dividend Income (from Trent, Inc.).	(40,000)	
Cost of Goods Sold	1,180,000	870,000
Operating Expenses (includes depreciation).	550,000	440,000
Net Income.	$ (210,000)	$ (190,000)
Retained Earnings:		
Retained Earnings, January 1, 2014.	$ (250,000)	$ (206,000)
Net Income	(210,000)	(190,000)
Dividends Paid.		40,000
Balance, December 31, 2014.	$ (460,000)	$ (356,000)
Balance Sheet:		
Cash	$ 285,000	$ 150,000
Accounts Receivable (net)	430,000	350,000
Inventories	530,000	410,000
Land, Building, and Equipment	660,000	680,000
Accumulated Depreciation	(185,000)	(210,000)
Investment in Trent Inc., (at cost)	750,000	
Accounts Payable and Accrued Expenses.	(670,000)	(544,000)
Common Stock ($10 par)	(1,200,000)	(400,000)
Additional Paid-In Capital in Excess of Par	(140,000)	(80,000)
Retained Earnings, December 31, 2014.	(460,000)	(356,000)
Totals	$ 0	$ 0

Additional information is as follows:

a. There have been no changes in the common stock and additional paid-in capital in excess of par accounts since the one necessitated in 2012 by Arther's acquisition of Trent, Inc.

b. At the acquisition date, the market value of Trent's machinery exceeded book value by $54,000. This excess is being amortized over the asset's estimated average remaining life of six years. The fair value of Trent's other assets and liabilities were equal to book value. Any remaining excess is goodwill.

c. On July 1, 2012, Arther sold a warehouse facility to Trent for $129,000 in cash. At the date of sale, Arther's book values were $33,000 for the land and $66,000 for the building. Trent allocated the $129,000 purchase price to the land for $43,000 and to the building for $86,000. Trent is depreciating the building over its estimated 5-year remaining useful life by the straight-line method with no salvage value.

d. During 2014, Arther purchased merchandise from Trent at an aggregate invoice price of $180,000, which included a 100% markup on Trent's cost. On December 31, 2014, Arther owed Trent $75,000 on these purchases, and $36,000 of the merchandise purchased remained in Arther's inventory.

Complete the vertical worksheet necessary to prepare the consolidated income statement
and retained earnings statement for the year ended December 31, 2014, and a consolidated
balance sheet as of December 31, 2014, for Arther Corporation and its subsidiary. Formal
consolidated statements and journal entries are not required. Include the determination and distribution of excess schedule and the income distribution schedules. ◄ ◄ ◄ ◄ ◄ **Required**

(*AICPA adapted*)

Problem 4A-2 *(LO 2, 3, 7)* **Vertical worksheet, 80%, cost, several excess distributions, merchandise, equipment sales.** (This is similar to Problem 4-10; it uses the simple equity method and vertical worksheet format.) On January 1, 2011, Peanut Company
acquired 80% of the common stock of Salt Company for $200,000. On this date, Salt had total
owners' equity of $200,000, which included retained earnings of $100,000. During 2011 and
2012, Peanut accounted for its investment in Salt using the simple equity method.

Any excess of cost over book value is attributable to inventory (worth $12,500 more than
cost), to equipment (worth $25,000 more than book value), and to goodwill. FIFO is used for
inventories. The equipment has a remaining life of four years, and straight-line depreciation is
used. Any remaining excess is attributed to goodwill.

On January 1, 2012, Peanut held merchandise acquired from Salt for $20,000. During
2012, Salt sold merchandise to Peanut for $40,000, $10,000 of which was still held by Peanut
on December 31, 2012. Salt's usual gross profit is 50%.

On January 1, 2011, Peanut sold equipment to Salt at a gain of $15,000. Depreciation is
being computed using the straight-line method, a 5-year life, and no salvage value.

The following condensed statements were prepared for the Peanut and Salt companies for
December 31, 2012.

	Peanut Company	Salt Company
Income Statement:		
Net Sales	$ (600,000)	$(315,000)
Cost of Goods Sold	350,000	150,000
Operating Expenses	150,000	60,000
Subsidiary Income	(84,000)	
Net Income.	$ (184,000)	$(105,000)
Retained Earnings Statement:		
Balance, January 1, 2012.	$ (320,000)	$(150,000)
Net Income (from above)	(184,000)	(105,000)
Dividends Declared	60,000	20,000
Balance, December 31, 2012.	$ (444,000)	$(235,000)
Consolidated Balance Sheet:		
Inventory, December 31	$ 130,000	$ 50,000
Other Current Assets	241,000	235,000
Investment in Salt Company.	308,000	
Other Long-Term Investments	20,000	
Land.	140,000	80,000
Building and Equipment.	375,000	200,000
Accumulated Depreciation	(120,000)	(30,000)
Other Intangible Assets		20,000
Current Liabilities.	(150,000)	(70,000)
Bonds Payable.		(100,000)
Other Long-Term Liabilities.	(200,000)	(50,000)
Common Stock.	(200,000)	(50,000)
Paid-In Capital in Excess of Par	(100,000)	(50,000)
Retained Earnings, December 31, 2012.	(444,000)	(235,000)
Totals	$ 0	$ 0

Complete the worksheet for consolidated financial statements for the year ended December 31, 2012. Include any necessary determination and distribution of excess schedule and
income distribution schedules. ◄ ◄ ◄ ◄ ◄ **Required**

Intercompany Transactions: Bonds and Leases

Learning Objectives

When you have completed this chapter, you should be able to

1. Explain the alternatives a parent company has if it wishes to acquire outstanding subsidiary bonds from outside owners.

2. Follow the procedures used to retire intercompany bonds on a consolidated worksheet.

3. Explain why a parent company would lease assets to the subsidiary.

4. Show how to eliminate intercompany operating lease transactions from the consolidated statements.

5. Eliminate intercompany capital leases on the consolidated worksheet.

6. Demonstrate an understanding of the process used to defer intercompany profits on sales-type leases.

7. Explain the complications caused by unguaranteed residual values with intercompany leases. (Appendix)

This chapter focuses on intercompany transactions that create a long-term debtor-creditor relationship between the members of a consolidated group. The usual impetus for these transactions is the parent's ability to borrow larger amounts of capital at more favorable terms than would be available to the subsidiary. In addition, the parent company may desire to manage all capital needs of the consolidated company for better control of all capital sources. Intercompany leasing with the parent as the lessor also may be motivated by centralized asset management and credit control.

Intercompany bond holdings will be analyzed first. Here, one member of the consolidated group, usually the subsidiary, has issued bonds that appear on its balance sheet as long-term liabilities. Another member, typically the parent company, may purchase the bonds and list them on its balance sheet as an investment. However, when consolidated statements are prepared, the intercompany purchase should be viewed as a retirement of the bonds. Only bonds that involve nonaffiliated companies may appear in the consolidated statements.

Consideration of intercompany leasing of assets will follow the bond coverage. In this case, one member of the consolidated group purchases the asset and leases it to another member. While the leasing transaction is recorded as such on the separate books of the affiliates, the lease has no substance from a consolidated viewpoint. Only a lease that involves a nonaffiliated company may appear in the consolidated statements.

INTERCOMPANY INVESTMENT IN BONDS

To secure long-term funds, one member of a consolidated group may sell its bonds directly to another member of the group. Clearly, such a transaction results in intercompany debt that must be eliminated from the consolidated statements. On the worksheet, the investment in bonds recorded by one company must be eliminated against the bonds payable of the other. In addition, the applicable interest expense recorded by one affiliate must be eliminated against

1

OBJECTIVE

Explain the alternatives a parent company has if it wishes to acquire outstanding subsidiary bonds from outside owners.

the applicable interest revenue recorded by the other affiliate. Interest accruals recorded on the books of the separate companies must be eliminated as well.

There are situations where one affiliate (usually the subsidiary) has outstanding bonds that have been purchased by parties that are not members of the affiliated group, and a decision is made by another affiliate (usually the parent) to purchase these bonds. The simplest way to acquire subsidiary bonds from outsiders is for the parent to loan money to the subsidiary so that the subsidiary can retire the bonds. From an accounting standpoint, this transaction is easy to record. The former debt is retired and a new, long-term intercompany debt originates. The only procedures required on future consolidated worksheets involve the elimination of the resulting intercompany debt.

A more complicated method is to have the parent purchase the subsidiary bonds from the outside parties and to hold them as an investment. This method creates an investment in subsidiary bonds. Each affiliate continues to accrue and record interest on the bonds. While the intercompany bonds are treated as a liability on the subsidiary books and as an investment on the parent's books, from a consolidated viewpoint the bonds have been retired and the debt to outside parties has been liquidated. The purchase of intercompany bonds has the following ramifications when consolidating:

1. Consolidated statements prepared for the period in which the bonds are purchased must portray the intercompany purchase as a retirement of the bonds. It is possible, but unlikely, that the bonds will be purchased at book value. There usually will be a gain or loss on retirement; this gain or loss is recognized on the consolidated income statement.

2. For all periods during which the intercompany investment exists, the intercompany bonds, interest accruals, and interest expense/revenue must be eliminated since the bonds no longer exist from a consolidated viewpoint.

The complexity of the elimination procedures depends on whether the bonds originally were issued at face value or at a premium or discount. Additionally, one must exercise extra care in the application of elimination procedures when only a portion of the outstanding subsidiary bonds is purchased by the parent company.

Bonds Originally Issued at Face Value

2

OBJECTIVE

Follow the procedures used to retire intercompany bonds on a consolidated worksheet.

When bonds are issued at face value by a subsidiary to outside parties, contract (nominal) interest agrees with the effective, or market, interest, and no amortizations of issuance premiums or discounts need to be recorded. However, subsequent to the issuance, the market rate of interest most likely will deviate from the contract rate. Thus, while there is no original issuance premium or discount, there will be what could be termed an *investment premium* or *discount* resulting from the intercompany purchase of the bonds.

To illustrate the procedures required for intercompany bonds originally issued at face value, assume a subsidiary, Company S, issued 5-year, 8% bonds at a face value of $100,000 to outside parties on January 1, 2011. Interest is paid on January 1 for the preceding year. On January 2, 2013, the parent, Company P, purchased the bonds from the outside parties for $103,600.

Company S will continue to list the $100,000 bonded debt and to record interest expense of $8,000 during 2013, 2014, and 2015. However, Company P will record a bond investment of $103,600 and will amortize $1,200 per year, for the remaining life of the bond, by reducing the investment account and adjusting interest revenue. Though the interest method of amortization is preferable, the straight-line method is permitted if results are not materially different. This initial example and most others in this chapter use the straight-line method in order to simplify analysis. A summary example is used to demonstrate the interest method of amortization.

Although the investment and liability accounts continue to exist on the separate books of the affiliated companies, retirement has occurred from a consolidated viewpoint. Debt with a book value of $100,000 was retired by a payment of $103,600, and there is a $3,600 loss on retirement. If a consolidated worksheet is prepared on the day the bonds are purchased, Bonds Payable would be eliminated against Investment in Company S Bonds, and a *loss on retirement* would be reported on the consolidated income statement. The following abbreviated worksheet prepared as of January 2, 2013, displays the procedures used to retire the bonds as part of the elimination process:

	Partial Trial Balance		Eliminations & Adjustments	
	Company P	Company S	Dr.	Cr.
Investment in Company S Bonds	103,600			(B) 103,600
Bonds Payable		(100,000)	(B) 100,000	
Loss on Bond Retirement			(B) 3,600	

This partial worksheet, prepared on January 2, 2013, is only hypothetical since, in reality, there will be no consolidated worksheet prepared until December 31, 2013, the end of the period. During 2013, Companies P and S will record the transactions for interest as follows:

Company P			Company S		
Interest Receivable...............	8,000		Interest Expense.............	8,000	
Investment in Company S Bonds ...		1,200	Interest Payable		8,000
Interest Income.................		6,800	To record interest expense.		
To record interest revenue, net of $1,200 per-year premium amortization.					

These entries will be reflected in the trial balances of the December 31, 2013 consolidated worksheet, shown in Worksheet 5-1 on pages 282 and 283. Note that Investment in Company S Bonds reflects the premium amortization since the balance is $102,400 ($103,600 original cost − $1,200 amortization). In this worksheet, it is assumed that Investment in Company S Stock reflects a 90% interest purchased at a price equal to the book value of the underlying equity, and the simple equity method is used by Company P to record the investment in stock.

Worksheet 5-1: page 282

Entries (CY1) and (EL) eliminate the intercompany stock investment. Entry (B1) eliminates the intercompany bonds at their year-end balances and the intercompany interest expense and revenue recorded during the year. In journal entry form, elimination entries are as follows:

(CY1) Eliminate current-year equity income:

Subsidiary Income.................................... 10,800

Investment in Company S Stock......................... 10,800

(EL) Eliminate 90% of subsidiary equity:

Common Stock ($10 par)—Company S.................... 72,000

Retained Earnings, January 1, 2013—Company S 18,000

Investment in Company S Stock......................... 90,000

(B1) Eliminate intercompany bonds and interest expense:

Bonds Payable....................................... 100,000

Investment in Company S Bonds 102,400

Interest Income..................................... 6,800

Interest Expense..................................... 8,000

Loss on Bond Retirement 3,600

(B2) Eliminate intercompany accrued interest:

Interest Payable.................................... 8,000

Interest Receivable.................................. 8,000

The amount of the gain or loss is the sum of the difference between the remaining book value of the investment on bonds compared to the debt and the difference between interest expense and debt. For this example:

Investment in Bonds Balance, December 31, 2013	$102,400	
Bonds Payable, December 31, 2013	100,000	$2,400
Interest Expense, 2013	$ 8,000	
Interest Revenue, 2013	6,800	1,200
Loss, January 2, 2013		$3,600

As a result of the elimination entries, the consolidated income statement will include the retirement loss but will exclude intercompany interest payments and accruals. The consolidated balance sheet will not list the intercompany bonds payable or investment in bonds accounts.

The only remaining problem is the distribution of consolidated net income to the controlling and noncontrolling interests. The income distribution schedule shows Company S absorbing all of the retirement loss. It is most common to view the purchasing affiliate as a mere agent of the issuing affiliate. Therefore, it is the issuer, not the purchaser, who must bear the entire gain or loss on retirement. Even though the debt is retired from a consolidated viewpoint, it still exists internally. Company P has a right to collect the interest as part of its share of Company S's operations. Based on the value of the debt on January 2, 2013, the interest expense/revenue is $6,800. The interest expense of $8,000 recorded by Company S must be corrected to reflect the internal interest expense of $6,800. The income distribution schedule increases the income of Company S to reflect the adjustment ($1,200) to interest expense. It should be noted that the retirement loss borne by Company S will entirely offset the adjustments to interest expense by the time the bonds mature. If the parent, Company P, had issued the bonds to outside parties and if the subsidiary, Company S, later had purchased them, the only change would be that the income distribution schedule of Company P would absorb the loss on retirement and the interest adjustment.

Worksheet 5-2: page 284

The worksheet procedures that would be needed at the end of 2014 are shown in Worksheet 5-2 on pages 284 and 285. The interest revenue and expense have been recorded on the books of the separate companies. The investment in Company S bonds account on the parent's books reflects its book value at the end of 2014.

The eliminations in journal entry form are as follows:

(CY1)	Eliminate current-year equity income:		
	Subsidiary Income.	19,800	
	Investment in Company S Stock.		19,800
(EL)	Eliminate 90% of subsidiary equity:		
	Common Stock ($10 par)—Company S	72,000	
	Retained Earnings, January 1, 2014—Company S	28,800	
	Investment in Company S Stock.		100,800
(B1)	Eliminate intercompany bonds and interest expense:		
	Bonds Payable.	100,000	
	Investment in Company S Bonds		101,200
	Interest Income.	6,800	
	Interest Expense		8,000
	Retained Earnings, January 1, 2014—Company P	2,160	
	Retained Earnings, January 1, 2014—Company S	240	
(B2)	Eliminate intercompany accrued interest:		
	Interest Payable.	8,000	
	Interest Receivable.		8,000

Entry (B1) eliminates the intercompany bonds at their year-end balances and the intercompany interest expense and revenue. Recall that the original retirement loss was $3,600 when the bonds had three years to maturity. By the start of the second period, 2014, $1,200 of that loss was already amortized on the separate books of the affiliates. The loss remaining is $2,400 [which is verified in the explanation to entry (B1) in Worksheet 5-2]. This remaining loss is debited to Retained Earnings since the retirement occurred in a prior period. The adjustment is allocated to noncontrolling and controlling beginning retained earnings since the bonds were issued by the subsidiary.

The 2014 consolidated income statement will not include intercompany interest expense or revenue. The income distribution schedules for Worksheet 5-2 reflect the fact that the debt still existed internally during the period. However, the interest expense recorded by Company S is reduced to reflect the interest cost based on the January 2, 2013, purchase price.

If Company S was the purchaser and Company P the issuer of the bonds, Worksheet 5-2 would differ as follows:

1. The January 1, 2014, retained earnings adjustment would be absorbed completely by the controlling retained earnings, since the parent company would be the issuer absorbing the loss.
2. The income distribution schedule of the parent would contain the interest adjustment.

Bonds Not Originally Issued at Face Value

The principles of eliminating intercompany investments in bonds are not altered by the existence of a premium or discount stemming from original issuance. The numerical calculations just become more complex. To illustrate, assume Company S issued $100,000 of 5-year, 8% bonds on January 1, 2011. The market interest rate approximated 9%, and, as a result, the bonds sold at a discount of $3,890. Interest is paid each December 31. On each interest payment date, the discount is amortized $778 ($3,890 ÷ 5 years) by decreasing the discount and increasing interest expense. On December 31, 2013, the balance of the discount is $1,556 [$3,890 − (3 × $778 annual amortization)].

The parent, Company P, purchased the bonds for $103,600 on December 31, 2013, after interest had been paid. The parent will amortize $1,800 of the investment each subsequent December 31, reducing the parent's interest income to $6,200 ($8,000 cash − $1,800 amortization) for 2014 and 2015.

The following abbreviated December 31, 2013 (date of purchase), worksheet lists the investment in Company S bonds account, the bonds payable account, and the remaining issuance discount. Eliminating the $103,600 price paid for the bonds by Company P against the book value of $98,444 ($100,000 − $1,556) creates a loss on retirement of $5,156, which is carried to consolidated net income. Worksheet procedures may be aided by linking the bonds payable and the related discount or premium on the worksheet. This is done on our worksheets by circling the amounts in the trial balance and in the eliminations.

	Partial Trial Balance		Eliminations & Adjustments	
	Company P	Company S	Dr.	Cr.
Investment in Company S Bonds	103,600			(B) 103,600
Bonds Payable (8%)		(100,000)	(B) 100,000	
Discount on Bonds Payable		1,556		(B) 1,556
Loss on Bond Retirement			(B) 5,156	
Interest Expense		8,778*		

*$8,000 cash + $778 straight-line amortization.

Interest expense on the books of Company S is extended to the consolidated income statement, since this interest was incurred as a result of transactions with outside parties. There would be no interest adjustment for 2013, since the bonds were not purchased by the parent until December 31, 2013. The income distribution schedules accompanying the worksheet would assess the retirement loss against the issuer, Company S.

Worksheet 5-3: page 286   The implications of these intercompany bonds on the 2014 consolidated worksheet are reflected in Worksheet 5-3 on pages 286 and 287. Assume Company P acquired a 90% interest in the common stock of Company S at a price equal to the book value of the underlying equity. The simple equity method is used by the parent to record the investment in the stock of Company S. The trial balances include the following items:

1. The investment in Company S bonds at its amortized December 31, 2014, balance of $101,800 ($103,600 − $1,800 amortization);

2. The interest revenue (adjusted for amortization) of $6,200 on the books of Company P;

3. The discount on bonds account at its amortized December 31, 2014, balance of $778; and

4. The interest expense (adjusted for discount amortization) of $8,778 ($8,000 cash + $778 amortization) on the books of Company S.

5. There is no accrued interest receivable/payable since interest was paid on December 31, 2014.

The eliminations in journal entry form are as follows:

(CY1)		Eliminate current-year equity income:		
		Subsidiary Income.	8,874	
		Investment in Company S Stock		8,874
(EL)		Eliminate 90% of subsidiary equity:		
		Common Stock ($10 par)—Company S	36,000	
		Retained Earnings, January 1, 2014—Company S	99,000	
		Investment in Company S Stock		135,000
(B)		Eliminate intercompany bonds and interest expense:		
		Bonds Payable.	100,000	
		Discount on Bonds		778
		Investment in Company S Bonds		101,800
		Interest Income.	6,200	
		Interest Expense		8,778
		Retained Earnings, January 1, 2014—Company P	4,640	
		Retained Earnings, January 1, 2014—Company S	516	

Entry (B) eliminates the investment in bonds against the bonds payable and the applicable remaining discount. Entry (B) also eliminates interest expense and revenue. Be sure to understand the calculation of the adjustment to beginning retained earnings that is explained in the entry (B) information. The loss at the start of the year is the sum of the loss remaining at year-end and the loss amortized on the books of the separate affiliates during the year.

Again, the consolidated income statement does not include intercompany interest. However, the Company S income distribution schedule does reflect the adjustment of Company S's interest expense. The original $8,778 interest expense has been replaced by a $6,200 expense, based on the purchase price paid by Company P. The smaller interest expense compensates the subsidiary for the retirement loss absorbed in a previous period.

Purchase of Only a Portion of the Bonds

The preceding examples assume that the parent company purchases all of the outstanding bonds of the subsidiary. In such cases, all of the bonds are retired on the worksheet. There may be cases, however, where the parent purchases only a portion of the subsidiary's outstanding bonds. Suppose, for example, that the parent purchased 80% of the subsidiary's outstanding bonds. Only the 80% interest in the bonds would be eliminated on the consolidated worksheet, and only the interest expense and revenue applicable to 80% of the bonds would be eliminated on the worksheet. **The 20% interest in the subsidiary bonds owned by persons outside the control group remains as a valid debt of the consolidated company and should not be**

eliminated. It is a common error for students to eliminate the 80% interest in intercompany bonds owned by a parent against 100% of the bonds issued by the subsidiary. Such a mistake improperly eliminates valid debt and greatly miscalculates the gain or loss on retirement. It also should be noted that the interest paid to persons outside the control group should remain a part of the consolidated statements. Only the interest paid to the affiliated company is to be eliminated.

Interest Method of Amortization

The procedures used to eliminate intercompany bonds are not altered by the interest method of amortization; only the dollar values change. To illustrate the calculations, assume that Company S issued $100,000 of 5-year, 8% bonds on January 1, 2011. The market interest rate on that date was 9%, so the bonds sold at a discount of $3,890. Interest on the bonds is paid each December 31. The discount amortization for the term of the bonds follows:

Year	Debt Balance, January 1	Effective Interest	Nominal Interest	Discount Amortization
2011	$96,110	$8,650 (0.09 × $96,110)	$8,000	$ 650
2012	96,760 ($96,110 + $650)	8,708 (0.09 × $96,760)	8,000	708
2013	97,468 ($96,760 + $708)	8,772 (0.09 × $97,468)	8,000	772
2014	98,240 ($97,468 + $772)	8,842 (0.09 × $98,240)	8,000	842
2015	99,082 ($98,240 + $842)	8,918* (0.09 × $99,082)	8,000	918
*Adjusted for rounding.				$3,890

On December 31, 2013, after interest had been paid, the bonds were purchased by parent Company P at a price to yield 6%. Based on present value computations, $103,667 was paid for the bonds. The premium on the bonds would be amortized by Company P as follows:

Year	Investment Balance, January 1	Effective Interest	Nominal Interest	Premium Amortization
2014	$103,667	$6,220 (0.06 × $103,667)	$8,000	$1,780
2015	101,887 ($103,667 − $1,780)	6,113 (0.06 × $101,887)	8,000	1,887
				$3,667

The following abbreviated December 31, 2013 (date of purchase) worksheet lists the investment in Company S bonds account, the bonds payable account, and the remaining issuance discount. Eliminating the $103,667 price paid by Company P against the book value of $98,240 ($100,000 − $1,760) creates a loss on retirement of $5,427 that is carried to consolidated net income.

	Partial Trial Balance		Eliminations & Adjustments	
	Company P	Company S	Dr.	Cr.
Investment in Company S Bonds	103,667			(B) 103,667
Bonds Payable, 8%		(100,000)	(B) 100,000	
Discount on Bonds Payable		1,760		(B) 1,760
Loss on Bond Retirement			(B) 5,427	
Interest Expense		8,772*		

*See preceding discount amortization schedule for issuer.

Worksheet 5-4: page 288

The differences in the 2014 consolidated worksheet caused by the interest method of amortization are shown in Worksheet 5-4 on pages 288 and 289. Note particularly the change in the Company S income distribution schedule. The original 9% interest, totaling $8,842, has been replaced by the $6,220 of interest calculated using the 6% rate.

The eliminations in journal entry form are as follows:

(CY1)	Eliminate current-year equity income:			
	Subsidiary Income		8,820	
	Investment in Company S Stock			8,820
(EL)	Eliminate 90% of subsidiary equity:			
	Common Stock ($10 par)—Company S		36,000	
	Retained Earnings, January 1, 2014—Company S		99,180	
	Investment in Company S Stock			135,180
(B)	Eliminate intercompany bonds and interest expense:			
	Bonds Payable		100,000	
	Discount on Bonds			918
	Investment in Company S Bonds			101,887
	Interest Income		6,220	
	Interest Expense			8,842
	Retained Earnings, January 1, 2014—Company P		4,884	
	Retained Earnings, January 1, 2014—Company S		543	

REFLECTION

- The parent can effectively retire subsidiary bonds by lending money to the subsidiary and letting the subsidiary purchase the bonds from existing owners or by simply buying the bonds from existing owners.

- When the parent buys subsidiary bonds, the bonds cease to exist from a consolidated viewpoint. They are retired on the consolidated worksheet by elimination.

- When the intercompany bonds are eliminated, there will be a difference between the amortized cost and the price paid; this creates a gain or loss on retirement.

- In periods subsequent to the intercompany purchase, the bonds must continue to be eliminated, and retained earnings is adjusted for the remaining retirement gain or loss that has not already been amortized.

- Intercompany interest expense/revenue and accrued interest receivable/payable are also eliminated.

INTERCOMPANY LEASES

Intercompany leases have become one of the most frequently encountered types of transactions between affiliated companies. It is particularly common for parent companies with substantial financial resources to acquire major assets and to lease the assets to their subsidiaries. This action may occur because the financially stronger parent may be able to both purchase and finance assets on more favorable terms. Also, the parent company may desire close control over plant assets and may prefer centralized ownership and management of assets. Leasing becomes a mechanism through which the parent can convey the use of centrally owned assets to subsidiaries. Some companies achieve centralized asset management by forming separate leasing subsidiaries whose major function is to lease assets to affiliated companies. When such subsidiaries exist, they are consolidated automatically with the parent regardless of the ownership percentage of the parent.[1]

3

OBJECTIVE

Explain why a parent company would lease assets to the subsidiary.

Operating Leases

Consolidation procedures for intercompany leases depend on the original recording of the lease by the separate companies. When an operating lease exists, the lessor has recorded the purchase of the asset and depreciates it. The lessor records rent revenue, while the lessee records rent expense. In such cases, it is necessary in the consolidation process to eliminate the intercompany rent expense/revenue and any related rent receivable/payable. The lessor's asset and related accumulated depreciation should be reclassified as a normal productive asset rather than as property under an operating lease. As an example, assume the parent, Company P, has both productive equipment used in its own operations and equipment that is under operating lease to a subsidiary, Company S. The following partial worksheet may be used to analyze required consolidation procedures:

4

OBJECTIVE

Show how to eliminate intercompany operating lease transactions from the consolidated statements.

	Partial Trial Balance		Eliminations & Adjustments	
	Company P	Company S	Dr.	Cr.
Equipment	800,000			
Accumulated Depreciation—Equipment	(300,000)			
Rent Receivable	1,200			(OL2) 1,200
Rent Payable		(1,200)	(OL2) 1,200	
Rent Income	(14,400)		(OL1) 14,400	
Rent Expense		14,400		(OL1) 14,400
Depreciation Expense	50,000			

Eliminations and Adjustments:

(OL1) Eliminate intercompany rent expense and revenue of $1,200 per month.
(OL2) Eliminate one month's accrued rent.

No adjustments are made in the income distribution schedules as a result of operating leases. The eliminations made on the worksheet do not change the amount of income or the distribution of income between the noncontrolling and controlling interests.

---

1 FASB 840-10-45-10, *Leases—Overall—Other Presentation Matters* (Norwalk CT, 2010).

Capitalized Leases

Consolidation procedures become more complicated when the lease is recorded as a capital lease by the lessee and as a direct-financing or sales-type lease by the lessor. The lessee records both an asset and intercompany long-term debt. Generally, the criteria for determining when a lease is a capital lease are the same for affiliated companies as for independent companies. However, when the terms of the lease are significantly affected by the fact that the lessee and lessor are affiliates, the usual criteria for classification of leases do not apply. Lease terms could be considered "significantly affected" when they could not reasonably be expected to occur between independent companies.[2] For example, a parent might lease to its subsidiary at a rent far below the market rate, or a parent might rent a highly specialized machine to its subsidiary on a month-to-month basis. Typically, such specialized machinery would be leased only on a long-term lease promising a full recovery of cost to the lessor, since there would be no use for the machine by other lessees if it were returned to the lessor. The month-to-month lease is possible only because the parent's control of the subsidiary assures a continued flow of rent payments. When, in the accountant's judgment, the terms of the lease are affected significantly by the parent-subsidiary relationship, the normal criteria are not used and the transaction is recorded so as to reflect its true economic substance.[3] Usually, in these circumstances, the lessee is viewed as having purchased the asset using funds borrowed from the lessor.

Consolidation Procedures for Direct-Financing Leases. A direct-financing lease is viewed as a unique type of asset transfer by the lessor, who accepts a long-term receivable from the lessee as consideration for the asset received by the lessee. There is no profit or loss to the lessor on the transfer, only future interest revenue as payments become due.

Prior to studying consolidated worksheet procedures, we will analyze the entries made by the affiliated lessee and lessor. In its simplest form, a direct-financing lease is recorded by the lessee as an asset and as debt. The lessor records the lease as a receivable from the lessee. If all payments to be received by the lessor will come from or are guaranteed by the original lessee, the present value of the net receivable recorded by the lessor will equal the present value of the payable recorded by the lessee, and the interest rates used to amortize the debt will be equal.

To illustrate, assume Company S is an 80%-owned subsidiary of Company P. On January 1, 2011, Company P purchased a machine for $5,851 and leased it to Company S. The terms of the direct-financing lease provide for rental payments of $2,000 per year at the beginning of each period and allow the lessee to exercise an option to purchase the machine for $1,000 at the end of 2013. The $1,000 purchase option is considered a bargain purchase option that will be exercised and is included in the minimum lease payments. The implicit interest rate (which equates all payments, including the bargain purchase option, to the lessor's purchase cost) is 16%. The lessee will depreciate the capitalized cost of the machine over five years, using the straight-line method. The lessee may use a 5-year life, despite the 3-year lease term, because it is assumed that the bargain purchase option will be exercised and that the asset will be used for five years.

The amortization of the debt at the implicit 16% interest rate is as follows:

Date	Payment	Interest at 16% on Previous Balance	Reduction of Principal	Principal Balance
January 1, 2011 . . .	$2,000		$2,000	$3,851*
January 1, 2012 . . .	2,000	$ 616	1,384	2,467
January 1, 2013 . . .	2,000	395	1,605	862
December 31, 2013	1,000	138	862	
Total	$7,000	$1,149	$5,851	

*Purchase price of $5,851 − $2,000 initial payment.

The journal entries for the separate companies would be as follows for the first two years:

Date	Company S (Lessee)			Company P (Lessor)		
2011						
Jan. 1	Assets Under Capital Lease	5,851		Minimum Lease Payments Receivable . .	5,000	
	Obligations Under Capital Lease . .		3,851	Cash	2,000	
	Cash		2,000	Unearned Interest Income		1,149
				Accounts Payable (for asset)		5,851
Dec. 31	Interest Expense (at 16%)	616		Unearned Interest Income	616	
	Interest Payable		616	Interest Income (at 16%)		616
	Depreciation Expense					
	($1/5 \times \$5,851$)	1,170				
	Accumulated Depreciation—Assets					
	Under Capital Lease.		1,170			
2012						
Jan. 1	Obligations Under Capital Lease	1,384		Cash	2,000	
	Interest Payable	616		Minimum Lease Payments		
	Cash		2,000	Receivable		2,000
Dec. 31	Interest Expense (at 16%)	395		Unearned Interest Income	395	
	Interest Payable		395	Interest Income (at 16%)		395
	Depreciation Expense	1,170				
	Accumulated Depreciation—Assets					
	Under Capital Lease.		1,170			

At the end of each period, consolidation procedures would be needed to eliminate the intercompany transactions. In substance, there appears on the separate records of the affiliates an intercompany transfer of a plant asset with resulting intercompany debt. The intercompany debt, related interest expense/revenue, and interest accruals must be eliminated. Also, it is necessary to reclassify the assets under capital leases as productive assets owned by the consolidated group. The adjusted partial worksheets (pages 274 and 275) illustrate consolidation procedures at the end of 2011 and 2012.

A review of the worksheet eliminations and adjustments reveals that **consolidated net income is not changed because equal amounts of interest expense and revenue were eliminated.** Therefore, no adjustments are required in the income distribution schedules.

Some capital leases will designate a portion of the annual rent as being applicable to executory costs, such as property taxes or maintenance, incurred by the lessor. Such payments for executory costs are not included in the obligation of the lessee or the minimum lease payments receivable recorded by the lessor. Instead, such payments are recorded as rent expense and revenue in each period. In the consolidation process, that portion of rent applicable to executory costs is eliminated like any other charge for intercompany services.

Partial Worksheet
Direct Financing Lease For Year Ended December 31, 2011

	Trial Balance		Eliminations & Adjustments			
	Company P	Company S	Dr.		Cr.	
Assets Under Capital Lease		5,851			(CL3)	5,851
Accumulated Depreciation—Assets						
Under Capital Lease		(1,170)	(CL3)	1,170		
Property, Plant, and Equipment	200,000	120,000	(CL3)	5,851		
Accumulated Depreciation—Property, Plant, and Equipment	(80,000)	(50,000)			(CL3)	1,170
Obligations Under Capital Lease		(3,851)	(CL2)	3,851		
Interest Payable		(616)	(CL2)	616		
Minimum Lease Payments Receivable	5,000				(CL2)	5,000
Unearned Interest Income	(533)		(CL2)	533*		
Interest Expense		616			(CL1)	616
Interest Income	(616)		(CL1)	616		

Eliminations and Adjustments:

(CL1)   Eliminate intercompany interest expense/revenue of $616.

(CL2)   Eliminate the intercompany debt recorded by the lessee (obligation under capital lease $3,851 plus accrued interest payable $616) against the net intercompany receivable of the lessor (minimum lease payments receivable $5,000 less unearned interest income $533).

(CL3)   Reclassify the asset under capital lease and its related accumulated depreciation as a productive asset owned by the consolidated company.

*From the amortization table on page 278; $533 = $395 + $138

The preceding example has a bargain purchase option. This means that all payments to be received by the lessor would come from the original lessee. Equality of payments for both parties to a lease between affiliates is the most common case. However, there may be intercompany leases where there is an unguaranteed residual value for the lessor. This means that a portion of the total payments to be received by the lessor will come from parties outside the control group. Therefore, the stream of payments to be received by the lessor exceeds the stream of payments to be paid by the lessee. This complicates the consolidation process. (The appendix to this chapter illustrates a revised version of the preceding example that deals with an unequal stream of payments.)

Consolidation Procedures for Sales-Type Leases. Under a sales-type lease, a lessor records a sales profit or loss at the inception of the lease. The sales profit or loss is the difference between the fair value of the asset at the inception of the lease and the cost of an asset purchased (or the net book value of an asset previously used by the seller) for the lessor. Consolidation procedures do not allow recognition of this intercompany profit or loss at the inception of the lease. This is exactly the same as the procedure for the deferral of gains and losses on fixed asset sales in Chapter 4. Instead, the profit or loss is deferred and then amortized over the lessee's period of usage. This period will be the lease term unless there is a bargain purchase or bargain renewal option, in which case the asset's useful life would be used.

6

OBJECTIVE

Demonstrate an understanding of the process used to defer intercompany profits on sales-type leases.

Partial Worksheet
Direct Financing Lease For Year Ended December 31, 2012

	Trial Balance		Eliminations & Adjustments			
	Company P	Company S	Dr.		Cr.	
Assets Under Capital Lease		5,851			(CL3)	5,851
Accumulated Depreciation—Assets						
Under Capital Lease		(2,340)	(CL3)	2,340		
Property, Plant, and Equipment	200,000	120,000	(CL3)	5,851		
Accumulated Depreciation—Property,						
Plant, and Equipment	(100,000)	(60,000)			(CL3)	2,340
Obligations Under Capital Lease		(2,467)	(CL2)	2,467		
Interest Payable		(395)	(CL2)	395		
Minimum Lease Payments Receivable	3,000				(CL2)	3,000
Unearned Interest Income	(138)		(CL2)	138		
Interest Expense		395			(CL1)	395
Interest Income	(395)		(CL1)	395		

Eliminations and Adjustments:

(CL1) Eliminate intercompany interest expense/revenue of $395.

(CL2) Eliminate intercompany debt and net receivable.

(CL3) Reclassify the asset under the capital lease and its related accumulated depreciation as a productive asset owned by the consolidated company.

To illustrate, assume that in the previous example the asset leased to Company S had a cost to Company P of $4,951. Company P would have recorded the following entry at the inception of the sales-type lease:

Minimum Lease Payments Receivable	5,000	
Cash	2,000	
Unearned Interest Income		1,149
Asset (cost of asset leased)		4,951
Sales Profit on Leases		900

This entry differs from that of the previous example only to the extent of recording the gain and transferring an existing asset. None of the lessor's subsequent entries recording the earning of interest and the payment of the receivable would change. The lessee's entries are unaffected by the existence of the sales profit.

Consolidation procedures for a sales-type lease, however, do require added steps to those already illustrated. The sales profit is similar to a profit on the sale of a plant asset. The $900 profit in this example must be deferred over the 3-year lease term. Thus, the asset and its related depreciation accounts must be adjusted to reflect the original sales profit.

The following added adjustments on the 2011 partial consolidated worksheet (page 274) would be needed for the original $900 sales profit:

(F1)	Sales Profit on Leases	900	
	Property, Plant, and Equipment		900
	To reduce cost of asset for gain on sales-type lease.		

(F2)	Accumulated Depreciation—Property, Plant, and Equipment.	300	
	Depreciation Expense		300
	To reduce depreciation expense at the rate of $300 per year.		

The income distribution schedule of the parent (lessor) would reflect the deferral of the original $900 profit in the year of the sale and would recognize $300 per year during the asset's life.

For the 2012 partial consolidated worksheet (page 275), the following added adjustments would be required if a sales-type lease were involved:

(F1)	Retained Earnings—Controlling Interest	600	
	Accumulated Depreciation—Property, Plant, and Equipment.	300	
	Property, Plant, and Equipment		900
	To adjust the remaining sales profit at the beginning of the period.		
(F2)	Accumulated Depreciation—Property, Plant, and Equipment.	300	
	Depreciation Expense		300
	To reduce depreciation expense at the rate of $300 per year.		

REFLECTION

- Intercompany leases provide the opportunity for the parent company to control the assets used by a subsidiary.

- Intercompany operating leases are the most common type of lease and are easy to eliminate. Intercompany rent expense/revenue is eliminated with no effect on consolidated income. The leased assets should also be reclassified as productive, rather than leased assets.

- An intercompany capital lease creates an intercompany receivable/payable that must be eliminated along with the resulting intercompany interest expense/revenue and the intercompany accrued interest, all of which must be eliminated. The asset under the capital lease must also be reclassified as a productive asset.

- An intercompany sales-type lease requires all of the same elimination procedures of a capital lease. In addition, the intercompany sales profit must be eliminated and deferred over the life of the asset in the same manner as was a profit on fixed assets in Chapter 4.

INTERCOMPANY TRANSACTIONS PRIOR TO BUSINESS COMBINATION

It is possible that the companies involved in a business combination may have had dealings with each other prior to the acquisition of one company by another. Under acquisition accounting procedures, profits made prior to the acquisition are allowed to stand and require no adjustment. However, debt and lease instruments between the parties change their nature on the acquisition date. Amounts that were due between separate entities now become intercompany debt or leases, and they must be eliminated. Consider the following examples:

1. Trade receivables/payables of the former independent companies become intercompany trade debt on the acquisition date. If still existing on the balance sheet date, they are eliminated. Only interest expense/revenue applicable to the period after the acquisition is eliminated.

2. Bonds of one of the affiliates that are owned by another affiliate were valid when the firms were not affiliated. Once the acquisition occurs, the bonds become intercompany bonds and are eliminated on the consolidated worksheet. Interest expense/revenue prior to the acquisition stands, but interest expense/revenue applicable to the period after the acquisition is eliminated.

3. Operating leases may have existed between the affiliated companies prior to the acquisition. Once the purchase occurs, rent expense/revenue for periods after the acquisition becomes intercompany and must be eliminated.

4. If there were capitalized leases between the companies prior to the acquisition date, the capital lease amounts remaining in each company's accounts must be eliminated after the acquisition date. The interest expense/revenue for periods after the acquisition is also eliminated.

All of the above eliminations of amounts that become intercompany, after the acquisition occurs, do not affect income or balance sheet amounts for periods prior to the acquisition. No restatement of prior-period statements is required.

REFLECTION

- When an acquisition occurs, prior sales between the two entities are not eliminated on the consolidated worksheet.

- Debt and lease instruments between the parties change their nature on the acquisition date and become intercompany relationships that must be eliminated when consolidating.

APPENDIX: INTERCOMPANY LEASES WITH UNGUARANTEED RESIDUAL VALUE

7

OBJECTIVE

Explain the complications caused by unguaranteed residual values with intercompany leases.

The intercompany lease may contain an unguaranteed residual value. This means that the original intercompany lessee will supply only a portion of the total cash flow to be received by the lessor. At the end of the original lease term, the lessor may lease the asset again or sell it. In either case, there is no obligation on the part of the lessee to renew the lease or to purchase the asset. Since the original lessee is contractually bound to provide only a portion of the payments to be received by the lessor, the lessee will record as its lease obligation only the present value of the minimum lease payments for which it is obligated. The lessee must calculate the present value of the minimum lease payments using its incremental borrowing rate, unless the lessee knows the lessor's implicit rate (and the implicit rate is lower). Since it is an intercompany lease, the interest rate used would normally be the implicit rate of the lessor. As part of the consolidation process, if any other rate is used, the present value of the payments would be adjusted to reflect the implicit lessor rate.

The lessor records the gross investment in the lease, which is the sum of the minimum lease payments receivable and the unguaranteed residual value. Unearned interest income is recorded as a contra account at an amount that reduces the gross investment to the market value of the asset at the inception of the lease. Unearned interest is amortized using the implicit rate of the lessor. The implicit rate of the lessor thus equates the present value of all payments expected, including the unguaranteed residual value, to the market value of the asset.

The recording methods used by the lessee and lessor for leases with an unguaranteed residual value present a complication to the consolidation process. The amount of the asset under the capital lease recorded by the lessee will be less than the asset's market value, since the present value of the lease payments recorded by the lessee will not include the asset's unguaranteed residual value. To understand this complication, the previous example may be used with one change. Instead of the $1,000 bargain purchase option that was included in the set of minimum lease payments, assume there is a $1,000 unguaranteed residual value. Since the residual value is not guaranteed, it is not part of the minimum lease payments. The revised facts are as follows:

1. Cost of asset to lessor: $5,851.
2. Lease terms: Three annual payments of $2,000, due at the start of each year. Unguaranteed residual value of $1,000 to lessor at the end of 2013.
3. Lessor implicit rate: 16% equates the three $2,000 payments plus the unguaranteed residual value to $5,851.
4. Lessee interest rate: 16% (lessor implicit rate) which, when applied only to the lease payments, results in a present value of $5,210.
5. Depreciation: Straight-line over the 3-year lease term, since the contractual use of the asset is for three years.
6. Amortization tables:

Lessor

Date	Payment	Interest at 16% on Previous Balance	Reduction of Principal	Principal Balance
January 1, 2011 . . .	$2,000		$2,000	$3,851*
January 1, 2012 . . .	2,000	$ 616	1,384	2,467
January 1, 2013 . . .	2,000	395	1,605	862
December 31, 2013	1,000	138	862	
Total	$7,000	$1,149	$5,851	

*Purchase price of $5,851 − $2,000 initial payment

Lessee (16%)

Date	Payment	Interest at 16% on Previous Balance	Reduction of Principal	Principal Balance
January 1, 2011 . . .	$2,000		$2,000	$3,210*
January 1, 2012 . . .	2,000	$514	1,486	1,724
January 1, 2013 . . .	2,000	276	1,724	
Total	$6,000	$790	$5,210	

*Present value of $5,210 − $2,000 initial payment.

The journal entries for the separate companies would be as shown on page 279 for the first two years.

Date	Company S (Lessee)			Company P (Lessor)		
2011						
Jan. 1	Assets Under Capital Lease	5,210		Minimum Lease Payments Receivable . .	4,000	
	Cash		2,000	Unguaranteed Residual Value.	1,000	
	Obligations Under Capital Lease . .		3,210	Cash	2,000	
				Unearned Interest Income		1,149
				Accounts Payable (for asset)		5,851
Dec. 31	Interest Expense (at 16%)	514		Unearned Interest Income	616	
	Interest Payable		514	Interest Income (at 16%)		616
	Depreciation Expense					
	(⅓ × $5,210)	1,737				
	Accumulated Depreciation—Assets					
	Under Capital Lease.		1,737			
2012						
Jan. 1	Obligations Under Capital Lease	1,486		Cash	2,000	
	Interest Payable	514		Minimum Lease Payments		
	Cash		2,000	Receivable		2,000
Dec. 31	Interest Expense (at 16%)	276		Unearned Interest Income	395	
	Interest Payable		276	Interest Income (at 16%)		395
	Depreciation Expense	1,737				
	Accumulated Depreciation—Assets					
	Under Capital Lease.		1,737			

A comparison of the lessor and lessee's amortization tables shows the following difference between the lessee's interest expense and the lessor's interest income each period:

Year Ending December 31	16% Lessor Implicit Interest	16% Lessee Interest	Difference
2011	$ 616	$514	$102
2012	395	276	119
2013	138		138
Total	$1,149	$790	$359

The difference is the interest on the unguaranteed residual value, which is recorded only by the lessor. This can be demonstrated as follows:

Date	16% Implicit Interest	Present Value of Unguaranteed Residual Value
January 1, 2011		$ 641*
December 31, 2011 . .	$102	743
December 31, 2012 . .	119	862
December 31, 2013 . .	138	1,000

*$5,851 − $5,210.

In the consolidation process, the intercompany debt and all interest applicable to the lease are eliminated. Even the interest income recorded on the unguaranteed residual value is eliminated, since it is a ramification of a lease that, from a consolidated viewpoint, does not exist. The asset recorded by the lessee and the unguaranteed residual value recorded by the lessor are eliminated and replaced by a productive asset recorded by the consolidated company.

Worksheet 5-5: page 290   Worksheet 5-5, page 290 and 291, contains the detailed steps for the elimination of the intercompany lease at the end of 2011. In this worksheet, it is assumed that the interest in the 80%-owned subsidiary was purchased at its book value.

The eliminations in journal entry form are as follows:

(CY1)	Eliminate current-year equity income:		
	Subsidiary Income......................................	15,634	
	Investment in Company S.............................		15,634
(EL)	Eliminate 80% of subsidiary equity:		
	Common Stock ($10 par)—Company S....................	32,000	
	Retained Earnings, January 1, 2014—Company S	40,000	
	Investment in Company S.............................		72,000
(CL1)	Eliminate intercompany interest and restore unearned interest on unguaranteed residual:		
	Interest Income..	616	
	Interest Expense.....................................		514
	Unearned Interest Income		102
(CL2)	Eliminate intercompany debt, unguaranteed residual value and restate asset as owned asset:		
	Property, Plant, and Equipment..........................	5,851	
	Asset Under Capital Lease............................		5,210
	Unearned Interest Income	635	
	Minimum Lease Payments Receivable		4,000
	Unguaranteed Residual Value..........................		1,000
	Obligation Under Capital Lease	3,210	
	Interest Payable......................................	514	
(CL3)	Adjust and reclassify depreciation:		
	Accumulated Depreciation—Asset Under Capital Lease	1,737*	
	Accumulated Depreciation—Property, Plant, and Equipment ..		1,617**
	Depreciation Expense		120

*$5,210/3 years = $1,737
**($5,851 cost − $1,000 residual)/3 = $1,617

Entry (CL1) eliminates the $616 of interest income against the $514 of interest expense. The $102 disparity reflects the interest applicable to the unguaranteed residual value and is returned to unearned interest income. Entry (CL2) eliminates the intercompany debt applicable to the lease. The $359 disparity reflects the interest applicable to the unguaranteed residual value over the life of the lease. This amount is used to reduce the unguaranteed residual value to its original present value of $641. The $641, combined with the $5,210 asset under capital lease, is eliminated and replaced by an owned asset and recorded at the $5,851 original cost to the consolidated company. Entry (CL3) adjusts the depreciation to reflect the cost and the residual value of the asset to the consolidated company. The accumulated depreciation also is reclassified as that applicable to an owned asset.

In Worksheet 5-6 on pages 294 and 295, the consolidation procedures for the second year of the lease term are illustrated.

Worksheet 5-6: page 294

REFLECTION

- An unguaranteed residual value causes the present value of the lease for the lessor to exceed that of the lessee. The interest applicable to the unguaranteed residual value is allowed to remain in the consolidated statements, since it will come from the outside world.

- All remaining procedures parallel those used for ordinary capital leases.

Worksheet 5-1

Intercompany Investment in Bonds, Year of Acquisition; Straight-Line Method of Amortization
Company P and Subsidiary Company S
Worksheet for Consolidated Balance Sheet
For Year Ended December 31, 2013

	(Credit balance amounts are in parentheses.)	Trial Balance	
		Company P	Company S
1	Other Assets	56,400	220,000
2	**Interest Receivable**	**8,000**	
3	Investment in Company S Stock (90%)	100,800	
4			
5	**Investment in Company S Bonds (100%)**	**102,400**	
6	**Interest Payable**		**(8,000)**
7	**Bonds Payable (8%)**		**(100,000)**
8	Common Stock ($10 par)—Company P	(100,000)	
9	Retained Earnings, January 1, 2013—Company P	(120,000)	
10	Common Stock ($10 par)—Company S		(80,000)
11	Retained Earnings, January 1, 2013—Company S		(20,000)
12	Operating Revenue	(100,000)	(80,000)
13	Operating Expense	70,000	60,000
14	**Interest Income**	**(6,800)**	
15	**Interest Expense**		**8,000**
16	Subsidiary Income	(10,800)	
17	**Loss on Bond Retirement**		
18		0	0
19	Consolidated Net Income		
20	To NCI (see distribution schedule)		
21	Balance to Controlling Interest (see distribution schedule)		
22	Total NCI		
23	Retained Earnings, Controlling Interest, December 31, 2013		
24			

Eliminations and Adjustments:

(CY1)   Eliminate the entry recording the parent's share of subsidiary net income for the current year. This entry returns the investment in Company S stock account to its January 1, 2013, balance to aid the elimination process.

(EL)   Eliminate 90% of the subsidiary equity balances of January 1, 2013, against the investment in stock account. No excess results.

(B1)   Eliminate intercompany interest revenue and expense. Eliminate the balance of the investment in bonds against the bonds payable. Note that the investment in bonds is at its year-end amortized balance. The loss on retirement at the date the bonds were purchased is calculated as follows:

Loss remaining at year-end:

Investment in bonds at December 31, 2013	$102,400	
Less: Carrying value of bonds at December 31, 2013	100,000	$2,400

Loss amortized during year:

Interest expense eliminated	$ 8,000	
Less: Interest revenue eliminated	6,800	1,200
Loss at January 2, 2013		$3,600

(B2)   Eliminate intercompany interest payable and receivable.

Worksheet 5-1 (see page 265)

Eliminations & Adjustments				Consolidated Income Statement	NCI	Controlling Retained Earnings	Consolidated Balance Sheet	
Dr.		Cr.						
							276,400	1
		(B2)	8,000					2
		(CY1)	10,800					3
		(EL)	90,000					4
		(B1)	102,400					5
(B2)	8,000							6
(B1)	100,000							7
							(100,000)	8
						(120,000)		9
(EL)	72,000				(8,000)			10
(EL)	18,000				(2,000)			11
				(180,000)				12
				130,000				13
(B1)	6,800							14
		(B1)	8,000					15
(CY1)	10,800							16
(B1)	3,600			3,600				17
	219,200		219,200					18
				(46,400)				19
				960	(960)			20
				45,440		(45,440)		21
					(10,960)		(10,960)	22
						(165,440)	(165,440)	23
							0	24

Subsidiary Company S Income Distribution

Loss on bond retirement ....(B1)	$3,600	Internally generated net income, **including**	
		interest expense	**$12,000**
		Interest adjustment ($3,600 ÷ 3) ...... (B1)	1,200
		Adjusted income	$ 9,600
		NCI share	× 10%
		NCI	$ 960

Parent Company P Income Distribution

		Internally generated net income, **including**	
		interest revenue........................	**$36,800**
		90% × Company S adjusted income of $9,600.....	8,640
		Controlling interest	$ 45,440

Worksheet 5-2

Intercompany Investment in Bonds, Year Subsequent to Acquisition; Straight-Line Method of Amortization
Company P and Subsidiary Company S
Worksheet for Consolidated Financial Statements
For Year Ended December 31, 2014

	(Credit balance amounts are in parentheses.)	Trial Balance	
		Company P	Company S
1	Other Assets	94,400	242,000
2	Interest Receivable	8,000	
3	Investment in Company S Stock (90%)	120,600	
4			
5	**Investment in Company S Bonds (100%)**	**101,200**	
6	Interest Payable		(8,000)
7	**Bonds Payable (8%)**		**(100,000)**
8	Common Stock ($10 par)—Company P	(100,000)	
9	**Retained Earnings, January 1, 2014—Company P**	**(167,600)**	
10	Common Stock ($10 par)—Company S		(80,000)
11	**Retained Earnings, January 1, 2014—Company S**		**(32,000)**
12			
13	Operating Revenue	(130,000)	(100,000)
14	Operating Expense	100,000	70,000
15	Subsidiary Income	(19,800)	
16	**Interest Expense**		**8,000**
17	**Interest Income**	**(6,800)**	
18		0	0
19	Consolidated Net Income		
20	To NCI (see distribution schedule)		
21	Balance to Controlling Interest (see distribution schedule)		
22	Total NCI		
23	Retained Earnings, Controlling Interest, December 31, 2014		
24			

Eliminations and Adjustments:

(CY1) Eliminate the entry recording the parent's share of subsidiary net income for the current year.

(EL)   Eliminate 90% of the subsidiary equity balances of January 1, 2014, against the investment in stock account. There is no excess to be distributed.

(B1)   Eliminate intercompany interest revenue and expense. Eliminate the balance of the investment in bonds against the bonds payable. Note that the investment in bonds is at its year-end amortized balance. The remaining unamortized loss on retirement at the start of the year is calculated as follows:

Loss remaining at year-end:

Investment in bonds at December 31, 2014 . . . . $101,200

Less: Carrying value of bonds at December 31, 2014 . . . .   100,000 $1,200

Loss amortized during year:

Interest expense eliminated . . . . $ 8,000

Less: Interest revenue eliminated   6,800   1,200

Remaining loss at January 1, 2014 . . . . $2,400

The remaining unamortized loss of $2,400 on January 1, 2014, is allocated 90% to the controlling retained earnings and 10% to the noncontrolling retained earnings since the bonds were issued by the subsidiary.

(B2)   Eliminate intercompany interest payable and receivable.

Worksheet 5-2 (see page 266)

Eliminations & Adjustments				Consolidated Income Statement	NCI	Controlling Retained Earnings	Consolidated Balance Sheet	
Dr.		Cr.						
							336,400	1
		(B2)	8,000					2
		(CY1)	19,800					3
		(EL)	100,800					4
		(B1)	**101,200**					5
(B2)	8,000							6
(B1)	**100,000**							7
							(100,000)	8
(B1)	**2,160**					(165,440)		9
(EL)	72,000				(8,000)			10
(EL)	28,800				(2,960)			11
(B1)	**240**							12
				(230,000)				13
				170,000				14
(CY1)	19,800							15
		(B1)	**8,000**					16
(B1)	**6,800**							17
	237,800		237,800					18
				(60,000)				19
				2,320	(2,320)			20
				57,680		(57,680)		21
					(13,280)		(13,280)	22
						(223,120)	(223,120)	23
							0	24

Subsidiary Company S Income Distribution

Internally generated net income, including interest expense	$22,000
Interest adjustment ($3,600 ÷ 3) . . . . **(B1)**	1,200
Adjusted income	$23,200
NCI share	× 10%
NCI	$ 2,320

Parent Company P Income Distribution

Internally generated net income, including interest revenue	$36,800
90% × Company S adjusted income of $23,200. . .	20,880
Controlling interest	$57,680

Worksheet 5-3

Intercompany Bonds, Subsequent Period; Straight-Line Method of Amortization
Company P and Subsidiary Company S
Worksheet for Consolidated Financial Statements
For Year Ended December 31, 2014

		Trial Balance	
	(Credit balance amounts are in parentheses.)	Company P	Company S
1	Other Assets	59,400	259,082
2	Investment in Company S Stock	143,874	
3			
4	**Investment in Company S Bonds**	**101,800**	
5	**Bonds Payable**		**(100,000)**
6	**Discount on Bonds**		**778**
7	Common Stock—Company P	(100,000)	
8	**Retained Earnings, January 1, 2014—Company P**	**(160,000)**	
9	Common Stock—Company S		(40,000)
10	**Retained Earnings, January 1, 2014—Company S**		**(110,000)**
11			
12	Sales	(80,000)	(50,000)
13	**Interest Income**	**(6,200)**	
14	Cost of Goods Sold	50,000	31,362
15	**Interest Expense**		**8,778**
16	Subsidiary Income	(8,874)	
17		0	0
18	Consolidated Net Income		
19	To NCI (see distribution schedule)		
20	Balance to Controlling Interest (see distribution schedule)		
21	Total NCI		
22	Retained Earnings, Controlling Interest, December 31, 2014		
23			

Eliminations and Adjustments:

(CY1) Eliminate the entry recording the parent's share of subsidiary net income for the current year.
(EL) Eliminate 90% of the January 1, 2014, subsidiary equity balances against the January 1, 2014, investment in Company S stock balance. No excess results.
(B) Eliminate intercompany interest revenue and expense. Eliminate the balance of the investment in bonds against the bonds payable. Note that the investment in bonds and the discount on bonds are at their year-end amortized balances. The remaining unamortized loss on retirement at the start of the year is calculated as follows:

Loss remaining at year-end:

Investment in bonds at December 31, 2014		$101,800	
Less: Bonds payable at December 31, 2014	$100,000		
Discount on bonds at December 31, 2014	(778)	99,222	$2,578

Loss amortized during year:

Interest expense eliminated		$ 8,778	
Less: Interest revenue eliminated		6,200	2,578
Remaining loss at January 1, 2014.			$5,156

Since from the consolidated viewpoint the bonds were retired in the prior year and since the bonds were issued by the subsidiary, the remaining unamortized loss of $5,156 on January 1, 2014, is allocated 90% to the controlling retained earnings and 10% to the noncontrolling retained earnings.

Worksheet 5-3 (see page 268)

Eliminations & Adjustments		Consolidated Income Statement	NCI	Controlling Retained Earnings	Consolidated Balance Sheet	
Dr.	Cr.					
					318,482	1
	(CY1) 8,874					2
	(EL) 135,000					3
	(B) 101,800					4
(B) 100,000						5
	(B) 778					6
					(100,000)	7
(B) 4,640				(155,360)		8
(EL) 36,000			(4,000)			9
(EL) 99,000			(10,484)			10
(B) 516						11
		(130,000)				12
(B) 6,200						13
		81,362				14
	(B) 8,778					15
(CY1) 8,874						16
255,230	255,230					17
		(48,638)				18
		1,244	(1,244)			19
		47,394		(47,394)		20
			(15,728)		(15,728)	21
				(202,754)	(202,754)	22
					0	23

Subsidiary Company S Income Distribution

Internally generated net income, including interest expense....................		$ 9,860
Interest adjustment ($8,778 − $6,200)... (B)		**2,578**
Adjusted income		$ 12,438
NCI share	×	10%
NCI		$ 1,244

Parent Company P Income Distribution

Internally generated net income, including interest revenue....................	$36,200
90% × Company S adjusted income of $12,438....	11,194
Controlling interest	$47,394

Worksheet 5-4

Intercompany Bonds; Interest Method of Amortization
Company P and Subsidiary Company S
Worksheet for Consolidated Financial Statements
For Year Ended December 31, 2014

	(Credit balance amounts are in parentheses.)	Trial Balance	
		Company P	Company S
1	Other Assets	59,333	259,082
2	Investment in Company S Stock	144,000	
3			
4	**Investment in Company S Bonds**	**101,887**	
5	**Bonds Payable**		**(100,000)**
6	**Discount on Bonds**		**918**
7	Common Stock—Company P	(100,000)	
8	**Retained Earnings, January 1, 2014—Company P**	**(160,180)**	
9	Common Stock—Company S		(40,000)
10	**Retained Earnings, January 1, 2014—Company S**		**(110,200)**
11			
12	Sales	(80,000)	(50,000)
13	**Interest Income**	**(6,220)**	
14	Cost of Goods Sold	50,000	31,358
15	**Interest Expense**		**8,842**
16			
17	Subsidiary Income	(8,820)	
18		0	0
19	Consolidated Net Income		
20	To NCI (see distribution schedule)		
21	Balance to Controlling Interest (see distribution schedule)		
22	Total NCI		
23	Retained Earnings, Controlling Interest, December 31, 2014		
24			

Eliminations and Adjustments:

(CY1)   Eliminate the entry recording the parent's share of subsidiary net income for the current year.
(EL)   Eliminate 90% of the January 1, 2014, subsidiary equity balances against the January 1, 2014, investment in Company S stock balance. No excess results.
(B)   Eliminate intercompany interest revenue and expense. Eliminate the balance of the investment in bonds against the bonds payable. Note that the investment in bonds and the discount on bonds are at their year-end amortized balances. The remaining unamortized loss on retirement at the start of the year is calculated as follows:

Loss remaining at year-end:			
Investment in bonds at December 31, 2014		$101,887	
Less: Bonds payable at December 31, 2014	$100,000		
Discount on bonds at December 31, 2014	(918)	99,082	$2,805
Loss amortized during year:			
Interest expense eliminated		$ 8,842	
Less: Interest revenue eliminated		6,220	2,622
Remaining loss at January 1, 2014.			$5,427

Since from the consolidated viewpoint the bonds were retired in the prior year and since the bonds were issued by the subsidiary, the remaining unamortized loss of $5,427 on January 1, 2014, is allocated 90% to the controlling retained earnings and 10% to the noncontrolling retained earnings.

Worksheet 5-4 (see page 270)

Eliminations & Adjustments		Consolidated Income Statement	NCI	Controlling Retained Earnings	Consolidated Balance Sheet	
Dr.	Cr.					
					318,415	1
	(CY1) 8,820					2
	(EL) 135,180					3
	(B) 101,887					4
(B) 100,000						5
	(B) 918					6
					(100,000)	7
(B) 4,884				(155,296)		8
(EL) 36,000			(4,000)			9
(EL) 99,180			(10,477)			10
(B) 543						11
		(130,000)				12
(B) 6,220						13
		81,358				14
	(B) 8,842					15
						16
(CY1) 8,820						17
255,647	255,647					18
		(48,642)				19
		1,242	(1,242)			20
		47,400		(47,400)		21
			(15,719)		(15,719)	22
				(202,696)	(202,696)	23
					0	24

Subsidiary Company S Income Distribution

Internally generated net income, including interest expense...................		$ 9,800
Interest adjustment ($8,842 − $6,220) .... **(B)**		2,622
Adjusted income		$ 12,422
NCI share	×	10%
NCI		$ 1,242

Parent Company P Income Distribution

Internally generated net income, including interest revenue	$36,220
90% × Company S adjusted income of $12,422...	11,180
Controlling interest	$47,400

Worksheet 5-5

Intercompany Capital Lease with Unguaranteed Residual Value
Company P and Subsidiary Company S
Worksheet for Consolidated Financial Statements
For Year Ended December 31, 2011

| | (Credit balance amounts are in parentheses.) | Trial Balance | |
		Company P	Company S
1	Accounts Receivable	30,149	44,793
2	**Minimum Lease Payments Receivable**	**4,000**	
3	**Unguaranteed Residual Value**	**1,000**	
4	**Unearned Interest Income**	**(533)**	
5	**Assets Under Capital Lease**		**5,210**
6	**Accumulated Depreciation—Assets Under Capital Lease**		**(1,737)**
7	**Property, Plant, and Equipment**	200,000	120,000
8	**Accumulated Depreciation—Property, Plant, and Equipment**	(80,000)	(50,000)
9	Investment in Company S	87,634	
10			
11	Accounts Payable	(21,000)	(5,000)
12	**Obligations Under Capital Lease**		**(3,210)**
13	**Interest Payable**		**(514)**
14	Common Stock ($10 par)—Company P	(50,000)	
15	Retained Earnings, January 1, 2011—Company P	(120,000)	
16	Common Stock ($5 par)—Company S		(40,000)
17	Retained Earnings, January 1, 2011—Company S		(50,000)
18	Sales	(120,000)	(70,000)
19	**Interest Income**	**(616)**	
20	Subsidiary Income	(15,634)	
21	Operating Expense	65,000	38,207
22	**Interest Expense**		**514**
23	**Depreciation Expense**	20,000	11,737
24		0	0
25	Consolidated Net Income		
26	To NCI (see distribution schedule)		
27	Balance to Controlling Interest (see distribution schedule)		
28	Total NCI		
29	Retained Earnings, Controlling Interest, December 31, 2011		
30			

Worksheet 5-5 (see page 280)

Eliminations & Adjustments				Consolidated Income Statement	NCI	Controlling Retained Earnings	Consolidated Balance Sheet	
Dr.		Cr.						
							74,942	1
		(CL2)	4,000					2
		(CL2)	1,000					3
(CL2)	635	(CL1)	102					4
		(CL2)	5,210					5
(CL3)	1,737							6
(CL2)	5,851						325,851	7
		(CL3)	1,617				(131,617)	8
		(CY1)	15,634					9
		(EL)	72,000					10
							(26,000)	11
(CL2)	3,210							12
(CL2)	514							13
							(50,000)	14
						(120,000)		15
(EL)	32,000				(8,000)			16
(EL)	40,000				(10,000)			17
				(190,000)				18
(CL1)	616							19
(CY1)	15,634							20
				103,207				21
		(CL1)	514					22
		(CL3)	120	31,617				23
	100,197		100,197					24
				(55,176)				25
				3,908	(3,908)			26
				51,268		(51,268)		27
					(21,908)		(21,908)	28
						(171,268)	(171,268)	29
							0	30

Eliminations and Adjustments:

(CY1)   Eliminate the parent company's entry recording its share of Company S net income. This step returns the investment account to its January 1, 2011, balance to aid the elimination process.

(EL)   Eliminate 80% of the January 1, 2011, Company S equity balances against the investment in Company S balance.

(CL1)   Eliminate the interest income recorded by the lessor, $616, and the interest expense recorded by the lessee, $514. The $102 disparity reflects the interest recorded on the unguaranteed residual value. This amount is returned to the unearned interest income.

(CL2)   Eliminate the intercompany debt and the unguaranteed residual value. Eliminate the asset under capital lease and record the owned asset. The amounts are reconciled as follows:

Disparity in recorded debt:

Lessor balance, **$4,000 − $635** unearned interest income	$ 3,365
Lessee balance, **$3,210 + $514** accrued interest	3,724
Interest applicable to unguaranteed residual value	$ (359)
Unguaranteed residual value	**1,000**
Net original present value of unguaranteed residual value	$ 641
Asset under capital lease	**5,210**
Owned asset at original cost	$ 5,851

(CL3)   Reclassify accumulated depreciation and adjust the depreciation expense to acknowledge cost of asset. The adjustment to depreciation expense is determined as follows:

Capitalized cost by lessee		$5,210
Depreciable cost:		
Cost	$5,851	
Less residual (salvage) value	1,000	4,851
Decrease in depreciable cost		$ 359
Adjustment to depreciation expense ($359 ÷ 3-year lease term)		**$ 120**

Subsidiary Company S Income Distribution

Internally generated net income, **including interest income on lease**	$19,542
Adjusted income	$19,542
NCI share	× 20%
NCI	$ 3,908

Parent Company P Income Distribution

Net interest eliminated. . . . . **(CL1)**	**$102**	Internally generated net income, **including interest income on lease**	$35,616
		80% × Company S adjusted income of $19,542. . .	15,634
		Decrease in depreciation . . . . **(CL3)**	**120**
		Controlling interest	$51,268

Worksheet 5-6

Intercompany Capital Lease with Unguaranteed Residual Value, Subsequent Period
Company P and Subsidiary Company S
Worksheet for Consolidated Financial Statements
For Year Ended December 31, 2012

	(Credit balance amounts are in parentheses.)	Trial Balance	
		Company P	Company S
1	Accounts Receivable	102,149	82,925
2	**Minimum Lease Payments Receivable**	**2,000**	
3	**Unguaranteed Residual Value**	**1,000**	
4	**Unearned Interest Income**	**(138)**	
5			
6	**Assets Under Capital Lease**		**5,210**
7	**Accumulated Depreciation—Assets Under Capital Lease**		**(3,474)**
8	**Property, Plant, and Equipment**	200,000	120,000
9	**Accumulated Depreciation—Property, Plant, and Equipment**	(100,000)	(60,000)
10	Investment in Company S	102,129	
11			
12	Accounts Payable	(41,000)	(15,000)
13	**Obligations Under Capital Lease**		**(1,724)**
14	**Interest Payable**		**(276)**
15	Common Stock ($10 par)—Company P	(50,000)	
16	**Retained Earnings, January 1, 2012—Company P**	**(171,250)**	
17	Common Stock ($5 par)—Company S		(40,000)
18	Retained Earnings, January 1, 2012—Company S		(69,542)
19	Sales	(150,000)	(80,000)
20	**Interest Income**	**(395)**	
21	Subsidiary Income	(14,495)	
22	Operating Expense	100,000	49,868
23	**Interest Expense**		**276**
24	**Depreciation Expense**	20,000	11,737
25		0	0
26	Consolidated Net Income		
27	To NCI (see distribution schedule)		
28	Balance to Controlling Interest (see distribution schedule)		
29	Total NCI		
30	Retained Earnings, Controlling Interest, December 31, 2012		
31			

Worksheet 5-6 (see page 281)

Eliminations & Adjustments				Consolidated Income Statement	NCI	Controlling Retained Earnings	Consolidated Balance Sheet	
Dr.		Cr.						
							185,074	1
		(CL2)	2,000					2
		(CL2)	1,000					3
(CL2)	359	(CL1a)	119					4
		(CL1b)	102					5
		(CL2)	5,210					6
(CL3)	3,474							7
(CL2)	5,851						325,851	8
		(CL3)	3,234				(163,234)	9
		(CY1)	14,495					10
		(EL)	87,634					11
							(56,000)	12
(CL2)	1,724							13
(CL2)	276							14
							(50,000)	15
(CL1b)	102	(CL3)	120			(171,268)		16
(EL)	32,000				(8,000)			17
(EL)	55,634				(13,908)			18
				(230,000)				19
(CL1a)	395							20
(CY1)	14,495							21
				149,868				22
		(CL1a)	276					23
		(CL3)	120	31,617				24
	114,310		114,310					25
				(48,515)				26
				3,624	(3,624)			27
				44,891		(44,891)		28
					(25,532)		(25,532)	29
						(216,159)	(216,159)	30
							0	31

Eliminations and Adjustments:

(CY1)   Eliminate the parent company's entry recording its share of Company S net income.
(EL)   Eliminate 80% of the January 1, 2012, Company S equity balances against the investment in Company S balance.
(CL1a) Eliminate the interest income recorded by the lessor, $395, and the interest expense recorded by the lessee, $276. The $119 disparity reflects the interest recorded on the unguaranteed residual value. This amount is returned to the unearned interest income.
(CL1b) Adjust the unearned income and the parent's retained earnings for the $102 interest recorded in 2011 on the unguaranteed residual value.
(CL2) Eliminate the intercompany debt and the unguaranteed residual value. Eliminate the asset under capital lease and record the owned asset. The amounts are reconciled as follows:

Disparity in recorded debt:	
Lessor balance, **$2,000 − $359** unearned interest income	$ 1,641
Lessee balance, **$1,724 + $276** accrued interest	2,000
Interest applicable to unguaranteed residual value	$ (359)
Unguaranteed residual value	**1,000**
Net original present value of unguaranteed residual value	$ 641
Asset under capital lease	**5,210**
Owned asset at original cost	$ 5,851

(CL3) Reclassify $3,474 depreciation and reduce it to depreciation based on cost ($3,234). This includes reducing current depreciation expense by $120 and prior year for $120 (credit to retained earning, contolling interest). The adjustment to the depreciation expense and the retained earnings is determined as follows:

Capitalized cost by lessee		$5,210
Depreciable cost:		
Cost	$5,851	
Less residual (salvage) value	1,000	4,851
Decrease in depreciable cost		$ 359
Adjustment to depreciation expense and retained earnings ($359 ÷ 3-year lease term)		**$ 120**

Subsidiary Company S Income Distribution

Internally generated net income, **including interest on lease**	$18,119
Adjusted income	$18,119
NCI share	× 20%
NCI	$ 3,624

Parent Company P Income Distribution

Net interest eliminated . . . . **(CL1a)** **$119**	Internally generated net income, **including interest income on lease**	$30,395
	80% × Company S adjusted income of $18,119	14,495
	Decrease in depreciation . . . . **(CL3)**	**120**
	Controlling interest	$44,891

UNDERSTANDING THE ISSUES

1. Subsidiary Company S has $1,000,000 of bonds outstanding. The bonds have 10 years to maturity and pay interest at 8% annually. The parent has an average annual borrowing cost of 6% and wishes to reduce the interest cost of the consolidated company. What methods could be used to maintain the subsidiary as the debtor?

2. Subsidiary Company S has $1,000,000 of bonds outstanding at 8% annual interest. The bonds have 10 years to maturity. If the parent, Company P, is able to purchase the bonds at a price that reflects 6% annual interest, what effect will the purchase have on consolidated income in the current and future years? What would the effects be if the purchase price reflected a 9% annual interest rate? Your response need not be quantified.

3. Subsidiary Company S has $1,000,000 of bonds outstanding at 8% annual interest. The bonds have 10 years to maturity. If the parent, Company P, is able to purchase the bonds at a price that reflects 6% annual interest, how will the noncontrolling interest be affected in the current and future years? Your response need not be quantified.

4. Company P purchased $100,000 of subsidiary Company S's bonds for $96,000 on January 1, 2011, when the bonds had five years to maturity. The bonds had been issued at face value and pay interest at 8% annually. What will the impact of this transaction be on consolidated net income for the current and future four years? Assuming a 20% noncontrolling interest, how will the NCI be affected in the current and next four years? Quantify your response.

5. Your friend is a noncontrolling interest shareholder in a large company. He knows that the subsidiary company leases most of its assets from the parent company under operating leases. He further believes that the lease rates are in excess of market rates. He made his concern known to the parent company management. Their response was: "Don't worry about it; it washes out in the consolidation process and ends up having no effect on income." Your friend wants to know if this is true and if he was wrong to be concerned.

6. A parent company may want to shift profits to the controlling interest and may use intercompany capital leases to accomplish that end. Is there an opportunity to do that with both direct financing and sales-type leases? What are the differences between the two types of leases with respect to income shifting?

7. A parent company is a producer of production equipment, some of which is acquired and used by the parent's subsidiary companies. The parent offers a discount to the subsidiaries but still earns a significant profit on the sales of equipment to a subsidiary. Is there any difference in the consolidated company's ability to recognize the profit on these sales if, instead of selling equipment to the subsidiaries, the equipment is leased to them under capital leases? Are there any other profit opportunities for the controlling interest in leasing as opposed to selling equipment to the subsidiaries?

EXERCISES

Exercise 1 *(LO 1)* **Effect of intercompany bonds on income.** Dennis Company is an 80%-owned subsidiary of Kay Industries. Dennis Company issued 10-year, 8% bonds in the amount of $1,000,000 on January 1, 2011. The bonds were issued at face value, and interest is payable each January 1. On January, 1, 2013, Kay Industries purchased all of the Dennis bonds for $968,000. Kay will amortize the discount on a straight-line basis. For the years ending (a) December 31, 2013, and (b) December 31, 2014, determine the effects of this transaction:

1. On consolidated net income.
2. On the distribution of income to the controlling and noncontrolling interests.

Exercise 2 *(LO 1)* **Options to lower interest cost.** Mode Engineering is a large corporation with the ability to obtain financing by selling its bonds at favorable rates. Currently, it pays 6% interest on its 10-year bond issues. In the past year, Mode acquired an 80% interest in Metel Industries. Metel Industries has $1,000,000 of bonds outstanding that mature in six years. Interest is paid annually at a stated rate of 9%. The bonds were issued at face value.

Interest rates have come down, but Metel Industries can still expect to pay 7% to 8.5% interest on a long-term issue. Metel Industries is a smaller company with a lower credit rating than Mode.

Mode would like to reduce interest costs on the Metel Industries debt. The company has asked your advice on whether it should purchase the bonds or loan Metel Industries the money to retire its own debt. Compare the options with a focus on the impact on consolidated statements.

Exercise 3 *(LO 2)* **Bond calculations, effective interest.** Linco Industries is a 90%-owned subsidiary of Sharp Incorporated. On January 1, 2015, Linco issued $100,000 of 10-year, 6% bonds for $86,580, to yield 8% interest. Interest is paid annually on January 1. The effective interest method is used to amortize the premium. Sharp purchased the bonds for $84,901 on January 2, 2018, when the market rate of interest was 9%. On the purchase date, the remaining discount on the bonds was $10,413. Linco's 2018 net income was $500,000.

1. Prepare the eliminations and adjustments required for this purchase on the December 31, 2018, consolidated worksheet. Amortization schedules will be needed to January 1, 2019.
2. Prepare the 2018 income distribution schedule for the NCI.

Exercise 4 *(LO 2)* **Bond eliminations, partial purchase.** Carlton Company is an 80%-owned subsidiary of Mirage Company. On January 1, 2011, Carlton sold $100,000 of 10-year, 7% bonds for $101,000. Interest is paid annually on January 1. The market rate for this type of bond was 9% on January 2, 2013, when Mirage purchased 60% of the Carlton bonds for $53,600. Discounts may be amortized on a straight-line basis.

1. Prepare the eliminations and adjustments required for this bond purchase on the December 31, 2013, consolidated worksheet.
2. Prepare the eliminations and adjustments required on the December 31, 2014, consolidated worksheet.

Exercise 5 *(LO 2)* **Bond eliminations, effective interest.** On January 1, 2014, Dunbar Corporation, an 85%-owned subsidiary of Garfield Industries, received $48,055 for $50,000 of 8%, 5-year bonds it issued when the market rate was 9%. When Garfield Industries purchased these bonds for $47,513 on January 2, 2016, the market rate was 10%. Given the following effective interest amortization schedules for both companies, calculate the gain or loss on retirement and the interest adjustments to the issuer's income distribution schedules over the remaining term of the bonds.

Dunbar (issuer):

Date	Effective Interest (9%)	Nominal Interest (8%)	Discount Amortization	Balance
1/1/14				$48,055
1/1/15	$4,325	$4,000	$325	48,380
1/1/16	4,354	4,000	354	48,734
1/1/17	4,386	4,000	386	49,120
1/1/18	4,421	4,000	421	49,541
1/1/19	4,459	4,000	459	50,000

Garfield (purchaser):

Date	Effective Interest (10%)	Nominal Interest (8%)	Discount Amortization	Balance
1/2/16				$47,513
1/1/17	$4,751	$4,000	$751	48,264
1/1/18	4,826	4,000	826	49,090
1/1/19	4,909	4,000	909	50,000*

*Adjusted for rounding

Exercise 6 *(LO 2)* **Bond eliminations, straight-line.** Cardinal Company is an 80%-owned subsidiary of Dove Corporation. Cardinal Company issued $100,000 of 8%, 10-year bonds for $96,000 on January 1, 2011. Annual interest is paid on January 1. Dove Corporation purchased the bonds on January 1, 2015, for $101,500. Both companies use the straight-line method to amortize the premium/discount on the bonds.

1. Prepare the eliminations and adjustments that would be made on the December 31, 2015, consolidated worksheet as a result of this purchase.
2. Prepare the eliminations and adjustments that would be made on the December 31, 2016, consolidated worksheet.

Exercise 7 *(LO 4)* **Operating lease, entries, and eliminations.** Grande Machinery Company purchased, for cash, a $60,000 custom machine on January 1, 2011. The machine has an estimated 5-year life and will be straight-line depreciated with no salvage value. The machine was then leased to Sunshine Engineering Company, an 80%-owned subsidiary, under a 5-year operating lease for $15,000 per year, payable each January.

1. Record the 2011 entries for the purchase of the machine and the lease to Sunshine Engineering Company on the books of Grande Machinery Company.
2. Record the 2011 entries for the transaction on the books of Sunshine Engineering Company.
3. Provide the elimination entries that would be made on the 2011 consolidated worksheet.

Exercise 8 *(LO 5)* **Direct-financing lease eliminations.** On January 1, 2011, Traylor Company, an 80%-owned subsidiary of Parker Electronics, Inc., signed a 4-year direct-financing lease with its parent for the rental of electronic equipment. The lease agreement requires a $12,000 payment on January 1 of each year, and title transfers to Traylor on January 1, 2015. The equipment originally cost $40,822 and had an estimated remaining life of five years at the start of the lease term. The lessor's implicit interest rate is 12%. The lessee also used the 12% rate to record the transaction.

1. Prepare a lease payment amortization schedule for the life of the lease.
2. Prepare the eliminations and adjustments required for this lease on the December 31, 2011, consolidated worksheet.
3. Prepare the eliminations and adjustments for the December 31, 2012, consolidated worksheet.

Exercise 9 *(LO 6)* **Sales-type lease eliminations.** The Auto Clinic is a wholly owned subsidiary of Fast-Check Equipment Company. Fast-Check Equipment sells and leases 4-wheel alignment machines. The usual selling price of each machine is $35,000; it has a cost to Fast-Check Equipment of $25,000. On January 1, 2011, Fast-Check Equipment leased such a machine to Auto Clinic. The lease provided for payments of $9,096 at the start of each year for five years. The payments include $1,000 per year for maintenance to be provided by the seller. There is a bargain purchase price of $2,000 at the end of the fifth year. The implicit interest rate in the lease is 10% per year. The equipment is being depreciated over eight years.

The amortization schedule for the lease prepared by Fast-Check Equipment is as follows:

Date	Payment	Interest at 10% on Previous Balance	Reduction of Principal	Principal Balance
				$35,000
1/1/11	$ 8,096		$ 8,096	26,904
1/1/12	8,096	$2,690	5,406	21,498
1/1/13	8,096	2,150	5,946	15,552
1/1/14	8,096	1,555	6,541	9,011
1/1/15	8,096	901	7,195	1,816
12/31/15	2,000	184*	1,816	0
Totals	$42,480	$7,480	$35,000	

*Adjusted for rounding

Prepare the eliminations and adjustments, in entry form, that would be required on a consolidated worksheet prepared on December 31, 2011.

PROBLEMS

Problem 5-1 *(LO 2)* **CPA Objective, equipment, merchandise, bonds.** The problem below is an example of a question of the CPA "Other Objective Format" type as it was applied to the consolidations area. A mark-sensing answer sheet was used on the exam. You may just supply the answer, which should be accompanied by calculations where appropriate.

Presented below are selected amounts from the separate unconsolidated financial statements of Pero Corporation and its 90%-owned subsidiary Sean Company at December 31, 2012. Additional information follows:

	Pero Corporation	Sean Company
Selected income statement amounts:		
Sales	$ 710,000	$ 530,000
Cost of goods sold	490,000	370,000
Gain on the sale of equipment		21,000
Earnings from investment in subsidiary (equity)	63,000	
Other expenses	48,000	75,000
Interest expense		16,000
Depreciation	25,000	20,000
Selected balance sheet amounts:		
Cash	30,000	18,000
Inventories	229,000	150,000
Equipment	440,000	360,000
Accumulated depreciation.	(200,000)	(120,000)
Investment in Sean (equity balance).	211,000	
Investment in bonds	(100,000)	
Discount on bonds	(9,000)	
Bonds payable.		(200,000)
Discount on bonds payable		3,000
Common stock.	100,000)	(10,000)
Additional paid-in capital in excess of par	(250,000)	(40,000)
Retained earnings	(402,000)	(140,000)

	Pero Corporation	Sean Company
Selected statement of retained earnings amounts:		
Beginning balance, December 31, 2011	$ 272,000	$ 100,000
Net income	210,000	70,000
Dividends paid.	80,000	30,000

Additional information is as follows:

1. On January 2, 2012, Pero purchased 90% of Sean's 100,000 outstanding common stock for cash of $175,000. On that date, Sean's stockholders' equity equaled $150,000, and the fair values of Sean's assets and liabilities equaled their carrying amounts. Any remaining excess is considered to be goodwill.
2. On September 4, 2012, Sean paid cash dividends of $30,000.
3. On December 31, 2012, Pero recorded its equity in Sean's earnings.

1. Items (a) through (c) shown below represent transactions between Pero and Sean during 2012. Determine the dollar amount effect of the consolidating adjustment on 2012 consolidated net income. Ignore income tax considerations. ◄ ◄ ◄ ◄ ◄ **Required**

Items to be answered:

a. On January 3, 2012, Sean sold equipment with an original cost of $30,000 and a carrying value of $21,000 to Pero for $36,000. The equipment had a remaining life of three years and was depreciated using the straight-line method by both companies.
b. During 2012, Sean sold merchandise to Pero for $60,000, which included a profit of $20,000. At December 31, 2012, half of this merchandise remained in Pero's inventory.
c. On December 31, 2012, Pero paid $94,000 to purchase 50% of the outstanding bonds issued by Sean. The bonds mature on December 31, 2018, and were originally issued at a discount. The bonds pay interest annually on December 31, and the interest was paid to the prior investor immediately before Pero's purchase of the bonds.

2. Items (a) through (l) below refer to accounts that may or may not be included in Pero's consolidated financial statements. The list on the right refers to the various possibilities of those amounts to be reported in Pero's consolidated financial statements for the year ended December 31, 2012. Consider all transactions stated above in determining your answer. Ignore income tax considerations.

Items to be answered:
a. Cash
b. Equipment
c. Investment in subsidiary
d. Bonds payable
e. NCI
f. Common stock
g. Beginning retained earnings
h. Dividends paid
i. Gain on retirement of bonds
j. Cost of goods sold
k. Interest expense
l. Depreciation expense

Responses to be selected:
1. Sum of amounts on Pero's and Sean's separate unconsolidated financial statements.
2. Less than the sum of amounts on Pero's and Sean's separate unconsolidated financial statements, but not the same as the amount on either.
3. Same as amount for Pero only.
4. Same as amount for Sean only.
5. Eliminated entirely in consolidation.
6. Shown in consolidated financial statements but not in separate unconsolidated financial statements.
7. Neither in consolidated nor in separate unconsolidated financial statements.

(AICPA adapted)

Problem 5-2 *(LO 2)* **80%, cost method, straight-line bonds, fixed asset sale.** On January 1, 2013, Appliance Outlets had the following balances in its stockholders' equity accounts: Common Stock ($10 par), $800,000; Paid-In Capital in Excess of Par, $625,000; and Retained Earnings, $450,000. General Appliances acquired 64,000 shares of Appliance

Outlets' common stock for $1,700,000 on that date. Any excess of cost over book value was attributed to goodwill.

Appliance Outlets issued $500,000 of 8-year, 11% bonds on December 31, 2012. The bonds sold for $476,000. General Appliances purchased one-half of these bonds in the market on January 1, 2015, for $256,000. Both companies use the straight-line method of amortization of premiums and discounts.

On July 1, 2016, General Appliances sold to Appliance Outlets an old building with a book value of $167,500, remaining life of 10 years, and $30,000 salvage value, for $195,000. The building is being depreciated on a straight-line basis. Appliance Outlets paid $20,000 in cash and signed a mortgage note with its parent for the balance. Interest, at 11% of the unpaid balance, and principal payments are due annually beginning July 1, 2017. (For convenience, the mortgage balances are not divided into current and long-term portions.)

The trial balances of the two companies at December 31, 2016, were as follows:

	General Appliances	Appliance Outlets
Cash	404,486	72,625
Accounts Receivable (net)	752,500	105,000
Interest Receivable	9,625	
Inventory	1,950,000	900,000
Investment in Appliance Outlets	1,700,000	
Investment in 11% Bonds	254,000	
Investment in Mortgage	175,000	
Property, Plant, and Equipment	9,000,000	2,950,000
Accumulated Depreciation	(1,695,000)	(940,000)
Accounts Payable	(670,000)	(80,000)
Interest Payable	(18,333)	(9,625)
Bonds Payable (11%)	(2,000,000)	(500,000)
Discount on Bonds Payable	10,470	12,000
Mortgage Payable		(175,000)
Common Stock ($5 par)	(3,200,000)	
Common Stock ($10 par)		(800,000)
Paid-In Capital in Excess of Par	(4,550,000)	(625,000)
Retained Earnings, January 1, 2016	(1,011,123)	(770,000)
Sales	(9,800,000)	(3,000,000)
Gain on Sale of Building	(27,500)	
Interest Income	(36,125)	
Dividend Income	(48,000)	
Cost of Goods Sold	4,940,000	1,700,000
Depreciation Expense	717,000	95,950
Interest Expense	223,000	67,544
Other Expenses	2,600,000	936,506
Dividends Declared	320,000	60,000
Totals	0	0

Required ▶ ▶ ▶ ▶ ▶   Prepare the worksheet necessary to produce the consolidated financial statements of General Appliances and its subsidiary for the year ended December 31, 2016. Include the determination and distribution of excess and income distribution schedules.

Problem 5-3 *(LO 2)* **Cost method, 90%, straight-line bonds.** On January 1, 2011, Patrick Company acquired 90% of the common stock of Stunt Company for $351,000. On this date, Stunt had common stock, other paid-in capital in excess of par, and retained earnings of $100,000, $40,000, and $210,000, respectively. The excess of cost over book value is due to goodwill. In both 2011 and 2012, Patrick accounted for the investment in Stunt using the cost method.

On January 1, 2011, Stunt sold $100,000 par value of 10-year, 8% bonds for $94,000. The bonds pay interest semiannually on January 1 and July 1 of each year. On December 31, 2011, Patrick purchased all of Stunt's bonds for $96,400. The bonds are still held on December 31, 2012. Both companies correctly recorded all entries relative to bonds and interest, using straight-line amortization for premium or discount.

The trial balances of Patrick Company and its subsidiary were as follows on December 31, 2012:

	Patrick Company	Stunt Company
Interest Receivable..	4,000	
Other Current Assets.....................................	248,200	315,200
Investment in Stunt Company............................	351,000	
Investment in Stunt Bonds...............................	96,800	
Land..	80,000	60,000
Buildings and Equipment.................................	400,000	280,000
Accumulated Depreciation	(120,000)	(60,000)
Interest Payable		(4,000)
Other Current Liabilities.................................	(98,000)	(56,000)
Bonds Payable (8%)		(100,000)
Discount on Bonds Payable		4,800
Other Long-Term Liabilities	(200,000)	
Common Stock—Patrick Company.......................	(100,000)	
Other Paid-In Capital in Excess of Par—Patrick Company	(200,000)	
Retained Earnings—Patrick Company	(365,000)	
Common Stock—Stunt Company		(100,000)
Other Paid-In Capital in Excess of Par—Stunt Company		(40,000)
Retained Earnings—Stunt Company		(260,000)
Net Sales...	(640,000)	(350,000)
Cost of Goods Sold	360,000	200,000
Operating Expenses	168,400	71,400
Interest Expense...		8,600
Interest Income..	(8,400)	
Dividend Income	(27,000)	
Dividends Declared......................................	50,000	30,000
Totals	0	0

Prepare the worksheet necessary to produce the consolidated financial statements of Patrick and its subsidiary Stunt for the year ended December 31, 2012. Round all computations to the nearest dollar. ◄ ◄ ◄ ◄ ◄ **Required**

Use the following information for Problems 5-4 and 5-5:

On January 1, 2014, Postman Company acquired Spartan Company. Postman paid $400,000 for 80% of Spartan's common stock. On the date of acquisition, Spartan had the following balance sheet:

Spartan Company
Balance Sheet
January 1, 2014

Assets		Liabilities and Equity	
Accounts receivable	$ 90,000	Accounts payable	$ 17,352
Inventory	50,000	Bonds payable	100,000
Land.....................	60,000	Premium on bonds payable...	2,648
Buildings	$100,000	Common stock ($1 par)......	$ 10,000
Accumulated depreciation ...	(30,000)	Paid-in capital in excess of par	90,000
Equipment	80,000	Retained earnings	100,000
Accumulated depreciation ...	(30,000)		
Total assets..............	$320,000	Total liabilities and equity ..	$320,000

Buildings, which have a 20-year life, are undervalued by $130,000. Equipment, which has a 5-year life, is undervalued by $50,000. Any remaining excess is considered to be goodwill.

Spartan issued $100,000 of 8%, 10-year bonds for $103,432 on January 1, 2011, when the market rate was 7.5%. Annual interest is paid on December 31. Postman purchased the bonds for $95,514 on January 1, 2015, when the market rate was 9%. Both companies use the effective interest method to amortize the premium/discount on the bonds. Postman and Spartan prepared the following bond amortization schedules:

	Spartan				Postman		
Period	Cash	Interest	Balance	Period	Cash	Interest	Balance
1/2011			$103,432	1/2011			
1/2012	$8,000	$7,757	103,189	1/2012			
1/2013	8,000	7,739	102,928	1/2013			
1/2014	8,000	7,720	102,648	1/2014			
1/2015	8,000	7,699	102,347	1/2015			$ 95,514
1/2016	8,000	7,676	102,023	1/2016	$8,000	$8,596	96,110
1/2017	8,000	7,652	101,675	1/2017	8,000	8,650	96,760
1/2018	8,000	7,626	101,301	1/2018	8,000	8,708	97,468
1/2019	8,000	7,598	100,899	1/2019	8,000	8,772	98,240
1/2020	8,000	7,567	100,466	1/2020	8,000	8,842	99,082
1/2021	8,000	7,534*	100,000	1/2021	8,000	8,918*	100,000

*Adjusted for rounding

Problem 5-4 *(LO 2)* **80%, equity, effective interest bonds purchased this year, inventory profits.** Refer to the preceding facts for Postman's acquisition of 80% of Spartan's common stock and the bond transactions. Postman uses the simple equity method to account for its investment in Spartan. On January 1, 2015, Postman held merchandise acquired from Spartan for $9,000. During 2015, Spartan sold $20,000 worth of merchandise to Postman. Postman held $12,000 of this merchandise at December 31, 2015. Postman owed Spartan $7,000 on December 31 as a result of these intercompany sales. Spartan has a gross profit rate of 25%.

Postman and Spartan had the following trial balances on December 31, 2015:

	Postman	Spartan
Cash	144,486	99,347
Accounts Receivable	90,000	60,000
Inventory	120,000	55,000
Land	200,000	60,000
Investment in Spartan	429,859	
Investment in Spartan Bonds	96,110	
Buildings	600,000	100,000
Accumulated Depreciation	(310,000)	(40,000)
Equipment	150,000	80,000
Accumulated Depreciation	(90,000)	(50,000)
Accounts Payable	(55,000)	(25,000)
Bonds Payable		(100,000)
Discount on Bonds Payable		(2,023)
Common Stock	(100,000)	(10,000)
Paid-In Capital in Excess of Par	(800,000)	(90,000)
Retained Earnings, January 1, 2015	(300,000)	(120,000)
Sales	(850,000)	(320,000)
Cost of Goods Sold	500,000	200,000
Depreciation Expense—Buildings	30,000	5,000
Depreciation Expense—Equipment	15,000	10,000
Other Expenses	140,000	70,000
Interest Revenue	(8,596)	
Interest Expense		7,676
Subsidiary Income	(21,859)	
Dividends Declared	20,000	10,000
Totals	0	0

Prepare the worksheet necessary to produce the consolidated financial statements for Postman Company and its subsidiary Spartan Company for the year ended December 31, 2015. Include the determination and distribution of excess and income distribution schedules.   ◄ ◄ ◄ ◄ ◄ **Required**

Problem 5-5 *(LO 2)* **80%, equity, effective interest bonds purchased last year, inventory profits.** Refer to the preceding facts for Postman's acquisition of 80% of Spartan's common stock and the bond transactions. Postman uses the simple equity method to account for its investment in Spartan. On January 1, 2016, Postman held merchandise acquired from Spartan for $12,000. During 2016, Spartan sold $25,000 worth of merchandise to Postman. Postman held $10,000 of this merchandise at December 31, 2016. Postman owed Spartan $6,000 on December 31 as a result of these intercompany sales. Spartan has a gross profit rate of 25%.

Postman and Spartan had the following trial balances on December 31, 2016:

	Postman	Spartan
Cash	290,486	99,347
Accounts Receivable	120,000	91,000
Inventory	140,000	55,000
Land	200,000	60,000
Investment in Spartan	435,737	
Investment in Spartan Bonds	96,760	
Buildings	600,000	100,000
Accumulated Depreciation	(340,000)	(45,000)

(continued)

	Postman	Spartan
Equipment	150,000	80,000
Accumulated Depreciation	(105,000)	(60,000)
Accounts Payable	(40,000)	(34,000)
Bonds Payable		(100,000)
Premium on Bonds Payable		(1,675)
Common Stock	(100,000)	(10,000)
Paid-In Capital in Excess of Par	(800,000)	(90,000)
Retained Earnings, January 1, 2016.	(475,455)	(137,324)
Sales	(900,000)	(350,000)
Cost of Goods Sold	530,000	230,000
Depreciation Expense—Buildings	30,000	5,000
Depreciation Expense—Equipment.	15,000	10,000
Other Expenses	155,000	80,000
Interest Revenue.	(8,650)	
Interest Expense.		7,652
Subsidiary Income	(13,878)	
Dividends Declared	20,000	10,000
Totals	0	0

Required ▶ ▶ ▶ ▶ ▶ Prepare the worksheet necessary to produce the consolidated financial statements for Postman Company and its subsidiary Spartan Company for the year ended December 31, 2016. Include the determination and distribution of excess and income distribution schedules.

Use the following information for Problems 5-6 and 5-7:

On January 1, 2014, Pontiac Company acquired an 80% interest in the common stock of Stark Company for $400,000. Stark had the following balance sheet on the date of acquisition:

Stark Company
Balance Sheet
January 1, 2014

Assets		Liabilities and Equity	
Accounts receivable	$ 40,000	Accounts payable	$ 42,297
Inventory	20,000	Bonds payable	100,000
Land.	35,000	Discount on bonds payable. . .	(2,297)
Buildings	250,000	Common stock ($10 par).	10,000
Accumulated depreciation . . .	(50,000)	Paid-in capital in excess of par	90,000
Equipment	120,000	Retained earnings	115,000
Accumulated depreciation . . .	(60,000)		
Total assets.	$355,000	Total liabilities and equity . .	$355,000

Buildings (20-year life) are undervalued by $80,000. Equipment (5-year life) is undervalued by $50,000. Any remaining excess is considered to be goodwill.

Stark issued $100,000 of 8%, 10-year bonds for $96,719 on January 1, 2011. Annual interest is paid on December 31. Pontiac purchased the bonds on January 1, 2015, for $104,770. Both companies use the straight-line method to amortize the premium/discount on the bonds. Pontiac and Stark used the following bond amortization schedules:

	Stark				Pontiac		
Period	Cash	Interest	Balance	Period	Cash	Interest	Balance
1/2011			$ 96,719	1/2011			
1/2012	$8,000	$8,328	97,047	1/2012			
1/2013	8,000	8,328	97,375	1/2013			
1/2014	8,000	8,328	97,703	1/2014			
1/2015	8,000	8,328	98,031	1/2015			$104,770
1/2016	8,000	8,328	98,359	1/2016	$8,000	$7,205	103,975
1/2017	8,000	8,328	98,687	1/2017	8,000	7,205	103,180
1/2018	8,000	8,328	99,015	1/2018	8,000	7,205	102,385
1/2019	8,000	8,328	99,343	1/2019	8,000	7,205	101,590
1/2020	8,000	8,328	99,671	1/2020	8,000	7,205	100,795
1/2021	8,000	8,328	100,000*	1/2021	8,000	7,205	100,000

*Adjusted for rounding

Problem 5-6 *(LO 2)* **80%, equity, straight-line bonds purchased this year, inventory profits.** Refer to the preceding facts for Pontiac's acquisition of 80% of Starks common stock and the bond transactions. Pontiac uses the simple equity method to account for its investment in Stark. On January 1, 2015, Stack held merchandise acquired from Pontiac for $15,000. During 2015, Pontiac sold $50,000 worth of merchandise to Stark. Stark held $20,000 of this merchandise at December 31, 2015. Stark owed Pontiac $10,000 on December 31 as a result of these intercompany sales. Pontiac has a gross profit rate of 30%. Pontiac and Stark had the trial balances on December 31, 2015, are as follows:

	Pontiac Company	Stark Company
Cash	17,870	32,031
Accounts Receivable	90,000	60,000
Inventory	100,000	30,000
Land.	150,000	45,000
Investment in Stark	435,738	
Investment in Stark Bonds	103,975	
Buildings	500,000	250,000
Accumulated Depreciation	(300,000)	(70,000)
Equipment	200,000	120,000
Accumulated Depreciation	(100,000)	(84,000)
Accounts Payable	(55,000)	(25,000)
Bonds Payable.		(100,000)
Discount on Bonds Payable		1,641
Common Stock	(100,000)	(10,000)
Paid-In Capital in Excess of Par	(600,000)	(90,000)
Retained Earnings, January 1, 2015.	(400,000)	(145,000)
Sales	(600,000)	(220,000)
Cost of Goods Sold	410,000	120,000
Depreciation Expense—Buildings.	30,000	10,000
Depreciation Expense—Equipment.	15,000	12,000
Other Expenses	109,360	45,000
Interest Revenue.	(7,205)	
Interest Expense.		8,328
Subsidiary Income.	(19,738)	
Dividends Declared	20,000	10,000
Totals	0	0

Required ▶ ▶ ▶ ▶ ▶   Prepare the worksheet necessary to produce the consolidated financial statements for Pontiac Company and its subsidiary Stark Company for the year ended December 31, 2015. Include the determination and distribution of excess and income distribution schedules.

Problem 5-7 *(LO 2)* **80%, equity, straight-line bonds purchased last year, inventory profits.** Refer to the preceding facts for Pontiac's acquisition of 80% of Stark's common stock and the bond transactions. Pontiac uses the simple equity method to account for its investment in Stark. On January 1, 2016, Stark held merchandise acquired from Pontiac for $20,000. During 2016, Pontiac sold $60,000 worth of merchandise to Stark. Stark held $25,000 of this merchandise at December 31, 2016. Stark owed Pontiac $12,000 on December 31 as a result of these intercompany sales. Pontiac has a gross profit rate of 30%. Pontiac and Stark had the following trial balances on December 31, 2016:

	Pontiac Company	Stark Company
Cash	49,150	61,031
Accounts Receivable	110,000	60,000
Inventory	120,000	45,000
Land.	150,000	45,000
Investment in Stark	453,075	
Investment in Stark Bonds	103,180	
Buildings	500,000	250,000
Accumulated Depreciation	(330,000)	(80,000)
Equipment	200,000	120,000
Accumulated Depreciation	(115,000)	(96,000)
Accounts Payable	(35,000)	(25,000)
Bonds Payable.		(100,000)
Discount on Bonds Payable		1,313
Common Stock	(100,000)	(10,000)
Paid-In Capital in Excess of Par	(600,000)	(90,000)
Retained Earnings, January 1, 2016.	(442,223)	(159,672)
Sales	(700,000)	(230,000)
Cost of Goods Sold	480,000	125,000
Depreciation Expense—Buildings	30,000	10,000
Depreciation Expense—Equipment.	15,000	12,000
Other Expenses	124,360	43,000
Interest Revenue.	(7,205)	
Interest Expense.		8,328
Subsidiary Income.	(25,337)	
Dividends Declared.	20,000	10,000
Totals	0	0

Required ▶ ▶ ▶ ▶ ▶   Prepare the worksheet necessary to produce the consolidated financial statements for Pontiac Company and its subsidiary Stark Company for the year ended December 31, 2016. Include the determination and distribution of excess and income distribution schedules.

Problem 5-8 *(LO 2)* **90%, cost, machine, merchandise, effective interest bonds.**
Princess Company acquired a 90% interest in Sundown Company on January 1, 2011, for $675,000. Any excess of cost over book value was due to goodwill.

Capital balances of Sundown Company on January 1, 2011, were as follows:

Common stock ($10 par).	$200,000
Paid-in capital in excess of par	100,000
Retained earnings	300,000
Total equity	$600,000

Sundown Company sold a machine to Princess for $30,000 on January 1, 2014. It cost Sundown $20,000 to build the machine, which had a 5-year remaining life on the date of the sale and is subject to straight-line depreciation.

Princess purchased one-half of the outstanding 9% bonds of Sundown for $89,186 (to yield 12%) on December 31, 2015. The bonds were sold originally by Sundown to yield 10% to outside parties. The discount on the entire set of bonds was $7,582 on December 31, 2015. The effective interest method of amortization is used.

During 2016, Princess Company sold merchandise to Sundown for $50,000. Princess recorded a 30% gross profit on the sales price. $20,000 of the merchandise purchased from Princess remains unsold at the end of the year.

The trial balances of Princess and its subsidiary, Sundown, are as follows on December 31, 2016:

	Princess Company	Sundown Company
Inventory	25,000	80,000
Equipment	371,190	1,522,413
Accumulated Depreciation	(200,000)	(600,000)
Investment in Sundown Stock	675,000	
Investment in Sundown Bonds	90,888	
Bonds Payable (9%)		(200,000)
Discount on Bonds Payable		6,345
Common Stock ($10 par)	(200,000)	(200,000)
Paid-In Capital in Excess of Par	(300,000)	(100,000)
Retained Earnings, January 1, 2016	(401,376)	(500,000)
Sales	(300,000)	(260,000)
Cost of Goods Sold	100,000	72,000
Interest Income	(10,702)	
Other Expenses	150,000	160,000
Interest Expense		19,242
Totals	0	0

Prepare the worksheet necessary to produce the consolidated financial statements of Princess Company and its subsidiary for the year ended December 31, 2016. Include the determination and distribution of excess and income distribution schedules. ◄ ◄ ◄ ◄ ◄ **Required**

Problem 5-9 *(LO 2)* **Eliminations, equity, 100%, bonds with straight-line.** Since its 100% acquisition of Dreger Corporation stock on December 31, 2012, Jayco Corporation has maintained its investment under the equity method. However, due to Dreger's earning potential, the price included a $40,000 payment for goodwill. At the time of the purchase, the fair value of Dreger's assets equaled their book value.

On January 2, 2014, Dreger Corporation issued 10-year, 7% bonds at a face value of $50,000. The bonds pay interest each December 31. On January 2, 2016, Jayco Corporation purchased all of Dreger Corporation's outstanding bonds for $46,000. The discount is amortized on a straight-line basis. They have been included in Jayco's long-term investment in bonds account. Below are the trial balances of both companies on December 31, 2016.

	Jayco Corporation	Dreger Corporation
Cash	72,500	67,500
Accounts Receivable	450,000	75,000
Inventory	200,000	65,000
Investment in Bonds	46,500	
Plant and Equipment (net)	2,420,000	196,000
Investment in Dreger Corporation	350,000	

	Jayco Corporation	Dreger Corporation
Accounts Payable	(275,000)	(18,000)
Bonds Payable (7%)		(50,000)
Common Stock ($10 par)—Jayco	(1,000,000)	
Paid-In Capital in Excess of Par—Jayco	(750,000)	
Retained Earnings, January 1, 2016—Jayco	(730,000)	
Common Stock ($10 par)—Dreger		(100,000)
Paid-In Capital in Excess of Par—Dreger		(130,000)
Retained Earnings, January 1, 2016—Dreger		(80,000)
Sales	(2,500,000)	(540,000)
Cost of Goods Sold	1,000,000	405,000
Other Expenses	720,000	106,000
Interest Income	(4,000)	
Interest Expense	0	3,500
Totals	0	0

Required ▶ ▶ ▶ ▶ ▶

1. Prepare the worksheet entries needed to eliminate the intercompany debt on December 31, 2016.
2. Prepare a consolidated income statement for the year ended December 31, 2016.

   Note: No worksheet is required.

Problem 5-10 *(LO 4, 5, 6)* **80%, cost, operating, sales-type and financing leases.**
Patter Inc. acquired an 80% interest in Swing Company for $480,000 on January 1, 2011, when Swing had the following stockholders' equity:

Common stock ($10 par)	$100,000
Additional paid-in capital in excess of par	300,000
Retained earnings	100,000
Total equity	$500,000

Any excess was attributed to goodwill.

The trial balances of Patter, Inc., and Swing Company were prepared on December 31, 2015, as follows:

	Patter, Inc.	Swing Company
Cash	91,013	26,050
Inventory	70,000	20,000
Property, Plant, and Equipment	320,000	50,000
Accumulated Depreciation—Property, Plant, and Equipment	(70,000)	(20,000)
Assets Under Capital Lease	40,676	
Accumulated Depreciation—Assets Under Capital Lease	(10,796)	
Assets Under Operating Lease		420,000
Accumulated Depreciation—Assets Under Operating Lease		(80,000)
Minimum Lease Payments Receivable		412,000
Unearned Interest Income on Leases		(4,000)
Investment in Swing Company	480,000	
Accounts Payable	(130,000)	(180,000)
Obligations Under Capital Lease	(24,560)	
Interest Payable	(4,440)	
Common Stock ($10 par)	(200,000)	(100,000)
Paid-In Capital in Excess of Par	(300,000)	(300,000)
Retained Earnings, January 1, 2015	(278,333)	(226,610)

	Patter, Inc.	Swing Company
Sales	(300,000)	(130,000)
Rent Income		(34,000)
Interest Income—Capital Lease		(4,440)
Depreciation Expense	41,000	23,000
Interest Expense	4,440	
Selling and General Expense	70,000	38,000
Cost of Goods Sold	190,000	90,000
Rent Expense	11,000	
Totals	0	0

The following intercompany leases have been written by Swing since the acquisition:

1. On January 1, 2013, Swing purchased for $140,000 land and a building, which it leased to Patter, Inc., under a 5-year operating lease. Payments of $11,000 per year are required at the beginning of each year. The $120,000 building cost is being depreciated over 20 years on a straight-line basis.
2. On January 1, 2014, Swing purchased a machine for $14,000 and leased it to Patter, Inc. The 4-year lease qualifies as a capital lease. The rentals are $5,000 per year, payable at the beginning of each year. There is a bargain purchase option whereby Patter will purchase the machine at the end of four years for $2,000.

    The fair value of the machine was $17,560 at the start of the lease term. The lease payments, including the purchase option, yield an implicit rate of 15% to the lessor. Patter is depreciating the machine over seven years on a straight-line basis with no salvage value.
3. January 1, 2015, Swing purchased a truck for $23,116 and leased it to Patter, Inc., under a 3-year capital lease. Payments of $8,000 per year are required at the beginning of each year. There is a bargain purchase agreement for $5,000. Patter, Inc., is depreciating the truck over four years, straight-line, with no salvage value. The lease has a lessor implicit rate of 20%.
4. Patter, Inc., has accrued interest in 2015 on its capital lease obligations. Swing has recognized earned interest for the year on its capital leases.

Prepare the worksheet necessary to produce the consolidated financial statements of Patter, Inc., and its subsidiary for the year ended December 31, 2015. Include the determination and distribution of excess and income distribution schedules.

◄ ◄ ◄ ◄ ◄ **Required**

Use the following information for Problems 5-11 through 5-14:

On January 1, 2011 Press Company acquired Simon Company. Press paid $450,000 for 80% of Simon's common stock. On the date of acquisition, Simon had the following balance sheet:

Simon Company
Balance Sheet
January 1, 2011

Assets		Liabilities and Equity	
Accounts receivable	$ 40,000	Accounts payable	$ 80,000
Inventory	60,000	Common stock ($1 par).........	10,000
Land.....................	100,000	Paid-in capital in excess of par ...	190,000
Buildings	400,000	Retained earnings	190,000
Accumulated depreciation ...	(200,000)		
Equipment	100,000		
Accumulated depreciation ...	(30,000)		
Total assets..............	$ 470,000	Total liabilities and equity	$470,000

Buildings, which have a 20-year life, are undervalued by $100,000. Any excess cost is considered to be goodwill.

Problem 5-11 *(LO 5)* **80%, equity, financing lease, merchandise.** Refer to the preceding facts for Press's acquisition of Simon common stock. Press uses the simple equity method to account for its investment in Simon. On January 1, 2012, Press held merchandise acquired from Simon for $10,000. During 2012, Simon sold $40,000 worth of merchandise to Press. Press held $12,000 of this merchandise at December 31, 2012. Press owed Simon $6,000 on December 31 as a result of this intercompany sale. Simon has a gross profit rate of 25%.

On January 1, 2012, Simon signed a 5-year lease with Press for the rental of equipment, which has a 5-year life. Payments of $23,363 are due each January 1, and there is a guaranteed residual value of $10,000 at the end of the five years. The market value of the equipment at the inception of the lease was $100,000. Press has a 12% implicit rate on the lease. The following amortization table was prepared for the lease.

Period	Payment	Interest	Principal	Balance
Jan. 1, 2012	$23,363		$(23,363)	$76,637
Jan. 1, 2013	23,363	$9,196	(14,167)	62,470
Jan. 1, 2014	23,363	7,496	(15,867)	46,603
Jan. 1, 2015	23,363	5,592	(17,771)	28,832
Jan. 1, 2016	23,363	3,460	(19,903)	8,929
Jan. 1, 2017	10,000	1,071	(8,929)	0

Press and Simon had the following trial balances on December 31, 2012:

	Press Company	Simon Company
Cash	72,363	73,637
Accounts Receivable	72,000	45,000
Inventory	120,000	56,000
Land	100,000	100,000
Investment in Simon	506,643	
Minimum Lease Payments Receivable	103,452	
Unearned Interest	(17,619)	
Buildings	800,000	400,000
Accumulated Depreciation	(220,000)	(220,000)
Equipment	150,000	100,000
Accumulated Depreciation	(90,000)	(50,000)
Equipment—Capital Lease		100,000
Accumulated Depreciation—Capital Lease		(18,000)
Accounts Payable	(60,000)	(40,000)
Obligation Under Capital Lease		(76,637)
Accrued Interest—Capital Lease		(9,196)
Common Stock	(100,000)	(10,000)
Paid-In Capital in Excess of Par	(800,000)	(190,000)
Retained Earnings, January 1, 2012	(450,000)	(230,000)
Sales	(800,000)	(400,000)
Cost of Goods Sold	450,000	240,000
Depreciation Expense—Buildings	30,000	10,000
Depreciation Expense—Equipment	15,000	28,000
Other Expenses	140,000	72,000
Interest Expense		9,196
Interest Revenue	(9,196)	
Subsidiary Income	(32,643)	
Dividends Declared	20,000	10,000
Totals	0	0

Required ▶ ▶ ▶ ▶ ▶   Prepare the worksheet necessary to produce the consolidated financial statements for Press Company and its subsidiary Simon Company for the year ended December 31, 2012. Include the determination and distribution of excess and income distribution schedules.

Problem 5-12 *(LO 5)* **80%, equity, financing lease, merchandise, later year.** Refer to the preceding facts for Press's acquisition of Simon common stock. Press uses the simple equity method to account for its investment in Simon. On January 1, 2013, Press held merchandise acquired from Simon for $12,000. During 2013, Simon sold $35,000 worth of merchandise to Press. Press held $8,000 of this merchandise at December 31, 2013. Press owed Simon $7,000 on December 31 as a result of this intercompany sale. Simon has a gross profit rate of 25%.

On January 1, 2012, Simon signed a 5-year lease with Press for the rental of equipment, which has a 5-year life. Payments of $23,363 are due each January 1, and there is a guaranteed residual value of $10,000 at the end of the five years. The market value of the equipment at the inception of the lease was $100,000. Press has a 12% implicit rate on the lease. The following amortization table was prepared for the lease:

Period	Payment	Interest	Principal	Balance
Jan. 1, 2012	$23,363		$(23,363)	$76,637
Jan. 1, 2013	23,363	$9,196	(14,167)	62,470
Jan. 1, 2014	23,363	7,496	(15,867)	46,603
Jan. 1, 2015	23,363	5,592	(17,771)	28,832
Jan. 1, 2016	23,363	3,460	(19,903)	8,929
Jan. 1, 2017	10,000	1,071	(8,929)	0

Press and Simon had the following trial balances on December 31, 2013:

	Press Company	Simon Company
Cash	140,000	78,274
Accounts Receivable	87,000	55,000
Inventory	170,000	66,000
Land	168,726	100,000
Investment in Simon	516,646	
Minimum Lease Payments Receivable	80,089	
Unearned Interest	(10,123)	
Buildings	800,000	400,000
Accumulated Depreciation	(250,000)	(230,000)
Equipment	150,000	100,000
Accumulated Depreciation	(105,000)	(60,000)
Equipment—Capital Lease		100,000
Accumulated Depreciation—Capital Lease		(36,000)
Accounts Payable	(60,000)	(30,000)
Obligation Under Capital Lease		(62,470)
Accrued Interest—Capital Lease		(7,496)
Common Stock	(100,000)	(10,000)
Paid-In Capital in Excess of Par	(800,000)	(190,000)
Retained Earnings, January 1, 2013	(636,839)	(260,804)
Sales	(900,000)	(450,000)
Cost of Goods Sold	550,000	290,000
Depreciation Expense—Buildings	30,000	10,000
Depreciation Expense—Equipment	15,000	28,000
Other Expenses	160,000	92,000
Interest Expense		7,496
Interest Revenue	(7,496)	
Subsidiary Income	(18,003)	
Dividends Declared	20,000	10,000
Totals	0	0

Required ▶ ▶ ▶ ▶ ▶   Prepare the worksheet necessary to produce the consolidated financial statements for Press Company and its subsidiary Simon Company for the year ended December 31, 2013. Include the determination and distribution of excess and income distribution schedules.

Problem 5-13 *(LO 5, 6)* **80%, equity, sales-type lease, merchandise.** Refer to the preceding facts for Press's acquisition of Simon common stock. Press uses the simple equity method to account for its investment in Simon. On January 1, 2012, Press held merchandise acquired from Simon for $10,000. During 2012, Simon sold $40,000 worth of merchandise to Press. Press held $12,000 of this merchandise at December 31, 2012. Press owed Simon $6,000 on December 31 as a result of this intercompany sale. Simon has a gross profit rate of 25%.

On January 1, 2012, Simon signed a 5-year lease with Press for the rental of equipment, which has a 5-year life. Payments of $23,363 are due each January 1, and there is a guaranteed residual value of $10,000 at the end of the five years. The market value of the equipment at the inception of the lease was $100,000. The cost of the equipment to Press was $85,000. Press has a 12% implicit rate on the lease. The amortization table shown on page 318 was prepared for the lease.

Period	Payment	Interest	Principal	Balance
Jan. 1, 2012	$23,363		$(23,363)	$76,637
Jan. 1, 2013	23,363	$9,196	(14,167)	62,470
Jan. 1, 2014	23,363	7,496	(15,867)	46,603
Jan. 1, 2015	23,363	5,592	(17,771)	28,832
Jan. 1, 2016	23,363	3,460	(19,903)	8,929
Jan. 1, 2017	10,000	1,071	(8,929)	0

Press and Simon had the following trial balances on December 31, 2012:

	Press Company	Simon Company
Cash	72,363	73,637
Accounts Receivable	72,000	45,000
Inventory	120,000	56,000
Land	100,000	100,000
Investment in Simon	506,643	
Minimum Lease Payments Receivable	103,452	
Unearned Interest	(17,619)	
Buildings	800,000	400,000
Accumulated Depreciation	(220,000)	(220,000)
Equipment	150,000	100,000
Accumulated Depreciation	(90,000)	(50,000)
Equipment—Capital Lease		100,000
Accumulated Depreciation—Capital Lease		(18,000)
Accounts Payable	(60,000)	(40,000)
Obligation Under Capital Lease		(76,637)
Accrued Interest—Capital Lease		(9,196)
Common Stock	(100,000)	(10,000)
Paid-In Capital in Excess of Par	(800,000)	(190,000)
Retained Earnings, January 1, 2012	(450,000)	(230,000)
Sales	(800,000)	(400,000)
Cost of Goods Sold	465,000	240,000
Depreciation Expense—Buildings	30,000	10,000
Depreciation Expense—Equipment	15,000	28,000
Other Expenses	140,000	72,000
Interest Expense		9,196
Interest Revenue	(9,196)	
Gain on Fixed Asset Sale	(15,000)	
Subsidiary Income	(32,643)	
Dividends Declared	20,000	10,000
Totals	0	0

Prepare the worksheet necessary to produce the consolidated financial statements for Press ◄ ◄ ◄ ◄ ◄ **Required**
Company and its subsidiary Simon Company for the year ended December 31, 2012. Include
the determination and distribution of excess and income distribution schedules.

Problem 5-14 *(LO 5, 6)* **80%, equity, sales-type lease, merchandise, later year.** Refer to the preceding facts for Press's acquisition of Simon common stock. Press uses the simple
equity method to account for its investment in Simon. On January 1, 2013, Press held merchandise
acquired from Simon for $12,000. During 2013, Simon sold merchandise to Press for $35,000.
Press held $8,000 of this merchandise at December 31, 2013. Press owed Simon $7,000 on
December 31 as a result of this intercompany sale. Simon has a gross profit rate of 25%.

On January 1, 2012, Simon signed a 5-year lease with Press for the rental of equipment,
which has a 5-year life. Payments of $23,363 are due each January 1, and there is a guaranteed
residual value of $10,000 at the end of the five years. The market value of the equipment at the
inception of the lease was $100,000. The cost of the equipment to Press was $85,000. Press has
a 12% implicit rate on the lease. The following amortization table was prepared for the lease:

Period	Payment	Interest	Principal	Balance
Jan. 1, 2012	$23,363		$(23,363)	$76,637
Jan. 1, 2013	23,363	$9,196	(14,167)	62,470
Jan. 1, 2014	23,363	7,496	(15,867)	46,603
Jan. 1, 2015	$23,363	$5,592	$(17,771)	$28,832
Jan. 1, 2016	23,363	3,460	(19,903)	8,929
Jan. 1, 2017	10,000	1,071	(8,929)	0

Press and Simon had the following trial balances on December 31, 2013:

	Press Company	Simon Company
Cash	140,000	78,274
Accounts Receivable	87,000	55,000
Inventory	170,000	66,000
Land	168,726	100,000
Investment in Simon	516,646	
Minimum Lease Payments Receivable	80,089	
Unearned Interest	(10,123)	
Buildings	800,000	400,000
Accumulated Depreciation	(250,000)	(230,000)
Equipment	150,000	100,000
Accumulated Depreciation	(105,000)	(60,000)
Equipment—Capital Lease		100,000
Accumulated Depreciation—Capital Lease		(36,000)
Accounts Payable	(60,000)	(30,000)
Obligation Under Capital Lease		(62,470)
Accrued Interest—Capital Lease		(7,496)
Common Stock	(100,000)	(10,000)
Paid-In Capital in Excess of Par	(800,000)	(190,000)
Retained Earnings, January 1, 2013	(636,839)	(260,804)
Sales	(900,000)	(450,000)
Cost of Goods Sold	550,000	290,000
Depreciation Expense—Buildings	30,000	10,000
Depreciation Expense—Equipment	15,000	28,000
Other Expenses	160,000	92,000
Interest Expense		7,496
Interest Revenue	(7,496)	
Subsidiary Income	(18,003)	
Dividends Declared	20,000	10,000
Totals	0	0

Required ▶ ▶ ▶ ▶ ▶   Prepare the worksheet necessary to produce the consolidated financial statements for Press Company and its subsidiary Simon Company for the year ended December 31, 2013. Include the determination and distribution of excess and income distribution schedules.

Problem 5-15 *(LO 4)* **100%, cost, operating lease.** Sym Corporation, a wholly owned subsidiary of Paratec Corporation, leased equipment from its parent company on August 1, 2016. The terms of the agreement clearly do not require the lease to be accounted for as a capital lease. Both entities are accounting for the lease as an operating lease. The lease payment is $12,000 per year, paid in advance each August 1.

Paratec purchased its investment in Sym on December 31, 2011, when Sym had a retained earnings balance of $150,000. Paratec is accounting for its investment in Sym under the cost method. Included in the original purchase price was a $50,000 premium attributable to Sym's history of exceptional earnings.

The December 31, 2018, trial balances of Paratec and its subsidiary are presented below.

	Paratec Corporation	Sym Corporation
Cash	190,000	40,000
Accounts Receivable (net)	738,350	142,000
Inventory	500,000	75,000
Prepaid Rent on Equipment		7,000
Investment in Bonds	250,000	65,000
Investment in Sym Corporation	400,000	
Land	250,000	85,000
Plant and Equipment	1,950,000	295,000
Accumulated Depreciation—Plant and Equipment	(250,000)	(60,000)
Equipment Under Operating Lease	120,000	
Accumulated Depreciation—Assets Under Operating Lease	(36,000)	
Accounts Payable	(385,000)	(52,000)
Deferred Rent Revenue	(7,000)	
Common Stock (no par)	(2,000,000)	(200,000)
Retained Earnings, January 1, 2018	(1,076,350)	(310,000)
Sales	(4,720,000)	(500,000)
Rent Income	(12,000)	
Cost of Goods Sold	3,068,000	300,000
Rent Expense		12,000
Other Expenses	725,000	101,000
Dividends Declared	295,000	
Totals	0	0

Required ▶ ▶ ▶ ▶ ▶   Prepare the worksheet necessary to produce the consolidated income statement and balance sheet of Paratec Corporation and its subsidiary for the year ended December 31, 2018.

Problem 5-16 *(LO 5, 6)* **80%, cost, financing and sales-type leases.** Plessor Industries acquired 80% of the outstanding common stock of Slammer Company on January 1, 2011, for $320,000. On that date, Slammer's book values approximated fair values, and the balance of its retained earnings account was $80,000. Any excess was attributed to goodwill. Slammer's net income was $20,000 for 2011 and $30,000 for 2012. No dividends were paid in either year.

On January 1, 2012, Slammer signed a 5-year lease with Plessor for the rental of a small factory building with a 10-year life. Payments of $25,000 are due at the beginning of each year on January 1, and Slammer is expected to exercise the $5,000 bargain purchase option at the end of the fifth year. The fair value of the factory was $103,770 at the start of the lease term. Plessor's implicit rate on the lease is 12%.

A second lease agreement, for the rental of production equipment with an 8-year life, was signed by Slammer on January 1, 2013. The terms of this 4-year lease require a payment of $15,000 at the beginning of each year on January 1. The present value of the lease payments at Plessor's 12% implicit rate was equal to the fair value of the equipment, $52,298, when the lease was signed. The cost of the equipment to Plessor was $45,000, and there is a $2,000 bargain purchase option. Eight-year, straight-line depreciation is being used, with no salvage value.

The following trial balances were prepared by the separate companies at December 31, 2013:

	Plessor Industries	Slammer Company
Cash	60,000	40,745
Accounts Receivable	97,778	76,000
Inventory	140,000	120,000
Minimum Lease Payments Receivable	127,000	
Unearned Interest Income	(14,417)	
Investment in Slammer Company	320,000	
Assets Under Capital Lease		156,068
Accumulated Depreciation—Assets Under Capital Lease		(27,291)
Property, Plant, and Equipment	1,900,000	310,000
Accumulated Depreciation—Property, Plant, and Equipment	(1,077,000)	(72,000)
Accounts Payable (includes accrued interest payable)	(148,000)	(45,065)
Obligations Under Capital Lease		(100,520)
Common Stock ($10 par)	(700,000)	(300,000)
Paid-In Capital in Excess of Par	(325,000)	
Retained Earnings, January 1, 2013	(295,000)	(130,000)
Sales	(1,400,000)	(600,000)
Sales Profit on Leases	(7,298)	
Interest Income	(12,063)	
Cost of Goods Sold	780,000	380,000
Interest Expense		12,063
Other Expenses	510,000	165,000
Dividend Income	(12,000)	
Dividends Declared	56,000	15,000
Totals	0	0

Prepare the worksheet necessary to produce the consolidated financial statements of Plessor Industries and its subsidiary for the year ended December 31, 2013. Include the determination and distribution of excess and income distribution schedules. ◄ ◄ ◄ ◄ ◄ **Required**

APPENDIX PROBLEMS

Problem 5A-1 *(LO 7)* **80%, equity, financing leases with unguaranteed residual value, fixed asset profit.** Steven Truck Company has been an 80%-owned subsidiary of Paulz Heavy Equipment since January 1, 2013, when Paulz acquired 128,000 shares of Steven common stock for $832,000, an amount equal to the book value of Steven's net assets at that date. Steven's net income and dividends paid since acquisition is shown on page 318:

Year	Net Income	Dividends
2013	$ 70,000	$25,000
2014	75,600	25,000
2015	81,650	30,000
Totals	$227,250	$80,000

On January 1, 2015, Paulz leased a truck from Steven. The 3-year financing-type lease provides for payments of $10,000 each January 1 (including present value of unguaranteed residual value of $4,763). On January 1, 2015, the present value of the truck at Steven's 8% implicit rate, including the unguaranteed residual value of $6,000 at the end of the third year, was $32,596. Paulz has used the 8% implicit rate to record the lease. The truck is being depreciated over three years on a straight-line basis.

On January 1, 2016, Steven signed a 4-year financing-type lease with Paulz for the rental of specialized production machinery with an 8-year life. There is a $7,000 purchase option at the end of the fourth year. The lease agreement requires lease payments of $30,000 each January 1 plus $1,500 for maintenance of the equipment. It also calls for contingent payments equal to 10% of Steven's cost savings through the use of this equipment, as reflected in any increase in net income (excluding gains or losses on sale of assets) above the previous growth rate of Steven's net income. The present value of the equipment on January 1, 2016, at Paulz's 10% implicit rate was $109,388.

On October 1, 2016, Steven sold Paulz a warehouse having a 20-year remaining life, a book value of $135,000, and an estimated salvage value of $20,000. Paulz paid $195,000 for the building, which is being depreciated on a straight-line basis.

The trial balances were prepared by the separate companies on December 31, 2016, as follows:

	Paulz Heavy Equipment	Steven Truck Company
Cash	90,485	123,307
Accounts Receivable (net)	228,000	120,000
Inventory	200,000	140,000
Minimum Lease Payments Receivable	97,000	10,000
Unguaranteed Residual Value		6,000
Unearned Interest Income	(9,673)	(444)
Assets Under Capital Lease	27,833	109,388
Accumulated Depreciation—Assets Under Capital Lease	(18,556)	(13,674)
Property, Plant, and Equipment	2,075,000	1,145,000
Accumulated Depreciation—Property, Plant, and Equipment	(713,000)	(160,000)
Investment in Steven Truck Company	1,045,800	
Accounts Payable	(100,000)	(85,000)
Interest Payable	(740)	(7,939)
Obligations Under Capital Lease	(9,260)	(79,388)
Common Stock ($5 par)	(1,800,000)	(800,000)
Retained Earnings, January 1, 2016	(864,834)	(387,250)
Sales	(3,200,000)	(1,400,000)
Gain on Sale of Assets		(60,000)
Interest Income	(7,939)	(1,152)
Rent Income	(2,182)	
Cost of Goods Sold	1,882,000	770,000
Interest Expense	740	7,939
Depreciation Expense	135,000	45,000
Other Expenses	924,326	483,213
Subsidiary Income	(124,000)	
Dividends Declared	144,000	35,000
Totals	0	0

Prepare the worksheet necessary to produce the consolidated financial statements of Paulz ◄ ◄ ◄ ◄ ◄ **Required** Heavy Equipment and its subsidiary for the year ended December 31, 2016. Include income distribution schedules.

Problem 5A-2 *(LO 7)* **Eliminations only, sales-type lease with unguaranteed residual value.** Penn Company leased a production machine to its 80%-owned subsidiary, Smith Company. The lease agreement, dated January 1, 2011, requires Smith to pay $18,000 each January 1 for three years. There is an unguaranteed residual value of $5,000. The machine cost $50,098. The present value of the machine at Penn's 16% implicit interest rate was $50,098 on January 1, 2011. Smith also uses the 16% lessor implicit rate to record the lease. The machine is being depreciated over three years on a straight-line basis with a $5,000 salvage value. Lease payment amortization schedules are as follows:

Penn

Date	Payment	Interest at 16% on Previous Balance	Reduction of Principal	Principal Balance
Jan. 1, 2011				$50,098
Jan. 1, 2011	$18,000		$18,000	32,098
Jan. 1, 2012	18,000	$5,136	12,864	19,234
Jan. 1, 2013	18,000	3,077	14,923	4,311
Jan. 1, 2014	5,000	689	4,311	
Totals	$59,000	$8,902	$50,098	

Smith

Date	Payment	Interest at 16% on Previous Balance	Reduction of Principal	Principal Balance
Jan. 1, 2011				$46,894
Jan. 1, 2011	$18,000		$18,000	28,894
Jan. 1, 2012	18,000	$4,623	13,377	15,517
Jan. 1, 2013	18,000	2,483	15,517	
Totals	$54,000	$7,106	$46,894	

1. Prepare the eliminations and adjustments required for this lease on the December 31, 2011, ◄ ◄ ◄ ◄ ◄ **Required** consolidated worksheet.
2. Prepare the eliminations and adjustments for the December 31, 2012, consolidated worksheet.

Learning Objectives

When you have completed this chapter, you should be able to

1. **Demonstrate an understanding of the effect of a business combination on cash flow in and subsequent to the period of the purchase.**

2. **Compute earnings per share for a consolidated firm.**

3. **Calculate and prepare a consolidated worksheet where the consolidated firm is an "affiliated group" and pays a single consolidated tax.**

4. **Prepare a consolidated worksheet where the parent and subsidiary are separately taxed by employing tax allocation procedures.**

We begin with the procedures necessary to prepare a consolidated statement of cash flows. Fortunately, this requires only minor changes in the procedures used in your prior accounting courses. Also, only minor adjustments of typical earnings per share procedures are needed for consolidated companies. The final consolidation issue is taxation of the consolidated company. Prior worksheets are now enhanced to include the provision for tax. This is quite simple when the affiliated companies are taxed as a single entity. Procedures are a bit more involved when the individual companies are taxed separately.

CONSOLIDATED STATEMENT OF CASH FLOWS

1

OBJECTIVE

Demonstrate an understanding of the effect of a business combination on cash flow in and subsequent to the period of the purchase.

FASB ASC 230-10 requires that a statement of cash flows accompany a company's published income statement and balance sheet. The process of preparing a consolidated statement of cash flows is similar to that which is used for a single company, a topic covered in depth in intermediate accounting texts. Since the analysis of changes in cash of a consolidated entity begins with consolidated balance sheets, intercompany transactions will have been eliminated and, thus, will not cause any complications. However, because of the parent-subsidiary relationship, some situations require special consideration. These situations are discussed in the following paragraphs.

Cash Acquisition of Controlling Interest

The cash acquisition of a controlling interest in a company is considered an *investing activity* and would appear as a cash outflow in the cash flows from investing activities section of the statement of cash flows. It also is necessary to explain the total increase in consolidated assets and the addition of the NCI to the consolidated balance sheet. This is a result of the requirement that the statement of cash flows disclose investing and *financing activities* that affect the company's financial position even though they do not impact cash.

To illustrate the disclosure required, consider an example of a cash acquisition of an 80% interest in Company S. Assume Company S had the balance sheet shown on page 322 on January 1, 2011, when Company P acquired an 80% interest for $540,000 in cash.

Assets		Liabilities and Equity	
Cash and cash equivalents	$ 50,000	Long-term liabilities	$150,000
Inventory	60,000	Common stock ($10 par).	200,000
Equipment (net)	190,000	Retained earnings	350,000
Building (net)	400,000		
Total assets.	$700,000	Total liabilities and equity	$700,000

Assume the fair values of the equipment and building are $250,000 and $425,000, respectively, and any remaining excess of cost is attributed to goodwill. The estimated remaining life of the equipment is five years and of the building is 10 years.

The following value analysis schedule and D&D schedule were prepared:

Value Analysis Schedule	Company Implied Fair Value	Parent Price (80%)	NCI Value (20%)
Company fair value.	$675,000	$540,000	$135,000
Fair value of net assets excluding goodwill	635,000	508,000	127,000
Goodwill.	**$ 40,000**	**$ 32,000**	**$ 8,000**

Based on the above information, the following D&D schedule is prepared:

Determination and Distribution of Excess Schedule			
	Company Implied Fair Value	Parent Price (80%)	NCI Value (20%)
Fair value of subsidiary	$ 675,000	$540,000	$135,000
Less book value of interest acquired:			
Common stock	$ 200,000		
Retained earnings	350,000		
Total stockholders' equity.	$ 550,000	$550,000	$550,000
Interest acquired		80%	20%
Book value.		$440,000	$110,000
Excess of fair value over book value	**$125,000**	$100,000	$ 25,000

Adjustment of identifiable accounts:

	Adjustment	Life	Amortization per Year	Worksheet Key
Equipment ($250,000 − $190,000)	$ 60,000	5	$ 12,000	**debit D1**
Building ($425,000 − $400,000).	25,000	10	2,500	**debit D2**
Goodwill ($675,000 − $635,000)	**40,000**			**debit D3**
Total	**$125,000**			

The effect of the purchase on the balance sheet accounts of the consolidated company for 2011 would be as follows:

	Debit	Credit
Cash ($540,000 paid − $50,000 subsidiary cash)		490,000
Inventory	60,000	
Equipment ($190,000 book value + $60,000 excess)	250,000	

	Debit	Credit
Building ($400,000 book value + $25,000 excess)	425,000	
Goodwill	40,000	
Long-term liabilities		150,000
Noncontrolling interest (20% × $550,000 subsidiary equity plus $25,000		
NCI adjustment)		135,000
Totals	775,000	775,000

The disclosure of the purchase on the statement of cash flows would be summarized as follows:

Under the heading "Cash flows from investing activities:"

Payment for purchase of Company S, net of cash acquired . . . . $(490,000)

In the supplemental schedule of noncash financing and investing activity:

Company P acquired 80% of the common stock of Company S for $540,000. In conjunction with the acquisition, liabilities were assumed and an NCI was created as follows:

Adjusted value of assets acquired ($700,000 book value + $125,000 excess)	$825,000
Cash paid for common stock	540,000
Balance (noncash)	$285,000
Liabilities assumed	$150,000
Noncontrolling interest	$135,000

Noncash Acquisition of Controlling Interest

Suppose that instead of paying cash for its controlling interest, Company P issued 10,000 shares of its $10 par stock for the controlling interest in Company S. Further assume the shares had a market value of $54 each. Since the acquisition price is the same ($540,000), the determination and distribution of excess schedule would not change. The analysis of balance sheet account changes would be as follows:

	Debit	Credit
Cash ($50,000 subsidiary cash received)	50,000	
Inventory	60,000	
Equipment ($190,000 book value + $60,000 excess)	250,000	
Building ($400,000 book value + $25,000 excess)	425,000	
Goodwill	40,000	
Long-term liabilities		150,000
Noncontrolling interest (20% × $550,000 subsidiary equity plus $25,000 NCI		
adjustment)		135,000
Common stock ($10 par)—Company P		100,000
Paid-in capital in excess of par—Company P		440,000
Totals	825,000	825,000

The disclosure of the purchase on the statement of cash flows would be summarized as follows:

Under the heading "Cash flows from investing activities:"

Cash acquired in purchase of Company S $50,000

In the supplemental schedule of noncash financing and investing activity:

Company P acquired 80% of the common stock of Company S in exchange for 10,000 shares of Company P common stock valued at $540,000. In conjunction with the acquisition, liabilities were assumed and a noncontrolling interest was created as follows:

Adjusted value of assets acquired ($700,000 book value + $125,000 excess)	$825,000
Common stock issued	$540,000
Liabilities assumed	$150,000
Noncontrolling interest	$135,000

Adjustments Resulting from Business Combinations

A business combination will have ramifications on the statements of cash flows prepared in subsequent periods. An acquisition may create amortizations of excess deductions (noncash items) that need to be adjusted. In addition, there may be changes resulting from additional purchases of subsidiary shares and/or dividend payments by the subsidiary. Intercompany bonds and nonconsolidated investments also need to be considered for their impact.

Amortization of Excesses. Income statements prepared for periods including or following an acquisition of another company will include depreciation based on the fair values assigned to the assets on the acquisition date. Using the facts of the preceding examples, the following adjustments would appear on the cash flows statement for 2011:

Cash from operating activities:	
Consolidated net income	$XXX,XXX
Add amortizations resulting from business combination:	
Depreciation on equipment [($190,000 book + $60,000 adj.) ÷ 5 years]	50,000
Depreciation on building [($400,000 book + $25,000 adj.) ÷ 10 years]	42,500

In addition, cash from operating activities would include adjustments for depreciation of book value recorded by the parent company.

Purchase of Additional Subsidiary Shares. The purchase of additional shares directly from the subsidiary results in no added cash flowing into the consolidated company. The transfer of cash within the consolidated company would not appear in the consolidated statement of cash flows. However, the purchase of additional shares from the noncontrolling interest does result in an outflow of cash. From a consolidated viewpoint, it is the equivalent of purchasing treasury shares. Thus, it would be listed under *financing activities.*

Subsidiary Dividends. Dividends paid by the subsidiary to the parent are a transfer of cash within the consolidated entity and thus would not appear in the consolidated statement of cash flows. However, dividends paid by the subsidiary to noncontrolling shareholders represent a flow of cash to parties outside the consolidated group and would appear as an outflow under the cash flows from financing activities heading of the consolidated statement of cash flows.

Purchase of Intercompany Bonds. The purchase of intercompany bonds from parties outside the consolidated company is a cash flow from a member of the consolidated group to parties outside the consolidated entity. The purchase of intercompany bonds is viewed as a retirement of the bonds on the consolidated worksheet (discussed in Chapter 5). The consolidated statement of cash flows also treats the purchase of the bonds as a retirement of the consolidated company's debt and includes the cash outflow under cash flows from financing activities. Since the process of constructing a cash flows statement starts with the consolidated income statement and balance sheet, intercompany interest payments and amortizations of premiums and/or discounts already are eliminated and will not enter into the analysis of consolidated cash flows. Only cash interest payments to bondholders outside the consolidated entity are important to the analysis and should be included in cash flows from *operating* activities.

Preparation of Consolidated Statement of Cash Flows

A complete example of the process of preparing a consolidated statement of cash flows is presented in this section. Assume Company P originally acquired an 80% interest in Company S on January 1, 2011. In addition, Company P purchased a 20% interest in Company E on January 2, 2012, and accounted for the investment under the sophisticated equity method. The following determination and distribution of excess schedules were prepared for each investment:

Determination and Distribution of Excess Schedule Investment in Company S			
	Company Implied Fair Value	Parent Price (80%)	NCI Value (20%)
Fair value of subsidiary	$ 456,250	$365,000	$ 91,250
Less book value of interest acquired:			
Common stock ($5 par)	$ 50,000		
Paid-in capital in excess of par	150,000		
Retained earnings	100,000		
Total stockholders' equity.	$ 300,000	$300,000	$300,000
Interest acquired		80%	20%
Book value.		$240,000	$ 60,000
Excess of fair value over book value	**$156,250**	$125,000	$ 31,250

Adjustment of identifiable accounts:

	Adjustment	Life	Amortization per Year	Worksheet Key
Equipment	$ 31,250	5	$ 6,250	**debit D1**
Goodwill.	125,000			**debit D2**
Total	**$156,250**			

The 20% investment is considered to be only an "influential investment." The price paid is compared to the interest purchased. There is no revaluation of the remaining 80% interest which was not acquired. The schedule is prepared as follows:

Determination and Distribution of Excess Schedule for Investment in Company E:		
Price paid for investment in Company E		$255,000
Less interest acquired:		
Common stock	$ 500,000	
Retained earnings	750,000	
Total equity.	$1,250,000	
Interest acquired	× 20%	250,000
Equipment (10-year life)		$ 5,000

Since this investment is not consolidated, there will be no recording of the increased value of the equipment. This information is used only to amortize the excess cost in future income statements. Because of this, there are no debits or credits accompanying the distribution of the excess. The following consolidated statements were prepared for Company P and its subsidiary, Company S, for 2013:

Company P and Subsidiary Company S
Consolidated Income Statement
For Year Ended December 31, 2013

Sales		$ 900,000
Less cost of goods sold		525,000
Gross profit		$ 375,000
Less expenses:		
General and administrative	$150,500	
Depreciation	**71,250***	**221,750**
Operating income		$ 153,250
Investment income (equity method)		**15,500****
Consolidated net income		$ 168,750
Distributed to:		
NCI		9,950
Controlling interest		$ 158,800

*Includes $6,250 of depreciation resulting from the excess of the subsidiary equipment's fair value over book value on January 1, 2011, the date on which the 80% interest was acquired.
**20% of Company E net income of $80,000 less $500 amortization of equipment. (Dividends received were $2,000.)

Company P and Subsidiary Company S
Consolidated Retained Earnings Statement
For Year Ended December 31, 2013

	NCI	Controlling
Retained earnings, January 1, 2013	$60,750	$440,000
Add distribution of consolidated net income	9,950	158,800
Less dividends declared	(4,000)	(50,000)
Balance, December 31, 2013	$66,700	$548,800

Company P and Subsidiary Company S
Consolidated Balance Sheet
December 31, 2012 and 2013

Assets	2013	2012
Cash and cash equivalents	$ 179,000	$ 160,000
Inventory	210,000	180,000
Accounts receivable	154,000	120,000
Property, plant, and equipment	1,336,250	1,256,250
Accumulated depreciation	(373,750)	(302,500)
Goodwill	125,000	125,000
Investment in Company E (20%)	333,500	320,000
Total assets	$1,964,000	$1,858,750

Liabilities and Stockholders' Equity		
Accounts payable	$ 156,500	$ 166,000
Bonds payable	300,000	300,000
Noncontrolling interest	106,700	100,750
Controlling interest:		
Common stock (par)	200,000	200,000
Paid-in capital in excess of par	652,000	652,000
Retained earnings	548,800	440,000
Total liabilities and stockholders' equity	$1,964,000	$1,858,750

The following additional facts are available to aid in the preparation of a consolidated statement of cash flows:

1. Company P purchased a new piece of equipment during 2013 for $80,000.
2. In 2013, Company P declared and paid $50,000 in dividends and Company S declared and paid $20,000 in dividends.

Illustration 6-1 is a worksheet approach to calculating a statement of cash flows under the *indirect method.* Explanations 1 through 6 use changes in balance sheet accounts to analyze cash from operations. This information is taken from the income statement and is implied from changes in current assets and current liabilities. Explanation 7 reflects the only investing activity in this example. Explanations 8 and 9 show the financing activities. The worksheet provides the information needed to develop the statement of cash flows that follows Illustration 6-1.

If the *direct method* of disclosing cash from operating activities is used, the cash flows from the operating activities section of the statement of cash flows would be prepared as follows:

Cash flows from operating activities:

Cash from customers ($900,000 sales − $34,000 increase in accounts receivable)	$ 866,000
Cash from investments (dividends received)	2,000
Cash to suppliers ($525,000 cost of goods sold + $30,000 inventory increase + $9,500 decrease in accounts payable)	(564,500)
Cash for general and administrative expenses	(150,500)
Net cash provided by operating activities	$ 153,000

Illustration 6-1
Company P and Subsidiary Company S
Worksheet for Analysis of Cash: Indirect Approach
For Year Ended December 31, 2013

	Account Change			Explanations			Balance
	Debit	Credit		Debit		Credit	
Inventory	30,000		(4)	30,000			0
Accounts receivable	34,000		(3)	34,000			0
Property, plant, and equipment........	80,000		(7)	80,000			0
Accumulated depreciation		71,250			(2)	71,250	0
Goodwill	0						0
Investment in Company E (20%)	13,500		(6)	13,500			0
Accounts payable	9,500		(5)	9,500			0
Bonds payable							0
Noncontrolling interest		5,950	(9)	4,000	(1)	9,950	0
Controlling interest:..................							
Common stock (par)...............							0
Paid-in capital in excess of par							0
Retained earnings		108,800	(8)	50,000	(1)	158,800	0
	167,000	186,000		221,000		240,000	
Net change in cash	19,000	0		19,000		0	
Cash from Operations:							
Consolidated net income..............			(1)	168,750			
Depreciation expense			(2)	71,250			
Increase in accounts receivable.........					(3)	34,000	
Increase in inventory					(4)	30,000	
Decrease in accounts payable					(5)	9,500	
Equity income in excess of dividends.....					(6)	13,500	
Net cash provided by operating activities.				153,000			
Cash from Investing:							
Purchase of equipment					(7)	80,000	
Net cash used in investing activities						80,000	
Cash from Financing:							
Dividend payment to controlling interest ..					(8)	50,000	
Dividend payment to noncontrolling interest.........................					(9)	4,000	
Net cash used in financing activities						54,000	
Net cash provided...................				19,000			

Company P and Subsidiary Company S
Consolidated Statement of Cash Flows
For Year Ended December 31, 2013

Cash flows from operating activities:		
Consolidated net income.................................		$168,750
Adjustments to reconcile net income to net cash:		
Depreciation expense	$ 71,250	
Increase in accounts receivable........................	(34,000)	
Increase in inventory	(30,000)	

Decrease in accounts payable........................	(9,500)
Equity income from Company E in excess of dividends Received	(13,500)
Total adjustments	(15,750)
Net cash provided by operating activities	$153,000
Cash flows from investing activities:	
Purchase of equipment...........................	(80,000)
Cash flows from financing activities:	
Dividend payment to controlling interest .... $(50,000)	
Dividend payment to noncontrolling interest .... (4,000)	
Net cash used in financing activities	(54,000)
Net increase in cash and cash equivalents	$ 19,000
Cash and cash equivalents at beginning of year..............	160,000
Cash and cash equivalents at year-end.....................	$179,000

REFLECTION

- The starting point for cash operations is consolidated net income, which includes the income attributed to the NCI.

- Subsequent to the period of acquisition, the only impact of consolidations on cash flow is the added amortization and depreciation caused by the acquisition.

- An acquisition of a subsidiary for cash is in the "investing" section of the cash flow statement. The cash outflow is net of the subsidiary's cash at acquisition.

- An acquisition of a subsidiary by issuing securities is a noncash investing/financing activity that must be disclosed in the notes to the cash flow statement. Any subsidiary cash received in the acquisition is a positive cash flow under "investing."

- The parent purchase of subsidiary bonds is treated as a retirement and is a financing activity.

- The parent purchase of additional shares of subsidiary stock is viewed as a treasury stock transaction and is considered a financing activity.

CONSOLIDATED EARNINGS PER SHARE

2

OBJECTIVE

Compute earnings per share for a consolidated firm.

The computation of *consolidated earnings per share (EPS)* remains virtually the same as that for single entities. For the purpose of this discussion, all calculations will be made only on an annual basis. *Basic earnings per share (BEPS)* is calculated as follows for the subsidiary and the consolidated firm:

Subsidiary BEPS = [Adjusted Subsidiary Net Income (as prepared on the income distribution schedule − Preferred Stock Dividends]/Subsidiary Weighted Average Common Shares Outstanding

$$
\text{Consolidated BEPS} = \frac{\begin{pmatrix}\text{Parent Adjusted Internally Generated Net Income}\end{pmatrix} - \begin{pmatrix}\text{Parent Preferred Stock Dividends}\end{pmatrix} + \begin{pmatrix}\text{Parent-Owned Subsidiary Common Shares} \times \text{Subsidiary BEPS}\end{pmatrix} + \begin{pmatrix}\text{Parent-Owned Subsidiary Preferred Shares} \times \text{Subsidiary Preferred Dividends per Share}\end{pmatrix}}{\text{Weighted Average Parent Company Common Shares Outstanding}}
$$

To illustrate the computation of consolidated BEPS, assume the following data concerning the subsidiary:

Net income (adjusted for intercompany profits) $22,000
Preferred stock cash dividend .... $ 2,000
Common stock shares outstanding 5,000

$$\text{Subsidiary BEPS} = \frac{\$22,000 - \overset{(1)}{\$2,000}}{5,000} = \$4.00$$

(1) Dividend on nonconvertible preferred stock, none of which is owned by the parent.

Now, assume the parent owns 80% of the subsidiary and has an adjusted internally generated net income of $40,000 and 10,000 shares of common stock outstanding.

$$\text{Consolidated BEPS} = \frac{\$40,000 + \overset{(1)}{\$16,000}}{10,000} = \$5.60$$

(1) Subsidiary common shares owned by parent (80% × 5,000)................... 4,000
Parent's interest in subsidiary income (4,000 shares × $4.00 subsidiary BEPS) $16,000

The calculation of *diluted earnings per share (DEPS)* is not complicated when applied to the consolidated company, provided that the subsidiary company has no dilutive securities. As long as no such securities exist, the controlling interest's share of consolidated net income is divided by the number of outstanding parent company shares. The numerator and denominator adjustments caused by parent company dilutive securities can be considered in the normal manner.

When the subsidiary has dilutive securities, the calculation of consolidated DEPS becomes a 2-stage process. First, the DEPS of the subsidiary must be calculated. Then, the consolidated DEPS is calculated using as a component of the calculation the adjusted DEPS of the subsidiary. This 2-stage process handles subsidiary dilutive securities which require the possible issuance of subsidiary company shares. A further complication occurs when the subsidiary has outstanding dilutive options, warrants, and/or convertible securities which may require the issuance of parent company shares.

First, consider the calculation of consolidated DEPS when the subsidiary has outstanding dilutive securities which may require the issuance of subsidiary company shares only. The EPS model for a single entity is modified in two ways:

1. Only the parent's adjusted internally generated net income, the parent's income adjusters, and the parent's share adjusters enter the formula directly.
2. The parent's share of the subsidiary's income is entered indirectly by multiplying the number of equivalent subsidiary shares owned by the parent by the subsidiary DEPS.

The basic model for computing consolidated DEPS in this situation is as follows:

$$\text{Consolidated DEPS} = \frac{\begin{pmatrix}\text{Parent's}\\\text{Adjusted}\\\text{Internally}\\\text{Generated}\\\text{Net Income}\end{pmatrix} + \begin{pmatrix}\text{Parent's DEPS}\\\text{Income}\\\text{Adjustments}\end{pmatrix} + \left(\begin{matrix}\text{Parent-}\\\text{Owned}\\\text{Equivalent}\\\text{Shares}\end{matrix} \times \begin{matrix}\text{Subsidiary}\\\text{DEPS}\end{matrix}\right)}{\begin{pmatrix}\text{Parent's Common}\\\text{Shares Outstanding}\end{pmatrix} + \begin{pmatrix}\text{Parent's DEPS Share}\\\text{Adjustments}\end{pmatrix}}$$

The parent's adjusted internally generated net income includes adjustments for unrealized profits (on sales to the subsidiary) recorded during the current period and for realization of profits deferred from previous periods. **This would be all of the adjustments that appear on the parent's income distribution schedule, except for the inclusion of the parent's share of**

subsidiary income. Likewise, the income used to compute the subsidiary DEPS must be adjusted for intercompany transactions and amortizations of excess (as shown in the subsidiary income distribution schedule). To illustrate the computation of consolidated DEPS, assume the following data concerning the subsidiary:

Net income (adjusted for intercompany profits)	$22,000
Preferred stock cash dividend	$ 2,000
Interest paid on convertible bonds	$ 3,000
Common stock shares outstanding	5,000
Warrants to purchase one share of common stock	1,000
Warrants held by parent	500
Convertible bonds outstanding (convertible into 10 shares of common stock)	200
Convertible bonds held by parent	180

$$\frac{\text{Subsidiary}}{\text{DEPS}} = \frac{\$22{,}000 - \overset{(1)}{\$2{,}000} + \overset{(2)}{\$3{,}000}}{\underset{(3)}{5{,}000} + \underset{(4)}{2{,}000} + 500} = \$3.07$$

(1) Dividend on nonconvertible preferred stock, none of which is owned by the parent.
(2) Income adjustment for convertible bonds, which are dilutive.
(3) Share adjustment associated with convertible debentures, 200 bonds × 10 shares per bond.
(4) Share adjustment (treasury stock method) associated with the warrants. It is assumed that, using the average fair value of the stock, 500 shares could be purchased with the proceeds of the sale and that 500 additional new shares would be issued.

Assume the parent owns 80% of the subsidiary and has an adjusted internally generated net income of $40,000 and 10,000 shares of common stock outstanding. Also assume the parent has dilutive bonds outstanding that are convertible into 3,000 shares of common stock and the interest paid on these bonds was $5,000. The consolidated DEPS would be computed as follows:

$$\frac{\text{Consolidated}}{\text{DEPS}} = \frac{\$40{,}000 + \overset{(1)}{\$5{,}000} + \overset{(2)}{\$18{,}574}}{10{,}000 + \underset{(3)}{3{,}000}} = \$4.89$$

(1) Income adjustment from interest on parent company convertible bonds, which are dilutive.

(2)		
	Subsidiary common shares owned by parent (80% × 5,000)	4,000
	Parent-owned equivalent shares applicable to convertible bonds (180 × 10 shares)*	1,800
	Parent-owned equivalent shares applicable to warrants (50% × 500)**	250
	Total parent-owned equivalent shares	6,050
	Parent's interest in subsidiary income (6,050 shares × $3.07 subsidiary DEPS)	$18,574

(3) Shares assumed to be issued in exchange for parent company convertible bonds (a common stock equivalent).

   *Parent owns 180 (or 90%) of 200 subsidiary bonds.
   **Parent owns 500 (or 50%) of 1,000 subsidiary warrants.

If the dilutive subsidiary securities enable the holder to acquire common stock of the parent, these securities are not included in the computation of subsidiary DEPS. However, these securities must be included in the parent's share adjustment in computing consolidated DEPS. The basic model by which to compute consolidated DEPS in this situation is as shown on page 332.

$$\text{Consolidated DEPS} = \frac{\begin{array}{c}\text{Parent's}\\\text{Adjusted}\\\text{Internally}\\\text{Generated}\\\text{Net Income}\end{array} + \begin{array}{c}\text{Parent's DEPS}\\\text{Income}\\\text{Adjustments}\end{array} + \left(\begin{array}{c}\text{Parent-}\\\text{Owned}\\\text{Equivalent}\\\text{Shares}\end{array} \times \begin{array}{c}\text{Subsidiary}\\\text{DEPS}\end{array}\right) + \begin{array}{c}\text{Income}\\\text{Adjustment}\\\text{Resulting}\\\text{from}\\\text{Subsidiary}\\\text{Securities}\\\text{that Enable}\\\text{Holder to}\\\text{Acquire}\\\text{Parent Stock}\end{array}}{\begin{array}{c}\text{Parent's Common}\\\text{Shares Outstanding}\end{array} + \begin{array}{c}\text{Parent's DEPS Share}\\\text{Adjustments}\end{array}}$$

To illustrate, assume the following facts for a parent owning 90% of the outstanding subsidiary shares:

Parent internally adjusted net income	$20,000
Parent company common stock shares outstanding	10,000
Parent company dilutive convertible bonds:	
Interest expense	$ 1,000
Shares to be issued in conversion	2,000
Subsidiary adjusted net income	$ 7,000
Subsidiary common stock shares outstanding	4,000
Subsidiary preferred stock convertible into parent common stock:	
Dividend requirement	$ 1,200
Number of preferred shares	1,000
Number of parent company common shares required	2,000
Subsidiary common stock warrants to acquire 100 parent shares	100

The first step is to calculate the subsidiary's DEPS as follows:

$$\frac{\text{Subsidiary}}{\text{DEPS}} = \frac{\$7,000 - \$1,200 \text{ preferred dividends}}{4,000 \text{ outstanding common shares}} = \$1.45$$

Note that the subsidiary convertible preferred stock and stock warrants are not satisfied with subsidiary shares and, thus, are not considered converted for the purpose of calculating subsidiary DEPS. The consolidated DEPS would be computed as follows:

$$\frac{\text{Consolidated}}{\text{DEPS}} = \frac{\$20,000 + \overset{(1)}{\$1,000} + \overset{(2)}{[3,600 \times \$1.45]} + \overset{(3)}{\$1,080}}{10,000 + \underset{(4)}{(2,000 + 2,000 + 50)}} = \$1.94$$

(1) $1,000 income adjustment associated with the parent company convertible security.

(2) The parent's share of subsidiary DEPS. Again, since the subsidiary's preferred stock and warrants are not convertible into subsidiary shares, the total parent-owned equivalent shares is 90% × 4,000.

(3) Income adjustment representing the dividend on subsidiary preferred shares that would not be paid if the shares were converted into common stock of the parent. Note that 90% of the $1,200 dividend adjustment is added back to the controlling share of income

(4) The parent's share adjustment consisting of 2,000 shares traceable to the parent company convertible security; 2,000 shares traceable to the subsidiary preferred stock that is convertible into parent common stock; and 50 incremental shares traceable to the subsidiary warrants to acquire parent common stock. It is assumed that 50 of the 100 shares required to satisfy the warrants can be purchased with the proceeds of the exercise and 50 new shares must be issued.

Special analysis is required in computing consolidated BEPS and DEPS when an acquisition occurs during a reporting period. In that case, only subsidiary income since the acquisition date is included, and the number of subsidiary shares is weighted for the partial period.

REFLECTION

- Prior to calculating consolidated EPS, the subsidiary's EPS (including dilution adjustments that add more subsidiary shares) is calculated.

- The parent's numerator for EPS includes its own internally generated net income plus its share of subsidiary EPS.

- The parent also adjusts its numerator and denominator for dilative parent company securities and subsidiary securities that are satisfied by issuing parent company shares.

TAXATION OF CONSOLIDATED COMPANIES

3

OBJECTIVE

Calculate and prepare a consolidated worksheet where the consolidated firm is an "affiliated group" and pays a single consolidated tax.

Consolidated companies that do not meet the requirements to be an *affiliated group*, as defined by the tax law, must pay their taxes as separate entities. The tax definition of an affiliated group is less inclusive than that used in accounting theory. Section 1504(a) of the Tax Code does not allow two or more corporations to file a consolidated return or to be considered an affiliated group for tax purposes unless the parent owns:

1. 80% of the voting power of all classes of stock *and*
2. 80% of the fair market value of all the outstanding stock of the other corporation.

For these provisions, preferred stock is not included if it (a) is not entitled to vote, (b) is limited and preferred as to dividends, (c) does not have redemption rights beyond its issue price plus a reasonable redemption or liquidation premium, and (d) is not convertible into the other class of stock. Comparison of these criteria with those required for consolidated financial reporting indicates that many consolidated companies have no choice but to submit to separate taxation of the member companies.

Consolidated companies that do meet the tax law requirements to be an affiliated group may elect to be taxed as a single entity or as separate entities. Once the election is made to file as a single entity, the permission of the Internal Revenue Service is required before the companies can be taxed separately again. Companies that elect to be taxed as a single entity file a consolidated tax return that may provide several tax advantages. For example, a consolidated return generally permits the offset of operating profits and losses and of capital gains and losses. Also, intercompany profits are not taxed until realized in later periods.

When companies that comprise an affiliated group elect not to file a consolidated return, each company within the group computes and pays its taxes independently. All members of the group must use the parent's tax year. However, the members may use different accounting methods.

Members of consolidated groups, when filing separate returns, must sum their incomes when applying graduated corporate tax rates. The lower tax rates available for low income levels can be used only once and cannot be applied by each of the companies individually.

Foreign corporations are not includible in consolidated tax returns. U.S. companies do not pay U.S. tax on foreign business profits of their foreign subsidiaries until the earnings are repatriated to the U.S. parent through a dividend distribution. This is not likely to happen if the U.S. company is trying to grow its business abroad. This policy is known as "deferral." Because of the current high U.S. corporate tax rate, deferral is perhaps the most important tax break available to U.S. multinational corporations. According to the Organization for Economic Cooperation and Development (OECD), in 2009 the average corporate income tax rate of the 29 OECD countries (excluding the United States) was 25.9%. The average U.S. rate, including state tax, was 39.1%. Only Japan had a higher rate.

Consolidated Tax Return

When an affiliated group elects to be taxed as a single entity, consolidated income as determined on the worksheet is the basis for the tax calculation. The affiliated companies should not record a provision for income tax based on their own separate incomes. Rather, the income tax expense is calculated as part of the consolidated worksheet process. The tax provision is based on consolidated income; intercompany profits will have been eliminated already. Thus, no special procedures are needed to deal with intercompany transactions when computing the tax provision. Once calculated, the tax provision may be recorded on the books of the separate companies.

As an example of an affiliated group's choosing to be taxed as a single entity, assume Company P acquired an 80% interest in Company S on January 1, 2011, at which time the following determination and distribution of excess schedule was prepared:

Determination and Distribution of Excess Schedule

	Company Implied Fair Value	Parent Price (80%)	NCI Value (20%)
Fair value of subsidiary	$993,750	$795,000	$198,750
Less book value of interest acquired:			
Common stock	$500,000		
Retained earnings	400,000		
Total stockholders' equity	$900,000	$900,000	$900,000
Interest acquired		80%	20%
Book value		$720,000	$180,000
Excess of fair value over book value	**$ 93,750**	$ 75,000	$ 18,750

Adjustment of identifiable accounts:

	Adjustment	Life	Amortization per Year	Worksheet Key
Patent	$ 93,750	15	$ 6,250	**debit D**

The following income statements are for Companies P and S for 2013. Since the companies desire to file a consolidated tax return, neither company has recorded a provision for income tax. The corporate tax rate is 30%.

	Company P	Company S
Sales	$600,000	$400,000
Less cost of goods sold	350,000	200,000
Gross profit	$250,000	$200,000
Less expenses:		
Depreciation expense	25,000	20,000
Other operating expenses	75,000	80,000
Operating income	$150,000	$100,000
Subsidiary income	80,000	
Income before tax	$230,000	$100,000

On January 1, 2012, Company P sold a piece of equipment, with a book value of $40,000, to Company S for $60,000. The equipment is depreciated by Company S on a straight-line basis over a 5-year life.

The following applies to 2013 intercompany merchandise sales to Company P by Company S:

Intercompany sales in beginning inventory of Company P	$ 50,000
Intercompany sales in ending inventory of Company P.	$ 70,000
Sales to Company P during 2013	$100,000
Gross profit rate.	50%

A 30% tax rate applies to both companies.

Worksheet 6-1, pages 344 to 345, contains the trial balances of Companies P and S on December 31, 2013. Since the income tax is to be calculated on the worksheet, no provision exists on the separate books. If separate provisions appear in the trial balances, they should be eliminated as an initial procedure in consolidating.

Worksheet 6-1: page 344

The balance of the investment in Company S account results from the use of the simple equity method. All eliminations should be made prior to calculating the provision for tax. This will assure that the consolidated income, upon which the provision is based, is adjusted for all intercompany transactions.

All worksheet entries, other than (T) are unchanged from procedures used in prior worksheets, and the same coding is used. In journal entry form, the entries are as follows:

(CY1)	Eliminate current-year equity income:		
	Subsidiary Income.	80,000	
	Investment in Company S.		80,000
(EL)	Eliminate 80% of subsidiary equity:		
	Common Stock—Company S	400,000	
	Retained Earnings—Company S.	560,000	
	Investment in Company S.		960,000
(D)/(NCI)	Distribute excess to patent:		
	Patent.	93,750	
	Investment in Company S.		75,000
	Retained Earnings—Company S (NCI adjustment)		18,750
(A)	Amortize patent for two prior years and the current year:		
	Patent Amortization Expense.	6,250	
	Retained Earnings—Company P	10,000	
	Retained Earnings—Company S.	2,500	
	Patent.		18,750
(F1)	Adjust retained earnings for fixed asset profit at start of year:		
	Retained Earnings—Company P	16,000	
	Accumulated Depreciation—Equipment.	4,000	
	Equipment		20,000
(F2)	Adjust current-year depreciation for gain on fixed asset sale:		
	Accumulated Depreciation—Equipment.	4,000	
	Depreciation Expense		4,000
(IS)	Eliminate intercompany merchandise sales:		
	Sales	100,000	
	Cost of Goods Sold		100,000
(BI)	Adjust January 1 retained earnings for inventory profit recorded by subsidiary:		
	Retained Earnings—Company S.	5,000	
	Retained Earnings—Company P	20,000	
	Cost of Goods Sold		25,000
(EI)	Adjust cost of goods sold for profit in ending inventory:		
	Cost of Goods Sold	35,000	
	Inventory, December 31, 2013.		35,000

Consolidated net income before tax is calculated on the worksheet and becomes the base for the tax provision. Entry **(T)** is not entered until this calculation is made. In journal entry form, the entry is as follows:

Consolidated Tax Provision	**71,700**	
Income Tax Payable		**71,700**

Explanation:

Consolidated income before tax (from the consolidated worksheet).....	$237,750
Nondeductible amortization of patent applicable to NCI (explained below)...	1,250
Adjusted reported income..	$239,000
Tax rate	× 30%
Tax provision and liability	$ 71,700

In this case, it was assumed that the acquisition was a taxable exchange to the seller. The parent's share of the patent amortization is deductible. However, the portion of the patent amortization applicable to the NCI is not deductible. The portion of the asset adjustment applicable to the NCI was not taxed and thus does not have the stepped-up basis. As indicated in Chapter 1, there are some combinations that are nontaxable exchanges and amortizations of excess are then not deductible.[1]

A new tax schedule is needed to aid the preparation of the subsidiary IDS. The complication is that the amortizations of excess attributable to the NCI are not deductible. The tax schedule is prepared as follows:

Subsidiary Tax Schedule	Controlling	NCI	Total
1. Total adjusted income	$ 67,000[c]	$ 16,750[b]	$ 83,750[a]
2. NCI share of asset adjustments		1,250	1,250
3. Taxable income (1. + 2.)	$ 67,000	$ 18,000	$ 75,000
4. Tax (30% × 3.)	**$20,100**	**$ 5,400**	**$25,500**
Net-of-tax share of income (1. − 4.)	**$46,900**	**$11,350**	**$58,250**

[a]Shown on the subsidiary's IDS as the internally generated income net of adjustments ($100,000 + $25,000 − $35,000 − $6,250). *Note: These are before-tax numbers.*
[b]$83,750 × 20%
[c]$83,750 × 80%

The IDS schedule of the subsidiary reflects the amounts in the above schedule. The parent's IDS schedule has two unique features.

1. The share of subsidiary income is already taxed and is entered on an after-tax basis using the amount shown in the subsidiary IDS schedule.
2. The parent's internally generated net income is taxed as part of the parent's IDS schedule.

It will be necessary for each member company to record its share of the tax provision on its own books. The subsidiary, Company S, would record the following:

Provision for Income Tax	25,500	
Income Tax Payable.......................................		25,500
To record the allocated portion of the tax provision.		

---

1 When there are nondeductible amortizations of excess cost, there also may be a recorded deferred tax liability. Recall that an excess of fair value over cost relative to an identifiable asset requires the recording of a deferred tax liability for the amount of the tax rate times the excess. This deferred tax liability would be amortized to tax expense in proportion to the amortization of the excess.

The parent, Company P, would record the following:

Subsidiary Income (80% × $25,500 tax provision)	20,400	
Investment in Company S.		20,400
To adjust Subsidiary Income for the tax expense recorded by		
Company S.		
Provision for Income Tax (from parent's IDS)	46,200*	
Income Tax Payable.		46,200
To record the allocated portion of the tax provision.		

*$154,000 internally generated income, net of adjustments × 30%

Complications Caused by Goodwill

The distribution of excess purchase price to goodwill creates a tax timing difference. Goodwill is no longer amortized for financial reporting but still is amortized for tax purposes over a 15-year life. Each year, the tax deduction taken for goodwill will result in a *deferred tax liability (DTL)*. The DTL will not be utilized until either the goodwill is impairment adjusted or the company purchased is later sold. For example, assume goodwill amortization is $5,000 per year for tax purposes, and the company has a 40% tax rate. Each year, the following adjustment would be made on the consolidated worksheet and on the parent company books:

Income Tax Payable	2,000	
Deferred Tax Liability.		2,000
To defer tax equal to 40% of $5,000 goodwill amortization for tax		
purposes only.		

After five years, there would be a $10,000 DTL. If, at the end of five years, the goodwill is reduced $20,000 for an impairment loss, the following adjustments would be made on the consolidated worksheet and on the parent company books:

Goodwill Impairment Loss	20,000	
Goodwill		20,000
To record loss on impairment of goodwill.		
Deferred Tax Liability.	8,000	
Provision for Income Taxes		8,000
To reduce tax provision for realization of tax liability resulting from prior		
amortization of goodwill for tax purposes.		

The amortization of goodwill built a DTL account that is reduced when the goodwill impairment loss is recorded. The DTL could also be removed if the company to which it relates is sold.

Consolidated returns are consistent with consolidated reporting procedures and do not alter in any way the procedures that have been discussed in previous chapters. It is necessary to add only new procedures to the worksheet to provide for income taxes. The procedures were explained in our example assuming the use of the simple equity method. There would not be any impact on the tax entry if the cost or sophisticated equity method were used.

Separate Tax Returns

When separate returns are required or are elected to be filed, each member of the consolidated group must base its provision for tax on its own reported income. For the parent, taxable income may include dividends received from other corporations. When the members of the consolidated company meet the requirements of an affiliated company (this requires at least an 80% ownership interest), 100% of the dividends received is excluded from reported income. For ownership interests of at least 20% but less than 80%, 80% of the dividends received is excluded from reported taxable income.[2] For ownership interests less than 20%, 70% of the

4

OBJECTIVE

Prepare a consolidated worksheet where the parent and subsidiary are separately taxed by employing tax allocation procedures.

----
2 The exclusion rate is determined by current tax law and is subject to change.

dividends received is excluded from reported income. The full or partial exclusion of dividends applies only to dividends from domestic corporations and is intended to reduce multiple taxation of the same income.

A major complication arises in consolidating. **The provision for tax recorded by each company is based on its reported separate net income prior to eliminating intercompany transactions.** This means that timing differences are created when consolidating. For example, suppose the parent sells inventory to the subsidiary at a price that includes a 25% gross profit. If $40,000 of intercompany sales remains in the subsidiary's ending inventory, consolidation procedures defer $10,000 of intercompany profit. The problem is that the parent already recorded a 30% or $3,000 tax provision on the profit as a separate company. This $3,000 now becomes a *deferred (prepaid) tax asset* (DTA) when the profit to which it attaches is deferred on the consolidated worksheet. In the following period, the intercompany profit on the inventory is realized (assuming the inventory is sold in that period). The deferred tax asset relative to the inventory profit is then expensed as part of the current year's provision for tax. The adjustments required as a result of these tax issues are examples of applying interperiod tax allocation procedures.

The use of separate tax returns for a consolidated group leads to a complicated application of interperiod tax allocation techniques. The calculations may become cumbersome when intercompany sales of plant assets and merchandise are involved. To illustrate, assume Company P purchased a 75% interest in Company S on January 1, 2011, at which time the following determination and distribution of excess schedule was prepared:

Determination and Distribution of Excess Schedule

	Company Implied Fair Value	Parent Price (75%)	NCI Value (25%)
Fair value of subsidiary	$380,000	$285,000	$ 95,000
Less book value of interest acquired:			
Common stock	$250,000		
Retained earnings	100,000		
Total stockholders' equity	$350,000	$350,000	$350,000
Interest acquired		75%	25%
Book value		$262,500	$ 87,500
Excess of fair value over book value	**$ 30,000**	$ 22,500	$ 7,500

Adjustment of identifiable accounts:

	Adjustment	Life	Amortization per Year	Worksheet Key
Patent	$ 30,000	15	$ 2,000	**debit D**

The patent amortization will not appear on the separate statements of the parent or the subsidiary. It will only arise in the consolidation process. Since it has not been included in the parent's determination of income, the parent has taken no tax deduction.

Further assume that on January 1, 2012, the subsidiary sold equipment with a cost of $60,000 to the parent for $100,000. This means that the subsidiary has included the $40,000 gain in 2012 income and has paid the tax on it. Meanwhile, the parent is depreciating the asset over five years on a straight-line basis. The parent is recording depreciation of $20,000 per year using a cost of $100,000. The parent's tax is computed using the $20,000 depreciation deduction.

In 2013 and 2014, the parent sold merchandise to the subsidiary to realize a gross profit of 40%. In 2014, the subsidiary had a beginning inventory of goods purchased from the parent for $60,000. The parent included this amount in its 2013 income and paid the taxes on it. During the 2014 year, sales by the parent to the subsidiary totaled $100,000. Intercompany goods of $40,000 remain in the subsidiary's 2014 ending inventory. Again, the parent has included the profit in its income and paid taxes on it.

The separate income statements of the parent and the subsidiary for 2014 are as follows:

	Company P	Company S
Sales (includes $100,000 intercompany sale by P)	$430,000	$240,000
Less cost of goods sold (includes $100,000 for intercompany purchase by S)	280,000	150,000
Gross profit	$150,000	$ 90,000
Less expenses:		
Depreciation expense (includes parent's $20,000 depreciation of equipment purchased from S)	20,000	10,000
Other operating expenses	50,000	20,000
Operating income	$ 80,000	$ 60,000

Taxation of Separate Entities. Before Companies P and S can be consolidated, it is necessary to calculate their separate tax liabilities since the 80% test of an affiliated group for tax purposes is not met. The tax provision of the subsidiary is $18,000 (30% × $60,000 Company S income before tax). Company S would record its tax provision as follows:

Provision for Income Tax	18,000	
Income Tax Payable		18,000

The tax provision for Company P requires consideration of the tax status of subsidiary income. When the conditions for an affiliated group are not met, the parent company must include in its taxable income 20% of the dividends it receives from a subsidiary. According to FASB ASC 740-30-25, subsidiary income included in the pretax income of a parent leads to a temporary difference between the earning of the income and its inclusion in the tax return as dividend income.[3] It is not necessary to account for the temporary difference if the tax law provides a means by which the investment can be recovered tax free. Company P will provide for tax expense equal to its tax rate times 20% of its share of the total subsidiary net income. It is assumed that the parent records its tax provision based on the income it records from the subsidiary. In this example, the parent records the investment under the simple equity method. Thus, the tax accrual is based on 20% of the simple equity income without any reduction for amortization of excesses. A parent using the cost method would record the tax only on dividends received and would need to accrue tax on the worksheet based on the cost-to-equity conversion.

This tax may be viewed as a secondary tax since it is the second taxation of subsidiary income. For 2014, this tax liability would be calculated as follows:

Subsidiary net income ($60,000 − $18,000 tax)	$42,000
Controlling interest (75% × $42,000)	31,500
Provision for tax on subsidiary income (30% × 20% × $31,500)	1,890

Company P would add this amount to the tax it has provided for its internally generated income to arrive at its total tax provision for the period as follows:

Tax on internally generated income (30% × $80,000)	$24,000
Secondary tax provision for subsidiary income	1,890
Total Company P provision for tax	$25,890

---

3 FASB ASC 740-30-25, *Income Taxes—Other Considerations or Special Areas—Recognition—General* (Norwalk, CT, 2010).

Since Company P has not received its share of the income of Company S, the secondary tax is not immediately payable, and a deferred tax liability for $1,890 is created. Assuming that the tax on internally generated income is currently payable, Company P would make the following entry to record its 2014 tax provision:

Provision for Income Tax	25,890	
Income Tax Payable.		24,000
Deferred Tax Liability.		1,890

If dividends had been paid by the subsidiary, the secondary tax applicable to the dividends received by Company P would be included in the current tax liability. Note that the secondary tax applies only to consolidated companies that do not qualify as an affiliated group. Companies that do meet the requirements would calculate only a single tax on each company's adjusted net income. When an affiliated group *elects* separate taxation, no dividends are included and no additional tax needs to be calculated.

Worksheet 6-2: page 348

Worksheet Procedures. Worksheet 6-2, on pages 348 to 349, includes the trial balances of Companies P and S. The companies do not qualify as an affiliated group for tax purposes. **Several observations should be made regarding the amounts listed in the trial balance before you study the elimination entries.**

1. The balance in Investment in Company S is computed according to the simple equity method, as follows:

Original cost		$285,000
Subsidiary income, 2011–2013 (*after tax*):		
Company S retained earnings, January 1, 2014	$350,000	
Company S retained earnings, January 1, 2011	100,000	
Net increase.	$250,000	
Controlling interest.	× 75%	187,500
Controlling interest in subsidiary net income, 2014 (75% × $42,000) .		31,500
Equity-adjusted balance, December 31, 2014.		$504,000

2. Since the parent's share of subsidiary undistributed income has been recorded from the date of acquisition, a deferred tax liability has been recorded by Company P each year to recognize the secondary tax provision. The total deferred tax liability on December 31, 2014, is calculated as follows:

Deferred tax liability on 2011–2013 income (20% × 30% × $187,500*	
on 2011–2013 undistributed income)	$11,250
Current year's additional deferment (20% × 30% × $31,500)	1,890
Total deferred tax liability	$13,140

    *75% × $250,000 increase in Company S retained earnings

3. The trial balances of both companies include their separate provisions for income tax and the current tax liabilities. **These provisions do not reflect adjustments for intercompany transactions.**

All worksheet entries, other than (T1) and (T2) are unchanged from procedures used in prior worksheets, and the same coding is used. In journal entry form, the entries for Worksheet 6-2 are as follows:

(CY1)	Eliminate current-year equity income:		
	Subsidiary Income.	31,500	
	Investment in Company S.		31,500

(EL)	Eliminate 75% of subsidiary equity:		
	Common Stock, Company S	187,500	
	Retained Earnings, Company S	262,500	
	Investment in Company S		450,000

(D)/(NCI)	Distribute excess to patent:		
	Patent	30,000	
	Investment in Company S		22,500
	Retained Earnings—Company S (NCI adjustment)		7,500

(A)	Amortize patent for three prior years and the current year:		
	Patent Amortization Expense	2,000	
	Retained Earnings—Company P	4,500	
	Retained Earnings—Company S	1,500	
	Patent		8,000

(F1)	Adjust retained earnings for fixed asset profit at start of year (two prior years):		
	Retained Earnings—Company P	18,000	
	Retained Earnings—Company S	6,000	
	Accumulated Depreciation—Equipment	16,000	
	Equipment		40,000

(F2)	Adjust current-year depreciation for gain on fixed asset sale:		
	Accumulated Depreciation—Equipment	8,000	
	Depreciation Expense		8,000

(IS)	Eliminate intercompany merchandise sales:		
	Sales	100,000	
	Cost of Goods Sold		100,000

(BI)	Adjust January 1 retained earnings for inventory profit recorded by parent:		
	Retained Earnings—Company P	24,000	
	Cost of Goods Sold		24,000

(EI)	Adjust cost of goods sold for profit in ending inventory:		
	Cost of Goods Sold	16,000	
	Inventory, December 31, 2014		16,000

(T1)	Record deferred tax asset applicable to prior adjustments:		
	Deferred Tax Liability	16,695	
	Retained Earnings—Company S		1,800
	Retained Earnings—Company P		14,895

(T2)	Record change in deferred tax asset during current period:		
	Provision for Income Tax	4,539	
	Deferred Tax Liability		4,539

Worksheet entries (T1) and (T2) are explained in the directions that accompany the worksheet, but let us expand on them. Entry (T1) takes the position that both companies have already paid a tax on the income recorded by the companies in prior periods. If consolidation procedures change the income, for example reduce income, then the taxes are considered to have been paid in advance and the taxes paid become a deferred tax asset.

It should be noted that only the controlling portion of excess amortizations are deductible since a tax deduction is allowed only for the interest in the assets that was actually purchased. The increase in the value of the assets attributed to the NCI are not subject to tax adjustments.

The adjustment to beginning retained earnings for taxes paid in prior periods, entry **(T1)**, is explained as follows:

DTA/DTL adjustments:

To beginning retained earnings:

Subsidiary transactions:	Total Tax	Parent Share	Subsidiary Share
Remaining fixed asset profit.	$ 24,000	$ 18,000	$ 6,000
Amortization of excess (patent, 75% × $6,000) . . .	4,500	4,500	
Total.	$ 28,500	$ 22,500	$ 6,000
1. First tax (30%)	8,550	6,750	1,800
Net income after tax	$ 19,950	**$15,750**	$ 4,200
2. 20% × 30% × $15,750.	$ 945	$ 945	
3. Total tax (1. + 2.)	$ 9,495	$ 7,695	$ 1,800
Parent transactions:			
Beginning inventory	$ 24,000	$ 24,000	
4. First tax (30% × $24,000)	$ 7,200	$ 7,200	
Total increase in DTA and retained earnings			
(3. + 4.).	**$16,695**	**$14,895**	**$1,800**

(T2)   Adjust current-year tax provision and adjust deferred tax asset for the effects of current-year income adjustments:

Subsidiary transactions:	Total Tax	Parent Share	Subsidiary Share
Realized fixed asset profit	$ (8,000)	$(6,000)	$(2,000)
Amortization of excess (patent, 75% × $2,000) . . .	1,500	1,500	
1. Total	$ (6,500)	$(4,500)	$(2,000)
First tax (30% × 1.)	$ (1,950)	$(1,350)	$ (600)
20% × 30 × ($4,500 − $1,350) first tax.	(189)	(189)	
2. Total tax.	$ (2,139)	$(1,539)	$ (600)
Parent transactions:			
Beginning inventory	$(24,000)		
Ending inventory	16,000		
Total.	$ (8,000)		
3. First tax (30% × $8,000)	$ (2,400)	$(2,400)	
Increase (decrease) in DTA (2. + 3.)	$ (4,539)	$(3,939)	$ (600)

This means that income of prior periods has been reduced by $52,500 ($24,000 + $4,500 + $24,000) and the taxes already paid on these reductions are $16,695. These tax payments now create a deferred tax asset that will be consumed in future periods.

Entry (T2) considers the tax effects of adjustments made to the current-year income. Let us consider an expanded version of the explanation to entry (T2) in the explanations to the worksheet.

When the entries in Worksheet 6-2 are completed, the resulting consolidated net income is $105,571, which is distributed to the controlling and noncontrolling interests.

Complications Caused by Goodwill

Since the firms are taxed separately, goodwill that results from a purchase has not been acknowledged for tax purposes and, thus, does not create a tax deduction for goodwill amortization and a resulting DTL as it did in the case of taxation of the consolidated company.

Let us revisit Worksheet 6-2 to discuss how it would be simplified if the consolidated company met the requirements of an affiliated company. The following procedures would be omitted from the worksheet:

1. Company P would not have recorded the deferred tax liability of $13,140 on its books. If the companies are an affiliated group, there is no tax due on the parent's share of subsidiary income. The parent's current-year provision for income tax would be only $24,000 since there would not be the secondary tax of $1,890 on the parent's share of subsidiary income.

2. Entry (T1) would not include the secondary tax applicable to the patent amortization and the intercompany equipment sale.

3. Entry (T2) would not include the secondary tax of $252 applicable to the patent amortization and the intercompany equipment sale.

4. The parent's income distribution schedule would not deduct the secondary tax on the parent's share of subsidiary income. Instead, the parent would just include 75% of the subsidiary's after-tax income of $46,050, or $34,538.

There are some additional minor worksheet modifications required if the cost or sophisticated equity methods are used by the parent company. If the cost method is used, there needs to be a recording of the deferred tax liability for prior years' subsidiary income. The adjustment would be to multiply the net amount of the cost-to-equity conversion adjustment by the effective tax rate, to debit the parent's retained earnings, and to credit a deferred tax liability account. If the sophisticated equity method is used, the parent company's retained earnings and current-year tax provision are correct and need no adjustment. The only entry needed in consolidating is to adjust the beginning retained earnings of the subsidiary for any intercompany profits on a net-of-tax basis. The adjustment of subsidiary retained earnings on the consolidated worksheet was covered in the partial worksheet on page 220. It still would be necessary to calculate the noncontrolling and controlling interests in combined net income on an after-tax basis when preparing the income distribution schedules. (Note that each income distribution schedule starts with net income *before tax*. This is done so that the tax provision may be recalculated on a consolidated basis.)

REFLECTION

- An "affiliated group" (under tax law) may prepare a consolidated tax return. The tax provision is computed based on the consolidated income computed on the worksheet. The provision is then allocated to the controlling and noncontrolling interests.

- When a consolidated company is subject to separate taxation, each firm has recorded its tax provision based on its own reported income. Taxes have already been paid on intercompany profits. The parent has paid the double tax on its share of subsidiary income.

- A worksheet prepared under separate taxation requires procedures for the adjustment of the separate taxes already present. The taxes applicable to intercompany gains, which are eliminated, become a deferred tax asset. Amortizations of excess (not deductible on separate tax returns) create additional deferred tax assets.

- As intercompany profits are realized through sale to the "outside world" or through amortization, the deferred tax asset is realized as an increase in the provision for taxes.

Worksheet 6-1

Affiliates File Consolidated Income Tax Return
Company P and Subsidiary Company S
Worksheet for Consolidated Financial Statements
For Year Ended December 31, 2013

	(Credit balance amounts are in parentheses.)	Trial Balance	
		Company P	Company S
1	Cash	205,000	380,000
2	Inventory	150,000	120,000
3	Investment in Company S	1,115,000	
4			
5			
6	Patent		
7	Plant and Equipment	900,000	1,100,000
8	Accumulated Depreciation	(440,000)	(150,000)
9			
10	Liabilities		(150,000)
11	Common Stock—Company S		(500,000)
12	Retained Earnings—Company S		(700,000)
13			
14			
15	Common Stock—Company P	(800,000)	
16	Retained Earnings, January 1, 2013—Company P	(900,000)	
17			
18			
19	Sales	(600,000)	(400,000)
20	Cost of Goods Sold	350,000	200,000
21			
22	Patent Amortization Expense		
23	Depreciation Expense	25,000	20,000
24	Other Expenses	75,000	80,000
25	Subsidiary Income	(80,000)	
26	Total	0	0
27	**Consolidated Income Before Tax**		
28	**Consolidated Tax Provision**		
29	**Income Tax Payable**		
30	Consolidated Net Income		
31	NCI Share		
32	Controlling Share		
33	NCI		
34	Controlling Retained Earnings		
35	Total		

Worksheet 6-1 (see page 335)

Eliminations & Adjustments				Consolidated Income Statement	NCI	Controlling Retained Earnings	Consolidated Balance Sheet	
Dr.		Cr.						
							585,000	1
		(EI)	35,000				235,000	2
		(CY1)	80,000					3
		(EL)	960,000					4
		(D)	75,000					5
(D)	93,750	(A)	18,750				75,000	6
		(F1)	20,000				1,980,000	7
(F1)	4,000							8
(F2)	4,000						(582,000)	9
							(150,000)	10
(EL)	400,000				(100,000)			11
(EL)	560,000	(NCI)	18,750					12
(A)	2,500							13
(BI)	5,000				(151,250)			14
							(800,000)	15
(A)	10,000							16
(BI)	20,000							17
(F1)	16,000					(854,000)		18
(IS)	100,000			(900,000)				19
		(IS)	100,000					20
(EI)	35,000	(BI)	25,000	460,000				21
(A)	6,250			6,250				22
		(F2)	4,000	41,000				23
				155,000				24
(CY1)	80,000							25
	1,336,500		1,336,500					26
				(237,750)				27
(T)	**71,700**			71,700				28
		(T)	**71,700**				(71,700)	29
				(166,050)				30
				11,350	(11,350)			31
				154,700		(154,700)		32
					(262,600)		(262,600)	33
						(1,008,700)	(1,008,700)	34
							0	35

Eliminations and Adjustments:

(CY1)   Eliminate the parent's entry recording its share of the current year's subsidiary income. This step returns the investment account to its balance on January 1, 2013.

(EL)   Eliminate 80% of the January 1, 2013, subsidiary equity balances against the investment in Company S account.

(D)   Record the NCI portion of excess of fair value over book value, distribute excess in investment account, and adjust patent to fair value.

(A)   Amortize the patent at an annual amount of $6,250 per year for the current and prior two years. Split retained earnings for prior years—80% controlling retained earnings and 20% NCI.

(IS)   Eliminate intercompany merchandise sales of $100,000 to avoid double-counting sale and purchase.

(BI)   Reduce the cost of goods sold by the $25,000 of intercompany profit included in the beginning inventory.
Since the sale was made by the subsidiary, the reduction of retained earnings is allocated 20% to the NCI and 80% to the controlling retained earnings.

(EI)   Reduce the ending inventory to its cost to the consolidated company by decreasing it $35,000, and increase the cost of goods sold by $35,000.

(F1)   Reduce retained earnings for the remaining undepreciated intercompany equipment gain on January 1, 2013.
Since the sale was by the parent, the entire retained earnings adjustment is debited to Controlling Retained Earnings.

(F2)   Adjust depreciation expense and accumulated for $4,000 over depreciation of equipment in current year.
This is the added depreciation caused by the $20,000 intercompany gain.

(T)   Record the provision for taxes, calculated as follows: ($237,750 + $1,250 adjustment for NCI share of asset adjustments) × 30% = $71,700.

Subsidiary Company S Income Distribution

Ending inventory profit	$35,000	Internally generated net income	$100,000
Amortizations	6,250	Beginning inventory profit	25,000
		Adjusted income before tax. . . .	$ 83,750
		Company S share of taxes (see tax schedule below the parent IDS schedule)	(25,500)
		Net income	$ 58,250
		NCI share (see schedule).	11,350
		Controlling share.	$ 46,900

Parent Company P Income Distribution

	Internally generated net income	$150,000
	Realized gain	4,000
	Adjusted income before tax. . . .	$154,000
	Company P share of taxes (30% × $154,000).	(46,200)
	Company P net income	$107,800
	Controlling share of subsidiary net income (see schedule) . . .	46,900
	Controlling interest	$154,700

Subsidiary Tax Schedule	Controlling	NCI	Total
1. Total adjusted income	$ 67,000[c]	$ 16,750[b]	$ 83,750[a]
2. NCI share of asset adjustments		1,250	1,250
3. Taxable income (1. + 2.)	$ 67,000	$ 18,000	$ 75,000
4. Tax (30% × 3.)	**$20,100**	**$ 5,400**	**$25,500**
Net-of-tax share of income (1. − 4.)	**$46,900**	**$11,350**	**$58,250**

[a]Shown on the subsidiary's IDS as the internally generated income net of adjustments ($100,000 + $25,000 − $35,000 − $6,250). *Note: These are before-tax numbers.*
[b]$83,750 × 20%.
[c]$83,750 × 80%.

Worksheet 6-2

Nonaffiliated Group for Tax Purposes
Company P and Subsidiary Company S
Worksheet for Consolidated Financial Statements
For Year Ended December 31, 2014

	(Credit balance amounts are in parentheses.)	Trial Balance	
		Company P	Company S
1	Cash	19,200	80,000
2	Inventory	170,000	150,000
3	Investment in Company S	504,000	
4			
5			
6	Patent		
7	Plant and Equipment	600,000	550,000
8	Accumulated Depreciation	(410,000)	(120,000)
9			
10	Current Tax Liability	(24,000)	(18,000)
11	**Deferred Tax Liability**	**(13,140)**	
12			
13	Common Stock—Company S		(250,000)
14	Retained Earnings, January 1, 2014—Company S		(350,000)
15			
16			
17			
18	Common Stock—Company P	(250,000)	
19	Retained Earnings—Company P	(510,450)	
20			
21			
22	Sales	(430,000)	(240,000)
23	Cost of Goods Sold	280,000	150,000
24			
25	Patent Amortization Expense		
26	Depreciation Expense	20,000	10,000
27	Other Expenses	50,000	20,000
28	**Provision for Income Tax**	**25,890**	**18,000**
29	Subsidiary Income	(31,500)	
30	Total	0	0
31	Consolidated Net Income		
32	NCI Share		
33	Controlling Share		
34	NCI		
35	Controlling Retained Earnings		
36	Total		

Worksheet 6-2 (see page 340)

Eliminations & Adjustments				Consolidated Income Statement	NCI	Controlling Retained Earnings	Consolidated Balance Sheet	
Dr.		Cr.						
							99,200	1
		(EI)	16,000				304,000	2
		(CY1)	31,500					3
		(EL)	450,000					4
		(D)	22,500					5
(D)	30,000	(A)	8,000				22,000	6
		(F1)	40,000				1,110,000	7
(F1)	16,000							8
(F2)	8,000						(506,000)	9
							(42,000)	10
(T1)	**16,695**	**(T2)**	**4,539**				(984)	11
								12
(EL)	187,500				(62,500)			13
(EL)	262,500	(NCI)	7,500					14
(A)	1,500	**(T1)**	**1,800**					15
(F1)	6,000							16
					(89,300)			17
							(250,000)	18
(A)	4,500							19
(BI)	24,000	**(T1)**	**14,895**					20
(F1)	18,000					(478,845)		21
(IS)	100,000			(570,000)				22
		(IS)	100,000					23
(EI)	16,000	(BI)	24,000	322,000				24
(A)	2,000			2,000				25
		(F2)	8,000	22,000				26
				70,000				27
(T2)	**4,539**			48,429				28
(CY1)	31,500							29
	728,734		728,734					30
				(105,571)				31
				11,400	(11,400)			32
				94,171		(94,171)		33
					(163,200)		(163,200)	34
						(573,016)	(573,016)	35
							0	36

Eliminations and Adjustments:

(CY1)   Eliminate the parent's entry recording its share of the current year's subsidiary income. This step returns the investment account to its balance on January 1, 2014.

(EL)   Eliminate 75% of the January 1, 2014, subsidiary equity balances against the investment in Company S account.

(D)   Record the NCI portion of excess of fair value over book value, distribute excess in investment account, and adjust patent to fair value.

(A)   Amortize the patent at an amount of $2,000 per year for the current and prior three years. Split retained earnings for prior years—75% controlling retained earnings and 25% NCI.

(IS)   Eliminate intercompany merchandise sales of $100,000 to avoid double-counting sale and purchase.

(BI)   Reduce the cost of goods sold by the $24,000 of intercompany profit included in the beginning inventory.
         Since the sale was made by the parent, the reduction of retained earnings is allocated only to the parent.

(EI)   Reduce the ending inventory to its cost to the consolidated company by decreasing it $16,000, and increase the cost of goods sold by $16,000.

(F1)   Reduce retained earnings for the remaining undepreciated intercompany equipment gain on January 1, 2014.
         Since the sale was by the subsidiary, the adjustment is allocated 25% to NCI and 75% to controlling retained earnings.

(F2)   Adjust depreciation expense and accumulated depreciation for $8,000 over depreciation of equipment in current year.
         This is the added depreciation caused by the $40,000 intercompany gain.

(T1)   Adjust beginning retained earnings and create a deferred tax asset on consolidated prior-period adjustments as follows:

DTA/DTL adjustments:
To beginning retained earnings:

Subsidiary transactions:	Total Tax	Parent Share	Subsidiary Share
Remaining fixed asset profit.	$ 24,000	$ 18,000	$ 6,000
Amortization of excess (patent, 75% × $6,000) . . .	4,500	4,500	
Total.	$ 28,500	$ 22,500	$ 6,000
1. First tax (30%)	8,550	6,750	1,800
Net income after tax	$ 19,950	**$15,750**	$ 4,200
2. 20% × 30% × $15,750.	$ 945	$ 945	
3. Total tax (1. + 2.)	$ 9,495	$ 7,695	$ 1,800
Parent transactions:			
Beginning inventory	$ 24,000	$ 24,000	
4. First tax (30% × $24,000)	$ 7,200	$ 7,200	
Total increase in DTA and retained earnings (3. + 4.)	**$16,695**	**$14,895**	**$1,800**

(T2)   Adjust current-year tax provision and adjust deferred tax asset for the effects of current-year income adjustments:

Subsidiary transactions:	Total Tax	Parent Share	Subsidiary Share
Realized fixed asset profit	$ (8,000)	$(6,000)	$(2,000)
Amortization of excess (patent, 75% × $2,000) . . .	1,500	1,500	
1. Total	$ (6,500)	$(4,500)	$(2,000)
First tax (30% × 1.)	$ (1,950)	$(1,350)	$ (600)
20% × 30 × ($4,500 − $1,350) first tax.	(189)	(189)	
2. Total tax.	$ (2,139)	$(1,539)	$ (600)
Parent transactions:			
Beginning inventory	$(24,000)		
Ending inventory	16,000		
Total.	$ (8,000)		
3. First tax (30% × $8,000)	$ (2,400)	$(2,400)	
Increase (decrease) in DTA (2. + 3.)	$ (4,539)	$(3,939)	$ (600)

Subsidiary Company S Income Distribution

Amortizations	$2,000	Internally generated net income	$ 60,000
		Realized gain	8,000
		Adjusted income before tax....	$ 66,000
		Company S share of taxes (see tax schedule below the parent IDS schedule)	(19,950)
		Net income	$ 46,050
		NCI share (see schedule)......	11,400
		Controlling share...........	$ 34,650

Parent Company P Income Distribution

Ending inventory profit	$16,000	Internally generated net income	$ 80,000
		Beginning inventory profit.....	24,000
		Adjusted income before tax....	$ 88,000
		Company P share of taxes (30% × $88,000).........	(26,400)
		Company P net income	$ 61,600
		Controlling share of subsidiary net income (see schedule) ...	34,650
		Second tax on subsidiary income (30% × 20% × $34,650)...	(2,079)
		Controlling interest	$ 94,171

Subsidiary Tax Schedule	Controlling	NCI	Total
1. Total adjusted income............................	$49,500	$16,500	$66,000
2. NCI share of asset adjustments		500	500
3. Taxable income (1. + 2.)	$49,500	$17,000	$66,500
4. Tax (30% × 3.)	$14,850	$ 5,100	$19,950
Net-of-tax share of income (1. − 4.)	$34,650	$11,400	$46,050

UNDERSTANDING THE ISSUES

1. Par Company acquires 100% of the common stock of Sub Company for an agreed-upon price of $900,000. The book value of the net assets is $700,000, which includes $50,000 of subsidiary cash equivalents. Existing fixed assets have fair values greater than their recorded book values. How will this transaction affect the cash flow statement of the consolidated firm in the period of the purchase, if:

   a. Par Company pays $900,000 cash to purchase the stock?
   b. Par Company pays $500,000 cash and signs 5-year notes for $400,000? All Sub Company shareholders receive notes.
   c. Par Company exchanges only common stock with the shareholders of Sub Company?

2. What will be the effect of the above acquisition on cash flow statements prepared in periods after the year of the purchase?

3. P Company acquires 80% of the common stock of S Company for an agreed-upon price of $640,000. The fair value of the NCI is $160,000. The book value of the net assets is $600,000, which includes $50,000 of subsidiary cash equivalents. Any excess is attributable to goodwill. (A D&D schedule is suggested to properly calculate the NCI.) How will this transaction affect the cash flow statement of the consolidated firm in the period of the purchase, if:

   a. P Company pays $640,000 cash to purchase the stock?
   b. P Company pays $400,000 cash and signs 5-year notes for $240,000? 80% of the Company S shareholders receives notes.
   c. P Company exchanges only common stock with 80% of the shareholders of Company S?

4. Company P has internally generated net income of $250,000 (excludes share of subsidiary income). Company P has 100,000 shares of outstanding common stock. Subsidiary Company S has a net income of $60,000 and 40,000 shares of outstanding common stock. What is consolidated basic EPS, if:

   a. Company P owns 100% of the Company S shares?
   b. Company P owns 80% of the Company S shares?

5. Company P has internally generated net income of $200,000 (excludes share of subsidiary income). Company P has 100,000 shares of outstanding common stock. Subsidiary Company S has a net income of $60,000 and 40,000 shares of outstanding common stock. Company P owns 100% of the Company S shares. What is consolidated diluted EPS, if:

   a. Company S has outstanding stock options for Company S shares, which cause a dilutive effect of 2,000 additional shares of Company S shares?
   b. Company S has outstanding stock options for Company P shares, which cause a dilutive effect of 2,000 additional shares of Company P shares?
   c. Company P has outstanding stock options for Company P shares, which cause a dilutive effect of 2,000 additional shares of Company P shares?

6. Company S is an 80% owned subsidiary of Company P. For 2011, Company P reports internally generated income before tax of $100,000. Company S reports an income before tax of $40,000. A 30% tax rate applies to both companies. Calculate consolidated net income (after taxes) and the distribution of income to the controlling and noncontrolling interests, if:

   a. The consolidated firm meets the requirements of an affiliated firm and files a consolidated tax return.
   b. The consolidated firm does not meet the requirements of an affiliated firm and files separate tax returns. Assume an 80% dividend exclusion rate.

7. Company S is an 80% owned subsidiary of Company P. On January 1, 2011, Company P sells equipment to Company S at a $50,000 profit. Assume a 30% corporate tax rate and an 80% dividend exclusion. The equipment has a 5-year life. The question is, would taxes be paid on this profit and what adjustments (if needed) for the tax would be made, if:

a. Companies P and S are an "affiliated firm" and file a consolidated tax return?
b. Companies P and S are not an "affiliated firm" and file separate tax returns?

EXERCISES

Exercise 1 *(LO 1)* **Cash flow, issue stock, year of purchase.** Duckworth Corporation purchases an 80% interest in Panda Corporation on January 1, 2013, in exchange for 5,000 Duckworth shares (market value of $18) plus $155,000 cash. The fair value of the NCI is proportionate to the price paid by Duckworth for its interest. The appraisal shows that some of Panda's equipment, with a 4-year estimated remaining life, is undervalued by $20,000. The excess is attributed to goodwill. Panda Corporation's balance sheet on December 31, 2012 is shown below.

Assets		Liabilities and Equity	
Cash	$ 30,000	Current liabilities	$ 30,000
Inventory	30,000	Long-term liabilities	40,000
Property, plant, and equipment . . .	300,000	Common stock ($10 par)	150,000
Accumulated depreciation	(90,000)	Retained earnings	50,000
Total assets	$270,000	Total liabilities and equity	$270,000

Comparative balance sheet data are as follows:

	December 31, 2012 (Parent Only)	December 31, 2013 (Consolidated)
Cash	$ 100,000	$ 95,000
Inventory	60,000	84,200
Property, plant, and equipment	950,000	1,346,000
Accumulated depreciation	(360,000)	(575,000)
Goodwill		86,250
Current liabilities	(80,000)	(115,000)
Long-term liabilities	(100,000)	(130,000)
Noncontrolling interest		(63,250)
Controlling interest:		
Common stock ($10 par)	(350,000)	(400,000)
Additional paid-in capital in excess of par	(50,000)	(90,000)
Retained earnings	(170,000)	(238,200)
Totals	$ 0	$ 0

The following information relates to the activities of the two companies for 2013:

a. Panda pays off $10,000 of its long-term debt.
b. Duckworth purchases production equipment for $76,000.
c. Consolidated net income is $103,200; the NCI's share is $5,000. Depreciation expense taken by Duckworth and Panda on their separate books is $92,000 and $28,000, respectively.
d. Duckworth pays $30,000 in dividends; Panda pays $15,000.

Prepare the consolidated statement of cash flows for the year ended December 31, 2013, for Duckworth Corporation and its subsidiary, Panda Corporation.

Exercise 2 *(LO 1)* **Cash flow, subsequent to year of purchase.** Paridon Motors purchases an 80% interest in Snap Battery Company on January 1, 2012, for $700,000 cash. At that date, Snap Battery Company has the following stockholders' equity:

Common stock ($10 par)......................	$100,000
Paid-in capital in excess of par	300,000
Retained earnings	250,000
Total stockholders' equity....................	$650,000

Any excess of cost over book value is attributed to goodwill. A statement of cash flows is being prepared for 2015. For each of the following situations, indicate the impact on the cash flow statement for 2015:

1. Adjustment resulting from the original acquisition of the controlling interest.
2. Snap Battery Company issues 2,000 shares of common stock for $90 per share on January 1, 2015. At the time, the stockholders' equity of Snap Battery is $800,000. Paridon Motors purchases 1,000 shares.
3. Paridon Motors purchases at 102, $100,000 of face value, 10% annual interest bonds issued by Snap Battery Company at face value on January 1, 2013. Paridon purchases the bonds on January 1, 2015.
4. Snap Battery purchases a production machine from Paridon Motors on July 1, 2015, for $80,000. Paridon's cost is $60,000, and accumulated depreciation is $20,000.

Exercise 3 *(LO 1)* **Cash flow, cash payment, year of acquisition.** Banner Company acquires an 80% interest in Roller Company for $640,000 cash on January 1, 2013. The NCI has a fair value of $160,000. Any excess of cost over book value is attributed to goodwill. To help pay for the acquisition, Banner Company issues 5,000 shares of its common stock with a fair value of $70 per share. Roller's balance sheet on the date of the purchase is as follows:

Assets		Liabilities and Equity	
Cash	$ 20,000	Current liabilities	$110,000
Inventory	140,000	Bonds payable	100,000
Property, plant, and		Common stock ($10 par)........	200,000
equipment (net)................	550,000	Retained earnings	300,000
Total assets	$710,000	Total liabilities and equity	$710,000

Controlling share of net income for 2013 is $150,000, net of the noncontrolling interest of $10,000. Banner declares and pays dividends of $10,000, and Roller declares and pays dividends of $5,000. There are no purchases or sales of property, plant, or equipment during the year. Based on the following information, prepare a statement of cash flows using the indirect method for Banner Company and its subsidiary for the year ended December 31, 2013. Any supporting schedules should be in good form.

	Banner Company December 31, 2012	Consolidated December 31, 2013
Cash	$ 300,000	$ 219,000
Inventory	220,000	454,000
Property, plant, and equipment (net)...............	800,000	1,230,000
Goodwill		300,000
Current liabilities	(160,000)	(284,000)
Bonds payable	(200,000)	(300,000)
Noncontrolling interest		(169,000)
Controlling common stock ($10 par)...............	(200,000)	(250,000)
Controlling paid-in capital in excess of par	(300,000)	(600,000)
Retained earnings	(460,000)	(600,000)
Totals	$ 0	$ 0

Exercise 4 *(LO 3)* **Consolidated taxation, intercompany profits.** Deko Company purchases an 80% interest in the common stock of Farwell Company for $850,000 on January 1, 2017. At the time of the purchase, the total stockholders' equity of Farwell is $968,750. The fair value of the NCI is $212,500. The excess of cost over book value is attributed to a patent with a 10-year life.

During 2019, Deko Company and Farwell Company report the internally generated income before taxes as shown below.

	Deko Company	Farwell Company
Sales	$ 300,000	$120,000
Cost of goods sold	(200,000)	(90,000)
Gain on machine	5,000	
Expenses	(40,000)	(20,000)
Income before taxes	$ 65,000	$ 10,000

Farwell Company sells goods to Deko Company for $50,000. Deko Company has $20,000 of Farwell Company's goods in its beginning inventory and $6,000 of Farwell's goods in its ending inventory. Farwell Company sells goods to Deko Company at a gross profit of 40%.

Deko Company sells a new machine to Farwell Company on January 1, 2019, for $30,000. The machine has a 5-year life, and its cost is $25,000. The affiliated group files a consolidated tax return and is taxed at 30%.

Prepare a determination and distribution of excess schedule and a consolidated income statement for 2019. Include income distribution schedules for both companies.

Exercise 5 *(LO 3)* **Taxation as consolidated company.** On May 1, 2016, Taft Company acquires a 80% interest in Marcus Company for $400,000. The fair value of the NCI is $100,000. The following determination and distribution of excess schedule is prepared:

Determination and Distribution of Excess Schedule

	Implied Company Fair Value	Parent Price (80%)	NCI Value (20%)
Fair value of subsidiary	$ 500,000	$400,000	$100,000
Less book value of interest acquired:			
Common stock	$ 300,000		
Retained earnings	100,000		
Total equity	$ 400,000	$400,000	$400,000
Interest acquired		80%	20%
Book value		$320,000	$ 80,000
Excess of fair value over book value	$100,000	$ 80,000	$ 20,000

Adjustment of identifiable accounts:

	Adjustment	Amortization per Year	Life	Worksheet Key
Goodwill	**$100,000**			**debit D**

Goodwill, applicable to the parent's interest ($64,000), will be amortized over 15 years *for tax purposes only.*

Taft Company and Marcus Company have the following separate income statements for the year ended December 31, 2018:

	Taft Company	Marcus Company
Sales	$750,000	$570,000
Less cost of goods sold.	440,000	350,000
Gross profit	$310,000	$220,000
Less other expenses	200,000	140,000
Income before dividends	$110,000	$ 80,000
Dividends received	17,500	
Income before tax	$127,500	$ 80,000

During 2018, Marcus Company pays cash dividends of $25,000.

Prepare the entry to record income tax payable on each company's books. Assume a 30% corporate income tax rate.

Exercise 6 *(LO 4)* **Tax allocation with separate taxation.** The separate income statements of Coors Company and its 60% owned subsidiary, Vespa Company, for the year ended December 31, 2017, are as follows:

	Coors Company	Vespa Company
Sales	$520,000	$370,000
Less cost of goods sold.	350,000	180,000
Gross profit	$170,000	$190,000
Less operating expenses	100,000	90,000
Operating income	$ 70,000	$100,000
Subsidiary (dividend) income	12,600	
Income before tax	$ 82,600	$100,000
Provision for income tax	21,756	30,000
Net income	$ 60,844	$ 70,000

The following additional information is available:

a. Coors Company acquires its interest in Vespa Company on July 1, 2015. The excess of cost over book value is attributable to machinery which is undervalued by a total amount of $100,000. The remaining life of the machine is 20 years.

b. Vespa Company sells a machine to Coors Company on December 31, 2016, for $10,000. This machine has a book value of $6,000 and an estimated future life of four years at the purchase date. Straight-line depreciation is assumed.

c. Coors Company sells $15,000 worth of merchandise to Vespa Company during 2017. Cooper sells its merchandise at a price that enables it to realize a gross profit of 25%.

Vespa Company has $2,000 worth of Coors merchandise in its ending inventory.

d. A corporate income tax rate of 30% is assumed.

Prepare the worksheet adjustments (in journal entry format) pertaining to the purchase cost amortization and the intercompany transactions, and prepare the interperiod tax allocations that result from the elimination of the intercompany transactions. The companies do not qualify as an affiliated group under the tax code.

Exercise 7 *(LO 4)* **Separate taxation, intercompany transactions.** *(This is the same as Exercise 4 but with separate taxation.)* Dunker Company purchases an 80% interest in the common stock of Fennig Company for $850,000 on January 1, 2017. The fair value of the NCI is $212,500. At the time of the purchase, the total stockholders' equity of Fennig is $968,750. The price paid is $75,000 in excess of the book value of the controlling portion of Fennig equity. The excess is attributed to a patent with a 10-year life.

During 2019, Dunker Company and Fennig Company report the following internally generated income before taxes:

	Dunker Company	Fennig Company
Sales	$ 300,000	$120,000
Cost of goods sold	(200,000)	(90,000)
Gain on machine	5,000	
Expenses	(40,000)	(20,000)
Income before taxes	$ 65,000	$ 10,000

Fennig Company sells goods to Dunker Company for $50,000. Dunker Company has $20,000 of Fennig Company's goods in its beginning inventory and $6,000 of Fennig's goods in its ending inventory. Fennig Company sells goods to Dunker Company at a gross profit of 40%.

Dunker Company sells a new machine to Fennig Company on January 1, 2019, for $30,000. The machine has a 5-year life, and its cost is $25,000. The companies file separate tax returns. Both are subject to a 30% tax rate. Dunker receives an 80% dividend deduction.

Prepare a consolidated income statement for 2019. Include income distribution schedules for both companies.

PROBLEMS

Problem 6-1 *(LO 1)* **Comprehensive cash flow, indirect method.** Presented below are the consolidated workpaper balances of Bush, Inc., and its subsidiary, Dorr Corporation, as of December 31, 2016 and 2015:

Assets	2016	2015	Net Change Incr. (Decr.)
Cash	$ 313,000	$ 195,000	$118,000
Marketable equity securities (at cost)	175,000	175,000	0
Allowance to reduce marketable equity securities to market	(13,000)	(24,000)	11,000
Accounts receivable (net)	418,000	440,000	(22,000)
Inventories	595,000	525,000	70,000
Land	385,000	170,000	215,000
Plant and equipment	755,000	690,000	65,000
Accumulated depreciation	(199,000)	(145,000)	(54,000)
Goodwill	60,000	60,000	0
Total assets	$2,489,000	$2,086,000	$403,000

Liabilities and Stockholders' Equity			
Current portion of long-term note	$ 150,000	$ 150,000	$ 0
Accounts payable and accrued liabilities	595,000	474,000	121,000
Note payable, long-term	300,000	450,000	(150,000)
Deferred income taxes	44,000	32,000	12,000

(continued)

Liabilities and Stockholders' Equity			
Noncontrolling interest in net assets of subsidiary . . .	179,000	161,000	18,000
Common stock ($10 par).	580,000	480,000	100,000
Additional paid-in capital in excess of par	303,000	180,000	123,000
Retained earnings	338,000	195,000	143,000
Treasury stock (at cost)		(36,000)	36,000
Total liabilities and stockholders' equity	$2,489,000	$2,086,000	$ 403,000

Additional information:

a. On January 20, 2016, Bush, Inc., issues 10,000 shares of its common stock for land having a fair value of $215,000.
b. On February 5, 2016, Bush reissues all of its treasury stock for $44,000.
c. On May 15, 2016, Bush pays a cash dividend of $58,000 on its common stock.
d. On August 8, 2016, equipment is purchased for $127,000.
e. On September 30, 2016, equipment is sold for $40,000. The equipment costs $62,000 and has a net book value of $34,000 on the date of the sale.
f. On December 15, 2016, Dorr Corporation pays a cash dividend of $50,000 on its common stock.
g. Deferred income taxes represent timing differences relating to the use of accelerated depreciation methods for income tax reporting and the straight-line method for financial reporting.
h. Net income for 2016 is as follows:

Controlling interest in consolidated net income.	$201,000
Dorr Corporation.	110,000

i. Bush, Inc., owns 70% of Dorr Corporation. There is no change in ownership interest in Dorr during 2015 and 2016. There are no intercompany transactions other than the dividend paid to Bush by its subsidiary.

Required ▶ ▶ ▶ ▶ ▶   Prepare the statement of cash flows for the consolidated company using the indirect method. A cash analysis worksheet should be prepared to aid in the development of the statement. Any other supporting schedules should be in good form.

Problem 6-2 *(LO 1)* **Cash flow, year subsequent to purchase.** Mario Company is an 80% owned subsidiary of Lois Company. The interest in Mario is purchased on January 1, 2011, for $680,000 cash. The fair value of the NCI was $170,000. At that date, Mario has stockholders' equity of $650,000. The excess price is attributed to equipment with a 5-year life undervalued by $25,000 and to goodwill.

The following comparative consolidated trial balances apply to Lois Company and its subsidiary, Mario:

	December 31, 2011	December 31, 2012
Cash	16,000	19,500
Inventory	120,000	160,000
Accounts Receivable	200,000	300,000
Property, Plant, and Equipment	3,005,000	3,425,000
Accumulated Depreciation	(1,081,000)	(1,282,000)
Investment in Charles Corporation (30%)		244,500
Goodwill	125,000	125,000
Accounts Payable	(117,000)	(200,000)
Bonds Payable.	(100,000)	(450,000)
Noncontrolling Interest	(167,000)	(179,000)

	December 31, 2011	December 31, 2012
Controlling Interest:		
Common Stock (par)	(1,000,000)	(1,000,000)
Additional Paid-In Capital in Excess of Par	(650,000)	(650,000)
Retained Earnings	(351,000)	(513,000)
Totals	0	0

The 2012 information shown below is available for the Lois and Mario companies.

a. Mario purchases equipment for $70,000.
b. Mario issues $350,000 of long-term bonds and later uses the proceeds to purchase a new building.
c. On January 1, 2012, Lois purchases 30% of the outstanding common stock of Charles Corporation for $230,000. This is an influential investment. Charles's stockholders' equity is $700,000 on the date of the purchase. Any excess cost is attributed to equipment with a 10-year life. Charles reports net income of $80,000 in 2012 and pays dividends of $25,000.
d. Controlling share of consolidated income for 2012 is $262,000; the noncontrolling interest in consolidated net income is $15,000. Lois pays $100,000 in dividends in 2012; Mario pays $15,000 in dividends in 2012.

Prepare the consolidated statement of cash flows for 2012 using the indirect method. Any supporting calculations (including a determination and distribution of excess schedule) should be in good form. ◄ ◄ ◄ ◄ ◄ **Required**

Problem 6-3 *(LO 1)* **Cash flow, year of partial noncash purchase.** Billing Enterprises purchases a 90% interest in the common stock of Rush Corporation on January 1, 2011, for an agreed-upon price of $495,000. Billing issues $400,000 of bonds to Rush shareholders plus $95,000 cash as payment. Rush's balance sheet on the acquisition date is as follows:

Assets		Liabilities and Equity	
Cash	$ 60,000	Accounts payable	$ 45,000
Accounts receivable	95,000	Long-term liabilities	120,000
Plant assets (net).	460,000	Common stock ($10 par).	150,000
		Retained earnings	300,000
Total assets.	$615,000	Total liabilities and equity	$615,000

Rush's equipment is understated by $20,000 and has a remaining depreciable life of five years. Any remaining excess is attributed to goodwill.

In addition to the bonds issued as part of the purchase, Billing sells additional bonds in the amount of $100,000.

Consolidated net income for 2011 is $92,300. The controlling interest is $87,700, and the noncontrolling interest is $4,600. Rush pays $10,000 in dividends to all shareholders, including Billing Enterprises.

No plant assets are purchased or sold during 2011.

Comparative balance sheet data are as follows:

	December 31, 2010 (Parent Only)	December 31, 2011 (Consolidated)
Cash	$ 82,000	$ 187,700
Accounts receivable	120,000	161,000
Plant assets (net).	870,000	1,277,600
Goodwill		80,000
Accounts payable	(52,000)	(80,000)
Bonds payable		(500,000)
		(continued)

	December 31, 2010 (Parent Only)	December 31, 2011 (Consolidated)
Long-term liabilities	(80,000)	(40,000)
Noncontrolling interest		(58,600)
Controlling interest:		
Common stock ($10 par)	(200,000)	(200,000)
Additional paid-in capital in excess of par	(300,000)	(300,000)
Retained earnings	(440,000)	(527,700)
Totals	$ 0	$ 0

Required ▶ ▶ ▶ ▶ ▶   Prepare a consolidated statement of cash flows using the indirect method for the year ended December 31, 2011. Supporting schedules (including a D&D schedule) should be in good form.

Problem 6-4 *(LO 2)* **Consolidated EPS.** On January 1, 2012, Peanut Corporation acquires an 80% interest in Sunny Corporation. Information regarding the income and equity structure of the two companies as of the year ended December 31, 2014, is as follows:

	Peanut Corporation	Sunny Corporation
Internally generated net income	$55,000	$56,000
Common shares outstanding during the year	20,000	12,000
Warrants to acquire Peanut stock, outstanding during the year	2,000	1,000
5% convertible (into Sunny's shares), $100 par preferred shares, outstanding during the year		800
Nonconvertible preferred shares outstanding	1,000	

Additional information is as follows:

a. The warrants to acquire Peanut stock are issued in 2013. Each warrant can be exchanged for one share of Peanut common stock at an exercise price of $12 per share.
b. Each share of convertible preferred stock can be converted into two shares of Sunny common stock. The preferred stock pays an annual dividend totaling $4,000. Peanut owns 60% of the convertible preferred stock.
c. The nonconvertible preferred stock is issued on July 1, 2014, and pays a 6-month dividend totaling $500.
d. Relevant market prices per share of Peanut common stock during 2014 are as follows:

	Average
First quarter	$10
Second quarter	12
Third quarter	13
Fourth quarter	16

Required ▶ ▶ ▶ ▶ ▶   Compute the basic and diluted consolidated EPS for the year ended December 31, 2014. Use quarterly share averaging.

Problem 6-5 *(LO 3)* **Worksheet, consolidated taxation, simple equity, inventory, fixed asset sale.** On January 1, 2011, Pillar Company purchases an 80% interest in Stark Company for $890,000. On the date of acquisition, Stark has total owners' equity of $800,000. Buildings, which have a 20-year life, are undervalued by $200,000. The remaining excess of cost over book value is attributable to goodwill. For tax purposes only, goodwill is amortized over 15 years.

On January 1, 2011, Stark sells equipment, with a net book value of $60,000, to Pillar for $100,000. The equipment has a 5-year remaining life. Straight-line depreciation is used.

During 2013, Pillar sells $70,000 worth merchandise to Stark. As a result of these intercompany sales, Stark holds beginning inventory $40,000 and ending inventory of $30,000. At December 31, 2013, Stark owes Pillar $8,000 from merchandise sales. Pillar has a gross profit rate of 50%. Neither company has provided for income tax. The companies qualify as an affiliated group and, thus, will file a consolidated tax return based on a 30% corporate tax rate. The original purchase is not a nontaxable exchange.

Trial balances of Pillar and Stark December 31, 2013, are as follows:

	Pillar Company	Stark Company
Cash	208,600	380,000
Accounts Receivable	130,000	150,000
Inventory	120,000	80,000
Investment in Stark	1,098,000	
Plant and Equipment ...	600,000	900,000
Accumulated Depreciation (amortization)	(350,000)	(300,000)
Liabilities	(205,000)	(150,000)
Deferred Tax Liability 2013	(3,600)	
Common Stock ...	(500,000)	(300,000)
Retained Earnings	(950,000)	(700,000)
Sales	(800,000)	(550,000)
Cost of Good	430,000	320,000
Depreciation	60,000	50,000
Other Exp	210,000	120,000
Subsidi	(48,000)	
	0	0

Consolidated worksheet based on the trial balances. Include a provision for income tax ◄ ◄ ◄ ◄ ◄ **Required**
...tion and distribution of excess schedule, and income distribution schedules.

---

following information for Problems 6-6 and 6-7:
January 1, 2011, Parson Company acquires an 80% interest in Solar Company for ...000. Solar had the following balance sheet on the date of acquisition:

Solar Company
Balance Sheet
January 1, 2011

Assets		Liabilities and Equity	
Accounts receivable	$ 60,000	Accounts payable	$ 70,000
Inventory	80,000	Bonds payable	100,000
Land	120,000	Common stock	10,000
Buildings	250,000	Paid-in capital in excess	
Accumulated depreciation	(50,000)	of par	190,000
Equipment	120,000	Retained earnings	170,000
Accumulated depreciation	(70,000)		
Goodwill	30,000		
Total assets	$540,000	Total liabilities and equity ...	$540,000

Buildings, which have a 20-year life, are undervalued by $70,000. Equipment, which has a 5-year life, is undervalued by $50,000. Any remaining excess of cost over book value is attributable to goodwill, which has a 15-year life for tax purposes only.

Problem 6-6 *(LO 3)* **Worksheet, consolidate taxation, simple equity, inventory, fixed asset sale.** Refer to the preceding facts for son's acquisition of Solar common stock. Parson uses the simple equity method to account for investment in Solar. During 2012, Solar sells $30,000 worth of merchandise to Parson. As a r t of these intercompany sales, Parson holds beginning inventory of $12,000 and ending ntory of $16,000 of merchandise acquired from Solar. At December 31, 2012, Parson ow ar $6,000 from merchandise sales. Solar has a gross profit rate of 30%.

On January 1, 2011, Parson sells equipment having a n k value of $50,000 to Solar for $80,000. The equipment has a 5-year useful life and is iated using the straight-line method.

Neither company has provided for income tax. The comp alify as an affiliated group and, thus, will file a consolidated tax return based on a 40% e tax rate. The original purchase is not a nontaxable exchange.

On December 31, 2012, Parson and Solar have the following ces:

	n	Solar Company
Cash	v	
Accounts Receivable		
Inventory	1	54,000
Land..	10	90,000
Investment in Solar................................	567	90,000
Buildings	800,	50,000
Accumulated Depreciation	(250,0	
Equipment	210,00	900
Accumulated Depreciation	(115,000	no)
Accounts Payable	(70,000)	
Bonds Payable.....................................		
Deferred Tax Liability (goodwill amortization)	(2,880)	
Common Stock	(100,000)	(
Paid-In Capital in Excess of Par	(600,000)	(19
Retained Earnings, January 1, 2012.................	(622,400)	(222,
Sales	(890,000)	(350,0
Cost of Goods Sold	480,000	220,00
Depreciation Expense—Buildings...................	30,000	10,000
Depreciation Expense—Equipment.................	25,000	10,000
Other Expenses	150,000	60,000
Interest Expense...................................		8,000
Subsidiary Income.................................	(33,600)	
Dividends Declared................................	20,000	10,000
Totals	0	0

Required ▶ ▶ ▶ ▶ ▶

1. Prepare a determination and distribution of excess schedule.
2. Prepare a consolidated worksheet for the year ended December 31, 2012. Include a provision for income tax and income distribution schedules.

Problem 6-7 *(LO 3)* **Worksheet, consolidated taxation, simple equity, inventory, fixed asset sale, later year.** Refer to the preceding facts for Parson's acquisition of Solar common stock. Parson uses the simple equity method to account for its investment in Solar. During 2013, Solar sells $40,000 worth of merchandise to Parson. As a result of these intercompany sales, Parson holds beginning inventory of $16,000 and ending inventory of $10,000 of merchandise acquired from Solar. At December 31, 2013, Parson owes Solar $8,000 from merchandise sales. Solar has a gross profit rate of 30%.

During 2013, Parson sells $60,000 worth of merchandise to Solar. Solar holds $15,000 of this merchandise in its ending inventory. Solar owes $10,000 to Parson as a result of these intercompany sales. Parson has a gross profit rate of 40%.

During 2013, Pillar sells $70,000 worth of merchandise to Stark. As a result of these intercompany sales, Stark holds beginning inventory of $40,000 and ending inventory of $30,000. At December 31, 2013, Stark owes Pillar $8,000 from merchandise sales. Pillar has a gross profit rate of 50%.

Neither company has provided for income tax. The companies qualify as an affiliated group and, thus, will file a consolidated tax return based on a 30% corporate tax rate. The original purchase is not a nontaxable exchange.

Trial balances of Pillar and Stark as of December 31, 2013, are as follows:

	Pillar Company	Stark Company
Cash	208,600	380,000
Accounts Receivable	130,000	150,000
Inventory	120,000	80,000
Investment in Stark	1,098,000	
Plant and Equipment	600,000	900,000
Accumulated Depreciation	(350,000)	(300,000)
Liabilities	(205,000)	(150,000)
Deferred Tax Liability (goodwill amortization)	(3,600)	
Common Stock	(500,000)	(300,000)
Retained Earnings, January 1, 2013	(950,000)	(700,000)
Sales	(800,000)	(550,000)
Cost of Goods Sold	430,000	320,000
Depreciation Expense	60,000	50,000
Other Expenses	210,000	120,000
Subsidiary Income	(48,000)	
Totals	0	0

Prepare a consolidated worksheet based on the trial balances. Include a provision for income tax, a determination and distribution of excess schedule, and income distribution schedules. ◄ ◄ ◄ ◄ ◄ **Required**

Use the following information for Problems 6-6 and 6-7:

On January 1, 2011, Parson Company acquires an 80% interest in Solar Company for $500,000. Solar had the following balance sheet on the date of acquisition:

Solar Company
Balance Sheet
January 1, 2011

Assets		Liabilities and Equity	
Accounts receivable	$ 60,000	Accounts payable	$ 70,000
Inventory	80,000	Bonds payable	100,000
Land	120,000	Common stock	10,000
Buildings	250,000	Paid-in capital in excess	
Accumulated depreciation	(50,000)	of par	190,000
Equipment	120,000	Retained earnings	170,000
Accumulated depreciation	(70,000)		
Goodwill	30,000		
Total assets	$540,000	Total liabilities and equity	$540,000

Buildings, which have a 20-year life, are undervalued by $70,000. Equipment, which has a 5-year life, is undervalued by $50,000. Any remaining excess of cost over book value is attributable to goodwill, which has a 15-year life for tax purposes only.

Problem 6-6 *(LO 3)* **Worksheet, consolidated taxation, simple equity, inventory, fixed asset sale.** Refer to the preceding facts for Parson's acquisition of Solar common stock. Parson uses the simple equity method to account for its investment in Solar. During 2012, Solar sells $30,000 worth of merchandise to Parson. As a result of these intercompany sales, Parson holds beginning inventory of $12,000 and ending inventory of $16,000 of merchandise acquired from Solar. At December 31, 2012, Parson owes Solar $6,000 from merchandise sales. Solar has a gross profit rate of 30%.

On January 1, 2011, Parson sells equipment having a net book value of $50,000 to Solar for $80,000. The equipment has a 5-year useful life and is depreciated using the straight-line method.

Neither company has provided for income tax. The companies qualify as an affiliated group and, thus, will file a consolidated tax return based on a 40% corporate tax rate. The original purchase is not a nontaxable exchange.

On December 31, 2012, Parson and Solar have the following trial balances:

	Parson Company	Solar Company
Cash	46,080	54,000
Accounts Receivable	150,600	90,000
Inventory	105,000	90,000
Land	100,000	150,000
Investment in Solar	567,200	
Buildings	800,000	250,000
Accumulated Depreciation	(250,000)	(70,000)
Equipment	210,000	120,000
Accumulated Depreciation	(115,000)	(90,000)
Accounts Payable	(70,000)	(40,000)
Bonds Payable		(100,000)
Deferred Tax Liability (goodwill amortization)	(2,880)	
Common Stock	(100,000)	(10,000)
Paid-In Capital in Excess of Par	(600,000)	(190,000)
Retained Earnings, January 1, 2012	(622,400)	(222,000)
Sales	(890,000)	(350,000)
Cost of Goods Sold	480,000	220,000
Depreciation Expense—Buildings	30,000	10,000
Depreciation Expense—Equipment	25,000	10,000
Other Expenses	150,000	60,000
Interest Expense		8,000
Subsidiary Income	(33,600)	
Dividends Declared	20,000	10,000
Totals	0	0

Required ▶ ▶ ▶ ▶ ▶

1. Prepare a determination and distribution of excess schedule.
2. Prepare a consolidated worksheet for the year ended December 31, 2012. Include a provision for income tax and income distribution schedules.

Problem 6-7 *(LO 3)* **Worksheet, consolidated taxation, simple equity, inventory, fixed asset sale, later year.** Refer to the preceding facts for Parson's acquisition of Solar common stock. Parson uses the simple equity method to account for its investment in Solar. During 2013, Solar sells $40,000 worth of merchandise to Parson. As a result of these intercompany sales, Parson holds beginning inventory of $16,000 and ending inventory of $10,000 of merchandise acquired from Solar. At December 31, 2013, Parson owes Solar $8,000 from merchandise sales. Solar has a gross profit rate of 30%.

During 2013, Parson sells $60,000 worth of merchandise to Solar. Solar holds $15,000 of this merchandise in its ending inventory. Solar owes $10,000 to Parson as a result of these intercompany sales. Parson has a gross profit rate of 40%.

On January 1, 2011, Parson sells equipment having a net book value of $50,000 to Solar for $80,000. The equipment has a 5-year useful life and is depreciated using the straight-line method.

On January 1, 2013, Solar sells equipment to Parson at a profit of $25,000. The equipment has a 5-year useful life and is depreciated using the straight-line method.

Neither company has provided for income tax. The companies qualify as an affiliated group and, thus, will file a consolidated tax return based on a 40% corporate tax rate. The original purchase is not a nontaxable exchange.

On December 31, 2013, Parson and Solar have the following trial balances:

	Parson Company	Solar Company
Cash	49,760	80,000
Accounts Receivable	150,600	100,000
Inventory	115,000	120,000
Land	100,000	150,000
Investment in Solar	604,000	
Buildings	900,000	250,000
Accumulated Depreciation	(290,000)	(80,000)
Equipment	210,000	120,000
Accumulated Depreciation	(140,000)	(100,000)
Accounts Payable	(50,000)	(40,000)
Bonds Payable		(100,000)
Deferred Tax Liability (goodwill amortization)	(5,760)	
Common Stock	(100,000)	(10,000)
Paid-In Capital in Excess of Par	(600,000)	(190,000)
Retained Earnings, January 1, 2013	(747,000)	(238,000)
Sales	(950,000)	(400,000)
Cost of Goods Sold	550,000	250,000
Depreciation Expense—Buildings	40,000	10,000
Depreciation Expense—Equipment	25,000	10,000
Other Expenses	176,000	75,000
Interest Expense		8,000
Gain on Sale of Fixed Asset		(25,000)
Subsidiary Income	(57,600)	
Dividends Declared	20,000	10,000
Totals	0	0

1. Prepare a determination and distribution of excess schedule.   ◄ ◄ ◄ ◄ ◄ **Required**
2. Prepare a consolidated worksheet for the year ended December 31, 2013. Include a provision for income tax and income distribution schedules.

Problem 6-8 *(LO 3)* **Consolidated income statement, affiliated firm for tax.** On January 1, 2011, Delta Corporation exchanges 12,000 shares of its common stock for an 80% interest in Morgan Company. The stock issued has a par value of $10 per share and a fair value of $20 per share. On the date of purchase, Morgan has the following balance sheet:

Common stock ($2 par)	$ 20,000
Paid-in capital in excess of par	50,000
Retained earnings	100,000
Total equity	$170,000

On the purchase date, Morgan has equipment with an 8-year remaining life that is undervalued by $20,000. Any remaining excess cost is attributed to goodwill.

There are intercompany merchandise sales. During 2012, Delta sells $20,000 of merchandise to Morgan. Morgan sells $30,000 of merchandise to Delta. Morgan has $2,000 of Delta goods in its beginning inventory and $4,200 of Delta goods in its ending inventory. Delta has

$2,500 of Morgan goods in its beginning inventory and $3,000 of Morgan goods in its ending inventory. Delta's gross profit rate is 40%; Morgan's is 25%.

On July 1, 2011, Delta sells a machine to Morgan for $90,000. The book value of the machine on Delta's books is $50,000 at the time of the sale. The machine has a 5-year remaining life. Depreciation on the machine is included in expenses.

The consolidated group meets the requirements of an affiliated group under the tax law and files a consolidated tax return. The original purchase is not structured as a nontaxable exchange.

Delta uses the cost method to record its investment in Morgan. Since Morgan has never paid dividends, Delta has not recorded any income on its investment in Morgan. The two companies prepare the following income statements for 2012:

	Delta Corporation	Morgan Company
Sales	$1,000,000	$600,000
Less cost of goods sold.	800,000	375,000
Gross profit	$ 200,000	$225,000
Less expenses	80,000	185,000
Income before tax	$ 120,000	$ 40,000

Required ▶ ▶ ▶ ▶ ▶ Prepare a determination and distribution of excess schedule. Prepare the 2012 consolidated net income in schedule form. Include eliminations and adjustments. Provide income distribution schedules to allocate consolidated net income to the controlling and noncontrolling interests.

Problem 6-9 *(LO 3)* **Worksheet, consolidated taxation, simple equity, inventory, land.** On January 1, 2011, Pepper Company purchases 80% of the common stock of Salty Company for $270,000. On this date, Salty has total owners' equity of $300,000. The excess of cost over book value is due to goodwill. For tax purposes, goodwill is amortized over 15 years.

During 2011, Pepper appropriately accounts for its investment in Salty using the simple equity method.

During 2011, Pepper sells merchandise to Salty for $50,000, of which $10,000 is held by Salty on December 31, 2011. Pepper's gross profit on sales is 40%.

During 2011, Salty sells some land to Pepper at a gain of $10,000. Pepper still holds the land at year-end. Pepper and Salty qualify as an affiliated group for tax purposes and, thus, will file a consolidated tax return. Assume a 30% corporate income tax rate.

The following trial balances are prepared on December 31, 2011:

	Pepper Company	Salty Company
Inventory, December 31	100,000	50,000
Other Current Assets	198,000	200,000
Investment in Salty Company.	302,000	
Land.	240,000	100,000
Buildings and Equipment.	300,000	200,000
Accumulated Depreciation	(80,000)	(60,000)
Current Liabilities.	(150,000)	(50,000)
Long-Term Liabilities	(200,000)	(100,000)
Common Stock	(100,000)	(50,000)
Paid-In Capital in Excess of Par	(180,000)	(100,000)
Retained Earnings	(320,000)	(150,000)
Sales	(500,000)	(300,000)
Cost of Goods Sold	300,000	180,000
Operating Expenses	100,000	80,000
Subsidiary Income.	(40,000)	
Gain on Sale of Land.		(10,000)
Dividends Declared.	30,000	10,000
Totals	0	0

Prepare a consolidated worksheet for Pepper Company and subsidiary Salty Company for the year ended December 31, 2011. Include the determination and distribution of excess schedule and the income distribution schedules. ◄ ◄ ◄ ◄ ◄ **Required**

Use the following information for Problems 6-10 and 6-11:

On January 1, 2011, Penske Company acquires an 80% interest in Stock Company for $450,000. Stock has the following balance sheet on the date of acquisition:

Stock Company
Balance Sheet
January 1, 2011

Assets		Liabilities and Equity	
Accounts receivable	$ 60,000	Accounts payable	$ 70,000
Inventory	80,000	Bonds payable	100,000
Land.....................	120,000	Common stock.............	10,000
Buildings	250,000	Paid-in capital in excess	
Accumulated depreciation ...	(50,000)	of par.................	190,000
Equipment	120,000	Retained earnings	170,000
Accumulated depreciation ...	(70,000)		
Goodwill	30,000		
Total assets..............	$540,000	Total liabilities and equity ..	$540,000

Buildings, which have a 20-year life, are undervalued by $100,000. Equipment, which has a 5-year life, is undervalued by $50,000. Any remaining excess of cost over book value is attributable to goodwill.

Problem 6-10 *(LO 4)* **Worksheet, separate tax, simple equity, inventory, fixed asset sale, analyze price.** Refer to the preceding facts for Penske's acquisition of Stock common stock. Penske uses the simple equity method to account for its investment in Stock. During 2012, Stock sells $30,000 worth of merchandise to Penske. As a result of these inter-company sales, Penske holds beginning inventory of $12,000 and ending inventory of $16,000 of merchandise acquired from Stock. At December 31, 2012, Penske owes Stock $6,000 from merchandise sales. Stock has a gross profit rate of 30%.

On January 1, 2011, Penske sells equipment having a net book value of $50,000 to Stock for $90,000. The equipment has a 5-year useful life and is depreciated using the straight-line method.

Penske and Stock do not qualify as an affiliated group for tax purposes and, thus, will file separate tax returns. Assume a 40% corporate tax rate and an 80% dividends received exclusion.

On December 31, 2012, Penske and Stock have the following trial balances:

	Penske Company	Stock Company
Cash	92,400	53,200
Accounts Receivable......................................	150,600	90,000
Inventory	105,000	90,000
Land..	100,000	120,000
Investment in Stock	503,120	
Buildings	800,000	250,000
Accumulated Depreciation	(250,000)	(70,000)
Equipment	210,000	120,000
Accumulated Depreciation	(115,000)	(90,000)

(continued)

	Penske Company	Stock Company
Goodwill		30,000
Accounts Payable	(70,000)	(40,000)
Current Tax Liability.	(82,640)	(16,800)
Bonds Payable.		(100,000)
Deferred Tax Liability (see note below)	(4,250)	
Common Stock	(100,000)	(10,000)
Paid-In Capital in Excess of Par	(600,000)	(190,000)
Retained Earnings, January 1, 2012.	(617,683)	(221,200)
Sales	(890,000)	(350,000)
Cost of Goods Sold	480,000	220,000
Depreciation Expense—Buildings.	30,000	10,000
Depreciation Expense—Equipment.	25,000	10,000
Other Expenses	150,000	60,000
Interest Expense.		8,000
Provision for Income Tax (see note below).	83,613	16,800
Subsidiary Income.	(20,160)	
Dividends Declared.	20,000	10,000
Totals	0	0

Note:

Provision for income taxes (Penske):

Current ($205,000 × 40%)	$82,000
Stock dividends ($8,000 × 20% × 40%)	640
	$82,640
Current deferred taxes [($20,160 − $8,000) × 20% × 40%].	973*
Provision for income taxes	$83,613

Deferred tax liability (Penske):

Current deferred taxes [($20,160 − $8,000) × 20% × 40%].	$ 973*
Change in Stock retained earnings [80% × ($221,200 − $170,000) × 20% × 40%]	3,277*
Deferred tax liability	$4,250

*Differences due to rounding.

Required ▶ ▶ ▶ ▶ ▶

1. Prepare a value analysis and a determination and distribution of excess schedule.
2. Prepare a consolidated worksheet for the year ended December 31, 2012. Include a provision for income tax and income distribution schedules.

Problem 6-11 *(LO 4)* **Worksheet, separate tax, simple equity, inventory, fixed asset sale, analyze price, later year.** Refer to the preceding facts for Penske's acquisition of Stock common stock. Penske accounts for its investment in Stock using the simple equity method, including income tax effects. During 2013, Stock sells $40,000 worth of merchandise to Penske. As a result of these intercompany sales, Penske holds beginning inventory of $16,000 and ending inventory of $10,000 of merchandise acquired from Stock. At December 31, 2013, Penske owes Stock $8,000 from merchandise sales. Stock has a gross profit rate of 30%.

During 2013, Penske sells $60,000 worth of merchandise to Stock. Stock holds $15,000 of this merchandise in its ending inventory. Stock owes $10,000 to Penske as a result of these intercompany sales. Penske has a gross profit rate of 40%.

On January 1, 2011, Penske sells equipment having a net book value of $50,000 to Stock for $90,000. The equipment has a 5-year useful life and is depreciated using the straight-line method.

On January 1, 2013, Stock sells equipment to Penske at a profit of $25,000. The equipment has a 5-year useful life and is depreciated using the straight-line method.

Penske and Stock do not qualify as an affiliated group for tax purposes and, thus, will file separate tax returns. Assume a 40% corporate tax rate and an 80% dividends received exclusion.

On December 31, 2013, Penske and Stock have the following trial balances:

	Penske Company	Stock Company
Cash	91,760	78,400
Accounts Receivable	150,600	100,000
Inventory	115,000	120,000
Land	100,000	120,000
Investment in Stock	529,680	
Buildings	900,000	250,000
Accumulated Depreciation	(290,000)	(80,000)
Equipment	210,000	120,000
Accumulated Depreciation	(140,000)	(100,000)
Goodwill		30,000
Accounts Payable	(50,000)	(40,000)
Current Tax Liability	(64,240)	(28,800)
Bonds Payable		(100,000)
Deferred Tax Liability (see note below)	(6,375)	
Common Stock	(100,000)	(10,000)
Paid-In Capital in Excess of Par	(600,000)	(190,000)
Retained Earnings, January 1, 2013	(739,230)	(236,400)
Sales	(950,000)	(400,000)
Cost of Goods Sold	550,000	250,000
Depreciation Expense—Buildings	40,000	10,000
Depreciation Expense—Equipment	25,000	10,000
Other Expenses	176,000	75,000
Interest Expense		8,000
Gain on Sale of Fixed Asset		(25,000)
Provision for Income Taxes (see note below)	66,365	28,800
Subsidiary Income	(34,560)	
Dividends Declared	20,000	10,000
Totals	0	0

Note:

Provision for income taxes (Penske):

Current ($159,000 × 40%)	$63,600
Stock dividends ($8,000 × 20% × 40%)	640
	$64,240
Current deferred taxes [($34,560 − $8,000) × 20% × 40%]	2,125[a]
Provision for income taxes	$66,365

Deferred tax liability (Penske):

Current deferred taxes [($34,560 − $8,000) × 20% × 40%]	$2,125[a]
Change in Stock retained earnings [80% × ($236,400 − $170,000) × 20% × 40%]	4,250[a]
Deferred tax liability	$6,375

[a]Differences due to rounding.

1. Prepare a value analysis and a determination and distribution of excess schedule.
2. Prepare a consolidated worksheet for the year ended December 31, 2013. Include a provision for income tax and income distribution schedules.

◀ ◀ ◀ ◀ ◀ **Required**

Problem 6-12 *(LO 4)* **Worksheet, separate tax, simple equity, inventory, fixed asset sale.** On January, 1, 2011, Perko Company acquires 70% of the common stock of Solan Company for $385,000 in a taxable combination. On this date, Solan has total owners' equity of $422,000, including retained earnings of $222,000. The excess of cost over book value is attributable to goodwill.

During 2011 and 2012, Solan Company reports the following information:

	2011	2012
Net income before taxes	$40,000	$40,000
Dividends.	0	30,000

During 2011 and 2012, Perko appropriately accounts for its investment in Solan using the simple equity method, including income tax effects.

On January 1, 2012, Perko holds merchandise acquired from Solan for $10,000. During 2012, Solan sells merchandise to Perko for $60,000, of which $20,000 is held by Perko on December 31, 2012. Solan's usual gross profit on affiliated sales is 30%.

On December 31, 2011, Perko sells some equipment to Solan, with a cost of $40,000 and a book value of $18,000. The sales price is $39,000. Solan is depreciating the equipment over a 3-year life, assuming no salvage value and using the straight-line method.

Perko and Solan do not qualify as an affiliated group for tax purposes and, thus, will file separate tax returns. Assume a 30% corporate tax rate and an 80% dividends received deduction.

The following trial balances are prepared by Perko and Solan on December 31, 2012:

	Perko Company	Solan Company
Accounts Receivable	282,576	295,000
Inventory	110,000	85,000
Land.	150,000	90,000
Investment in Solan	422,800	
Buildings	200,000	200,000
Accumulated Depreciation	(100,000)	(50,000)
Equipment	120,000	80,000
Accumulated Depreciation	(35,000)	(20,000)
Goodwill		
Accounts Payable	(120,000)	(80,000)
Current Tax Liability.	(31,260)	(24,000)
Bonds Payable.	(200,000)	(100,000)
Discount (premium)		
Deferred Tax Liability.	(2,268)	
Common Stock—Solan		(10,000)
Paid-In Capital in Excess of Par—Solan.		(190,000)
Retained Earnings—Solan.		(250,000)
Common Stock—Perko	(100,000)	
Paid-In Capital in Excess of Par—Perko.	(200,000)	
Retained Earnings—Perko.	(450,000)	
Sales	(590,000)	(370,000)
Cost of Goods Sold	340,000	220,000
Depreciation Expense—Buildings.	15,000	8,000
Depreciation Expense—Equipment.	20,000	12,000
Other Expenses	115,000	50,000
Interest Expense.		
Provision for Tax	32,352	24,000
Subsidiary Income.	(39,200)	
Dividends Declared—Solan		30,000
Dividends Declared—Perko	60,000	
Totals	0	0

Note:

Provision for income taxes (Perko):

Current ($100,000 × 30%)	$30,000
Solan dividends ($21,000 × 20% × 30%).................................	1,260
	$31,260
Current deferred taxes [($39,200 − $21,000) × 20% × 30%]...................	1,092
Provision for income taxes	$32,352

Deferred tax liability (Perko):

Current deferred taxes [($39,200 − $21,000) × 20% × 30%]...................	$1,092
Change in Solan retained earnings [70% × ($250,000 − $222,000) × 20% × 30%]	1,176
Deferred tax liability	$2,268

Prepare a consolidated worksheet for Perko Company and subsidiary Solan Company for the ◄ ◄ ◄ ◄ ◄ **Required** year ended December 31, 2012. Include the determination and distribution of excess schedule and the income determination schedules.

Special Issues in Accounting for an Investment in a Subsidiary

Learning Objectives

When you have completed this chapter, you should be able to

1. **Consolidate a subsidiary when a parent purchases stock directly from the subsidiary.**

2. **Account for purchases of additional shares of a subsidiary by the parent.**

3. **Demonstrate the accounting procedures for a complete or partial sale of the investment in a subsidiary.**

4. **Explain the issues surrounding preferred stock in the equity structure of the subsidiary, and follow the procedures used when the parent owns subsidiary preferred stock.**

5. **Solve balance-sheet-only problems (CPA Exam issue). (Appendix)**

This chapter considers several issues concerning the acquisition and sale of a parent's interest in a subsidiary. The first concern is special purchase situations. A parent may purchase its controlling interest directly from the subsidiary at the time of original issue. Procedures also are developed for parent ownership interests that are acquired in a series of separate purchases over time.

This chapter then will consider the issues involved when a parent company sells all or a portion of its controlling interest in a subsidiary. Not only must the sale be properly recorded, but special care must also be taken in accounting for any portion of the investment retained.

The final equity concern of the chapter is the procedure needed in consolidation when the subsidiary has preferred stock in its equity structure. An apportionment of retained earnings may be needed in order to properly account for the parent's interest in common stock. If the parent owns any subsidiary preferred stock, it must be treated as retired in the consolidation process.

The chapter concludes with an appendix that provides the consolidation procedures needed when a worksheet is used to produce only a consolidated balance sheet. These procedures are really only of concern when preparing for the CPA Exam. The Exam may use this approach to save time and space. It is not a worksheet that is used in practice since the accountant must prepare a consolidated income statement, a consolidated statement of retained earnings, and a consolidated balance sheet. There would be no practical reason to use a worksheet for only one of the three statements.

PARENT ACQUISITION OF STOCK DIRECTLY FROM SUBSIDIARY

1

OBJECTIVE

Consolidate a subsidiary when a parent purchases stock directly from the subsidiary.

A parent company may organize a new corporation and supply all of the common stock equity funds in exchange for all of the newly organized company's common stock. Since the newly formed corporation receives the funds directly, there will be no difference between the price paid for the shares and the equity in assets acquired. Thus, the determination and distribution of excess (D&D) schedule will show no excess of cost over book value or excess of book value over cost.

In other cases, the parent company will allow the newly organized subsidiary to sell a portion of the shares to persons outside the consolidated group. If the shares are sold to outsiders at a price equal to the price paid by the parent, the cost and book value again will be equal. However, if a price greater or less than the price paid by the parent is charged to outside parties, an excess of cost or book value will result. This excess occurs because the total price paid by the parent will not equal its ownership interest multiplied by the total subsidiary common stockholders' equity. Normally, the excess of cost is recorded as goodwill, and an excess of book value is recorded as a gain.

An existing corporation might sell a sufficient number of new shares to grant a controlling interest to the buying company. For example, assume Company S had the following equity balances prior to a sale of shares to Company P:

Common stock ($10 par, 10,000 shares)	$100,000
Paid-in capital in excess of par	150,000
Retained earnings	220,000
Total stockholders' equity.	$470,000

Assume Company S sells 30,000 additional shares directly to Company P at $50 per share, for a total of $1,500,000. Subsequent to the sale, the equity balances of Company S appear as follows:

Common stock ($10 par, 40,000 shares)	$ 400,000
Paid-in capital in excess of par	1,350,000
Retained earnings	220,000
Total stockholders' equity.	$1,970,000

A determination and distribution of excess schedule must be prepared for this investment as it would be for any acquisition of a controlling interest. There is no direct connection between the price paid and the interest in subsidiary equity received. It is assumed that the NCI shares are also worth $40 per share. The monies paid become a part of the subsidiary's total equity. The interest purchased is a 75% interest (30,000 of 40,000 shares) in the total equity after the sale of the new shares, not a 100% interest in the funds provided by the specific sale of the new shares purchased by the parent. The following determination and distribution of excess schedule would be prepared for the interest purchased by the parent:

Determination and Distribution of Excess Schedule

	Company Implied Fair Value	Parent Price (75%)	NCI Value (25%)
Fair value of subsidiary	$2,000,000*	$1,500,000	$ 500,000
Less book value of interest acquired:			
Common stock ($10 par).	$ 400,000		
Paid-in capital in excess of par	1,350,000		
Retained earnings	220,000		
Total stockholders' equity.	$1,970,000	$1,970,000	$1,970,000
Interest acquired		75%	25%
Book value.		$1,477,500	$ 492,500
Excess of fair value over book value	**$ 30,000**	$ 22,500	$ 7,500

Adjustment of identifiable accounts:

	Adjustment	Worksheet Key
Goodwill.	**$ 30,000**	**debit D**

*$1,500,000/75%

The excess would be distributed to identifiable accounts using normal purchase rules. Any remaining excess, as in this example, would be considered goodwill.

REFLECTION

- The purchase of a controlling interest directly from the subsidiary still requires the preparation of a D&D schedule.

Parent Purchase of Additional Subsidiary Shares

Chapter 2 included consideration of a situation where a potential parent company may own less than a controlling interest in another company and then buy additional shares to obtain control. The previously owned shares are adjusted to fair values and are combined with the newly acquired shares to create a single D&D schedule for the combined set of shares.

The current concern is that of a parent company that already owns a controlling interest in a subsidiary Company B and then purchases additional shares. For example, Company P may already own a 60% interest in a subsidiary and already be consolidating its financial statements since it has control over Company S. If Company P acquires another 20% interest, how is it accounted for? The purchase is viewed as the retirement of existing outstanding shares by the consolidated entity. Since the consolidated firm is a single reporting entity, the reacquisition of parent or subsidiary shares is a reduction of total equity.

Applying the retirement theory means that the rules for retirement are the same as for any retirement of shares.

- There can never be an income statement gain or loss.
- If the price paid to reacquire the shares is less than their book value, there is a credit to paid-in capital in excess of par from retirement.
- If the price paid to reacquire the shares exceeds their book value, the debit first is used to reduce existing paid-in capital in excess of par from retirement and the balance is a debit to Retained Earnings.

The complication in applying this approach is that you cannot compare the price paid for the reacquired shares to the subsidiary book value. Instead, **the price paid has to be compared to the NCI value as established on the day control was achieved.**

As an example, assume that Company P purchased its original 60% (6,000 shares) controlling interest in Company S on January 1, 2011, for $126,000. On that date, Company S had the following balance sheet:

Assets		Liabilities and Equity	
Current assets	$ 50,000	Liabilities	$ 40,000
Equipment (net)	150,000	Common stock ($10 par,	
		10,000 shares)	100,000
		Retained earnings	60,000
Total assets.	$200,000	Total liabilities and equity . . .	$200,000

Assume that equipment has a fair value of $180,000 with a 5-year remaining life. Any remaining excess is attributed to goodwill. The D&D schedule shown on page 374 would be prepared for the 60% purchase.

2

OBJECTIVE

Account for purchases of additional shares of a subsidiary by the parent.

Determination and Distribution of Excess Schedule

	Company Implied Fair Value	Parent Price (60%)	NCI Value (40%)
Fair value of subsidiary	$210,000*	$126,000	$ 84,000
Less book value of interest acquired:			
Common stock ($10 par)	$100,000		
Retained earnings	60,000		
Total stockholders' equity	$160,000	$160,000	$160,000
Interest acquired		60%	40%
Book value		$ 96,000	$ 64,000
Excess of fair value over book value	**$ 50,000**	$ 30,000	$ 20,000

Adjustment of identifiable accounts:

	Adjustment	Amortization per Year	Life	Worksheet Key
Equipment	$ 30,000	$ 6,000	5	**debit D1**
Goodwill	**20,000**			**debit D2**
Total	**$ 50,000**			

*$126,000/60% (assumes value of NCI is proportionate to price paid by parent)

On January 1, 2013, Company P acquired another 2,000 shares from NCI shareholders for $25 each, for a total of $50,000. Further assume that the Company S retained earnings on that date was $100,000, a $40,000 increase since the date of the purchase of the original 60% interest. The difference between the $50,000 price paid and the January 1, 2013, NCI balance is the adjustment of parent company equity caused by the acquisition of the shares. The following analysis is prepared for the new 20% interest:

Price paid for 20% interest, 50% of then existing 40% NCI		$50,000
Less book value of NCI interest purchased:		
Common stock ($10 par, 2,000 shares)	$ 20,000	
Retained earnings, January 1, 2013 (20% × $100,000)	20,000	
Total book value of interest purchased		40,000
Excess of cost over book value		$10,000
Excess attributed to change in NCI:		
Original excess cost for company	$ 50,000	
Amortizations to date (2 years × $6,000)	(12,000)	
Balance	$ 38,000	
NCI adjustment applicable to shares purchased	× 20%	7,600
Balance, adjustment to parent paid-in capital in excess of par (unless there is none, then adjustment is to parent retained earnings)		$ 2,400

This $2,400 adjustment becomes a part the distribution of the excess on future worksheets. This adjustment to the parent's paid-in capital in excess of par would be made on each subsequent consolidated worksheet.

Worksheet 7-1: page 396   The additional worksheet procedures that arise from this piecemeal acquisition are shown in Worksheet 7-1 on pages 396 to 397. The trial balances of Companies P and S are shown as they would appear on December 31, 2013. The investment in Company S account is based on the use of the simple equity method during the current and previous years. The December 31, 2013, balance was determined as shown on page 375.

Cost of **60%** investment (January 1, 2011)		$ 126,000
Add equity share of change in Company S retained earnings as of January 1, 2013:		
Balance, January 1, 2013 . . . . **$100,000**		
Balance, January 1, 2011 . . . . **60,000**		
Increase in retained earnings . . . . **$ 40,000 × 60%** =		24,000
Cost of **20%** investment (January 1, 2013)		50,000
Add equity share of Company S 2013 net income (**80%** × $35,000)		28,000
Investment account balance, December 31, 2013		**$228,000**

In journal entry form, the eliminations are as follows:

(CY)	Eliminate current-year entries to record subsidiary income:		
	Subsidiary Income	28,000	
	Investment in Company S		28,000
(EL)	Eliminate 80% of subsidiary equity against investment account:		
	Common Stock—(Company S)	80,000	
	Retained Earnings, January 1, 2013—Company S	80,000	
	Investment in Company S		160,000
(D/NCI)	Distribute excess on 2011, 60% investment and the NCI adjustment:		
(D1)	Equipment	30,000	
(D2)	Goodwill	20,000	
	Investment in Company S		30,000
	Retained Earnings—Company S (for NCI)		20,000
(A1)	Adjust depreciation on equipment for 60% purchase:		
	Retained Earnings—Company P (2 years × 60% × $6,000) . .	7,200	
	Retained Earnings—Company S (2 years × 40% × $6,000) . .	4,800	
	Expenses	6,000	
	Accumulated Depreciation—Equipment		18,000
(D3)	Distribute excess on 2013, 20% investment:		
	Retained Earnings—Company S (NCI)	7,600	
	Retained Earnings—Company P (adjustment for retirement) . . .	2,400	
	Investment in Company S		10,000

The correctness of the $7,600 debit to NCI is confirmed as follows:

NCI adjustment on January 1, 2011	$20,000
Depreciation adjustment (2 years × $6,000 × 40% NCI share)	(4,800)
Balance on January 1, 2013	$15,200
½ of 40% NCI share	× 50%
Applicable to 20% total retired	$ 7,600

The consolidated net income of $79,000 is distributed to the controlling and noncontrolling interests as shown in the income distribution schedules (IDS) that accompany Worksheet 7-1. The $6,000 amortization of excess attributed to equipment depreciation is a debit on the subsidiary's IDS.

When investment blocks are carried at cost, each investment must be converted separately to its simple equity balance as of the beginning of the year. For each investment, the adjustment is based on the change in subsidiary retained earnings between the date of acquisition of the individual investment and the beginning of the current year.

The determination and distribution of excess schedule for the second purchase should consider existing unrealized intercompany profits recorded by the subsidiary. Suppose the subsidiary of the previous example sold merchandise to the parent during 2012, and a $2,000 subsidiary profit is included in the parent's ending inventory of merchandise and in the subsidiary retained earnings. *In theory*, the determination and distribution of excess schedule prepared for the 20% investment purchased on January 1, 2013, should reflect the unrealized gross profit on sales applicable to the 20% interest purchased. Thus, the determination and distribution of excess schedule would be revised to distribute the excess as follows:

Excess of cost over book value.			$10,000
Excess attributed to change in NCI:			
Original excess cost for company	$ 50,000		
Amortizations to date (2 years × $6,000)	(12,000)		
Balance	$ 38,000		
NCI adjustment applicable to shares purchased	× 20%	$7,600	
Adjustment for unrealized inventory profit ($2,000 × 20%).		(400)	7,200
Balance, adjustment to parent paid-in capital in excess of par (unless			
there is none, then adjustment is to parent retained earnings)			$ 2,800

The deferred gross profit on the inventory sale means that the NCI just acquired is overstated since the profit already is included in retained earnings. The decrease in the equity acquired increases the excess of cost over book value and increases the negative impact of the retirement on equity.

The following entry would distribute the revised excess on the 2013 worksheet:

Retained Earnings—Company S (NCI)	7,600	
Retained Earnings—Company P	2,800	
Deferred Gross Profit on Inventory Sale		400
Investment in Company S		10,000

The following elimination for the $2,000 profit in the beginning inventory then would be made:

Retained Earnings—Controlling Interest (60% interest at time of original sale) . . .	1,200	
Retained Earnings—NCI (20%)	400	
Deferred Gross Profit on Inventory Sale	400	
Cost of Goods Sold (beginning inventory)		2,000

In practice, the concept of materiality often will prevail, and the above procedure may not be followed. The determination and distribution of excess schedule may not recognize the deferred inventory profit, which will result in the lesser debit to Retained Earnings. Under this practical approach, worksheets for periods subsequent to the second purchase will ignore the deferred profit existing on the purchase date and will distribute the retained earnings adjustment according to the ownership percentages existing at the time the worksheet is prepared. In this example, the 20% profit applicable to the inventory on the second purchase date would be allocated to the parent with the following adjustment on the worksheet:

Retained Earnings—Controlling Interest (80%)	1,600	
Retained Earnings—NCI (20%)	400	
Cost of Goods Sold (beginning inventory)		2,000

REFLECTION

- The acquisition of additional shares of a subsidiary is viewed as the retirement of those shares.

- When control already exists at the time the parent purchases another block of subsidiary stock, a second D&D schedule is prepared. The purpose of the schedule is to determine the impact of the "retirement" on controlling equity.

SALE OF PARENT'S INVESTMENT IN COMMON STOCK

3

OBJECTIVE

Demonstrate the accounting procedures for a complete or partial sale of the investment in a subsidiary.

A parent may sell some or all of its subsidiary interest. When control is lost through the sale of enough shares to fall below the 50% interest generally required for consolidated reporting, a gain or loss on the transaction is recorded. There may be other subsidiary stock sales where the parent reduces its percentage interest but still has control after the sale. Such a sale is considered to be the sale of the shares to NCI shareholders.

Sale of Entire Investment

The sale of the entire investment in a subsidiary terminates the need for consolidated financial statements. In fact, when a sale occurs during the parent's fiscal year, the results of the subsidiary operations prior to the sale date are not consolidated. In recording the sale of the investment in a subsidiary, the accountant's primary concern is to adjust the carrying value of the investment so that the correct dollar effect on the sale can be recorded. The results of the subsidiary's operations up to the date of sale must be reported in one of two ways: (a) the net results of operations as a separate line item in the determination of income from continuing operations or (b) as a disposal of a component of an entity.

The accountant must determine if the sale of the investment in a subsidiary constitutes a disposal of a component of an entity. FASB ASC 205-20-20 states:

> *A component of an entity comprises operations and cash flows that can be clearly distinguished, operationally and for financial reporting purposes, from the rest of the entity. A component of an entity may be a reportable segment or an operating segment, a reporting unit, a subsidiary, or an asset group.*[1]

Not all subsidiaries qualify as components of an entity. For example, a parent may own several subsidiaries engaged in mining coal. If one subsidiary is sold, that would not constitute a sale of a component on an entity since the parent still is involved in coal mining. When the sale of a subsidiary qualifies as a disposal of a component of an entity, both the gain or loss on the sale and the results of operations for the period are shown net of tax in a separate discontinued operations section of the income statement. When the sale does not qualify as a disposal of a component on an entity, the gain or loss and the results of operations for the period usually are shown on the income statement as a part of the normal recurring operations.

The complexities of properly recording the sale of an entire subsidiary investment are shown in the following example. Suppose Company P purchased an 80% interest in Company S on January 1, 2011, for $250,000, and the determination and distribution of excess schedule was prepared as shown on page 378.

---

1 FASB ASC 205-20-20 *Presentation of Financial Statements—Discontinued Operations—Glossary* (Norwalk, CT).

Determination and Distribution of Excess Schedule

	Company Implied Fair Value	Parent Price (80%)	NCI Value (20%)
Fair value of subsidiary	$312,500	$250,000	$ 62,500
Less book value of interest acquired:			
Common stock	$100,000		
Retained earnings	150,000		
Total equity	$250,000	$250,000	$250,000
Interest acquired		80%	20%
Book value		$200,000	$ 50,000
Excess of fair value over book value	**$ 62,500**	$ 50,000	$ 12,500

Adjustment of identifiable accounts:

	Adjustment	Life	Amortization per Year	Worksheet Key
Equipment	$ 25,000	5	5,000	**debit D1**
Goodwill.	37,500			**debit D2**
Total	**$ 62,500**			

Company S earned $40,000 in 2011 and $25,000 in 2012. Company P sells the entire 80% interest on January 1, 2013, for $320,000. Assuming the use of the simple equity method, Company P's separate statements reflect the following:

Purchase price	$250,000
Share of subsidiary income, 2011, 80% × $40,000	32,000
Share of subsidiary income, 2012, 80% × $25,000	20,000
Investment in Company S, December 31, 2012	$302,000

The investment account and the parent's January 1, 2013, retained earnings balance reflect a $52,000 increase as a result of subsidiary operations in 2011 and 2012. On this basis, it appears that there is an $18,000 gain on the sale of the investment ($320,000 selling price less $302,000 simple-equity-adjusted cost). This result does not agree, however, with the consolidated financial statements prepared for 2011 and 2012, which included as expenses the amortizations of excess required by the determination and distribution of excess schedule. The parent's share of subsidiary income appeared as follows in the consolidated statements:

	2011	2012	Total
Share of subsidiary income to Company P (80%)	$32,000	$20,000	$52,000
Less amortization of excess of cost of investment over book value:			
Adjustment for depreciation on equipment: ($25,000 ÷ 5 = $5,000 per year) × 80% interest	(4,000)	(4,000)	(8,000)
Net increase in Company P income due to ownership of Company S investment	$28,000	$16,000	$44,000

Thus, while Company P's investment account shows a $52,000 share of Company S income, the consolidated statements reflect only $44,000, the difference being caused by the $8,000 of amortizations indicated by the determination and distribution of excess schedule. Clearly, the recording of the sale of the parent's interest must be based on the $44,000 share of income, since that amount of income is shown on the prior income statements of the consolidated company. Before recording the sale of the investment, Company P must adjust its books to be consistent with prior consolidated statements. In other words, it must adjust its investment to show the balance under the sophisticated equity method. The entry needed will adjust the January 1, 2013, retained earnings account on the separate books of the parent to the December 31, 2012, balance of the controlling interest in retained earnings shown on the consolidated statements. The adjusting entry on the books of Company P is as follows:

Retained Earnings, January 1, 2013.	8,000	
Investment in Company S.		8,000
To adjust the investment account and Company P retained earnings		
account for the parent's share of amortizations made on past		
consolidated statements.		

If the sophisticated equity method was used, the amortizations would be reflected already in the investment account and no adjustment would be needed.

Under either equity method, the entry to record the sale then would be as follows:

Cash	320,000	
Investment in Company S ($302,000 – $8,000)		294,000
Gain on Disposal of Subsidiary		26,000
To record the gain on the sale of the 80% interest in Company S.		

Note that the $8,000 adjusting entry for the past years' amortizations of excess normally would have been made on the consolidated worksheet for 2013. However, since there will be no further consolidations, the adjustment must be made directly on Company P's books. The gain (net of tax) on the disposal of the subsidiary will appear as a separate item on the income statement for 2013 if the sale of the subsidiary meets the criteria for a disposal of a component on an entity.

Since there will no longer be a consolidation, the NCI adjustments will no longer be made. The former subsidiary company will report as an independent entity, and its equity balances will not be affected by the prior adjustments that were required as part of the consolidation process.

In this example, if Company P had used the cost method, the investment account still would be shown at the original cost of $250,000. It then would be necessary to update the investment and retained earnings accounts on the separate books of Company P to include its $44,000 (net of amortizations) share of subsidiary income for 2011 and 2012. This adjustment would allow the accounts of the parent on January 1, 2013, to conform to past consolidated statements. The following entries would be made on the books of Company P to record the sale of the parent's 80% interest:

Investment in Company S	44,000	
Retained Earnings, January 1, 2013		44,000
To record the parent's share of subsidiary income as shown on		
prior years' consolidated statements.		

Cash	320,000	
Investment in Company S ($250,000 + $44,000).		294,000
Gain on Disposal of Subsidiary		26,000

It also is necessary to adjust the investment account for any unrealized intercompany gains and losses. These profits would have been deferred in the most recent consolidated statement, but under the cost or simple equity method they are not reflected in the investment account. Again, we must adjust the investment account to reflect the income reported in past consolidated statements. Suppose the parent had on hand at the sale date inventory on which the subsidiary recorded a $1,000 profit. Since the parent owns an 80% interest, the adjusting entry on the day the investment is sold would be as follows:

Retained Earnings	800	
Investment in Company S.		800

Assume the investment in the previous example was sold for $320,000 on July 1, 2013, and Company S reported income of $12,000 for the first six months of 2013. Since Company S will not be a part of the consolidated group at the end of the period, the results of its operations will not be consolidated with those of the parent. Therefore, the parent must record its share of subsidiary income for the current period to the date of disposal. The parent's net share of subsidiary income would be calculated on a basis consistent with past consolidated statements, as follows:

Share of subsidiary income for first six months to Company P (80%)	$ 9,600
Less amortization of excess of cost over book value that would have been made on	
consolidated statements:	
Equipment depreciation adjustment ($5,000 per year × ½ year × 80% interest)	(2,000)
Net share of subsidiary income.	$ 7,600

The parent would proceed to record the July 1, 2013, sale of its subsidiary investment as follows:

1. Assuming the past use of the simple equity method, the parent's investment account on January 1, 2013, is adjusted to reflect the amortizations made on past consolidated statements (as calculated on page 378).

Retained Earnings, January 1, 2013.	8,000	
Investment in Company S.		8,000

2. The parent's share of subsidiary income for the partial year is recorded. This amount is the $7,600 income net of amortizations (as calculated above).

Investment in Company S	7,600	
Investment income		7,600

3. The sale of the investment for $320,000 is recorded.

Cash	320,000	
Investment in Company S.		301,600
Gain on Disposal of Subsidiary		18,400

The adjusted cost of the investment is determined as follows:

Original cost, January 1, 2011.	$250,000
Simple equity income adjustments for 2011 and 2012	52,000
Amortization of excess (entry 1)	(8,000)
Share of Company S income for six months (entry 2)	7,600
Net cost, July 1, 2013	$301,600

Sale of Portion of Investment

The sale of a portion of an investment in a subsidiary requires unique treatment, depending on whether effective control is lost as a result of the sale. Special procedures must also be used when a sale of a partial interest occurs during a reporting period.

Loss of Control. A parent may sell a portion of its investment in a subsidiary so that it loses control. This situation may occur for foreign subsidiaries when the foreign government passes a law forbidding control of its companies by nonresidents. Such a sale also may be made to avoid consolidating affiliated companies. For example, a parent company may not want to include in its statements, the results of financing units that have large amounts of debt. If control is lost, consolidation procedures no longer will apply. This situation would require that the parent company books be adjusted to make them consistent with prior consolidated statements. Exactly the same adjusting entries as in the immediately preceding section are needed to adjust the parent's investment account. Note that the adjustments are made for the *entire interest* previously owned, not just the portion sold. If, in the preceding example, Company P sells one-half instead of all of its 80% interest, the investment account should be adjusted for the entire 80% interest in past and current years' subsidiary income, net of amortizations. The 40% interest sold must be adjusted to properly record the sale, and the 40% interest retained also must be adjusted, since it no longer will be consolidated. Past adjustments that would be handled as part of the annual consolidation process now must be made directly to the investment account, so that the investment remaining conforms with FASB ASC 323, *Investments—Equity Method and Joint Ventures*. The sophisticated equity method should be applied to remaining interests of 20% or more.[2]

If one-half of Company P's investment of the preceding section is sold for $160,000 on July 1, 2013, the following entries would be recorded:

1. Assuming the past use of the simple equity method, the parent's investment account on January 1, 2013, is adjusted to reflect the amortizations made on past consolidated statements.

Retained Earnings, January 1, 2013.	8,000	
Investment in Company S.		8,000

2. The parent's share of subsidiary income for the partial year is recorded. This amount is the $7,600 income net of amortizations.

Investment in Company S	7,600	
Operating Income of Former Subsidiary		7,600

3. The sale of one-half of the investment for $160,000 is recorded. The resulting gain is always ordinary income and never a gain from a "discontinued segment."

Cash	160,000	
Investment in Company S (½ of $301,600 adjusted cost calculated on page 380).		150,800
Gain on Sale of Investment		9,200

The remaining 40% investment will not be consolidated. It will be accounted for as an "influential" investment under the sophisticated equity method.

Control Retained. A parent company may sell a portion of its investment in a subsidiary but still have an interest that provides control even after the sale. For example, assume that on January 1, 2011, a parent purchased from outside parties 8,000 of the total 10,000 shares of a subsidiary. On January 1, 2013, the parent sold 2,000 shares and thereby lowered its percentage of ownership to 60%. Since the parent still had control, the 2,000 shares were sold, in essence, to NCI shareholders. Such a sell-down is considered to be a sale of additional shares to NCI shareholders. The parent has chosen to sell subsidiary shares, instead of parent shares, to raise additional equity capital. **There can be no income statement gains or losses resulting from any stock issuances by the consolidated entity.** This transaction would impact only paid-in capital in excess of par.

To illustrate the recording of such a partial sale, return to the example for which a determination and distribution of excess schedule was prepared on page 378. Assume that on January 1, 2013, Company P sells 2,000 subsidiary shares to lower its total interest to 60%. **Only the portion of the investment account sold is to be adjusted to the sophisticated equity method** to allow the

---

2 ASC 323-10-15-8, *Investments, Equity Method and Joint Ventures*, FASB (Norwalk, CT).

proper recording of the sale. The 60% remaining interest need not be adjusted on Company P's books since all amortization adjustments on the 60% interest will be made on future consolidated statements. The adjustment of the 20% interest on the separate books of Company P must agree with the treatment of that interest in prior consolidated statements. Assuming the use of the simple equity method, the portion of the investment sold must be adjusted for its share of the past amortizations made on consolidated statements. The annual amortization of the excess attributable to the equipment is $5,000. The amount applicable to the 20% interest sold is 20% of $5,000, or $1,000 per year. The adjustment for the prior two years would be as follows:

Retained Earnings, January 1, 2013.	2,000	
Investment in Company S.		2,000
To adjust for amortizations made on previous consolidated statements		
for the portion of the subsidiary investment sold.		

To record the sale of the investment, the parent would remove from its books **one-fourth** of the simple-equity-adjusted cost of January 1, 2013, as follows:

Simple equity adjusted cost of investment (page 378).	$302,000
	× 25%
¼ of 80% interest sold.	$ 75,500
Less amortizations of excess on 20% interest	(2,000)
Adjusted investment balance.	$ 73,500

If the sale price is greater than $73,500, then an increase in the paid-in capital in excess of par would be recorded, as shown in the following entry to record the sale of the investment for $80,000:

Cash	80,000	
Investment in Company S [(¼ × $302,000) – $2,000		
amortization adjustment]		73,500
Paid-In Capital in Excess of Par, Company P		6,500

If the sale price is less than $73,500, then a reduction of the paid-in capital in excess of par would be recorded. If there is not an adequate amount of paid-in capital in excess of par, Retained Earnings is debited.

If the parent in the previous example had used the cost method, only the portion of the investment sold would be adjusted to the sophisticated equity method on the parent's books. The analysis on page 378 shows that the parent's 80% share of income for 2011 and 2012 was $44,000 on a consolidated basis, net of amortizations. The interest sold must be adjusted by **one-fourth** (20% out of 80%) of $44,000, or $11,000. The remaining 60% will be adjusted in future worksheets. The entry to adjust the 20% interest would be as follows:

Investment in Company S	11,000	
Retained Earnings, January 1, 2013.		11,000
To adjust for the parent's share of past consolidated income		
pertaining to the interest sold.		

The parent then would proceed to record the sale of the investment for $80,000 as follows:

Cash	80,000	
Investment in Company S (¼ of original $250,000 cost + $11,000		
equity income)		73,500
Paid-In Capital in Excess of Par, Company P		6,500

Intraperiod Sale of a Partial Interest. When a sale of an interest during the reporting period does not result in loss of control, careful analysis is needed to ensure that the worksheet adheres to consolidation theory. Referring to the situation on pages 381–382, assume Company P sells **one-fourth** of its 80% interest for $80,000 on July 1, 2013, and subsidiary income for the first half of the year is $12,000. Assuming the use of the simple equity method, the parent would adjust its own investment and the beginning-of-year retained earnings accounts for the amortizations of excess cost recorded on the prior years' consolidated worksheets. The adjustment would be recorded as follows:

Retained Earnings, January 1, 2013.	2,000	
Investment in Company S.		2,000
To record 20% of the $10,000 amortizations for 2011 and 2012.		

A parent using the cost method would adjust the retained earnings for the subsidiary income, net of amortizations, for 2011 and 2012 (1/4 × $44,000 income on a consolidated basis).

Next, the parent would calculate its share of subsidiary income for the first half of 2013 applicable to the 20% interest sold and adjusted for partial-year amortizations of excess relating to that portion of the investment as follows:

Income on 20% interest in Company S sold (20% × $12,000)	$2,400
Less amortizations of excess of cost over book value that would be	
necessary on consolidated statements:	
Equipment depreciation adjustment ($5,000 per year × ½ year ×	
20% interest sold)	(500)
Net share of income on interest sold	$1,900

The parent then would make a sophisticated equity method adjustment for this income and record the sale as follows:

Investment in Company S	1,900	
Subsidiary Income.		1,900
To record share of first six months' subsidiary income applicable to the		
20% interest sold and adjusted for partial-year amortizations of excess		
relating to that portion of the investment.		
Cash	80,000	
Investment in Company S [(¼ × $302,000) – $2,000 amortizations +		
$1,900 income]		75,400
Paid-In Capital in Excess of Par—Company P		4,600
To record sale of 20% interest in subsidiary.		

The sale of a partial interest that does not result in loss of control requires special procedures on the consolidated worksheet for the period in which the sale occurs. Worksheets of later periods would not include any complications resulting from the sale. In Worksheet 7-2 on pages 400 to 401, the following should be noted: **Worksheet 7-2:** page 400

1. The investment in Company S account reflects its simple equity balance on December 31, 2013, for the remaining 60% interest held. The balance is computed as follows:

December 31, 2012, balance applicable to remaining (60%) interest held at	
year-end, ¾ × $302,000.	$226,500
Add **60%** of subsidiary reported income of $30,000* for 2013	18,000
Simple equity balance, December 31, 2013	$244,500

*This is for all of 2013 and includes the $12,000 reported in the first half of the year.

2. The balance in Paid-In Capital in Excess of Par—Company P is the increase in equity from the parent's ¼ interest sold.
3. The balance in Subsidiary Income includes **60%** of the subsidiary's $30,000 2013 income, plus the $1,900 earned on the **20%** interest prior to its sale.

In journal entry form, the eliminations are as follows:

(NCI)	Transfer income on interest sold to NCI and record amortizations of excess on interest sold:		
	Subsidiary Income......................................	1,900	
	Income Sold to NCI		1,900
(CY)	Eliminate current-year entries to record subsidiary income:		
	Subsidiary Income......................................	18,000	
	Investment in Company S............................		18,000
(EL)	Eliminate subsidiary equity against investment account on 60% investment still owned:		
	Common Stock—Company S	60,000	
	Retained Earnings, January 1, 2013—Company S	129,000	
	Investment in Company S.............................		189,000
(D)/(NCI)	Distribute excess and NCI adjustment:		
(D1)	Equipment	25,000	
(D2)	Goodwill	37,500	
	Investment in Company S (60% of original total excess on D&D)		37,500
	Retained Earnings—Company S (NCI) (40% of original total excess on D&D)		25,000
(A)	Adjust depreciation on equipment:		
	Retained Earnings—Company P (2 years × $5,000 × 60% remaining interest)	6,000	
	Retained Earnings—Company S (2 years × $5,000 × 40% current NCI)	4,000	
	Expenses	5,000	
	Accumulated Depreciation—Equipment		15,000

Carefully study the income distribution schedules for Worksheet 7-2. The NCI receives its 40% interest in subsidiary adjusted income of $25,000 for the entire year, but there is a deduction for the income purchased from the parent for the first six months. The parent company income distribution schedule claims 60% of the subsidiary income for the entire year plus a 20% interest in the first six months' income.

If the parent had used the cost method, there would be few changes in Worksheet 7-2. Entry (NCI) would be unchanged; however, an entry would be needed to convert the remaining 60% interest to the simple equity method at the beginning of the year. Entry (CY) would not be applicable since there would be no current-year equity adjustment to reverse. Remaining entries would remain the same.

Complications Resulting from Intercompany Transactions. When a sale of subsidiary stock results in loss of control, the parent should adjust its investment account on the date of the sale for its share of unrealized subsidiary gains and losses resulting from intercompany transactions. When control is not lost as the result of a sale of subsidiary shares, the adjustment on the consolidated worksheet for unrealized gains and losses resulting from previous intercompany transactions need be recorded only as it applies to the interest sold. The remaining controlling interest's share of these gains and losses can be adjusted on subsequent consolidated worksheets. On these worksheets, retained earnings adjustments for unrealized gains and losses would be distributed according to the relative ownership interests existing on the dates the worksheets are prepared.

REFLECTION

- When the parent's entire investment in a subsidiary is sold, the investment must be adjusted to the sophisticated equity method to properly record the gain or loss. The gain or loss may qualify as a gain or loss on a discontinued operation.

- If a portion of the investment in a subsidiary is sold and control is lost, the entire investment is still adjusted to the sophisticated equity method. This allows the correct gain or loss to be calculated on the interest sold. The remaining investment is also then restated at the sophisticated equity balance.

- If a portion of the investment in a subsidiary is sold, but control is retained, only the block sold is adjusted to the sophisticated equity balance. This allows the correct calculation of the increases or decreases of the parent's paid-in capital in excess of par resulting from the sale of the interest. The remaining investment will still be consolidated and may be accounted for under the cost, equity, or sophisticated equity method. Special procedures are needed for the current-year portion of income on the interest sold.

SUBSIDIARY PREFERRED STOCK

4

OBJECTIVE

Explain the issues surrounding preferred stock in the equity structure of the subsidiary, and follow the procedures used when the parent owns subsidiary preferred stock.

The existence of preferred stock in the capital structure of a subsidiary complicates the calculation of a parent's claim on subsidiary retained earnings, both at the time of acquisition and in the preparation of subsequent consolidated statements. In previous examples, the subsidiary had only common stock outstanding, so that all retained earnings were associated with common stock, and the parent had a claim on subsidiary retained earnings in proportion to its ownership interest. When a subsidiary has preferred stock outstanding, however, the preferred stock also may have a claim on retained earnings. This claim may be caused by a liquidation value in excess of par value and/or by participation and cumulative dividend rights. When these conditions exist, the retained earnings must be divided between the preferred and common stockholder interests.

Once retained earnings are allocated between the common and preferred stockholders, the intercompany investments can be eliminated. The investment in subsidiary common stock account will be eliminated against the total equity claim of the common stockholders. If there is an investment in subsidiary preferred stock account, it will be eliminated against the preferred stockholders' total equity.

Determination of Preferred Shareholders' Claim on Retained Earnings

The allocation of the retained earnings to the preferred and common stockholder interests is accomplished by employing the procedures used to calculate the book value of preferred and common stock. Although typically covered in intermediate accounting, the topic will be reviewed briefly in the following paragraphs.

The preferred shareholders' claim on retained earnings equals the claim they would have if the company was dissolved. In addition to the par value of the preferred shares, there may be a stipulated liquidation value in excess of par and/or dividend preferences. In the rare case of a liquidation value in excess of par, an amount equal to the liquidation bonus (liquidation value less par value) must be segregated from retained earnings as a preferred shareholder claim. Liquidation values should not be confused with paid-in capital in excess of par, which results from the sale of preferred shares. Such paid-in capital is not available to preferred shareholders in liquidation and is not part of the book value of preferred shares. Instead, it becomes part of the total paid-in capital in excess of par that is available to common shareholders.

In addition to a liquidation bonus, there must be an analysis of any cumulative and/or participation clauses applicable to the preferred stock. Other than the effect of a liquidation bonus, if the preferred stock is noncumulative and nonparticipating, the preferred stockholders would have no claim and all the retained earnings attach to the common stock. However, if there are preferred shareholder claims resulting from cumulative and/or participation clauses, these claims reduce the retained earnings applicable to the common stock. For example, if the preferred stock is noncumulative but fully participating, the retained earnings are allocated pro rata according to the total par or stated values of the preferred and common stock. If the preferred stock is cumulative but nonparticipating and, for example, has two years' dividends in arrears, a claim on retained earnings equal to the two years of dividends exists, although there is no liability to pay the preferred dividends until a dividend is declared.

When preferred stock is both cumulative and fully participating, the arrearage for prior periods is met first. The remaining retained earnings are allocated pro rata according to the total par values of the preferred and common stock. When preferred stock is cumulative and participating but no dividends are in arrears, the analysis is the same as if the preferred stock were noncumulative but participating.

When preferred stock is cumulative and limited in participation to a percentage of par value, the arrearage for prior periods is met first and is excluded from the limited participation. The lesser of a pro rata share of the remaining retained earnings or the limiting percentage of the preferred stock's par value is allocated to the preferred claim. Any retained earnings remaining after this allocation are assigned to the common stock.

Apportionment of Retained Earnings

Additional procedures are required when a subsidiary with preferred stock that has liquidation and/or dividend preferences is consolidated, even if none of the preferred shares are owned by the parent. In this situation, allocation of retained earnings to the preferred and common stock is as follows:

1. The determination and distribution of excess schedule prepared as of the date of the parent's investment in common stock must include only that portion of retained earnings that is allocable to the common stock on the purchase date.
2. Periodic equity adjustments for the parent's investment in common stock are made only for the common shareholders' claim on income. The preferred shareholders' claim on the current year's income, including dividends paid or accumulated and any participation rights for the current year, must be deducted to arrive at income available to common shareholders. When the cost method is used, the worksheet's simple equity conversion adjustment is made for the parent's share of change in the retained earnings applicable to common stock since the date of acquisition.
3. Subsidiary retained earnings must be allocated between preferred and common stockholders on consolidated worksheets. The parent's investment in common stock account then is eliminated against the parent's pro rata share of only the equity attaching to common stock.

To illustrate these procedures, assume Company S has the following stockholders' equity on January 1, 2013, the date on which Company P purchases an 80% interest in the common stock for $150,000:

Preferred stock ($100 par, 6% cumulative)	$100,000
Common stock ($10 par)	100,000
Retained earnings	80,000
Total equity	$280,000

The preferred stock has a liquidation value equal to par value, and dividends are two years in arrears as of January 1, 2013. Company S assets have a fair value equal to book value. Any excess purchase price is attributable to goodwill. The determination and distribution of excess schedule would be prepared as shown on page 387.

Determination and Distribution of Excess Schedule

	Company Implied Fair Value	Parent Price (80%)	NCI Value (20%)
Fair value of subsidiary	$187,500	$150,000	$ 37,500
Less book value of interest acquired:			
Common stock	$100,000		
Retained earnings	80,000		
Preferred dividends in arrears (2 yrs. × $6,000).	(12,000)		
Total common equity	$168,000	$168,000	$168,000
Interest acquired		80%	20%
Book value		$134,400	$ 33,600
Excess of fair value over book value	**$ 19,500**	$ 15,600	$ 3,900

Adjustment of identifiable accounts:

	Adjustment	**Worksheet Key**
Goodwill.	**$ 19,500**	**debit D**

Assume that income is exactly $25,000 per year in future years and no dividends are paid. Each year, the following entry would be made by Company P using the simple equity method of accounting for its subsidiary investment:

Investment in Company S	15,200	
Subsidiary Income		15,200

To adjust for 80% of Company S income applicable to common stock ($25,000 reported income – $6,000 cumulative claim of preferred stock)

Worksheet 7-3, pages 404 to 405, is a consolidated financial statements worksheet for the year ended December 31, 2015 (3 years subsequent to the purchase). The investment in Company S common stock account includes the original cost of the investment plus three years (3 × $15,200 = $45,600) of simple equity adjustments for income and dividends. The worksheet is unique in that it subdivides the subsidiary retained earnings into two parts: one for the common portion and one for the preferred portion of retained earnings. Entry (PS) of Worksheet 7-3 accomplishes this apportionment.

Worksheet 7-3: page 404

In journal entry form, the eliminations are as follows:

(PS)	Distribute portion of retained earnings to preferred stockholders as of January 1, 2015 (original arrearages totaling $12,000 plus $12,000 for 2013 and 2014):		
	Retained Earnings, January 1, 2015—Company S	24,000	
	Retained Earnings Allocated to Preferred Stock, January 1, 2015— Company S		24,000
(CY)	Eliminate current-year entries to record subsidiary income:		
	Subsidiary Income	15,200	
	Investment in Company S		15,200

(continued)

(EL)   Eliminate subsidiary common stock equity against investment in
          common stock account:

Common Stock, Company S	80,000	
Retained Earnings, January 1, 2015—Company S	84,800*	
Investment in Common Stock of Company S		164,800

*(Retained earnings of $130,000 – $24,000 allocated to preferred stock) × 80%.

(D)   Distribute excess on 80% investment in common stock:

Goodwill	19,500	
Investment in Common Stock of Company S		15,600
Retained Earnings—Company S (NCI)		3,900

This division of retained earnings is only for worksheet purposes; the subsidiary will maintain only one retained earnings account.

After the eliminations and adjustments are completed, the resulting consolidated net income of $175,000 is allocated as shown in the income distribution schedules. Since none of the preferred stock is owned by controlling shareholders, the NCI receives all applicable preferred income plus 20% of the income allocable to common stock. It should be observed that the NCI column, as well as the NCI shown on a formal balance sheet, includes the NCI in both preferred and common shares.

The worksheet just analyzed can handle all types of subsidiary preferred stockholder claims. Once the claim is determined, with supporting calculations, it can be isolated in a separate worksheet account, *Retained Earnings Allocated to Preferred Stock*.

When a parent uses the cost method to record its investment in a subsidiary, slightly different worksheet procedures are used. In the previous illustration, if Company P had used the cost method, the investment account still would be at the $150,000 original cost. In addition, there would be no subsidiary income shown, and the January 1, 2015, retained earnings of Company P would not reflect the 2013 and 2014 simple equity adjustments. As described earlier, a conversion to the simple equity method is made on the worksheet. Since the beginning-of-the-period investment balance is needed for elimination, the equity adjustment converts the investment account to the January 1, 2015, balance, as follows:

Retained earnings, January 1, 2015—Company S		$130,000	
Less four years' arrearage of preferred dividends		24,000	
Retained earnings applicable to common stock, January 1, 2015			**$106,000**
Retained earnings, January 1, 2013—Company S		$ 80,000	
Less two years' arrearage of preferred dividends		12,000	
Retained earnings applicable to common stock, January 1, 2013			**68,000**
Increase in common stock portion of retained earnings			$ 38,000
Controlling interest (80%)			$ 30,400

The conversion (CV) entry for $30,400 would debit the investment account and credit the Company P retained earnings account. The investment account now would be stated at its simple-equity-adjusted, January 1, 2015, balance. Worksheet entries (PS), (EL), (D), and (NCI) would be made just as in Worksheet 7-3. Only entry (CY) would be omitted, since it is not applicable to the cost method. The following partial worksheet includes the conversion and subsequent eliminations and adjustments under the cost method. All remaining procedures for this example would be identical to those used in Worksheet 7-3.

Subsidiary Preferred Stock, None Owned by Parent
Cost Method Used for Investment in Common Stock

	Partial Trial Balance		Eliminations & Adjustments			
	Company P	Company S	Dr.		Cr.	
Investment in Common Stock of Company S	150,000		**(CV)**	**30,400**	(EL)	164,800
					(D)	15,600
Goodwill			(D)	19,500		
Retained Earnings, January 1, 2015—Company P	(309,600)				**(CV)**	**30,400**
Preferred Stock ($100 par)—Company S		(100,000)				
Retained Earnings, Allocated to Preferred Stock, January 1, 2015, Company S					(PS)	24,000
Common Stock ($10 par)—Company S		(100,000)	(EL)	80,000		
Retained Earnings, January 1, 2015—Company S		(130,000)	(PS)	24,000	(NCI)	3,900
			(EL)	84,800		
Expenses	100,000	25,000				

Eliminations and Adjustments:

(CV) The cost-to-equity conversion entry was explained prior to the partial worksheet.

(PS) Distribute the beginning-of-period subsidiary retained earnings into the portions allocable to common and preferred stock. The typical procedure would be to consider the stated subsidiary retained earnings as applicable to common and to remove the preferred portion. This distribution reflects four years of arrearage (as of January 1, 2015) at $6,000 per year.

(EL) Eliminate the pro rata subsidiary common stockholders' equity at the beginning of the period against the investment account. This entry includes elimination of the 80% of subsidiary retained earnings applicable to common stock.

(D)/(NCI) Distribute the excess of cost and the NCI adjustment according to the determination and distribution of excess schedule.

Parent Investment in Subsidiary Preferred Stock

A parent may purchase all or a portion of the preferred stock of a subsidiary. Normally, preferred stock is nonvoting; therefore, it is not considered in determining whether the parent owns a controlling interest in the subsidiary. Thus, a 100% ownership of nonvoting preferred stock and a 49% interest in voting common stock may not require the preparation of consolidated statements.

From a consolidated viewpoint, the parent's purchase of subsidiary preferred stock is viewed as a retirement of the stock.[3] The amount paid is compared to the sum of the original proceeds resulting from the issuance of the shares and any claim the shares have on retained earnings, and an increase or decrease in equity as a result of the retirement is calculated. When the price paid is less than the preferred equity retired, the resulting increase in equity is credited to the controlling paid-in capital in excess of par account, not the retained earnings account, because it results from a transaction with the consolidated company's shareholders. A decrease in equity, which occurs when the price paid exceeds the preferred equity, would offset against the paid-in capital in excess of par applicable to the preferred stock. If not enough of the preferred stock paid-in capital in excess of par exists, the remaining decrease would be taken from the controlling retained earnings and viewed as a retirement dividend.

---

3 It also would be possible to view the investment as treasury shares, in which case they would appear as a contra account to the preferred stock in the minority interest section of the consolidated balance sheet. This approach, however, does not have popular support. It could be justified only if there were intent to reissue the shares.

To illustrate this type of investment, assume Company P in the previous example purchased 600 shares (60%) of Company S preferred stock on January 1, 2013, for $65,000. The increase or decrease in equity resulting from the retirement would be calculated as follows:

Price paid		$65,000
Less **preferred** interest acquired:		
Preferred stock ($100 par)...............................	$100,000	
Claim on dividends (2 years in arrears × $6,000 per year)	12,000	
Total preferred interest...	$112,000	
Interest acquired	× 60%	67,200
Increase in equity (credit parent's Paid-In Capital in Excess of Par) .		**$ 2,200**

Though viewed as retired, the preferred stock investment account will continue to exist on the books of the parent in subsequent periods. At the end of each period, the investment must be "retired" on the consolidated worksheet. The procedures used depend on whether the parent accounts for the investment in preferred stock under the equity method or the cost method. Under the equity method, the parent adjusts the investment in preferred stock account each period for any additional claim on the subsidiary retained earnings, including any continued arrearage or participation privilege. In this example, the arrearage of dividends would be recorded each year, 2013 to 2015, as follows:

Investment in Company S Preferred Stock	3,600	
Subsidiary Income		3,600
To acknowledge 60% of the annual increase in the Company S preferred stock dividend arrearage.		

Assuming the equity adjustments are properly made, any original discrepancy between the price paid for the preferred shares and their book value would be maintained. The equity method also acknowledges that, even though the shares are viewed as retired in consolidated reports, the controlling interest is entitled to its proportionate share of consolidated net income based on both its common and preferred stock holdings.

Worksheet 7-4: page 406
Worksheet 7-4, pages 406 to 407, displays the consolidation procedures that would be used for the ownership interest in preferred stock described above. This worksheet parallels Worksheet 7-3 except that the parent owns 60% of the subsidiary preferred stock. The investment is listed at its $65,000 cost plus three years of equity adjustments to reflect the increasing dividend arrearage.

All of the eliminations from Worksheet 7-3 are repeated in Worksheet 7-4. The following additional eliminations are added in Worksheet 7-4:

(CYP)	Eliminate the income reported during the current year on the interest in preferred stock:		
	Subsidiary Income—Preferred...........................	3,600	
	Investment in Company S Preferred Stock		3,600
(ELP)	Eliminate investment in preferred stock against equity applicable to parent's share of subsidiary preferred stock equity; excess of equity over investment is an increase in parent's paid-in capital in excess of par:		
	Preferred Stock ($100 par)—Company S...................	60,000	
	Retained Earnings Allocated to Preferred Stock, January 1, 2015— Company S......................................	14,400*	
	Investment in Company S Preferred Stock		72,200
	Paid-In Capital in Excess of Par—Company P		2,200

*$24,000 × 60%

Consolidated net income is distributed as shown in the income distribution schedules that accompany the worksheet. The distributions respect the controlling/NCI ownership of both common and preferred shares. The common and preferred equity interests of the NCI again are summarized on the worksheet and for presentation on the formal balance sheet.

If a parent uses the cost method for its investment in subsidiary preferred stock, the investment should be converted to its equity balance as of the beginning of the period. In this example, if the cost method is used for the investment in preferred stock, the following conversion adjustment would be made on the worksheet:

(CVP)	Preferred stock cost-to-equity conversion:		
	Investment in Company S Preferred Stock	7,200	
	Retained Earnings, January 1, 2015—Company P		7,200

The adjustment reflects two years of arrearage at $6,000 per year times the 60% ownership interest. Eliminations and adjustments would proceed as in Worksheet 7-4, except that there would be no need for entry (CY).

This example contains only cumulative preferred stock. However, the same principles would apply to participating preferred stock, and the allocation procedures outlined earlier in this chapter would be used. Only the subdivision of the subsidiary retained earnings and the amounts of the equity adjustments would differ.

R E F L E C T I O N

- If a subsidiary has preferred stock with a claim on retained earnings (because it is cumulative and/or participating), the subsidiary retained earnings must be allocated between the preferred and common stock. The investment in common stock is eliminated only against the retained earnings allocated to the common stock.

- In addition, if the parent owns subsidiary preferred stock, the investment is eliminated on the worksheet against the applicable subsidiary preferred stock.

APPENDIX: WORKSHEET FOR A CONSOLIDATED BALANCE SHEET

5

OBJECTIVE

Solve balance-sheet-only problems (CPA Exam issue).

Previous chapters displayed procedures applicable to worksheets that produced a consolidated income statement, retained earnings statement, and balance sheet. However, there may be occasions when only consolidated balance sheets are required, and the separate balance sheets of the affiliates form the starting point for consolidation procedures. Such occasions are rare in practice but are of concern to students desiring to take the CPA Exam. Past examinations have used balance-sheet-only consolidation problems as an expedient method for testing purposes. This type of problem requires less time to solve while still testing the candidates' knowledge of consolidations.

A balance sheet worksheet requires only adjustments to balance sheet accounts. No adjustments for nominal accounts are required. Your past experience often will lead you to consider the impact of an elimination on the nominal accounts, but you must adjust your thinking to cover only the remaining impact of an elimination on the balance sheet. For example, intercompany merchandise sales no longer will require an elimination of the sales and cost of goods sold relative to the transaction. The only balance sheet adjustment would be for intercompany profit on the ending inventory. The following sections examine the simplified procedures that are used on a consolidated balance sheet worksheet.

Investment Account

When the investment account is maintained under the simple equity method, it will reflect the same point in time as do the subsidiary equity balances. There is no need to eliminate the parent's entry for its share of subsidiary income. Instead, the pro rata share of subsidiary equity balances may be eliminated directly against the investment account.

Investments maintained under the sophisticated equity method are also at a common point in time and, thus, can be eliminated directly against the underlying subsidiary equity. The distributable excess, however, will be only that which remains net of the amortizations made in the current and previous periods.

Investments maintained at cost should be converted to the simple equity method as of the *end of the year* to agree in time with the subsidiary equity balances. The entire conversion adjustment is carried to the controlling retained earnings.

Excesses and the NCI adjustment are distributed according to the determination and distribution of excess schedules. Once distributed, the excesses are amortized to the balance sheet date and the entire amortization is carried to the controlling retained earnings and the NCI.

Merchandise Sales

Only the intercompany profit in the ending inventory needs adjustment. The profit is eliminated from the inventory and from retained earnings. The adjustment to retained earnings is allocated according to the NCI/controlling ownership percentages in effect when the subsidiary made the intercompany sale. If the parent made the sale, the adjustment is made only to the controlling retained earnings. The intercompany profit in the beginning inventory either has been realized through the subsequent sale of the merchandise to an outside party, or, if the units in the beginning inventory are still on hand at year-end, they would be included in the adjustment for intercompany profit in the ending inventory.

Plant Asset Sales

The only matter for concern in the case of intercompany plant asset sales is the adjustment of the asset and retained earnings accounts for the undepreciated portion of the intercompany gain or loss as of year-end. The asset account is adjusted to its cost to the consolidated firm; accumulated depreciation is adjusted for all periods to date; and retained earnings are adjusted for the undepreciated profit or loss that is to be deferred to future periods. If the subsidiary sold to the parent, the retained earnings adjustment is allocated to the NCI and controlling interests that existed at the time of the sale.

Investment in Bonds

The amortized balance in Investment in Company S Bonds is eliminated against the bonds payable and any related discount or premium balance. The net disparity in amounts is the net retirement gain or loss remaining at year-end, which is carried to retained earnings. When the subsidiary is the issuer, the retained earnings adjustment is allocated to the NCI and controlling interests.

Leases

For operating leases, it is necessary only to reclassify the asset and accumulated depreciation as owned assets rather than assets under operating leases. Where direct financing leases exist, the intercompany debt resulting from the capitalized lease must be eliminated. Also, it is necessary to reclassify the asset and accumulated depreciation as owned assets rather than assets under capital leases. An intercompany sales-type lease requires the same procedures as a direct-financing lease plus an additional adjustment to defer the remaining undepreciated intercompany profit on the lease. If the subsidiary leased the asset to the parent, the retained earnings adjustment is allocated to the NCI and controlling interest that existed at the inception of the lease.

Illustration

To illustrate the procedures used for the balance sheet worksheet, assume Company P purchased an 80% interest in Company S on January 1, 2011. Company P uses the cost method to record its investment in Company S. The determination and distribution of excess schedule prepared for this purchase is as follows:

	Determination and Distribution of Excess Schedule		
	Company Implied Fair Value	Parent Price (80%)	NCI Value (20%)
Fair value of subsidiary	$ 937,500	$750,000	$187,500
Less book value of interest acquired:			
Common stock	$ 200,000		
Retained earnings	600,000		
Total stockholders' equity	$ 800,000	$800,000	$800,000
Interest acquired		80%	20%
Book value		$640,000	$160,000
Excess of fair value over book value	**$137,500**	$110,000	$ 27,500

Adjustment of identifiable accounts:

	Adjustment	Life	Amortization per Year	Worksheet Key
Building	$ 37,500	10	$ 3,750	**debit D1**
Goodwill	**100,000**			**debit D2**
Total	**$137,500**			

The facts pertaining to intercompany sales by Company S to Company P are as follows:

	2013	2014
Intercompany sales	$80,000	$100,000
Gross profit	30%	40%
Intercompany sales in ending inventory	$20,000	$ 40,000
Unpaid balance, end of the year	$30,000	$ 35,000

On January 1, 2012, Company P sold a new piece of equipment that cost $10,000 to Company S for $15,000. Company S is depreciating the equipment over five years on a straight-line basis.

Company S has outstanding $100,000 of 20-year, 5% bonds due January 1, 2019. Interest is payable on January 1 for the previous year. The bonds originally were sold to yield 6%. On January 1, 2013, Company P purchased the bonds on the open market at a price to yield 8%.

Worksheet 7-5: page 410   Worksheet 7-5, pages 410 to 411, contains the balance sheets and eliminations and adjustments for Companies P and S on December 31, 2014. After the worksheet entries are completed, the amounts are combined to produce the consolidated balance sheet.

In journal entry form, the eliminations for Worksheet 7-5 are as follows:

(CV)   Convert investment to simple equity balance on
            December 31, 2014 (end of year):
            Investment in Company S Stock   240,000
                Retained Earnings, December 31, 2014—Company P   240,000
            Adjustment = 80% × $300,000 increase in retained earnings of
                Company S.

(EL)   Eliminate 80% of subsidiary equity against the investment account:
            Common Stock—Company S   160,000
            Retained Earnings, December 31, 2014—Company S   720,000
                Investment in Company S Stock   880,000

(D)/(NCI)   Distribute excess and NCI adjustment to buildings and goodwill:
            Buildings   37,500
            Goodwill   100,000
                Investment in Company S Stock   110,000
                Retained Earnings, December 31, 2014—Company S (NCI) . .   27,500

(A)   Adjust depreciation on buildings through end of year:
            Retained Earnings, December 31, 2014—Company P (4 years ×
                $3,750 × 80%)   12,000
            Retained Earnings, December 31, 2014—Company S (4 years ×
                $3,750 × 20%)   3,000
                Accumulated Depreciation—Buildings (4 × $3,750)   15,000

(IA)   Eliminate intercompany trade balances:
            Accounts Payable   35,000
                Accounts Receivable   35,000

(EI)   Defer ending inventory profit (40% × $40,000):
            Retained Earnings, December 31, 2014—Company P   12,800
            Retained Earnings, December 31, 2014—Company S (20%)   3,200
                Inventory, December 31, 2014   16,000

(F)   Defer remaining profit on equipment sale (2/5 of $5,000):
            Retained Earnings, December 31, 2014—Company P   2,000
            Accumulated Depreciation (3 years × $1,000)   3,000
                Equipment   5,000

(B)   Retire intercompany bonds on the worksheet:

Bonds Payable..	100,000	
Discount on Bonds Payable		3,465
Investment in Company S Bonds		90,064
Retained Earnings, December 31, 2014—Company P		
(80% × $6,471*)		5,177
Retained Earnings, December 31, 2014, Company S		
(20% × $6,471)		1,294

    *($100,000 – $3,465) – $90,064

The time savings from the balance sheet worksheet stems from the fact that there is no consolidated net income to calculate and distribute.

Worksheet 7-1

Acquisition of Additional Shares of Subsidiary
Company P and Subsidiary Company S
Worksheet for Consolidated Financial Statements
For Year Ended December 31, 2013

	(Credit balance amounts are in parentheses.)	Trial Balance	
		Company P	Company S
1	Current Assets	60,000	130,000
2	Investment in Company S	228,000	
3			
4			
5			
6	Building	400,000	80,000
7	Accumulated Depreciation—Building	(100,000)	(5,000)
8	Equipment		150,000
9			
10	**Accumulated Depreciation—Equipment**		(90,000)
11			
12	Goodwill		
13			
14	Liabilities	(100,000)	(30,000)
15	Common Stock—Company P	(200,000)	
16	**Retained Earnings, January 1, 2013—Company P**	**(210,000)**	
17			
18	Common Stock—Company S		(100,000)
19	**Retained Earnings, January 1, 2013—Company S**		(100,000)
20			
21			
22	Sales	(400,000)	(200,000)
23	Cost of Goods Sold	300,000	120,000
24	**Expenses**	**50,000**	**45,000**
25			
26	Subsidiary Income	(28,000)	
27		0	0
28	Consolidated Net Income		
29	To NCI (see distribution schedule)		
30	Balance to Controlling Interest (see distribution schedule)		
31	Total NCI		
32	Retained Earnings, Controlling Interest, December 31, 2013		
33			

Worksheet 7-1 (see page 374)

Eliminations & Adjustments			Consolidated Income Statement	NCI	Controlling Retained Earnings	Consolidated Balance Sheet	
Dr.	Cr.						
						190,000	1
	(CY)	28,000					2
	(EL)	160,000					3
	(D)	30,000					4
	(D3)	10,000					5
						480,000	6
						(105,000)	7
(D1)	30,000					180,000	8
							9
	(A1)	18,000				(108,000)	10
							11
(D2)	20,000					20,000	12
							13
						(130,000)	14
						(200,000)	15
(A1)	7,200				(200,400)		16
(D3)	2,400						17
(EL)	80,000			(20,000)			18
(EL)	80,000	(NCI)	20,000	(27,600)			19
(A1)	4,800						20
(D3)	7,600						21
			(600,000)				22
			420,000				23
(A1)	6,000		101,000				24
							25
(CY)	28,000						26
	266,000		266,000				27
			(79,000)				28
			5,800	(5,800)			29
			73,200		(73,200)		30
				(53,400)		(53,400)	31
					(273,600)	(273,600)	32
						0	33

Eliminations and Adjustments:

(CY)   Eliminate the parent's entry recognizing 80% of the subsidiary net income for the current year. This entry restores the investment account to its balance at the beginning of the year, so that it can be eliminated against Company S beginning-of-year equity balances.

(EL)   Eliminate the 80% controlling interest in beginning-of-year subsidiary accounts against the investment account. The 60% and 20% investments could be eliminated separately if desired.

(D1/NCI) The $30,000 excess of cost on the original 60% investment and the NCI adjustment on the purchase date is distributed to the equipment (D1) and goodwill (D2) accounts according to the determination and distribution of excess schedule prepared on January 1, 2011.

(A1)   Since the equipment has a 5-year remaining life on January 1, 2011, the depreciation should be increased $6,000 per year for three years. This entry corrects the controlling retained earnings for the past two years by $7,200 (60%) and the NCI for $4,800 (40%) and adjusts the current depreciation expense by $6,000.

(D3)   The $10,000 excess of cost on the 20% block is distributed to the NCI for $7,600, which was the portion of the NCI adjustment applicable to the 20% interest on January 1. The $2,400 is the adjustment to parent retained earnings resulting from the retirement of the subsidiary shares.

Subsidiary Company S Income Distribution

Equipment depreciation	$6,000	Internally generated net income	$35,000
		Adjusted income	$29,000
		NCI share	× 20%
		NCI	$ 5,800

Parent Company P Income Distribution

	Internally generated net income	$50,000
	80% × Company S adjusted income of $29,000....	23,200
	Controlling interest	$73,200

Worksheet 7-2

Sale of Subsidiary Interest During Period; No Loss of Control
Company P and Subsidiary Company S
Worksheet for Consolidated Financial Statements
For Year Ended December 31, 2013

	(Credit balance amounts are in parentheses.)	Trial Balance	
		Company P	Company S
1	Investment in Company S (60%)	244,500	
2			
3			
4	Equipment	600,000	100,000
5	Accumulated Depreciation—Equipment	(100,000)	(60,000)
6	Other Assets	581,500	305,000
7	Goodwill		
8	Common Stock—Company P	(500,000)	
9	Retained Earnings, January 1, 2013—Company P	(701,500)	
10			
11	Common Stock—Company S		(100,000)
12	Retained Earnings, January 1, 2013—Company S		(215,000)
13			
14	Sales	(500,000)	(200,000)
15	Cost of Goods Sold	350,000	140,000
16	Expenses	50,000	30,000
17			
18	**Paid-In Capital in Excess of Par—Company P**	**(4,600)**	
19	**Subsidiary Income**	**(19,900)**	
20			
21	**Income Sold to NCI (second 20% block)**		
22		0	0
23			
24	Consolidated Net Income		
25	To NCI (see distribution schedule)		
26	Balance to Controlling Interest (see distribution schedule)		
27	Total NCI		
28	Retained Earnings, Controlling Interest, December 31, 2013		
29			

Worksheet 7-2 (see page 383)

Eliminations & Adjustments			Consolidated Income Statement	NCI	Controlling Retained Earnings	Consolidated Balance Sheet	
Dr.		Cr.					
		(CY)	18,000					1
		(EL)	189,000					2
		(D)	37,500					3
(D1)	25,000						725,000	4
		(A)	15,000				(175,000)	5
							886,500	6
(D2)	37,500						37,500	7
							(500,000)	8
(A)	6,000					(695,500)		9
								10
(EL)	60,000				(40,000)			11
(EL)	129,000	(NCI)	25,000		(107,000)			12
(A)	4,000							13
				(700,000)				14
				490,000				15
				85,000				16
(A)	5,000							17
							(4,600)	18
(NCI)	**1,900**							19
(CY)	18,000							20
		(NCI)	**1,900**		(1,900)			21
	286,400		286,400					22
								23
				(125,000)				24
				8,100	(8,100)			25
				116,900		(116,900)		26
					(157,000)		(157,000)	27
						(812,400)	(812,400)	28
							0	29

Eliminations and Adjustments:

(NCI)   The income earned by the parent on the 20% interest sold on July 1, though earned by the controlling interest, now belongs to the NCI. The NCI owns 20% of the reported subsidiary income for the half-year ($12,000), which is $2,400. Note that this entry credits the account, Income Sold to NCI, to accomplish the transfer of the income to the NCI. The offsetting debit is explained as follows:
20% of subsidiary income for the first six months, adjusted for one-fourth of the parent's half-year amortization of excess or $(20\% \times \$12,000) - (20\% \times \frac{1}{2} \times \$5,000) = \$1,900$.

(CY)   Eliminate the parent's entry recording its 60% share of subsidiary net income of $30,000. This entry restores the 60% interest to its simple-equity-adjusted cost at the beginning of the year so that the investment can be eliminated against subsidiary equity balances at the beginning of the year.

(EL)   Eliminate 60% of the subsidiary equity balances at the beginning of the year against the investment account. An excess cost of $37,500 remains. This amount is 60% of the original $62,500 total excess shown on page 378, since only a 60% interest is retained.

(D)/(NCI)   Distribute $62,500 total adjustment to equipment (D1) and goodwill (D2) according to the D&D schedule. 60% of the excess ($37,500) applies to the remaining investment and 40% ($25,000) now applies to the 40% NCI.

(A)   Amortize equipment $5,000 for two prior years and the current year. Prior-year amortization is distributed 60% to controlling interest and 40% to the NCI.

Subsidiary Company S Income Distribution

Depreciation adjustment . . . . (A)	$5,000	Internally generated net income	$ 30,000
		Adjusted income	$ 25,000
		NCI share	× 40%
		NCI for full year	$ 10,000
		Less income purchased.	**1,900**
		NCI	$ 8,100

Parent Company P Income Distribution

		Internally generated net income	$100,000
		60% × Company S adjusted income of $25,000.	15,000
		20% × Company S adjusted income for first six months (net of amortization)	**1,900**
		Controlling interest	$116,900

Worksheet 7-3

Subsidiary Preferred Stock, None Owned by Parent
Company P and Subsidiary Company S
Worksheet for Consolidated Financial Statements
For Year Ended December 31, 2015

	(Credit balance amounts are in parentheses.)	Trial Balance	
		Company P	Company S
1	Current Assets	259,600	150,000
2	Property, Plant, and Equipment (net)	400,000	250,000
3	Investment in Company S Common Stock	195,600	
4			
5			
6	Goodwill		
7	Liabilities	(150,000)	(45,000)
8	Common Stock—Company P	(200,000)	
9	Retained Earnings, January 1, 2015—Company P	(340,000)	
10	Preferred Stock ($100 par)—Company S		(100,000)
11	**Retained Earnings Allocated to Preferred Stock, January 1, 2015—Company S**		
12	Common Stock ($10 par)—Company S		(100,000)
13	Retained Earnings, January 1, 2015—Company S		(130,000)
14			
15	Sales	(450,000)	(200,000)
16	Cost of Goods Sold	200,000	150,000
17	Expenses	100,000	25,000
18	Subsidiary Income	(15,200)	
19		0	0
20			
21	Consolidated Net Income		
22	To NCI (see distribution schedule)		
23	Balance to Controlling Interest (see distribution schedule)		
24	Total NCI		
25	Retained Earnings, Controlling Interest, December 31, 2015		
26			

Eliminations and Adjustments:

(PS)   Distribute the beginning-of-period subsidiary retained earnings into the portions allocable to common and preferred stock. The typical procedure would be to consider the stated subsidiary retained earnings as applicable to common and to remove the preferred portion. This distribution reflects four years of arrearage (as of January 1, 2015) at $6,000 per year.

(CY)   Eliminate the parent's entry recording its share of subsidiary current income.

(EL)   Eliminate the pro rata subsidiary common stockholders' equity at the beginning of the period against the investment account. This entry includes elimination of the 80% of subsidiary retained earnings applicable to common stock.

(D)/(NCI)   Distribute the excess of cost and the NCI adjustment according to the determination and distribution of excess schedule.

Worksheet 7-3 (see page 387)

Eliminations & Adjustments		Consolidated Income Statement	NCI	Controlling Retained Earnings	Consolidated Balance Sheet	
Dr.	Cr.					
					409,600	1
					650,000	2
	(CY) 15,200					3
	(EL) 164,800					4
	(D) 15,600					5
(D) 19,500					19,500	6
					(195,000)	7
					(200,000)	8
				(340,000)		9
			(100,000)			10
	(PS) 24,000		(24,000)			11
(EL) 80,000			(20,000)			12
(PS) 24,000	(NCI) 3,900		(25,100)			13
(EL) 84,800						14
		(650,000)				15
		350,000				16
		125,000				17
(CY) 15,200						18
223,500	223,500					19
						20
		(175,000)				21
		9,800	(9,800)			22
		165,200		(165,200)		23
			(178,900)		(178,900)	24
				(505,200)	(505,200)	25
					0	26

Subsidiary Company S Income Distribution

Internally generated net income (no adjustments) . . .	$ 25,000
Less preferred cumulative claim to NCI	**(6,000)**
Common stock income	$ 19,000
NCI share	× 20%
NCI in common income.	$ 3,800
Total NCI ($6,000 + $3,800)	**$ 9,800**

Parent Company P Income Distribution

Internally generated net income	$ 150,000
80% × Company S adjusted income on common stock of $19,000	15,200
Controlling interest	$ 165,200

Worksheet 7-4

Subsidiary Preferred Stock Owned by Parent
Company P and Subsidiary Company S
Worksheet for Consolidated Financial Statements
For Year Ended December 31, 2015

	(Credit balance amounts are in parentheses.)	Trial Balance	
		Company P	Company S
1	Current Assets	194,600	150,000
2	Property, Plant, and Equipment (net)	400,000	250,000
3	Investment in Company S Common Stock	195,600	
4			
5			
6	**Investment in Company S Preferred Stock**	**75,800**	
7			
8	Goodwill		
9	Liabilities	(150,000)	(45,000)
10	Common Stock—Company P	(200,000)	
11	**Paid-In Capital in Excess of Par—Company P**		
12	Retained Earnings, January 1, 2015—Company P	(347,200)	
13	Preferred Stock ($100 par)—Company S		(100,000)
14	Retained Earnings Allocated to Preferred Stock, January 1, 2015—Company S		
15	Common Stock ($10 par)—Company S		(100,000)
16	Retained Earnings, January 1, 2015—Company S		(130,000)
17			
18	Sales	(450,000)	(200,000)
19	Cost of Goods Sold	200,000	150,000
20	Expenses	100,000	25,000
21	Subsidiary Income—Common	(15,200)	
22	**Subsidiary Income—Preferred**	**(3,600)**	
23		0	0
24			
25	Consolidated Net Income		
26	To NCI (see distribution schedule)		
27	Balance to Controlling Interest (see distribution schedule)		
28	Total NCI		
29	Retained Earnings, Controlling Interest, December 31, 2015		
30			

Worksheet 7-4 (see page 390)

Eliminations & Adjustments				Consolidated Income Statement	NCI	Controlling Retained Earnings	Consolidated Balance Sheet	
Dr.		Cr.						
							344,600	1
							650,000	2
		(CY)	15,200					3
		(EL)	164,800					4
		(D)	15,600					5
		(CYP)	**3,600**					6
		(ELP)	**72,200**					7
(D)	19,500						19,500	8
							(195,000)	9
							(200,000)	10
		(ELP)	**2,200**				(2,200)	11
						(347,200)		12
(ELP)	**60,000**				(40,000)			13
(ELP)	**14,400**	(PS)	24,000		(9,600)			14
(EL)	80,000				(20,000)			15
(PS)	24,000	(NCI)	3,900		(25,100)			16
(EL)	84,800							17
				(650,000)				18
				350,000				19
				125,000				20
(CY)	15,200							21
(CYP)	**3,600**							22
	301,500		301,500					23
								24
				(175,000)				25
				6,200	(6,200)			26
				(168,800)		(168,800)		27
					(100,900)		(100,900)	28
						(516,000)	(516,000)	29
							0	30

Eliminations and Adjustments:

(PS), (CY), (EL), and (D)	Same as Worksheet 7-3; the common stock investment elimination procedures are unaffected by the investment in preferred stock.
(CYP)	Eliminate the entry recording the parent's share of income allocable to preferred stock. If declared, intercompany preferred dividends would also have been eliminated. This adjustment restores the investment account to its beginning-of-period equity balance.
(ELP)	The parent's ownership portion of the par value and beginning-of-period retained earnings applicable to preferred stock is eliminated against the balance in the investment in preferred stock account. The difference in this case was an increase in equity, and it was carried to the controlling paid-in capital in excess of par.

Subsidiary Company S Income Distribution

Internally generated net income (no adjustments) .	$ 25,000
Less preferred cumulative claim:	
to NCI, 40% × $6,000	(2,400)
to controlling, 60% × $6,000	**(3,600)**
Common stock income	$ 19,000
NCI share	× 20%
NCI in common income.	$ 3,800
Total NCI ($2,400 + $3,800)	$ 6,200

Parent Company P Income Distribution

Internally generated net income	$ 150,000
60% × Company S income attributable	
to preferred stock	**3,600**
80% × Company S adjusted income on	
common stock of $19,000.	15,200
Controlling interest	$ 168,800

Worksheet 7-5

Balance Sheet Only
Company P and Subsidiary Company S
Worksheet for Consolidated Balance Sheet
December 31, 2014

	(Credit balance amounts are in parentheses.)	Trial Balance	
		Company P	Company S
1	Cash	61,936	106,535
2	Accounts Receivable	80,000	200,000
3	Inventory, December 31, 2014	60,000	150,000
4	Land	300,000	250,000
5	Building	800,000	600,000
6	Accumulated Depreciation—Building	(400,000)	(100,000)
7	Equipment	120,000	95,000
8	Accumulated Depreciation—Equipment	(70,000)	(30,000)
9	Investment in Company S Bonds	90,064	
10	Investment in Company S Stock	750,000	
11			
12	Goodwill		
13	Accounts Payable	(92,000)	(75,000)
14	Bonds Payable		(100,000)
15	Discount on Bonds Payable		3,465
16	Common Stock—Company P	(500,000)	
17	Retained Earnings, December 31, 2014—Company P	(1,200,000)	
18			
19			
20	Common Stock—Company S		(200,000)
21	Retained Earnings, December 31, 2014—Company S		(900,000)
22			
23			
24		0	0
25	Total NCI		
26			

Eliminations and Adjustments:

(CV)   Investment in Company S Stock is converted to the simple equity method as of December 31, 2014, as follows: 80% × $300,000 increase in retained earnings = $240,000.

(EL)   80% of the subsidiary equity balances is eliminated against the investment in stock account.

(D)/(NCI)   The $110,000 excess of cost and $27,500 NCI adjustment is distributed according to the determination and distribution of excess schedule. Entry (D1) adjusts the building account and (D2) adjusts goodwill.

(A)   The excess attributable to the building is amortized for four years at $3,750 per year. The retained earnings adjustment is allocated 80% to Company P retained earnings and 20% to Company S retained earnings.

(IA)   The intercompany trade balance is eliminated.

(EI)   The gross profit of $16,000 (40% × $40,000) recorded by Company S and applicable to merchandise in Company P's ending inventory is deferred by reducing the inventory and retained earnings. Since the sale was made by Company S, the adjustment is allocated to the NCI and controlling retained earnings.

(F)   As of December 31, 2014, $2,000 ($5,000 × 2/5) of the profit on the equipment sale is still to be deferred. Since the sale was made by Company P, the controlling retained earnings absorb this adjustment, and the equipment and accumulated depreciation accounts are adjusted.

(B)   Investment in Company S Bonds is eliminated against the net book value of the bonds. The remaining gain on the worksheet retirement is allocated to the NCI and controlling retained earnings, since the subsidiary originally issued the bonds.

Worksheet 7-5 (see page 394)

Eliminations & Adjustments				NCI	Consolidated Balance Sheet	
Dr.		Cr.				
					168,471	1
		(IA)	35,000		245,000	2
		(EI)	16,000		194,000	3
					550,000	4
(D1)	37,500				1,437,500	5
		(A)	15,000		(515,000)	6
		(F)	5,000		210,000	7
(F)	3,000				(97,000)	8
		(B)	90,064			9
(CV)	**240,000**	(EL)	880,000			10
		(D)	110,000			11
(D2)	100,000				100,000	12
(IA)	35,000				(132,000)	13
(B)	100,000					14
		(B)	3,465			15
					(500,000)	16
(A)	12,000	**(CV)**	**240,000**		(1,418,377)	17
(EI)	12,800	(B)	5,177			18
(F)	2,000					19
(EL)	160,000			(40,000)		20
(EL)	720,000	(B)	1,294	(202,594)		21
(EI)	3,200	(NCI)	27,500			22
(A)	3,000					23
	1,428,500		1,428,500			24
				(242,594)	(242,594)	25
					0	26

UNDERSTANDING THE ISSUES

1. Company S has 4,000 shares outstanding and a total stockholders' equity of $200,000. It is about to issue 6,000 new shares to the prospective parent company. The shares will be sold for a total of $650,000. Will there be an excess of cost over book value? If so, how will it likely be accounted for?

2. Company P purchases an 80% interest in Company S on January 1, 2011, for $480,000. Company S had equity of $450,000 on that date. Any excess of cost over book value was attributed to equipment with a 10-year life. On July 1, 2016, Company P purchased another 10% interest for $160,000. Company S's equity was $550,000 on January 1, 2016, and it earned $50,000 evenly during 2016. Company P had internally generated net income of $120,000 during 2016. Calculate consolidated income for 2016 and the distribution of consolidated income to the noncontrolling and controlling interests.

3. Company P purchased an 80% interest (8,000 shares) in Company S for $800,000 on January 1, 2011. Company S's equity on that date was $900,000. Any excess of cost over book value was attributed to equipment with a 10-year life. On January 1, 2015, Company S's equity was $1,200,000. Company S earned $200,000, evenly, during 2015. In December 2015, Company S paid $10,000 in dividends. Company P had internally generated net income of $150,000. On July 1, 2015, there was a sale of Company S stock, for $150 per share, to outside interests by Company P. Consider these situations:

   ◆ Company P sells all 8,000 shares.
   ◆ Company P sells 2,000 shares.
   ◆ Company P sells 6,000 shares.

   For each of these situations:

   a. How will the sale be recorded?
   b. Will consolidated statements be prepared for 2015? If so, what will be consolidated net income, and what will be the distribution to the NCI?
   c. If consolidated statements will not be prepared, what will be reported by the parent for its income from Company S?

4. Company S has the following stockholders' equity on January 1, 2015:

Common stock ($1 par, 100,000 shares)	$100,000
6% preferred stock ($100 par, 2,000 shares)	200,000
Paid-in capital in excess of par	900,000
Retained earnings	500,000

The preferred stock is cumulative and has dividends one year in arrears on January 1, 2015.

Company P purchased an 80% interest in the common stock of Company S on January 1, 2015, for $1,400,000. Any excess of cost over book value was attributed to goodwill. Company S earned $80,000 during 2015 and paid no dividends. Company P had internally generated net income of $120,000.

What is consolidated net income for 2015, and how is it distributed to the controlling and noncontrolling interests?

How would the answer differ if Company P also purchases one-half of the preferred stock of Company S for $120,000?

EXERCISES

Exercise 1 *(LO 1)* **Purchase of shares directly from subsidiary.** Prior to January 2, 2014, Penstar and Sargio are separate corporations. Sargio Corporation is contemplating a major expansion and seeks to be purchased by a larger corporation with available cash. Penstar Corporation issues $1,320,000 of bonds and uses the proceeds to buy 30,000 newly issued Sargio shares for $44 per share. The price reflects a control premium since the fair value of the NCI shares is $40. Just prior to the issue of the bonds and the issue and purchase of Sargio stock, Penstar and Sargio have the following separate balance sheets:

Assets	Penstar Corporation	Sargio Corporation
Current assets	$ 600,000	$100,000
Land.	150,000	60,000
Property, plant, and equipment.	700,000	400,000
Total assets.	$1,450,000	$560,000
Liabilities and Stockholders' Equity		
Current liabilities	$ 250,000	$100,000
Common stock ($5 par).	400,000	100,000
Retained earnings	800,000	360,000
Total liabilities and equity	$1,450,000	$560,000

Purchasing the 30,000 new shares gives Penstar Corporation a 60% controlling interest (30,000 of a total 50,000 common shares). On the purchase date, Sargio's property is undervalued by $200,000 and has a remaining life of 20 years. Any remaining excess cost can be attributed only to goodwill.

Prepare a determination and distribution of excess schedule for Penstar Corporation's investment in Sargio. Prepare a consolidated balance sheet for the consolidated firm immediately after the acquisition by Penstar Corporation.

Exercise 2 *(LO 2)* **Block purchase, control with first block.** Barker Corporation purchases a 60% interest in Hardwood Company on January 1, 2011, for $150,000. On that date, Hardwood Company has the following stockholders' equity:

Common stock ($10 par).	$100,000
Retained earnings	20,000
	$120,000

Any excess of cost over fair value is due to equipment with a 10-year life.

Barker Corporation purchases another 20% interest in Hardwood Company for $40,000 on January 1, 2013, when Hardwood Company has the following stockholders' equity:

Common stock ($10 par).	$100,000
Retained earnings	50,000
	$150,000

On December 31, 2015, Barker Corporation and Hardwood Company have the following balance sheets:

Assets	Barker Corporation	Hardwood Company
Current assets	$ 270,000	$ 80,000
Investment in Hardwood Company.	190,000	
Property, plant, and equipment.	740,000	240,000
Total assets.	$1,200,000	$320,000

Liabilities and Stockholders' Equity	Barker Corporation	Hardwood Company
Current liabilities	$ 400,000	$100,000
Stockholders' equity:		
Common stock ($10 par)	500,000	100,000
Retained earnings	300,000	120,000
Total liabilities and stockholders' equity	$1,200,000	$320,000

Prepare a determination and distribution of excess schedule for the January 1, 2011, acquisition and analysis of the 20% acquisition on January 1, 2013. Prepare the consolidated balance sheet of Barker Corporation and subsidiary Hardwood Company on December 31, 2015.

Exercise 3 *(LO 3)* **Sale of interest, control maintained.** Carpenter Company has the following balance sheet on December 31, 2015:

Assets		Liabilities and Equity		
Current assets	$150,000	Liabilities		$100,000
Investment in Hinckley		Equity:		
Company	160,000	Common stock ($10 par)	$500,000	
Property, plant, and		Retained earnings	100,000	600,000
equipment (net)	390,000			
Total assets.	$700,000	Total liabilities and equity		$700,000

The investment in Hinckley Company account reflects the original cost of an 80% interest (40,000 shares) purchased on January 1, 2012. On the date of the purchase, Hinckley stockholders' equity has a book value of $150,000. Hinckley's other book values approximate fair values, except for a machine with a 5-year remaining life that is undervalued by $20,000. Any additional excess is attributed to goodwill.

A review of Hinckley's past financial statements reveals the following:

	Income	Dividends Paid
2012	$ 10,000	$ 5,000
2013	25,000	5,000
2014	40,000	5,000
2015	35,000	5,000
Total.	$110,000	$20,000

Carpenter sells 2,000 shares of Hinckley common stock on January 1, 2016, for $40,000.

Prepare the necessary entries on Carpenter's books to account accurately for the sale of the 2,000 Hinckley shares. Provide a determination and distribution of excess schedule along with all other necessary computations as support.

Exercise 4 *(LO 3)* **Sale of interest, alternative remaining interests.** Center, Inc., purchases 24,000 shares of Bruce Corporation, which equates to an 80% interest, on January 1, 2015. The following determination and distribution of excess schedule is prepared:

	Company Implied Fair Value	Parent Price (80%)	NCI Value (20%)
Determination and Distribution of Excess Schedule			
Fair value of subsidiary	$1,000,000	$800,000	$200,000
Less book value of interest acquired:			
Common stock ($10 par)	$ 300,000		
Retained earnings	400,000		

Determination and Distribution of Excess Schedule

	Company Implied Fair Value	Parent Price (80%)	NCI Value (20%)
Total stockholders' equity...............	$ 700,000	$700,000	$700,000
Interest acquired		80%	20%
Book value............................		$560,000	$140,000
Excess of fair value over book value	**$ 300,000**	$240,000	$ 60,000

Adjustment of identifiable accounts:

	Adjustment	Amortization per Year	Life	Worksheet Key
Building	$ 50,000	$ 5,000	10	**debit D1**
Goodwill............................	**250,000**			**debit D2**
Total	**$ 300,000**			

Bruce Corporation reports net income of $35,000 for the six months ended July 1, 2018. Center's simple-equity-adjusted investment balance is $864,000 as of December 31, 2017.

Prepare all entries for the sale of the Brown Corporation shares on July 1, 2018, for each of the following situations:

1. 24,000 shares are sold for $890,000.
2. 12,000 shares are sold for $455,000.
3. 6,000 shares are sold for $232,500.

Exercise 5 *(LO 3)* **Sale of interest, loss of control.** Rob Company purchases a 90% interest in Venus Company for $418,500 on January 1, 2013. Any excess of cost over book value is attributed to equipment, which is being depreciated over 20 years. Both companies end their reporting periods on December 31. Since the investment in Venus Company is consolidated, Rob Company chooses to use the cost method to maintain its investment.

On December 31, 2016, Rob Company sells 8,000 shares of Venus Company for $700,000. The following stockholders' equity balances of Venus Company are available:

	January 1, 2013	January 1, 2016
Common stock ($10 par)..	$100,000	$100,000
Retained earnings	250,000	420,000
Total equity	$350,000	$520,000

Venus Company earns $70,000 during 2016. Prepare a determination and distribution of excess schedule. Record the sale of the shares of Venus Company and any other adjustments needed to the investment account.

Exercise 6 *(LO 4)* **Equity adjustments with preferred stock.** Brian Construction Company has the following stockholders' equity on January 1, 2011, the date on which Roller Company purchases an 80% interest in the common stock for $720,000:

8% cumulative preferred stock (5,000 shares, $100 par)	$ 500,000
Common stock (40,000 shares, $20 par)......................................	800,000
Retained earnings	200,000
Total stockholders' equity..	$1,500,000

Brian Construction Company did not pay preferred dividends in 2010.

1. Prepare a determination and distribution of excess schedule. Assume that the preferred stock's liquidation value is equal to par and that any excess of cost is attributable to goodwill.
2. Assume Ace Construction has the following net income (loss) for 2011 and 2012 and does not pay any dividends:

2011 income	$70,000
2012 income	40,000

Roller maintains its investment account under the cost method. Prepare the cost-to-equity conversion entries necessary on Roller Company's books to adjust its investment account to the simple equity balance as of January 1, 2013.

Exercise 7 *(LO 4)* **Cost-to-equity conversion with preferred stock.** On December 31, 2014, Zigler Corporation purchases an 80% interest in the common stock of Kim Company for $420,000. The stockholders' equity of Kim Company on December 31, 2014, is as follows:

8% Cumulative preferred stock (2,000 shares, $100 par)	$200,000
Common stock (30,000 shares, $10 stated value)	300,000
Retained earnings	160,000
Total stockholders' equity	$660,000

Any excess of cost over book value is attributable to goodwill. The common stock investment is accounted for under the cost method.

Zigler Corporation purchases 1,000 shares of the cumulative preferred stock of Kim Company on January 1, 2015, for $90,000. Kim Company issues a total of 2,000 preferred shares on January 1, 2011. Dividends on preferred stock are paid in 2011 and 2012, but not in subsequent years. Zigler Corporation accounts for its investment using the cost method.

During 2015 and 2016, Kim Company pays no dividends, and its retained earnings balance on December 31, 2016, is $210,000. Kim Company income during 2017 is $60,000.

1. Calculate the preferred and common stockholders' equity claim on Kim Company's retained earnings balance at January 1, 2017.
2. Prepare the cost-to-simple-equity conversion and the elimination as of January 1, 2017, that would be made on the December 31, 2017, consolidated trial balance worksheet for the investment in preferred stock.
3. Prepare the cost-to-simple-equity conversion and the eliminations that would be made on the December 31, 2017, consolidated trial balance worksheet for the investment in common stock. Provide a determination and distribution of excess schedule as support.

Exercise 8 *(LO 4)* **D&D with preferred stock.** On January 1, 2012, Boelter Company purchases 80% of the outstanding common stock of Mill Corporation for $280,000. On this date, Mill Corporation stockholders' equity is as follows:

6% Preferred stock (1,000 shares, $100 par)	$100,000
Common stock (20,000 shares, $10 par)	200,000
Retained earnings	90,000
Total stockholders' equity	$390,000

Prepare a determination and distribution of excess schedule under each of the following situations (any excess of cost over book value is attributable to goodwill):

1. The preferred stock is cumulative, with dividends one year in arrears at January 1, 2012, and has a liquidation value equal to par.
2. The preferred stock is noncumulative but fully participating.
3. The preferred stock is cumulative, with dividends two years in arrears as of January 1, 2012, and has a liquidation value equal to 110% of par.

PROBLEMS

Problem 7-1 *(LO 2)* **Worksheet, blocks, control with first block, loans, fixed asset sales, intercompany merchandise.** During 2017, Away Company acquires a controlling interest in Stallward, Inc. Trial balances of the companies at December 31, 2017, are as follows:

	Away Company	Stallward, Inc.
Cash	99,500	78,000
Notes Receivable	100,000	
Accounts Receivable	200,000	100,000
Interest Receivable	3,000	
Dividends Receivable	4,500	
Inventories	924,000	125,000
Investment in Stallward, Inc.	469,200	
Property, Plant, and Equipment	1,250,000	500,000
Accumulated Depreciation	(500,000)	(150,000)
Deferred Charges	25,000	
Patents and Licenses		50,000
Accounts Payable	(425,000)	(80,000)
Notes Payable		(75,000)
Dividends Payable		(5,000)
Capital Stock	(300,000)	(100,000)
Retained Earnings, January 1, 2017	(1,605,000)	(400,000)
Sales and Services	(1,800,000)	(750,000)
Subsidiary Income	(43,200)	
Interest Income	(3,000)	
Cost of Goods Sold	1,350,000	525,000
Administrative and Selling Expenses	251,000	174,000
Interest Expense		3,000
Dividends Declared		5,000
Totals	0	0

The following information is available regarding the transactions and accounts of the two companies:

a. An analysis of the investment in Stallward, Inc., account follows:

	Description	Amount	Interest Acquired
January 1, 2017	Investment	$325,000	70%
September 30, 2017	Investment	105,000	20%
Total		$430,000	90%
December 31, 2017	90% of Stallward income for 2017	43,200	
December 31, 2017	90% of Stallward dividends for 2017	(4,500)	
Total		$468,700	

b. The net income of Stallward, Inc., for the nine months ended September 30, 2017, is $25,000.

c. The price paid by the parent on January 1, 2017, to achieve control is considered to be a bargain and will result in a gain (only for the parent).

d. On September 30, 2017, Away Company loans its subsidiary $100,000 on a 1-year, 12% note. Interest and principal are payable in quarterly installments beginning December 31, 2017. The December 31, 2017, payment is made by Stallward but is not received by Away. Away Company has no other notes receivable outstanding.

e. Stallward, Inc.'s sales principally are engineering services billed at cost plus 50%. During 2017, Away Company is billed for $40,000, of which $16,500 is treated as a deferred charge at December 31, 2017.

f. During the year, parent company sales to the subsidiary total $60,000, of which $10,000 remains in the inventory of Stallward, Inc., at December 31, 2017.

g. In 2017, Away constructs certain tools at a cost of $15,000 and sells them to Stallward, Inc., for $25,000. Stallward, Inc., depreciates such tools using the straight-line method over a 5-year life. One-half year's depreciation is taken in the year of acquisition.

Required ▶ ▶ ▶ ▶ ▶   Prepare the worksheet necessary to produce the consolidated financial statements of Away Company and its subsidiary for the year ended December 31, 2017. Include the determination and distribution of excess and income distribution schedules.

(AICPA adapted)

Problem 7-2 *(LO 2)* **Worksheet, blocks, control with first block.** The following determination and distribution of excess schedule is prepared on January 1, 2012, the date on which Parker Company purchases a 60% interest in Share Company:

Determination and Distribution of Excess Schedule

	Company Implied Fair Value	Parent Price (60%)	NCI Value (40%)
Fair value of subsidiary	$ 300,000	$180,000	$120,000
Less book value of interest acquired:			
Common stock	$ 100,000		
Retained earnings	60,000		
Total equity	$ 160,000	$160,000	$160,000
Interest acquired		60%	40%
Book value		$ 96,000	$ 64,000
Excess of fair value over book value	**$140,000**	$ 84,000	$ 56,000

Adjustment of identifiable accounts:

	Adjustment	Amortization per Year	Life	Worksheet Key
Equipment	$ 100,000	$100,000	10	**debit D1**
Goodwill	40,000			**debit D2**

On December 31, 2013, Parker Company purchases an additional 20% interest in Share Company for $70,000. Share's stockholders' equity is determined to be the following at that date:

Common stock	$100,000
Retained earnings	85,000
Total stockholders' equity	$185,000

On December 31, 2015, the following trial balances are available:

	Parker Company	Share Company
Current Assets	160,000	80,000
Investment in Share Company	301,000	
Property, Plant, and Equipment (net)	450,000	170,000
Current Liabilities	(110,000)	(20,000)
Common Stock ($10 par)	(500,000)	(100,000)
Retained Earnings, January 1, 2015	(198,000)	(100,000)

	Parker Company	Share Company
Sales	(400,000)	(110,000)
Subsidiary Income	(28,000)	
Cost of Goods Sold	200,000	60,000
Other Expenses	100,000	15,000
Dividends Declared	25,000	5,000
Totals	0	0

1. Prepare an analysis for the second purchase of Share stock by Parker Company on December 31, 2013.
2. Prepare the worksheet necessary to produce the consolidated financial statements of Parker Company and its subsidiary as of December 31, 2015. Include an income distribution schedule.

Problem 7-3 *(LO 2)* **Worksheet, blocks, control with first block, merchandise sales.** On January 1, 2011, James Company purchases 70% of the common stock of Craft Company for $245,000. On this date, Craft has common stock, other paid-in capital in excess of par, and retained earnings of $50,000, $100,000, and $150,000, respectively.

On May 1, 2012, James Company purchases an additional 20% of the common stock of Craft Company for $92,000.

Net income and dividends for two years for Craft Company are as follows:

	2011	2012
Net income for year	$60,000	$90,000
Dividends, declared in December	20,000	30,000

In 2012, the net income of Craft from January 1 through April 30 is $30,000.

On January 1, 2011, the only tangible asset of Craft that is undervalued is equipment, which is worth $20,000 more than book value. The equipment has a remaining life of four years, and straight-line depreciation is used. Any remaining excess is goodwill.

In the last quarter of 2012, Craft sells $50,000 in goods to James, at a gross profit rate of 30%. On December 31, 2012, $10,000 of these goods are in James's ending inventory.

The trial balances for the companies on December 31, 2012, are as follows:

	James Company	Craft Company
Inventory, December 31	100,000	50,000
Other Current Assets	126,000	180,000
Investment in Craft Company	*	
Land	50,000	50,000
Buildings and Equipment	350,000	320,000
Accumulated Depreciation	(100,000)	(60,000)
Other Intangibles	20,000	
Current Liabilities	(120,000)	(40,000)
Bonds Payable		(100,000)
Other Long-Term Liabilities	(200,000)	
Common Stock—James	(200,000)	
Other Paid-In Capital in Excess of Par—James	(100,000)	
Retained Earnings—James	(214,000)	
Common Stock—Craft		(50,000)
Other Paid-In Capital in Excess of Par—Craft		(100,000)
Retained Earnings—Craft		(190,000)

	James Company	Craft Company
Net Sales	(520,000)	(450,000)
Cost of Goods Sold	300,000	260,000
Operating Expenses	121,000	100,000
Subsidiary Income	*	
Dividends Declared	50,000	30,000
Totals	0	0

* To be calculated and inserted.

Required ▶ ▶ ▶ ▶ ▶ 1. Using this information, prepare a determination and distribution of excess schedule. Prepare an analysis of the later purchase of a 20% interest.
2. James Company carries the investment in Craft Company under the simple equity method. In general journal form, record the entries that would be made to apply the equity method in 2011 and 2012.
3. Compute the balance that should appear in Investment in Craft Company and in Subsidiary Income on December 31, 2012 (the second year). Fill in these amounts on James Company's trial balance on the worksheet for 2012.
4. Complete the worksheet for consolidated financial statements for 2012.

Problem 7-4 *(LO 3)* **Sale of partial, then balance of interest.** On January 1, 2013, Carlos Corporation purchases 90% (18,000 shares) of the outstanding common stock of Dower Company for $504,000. Just prior to Carlos Corporation's purchase, Dower Company has the following stockholders' equity:

Common stock ($5 par)	$100,000
Paid-in capital in excess of par	300,000
Retained earnings	100,000
Total stockholders' equity	$500,000

At this time, Dower Company's book values approximate fair values except for buildings with a 20-year life.

On January 1, 2017, Dower Company's retained earnings balance amounts to $200,000. No changes have taken place in the paid-in capital in excess of par accounts since the original sale of common stock on July 10, 2010.

On July 1, 2017, Carlos Corporation sells 2,000 of its Dower Company shares to Tanner Corporation for $100,000. At the time of this sale, Carlos has no intention of selling the balance of its holding in Dower Company.

In an unexpected move on December 31, 2017, Carlos Corporation sells its remaining 80% interest in Dower Company to Tanner Corporation for $540,000.

Dower Company's reported income and dividends for 2017 are as follows:

	Income	Dividends
January 1, 2017–July 1, 2017	$30,000	$0.50/share
July 1, 2017–December 31, 2017	40,000	0.50/share

Required ▶ ▶ ▶ ▶ ▶ Prepare the determination and distribution of excess schedule for Carlos Corporation's purchase of Dower Company common stock on January 1, 2013. Then, prepare all the entries on Carlos's books needed to reflect the changes in its investment account from January 1, 2017, to December 31, 2017. (Assume Carlos uses the cost method to report its investment in Dower Company.)

Problem 7-5 *(LO 2, 3, 4)* **Analysis of block acquisitions, sale of interest, preferred stock.** The information shown on page 421 is available regarding the investments of Billings Corporation in Channel Company for the years 2011–2015.

Date	Transaction	Interest	Price
January 1, 2011	Purchased common	10%	$ 25,000
January 1, 2012	Purchased preferred	60	30,000
January 1, 2013	Purchased common	50	140,000
January 1, 2015	Purchased common	20	60,000
December 31, 2015	Sold common	10	(35,000)

The stockholders' equity section of Channel Company's balance sheet has not changed since the January 1, 2010, original sale of preferred stock to the public, except for the balance in the retained earnings account. The stockholders' equity as of January 1, 2013, is as follows:

6% Cumulative preferred stock ($50 par, liquidation value equals par value)	$ 50,000
Common stock ($10 par).	100,000
Paid-in capital in excess of par	20,000
Retained earnings	103,000
Total stockholders' equity.	$273,000

Other relevant facts are as follows:

a. On January 1, 2011, Channel has a $60,000 retained earnings balance and there are no dividends in arrears on the preferred stock.
b. Any excess of cost over book value on the investment in common stock is viewed as goodwill.
c. The 10% interest sold on January 1, 2016, is the interest purchased on January 1, 2011.
d. Channel Company income and dividends are as follows for 2011–2015:

	Net Income	Preferred Dividends	Common Dividends
2011	$25,000	$3,000	None
2012	30,000	3,000	$6,000
2013	30,000	3,000	5,000
2014	25,000	None	None
2015	20,000	None	None

Billings's investment account balances for its interests in Channel Company are calculated as follows on December 31, 2015:

Investment in preferred stock:	
Original cost	$ 30,000
Plus dividends in arrears for 2014.	1,800
Balance, December 31, 2015.	$ 31,800
Investment in common stock:	
January 1, 2011, purchase	$ 25,000
January 1, 2013, purchase	140,000
2013 Channel income ($30,000 × 60%)	18,000
2013 Channel dividends ($5,000 × 60%).	(3,000)
2014 Channel income ($25,000 × 60%)	15,000
January 1, 2015 purchase	60,000
2015 Channel income ($20,000 × 80%)	16,000
December 31, 2015, sale.	(35,000)
Balance, December 31, 2015.	$236,000

Assume the investment accounts are to be properly maintained under the simple equity ◀ ◀ ◀ ◀ ◀ **Required** method. Prepare all necessary correcting entries on the books of Billings Corporation as of

January 1, 2016. (Assume nominal accounts are open.) All supporting computations and schedules should be in good form.

Problem 7-6 *(LO 4)* **Worksheet, two subsidiaries, preferred stock, intercompany merchandise and fixed assets, bonds.** The following information pertains to Titan Corporation and its two subsidiaries, Boat Corporation and Engine Corporation:

a. The three corporations are all in the same industry and their operations are homogeneous. Titan Corporation exercises control over the boards of directors of Boat Corporation and Engine Corporation and has installed new principal officers in both.

b. Boat Corporation has a retained earnings balance of $92,000 at January 1, 2017, and has income of $15,000 for the first three months of 2017 and $20,000 for the first six months of 2018.

c. Titan Corporation acquires 250 shares of fully participating Engine preferred stock for $7,000 and 14,000 shares of Engine common stock for $196,000 on January 2, 2018. Engine Corporation has a net income of $20,000 in 2018 and does not declare any dividends.

d. Engine Corporation's inventory includes $22,400 of merchandise acquired from Boat Corporation subsequent to July 2018, for which no payment has been made. Boat Corporation marks up the merchandise 40% on cost.

e. Titan Corporation acquires in the open market twenty-five $1,000, 6% bonds of Boat Corporation for $21,400 on January 1, 2015. Boat Corporation bonds mature December 31, 2020. Interest is paid each June 30 and December 31. Straight-line amortization is allowed on the basis of materiality.

f. The 2018 year-end balance in the investment in Boat Corporation stock account is composed of the items shown in the following schedule:

Date	Description	Amount
April 1, 2017	Cost of 5,000 shares of Boat Corporation stock	$ 71,400
December 31, 2017	20% of the dividends declared in December 2017 by Boat Corporation	(9,000)
December 31, 2017	20% × 2017 annual net income of $60,000 for Boat Corporation.	12,000
July 1, 2018	Cost of 15,000 shares of Boat Corporation	226,200
December 31, 2018	80% of the dividends declared in December 2018 by Boat Corporation	(24,000)
December 31, 2018	80% of the 2018 June–December net income of Boat Corporation.	16,000
December 31, 2018	Total.	$292,600

g. Titan Corporation does not properly adjust the prior 20% investment when it acquires the 60% interest on July 1, 2018.

h. The December 31, 2018, trial balances for the three corporations appear as follows:

	Titan Corporation	Boat Corporation	Engine Corporation
Cash	100,000	87,000	95,000
Accounts Receivable	158,200	210,000	105,000
Inventories	290,000	90,000	115,000
Advance to Boat Corporation	17,000		
Dividends Receivable	24,000		
Property, Plant, and Equipment	777,600	325,000	470,000
Accumulated Depreciation	(180,000)	(55,000)	(160,000)
Investment in Boat Corporation:			
6% Bonds.	23,800		
Common Stock.	292,600*		

	Titan Corporation	Boat Corporation	Engine Corporation
Investment in Engine Corporation:			
Preferred Stock.	7,400		
Common Stock.	207,200		
Notes Payable	(45,000)	(14,000)	(44,000)
Accounts Payable	(170,000)	(96,000)	(86,000)
Bonds Payable.	(285,000)	(150,000)	(125,000)
Discount on Bonds Payable	8,000		
Dividends Payable.	(22,000)	(30,000)	
Preferred Stock ($20 par)	(400,000)		(50,000)
Common Stock ($10 par)	(600,000)	(250,000)	(200,000)
Retained Earnings, January 1, 2018.	(154,600)	(107,000)	(100,000)
Sales	(1,050,000)	(500,000)	(650,000)
Other Revenue.	(2,100)		
Subsidiary Income:			
Common Stock—Boat	(16,000)		
Preferred Stock—Engine	(400)		
Common Stock—Engine	(11,200)		
Cost of Goods Sold	650,000	300,000	400,000
Other Expenses	358,500	160,000	230,000
Dividends Declared.	22,000	30,000	
Totals	0	0	0

*Correction required.

1. Prepare any adjustment needed to the investment account as a result of the July 1, 2018, acquisition. ◀ ◀ ◀ ◀ ◀ **Required**

2. Prepare the worksheet necessary to produce the consolidated financial statements of Titan Corporation and its subsidiaries as of December 31, 2018. Correct the trial balances prior to consolidating. Consolidated retained earnings should be allocated to Titan Corporation, and the NCIs should be shown separately in the Consolidated Balance Sheet column. All supporting computations and schedules should be in good form.

(AICPA adapted)

Problem 7-7 *(LO 4)* **Worksheet, preferred stock, intercompany fixed assets and merchandise, sale of interest.** On January 1, 2017, Black Jack Corporation purchases all of the preferred stock and 60% of the common stock of Zeppo Company for $56,000 and $111,000, respectively. Immediately prior to the purchases, Zeppo Company has the following stockholders' equity:

8% Cumulative preferred stock ($100 par, two years in arrears)	$ 50,000
Common stock ($10 par).	100,000
Paid-in capital in excess of par (common stock).	20,000
Retained earnings	30,000
Total stockholders' equity.	$200,000

The December 31, 2018, trial balances of the two companies are as follows:

	Black Jack Corporation	Zeppo Company
Cash	30,400	10,000
Accounts Receivable (net)	80,000	76,000
Inventories	230,000	44,000

(continued)

	Black Jack Corporation	Zeppo Company
Other Current Assets	20,000	8,000
Property, Plant, and Equipment	1,450,000	122,000
Accumulated Depreciation	(420,000)	(25,000)
Investment in Zeppo Preferred Stock	56,000	
Investment in Zeppo Common Stock	121,200	
Liabilities	(350,000)	(18,000)
Common Stock—Black Jack	(1,000,000)	
Retained Earnings—Black Jack	(195,000)	
Preferred Stock—Zeppo ($100 par)		(50,000)
Common Stock—Zeppo		(100,000)
Paid-In Capital in Excess of Par—Zeppo		(20,000)
Retained Earnings—Zeppo		(41,000)
Sales	(420,000)	(96,000)
Cost of Goods Sold	300,000	60,000
Other Expenses	80,000	26,000
Dividends Declared	25,000	4,000
Subsidiary Income—Preferred	(4,000)	
Subsidiary Income—Common	(3,600)	
Totals	0	0

Additional information is as follows:

a. Any excess of cost over book value on the investment in common stock is attributed to equipment with an 8-year life.
b. On December 30, 2017, and December 30, 2018, Zeppo Company pays preferred stock dividends of $8 per share.
c. Zeppo Company has a net income of $15,000 in 2017 and $10,000 for 2018.
d. Zeppo Company sells a piece of equipment with a book value of $8,000 to Black Jack Corporation for $13,000 on January 2, 2017. The machine has an estimated future life of five years, and straight-line depreciation is being used.
e. During 2018, Black Jack sells $20,000 of goods to Zeppo for cost plus 40%. Zeppo has $2,800 of such purchases in its beginning inventory and $7,000 of such purchases in its ending inventory. Zeppo owes Black Jack $2,000 for purchases at year-end. During 2018, Zeppo sells $8,000 of goods to Black Jack at cost plus 60%. Of these goods, $1,200 are in Black Jack's beginning inventory, and $1,600 of such goods are in its ending inventory. Black Jack owes Zeppo $6,000 for purchases at year-end.
f. On January 1, 2019, Black Jack Corporation sells its 60% interest in Zeppo Company common stock for $130,000.

Required ▶ ▶ ▶ ▶ ▶

1. Prepare the worksheet necessary to produce the consolidated financial statements of Black Jack Corporation and its subsidiary for the year ended December 31, 2018. Include the determination and distribution of excess and income distribution schedules.
2. Prepare the entries on Black Jack Corporation's books to reflect the sale of its investment in Zeppo Company common stock on January 1, 2019.

Problem 7-8 *(LO 4)* **Worksheet, preferred stock, fixed asset sale.** Marsha Corporation purchases an 80% interest in the common stock of Transam Corporation on December 31, 2013, for $720,000, when Transam has the following condensed balance sheet:

Assets		Liabilities and Stockholders' Equity	
Current assets	$ 500,000	Liabilities	$ 600,000
Land	100,000	Preferred stock (8% cumulative, $100 par)	100,000

Assets		Liabilities and Stockholders' Equity	
Building (net)	400,000	Common stock ($20 par)	750,000
Equipment (net)	500,000	Retained earnings	50,000
Total assets.	$1,500,000	Total liabilities and equity	$1,500,000

On the December 31, 2013, purchase date, the dividends on the preferred stock are two years in arrears. Also on this date, the book values of Transam's assets approximate fair values, except for the building which is undervalued by $28,000 and has a 20-year remaining life. Any remaining excess is considered to be goodwill.

For 2014–2016, earnings and dividends for Transam Corporation are as follows:

	Income	Preferred Dividends	Common Dividends
2014	$40,000		
2015	50,000	$16,000	
2016	80,000	24,000	$26,750

The following trial balances of the two companies are prepared on December 31, 2016:

	Marsha Corporation	Transam Corporation
Current Assets	806,400	463,250
Investment in Transam Corporation	720,000	
Land	400,000	210,000
Building	950,000	500,000
Accumulated Depreciation—Building	(200,000)	(160,000)
Equipment	1,500,000	740,000
Accumulated Depreciation—Equipment	(400,000)	(200,000)
Liabilities	(800,000)	(550,000)
Preferred Stock, 8%		(100,000)
Common Stock ($20 par)	(2,000,000)	(750,000)
Retained Earnings, January 1, 2016	(860,000)	(124,000)
Sales	(2,100,000)	(1,000,000)
Subsidiary Dividend Income	(21,400)	
Cost of Goods Sold	1,155,000	600,000
Other Expenses	650,000	320,000
Dividends Declared	200,000	50,750
Totals	0	0

On January 1, 2015, Marsha sells production equipment to Transam for $55,000 with a 5-year remaining life. Marsha's original cost is $80,000, and accumulated depreciation on the date sold is $50,000.

Prepare the worksheet necessary to produce the consolidated financial statements of Marsha Corporation and its subsidiary as of December 31, 2016. Include the determination and distribution of excess and income distribution schedules.   ◄ ◄ ◄ ◄ ◄ **Required**

APPENDIX PROBLEMS

Problem 7A-1 *(LO 5)* **Balance sheet worksheet, blocks, control with first, inventory, fixed asset sales.** The December 31, 2019, post-closing trial balances of Marley Corporation and its subsidiary, Foster Corporation, are as follows:

	Marley Corporation	Foster Corporation
Cash	167,250	101,000
Accounts Receivable	170,450	72,000
Notes Receivable.	87,500	28,000
Dividends Receivable	36,000	
Inventories	122,000	68,000
Property, Plant, and Equipment	487,000	252,000
Accumulated Depreciation	(117,000)	(64,000)
Investment in Foster Corporation	248,800	
Accounts Payable	(222,000)	(76,000)
Notes Payable	(79,000)	(89,000)
Dividends Payable.		(40,000)
Common Stock ($10 par)	(400,000)	(100,000)
Retained Earnings	(501,000)	(152,000)
Totals	0	0

The following additional information is available:

a. Marley initially acquires 60% of the outstanding common stock of Foster in 2017. There is no difference between the cost and book value of the net assets acquired. As of December 31, 2019, the percentage owned is 90%. An analysis of the investment in Foster Corporation account is as follows:

Date	Description	Amount
December 31, 2017	Acquired 6,000 shares	$ 70,800
December 31, 2018	60% of 2018 net income of $78,000	46,800
September 1, 2019	Acquired 3,000 shares	100,000
December 31, 2019	Subsidiary income for 2019	67,200*
December 31, 2019	90% of dividends declared	(36,000)
	Investment balance, December 31, 2019	$248,800

*Subsidiary income for 2019:

60% × $96,000	$57,600
30% × $96,000 × 33½%	9,600
Total	$67,200

Foster net income is earned ratably during the year.

On December 15, 2019, Foster declares a cash dividend of $4 per share of common stock, payable to shareholders on January 7, 2020.

b. During 2019, Marley sells merchandise to Foster. Marley has a 25% gross profit, and the sale is made at $80,000. Foster's inventory at December 31, 2019, includes merchandise purchased from Marley for $40,000.

c. On October 1, 2019, Marley sells excess equipment to Foster for $45,000. Data relating to this equipment are as follows:

Book value on Marley's records	$36,000
Method of depreciation.	Straight-line
Estimated remaining life on October 1, 2019.	10 years

d. Near the end of 2019, Foster reduces the balance of its intercompany account payable to zero by transferring $8,000 to Marley. This payment is still in transit on December 31, 2019.

Prepare the worksheet necessary to produce the consolidated balance sheet of Marley Corporation and its subsidiary as of December 31, 2019. Include an analysis for Marley's purchase of Foster common stock on September 1, 2019. ◀ ◀ ◀ ◀ ◀ **Required**

(AICPA adapted)

Problem 7A-2 *(LO 5)* **Balance sheet worksheet, mid-year purchase, intercompany bonds and inventory.** Book, Inc., acquires all of the outstanding $25 par common stock of Cray, Inc., on June 30, 2014, in exchange for 40,000 shares of its $25 par common stock. On June 30, 2014, Book, Inc., common stock closes at $65 per share on a national stock exchange. Any excess of cost over book value is attributed to goodwill. Both corporations continue to operate as separate businesses, maintaining separate accounting records with years ending December 31.

Additional information is as follows:

a. Book, Inc., uses the simple equity method to account for its investment in Cray.
b. On June 30, 2014, Cray pays cash dividends of $4 per share on its common stock.
c. On December 10, 2014, Book pays a cash dividend totaling $256,000 on its common stock.
d. On June 30, 2014, immediately before the combination, the stockholders' equities are as follows:

	Book, Inc.	Cray, Inc.
Common stock.	$2,200,000	$1,000,000
Additional paid-in capital in excess of par	1,660,000	190,000
Retained earnings	3,036,000	980,000
Totals	$6,896,000	$2,170,000

e. Cray's long-term debt consists of 10-year, 10% bonds issued at face value on March 31, 2011. Interest is payable semiannually on March 31 and September 30. Book purchases Cray's bonds at the face value of $320,000 in 2011, and there is no change in ownership.
f. During October 2014, Book sells merchandise to Cray at a total invoice price of $720,000, which includes a profit of $180,000. At December 31, 2014, one-half of the merchandise remains in Cray's inventory, and Cray has not paid Book for the merchandise purchased.
g. The 2014 net income amounts per the separate books of Book and Cray are $890,000 (exclusive of equity in Cray earnings) and $580,000 ($320,000 in the first six months and $260,000 in the second six months), respectively.
h. The retained earnings balances at December 31, 2013, are $2,506,000 and $820,000 for Book and Cray, respectively.
i. On December 31, 2014, the companies have the following post-closing trial balances:

	Book, Inc.	Cray, Inc.
Cash	825,000	330,000
Accounts and Other Current Receivables	2,140,000	835,000
Inventories.	2,310,000	1,045,000
Land.	650,000	300,000
Depreciable Assets (net)	4,575,000	1,980,000
Investment in Cray, Inc..	2,860,000	
Long-Term Investments and Other Assets.	865,000	385,000
Accounts Payable and Other Current Liabilities	(2,465,000)	(1,145,000)
Long-Term Debt	(1,900,000)	(1,300,000)

(continued)

	Book, Inc.	Cray, Inc.
Common Stock ($25 par)	(3,200,000)	(1,000,000)
Additional Paid-In Capital in Excess of Par	(3,260,000)	(190,000)
Retained Earnings	(3,400,000)	(1,240,000)
Totals	0	0

Required ▶ ▶ ▶ ▶ ▶

1. Prepare the worksheet necessary to produce the consolidated balance sheet of Book, Inc., and its subsidiary for the year ended December 31, 2014. Include a determination and distribution of excess schedule.
2. Prepare the formal consolidated statement of retained earnings for December 31, 2014.

Problem 7A-3 *(LO 5)* **Balance sheet worksheet, intercompany inventory, bonds and capital lease.** On January 1, 2011, Press Company acquires 90% of the common stock of Soap Company for $324,000. On this date, Soap has total owners' equity of $270,000, including retained earnings of $100,000.

On January 1, 2011, any excess of cost over book value is attributable to the undervaluation of land, building, and goodwill. Land is worth $20,000 more than cost. Building is worth $40,000 more than book value. It has a remaining useful life of 20 years and is depreciated using the straight-line method.

During 2011 and 2012, Press has appropriately accounted for its investment in Soap using the simple equity method.

During 2012, Soap sells merchandise to Press for $40,000, of which $15,000 is held by Press on December 31, 2012. Soap's usual gross profit on affiliated sales is 40%. On December 31, 2012, Press still owes Soap $8,000 for merchandise acquired in December.

On October 1, 2010, Soap sells $100,000 par value of 10-year, 10% bonds for $102,000. The bonds pay interest semiannually on April 1 and October 1. Straight-line amortization is used. On October 2, 2011, Press repurchases $60,000 par value of the bonds for $59,100. Straight-line amortization is used.

On January 1, 2012, Press purchases equipment for $111,332 and immediately leases the equipment to Soap on a 3-year lease. The minimum lease payments of $40,000 are to be made annually on January 1, beginning immediately, for a total of three payments. The implicit interest rate is 8%. The useful life of the equipment is three years. The lease has been capitalized by both companies. Soap is depreciating the equipment using the straight-line method and assuming a salvage value of $6,332. A lease amortization schedule, applicable to both companies, follows:

Carrying Value on	Carrying Value	Interest Rate	Interest	Payment	Principal Reduction
January 1, 2011	111,332				
	(40,000)				
January 1, 2012	71,332	8%	$5,707	$40,000	$34,293
	(34,293)				
January 1, 2013	37,039	8%	2,961*	40,000	37,039
	(37,039)				
January 1, 2014	0				

*Adjusted for rounding error

The balance sheet for the companies on December 31, 2012, is as follows:

Assets	Press Company	Soap Company
Accounts receivable	$ 65,000	$ 50,000
Bond interest receivable	1,500	
Minimum lease payments receivable	80,000	
Unearned interest income	(2,961)	
Inventory	86,000	80,000
Other current assets.	60,236	183,668
Investment in Soap Company	351,000	
Investment in Soap bonds	59,225	
Land.	60,000	30,000
Building and equipment	300,000	230,000
Accumulated depreciation	(100,000)	(50,000)
Equipment under capital lease		111,332
Accumulated depreciated equipment under lease		(35,000)
Totals	$ 960,000	$600,000

Liabilities and Equity	Press Company	Soap Company
Accounts payable	$ 78,000	$ 70,000
Bond interest payable		2,500
Lease interest payable.		5,707
Other current liabilities	57,000	48,911
Lease obligation payable		71,332
Bonds payable	150,000	100,000
Premium on bonds.		1,550
Common stock—Press.	200,000	
Other paid-in capital in excess of par—Press	150,000	
Retained earnings—Press	325,000	
Common stock—Soap.		100,000
Other paid-in capital in excess of par—Soap		70,000
Retained earnings—Soap		130,000
Totals	$960,000	$600,000

Complete the worksheet for a consolidated balance sheet as of December 31, 2012. Include ◄ ◄ ◄ ◄ ◄ **Required** a determination and distribution of excess schedule. Round all computations to the nearest dollar.

Subsidiary Equity Transactions, Indirect Subsidiary Ownership, and Subsidiary Ownership of Parent Shares

CHAPTER

8

Learning Objectives

When you have completed this chapter, you should be able to

1. Explain the effect of subsidiary stock dividends on elimination procedures.

2. Account for the effect of the subsidiary's sale of its own common stock on the parent's investment in the subsidiary.

3. Account for the effect of subsidiary treasury stock transactions on the parent's investment in the subsidiary.

4. Demonstrate accounting procedures for multilevel holdings.

5. Demonstrate an understanding of the alternatives used for accounting for investments in the parent company owned by the subsidiary.

This chapter is concerned with subsidiary equity transactions and complicated parent ownership arrangements that affect the recording and consolidations of the parent's investment in a subsidiary. First, we will consider the impact of subsidiary equity transactions on the parent's recording and consolidation of the investment in the subsidiary. We will consider the subsidiary declaration of stock dividends, subsidiary sales of additional shares of stock, and the subsidiary repurchase of its outstanding shares.

Second, this chapter will deal with more complex ownership structures. Accounting procedures will be developed for indirect holdings and ownership of parent shares by a subsidiary. Indirect holdings are situations where a parent holds a controlling interest in a subsidiary and the subsidiary is, in turn, a parent of another company. A mutual holding exists when the subsidiary also owns voting common stock of the parent company.

SUBSIDIARY STOCK DIVIDENDS

1

OBJECTIVE

Explain the effect of subsidiary stock dividends on elimination procedures.

A subsidiary may issue stock dividends to convert retained earnings into paid-in capital. The minimum amount to be removed from retained earnings is the par value or stated value of the shares distributed. However, according to accounting principles, when the distribution does not exceed 20% to 25% of the previously outstanding shares, an amount equal to the fair value of the shares should be removed from retained earnings and transferred to paid-in capital in excess of par. The recording of stock dividends at fair value is defended by FASB ASC 505-20-05-2:

> *Many recipients of stock dividends look upon them as distributions of corporate earnings, and usually in an amount equivalent to the fair value of the additional shares received. If the issuances of stock dividends are so small in comparison with the shares previously outstanding,*

such issuances generally do not have any apparent effect on the share market price and, consequently, the market value of the shares previously held remains substantially unchanged.

Accounting theory, however, is not consistent when it comes to recording the receipt of dividends by an investor. Even though the false impression of the "typical" investor is sufficient reason to allow the issuing corporation to record the market value of the shares distributed, the investor is not permitted to do likewise. In fact, the investor must not record income when stock dividends are received but must acknowledge the true impact of the transaction, which is that nothing of substance has been given or received. Thus, the investor merely makes a memo entry indicating that the cost of the original investment now is allocated to a greater number of shares. The revised number of shares is important in computing cost per share if there is a subsequent partial sale of the investment.

To review the recording of a stock dividend and to provide a basis for worksheets, assume that Company P acquired an 80% interest in Company S on January 1, 2011, at which time the following determination and distribution of excess schedule was prepared:

Determination and Distribution of Excess Schedule

	Company Implied Fair Value	Parent Price (80%)	NCI Value (20%)
Fair value of subsidiary	$250,000	$200,000	$ 50,000
Less book value of interest acquired:			
Common stock	$100,000		
Retained earnings	80,000		
Total equity.	$180,000	$180,000	$180,000
Interest acquired		80%	20%
Book value.		$144,000	$ 36,000
Excess of fair value over book value	$ 70,000	$ 56,000	$ 14,000

Adjustment of identifiable accounts:

	Adjustment	Life	Amortization per Year	Worksheet Key
Equipment	$ 70,000	10	$ 7,000	**debit D**

On January 2, 2013, Company S declared and distributed a 10% stock dividend. Prior to declaration of the dividend, its stockholders' equity appeared as follows:

Common stock ($10 par).	$100,000
Retained earnings	120,000
Total stockholders' equity.	$220,000

In the following entry to record the stock dividend, Company S acknowledged the $25 fair value of the 1,000 shares distributed:

Retained Earnings (or Stock Dividends Declared) ($25 fair value × 1,000 shares) . . .	25,000	
Common Stock ($10 par × 1,000 shares)		10,000
Additional Paid-In Capital in Excess of Par from Stock Dividend		
(1,000 shares × $15 excess over par)		15,000

Parent Using the Simple Equity Method

Continuing the example, on January 1, 2013 (prior to the dividend), Company P has a simple-equity-adjusted balance of $232,000 in its investment in Company S account, derived as shown on page 433.

Original cost		$200,000
Share of undistributed income:		
Company S retained earnings, January 1, 2013	$120,000	
Company S retained earnings, January 1, 2011	80,000	
Increase in retained earnings...........................	$ 40,000	
Ownership interest......................................	× 80%	32,000
Simple-equity-adjusted balance, January 1, 2013		$232,000

During 2013, Company S earned $20,000 and made no other dividend declarations. Company P would make the following entries during 2013, under the simple equity method:

Receipt of stock dividend:

Jan. 2, 2013   Memo: Investment in Company S now includes 800 added shares for a total of 8,800 shares. The parent's interest remains at 80%.

Recording of equity income:

Dec. 31, 2013   Investment in Company S   16,000
                    Subsidiary Income...........................   16,000
              To record the 80% interest in Company S
              $20,000 reported net income for 2013.

The partial worksheet below lists the investment in Company S account at the December 31, 2013, simple-equity-adjusted cost of $248,000. Note that the partial worksheet includes the redistributed capital structure of Company S, which resulted from the stock dividend. It should be clear that the complications arising from stock dividends pertain primarily to their recording by the separate affiliated firms. There is only a minimal effect on the consolidated worksheet.

	Trial Balance		Eliminations & Adjustments			
	Company P	Company S	Dr.		Cr.	
Investment in Company S	248,000				(CY)	16,000
					(EL)	176,000
					(D)	56,000
Equipment			(D)	70,000	(A)	21,000
Common Stock—Company P	(500,000)					
Retained Earnings—Company P	(420,000)		(A)	11,200		
Common Stock ($10 par)—Company S		(110,000)	(EL)	88,000		
Additional Paid-In Capital in Excess of Par from Stock						
Dividend—Company S		(15,000)	(EL)	12,000		
Retained Earnings—Company S (reduced $25,000 for stock dividend)		(95,000)	(EL)	76,000	(NCI)	14,000
			(A)	2,800		
Subsidiary Income	(16,000)		(CY)	16,000		
Expenses	30,000	18,000	(A)	7,000		

Eliminations and Adjustments:

(CY)   Eliminate the parent's entry recording its share of subsidiary income for the current year. There is no complication caused by the stock dividend since it does not constitute income to Company P.

(EL)   Eliminate 80% of Company S equity balances as restructured by the stock dividend. If the subsidiary recorded the stock dividend with a debit to Stock Dividends Declared, 80% of that account would be eliminated in this step.

(D)/NCI   Distribute the excess cost and NCI adjustment to the equipment account as required by the determination and distribution of excess schedule.

(A)   Depreciate the equipment for three years. Depreciation for the two prior years reduces the controlling and noncontrolling interest in retained earnings (80%/20%), while the current-year depreciation reduces current consolidated net income.

Parent Using the Sophisticated Equity Method

Using the sophisticated equity method, the parent would have a balance in its investment in Company S account of $220,800, derived as follows:

Original cost		$200,000
Share of undistributed income:		
Company S retained earnings, January 1, 2013	$120,000	
Company S retained earnings, January 1, 2011	80,000	
Increase in retained earnings.	$ 40,000	
Ownership interest.	× 80%	32,000
Equipment depreciation, 2 years × 80% × $7,000.		(11,200)
Sophisticated-equity-adjusted balance, January 1, 2013.		$220,800

During 2013, Company P would make the same memo entry as under the simple equity method to record the stock dividend. The following entry would be made to record equity income for 2013:

Dec. 31, 2013	Investment in Company S	10,400	
	Subsidiary Income		10,400
	To record the 80% interest in Company S reported		
	income for 2013 less 80% × $7,000 equipment		
	depreciation.		

The following partial worksheet would apply to the investment maintained under the sophisticated equity method:

	Trial Balance		Eliminations & Adjustments			
	Company P	Company S	Dr.		Cr.	
Investment in Company S	231,200				(CY)	10,400
					(EL)	176,000
					(D)	**44,800**
Equipment			**(D)**	**56,000**	(A)	7,000
Common Stock—Company P	(500,000)					
Retained Earnings, January 1, 2013—Company P	(408,800)					
Common Stock ($10 par)—Company S		(110,000)	(EL)	88,000		
Additional Paid-In Capital in Excess of Par from Stock						
Dividend—Company S		(15,000)	(EL)	12,000		
Retained Earnings (reduced $25,000 for stock dividend), January 1, 2013—Company S		(95,000)	(EL)	76,000	**(NCI)**	**11,200**
Subsidiary Income	(10,400)		(CY)	10,400		
Expenses	30,000	18,000	(A)	7,000		

Eliminations and Adjustments:

(CY)   Eliminate the parent's entry recording its share of subsidiary income for the current year. There is no complication caused by the stock dividend since it does not constitute income to Company P.

(EL)   Eliminate 80% of Company S equity balances as restructured by the stock dividend. If the subsidiary recorded the stock dividend with a debit to Stock Dividends Declared, 80% of that account would be eliminated in this entry.

(D)/(NCI) Distribute the excess cost and NCI adjustment to the equipment account as required by the determination and distribution of excess schedule. Since the parent is amortizing the excess on its books, this is the remaining balance at the start of the year ($70,000 less two years' amortization at $7,000 per year).

(A)   Depreciate the equipment for the current year. The parent retained earnings is already adjusted for prior-year depreciation. The NCI adjustment is the net amount remaining at the start of the year; no depreciation for prior years is needed.

Note the following special features:

1. The investment is at the sophisticated equity balance of $231,200 ($220,800 balance on January 1, 2013, plus $10,400 equity income for 2013).
2. The retained earnings of Company P are $408,800. This is $11,200 less than under the simple equity method since there is $5,600 per year of equipment depreciation subtracted for 2011 and 2012.
3. Subsidiary income is the sophisticated equity amount of $10,400.
4. Only the equipment adjustment remaining on January 1, 2013, is entered when distributing the excess in entry (D). Recall that the prior years' depreciation has already reduced the investment account and the parent retained earnings. Note that only the current-year depreciation is made in entry (A).

Parent Using the Cost Method

In the preceding example, if the parent, Company P, had used the cost method to record its investment in Company S, no adjustments would have been made to the investment account. The investment in Company S still would be carried at its original cost of $200,000 on the December 31, 2013, worksheet.

The declaration of a stock dividend by a subsidiary requires a more difficult process for the conversion of the parent's investment account from a cost to a simple-equity basis. The conversion must reflect all the changes in subsidiary retained earnings since acquisition, including the retained earnings transferred to paid-in capital in excess of par as a result of a stock dividend. The correct simple-equity conversion would be made as follows for the preceding example:

Retained earnings, January 2, 2013 (after stock dividend)	$95,000
Retained earnings, January 1, 2011	80,000
Change in retained earnings balance	$15,000
Retained earnings transferred to paid-in capital in excess of par ($25 × 1,000 shares) as a result of stock dividend	25,000
Total change in retained earnings	$40,000
Ownership interest	× 80%
Simple-equity conversion	$32,000

A faster approach to the simple-equity conversion is to consider the change in total subsidiary stockholders' equity available to common stockholders as follows:

Subsidiary total equity, January 1, 2013	$220,000
Subsidiary total equity, January 1, 2011	180,000
Net change	$ 40,000
Ownership interest	× 80%
Simple-equity conversion	$ 32,000

Normally, a parent will maintain a permanent file with the needed information for this adjustment. This faster method, however, could be useful in later years if facts surrounding the stock dividend were not readily available. The faster procedure will work well, provided in the interim periods there have been no other changes in subsidiary paid-in capital in excess of par, such as a subsidiary sale or retirement of its shares.

The $32,000 simple-equity conversion would be the first step on a worksheet when the cost method is used for the subsidiary investment. This step converts the investment in subsidiary account to its simple-equity balance at the beginning of 2013. The entry would be as follows:

Investment in Company S	32,000	
Retained Earnings, January 1, 2013		32,000

The remaining worksheet procedures would not include the elimination of the current year's subsidiary income, but otherwise it would be identical to entries (D), (NCI), (EL), and (A) of the partial worksheet on page 434.

REFLECTION

- The receipt of subsidiary stock dividends requires no entry by the parent.
- Care needs to be taken when converting from cost to equity. The adjustment for the increase in equity includes amounts moved from retained earnings to paid-in capital in excess of par as a result of subsidiary stock dividends.

2

OBJECTIVE

Account for the effect of the subsidiary's sale of its own common stock on the parent's investment in the subsidiary.

SUBSIDIARY SALE OF ITS OWN COMMON STOCK

In virtually all cases where the subsidiary issues additional shares of stock, the transaction impacts the parent's investment in the subsidiary account. Even though the parent purchases none of the newly issued shares, its share of subsidiary equity has changed, and consolidation procedures must acknowledge the change. When the parent purchases some of the newly issued shares, the adjustment needed depends on whether the ownership interest after the purchase is equal to, less than, or greater than the ownership interest prior to the purchase. The adjustments resulting from a subsidiary stock sale are made at the time of the sale when the equity method is used, or they are part of the cost-to-equity conversion process when the cost method is used. In all cases, a comparison is made of the parent's position before and after the subsidiary transaction occurs. Thus, the term that will be used is "before and after" analysis.

Sale of Subsidiary Stock to Noncontrolling Shareholders

A parent may allow a subsidiary to sell additional shares of stock in order to raise additional equity. A sale of stock by the subsidiary to new or existing noncontrolling shareholders results in an increase in the total subsidiary stockholders' equity against which the controlling interest has a claim. However, the effect of increasing the number of subsidiary shares in the hands of noncontrolling stockholders is to lower the controlling interest ownership percentage. Thus, the controlling ownership receives a smaller percentage of a larger subsidiary equity. The net effect on the value of the controlling interest depends on the price at which the shares are sold.

A change in the equity of the subsidiary is recorded as a capital transaction, and it never has an impact on income. In most cases, the subsidiary equity change would be recorded as a change in the paid-in capital in excess of par of the parent company (debit effect could impact retained earnings when no paid-in capital in excess of par exists).[1]

Parent Using the Equity Method. A parent company using either the simple or sophisticated equity method usually will need to make an adjustment to its investment account when its subsidiary sells additional shares of stock to NCI shareholders. To illustrate, assume Company P has a 90% interest in Company S. The interest was purchased on January 1, 2011, at which time the determination and distribution of excess schedule was prepared, as shown on page 437.

---

1 FASB ASC 810-10-45-23.

Determination and Distribution of Excess Schedule

	Company Implied Fair Value	Parent Price (90%)	NCI Value (10%)
Fair value of subsidiary	$160,000	$144,000	$ 16,000
Less book value of interest acquired:			
Common stock.	$100,000		
Retained earnings	50,000		
Total equity.	$150,000	$150,000	$150,000
Interest acquired		90%	10%
Book value.		$135,000	$ 15,000
Excess of fair value over book value	**$ 10,000**	$ 9,000	$ 1,000

Adjustment of identifiable accounts:

	Adjustment	Life	Amortization per Year	Worksheet Key
Equipment	$ 10,000	10	$ 1,000	**debit D**

Assume that Company S will issue additional shares on January 1, 2014. The equity of Company S is based on the recorded equity amounts as adjusted by the fair value adjustments made on the acquisition date. That amount is calculated as follows:

Common stock ($10 par).	$100,000
Retained earnings, January 1, 2014.	140,000
Company S equity.	$240,000
Remaining fair value adjustment [$10,000 − (3 years × $1,000)]	7,000
Equity adjusted for fair value adjustment on acquisition date	$247,000

The "before and after" analysis will be applied to the following example. On January 1, 2014, 2,000 shares of previously unissued common stock are sold to the noncontrolling interest. As a result, the parent's interest is reduced to 75% ($9,000 ÷ $12,000). An analysis of the controlling interest before and after the sale of 2,000 new subsidiary shares to noncontrolling shareholders follows. The "before and after" analysis shows the three possibilities: shares sold at book value (Case 1), at more than book value (Case 2), and at less than book value (Case 3).

	Case 1 (sold at book value)	Case 2 (sold at price greater than book value)	Case 3 (sold at price less than book value)
Sale price per share.	$ 24.70	$ 30.00	$ 20.00
Company S shareholders' equity prior to sale			
Adjusted for fair value adjustments (see above)	$247,000	$247,000	$247,000
Add to common stock ($10 par × 2,000 shares)	20,000	20,000	20,000
Add to paid-in capital in excess of par	29,400	40,000	20,000
Company S shareholders' equity after the sale	$296,400	$307,000	$287,000
Controlling interest after the sale (75%).	$222,300	$230,250	$215,250
Controlling interest before the sale (90% × $247,000) .	222,300	222,300	222,300
Net increase (decrease) in controlling interest.	$ 0	$ 7,950	$ (7,050)

Based on the results of the three cases in the above table, it should be noted that no change in controlling interest occurs when a subsidiary sells new stock to noncontrolling shareholders at adjusted book value (as adjusted for fair value adjustments on acquisition date). An increase occurs when the stock is sold above adjusted book value, and a decrease results when the stock is sold below adjusted book value.

The parent would adjust its investment in subsidiary account to record the effect on controlling interest in each of the three cases as follows:

Case 1: Memo entry only to record a change from a 90% to a 75% interest.

Case 2: Investment in Company S 7,950
            Paid-In Capital in Excess of Par   7,950
               To record increase in ownership interest and change from 90%
               to 75% interest.

Case 3: Paid-In Capital in Excess of Par* 7,050
            Investment in Company S.................................   7,050
               To record decrease in ownership interest. It is assumed that
               parent additional paid-in capital in excess of par exists to offset
               the decrease. Also record change from 90% to 75% interest.

*Or Retained Earnings if there is no paid-in capital in excess of par.

Note that when the equity method is used, these entries would be made directly on the books of the parent; they are not worksheet adjustments.

To illustrate the effect of Case 2 on consolidation, assume subsidiary income for 2014 was $40,000 and no dividends were declared. The investment account balance under the simple equity method would be determined as follows:

Original cost	$144,000
Simple-equity income adjustments (2011 through 2013, 90% × $90,000	
increase in retained earnings)..	81,000
Increase from stock sale to NCI on January 1, 2014............................	7,950
Simple-equity adjustment for 2014 subsidiary income (75% × $40,000 income).......	30,000
Balance, December 31, 2014	$262,950

In the partial worksheet shown below, for the year ended December 31, 2014, the trial balances of Company P and Company S reflect the sale of 2,000 additional shares at $30 per share (Case 2).

	Trial Balance		Eliminations & Adjustments			
	Company P	Company S	Dr.		Cr.	
Investment in Company S (75%)	262,950				(CY)	30,000
					(EL)	225,000
					(D)	7,500
					(adj)	450
Equipment			(D)	10,000	(A)	4,000
Common Stock—Company P	(400,000)					
Paid-In Capital in Excess of Par—Company P	(7,950)					
Retained Earnings—Company P	(320,000)		(A)	2,250		
			(adj)	450		
Common Stock—Company S		(120,000)	(EL)	90,000		
Paid-In Capital in Excess of Par—Company S		(40,000)	(EL)	30,000		
Retained Earnings, January 1, 2014—Company S		(140,000)	(EL)	105,000	(NCI)	2,500
			(A)	750		
Subsidiary Income	(30,000)		(CY)	30,000		
Expenses	40,000	27,000	(A)	1,000		

Eliminations and Adjustments:

(CY)	Eliminate the parent's entry recording subsidiary income for the current year. The parent's share is now **75%** of the subsidiary undistributed net income. If the sale had occurred during the year, the old percentage of ownership would be applied to income earned prior to the sale date.
(EL)	Eliminate the parent's **75%** share of subsidiary equity balances at the beginning of the year against the investment account.
(D)/(NCI)	Distribute to the equipment account the original excess of cost over book value and NCI adjustment, as required by the January 1, 2011, determination and distribution of excess schedule. The adjustment is now allocated 75%/25% to the investment account and to the NCI.
(A)	Depreciate equipment for the past three years and the current year. The prior-year amortizations are allocated 75%/25% to controlling and noncontrolling retained earnings.
(adj)	The "amortization adjustment" is to adjust parent retained earnings for the fact that the amortization in prior years was allocated 90% to the parent, as opposed to the current 75% allocation. It is calculated as (15% change × $1,000 annual depreciation × 3 years).

The consolidated worksheet may require the adjustment of both the controlling and non-controlling interests in beginning retained earnings for intercompany transactions originating in previous periods. When such adjustments are necessary, the current, not the original, owner-ship interest percentages are used.

Parent Using the Cost Method. A parent using the cost method records only dividends received from a subsidiary. Usually, no adjustment is made for any other changes in the subsidiary stock-holders' equity, including changes caused by sales of subsidiary stock. As a result, the entry to convert from the cost method to the equity method on future worksheets must consider not only the equity adjustments for the subsidiary undistributed income but also adjustments in the parent's ownership interest caused by subsidiary stock sales. A parent using the cost method still would list the subsidiary investment at its original cost.

The partial worksheet on page 440 demonstrates the consolidation procedures needed for Case 2 when the cost method is used.

To review this process, the cost-to-simple-equity conversion amount for Case 2 is deter-mined as it would apply to the December 31, 2014, worksheet.

Undistributed income:		
90% of change in retained earnings of Company S from		
January 1, 2011, to January 1, 2014 (90% × $90,000)		$81,000
Adjustment to paid-in capital in excess of par:		
Controlling interest in Company S equity subsequent to sale on		
January 1, 2014 (75% × $307,000)	$230,250	
Controlling interest in Company S equity prior to sale on		
January 1, 2014 (90% × $247,000)	222,300	
Net increase in paid-in capital in excess of par		7,950
Total increase in investment account		$88,950

This adjustment becomes (CV) in the cost method worksheet. In later years, the conversion entry would include only 75% of the change in subsidiary retained earnings that occurs after the January 1, 2014, sale of stock.

Company P and Subsidiary Company S
Partial Worksheet (Cost Method)
For Year Ended December 31, 2014

	Trial Balance		Eliminations & Adjustments			
	Company P	Company S	Dr.		Cr.	
Investment in Company S (75%)	144,000		(CV)	88,950	(EL)	225,000
					(D)	7,500
					(adj)	450
Equipment			(D)	10,000	(A)	4,000
Common Stock—Company P	(400,000)					
Paid-In Capital in Excess of Par—Company P					(CV)	7,950
Retained Earnings ($81,000 less since no equity income was recorded), January 1, 2014—Company P	(239,000)		(A)	2,250	(CV)	81,000
			(adj)	450		
Common Stock—Company S		(120,000)	(EL)	90,000		
Paid-In Capital in Excess of Par—Company S		(40,000)	(EL)	30,000		
Retained Earnings, January 1, 2014—Company S		(140,000)	(EL)	105,000	(NCI)	2,500
			(A)	750		
Expenses	40,000	27,000	(A)	1,000		

Eliminations and Adjustments:

(CV) The simple-equity conversion is recorded:
(EL) Eliminate the parent's **75%** share of subsidiary equity balances at the beginning of the year against the investment account.
(D)/(NCI) Distribute to the equipment account the original excess of cost over book value and NCI adjustment, as required by the January 1, 2011, determination and distribution of excess schedule. The adjustment is now allocated 75%/25% to the investment account and to the NCI.
(A) Depreciate equipment for the past three years and the current year. The prior-year amortizations are allocated 75%/25% to controlling and noncontrolling retained earnings.
(adj) The "amortization adjustment" is to adjust parent retained earnings for the fact that the amortization in prior years was allocated 90% to the parent, as opposed to the current 75% allocation. It is calculated as (15% change × $1,000 annual depreciation × 3 years).

A dangerous shortcut might be attempted whereby the net change in the controlling ownership interest is calculated by comparing 90% of the total subsidiary equity (adjusted for fair value adjustments) on January 1, 2011, to 75% of the total subsidiary equity (adjusted for fair value adjustments) on January 1, 2015. This shortcut will produce the correct adjustment to the investment in subsidiary account, but it will not provide the analysis needed to distribute the adjustment to the parent's paid-in capital in excess of par and retained earnings.

Parent Purchase of Newly Issued Subsidiary Stock

A parent may purchase all or a portion of the newly issued stock. The general approach in such cases is to compare the change resulting from the sale to the price paid for the additional interest:

◆ When the ownership interest remains the same, there will be no adjustment.
◆ When the ownership interest increases or decreases, the difference between the change in equity and the price paid is viewed as a change in paid-in capital in excess of par. (In some cases, there may be a debit to Retained Earnings.)

Presented in the following table are three cases based on the previous example for which the determination and distribution of excess schedule was shown on page 437. Recall that the subsidiary is issuing 2,000 new shares of common stock for $30 per share.

	Case A (maintain interest)		Case B (increase interest)		Case C (decrease interest)	
1 Shares purchased by parent	1,800		2,000		1,000	
2 Total shares owned by parent after purchase	10,800		11,000		10,000	
3 Total subsidiary shares outstanding after issue	12,000		12,000		12,000	
4 Subsidiary equity after the sale (includes fair value adjustment from Case 2, page 437)	$307,000		$307,000		$307,000	
5 Parent's ownership percent after purchase **(2 ÷ 3)**.	× 90%		× 91.67%		× 83.33%	
6 Parent's new equity interest after purchase **(4 × 5)**		$276,300		$281,427		$255,823
7 Subsidiary equity before the sale (from page 437).	$247,000		$247,000		$247,000	
8 Parent's ownership percent before the purchase	× 90%		× 90%		× 90%	
9 Parent's equity interest before the purchase **(7 × 8)**		222,300		222,300		222,300
10 Change in parent's equity interest due to purchase **(6 − 9)**		$ 54,000		$ 59,127		$ 33,523
11 Price paid **($30 × 1)**		54,000		60,000		30,000
12 Increase (decrease) in parent's equity interest over price paid **(10 − 11)**		$ 0		$ (873)		$ 3,523

In Case A, the parent maintains its ownership interest by purchasing 90% of the newly issued shares. Note that there is no difference between the price paid by the parent for the new shares and the dollar change in the parent's ownership interest due to the purchase. Thus, no entry is needed other than to record the purchase of the shares as follows:

Investment in Company S (1,800 shares × $30)	54,000	
Cash		54,000

No new disparity between cost and underlying equity is created. As a result, **no additional equity adjustment is needed when the parent maintains its ownership interest and the same price is paid by all buyers**.

In Case B, the parent has increased its ownership interest to 91.67%. The price paid in excess of the additional interest is a reduction of equity that is charged against existing parent paid-in capital in excess of par, unless it does not exist. In that case, it is a debit to the parent's Retained Earnings.

The entry at the time of the purchase of the additional shares would be as follows:

Investment in Company S	59,127	
Retained Earnings—Parent (assumes no paid-in capital in excess of par). . .	873	
Cash (2,000 shares × $30)		60,000
Future eliminations would be based on the 91.67% interest		

In Case C, the parent did not buy enough shares to maintain its ownership interest. However, the parent's investment account increased by $3,523 more than the price paid for the new interest. The increase would be an addition to paid-in capital in excess of par. A decrease would be a debit to existing Paid-In Capital in Excess of Par. If there is no existing paid-in capital in excess of par on the parent's books, retained earnings would be reduced. In Case C, the investment account increased $33,523, and the price paid was only $30,000. In addition to recording the purchase of the shares, the entry records the $3,523 increase in the parent's ownership interest. The entry for the transactions discussed would be as follows:

Investment in Company S	33,523	
Cash (1,000 shares × $30)		30,000
Paid-In Capital in Excess of Par—Parent		3,523

This entry is made at the time of the purchase and assumes the use of the equity method. If the cost method were used, it would be made as part of the cost-to-equity conversion process.

REFLECTION

- The subsidiary may increase its equity by issuing additional shares to noncontrolling shareholders.

- A "before and after" analysis is used to calculate the effect of stock issuance by the subsidiary on the parent's interest.

- The adjustment is made to the paid-in capital in excess of par account of the parent. (A decrease in equity would be a reduction of the parent's retained earnings if no paid-in capital in excess of par is available.)

3

OBJECTIVE

Account for the effect of subsidiary treasury stock transactions on the parent's investment in the subsidiary.

SUBSIDIARY PURCHASE OF ITS OWN COMMON STOCK

When a subsidiary acquires some of its own shares from the noncontrolling interest, the subsidiary equity is reduced. The parent will now own a larger percentage of a smaller equity. As is the case when subsidiary equity increases, a "before and after" analysis is needed. When the parent's interest increases, the increase is credited to the parent's Paid-In Capital in Excess of Par. When the parent's interest is reduced, the decrease is debited to the parent's Paid-In Capital in Excess of Par, if available. If paid-in capital in excess of par is not available, then the parent's retained earnings is reduced.

Purchase of Shares as Treasury Stock

To illustrate a subsidiary treasury stock purchase, assume the parent, Company P, owned a 70% interest in Company S. On January 1, 2011, Company S had the following stockholders' equity:

Capital stock ($10 par)	$100,000
Paid-in capital in excess of par	50,000
Retained earnings	90,000
Total stockholders' equity....................	$240,000

Further assume that the remaining fair value adjustment resulting from the original acquisition is $15,000. Thus, the adjusted equity of the subsidiary was as follows:

Total stockholder's equity from above	$240,000
Remaining fair value adjustment	15,000
Adjusted subsidiary equity..................	$255,000

On this date, the subsidiary purchased 2,000 of its 10,000 outstanding shares. The entry (shown on page 443) then was recorded by Company S as a result of this purchase from noncontrolling shareholders at a cost of $26 each.

| Treasury Stock (at cost) | 52,000 | |
| Cash | | 52,000 |

As a result of the purchase, Company S had the following stockholders' equity:

Capital stock ($10 par)	$100,000
Paid-in capital in excess of par	50,000
Retained earnings	90,000
Total	$240,000
Less treasury stock (at cost)	52,000
Total stockholders' equity	$188,000
Add remaining fair value adjustment	15,000
Adjusted subsidiary equity after treasury stock purchase	$203,000

The parent now owns 7,000 of 8,000 outstanding subsidiary shares (87.5% interest). The "before and after" analysis is as follows:

Parent interest after treasury stock purchase (87.5% × $203,000)	$177,625
Parent interest prior to treasury stock purchase (70% × $255,000)	178,500
Increase (decrease) in parent company equity	$ (875)

An increase would be credited to the parent's Paid-In Capital in Excess of Par. A decrease is debited to the available parent Paid-In Capital in Excess of Par, otherwise to the parent's Retained Earnings. In this case (assuming no parent paid-in capital in excess of par), the entry for a parent using either equity method would be as follows:

| Retained Earnings—Parent | 875 | |
| Investment in Subsidiary | | 875 |

Eliminations in future periods would be based on the resulting 87.5% parent interest. Eliminations would include eliminating 87.5% of the subsidiary treasury stock account.

A parent using the cost method would include the above adjustment in its cost-to-equity conversion worksheet adjustment (CV).

Resale of Shares Held in Treasury

The purchase and resale of treasury stock by a subsidiary would be handled as two separate events using the previously described "before and after" comparison method. Alternative procedures might be used if there is any intent to resell the treasury shares in the near future. When, for example, the treasury stock is purchased and resold within the consolidated company's fiscal period, a shortcut is possible. Since there would be no change in the parent's percentage of ownership by the end of the period, the parent only needs to make an adjustment equal to its ownership interest multiplied by the subsidiary's increase or decrease in equity as a result of the treasury stock transaction. This adjustment should be carried to the additional paid-in capital in excess of par of the parent and is not viewed as an operating gain or loss since it results from dealings with the company's own shareholders. Using the same reasoning, a decrease in equity reduces the parent's retained earnings only when no additional paid-in capital in excess of par is available.

REFLECTION

- The repurchase of shares by a subsidiary is treated as a change in subsidiary equity that is accounted for by employing "before and after" analysis.

4

OBJECTIVE

Demonstrate accounting procedures for multilevel holdings.

INDIRECT HOLDINGS

A parent company may own a controlling interest in a subsidiary that, in turn, owns a controlling interest in another company. For example, Company A may own a 75% interest in Company B, which owns an 80% interest in Company C. Thus, A has indirect holdings in C. This situation could be diagrammed as follows:

The treatment of the *level one* investment in B and the *level two* investment in C can be mastered with the methods we have used, but the procedures must be applied carefully. The procedures are applied easily to indirect holdings when the level one investment already exists at the time of the level two acquisition. Complications arise in preparing the determination and distribution of excess schedule for the new investment when the level two investment exists prior to the time that the parent achieves control over the subsidiary (level one investment). These complications result because the level two investment held by the subsidiary represents one of the subsidiary's assets that may require adjustment to fair value on the determination and distribution of excess schedule prepared at the time of the parent's level one acquisition. **The use of separate and distinct determination and distribution of excess schedules for each level of investment should facilitate the maintaining of proper accounting when two or more levels are involved.**

Level One Holding Acquired First

Assume Company A purchased a 75% interest in Company B on January 1, 2011, at which time the following determination and distribution of excess schedule was prepared:

Determination and Distribution of Excess Schedule

	Company Implied Fair Value	Parent Price (75%)	NCI Value (25%)
Fair value of subsidiary	$ 550,000	$412,500	$137,500
Less book value of interest acquired			
Common stock	$ 200,000		
Retained earnings	100,000		
Total equity	$ 300,000	$300,000	$300,000
Interest acquired		75%	25%
Book value		$225,000	$ 75,000
Excess of fair value over book value	**$250,000**	$187,500	$ 62,500

Adjustment of identifiable accounts:

	Adjustment	Life	Amortization per Year	Worksheet Key
Equipment	$ 250,000	10	$ 25,000	**debit D₁**

On January 1, 2012, the subsidiary, Company B, purchased an 80% interest in Company C, and the following schedule was prepared:

Determination and Distribution of Excess Schedule

	Company Implied Fair Value	Parent Price (80%)	NCI Value (20%)
Fair value of subsidiary	$ 337,500	$270,000	$ 67,500
Less book value of interest acquired:			
Common stock	$ 100,000		
Retained earnings	120,000		
Total equity.	$ 220,000	$220,000	$220,000
Interest acquired		80%	20%
Book value.		$176,000	$ 44,000
Excess of fair value over book value	**$117,500**	$ 94,000	$ 23,500

Adjustment of identifiable accounts:

	Adjustment	Life	Amortization per Year	Worksheet Key
Building	$ 117,500	20	$ 5,875	**debit Dc**

Equity adjustments must be made carefully. Company A must be sure that Company B has included its equity income from Company C in its net income before Company A records its percentage share of Company B income.

Assume the following internally generated net incomes:

	Company A	Company B	Company C
2011	$100,000	$100,000	$20,000
2012	70,000	76,000	30,000
2013	90,000	100,000	30,000

On this basis, the following simple-equity adjustments would be required:

Date	Company B's Books		Company A's Books	
2011 Dec. 31	None (interest in Company C not yet acquired)		Investment in Company B . . . . 75,000 Subsidiary Income . . . . 75,000 To adjust for 75% of Company B reported income.	
2012 Dec. 31	Investment in Company C . . . . 24,000 Subsidiary Income . . . . 24,000 To adjust for 80% of Company C reported income.		Investment in Company B . . . . 75,000 Subsidiary Income . . . . 75,000 To adjust for 75% of Company B total income ($76,000 plus $24,000 subsidiary income).	
2013 Dec. 31	Investment in Company C . . . . 24,000 Subsidiary Income . . . . 24,000 To adjust for 80% of Company C reported income.		Investment in Company B . . . . 93,000 Subsidiary Income . . . . 93,000 To adjust for 75% of Company B total income ($100,000 plus $24,000 subsidiary income).	

Worksheet 8-1, pages 454 and 455, is based on the trial balances of the three separate companies on December 31, 2013. The investment account balances reflect the equity adjustments previously shown. The additional information for 2013, shown on page 446, is assumed.

Worksheet 8-1: page 454

	Intercompany Sales by B to A	Intercompany Sales by C to B
Selling company goods in buyer's January 1, 2013, inventory	$ 8,000	$ 6,000
Sales during 2013	$50,000	$40,000
Selling company goods in buyer's December 31, 2013, inventory	$10,000	$10,000
Gross profit on all sales	25%	30%

The investment accounts must be handled carefully when any eliminations are made in order to ensure that the NCI accounts are available to receive applicable amortizations of excess. It is suggested that the level one investment be eliminated first, thereby reducing Company B retained earnings to the NCI. Then, it will be possible to allocate the amortizations of excess resulting from the level two (Company C) holding to the controlling interest (Company A) and the Company B NCI. Since Company B owns the interest in Company C, the Company B NCI must share in the amortizations of excess resulting from the investment in Company C.

The eliminations for Worksheet 8-1 in journal entry form are as follows:

Entries to eliminate investment in Company B:

(CYb)   Eliminate current-year equity income:
Subsidiary Income	93,000	
Investment in Company B		93,000

(ELb)   Eliminate subsidiary B equity:
Common Stock ($10 par)—Company B	150,000	
Retained Earnings, January 1, 2013—Company B	225,000	
Investment in Company B		375,000

(Db)/(NCIb)   Distribute excess to buildings and equipment:
Buildings and Equipment	250,000	
Investment in Company B		187,500
Retained Earnings, January 1, 2013—Company B (NCI)		62,500

(Ab)   Amortize excess:
Retained Earnings, January 1, 2013—Company A	37,500	
Retained Earnings, January 1, 2013—Company B	12,500	
Expenses	25,000	
Accumulated Depreciation		75,000

Entries to eliminate investment in Company C:

(CYc)   Eliminate current-year equity income:
Investment Income	24,000	
Investment in Company C		24,000

(ELc)   Eliminate subsidiary C equity:
Common Stock ($10 par)—Company C	80,000	
Retained Earnings, January 1, 2013—Company C	120,000	
Investment in Company C		200,000

(Dc)/(NCIc)   Distribute excess and NCI adjustment to buildings and equipment:
Buildings and Equipment	117,500	
Investment in Company C		94,000
Retained Earnings, January 1, 2013—Company C (NCI)		23,500

(Ac) Amortize excess:

Retained Earnings, January 1, 2013—Company A	3,525	
Retained Earnings, January 1, 2013—Company B	1,175	
Retained Earnings, January 1, 2013—Company C	1,175	
Expenses	5,875	
Accumulated Depreciation		11,750

(IS) Eliminate intercompany sales:

Sales	90,000	
Cost of Goods Sold		90,000

(BIb) Beginning inventory profit, Company B sales:

Retained Earnings, January 1, 2013—Company A	1,500	
Retained Earnings, January 1, 2013—Company B	500	
Cost of Goods Sold		2,000

(EIb) Ending inventory profit, Company B sales:

Cost of Goods Sold	2,500	
Inventory, December 31, 2013		2,500

(BIc) Beginning inventory profit, Company C sales:

Retained Earnings, January 1, 2013—Company A	1,080	
Retained Earnings, January 1, 2013—Company B	360	
Retained Earnings, January 1, 2013—Company C	360	
Cost of Goods Sold		1,800

(EIc) Ending inventory profit, Company C sales:

Cost of Goods Sold	3,000	
Inventory, December 31, 2013		3,000

In Worksheet 8-1, the consolidated net income is $187,425, which must be distributed to the two NCIs and to the controlling interest. Distribution must proceed from the lowest level (level two) to ensure proper distribution. Company B adjusted income includes 80% of Company C adjusted income. Thus, the Company C IDS must be completed first, followed by the distribution schedules for Companies B and A. These schedules accompany Worksheet 8-1.

If the cost method was used in the previous example, the investment account balances still would contain the January 1, 2011, $412,500 cost of the Company B investment and the January 1, 2012, $270,000 cost of the Company C investment. Conversion entries would be made on the consolidated worksheet to update both investment accounts to their January 1, 2013, simple-equity balances. It is advisable to make equity adjustments at the lowest level of investment first, because the retained earnings of the mid-level firm must be adjusted for its share of investment income before the parent can adjust for the change in its subsidiary's retained earnings. The following simple-equity conversion entry would be made first for Company B's investment in Company C:

Investment in Company C	24,000	
Retained Earnings—Company B		24,000
To record 80% of $30,000 increase in Company C retained earnings		
between January 1, 2012, and January 1, 2013.		

The following conversion entry then would be made for Company A's investment in Company B:

Investment in Company B	150,000	
Retained Earnings—Company A.		150,000
To record 75% of $200,000 increase in Company B retained		
earnings (including previous equity adjustment for Company B)		
between January 1, 2011, and January 1, 2013.		

Eliminations and adjustments would be made as on Worksheet 8-1, except that there would be no need to eliminate the current year's equity adjustment.

Level Two Holding Exists at Time of Parent's Purchase

When a parent acquires a controlling interest in another parent company, the determination and distribution of excess schedule must compare the price paid with the interest in the parent acquired. For example, assume that in a period before January 1, 2011, Company Y purchased an 80% interest in Company Z for a price equal to book value. Also assume that on January 1, 2011, Company Z's book value is $200,000 and its fair value is $300,000. The $100,000 is attributable to one of Company Z's buildings. On January 1, 2011, Company X purchased a 70% interest in Company Y for $700,000. On that date, Company Y had a stockholders' equity of $740,000 (including its interest in Company Z), and it had equipment that was understated by $40,000. Based on these facts, the following determination and distribution of excess schedule would be prepared:

Determination and Distribution of Excess Schedule

	Company Implied Fair Value	Parent Price (70%)	NCI (Y) Value (30%)
Fair value of subsidiary	$1,000,000	$700,000	$300,000
Less book value of interest acquired:			
Common stock	$ 400,000		
Retained earnings	340,000		
Total equity.	$ 740,000	$740,000	$740,000
Interest acquired		70%	30%
Book value.		$518,000	$222,000
Excess of fair value over book value	**$ 260,000**	$182,000	$ 78,000

Adjustment of identifiable accounts:

	Adjustment	**Life**	**Amortization per Year**	**Worksheet Key**
Company Z building (80%)	$ 80,000	20	$ 4,000	**debit D1**
Company Y equipment	40,000	5	8,000	**debit D2**
Goodwill.	**140,000**			**debit D3**
Total	**$ 260,000**			

The distribution of the excess and NCI adjustments would be made on the worksheet as follows:

Company Z Building ($80,000 parent share + $20,000 NCI —		
Company Z share)	100,000	
Company Y Equipment	40,000	
Company Y Goodwill	140,000	
Investment in Company Y (excess remaining after elimination)		182,000
NCI—Company Y		78,000
NCI—Company Z (for building)		20,000

In future years, amortization adjustments would be distributed to retained earnings in the following percentages:

	Controlling	NCI Company Y	NCI Company Z
(A1) Building	70% × 80% = 56%	30% × 80% = 24%	20%
(A2) Equipment	70%	30%	

The above example assumes that the investment in Company Z was acquired at book value. If that were not the case, the Company Z equity would be adjusted for the remaining excess, prior to multiplying by the Company X ownership interest.

When the simple equity method is used for the investments, the procedures illustrated in Worksheet 8-1 apply without modification. When the cost method is used, simple-equity conversion adjustments again proceed from the lowest level. Be sure to note, however, that in this example Company X would convert to the equity basis for the change in Company Y retained earnings after January 1, 2013.

Connecting Affiliates

A business combination involving connecting affiliates exists when a parent company has a direct (level one) investment in a company and an indirect (level two) investment in the same company sufficient to result in control. For example, the following diagram illustrates a connecting affiliate structure:

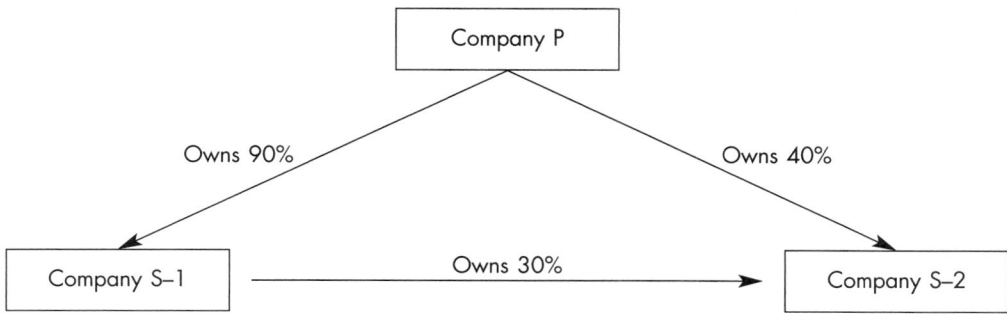

Not only does Company P have a 90% interest in Company S–1, but it also has, in effect, a 67% interest in Company S–2, calculated as follows:

Direct.	40%
Indirect (90% × 30%)	27%
Total	67%

This type of structure is consolidated more readily once the determination and distribution of excess schedule has been prepared. Referring to the diagram, the special concerns in consolidating connecting affiliates are as follows:

1. Company S–2 generally is not included in the consolidation process until the total percentage of S–2 shares held by the parent and its subsidiaries (70% in this example) exceeds 50%. Prior to that time, an investment of 20% or more is accounted for under the sophisticated equity method, and a less-than-20% investment is accounted for under the cost method.

2. Company S–2 accounts are adjusted to fair value on the date that control of Company S–2 is achieved. The amortizations resulting from the D&D schedule would be distributed to the ownership groups by including them in the Company S–2 IDS schedule. Prior-period amortizations on the worksheet would be distributed as follows:
   - 30% (NCI %) to S–2 retained earnings
   - 3% (10% NCI × 30% interest) to S–1 retained earnings
   - 67% [(90% interest × 30% Company S–1 interest) + 40% interest in Company S–2] to the controlling interest.

   The above percentages are also used for prior-period intercompany profits originated by Company S–2.

3. Company S–1 accounts are adjusted to fair value on the date that control of Company S–1 is achieved. The amortizations resulting from the D&D schedule would be distributed to the ownership groups by including them in the Company S–1 IDS schedule. Prior-period amortizations on the worksheet would be distributed as follows:
   - 10% to S–1 retained earnings
   - 90% to the controlling interest

The percentages shown on page 449 are also used for prior-period intercompany profits originated by Company S–2.

4. Income distributions would begin with Company S–2: 30% of its income would go to NCI S–2, 30% would flow to the Company S–1 distribution schedule, and 40% would flow to the Company P schedule. Company P will receive 90% of the Company S–1 adjusted income (including the 30% share of Company S–2).

5. When either equity method is used, Companies P and S–1 each must adjust for their interest in Company S–2, even though neither company's interest by itself would merit consolidation techniques.

6. When the cost method is used, each investment is converted to the simple equity method from the purchase date forward. Again, equity conversions must begin at the lowest level. For example, the Company S–1 investment in Company S–2 must be converted first, so that Company S–1 retained earnings are updated before the Company P investment in Company S–1 is converted to the simple equity method.

REFLECTION

- Indirect holdings have three or more ownership tiers and create the ownership of the shares of one subsidiary by another subsidiary.

- Equity adjustments must proceed from the lowest level to the highest to ensure that upper-level investments include the effect of income earned by the subsidiary being analyzed.

- Eliminations should begin at the highest level. This makes the NCI available to receive adjustments from the elimination of lower-level investments.

- Retained earnings and IDS adjustments must be made carefully to assign adjustments to the appropriate ownership group.

5

OBJECTIVE

Demonstrate an understanding of the alternatives used for accounting for investments in the parent company owned by the subsidiary.

PARENT COMPANY SHARES PURCHASED BY SUBSIDIARY

The subsidiary may use its resources to purchase shares of the parent. When this occurs, the subsidiary is viewed as the parent's agent purchasing treasury shares for the parent. The shares purchased are recorded at cost. When the shares are resold, an excess received over cost is carried to additional paid-in capital in excess of par. If cost exceeds proceeds on resale, the difference is offset against existing paid-in capital in excess of par. If there is no additional paid-in capital in excess of par, retained earnings are reduced. There is never an income statement effect, and the resulting capital account adjustments fall entirely upon the parent

An important requirement of the treasury stock approaches is that the subsidiary investment in the parent be maintained at its original cost. Since the stock is not to be viewed as outstanding, it has no claim on income. If equity adjustments have been made in error, they must be reversed on the consolidated worksheet.

To illustrate the treasury stock method, consider the following example. Suppose Company P acquired an 80% interest in Company S on January 1, 2011, at which time the following determination and distribution of excess schedule was prepared:

Determination and Distribution of Excess Schedule

	Company Implied Fair Value	Parent Price (80%)	NCI Value (20%)
Fair value of subsidiary	$ 250,000	$200,000	$ 50,000
Less book value of interest acquired:			
Common stock......................	$ 100,000		
Retained earnings	50,000		
Total equity	$ 150,000	$150,000	$150,000
Interest acquired		80%	20%
Book value..........................		$120,000	$ 30,000
Excess of fair value over book value	**$100,000**	$ 80,000	$ 20,000

Adjustment of identifiable accounts:

	Adjustment	Life	Amortization per Year	Worksheet Key
Equipment	$ 100,000	20	$ 5,000	**debit D**

Further assume that on January 1, 2013, Company S purchases a 10% interest (1,000 shares) in the parent for $80,000. There would be no need for a determination and distribution of excess schedule for the subsidiary investment, since no excess of cost or book value is acknowledged or distributed. For 2013, the parent will make the normal simple-equity adjustment to acknowledge its 80% interest in subsidiary income of $20,000 as follows:

Investment in Company S	16,000	
Subsidiary Income......................................		16,000
To record 80% of subsidiary reported income of $20,000.		

There is no equity adjustment for the Company S investment in the parent since it must remain at cost.

The trial balances of the two companies on December 31, 2013, are contained in the first two columns of Worksheet 8-2 on pages 458 and 459. The investment in Company S account on Worksheet 8-2 is computed as follows:

Worksheet 8-2: page 458

Original cost	$200,000
80% × 2011 and 2012 undistributed income of $40,000	32,000
2013 simple-equity adjustment	16,000
Balance, December 31, 2013	$248,000

The eliminations for Worksheet 8-2 in journal entry form are as follows:

(CY)	Eliminate current-year equity income:		
	Subsidiary Income	16,000	
	Investment in Company S		16,000

(EL)	Eliminate subsidiary S equity:		
	Common Stock—Company S	80,000	
	Retained Earnings, January 1, 2013—Company S	72,000	
	Investment in Company S		152,000

(D)/(NCI)	Distribute excess and NCI adjustment to equipment:		
	Equipment	100,000	
	Investment in Company S		80,000
	Retained Earnings—Company S		20,000

(A)	Amortize excess:		
	Retained Earnings, January 1, 2013—Company P	8,000	
	Retained Earnings, January 1, 2013—Company S	2,000	
	Expenses	5,000	
	Accumulated Depreciation		15,000

(TS)	Restate investment in Company P as treasury stock:		
	Treasury Stock (at cost)	**80,000**	
	Investment in Company P (10%, at cost)		**80,000**

Examination of the formal statements of the consolidated company reveals that the treasury shares are held by the consolidated company and no income accrues to them. These statements, based on Worksheet 8-2, are as follows:

Company P and Subsidiary Company S
Consolidated Income Statement
For Year Ended December 31, 2013

Sales	$500,000
Less cost of goods sold	300,000
Gross profit	$200,000
Less expenses	145,000
Consolidated net income	$ 55,000
Noncontrolling interest of Company S	$ 3,000
Controlling interest	$ 52,000

Company P and Subsidiary Company S
Retained Earnings Statement
For Year Ended December 31, 2013

	Noncontrolling Interest	Controlling Interest
Balance, January 1, 2013	$36,000	$192,000
Net income	3,000	52,000
Balance, December 31, 2013	$39,000	$244,000

Company P and Subsidiary Company S
Consolidated Balance Sheet December 31, 2013

Assets		Stockholders' Equity		
Equipment	$888,000	Noncontrolling interest		$ 59,000
Less accumulated		Controlling interest:		
depreciation	165,000	Common stock	$500,000	
		Retained earnings	244,000	744,000
		Total		$803,000
		Less treasury stock (at cost)		80,000
Total assets	$723,000	Net stockholders' equity		$723,000

REFLECTION

- If a subsidiary purchases parent company shares, the transaction is viewed as the purchase of parent company treasury shares.

- The treasury stock method allows the parent shares, owned by the subsidiary, to remain on the balance sheet as treasury stock.

Worksheet 8-1

Indirect Holdings; Intercompany Sales
Company A and Subsidiary Companies B and C

Worksheet for Consolidated Financial Statements
For Year Ended December 31, 2013

	(Credit balance amounts are in parentheses.)	Trial Balance		
		Company A	Company B	Company C
1	Inventory, December 31, 2013	80,000	20,000	30,000
2				
3	Other Assets	47,500	146,000	130,000
4	Building and Equipment	300,000	200,000	150,000
5				
6	Accumulated Depreciation	(100,000)	(60,000)	(30,000)
7				
8	Investment in Company B	655,500		
9				
10				
11	Investment in Company C		318,000	
12				
13				
14	Common Stock ($10 par)—Company A	(300,000)		
15	**Retained Earnings, January 1, 2013—Company A**	**(500,000)**		
16				
17				
18				
19	Common Stock ($10 par)—Company B		(200,000)	
20	**Retained Earnings, January 1, 2013—Company B**		**(300,000)**	
21				
22				
23				
24				
25	Common Stock ($10 par)—Company C			(100,000)
26	**Retained Earnings, January 1, 2013—Company C**			**(150,000)**
27				
28				
29	Sales	(400,000)	(300,000)	(150,000)
30	Cost of Goods Sold	250,000	160,000	80,000
31				
32				
33	Expenses	60,000	40,000	40,000
34				
35	Subsidiary or Investment Income	(93,000)	(24,000)	
36				
37		0	0	0
38	Consolidated Net Income			
39	To NCI, Company C (see distribution schedule)			
40	To NCI, Company B (see distribution schedule)			
41	To Controlling Interest (see distribution schedule)			
42	Total NCI			
43	Retained Earnings, Controlling Interest, December 31, 2013			
44				

Worksheet 8-1 (see page 445)

Eliminations & Adjustments				Consolidated Income Statement	NCI	Controlling Retained Earnings	Consolidated Balance Sheet	
Dr.		Cr.						
		(Elb)	2,500				124,500	1
		(Elc)	3,000					2
							323,500	3
(Db)	250,000						1,017,500	4
(Dc)	117,500							5
		(Ab)	75,000				(276,750)	6
		(Ac)	**11,750**					7
		(CYb)	93,000					8
		(ELb)	375,000					9
		(Db)	187,500					10
		(CYc)	24,000					11
		(ELc)	200,000					12
		(Dc)	94,000					13
							(300,000)	14
(Ab)	37,500					(456,395)		15
(Ac)	**3,525**							16
(Blb)	1,500							17
(Blc)	**1,080**							18
(ELb)	150,000				(50,000)			19
(ELb)	225,000	(NClb)	62,500		(122,965)			20
(Ab)	12,500							21
(Ac)	**1,175**							22
(Blb)	500							23
(Blc)	**360**							24
(ELc)	80,000				(20,000)			25
(ELc)	120,000	(NClc)	23,500		(51,965)			26
(Ac)	**1,175**							27
(Blc)	**360**							28
(IS)	90,000			(760,000)				29
(Elb)	2,500	(IS)	90,000	401,700				30
(Elc)	3,000	(Blb)	2,000					31
		(Blc)	**1,800**					32
(Ac)	**5,875**							33
(Ab)	25,000			170,875				34
(CYb)	93,000							35
(CYc)	24,000							36
	1,245,550		1,245,550					37
				(187,425)				38
				4,585	(4,585)			39
				23,210	(23,210)			40
				159,630		(159,630)		41
					(272,725)		(272,725)	42
						(616,025)	(616,025)	43
							0	44

Eliminations and Adjustments:

(CYb)	Eliminate the entry made by Company A to record its share of Company B income. This step returns the investment in the Company B account to its January 1, 2013, balance to aid the elimination process.
(ELb)	Eliminate 75% of the January 1, 2013, Company B equity balances against the investment in Company B.
(Db)/(NCIb)	Distribute the $187,500 excess of cost and $62,500 NCI adjustment to the building and equipment account according to the determination and distribution of excess schedule applicable to the level one investment.
(Ab)	Amortize the excess (added depreciation) according to the determination and distribution of excess schedule. This step requires adjustment of Company A and B retained earnings for 2011 and 2012, plus adjustment of 2013 expenses.
(CYc)	Eliminate the entry made by Company B to record its share of Company C income. This returns the investment in Company C account to its January 1, 2013, balance to aid elimination.
(ELc)	Eliminate 80% of the January 1, 2013, Company C equity balances against the investment in Company C.
(Dc)/(NCIc)	Distribute the $94,000 excess of cost and the $23,500 NCI adjustment to the building and equipment account according to the determination and distribution of excess schedule applicable to the level two investment.
(Ac)	Amortize the excess (added depreciation) according to the determination and distribution of excess schedule. Since it is created by actions of subsidiary Company B, the 2012 amortization must be prorated 20% ($1,175) to the Company B NCI, 20% ($1,175) to the Company C NCI and 75% × 80% = 60% ($3,525) to the controlling interest. Note that the Company B NCI appears on the worksheet only after the first level investment has been eliminated, again pointing to the need to eliminate the level one investment first.
(IS)	Eliminate intercompany sales to prevent double counting in the consolidated sales and cost of goods sold.
(BIb)	Eliminate the Company B profit contained in the beginning inventory. Since Company B generated the sale, the correction of beginning retained earnings is split 75% to the controlling interest and 25% to the noncontrolling interest. The cost of goods sold is decreased since the beginning inventory was overstated.
(EIb)	The cost of goods sold is adjusted and the ending inventory is reduced by the $2,500 of Company B profit contained in the ending inventory.
(BIc)	Eliminate the Company C profit contained in the beginning inventory. Since Company C generated the retained earnings adjustment, it is apportioned as follows:

To NCI in Company C (20%)	$ 360
To NCI in Company B (25% of 80%).	360
To controlling interest (75% of 80%)	1,080
Total.	$1,800

(EIc)	The cost of goods sold is adjusted, and the ending inventory is reduced by the $3,000 of Company C profit.

Company C Income Distribution

Ending inventory profit . . . . (EIc)	$ 3,000	Internally generated net income	$30,000
Building depreciation . . . . **(Ac)**	**5,875**	Beginning inventory profit . . . . **(BIc)**	**1,800**
		Adjusted income	$22,925
		Company C NCI share	× 20%
		Company C NCI	$ 4,585

Company B Income Distribution

Ending inventory profit . . . . (EIb)	$ 2,500	Internally generated net income	$100,000
Equipment depreciation . . . . (Ab)	25,000	Beginning inventory profit . . . . (BIb)	2,000
		80% of Company C adjusted income	18,340
		Adjusted income	$ 92,840
		Company B NCI share	× 25%
		Company B NCI	$ 23,210

Company A Income Distribution

		Internally generated income	$ 90,000
		75% of Company B adjusted income	69,630
		Controlling interest	$159,630

Worksheet 8-2

Treasury Stock Method for Parent Shares Owned by Subsidiary
Company P and Subsidiary Company S
Worksheet for Consolidated Financial Statements
For Year Ended December 31, 2013

| | (Credit balance amounts are in parentheses.) | Trial Balance | |
		Company P	Company S
1	Investment in Company S (80%)	248,000	
2			
3			
4	**Investment in Company P (10%, at cost)**		**80,000**
5	Equipment	608,000	180,000
6	Accumulated Depreciation	(100,000)	(50,000)
7	Common Stock—Company P	(500,000)	
8	Retained Earnings, January 1, 2013—Company P	(200,000)	
9	Common Stock—Company S		(100,000)
10	Retained Earnings, January 1, 2013—Company S		(90,000)
11			
12	Sales	(300,000)	(200,000)
13	Cost of Goods Sold	180,000	120,000
14	Expenses	80,000	60,000
15	Subsidiary Income	(16,000)	
16	**Treasury Stock (at cost)**		
17		0	0
18	Consolidated Net Income		
19	To NCI (see distribution schedule)		
20	Balance to Controlling Interest (see distribution schedule)		
21	Total NCI		
22	Retained Earnings, Controlling Interest, December 31, 2013		
23			

Eliminations and Adjustments:

(CY)   Eliminate the entry made by the parent during the current year to record its share of Company S income.
(EL)   Eliminate 80% of the January 1, 2013, subsidiary equity balances against the investment in Company S account.
(D)/(NCI) Distribute the excess of cost over book value and the NCI adjustment to the equipment account as specified by
                 the determination and distribution of excess schedule applicable to the Investment in Company S.
(A)   Amortize the excess of $100,000 for the past two years and the current year at the rate of $5,000 per year.
(TS)   The investment in Company P must be at cost. If any equity adjustments have been made, they must be reversed and
                 the investment in the parent returned to cost. If the shares are to be reissued, as is the case in this example, the investment
                 is then transferred to the treasury stock account, a contra account to total consolidated stockholders' equity.

As an alternative to entry **(TS)**, the cost of the treasury shares could be used to retire them on the worksheet as follows:

Common Stock—Company P   50,000
Retained Earnings—Company P   30,000
    Investment in Company P   80,000

Worksheet 8-2 (see page 451)

Eliminations & Adjustment		Consolidated Income Statement	NCI	Controlling Retained Earnings	Consolidated Balance Sheet	
Dr.	Cr.					
	(CY) 16,000					1
	(EL) 152,000					2
	(D) 80,000					3
	(TS) 80,000					4
(D) 100,000					888,000	5
	(A) 15,000				(165,000)	6
					(500,000)	7
(A) 8,000				(192,000)		8
(EL) 80,000			(20,000)			9
(EL) 72,000	(NCI) 20,000		(36,000)			10
(A) 2,000						11
		(500,000)				12
		300,000				13
(A) 5,000		145,000				14
(CY) 16,000						15
(TS) 80,000					80,000	16
363,000	363,000					17
		(55,000)				18
		3,000	(3,000)			19
		52,000		(52,000)		20
			(59,000)		(59,000)	21
				(244,000)	(244,000)	22
					0	23

Subsidiary Company S Income Distribution

Depreciation of excess for current year . . . . (A) $5,000	Internally generated net income	$20,000
	Adjusted income	$15,000
	NCI share	× 20%
	NCI	$ 3,000

Parent Company P Income Distribution

	Internally generated net income	$40,000
	80% × Company S adjusted income of $15,000. . .	12,000
	Controlling interest	$52,000

UNDERSTANDING THE ISSUES

1. Subsidiary Company S had the following stockholders' equity on December 31, 2013, prior to distributing a 10% stock dividend:

Common stock ($1 par), 100,000 shares issued and outstanding	$ 100,000
Paid-in capital in excess of par	1,900,000
Retained earnings	2,000,000
Total equity	$4,000,000

The fair value of the shares distributed is $50 each. What is the effect of this dividend on the subsidiary equity, the investment account, and the December 31, 2013, elimination procedures? Assume the parent uses the simple equity method to account for its investment in the subsidiary.

2. Subsidiary Company S had the following stockholders' equity on January 1, 2014, prior to issuing 20,000 additional new shares to noncontrolling shareholders:

Common stock ($1 par), 100,000 shares issued and outstanding	$ 100,000
Paid-in capital in excess of par	1,900,000
Retained earnings	2,000,000
Total equity	$4,000,000

At that time, the parent company owned 90,000 Company S shares. Assume that the parent acquired the shares at a price equal to their book value. What is the impact on the parent's investment account of the sale of 20,000 additional shares by the subsidiary for $45 per share?

3. Subsidiary Company S had the following stockholders' equity on January 1, 2014, prior to issuing 5,000 additional new shares:

Common stock ($1 par), 100,000 shares issued and outstanding	$ 100,000
Paid-in capital in excess of par	1,900,000
Retained earnings	2,000,000
Total equity	$4,000,000

Prior to the sale of additional shares, the parent owned 90,000 shares. Assume that the parent acquired the shares at a price equal to their book value. Assume that the new shares are sold for $45 each. Describe the general impact (no calculations required) the sale will have on the parent's investment account if:

   a. The parent buys less than 90% of the new shares.
   b. The parent buys 90% of the new shares.
   c. The parent buys all the new shares.

4. Company A owns 80% of Company B. Company B owns 60% of Company C. From a consolidated viewpoint, does A control C? How will $10,000 of Company C income flow to the members of the consolidated firms when it is distributed at year-end?

5. Company P owns 90% of Company S's shares. Assume Company S then purchases 2% of Company P's outstanding shares of common stock. When consolidating, what happens to the 2% holding in the consolidated financial statements?

EXERCISES

Exercise 1 *(LO 1)* **Subsidiary stock dividend.** On January 1, 2011, Tibor Company acquires 90% of the outstanding stock of Largo Company for $800,000. At the time of the acquisition, Largo Company has the following stockholders' equity:

Common stock ($10 par).................	$300,000
Paid-in capital in excess of par	150,000
Retained earnings	200,000
Total stockholders' equity..............	$650,000

It is determined that Largo Company's book values approximate fair values as of the purchase date. Any excess of cost over book value is attributed to goodwill.

On July 1, 2011, Largo Company distributes a 10% stock dividend when the fair value of its common stock is $30 per share. A cash dividend of $0.50 per share is distributed on December 31, 2011. Largo Company's net income for 2011 amounts to $108,000 and is earned evenly throughout the year.

1. Prepare the entry required on Largo Company's books to reflect the stock dividend distributed on July 1, 2011. Prepare the stockholders' equity section of the Largo Company balance sheet as of December 31, 2011.
2. Prepare the simple equity method entries that Tibor Company would make during 2011 to record its investment in Largo Company.
3. Prepare the eliminations that would be made on the December 31, 2011, consolidated worksheet. (Assume the use of the simple equity method.) Prepare a determination and distribution of excess schedule to support the elimination.

Exercise 2 *(LO 2)* **Subsidiary sale of shares to noncontrolling interest.** Track Company owns a 90% interest in Trail Company on January 1, 2011, when Trail has the following stockholders' equity:

Common stock ($10 par)....................	$100,000
Paid-in capital in excess of par	250,000
Retained earnings	200,000
Total stockholders' equity..................	$550,000

The investment is purchased for book value, $495,000.

On July 1, 2011, Trail sells 2,000 additional shares to noncontrolling shareholders in a private offering for $80 per share. Trail's net income for 2011 is $70,000, and the income is earned evenly during the year.

Track uses the simple equity method to record the investment in Trail. Summary entries are made each December 31 to record the year's activity.

Prepare Track's equity adjustments for 2011 that result from the above activities of Trail Company during 2011. Assume Track has $500,000 of paid-in capital in excess of par.

Exercise 3 *(LO 2)* **Subsidiary sale of shares, alternative amounts purchased by parent.** On January 1, 2011, Artic Company acquires an 80% interest in Calco Company for $400,000. On the acquisition date, Calco Company has the following stockholders' equity:

Common stock ($10 par).................	$200,000
Paid-in capital in excess of par	100,000
Retained earnings	150,000
Total stockholders' equity..............	$450,000

Assets and liabilities have fair values equal to book values. Goodwill totals $50,000.

Calco Company has net income of $60,000 for 2011. No dividends are paid or declared during 2011.

On January 1, 2012, Calco Company sells 10,000 shares of common stock at $60 per share in a public offering.

Assuming the parent uses the simple equity method, prepare all parent company entries required for the issuance of the shares.

Assume the following alternative situations:

1. Artic Company purchases 8,000 shares.
2. Artic Company purchases 9,000 shares.
3. Artic Company purchases 5,000 shares.

Suggestion: It is helpful to use a 3-column table which, for each case, organizes the changes in ownership interest. See the schedule on page 437.

Exercise 4 *(LO 3)* **Subsidiary treasury stock.** The following comparative statements of stockholders' equity are prepared for Nolan Corporation:

	Jan.1,2011	Jan.1,2013	Jan.1,2015
Common stock ($10 par).........................	$300,000	$300,000	$300,000
Paid-in capital in excess of par	60,000	60,000	60,000
Retained earnings		42,000	120,000
Total......................................	$360,000	$402,000	$480,000
Less treasury stock (at cost)		(75,000)	(75,000)
Total stockholders' equity.......................	$360,000	$327,000	$405,000

Tarman Corporation acquires 60% of Nolan Corporation common stock for $12 per share on January 1, 2011, when the latter corporation is formed.

On January 1, 2013, Nolan Corporation purchases 5,000 shares of its own common stock from noncontrolling interests for $15 per share. These shares are accounted for as treasury stock at cost.

Assuming Tarman Corporation uses the cost method to record its investment in Nolan Corporation, prepare the necessary cost-to-simple-equity conversion and the eliminations and adjustments required on the consolidated worksheet as of December 31, 2015. Include all pertinent supporting calculations in good form.

Exercise 5 *(LO 4)* **Acquisition of a company with a subsidiary.** On January 1, 2011, Bell Company acquires an 80% interest in Carter Company for $140,000. The purchase price results in a $30,000 (including NCI adjustment) increase in the patent which has a 10-year life. The investment is recorded under the simple equity method.

On January 1, 2013, Ace Company purchases a 60% interest in Bell Company for $420,000. Ace Company believes that the patent value remaining on the investment by Bell in Carter is stated correctly. Comparative equities of Bell Company and Carter Company immediately prior to the purchase reveal the following:

Stockholders' Equity	Bell Company	Carter Company
Common stock ($5 par)...	$200,000	
Common stock ($10 par)..		$100,000
Paid-in capital in excess of par	100,000	20,000
Retained earnings	150,000	80,000
Total stockholders' equity.....................................	$450,000	$200,000

An analysis of the separate accounts of Bell and Carter on January 1, 2013, reveals that Carter's inventory is undervalued by $20,000 and that Bell's equipment with a 5-year future life is undervalued by $30,000. All other book values approximate fair values for Bell and Carter.

Prepare the determination and distribution of excess schedule for Ace's purchase of Bell Company on January 1, 2013.

Exercise 6 *(LO 4)* **Direct and indirect holdings.** The following diagram depicts the investment affiliations among Companies M, N, and O:

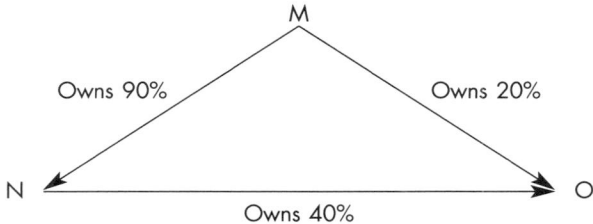

The following facts apply to 2013 operations:

	M	N	O
Internally generated net income	$200,000	$90,000	$40,000
Dividends declared and paid	40,000	10,000	5,000

All investments are made at a price equal to book value.

1. Prepare the simple equity method adjustments that would be made for the investments owned by Companies M and N during the year 2013.
2. Intercompany inventory transactions affecting 2013 are as follows:

	Sold by N to O	Sold by O to M
Profit on sales	25%	30%
Beginning inventory of intercompany goods	$10,000	$15,000
2013 sales	$50,000	$75,000
Ending inventory of intercompany goods	$12,000	$20,000

Using the facts given, determine the consolidated income of the consolidated company, the noncontrolling interest, and the controlling interest net income. Income distribution schedules may be used for support.

Exercise 7 *(LO 4)* **Three-level acquisition, intercompany asset sale.** Baker Company acquires an 80% interest in the common stock of Cain Company for $440,000 on January 1, 2011. The price is equal to the book value of the interest acquired. Baker Company maintains its investment in Cain Company under the cost method.

Able Company acquires a 60% interest in the common stock of Baker Company on January 1, 2015, for $2,700,000. Any excess of cost is attributable to Cain Company equipment, which is understated by $80,000, and a Baker Company building, which is understated by $200,000. Any remaining excess is considered goodwill. Relevant stockholders' equities are as follows:

	Baker Company	Cain Company	
	Jan.1, 2015	Jan.1, 2011	Jan.1, 2015
Common stock	$ 400,000	$100,000	$100,000
Paid-in capital in excess of par	1,100,000	150,000	150,000
Retained earnings	2,000,000	300,000	450,000

1. Prepare a determination and distribution of excess schedule for Able Company's investment in Baker Company.

2. On January 1, 2016, Cain Company sells a machine with a net book value of $35,000 to Able Company for $60,000. The machine has a 5-year life. Prepare the eliminations and adjustments needed on the December 31, 2017, trial balance worksheet that relate to this intercompany sale.

Exercise 8 *(LO 4)* **Three-level acquisition, inventory and fixed asset sales.** Companies A, B, and C produce the following separate internally generated net incomes during 2015:

	A	B	C
Sales	$300,000	$400,000	$100,000
Less cost of goods sold	200,000	300,000	60,000
Gross profit	$100,000	$100,000	$ 40,000
Expenses	60,000	30,000	10,000
Internally generated net income	$ 40,000	$ 70,000	$ 30,000

Company A acquires an 80% interest in Company B on January 1, 2012, and Company B acquires a 60% interest in Company C on January 1, 2013. Each investment is acquired at a price equal to the book value of the stock purchased.

Additional information is as follows:

a. Company A purchases goods billed at $30,000 from Company C during 2015. The price includes a 40% gross profit. One-half of the goods are held in Company A's year-end inventory.
b. Company B purchases goods billed at $30,000 from Company A during 2015. Company A always bills Company B at a price that includes a 30% gross profit. Company B has $6,000 of Company A goods in its beginning inventory and $2,400 of Company A goods in its ending inventory.
c. Company C purchases goods billed at $15,000 from Company B during 2015. Company B bills Company C at a 20% gross profit. At year-end, $7,500 of the goods remains unsold. The goods are inventoried at $5,000, under the lower-of-cost-or-market procedure.
d. Company B sells a machine to Company C on January 1, 2014, for $50,000. Company B's cost is $70,000, and accumulated depreciation on the date of sale is $40,000. The machine is being depreciated on a straight-line basis over five years.

Prepare the consolidated income statement for 2015, including the distribution of consolidated net income supported by distribution schedules.

Exercise 9 *(LO 4)* **Three-level acquisition.** You have secured the following information for Companies A, B, and C concerning their internally generated net incomes (excluding subsidiary income) and dividends paid:

		A	B	C
2011	Internally generated net income	$30,000	$20,000	$10,000
	Dividends declared and paid	10,000	5,000	
2012	Internally generated net income	50,000	30,000	25,000
	Dividends declared and paid	10,000	5,000	5,000
2013	Internally generated net income	40,000	40,000	30,000
	Dividends declared and paid	10,000	5,000	5,000

1. Assume Company A acquires an 80% interest in Company B on January 1, 2011, and Company B acquires a 60% interest in Company C on January 1, 2012. Prepare the simple equity method adjusting entries made by Companies A and B for subsidiary investments for the years 2011 through 2013.
2. Assume Company B acquires a 70% interest in Company C on January 1, 2011, and Company A acquires a 90% interest in Company B on January 1, 2013. Prepare the simple equity method adjusting entries made by Companies A and B for subsidiary investments for the years 2011 through 2013.

Exercise 10 *(LO 5)* **Treasury stock method.** Myles Corporation and its subsidiary, Downer Corporation, have the following trial balances as of December 31, 2013:

	Myles Corporation	Downer Corporation
Current Assets	402,000	182,000
Investment in Downer Corporation	396,000	
Investment in Myles Corporation		150,000
Property, Plant, and Equipment (net)	850,000	400,000
Liabilities	(200,000)	(100,000)
Common Stock ($10 par)	(1,000,000)	(500,000)
Retained Earnings, January 1, 2013	(400,000)	(100,000)
Sales	(800,000)	(350,000)
Dividend Income		(2,000)
Subsidiary Income	(18,000)	
Cost of Goods Sold	600,000	240,000
Expenses	150,000	80,000
Dividends Declared	20,000	
Totals	0	0

Myles Corporation acquires its 60% interest in Downer Corporation for $348,000 on January 1, 2011. At that time, Downer's retained earnings balance is $50,000. Any excess of cost over book value is attributed to equipment and given a 20-year life.

Downer Corporation purchases a 10% interest in Myles Corporation on January 1, 2013, for $150,000.

No intercompany transactions occur during 2013.

1. Prepare determination and distribution of excess schedules for the investment in Downer.
2. Prepare the 2013 consolidated income statement, including the consolidated net income distribution, using the treasury stock method for mutual holdings. Prepare the supporting income distribution schedules.

PROBLEMS

Problem 8-1 *(LO 1)* **Stock dividend, subsidiary stock sales, cost method.** On January 1, 2011, Bear Corporation acquires a 60% interest in Kelly Company and an 80% interest in Samco Company. The purchase prices are $225,000 and $250,000, respectively. The excess of cost over book value for each investment is considered to be goodwill.

Immediately prior to the purchases, Kelly Company and Samco Company have the following stockholders' equities:

	Kelly Company	Samco Company
Common stock ($10 par)	$200,000	
Common stock ($20 par)		$200,000
Paid-in capital in excess of par	50,000	
Retained earnings	100,000	100,000
Total stockholder' equity	$350,000	$300,000

Additional information:

a. Kelly Company and Samco Company have the following net incomes for 2011 through 2013 (incomes are earned evenly throughout the year):

	2011	2012	2013
Kelly Company	$50,000	$60,000	$60,000
Samco Company	40,000	30,000	55,000

b. Kelly Company has the following equity-related transactions for the first three years after it becomes a subsidiary of Bear Corporation:

July 1, 2011	Sells 5,000 shares of its own stock at $20 per share. Bear purchases 3,000 of these shares.
December 31, 2012	Pays a cash dividend of $1 per share.
July 1, 2013	Purchases 5,000 shares of NCI-owned stock as treasury shares at $27 per share.

c. Samco Company has the following equity-related transactions for the first three years after it becomes a subsidiary of Bear Corporation:

December 31, 2011 . .	Issues a 10% stock dividend. The estimated fair value of Samco common stock is $30 per share on the declaration date.
October 1, 2012	Sells 4,000 shares of its own stock at $30 per share. Of these shares, 200 are purchased by Bear.

d. Bear Corporation has $200,000 of additional paid-in capital in excess of par on December 31, 2013.

Required ▶ ▶ ▶ ▶ ▶

Bear Corporation uses the cost method to account for its investments in subsidiaries. Convert its investments to the simple equity method as of December 31, 2013, and provide adequate support for the entries. Assume that the 2013 nominal accounts are closed. Prepare D&D schedules for each investment.

Problem 8-2 *(LO 1)* **Stock dividend, subsidiary stock sales, equity method.** On January 1, 2011, Wells Corporation acquires 8,000 shares of Towne Company stock and 18,000 shares of Sara Company stock for $176,000 and $240,000, respectively. Each investment is acquired at a price equal to the subsidiary's book value, resulting in no excesses.

Towne Company and Sara Company have the following stockholders' equities immediately prior to Wells's purchases:

	Towne Company	Sara Company
Common stock ($5 par)	$ 50,000	
Common stock ($10 par)		$300,000
Paid-in capital in excess of par	100,000	
Retained earnings	70,000	100,000
Total stockholder's equity	$220,000	$400,000

Additional information is as follows:

a. Net income for Towne Company and Sara Company for 2011 and 2012 follows (income is assumed to be earned evenly throughout the year):

	2011	2012
Towne Company	$50,000	$50,000
Sara Company	40,000	40,000

b. No cash dividends are paid or declared by Towne or Sara during 2011 and 2012.
c. Towne Company distributes a 10% stock dividend on December 31, 2011. Towne stock is selling at $25 per share when the stock dividend is declared.

d. On July 1, 2012, Towne Company sells 2,750 shares of stock at $35 per share. Wells Corporation purchases none of these shares.

e. Sara Company sells 5,000 shares of stock on July 1, 2011, at $25 per share. Wells Corporation purchases 3,700 of these shares.

f. On January 1, 2012, Sara Company purchases 5,000 shares of its common stock from noncontrolling interests at $20 per share.

Assume Wells Corporation uses the simple equity method for its investments in subsidiaries. ◄ ◄ ◄ ◄ ◄ **Required**
For 2011 and 2012, record each of the adjustments to the investment accounts. Provide all supporting calculations in good form.

Problem 8-3 *(LO 2)* **Worksheet, two subsidiaries, subsidiary stock sales, intercompany merchandise, fixed assets, bonds.** The audit of Barns Company and its subsidiaries for the year ended December 31, 2012, is completed. The working papers contain the following information:

a. Barns Company acquires 4,000 shares of Webo Company common stock for $320,000 on January 1, 2011. Webo Company purchases 500 shares of its own stock from NCI shareholders as treasury shares for $48,000 on January 1, 2012.

b. Barns Company acquires all 8,000 outstanding shares of Elcam Company stock on January 1, 2011, for $600,000. On January 1, 2012, Elcam Company issues through a private sale 2,000 additional shares to new noncontrolling shareholders at $85 per share. Barns has no investments other than the stock of Webo and Elcam.

c. Elcam Company originally issues $200,000 of 10-year, 8% mortgage bonds at 98, due on January 1, 2015. On January 1, 2012, Webo Company purchases $150,000 of these bonds in the open market at 98. Interest on the bonds is paid each June 30 and December 31.

d. Condensed balance sheets of Webo and Elcam on January 1, 2011, and January 1, 2012, are as follows:

	Webo Company		Elcam Company	
	Jan. 1, 2011	Jan. 1, 2012	Jan. 1, 2011	Jan. 1, 2012
Current assets	$195,000	$225,000	$280,400	$205,000
Property, plant, and equipment.........	305,000	350,000	613,000	623,800
Unamortized bond discount			1,600	1,200
Total	$500,000	$575,000	$895,000	$830,000
Current liabilities....................	$100,000	$125,000	$ 95,000	$105,000
Bonds payable			200,000	200,000
Capital stock ($50 par)...............	250,000	250,000	400,000	400,000
Retained earnings	150,000	200,000	200,000	125,000
Total	$500,000	$575,000	$895,000	$830,000

e. Total dividends declared and paid during 2012 are as follows:

Barns Company............................	$24,000
Webo Company	22,500
Elcam Company	10,000

f. On June 30, 2012, Barns sells equipment with a book value of $8,000 to Webo for $10,000. Webo depreciates equipment by the straight-line method based on a 10-year life.

g. Barns Company consistently sells to its subsidiaries at prices that realize a gross profit of 25% on sales. Webo and Elcam companies sell to each other and to Barns Company at cost. Prior to 2012, intercompany sales are negligible, but the following sales are made during 2012:

	Total Sales	Included in Purchaser's Inventory at December 31, 2012
Barns Company to Webo Company...............	$172,000	$20,000
Barns Company to Elcam Company	160,000	40,000
Webo Company to Elcam Company	25,000	5,000
Webo Company to Barns Company...............	28,000	8,000
	$385,000	$73,000

h. At December 31, 2012:

Barns Company owes Webo Company	$24,000
Webo Company owes Elcam Company......	16,000
Elcam Company owes Barns Company	12,000
Total	$52,000

i. The following trial balances as of December 31, 2012, are prepared:

	Barns Company	Webo Company	Elcam Company
Cash	110,000	26,000	165,200
Accounts Receivable	85,000	73,500	105,000
Inventories...........................	138,000	163,000	150,000
Investment in Webo Company Stock........	320,000		
Investment in Elcam Company Stock	600,000		
Investment in Elcam Company Bonds		148,000	
Property, Plant, and Equipment	700,000	525,000	834,000
Accumulated Depreciation	(402,000)	(325,000)	(240,000)
Accounts Payable	(202,000)	(150,500)	(86,900)
Dividends Payable....................	(12,000)		
Bonds Payable.......................	(400,000)		(200,000)
Unamortized Bond Discount			800
Capital Stock ($50 par).................	(600,000)	(250,000)	(500,000)
Paid-In Capital in Excess of Par			(70,000)
Retained Earnings, January 1, 2012........	(302,200)	(200,000)	(125,000)
Dividends declared	24,000	22,500	10,000
Treasury Stock (at cost)		48,000	
Gain on Sale of Equipment	(2,000)		
Sales	(2,950,000)	(1,550,000)	(1,750,000)
Interest Income on Bonds................		(13,000)	
Dividend Income	(28,000)		
Cost of Goods Sold	2,500,000	1,200,000	1,400,000
Operating Expenses	405,000	280,000	290,500
Interest Expense......................	16,200	2,500	16,400
Totals...........................	0	0	0

Required ▶ ▶ ▶ ▶ ▶   Prepare the worksheet necessary to produce the consolidated financial statements of Barns Company and its subsidiaries for the year ended December 31, 2012. Include the determination and distribution of excess and income distribution schedules. Any excess of cost over book value is attributable to goodwill. All bond discounts are assumed to be amortized on a straight-line basis.

(AICPA adapted)

Problem 8-4 *(LO 2)* **Worksheet, subsidiary stock sale, intercompany merchandise.**
On January 1, 2012, Palo Company acquires 80% of the outstanding common stock of Sheila
Company for $700,000.

On January 1, 2014, Sheila Company sells 25,000 shares of common stock to the public at
$12 per share. Palo Company does not purchase any of these shares. No entry has been made by
the parent. Sheila Company has the following stockholders' equity at the end of 2011 and 2013:

	December 31,	
	2011	2013
Common stock ($2 par)	$200,000	$200,000
Paid-in capital in excess of par	400,000	400,000
Retained earnings	100,000	180,000
Total stockholders' equity	$700,000	$780,000

On the January 1, 2012, acquisition date, Sheila Company's book values approximate fair
values, except for a building that is undervalued by $80,000. The building has an estimated
future life of 20 years. Any additional excess is attributed to goodwill.

Trial balances of the two companies as of December 31, 2014, are as follows:

	Palo Company	Sheila Company
Cash	179,040	105,000
Accounts Receivable (net)	280,000	190,000
Inventory	325,000	175,000
Investment in Sheila Company	700,000	
Property, Plant, and Equipment	2,450,000	1,400,000
Accumulated Depreciation	(1,256,000)	(536,000)
Liabilities	(750,000)	(210,000)
Common Stock ($10 par)	(1,500,000)	
Common Stock ($2 par)		(250,000)
Paid-In Capital in Excess of Par		(650,000)
Retained Earnings, January 1, 2014	(375,000)	(180,000)
Sales	(1,600,000)	(750,000)
Subsidiary Dividend Income	(23,040)	
Cost of Goods Sold	1,120,000	450,000
Other Expenses	405,000	220,000
Dividends Declared	45,000	36,000
Totals	0	0

During 2014, Sheila Company sells $50,000 of merchandise to Palo Company at a price
that includes a 20% gross profit. This is their first intercompany sale. $10,000 of the goods
remains in Palo's ending inventory.

Prepare the worksheet necessary to produce the consolidated financial statements of Palo ◄ ◄ ◄ ◄ ◄ **Required**
Company and its subsidiary as of December 31, 2014. Include the determination and distribution of excess and income distribution schedules.

Problem 8-5 *(LO 2)* **Worksheet, subsidiary stock sale with parent purchase, intercompany merchandise.** On January 1, 2012, Mitta Corporation acquires a 60% interest
(12,000 shares) in Train Company for $156,000. Train stockholders' equity on the purchase
date is as follows:

Common stock ($5 par)	$100,000
Paid-in capital in excess of par	50,000
Retained earnings	80,000
Total stockholders' equity	$230,000

At the purchase date, Train's book values for assets and liabilities closely approximate fair values. Any excess of cost over book value is attributed to goodwill.

On January 1, 2013, Train Company sells 5,000 shares of common stock in a public offering at $20 per share. Mitta Corporation purchases 4,000 shares.

During 2013, Mitta sells $30,000 of goods to Train at a gross profit of 25%. There are $6,000 of Mitta goods in Train's beginning inventory and $8,000 of Mitta goods in Train's ending inventory.

Merchandise sales by Train to Mitta are $20,000 during 2013 at a gross profit of 30%. There are $6,000 of Train goods in Mitta's beginning inventory and $2,000 of Train goods in Mitta's ending inventory.

Intercompany gross profit rates have been constant for many years. There are no intercompany payables/receivables.

Mitta's investment in Train Company balance is determined as follows:

Original cost	$156,000
60% of Train 2012 income ($40,000 × 60%)	24,000
Subtotal	$180,000
Less 60% of Train dividends declared in 2012 (60% × $8,000)	(4,800)
Subtotal	$175,200
Cost to acquire additional shares (new issue)	80,000
64% of Train 2013 income ($50,000 × 64%)	32,000
Subtotal	$287,200
Less 64% of Train dividends declared in 2013 (64% × $10,000)	(6,400)
Investment balance, December 31, 2013	$280,800

The trial balances of the two companies as of December 31, 2013, are as follows:

	Mitta Corporation	Train Company
Cash	106,200	63,500
Accounts Receivable	113,600	60,000
Inventory	350,000	80,000
Investment in Train Company	280,800	
Property, Plant, and Equipment	1,800,000	360,000
Accumulated Depreciation	(600,000)	(89,500)
Accounts Payable	(180,000)	(64,000)
Other Current Liabilities	(26,000)	(8,000)
Bonds Payable	(500,000)	
Common Stock ($10 par)	(1,000,000)	
Common Stock ($5 par)		(125,000)
Paid-In Capital in Excess of Par		(125,000)
Retained Earnings, January 1, 2013	(212,600)	(112,000)
Sales	(1,950,000)	(600,000)
Subsidiary Income	(32,000)	
Cost of Goods Sold	1,170,000	420,000
Other Expenses	630,000	130,000
Dividends Declared	50,000	10,000
Totals	0	0

Required ▶ ▶ ▶ ▶ ▶   Prepare the worksheet necessary to produce the consolidated financial statements of Mitta Corporation and its subsidiary as of December 31, 2013. Include the determination and distribution of excess and income distribution schedule.

Problem 8-6 *(LO 4)* **Worksheet, three-level holding, intercompany merchandise, plant assets.** Shelby Corporation purchases 90% of the outstanding stock of Borner Company on January 1, 2011, for $603,000 cash. At that time, Borner Company has the following

stockholders' equity balances: common stock, $200,000; paid-in capital in excess of par, $80,000; and retained earnings, $300,000.

All book values approximate fair values except for the plant assets (undervalued by $50,000 and with an estimated remaining life of 10 years). Any remaining excess is goodwill.

DeNoma Company acquires a 60% interest in Shelby on January 1, 2013, for $750,000. At this time, Shelby has consolidated shareholders' equity of common stock, $500,000; paid-in capital in excess of par, $150,000; and controlling retained earnings, $500,000 (not including amortization of excess price applicable to investment in Borner).

At that time, it is also determined that Shelby's plant assets are undervalued by $50,000 and have a 10-year remaining life. Any remaining excess is goodwill.

Intercompany merchandise sales from Borner to Shelby for 2014 are (1) seller's goods in buyer's beginning inventory, $7,500; (2) sales during 2014, $125,000; (3) seller's goods in buyer's ending inventory, $10,000; and (4) gross profit on intercompany sales, 80%.

On January 1, 2013, Shelby sells plant assets with a cost of $80,000 and accumulated depreciation of $45,000 to DeNoma for $50,000. Remaining life on the date of sale is estimated to be five years.

Shelby and DeNoma use the simple equity method to account for their investments. The trial balances on December 31, 2014, are as follows:

	DeNoma Company	Shelby Corporation	Borner Company
Inventory	75,000	60,000	40,000
Other Current Assets	900,000	2,000	390,000
Plant Assets	1,200,000	800,000	600,000
Accumulated Depreciation	(450,000)	(300,000)	(200,000)
Investment in Shelby Corporation	894,000		
Investment in Borner Company		828,000	
Common Stock	(1,500,000)	(500,000)	(200,000)
Paid-In Capital in Excess of Par		(150,000)	(80,000)
Retained Earnings	(922,000)	(620,000)	(500,000)
Sales	(900,000)	(700,000)	(600,000)
Cost of Goods Sold	570,000	425,000	400,000
Expenses	205,000	200,000	150,000
Subsidiary Income	(72,000)	(45,000)	
Totals	0	0	0

Prepare the determination and distribution of excess schedule for Shelby's investment in Borner and DeNoma's investment in Shelby. Prepare the December 31, 2014, consolidated worksheet and income distribution schedules.   ◄ ◄ ◄ ◄ ◄ **Required**

Suggestion: The determination and distribution of excess schedule must show an adjustment to Shelby's retained earnings for the amortization of excess applicable to Shelby's investment in Borner. [*Hint* (for consolidated balance sheet): The reduced retained earnings in the determination and distribution of excess schedule must be adjusted before eliminating the pro rata share of equity balances.]

Problem 8-7 *(LO 4)* **Worksheet, direct and indirect holding, intercompany merchandise, machine.** The following diagram depicts the relationships among Mary Company, John Company, and Joan Company on December 31, 2014:

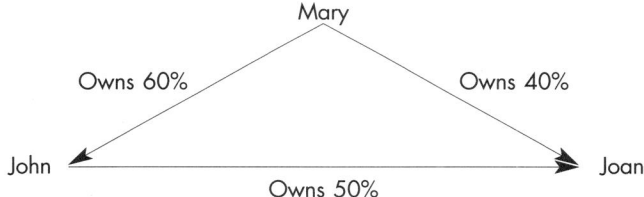

Mary

Owns 60%   Owns 40%

John   Joan

Owns 50%

Mary Company purchases its interest in John Company on January 1, 2012, for $204,000. John Company purchases its interest in Joan Company on January 1, 2013, for $75,000. Mary Company purchases its interest in Joan Company on January 1, 2014, for $72,000. All investments are accounted for under the equity method. Control over Joan Company does not occur until the January 1, 2014, acquisition. Thus, a D&D schedule will be prepared for the investment in Joan as of January 1, 2014.

The following stockholders' equities are available:

	John Company December 31,	Joan Company December 31,	
	2011	2012	2013
Common stock ($10 par)........................	$150,000		
Common stock ($10 par)........................		$100,000	$100,000
Paid-in capital in excess of par	75,000		
Retained earnings	75,000	50,000	80,000
Total equity	$300,000	$150,000	$180,000

On January 2, 2014, Joan Company sells a machine to Mary Company for $20,000. The machine has a book value of $10,000, with an estimated life of five years and is being depreciated on a straight-line basis.

John Company sells $20,000 of merchandise to Joan Company during 2014 to realize a gross profit of 30%. Of this merchandise, $5,000 remains in Joan Company's December 31, 2014, inventory. Joan owes John $3,000 on December 31, 2014, for merchandise delivered during 2014.

Trial balances of the three companies prepared from general ledger account balances on December 31, 2014, are as follows:

	Mary Company	John Company	Joan Company
Cash	62,500	60,000	30,000
Accounts Receivable	200,000	55,000	30,000
Inventory	360,000	80,000	50,000
Investment in John Company	270,000		
Investment in Joan Company	86,000	107,500	
Property, Plant, and Equipment	2,250,000	850,000	350,000
Accumulated Depreciation	(938,000)	(377,500)	(121,800)
Intangibles.................................	15,000		
Accounts Payable	(215,500)	(61,000)	(22,000)
Accrued Expenses	(12,000)	(4,000)	(1,200)
Bonds Payable..............................	(500,000)	(300,000)	(100,000)
Common Stock ($5 par)	(500,000)		
Common Stock ($10 par)		(150,000)	
Common Stock ($10 par)			(100,000)
Paid-In Capital in Excess of Par	(700,000)	(75,000)	
Retained Earnings, January 1, 2014..............	(290,000)	(130,000)	(80,000)
Sales	(1,800,000)	(500,000)	(300,000)
Gain on Sale of Equipment			(10,000)
Subsidiary Income...........................	(58,000)	(20,000)	
Cost of Goods Sold	1,170,000	350,000	180,000
Other Expenses	525,000	100,000	90,000
Dividends Declared..........................	75,000	15,000	5,000
Totals	0	0	0

Prepare the worksheet necessary to produce the consolidated financial statements of Mary   ◄ ◄ ◄ ◄ ◄ **Required**
Company and its subsidiaries as of December 31, 2014. Include the determination and distribution of excess and income distribution schedules. Any excess of cost is assumed to be attributable to goodwill.

Problem 8-8 *(LO 5)* **Worksheet, purchase in blocks, subsidiary stock dividend, subsidiary purchase of parent shares, machinery sale, merchandise.** On
January 1, 2013, Heckert Company purchases a controlling interest in Aker Company. The
following information is available:

a. Heckert Company purchases 1,600 shares of Aker Company outstanding stock on
January 1, 2012, for $48,000 and purchases an additional 1,400 shares on January 1, 2013,
for $51,800.
b. An analysis of the stockholders' equity accounts at December 31, 2012, and 2011, follows:

	Heckert Company December 31,		Aker Company December 31,	
	2012	2011	2012	2011
Common stock ($10 par)...........	$150,000	$150,000		
Common stock ($5 par)............			$ 20,000	$ 20,000
Paid-in capital in excess of par	36,000	36,000	10,000	10,000
Retained earnings	378,000	285,000	112,000	82,000
Total	$564,000	$471,000	$142,000	$112,000

c. Aker Company's marketable securities consist of 1,500 shares of Heckert Company stock
purchased on June 15, 2013, in the open market for $18,000. The securities are purchased
as a temporary investment and are sold on January 15, 2014, for $25,000.
d. On December 10, 2013, Heckert Company declares a cash dividend of $0.50 per share, pay-
able January 10, 2014, to stockholders of record on December 20, 2013. Aker Company
pays a cash dividend of $1 per share on June 30, 2013, and distributes a 10% stock dividend on
September 30, 2013. The stock is selling for $15 per share ex-dividend on September 30, 2013.
Aker Company pays no dividends in 2012.
e. Aker Company sells machinery, with a book value of $4,000 and a remaining life of five
years, to Heckert Company for $4,800 on December 31, 2013. The gain on the sale is cred-
ited to the other income account.
f. Aker Company includes all intercompany receivables and payables in its trade accounts receivable and trade accounts payable accounts.
g. During 2013, the following intercompany sales are made:

	Net Sales	Included in Purchaser's Inventory at December 31, 2013
Heckert Company to Aker Company...................	$ 78,000	$24,300
Aker Company to Heckert Company..................	104,000	18,000
	$182,000	$42,300

Heckert Company sells merchandise to Aker Company at cost. Aker Company sells merchandise to Heckert at the regular selling price to make a normal profit margin of 30%. There
were no intercompany sales in prior years.

The trial balances of the two companies at December 31, 2013, are as follows:

	Heckert Company	Aker Company
Cash	38,100	29,050
Marketable Securities	33,000	18,000
Trade Accounts Receivable	210,000	88,000
Allowance for Doubtful Accounts	(6,800)	(2,300)
Intercompany Receivables	24,000	
Inventories	275,000	135,000
Machinery and Equipment	514,000	279,000
Accumulated Depreciation	(298,200)	(196,700)
Investment in Aker Company (at cost)	99,800	
Patents	35,000	
Dividends Payable	(7,500)	
Trade Accounts Payable	(195,500)	(174,050)
Intercompany Payables	(8,000)	
Common Stock ($10 par)	(150,000)	
Common Stock ($5 par)		(22,000)
Paid-In Capital in Excess of Par	(36,000)	(14,000)
Retained Earnings	(378,000)	(106,000)
Dividends Declared (cash)	7,500	4,000
Sales and Services	(850,000)	(530,000)
Dividend Income	(3,000)	
Other Income	(9,000)	(3,700)
Cost of Goods Sold	510,000	374,000
Depreciation Expense	65,600	11,200
Administrative and Selling Expenses	130,000	110,500
Totals	0	0

Required ▶ ▶ ▶ ▶ ▶   Prepare the worksheet necessary to produce the consolidated financial statements of Heckert Company and its subsidiary for the year ended December 31, 2013. Include the determination and distribution of excess and income distribution schedules. Assume any excess of cost over book value is attributable to goodwill.

(AICPA adapted)

Problem 8-9 *(LO 5)* **Worksheet, subsidiary owns parent shares, merchandise.** On January 1, 2011, Parson Company purchases 80% of the common stock of Salary Company for $450,000. On this date, Salary has common stock, other paid-in capital in excess of par, and retained earnings of $50,000, $140,000, and $220,000, respectively.

Any excess of cost over book value is due to goodwill.

In both 2011 and 2012, Parson has accounted for the investment in Salary using the cost method.

On January 1, 2012, Salary purchases 1,000 shares (10%) of the common stock of Parson Company from outside investors for $100,000 cash. It is expected that the shares may be resold later. Salary uses the cost method in accounting for the investment.

During the last quarter of 2012, Parson sells merchandise to Salary for $48,000, one-fourth of which is still held by Salary on December 31, 2012. Parson's usual gross profit on intercompany sales is 40%.

The trial balances for Parson and Salary on December 31, 2012, are as follows:

	Parson Company	Salary Company
Inventory	170,000	120,000
Other Current Assets	166,000	196,000
Investment in Salary Company	450,000	

(continued)

	Parson Company	Salary Company
Investment in Parson Company		100,000
Land.	80,000	70,000
Buildings and Equipment.	400,000	280,000
Accumulated Depreciation	(180,000)	(90,000)
Current Liabilities.	(98,000)	(74,000)
Long-Term Liabilities	(250,000)	(100,000)
Common Stock—Parson Company ($10 par).	(100,000)	
Paid-In Capital in Excess of Par—Parson Company	(200,000)	
Retained Earnings—Parson Company	(350,000)	
Common Stock—Salary Company ($10 par).		(50,000)
Paid-In Capital in Excess of Par—Salary Company.		(140,000)
Retained Earnings—Salary Company.		(260,000)
Net Sales.	(640,000)	(350,000)
Cost of Goods Sold	360,000	200,000
Operating Expenses	160,000	90,000
Dividend Income	(8,000)	(2,000)
Dividends Declared.	40,000	10,000
Totals	0	0

Complete the worksheet for consolidated financial statements for the year ended December   ◄ ◄ ◄ ◄ ◄ **Required**
31, 2012. Shares of Parson owned by Salary are to be treated as treasury stock. Round all computations to the nearest dollar. Include a determination and distribution of excess schedule and income distribution schedule.

(AICPA adapted)

Accounting for Influential Investments

In practical terms, an influential investment is generally an investment of 20% or more in the voting common stock of a company, but not more than 50%, which would require consolidation. *Influence* is defined as follows by the FASB:

> *The equity method tends to be most appropriate if an investment enables the investor to influence the operating or financial decisions of the investee. The investor then has a degree of responsibility for the return on its investment, and it is appropriate to include in the results of operations of the investor its share of the earnings or losses of the investee. Influence tends to be more effective as the investor's percent of ownership in the voting stock of the investee increases. Investments of relatively small percentages of voting stock of an investee tend to be passive in nature and enable the investor to have little or no influence on the operations of the investee.* [1]

The use of the sophisticated equity method is required for the following types of investments:

1. *Influential investments*. The FASB defines influence as "representation on the board of directors, participation in policy-making processes, material intercompany transactions, interchange of managerial personnel, or technological dependency." [2] When the investor holds 20% or more of the voting shares of an investee, influence is assumed and the sophisticated equity method is required unless the investor takes on the burden of proof to show that influence does not exist, in which case the cost method would be used. [3] When the investment falls below 20%, the presumption is that influence does not exist, and the cost method is to be used unless the investor can show that influence does exist despite the low percentage of ownership. Since the most common use of the sophisticated equity method is for influential (20% to 50%) investments, such investments are used in subsequent illustrations.

2. *Corporate joint ventures.* A corporate joint venture is a separate, specific project organized for the benefit of several corporations. An example would be a research project undertaken jointly by several members of a given industry. The member corporations typically participate in the management of the venture and share the gains and losses. Since such an arrangement does not involve passive investors, the sophisticated equity method is required.

3. *Unconsolidated subsidiaries.* A parent may own over 50% of the shares of a subsidiary but may meet one of the exceptions (control is temporary or does not rest with the majority owner) to the requirement that subsidiaries be consolidated. However, if influence does exist, the sophisticated equity method would be used for the investment.

---

1 FASB ASC 323-10-05-5.
2 FASB ASC 323-10-15-6.
3 FASB ASC 323-10-15-8.

The use of the equity method requires that the investment in common stock appear as a single, equity-adjusted amount on the balance sheet of the investor. The investor's income statement will include the investor's share of the investee ordinary income as a single amount in the ordinary income section. The investor's share of investee discontinued operations, extraordinary items, and cumulative effects of changes in accounting principles will appear as single amounts in the sections of the investor's income statement that correspond to the placement of these items in the investee's statement.

In 2007, the FASB allowed investors to opt for the use of the fair value method for influential investments that would normally be accounted for under the equity method. This option will be discussed after our study of the equity method.

CALCULATION OF EQUITY INCOME

The equity method requires the investor to recognize its pro rata share of investee reported income. Dividends, when received, do not constitute income but are viewed instead as a partial liquidation of the investment. In reality, however, the price paid for the investment usually will not agree with the underlying book value of the investee, which requires that any amortization of an excess of cost or book value be treated as an adjustment of the investor's pro rata share of investee income. It is very likely that the reported income of the investee will include gains and losses on transactions with the investor. As was true in consolidations, these gains and losses must be deferred until they are confirmed by a transaction between the affiliated group and unrelated parties. The proper application of the sophisticated equity method will mean that the income recognized by the investor will be the same as it would be under consolidation procedures. In fact, the sophisticated equity method sometimes is referred to as "one-line consolidation."

In the next two sections, the sophisticated equity method will be presented without consideration of the tax implications. Following that, the tax effect on such an investment will be addressed.

Amortization of Excesses

A determination and distribution of excess schedule is prepared for a sophisticated equity method investment. It compares the price paid for the investment to only the equity interest that was purchased. **In the absence of control, there is no fair value adjustment for the shares not purchased.** For example, assume the following schedule was prepared by Excel Corporation for a 25% interest in Flag Company acquired on January 1, 2011:

Price paid		$250,000
Less interest acquired:		
Common stock ($10 par).	$200,000	
Retained earnings, January 1, 2011.	600,000	
Total stockholders' equity.	$800,000	
Interest acquired	× 25%	200,000
Excess of cost over book value.		$ 50,000
Less excess attributable to equipment with a 5-year remaining		
life and undervalued by $80,000 (25% × $80,000)		20,000
Goodwill		$ 30,000

As a practical matter, it may not be possible to relate the excess to specific assets, in which case the entire excess may be considered goodwill. However, an attempt should be made to allocate the excess in the same manner as would be done for the purchase of a controlling interest in a subsidiary.[4]

The determination and distribution of excess schedule indicates the pattern of amortization to be followed. The required amortizations must be made directly through the investment account since the distributions shown on the schedule are not recorded in the absence of consolidation procedures. Assuming Flag Company reported net income of $60,000 for 2011, Excel Corporation would make the following entry for 2011:

Investment in Flag Company	11,000	
Investment Income		11,000

Income is calculated as follows:

25% × Flag reported net income of $60,000	$15,000
Less amortizations of excess cost:	
Equipment ($20,000 ÷ 5)	4,000
Investment income, net of amortizations	$11,000

If an investment is acquired for less than book value, the excess of book value over cost would be amortized based on the life of assets to which it pertains. This procedure would increase investment income in the years of amortization.

Intercompany Transactions by Investee

The investee may sell inventory to the investor. As would be true if the investment were consolidated, the share of the investee's profit on goods still held by the investor at the end of a period cannot be included in income of that period. Instead, the profit must be deferred until the goods are sold by the investor. Since the two firms are separate reporting entities, the intercompany sales and related debt cannot be eliminated. Only the investor's share of the investee's profit on unsold goods in the hands of the investor is deferred. In a like manner, the investor may have plant assets that were purchased from the investee. The investor's share of the investee's gains and losses on these sales also must be deferred and allocated over the depreciable life of the asset. Profit deferments should be handled in an income distribution schedule similar to that used for consolidated worksheets. To illustrate, assume the following facts for the example of the 25% investment in Flag by Excel. Again, note that income tax is not being considered in this illustration:

1. Excel had the following merchandise acquired from Flag Company in its ending inventories:

Year	Amount	Gross Profit of Flag Company
2011	$30,000	40%
2012	40,000	45

2. Excel purchased a truck from Flag Company on January 1, 2011, for $20,000. The truck is being depreciated over a 4-year life on a straight-line basis with no salvage value. The truck had a net book value of $16,000 when it was sold by Flag.
3. Flag Company had an income of $60,000 in 2011 and $70,000 in 2012.
4. Flag declared and paid $10,000 in dividends in 2012.

Based on these facts, Excel Corporation would prepare the income distribution schedules shown on page 480.

---

4 FASB ASC 323-10-35-34.

2011 Income Distribution for Investment in Flag Company

Gain on sale of truck, to be amortized over 4 years	$ 4,000	Reported income of Flag Company	$60,000
Profit in Excel ending inventory (40% × $30,000)	12,000	Realization of ¼ of profit on sale of truck	1,000
		Adjusted income of Flag Company	$45,000
		Ownership interest (25%)	$11,250
		Less amortization of excess cost:	
		Equipment	4,000
		Investment income, net of amortizations	$ 7,250

2012 Income Distribution for Investment in Flag Company

Profit in Excel ending inventory (45% × $40,000)	$18,000	Reported income of Flag Company	$70,000
		Profit in Excel beginning inventory (40% × $30,000)	12,000
		Realization of ¼ of profit on sale of truck	1,000
		Adjusted income of Flag Company	$65,000
		Ownership interest (25%)	$16,250
		Less amortization of excess cost:	
		Equipment	4,000
		Income from investment	$12,250

The schedules would lead to the following entries to record investment income:

2011	Investment in Flag Company	7,250	
	Investment Income		7,250
2012	Investment in Flag Company	12,250	
	Investment Income		12,250

In addition, the following entry would be made in 2012 to record dividends received:

Cash	2,500	
Investment in Flag Company		2,500

It should be noted that only the investor's share of intercompany gains and losses is deferred. The investee's remaining stockholders are not affected by the Excel Corporation investment.

TAX EFFECTS OF EQUITY METHOD

The investor not meeting the requirements of affiliation as defined by tax law pays income taxes on dividends received. In the case of a domestic corporation, 20% of the dividends are includable in taxable income. However, a temporary difference is created through the use of the equity method for financial reporting.[5] As a result, **the provision for tax is based on the equity income, and a deferred tax liability is created for undistributed investment income.**

---

5 FASB ASC 740-20-20.

The provision may be based on the assumption that investment income will be distributed in dividends, or it will be realized via the sale of the investment. In the latter case, it is likely that the income would be taxed in the form of a capital gain. The assumption used will determine the rate to be applied to the undistributed income. The provision for tax is based on the investor's net investment income after adjustments and amortizations. However, **amortizations of excess cost are not deductible** since they have no impact on the income that could be distributed to the investor and, thus, must be added back to the net investment income to compute the tax.

The following entries are based on the previous example of Flag Company and Excel Corporation, but it is assumed that each company is subject to a 30% income tax. Excel Corporation's share of Flag Company net income would now be calculated as follows:

	2011	2012
Adjusted income of Flag Company (before tax)*	$45,000	$65,000
Tax provision (30%)	13,500	19,500
Adjusted net income of Flag Company	$31,500	$45,500
Ownership interest in adjusted net income (25%)	$ 7,875	$11,375
Less amortizations of excess*	4,000	4,000
Net income from investment	$ 3,875	$ 7,375

*See the income distribution schedules in the previous section.

Note that the tax provision calculated by the investor will not agree with the provision for tax on the books of the investee. This is due to the adjustments made in the income distribution schedules to recognize the profit deferrals.

The 2011 and 2012 entries to record investment income and the applicable tax provision would be as follows:

2011	Investment in Flag Company	3,875	
	Investment Income		3,875
	Provision for Income Tax [20% included × 30% tax rate × ($3,875 net income + $4,000 nondeductible amortizations of excess)]	473	
	Deferred Tax Liability.		473
2012	Investment in Flag Company	7,375	
	Investment Income		7,375
	Cash	2,500	
	Investment in Flag Company		2,500
	Provision for Income Tax [20% included × 30% tax rate × ($7,375 net income + $4,000 nondeductible amortizations of excess)]	683	
	Income Tax Payable (20% included × 30% tax rate × $2,500 dividends)		150
	Deferred Tax Liability ($683 – $150)		533

UNUSUAL EQUITY ADJUSTMENTS

There are several unusual situations involving the investee that require special procedures for the proper recording of investment income. These situations are described in the following paragraphs.

Investee with Preferred Stock

In the absence of consolidation, an investment in preferred stock does not require elimination. However, the existence of preferred stock in the capital structure of the investee requires that the investor's equity adjustment be based on only that portion of investee income available for common stockholders. Dividends declared on preferred stock must be subtracted from income of the investee. When the preferred stock has cumulative or participation rights, the claim of preferred stockholders must be subtracted from the investee income each period to arrive at the income available for common stockholders. The procedures for calculating this income are contained in Chapter 7.

Investee Stock Transactions

The investee corporation may engage in transactions with its common stockholders, such as issuing additional shares, retiring shares, or engaging in treasury stock transactions. Each of these transactions affects the investor's equity interest. A comparison is made of the investor's ownership interest before and after the investee stock transaction. An increase in the investor's interest is treated as a gain, while a decrease is recorded as a loss.

Write-Down to Market Value

The investment in another company is subject to reduction to a lower market value if it appears that a relatively permanent fall in value has occurred. The fact that the current market value of the shares is temporarily less than the equity-adjusted cost of the shares is not sufficient cause for a write-down. When the sophisticated equity method is used and a permanent decline in value occurs, a reduction would be made to the equity-adjusted cost. The equity method would continue to be applied subsequent to the write-down. There can be no subsequent write-ups, however, other than through normal equity adjustments.

Zero Investment Balance

It is possible that an investee will suffer losses to the extent that the continued application of the equity method could produce a negative balance in the investment account. Equity adjustments are to be discontinued when the investment balance becomes zero. Further losses are acknowledged only by memo entries, which are needed to maintain the total unrecorded share of losses. If the investee again becomes profitable, the investor must not record income on the investment until its subsequent share of income equals the previously unrecorded share of losses.

To illustrate these procedures, assume Grate Corporation has a 35% investment in Dittmar Company, with a sophisticated equity-adjusted cost of $30,000 on January 1, 2011, and Dittmar reports the following results:

Period	Income (Loss)
2011	$(80,000)
2012	(50,000)
2013	(20,000)
2014	90,000

The following T account summarizes entries for 2011 through 2014 (taxes are ignored):

Investment in Dittmar Company

Equity-adjusted balance, January 1, 2011....................................	$30,000	Equity loss for 2011 (35% × $80,000 Dittmar loss)...............................	$28,000
		Recorded equity loss for 2012 (35% × $50,000 Dittmar loss = $17,500; loss limited to investment balance).............	2,000
Balance, January 1, 2012..............	$ 0	Memo entries:	
Memo entry:		Unrecorded 2012 loss ($17,500 – $2,000)	$15,500
Unrecorded share of 2014 Dittmar income	22,500	Unrecorded loss for 2013 (35% × $20,000 Dittmar loss)......................	7,000
Actual entries resumed:			
Recorded equity income, 2014 [35% × $90,000 Dittmar income = $31,500, less amount to cover unrecorded losses ($15,500 + $7,000)].........................	9,000		
Balance, December 31, 2014	$ 9,000		

Intercompany Asset Transactions by Investor

An investor may sell merchandise and/or plant assets to an investee at a gain or loss. When influence is deemed to exist, it might seem appropriate to defer the entire gain or loss until the asset is resold or depreciated by the investee. However, the entire gain or loss is to be deferred only when the transaction is with a controlled (over 50% owned) investee and is not at arm's length. In all other cases, it is appropriate to defer only a gain or loss that is in proportion to the investor's ownership interest.[6]

To illustrate, assume Grant Corporation, which owns a 35% interest in Hartwig Company sold $50,000 of merchandise to Hartwig at a gross profit of 40%. Of this merchandise, $20,000 is still in Hartwig's 2011 ending inventory. Grant needs to defer only profit equal to the $8,000 (40% × $20,000) unrealized gross profit multiplied by its 35% interest, or $2,800. Grant would make the following entry on December 31, 2011:

Sales	2,800	
Deferred Gross Profit on Sales to Investee		2,800

Assuming the investor recorded the provision for income tax prior to this adjustment, the tax applicable to the unrealized gain would be deferred by the following entry, which is based on a 30% tax rate:

Deferred Tax Expense (30% × $2,800)	840	
Provision for Income Tax		840

The deferred gross profit and the related tax deferment would be realized in the period in which the goods are sold to outside parties. The deferred profit and related tax effects on plant asset sales would be realized in proportion to the depreciation recorded by the investee company.

Intercompany Bond Transactions by Investor

Unlike consolidation procedures, when the investor purchases outstanding bonds of the investee, the bonds are not assumed to be retired since the investor and investee are separate reporting entities.

---

6 FASB ASC 323-10-35 & 36.

Similarly, a purchase of investor bonds by the investee is not a retirement of the bonds. Thus, no adjustments to income are necessary as a result of intercompany bond holdings.

Gain or Loss of Influence

An investor may own less than a 20% interest in an investee, in which case the cost method or fair value method would be used to record the investment. If the investor subsequently buys sufficient additional shares to have its total interest equal or exceed 20%, the investor must *retroactively* apply the sophisticated equity method to the total holding period of the investment.

It is possible that an investor will own 20% or more of the voting shares of the investee but will sell a portion of the shares so that the ownership interest falls below 20%. In such a case, the sophisticated equity method is discontinued as of the sale date. However, there is no adjustment back to the cost method. The balance of the investment account remains at its equity-adjusted balance on the sale date. Should influence be attained again, a retroactive ("catch-up") equity adjustment would be made.

When all or part of an investment recorded under the sophisticated equity method is sold, the gain or loss is based on the equity-adjusted balance as of the sale date. An adjustment also would be necessary for deferred tax balances applicable to the investment.

DISCLOSURE REQUIREMENTS

Since a significant portion of the investor's income may be derived from investments, added disclosures are required in order to properly inform the readers of the financial statements. For investments of 20% or more, the investor must disclose the name of each investee, the percentage of ownership in each investee, and the disparity between the cost and underlying book value for each investment. If the sophisticated equity method is not being applied, the reasons must be given. When investments are material with respect to the investor's financial position or income, the financial statements of the investees should be included as supplemental information.

When a market value for the investment is available, it should be disclosed. However, if the investor owns a relatively large block of a subsidiary's shares, quoted market values would have little relevance because the sale of an entire controlling interest would involve different motivations and would result in a unique value.

REFLECTION

- The sophisticated equity method is used for "influential" investments.

- The sophisticated equity income is based on the investee's adjusted (for intercompany profits) income less amortizations of excess from the D&D. Note that this process includes adjustment for only investee-generated intercompany transactions.

- The investor is liable for the tax on its share of investee income.

- The investor must make a separate adjustment for its share of unrealized profits on sales to the investee. These adjustments also create a deferred tax asset.

- The investor cannot adjust its investment below a zero balance by recording its share of investee losses. If the investee becomes profitable, income equal to the unrecorded losses must be excluded from income.

- An initial ownership interest may not be "influential." If a second block is purchased, so as to make the total interest "influential," the prior block is retroactively converted to the sophisticated equity method.

- If an interest is sold down to a level that is no longer influential, the remaining interest stays at its equity-adjusted cost. The use of the equity method is discontinued in future periods.

FAIR VALUE OPTION

The investor may elect to record an influential investment using fair value at each recording date. The election is made on the date the investment is purchased. The election once made, may not be revoked.

The fair value option is applied as follows:

1. The investment is recorded at the price paid.
2. At the end of each accounting period, the investment is adjusted to fair value, and the adjustment is recorded as income.
3. Dividends are recorded as income when declared by the investee.

The following example applies the fair value option to the investment in Flag Company that starts on page 478. Assume that the fair value of the investment is $270,000 on December 31, 2011, and $310,000 on December 31, 2012.

2011	Purchase Date	Investment in Flag Company	250,000	
		Cash		250,000
		To record purchase of investment		
2011	Year-end adjustment	Investment in Flag Company	20,000	
		Unrealized Gain on Investment		20,000
2012	Year-end adjustment	Investment in Flag Company	40,000	
		Unrealized Gain on Investment		40,000
	Dividend declared	Cash	2,500	
		Dividend Income		2,500

The unrealized gain is recorded as income as is the investor's share of dividends. There would be no adjustments for unrealized intercompany gains and losses. The unrealized gains will require the recording of a deferred income tax liability since the income is not taxable.

UNDERSTANDING THE ISSUES

1. Company R pays $170,000 for a 30% interest in Company E on January 1, 2011. Company E's total stockholders' equity on that date is $500,000. The excess price is attributed to equipment with a 5-year life. During 2011, Company E reports net income of $35,000 and pays total dividends of $10,000. Answer the following questions assuming the investment is recorded under the equity method:

   a. What is Company R's investment income for 2011?
   b. What is Company R's investment balance on December 31, 2011?
   c. Explain, in words, the investment balance on December 31, 2011.

2. Assume the same facts as for Question 1 above. The fair value of the investment in Company E is $220,000 on December 31, 2011. Answer the following questions assuming the investment is recorded using the fair value option:

   a. What is Company R's investment income for 2011?
   b. What is Company R's investment balance on December 31, 2011?
   c. Explain in words the investment balance on December 31, 2011.

3. Company R owns a 30% interest in Company E, which it acquires at book value. Company E reports net income of $50,000 for 2011 (ignore taxes). There is an intercompany sale of equipment at a gain of $20,000 on January 1, 2011. The equipment has a 5-year life. What is Company R's investment income for 2011, and what adjusting entry (if any) does Company R need to make as a result of the equipment sale, if:

   a. Company E made the sale?
   b. Company R made the sale?

4. Company E reports net income of $100,000 for 2011. Assume the income is earned evenly throughout the year. Dividends of $10,000 are paid on December 31. What will Company R report as investment income under the following ownership situations, if:

    a. Company R owns a 10% interest from July 1 to December 31?

    b. Company R owns a 10% interest from January 1 to June 30 and a 25% interest from July 1 to December 31?

    c. Company R owns a 30% interest from January 1 to June 30 and a 10% interest from July 1 to December 31?

5. Company R purchases a 25% interest in Company E on January 1, 2010, at its book value of $20,000. From 2010 through 2014, Company E earns a total of $200,000. From 2015 through 2019, it loses $300,000. In 2020, Company E reports net income of $30,000. What is Company R's investment income for 2020, and what is its balance in the investment in Company E account on December 31, 2020?

EXERCISES

Exercise SA-1 Income recording. Tucker Corporation purchases a 25% interest in Lincoln Company for $120,000 on January 1, 2017. The following determination and distribution of excess schedule is prepared:

Price paid		$120,000
Less interest acquired:		
Common stock ($10 par).............................	$200,000	
Retained earnings	100,000	
Total stockholders' equity...........................	$300,000	
Interest acquired	× 25%	75,000
Excess of cost over book value.............................		$ 45,000
Less excess attributable to equipment [25% × $40,000 (5-year life)].		10,000
Goodwill		$ 35,000

    Lincoln Company earns income of $25,000 in 2017 and $30,000 in 2018. Lincoln Company declares a 25-cent per-share cash dividend on December 22, 2018, payable January 12, 2019, to stockholders of record on December 30, 2018.

    During 2018, Lincoln sells merchandise costing $10,000 to Tucker for $15,000. Twenty percent of the merchandise is still in Tucker's ending inventory on December 31, 2018. The fair value of the investment is $135,000 on December 31, 2017, and $145,000 on December 31, 2018.

1. Assuming the use of the equity method, prepare the adjustment on Tucker's books on December 31, 2017, and December 31, 2018, to account for its investment in Lincoln Company. Assume Tucker Corporation makes no adjustment except at the end of each calendar year. Ignore income tax considerations.

2. Assuming the use of the fair value option, prepare the adjustment on Tucker's books on December 31, 2017, and December 31, 2018, to account for its investment in Lincoln Company. Assume Tucker Corporation makes no adjustment except at the end of each calendar year. Ignore income tax considerations.

Exercise SA-2 Equity method investment with intercompany profits. Turf Company purchases a 30% interest in Minnie Company for $90,000 on January 1, 2011, when Minnie has the following stockholders' equity:

Common stock ($10 par)................................	$100,000
Paid-in capital in excess of par	20,000
Retained earnings	130,000
Total......................................	$250,000

The excess cost was due to a building that is being amortized over 20 years.

Since the investment, Minnie has consistently sold goods to Turf to realize a 40% gross profit. Such sales total $50,000 during 2013. Turf has $10,000 of the goods in its beginning inventory and $40,000 in its ending inventory.

On January 1, 2013, Turf sells a machine with a book value of $15,000 to Minnie for $20,000. The machine has a 5-year life and is being depreciated on a straight-line basis. Minnie reports a net income of $60,000 for 2013 and pays $5,000 in dividends in 2013.

Prepare all 2013 entries caused by Turf's investment in Minnie. Assume that Turf has recorded the tax on its internally generated income. Turf has properly recorded the investment using the equity method in previous periods. Ignore income tax considerations.

Exercise SA-3 Equity income with intercompany profits.
Spancrete Corporation acquires a 30% interest in the outstanding stock of Werl Corporation on January 1, 2015. At that time, the following determination and distribution of excess schedule is prepared:

Price paid		$125,000
Less interest acquired:		
Common stock.......................................	$150,000	
Retained earnings	160,000	
Total stockholders' equity.............................	$310,000	
Interest acquired	× 30%	93,000
Excess of cost over book value attributable to equipment (10-year life)		$ 32,000

During 2015, Spancrete purchases $200,000 of goods from Werl. $20,000 of these purchases are in the December 31, 2015, ending inventory. During 2016, Spancrete purchases $250,000 of goods from Werl. $30,000 of these purchases are in the December 31, 2016, ending inventory. Werl's gross profit rate is 30%. Also, Spancrete purchases a machine from Werl for $15,000 on January 1, 2016. The machine has a book value of $10,000 and a 5-year remaining life. Werl reports net income of $90,000 and pays $20,000 on dividends during 2016.

Prepare an income distribution schedule for Werl, and record the entries to adjust the investment in Werl for 2016 using the equity method.

Exercise SA-4 Equity method, change in interest.
Hanson Corporation purchases a 10% interest in Novic Company on January 1, 2016, and an additional 15% interest on January 1, 2018. These investments cost Hanson Corporation $80,000 and $110,000, respectively.

The following stockholders' equities of Novic Company are available:

	December 31, 2015	December 31, 2017
Common stock ($10 par)...................	$500,000	$500,000
Retained earnings	250,000	300,000
Total equity	$750,000	$800,000

Any excess of cost over book value on the original investment is attributed to goodwill. Any excess on the second purchase is attributable to equipment with a 4-year life.

Novic Company has income of $30,000, $30,000, and $40,000 for 2016, 2017, and 2018, respectively. Novic pays dividends of $0.20 per share in 2017 and 2018.

Ignore income tax considerations, and assume equity method adjusting entries are made at the end of the calendar year only.

1. Prepare the cost-to-equity conversion entry on January 1, 2018, when Hanson's investment in Novic Company first exceeds 20%. Any supporting schedules should be in good form.
2. Prepare the December 31, 2018, equity adjustment on Hanson's books. Provide supporting calculations in good form.

Exercise SA-5 Sale of equity method investment. On January 1, 2017, Lund Corporation purchases a 30% interest in Aluma-Boat Company for $200,000. At the time of the purchase, Aluma-Boat has total stockholders' equity of $400,000. Any excess of cost over the equity purchased is attributed in part to machinery worth $50,000 more than book value with a remaining useful life of five years. Any remaining excess would be allocated to goodwill.

Aluma-Boat reports the following income and dividend distributions in 2017 and 2018:

	2017	2018
Income.	$50,000	$45,000
Dividends declared and paid	10,000	10,000

Lund sells its investment in Aluma-Boat Company on January 2, 2019, for $230,000. Record the sale of the investments assuming the use of the equity method. You may ignore income taxes. Carefully schedule the investment account balance at the time of the sale.

PROBLEMS

Problem SA-1 Equity income, inventory, fixed asset sale. Schinzer Company purchases an influential 25% interest in Fowler Company on January 1, 2016, for $300,000. At that time, Fowler's stockholders' equity is $1,000,000.

Fowler Company assets have fair value similar to book value except for a building that is undervalued by $40,000. The building has an estimated remaining life of 10 years. Any remaining excess is attributed to goodwill.

The following additional information is available:

a. On July 1, 2016, Schinzer sells a machine to Fowler for $25,000. The cost of the machine to Schinzer is $16,000. The machine is being depreciated on a straight-line basis over five years.
b. Schinzer provides management services to Fowler at a billing rate of $15,000 per year. This arrangement starts in 2016.
c. Fowler has sold merchandise to Shinzer since 2017. Sales are $15,000 in 2017 and $20,000 in 2018. The merchandise is sold to provide a gross profit rate of 25%. Schinzer has $2,000 of these goods in its December 31, 2017, inventory and $3,000 of such goods in its December 31, 2018, inventory.
d. The income earned and dividends paid by Fowler are as follows:

Year	Income	Dividends
2016	$52,000	$60,000
2017	50,000	10,000
2018	65,000	10,000

Required ▶ ▶ ▶ ▶ ▶   Prepare all entries required by Schinzer's investment in Fowler Company for 2016 through 2018 using the equity method. Supporting schedules should be in good form. Ignore taxes.

Problem SA-2 Fair value option for influential investment. Assume the same information as for Problem SA-1. Instead of using the equity method, Schinzer uses the fair value option to record the investment in Fowler. The fair value of the investment in Fowler is as follows:

Date	Fair Value
December 31, 2016	$360,000
December 31, 2017	425,000
December 31, 2018	410,000

Required ▶ ▶ ▶ ▶ ▶   Prepare all entries required by Schinzer's investment in Fowler Company for 2016 through 2018 using the fair value option.

Problem SA-3 Equity income, taxation, inventory, fixed asset sale. On January 1, 2016, Ashland Company purchases a 25% interest in Cramer Company for $195,000. Ashland Company prepares the following determination and distribution of excess schedule:

Price paid for investment		$195,000
Less book value of interest acquired:		
Common stock ($5 par)	$100,000	
Paid-in capital in excess of par	200,000	
Retained earnings	150,000	
Total stockholders' equity	$450,000	
Interest acquired	× 25%	112,500
Excess of cost over book value (debit)		$ 82,500
Equipment [25% × $30,000 (10-year life)]		7,500 Dr
Goodwill		$ 75,000 Dr

The following additional information is available:

a. Cramer Company sells a machine to Ashland Company for $30,000 on July 1, 2017. At this date, the machine has a book value of $25,000 and an estimated future life of five years. Straight-line depreciation (to the nearest month) is being used. For income tax purposes, the gain on the sale is taxable in the year of the sale.

b. The following applies to Ashland Company sales to Cramer Company for 2017 and 2018:

	2017	2018
Intercompany merchandise in beginning inventory		$ 4,000
Sales for the year	$10,000	$15,000
Intercompany merchandise in ending inventory	$ 4,000	$ 5,000
Gross profit on sales	40%	40%

c. Internally generated income (before tax) for the two companies is as follows:

	2016	2017	2018
Ashland Company	$140,000	$150,000	$155,000
Cramer Company	60,000	80,000	100,000

d. Cramer pays dividends of $5,000, $10,000, and $10,000 in 2016, 2017, and 2018, respectively.

e. The corporate income tax rate of 30% applies to both companies. Assume an 80% dividend exclusion.

Prepare all equity method adjustments for Ashland Company's investment in Cramer Company on December 31, 2016, 2017, and 2018. Consider income tax implications. Supporting calculations and schedules should be in good form.   ◄ ◄ ◄ ◄ ◄ **Required**

Multinational Accounting and Other Reporting Concerns

In today's evolving global economy, companies buy goods and services from foreign sources, manufacture goods in a number of different countries, and sell their products to customers throughout the world. The complexities of the many international transactions have required accounting to become more international in nature. Efforts are underway to develop accounting principles that are comparable or harmonious between trading nations.

As international trading expands, accounting principles must address how to account for transactions involving different currencies. Since changes in currency exchange rates expose trading parties to potential gains or losses, the economic consequences of such rate changes must be measured. Also, companies often use different strategies to reduce risk. Hedging strategies, including the use of such derivatives as forward contracts, options, and currency swaps, add complexity to accounting for these transactions.

Companies also invest in foreign entities. These investments create a need to translate foreign entity financial statements from one currency to another. Specialized accounting procedures are used for the required translation or remeasurement from the foreign currency into the domestic currency of the investor.

Interim reporting and segmental reporting are designed to provide timely and relevant information for decision making. Both types of reporting involve the application of special accounting principles. Timely reporting of interim information serves as an indicator of annual results. Segmental reports, arising from growing diversification in companies domestically and globally, communicate useful financial information about segmental assets and performance.

The International Accounting Environment

Learning Objectives

When you have completed this chapter, you should be able to

1. **Describe the international business environment.**

2. **Describe the accounting issues associated with foreign currency transactions.**

3. **Describe the accounting issues associated with foreign currency translation.**

4. **Describe the factors and parties influencing the development of International Financial Reporting Standards (IFRS).**

5. **Understand the U.S. initiatives to converge with International Accounting Standards (IAS).**

Jacob Corporation (a fictitious company) began with a small facility in central Wisconsin, where it manufactured precision measuring equipment to be used primarily in the food industry. As the company began to grow, its sales extended throughout the continental United States. While attending a trade show in Atlanta, Georgia, company representatives had the opportunity to arrange a sale to a foreign customer in Germany, and that was the beginning of the company's venture into export sales. The sale to the German company was collected in U.S. dollars, and the company began to expand its sales to other foreign customers. However, as these sales increased, a number of customers settled their accounts by payment in foreign currencies, such as the euro, rather than U.S. dollars. The company quickly realized that this could be good news or bad news, depending on how the U.S. dollar performed against the respective foreign currencies. For example, if the dollar strengthened against the euro, the euros collected by Jacob when the customer paid their account were actually worth fewer dollars than their value at the time of sale. Assume a dollar was equal to 1.5 euros at the time of the sale and goods were sold for 1,500 euros or $1,000. If the customer paid its balance due of 1,500 euros when a dollar was equal to 2.0 euros, the 1,500 euros collected would only be worth $750 at the time of collection. Jacob Corporation recognized that steps might have to be taken that would reduce the risk associated with settling accounts in a currency other than the U.S. dollar.

As sales continued to grow, the company decided to construct a manufacturing facility in France. This new facility was established as a separate French company subject to the laws of France but owned 90% by the U.S. company. The social, language, legal, taxation, and cultural differences of operating in a foreign country were just a few of the challenges with which the company was now dealing. In order to finance the construction of the French facility, Jacob sought financing from both French and German banks. Recognizing that financial statements would have to be submitted as part of any loan application, Jacob became aware of the fact that its financial statements followed generally accepted accounting principles (GAAP) that were recognized in the United States but may not account for transactions the same way that French or German accounting principles would. The French facility sells approximately 40% of its production to a Brazilian company that is a wholly owned subsidiary of Jacob. The pricing of sales between the French and Brazilian companies is designed to take advantage of the higher tax rate in France without violating any tax laws that discourage the manipulation of taxable income through intercompany pricing policies. Both the French and Brazilian company measure their operations in terms of the euro and follow the accounting principles established in their respective countries. However, Jacob prepares consolidated financial statements, in conformity with U.S. GAAP as measured in dollars, that reflect its ownership in these foreign companies. Therefore, Jacob must first make sure that the foreign company's transactions are recorded in conformity with U.S. GAAP and then translate the euro-based financial statements of its foreign subsidiaries into dollars before such statements can be consolidated with those of the U.S. parent company.

Today, we find our U.S. company constructing its sixth manufacturing facility—this one in Africa. As part of its agreement with the government of the African country, the U.S. company will be constructing a health clinic and school in the community and guaranteeing a minimum employment level for the next five years. Thus, Jacob Corporation has come a long way from central Wisconsin. It may be a fictitious company, but the scenario described is common in companies today. Welcome to international business and the global economy. All of this is possible when a commercial activity transcends national boundaries or borders.

In this chapter, the Derivatives Module, and the following two chapters, several issues relating to international accounting will be explored, including the following:

1. Derivative instruments and their use in hedge transactions
2. Accounting for transactions denominated or settled in foreign currencies
3. The translation and remeasurement of financial statements prepared in a foreign currency
4. The international standard-setting process.

1
OBJECTIVE

Describe the international business environment.

THE SCOPE OF INTERNATIONAL BUSINESS ACTIVITIES

An entity's involvement in international business can range from export or import activity to that of a multinational or transnational enterprise with a global approach to manufacturing, distribution, and sales. Trade between different nations certainly is not new. It has existed before biblical times and has provided the means by which certain nations have evolved into world powers. The United Kingdom and the Netherlands are just two examples of countries that have been active in international trade for centuries. However, it has been since World War II that international trade has increased significantly, and many more goods and services are becoming part of a global economy.

Dramatic changes occurring in recent times have allowed a global economy to become a reality for an increasing number of entities. The restructuring of Eastern Europe and the former Soviet Union has opened the door for free enterprise. The growth of the European Union (EU) has been responsible for reducing the economic barriers between nations by forming a single market with its own common currency, the euro. Comprehensive free trade agreements such as the North American Free Trade Agreement (NAFTA) and the American Free Trade Agreement (AFTA) as well as the World Trade Organization (WTO) are committed to reducing trade barriers through multilateral agreements.

As the barriers to world trade are reduced, the world becomes smaller in a number of ways. For example, modern communications technology makes it much easier to transact business between countries. The credit card purchase you made today may be processed in a center located in Ireland, and tomorrow you will be able to inquire about your account balance which will include your recent purchase. The Internet also is proving to be a significant tool through which entities make their goods and services available to consumers on an international scale.

Not only are goods and services trading in international markets, but the stocks of these companies are also traded internationally. International securities trading has increased rapidly due to a number of forces. As companies expand into different international markets, they need to acquire the factors of production in those markets and, thus, need to raise additional capital. International securities trading also offers investors the opportunity to diversify their portfolios against loss from currency fluctuations, political instabilities, and economic downturns.

R E F L E C T I O N

- The increasing international business activity includes trading in goods, services, and securities.

FOREIGN CURRENCY TRANSACTIONS

There are many businesses of all sizes within a country that operate on an international scale by exporting and/or importing goods and services. For example, in 2009 the United States exported approximately $1,056 billion of goods and imported approximately $1,560 billion of goods. The United States exported $258 billion of goods to Europe alone and $255 billion to Pacific Rim countries. On the other hand, we imported $331 billion from Europe, $533 billion from Pacific Rim countries, and $112 billion from the Organization of Petroleum Exporting Countries (OPEC). During this period of time, trading levels with the top five trading nations were as follows:

2

OBJECTIVE

Describe the accounting issues associated with foreign currency transactions.

	Exports			Imports	
Nation	(in millions)	% of Total	Nation	(in millions)	% of Total
Canada	$ 204,658	19.4	China	$ 296,374	19.0
Mexico	128,892	12.2	Canada	226,248	14.5
China	69,497	6.6	Mexico	176,654	11.3
Japan	51,134	4.8	Japan	95,804	6.1
United Kingdom	45,704	4.3	Germany	71,498	4.6
Total all nations	1,056,043	100.0	Total all nations	1,559,625	100.0

Think of some large U.S. companies, and you will be surprised at the scale of their international sales. Consider some of the information as shown below.

	Boeing	Kraft Foods	The Coca-Cola Company	Johnson Controls
Year-end	December 31, 2009	December 31, 2009	December 31, 2009	September 30, 2009
Total revenues (in millions).	$68,281	$40,386	$30,990	$28,497
Non-U.S. revenues (in millions)	$28,783	$20,811	$22,979	$17,398
Percent traceable to non-U.S	42.2%	51.5%	74.1%	61.1%

Today, there are almost 200 countries in the world and there are well over 150 different currencies in use throughout the world (even the Vatican has its own currency). It is simplistic to think that business activities within a given country are only settled or denominated within their domestic currency (home country). In fact, in some instances, businesses within a country may prefer to settle transactions in a currency other than their domestic currency. Business transactions that are settled in a currency other than that of the domestic currency are referred to, in this text, as *foreign currency transactions*. One of the transacting parties will settle the transaction in its own domestic currency and also measure the transaction in its domestic currency. For example, a German company may sell inventory to a U.S. company and require payment in euros. The currency used to settle the transaction is referred to as the *denominated currency* and would be the euro in this case. The other transacting party will settle the transaction in a foreign currency but will need to measure the transaction in its domestic currency. For example, a U.S. company that purchases inventory from a German company must settle the resulting accounts payable in euros and yet must measure the purchase of inventory and the accounts payable in terms of U.S. dollars. The currency used to measure or record the transaction is referred to as the *measurement currency* and would be the U.S. dollar in this case. Whenever a transaction is denominated in a currency different from the measurement currency, exchange rate risk exists, and exchange rates must be used for measurement purposes. The process of expressing a transaction in the measurement currency when it is denominated in a different currency is referred to as a *foreign currency translation*.

Continuing with our example involving a purchase of inventory from a German company, assume that inventory was purchased for 13,200 euros when $1 was equal to 1.20 euros. At the time of the purchase, the respective parties would recognize the following:

German company	
Sales revenue of.	€13,200
Accounts receivable of.	€13,200
U.S. company	
Inventory of	$11,000
Accounts payable of	$11,000

Assume that $1 was equal to 1.10 euros at the time of settling the transaction. At that time, the German company would still receive 13,200 euros in settlement of its receivable. However, the U.S. company would have to spend $12,000 (13,200 euros divided by 1.10) in order to settle its account payable rather than the $11,000 that was recorded at the time of the purchase. The U.S. company has experienced an economic loss due to changes in the exchange rates over time. Whenever a transaction is denominated in a currency different than the measurement currency, one of the parties to the transaction is exposed to either economic gain or loss if exchange rates change between the date of the transaction and the date of settlement. The change in exchange rates over time did not expose the German company to exchange risk because the transaction is both denominated and measured in its domestic currency. However, the U.S. company was exposed to exchange risk because the transaction was denominated in euros but measured in dollars. The above example brings to light two issues: first, business strategies may need to be developed to reduce or hedge against this economic impact and second, accounting principles must be developed to account for the economic impact of changing exchange rates. Both of these issues will be explored in the following Derivative Module and in Chapter 10.

REFLECTION

- Strategies may be developed to reduce or hedge against the economic impact associated with changes in rates of exchange between currencies.

- Specialized accounting principles must be developed to account for the economic impact associated with changes in rates of exchange between currencies.

3

OBJECTIVE

Describe the accounting issues associated with foreign currency translation.

FOREIGN CURRENCY TRANSLATION

Foreign currency transactions are not dependent on the domestic entity having an ownership interest in a foreign entity. However, as a company's international activities increase in scale and scope, they often acquire some form of ownership interest or control over a foreign entity and truly become multinational companies, also known as *transnational companies*. The magnitude of U.S. investment abroad has increased significantly in response to a more global economy, a reduction in trade barriers, and the growth of international capital markets. Similarly, these same factors have encouraged an increase in foreign investment in the United States. The size and growth of these investment patterns are suggested by the following statistics.

U.S. Direct Investment Position and U.S. Direct Investment Abroad for Capital Outflows

	U.S. Direct Investment Position[a] (in millions)	U.S. Financial Outflows[b] (in millions)
2005	$2,241,656[c]	$ 15,369[d]
2006	2,477,268	224,220
2007	2,993,980	393,518
2008	3,219,725	330,491
2009	3,508,142	248,074

[a]U.S. Direct Investment Position—Value of U.S. direct investors' equity in, and net outstanding loans to, their foreign affiliates. Values are not adjusted to reflect current costs or the replacement costs.

[b]U.S. Financial Outflows—Increases in U.S. assets invested in foreign affiliates traceable to equity capital, intercompany debt, and reinvested earnings.

[c]Private assets on a historical cost basis. The market value of the 2009 position was $4,302,851 (in millions).

[d]Outflows without current-cost adjustment.

Source: U.S. Department of Commerce, Bureau of Economic Analysis.

The accounting treatments of domestic and foreign entity relationships that involve some degree of ownership are summarized as follows:

Domestic Entity	Foreign Entity	Accounting Treatment
Home office	Branch	Branch accounting
Parent	Subsidiary	Consolidated financial statements or separate financial statements
Investor	Investee	Investment in foreign entity at market or equity

The above relationships suggest the need to combine or consolidate the foreign entity financial statements with those of the domestic entity. The financial statements of a foreign entity typically are measured in the currency of that foreign country. This currency usually is different from the reporting currency of the domestic entity. Therefore, a methodology must be developed to express the foreign entity's financial statements in the reporting currency of the domestic entity. The process of expressing amounts denominated or measured in foreign currencies into amounts measured in the reporting currency (dollars) of the domestic entity (U.S.) is referred to as foreign currency translation.

Continuing the example from earlier in the chapter, assume that a U.S. company (the domestic entity) has a 100% interest in a German company (the foreign entity) and that the German company conducts business in euros and also records those transactions in euros. In order for the domestic company to prepare consolidated financial statement that reflect its 100% interest in the foreign subsidiary, the domestic company must translate the financial statement amounts from the euro into the U.S. dollar using rates of exchange between the two respective currencies. Several issues come to mind concerning this translation process: first, what impact will changes in exchange rates between the currencies have on the parent company's cash flows and second, what rates of exchange should be used to properly capture the impact of exchange rate changes? For example, should the equipment of the foreign company be translated from euros into dollars using the rate of exchange when the equipment was acquired or at the exchange rate at the date of the balance sheet? These issues will be addressed in Chapter 11 of this text. In addition to these issues, what about the possibility that the accounting principles used by the foreign entity are not the same as those of the domestic entity? If the principles were different, it would seem that the recorded transactions would have to be adjusted to reflect the domestic GAAP. Perhaps a more fundamental question should be whether a common transaction such as the recording of cost of goods sold should have a different recorded impact depending on what country is recording the transaction. Given the global economy, would it not be better to have a single set of global accounting standards?

REFLECTION

- Certain investment and/or control relationships require that a foreign entity's financial statements be consolidated with the statements of a domestic entity.

- The translation of foreign currency financial statements into a domestic entity's currency should capture the economic impact of exchange rate changes on the domestic entity's cash flows.

- Selection of the appropriate rate of exchange is necessary to properly capture the economic impact on cash flows.

4

OBJECTIVE

Describe the factors and parties influencing the development of International Financial Reporting Standards (IFRS).

HARMONIZATION OF ACCOUNTING STANDARDS

It seems that life would be simpler if there were more consistency and uniformity in certain respects. Why doesn't my cell phone charger plug into the outlet in South America as it does when I travel in the United States? Why don't all 2-cycle engines use the same size spark plug? Why don't two identical economic transactions, one occurring in the United States and one occurring in China, receive identical accounting treatment? In a perfect world, identical transactions should receive identical accounting treatment regardless of where the transactions occur, whether it is the United States or China. In reality, this has not been the case and a number of factors have and continue to influence the development of accounting. Harmonization of accounting standards has as its goal the development of consistent accounting standards that will improve comparability of financial information.

Multinational companies must have comparable accounting standards with which to measure the effectiveness and efficiency of their various international subsidiaries, branches, and/or other equity investments. Also, in order to efficiently allocate and regulate the exchange of capital, international capital markets need to evaluate the adequacy of financial statements and disclosures made by those companies seeking to raise capital. Comparable standards of accounting and financial disclosure for companies competing for capital on an international scale are critical to the functioning of such markets. Finally, other users, such as suppliers and customers, exposed to opportunities on an international scale need comparable financial information upon which to base their decisions. Evaluating the profitability or financial position of two competing business opportunities will have meaning only if comparable accounting standards are in place. The international growth of business and investing naturally creates a need for the international development of accounting. Thus, the development of International Accounting Standards must be based on an understanding of international business and markets and the factors that affect accounting in various countries.

Factors Influencing the Development of Accounting

Accounting is not defined by nature but, rather, is made by humans. It evolves from the environment in which humans exist and defines itself in a way which serves the needs of that environment. Given the differences in various environments, it is not surprising that accounting principles may differ between nations. The development of accounting principles and standards is an extremely complex process involving a social and cultural environment, various special interest groups, and varying degrees of due process. By studying the standard-setting process in the United States, one realizes how complex the process can be. This complexity holds true in the development of accounting principles and standards in other nations, too. It is the factors influencing the process, however, that vary from nation to nation.

A number of environmental factors such as the following may explain these differences to varying degrees:

1. Social and cultural values
2. Political and legal systems

3. Business activities and economic conditions
4. Standard-setting processes
5. Forms of ownership and capital markets
6. Cooperative efforts between nations

For example, consider the impact that political and legal systems have had on the development of accounting over time. Nations that previously were ruled or colonized by another country tend to have developed principles similar to those of the ruling nation. Nations such as the United States, Canada, and the Bahamas have accounting principles that historically were patterned after those found in the United Kingdom. Those nations that have more democratic political environments tend to develop principles more through private standard-setting groups than through government decree or regulation. The tax laws and legal requirements of a country also may influence the development of accounting to the extent that differences between accounting income and taxable income are rare or nonexistent.

Although a number of environmental factors have influenced the development of accounting standards throughout the world, there is growing momentum to move toward a single set of International Accounting Standards. A number of professional organizations throughout the world have cooperated in this initiative with the International Accounting Standards Board (IASB) being the major force.

The International Accounting Standards Board

It is understandable that a variety of users of accounting information would be interested in ensuring that the accounting for particular types of transactions is consistent between nations for the purpose of improving comparability. Several approaches to harmonization have been pursued including bilateral agreements between nations and international standard setting on a worldwide scale. The initiatives of the European Union to harmonize accounting standards among member nations are an example of a bilateral approach to harmonization. Standard setting on a worldwide scale obviously represents a monumental task. The leaders of this movement must be sensitive to the variety of cultural, ethical, and economic differences that exist among countries. This approach to harmonization is the dominant approach and major forces behind the effort have been the International Accounting Standards Board and the International Federation of Accountants (IFAC). The IASB is concerned with the promulgation and harmonization of International Accounting Standards. The IFAC is concerned with a variety of issues affecting the professional practice of accounting on a worldwide basis, including quality control standards and international auditing standards.

The IASB was created in 2001 as a result of a restructuring of its predecessor, the International Accounting Standards Committee (IASC). The IASC was formed in 1973 and had two primary objectives: (1) formulate and publish standards on financial accounting and reporting and promote their worldwide acceptance and (2) work for the harmonization of accounting standards and procedures relating to the presentation of financial statements. Rather than each nation establishing its own accounting standards, the IASC recognized the importance of taking a global approach toward standard setting in order to best serve the global economy. The IASC issued 41 International Accounting Standards of which the majority are still in effect.

In the late 1990s, the IASC engaged in a strategy review that resulted in its restructuring. In early 2001, the restructured IASC became the International Accounting Standards Board. The IASB assumed responsibility for establishing a single set of International Financial Reporting Standards and achieving convergence of national accounting standards and IFRS.

The International Accounting Standards Committee (IASC) Foundation. The IASC Foundation was formed in 2001 as the parent entity of the IASB, which is based in London. The structure of the Foundation consists of the Trustees, the Board, the Standing Interpretations Committee, and the Standards Advisory Council. Objectives of the Foundation as set forth in its constitution are:

a. To develop, in the public interest, a single set of high quality, understandable and enforceable global accounting standards that require high quality, transparent and comparable information in financial statements and other financial reporting to help participants in the world's capital markets and other users make economic decisions;

b. To promote the use and rigorous application of those standards;

c. To fulfill the objectives associated with (a) and (b), to take account of, as appropriate, the special needs of small and medium-sized entities and emerging economies; and

d. To bring about convergence of national accounting standards and International Accounting Standards and International Financial Reporting Standards to high quality solutions.

The trustees of the IASC Foundation are the ultimate governing body and appoint the members of the IASB, the Standing Interpretations Committee, and the Standards Advisory Council. The 22 trustees come from a variety of countries (6 from North America, 6 from Europe, 6 from Asia/Oceania region, 4 from any area being sensitive to geographical balance) and have diverse professional backgrounds. Although not responsible for setting international standards, the trustees are responsible for developing and implementing the strategy and operating policies of the IASB and other committees. The trustees also appoint members of the IASB and other committees. The chairperson of the IASB serves as the chief executive of the Foundation and is supervised by the trustees. Decisions are made by simple majority except for certain actions (e.g., amendments to the constitution) which require a three-fourths majority of all trustees.

International Accounting Standards Board. Appointed by the trustees of the IASC Foundation, the Board consists of 15 members, but will increase to 16 members no later than July 2012, from nine countries including the United States. The Board must consist of competent individuals with practical experience as auditors, preparers, users, and academics. Although there is no requirement regarding geographical representation, the trustees must ensure that no particular constituency or geographical area dominates the Board. Each Board member has one vote and may serve a term of up to five years, renewable once. The Board has full discretion over the technical agenda and complete responsibility for all technical matters including preparing and issuing International Financial Reporting Standards and Exposure Drafts and approving Interpretations presented by the International Financial Reporting Interpretations Committee.

The Board has responsibility for establishing a single set of International Accounting Standards now designated as International Financial Reporting Standards. However, the International Accounting Standards issued by the IASC have been adopted by the IASB and continue to be referred to as IAS. The IASB has followed a conceptual accounting framework, "Framework for the Preparation and Presentation of Financial Statements," which was approved in 1989 by the IASC and adopted by the IASB in 2001.[1] The framework sets forth the concepts that underlie the preparation and presentation of financial statements for external users and serves as a platform against which future standards are developed and existing standards are reviewed. The Board follows a rigorous due process leading to the issuance of IFRS. This process includes open meetings, webcasts, the possible use of an Advisory Committee, and the publication of Discussion Documents and Exposure Drafts for public comment. The Board has the discretion to use field tests and to hold public hearings regarding proposed standards. The publication of IFRS, Exposure Drafts, or Interpretations requires approval by at least nine members of the Board if there are fewer than 16 members currently serving, and by 10 members if there are 16 members. Other decisions of the Board require a simple majority of the members present at a meeting (at least 60% of the members must be present in person or by telecommunication link).

International Financial Reporting Interpretations Committee. The trustees also appoint 14 individuals to the International Financial Reporting Interpretations Committee. The Committee is responsible for reviewing accounting issues that arise in the context of IFRS and to provide authoritative guidance in the form of interpretations known as IFRIC.

---

1 In September 2010, the IASB and the FASB announced completion of the first phase of a joint project to develop a new conceptual framework. The framework will serve as the foundation for the development of future accounting principles that are principles-based and lead to the convergence of international and U.S. accounting principles.

REFLECTION

- A number of factors may explain why accounting principles between nations differ. Factors include social/cultural values, political/legal systems, types of business activities, economic conditions, the standard-setting process, forms of ownership, the extent of capital markets, and cooperation among nations.

- Harmonization is concerned with developing a single set of high-quality worldwide accounting standards that result in comparable information in financial statements and reports.

- The IASB and the IFAC are critical international organizations involved in the harmonization of accounting and professional standards.

CONVERGENCE TO INTERNATIONAL ACCOUNTING STANDARDS

5

OBJECTIVE

Understand the U.S. initiatives to converge with International Accounting Standards (IAS).

The factors that have influenced the development of accounting standards within nations continue to exist and yet there is a recognized need to move toward a single set of International Accounting Standards. The goals of the international standard-setting organizations are ambitious, and it is clear that the harmonization of accounting standards is a complex process that will challenge accountants and professional accountancy organizations within nations. Accountants may be asked to learn new standards and reporting formats that may replace tried and true past practice. Without question, accountants will resist or reject change in certain instances based on theoretical and/or practical considerations. Issuers of financial information will have to modify their accounting systems and educate users of such information regarding new standards and reporting formats. Fortunately, a significant number of national accountancy organizations recognize the importance of harmonization and nearly 120 countries have either adopted or agreed to adopt IFRS.

The EU has converged to international standards with qualification. The EU and the IASB have disagreed on how financial instruments such as derivatives should be accounted for. This has resulted in the EU adopting IFRS as "adopted in Europe," which means that the standard on financial instruments is optional.[2] China is a major economic power that has more recently recognized the importance of embracing international standards and the role they play in capital markets. IFRS is more principles based rather than rules based; transitioning to principles-based standards itself may present major challenges.

Initiatives of the Financial Accounting Standards Board. The FASB believes in the ultimate goal of a single set of International Accounting Standards that would be used worldwide for domestic and international financial reporting. In keeping with this commitment, the FASB and the IASB in 2002 signed a memorandum of understanding (MoU), known as the Norwalk Agreement, formalizing their commitment to the convergence of U.S. GAAP and International Accounting Standards. Convergence means that the FASB and IASB will work together to develop standards rather than the FASB merely agreeing to adopt IFRS. In essence, this will be a collaborative effort whereby IFRS may converge with U.S. GAAP, U.S. GAAP may converge with IFRS, or an entirely new standard may be generated. The parties have agreed to move toward common standards in areas that are not in need of significant improvement. For example, recent changes to the U.S. GAAP standard regarding the calculation of earnings per share are examples of converging to the international standard. Other topics in this category include

---

2 As part of the IASB's ongoing project on financial instruments, new principles regarding hedging transactions are being proposed which may resolve these disagreements.

accounting for impairments, segmental reporting, subsequent events, and accounting for income taxes. If a standard is in need of significant change or improvement, the two Boards will work together to develop a new common standard. Examples of topics in this category include: fair value measurement, postretirement benefits, revenue recognition, and accounting for leases.

In 2006, the FASB and the IASB published a MoU that reaffirmed their mutual commitment, set forth a "roadmap" identifying convergence topics, and encouraged the Securities and Exchange Commission (SEC) to allow public foreign companies to file statements according to IFRS without reconciliation to U.S. GAAP. Joint projects between the FASB and the IASB are in place, with full sharing of staff and research resources. In 2010, both parties reaffirmed their earlier commitment to the 2006 MoU and also expanded their efforts to create new accounting standards where existing standards were deemed to be in need of significant improvement. June 2011 is the target date for completing the major projects identified in the 2006 MoU. Both the FASB and the IASB still are committed to that date, noting that a few projects have been extended into the second half of 2011. Clearly, the response to Exposure Drafts issued will influence the timeline, but the goal remains high-quality, compatible, and accepted converged standards.

U.S. GAAP has historically been more rules based than IFRS, which is more principles based; this will certainly introduce much more subjectivity into financial reporting. The impact that the adoption of certain IFRS will have on U.S. companies varies, in part, depending on what industry the company is in. Adoption of international standards will also come at significant cost to some companies. It is interesting to note that the SEC has estimated that a large SEC registrant could incur $32 million in additional costs in order to prepare their first annual report according to IFRS. It is also estimated that the average U.S. company would incur costs of approximately 0.12% of revenues for such preparation. There may also be certain areas where convergence might not be achieved. For example, the LIFO inventory method is a common and popular method within the United States. However, IFRS does not allow LIFO. Will this become the subject of an "adopted in U.S." qualification, or will the United States fully converge? Although it is certain that convergence to International Accounting Standards will not be seamless and many challenges certainly lay ahead, the FASB and the IASB have pledged to make their accounting standards fully compatible and maintain such compatibility over time.

Initiatives of the Securities and Exchange Commission. The SEC continues to believe that IFRS will serve as the best source of high-quality International Accounting Standards. In 2007, the SEC agreed to accept financial statements from foreign registrants to be prepared in accordance with IFRS without reconciliation to U.S. GAAP. In early 2010, the SEC adopted a new timeline that anticipates the year 2015 as the earliest date for requiring U.S. companies to use IFRS in filings with the SEC. However, the SEC will not make a final decision regarding the requirement to use IFRS until the year 2011, further illustrating the importance of maintaining the FASB and IASB timetable for convergence. Furthermore, the SEC is not pursuing the option of early adoption.

REFLECTION

- The IASB and the IFAC are critical international organizations involved in the convergence of accounting principles.

- Convergence to International Accounting Standards has already taken place on a worldwide scale, and the FASB, IASB, and SEC are actively involved in the process.

UNDERSTANDING THE ISSUES

1. Identify several environmental factors that may explain why accounting principles differ among countries.

2. What are the objectives of the International Accounting Standards Committee Foundation, and does the FASB support those objectives?

3. Identify the unique accounting issues associated with consolidating a foreign subsidiary with the operations of its U.S. parent company.

EXERCISES

Exercise 1 *(LO 3)* **The accounting issues associated with foreign currency transactions.** Assume that a U.S. company has made three purchases of inventory from three different foreign vendors. One of the purchases is denominated in U.S. dollars, and the other two purchases are denominated in foreign currency, FC-A and FC-B, respectively. Furthermore, between the time of the purchase and payment to the vendor, the U.S. dollar has strengthened relative to FC-A and weakened relative to FC-B.

Discuss how exchange rate changes would impact each of the three purchases.

Exercise 2 *(LO 4)* **International accounting organizations.** Several organizations are actively involved in international standard setting.

1. Discuss the relationship between the IASB and the International Accounting Standards Committee Foundation.
2. Discuss the position of the SEC with respect to convergence to International Accounting Standards.

Exercise 3 *(LO 5)* **Harmonization effect.** Harmonization of accounting standards through a private standard-setting process will have both advantages and disadvantages to American investors and businesses.

1. Discuss the advantages of harmonization to American investors.
2. Discuss why differences in accounting principles and disclosure requirements may place American businesses at a competitive disadvantage.
3. Discuss how the U.S. accounting profession can influence the process of harmonization.

Exercise 4 *(LO 4, 5)* **Convergence.** One of your clients has recently read about the goal of converging to International Accounting Standards and they are concerned about what impact it may have on their company.

1. Discuss some of the costs that a company might incur as part of its converging with International Accounting Standards.
2. Discuss why it might be important to your client to adopt International Accounting Standards even though they are currently only operating domestically throughout the central part of the United States.

Derivatives and Related Accounting Issues

Learning Objectives

When you have completed this module, you should be able to

1. State the general characteristics of a derivative instrument, and define *underlying* and *notional amount*.

2. Explain the basic features of common derivative instruments, including forward contracts, futures contracts, options, and interest rate swaps.

3. Determine and account for the change in value over time of forward and futures contracts.

4. Determine and account for the intrinsic and time value components of an option.

5. Appreciate the basic objectives of an interest rate swap.

6. Explain how a derivative instrument may be used to reduce or avoid the exposure to risk associated with other transactions.

7. Demonstrate how a fair value hedge is used, and account for such hedges.

8. Demonstrate how a cash flow hedge is used, and account for such hedges.

9. Identify the various types of information that should be included in disclosures regarding derivative instruments and hedging activities.

The use of derivative instruments has increased significantly among both financial and non-financial corporations. These instruments derive their value from changes in the price or rate of a related asset or liability. For example, the option or right to buy a share of stock at a fixed price derives its value from the price of the related stock. If you could buy the stock at a fixed price of $50 when the stock is trading at $55, the option has value.

Derivative instruments may be held as: (a) investments or (b) part of a strategy to reduce or hedge against exposure to risk associated with some other transaction. The use of derivatives is most common among large corporations with foreign currency exchange and interest rate exposures. Derivatives received a lot of attention during the mid-1990s due to their use as an investment instrument by large governmental units. These investments were extremely volatile and resulted in huge losses for a number of entities. At that time, derivative instruments were not recorded on the balance sheets. This *off-balance-sheet* treatment made financial analysis even more difficult. Since that time, the Financial Accounting Standards Board (FASB) has issued multiple standards for derivatives that require them to be recorded as assets or liabilities at fair value. These standards are extremely complex and are contained in the FASB Accounting Standards Codification (ASC) Topic 815 (Derivatives and Hedging). These standards are developed from two critical underpinnings: (1) derivatives represent assets or liabilities, and (2) derivatives are to be measured at fair value.

DERIVATIVES: CHARACTERISTICS AND TYPES

A financial instrument represents a right, through a contractual agreement between two opposite parties called *counterparties,* to receive or deliver cash or another financial instrument on potentially favorable or unfavorable terms. Financial instruments include cash, equity and debt investments, and derivatives. A derivative is a type of financial instrument that has several distinguishing characteristics that have been set forth by the FASB. These characteristics are that a derivative:

1. Derives its value from changes in the rate or price of a related asset or liability. The rate or price is known as an *underlying*.
2. The quantity or number of units specified by a derivative is known as the *notional amount*.
3. Requires little or no initial investment upon inception.
4. Allows for *net settlement* in that the derivative contract can be settled in exchange for cash, without having to actually buy or sell the related asset or liability.

Characteristics of Derivatives

A critical characteristic of a derivative and the basis for its name is that the instrument derives its value from changes in the value of a related asset or liability. The rates or prices that relate to the asset or liability underlying the derivative are referred to as *underlyings*. The underlying may take a variety of forms, including a commodity price, stock price, foreign currency exchange rate, or interest rate. **It is important to note that the underlying is not the asset or liability itself, but rather its price or rate.** For example, the underlying in an option to buy a share of stock at a fixed price of $50 is not the stock itself; it is the $50 price of the stock, and it determines the value of the derivative. Changes in the underlying price or rate cause the value of the derivative to change. For example, if the price of a stock underlies the value of an option to buy that stock, changes in the price of the stock relative to the option price will cause the value of the option to change. If the underlying price of the stock changes from $50 to $52, then the option to buy at $50 has increased in value by $2 (one could buy the stock for $50 when it has a fair value of $52).

In order to fully value a derivative, one must know the number of units (quantity) that is specified in the derivative instrument. This is called the *notional amount*, and it determines the total dollar value of a derivative, traceable to movement or changes in the underlying. For example, if the option to buy stock for $50 increases in value because the underlying price of the stock moves from $50 to $52, the total magnitude of this increase in value depends on how many shares can be purchased under the terms of the option. If the option applies to 1,000 shares, then the total intrinsic value of the option is $2,000 (a $2 change in the underlying price of $50 to $52 times a notional amount of 1,000 shares). The notional amount of a derivative might refer to so many bushels of a commodity, number of shares, foreign currency units, or principal amount of debt. **Both the underlying price or rate and the notional amount are necessary in order to determine the total value of a derivative at any point in time.**

Typically, a derivative requires little or no initial investment because it is *an investment in a change* in value traceable to an underlying, rather than an investment in the actual asset or liability to which the underlying relates. For example, if the price of a stock increases, the value of an option to buy that stock also increases. If one actually owned the stock, an increase in the price of the stock would also result in increased value. However, the important difference is that in order to experience the increase in value an option holder needs to make little or no initial investment, whereas the owner of the stock has to make a significant investment to acquire the stock in the first place.

Many derivatives do not require the parties to the contract, the counterparties, to actually deliver an asset that is associated with the underlying in order to realize the value of a derivative. For example, the option to buy a share of stock at a fixed price would allow the holder to sell the option rather than requiring the other counterparty to actually transfer stock to them at the option price. Assume that a stock is trading at $52 per share and that one holds an option to buy stock at $50 per share. The holder could sell the option for $2 or require the counterparty to sell them stock at $50. If the stock were purchased for $50, it could readily be converted into cash by selling at $52, thereby realizing a gain of $2. The ability to settle the contract in exchange for cash, without actually buying or selling the related asset or liability, is referred to as *net settlement*.

A derivative may be a separate, distinct financial instrument, or it may be *embedded* in another financial instrument. An embedded derivative has economic characteristics and risks that are not clearly and closely related to those of the host instrument. For example, a convertible bond is a host contract that also contains an embedded derivative. That derivative represents the option to convert the bond into common stock; its underlying is the price of the respective stock. The conversion feature's economic value is more closely related to the underlying stock than the bond. If the embedded derivative meets certain criteria, it may be separated, or *bifurcated*, from the host contract and be accounted for as a separate instrument. The discussion of bifurcation is beyond the scope of this text.

Common Types of Derivatives

The number of financial instruments that have the characteristics of a derivative has continued to expand, and, in turn, these instruments have become increasingly complex. In spite of the diversity and/or complexity that characterizes them, most derivatives are variations of four basic types, including forwards, futures, options, and swaps. Other more complex derivative instruments are not described here.

Derivatives are often part of a trading portfolio and are held primarily for sale in the short term. As with other trading investments, derivatives are marked-to-market, and the resulting gain or loss is recognized currently in earnings. A specific discussion of each type of derivative follows. In this section, we cover derivatives as investments made for speculative purposes. The use of derivatives as a hedging instrument is discussed in a separate section. Transaction costs (e.g., brokers' fees), which are typically included as part of the original cost or basis of the derivative as with all investments, are ignored for purposes of discussion.

Forward Contracts. A *forward contract* is an executory contract to buy or sell a specified amount of an asset, such as foreign currency, at a specified fixed price with delivery at a specified future point in time. The party that agrees to sell the asset is said to be in a *short position,* and the party that agrees to buy the asset is said to be in a *long position.* The specified fixed price in the contract is known as a *forward price* or *forward rate.* The current price or rate for the asset is known as the *spot rate.* The specified future point is referred to as the *forward date.* Forward contracts are not formally regulated on an organized exchange, and the parties are exposed to a risk that default of the contract could occur. However, the lack of formal regulation means that such contracts can be customized in response to specialized needs regarding notional amounts and forward dates.

The value of a forward contract is zero at inception and typically does not require an initial cash outlay. However, over time, movement in the price or rate of the underlying results in a change in value of the forward contract. **The total change in the value of a forward contract is measured as the difference between the forward rate and the spot rate "at the forward date."**

For example, on April 1, a party (called the *writer*) writes a contract in which she/he agrees to sell (short position) to another party (called the *holder*) who agrees to buy (long position) 1,000,000 foreign currencies (for example, euros) at a specific price of $0.16 per foreign currency (FC) with delivery in 90 days (June 29). The relationship between the parties is as follows:

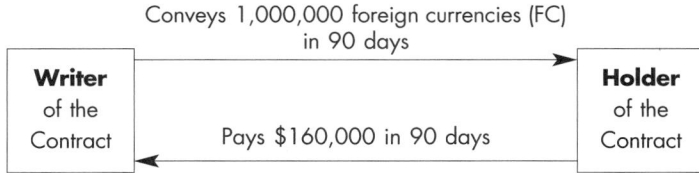

If the spot rate at the end of the forward period is $0.18, the total change in value is determined as follows:

1,000,000 FC at a forward rate (on April 1) of $0.16 (1,000,000 × $0.16)	$160,000
1,000,000 FC at a spot rate (on June 29) of $0.18 (1,000,000 × $0.18)	180,000
Gain in value to holder	$ 20,000

2

O B J E C T I V E

Explain the basic features of common derivative instruments, including forward contracts, futures contracts, options, and interest rate swaps.

3

O B J E C T I V E

Determine and account for the change in value over time of forward and futures contracts.

This is a gain because on June 29 the holder received something with a fair value greater than the fair value given up that day. (Conversely, this would be a loss to the writer.) The holder of the forward contract could buy foreign currencies for $160,000 on the forward date compared to the spot value of $180,000 at that time and experience an immediate $20,000 gain. It is important to note that the value of the currency at the final spot rate could have been less than $160,000. In that case, the holder would have experienced a loss and the writer a gain. When the value of a derivative can change in both directions (gain or loss), it is said to have a *symmetric return profile*. It is also important to note that in the case of a forward contract, if the holder of the contract experiences a gain (loss) in value, then the writer of the contract simultaneously experiences a loss (gain) in value.

The forward price or rate is a function of a number of variables, including the length of the forward period and the current spot rate. As these variables change over the life of the contract, the value of the forward contract also changes. Also, because *the forward prices or rates represent values in the future, the current value is represented by the present value of the future rates.* Continuing with the example involving foreign currencies, assume the following forward rates information throughout the 90-day term of the contract:

Remaining Term of Contract	Forward Rate	Notional Amount	Total Forward Value	Change in Forward Value
90 days	$0.160	1,000,000	$160,000	
60 days	0.170	1,000,000	170,000	$10,000
30 days	0.170	1,000,000	170,000	10,000
0 days	0.180	1,000,000	180,000	20,000

Assuming a 6% discount rate, the change in value of the forward contract over time is as follows:

	60 Days Remaining	30 Days Remaining	Total Life of Contract
Cumulative change in forward value.................	$10,000	$10,000	$20,000
Present value of cumulative change:			
60 days at 6%...............................	$ 9,901		
30 days at 6%...............................		$ 9,950	
0 days at 6%................................			$20,000
Previously recognized gain or loss	0	(9,901)	(9,950)
Current period gain or loss	$ 9,901	$ 49	$10,050

Note that the total change in the value of the forward contract is $20,000 ($9,901 + $49 + $10,050), which is recognized over the term of the contract as the net present value of changes in the forward rates. Even if the forward rates did not change between two valuation dates (there was no change between 60 and 30 days here), the value of the contract would change because the remaining term of the forward contract continues to decrease and the present value of the forward value increases. Also, note that *the stated forward rate at the expiration date of the contract is equal to the spot rate at that date.* This is due to the fact that at expiration of the contract the forward date is the same as the current date.

Investors could acquire forward contracts to purchase foreign currencies, even though they have no need for the foreign currencies, hoping that the value of the contract increases and results in investment income. Of course, holding the contract as an investment could also expose them to the risk that the value would decrease over time. As previously stated, the value of a forward contract can move in both directions resulting in a symmetric return profile. Investors in forward contracts would typically settle them by selling prior to the forward date because they do not actually need to buy or sell the foreign currencies. If the above forward contract were held as an investment and settled with 30 days remaining, the entries to account for the contract would be as shown on page 509.

Event	Entry		
Initial acquisition.	A memo entry to record acquisition of the contract. At inception, the value of the contract is zero.		
60 days remaining.	Investment in Forward Contract..............................	9,901	
	Gain on Contract.......................................		9,901
	To record the change in value of the contract. (This entry is necessary only when financial statements are being prepared.)		
30 days remaining.	Cash	9,950	
	Investment in Forward Contract............................		9,901
	Gain on Contract.......................................		49
	To record the settlement of the contract.		

Futures Contracts. A *futures contract* is exactly like a forward contract in that it too provides for the receipt or payment of a specified amount of an asset at a specified price with delivery at a specified future point in time. However, the futures contract has the following distinguishing characteristics:

- Unlike forward contracts, futures are traded on organized exchanges. The exchanges help ensure that the trading partners honor their obligations. The exchange clearinghouse actually becomes an intermediary between the buyer and seller of the contract. In essence, the clearinghouse becomes the seller for each buyer and the buyer for each seller.

- The formal regulation of futures contracts results in contracts that are standardized in nature versus customized. For example, the exchange specifies the quantity and quality of commodities traded, as well as the delivery place and date.

- A futures contract requires an initial deposit of funds with the transacting broker. This deposit is referred to as a *margin account*; it serves as collateral to help ensure that the parties to the contract are able to perform. Each day, the contract is valued and marked-to-market. If the contract loses too much value, the holder will have to contribute additional cash to the margin account. If the margin account balance falls below a minimum balance, called the *maintenance margin*, the investor is required to replenish the account through what is called a *margin call*.

- Forward contracts represent cash amounts settled only at delivery and therefore represent future amounts that must be discounted to yield a current present value. However, future prices are marked-to-market each day. At the close of each trading day, a new futures price or settlement price is established. Therefore, the futures price represents a current versus future value, and no discounting is necessary. This new futures price is used to compute the gain or loss on the contract over time.

- The party that has written a futures contract is said to be *short*, and the party that owns the contract is said to be *long*.

For example, assume one buys 50 contracts on the Chicago Board of Trade (CBT) to receive November delivery of corn to a certified warehouse. Each contract is in units of 5,000 bushels at a *futures* price of $2.50 per bushel. Notice that the terms of the contract are standardized. Obviously, a second party must agree to sell corn at a November futures price of $2.50. Acting as an intermediary between the counterparties, the CBT, in essence, writes a contract to sell a corn future to the first party and buys a contract to purchase a corn future from the second party. The relationship between the parties is as follows:

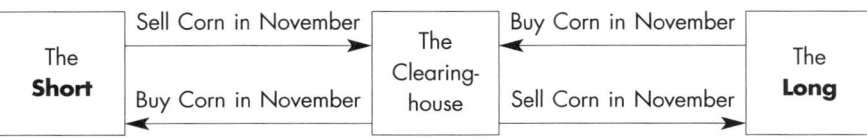

Assume that the initial margin on the above contract is set at $20,000, with a maintenance margin of $15,000, and that future prices are as follows:

	Day 1	Day 2	Day 3	Day 4
	$2.50	$2.51	$2.49	$2.47

The following entries illustrate the valuation of the futures contracts and the use of a margin account for the long (the owner of the contract).

Day 1	Futures Contract—Margin Account.	20,000	
	Cash		20,000
	To record establishment of margin account.		
Day 2	Futures Contract—Margin Account.	2,500	
	Gain on Contract.		2,500
	To record gain in fair value of contract		
	[50 contracts × 5,000 bushels × ($2.51 vs. $2.50)].		
Day 3	Loss on Contract	5,000	
	Futures Contract—Margin Account.		5,000
	To record loss in fair value of contract		
	[50 contracts × 5,000 bushels × ($2.49 vs. $2.51)].		
Day 4	Loss on Contract	5,000	
	Futures Contract—Margin Account.		5,000
	To record loss in fair value of contract		
	[50 contracts × 5,000 bushels × ($2.47 vs. $2.49)].		
	Futures Contract—Margin Account.	7,500	
	Cash		7,500
	To meet margin call and reestablish initial margin balance of $20,000 (balance before call = $20,000 + $2,500 − $5,000 − $5,000 = $12,500, which is less than $15,000 maintenance margin).		

The value of the futures contract is influenced by either positive or negative movements in the underlying price. Therefore, the risk associated with the contract is symmetrical. Unlike forward contracts, the value of futures contracts, which typically change on a daily basis, can be easily monitored since such contracts are traded on the open market. Futures prices can be found in several different places such as *The Wall Street Journal* or online at http://www.wsjmarkets.com.

4

OBJECTIVE

Determine and account for the intrinsic and time value components of an option.

Option Contracts. An *option* represents a right, rather than an obligation, to either buy or sell some quantity of a particular underlying. Common examples include options to buy or sell stocks, a stock index, an interest rate, foreign currency, oil, metals, and agricultural commodities. The option is valid for a specified period of time and calls for a specified buy or sell price, referred to as the *strike price* or *exercise price*. If an option allows the holder to *buy* an underlying, it is referred to as a *call option*. An option that allows the holder to *sell* an underlying is referred to as a *put option*. Options are actively traded on organized exchanges or may be negotiated on a case-by-case basis between counterparties (over-the-counter contracts). Option contracts require the holder to make an initial nonrefundable cash outlay, known as the *premium,* as represented by the option's current value. The premium is paid, in part, because the writer of the option takes more risk than the holder of the option. The holder can allow the option to expire, while the writer must comply if the holder chooses to exercise it.

During the option period, the strike price of the option on the underlying is generally different from the current value of an underlying. The following terms are used to describe the relationship between the strike price and the current price (note that the premium is not considered in these relationships):

Option Type	Strike Price Is Equal to Current Price	Strike Price Is Greater Than Current Price	Strike Price Is Less Than Current Price
Call (buy) option	At-the-money	Out-of-the-money	In-the-money
Put (sell) option	At-the-money	In-the-money	Out-of-the-money

As the table suggests, in-the-money is a favorable condition as compared to being out-of-the-money, which is an unfavorable condition. The original premium is not considered when describing whether an option is or is not in-the-money. However, it is important to note that the original premium certainly is considered when determining whether an investment in an option has experienced an overall profit. The holder of an option has a right, rather than an obligation, and will not exercise the option unless it is in-the-money. In that case, the holder will experience a gain, and the writer will experience a loss. However, if the option is not in-the-money, the option will not be exercised, the holder will limit her/his loss to the amount of the option premium, and the writer will limit her/his gain to the amount of the premium. Therefore, in theory, the opportunities for gain and loss are characterized as follows:

	Potential for	
	Gain	Loss
Holder of option	Unlimited	Limited to amount of premium
Writer of option	Limited to amount of premium	Unlimited

Because the counterparties do not have equal opportunity for both upside and downside changes in value, options are said to have an *asymmetric* or one-sided *return profile*.

Options are traded on an organized exchange and over the counter; therefore, their current value is quoted in terms of present dollars on a frequent basis. The current value of an option depends on forward periods and spot prices. The difference between the strike and spot price, at any point in time, measures the *intrinsic value* of the option, so changes in spot prices will change the intrinsic value of the option. Changes in the length of the remaining forward period will affect the *time value* of the option. The time value is measured as the difference between an option's current value and its intrinsic value as in the following illustration:

- If the option is in-the-money, the option has intrinsic value. For example, if an investor has an April call (buy) option to buy IBM stock at a strike price of $110 and the current stock price is $112, the option is in-the-money and has an intrinsic value of $2. An option that is out-of-the-money or at-the-money has no intrinsic value.

- The difference between the current value of an option and its intrinsic value represents time value. For example, if the IBM April call (buy) option has a current value of $8 and an intrinsic value of $2, the time value component is $6 (the current value of $8, less the intrinsic value of $2). The time value of an option represents a discounting factor and a volatility factor.

- The *discounting factor* relates to the fact that the strike price does not have to be paid currently, but rather at the time of exercise. Therefore, the holder of an option to buy stock could benefit from an appreciation in stock value without actually having to currently pay out the cash to purchase the stock. For example, assume that a 30-day, at-the-money option has a strike price of $100 and that a discount rate of 12% is appropriate. The ability to use the $100 for 30 days at an assumed discount rate of 12%, rather than having to buy the stock at the current price of $100, is worth $1 ($100 × 12% × $1/12$ year). Thus, the ability to have the alternative use of the cash equal to the strike price until exercise date of the option has value.

◆ The *volatility factor* relates to the volatility of the underlying relative to the fixed strike price and reflects the potential for gain on the option. Underlyings with more price volatility present greater opportunities for gains if the option is in-the-money. Therefore, higher volatility increases the value of an option. Note that volatility could also lead to an out-of-the-money situation. However, this possibility can be disregarded because, unlike forward or futures contracts, the risk for an option is asymmetric since the holder can avoid unfavorable outcomes by allowing the option to expire.

To illustrate the value components of an option, assume that a put (sell) option allows for the sale of a share of stock in 60 days at a strike or exercise price of $50 per share. The value of the option would consist of the following:

	Initial Date of Purchase	End of 30 Days	End of 60 Days
Market value of stock	$51	$49	$48
Assumed total value of option	1.30	1.65	2.00
Intrinsic value (never less than zero)	0 (option is out-of-the-money)	1 (in-the-money = $50 − $49)	2 (in-the-money = $50 − $48)
Time value (total value less intrinsic value)	1.30	0.65	0

The value of an option can be realized either through exercise of the option or through cash settlement. If the option can be exercised any time during the specified period, it is referred to as an *American option*; if it is exercisable only at the maturity date/expiration of the contract, it is referred to as a *European option*.

To illustrate the use of an option, assume that a call (buy) option on 10,000 bushels of corn with delivery in April is purchased in February for a premium of $1,000 and has a strike price of $2.20 per bushel. The values of the option at the end of February and March are $1,050 and $700, respectively. It is sold in early April, prior to expiration, for $750. The relationship between the parties is as follows:

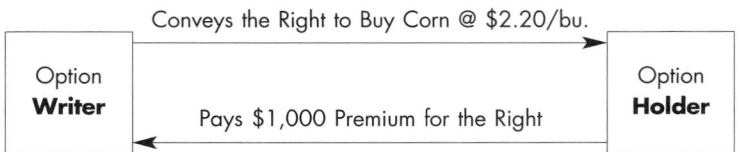

The following entries account for the holder's investment in the option, given various values over time:

Feb. 1	Investment in Call Option		1,000	
	Cash			1,000
	To record purchase of call option.			
28	Investment in Call Option		50	
	Gain on Option			50
	To record change in total value of option ($1,050 − $1,000).			
Mar. 31	Loss on Option		350	
	Investment in Call Option			350
	To record change in total value of option ($700 − $1,050).			
Apr. 2	Cash		750	
	Investment in Call Option (book value)			700
	Gain on Call Option			50
	To record sale of option.			

The basic concepts related to both call (buy) and put (sell) options are set forth in Exhibit M-1.

Exhibit M-1
Basic Concepts Related to Options

Call Options	Holder	Holder
Rights	Right to buy an underlying asset at a set exercise or strike price.	Obligation to sell an underlying asset at a set exercise or strike price.
Type	European or American—European can be exercised only at maturity date. American can be exercised any time up to and including maturity date.	European or American—European can be exercised only at maturity date. American can be exercised any time up to and including maturity date.
Cost	Pays an initial fixed cost referred to as a premium.	Receives an initial premium.
Value of the call option:		
Net gain	Experienced when the strike price is less than fair value of the underlying asset. In theory, the gain is unlimited. This is referred to as being in-the-money. The value of this difference must exceed the initial premium to produce a net gain.	Experienced when the strike price is more than or equal to the fair value of the underlying asset. The gain is limited to the initial premium.
Net loss	Experienced when the strike price is more than or equal to the fair value of the underlying asset. The loss is limited to the initial premium.	Experienced when the strike price is less than fair value of the underlying asset. In theory, the loss is unlimited. The value of this difference must exceed the initial premium to produce a net loss.
Components of value	The value consists of intrinsic value and time value.	The value consists of intrinsic value and time value.

Put Options	Holder	Writer
Rights	Right to sell an underlying asset at a set exercise or strike price.	Obligation to buy an underlying asset at a set exercise or strike price.
Type	European or American—European can be exercised only at maturity date. American can be exercised any time up to and including maturity date.	European or American—European can be exercised only at maturity date. American can be exercised any time up to and including maturity date.
Cost	Pays an initial fixed cost referred to as a premium.	Receives an initial premium.
Value of the put option:		
Net gain	Experienced when the strike price is more than fair value of the underlying asset. In theory, the gain is unlimited. This is referred to as being in-the-money. The value of this difference must exceed the initial premium to produce a net gain.	Experienced when the strike price is less than or equal to the fair value of the underlying asset. The gain is limited to the initial premium.
Net loss	Experienced when the strike price is less than or equal to the fair value of the underlying asset. The loss is limited to the initial premium.	Experienced when the strike price is more than fair value of the underlying asset. The value of this difference must exceed the initial premium. The maximum loss is limited to the strike price, less the initial premium.
Components of value	The value consists of intrinsic value and time value.	The value consists of intrinsic value and time value.

Swaps. A *swap* is a type of forward contract represented by a contractual obligation, arranged by an intermediary that requires the exchange of cash flows between two parties. Swaps are customized to meet the needs of the specific parties and are not traded on regulated exchanges. Most often, swaps are used to hedge against unfavorable outcomes and are explained more fully in the later discussion of hedging. However, it is important to understand the basic format of a swap. Common examples include foreign currency swaps and interest rate swaps. For example,

5

OBJECTIVE

Appreciate the basic objectives of an interest rate swap.

assume a U.S. company has an opportunity to invest in a German joint venture that is expected to last six months. The U.S. company must invest euros in the venture, and its investment will be returned in euros at the end of the 6-month period. Through an intermediary, the U.S. company could contract with a German company that needs U.S. dollars for a similar period of time. Each of the companies would have available or borrow their respective currencies and then swap the currencies, dollars for euros and euros for dollars. At the end of the 6-month investment period, the U.S. company would return euros to the German company, and the German company would return dollars to the U.S. company.

Rather than involving the swap of different currencies, an interest rate swap involves exchanging variable or floating (fixed) interest rates for fixed (variable or floating) rates. For example, assume a Company issued $10,000,000 of variable interest debt when rates were 6% and is now concerned that interest rates will increase. In order to protect against rising rates, the Company contracts with a Bank and agrees to pay a fixed rate of interest of 6.5% to the Bank in exchange for receiving variable rates. The Company is referred to as the *pay fixed* or *receive floating* party, and the Bank is referred to as the *pay floating* or *receive fixed* party. In essence, the Company has converted its floating or variable rate debt into fixed rate debt. The relationship between the parties is as follows:

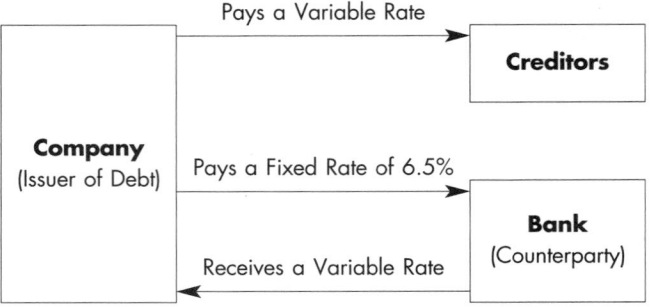

If the variable rate increased to 6.7% on the $10,000,000 of variable interest debt, the Company's semiannual net interest expense would be determined as follows:

Variable interest paid to creditors (6.7% × $10,000,000 × ½ year) . . . . $ 335,000
Fixed interest paid to the Bank (6.5% × $10,000,000 × ½ year) 325,000*
Variable interest received from the Bank (6.7% × $10,000,000 × ½ year)* . . . . (335,000)
Net interest paid [(−6.7% − 6.5% + 6.7%) × $10,000,000 × ½ year] . . . . $ 325,000

*Rather than actually paying and receiving, the entities exchange the net difference between the rates (fixed vs. variable) in the amount of $10,000 ($325,000 vs. $335,000). This results in a net interest expense of $325,000 ($335,000 paid to creditors less $10,000 received from the Bank).

The interest swap was entered into because the Company feared that variable rates would increase. In essence, the swap allowed the Company to exchange a variable interest rate for a fixed interest rate as though it had actually issued fixed debt. As the swap continues, new variable rates will be determined and applied to subsequent semiannual interest payments. This process of determining a new rate for the swap is referred to as *resetting* the rate. Generally, the variable interest rate is reset at each interest date and is applied to the subsequent period's interest calculations.

In the above example, if the variable rate increased to more than the 6.5% fixed rate paid to the Bank, the Company received a net cash amount from the bank and realized a gain as a result of entering into the swap. Therefore, the value of the swap, represented by the payment of a fixed rate in exchange for a higher variable rate, has increased. If the variable rate had decreased below the 6.5% fixed rate paid to the Bank, the Company would have made a net cash settlement payment to the Bank, and the swap would have lost value. Changes in the variable interest rates expose one party to potential loss and the other party to potential gain. Therefore, swaps, like other forward contracts, are characterized by symmetric risk. In the above example, the Bank is acting as the counterparty and lost value on the swap. However, acting as a counterparty, the Bank will attempt to match the notional amount of the current swap with the notional amount of another swap with a party that is seeking to pay floating/receive fixed. This results in the counterparty Bank having one swap where it pays floating (receive fixed) and another swap where it pays fixed (receive floating). The counterparty will have a spread between the pay and receive floating rate or the pay and receive fixed rate that compensates it for its services. For example, assume a notional amount of $10,000,000. If the counterparty has a pay floating rate of 3.5% and a receive floating rate of 3.7%, then the spread will result in compensation of $20,000 [(−3.5% + 3.7%) × $10,000,000].

The valuation of swaps is complex and dependent on assumptions regarding future rates or prices. For example, if a fixed interest payment is swapped for a variable interest payment, the value of the swap is a function of how future variable rates are expected to compare to the fixed rate. Therefore, an estimate of future variable rates is required. Furthermore, the differences between the future variable rates and the fixed rate represent future differences that need to be discounted in order to produce a present value of the differences.

The above example involved a swap of fixed interest payments to a counterparty in exchange for the receipt of a variable rate of interest. It is also possible to swap a variable interest payment in exchange for a fixed rate of interest. The use of these swaps and the resulting accounting will be discussed in greater detail in a subsequent section of this chapter.

Summary of Derivative Instruments

Exhibit M-2 presents a summary and comparison of the four basic types of derivative instruments discussed in the preceding sections. The most important differences are between options and the other three types of derivatives. Futures, forwards, and swaps each provide symmetric risk to a holder because the value of the derivative can change in both directions (gains or losses) without limits. This symmetric risk profile requires both counterparties to execute the contract whether the effect is favorable or unfavorable. In contrast, the holder of an option is not required or obligated to exercise the option and, in fact, will not do so if the option is at- or out-of-the-money. This provides asymmetric risk for the holder who may want to avoid downside risk. Options also differ from the other derivative instruments described here in the requirement for an initial cash outlay, which represents the initial intrinsic and time values of the option.

Exhibit M-2
Basic Concepts Related to Selected Derivative Instruments

	Forward Contracts	**Futures Contracts**	**Options**	**Swaps**
Basic design	An obligation to buy or sell an asset at a specified forward price/rate with delivery at a specified forward date.	An obligation to buy or sell an asset at a specified forward price/rate with delivery at a specified future date.	A right to buy or sell an asset at a specified strike price. The strike price is valid for a specified period of time.	A contract that exchanges cash flows between two parties. In substance, a type of forward contract.
Trading and regulation	Not traded on an organized exchange. Trading is not formally regulated.	Traded on an organized exchange (e.g., Chicago Board of Trade). Trading is formally regulated.	Traded on an organized exchange (e.g., Chicago Board Options Exchange) and in the over-the-counter (OTC) market. Trading is formally regulated.	Not traded on an organized exchange. Trading is not formally regulated.
Counterparty default risk	Parties are exposed to default risk.	The exchange clearinghouse acts as an intermediary between the counterparties. It helps to ensure that the parties honor their obligations.	Because of the involvement of the exchange, there is no default risk.	Parties are exposed to default risk.

(continued)

Exhibit M-2 *(concluded)*

	Forward Contracts	**Futures Contracts**	**Options**	**Swaps**
Derivative form	Customized contracts to meet the specialized needs of the counterparties.	The formal regulation of contracts results in standardized contracts.	The formal regulation of options results in standardized contracts.	Swaps are customized to meet the needs of the specific parties.
Initial cash outlay	No initial cash outlay required.	Typically, no initial cash outlay. However, holders of a contract must establish a cash margin account.	Holders are required to make an initial cash outlay known as a premium.	No initial cash outlay required.
Return profile	Symmetric.	Symmetric.	Assymmetric.	Symmetric.

REFLECTION

- An underlying, a notional amount, and the opportunity for net settlement characterize derivatives.

- Major types of derivative instruments include forward contracts, futures contracts, options, and swaps.

- Derivative instruments may be held as an investment, and changes in their value should be recognized in current earnings. The value of a derivative is a function of the movement or changes in the underlying and the notional amount.

6

OBJECTIVE

Explain how a derivative instrument may be used to reduce or avoid the exposure to risk associated with other transactions.

ACCOUNTING FOR DERIVATIVES THAT ARE DESIGNATED AS A HEDGE

Changes in the value of a derivative held as an investment are recognized currently in earnings, and the derivative is carried on the balance sheet at its current value. The value of the asset or liability that the underlying related to also changes over time. Furthermore, if the change in the value of the underlying asset or liability is negative, one would want to protect against the adverse effect of the change. One way to protect against such adverse changes is to hedge against the change through the use of a derivative. If the asset or liability (the hedged item) experiences an unfavorable change in value, a properly structured hedge (the hedging instrument) could be effective in providing a change in value in the opposite direction such that there is no adverse effect. If a derivative is properly structured for this purpose, it seems that the change in the value of the derivative (the hedging instrument) should be recognized in the same accounting period as is the change in the value of the related asset or liability (the hedged item). Hedges are generally designated as either *fair value* or *cash flow*. A **fair value** hedge is used to offset changes in the fair value of items with fixed prices or rates. Fair value hedges include hedges against a change in the fair value of:

- A recognized asset or liability.
- An unrecognized firm commitment.

A **cash flow hedge** is used to establish fixed prices or rates when future cash flows could vary due to changes in prices or rates. Cash flow hedges include hedges against the change in cash flows associated with:

- A forecasted transaction.
- The variability in the cash flows associated with a recognized asset or liability.

Derivative instruments are frequently used as hedges with respect to the exposure to risk associated with foreign currency transactions and investments in foreign companies. The use of derivatives in this context is discussed in Chapter 10, which deals with multinational accounting. The following sections deal with the accounting for hedges employed in other contexts.

Special Accounting for Fair Value Hedges

The hedged item in a fair value hedge is either a recognized asset or liability or a firm commitment. Recognized assets or liabilities in a fair value hedge result from actual past transactions such as a purchase of inventory or a note payable. Commitments relate to transactions that have not yet occurred, such as a contract to purchase inventory or incur debt. A commitment is a binding agreement between two parties that specifies all significant terms related to the prospective transaction. The price of the prospective transaction is fixed or it may involve a specified fixed rate such as a rate of interest. The agreement also includes a large enough disincentive to make performance of the contract probable.

Because the prices or rates are fixed, subsequent changes in prices or rates affect the value of a recognized asset, liability, or commitment. For example, if a company holds an inventory of crude oil, changes in the price of crude oil will affect the fair value of the asset. Similarly, if a company has committed to acquire crude oil for a fixed price, changes in the price of crude oil will affect the value of the commitment. If the price of crude oil increased, the value of the asset or commitment would increase favorably. The existing inventory would be worth more, or the commitment to acquire crude at previously fixed lower prices would have more value. However, if crude oil prices decreased, the resulting effect would be unfavorable.

To avoid the potential unfavorable effect associated with changes in prices or rates on recognized transactions or commitments with fixed terms, an entity could acquire a derivative instrument as a hedge against unfavorable outcomes. For example, in order to hedge against a decrease in the value of crude oil, an entity could acquire a futures contract to sell crude. Many accounting principles do not allow for the *recognition in current earnings of both increases and decreases* in the value of recognized assets, liabilities, or firm commitments. However, if the risk of such changes in value is covered by a fair value hedge, special accounting treatment is allowed that provides for the recognition of such changes in earnings. In a qualifying fair value hedge, the gain or loss on the derivative hedging instrument and the offsetting loss or gain on the hedged item are both recognized currently in earnings. For instance, assume an existing liability has a fixed interest rate. A decrease in interest rates will result in a higher fair value of the debt (lower interest rates result in larger present values). If the debt is not hedged, the increase in the value of the debt is not recognized in earnings. However, if the liability is hedged, both the increase in the value of the debt and the change in the value of the derivative instrument used as a hedge are recognized in earnings.

It is important to note that if both increases and decreases in the value of a recognized asset or liability are recognized in current earnings according to existing accounting principles, special hedge accounting is not necessary. For example, if a trading portfolio consisted of debt instruments, such investments would be marked-to-market, and both increases and decreases in value would be recognized in current earnings. Therefore, if the portfolio were hedged, special accounting treatment would not be necessary. Changes in the value of both the hedged item and the hedging instrument are already being recognized in earnings. However, if a debt instrument is part of an *available-for-sale portfolio* and the debt is marked-to-market, the resulting changes in value are not recognized in current earnings. Therefore, if the portfolio were hedged, special accounting treatment would be allowed and would result in recognizing in earnings the change in value of the debt instrument.

Qualifying Criteria for Fair Value Hedges. In order to qualify for special fair value hedge accounting, the derivative hedging instrument and the hedged item must satisfy a number of criteria. A critical criterion is that an entity must have formal documentation of the hedging relationship and the entity's risk-management objective and strategy. The entity must indicate the reason for undertaking the designated hedge, identify the hedged item and the derivative hedging instrument, and explain the nature of the risk being hedged. This criterion must be satisfied at inception and cannot be retroactively applied after an entity has determined whether hedging would be appropriate.

7

OBJECTIVE

Demonstrate how a fair value hedge is used, and account for such hedges.

Another important criterion is that the hedging relationship must be assessed both at inception and on an ongoing basis to determine if it is highly effective in offsetting the identified risks. Although specific quantitative guidelines are not available to define *highly effective,* the FASB expects a high correlation to exist between changes in the value of the derivative instrument and in the fair value of the hedged item such that the respective changes in value would be substantially offset. Generally speaking, a hedge would be totally effective if the terms (such as notional amount, maturity dates, quality/condition, delivery locations) of the hedging instrument and the hedged item are the same. This approach is known as *critical terms analysis.* It is important to note that in practice the terms of a derivative do not always align with the terms of the related asset or liability. For example, a corn future may call for delivery at a different location than where the related inventory of hedged corn is located.

Another approach to assessing effectiveness is known as *statistical analysis.* This approach statistically measures the correlation between the value of the derivative and the related asset or liability. For example, if you are hedging an inventory of 200 tons of flour with a wheat future for 5,000 bushels of wheat, you would measure the correlation between prices for flour and wheat. You could also examine the relationship between changes in the value of the wheat future derivative and the changes in the value of flour over a period of time. This approach is known as *frequency analysis,* and the ratio between these price changes is known as the *delta ratio.* Although the FASB requires that the hedge be highly effective, it has not set specific quantitative levels of effectiveness that must be satisfied by the hedging relationship. However, practical standards have developed, which suggest target values that must be satisfied in order to be considered highly effective. For example, if the change in the value of a derivative is 80% to 125% of the change in the value of the hedged item, the hedge is considered to be highly effective.

Management must also describe how it will assess hedge effectiveness. Generally, hedge ineffectiveness is the difference between the gains or losses on the derivative and the hedged item. However, the portion of the gain or loss representing time value may be excluded from the assessment of effectiveness and included in current earnings. For example, the hedge of an inventory of corn with an option might only consider changes in the intrinsic value of the option for purposes of assessing effectiveness. The exclusion of a portion of the change in the value of a derivative instrument from the assessment of effectiveness will be illustrated in subsequent discussions.

Although set out in greater detail in the Accounting Standards Codification,[1] selected qualifying criteria for fair value hedges are listed in Exhibit M-3.

Accounting for a Fair Value Hedge. If the derivative instrument and the hedged item satisfy the above criteria, then the fair value hedge will qualify for special accounting. The gain or loss on the derivative hedging instrument will be recognized currently in earnings, along with the change in value on the hedged item, and an appropriate adjustment to the basis of the hedged item will be recorded. If the cumulative change in the value of the derivative instrument does not exactly offset the cumulative change in the value of the hedged item, the difference is recognized currently in earnings. Because both hedge effectiveness and ineffectiveness are recognized currently in earnings, it is not necessary to separately account for that portion of the hedge that is considered to be ineffective.

Examples of fair value hedges against inventory, a firm commitment, and a fixed interest notes payable follow. Entries for the transaction/commitment are presented side by side with entries for the hedges. All transaction costs are ignored. The examples include the use of derivatives in the form of a futures contract, forward contract, and swap. Note, however, that other types of derivatives could have been used in some of these examples.

The special accounting treatment given a fair value hedge should continue unless:

◆ The criteria necessary for special accounting treatment are no longer satisfied,

◆ The derivative instrument expires or is sold, terminated, or exercised,

◆ The entity no longer designates the derivative instrument as a fair value hedge, or

◆ The hedging relationship is no longer considered highly effective based on management's policies.

---

1 FASB ASC Section 815-25-25, *Derivatives and Hedging—Fair Value Hedges—Recognition.*

Exhibit M-3
Selected Qualifying Criteria for Fair Value Hedges

1. At inception of the hedge, there must be formal documentation of the hedging relationship and the entity's risk-management objective and strategy. Documentation should also identify the hedging instrument, the hedged transaction, the nature of the risk being hedged, and a plan for assessing the effectiveness of the hedge.

2. Both at inception and on an ongoing basis, the hedging relationship must be assessed to determine if it is highly effective in offsetting the risk exposure associated with changes in the hedged item's fair value. The effectiveness of the hedging instrument must be assessed whenever financial statements or earnings are reported and at least every three months.

3. The hedged item is specifically identified as part or all of a recognized asset, recognized liability, or unrecognized firm commitment. The hedged item may be a single asset or liability or a portfolio of similar assets or liabilities.

4. The hedged item has exposure to changes in fair value, due to the hedged risk, that could affect earnings. For example, decreasing prices could affect an existing inventory of materials and result in lower gross profits.

5. The hedged item is not an asset or a liability that is being measured at fair value, with changes in fair value, both positive and negative, being currently recognized in earnings. For example, an investment in securities, classified as a trading portfolio, would not qualify for special hedge accounting. The unrealized gains and losses on the portfolio would already be recognized in earnings, and changes in the value of a designated derivative would also be recognized currently in earnings. Therefore, special hedge accounting would only be allowed if generally accepted accounting principles (GAAP) do not already require the hedged item to be measured at fair value.

6. For nonfinancial assets (such as inventory) or liabilities, the risk being hedged against is the change in value of the entire item at its actual location rather than a change in value due to a different location or a component part. Therefore, you could not hedge an inventory of butter by designating price changes of milk as the risk being hedged.

7. Financial assets or liabilities and nonfinancial commitments with a financial component can be designated as hedged items if certain types of risks, such as those related to benchmark interest rate risk, foreign currency exchange rates, and creditworthiness are being hedged. Two or more of the above risks may be hedged simultaneously. Prepayment risk may not be designated as the risk being hedged.

An Example of a Fair Value—Inventory Transaction Hedge Using a Futures Contract

Assume that a Midwest hog producer has an inventory of hogs. On April 1, the producer decides to hedge the fair value of the hog inventory by acquiring two July futures contracts to sell hogs (each contract has a notional amount of 40,000 pounds) at $0.65 per pound. Assume the contracts are settled on July 15. It is assumed that the terms of the futures contracts and the hedged assets match with respect to the delivery location, quantity, and quality of hogs. (Margin amounts and brokers' fees are ignored for purposes of discussion.) On July 20, the producer sells 80,000 pounds of hogs at the current market price of $0.611 per pound and offsets the contract. Assume that the producer's carrying basis (book value) of the hogs is $40,000 before any adjustments related to the hedging transaction. The producer designates the futures contracts as a hedge against changes in the fair value of hogs.

The fair value of the futures contracts will be based on changes in the futures prices over the life of the contract. As previously stated, this difference represents current marked-to-market value and no discounting is required. Effectiveness of the hedging relationship will be assessed by comparing changes over time in the current spot prices for hogs and changes in the value of the futures contracts attributable to changes in spot prices. The time value of the futures contract will be excluded from the assessment of hedge effectiveness. The time value component of the futures contract is the difference between the original spot rate and the original futures rate and is referred to as the *spot-forward difference*. The time value will periodically be recognized over the life of the contract and is measured in one of two ways. The change in the time value, spot-forward difference, may be calculated as either (1) the difference between the change in fair value of the contract and the change in spot rates or (2) directly as the change in spot-forward rates over time. Relevant values are as follows:

	April 1	May 1	June 1	July 15
Number of lbs.	80,000	80,000	80,000	80,000
Spot price/lb.	$0.640	$0.628	$0.622	$0.610
Futures price/lb.	$0.650	$0.635	$0.624	$0.610
Fair value of contract		$1,200 = ($0.650 − $0.635) × 80,000	$2,080 = ($0.650 − $0.624) × 80,000	$3,200 = ($0.650 − $0.610) × 80,000
(a) Current period change in above fair value of contract – gain (loss)		$1,200 = $1,200 − $0	$880 = $2,080 − $1,200	$1,120 = $3,200 − $2,080
(b) Current period change in intrinsic (spot rates) – gain (loss)		$960 = ($0.640 − $0.628) × 80,000	$480 = ($0.628 − $0.622) × 80,000	$960 = ($0.622 − $0.610) × 80,000
(a) − (b) = Current period change in time value, (spot-forward difference) – gain (loss)		$240 = ($0.650 − $0.640) − ($0.635−$0.628) × 80,000 or $1,200 − $960	$400 = ($0.635 − $0.628) − ($0.624 − $0.622) × 80,000 or $880 − $480	$160 = ($0.624 − $0.622) − ($0.610 − $0.610) × 80,000 or $1,120 − $960

The following entries to record the hedging relationship are on the producer's books:

Accounting for Hog Inventory			Accounting for Derivative Hedge		
Apr. 1			Memo entry to record the acquisition of the futures contracts.		
May 1 Loss on Inventory	960		Futures Contract*	960	
Inventory of Hogs		960	Gains on Futures Contract		960
To record the change in the value of the inventory.			To record the change in the value of the contract included in hedge effectiveness.		
			Futures Contract*	240	
			Gains on Futures Contract		240
			To record the change in time value excluded from hedge effectiveness.		
			*Note: The two previous entries regarding the change in the value of the futures contract could be combined into one single entry.		
June 1 Loss on Inventory	480		Futures Contract	480	
Inventory of Hogs		480	Gains on Futures Contract		480
To record the change in the value of the inventory.			To record the change in the value of the contract included in hedge effectiveness.		
			Futures Contract	400	
			Gains on Futures Contract		400
			To record the change in time value excluded from hedge effectiveness.		
July 15 Loss on Inventory	960		Futures Contract	960	
Inventory of Hogs		960	Gains on Futures Contract		960
To record the change in the value of the inventory.			To record the change in the value of the contract included in hedge effectiveness.		
			Futures Contract	160	
			Gains on Futures Contract		160
			To record the change in time value excluded from hedge effectiveness.		

(continued)

Accounting for Hog Inventory			Accounting for Derivative Hedge		
July 20 Cash	48,880		Cash	3,200	
Sales Revenue		48,880	Futures Contract		3,200
To record the sale of 80,000 pounds of hogs at $0.611 per pound.			To record settlement of the futures contract.		
Cost of Sales	37,600				
Inventory of Hogs		37,600			
To record the cost of sales consisting of original carrying value of $40,000 less decline in value of $2,400 [($0.640 − $0.610) × 80,000] due to price changes.					

In this example, the hedge totally offsets the adverse effect of price changes on the fair value of the hog inventory. The hedge was highly effective because:

1. The terms of the futures contract and the hedged inventory match regarding quantity, location, and quality.
2. The assessment of the effectiveness of the hedge excludes the time value of the futures contract.

The benefit of the hedge can best be understood by evaluating the situation as follows:

	Desired Position	Without the Hedge	With the Hedge
Sales price of hogs	$ 51,200	$ 48,880	$ 48,880
Cost of sales	(40,000)	(40,000)	(37,600)
Gross profit	$ 11,200	$ 8,880	$ 11,280
Hedging gain on derivative ($960 + $480 + $960)			2,400
Loss on inventory ($960 + $480 + $960)			(2,400)
Subtotal	$ 11,200	$ 8,880	$ 11,280
Gain excluded from hedge effectiveness ($240 + $400 + $160)			800
Net effect on earnings	$ 11,200	$ 8,880	$ 12,080

The hedge was highly effective in achieving the desired position which was to maintain the sales value of the inventory at the April 1 spot rate (80,000 pounds × $0.64 = $51,200) and realize a gross profit of at least $11,200. The hedge allowed the producer to avoid the exposure to decreases in the value of the inventory due to adverse price changes (decreasing spot rates). Excluding the $800 gain from the time value component, the net effect on earnings of $11,280 ($12,080 − $800) resulting from the use of the hedge was basically the same as the desired position of $11,200. The $80 difference was due to the increase in the spot rate from the expiration date of the futures contracts (July 15) to the actual sale date (July 20).

An Example of a Fair Value—Firm Commitment Hedge Using a Forward Contract

The special accounting treatment given a fair value hedge is also applicable to a hedge on a firm commitment. By way of example, assume that on April 14, when the current spot rate is $172, a company makes a firm commitment to sell 3,000 tons of inventories at the end of June for $172 per ton. It is estimated that the cost of inventory sold under the contract will be $430,000. Concerned that prices may increase and that the firm commitment will prevent the company from realizing even a higher sales value, on April 14 the company enters into a forward contract to buy 3,000 tons of identical inventory at the current forward rate of $173 per ton. The forward contract expires on June 30. The forward contract will gain in value if prices increase, because the holder will be able to buy inventory at the lower price of $173 per ton. Therefore, if prices increase, the loss associated with the firm commitment will be offset by the gain traceable to the forward contract.

Changes in the value of the commitment may be measured in several ways. One way to measure the change in value is to measure changes in the spot rates over time and then discount that value at an appropriate discount rate. It is also possible to measure the change in the value of a commitment based on changes in forward rates over time and then discount that value.

Changes in the fair value of the contract that are attributable to changes in the time value, that is changes in the spot-forward difference, are excluded from the assessment of hedge effectiveness and reported directly in current earnings.[2] Because changes in the time value are reported in earnings along with changes in the intrinsic value of the hedging instrument, it is not necessary to separately account for the change in time value.

The change in the value over time of the forward contract used to hedge the firm commitment is calculated as follows:

	April 14	April 30	May 31	June 30
Notional amount in tons	3,000	3,000	3,000	3,000
Spot rate per ton	$172	$174	$174	$176
Forward rate per ton for remaining time	$173	$175	$174	$176
Initial forward rate		$173	$173	$173
Change from original forward rate		$2	$1	$3
Fair value of forward contract in future dollars:				
Original forward value		$519,000	$519,000	$519,000
Current forward value		525,000	522,000	528,000
Change – gain (loss) in forward value		$ 6,000	$ 3,000	$ 9,000
Discount rate		6%	6%	6%
Present value of the fair value of the contract:				
FV = $6,000, n = 2, i = 0.5%		$ 5,940		
FV = $3,000, n = 1, i = 0.5%			$ 2,985	
FV = $9,000, n = 0, i = 0.5%				$ 9,000
Change in above fair value of the contract – gain (loss):				
Current present value		$ 5,940	$ 2,985	$ 9,000
Prior present value		0	5,940	2,985
Change in present value		$ 5,940	$ (2,955)	$ 6,015

Assume that management has decided to measure changes in the value of the commitment based on changes in the forward rates over time and that the suggested change in value is then discounted. Therefore, the change in value of the commitment will equal the change in the value of the forward contract. Based on the above relevant information, the entries to record the commitment, hedge, and sales transaction follow on page 523.

---

2 Management has the discretion to either include or exclude the time value of the futures contract from the assessment of effectiveness. However, excluding the time value of the contract increases the likelihood that there will be no ineffectiveness in the hedge. Generally speaking, if the terms of the forward contract and the commitment are the same (in terms of notional amount, expiration date, location, etc.) and the time value is excluded, there will be no hedge ineffectiveness.

Apr. 30	Loss on Firm Commitment	5,940		Forward Contract*	5,940	
	Firm Commitment.		5,940	Gain on Forward Contract.		5,940
	To record change in fair value of firm commitment.			To record the change in value of forward contract.		

*Note: The above entry records the total change in the value of the contract including both the intrinsic value and the time value.

May 31	Firm Commitment.	2,955		Loss on Forward Contract	2,955	
	Gain on Firm Commitment.		2,955	Forward Contract.		2,955
	To record change in fair value of firm commitment.			To record the change in value of forward contract.		

June 30	Loss on Firm Commitment	6,015		Forward Contract	6,015	
	Firm Commitment.		6,015	Gain on Forward Contract.		6,015
	To record change in value forward.			To record the change in value of contract.		
	Cash	516,000		Cash	9,000	
	Firm Commitment.	9,000		Forward Contract.		9,000
	Sales		525,000	To record settlement of forward contract.		
	To record the sale of inventory covered by the firm commitment (3,000 tons sold at $172).					
	Cost of Sales	430,000				
	Inventory		430,000			
	To record the cost of sales.					

The concern with the firm commitment was that prices would increase above the firm sales price and reduce the value of the commitment. A forward contract to buy is an appropriate strategy if prices are expected to increase, because as prices increase, the value of the forward contract would increase. After excluding the time value of the contract, the forward contract was expected to be highly effective as a hedge because the derivative instrument had the same type of inventory, notional amount, and forward rate as the hedged commitment. The effectiveness of the hedge is as follows:

	Desired Position	Without the Forward Contract	With the Forward Contract
Sales value of firm commitment	$ 528,000	$ 516,000	$ 525,000
Cost of sales.	(430,000)	(430,000)	(430,000)
Gross profit	$ 98,000	$ 86,000	$ 95,000
Loss on firm commitment			(9,000)
Gain in value of forward contract			9,000
Net effect on earnings	$ 98,000	$ 86,000	$ 95,000

The hedge on the firm commitment was highly effective in that the loss in the value of the firm commitment was totally offset by the gain in the value of the forward contract. This resulted in establishing a sales value that reflected the rate at the actual date of the sale (3,000 tons at $176 = $528,000) less the $3,000 [3,000 × ($172 − $173)] spot forward difference rather than the lower value (3,000 tons at $172 = $516,000) that was established at the date of the commitment. Note that the account Firm Commitment serves the purpose of adjusting the sales value of the commitment. In essence, through the use of a hedge, the firm commitment did not prevent the company from realizing even a higher sales value.

An Example of a Fair Value—Hedge against a Fixed Interest Notes Payable Using an Interest Rate Swap

If a company has borrowed at a fixed rate of interest, the fair value of the resulting liability will change if benchmark interest rates change.[3] Although the cash flows are fixed, the discount (current interest) rate changes, resulting in a change in present value. For example, if interest rates decrease, the net present value of the cash flows and the liability will increase. Furthermore, if the debtor company anticipates that variable rates will fall below the original fixed rate, it would have preferred to structure the debt with a variable rate rather than a fixed rate of interest. An interest rate swap would allow the company to accomplish this if it paid a variable rate of interest to a counterparty in exchange for the receipt of a fixed rate of interest. In essence, the debt with a fixed rate of interest is converted into debt with a variable rate of interest.

For example, assume that on January 1, 2011, a company had taken out an 18-month, $20,000,000 note from a bank at a fixed rate of 7% with interest due on a semiannual basis. On January 1, 2011, believing that interest rates are likely to drop, the company arranged to receive a 7% fixed rate of interest from another financial institution in exchange for the payment of variable rates. Differences between the fixed and variable rates are to be settled on a semiannual basis. The variable rates are based on the London Interbank Offered Rate (LIBOR) rate + 1.25% (125 basis points) and are reset semiannually in order to determine the interest rate to be used for the next semiannual payment. The notional amount of the interest rate swap is $20,000,000, and the expiration date of the swap matches the maturity date of the original bank loan. Relevant values are as follows:

Reset Dates	LIBOR +1.25% Rates for Next Period	Assumed Fair Value of Swap	Change in Fair Value
Jan. 1, 2011	7.0%		
June 30, 2011	6.8	$38,000	$38,000
Dec. 31, 2011	6.7	29,000	(9,000)

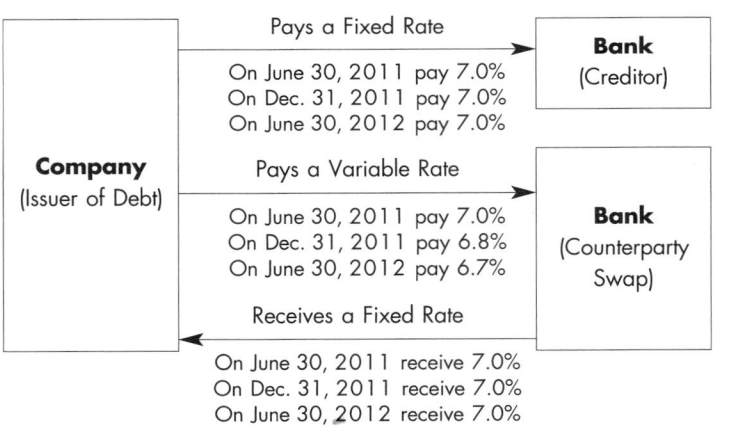

---

3 Per FASB ASC subparagraph 815-20-25-6A, in the United States, currently only the interest rates on direct Treasury obligations of the U.S. government and, for practical reasons, the London Interbank Offered Rate (LIBOR) swap rate are considered to be benchmark interest rates.

Based on the above relevant information, the entries to record the note payable and the interest rate swap are as follows:

2011

Jan. 1

Cash	20,000,000		
7% Note Payable.		20,000,000	
To record receipt of note proceeds.			

June 30

Interest Expense.	700,000		
Cash		700,000	
To record semiannual interest payment ($20,000,000 × 7% × ½ year).			

Loss on Debt.	38,000		Interest Rate Swap Asset	38,000	
7% Note Payable.		38,000	Gain on Swap		38,000
To recognize the change in the value of the debt.			To recognize the change in the value of the swap.		

Dec. 31

Interest Expense.	700,000		Cash	20,000	
Cash		700,000	Interest Expense.		20,000
To record semiannual interest payment ($20,000,000 × 7% × ½ year).			To record settlement of interest rate difference on swap (6.8% vs. 7% on $20,000,000 × ½ year).		

7% Note Payable	9,000		Loss on Swap.	9,000	
Gain on Debt		9,000	Interest Rate Swap Asset		9,000
To recognize the change in the value of the debt.			To recognize the change in the value of the swap.		

2012

June 30

Interest Expense.	700,000		Cash	30,000	
Cash		700,000	Interest Expense.		30,000
To record semiannual interest payment ($20,000,000 × 7% × ½ year).			To record settlement of interest rate difference on swap (6.7% vs. 7% on $20,000,000 × ½ year).		

7% Note Payable	29,000		Loss on Swap.	29,000	
Gain on Debt		29,000	Interest Rate Swap Asset		29,000
To recognize the change in the value of the debt.			To write down swap value to zero at end of contract.		

7% Note Payable	20,000,000		
Cash		20,000,000	
To record repayment of debt.			

During the period covered by the interest rate swap, the carrying amount of the debt was adjusted to reflect changes in the value traceable to movement in benchmark interest rates. In essence, these adjustments represent a discount or premium on the debt. However, while the hedge is in effect, the discount or premium does not have to be amortized. After termination of the swap, any remaining discount or premium must be amortized over the remaining life of the debt.

The interest rate swap was highly effective in replacing a 7.0% fixed rate of interest on the debt with a variable or floating rate of interest equal to LIBOR + 1.25%. The variable rate of interest is derived as follows:

Rate paid on original debt.	−7.00%
Receive fixed rate on swap	+7.00%
Pay floating rate on swap	− LIBOR +1.25%
Net pay rate [− 7.00% + 7.00% − (LIBOR +1.25%)]	= LIBOR +1.25%

Given the decreasing pattern of the floating rates, the company experienced a reduction in interest expense and cash outflows as follows:

Total interest expense at fixed rate.	$2,100,000
Total interest expense at floating rate	2,050,000
Reduction in interest expense and cash flows	$ 50,000

The change in the value of the swap offsets the change in the value of the debt. The fair value hedge was expected to be highly effective (in this case perfectly effective) in offsetting changes in the fair value of the debt due to the fact that:

- The notional amount of the swap matches that of the debt.
- The maturity date of the swap matches that of the debt.
- The fair value of the swap at inception is zero.
- The fixed rate is the same over the life of the note, and the variable rate is based on the same index (LIBOR) over the life of the note.
- The debt is not prepayable.
- There is no floor or ceiling on the variable interest rate.
- The intervals between reset dates are frequent enough to justify an assumption that the settlement amounts are based on market rates.

Special Accounting for Cash Flow Hedges

8

OBJECTIVE

Demonstrate how a cash flow hedge is used, and account for such hedges.

The hedged item in a cash flow hedge is one in which future cash flows could be affected due to a particular risk. These hedges involve cash flows associated with a forecasted transaction, forecasted cash flows associated with a recognized asset or liability, or an unrecognized firm commitment. A forecasted transaction is one that is expected to occur in the future at a market price that will be in existence at the time of the transaction. This is in contrast to a commitment, which involves market prices that have been previously determined at the time of the commitment. Unlike a commitment, a forecasted transaction does not provide an entity with any present rights or obligations and therefore does not have any fixed prices or rates. Because fixed prices or rates are not present in a forecasted transaction, an entity is exposed to the risk that future cash flows may vary due to changes in prices/rates. In order to reduce the risk associated with unfavorable cash flow variability, a strategy is developed to hedge the variable cash flows. These hedges are known as cash flow hedges. For example, assume that a food processor forecasts that it will need to purchase corn in 60 days. Absent a fixed commitment, the producer is exposed to the risk that corn prices may increase and more cash will be needed to acquire the inventory. In order to reduce the risk associated with uncertain variable cash flows, the producer could acquire a futures contract to buy corn or perhaps a call option to buy corn. The objective of the hedge is to allow the entity to fix the price or rate and reduce the variability of cash flows.

Qualifying Criteria for Cash Flow Hedges. As is the case with a fair value hedge, special hedge accounting is not available for a cash flow hedge unless a number of criteria are satisfied. Cash flow hedges must also meet the criteria regarding documentation and assessment of effectiveness. Although set forth in greater detail in the FASB's Accounting Standards Codification, selected qualifying criteria for a cash flow hedge are set forth in Exhibit M-4.[4]

Accounting for a Cash Flow Hedge. If the derivative instrument and the hedged item satisfy the criteria, then the cash flow hedge will qualify for special accounting. The gain or loss on the derivative instrument will be reported in **other comprehensive income (OCI)**, and the ineffective portion, if any, will be recognized currently in earnings.[5] As with fair value hedges, a portion of the derivative instrument's gain or loss may be excluded from the assessment of effectiveness. That portion of the gain or loss will be recognized currently in earnings rather than as a component of other comprehensive income.

The gain or loss on a cash flow hedge is reported as OCI, rather than recognized currently in earnings, because the hedged forecasted cash flows have not yet occurred or been recognized in the financial statements. The hedge is intended to establish the values that will be recognized once the forecasted transaction occurs and is recognized. Once the forecasted transaction has actually occurred, the OCI gain or loss will be reclassified into earnings in the same period(s) as the

---

4 FASB ASC 815-20-25.

5 Other comprehensive income is not included in the income statement; it bypasses the traditional income statement but is shown as a component of equity.

forecasted transaction affects earnings. For example, assume that a forecasted sale of inventory is hedged. Once the inventory is sold and recognized in earnings, the applicable amount, the OCI gain or loss, will also be recognized in earnings. If the forecasted transaction were a purchase of a depreciable asset, the applicable portion of the OCI would be recognized in earnings when the asset's depreciation expense is recognized.

Exhibit M-4
Selected Qualifying Criteria for Cash Flow Hedges

1. At inception of the hedge, there must be formal documentation of the hedging relationship and the entity's risk-management objective and strategy. Documentation should also identify the hedging instrument, the hedged transaction, the nature of the risk being hedged, and a plan for assessing the effectiveness of the hedge.

2. Both at inception and on an ongoing basis, the hedging relationship must be assessed to determine if it is highly effective in achieving offsetting cash flows attributable to the hedged item's fair value. The effectiveness of the hedging instrument must be assessed whenever financial statements or earnings are reported and at least every three months.

3. If a hedging instrument is used to modify variable interest rates on a recognized asset or liability to another variable interest rate (such instruments are known as basis swaps), the hedging instrument must be a link between a recognized asset with variable rates and a recognized liability with variable rates. For example, an entity with a variable rate loan receivable (e.g., prime rate + 1%) and a variable rate loan payable (e.g., LIBOR) may use a hedging instrument (e.g., swap prime rate + 1% for LIBOR) to link the two variable rate instruments.

4. The forecasted transaction is specifically identified as a single transaction or a group of individual transactions.

5. The forecasted transaction is with an external party, probably will occur, and presents exposure to variability in cash flows that could affect earnings.

6. The forecasted transaction is not the acquisition of an asset or incurrence of a liability that will subsequently be measured at fair value with changes in fair value being currently recognized in earnings. If the forecasted transaction relates to a recognized asset or liability, such asset or liability is not remeasured with changes in fair value being reported in current earnings.

7. For the forecasted purchase or sale of a nonfinancial item (such as inventory), the risk being hedged against is the change in cash flows due to price/rate changes rather than a change in cash flows due to a different location or a component part.

8. The forecasted purchase or sale of a financial asset or liability (or the interest payments on that asset or liability) or the variable cash flows associated with an existing financial asset or liability can be designated as a hedged item if certain types of risks, such as those related to changes in cash flows, benchmark interest rates, foreign currency exchange rates, and creditworthiness are being hedged. Two or more of the above risks may be hedged simultaneously. Prepayment risk may not be designated as the risk being hedged.

The deferral of a loss on a cash flow hedge as a component of OCI is not appropriate if it is likely to result in a combined basis/cost that exceeds the fair value of the resulting asset or liability. For example, assume a derivative loss associated with a forecasted purchase of equipment will, when combined with the expected cost of the equipment, result in a total cost in excess of the item's fair value. If this is expected, the derivative's loss should be recognized immediately in earnings, to the extent that it exceeds the equipment's fair value.

The change in the value of a derivative instrument that equals the change in the value of the forecasted cash flows is recognized as OCI. If the change in the value of the derivative is less than the change in forecasted cash flows, only the lesser amount is recorded. However, if the change in the value of the derivative exceeds the change in forecasted cash flows, the excess (ineffective portion of the derivative) is recognized in current earnings. For example, if a derivative instrument increases $1,000 in value and the forecasted cash flows decrease in value by $900, a $900 gain will be shown as OCI, and a $100 gain will be recognized in current earnings.

If the change in value of a derivative instrument is less than the change in value of the forecasted transaction, all of the change in value of the derivative instrument is recognized as a component of other comprehensive income. However, the excess change in value of the forecasted transaction is not recognized. To do so would allow partial recognition of a transaction that has not yet occurred. For example, assume a derivative instrument changes $1,000 in value and the forecasted cash flows change in value by $1,200. Only $1,000 of the change in value is recognized as a component of other comprehensive income and the $200 difference is not accounted for.

If all or part of a transaction is still forecasted, there may be some gain or loss on a corresponding derivative that is still being classified as a component of OCI. On an ongoing basis, it is important to make sure that the gain (loss) on a derivative that remains as a component of OCI does not more than offset the cumulative loss (gain) in the value of the remaining forecasted transaction. If excessive amounts are classified as OCI, such excess amounts must be reclassified as a component of current earnings. By way of illustration, consider the following independent cases:

	Case A	Case B	Case C
Amount of gain (loss) on derivative that is still being classified as OCI..............	$ 10,000	$10,000	$(10,000)
Cumulative gain (loss) on remaining forecasted transaction.......................	(12,000)	(8,000)	8,000
Extent to which OCI gain (loss) more than offsets the cumulative loss (gain) in the value of the remaining forecasted transaction	Not applicable	2,000	(2,000)
Amount of OCI to be reclassified as a component of current earnings	Not applicable	2,000	(2,000)

The accounting treatment given a cash flow hedge should continue unless:

◆ The criteria identified above are no longer satisfied,

◆ The derivative instrument expires or is sold, terminated, or exercised,

◆ The entity no longer designates the derivative instrument as a cash flow hedge, or

◆ The hedging relationship is no longer considered highly effective based on management's policies.

If any of the above conditions occur, the cumulative balance remaining in other comprehensive income should be reclassified into earnings in the same period or periods as the forecasted transaction affects earnings. Furthermore, if it is probable that a forecasted transaction will not occur by the end of the original anticipated time or within an additional 2-month period thereafter, the cumulative balance remaining in other comprehensive income should generally be immediately reclassified into earnings.

Examples of cash flow hedges against a forecasted transaction and a variable interest notes payable follow. Entries for the transactions are presented side by side with entries for the hedges for clarity. All transaction costs are ignored. The examples include the use of derivatives in the form of an option and a swap.

An Example of a Cash Flow—Hedge against a Forecasted Transaction Using an Option

Assume that in March, a processor of cereals and other food forecasts a purchase of 300 tons of soybean meal for June delivery. Concerned that prices may increase, the processor purchases three at-the-money, June call options on March 10. On the Chicago Board of Trade, the options are trading at $800 per option with a strike price of $165 per ton. Note that the option was trading at-the-money, which means that the strike price ($165) and current spot price ($165) are equal and that the option has no intrinsic value. The $800 paid for the option reflects time value. Each option is for a 100-ton unit with delivery at a warehouse specified by the CBT and a settlement date of June 25. Effectiveness of the hedge is measured by comparing changes in the option's intrinsic value with changes in the forecasted cash flows based on spot rates for soybean meal. Therefore, the change in time value of the option is excluded from the assessment of hedge effectiveness. In addition to the information given above, the data shown on page 529 are relevant to the hedging strategy.

Given:	March 10	March 31	April 30	May 31	June 25
Spot price per ton	$165	$167	$164	$172	$178
Strike price.	$165	$165	$165	$165	$165
Number of tons per option.	100	100	100	100	100
Fair value per option (given)	$800	$920	$700	$1,100	$ 1,300
Calculations per Option:					
Intrinsic value (Spot minus strike × number of tons)[a]	$ 0	$200	$ 0	$ 700	$ 1,300
Time value	800	720	700	400	0
Total (intrinsic + time)	$800	$920	$700	$1,100	$ 1,300
Value of expected cash flows					
[change in spot rates – gain (loss)]		$(200)[b]	$100[c]	$ (700)[d]	$(1,300)[e]
OCI balance after adjustments Dr (Cr)					
(lesser of intrinsic value or expected cash flows		(200)	0	(700)	(1,300)
Adjustment to OCI – Dr (Cr) (change in OCI balance)		(200)	200	(700)	(600)
Adjustment to income – Dr (Cr) (change in time value)		80	20	300	400

[a]The intrinsic value is never less than zero because the holder does not have to exercise the option if it is not in-the-money.
[b]($165 – $167) × 100 = $(200)
[c]($165 – $164) × 100 = $100
[d]($165 – $172) × 100 = $(700)
[e]($165 – $178) × 100 = $(1,300)

The following entries relate only to the hedge because no transaction has yet occurred. The recorded amounts are based on the above calculations:

Mar. 10 Investment in Call Option	2,400	
Cash		2,400
To record purchase of three options at $800 each.		
31 Investment in Call Option [($920 – $800) × 3]	360	
Loss on Option ($80 × 3)	240	
Other Comprehensive Income ($200 × 3)		600
To record the change in the value of the option. The change in time value is excluded from the assessment of hedge effectiveness.		
Apr. 30 Loss on Option ($20 × 3)	60	
Other Comprehensive Income [($0 – $200) ×3]	600	
Investment in Call Option [($700 – $920) × 3]		660
To record the change in the value of the option (note the absence of intrinsic value).		
May 31 Investment in Call Option [($1,100 – $700) × 3]	1,200	
Loss on Option ($300 × 3)	900	
Other Comprehensive Income [($700 – $0) × 3]		2,100
To record the change in the value of the option.		
June 25 Investment in Call Option [($1,300 – $1,100) × 3]	600	
Loss on Option ($400 × 3)	1,200	
Other Comprehensive Income [($1,300 – $700) × 3]		1,800
To record the change in the value of the option.		
Cash ($1,300 × 3)	3,900	
Investment in Call Option.		3,900
To record settlement of option.		
Inventory—Soybean Meal.	53,400	
Cash		53,400
To record purchase of 300 tons at the spot rate of $178 per ton.		

When the inventory of soybean meal is recognized as a component of cost of sales and thereby affects earnings, the applicable amount of other comprehensive income will also be recognized in earnings. Entries to reflect this are as follows:

Cost of Sales—Soybean Meal	53,400	
Inventory—Soybean Meal		53,400
To recognize cost of sales.		
Other Comprehensive Income	3,900	
Cost of Sales—Soybean Meal		3,900
To adjust cost of sales by the gain accumulated in other		
comprehensive income.		

There are several important points to note about the above entries regarding the cash flow hedge.

◆ Changes in the time value of the option are recognized currently in earnings, not OCI, as an unrealized loss of $2,400 ($240 + $60 + $900 + $1,200) on the hedge.

◆ At the end of April, the cumulative change in the value of the expected cash flows associated with the forecasted purchase of inventory was a $300 gain ($100 × 3), but the intrinsic value of the derivative hedge was $0. Therefore, the balance in OCI must be the lesser of the absolute value of these two values. At the end of April, the OCI balance is zero even though there is a cumulative loss due to changes in the spot rates.

◆ The cumulative balance in OCI will be reclassified into earnings in the same periods(s) in which the inventory of soybean meal affects earnings (as cost of sales). As shown above, this occurred through the entry that reduced the cost of goods sold by the OCI balance amount.

Note that this example contained no hedge ineffectiveness because of the following:

1. The terms of the derivative option and the forecasted transaction match in terms of commodity, quantities, qualities, location, and timing.
2. The time value of the option was excluded from an assessment of the hedge effectiveness.
3. The call option was in-the-money;, therefore, the changes in intrinsic value could offset the changes in the forecasted cash flows based on spot rates. If an option is out-of-the-money, it has no intrinsic value and cannot offset the changes in the forecasted cash flows.

The hedge was effective against adverse effects of increases in the spot price. By entering into the hedging relationship, the cost of the inventory, and ultimately the resulting cost of sales, was fixed at the strike price of $49,500 (300 tons at the strike price of $165 per ton). This was accomplished by incurring a cost of $2,400, represented by the initial premium on the three options (3 × $800 = $2,400). The effect the cash flow hedge had on the forecasted transaction is summarized as follows:

	Without the Call Option	With the Call Option
Cost of inventory to be included in cost of sales based on spot prices (300 tons @ $178 per ton)	$53,400	$53,400
Gain included in other comprehensive income and reclassified as an adjustment to cost of sales [300 tons × ($165 − $178)]		(3,900)
Adjusted basis of inventory to be included in cost of sales	$53,400	$49,500
Time value of the option recognized as a loss on hedge equal to the premium (3 options @ $800)		2,400
Net cost to be recognized in income statement	$53,400	$51,900

Although this hedge was effective, it is important to note that if the spot rate on June 25 had been less than the strike price, the hedge would not have been effective.

An Example of a Cash Flow—Hedge against a Variable Interest Notes Payable Using an Interest Rate Swap

If an entity has a note receivable or payable that is based on a variable rate of interest, the entity may hedge the variable interest cash flows. Note that a hedge of an asset or liability involving a fixed rate of interest would be a fair value hedge, but if the interest rate is variable, it is a cash flow hedge. The purpose of the cash flow hedge is to offset the risk associated with uncertain variable cash flows by establishing a fixed interest rate.

For example, assume that on January 1, 2011, an entity has loaned $10,000,000 for two years with semiannual interest due based on a variable rate of LIBOR + 1% (100 basis points). On June 30, 2011, concerned that variable interest rates will decline, the entity enters into a swap to receive a fixed rate of 7% in return for payment of a variable LIBOR + 1.25% (125 basis points) rate. The notional amount of the swap is $10,000,000. At each semiannual period, the swap is settled, and the variable rate is reset for the following semiannual interest payment. Relevant values are as follows:

Reset Dates	Receive LIBOR + 1% for Next Period	Pay LIBOR + 1.25% for Next Period	Fair Value of Swap	Change in Fair Value
June 30, 2011	6.75%	7.0%		
Dec. 31, 2011	6.65%	6.9	$ 9,505	$9,505
June 30, 2012	6.35%	6.6	19,361	9,856*

*Note that the loan is for two years and matured on December 31, 2012. Therefore, the swap does not exist after that point in time.

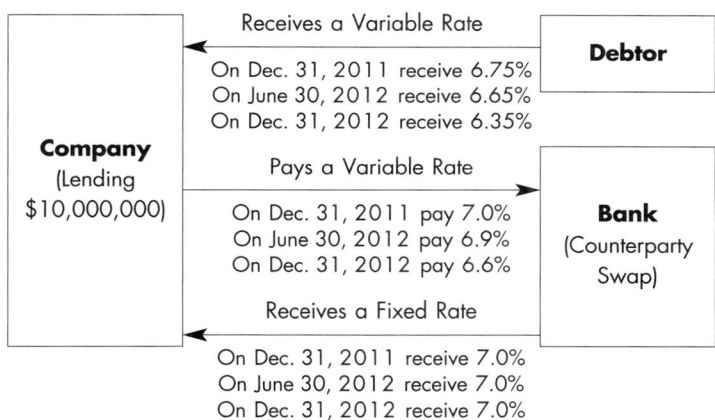

The entries to record the interest rate swap are as follows:

```
2011
Dec. 31   Cash ..........................................    337,500
              Interest Income...............................              337,500
                  To record interest income at the variable rate
                  ($10,000,000 × 6.75% × ½ year).

          Interest Rate Swap Asset ............................      9,505
              Other Comprehensive Income*......................               9,505
                  To record settlement of the swap [$10,000,000 ×
                  (7.0% − 7.0%) × ½ year] plus the change in the value
                  of the swap.
```

2012

June 30   Cash 332,500

    Interest Income.. 332,500

        To record interest income at the variable rate

        ($10,000,000 × 6.65% × ½ year).

    Cash 5,000

    Interest Rate Swap Asset 9,856

        Other Comprehensive Income.................................. 14,856

            To record settlement of the swap [$10,000,000 ×

            (7.0% − 6.9%) × ½ year] plus the change in the value

            of the swap.

    Other Comprehensive Income* 5,000

        Interest Income... 5,000

            To reclassify other comprehensive income to earnings

            (equal to the cash settlement associated with interest

            currently being recognized in earnings).

Dec. 31   Cash 317,500

    Interest Income.. 317,500

        To record interest income at the variable rate

        ($10,000,000 × 6.35% × ½ year).

    Cash 20,000

        Interest Rate Swap Asset 19,361

        Other Comprehensive Income................................. 639

            To record settlement of the swap [$10,000,000 ×

            (7.0% − 6.6%) × ½ year] plus the change in the value

            of the swap.

    Other Comprehensive Income...................................... 20,000

        Interest Income... 20,000

            To reclassify other comprehensive income to earnings.

*The two previous entries could be combined into one entry. However, it is important to note that other comprehensive income is reclassified into earnings only in the period in which the forecasted transaction affects earnings (i.e., interest income is recognized).

The swap was not a hedge against changing values of the debt but rather a hedge against the changing cash values of the variable interest payments. The interest rate swap was highly effective in replacing a LIBOR + 1.00% variable or floating rate of interest on the note receivable with a fixed rate of interest equal to 6.75%. The fixed rate of interest is derived as follows:

Rate received on original debt..................................	LIBOR + 1.00%
Pay floating rate on swap	−LIBOR + 1.25%
Receive fixed rate on swap	+ 7.00%
Net receive rate [(LIBOR + 1.00%) − (LIBOR + 1.25%) + 7.00%]	= 6.75%

Given the decreasing pattern of the floating rates, the company experienced an increase in interest income and cash inflows with a swap to pay floating for receive fixed as follows:

Total interest income from receive fixed rate swap (net rate of 6.75% × $10,000,000 × 1.5 years)	$1,012,500
Total interest income at floating rate	987,500
Increase in interest income and cash inflows.	$ 25,000

The $25,000 increase in interest income was initially recorded in OCI and was then reclassified into earnings when interest on the loan receivable affected earnings.

REFLECTION

- Fair value hedges apply to recognized assets and liabilities or firm commitments. The terms, prices, and/or rates for these items are fixed. Therefore, changes in the prices or rates affect the fair value of the recognized item or commitment.

- Cash flow hedges apply to existing assets or liabilities with variable future cash flows and to forecasted transactions. The prices or rates for these items are not fixed, and, therefore, future cash flows may vary due to changes in prices or rates.

- In a fair value hedge, both the derivative instrument and the hedged item are measured at fair value. Changes in the fair value of the respective items are recognized currently in earnings.

- In a cash flow hedge, the derivative instrument is measured at fair value with changes in value being recognized in other comprehensive income. The amounts in other comprehensive income are recognized in current earnings in the same period(s) as are the gains or losses on the hedged cash flow.

IASB PERSPECTIVES

As part of the IASB's financial instruments project, an Exposure Draft on hedge accounting was issued in the fall of 2010 with the adoption of IFRS scheduled for the second quarter of 2011. It is hoped that the principles adopted for hedge accounting will be more widely accepted, especially by some European leaders. The critical and complex issue of assessing hedge effectiveness will be reassessed allowing for more qualitative assessment in order to reflect a company's hedging strategies. It is anticipated that the "bright line rule," which suggested that the change in the value of a derivative had to be with 80% to 125% of the change in the value of hedged in order to be effective would be discarded. Effectiveness of the hedge will still have to be assessed at inception and on an ongoing basis. In all cases, the ineffectiveness of a hedge will have to be recognized in earnings. Accounting for cash flow hedges will basically be unchanged although there will be changes to the way fair value hedges are currently accounted for. It is hoped that aligning the way a cash flow hedge and a fair value hedge are accounted for will reduce complexity. Proposed changes in the accounting for a fair value hedge would include:

IASB *standards*

- Disclosing the cumulative gain or loss on the hedged item traceable to the hedged risk as a separate item on the balance sheet.

- Not adjusting the hedged item's carrying basis.

- Recording the fair value changes, attributable to the hedged risk, in the hedged item and the related hedging instrument as a component of other comprehensive income.

DISCLOSURES REGARDING DERIVATIVE INSTRUMENTS AND HEDGING ACTIVITIES

The FASB requires entities that hold or issue derivative instruments that are designated and qualify as hedging instruments to disclose information that allows users to understand:

1. How and why the reporting entity uses derivative instruments.
2. In the case of both fair value and cash flow hedges, how to account for the derivative instruments and the related hedged items.
3. In the case of both fair value and cash flow hedges, how the derivative instruments and the related hedged items affect the reporting entity's financial position, financial performance, and cash flows.

9

OBJECTIVE

Identify the various types of information that should be included in disclosures regarding derivative instruments and hedging activities.

The above disclosures must be made on an annual basis as well as on an interim reporting basis when a statement of financial position and a statement of financial performance are presented. The complete disclosure requirements are contained in FASB ASC 815-10-50.

Certain other disclosures are required for hedges relating to the foreign currency exposure of a net investment in a foreign operation. These disclosures will be discussed in Chapter 11.

REFLECTION

- The FASB requires general and specific financial statement disclosures by companies holding or issuing derivative instruments.

UNDERSTANDING THE ISSUES

1. Explain how both the intrinsic value and the time value are measured for a forward contract to sell and for a put option.

2. What is the exposure to risk associated with a firm commitment to sell inventory that a fair value hedge is intended to reduce?

3. A regional bakery is forecasting a major purchase of flour and is considering the use of a cash flow hedge. Explain how a cash flow hedge affects operating income currently and in the future as well as how such amounts are calculated.

4. Why might an option be preferred over a futures contract?

5. Using an example, explain how an interest swap works.

EXERCISES

Exercise 1 *(LO 4, 5)* **Impact on earnings of an option and an interest rate swap.** Millikin Corporation decided to hedge two transactions. The first transaction is a forecasted transaction to buy 500 tons of inventory in 60 days. The company was concerned that selling prices might increase, and it acquired a 60-day option to buy inventory at a price of $1,200 per ton. Upon acquiring the option, the company paid a premium of $10 per ton when the spot price was $1,201. At the end of 30 days, the option had a value of $19 per ton and a current spot price of $1,214 per ton. Upon expiration of the option, the spot price was $1,216 per ton.

In another transaction, the company borrowed $3,000,000 at a fixed rate of 8%; after three months, the company became concerned that variable rates would be lower than 8%. In response, the company entered into an interest rate swap whereby it paid variable rates to a counterparty in exchange for a fixed rate of 8%. The reset rate for the first 30 days of the swap was 8.1% and was 7.8% for the second 30 days of the swap. The fair value of the swap was $3,000 after the first 30 days and $3,300 after 60 days.

Determine the impact on earnings of the above hedges for the first and second 30-day period.

Exercise 2 *(LO 3)* **Fair value hedges using futures.** A large corporate farming operation is holding an inventory of corn and wheat and is concerned that excess harvests this season will lower the value of the commodities. In order to hedge against adverse market changes, the corporation acquired the following contracts on June 1:

◆ 30 contracts to sell 5,000 bushels of corn in December at a future price of $3.56 per bushel.

◆ 30 contracts to sell 5,000 bushels of wheat in December at a future price of $6.35 per bushel.

Spot and future prices are as follows:

	Corn—Dollars per Bushel		Wheat—Dollars per Bushel	
	Spot Price	Future Price	Spot Price	Future Price
June 1	$3.42	$3.56	$6.20	$6.35
June 30	3.41	3.53	6.19	6.33
July 31	3.43	3.54	6.175	6.32

For each of the fair value hedges, determine, by month, the change in the value of the respective inventories and the gain or loss on the futures contracts.

Exercise 3 *(LO 3, 7)* **Fair value hedge—an interest rate swap's effect on interest and the carrying value of a note.** On July 1, 2012, Hargrove Corporation issued a 2-year note with a face value of $4,000,000 and a fixed interest rate of 9%, payable on a semiannual basis. On January 15, 2013, the company entered into an interest rate swap with a financial institution in anticipation of lower variable rates. At the initial date of the swap, the company paid a premium of $9,200. The swap had a notional amount of $4,000,000 and called for the payment of a variable rate of interest in exchange for a 9% fixed rate. The variable rates are reset semiannually beginning with January 1, 2013, in order to determine the next interest payment. Differences between rates on the swap will be settled on a semiannual basis. Variable interest rates and the value of the swap on selected dates are as follows:

Reset Date	Variable Interest Rate	Value of the Swap
January 1, 2013	8.75%	
June 30, 2013.	8.50	$14,000
December 31, 2013	8.85	3,500

For each of the above dates, determine:

1. The net interest expense.
2. The carrying value of the note payable.
3. The net unrealized gain or loss on the swap.

Exercise 4 *(LO 6, 7)* **Evaluating a hedge of a firm commitment with a put option.** A major cattle feeding operation has entered into a firm commitment to buy 100,000 bushels of corn to be delivered to its feed lot in Kansas. The corn is expected to be delivered in 90 days. The company is committed to pay $1.50 per bushel. If corn yields are greater than expected, the price of corn could decline and the company would experience higher operating costs than necessary as a result of the commitment.

In order to protect itself against falling corn prices, the company purchased an option to sell corn in 90 days at a strike price of $1.51 per bushel delivered to a facility in Nebraska.

1. Assuming that the company designated the swap as a fair value hedge, identify several critical criteria that would need to be satisfied in order to justify this classification.
2. Identify several factors that would suggest that the company's hedge would qualify as being highly effective in reducing the risk associated with the firm's commitment to buy 100,000 bushels of corn.
3. Explain why an option to sell corn rather than corn futures may provide the company with more flexibility.

4. Assume that at the time of acquiring the put option, the price of corn was less than $1.51. Explain why the option had a value of more than zero at inception.
5. Assume that one of your colleagues made the following comment: "An option can never have a negative value; therefore, you can never lose money on an option." Discuss whether or not you agree with your colleague.
6. Assuming that only the intrinsic value is used to assess effectiveness, explain how the option's time value affects earnings prior to the end of the commitment.

Exercise 5 *(LO 4, 8)* **Evaluating the impact of hedging a forecasted transaction with an option.** Casper Enterprises is forecasting two significant transactions and is concerned that adverse price movements could negatively impact these transactions. In order to hedge against adverse movements, Casper has acquired two options as described below.

The first forecasted transaction involves the purchase of a commodity with the concern being that commodity prices could increase prior to the transaction actually taking place. As a defensive move, Casper acquired Option A. The option is a call option involving 200 tons of a commodity with a strike price of $1,500 per ton with delivery of the commodity in 90 days.

The other forecasted transaction involves the sale of 100,000 bushels of a harvested commodity with the concern that the price of the commodity may decrease prior to the transaction actually taking place. As a defensive move, Casper acquired Option B. The option is a put option involving 100,000 bushels of the commodity with a strike price of $2.50 per bushel and delivery in 90 days.

Effectiveness of the hedge is measured by comparing the changes in the intrinsic value of the option with changes in the forecasted cash flows based on spot rates. Information concerning the options is as follows:

	At Inception of Option	30 Days Later	60 Days Later
Option A:			
Spot price per ton	$1,490	$1,498	$1,510
Strike price per ton	$1,500	$1,500	$1,500
Number of tons per option	200	200	200
Fair value of option	$900	$700	$2,500
Option B:			
Spot price per bushel	$2.52	$2.48	$2.45
Strike price per bushel	$2.50	$2.50	$2.50
Number of bushels per option	100,000	100,000	100,000
Fair value of option	$1,200	$3,300	$5,200

For each option, determine the following balances at both 30 days and 60 days after inception of the option: Investment in Option, Other Comprehensive Income, and Gain or Loss on Option (the change in time value).

Exercise 6 *(LO 4, 8)* **Entries to record a hedge of a forecasted purchase with an option.** A Midwest food processor forecasts purchasing 300,000 pounds of soybean oil in May. On February 20, the company acquires an option to buy 300,000 pounds of soybean oil in May at a strike price of $1.60 per pound. Information regarding spot prices and option values at selected dates is as follows:

	February 20	February 28	March 31	April 20
Spot price per pound	$ 1.61	$ 1.59	$ 1.62	$ 1.64
Fair value of option	3,800	1,200	6,800	12,500

The company settled the option on April 20 and purchased 300,000 pounds of soybean oil on May 3 at a spot price of $1.63 per pound. During May, the soybean oil was used to produce food. One-half of the resulting food was sold in June. The change in the option's time value is excluded from the assessment of hedge effectiveness.

1. Prepare all necessary journal entries through June to reflect the above activity.
2. What would the effect on earnings have been had the forecasted purchase not been hedged?

Exercise 7 *(LO 5, 7)* **Interest rate swap with variable for fixed.** At the beginning of the current year, Skeeba Manufacturing borrowed $10 million to be repaid over the next five calendar quarters with quarterly payments of $2,090,893.23 based on a fixed annual interest rate of 6.0%. Concerned that variable interest rates would be lower than the 6.0% fixed interest rate, on March 31 Skeeba secured an interest rate swap whereby it would receive a 6.0% fixed rate of interest in exchange for the payment of a variable rate. The notional amount of the swap is $10 million, and the maturity date of the swap matches the maturity date of the original borrowing.

Reset dates are March 31, June 30, September 30, and December 31, with variable rates for the next quarter of 5.8%, 5.5%, 5.6%, and 5.4%, respectively. Assumed fair values of the swap are $14,954, $6,037, and $3,049, as of June 30, September 30, and December 31, respectively.

Determine the basis of the 6% note payable on June 30, September 30, and December 31 along with the interest expense for each of those calendar quarters.

PROBLEMS

Problem M-1 *(LO 4, 7)* **Entries to record a commitment and the impact on earnings.** On March 17, Kennedy Baking, Inc., committed to buy 1,000 tons of commodity A for delivery in May at a cost of $118 per ton. Concerned that the price of commodity A might decrease, on March 29 the company purchased a May put option for 1,000 tons of commodity A at a strike price of $119 per ton. The change in the time value of the option is excluded from the assessment of hedge effectiveness, and the option was settled on May 18. After processing all 1,000 tons of commodity A at a cost of $25 per ton, one-half of the resulting inventory was sold for $180 per ton on June 16. Relevant values are as follows:

Number of tons per option................	1,000	1,000	1,000	1,000
Spot price per ton	$118	$118	$116	$115
Strike price per ton......................	$119	$119	$119	$119
Value of option	$2,400	$2,200	$3,300	$4,000

1. Prepare all applicable entries for the months of March through June regarding the inventory and the hedging instrument assuming qualification as a fair value hedge. Record the changes in the intrinsic value and time value of the option with separate entries.
2. For the entire 1,000 tons of processed commodity A, prepare a schedule regarding the cost of the processed commodity available for sale in terms of the desired cost, the cost without the hedge, and the cost with the hedge.

◀ ◀ ◀ ◀ ◀ **Required**

Problem M-2 *(LO 3, 8)* **Cash flow hedge of a forecasted purchase of wheat.** Custom Brand Bakeries, Inc. (CBBI), located in Erie, Pennsylvania, bakes a variety of products for various parties on a contract basis. For example, a food company may contract with CBBI to make energy bars that are then sold under the food company's private label. Contracts are typically signed several months in advance of actual production and set forth a fixed sales price. Because sales prices are fixed by contact, CBBI is concerned that materials costs do not increase and further reduce profits. However, CBBI does not want to guard against increasing costs by purchasing materials in advance of their scheduled production. Corn and wheat flour are two major ingredients used in the production process where increasing costs are of concern. CBBI wants to hedge against these costs increasing but cannot buy flour futures. However, buying corn and wheat futures can provide an effective hedge against changing flour prices. Changes in the price of corn flour and wheat flour often correlate highly with changes in the price of corn and wheat.

On September 1, 2015, the company purchased, on the Chicago Board of Trade, futures for delivery of the commodities in November. The CBT required a deposit of $70,000 toward a margin account.

	Corn Futures		
Date	Spot Price per Bushel	Futures Price per Bushel	Notional Amount
September 1	$2.5000	$2.5100	1,000,000 bushels
September 30	2.5380	2.5420	1,000,000
October 31	2.5680	2.5700	1,000,000
November 5	2.5685	2.5710	1,000,000

	Wheat Futures		
Date	Spot Price per Bushel	Futures Price per Bushel	Notional Amount
September 1	$3.5150	$3.5210	2,000,000 bushels
September 30	3.5480	3.5520	2,000,000
October 31	3.5700	3.5710	2,000,000
November 5	3.5700	3.5705	2,000,000

CBBI properly documents the hedging relationship, and all criteria for special accounting as a hedge are satisfied. The hedging instruments are determined to be highly effective as a hedge against changing flour prices. The changes in the time value of the futures contracts are to be excluded from the assessment of hedge effectiveness.

In early November, CBBI actually purchased both corn flour and wheat flour used in products sold to contracting parties on November 21. The futures contracts are settled net on November 5.

Required ▶ ▶ ▶ ▶ ▶

1. Prepare all monthly entries to record hedging activity.
2. Identify and discuss several factors that might cause the futures contracts to not be perfectly effective as a hedge against changes in the price of flour used by CBBI.

Problem M-3 *(LO 3, 4, 7, 8)* **Impact on earnings of various hedged relationships.** The chief financial officer (CFO) of Baxter International has employed the use of hedges in a variety of contexts over the first quarter of the current calendar year as follows:

Futures Contract—The company hedged against a possible decline in the value of inventory represented by commodity A. At the beginning of February, an April futures contract to sell 10,000 units of commodity A for $3.50 per unit was acquired. It is assumed that the terms of the futures contract and the hedged assets match with respect to delivery location, quantity, and quality. The fair value of the futures contract will be measured by changes in the futures prices over time, and the time value component of the futures contract will be excluded from the assessment of hedge effectiveness. Relevant values are as follows:

	February 28	March 31
Number of units per contract	10,000	10,000
Spot price per unit	$3.45	$3.40
Futures price per unit	$3.50	$3.44

Forward Contract—On January 15, the company committed to sell 5,000 units of inventory for $90 per unit on March 15. Concerned that selling prices might increase over time, the company entered into a March 15 forward contract to buy 5,000 units of identical inventory at a forward rate of $92 per unit. Changes in the value of the commitment are measured based on the changes in the forward rates over time discounted at 6%. On March 15, the inventory, with a cost of $360,000, was sold, and the forward contract was settled. Relevant values are as shown on page 539.

	January 15	January 31	February 28	March 15
Number of units per contract........	5,000	5,000	5,000	5,000
Spot price per unit................	$90.00	$90.20	$90.50	$90.60
Forward rate per unit.............	$92.00	$91.50	$91.20	$90.60

Option—In January, the company forecasted the purchase of 100,000 units of commodity B with delivery in February. Upon receipt, the commodity was processed further and sold for $12 per unit on March 17. On January 15, the company purchased a February 20 call option for 100,000 units of commodity B at a strike price of $8 per unit. Changes in the time value of the option are excluded from the assessment of hedge effectiveness. Relevant values are as follows:

	January 15	January 31	February 20	March 17
Number of units per option	100,000	100,000	100,000	
Spot price per unit................	$8.05	$8.02	$7.95	
Strike price per unit	$8.00	$8.00	$8.00	
Fair value of option	$6,000	$2,400	$—	
Processing costs per unit				$1.10

For each of the above hedged events and the related hedging instruments, prepare a schedule to reflect the effect on earnings for each of the months of January through March of the current year. Clearly identify each component account impacting earnings. ◄ ◄ ◄ ◄ ◄ **Required**

Problem M-4 *(LO 5)* **Hedging both fixed and floating interest rates.**

Pasu International purchased a plant in Louisiana on December 31, 2015, and financed $20,000,000 of the purchase price with a 5-year note. The note bears interest at the fixed rate of 5%, and payments on the note are made quarterly in the amount of $1,136,408. The note has a balance of $12,590,619 as of December 31, 2017. At the beginning of 2018, Pasu became concerned that variable or floating interest rates would be less than its fixed rate on the above note. Given this concern, Pasu arranged an interest rate swap on a notional amount equal to the outstanding balance of the note at the beginning of each quarter beginning with the January 1, 2018, balance of the note. The swap calls for the payment of a variable or floating interest rate on the principal balance of the note to a counterparty in exchange for a fixed rate of 4.75%. The floating rate is LIBOR plus 1.5% and is reset at the beginning of each quarter for that quarter's calculations.

In an unrelated transaction, on June 30, 2018, Pasu sold its plant in Europe and as part of the transaction received an 18-month $10,000,000 note receivable from the buyer. The note bears interest at a rate of LIBOR plus 2.0%, and interest-only payments are made each quarter during 2018. The floating rate is reset at the beginning of each quarter. Concerned that declining floating interest rates will decrease the value of the note, Pasu has arranged an interest rate swap with a counterparty effective July 1, 2018. The swap calls for the payment by Pasu of floating rate of LIBOR plus 1.7% in exchange for a fixed rate of 4.5%.

LIBOR rates at the beginning of each calendar quarter of 2018 are as follows:

January 1......................	3.25%
April 1	3.15
July 1	2.90
October 1	2.65

All interest rates are stated as annual interest rates. As of December 31, 2018, calculate each of the following: ◄ ◄ ◄ ◄ ◄ **Required**

1. Annual fixed interest paid on the note resulting from the purchase of the Louisiana plant.
2. Annual floating interest paid to the counterparty on the note resulting from the sale of the European plant.
3. Annual net interest expense on the note resulting from the purchase of the Louisiana plant.
4. Annual net interest income on the note receivable.

5. Assuming that the LIBOR rate at October 1, 2018, will continue into the future, determine the December 31, 2018, value of the interest rate swap associated with the note receivable. (*Hint*: Compare the year-end present value of paying a floating rate on the notional amount with the year-end present value of receiving a fixed rate on the notional amount.)
6. If the note receivable had been denominated in euros versus U.S. dollars, determine to what additional risks Pasu would have been exposed.

Problem M-5 *(LO 8)* **Prepare entries to account for a cash flow hedge involving an option.** Industrial Plating Corporation coats manufactured parts with a variety of coatings such as Teflon, gold, and silver. The company intends to purchase 100,000 troy ounces of silver in September. The purchase is highly probable, and the company has become concerned that the prices of silver may increase, and, therefore, the forecasted purchase will become even more expensive. In order to reduce the exposure to rising silver prices, on July 10 the company purchased 20 September call (buy) options on silver. Each option is for 5,000 troy ounces and has a strike price of $5.00 per troy ounce. The company excludes from hedge effectiveness changes in the time value of the option. Spot prices and option value per troy ounce of silver are as follows:

	July 10	July 31	August 31	September 10
Spot price	$5.10	$5.14	$5.35	$5.32
Option value	0.20	0.23	0.37	0.33

On September 10, the company settled the option and on September 15 purchased 100,000 troy ounces of silver on account at $5.33 per ounce. The silver was used in the company's production process over the next three months. In September and October, plating services were provided as follows:

	September	October
Units of silver used	15,000	50,000
Other costs.	$105,000	$350,000
Plating revenues	$225,000	$750,000

Required ▶ ▶ ▶ ▶ ▶ Prepare all necessary entries to account for the above activities through October. Assume that the hedge satisfies all necessary criteria for special hedge accounting.

Problem M-6 *(LO 4)* **Prepare a schedule to determine the earnings effect of various hedging relationships.** During the third quarter of the current year, Beamer Manufacturing Company invested in derivative instruments for a variety of reasons. The various investments and hedging relationships are as follows:

a. Call Option A—This option was purchased on July 10 and provided for the purchase of 10,000 units of commodity A in October at a strike price of $45 per unit. The company designated the option as a hedge of a commitment to sell 10,000 units of commodity A in October at a fixed price of $45 per unit. Information regarding the option and commodity A is as follows:

	July 10	July 31	August 31	September 30
Spot price	$ 45	$ 46	$ 44	$ 46.50
Value of option	2,000	12,400	1,000	16,000

b. Call Option B—This option provided for the purchase of 10,000 units of commodity B in October at a strike price of $30 per unit. The company designated the option as a hedge of a forecasted purchase of commodity B in October. Information regarding the option and commodity B is as follows:

	July 1	July 31	August 31	September 30
Spot price	$ 29	$29.50	$ 29	$28.75
Value of option	1,100	900	600	200

c. Put Option C—This option provided for the sale of 10,000 units of commodity C in September at a strike price of $30 per unit. The company designated the option as a hedge of a forecasted sale of 10,000 units of commodity C on September 10. Information regarding the option and commodity C is as follows:

	July 1	July 31	August 31	September 10
Spot price	$ 30	$29.50	$ 29	$ 28.75
Value of option	500	5,600	10,200	12,600

The company settled the option on September 10 and sold 10,000 units of commodity C at the spot price. The manufacturing cost of the units sold was $20 per unit.

d. Futures Contract D—The contract calls for the sale of 10,000 units of commodity D in October at a future price of $10 per unit. The company designated the contract as a hedge on a forecasted sale of commodity D in October. Information regarding the contract and commodity D is as follows:

	July 1	July 31	August 31	September 10
Spot price	$9.95	$9.92	$9.89	$9.85
Futures price	9.94	9.90	9.87	9.84

e. Interest Rate Swap—The company has a 12-month note receivable with a face value of $10,000,000 that matures on June 30 of next year. The note calls for interest to be paid at the end of each month based on the LIBOR variable interest rate at the beginning of each month. On July 31, the company entered into an agreement to receive a 7% fixed rate of interest beginning in August in exchange for payment of a variable rate based on LIBOR. The reset date is at the beginning of each month, and net settlement occurs at the end of each month. LIBOR rates and swap values are as follows:

	July	August	September
LIBOR for month	6.8%	6.8%	6.7%
Swap value at end of month	$17,729	$24,249	$21,884

In all of the above cases, the change in the time value of the derivative instrument is excluded from the assessment of hedge effectiveness. Furthermore, the company assesses hedge effectiveness on a continuing basis. Such an assessment at the end of June concluded that call option B was not effective.

Prepare a schedule to reflect the effect on current earnings of the above hedging relationships. ◄ ◄ ◄ ◄ ◄ **Required**
The schedule should show relevant amounts for each month from July through September.

Problem M-7 *(LO 4)* **Prepare entries to record a variable for fixed interest rate swap.** Hauser Corporation has $20,000,000 of outstanding debt that bears interest at a variable rate and matures on June 30, 2014. At inception of the debt, the company had a lower credit rating, and most available financing carried a variable rate. The company's variable rate is the LIBOR rate plus 1%. However, the company's credit rating has improved, and the company feels that a fixed, lower rate of interest would be most appropriate. Furthermore, the company is of the opinion that variable rates will increase over the next 24 months. In May 2012, the company negotiated with First Bank of Boston an interest rate swap that would allow the company to pay a fixed rate of 7% in exchange for receiving interest based on the LIBOR rate. The terms of the swap call for settlement at the end of June and December, which coincides with the company's interest payment dates. The variable rates are reset at the end of each 6-month period for the following 6-month period. The terms of the swap are effective for the 6-month period beginning July 2012.

The hedging relationship has been properly documented, and management has concluded that the hedge will be highly effective in offsetting changes in the cash flows due to changes in interest rates. The criteria for special accounting have been satisfied.

Relevant LIBOR rates and swap values are as follows:

	June 30, 2012	Dec. 31, 2012	June 30, 2013	Dec. 31, 2013
LIBOR rate	7.0%	7.1%	6.9%	6.8%
Swap value		$27,990	$(19,011)	$(19,342)

Required ▶ ▶ ▶ ▶ ▶

1. Prepare the necessary entries to record the activities related to the debt and the hedge from July 1, 2012, through June 30, 2014.
2. Prepare a schedule to evaluate the positive or negative impact the hedge had on each 6-month period of earnings.
3. What would the LIBOR rate on December 31, 2013, have had to be in order for the interest expense to be the same whether or not there was a cash flow hedge?

Foreign Currency Transactions

Learning Objectives

When you have completed this chapter, you should be able to

1. Explain the floating international monetary system, and identify factors that influence rates of exchange between currencies.

2. Define the various terms associated with exchange rates, including spot rates, forward rates, premiums, and discounts.

3. Account for a foreign currency transaction, including the measurement of exchange gain or loss.

4. Identify the contexts in which a company may be exposed to foreign currency exchange risk.

5. Understand the characteristics of derivatives and the common types used to hedge foreign currency exchange rate risk.

6. Explain the accounting treatment given various types of foreign currency hedges.

As discussed in Chapter 9, companies in the United States are engaged in significant export and import activity. Such transactions must be denominated or settled in a currency agreed upon by the transacting parties. Each party would often like to use its own national currency. Since it is impossible to use more than one currency as the medium of exchange, a currency must be selected, and rates of exchange must be established between the two competing currencies. For example, if a U.S. footwear manufacturer purchases leather from a German supplier, the transaction would usually be settled in either U.S. dollars or euros. If euros are chosen, a rate of exchange between the U.S. dollar and the euro must be determined in order to record the transaction on the American company's books in dollars. Given that rates of exchange vary, the number of U.S. dollars needed to acquire the necessary euros also could change between the time the order is placed and when payment is made for the goods. If, during this time, more dollars are needed to acquire the necessary euros to pay for the leather, the U.S. purchaser is exposed to an additional business risk. The more volatility there is in exchange rates, the more risk to which the party is exposed. Similarly, if the dollar is used as the medium of exchange, this risk would still exist, but it would be transferred to the German vendor.

It is readily apparent that the currency decision becomes an important factor in negotiating such transactions. Due to the volatility of currency exchange rates, companies transacting business in foreign markets should aggressively control and measure exchange risk. Management should develop a model that enables them to forecast the direction, magnitude, and timing of exchange rate changes. This model, in turn, can be used to develop a strategy to minimize foreign exchange losses and maximize foreign exchange gains.

Business transactions that are settled in a currency other than that of the domestic (home country) currency are referred to, in this text, as *foreign currency transactions*. One of the transacting parties will settle the transaction in its own domestic currency and also measure the transaction in its domestic currency. For example, a German company may sell inventory to a U.S. company and require payment in euros. The currency used to settle the transaction is referred to as the *denominated currency* and would be the euro in this case. The other transacting party will settle the transaction in a foreign currency but will need to measure the transaction in its domestic currency. For example, a U.S. company that purchases inventory from a German company must settle the resulting accounts payable in euros and yet must measure the purchase of inventory and the accounts payable in terms of U.S. dollars. The currency used to measure or record the transaction is referred to as the *measurement currency* and would be the U.S. dollar in this case. Whenever a transaction is denominated in a currency different from the measurement currency, exchange rate risk exists, and exchange rates must be used for measurement purposes. The process of expressing a transaction in the measurement currency when it is denominated in a different currency is referred to as a *foreign currency translation.*

<table>
<tr><td>

1

OBJECTIVE

Explain the floating international monetary system, and identify factors that influence rates of exchange between currencies.

</td></tr>
</table>

THE INTERNATIONAL MONETARY SYSTEM

Denominating a transaction in a currency other than the entity's domestic currency requires the establishment of a rate of exchange between the currencies. The international monetary system establishes rates of exchanges between currencies through the use of a variety of systems. The selection of a particular monetary system and the resulting exchange rates have a significant effect on international business and the risk associated with such business.

Alternative International Monetary Systems

Several major international monetary systems have been employed over time, and previous systems have occasionally been reestablished. Prior to 1944, the *gold system* provided a strict apolitical system based on gold. The currencies of nations were backed by or equivalent to some physical measure of gold. To illustrate, suppose Nation A has 1 million currency units backed by 1,000 ounces of gold and Nation B has 2 million currency units also backed by 1,000 ounces of gold. With gold as the common denominator, exchange rates between currencies could be established. In the above example, one unit of Nation A's currency could be exchanged for two units of Nation B's currency. A nation's supply of gold, therefore, influenced its money supply, rates of exchange, prices, and international trading levels (imports and exports).

In 1944, the *Bretton Woods Agreement*, which created the International Monetary Fund (IMF) and a *fixed rate exchange system*, was signed. The fixed rate system required each nation to set a par value for its currency in terms of gold or the U.S. dollar. In turn, the U.S. dollar's value was defined in terms of gold. Modest variations from a currency's par value were allowed, and each nation could adjust its money supply in order to maintain its par value. The IMF could provide support to a nation in order to maintain its par value. Changes in a currency's par value were referred to as *devaluations* and *revaluations*.

As pressures to maintain the par values established by the fixed rate system increased, pressure was placed on the U.S. dollar. The ability of the dollar to support the system became questionable, and fears arose that countries with dollar surpluses might seek to convert these dollars into gold. In 1971, the U.S. government, for all practical purposes, terminated the Bretton Woods Agreement by suspending the convertibility of the dollar into gold.

Currencies temporarily became part of a *floating system* where rates of exchange were in response to the supply and demand factors affecting a currency. Shortly thereafter, the IMF accepted the *Smithsonian Agreement* which devaluated the U.S. dollar and did not allow for the convertibility of the dollar into gold. Par values of currencies were established along with a wider margin of acceptable values around the par value. The Smithsonian Agreement was short-lived, and in response to increasing pressures on the U.S. dollar, the fixed rate system was abandoned in 1973.

Today, the international monetary system is a floating system whereby the factors of supply and demand primarily define currency exchange rates. Each nation's central bank may intervene in order to move its currency toward a target rate of exchange. This intervention results in a managed, or "dirty" float, versus an unmanaged, or "clean" float. Supply and demand factors along with possible central bank intervention result in much more uncertainty and risk than that experienced in a fixed rate system. A number of factors beyond supply and demand affect exchange rates including but not limited to a nation's trade balances, money supply, economic stability, interest rates, and governmental intervention.

Although the present international monetary system is best described as a floating system, there are a number of special variations within the system. Some nations still maintain a fixed system whereby the rate of exchange is established by their central bank. However, because these fixed rates are changed frequently, sometimes daily, they may be viewed as a controlled or "dirty" float. A currency that is frequently adjusted downward, such as those in less-developed nations, is referred to as a "crawling peg" currency. Tiered systems also exist whereby special rates are established for certain types of transactions, such as import and export sales and dividend payments, to accomplish desired political and economic objectives. For example, to encourage exports and to discourage capital withdrawal, a foreign government may establish favorable official rates for export sales and less favorable exchange rates for the payment of dividends to investors in other countries. The forces of supply and demand, however, occasionally make it difficult for a government to maintain an official exchange rate. In response, the government either devalues or revalues its currency.

The Mechanics of Exchange Rates

An exchange rate is a measure of how much of one currency may be exchanged for another currency. These rates may be in the form of either *direct* or *indirect quotes* made by a foreign currency trader who is usually employed by a large commercial bank. A direct quote measures how much of the domestic currency must be exchanged to receive one unit of the foreign currency (1 FC). Direct quotes allow the party using the quote to understand the price of the foreign currency in terms of its own "base" or domestic currency. This method is frequently used in the United States, and direct quotes are published daily in financial papers such as *The Wall Street Journal* or on Web sites such as http://www.x-rates.com/. Indirect quotes, also known as European terms, measure how many units of foreign currency will be received for one unit of the domestic currency. Thus, if the direct quote for a foreign currency (FC) is $0.25, then 1 FC would cost $0.25. The indirect quote would be the reciprocal of the direct quote, or 4 FC per dollar ($1.00 divided by $0.25).

2

OBJECTIVE

Define the various terms associated with exchange rates, including spot rates, forward rates, premiums, and discounts.

Exchange Rate Quotes	
Direct Quote	Indirect Quote
1 FC = $0.25	$1 = 4 FC

The business news often reports that a currency has strengthened (gained) or weakened (lost) relative to another currency. Assuming a direct quote system, such changes measure the difference between the new rate and the old rate, as a percentage of the old rate. For example, if the dollar strengthened or gained 20% against a foreign currency from its previous rate of $0.25, the dollar would now command more FC (i.e., the FC would be cheaper to buy). To be exact, the new exchange rate would be $0.20 [$0.25 − (20% × 0.25)]. Therefore, *the strengthening currency would be evidenced by a reduction in the directly quoted amount and an increase in the indirectly quoted amount.* The opposite would be true for a weakening of the domestic currency. Reaction to the strengthening or weakening of a currency depends on what type of transaction is contemplated. For example, an American exporter would want a weaker dollar because the foreign importer would need fewer of its currency units to acquire a dollar's worth of U.S. goods. Thus, U.S. goods would cost less in terms of the foreign currency. If the dollar strengthened so that one could acquire more foreign currency units for a dollar, importers would benefit. Therefore, U.S. companies and citizens would have to spend fewer U.S. dollars to buy the imported goods.

Changes Relative to Another Currency			
A Strengthening U.S Currency		**A Weakening U.S. Currency**	
Before:	1 FC = $0.25	Before:	1 FC = $0.25
After:	1 FC = $0.20	After:	1 FC = $0.30
Result:	The dollar gained 20%.	Result:	The dollar lost 20%.
	($0.25 − $0.20 = $0.05;		($0.25 − $0.30 = −$0.05;
	$0.05 ÷ $0.25 = 20%)		−$0.05 ÷ 0.25 = −20%)

Exchange rates often are quoted in terms of a buying rate (the bid price) and a selling rate (the offered price). The buying and selling rates represent what the currency broker (normally a large commercial bank) is willing to pay to acquire or sell a currency. The difference or spread between these two rates represents the broker's commission and is often referred to as the points. The spread is influenced by several factors, including the supply of and demand for the currency, the number of transactions taking place, currency risk, and the overall volatility of the market. For example, assume a currency broker agrees to pay $0.20 to a holder of a foreign currency and agrees to sell that currency to a buyer of foreign currency for $0.22. In this case, the broker will receive a commission of $0.02 ($0.22 − $0.20). In the United States, rates generally are quoted between the U.S. dollar and a foreign currency. However, rates between two foreign currencies are also quoted and are referred to as cross rates.

Exchange rates fall into two primary groups. A *spot rate* is the current rate of exchange between two currencies. In addition to current exchange rates governing the immediate delivery of currency, *forward rates* apply to the exchange of different currencies at a future point in time. An agreement to exchange currencies at a specified price with delivery at a specified future point in time is a *forward contract*. Although not all currencies are quoted in forward rates, virtually all major trading nations have forward rates.

Although future exchange dates typically are quoted in 30-day intervals, contracts can be written to cover any number of days. To illustrate a forward contract, assume the forward rate to buy one FC to be delivered in 90 days is $1.650. This means that, after the specified time from the inception of the contract date (90 days), one FC will be exchanged for $1.650, regardless of what the spot rate is at that time.

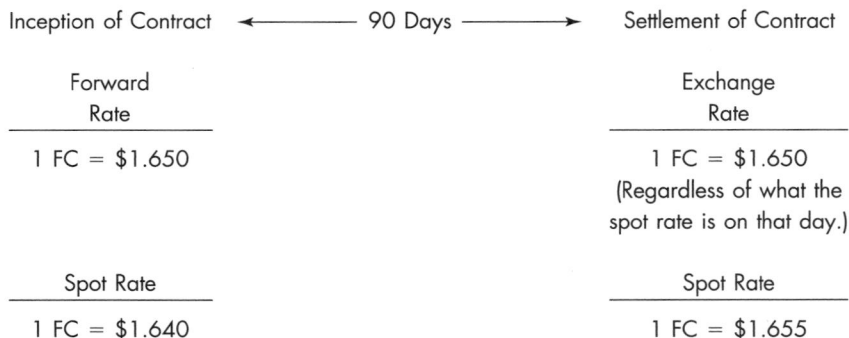

Several aspects of spot rates and forward rates are noteworthy. First, typically, both rates are constantly changing. Spot rates are revised daily; as they change, forward rates for the *remaining time* covered by a given forward contract also change even though the forward rate at inception is fixed. At the expiration date of the contract, the forward date is the current date and, therefore, the forward rate at that time is the current spot rate. Thus, the value of a forward contract changes over the forward period. For instance, in the above example, if the forward rate is 1 FC = $1.652 with 30 days remaining, the right to *buy* FC at the original fixed forward rate of 1 FC = $1.650 suggests that the value of the forward contract has increased. Rather than paying a forward rate of $1.652 to acquire FC in 30 days, the holder of the original forward contract must only pay the fixed rate of $1.650. Second, the ultimate value of the forward contract must be assessed by comparing the original fixed forward rate against the spot rate at the settlement date. In the above example, at the settlement date, the holder of the contract will pay the fixed rate of 1 FC = $1.650 to buy an FC rather than the spot rate of 1 FC = $1.655. The total change in value is represented by the difference between the original fixed forward rate and the spot rate at settlement date ($1.650 vs. $1.655). Finally, the difference between the original forward rate and the spot rate at inception of the contract ($1.650 vs. $1.640) represents a premium or discount which is traceable to a number of factors. This difference between the spot and original fixed forward rate represents the time value of the forward contract.

If the original fixed forward rate is greater than the spot rate at inception of the contract, the contract is said to be at a *premium* (as in the above example). The opposite situation results in a discount. Quoting premiums or discounts (known as forward differentials) relative to the spot rate, rather than forward rates, is common industry practice.

Forward Rates
Employ a Forward Exchange Contract

At a Premium	At a Discount
Forward Rate > Spot Rate	Forward Rate < Spot Rate
(At inception of contract)	(At inception of contract)

At inception, the difference between the forward and spot rates represents a contract expense or contract income to the purchaser of the forward contract. A number of factors influence forward rates and, thus, account for the difference between a forward rate and a spot rate. A primary factor is the interest rate differential between holding an investment in foreign currency and holding an investment in domestic currency over a period of time. It is for this reason that the difference between a forward rate is referred to as the *time value* of the forward contract. For example, if a broker sold a contract to deliver foreign currency in 30 days, the interest differential would be the difference between:

1. The interest earned on investing foreign currency for the 30 days prior to delivery date and
2. The 30 days of interest lost on the domestic currency that was not invested but was used to acquire the foreign currency needed for delivery.

Assume that the spot rate is 1 FC = $0.60 and that you want to determine a 6-month forward rate. Further, assume that the dollar could be invested at 4.5% and the FC could be invested at 7.25%. The forward rate would be calculated as follows:

	U.S. Dollars	Foreign Currency (FC)
Value today	$600.00	1,000 FC
Interest rate	4.5%	7.25%
Six months of interest	$ 13.50	36.25 FC
Value in six months	$613.50	1,036.25 FC

6-month forward rate = $613.50 ÷ 1,036.25 FC = 1 FC = $0.592

The forward rate for a currency can also be derived by the following formula:

$$\text{Forward Rate} = \text{Direct Spot Rate at the Beginning of Period } t \times \frac{1 + \text{ Interest Rate for Domestic Investment During Period } t}{1 + \text{Interest Rate for Foreign Country Investment During Period } t}$$

Using the formula to solve the previous example results in the following, based on six-month interest rates:

$$\text{Forward rate of } \$0.592 = \$0.60 \times \frac{1 + 0.0225}{1 + 0.03625}$$

If the interest yield on the FC is greater than the yield on the U.S. dollar, the forward rate will be less than the spot rate (contract sells at a discount). The forward contract will sell at a premium if the opposite is true. The forward rate based on interest differentials will be slightly different from the quoted forward rate because the quoted rate includes a commission to the foreign currency broker. Furthermore, other factors in addition to interest differentials could be incorporated into the forward rate. These other factors include the volatility of the spot rates, the time period covered by the contract, expectations of future exchange rate changes, and the political and economic environments of a given country.

The student of international accounting should have an understanding of the international monetary system and exchange rates. As previously mentioned, changes in exchange rates represent an additional business risk when transactions are denominated in a foreign currency. The accounting for foreign currency transactions measures this risk and demonstrates the use of both spot and forward rates.

REFLECTION

- The current international monetary system is a floating system in which rates of exchange between currencies change in response to a variety of factors including trade balances, interest rates, money supply, and other economic factors.

- Spot rates represent the current rate of exchange between two currencies. A forward rate represents a future rate of exchange at a future point in time. If the forward rate exceeds the spot rate, the contract is at a premium rather than a discount.

<table>
<tr><td>**3**</td></tr>
<tr><td>**OBJECTIVE**</td></tr>
</table>

Account for a foreign currency transaction, including the measurement of exchange gain or loss.

ACCOUNTING FOR FOREIGN CURRENCY TRANSACTIONS

Assume a U.S. company sells mining equipment to a foreign company and the equipment must be paid for in 30 days with U.S. dollars. This transaction is denominated in dollars and will be measured by the U.S. company in dollars. Changes in the exchange rate between the U.S. dollar and the foreign currency from the transaction date to the settlement date will not expose the U.S. company to any risk of gain or loss from exchange rate changes. Now assume that the same transaction occurs except that the transaction is to be settled in the foreign currency. Because this transaction is denominated in the foreign currency and will be measured by the U.S. company in dollars, changes in the exchange rate subsequent to the transaction date expose the U.S. company to the risk of an exchange rate loss or gain. If the U.S. dollar strengthens, relative to the foreign currency, the U.S. company will experience a loss because it is holding an asset (a receivable of foreign currency) whose price and value have declined. If the dollar weakens, the opposite effect would be experienced. For example, assume the U.S. company sells the mining equipment for 1,000,000 FC when the spot rate is 1 FC = $0.50 and that the dollar subsequently strengthens 10% (1 FC = $0.45).

Time	Spot Rate	Value of Receivable
Originally	1 FC = $0.50	$500,000
Subsequent strengthening	1 FC = $0.45	$450,000
Decline in value of receivable resulting in a loss . .		$ 50,000

Whether a transaction is settled in dollars versus a foreign currency is a matter that is negotiated between the transacting parties and is influenced by a number of factors. For one of the parties, the currency will be a foreign currency; for the other party, the currency will be its domestic currency. A bank wire transfer is generally used to transfer currency between parties in different countries. When a bank wire transfer is used, the owing party instructs its bank to reduce its bank account by the appropriate amount. Its bank, in turn, notifies the receiving party's bank to add a corresponding translated amount to the receiving party's bank account. Therefore, the bank wire transfer, through the use of electronic means, eliminates the need to physically transfer currencies between transacting parties.

To summarize, *changes in exchange rates do not affect transactions that are both denominated and measured in the reporting entity's currency.* Therefore, these transactions require no special accounting treatment. However, if a transaction is denominated in a foreign currency and measured in the reporting entity's currency, changes in the exchange rate between the transaction date and settlement date result in a gain or loss to the reporting entity. These gains or losses are referred to as exchange gains or losses, and their recognition requires special accounting treatment.

Effect of Rate Changes	
No Exchanges Gain or Loss	Exchange Gain or Loss
Transactions are denominated and measured in the reporting entity's currency.	Transactions are denominated in the foreign currency and measured in the reporting entity's currency.

Originally, two methods were proposed for the treatment of exchange gains or losses arising from foreign currency transactions. After considering the merits of these two methods, the FASB adopted the *two-transactions method* which views the initial foreign currency transaction as one transaction. The effect of any subsequent changes in the exchange rates and the resulting exchange gain or loss are viewed as a second transaction. Therefore, the initial transaction is recorded independently of the settlement transaction. This method is consistent with accepted accounting techniques, which normally account for the financing of a transaction as a separate and distinct event. (The required two-transactions method is used in all instances with one exception. The exception relates to a hedge on a foreign currency commitment that is discussed later in this chapter. Therefore, unless otherwise stated, the two-transactions method will be used throughout the chapter.)

In order to illustrate the two-transactions method, assume that a U.S. company sells mining equipment on June 1 of the current year to a foreign company, with the corresponding receivable to be paid or settled on July 1 of the current year. The equipment has a selling price of $306,000 and a cost of $250,000. On June 1, the foreign currency is worth $1.70, and on July 1, the foreign currency is worth $1.60. Illustrations 10-1 and 10-2 present the entries to record the sale of the mining equipment, assuming that the transaction is denominated in dollars ($306,000) and then in foreign currency (180,000 FC = $306,000/$1.70). Note that, when the transaction is denominated in dollars (in Illustration 10-1), the U.S. company does not experience an exchange gain or loss. However, because the foreign company measures the transaction in foreign currency but denominates the transaction in dollars, it experiences an exchange loss. In substance, the value of the foreign company's accounts payable changed because it was denominated in a foreign currency (dollars, in this case), that is, in a currency other than its own. In order to emphasize that the value of certain asset or liability balances is not fixed and will change over time, these changing accounts are identified in **boldface type** throughout the text.

When the transaction is denominated in foreign currency, as in Illustration 10-2, the U.S. company experiences an exchange loss (or gain). The exchange loss (or gain) is accounted for separately from the sales transaction and does not affect the U.S. company's gross profit on the sale. This separately recognized exchange gain or loss is not viewed as an extraordinary item, but should be included in determining income from continuing operations for the period and, if material, should be disclosed in the financial statements or in a note to the statements. Finally, it is important to note in Illustration 10-2 that the foreign company does not experience an exchange gain or loss. This is because the foreign company both measured and denominated the transaction in foreign currency.

Unsettled Foreign Currency Transactions

If a foreign currency transaction is unsettled at year-end, an unrealized gain or loss should be recognized to reflect the change in the exchange rate occurring between the transaction date and the end of the reporting period (e.g., year-end). This treatment focuses on accrual accounting and the fact that exchange gains and losses occur over time rather than only at the date of settlement or payment. Therefore, at any given time the asset or liability arising from a foreign currency transaction that is denominated in a foreign currency *should be measured at its fair value* as suggested by current spot rates. The changes in fair value, both positive and negative, are recognized in current earnings. In essence, the asset or liability is *marked-to-market*.

Illustration 10-1
Transaction Denominated in **Dollars:** Two-Transactions Method

U.S. Company (dollars)			Foreign Company (foreign currency—FC)		
June 1					
Accounts Receivable	306,000		Equipment	180,000*	
Sales Revenue		306,000	**Accounts Payable—FC** . . .		**180,000**
Cost of Goods Sold	250,000				
Inventory		250,000			
July 1					
Cash	306,000		**Accounts Payable—FC**	**180,000**	
Accounts Receivable		306,000	Exchange Loss	11,250	
			Cash		191,250**

Note: The U.S. company experienced no exchange gain or loss because its transaction was both denominated and measured in dollars. However, under the two-transactions method, the foreign company did experience an exchange loss since its transaction was measured in foreign currency and denominated in dollars. The decrease in the value of the foreign currency relative to the U.S. dollar means more foreign currency must be paid to cover the liability.

*$306,000 ÷ $1.70 = 180,000 FC
**$306,000 ÷ $1.60 = 191,250 FC

Illustration 10-2
Transaction Denominated in **Foreign Currency (FC):** Two-Transactions Method

U.S. Company (dollars)			Foreign Company (foreign currency)		
June 1					
Accounts Receivable—FC	**306,000**		Equipment	180,000	
Sales Revenue		306,000	Accounts Payable		180,000
Cost of Goods Sold	250,000				
Inventory		250,000			
July 1					
Cash	288,000*		Accounts Payable	180,000	
Exchange Loss	18,000**		Cash		180,000
Accounts Receivable—FC . .		**306,000**			

Note: The loss is considered to be part of a separate financing decision and unrelated to the original sales transaction.

*The company received 180,000 FC when the exchange rate was 1 FC = $1.60 (180,000 FC × $1.60 = $288,000). Normally, the company would not physically receive FC but would have the dollar equivalent wired to its bank account. Through the use of a bank wire transfer, the foreign company's account would be debited for the number of FC, and the U.S. company's bank account would be credited for the applicable number of dollars, given the exchange rate.
**The decrease in the value of the FC from $1.70 to $1.60 results in an exchange loss to the U.S. company since the FC it received is less valuable than it was at the transaction date [180,000 × ($1.60 − $1.70) = −$18,000].

To illustrate the accounting for unsettled transactions, assume a U.S. company purchases goods from a foreign company on November 1, 2011. The purchase in the amount of 1,000 foreign currencies (FC) is to be paid for on February 1, 2012, in foreign currency. To record or measure the transaction, the domestic company would make the following entry, assuming an exchange rate of 1 FC = $0.50:

Inventory	500	
Accounts Payable—FC		500
Purchase of inventory for 1,000 FC when the exchange rate is 1 FC = $0.50.		

Assuming the exchange rate on the December 31, 2011, year-end is 1 FC = $0.52, the following entry would be necessary:

Exchange Loss [1,000 × ($0.52 − $0.50)]*	20	
Accounts Payable—FC		20
To accrue the exchanges loss on the unperformed portion of the foreign currency transaction when 1 FC = $0.52.		

*The increase in the value of each FC from $0.50 to $0.52 results in a loss to the domestic company since, as of year-end, the company would have to pay out more dollars than originally recorded in order to eliminate the liability.

If the transaction had been settled at year-end, the domestic company would have had to expend $520 to acquire 1,000 FC. Therefore, a loss of $20 is traceable to the unperformed portion of the transaction. Some theorists have suggested that an exchange gain or loss should not be recognized prior to settlement because the gain or loss has not been "realized" through settlement. This position fails to recognize the merits of accrual accounting and is in conflict with the position of the FASB, which requires that the assets or liabilities that are denominated in a foreign currency be measured at fair value with the recognition of resulting unrealized gains or losses being recognized in current earnings.

Finally, assuming an exchange rate of 1 FC = $0.55 on the settlement date (February 1, 2012), the domestic entity would make the following entry to record the settlement:

Accounts Payable—FC ($500 + $20)	520	
Exchange Loss [1,000 × ($0.55 − $0.52)]	30	
Cash		550
To accrue payment of liability for 1,000 FC, when 1 FC = $0.55.		

Note that the company experiences a $50 loss due to changes in the exchange rate. This is allocated between 2011 and 2012 in accordance with accrual accounting.

R E F L E C T I O N

- If a transaction is denominated in a foreign currency, there is exposure to risk associated with exchange rate changes.

- Assets or liabilities that are denominated in foreign currency are to be measured at fair value using spot exchange rates at the date of measurement. In essence, such accounts are marked-to-market. Exchange gains and losses are recorded in current earnings even if not yet realized.

THE EXPOSURE TO FOREIGN CURRENCY EXCHANGE RISK AND THE USE OF DERIVATIVES

4

OBJECTIVE

Identify the contexts in which a company may be exposed to foreign currency exchange risk.

When business transactions are measured in one currency and settled in another currency, one of the transacting parties will be exposed to the exchange rate risk associated with having a transaction denominated in a foreign currency. Companies may be exposed to foreign currency exchange risk in several situations including the following:

1. *An actual existing foreign currency transaction that results in the recognition of assets or liabilities.* As previously illustrated, the risk to be hedged against is the risk that exchange rates may change between the transaction date and the settlement date.

2. *A firm commitment to enter into a foreign currency transaction.* Such a commitment is an agreement between two parties that specifies all significant terms related to the prospective transaction including prices or amounts of consideration stated in foreign currency units. Beginning at the date of the commitment, the risk to be hedged against is the risk that the value of the commitment, which is fixed in a foreign currency amount, could be adversely affected by subsequent changes in exchange rates. For example, a commitment to purchase inventory for a fixed amount of foreign currency could have a value of $100,000 at the commitment date but, due to exchange rate changes, have a value of $110,000 at the transaction date thus resulting in a higher inventory cost than anticipated.

3. *A forecasted foreign currency transaction that has a high probability of occurrence.* Such a forecasted transaction, unlike a commitment or an existing transaction, does not provide an entity with any present rights or obligations and does not have any fixed prices or rates. Because fixed prices or rates are not present, an entity is exposed to the risk that future cash flows may vary due to changes in prices and exchange rates. The risk being hedged against is the risk associated with exchange rate changes. For example, if a manufacturer forecasted needing raw materials to meet future production, even if material prices to be paid in foreign currency did not change in the future, the dollar equivalent cash flows associated with the forecasted purchase could change over time due to changes in exchange rates.

4. *An investment in a foreign subsidiary.* Translating the financial statements of a foreign subsidiary expressed in foreign currency into the domestic currency of the investor entity can affect the equity of the investor entity. The risk being hedged against is the risk that the translation will reduce the investor's equity due to adverse changes in exchange rates. Such a hedge is known as a *hedge of a net investment.*

The risk associated with (4) above will be discussed in the next chapter. However, the risk associated with the first three situations above is traceable to the risk of changes in exchange rates over the time periods prior to when payment is made on a transaction as shown in the following illustration:

Situation 3	Situation 2	Situation 1	
Company forecasts a transaction	Company commits to a transaction	Transaction occurs	Payment is made on the transaction

Characteristics of Derivatives

5

OBJECTIVE

Understand the characteristics of derivatives and the common types used to hedge foreign currency exchange rate risk.

As stated, a company can be exposed to the risk associated with changes in currency exchange rates in a number of contexts. Common strategies to hedge against such risks involve the use of derivative financial instruments. A financial instrument represents a right, through a contractual agreement between two opposite parties called *counterparties*, to receive or deliver cash or another financial instrument on potentially favorable or unfavorable terms. Financial instruments include cash, equity and debt investments, and derivatives. A derivative is a type of financial instrument that has several distinguishing characteristics that have been set forth by the FASB. These are the characteristics of a derivative.

1. It derives its value from changes in the rate or price of a related asset or liability. The rate or price is known as an underlying.

2. The quantity or number of units specified by a derivative is known as the notional amount.

3. It requires little or no initial investment upon inception.

4. It allows for net settlement in that the derivative contract can be settled in exchange for cash, without having to actually buy or sell the related asset or liability.

A critical characteristic of a derivative and the basis for its name is that the instrument derives its value from changes in the value of a related asset or liability. The rates or prices that relate to the asset or liability underlying the derivative are referred to as *underlyings*. The underlying may take a variety of forms, including a commodity price, stock price, foreign currency exchange rate, or interest rate. **It is important to note that the underlying is not the asset or liability itself, but rather its price or rate**. For example, the underlying in a forward contract is not the foreign currency itself but rather the currency exchange rate. Changes in the underlying price or rate cause the value of the derivative to change. For example, if the forward exchange rate underlies the value of the forward contract, an increase in the forward rate will cause a forward contract to buy foreign currency to increase in value.

In order to fully value a derivative, one must know the number of units (quantity) that is specified in the derivative instrument. This is called the *notional amount*, and it determines the total dollar value of a derivative, traceable to movement or changes in the underlying. For example, if the forward contract to buy foreign currency increases in value, the total magnitude of this increase in value depends on how many foreign currency units, for example 100,000 units, can be sold under the terms of the contract. **Both the underlying price or rate and the notional amount are necessary in order to determine the total value of a derivative at any point in time.**

Typically, a derivative requires little or no initial investment because it is an investment in a change in value traceable to an underlying, rather than an investment in the actual asset or liability to which the underlying relates. The holder of a forward contract to buy foreign currency to be used at a future date involves no initial investment, whereas the holder of actual foreign currency to be used at a future date has already made an investment in the currency.

Many derivatives do not require the parties to the contract, the counterparties, to actually deliver an asset that is associated with the underlying in order to realize the value of a derivative. For example, the holder of a forward contract to buy foreign currency could sell the contract. The ability to settle the contract in exchange for cash, without actually buying or selling the related asset or liability, is referred to as *net settlement*.

Common Types of Derivatives

The number of financial instruments that have the characteristics of a derivative has continued to expand, and, in turn, these instruments have become increasingly complex. However, within the context of hedging the risk associated with foreign currency exchange rate risk, two common types of derivatives are forward contracts and options (the use of foreign currency swaps are beyond the scope of this chapter).

Foreign Currency Forward Contract. A *foreign currency forward contract* is an executory contract to buy or sell a specified amount of foreign currency, at a specified fixed rate with delivery at a specified future point in time. The party that agrees to sell the asset is said to be in a *short position*, and the party that agrees to buy the asset is said to be in a *long position*. The specified fixed rate in the contract is known as a *forward rate*. The specified future date is referred to as the *forward date*. Forward contracts are not formally regulated on an organized exchange, and the parties are exposed to a risk that default of the contract could occur. However, the lack of formal regulation means that such contracts can be customized in response to specialized needs regarding notional amounts and forward dates.

The value of a forward contract is zero at inception and typically does not require an initial cash outlay. However, over time, movement in the rate of the underlying results in a change in value of the forward contract. **The total change in the value of a forward contract is measured as the difference between the forward rate and the spot rate at the forward date**. For example, on April 1, a party (called the *writer*) writes a contract in which she/he agrees to sell (short position) to another party (called the *holder*) who agrees to buy (long position) 1,000,000 FC (for example, euros) at a specific price of $0.16 per FC with delivery in 90 days (June 29). The relationship between the parties is as shown on page 554.

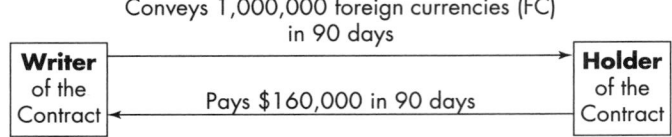

If the spot rate at the end of the forward period is $0.18, the total change in value is determined as follows:

1,000,000 FC at a forward rate (on April 1) of $0.16 (1,000,000 × $0.16)	$160,000
1,000,000 FC at a spot rate (on June 29) of $0.18 (1,000,000 × $0.18)	180,000
Gain in value to holder	$ 20,000

This is a gain because on June 29 the holder received something with a fair value greater than the fair value given up that day. (Conversely, this would be a loss to the writer.) The holder of the forward contract could buy foreign currencies for $160,000 on the forward date compared to the spot value of $180,000 at that time and experience an immediate $20,000 gain. It is important to note that the value of the currency at the final spot rate could have been less than $160,000. In that case, the holder would have experienced a loss and the writer a gain. When the value of a derivative can change in both directions (gain or loss), it is said to have a *symmetric return profile*. It is also important to note that in the case of a forward contract, if the holder of the contract experiences a gain (loss) in value, then the writer of the contract simultaneously experiences a loss (gain) in value.

The forward rate is a function of a number of variables and as these variables change over the life of the contract, the value of the forward contract also changes. Also, because the forward rates represent values in the future, the current value is represented by the present value of the future rates. Continuing with the example involving foreign currencies, assume the following forward rate information throughout the 90-day term of the contract:

Remaining Term of Contract	Forward Rate	Notional Amount	Total Forward Value	Cumulative Change in Forward Value
90 days	$0.160	1,000,000	$160,000	
60 days	0.170	1,000,000	170,000	$10,000
30 days	0.170	1,000,000	170,000	10,000
0 days	0.180	1,000,000	180,000	20,000

Assuming a 6% discount rate, the change in value of the forward contract over time is as follows:

	60 Days Remaining	30 Days Remaining	Total Life of Contract
Cumulative change in forward value	$10,000	$10,000	$20,000
Present value of cumulative change:			
60 days at 6%	$ 9,901		
30 days at 6%		$ 9,950	
0 days at 6%			$20,000
Previously recognized gain or loss.	0	(9,901)	(9,950)
Current period gain or loss	$ 9,901	$ 49	$10,050

Note that the total change in the value of the forward contract is $20,000 ($9,901 + $49 + $10,050), which is recognized over the term of the contract as the net present value of changes in the forward rates. Even if the forward rates did not change between two valuation dates (as is the case here between 60 and 30 days), the value of the contract would change because the remaining term of the forward contract continues to decrease and the present value of the forward value increases. *Also, note that the stated forward rate at the expiration date of the contract is equal to the spot rate at that date.* This is due to the fact that at expiration of the contract the forward date is the same as the current date.

Foreign Currency Option. A *foreign currency option* represents a right, rather than an obligation, to either buy or sell some quantity of a particular foreign currency. The option is valid for a specified period of time and calls for a specified buy or sell rate or price, referred to as the *strike price* or *exercise price.* If an option allows the holder to *buy* an underlying, it is referred to as a *call option.* An option that allows the holder to *sell* an underlying is referred to as a *put option.* Options are actively traded on organized exchanges or may be negotiated on a case-by-case basis between counterparties (over-the-counter contracts). Option contracts require the holder to make an initial nonrefundable cash outlay, known as the *premium,* as represented by the option's current value. The premium is paid, in part, because the writer of the option takes more risk than the holder of the option. The holder can allow the option to expire, while the writer must comply if the holder chooses to exercise it.

During the option period, the strike price of the option on the underlying is generally different from the current value of an underlying. The following terms are used to describe the relationship between the strike price and the current price (note that the premium is not considered in these relationships):

Option Type	Strike Price Is Equal to Current Price	Strike Price Is Greater Than Current Price	Strike Price Is Less Than Current Price
Call (buy) option	At-the-money	Out-of-the-money	In-the-money
Put (sell) option	At-the-money	In-the-money	Out-of-the-money

As the above table suggests, in-the-money is a favorable condition as compared to being out-of-the-money, which is an unfavorable condition. The original premium is not considered when describing whether an option is or is not in-the-money. However, it is important to note that the original premium certainly is considered when determining whether an investment in an option has experienced an overall profit. The holder of an option has a right, rather than an obligation, and will not exercise the option unless it is in-the-money. In that case, the holder will experience a gain, and the writer will experience a loss. However, if the option is not in-the-money, the option will not be exercised, the holder will limit her/his loss to the amount of the option premium, and the writer will limit her/his gain to the amount of the premium. Therefore, in theory, the opportunities for gain and loss are characterized as follows:

	Potential for	
	Gain	Loss
Holder of option	Unlimited	Limited to amount of premium
Writer of option	Limited to amount of premium	Unlimited

Because the counterparties do not have equal opportunity for both upside and downside changes in value, options are said to have an *asymmetric* or one-sided return profile.

Options are traded on an organized exchange and over the counter; therefore, their current value is quoted in terms of present dollars on a frequent basis. The current value of an option depends on forward periods and spot prices. The difference between the strike and spot prices, at any point in time, measures the intrinsic value of the option, so changes in spot prices will change the intrinsic value of the option. Changes in the length of the remaining forward period will affect the time value of the option. The time value is measured as the difference between an option's current value and its intrinsic value as in the following illustration:

◆ If the option is in-the-money, the option has intrinsic value. For example, if an investor has a 90-day call (buy) option to buy 100,000 FC at a strike price of $1.10 per FC and the current spot rate is $1.12 FC, the option is in-the-money and has an intrinsic value of $2,000 (100,000 × $0.02). An option that is out-of-the-money or at-the-money has no intrinsic value.

◆ The difference between the current value of an option and its intrinsic value represents time value. For example, if the 90-day call (buy) option has a current value of $2,200 and an intrinsic value of $2,000, the time value component is $200 (the current value of $2,200, less the intrinsic value of $2,000). The time value of an option represents a discounting factor and a volatility factor.

◆ The discounting factor relates to the fact that the strike price does not have to be paid currently, but rather at the time of exercise. Therefore, the holder of an option to buy FC could benefit from an appreciation in the value of FC without actually having to currently pay out the cash to purchase the FC. Thus, the ability to have the alternative use of the cash equal to the strike price until exercise date of the option has value and is a component of the time value.

◆ The volatility factor relates to the volatility of the underlying relative to the fixed strike price and reflects the potential for gain on the hedge option. Underlyings with more price volatility present greater opportunities for gains if the option is in-the-money. Therefore, higher volatility increases the value of an option and this is a component of the time value. Note that volatility could also lead to an out-of the-money situation. However, this possibility can be disregarded because, unlike forward contracts, the risk for an option is asymmetric since the holder can avoid unfavorable outcomes by allowing the option to expire.

To illustrate the value components of an option, assume that a put (sell) option allows for the sale of 100,000 FC in 60 days at a strike or exercise price of $0.50 per FC. The value of the option would consist of the following:

	Initial Date of Purchase	End of 30 Days	End of 60 Days
Value of 100,000 FC at the current spot rate	$51,000	$49,000	$48,000
Assumed total value of option	$ 1,300	$ 1,650	$ 2,000
Intrinsic value (never less than zero)	0 (option is out-of-the-money)	1,000 [in-the-money ($50,000 vs. $49,000)]	2,000 [in-the-money ($50,000 vs. $48,000)]
Time value (total value less intrinsic value)	$ 1,300	$ 650	$ 0

R E F L E C T I O N

• Derivatives have a number of characteristics including: value derived from a change in the rate or price of a related asset or liability, a notional amount, little or no initial investment, and allowance for net settlement.

• Common types of derivatives include a foreign currency forward contract and a foreign currency option.

ACCOUNTING FOR DERIVATIVES THAT ARE DESIGNATED AS A HEDGE

As previously discussed, transactions that are denominated in a foreign currency and measured in an entity's domestic currency are exposed to risk associated with exchange rate changes. In turn, the rate changes result in exchange gains or losses associated with the related asset or liability denominated in foreign currency. Derivative instruments can be used to hedge against the exchange risk associated with these transactions. If the asset or liability (the hedged item) experiences an unfavorable change in value, a properly structured hedge (the hedging instrument) could be effective in providing a change in value in the opposite direction such that there is no adverse effect. If a derivative is properly structured for this purpose, it seems that the change in the value of the derivative (the hedging instrument) should be recognized in the same accounting period as is the change in the value of the related asset or liability (the hedged item). Hedges are generally designated as either *fair value* or *cash flow*. A **fair value hedge** is used to offset changes in the fair value of items with fixed exchange prices or rates. Fair value hedges include hedges against a change in the fair value of:

◆ A recognized foreign-currency-denominated asset or liability.

◆ An unrecognized foreign currency firm commitment.

A **cash flow hedge** is used to establish fixed prices or rates when future cash flows could vary due to changes in prices or rates. Cash flow hedges include hedges against the change in cash flows associated with:

◆ A forecasted foreign currency transaction.

◆ The forecasted functional-currency-equivalent cash flows associated with a recognized asset or liability.

◆ An unrecognized foreign currency firm commitment.

Special Accounting for Fair Value Hedges

The hedged item in a fair value hedge is either a recognized asset or liability or a firm commitment. Recognized assets or liabilities in a fair value hedge result from actual past transactions such as a purchase of inventory denominated in foreign currency. Commitments relate to transactions that have not yet occurred, such as a contract to purchase inventory denominated in foreign currency. A commitment is a binding agreement between two parties that specifies all significant terms related to the prospective transaction. Such terms include the quantity to be exchanged, the timing of the transaction, and a fixed price (e.g., the number of foreign currency units). The agreement also includes a large enough disincentive to make performance of the contract probable.

Because the number of foreign currency units in an existing transaction or a firm commitment is fixed, subsequent changes in currency exchange rates affect the value of a recognized asset, liability, or commitment. For example, if an entity has purchased inventory and has a recognized accounts payable to be settled in FC, changes in exchange rates will change the value of the payable. Similarly, if an entity has a firm commitment to purchase inventory, changes in the exchange rates will change the value of the commitment.

Many accounting principles do not allow for the recognition in current earnings of both increases and decreases in the value of recognized assets, liabilities, or firm commitments. However, if the risk of such changes in value is covered by a fair value hedge, special accounting treatment is allowed that provides for the recognition of such changes in earnings. In a qualifying fair value hedge, the gain or loss on the derivative hedging instrument and the offsetting loss or gain on the hedged item are both recognized currently in earnings. For instance, assume a recognized account payable is to be settled in FC. If the domestic currency weakens relative to the FC, it will require more domestic currency to settle the account payable than previously thought, resulting in an exchange loss. If the payable is hedged, both the exchange loss on the payable and the change in the value of the derivative instrument used as a hedge are recognized in earnings.

In order to qualify for special fair value hedge accounting, the derivative hedging instrument and the hedged item must satisfy a number of criteria. A critical criterion is that an entity must have formal documentation of the hedging relationship and the entity's risk-management objective and strategy. The entity must indicate the reason for undertaking the designated hedge, identify the hedged item and the derivative hedging instrument, and explain the nature of the risk being hedged. This criterion must be satisfied at inception and cannot be retroactively applied after an entity has determined whether hedging would be appropriate. Another important criterion is that the hedging relationship must be assessed both at inception and on an ongoing basis to determine if it is highly effective in offsetting the identified risks. Generally speaking, a hedge would be totally effective if the terms (such as notional amount, maturity dates, quality/condition, delivery locations, etc.) of the hedging instrument and the hedged item are the same. This approach is known as *critical terms analysis*. It is important to note that in practice the terms of a derivative do not always align with the terms of the related asset or liability, and, therefore, other approaches to assessing effectiveness must be employed. Management must also describe how it will assess hedge effectiveness. Generally, hedge ineffectiveness is the difference between the gains or losses on the derivative and the hedged item.

Assuming the necessary criteria are satisfied for treatment as a fair value hedge, the hedge will qualify for special accounting treatment. The gain or loss on the derivative hedging instrument will be recognized currently in earnings, along with the change in value on the hedged item, and an appropriate adjustment to the basis of the hedged item will be recorded. If the cumulative change in the value of the derivative instrument does not exactly offset the cumulative change in the value of the hedged item, the difference is recognized currently in earnings. Because both hedge effectiveness and hedge ineffectiveness are recognized currently in earnings, it is not necessary to separately account for that portion of the hedge which is considered to be ineffective.

IASB PERSPECTIVES

IASB *standards*

As part of the IASB's financial instruments project, an Exposure Draft on hedge accounting was issued in the fall of 2010 with the adoption of IFRS scheduled for the second quarter of 2011. As set forth in the Derivative Module, the IASB is proposing several changes that will impact the accounting for derivatives including those used to hedge the risk associated with exchange rate changes. In a later section of this chapter, another IASB Perspective illustrates one of the major proposals impacting the accounting for fair value hedges.

Special Accounting for Cash Flow Hedges

The hedged item in a cash flow hedge is one in which future cash flows could be affected due to a particular risk such as the change in foreign currency exchange rates. A forecasted transaction is well suited to the use of a cash flow hedge. Because fixed prices or rates are not present in a forecasted transaction, an entity is exposed to the risk that future cash flows may vary due to changes in prices/rates. For example, if an entity forecasted purchasing raw materials from a foreign vendor with the invoice payable in FC, the cash flows needed to acquire the materials could change because the price of the materials could change between the forecast date and the purchase date. However, even if that did not occur, the necessary cash flows could also be affected because of changes in the exchange rate between the foreign and domestic currencies. Another application of a cash flow hedge could involve an existing liability, denominated in FC, which bears interest at a variable rate of interest. The cash flows associated with interest could be affected due to not only the variability of interest rates but also changes in the exchange rate.

A nonderivative financial instrument may not be used as the hedging instrument in a foreign currency cash flow hedge. Furthermore, as is the case with a fair value hedge, special hedge accounting is not available for a cash flow hedge unless a number of criteria are satisfied. Cash flow hedges must also meet the criteria regarding documentation and assessment of effectiveness. If the derivative instrument and the hedged item satisfy the criteria, then the cash flow hedge will qualify for special accounting. The effective portion of the gain or loss on the derivative instrument will be reported in *other comprehensive income (OCI)*, and the ineffective portion, if any, will be recognized currently in earnings.[1] As with fair value hedges, a portion of the derivative instrument's gain or loss may be excluded from the assessment of effectiveness. That portion of the gain or loss will be recognized currently in earnings rather than as a component of other comprehensive income. The amounts reported in OCI will be reclassified into recognized earnings in the same period in which the hedged item affects earnings. For example, assume that a forecasted sale of inventory is hedged. Once the inventory is sold and recognized in earnings, the applicable amount, the OCI gain or loss, will also be recognized in earnings. If the forecasted transaction were a purchase of a depreciable asset, the applicable portion of the OCI would be recognized in earnings when the asset's depreciation expense is recognized.

REFLECTION

- Hedges are generally designated as either fair value or cash flow hedges.

- The hedged item in a fair value hedge is either a recognized asset or liability or a firm commitment. The value of the hedged item changes over time and such changes in value are recognized currently in earnings.

- The hedged item in a cash flow hedge is either a forecasted foreign currency transaction, forecasted cash flows associated with a recognized asset or liability, or an unrecognized foreign currency commitment. The effective portion of the gain or loss on the derivative instrument will be reported in other comprehensive income and subsequently reclassified into earnings.

EXAMPLES OF THE ACCOUNTING FOR FAIR VALUE HEDGES

As previously stated, fair value hedges may be used to hedge against changes in the fair value of either a recognized foreign-currency-denominated asset or liability or an unrecognized foreign currency firm commitment. Assuming the necessary criteria are satisfied, the fair value hedge will be given special accounting treatment. This special treatment allows for the recognition in current earnings of both the gain or loss on the derivative hedging instrument and the offsetting loss or gain on the hedged item.

Hedging an Existing Foreign-Currency-Denominated Asset or Liability

The gain or loss associated with the foreign currency exposure of a recognized, foreign-currency-denominated asset or liability as measured by changes in the spot rate is generally recognized in earnings. However, this recognition does not prevent such exposed positions from being hedged with a fair value hedge. It is important to note that only derivative instruments can be designated as a hedge of a foreign-currency-denominated asset or liability.

Illustration of Hedging with a Forward Contract. Assume that a U.S. company purchases inventory from a foreign vendor with subsequent payment due in FC, a foreign-currency-denominated liability, and that the company acquires a forward contract to buy FC. If prior to settlement, the dollar weakens relative to the FC, the accounts payable will increase in value resulting in an exchange loss. However, the forward contract to buy FC (an asset) will increase in value if the dollar weakens.

6

OBJECTIVE

Explain the accounting treatment given various types of foreign currency hedges.

---

1 Other comprehensive income is not included in the income statement; it bypasses the traditional income statement but is shown as a component of equity.

Additional information supporting this illustration is as follows:

1. On November 1, 2011, the company bought inventory from a foreign vendor with payment due on February 1, 2012, in the amount of 100,000 FC.
2. On November 1, 2011, the company purchased a forward contract to buy 100,000 FC on February 1, 2012, at a forward rate of 1 FC = $0.506.
3. Selected spot and forward rates are as follows:

Date	Spot Rate	Forward Rate for Remaining Term of Contract
November 1, 2011	1 FC = $0.500	1 FC = $0.506
December 31, 2011	1 FC = 0.520	1 FC = 0.530
February 1, 2012	1 FC = 0.550	1 FC = 0.550

4. Changes in the value of the forward contract are to be discounted at a 6% rate.
5. Changes in the value of the forward contract over time are as follows:

	November 1— 90 Days Remaining	December 31— 30 Days Remaining	Transaction Date
Number of FC	100,000	100,000	100,000
Spot rate — 1 FC	$0.500	$0.520	$0.550
Forward rate for remaining time — 1 FC	$0.506	$0.530	$0.550
Initial forward rate — 1 FC		$0.506	$0.506
Fair value of forward contract:			
Original forward value		$50,600	$50,600
Current forward value		53,000	55,000
Change—gain (loss) in forward value		$ 2,400	$ 4,400
Present value of change:			
$n = 1, i = 6\%/12$		$ 2,388	
$n = 0, i = 6\%/12$			$ 4,400
Change in value from prior period:			
Current present value		$ 2,388	$ 4,400
Prior present value		0	2,388
Change in present value		$ 2,388	$ 2,012

Illustration 10-3 presents the entries to record the foreign currency transaction and the related forward contract. Once again, in order to emphasize that the value of certain account balances is not fixed and will change over time, these accounts are identified in boldface type.

Illustration 10-3
Hedging a Foreign-Currency-Denominated Liability

Relating to the Purchase of Inventory			Relating to the Forward Contract		
November 1, 2011					
Inventory	50,000		Memo: Company acquires a forward		
Accounts Payable—FC		50,000	contract to buy 100,000 FC at a forward		
Purchase of inventory			rate of 1 FC = $0.506.[a]		
for 100,000 FC when					
1 FC = $0.500.					
December 31, 2011					
Exchange Loss	2,000		**Forward Contract**	2,388	
Accounts Payable—FC		2,000	Gain on Contract		2,388
To accrue the exchange loss on			To record change in the value		
the FC denominated payable			of the forward contract.		
when the spot rate is $0.520.					
			Note that the above entry includes the entire		
			change in the value of the contract including both		
			the effective and ineffective portion of the		
			contract.		
February 1, 2012					
Accounts Payable—FC	52,000		**Forward Contract**	2,012	
Exchange Loss	3,000		Gain on Contract		2,012
Foreign Currency		55,000	To record change in value		
To record settlement			of the forward contract.		
of the liability when					
1 FC = $0.550.					
			Foreign Currency[b]	55,000	
			Forward Contract Receivable		4,400
			Cash		50,600
			To record settlement of contract.		

[a]Noting the executory nature of the contract, a memo entry is made to describe the derivative.
[b]Generally, the company would not physically receive the foreign currency. Instead, a bank wire transfer would be used to settle the transaction. The currency broker would debit the domestic company's bank account for the necessary number of dollars and credit the foreign company's bank account for the necessary number of foreign currencies.

To summarize, the accounting for the hedge of a foreign-currency-denominated asset or liability is characterized as follows:

1. The accounting for the hedging instrument is separate from the accounting for the foreign-currency-denominated asset or liability.
2. The hedging instrument will be carried at fair value, and changes in value over time will be recognized as an unrealized gain or loss and be reported in earnings.

3. The change in value of the hedging instrument consists of a change in the instrument's intrinsic value and its time value. The total change in value of the instrument, including both hedge effectiveness and hedge ineffectiveness, is reported currently in earnings.

4. Changes in the value of the hedging instrument should be accrued at the end of a reporting period.

5. The gains (losses) on the hedging instrument will offset or net against the losses (gains) on the foreign currency transaction (the hedged item).

6. A hedge would be fully effective or "perfect" if the critical terms (nature of the underlying, notional amount, delivery dates, settlement date, type of currency, etc.) of the hedging instrument matched the terms of the hedged item. In a perfect hedge, the net offset amount will merely equal the change in the time value of the hedging instrument.

7. In the case of a forward contract, technically there is no need to record the contract at inception because it is an executory contract. In reality, most companies follow this no recording practice but do keep supporting schedules detailing contracts. Even if this practice is followed, the forward contract is marked-to-market in order to reflect changes in the value of the underlying foreign currency. These changes in fair value are recorded by the company. Note, however, that the forward contract receivable and forward contract payable accounts will be netted against each other for presentation purposes. This netting results in balance sheet amounts equal to those that would have existed if no entry had been made at inception to record the hedging instrument.

The hedge accounted for in Illustration 10-3 was effective in that the losses associated with the changing value of the FC-denominated account payable were offset by the positive changes in the value of the forward contract. Instead of a $5,000 exchange loss, the company incurred only a $600 loss, which represents the premium on the forward rate of $0.506 versus the spot rate of $0.500 on the inception date of the forward contract (100,000 FC × ($0.506 − $0.500). The net loss of $600 consists of the $5,000 exchange loss ($2,000 + $3,000) offset by the gain on the derivative of $4,400 ($2,388 + $2,012). The $600 loss is the ineffective portion of the hedge. If financial statements were presented on December 31, 2011, the purchase and hedge would be reported as follows:

Income Statement		Balance Sheet	
		Assets:	
Exchange loss	$(2,000)	Inventory	$50,000
Unrealized gain on contract	2,388	Forward contract	$ 2,388
Net gain	$ 388		
		Liabilities:	
		Accounts payable—FC	$52,000

The overall effect of the hedge presented in Illustration 10-3 is summarized as follows:

	Without the Hedge	With the Hedge
Exchange gain (loss) on foreign-currency-denominated asset or liability [100,000 FC × ($0.550 − $0.500)]	$(5,000)	$(5,000)
Gain on forward contract [100,000 FC × ($0.550 − $0.506)]		
Effective portion of hedge.........$5,000		
Ineffective portion of hedge....... (600)		4,400
Net income effect	$(5,000)	$ (600)

The net effect on income represents the original premium on the forward contract of $600 [100,000 × (forward rate of $0.506 versus original spot rate of $0.500)].

It is important to note that a hedge may also eliminate exchange gains associated with a foreign-currency-denominated asset or liability. For instance, when a forward contract establishes a forward rate, it is possible that changes in the spot rate may not move in the same direction or may not move as much as had been expected. Considering the previous transactions, assume the same facts except that the spot rates are as follows:

Date	Spot Rate
November 1, 2011	1 FC = $0.50
December 31, 2011	1 FC = $0.49
February 1, 2012	1 FC = $0.48

In effect, the hedge eliminated potential exchange gains, and the company paid the same $600 premium for the forward contract:

	Without the Hedge	With the Hedge
Exchange gain (loss) on foreign currency transaction [100,000 FC × ($0.480 − $0.500)]	$2,000	$ 2,000
Loss on forward contract [100,000 FC × ($0.480 − $0.506)]:		
Effective portion of hedge..........$(2,000)		
Ineffective portion of hedge........ (600)		(2,600)
Net income effect	$2,000	$ (600)

Although this hedge had a negative impact on earnings, it did eliminate the uncertainty associated with exchange rate risk. By entering into a forward contract on the date of the transaction, the company established a known payment amount of $50,600. Illustration 10-3 involved the use of a forward contract to buy FC in order to settle the FC-denominated accounts payable. A forward contract may also be used to sell FC when an FC-denominated receivable is settled. For example, if a U.S. company sold inventory to a foreign customer and the resulting account receivable was denominated in FC, the company would receive FC. The company could acquire a forward contract to sell FC upon receipt from the foreign customer. If the dollar strengthened relative to the FC, the U.S. company's receivable would decrease in value. However, a forward contract to sell FC in this scenario would increase in value and serve as a hedge against the losses on the receivable.

Illustration of Hedging with a Foreign Currency Option. Assume that a U.S. company sold inventory to a foreign customer with subsequent collection due in FC, a foreign-currency-denominated asset, and that the company acquired a put option to sell FC.

Additional information supporting this illustration is as follows:

1. On November 1, 2011, the company sold inventory, with a cost of $32,000, to a foreign customer with payment due on February 1, 2012, in the amount of 100,000 FC.

2. On November 1, 2011, the company purchased an out-of-the-money put option to sell 100,000 FC on February 1, 2012, at a strike price of 1 FC = $0.510. An option premium of $400 was paid.

3. Spot rates, option values, and changes in value over time are as follows:

	November 1, 2011	December 31, 2011	February 1, 2012
Strike price 1 FC	$0.510	$0.510	$0.510
Spot rate 1 FC	$0.515	$0.498	$0.495
Fair value of options	$ 400	$1,300	$1,500
Intrinsic value of option	0	1,200	1,500
Time value of option	$ 400	$ 100	$ 0

Illustration 10-4 presents the entries to record the foreign currency transaction and the related option. Once again, in order to emphasize that the value of certain account balances is not fixed and will change over time, these accounts are identified in boldface type.

Illustration 10-4
Hedging a Foreign-Currency-Denominated Asset

Relating to the Sale of Inventory			Relating to the Put Option		
November 1, 2011					
Accounts Receivable—FC . . .	51,500		Investment in Put Option.	400	
Sales Revenue		51,500	Cash.		400
			To record purchase of option.		
Cost of Sales	32,000				
Inventory		32,000			
To record sale of inventory.					
December 31, 2011					
Exchange Loss	1,700		**Investment in Put Option**	900	
Accounts Receivable—FC . . .		1,700	Gain on Option		900
To accrue the exchange loss on			To record change in the value		
the FC-denominated receivable			of the put option.		
when the spot rate is $0.498.					
			Note that the above entry includes the entire		
			change in the value of the option including both		
			the effective (intrinsic value) and ineffective		
			(time value) portion.		
February 1, 2012					
Foreign Currency.	49,500		Investment in Put Option	200	
Exchange Loss	300		Gain on Option		200
Accounts Receivable—FC . . .		49,800	To record change in the value		
To record settlement			of the put option.		
of the receivable when					
1 FC = $0.495.					
			Cash	51,000	
			Foreign Currency.		49,500
			Investment in Put Option.		1,500
			To record settlement of the option.		

The overall effect of the hedge presented in Illustration 10-4 is summarized as follows:

	Without the Hedge	With the Hedge
Exchange gain (loss) on foreign-currency-denominated asset or liability [100,000 FC × ($0.515 − $0.495)]	$(2,000)	$(2,000)
Gain on option ($1,500 − $400).		1,100
Net income effect	$(2,000)	$ (900)

As a result of the hedge, the net effect on income represents two components: (a) the fact that the option's intrinsic value of $1,500 only offsets $2,000 of the exchange loss on the receivable (traceable to the fact that the option was originally out-of-the-money) and (b) the $400 cost of the original premium on the option.

Special Hedging Complications

The previous examples assumed that the term of the hedging instrument covered the same period of time as the settlement period, which is defined as the period of time between the transaction date and the settlement date of the foreign-currency-denominated asset or liability. However, it is possible that a hedging instrument could cover a period of time different from the settlement period. The previous examples also assumed that the hedging instrument was for the same number of foreign currency units as required by the foreign currency transaction. It also is possible that a hedging instrument could be for a number of foreign currency units different from the number of units required by the transaction.

Hedging Instrument Expires Before Settlement Date. Prior to the expiration date of a hedging instrument, it is possible for the holder of the contract to settle the contract in exchange for cash. Net settlement is a characteristic of all derivatives such as a forward contract. However, if the contract expires before the settlement date of the underlying hedged transaction, the holder of the hedging instrument has several alternatives for dealing with the contract. For example, assuming that a forward contract to sell foreign currency expires before the customer remits the foreign currency, the seller may: (a) roll over the forward contract, (b) purchase the necessary foreign currency to satisfy the contract and acquire a new forward contract to sell the foreign currency when the customer pays, or (c) simply purchase the necessary foreign currency to satisfy the contract and deal with the foreign currency when it is received.

Transactions and hedging instruments may be settled on different dates. For example, some currency brokers will extend a forward contract for a short time at the original forward rate as a courtesy to their clients. However, if settlement is not expected soon, the original contract may be rolled over into a new contract to settle on the anticipated date of payment. Rather than rolling over a forward contract, the needed FC can be purchased to settle the forward contract. When the hedged transaction is ultimately settled, the FC received could then be sold at the spot rate. Obviously, this route creates exposure to the risk that spot rates will change between the time of purchasing FC and receiving FC from the customer. In order to avoid this exposure, a new forward contract to sell FC could be employed.

Hedging Instrument Expires After Settlement Date. Hedging instruments can also expire after the settlement date. For example, suppose a customer paying in foreign currency accelerates the payment date in order to improve his/her current ratio. Assuming the seller has hedged the transaction with a forward contract, they once again have several options: (a) hold the foreign currency until the date of the original forward contract, (b) roll the contract back and sell the foreign currency immediately, (c) sell the foreign currency immediately and sell the forward contract to another party, and (d) sell the foreign currency immediately and acquire FC at the spot rate when the forward contract is settled. Alternative (d) results in a speculative position. (There is no hedged transaction, and it is discouraged by many company policy statements.) If a forward contract expires after the settlement date, any gain or loss that accrues on the forward contract after the transaction settlement date is recognized as a component of current operating income.

Hedging Instrument's Notional Amount Different from Transaction Amount. If a hedging instrument is for a smaller number of foreign currency units than the foreign currency transaction, the contract gain or loss is recognized as a partial hedge on the exposed position. However, if the forward contract is for a greater number of foreign currency units than the exposed asset or liability position, special treatment is required. That portion of the hedging instrument which exceeds the exposed position is considered to be a speculative hedge and is accounted for as an investment. The gain or loss on that portion of the contract which exceeds the exposed position is accordingly accounted for as an investment gain or loss.

Hedging an Identifiable Foreign Currency Firm Commitment

An identifiable firm commitment is a binding agreement between two parties that specifies all significant terms related to a yet-to-be-executed transaction. If the commitment requires ultimate settlement in a fixed amount of FC, then exposure to exchange rate risk exists. Because the terms and prices of the commitment in FC are fixed, changes in FC exchange rates affect the value of the commitment or the cash flows associated with the commitment. For example, assume a commitment to buy inventory in 60 days for 500,000 FC. If at the date of the commitment the spot rate is 1 FC = $0.250 and the 60-day forward rate is 1 FC = $0.258, changes in these rates could be used to suggest the change in the relative dollar value of the commitment. If 30 days after the commitment date the spot rate is 1 FC = $0.254 and the remaining 30-day forward rate is 1 FC = $0.264, it would appear that the commitment has lost value. Clearly, it appears that the commitment will require more dollars to settle than previously estimated. Using spot rates to suggest that the commitment has lost value, consider the following:

Number of dollars needed to satisfy commitment at commitment date equals	$125,000 (500,000 FC × $0.250)
Number of dollars needed to satisfy commitment 30 days later equals	$127,000 (500,000 FC × $0.254)

As suggested above, given changes in the spot rate it will take more U.S. dollars to satisfy the commitment than anticipated; therefore, the commitment has lost value. Furthermore, because the commitment terms (e.g., pay 500,000 FC) are fixed, the commitment cannot be renegotiated to take into consideration the fact that the dollar has weakened relative to the FC. Changes in the value of a commitment can be suggested by either changes in spot rates or forward rates over time. In either case, the suggested change reflects value at the transaction date, versus commitment date, and therefore must be discounted to reflect the change in value at the present time. Using the above example and a discount rate of 6%, the change in value of the above commitment after the first 30 days would be measured as follows:

	Based on Spot Rates	Based on Forward Rates
Rate at:		
Commitment date.	$0.250	$0.258
30 days later	$0.254	$0.264
Change in rate.	$0.004	$0.006
Number of FC	500,000	500,000
Change in value	$2,000	$3,000
Present value of change where n = 1 month and i = 6%/12	$1,990	$2,985

In order to avoid the unfavorable effect of exchange rate changes on the firm commitment, an entity could designate a derivative instrument as a hedge against unfavorable outcomes. The hedge of a firm commitment can be designated as either a fair value hedge or a cash flow hedge assuming the necessary respective criteria are satisfied. More often than not, a fair value hedge will be employed, and such a hedge will be illustrated below.

The special accounting for a fair value hedge of a firm foreign currency commitment is characterized as follows:

1. The accounting for the hedge (the hedging instrument) is separate from the accounting for the foreign currency commitment (the hedged item). If the commitment were not hedged, no special accounting treatment would be given the commitment.

2. The hedging instrument will be carried at fair value, and changes in value over time will be recognized as an unrealized gain or loss and be reported currently in earnings.

3. The change in the value of the hedging instrument consists of a change in the instrument's intrinsic value and its time value. Changes in both the intrinsic and time values are reported currently in earnings and therefore will not be separately accounted for.

4. Changes in the value of the hedging instrument should be accrued at the end of a reporting period.

5. A hedge would be fully effective or "perfect" if the critical terms (nature of the underlying, notional amount, delivery dates, settlement date, type of currency, etc.) of the hedging instrument matched the terms of the hedged item. It is permitted, but not required, to exclude the time value of the derivative instrument from the assessment of hedge effectiveness.

6. Management must set forth how the gain or loss on the firm commitment will be measured. The resulting gain or loss in value will be reported currently in earnings. The change in the value of the firm commitment from the time of the commitment to the transaction date is recognized as a firm commitment asset or liability. This recognized change in value will result in an adjustment to the basis of the committed item. The gains (losses) on the hedging instrument will offset or net against the losses (gains) on the commitment (the hedged item).

7. If the hedge is perfectly effective, the change in the value of the firm commitment will result in an adjustment, at the date of the transaction, to the basis of the committed item so that the effect of exchange rate changes on fixed prices can be offset. The result is that the dollar basis of the transaction is established at the commitment date rather than the later transaction date, and the targeted values at the date of the commitment can be realized.

8. That portion of the hedging instrument which exceeds the notional amount of the commitment is considered to be a speculative hedge and is accounted for accordingly. Therefore, the special accounting treatment given a fair value hedge is not extended to the portion of the hedge which is deemed to be ineffective.

To illustrate, assume that on March 31, a U.S. company commits to selling specialty equipment to a foreign customer with delivery and payment in 90 days. The firm commitment calls for a selling price of 100,000 FC, and it is estimated that the cost to manufacture the equipment will be $55,000. Assume that the spot rate at the date of the commitment is 1 FC = $0.850. If the spot rate were to remain constant over time, management would be able to realize a target gross profit on the sale of $30,000 [(100,000 FC × $0.850) − $55,000]. However, management fears that the FC could weaken relative to the dollar and the target gross profit margin could be reduced. For example, if the rate of exchange at the transaction date were 1 FC = $0.800, the gross profit would be reduced to $25,000 [(100,000 FC × $0.800) − $55,000]. Recognizing that it may be desirable to establish the dollar basis of a transaction at the commitment date rather than the later transaction date, management could enter into a hedge.

To continue the above example, assume that at the date of the commitment, management decides to hedge the commitment by acquiring a forward contract to sell FC in 90 days. Management has elected to include both the change in intrinsic value and time value in the measurement of hedge effectiveness. The change in the value of the firm commitment will be measured by changes in the forward rates. Assume that a 6% discount rate is to be used.

Selected rates and changes in value are presented in the table below. It is important to note the following:

1. The forward contract calls for the sale of FC. Therefore, as remaining forward rates fall below the original forward rate (FC can be sold forward for fewer dollars), the forward contract increases in value and gains are experienced.

2. The difference between the initial spot and forward rates, referred to as the spot-forward difference, represents the time value of the contract and is either a premium or discount. In the present case, the spot-forward difference is a discount that represents a loss. The initial forward rate to sell is less than the initial spot value of the FC. This loss is included in the assessment of hedge effectiveness as so elected at inception of the hedge although management could have elected to exclude it from hedge effectiveness. The hedge is expected to be fully effective or "perfect" because the critical terms (nature of the underlying, notional amount,

delivery dates, settlement date, type of currency, etc.) of the hedging instrument match the terms of the hedged item.

3. Changes in the value of the firm commitment are measured as changes in the forward rate over time. As the forward rates decrease over time, the commitment to sell becomes less valuable.

	March 31— 90 Days Remaining	60 Days Remaining	30 Days Remaining	Transaction Date
Number of FC	100,000	100,000	100,000	100,000
Spot rate 1 FC	$0.850	$0.840	$0.820	$0.800
Forward rate for remaining time — 1 FC.	$0.845	$0.838	$0.814	$0.800
Initial forward rate — 1 FC		$0.845	$0.845	$0.845
Fair value of forward contract:				
Original forward value		$ 84,500	$ 84,500	$ 84,500
Current forward value		83,800	81,400	80,000
Change—gain (loss)—in forward value		$ 700	$ 3,100	$ 4,500
Present value of change:				
$n = 2, i = 6\%/12$.		$ 693		
$n = 1, i = 6\%/12$.			$ 3,085	
$n = 0, i = 6\%/12$.				$ 4,500
Change in value from prior period:				
Current present value.		$ 693	$ 3,085	$ 4,500
Prior present value		0	693	3,085
Change in present value		$ 693	$ 2,392	$ 1,415

Entries by the U.S. company to record the fair value hedge are set forth in Illustration 10-5. An analysis of the entries in Illustration 10-5 reveals that the fair value hedge was effective in accomplishing the concerns of the U.S. company. At the commitment date, the commitment to receive FC had a value of $85,000 (ignoring the time value of money), represented by 100,000 FC at a then spot rate of 1 FC = $0.850. Nevertheless, the company was concerned that the FC would weaken, resulting in a reduction of the targeted gross profit. In fact, the value of the commitment to receive FC did lose value over time as evidenced by a declining spot rate. However, by hedging the commitment, the company was able to ultimately adjust the basis of the sales transaction and, with the exception of the forward contract discount, attain the targeted gross profit. Note that the account "Firm Commitment" serves the purpose of fixing the basis of the sale by the amount of the loss on the firm commitment recognized during the commitment period. The effect of the above fair value hedge on reported income can be summarized as follows:

	Targeted Position	Without the Hedge	With the Hedge
Sales price.	$85,000	$80,000	$84,500
Cost of sales.	55,000	55,000	55,000
Gross profit	$30,000	$25,000	$29,500

Illustration 10-5
Hedge of an Identifiable Foreign Currency Commitment

Relating to the Commitment and Sale of Equipment			Relating to the Forward Contract		

March 31
Memo: Company commits to sell equipment.

Memo: Company acquires a forward contract to sell 100,000 FC at a forward rate of 1 FC = $0.845

60 days remaining

Loss on Firm Commitment	693		**Forward Contract**	693	
Firm Commitment		693	Gain on Contract		693
To record the loss on commitment measured by change in the forward rates.			To record change in value due to forward rate changes.		

30 days remaining

Loss on Firm Commitment	2,392		**Forward Contract**	2,392	
Firm Commitment		2,392	Gain on Contract		2,392
To record the loss on commitment.			To record change in value due to forward rate changes.		

0 days remaining

Loss on Firm Commitment	1,415		**Forward Contract**	1,415	
Firm Commitment		1,415	Gain on Contract		1,415
To record the loss on commitment.			To record change in value due to forward rate changes.		

Foreign Currency	80,000		**Cash**	84,500	
Firm Commitment	4,500		Foreign Currency		80,000
Sales Revenue		84,500	**Forward Contract**		4,500
To record sale and adjustment to basis of sale.			To record settlement of contract.		

Cost of Sales	55,000	
Equipment Inventory		55,000
To record cost of sales.		

If the commitment had not been hedged, the actual gross profit on the sale would have been reduced from the targeted gross profit of $30,000 to $25,000. However, the fair value hedge was effective in maintaining the targeted gross profit. This was accomplished at a cost of $500, which represents the time value (the original discount – a forward rate less than the spot rate) on the forward contract [($0.845 – $0.850) × 100,000 FC]. This hedge was highly effective in that the loss on the commitment ($4,500) was perfectly offset by the gain on the forward contract ($4,500). Although this hedge was highly effective in offsetting losses on the commitment, it is important to remember that forward rates could have increased over time, and the hedge would have effectively eliminated gains on the commitment.

If financial statements were presented on April 30, with 60 days remaining on the hedge, the sale and hedge would be reported as follows:

Income Statement		Balance Sheet	
		Assets:	
Loss on firm commitment	$(693)	Forward contract	$693
Gain on contract	693		
Net loss	$ (0)	Liabilities:	
		Firm commitment	$693

The special accounting treatment given a fair value hedge of a firm commitment continues during the commitment period unless:

- The necessary criteria to qualify as a fair value hedge are no longer satisfied,
- The derivative instrument expires or is sold, terminated, or exercised,
- The entity no longer designates the derivative as a fair value hedge, or
- The hedging relationship is no longer considered highly effective based on management's policies.

Furthermore, note that the treatment given a fair value hedge does not continue beyond the point in time where the commitment actually becomes a transaction. If the term of the derivative instrument extends beyond the transaction date, any exchange gains or losses after the transaction date are treated, as shown in Illustration 10-3, as a hedge of an existing foreign-currency-denominated asset or liability assuming proper documentation.

Foreign currency commitments are frequently hedged through the use of forward contracts. However, other forms of derivative and nonderivative instruments may be effective. For example, in the above illustration, management could have acquired a put option to sell foreign currency at the transaction date. Alternatively, management could have borrowed dollars for a short term with a promise to repay the loan with a fixed number of FC. The FC received from the sales transaction could have been used to settle the loan denominated in FC. Regardless of the instrument used, the goal of a hedge of a commitment is to reduce the exposure that exchange rate changes may have on the value or amount of the U.S. (domestic) currency to be received or paid. Although the above illustration focused on a commitment involving the receipt of FC in connection with a sale, it is also possible that a commitment might involve the payment of FC. For example, if a company was committed to acquire inventory to be paid for in FC, changes in exchange rates could result in the inventory costing more than anticipated. Such increases in the cost of inventory could reduce gross profits associated with the subsequent sale of the inventory.

R E F L E C T I O N

- In a hedge of an existing foreign currency transaction, both the hedging instrument and the hedged transaction are measured at fair value with resulting gains or losses being recognized currently in earnings.

- A hedge of a foreign currency commitment is a fair value hedge that is given special accounting treatment. Changes in the fair value of both the hedging instrument and the commitment are recognized currently in earnings. When the transaction occurs, the hedged item is adjusted for the accumulated gain or loss on the commitment.

EXAMPLES OF THE ACCOUNTING FOR CASH FLOW HEDGES

As previously stated, cash flow hedges may be used to hedge against changes in the cash flows of either a forecasted foreign currency transaction, the forecasted functional currency equivalent cash flows associated with a recognized asset or liability, and an unrecognized foreign currency firm commitment. Assuming the necessary criteria are satisfied, the cash flow hedge will be given special accounting treatment. This special treatment is characterized as follows:

1. The effective portion of the gain or loss on the derivative instrument will be reported in other comprehensive income.
2. Although not required, a portion of the derivative instrument's gain or loss represented by the time value may be excluded from the assessment of hedge effectiveness. If the time value is excluded, changes in time value will be recognized currently in earnings rather than as a component of other comprehensive income.
3. The amounts reported in OCI will be reclassified into recognized earnings in the same period in which the hedged item affects earnings.
4. Given a hedge of a forecasted transaction, special rules relate to how much of the change in the value of the derivative instrument can be recognized in OCI relative to the change in the forecasted transaction. These rules will be discussed in a subsequent section.

Hedging a Foreign Currency Forecasted Transaction

A forecasted transaction is one that is expected to occur in the future at market prices that will be in existence at the time of the transaction. This is in contrast to a foreign currency commitment, which involves market prices that have been previously determined or committed to at the time of the commitment. Because the transaction is forecasted and has not yet occurred, a forecasted transaction does not provide an entity with any present rights or obligations and therefore does not have any fixed prices or rates. Because, unlike a firm commitment, no terms are fixed, an entity is exposed to the risk that future cash flows associated with the forecasted transaction could change. For example, if a company forecasted a purchase of inventory, the cost of the inventory could change. Furthermore, if the forecasted transaction were denominated in FC, not only could the FC price change, but the number of dollars needed to acquire the necessary FC could also change. To illustrate, assume that a company forecasts purchasing inventory for 100,000 FC and that the current spot rate is 1 FC = $1.100. The entity is exposed to the risk that the actual cost of the inventory could exceed 100,000 FC and that the FC could strengthen relative to the dollar. For example, if it turned out that the inventory actually cost 105,000 FC and that 1 FC = $1.140, then the transaction that was forecasted to cost \$110,000 (100,000 FC × \$1.100) would actually cost \$119,700 (105,000 FC × \$1.140).

The objective of a hedge of a forecasted transaction is to reduce the variability of cash flows associated with the transaction by fixing exchange rates. As previously stated, qualifying cash flow hedges are given special accounting treatment and in the case of a forecasted transaction it is important to note the following:

1. The accounting for the hedge (the hedging instrument) is separate from the accounting for the forecasted foreign currency transaction (the hedged item). Furthermore, since the hedged item is a forecasted transaction, which obviously has not yet occurred or been firmly committed to, no accounting is necessary until the forecasted transaction actually takes place. Therefore, there are no recognized gains or losses in the value of the forecasted transaction being concurrently recognized along with changes in the value of the hedging instrument.

2. The cumulative amount of OCI, resulting from changes in the value of the hedging instrument, cannot exceed the cumulative change in the value of expected/forecasted cash flows. If the cumulative amount of OCI exceeds the cumulative change in the value of expected/forecasted cash flows, the difference is removed from OCI and recognized currently as earnings. For example, if a derivative instrument increases \$1,000 in value and the forecasted cash flows decrease in value by \$900, a \$900 gain will be shown as OCI, and a \$100 gain will be recognized in current earnings. In essence, if the hedge is over effective, that amount will be taken to earnings rather than OCI.

3. If the change in value of a derivative instrument is less than the change in value of the forecasted transaction, all of the change in value of the derivative instrument is recognized as a component of other comprehensive income. However, the excess change in value of the forecasted transaction is not recognized. To do so would allow partial recognition of a transaction that has not yet occurred. For example, assume a derivative instrument changes \$1,000 in value and the forecasted cash flows change in value by \$1,200. Only \$1,000 of the change in value is recognized as a component of other comprehensive income and the \$200 difference is not accounted for.

4. Changes in the value of the hedging instrument should be accrued at the end of a reporting period.

5. When the forecasted transaction actually affects earnings (versus occurs), the change in the hedging instrument's value recognized as a component of OCI is reclassified into current earnings.

6. If the hedge is perfectly effective, the variability of forecasted cash flows due to changes in exchange rates will be reduced. The component of OCI that is reclassified into current earnings, when the forecasted transaction actually affects earnings, will reduce the effect that changes in exchange rates have had on the underlying cash flows. The result of the hedge is that resulting cash flows are fixed at an exchange rate rather that being allowed to vary as would be the case without a hedge.

7. The deferral of a loss on a cash flow hedge as a component of OCI is not appropriate if it is likely to result in a combined basis/cost that exceeds the fair value of the resulting asset or liability. For example, assume a derivative loss associated with a forecasted purchase of equipment will, when combined with the expected cost of the equipment, result in a total cost in excess of the item's fair value. If this is expected, the derivative's loss should be recognized immediately in earnings, to the extent that it exceeds the equipment's fair value.

8. If all or part of a transaction is still forecasted, there may be some gain or loss on a corresponding derivative that is still being classified as a component of OCI. On an ongoing basis, it is important to make sure that the gain (loss) on a derivative that remains as a component of OCI does not more than offset the cumulative loss (gain) in the value of

the remaining forecasted transaction. If excessive amounts are classified as OCI, such excess amounts must be reclassified as a component of current earnings. For example, if the balance in OCI related to a forecasted transaction represents a gain on the hedging instrument of $10,000 and the loss in value of the remaining forecasted transaction is $8,000, the excess OCI balance of $2,000 must be reclassified as a component of current earnings.

Illustration of Hedging a Forecasted Transaction with an Option. To illustrate the special accounting for a cash flow hedge of a forecasted transaction, assume the following:

1. On June 1, a company forecasted the purchase of 5,000 units of inventory from a foreign vendor. The purchase would probably occur on September 1 and require the payment of 100,000 FC.

2. Upon purchase of the inventory, it is anticipated that the inventory could be further processed and delivered to customers by early October.

3. On June 1, the company purchased an out-of-the-money call option to buy 100,000 FC at a strike price of 1 FC = $0.550 during September. An option premium of $900 was paid.

4. Effectiveness of the hedge is measured by comparing changes in the option's intrinsic value with changes in the forecasted cash flows based on changes in the spot rates for FC. Changes in the time value of the option will be excluded from the assessment of hedge effectiveness and recognized currently in earnings rather than as a component of other comprehensive income. The hedge is expected to be fully effective because the critical terms (nature of underlying, notional amounts, delivery dates, settlement date, type of currency, etc.) of the hedging instrument match the terms of the hedged item.

5. Spot rates, option values, and changes in value over time are as follows:

	June 1	June 30	July 31	September 1
Strike price — 1 FC	$0.550	$ 0.550	$ 0.550	$ 0.550
Spot rate — 1 FC	$0.530	$ 0.552	$ 0.570	$ 0.575
Fair value of options	$ 900	$ 1,350	$ 2,400	$ 2,600
Intrinsic value of option	0	200	2,000	2,500
Time value of option	$ 900	$ 1,150	$ 400	$ 100
Cumulative change — gain/(loss) in:				
(a) Intrinsic value		$ 200	$ 2,000	$ 2,500
(b) Value of forecasted cash flows (change in spot rates over time)		$(2,200)	$(4,000)	$(4,500)
Lesser (in absolute amount) of (a) or (b) above				
		$ 200	$ 2,000	$ 2,500

6. On September 1, the company purchased 5,000 units of inventory at a cost of 103,000 FC. The option was settled/sold on September 1 at its fair value of $2,600.

7. After incurring further processing costs of $20,000, the inventory was sold for $95,000 on October 5.

Illustration 10-6 presents the necessary entries to account for the cash flow hedge of the above forecasted transaction and the subsequent actual transactions.

Illustration 10-6
Using an Option as a Cash Flow Hedge of a Forecasted Transaction

The following entries relate to the hedge. There is no corresponding transaction.

June 1
Investment in Call Option	900	
Cash		900
To record purchase of option.		

June 30
Investment in Call Option ($1,350 − $900)	450	
Gain on Option (change in time value)		250
OCI [($0.552 − $0.550) × 100,000 FC]		200
To record change in the value of the option.		

The change in the time value is excluded from the assessment of hedge effectiveness. The portion of the gain recorded in OCI equals the change in the option's intrinsic value, which was zero on June 1 because the strike price of $0.550 was greater than the spot rate of $0.530.

July 31
Investment in Call Option ($2,400 − $1,350)	1,050	
Loss on Option (change in time value)	750	
OCI [($0.570 − $0.552) × 100,000 FC]		1,800
To record change in the value of the option.		

September 1
Investment in Call Option	200	
Loss on Option (change in time value)	300	
OCI		500
To record change in value of the option.		

Cash	2,600	
Investment in Call Option		2,600
To record net settlement of option.		

The remaining entries relate to the inventory purchase and subsequent sale. There is no hedge outstanding.

Inventory	59,225	
Cash		59,225
To record payment of 103,000 FC × $0.575.		

Inventory	20,000	
Cash		20,000
To record additional processing costs.		

October 5
Cash	95,000	
Sales Revenue		95,000
To record sale of inventory.		

Cost of Sales ($59,225 + $20,000)	79,225	
Inventory		79,225
To recognize cost of sales.		

OCI (balance)	2,500	
Cost of Sales		2,500
To adjust cost of sales by the gain accumulated in OCI.		

An analysis of the entries in Illustration 10-6 reveals that the cash flow hedge was effective in accomplishing the concerns of the U.S. company. At the time of the forecasted transaction, the company anticipated purchasing inventory for 100,000 FC. At a current spot rate of 1 FC = $0.530, the cash outflow would have been $53,000. However, as the spot rate began to increase, the cost of the inventory would increase, and the potential gross profit on its eventual sale would decrease. At the date of the transaction, the spot rate was 1 FC = $0.575. If the price of the inventory had remained at 100,000 FC, the cost of the inventory would have been $57,500. Acquiring an option to buy FC allowed the company to reduce the variability of cash flows and acquire FC at a fixed strike price of 1 FC = $0.550. The effect of the cash flow hedge of the forecasted transaction can be summarized as follows:

	Without the Call Option	With the Call Option
Sales price of inventory	$ 95,000	$ 95,000
Cost of sales—Raw materials	(59,225)	(59,225)
Cost of sales—Processing costs	(20,000)	(20,000)
Gross profit	$ 15,775	$ 15,775
Adjustment to cost of sales due to change in the intrinsic value of the option		2,500
Adjusted gross profit	$ 15,775	$ 18,275
Unrealized loss on hedge excluded from assessment of hedge effectiveness (change in time value)		(800)
Net income effect	$ 15,775	$ 17,475

The adjusted gross profit resulting from the use of a hedge results from the following:

Sales revenue	$ 95,000
Locked in cost of sales on 100,000 FC at the strike price of $0.550	(55,000)
No hedge on the additional cost of 3,000 FC at the transaction date spot rate of $0.575	(1,725)
Processing costs	(20,000)
Adjusted gross profit	$ 18,275

An analysis of the entries also shows that the balance in OCI at any point in time never exceeded the lesser (in absolute amounts) of the derivative's cumulative gain (loss) in intrinsic value or the loss (gain) in the value of the expected/forecasted cash flows (as measured by changes in spot rates).

The cash flow hedge was effective in reducing the variability of cash flows and was accomplished at a cost of $800, which represents the change in the time value of the option over the holding period ($900 − $100). Once again, remember that the variability of cash flows may also produce a positive effect. For example, if the spot rate had decreased, the purchase of inventory would have required even less cash flow than originally forecasted, and additional gross profit may have resulted. However, an option is a useful derivative to employ in such situations. Remember that the option represents a right, rather than an obligation, to buy FC. If spot rates had declined below the strike price, the holder of the out-of-the-money option could have elected not to exercise and merely recognized the option premium of $900 as a loss. If a forward contract to buy FC had been employed, the holder would have been obligated to exercise or settle the contract. In that case, the hedging instrument would have had an unfavorable effect, offsetting the positive effects associated with variable cash flows.

If financial statements were presented at June 30, the hedge would be reported as follows:

Income Statement		Balance Sheet	
		Assets:	
Gain on option	$250	Investment in options	$1,350
		Stockholders' Equity:	
		Other comprehensive income—Gain on option	$ 200

The special accounting treatment given a cash flow hedge of a forecasted transaction continues unless:

◆ The necessary criteria to qualify as a cash flow hedge are no longer satisfied,
◆ The derivative instrument expires or is sold, terminated, or exercised,
◆ The derivative instrument is no longer designated as a hedge on a forecasted transaction, or
◆ The hedging relationship is no longer highly effective based on management's policies.

If a forecasted transaction is no longer probable, the gain or loss accumulated in OCI should be recognized immediately in earnings. Once a forecasted transaction actually occurs, however, it is possible at that time to designate the original derivative, if not expired, or a new derivative as a hedge on any exposed asset or liability resulting from the actual transaction.

Illustration of Hedging a Forecasted Transaction with a Forward Contract. To illustrate the special accounting for a cash flow hedge of a forecasted transaction with a forward contract, assume the same facts as presented above in the case of hedging with an option except the following:

1. On June 1, the company purchased a forward contract to buy 100,000 FC at a forward rate of 1 FC = $0.542 on September 1.
2. Effectiveness of the hedge is measured by comparing changes in the spot rates (intrinsic value) with changes in the forecasted cash flows based on changes in the spot rates for FC. Changes in the time value of the forward will be excluded from the assessment of hedge effectiveness and recognized currently in earnings rather than as a component of other comprehensive income. The hedge is expected to be fully effective because the critical terms (nature of underlying, notional amounts, delivery dates, settlement date, type of currency, etc.) of the hedging instrument match the terms of the hedged item.
3. Spot rates, forward rates, and changes in value over time are as follows:

	June 1	June 30	July 31	September 1
Number of FC	100,000	100,000	100,000	100,000
Spot rate — 1 FC	$0.530	$0.552	$0.570	$0.575
Forward rate for remaining time — 1 FC	$0.542	$0.560	$0.572	$0.575
Initial forward rate — 1 FC		$0.542	$0.542	$0.542
Fair value of forward contract:				
Original forward value		$54,200	$54,200	$ 54,200
Current forward value		56,000	57,200	57,500
Change—gain (loss)—in forward value		$ 1,800	$ 3,000	$ 3,300
Present value of change:				
n = 2, i = 6%/12		$ 1,782		
n = 1, i = 6%/12			$ 2,985	
n = 0, i = 6%/12				$ 3,300
Change in value from prior period:				
Current present value		$ 1,782	$ 2,985	$ 3,300
Prior present value		0	1,782	2,985
Change in present value		$ 1,782	$ 1,203	$ 315
Amortization of time value		400*	400	400
Increase (decrease) in OCI		$ 2,182	$ 1,603	$ 715

*The time value of the forward contract is represented by the original contract premium or discount. In the present case, the premium is $1,200 [100,000 × ($0.542 forward rate − $0.530 spot rate)]. Amortization of the contract premium or discount over the life of the contract can be accomplished using several methods. However, straight-line amortization is allowed and is used throughout the text examples and end-of-chapter materials. Furthermore, other available methods are more complex than straight-line.

Using a forward contract as the hedging instrument, Illustration 10-7 presents the necessary entries to account for the cash flow hedge of the above forecasted transaction and the subsequent actual transactions.

Illustration 10-7
Using a Forward Contract as a Cash Flow Hedge of a Forecasted Transaction

The following entries relate to the hedge. There is no corresponding transaction.

June 1
Memo: Company acquires a forward contract to buy 100,000 FC at a forward rate of 1 FC = $0.542.

June 30
Forward Contract.	1,782	
Premium Expense	400	
OCI		2,182

To record change in value of the forward contract and record the amortization of the contract premium.

July 31
Forward Contract.	1,203	
Premium Expense	400	
OCI		1,603

To record change in value of the forward contract and record the amortization of the contract premium.

September 1
Forward Contract.	315	
Premium Expense	400	
OCI		715

To record change in value of the forward contract and record the amortization of the contract premium.

Foreign Currency.	57,500	
Forward Contract.		3,300
Cash.		54,200

To record settlement of the forward contract.

The remaining entries relate to the inventory purchase and subsequent sale. There is no hedge outstanding.

Inventory	59,225	
Cash		1,725
Foreign currency		57,500

To record payment of 103,000 FC × $0.575.

Inventory	20,000	
Cash		20,000

To record additional processing costs.

October 5
Cash	95,000	
Sales Revenue		95,000

To record sale of inventory.

Cost of Sales ($59,225 + $20,000)	79,225	
Inventory		79,225

To recognize cost of sales.

OCI (balance)	4,500	
Cost of Sales		4,500

To adjust cost of sales by the gain accumulated in OCI.

An analysis of the entries in Illustration 10-7 reveals that the cash flow hedge was effective in accomplishing the concerns of the U.S. company. Given the use of a forward contract, the effect of the cash flow hedge of the forecasted transaction can be summarized as follows:

	Without the Forward Contract	With the Forward Contract
Sales price of inventory	$ 95,000	$ 95,000
Cost of sales—Raw materials	(59,225)	(59,225)
Cost of sales—Processing costs	(20,000)	(20,000)
Gross profit	$ 15,775	$ 15,775
Adjustment to cost of sales		4,500
Adjusted gross profit	$ 15,775	$ 20,275
Unrealized loss on hedge excluded from assessment of hedge effectiveness		(1,200)
Net income effect	$ 15,775	$ 19,075

The adjusted gross profit resulting from the use of a hedge results from the following:

Sales revenue	$ 95,000
Locked in cost of sales on 100,000 FC at the spot rate of $0.530	(53,000)
No hedge on the additional cost of 3,000 FC at the transaction date spot rate of $0.575	(1,725)
Processing costs	(20,000)
Adjusted gross profit	$ 20,275

The above gross profit of $20,275 based on the use of a forward contract is $2,000 greater than the gross profit of $18,275 traceable to the earlier hedge of a forecasted transaction using an option (Illustration 10-5). The difference is traceable to the fact that the forward contract was able to lock in the purchase of inventory at a cost of $53,000 (100,000 × $0.530 spot rate) compared to the option that locked in a cost of inventory of $55,000 (100,000 × $0.550 strike price).

Illustration of Hedging the Cash Flows Associated with a Recognized Asset of Liability. As previously discussed in the section dealing with fair value hedges, the risk associated with recognized assets or liabilities can be hedged with a fair value hedge. However, the cash flows associated with a recognized asset or liability denominated in foreign currency may also be designated as a cash flow hedge. However, in order to be designated as a cash flow hedge, all of the variability in the hedged item's foreign currency cash flows must be eliminated by the hedging instrument. In the case of a cash flow hedge, the risk is that the cash flows associated with the recognized asset or liability could be affected due to changes in the foreign currency exchange rates. In order to demonstrate the treatment as a cash flow hedge, the facts of the illustration involving the hedge of a foreign currency asset with a fair value hedge set forth on page 560 will be used. Those facts are as follows:

1. On November 1, 2011, the company bought inventory from a foreign vendor with payment due on February 1, 2012, in the amount of 100,000 FC.

2. On November 1, 2011, the company purchased a forward contract to buy 100,000 FC on February 1, 2012, at a forward rate of 1 FC = $0.506.

3. Selected spot and forward rates are as follows:

Date	Spot Rate	Forward Rate for Remaining Term of Contract
November 1, 2011	1 FC = $0.500	1 FC = $0.506
December 31, 2011	1 FC = 0.520	1 FC = 0.530
February 1, 2012	1 FC = 0.550	1 FC = 0.550

4. Changes in the value of the forward contract are to be discounted at a 6% rate.

5. The contract premium or discount is excluded from assessment of hedge effectiveness and is recognized currently in earnings rather than as a component of other comprehensive income.

6. Changes in the value of the forward contract over time are as follows:

	November 1—90 Days Remaining	December 31—30 Days Remaining	Transaction Date
Number of FC	100,000	100,000	100,000
Spot rate — 1 FC	$0.500	$0.520	$0.550
Forward rate for remaining time — FC	$0.506	$0.530	$0.550
Initial forward rate — FC		$0.506	$0.506
Fair value of forward contract:			
Original forward value		$50,600	$50,600
Current forward value		53,000	55,000
Change—gain (loss)—in forward value		$ 2,400	$ 4,400
Present value of change:			
$n = 1, i = 6\%/12$		$ 2,388	
$n = 0, i = 6\%/12$			$ 4,400
Change in value from prior period:			
Current present value		$ 2,388	$ 4,400
Prior present value		0	2,388
Change in present value		$ 2,388	$ 2,012

Illustration 10-8 presents the entries to record the foreign currency transaction and the related forward contract as a cash flow hedge. Once again, in order to emphasize that the value of certain account balances is not fixed and will change over time, these accounts are identified in boldface type.

Illustration 10-8
Using a Cash Flow Hedge to Hedge a Foreign-Currency-Denominated Liability

Relating to the Purchase of Inventory

November 1, 2011

Inventory	50,000	
Accounts Payable—FC		50,000

To record purchase of inventory for 100,000 FC when 1 FC = $0.500.

December 31, 2011

Exchange Loss	2,000	
Accounts Payable—FC		2,000

To accrue exchange loss on the FC-denominated payable when the spot rate is $0.520.

Relating to the Forward Contract

Memo: Company acquired a forward contract to buy 100,000 FC at a forward rate of 1 FC = $0.506.

Forward Contract	2,388	
Premium Expense	400	
OCI		2,788

To record change in the value of the forward contract and premium expense.

OCI	2,000	
Gain on Contract		2,000

To offset impact on earnings of exchange loss on accounts payable.

(continued)

February 1, 2012

Accounts Payable—FC	52,000	
Exchange Loss	3,000	
Foreign Currency		55,000
To record settlement of the liability		
when 1 FC = $0.550.		

Forward Contract Receivable—FC	2,012	
Premium Expense	200	
OCI		2,212
To record change in the value of the forward		
contract and premium expense.		
OCI	3,000	
Gain on Contract		3,000
To offset impact on earnings of exchange loss		
on accounts payable.		
Foreign Currency	55,000	
Forward Contract Receivable		4,400
Cash		50,600
To record settlement of contract.		

In order to understand the impact of treating a hedge on an existing foreign-currency-denominated asset or liability as a fair value hedge versus a cash flow hedge, the financial statement impact of Illustration 10-3 is compared to Illustration 10-8 as follows:

Debit (Credit)	Fair Value Hedge (Illustration 10-3)	Cash Flow Hedge (Illustration 10-8)
December 31, 2011, balance sheet values:		
Inventory	$ 50,000	$ 50,000
Forward contract	2,388	2,388
Accounts payable	(52,000)	(52,000)
Other comprehensive income	0	(788)
2011 income statement values:		
Exchange loss	2,000	2,000
Gain on contract	(2,388)	(2,000)
Premium expense	0	400
Impact on net earnings	(388)	400
February 1, 2012, balance sheet values	No balances	No balances
2012 income statement values:		
Exchange loss	3,000	3,000
Gain on contract	(2,012)	(3,000)
Premium expense	0	200
Impact on net earnings	988	200
Total impact on net earnings—2011 and 2012 . .	600	600

Based on the above table, the balance sheet difference between the alternative hedging classifications relates only to the balance in other comprehensive income resulting from the cash flow treatment. However, the big differences in classifications relate to the income statement. Under the fair value classification, there is significantly more volatility in reported earnings between periods than under the cash flow treatment. In fact, under the cash flow treatment, the only periodic net impact on earnings will be traceable to the amortization of the contract premium or discount that is excluded from hedge effectiveness. In fact, the periodic impact on net earnings will be known in advance because the contract premium or discount is known at inception of the contract. Although the overall impact on net earnings is the same ($600) regardless of the classification of the hedge, the predictability of the periodic impact on net earnings associated with the cash flow treatment is a clear advantage.

Summary of Hedging Transactions

When transactions are denominated in one currency and measured in another, changes in currency exchange rates can expose the transacting party to potential exchange gains or losses. In order to reduce the uncertainty associated with exchange rate changes, forward contracts and other derivatives are often used to hedge against the exposure associated with:

- A forecasted foreign currency transaction,
- An unrecognized foreign currency commitment, or
- A recognized foreign currency denominated asset or liability.

The following table summarizes some of the details relating to these risk-management techniques:

	Transaction Is Forecasted	Commit to Transaction	Transaction Occurs
	Hedge of a Forecasted Transaction	Hedge of an Identifiable Firm Commitment	Hedge of a Denominated FC Asset or Liability
1. Type of hedge.	Cash flow hedge.	Fair value hedge or cash flow hedge.	Fair value hedge or cash flow hedge.
2. Basic purpose of hedge.	Hedge against changes in the cash flows due to exchange rate risk occurring between the time of the probable forecasted transaction and the resulting actual transaction.	Hedge against exchange rate risk occurring between the commitment date and the transaction date.	Hedge the exchange rate risk between the transaction date and the payment/settlement date.
3. Measurement of the value of a forward contract at a point in time.	Measured as the net present value of the difference between the notional amount at the forward rate at inception and the notional amount at the now current forward rate.	Measured as the net present value of the difference between the notional amount at the forward rate at inception and the notional amount at the now current forward rate.	Measured as the net present value of the difference between the notional amount at the forward rate at inception and the notional amount at the now current forward rate.
4. Measurement of the value of an option at a point in time.	Measured as the quoted option value.	Measured as the quoted option value.	Measured as the quoted option value.
5. Recognition over time of changes in the value of the derivative.	Changes in value are recognized as a component of other comprehensive income. When the resulting transaction affects earning, an offsetting amount of OCI is also recognized currently in earnings.	Changes in value are recognized currently as a component of income.	Changes in value are recognized currently as a component of income.
6. Portion of the change in value of a derivative that is excluded from assessment of hedge effectiveness.	May exclude that portion traceable to the time value of the derivative.	May exclude that portion traceable to the time value of the derivative.	May exclude that portion traceable to the time value of the derivative.
7. Measurement of the time value of a derivative at inception.	For a forward contract, the difference between the initial forward rate and the initial spot rate times the notional amount. For an option, the total value of the option at inception less the intrinsic value at inception.	For a forward contract, the difference between the initial forward rate and the initial spot rate times the notional amount. For an option, the total value of the option at inception less the intrinsic value at inception.	For a forward contract, the difference between the initial forward rate and the initial spot rate times the notional amount. For an option, the total value of the option at inception less the intrinsic value at inception.
8. If excluded from the assessment of hedge effectiveness, recognition of the change in time value.	Recognized currently in earnings with an offsetting amount being recorded in OCI.	Recognized currently in earnings. There is no need to separately account for the ineffective portion.	Recognized currently in earnings. There is no need to separately account for the ineffective portion.

(continued)

	Transaction Is Forecasted	Commit to Transaction	Transaction Occurs
	Hedge of a Forecasted Transaction	Hedge of an Identifiable Firm Commitment	Hedge of a Denominated FC Asset or Liability
9. Recognition of the gain or loss on the hedged item.	No gain or loss—forecasted transaction is not recorded.	Recognized currently in earnings and results in an adjustment to the basis of the hedged transaction.	Recognized currently in earnings.
10. Measurement of the gain or loss on the hedged item.	No gain or loss—forecasted transaction is not recorded.	Measured as the change in spot or forward rates between the date of the commitment and the transaction date.	Measured as the change in spot rates between the date of the transaction date and the settlement date.
11. Effect on the basis of the resulting transaction.	Fixes the dollar basis of the actual transaction.	Fixes the dollar basis of the actual transaction.	None.

IASB PERSPECTIVES

The effective date for application of the new hedging standards would likely be for annual periods beginning on or after January 1, 2013. Accounting for cash flow hedges will basically be unchanged although there will be changes to the way fair value hedges are currently accounted for. It is hoped that aligning the way a cash flow hedge and a fair value hedge are accounted for will reduce complexity. Proposed changes in the accounting for a fair value hedge would include:

- Disclosing the cumulative gain or loss on the hedged item traceable to the hedged risk as a separate item on the balance sheet—for example as a "Hedge Adjustment."

- Not adjusting the hedged item's carrying basis. If the basis is adjusted, the resulting measurement does not represent either cost or market. Therefore, no adjustment of the basis is deemed preferable.

- Recording the fair value changes, attributable to the hedged risk, in the hedged item and the related hedging instrument as a component of other comprehensive income. The change in value, which is deemed to be related to hedge ineffectiveness, will be immediately recognized in profit or loss rather than as a component of OCI.

In order to illustrate the changes proposed in the above IASB Perspectives feature, the information supporting Illustration 10-5 will be assumed. Given the proposed changes, the accounting for this information would be as presented in Illustration 10-9.

Illustration 10-9
Based on Proposed Changes—Hedge of an Identifiable Foreign Currency Commitment

Relating to the Commitment and Sale of Equipment		Relating to the Forward Contract	

March 31
Memo: Company commits to sell equipment.

Memo: Company acquires a forward contract to sell 100,000 FC at a forward rate of 1 FC = $0.845.

60 days remaining

OCI	693		**Forward Contract**	693	
Hedge Adjustment		693	OCI		693
To record the loss on commitment measured by change in the forward rates.			To record change in value due to forward rate changes.		

30 days remaining

OCI	2,392		**Forward Contract**	2,392	
Hedge Adjustment		2,392	OCI		2,392
To record the loss on commitment.			To record change in value due to forward rate changes.		

0 days remaining

OCI	1,415		**Forward Contract**	1,415	
Hedge Adjustment		1,415	OCI		1,415
To record the loss on commitment.			To record change in value due to forward rate changes.		

Foreign Currency	80,000		**Cash**	84,500	
Hedge Adjustment	4,500		Foreign Currency		80,000
Sales Revenue		84,500	**Forward Contract**		4,500
To record sale and adjustment to basis of sale.			To record settlement of contract.		

Cost of Sales	55,000	
Equipment Inventory		55,000
To record cost of sales.		

Disclosures Regarding Hedges of Foreign Currency Exposure

Disclosures regarding foreign currency hedges are required as part of the broader disclosure requirements for derivative instruments and hedging activity. More specific disclosure requirements also exist for fair value and cash flow hedges.

REFLECTION

- A hedge of a forecasted foreign currency transaction is a cash flow hedge that is given special accounting treatment. Changes in the fair value of the hedging instrument are recognized as a component of other comprehensive income. Components of OCI are subsequently recognized in earnings in the same period(s) as the actual transaction affects earnings.

- The risk associated with a recognized asset or liability may be hedged with either a fair value hedge or a cash flow hedge. Hedging with a cash flow hedge results in less volatility in reported earnings over time as compared to if a fair value hedge were used.

- A company may be exposed to foreign currency exchange risk in several contexts including forecasted transactions, commitments, and foreign currency transactions. The hedge used in each area of risk has a unique purpose and requires special measurement principles.

UNDERSTANDING THE ISSUES

1. If the U.S. dollar was expected to strengthen relative to a foreign currency (FC), what effect might this have on a U.S. exporter?

2. A U.S. company purchases inventory from a foreign vendor, and purchases are denominated in the foreign currency (FC). The U.S. dollar is expected to weaken against the FC. Explain how a forward contract might be employed as a hedge against exchange rate risk.

3. Explain how a U.S. company's commitment to purchase inventory with settlement in foreign currency (FC) might become less attractive over time and how adverse effects on earnings could be reduced.

4. A company is forecasting the purchase of inventory from an overseas vendor with payment to be made in a foreign currency (FC). Assume an option were used as a hedging instrument for this forecasted transaction. Explain how changes in the time value of the option would be measured and accounted for.

EXERCISES

Exercise 1 *(LO 2)* **Spot rates and forward rates.** On January 1, 2015, one U.S. dollar can be exchanged for eight foreign currencies (FC). The dollar can be invested short term at a rate of 4%, and the FC can be invested at a rate of 5%.

1. Calculate the direct and indirect spot exchange rates as of January 1, 2015.
2. Calculate the 180-day forward rate to buy FC (assume 365 days per year).
3. If the spot rate is 1 FC = $0.740 and the 90-day forward rate is $0.752, what does this suggest about interest rates in the two countries?
4. Explain why a weak dollar relative to the FC would likely increase U.S. exports.
5. Discuss what would happen to the forward rate if the dollar strengthened relative to the FC.

Exercise 2 *(LO 3)* **Foreign currency transactions involving a building and loan payable.** Regber International is building an addition to one of its overseas manufacturing facilities with all construction costs being paid in foreign currency (FC) as follows: 200,000 FC, 300,000 FC, 400,000 FC, and 100,000 FC on March 1, June 30, August 31, and September 30, respectively.

The initial payment was financed by a 2-month note in the amount of 200,000 FC. The note bears interest at the rate of 4.8% and principal and interest are to be paid on April 30. On April 30, the company secured a 6-month note in order to finance ongoing construction costs. This 300,000 FC note bears interest at 6% and calls for quarterly interest payments. On June 1, the company forecasted remaining construction payments and acquired a forward contract to buy 400,000 FC at a forward rate of $1.53 with settlement on August 31. Various spot and forward rates are as shown on page 585.

	Spot Rate	Forward Rate		Spot Rate	Forward Rate
March 1........	$1.50		June 30	$1.55	$1.57
April 30........	$1.48		July 31.........	$1.58	$1.59
June 1	$1.52	$1.53	August 31	$1.60	$1.60
			September 30 ...	$1.65	

Calculate the basis of the building addition including capitalized interest and financing costs associated with the forward contract. Assume that the construction was completed on September 30.

Exercise 3 *(LO 3, 6)* **Hedging a foreign currency liability with an option designated as a fair value hedge.** Williams Corporation imports, from a number of German manufacturers, large machining equipment used in the tooling industry. On June 1, the company received delivery of a piece of machinery with a cost of 450,000 euros when the spot rate was 1 euro equals $1.370. Williams had already paid 50,000 euros, when the spot rate was 1 euro equals $1.350, to the German company at the time of placing the order, and the balance of the invoice was due in 60 days after delivery. On June 15, the company became concerned that the dollar would weaken relative to the euro and proceeded to purchase an option to buy euros on July 31 at a strike price of 1 euro equals $1.375. The hedge was designated as a fair value hedge. At the time of purchase, the out-of-the-money option had a value of $1,400 and a value of $2,600 at June 30. Euro spot rates are as follows:

	1 euro =
June 15	$1.373
June 30	1.381
July 31	1.385

On July 31, the option was settled and the foreign currency was remitted to the German vendor.

Assuming that financial statements are prepared for June and July, identify all relevant income statement and balance sheet accounts for the above transactions and determine the appropriate monthly balances.

Exercise 4 *(LO 3, 6)* **Hedging a commitment with an option.** Wellington Manufacturing manufactures industrial ovens used primarily in the process of coating or painting metals. The ovens are sold throughout the world, and units are manufactured to customers' specifications. On June 15, the company committed to sell two ovens to a major transnational customer. One of the ovens has a selling price of $549,600 and is to be paid for with foreign currency A (FCA). The other unit has a selling price of $297,975 and is to be paid for with foreign currency B (FCB). Both units were shipped, FOB shipping point, on September 15, and payment is due within 30 days of shipment. In order to hedge against exchange rate risks, Wellington acquired two put options on June 15 with notional amounts equal to the respective foreign currency selling prices. The options expire on October 15, and customer remittances are also received on October 15. Relevant information concerning the options and exchange rates is as shown:

Fair Value of Option	June 15	September 15	October 15
FCA option (strike price = $1.200).	$5,000	$21,000	
FCB option (strike price = $0.700) .	$8,500	$ 4,300	

Spot Rates			
FCA........................	$1.200	$1.160	$1.170
FCB	$0.685	$0.692	$0.720

1. Assuming that the time value of the options is excluded from the determination of hedge effectiveness, determine the gain or loss to be recognized on each of the commitments. The

firm commitment is measured based on changes in the spot rate over time, and all discounting is based on a 6% discount rate.

2. Assuming that the costs of the FCA unit and the FCB unit are $440,000 and $235,000, respectively, calculate the gross profit margin on each of the units that would have been experienced with and without the hedge.

3. Calculate the exchange gain or loss on the receivables resulting from the two sales transactions.

Exercise 5 *(LO 3, 6)* **Fair value hedge with forward contract.** Stark, Inc., placed an order for inventory costing 500,000 FC with a foreign vendor on April 15 when the spot rate was 1 FC = $0.683. Stark received the goods on May 1 when the spot rate was 1 FC = $0.687. Also on May 1, Stark entered into a 90-day forward contract to purchase 500,000 FC at a forward rate of 1 FC = $0.693. Payment was made to the foreign vendor on August 1 when the spot rate was 1 FC = $0.696. Stark has a June 30 year-end. On that date, the spot rate was 1 FC = $0.691, and the forward rate on the contract was 1 FC = $0.695. Changes in the current value of the forward contract are measured as the present value of the changes in the forward rates over time. The relevant discount rate is 6%.

1. Prepare all relevant journal entries suggested by the above facts assuming that the hedge is designated as a fair value hedge.
2. Prepare a partial income statement and balance sheet as of the company's June 30 year-end that reflect the above facts.

Exercise 6 *(LO 4, 5)* **Income statement effects with and without hedging.** In the past, Baxter Manufacturing has engaged in a number of foreign currency transactions but has never before attempted to hedge these transactions. Baxter has given you three past events and asked you to illustrate how hedging could have been employed. The events are as follows:

Event A: Purchased raw materials from a foreign supplier for 100,000 FC when 1 FC = $1.100. The supplier was paid 60 days later when 1 FC = $1.150. When the goods were purchased, a 60-day forward contract to buy FC had a forward rate of 1 FC = $1.110.

Event B: Committed to sell inventory (with a cost of $120,000) to a foreign buyer for 200,000 FC when 1 FC = $1.130. Sixty days later, when the inventory was shipped, 1 FC = $1.170, and 90 days later, when the customer paid, 1 FC = $1.180. At the date of the commitment, the 90-day forward rate to sell was 1 FC = $1.150, and at the date of shipment, a 30-day forward rate was 1 FC = $1.172. Changes in the value of the commitment are based on changes in forward rates. Assume a 6% discount rate.

Event C: Forecasted needing to buy inventory with a cost of 60,000 FC in 60 days in order to meet a sale in the amount of $100,000. When the inventory was actually purchased, it had a cost of 68,000 FC. At the time of the forecast, the spot rate was 1 FC = $1.160, and a 60-day forward contract to buy FC was 1 FC = $1.150. At the time the goods were actually purchased, the spot rate was 1 FC = $1.170.

For each of the above events, indicate how income would have been affected with and without the accompanying hedge.

Exercise 7 *(LO 4, 5)* **Hedging a commitment; forecasted transaction—forward contract vs. option.** Jackson, a U.S. company, acquires a variety of raw materials from foreign vendors with amounts payable in foreign currency (FC). The company needs to acquire 20,000 units of raw materials, and the goods are expected to have a price of 100,000 FC. Assume that the inventory can be subsequently sold to U.S. customers for $160,000.

Jackson is contemplating committing to the purchase of the inventory on September 1 with delivery on November 1. However, rather than making a commitment, the company could forecast a probable purchase of inventory with delivery on November 1. In either case, assume that on September 1 the company would either (a) acquire a forward contract to buy 100,000 FC with a forward date of November 1 or (b) acquire an option to buy FC in November at a strike price of $1.250. The option premium is expected to cost $2,100.

Various spot rates, forward rates, and option values are as follows:

	Spot Rate	Forward Rate for November 1	Time Value of Option
September 1	1 FC = $1.250	1 FC = $1.270	$2,100
November 1	1 FC = $1.320	1 FC = $1.320	0

1. Prepare a schedule that would compare the effect on current earnings of the two alternatives (commit or forecast), given the alternative hedging instruments. Show the effect on earnings for the period prior to the transaction date separately from the effect after the transaction date. The time value component of the hedging instruments is excluded from the assessment of hedge effectiveness. Changes in the value of the commitment are measured by changes in the spot rates.
2. Discuss your conclusion, and explain to Jackson why one alternative might be preferable over the other.

Exercise 8 *(LO 5, 6)* **Measuring changes in the value of derivatives and accounting for such changes.** A company has acquired two derivatives: an option to buy foreign currency (FC) and a forward contract to buy FC. Both derivatives were acquired on the same day, for the same notional amount and expire on May 31. Relevant information involving the derivatives is as follows:

	February 1	April 30	May 31
Notional amount in FC . . .	100,000	100,000	100,000
Spot rate	$ 2.05	$ 2.08	$ 2.10
Forward rate	$ 2.07	$ 2.09	$ 2.10
Strike price.	$ 2.05	$ 2.05	$ 2.05
Value of option	$ 1,000	$ 3,400	$ 5,000

1. Calculate the intrinsic and the time value of the option for each of the above dates and indicate how the changes in each of these values would be accounted for if the option hedged: (a) a forecasted FC transaction and (b) a recognized FC-denominated liability.
2. Calculate the value of the forward contract at each of the above dates and indicate how the changes in each of these values would be accounted for if the contract hedged: (a) an unrecognized FC firm commitment (b) a recognized FC-denominated liability. Assume a 6% interest rate for any discounting purposes.
3. In part (2), assume that the two hedged items involved the purchase of inventory. Explain how the changes in value of the hedging instruments would affect the basis of the inventory.

PROBLEMS

Problem 10-1 *(LO 5)* **FC transactions, commitments, forecasted transactions— earnings impact.** Jarvis Corporation transacts business with a number of foreign vendors and customers. These transactions are denominated in FC, and the company uses a number of hedging strategies to reduce the exposure to exchange rate risk. Several such transactions are as follows:

Transaction A: On November 30, the company purchased inventory from a vendor in the amount of 100,000 FC with payment due in 60 days. Also on November 30, the company purchased a forward contract to buy FC in 60 days.

Transaction B: On November 1, the company committed to provide services to a foreign customer in the amount of 100,000 FC. The services will be provided in 30 days. On November 1, the company also purchased a forward contract to sell 100,000 FC in 30 days. Changes in the value of the commitment are based on changes in forward rates.

Transaction C: On November 1, the company forecasted a purchase of equipment in 30 days. The forecasted cost is 100,000 FC, and the equipment is to be depreciated over five years using the straight-line method of depreciation. On November 1, the company acquired a forward contract to buy 100,000 FC in 30 days.

Transaction D: On November 30, the company purchased an option to sell 100,000 FC in 60 days to hedge a forecasted sale to a customer in 60 days. The option sold for a premium of $1,200 and had a strike price of $1.155. The value of the option on December 31 was $2,000.

The time value of all hedging instruments is excluded from the assessment of hedge effectiveness. Relevant spot and forward rates is as shown:

	Spot Rate	Forward Rate for 30 Days from November 1	Forward Rate for 60 Days from November 30
November 1	1 FC = $1.120	1 FC = $1.132	
November 15	1 FC = $1.130		
November 30	1 FC = $1.150		1 FC = $1.146
December 31.	1 FC = $1.140		1 FC = $1.138

Required ▶ ▶ ▶ ▶ ▶   Assuming that the company's year-end is December 31, for each of the above transactions determine the current-year effect on earnings. All necessary discounting should be determined by using a 6% discount rate. For transactions C and D, the time value of the hedging instrument is excluded from hedge effectiveness and is to be separately accounted for.

Problem 10-2 *(LO 6)* **Cash flow hedges of a commitment, a forecasted transaction and a recognized liability.** On March 1, a company committed to acquire 10,000 units of inventory to be delivered on May 31. The purchase price is to be paid in foreign currency (FC) in the amount of 200,000 FC. Changes in the value of the commitment are measured as the difference between spot rates over time with appropriate discounting. Assume that the commitment's negative values are $7,960 and $14,000 as of March 31 and May 31, respectively. Also assume that the inventory will be processed further during the month of June at a cost of $12.50 per unit and will be sold on July 10 to a customer for $90 per unit. On March 1, the company also forecasted the purchase of a piece of equipment to be delivered on May 31 with a cost of 200,000 FC. The equipment was placed into service at the beginning of July and has a useful life of 12 years and a salvage value of $74,000. On March 1, the company borrowed 200,000 FC from a foreign bank at an interest rate of 6.0% with interest and principal to be repaid on May 31.

Assume that on March 1 the company acquired three identical options to buy FC on May 31 with each option to be designated as a hedge for each of the three situations described above. Information relating to each option is as follows:

For each option	March 1	March 31	May 31
Notional amount	200,000	200,000	200,000
Strike price.	$ 2.52	$ 2.52	$ 2.52
Spot price	$ 2.50	$ 2.54	$ 2.57
Value of option	$ 1,300	$ 5,000	$ 10,000

Required ▶ ▶ ▶ ▶ ▶   For each of the three hedged situations, prepare a schedule to show the impact on earnings for each of the first three calendar quarters of the year noting that all hedges are to be considered cash flow hedges.

Problem 10-3 *(LO 6)* **Hedging a forecasted transaction with a forward contract.** In the process of preparing a budget for the second quarter of the current fiscal year, Anderson Welding, Inc., has forecasted foreign sales of 1,200,00 foreign currency (FC). The company is concerned that the dollar will strengthen relative to the FC and has decided to hedge one-half of the forecasted foreign sales with a forward contract to sell FC in 90 days. Assume that all 1,200,000 of the forecasted sales are shipped 60 days after acquiring the contract and that payment of the sales invoices occurs 30 days after shipment, with terms FOB shipping point. Selected rate information is as shown on page 589.

Days remaining on forward contract	90 days	60 days	30 days	0 days
Spot rate	$1.900	$1.920	$1.880	$1.850
Forward rate	1.890	1.910	1.900	1.850

Assume that contract premiums or discounts are to be amortized on a straight-line basis over the term of the contract. All discounting is to be based on a 6% interest rate.

1. Prepare all entries to record the forecasted sales and the related hedging activity. Assume that financial statements are prepared every month and that entries should be made monthly.   ◄ ◄ ◄ ◄ ◄ **Required**
2. Prepare a schedule to compare the impact on earnings of hedging half of the forecasted sales versus not hedging the other half. Assume that the total cost of goods sold was $1,800,000, evenly divided among the sales.

Problem 10-4 *(LO 3, 5)* **Income statement effects of transactions, commitments, and hedging.**

Clayton Industries sells medical equipment worldwide. On March 1 of the current year, the company sold equipment, with a cost of $160,000, to a foreign customer for 200,000 euros payable in 60 days. At the same time, the company purchased a forward contract to sell 200,000 euros in 60 days. In another transaction, the company committed, on March 15, to deliver equipment in May to a foreign customer in exchange for 300,000 euros payable in June. This equipment is anticipated to have a completed cost of $210,000. On March 15, the company hedged the commitment by acquiring a forward contract to sell 300,000 euros in 90 days. Changes in the value of the commitment are based on changes in forward rates, and all discounting is based on a 6% discount rate.

Various spot and forward rates for the euro are as follows:

	Spot Rate	Forward Rate for 60 Days from March 1	Forward Rate for 90 Days from March 15
March 1	$1.180	$1.181	
March 15	1.181	1.180	$1.179
March 31	1.179	1.178	1.177
April 30	1.175		1.174

For individual months of March and April, calculate the income statement effect of: ◄ ◄ ◄ ◄ ◄ **Required**

1. The foreign currency transaction.
2. The hedge on the foreign currency transaction.
3. The foreign currency commitment.
4. The hedge on the foreign currency commitment.

Problem 10-5 *(LO 3, 6)* **Hedge with forward contract a commitment and subsequent transaction.**

Kaiser Exporters buys used medical equipment and sells it to various foreign health care institutions. On June 15, the company committed to sell medical equipment to a foreign hospital for 800,000 FC. The equipment, with a cost of $325,000, was shipped to the customer on August 15 with terms FOB shipping point and payment due on October 15. At the time of the commitment, Kaiser acquired a forward contract to sell 800,000 FC in 120 days. Selected spot and forward rates are as follows:

	June 15	June 30	August 15	September 30
Spot rate	$0.500	$0.485	$0.480	$0.470
Forward rate	0.510	0.490	0.475	0.468

The relevant discount rate is 6% and changes in the value of the firm commitment are measured as changes in the forward rate over time.

Required ▶ ▶ ▶ ▶ ▶   Assuming that financial statements are prepared for the second and third quarters, identify all relevant income statement and balance sheet accounts for the above transactions and determine the appropriate quarterly balances.

Problem 10-6 *(LO 3, 6)* **Hedging foreign currency transactions and commitments.** Medical Distributors, Inc., is a U.S. company that buys and sells used medical equipment throughout the United States and Canada. During the month of June, the company had the following transactions with Canadian parties:

1. Purchased used equipment on June 1 from a hospital located in Toronto for 220,000 Canadian dollars (CA$) payable in 45 days. On the same day, the company paid $1,000 for a call option to buy 220,000 Canadian dollars during July at a strike price of 1 CA$ = $0.726. The option had a fair value of $3,200 on June 30. The hedge was designated as a fair value hedge.
2. Sold equipment on June 1 for 300,000 Canadian dollars to be paid in 30 days. At the same time, the company purchased a forward contract to sell the Canadian dollars in 30 days and the hedge was designated as a fair value hedge.
3. Committed to buy equipment on June 15 from a Montreal health care provider for 400,000 Canadian dollars in 45 days. At the same time, the company purchased a forward contract to buy 400,000 Canadian dollars in 45 days.
4. Paid 30,000 Canadian dollars on June 20 to refurbish the equipment purchased on June 1.
5. Sold the equipment purchased on June 1 on June 20 for 310,000 Canadian dollars to be received in 30 days.
6. Collected the 300,000 Canadian dollars on June 30 from the sale on June 1.

Selected spot and forward rates are as follows:

	Spot Rate 1 CA$	Forward Rate 1 CA$ =
June 1	$0.720	30-day sell rate = $0.729
June 15	0.729	45-day buy rate = $0.731
June 20	0.732	
June 30	0.735	30-day buy rate = $0.737

Required ▶ ▶ ▶ ▶ ▶   Prepare all of the necessary journal entries to record the above activities during the month of June. Changes in the value of the commitment are based on changes in forward rates. All necessary discounting should be determined using a 6% discount rate.

Problem 10-7 *(LO 5, 6)* **The impact of no hedging versus hedging.** In several instances, Neibler Corporation has been engaged in transactions that were denominated or settled in foreign currencies (FC). Given recent volatility in exchange rates between the U.S. dollar and the FC, the company is considering using FC derivatives in a number of instances. In order to communicate to management the impact of hedging, you have been asked to develop a schedule relating to several hypothetical situations.

Hypothetical A involves the purchase of inventory in the amount of 100,000 FC with payment due in 60 days. Assume that the hedge would involve: (a) an option to buy 100,000 FC in 60 days and (b) a forward contract to buy 100,000 FC in 60 days. In both cases, the hedge is to be considered a fair value hedge.

Hypothetical B involves the same facts as Hypothetical A except that the hedge is to be considered a cash flow hedge.

Hypothetical C involves a commitment to sell inventory in 90 days for 100,000 FC. Assume that the hedge would involve: (a) an option to sell 100,000 FC in 90 days and (b) a forward contract to sell 100,000 FC in 90 days. In both cases, the hedge is to be considered a cash flow hedge. In the case of the option, changes in the value of the commitment are to be measured by changes in spot rates over time, whereas in the case of the forward contract, changes in the value of commitment are measured based on changes in forward rates. The inventory sold has a cost of $100,000.

Hypothetical D involves a 90-day 100,000 FC note receivable bearing interest at 6%. Both principal and interest are payable at maturity, and it is assumed that an option to sell 100,000 FC will be employed as a cash flow hedge.

Hypothetical E involves a forecasted sale of inventory in 90 days for 100,000 FC. Assume that the inventory has a cost of $110,000 and a forward contract to sell 100,000 FC in 90 days is the hedging instrument.

Selected rate information is as follows:

	At Inception	After 60 days	After 90 days
Derivatives to buy FC			
Spot rate	$ 1.50	$ 1.55	
Forward rate	$ 1.52	$ 1.55	
Strike price	$ 1.51	$ 1.51	
Option value	$ 800	$4,000	
Derivates to sell FC			
Spot rate	$ 1.50		$ 1.40
Forward rate	$ 1.48		$ 1.40
Strike price	$ 1.50		$ 1.50
Option value	$1,000		$10,000

For each of the above hypothetical situations, prepare a schedule to show the activity in balance sheet accounts and income statement accounts over the course of the events assuming: (1) no hedging and (2) hedging. With respect to the balance sheet accounts, show the balance in the derivative just prior to settlement and ignore an analysis of cash or foreign currency balances.

◄ ◄ ◄ ◄ ◄ **Required**

Translation of Foreign Financial Statements

Learning Objectives

When you have completed this chapter, you should be able to

1. **Define the functional currency, and identify factors suggesting the functional currency.**

2. **Explain the objectives of the translation process.**

3. **Apply the functional currency translation process to a trial balance, and calculate the translation adjustment.**

4. **Explain how the translation adjustment is accounted for and how a hedge may be employed.**

5. **Describe the consolidation process and the sophisticated equity method, giving particular attention to modifications due to translation.**

6. **Apply the remeasurement process to a trial balance, and explain how to account for the remeasurement gain or loss.**

7. **Differentiate between the two methods for converting functional currency to the parent/investor's currency, and explain the circumstances under which each should be used.**

The previous chapter identified a variety of transactions that may occur between a domestic (U.S.) company and a foreign entity. These transactions were not dependent on the domestic company's having any type of ownership interest in the foreign entity. However, many domestic companies do have an ownership interest in or control of foreign companies, and accounting for these interests presents special problems. The accounting treatments of domestic and foreign entity relationships that involve some degree of control are summarized as follows:

Domestic Entity	Foreign Entity	Accounting Treatment
Home office	Branch	Branch accounting
Parent	Subsidiary	Consolidated financial statements or separate financial statements
Investor	Investee	Investment in foreign entity at market or equity

The above relationships suggest the need to combine or consolidate the foreign entity financial statements with those of the domestic entity. The financial statements of a foreign entity typically are measured in the currency of that foreign country. This currency usually is different from the reporting currency of the domestic entity. Therefore, a methodology must be developed to express the foreign entity's financial statements in the reporting currency of the domestic entity. The process of expressing amounts denominated or measured in foreign currencies into amounts measured in the reporting currency (dollars) of the domestic entity (U.S.) is referred to as *foreign currency translation*.

In addition to establishing a methodology for translation, the process is complicated by the reality that the foreign financial statements may have been prepared using accounting principles that are different from those of the domestic reporting entity. Although becoming fewer in number, due to significant efforts to converge various alternative accounting standards into a worldwide set of recognized standards, differences in standards continue to exist. Therefore, prior to translation, the statements of a foreign entity must be adjusted to reflect the generally accepted accounting principles (GAAP) employed by the domestic reporting entity. For example, a foreign subsidiary may not be required to capitalize leases although the lease would be capitalized if GAAP followed by the parent company were employed. Before proceeding with translation, the accounting for these leases must be adjusted to conform to the principles employed by the reporting entity.

1

OBJECTIVE

Define the functional currency, and identify factors suggesting the functional currency.

STATEMENT OF FINANCIAL ACCOUNTING STANDARDS NO. 52

A central question to the process of translating foreign currency financial statements into the currency of the domestic reporting entity is what effect exchange rate changes will have on the domestic reporting entity. The FASB adopted a *functional currency* approach which focuses on whether the domestic reporting entity's cash flows will be indirectly or directly affected by changes in the exchange rates of the foreign entity's currency.

IASB standards

IASB PERSPECTIVES

IAS 21, *The Effects of Changes in Foreign Exchange Rates*, addresses the translation of foreign financial statements. The concept of a functional currency is applied, and the term "presentation currency" (rather than "reporting currency") is used to describe the currency in which financial statements are prepared.

Assume a foreign entity operates exclusively in its own country using only its currency (see Illustration 11-1a). It is questionable whether changes in the exchange rate between its currency and that of the parent entity would directly affect either the subsidiary's or the parent's cash flows. After all, how could changes in the rate of exchange between the foreign currency and the dollar affect you if your transactions were primarily denominated in the foreign currency and not exposed to exchange rate risk? If you transact business only in your own currency, how your currency changes relative to another currency does not impact you. However, if a foreign entity operates or functions in a currency other than its own, exchange rate changes between these currencies presumably will directly affect cash flows of the foreign entity and ultimately the cash flows of the parent (see Illustration 11-1b). For example, if the foreign subsidiary has to convert one foreign currency into another type of foreign currency (FCA) in order to pay a foreign supplier, the exposure to exchange rate risk may affect cash flows of the subsidiary and in turn the parent. If the foreign subsidiary has less cash due to exchange rate changes, then the parent would, in turn, expect to receive less cash from its investment in the subsidiary. In this instance, the resulting effect on the parent would be the same as if the parent had engaged in transactions that were denominated in a foreign currency.

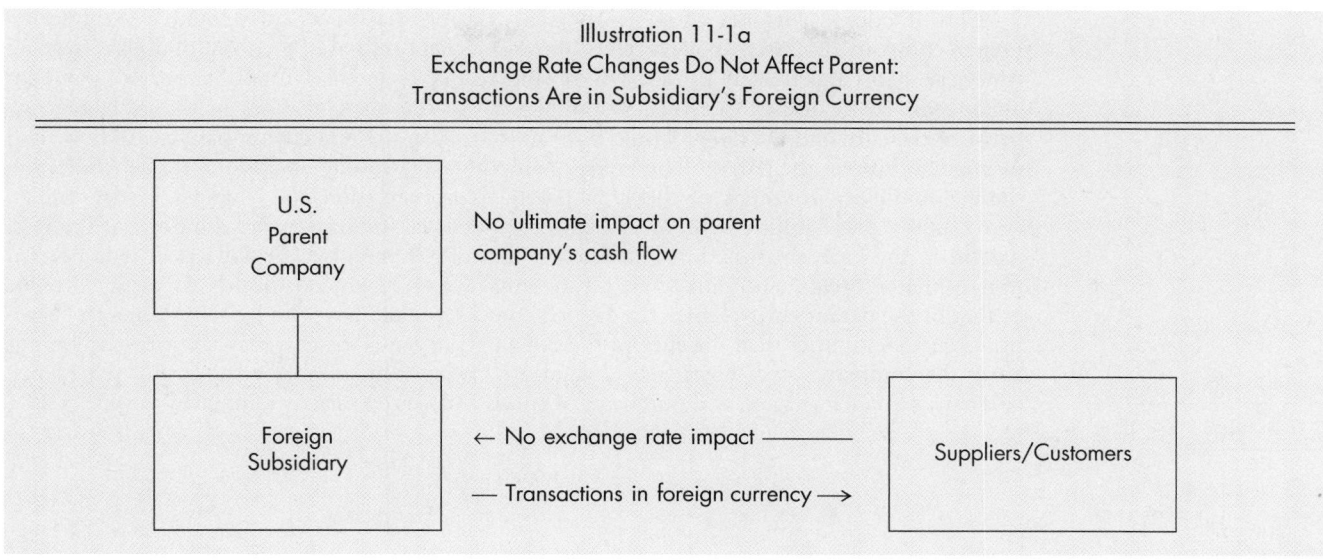

Illustration 11-1a
Exchange Rate Changes Do Not Affect Parent:
Transactions Are in Subsidiary's Foreign Currency

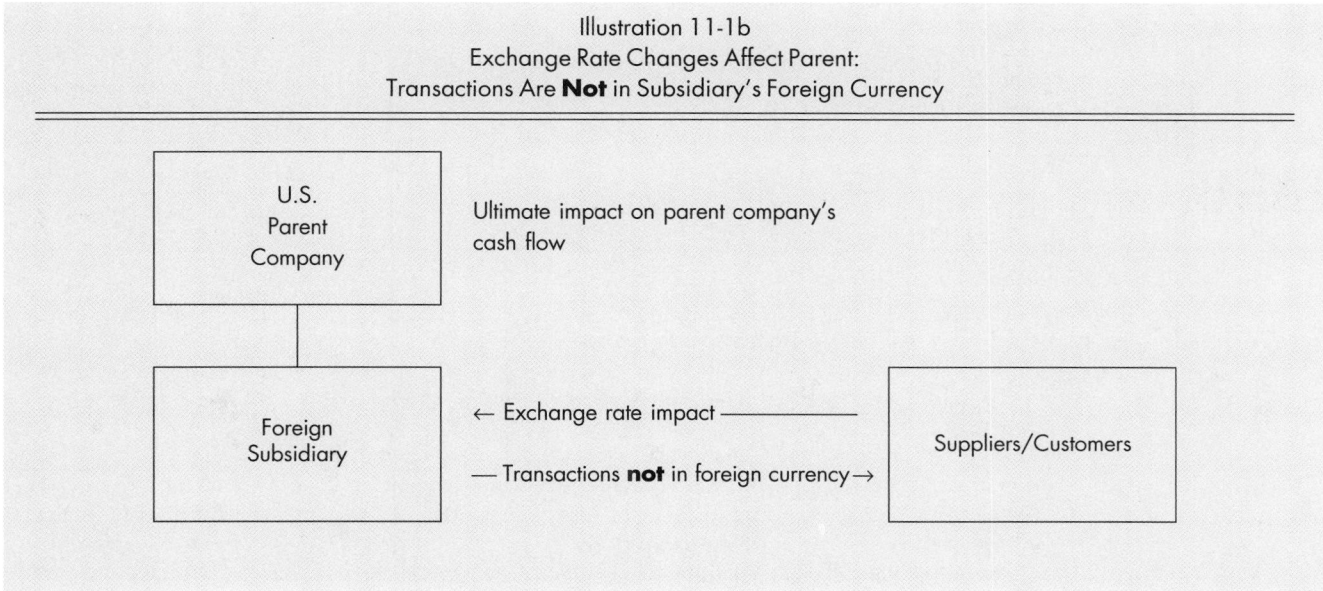

Illustration 11-1b
Exchange Rate Changes Affect Parent:
Transactions Are **Not** in Subsidiary's Foreign Currency

Functional Currency Identification

In order to achieve the objectives of the translation process, it is critical to identify the foreign entity's functional currency. The functional currency is the currency of the primary economic environment in which the entity generates and expends cash. For example, assume a French company that is a subsidiary of a U.S. company purchases labor and materials and pays for these items with euros (see Illustration 11-2a). The finished product of the company is sold, and payment is received in euros. In this situation, the French company operates or functions in euros and is therefore not exposed to exchange rate risk between the euro and the dollar. Therefore, changes in the exchange rate between the euro and the dollar of the U.S. parent do not have an economic impact on the French company or its U.S. parent. Because of this, the French company's day-to-day operations are not dependent on the economic environment of the U.S. parent's currency (dollars). Therefore, the euro would be considered the functional currency of the French company.

The functional currency of an entity is not always that of its own country. Assume the French company discussed above received most of its debt capital in the form of dollars from an American bank and that its products were sold primarily in the United States with payment being received in dollars (see Illustration 11-2b). In this case, changes in the exchange rate between the euro and the dollar would have an impact on the French company's cash flows and ultimately those of the parent. The French company's day-to-day operations are dependent on the economic environment of the U.S. parent's currency (dollars). Changes in the foreign entity's assets and liabilities will, or will have the potential to, impact the cash flows of the U.S. parent. In this case, the functional currency is that of the parent (U.S. dollars). It is important to note that a foreign entity may have a functional currency which is not its domestic currency or that of the parent entity. Thus, the French company could have the Japanese yen as its functional currency, rather than the euro or the dollar, if the yen is the currency that primarily influences the company's cash flows (see Illustration 11-2c). This might be the case if the French company's financing, sales, and purchases of goods and services are denominated in yen.

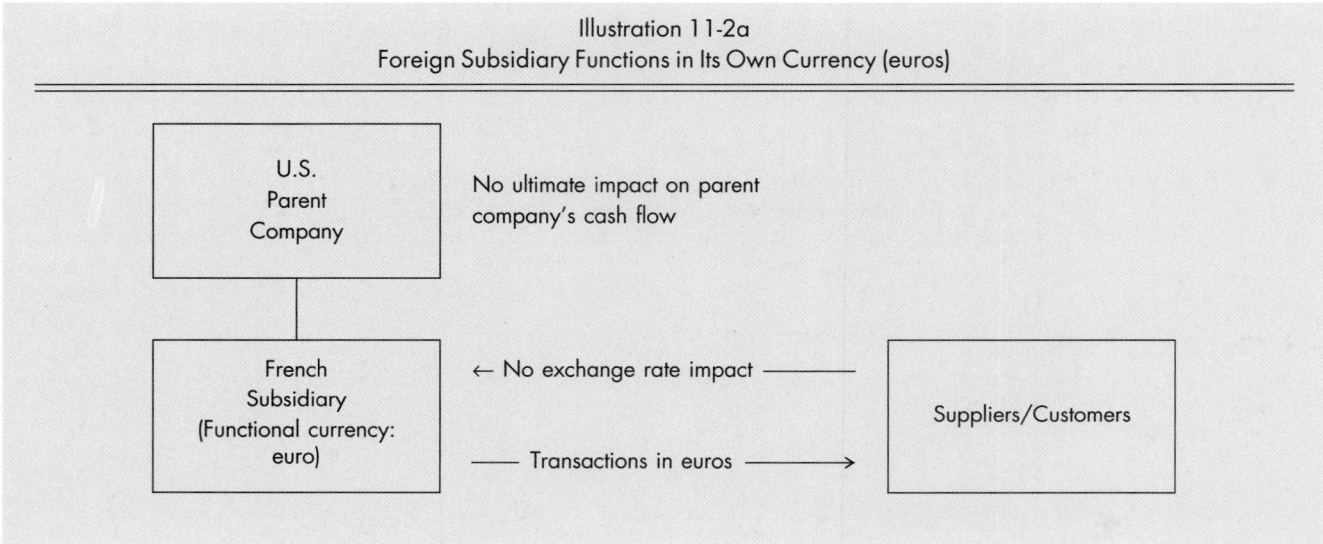

Illustration 11-2a
Foreign Subsidiary Functions in Its Own Currency (euros)

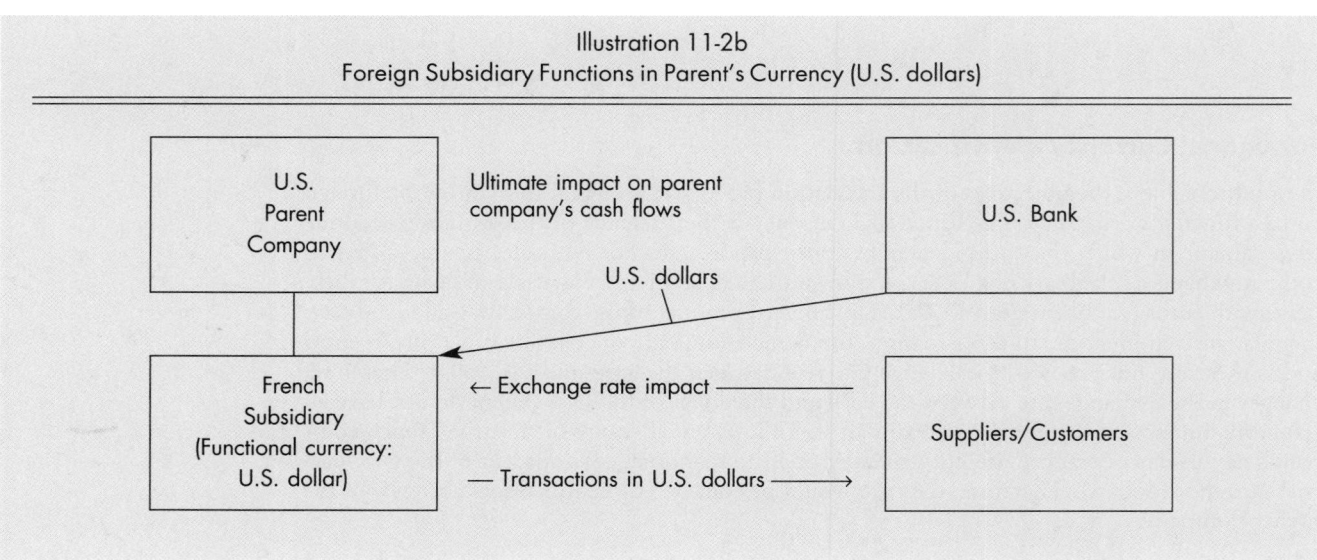

Illustration 11-2b
Foreign Subsidiary Functions in Parent's Currency (U.S. dollars)

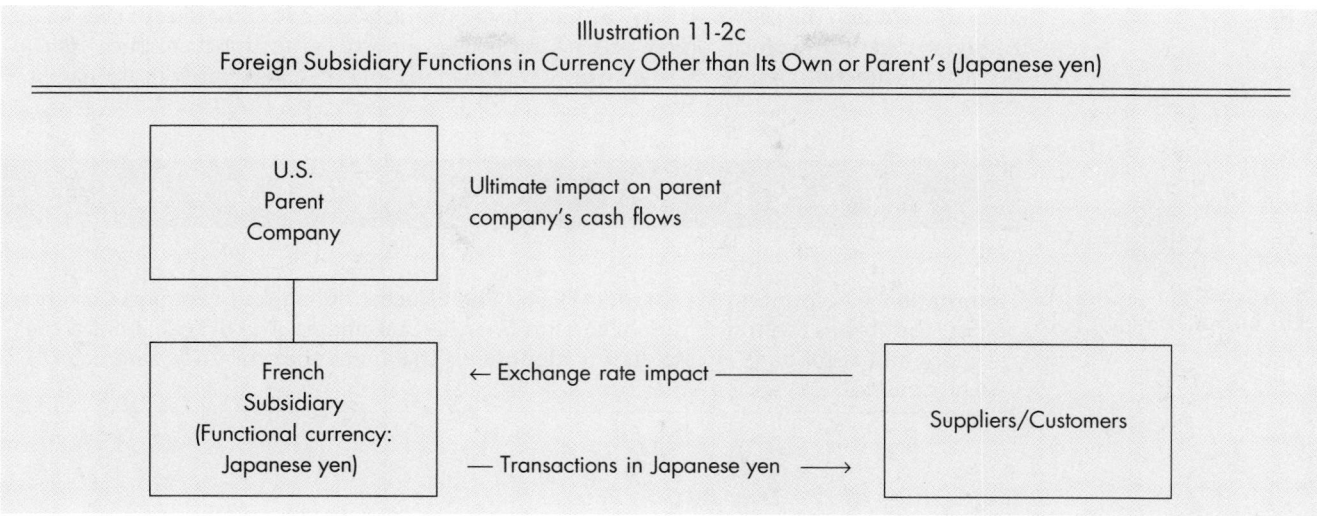

Illustration 11-2c
Foreign Subsidiary Functions in Currency Other than Its Own or Parent's (Japanese yen)

Identification of the functional currency is not subject to definitive criteria. However, certain basic economic factors should be considered in making this identification.[1] Some of these factors are summarized in Exhibit 11-1.

Exhibit 11-1
Factors Suggesting the Functional Currency

Indicator	Foreign Entity's Currency Is the Functional Currency	Parent's Currency Is the Functional Currency
Cash flows	Cash flows are primarily in the currency of the foreign entity. Such flows do not impact the parent's cash flows.	Cash flows directly impact the parent's cash flows and are readily available to the parent.
Sales price	Sales prices are influenced by local factors rather than exchange rates.	Sales prices are influenced by international factors and exchange rate changes.
Sales market	There is an active and primarily local market.	The sales market is primarily in the parent's country.
Expenses	Goods and services are acquired locally and denominated in local currencies.	Goods and services are acquired from the parent's country.
Financing	Financing is secured locally and denominated in local currencies. Debt is serviced through local operations.	Financing is secured primarily from the parent or is denominated in the parent's currency.
Intercompany transaction and arrangements	Intercompany transaction volume is low. Major interrelationships between foreign and parent operations do not exist.	Intercompany transaction volume is high. There are major interrelationships between entities. A foreign entity holds major assets and obligations of the parent.

These factors should be considered both individually and collectively in order to identify the functional currency. The selection of a functional currency should be applied consistently over time, unless significant changes suggest that the functional currency has changed. Changes should not be accounted for on a retroactive basis but rather prospectively. Therefore, all items

---

1 FASB ASC 830-10-55-5, *Foreign Currency Matters—Overall—Implementation Guidance—The Functional Currency.*

are translated into the new functional currency using the exchange rate at the date of the change. Although these factors focus on the parent's currency as a possible functional currency, remember that the functional currency may be one other than that of the foreign entity or the parent.

IASB PERSPECTIVES

IASB *standards*

International Accounting Standard (IAS) 21, "The Effects of Changes in Foreign Currency Rates," addresses the translation of foreign financial statements. The IAS has a hierarchy, primary and secondary, of factors for identifying the functional currency whereas U.S. GAAP does not.

2

OBJECTIVE

Explain the objectives of the translation process.

Objectives of the Translation Process

The compatibility resulting from translating various financial statements into a common reporting currency is a practical necessity. However, this process should not alter the significance of the results and relationships experienced by the individual consolidated entity. Consistent with this underlying concern, the translation process should accomplish the following objectives. The first objective is explained in this section. The second objective is explained later in the chapter.

1. Provide information that is generally compatible with the expected economic effects of a rate change on an enterprise's cash flows and equity.
2. Reflect in consolidated statements the financial results and relationships of the individual consolidated entities as measured in their functional currencies in conformity with U.S. generally accepted accounting principles.[2]

The first objective recognizes that exchange rate changes may or may not have any substantial or direct effect on the cash flows and economic well-being of the related entities (e.g., subsidiary and parent). If the foreign entity conducts business in its own currency, exchange rate changes relative to the parent's currency would not affect the cash flow or economic well-being of the foreign entity. Therefore, the process of translating the foreign entity's financial statements into U.S. dollars should not currently impact net income. For example, assume that a foreign subsidiary borrows 1,000 foreign currencies (FC) from a bank in order to purchase a tract of land for 1,000 FC when the rate of exchange is 1 FC = $1 (see Illustration 11-3a). If the land were to be sold for 1,000 FC when the rate of exchange is 1 FC = $0.80, then 1,000 FC would be available to repay the loan. Neither the foreign entity's nor the parent's cash flows, or their economic well-being, would have been adversely affected by the change in exchange rates because the foreign subsidiary functions in foreign currency, not the U.S. dollar.

However, if the foreign entity conducts business primarily in another currency (e.g., the parent's currency), changes in the exchange rate would affect the cash flow or economic well-being of the foreign entity. Therefore, the effect of translation should be included in reported income. To illustrate, assume the same facts as in the above example except that the funds necessary to purchase the land were borrowed from a U.S. bank in dollars and then converted to FC with ultimate repayment of the loan due in dollars (see Illustration 11-3b). If the land were to be sold for 1,000 FC and the proceeds converted to U.S. dollars when 1 FC = $0.80, only $800 would be available to repay the loan. The French subsidiary would then need to use more cash in order to pay off the remaining $200 of debt. This would have a negative impact on the cash flows of the subsidiary and ultimately on those of the U.S. parent. Therefore, the change in exchange rates would have an effect on both the potential cash flows available to the parent and the

---

2 FASB ASC 830-10-10, *Foreign Currency Matters—Overall—Objectives.*

parent's economic well-being. This adverse effect of the exchange rate changes should be reflected in the current-period net income.

The expected economic effects of rate changes must be properly reflected in financial statements and may be analyzed as follows:

Expected Economic Effect of Rate Changes	Accounting Response to Effect of Rate Changes
Cash inflows increase, and/or cash outflows decrease. Economic well-being is affected.	Translation gains should be included in net income.
Cash inflows decrease, and/or cash outflows increase. Economic well-being is affected.	Translation losses should be included in net income.
Cash inflows and/or outflows are not affected. Economic well-being is not affected.	No translation gain or loss should be included in net income. The effect of rate changes will not be realized until the parent's investment in the foreign entity is disposed of or liquidated. Therefore, the effect of translation does not affect current net income and is shown as a separate component of other comprehensive income.

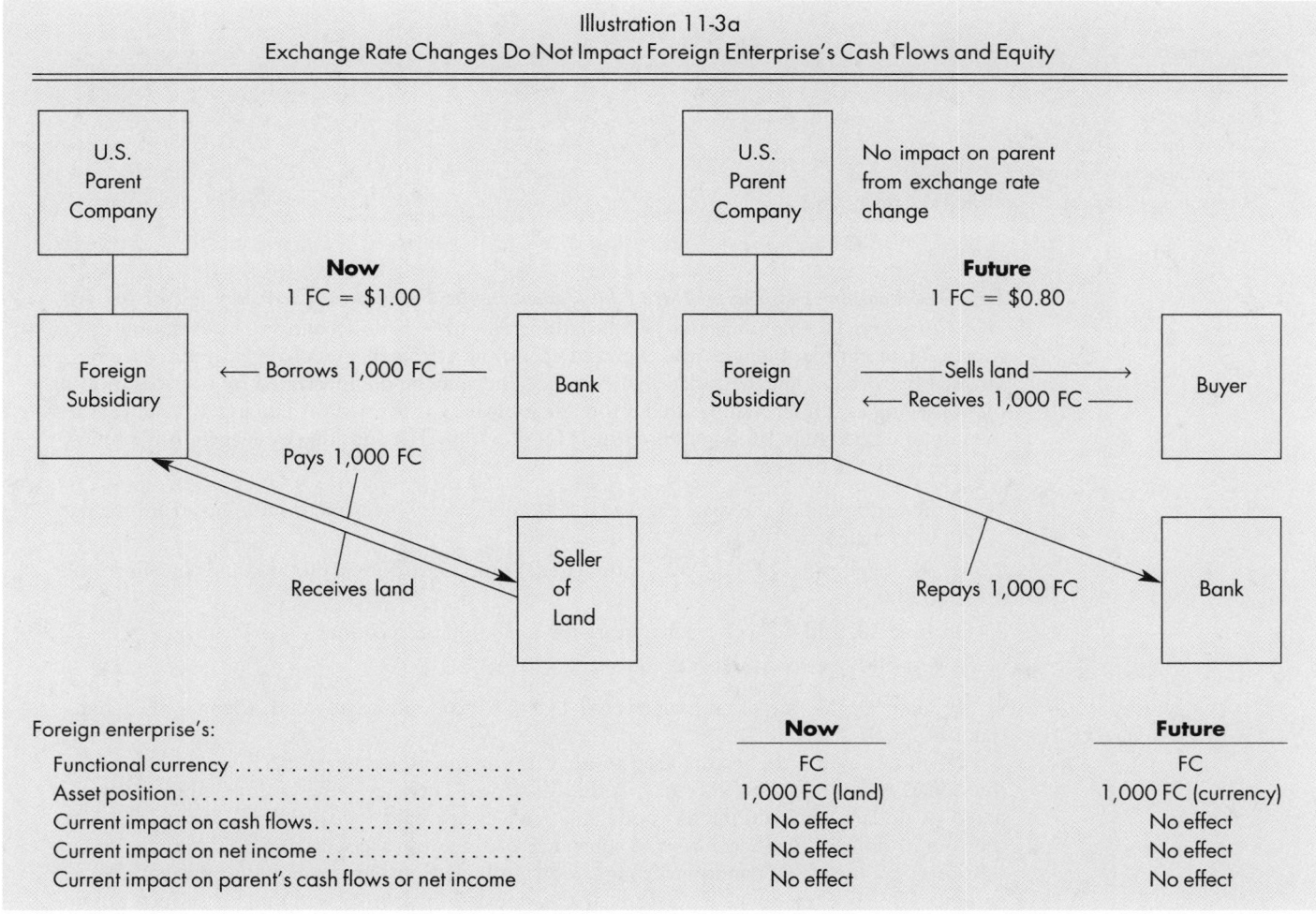

Illustration 11-3a
Exchange Rate Changes Do Not Impact Foreign Enterprise's Cash Flows and Equity

Foreign enterprise's:	Now	Future
Functional currency	FC	FC
Asset position.	1,000 FC (land)	1,000 FC (currency)
Current impact on cash flows.	No effect	No effect
Current impact on net income	No effect	No effect
Current impact on parent's cash flows or net income	No effect	No effect

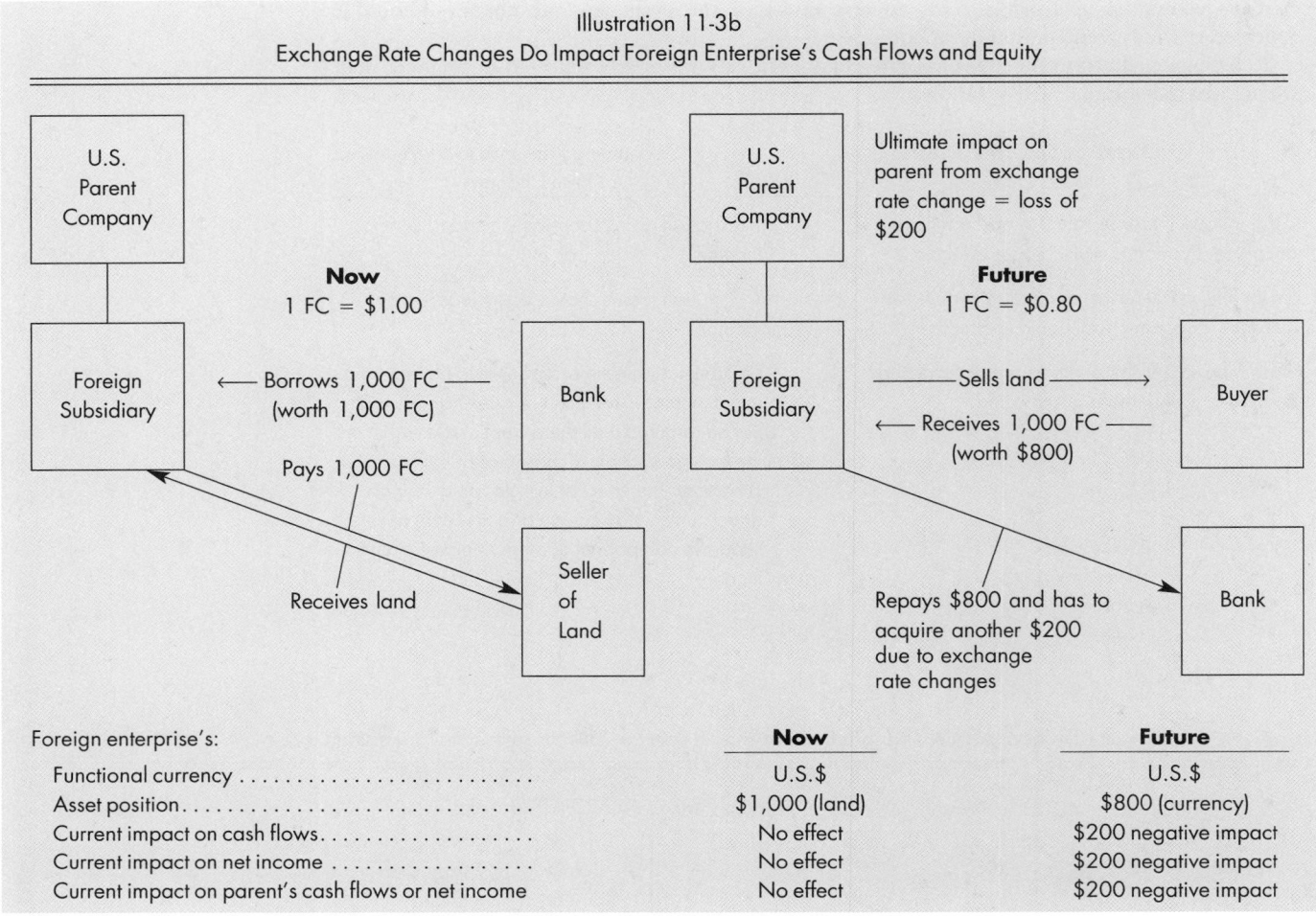

Illustration 11-3b
Exchange Rate Changes Do Impact Foreign Enterprise's Cash Flows and Equity

Foreign enterprise's:	Now	Future
	U.S.$	U.S.$
Functional currency		
Asset position	$1,000 (land)	$800 (currency)
Current impact on cash flows	No effect	$200 negative impact
Current impact on net income	No effect	$200 negative impact
Current impact on parent's cash flows or net income	No effect	$200 negative impact

Expected Economic Effects of Rate Changes when the Functional Currency Is Not the Foreign Currency. The first objective of translation seeks to provide accounting information that is consistent or compatible with the expected economic effects of rate changes. This objective is satisfied by focusing on the functional currency and may be demonstrated by consideration of the following example. Assume that a foreign subsidiary is formed on January 1, Year 1, when the rate of exchange is 1 foreign currency (FC) = $1.00. The subsidiary engaged in the following activity in the first year:

1. At the beginning of the year, received a $300,000 equity investment in dollars from the parent in exchange for stock.
2. At the beginning of the year, purchased equipment for $100,000 and inventory for $200,000.
3. On June 30, sold 40% of the inventory for $120,000 on account.
4. At year-end, the receivable was collected.

At June 30, the rate of exchange was 1 FC = $1.20, and at year-end, the rate of exchange was 1 FC = $1.25.

When evaluating the factors used to identify the functional currency, it would appear that the dollar, not the foreign currency, is the functional currency, because financing is denominated in dollars, acquisitions of goods and services are paid for in dollars, and sales are receivable in dollars. Furthermore, the substance of these transactions suggests that the foreign subsidiary is merely a conduit through which the U.S. parent conducts business and experiences dollar cash flows. Therefore, if the translation process is sound, it should provide information that is compatible with the expected economic effects of rate changes. In this particular example, the translated dollar amounts for the subsidiary should be identical to the dollar balances that would have resulted had the U.S. parent engaged in these transactions without the foreign subsidiary serving as a conduit. If the parent, rather than the subsidiary, had engaged in the above activities, it would have made the following entries shown in column A as compared to the entries in column B which were made by the foreign subsidiary as measured in FC:

		Column A in U.S.$		Column B in FC	
Jan. 1	Cash	300,000		300,000	
	Common Stock		300,000		300,000
	To record initial investment when 1 FC = $1.00.				
	Equipment	100,000		100,000	
	Inventory	200,000		200,000	
	Cash		300,000		300,000
	To record initial cash expenditures when 1 FC = $1.00.				
June 30	Accounts Receivable	120,000		100,000	
	Sales Revenue		120,000		100,000
	To record sale when 1 FC = $1.20, which is the equivalent of 100,000 FC ($120,000 ÷ $1.20).				
	Cost of Sales	80,000		80,000	
	Inventory		80,000		80,000
	To record cost of sales (40% of available inventory of $200,000).				
Dec. 31	Cash	120,000		96,000	
	Exchange Loss	0		4,000	
	Accounts Receivable		120,000		100,000
	To record collection of receivable when 1 FC = $1.25. The $120,000 receivable has a 96,000 FC equivalent ($120,000 ÷ $1.25).				

Resulting year-end trial balances and analytics measured in dollars and FC are as follows:

Trial Balances	Column A in U.S.$	Column B in FC
Cash	$ 120,000	96,000 FC
Inventory	120,000	120,000
Equipment	100,000	100,000
Common stock	(300,000)	(300,000)
Sales revenue	(120,000)	(100,000)
Cost of sales	80,000	80,000
Exchange loss		4,000
Total	$ 0	0 FC
Net income	$ 40,000	16,000 FC
Current assets to total assets	0.71 to 1 (240/340)	0.68 to 1 (216/316)
Gross profit margin	33.33%	20%

In this example, remember that the subsidiary is merely a conduit through which the U.S. parent conducts business and experiences dollar cash flows because the dollar is the functional currency. Therefore, the subsidiary's financial statements when translated into U.S. dollars should be the same as what the financial statements would have been had the U.S. parent recorded the transactions (values per column A above). The translation process should translate the values in FC (the column B values) at exchange rates so that the resulting values in dollars are equal to the column A values. The following translated trial balances accomplish this goal based on the suggested relevant exchange rates:

Trial Balances	Column B in FC	Relevant Exchange Rate	Column A in U.S.$
Cash	96,000 FC	1.25	$ 120,000
Inventory	120,000	1.00	120,000
Equipment	100,000	1.00	100,000
Common stock	(300,000)	1.00	(300,000)
Sales revenue	(100,000)	1.20	(120,000)
Cost of sales	80,000	1.00	80,000
Exchange loss	4,000	1.25	5,000
Subtotal	0 FC		$ 5,000
Translation adjustment (to balance) a component of net income			(5,000)
Total	0 FC		$ 0
Net income	16,000 FC		$ 40,000
Current assets to total assets			0.71 to 1 (240/340)
Gross profit margin			33.33%

Note the exchange rates that were necessary to achieve the above desired outcome. Monetary net assets (cash in this example) were translated at current rates, historical values (inventory and equipment) were translated at historical rates, common stock was translated at historical rates, revenues and expenses not involving historical values (sales revenue and exchange loss) were translated at the rate in existence when the income transaction occurred, and revenues and expenses representing historical values (cost of inventory sold) were translated at historical rates.

The objective of the translation process was to produce financial statements that reflected the economic effects of exchange rate changes on an enterprise's cash flows and equity. In this example, the U.S. dollar was the functional currency, not the FC. Therefore, the subsidiary was exposed to exchange rate risk and merely functioned as a conduit through which the U.S. parent conducted business. The goal of translating the FC statements was to produce identical values to those that would have resulted if the U.S. parent had engaged in the same transactions. A comparison of the above financial statements compared to those that would have resulted had the U.S. parent recorded the transactions reveals that the values are identical. The relevant exchange rates necessary to accomplish this goal are dependent upon a proper identification of the functional currency. The first objective of the translation process has been satisfied, and the results confirm the following:

1. The foreign subsidiary merely acted as a conduit through which the U.S. parent operated.
2. The foreign subsidiary's translated financial statements are identical to those statements that would have resulted had the transactions been originally recorded in the dollar functional currency (translated statements into dollars are the same as the original column A values as though the parent had recorded the transactions).
3. The financial statement relationships (current assets as a percentage of total assets and return on original equity) for the translated financial statements are identical to those that would have resulted had the transactions been originally recorded in the dollar functional currency.
4. The transactions of the foreign entity had an immediate or potentially immediate impact on the dollar cash flows and equity; therefore, the impact was included in net income. Including the translation adjustment in the translated income results in net income of $40,000 which is identical to what would have resulted had the transactions been originally recorded in the dollar functional currency. If the translation adjustment were not included as a component of net income, then the translated net income would have been only $35,000 which is not the same as what would have resulted had the transactions been originally recorded in the dollar functional currency.

In this example, the translation process produced financial statements that reflect the economic effects of exchange rate risk and include the effects of that risk as a component of net income. The total value of the translated assets is $340,000 which is $40,000 more than the initial $300,000 of assets invested into the subsidiary. Clearly, the $40,000 change could be distributed as increased cash flow to the parent. This increase has impacted the enterprise's cash flows and equity. Therefore, the exchange rate change did have a potentially immediate effect on the cash flows and economic well-being of the parent and should be included in net income of the period in which exchange rates change. (This example parallels the one in Illustration 11-2b.)

Expected Economic Effects of Rate Changes when the Functional Currency Is the Foreign Currency. If the foreign currency (FC) is the functional currency, rate changes are not expected to have an immediate impact on the parent's cash flows (as shown in Illustration 11-3a). Therefore, in response to rate changes, the accounting information should not include any translation adjustment in the determination of current net income. Instead, translation adjustments should be classified as a separate component of other comprehensive income. This component would be recognized as a component of net income when realized through the liquidation or disposition of the foreign entity. In order to demonstrate these concepts, consider the following example:

Assume the facts of the previous example except that all transactions are denominated in FC as follows:

1. At the beginning of the year, received a 300,000 FC equity investment from the parent in exchange for stock.
2. At the beginning of the year, purchased equipment for 100,000 FC and inventory for 200,000 FC.
3. On June 30, sold 40% of the inventory for 100,000 FC on account.
4. At year-end, the receivable was collected.

When evaluating the factors used to identify a functional currency, it would appear that the FC is the functional currency because financing is denominated in FC, acquisitions of goods and services are paid for in FC, and sales prices are based on local economics and are collected in FC. Furthermore, the substance of these transactions suggests that the foreign subsidiary operates independently of the U.S. parent (not as a conduit), and its day-to-day operations are not dependent on the economic environment of the U.S. parent's currency but on that of the foreign country. Therefore, changes in the exchange rate between the FC and the U.S. dollar would not impact the enterprise's cash flows or equity. Entries to record the activity on the books of the foreign subsidiary as measured and denominated in FC are as follows:

Jan. 1	Cash	300,000	
	Common Stock		300,000
	To record initial investment of 300,000 FC.		
	Equipment	100,000	
	Inventory	200,000	
	Cash		300,000
	To record initial cash expenditures of 300,000 FC.		
June 30	Accounts Receivable	100,000	
	Sales Revenue		100,000
	To record sale for 100,000 FC.		
	Cost of Sales	80,000	
	Inventory		80,000
	To record cost of sales (40% of available inventory of 200,000 FC).		
Dec. 31	Cash	100,000	
	Accounts Receivable		100,000
	To record collection of receivable.		

Since the subsidiary is not exposed to exchange rate risk, it would seem that the relationships that existed as measured in FC should continue to be the same after the FC are translated into U.S. dollars. The translation process should not make an entity look fundamentally different if exchange rate risk does not impact it. Resulting trial balances and analytics measured in FC and translated into U.S. dollars are as follows:

Trial Balances	In FC	Relevant Exchange Rate	In U.S.$
Cash	100,000 FC	1.25	$ 125,000
Inventory	120,000	1.25	150,000
Equipment	100,000	1.25	125,000
Common stock	(300,000)	1.00	(300,000)
Sales revenue	(100,000)	1.20	(120,000)
Cost of sales	80,000	1.20	96,000
Subtotal	0 FC		$ 76,000
Translation adjustment (to balance) a component of other comprehensive income			(76,000)
Total	0 FC		$ 0
Net income	20,000 FC		$ 24,000
Current assets to total assets	0.69 to 1 (220/320)		0.69 to 1 (275/400)
Gross profit margin	20%		20%

Note the exchange rates that were necessary to achieve the above desired outcome. All assets and liabilities were translated at the current rate, common stock was translated at historical rates, and all revenues and all expenses were translated at the rate in existence when the income transaction occurred.

Given the above translated trial balance, it is clear that a translation adjustment is needed in order for the trial balance to balance. The question is how the translation adjustment should be classified on financial statements. Since the foreign subsidiary's functional currency is the FC, it is not exposed to exchange rate risk. Changes in the exchange rates between the FC and the U.S. dollar have no immediate economic impact on the subsidiary. Therefore, it would not make sense to include the translation adjustment as a component of current-period net income. However, it is a balancing amount that needs to be classified somewhere. Since there does not appear to be any immediate impact on earnings related to exchange rate risk, the translation adjustment is to be included as a component of other comprehensive income. This solution does not impact current-period earnings but does allow for the balance sheet to balance.

In comparing the results of the above example to that of the prior example, where the foreign entity was merely a conduit and the functional currency was the U.S. dollar, several important differences surface.

◆ The exchange rate change requires an adjustment to the accounts receivable when the dollar is the functional currency but not when the foreign currency is the functional currency.

◆ When the FC is the functional currency, changes in the exchange rate do not produce an exchange gain or loss with respect to the accounts receivable because it is denominated in FC and rate changes have no impact on the settlement value of the receivable.

◆ When the FC is the functional currency, there is no indication that the exchange rate changes will immediately impact the subsidiary's or the parent's cash flows or equity. Therefore, to include the translation adjustment as a component of net income would not be compatible with the economic effects of the rate change. Because the impact on the cash flows is unclear, the translation adjustment is included as a separate component of other comprehensive income rather than as net income.

◆ It is important to note that the translation adjustment included as a component of other comprehensive income is a balance sheet account that may change in value over time as subsequent exchange rate changes occur. For example, if the trial balance for the subsidiary changes in year 2 and exchange rates change, the necessary translation adjustment needed to balance will also change.

If there is a balance in the cumulative translation adjustment included as a component of other comprehensive income, its impact on the parent's cash flows and/or economic well-being is normally not considered to be immediate or potentially immediate unless the parent liquidates or disposes of its investment in the foreign subsidiary. At that time, the separate component of other comprehensive income should be transferred to the income statement and recognized as a component of net income. To illustrate, assume that in the above example the foreign subsidiary is liquidated after the first year and all noncash assets (inventory of 120,000 FC plus equipment of 100,000 FC) are disposed of at book value in FC. After converting all assets into cash, 320,000 FC of cash would be remitted to the parent in exchange for its equity investment. The 320,000 FC received by the parent have a value of $400,000 (assuming the exchange rate remains at 1 FC = $1.25). When compared to the historical basis of the parent's original $300,000 investment in the equity of the subsidiary, the current equity of $400,000 represents a $100,000 realized gain. The $100,000 gain over time is represented by the year 1 net income of $24,000 and the realization of the $76,000 translation adjustment which was previously classified as a component of other comprehensive income.

I A S B   P E R S P E C T I V E S

IAS 21, *The Effects of Changes in Foreign Currency Rates*, addresses the translation of foreign financial statements. The standard does not use the term "translation adjustment" but rather "exchange difference" to describe the difference resulting from translating a number of units of one currency into another currency. The methodology for translating from the functional currency into the presentation currency is the same, and the exchange difference is recognized in other comprehensive income. In addition to the disposal of an interest in a foreign entity, the international standard identifies other factors that may result in the recognition of the exchange differences as a component of income even if the parent retains an interest in the foreign entity.

As a second objective of the translation process, the FASB stated that the translation process should produce (consolidated) financial statements that reflect the financial results and relationships of the individual entities as measured in their functional currency. In both of the above examples, this objective was accomplished as evidenced by the following financial relationships:

	First Example: U.S. Dollar = Functional Currency			Second Example: FC = Functional Currency	
	As Measured in Functional Currency	As Measured in Foreign Currency	Translated Statements	As Measured in Functional Currency	Translated Statements
Current assets to total assets	0.71 to 1	0.68 to 1	0.71 to 1	0.69 to 1	0.69 to 1
Gross profit margin	33.33%	20%	33.33%	20%	20%

The above illustrations emphasize the importance of properly identifying the functional currency. The expected economic effects of rate changes vary, and the foreign subsidiary's financial statements differ significantly, depending upon the identification of the functional currency. The translation process set forth by the FASB achieves its objectives when the functional currency is properly identified.

Relative to a parent/subsidiary relationship, a summary of the critical observations associated with the identification of the functional currency is as shown on page 606.

	When the Functional Currency	
	Is Not the Foreign Currency	Is the Foreign Currency
Nature of the subsidiary entity.	Operates as a conduit through which transactions occur in the parent's functional currency.	Operates as an independent entity through which transactions occur in the subsidiary's functional currency.
Exchange rate changes.	Affect the economic well-being of the parent.	Do not affect the economic well-being of the parent.
Effect of exchange rate changes on net income.	The effect is a gain or loss which is recognized as a component of net income.	The effect is not currently recognized as a component of net income but rather as a component of other comprehensive income.
Effect of exchange rate changes on the parent's cash flows.	Changes have an immediate or potentially immediate impact on cash flows.	Changes do not have an immediate or potentially immediate impact on cash flows. The impact on cash flows is currently unclear.
When the translation adjustment is recognized as a component of current-period net income.	The translation adjustment is recognized immediately in current-period net income.	The translation adjustment is recognized when there is a partial or complete sale or complete or substantially complete liquidation of the investment in the foreign entity.
The subsidiary's financial relationships between accounts.	Relationships subsequent to translation are different than they were prior to translation, therefore reflecting the economic effect of exchange rate changes.	Relationships subsequent to translation retain the same values as they had prior to translation. Exchange rate changes do not have an economic effect on the parent.

REFLECTION

- The functional currency is the primary currency in which an entity experiences cash inflows and outflows. Evaluating cash flows, marketing practices, financing arrangements, and procurement of necessary factors of production may identify this currency.

- Given a functional currency, the objectives of translation are to provide information that is reflective of the economic effects of exchange rate changes. Translation should also reflect the financial results and relationships of entities consistent with their functional currency and U.S. GAAP.

3
OBJECTIVE

Apply the functional currency translation process to a trial balance, and calculate the translation adjustment.

BASIC TRANSLATION PROCESS: FUNCTIONAL CURRENCY TO REPORTING CURRENCY

Before beginning the translation process, **the financial statements of the foreign entity must be adjusted to conform to generally accepted accounting principles.** Although this is a very important step in the accounting process, the specifics are not covered in this text. It is assumed that all of the adjustments to GAAP have already been made. The next step in the translation process is to identify the functional currency of the foreign entity.

- If the functional currency is determined to be the foreign entity's local currency, the *current rate method* is used to translate. This is also called the *functional* or *translation method.*
- If the foreign entity's local currency is not the functional currency, the *historical rate method* is used to translate. This is also called the *temporal* or *remeasurement method.*

In the following pages, both the current rate/functional method and the historical rate/temporal method will be fully illustrated.

The basic translation process is applied to a foreign subsidiary's trial balance prior to its inclusion in consolidated financial statements, home and branch combined statements, or the computation of equity income for influential foreign investments.

With respect to consolidated financial statements, recall that one of the primary criteria to determine if consolidation is appropriate deals with the extent of control the parent entity exercises over the subsidiary. For foreign subsidiaries, effective control is determined, in part, by currency restrictions and the possibility of nationalization of the operations by foreign governments. Assuming consolidation is appropriate, the financial statements of the foreign entity must be translated into dollars. Then intercompany eliminations are made, and the statements are consolidated according to the principles of consolidation discussed earlier in this text.

Demonstrating the Current Rate/Functional Method

If the foreign entity's currency is the functional currency, then the current rate method would be used for translation. The current rate/functional method requires that:

1. All assets and liabilities are translated at the current exchange rate at the date of translation.
2. Elements of income are translated at the current exchange rates that existed at the time the revenues and expense were recognized. As a practical consideration, income elements normally are translated at a weighted-average exchange rate for the period.
3. Equity accounts other than retained earnings are translated at the historical exchange rate on the date of investment in the subsidiary.
4. Retained earnings are translated in layers.

   a. Retained earnings that exist on the date of investment are translated at the historical rate on the date of investment.
   b. Income additions to retained earnings since the initial acquisition are included as translated in item (2).
   c. Reductions for dividends are translated at the historical exchange rates at the date of declaration.

5. Components of the statement of cash flows are translated at the exchange rates in effect at the time of the cash flows. Operations are translated at the rate used for income elements [see item (2) above]. The reconciliation of the change in cash and cash equivalents during the period should include the effect of exchange rate changes on cash balances.
6. The translation process will result in a cumulative translation adjustment which is classified as a component of other comprehensive income (OCI) expressed in the parent/investor's currency (U.S. dollars) rather than as a component of net income.

Illustration 11-4 demonstrates the translation of a subsidiary's financial statements, measured in its local currency (the functional currency), into U.S. dollars for the purpose of preparing consolidated financial statements and is based on the following facts:

1. Sori Corporation, a foreign corporation, began operations on January 1, 2010. On January 1, 2011, when net assets totaled 100,000 FC, 90% of Sori stock was acquired by Pome Corporation, a U.S. corporation. Sori's functional currency is the foreign currency, and it maintains its records in the functional currency.
2. Sales to Pome are billed in the foreign currency, and all receivables from Pome have been collected except for the amount shown in the account Due from Pome. All other sales are billed in the foreign currency as well. The level of sales and purchases was constant over the year. None of the inventory purchased from Sori remains in Pome's ending inventory.
3. Selected exchange rates between the functional currency and the dollar are as follows:

Date	Rate
January 1, 2010	1 FC = $0.98
January 1, 2011	1 FC = 1.00
December 31, 2011	1 FC = 1.05
2011 average	1 FC = 1.03

Illustration 11-4
Sori Corporation
Trial Balance Translation
December 31, 2011

Account	Balance in Functional Currency	Relevant Exchange Rate (Dollars/FC)	Balance in Dollars
Cash	10,000 FC	1.05	$ 10,500
Accounts Receivable	21,000	1.05	22,050
Allowance for Doubtful Accounts	(1,000)	1.05	(1,050)
Due from Pome	14,000	1.05	14,700
Inventory (at market, cost = 32,000)	30,000	1.05	31,500
Prepaid Insurance	3,000	1.05	3,150
Land	18,000	1.05	18,900
Depreciable Assets	120,000	1.05	126,000
Accumulated Depreciation	(15,000)	1.05	(15,750)
Cost of Goods Sold	180,000	1.03	185,400
Depreciation Expense	10,000	1.03	10,300
Income Tax Expense	30,000	1.03	30,900
Other Expenses	23,000	1.03	23,690
Total (Note B)	443,000 FC		$460,290
Accounts Payable	20,000 FC	1.05	$ 21,000
Taxes Payable	30,000	1.05	31,500
Accrued Interest Payable	1,000	1.05	1,050
Mortgage Payable—Land	10,000	1.05	10,500
Common Stock	80,000	1.00	80,000
Retained Earnings (January 1, 2011)	20,000	Note A	20,000
Sales—Pome	80,000	1.03	82,400
Sales—Other	200,000	1.03	206,000
Gain on Sale of Depreciable Assets	2,000	1.03	2,060
Cumulative Translation Adjustment (to balance)			**5,780**
Total (Note B)	443,000 FC		$460,290

Note A: The beginning balance of retained earnings normally is equal to the translated value of the previous period's ending retained earnings. However, since 2011 is the first year Pome has owned Sori, the beginning balance is set equal to the January 1, 2011 (acquisition date), balance of retained earnings in foreign currency translated at the January 1, 2011, spot rate (in this case, 1.00). The balance sheet for year-end 2011 would show a translated value for retained earnings equal to the translated beginning balance of retained earnings plus the translated value of net income less dividends translated at the rate existing on the declaration date.

Note B: If the accounts in this trial balance were arranged in balance sheet and income statement order, the following totals would be calculated:

Total revenues and gains	282,000 FC	$290,460
Total expenses	243,000	250,290
Net income (NI)	39,000 FC	$ 40,170
Total assets	200,000 FC	$210,000
Total liabilities	61,000 FC	$ 64,050
Total equity (including NI)	139,000	140,170
Total liabilities and equity (including NI)	200,000 FC	$204,220
Cumulative translation adjustment to balance		5,780
Total liabilities and equity (December 31, 2011)	200,000 FC	$210,000

Accounting for the Cumulative Translation Adjustment. Translation adjustments result from the process of translating foreign financial statements from their functional currency into the domestic entity's reporting currency. Because various exchange rates (current, historical, and weighted-average) are used in the translation process, the basic equality of the balance sheet equation is not preserved. Therefore, from a mechanical viewpoint, the translation adjustment is an amount necessary to balance a translated entity's trial balance. Translation adjustments do not exist in terms of the functional currency and have no immediate effect on the cash flows of the foreign or domestic entity. At the time of the translation, exchange rate fluctuations do not have an economic impact on the foreign entity or its domestic parent. Furthermore, any potential impact on the reporting (parent) entity is uncertain and remote. Therefore, as discussed above, it would be improper to include the translation adjustment in current reported net income. However, the translation adjustment must be reported somewhere. Rather than being included as a component of reported earnings, the translation should be included as a component of other comprehensive income. It is important to remember that the translation adjustment on the trial balance is a cumulative amount which changes from period to period.

Direct Calculation of the Current-Period Translation Adjustment. Although the translation adjustment is a balancing amount necessary to satisfy the balance sheet equation, the current period's (not cumulative) adjustment may be calculated directly as follows:

1. The change in exchange rates during the period multiplied by the amount of net assets (i.e., owners' equity) held by the domestic investor at the beginning of the period; plus
2. The difference between the weighted-average exchange rate used in translating income elements and the end-of-period exchange rate multiplied by the increase or decrease in net assets for the period traceable to net income, excluding capital transactions; plus (minus)
3. The increase (decrease) in net assets as a result of capital transactions, including investments by the domestic investor during the period (e.g., stock issuances, retirements, and dividends), multiplied by the difference between the end-of-period exchange rate and the exchange rate at the time of the transaction.

Based on the information given in Illustration 11-4, the direct calculation of the translation adjustment is as follows:

Reconciliation of Annual Translation Adjustment

Net assets at beginning of period multiplied by the change in exchange rates during the period [$0^a \times$ ($\$1.05 - \$1.00$)]	\$ 0
Increase in net assets (excluding capital transactions) multiplied by the difference between the current rate and the average rate used to translate income [39,000 FC$^b \times$ ($\$1.05 - \$1.03$)]	780
Increase in net assets due to capital transactions (including investments by the domestic investor) multiplied by the difference between the current rate and the rate at the time of the capital transaction [100,000 FC$^c \times$ ($\$1.05 - \$1.00$)]	5,000
Translation adjustment	\$5,780

^{a}Although Sori Corporation began operations in 2010, the parent company, Pome Corporation, had not acquired an interest until 2011. Therefore, Pome had no investment in Sori as of the beginning of 2011.
^{b}This is the net income for the period (see Illustration 11-4).
^{c}This is the original capital balance as of the date of the parent's acquisition.

The above reconciliation is not a required disclosure but may help in understanding the factors which contribute to the translation adjustment. Note that the reconciliation explains only the $5,780 translation adjustment traceable to 2011. After the first year of operation, the annual translation adjustments will be accumulated and presented as a component of other comprehensive income. For example, if Sori Corporation has a translation adjustment of $4,400 traceable to 2012, the accumulated other comprehensive income portion of equity on the balance sheet at the end of 2012 will show a cumulative translation adjustment of $10,180 ($5,780 + $4,400).

4

OBJECTIVE

Explain how the translation adjustment is accounted for and how a hedge may be employed.

Accomplishing the Objectives of Translation. The translation demonstrated in Illustration 11-4 has accomplished the objectives of translation. The economic effect of the exchange rate change (i.e., translation adjustment) has been presented as an increase in stockholders' equity, as a component of other comprehensive income, rather than as net income. The spot rate had increased from a beginning-of-year rate of 1 FC = $1.00 to an end-of-period rate of 1 FC = $1.05. This change indicates that the foreign currency strengthened relative to the dollar. Therefore, the domestic company's investment in the net assets of the foreign subsidiary has increased as evidenced by the increase in stockholders' equity. However, because the foreign entity's currency is the functional currency, exchange rate changes do not have an immediate effect on the cash flows of the foreign or domestic entity. Thus, the translation adjustment is not reported as a component of current net income but rather as a component of other comprehensive income. Therefore, the presentation is compatible with the expected economic effects of exchange rate changes. In addition, the translated financial statements reflect the same financial results and relationships of the foreign company as originally measured in its functional currency. For instance, the following ratios indicate that the original relationships have been preserved after translation:

Ratio	Before Translation	After Translation
Current	1.51 (77,000 ÷ 51,000)	1.51 (80,850 ÷ 53,550)
Debt-to-equity	0.44 (61,000 ÷ 139,000)*	0.44 (64,050 ÷ 145,950)**
Gross profit percent	36% (100,000 ÷ 280,000)	36% (103,000 ÷ 288,400)

  *See Illustration 11-4, Note B.
**After translation equity includes the cumulative translation adjustment ($140,170 + $5,780).

Subsequent Recognition of the Translation Adjustment. Although translation adjustments have no immediate effect on reported earnings, they may ultimately affect income when there is a *partial or complete sale or complete or substantially complete liquidation of the investment in the foreign entity.*[3] Unfortunately, the FASB has not defined what constitutes a substantially complete liquidation. Given such a sale or liquidation, some or all of the accumulated translation adjustment included in equity would be removed and included as part of the gain or loss on disposition of the investment. For example, assume a company owns 100% of a foreign entity, its investment account has a balance of $4,200,000, and its owners' equity includes accumulated other comprehensive income containing a debit of $320,000 representing the accumulated translation adjustment. If the entire investment in the subsidiary is sold for $4,750,000, the translation adjustment does affect the gain on sale as follows:

Proceeds from sale of investment.................	$ 4,750,000
Basis of investment account......................	(4,200,000)
	$ 550,000
Balance in cumulative translation adjustment	(320,000)
Gain on sale of investment......................	$ 230,000

    The cumulative translation adjustment did ultimately affect reported earnings as a component of the gain on the sale of the investment. It is important to note that if only a portion of the investment in the subsidiary were sold, then only a pro rata portion of the translation adjustment would have been allocated to the sale.

Consolidating the Foreign Subsidiary

Once a foreign subsidiary's financial statements have been translated into the reporting currency, certain eliminations and adjustments due to intercompany transactions generally will be required. With regard to the exchange rate that should be used to translate such transactions, the FASB concluded that **all intercompany balances, except for intercompany profits and losses, should be translated at the rates used for all other accounts. Intercompany profits and losses should be translated using the exchange rate that existed at the date of the sale or transfer.** As a practical matter, however, average rates or approximations may be used to translate such profits and losses.

5

OBJECTIVE

Describe the consolidation process and the sophisticated equity method, giving particular attention to modifications due to translation.

---

3 FASB ASC 830-30-40, *Foreign Currency Matters—Translation of Financial Statements—Derecognition.*

The facts of Illustration 11-4 are used here to demonstrate the consolidation process. Assume Pome Corporation paid 103,500 FC for its 90% interest in Sori Corporation. Recall that at the time of acquisition (January 1, 2011), Sori equity consisted of 80,000 FC of common stock and 20,000 FC of retained earnings. Upon acquisition of Sori, Pome recorded its investment as follows:

Investment in Sori..	103,500	
Cash (103,500 × $1.00)		103,500

Assuming that any excess is traceable to patents with a 10-year useful life, the excess of cost over book value is determined as follows:

Determination and Distribution of Excess Schedule (In FC)

	Company Implied Fair Value	Parent Price (90%)	NCI Value (10%)
Fair value of subsidiary	115,000	103,500	11,500
Less book value of interest acquired:			
Common stock....................................	80,000		
Retained earnings	20,000		
Total equity.....................................	100,000	100,000	100,000
Interest acquired		90%	10%
Book value......................................		90,000	10,000
Excess of fair value over book value	15,000	13,500	1,500

Adjustment of identifiable accounts:

	Adjustment	Amortization per Year	Life
Patent.......................................	15,000	1,500	10

Notice that the determination of excess is calculated in the foreign currency. The excess will be translated into the parent's currency separately. Assume that Pome used the simple equity method to account for its investment in Sori. The following translation would be required to determine the subsidiary income recorded by Pome. Note that under the current rate method the weighted-average exchange rate for the year is used to translate income items.

Account	Balance in Functional Currency	Relevant Exchange Rate (Dollars/FC)	Balance in Dollars
Sales—Pome..............................	80,000 FC	1.03	$ 82,400
Sales—Other..............................	200,000	1.03	206,000
Gain on Sale of Depreciable Assets	2,000	1.03	2,060
Cost of Goods Sold	(180,000)	1.03	(185,400)
Depreciation Expense	(10,000)	1.03	(10,300)
Income Tax Expense	(30,000)	1.03	(30,900)
Other Expenses (including interest)	(23,000)	1.03	(23,690)
Net Income	39,000		$ 40,170
Pome's share...............................			× 90%
Pome's interest in Sori net income (in dollars)			$ 36,153

The parent's entry to record its interest in the foreign subsidiary's undistributed income would be as follows:

Investment in Sori..	36,153	
Subsidiary Income......................................		36,153

Worksheet 11-1: page 632

Worksheet 11-1, pages 632 and 633, shows the consolidated financial statements of the Pome and Sori corporations. The trial balance amounts for Pome are assumed, and Sori's balances are based on Illustration 11-4. Entries (CY1) and (EL) in the worksheet follow the usual procedures of eliminating the current-period entry recording the parent's share of the subsidiary net income and its share of the subsidiary equity accounts as of the beginning of the period. Entry (CT) allocates 90% of Sori's cumulative adjustment to the controlling interest. These entries do not require any translating because the balances being eliminated have already been translated into U.S. dollars.

The asset markup is traceable to the parent's 90% investment. However, 100% of the suggested markup must be reflected on the consolidated financial statements, with 10% of the markup being traceable to the noncontrolling interest. The total markup is 15,000 FC (13,500 FC ÷ 90% = 15,000 FC) of which 10% is traceable to the noncontrolling interest. Entries to record 100% of the excess of cost over book value and appropriate depreciation/amortization of excess are based on translated values and are determined as follows:

Calculations for entry (D)/(NCI):

Distribution of Asset Markup	FC	Exchange Rate	U.S. Dollars
Accounts:			
Depreciable Assets and Patents....................	15,000	1.05[a]	$15,750 DR
Investment in Sori Corporation	13,500	1.00[b]	13,500 CR
Retained Earnings—Sori.........................	1,500	1.00	1,500 CR
Cumulative Translation Adjustment (to balance)			750 CR[c]

[a]Use the current exchange rate for asset markup as used in the current rate method for all asset accounts.
[b]Use the date of investment exchange rate for crediting the investment account because the objective of the entry is to eliminate this balance, and it was initially recorded at a 1.00 exchange rate.
[c]To be allocated 90% to parent and 10% to subsidiary.

Calculations for entry (A):

Amortization of Asset Markups	FC	Exchange Rate	U.S. Dollars
Accounts:			
Accumulated Depreciation and Amortization (15,000/10).	1,500	1.05[a]	$1,575 CR
Depreciation and Amortization Expense................	1,500	1.03[b]	1,545 DR
Cumulative Translation Adjustment (to balance)			30 DR[c]

[a]Use the current exchange rate for accumulated depreciation and amortization as used in the current rate method for all asset accounts.
[b]Use the weighted-average exchange rate for expenses as used in the current rate method for all income items.
[c]To be allocated 90% to parent and 10% to subsidiary.

Entries (IA) and (IS) follow the usual worksheet eliminations and adjustments for intercompany transactions and require no additional translation.

The consolidation procedures just discussed also are applicable to periods subsequent to the first year of acquisition. Although the methodology is the same, the following should be noted:

1. The parent and noncontrolling interest must both continue to recognize their interests in the amortization of any original excess of cost over book value.
2. Any additional cumulative adjustment traceable to the excess of cost over book value should continue to be recognized.

When consolidating a foreign subsidiary, special attention must be paid to the elimination of intercompany profits. This is true only when the foreign entity's currency is the functional currency. The problem arises because the exchange rates used to translate receivables and payables resulting from intercompany transactions are different from the rates that existed at the date of the intercompany transaction. In order to illustrate this point, assume that a U.S. parent sold inventory to a foreign subsidiary and that none of the inventory had been sold by the subsidiary as of the end of the period. In the consolidation process, it would be appropriate to eliminate the parent's receivable and the subsidiary's corresponding payable. Furthermore, the unrealized intercompany profit on the unsold inventory must also be eliminated. For purposes of discussion, assume that the intercompany transaction is denominated in foreign currencies in the amount of 1,000 FC and that relevant exchange rates are as follows:

| Date of sale | 1 FC = $1.00 | End of period | 1 FC = $1.20 |

Relevant balances at the end of the period would be as follows:

	Value in FC	Exchange Rate	Value in U.S. Dollars
Parent's Accounts:			
Accounts Receivable	1,000	1.20	$1,200
Sales Revenue	1,000	1.00	1,000
Cost of Sales (assume 80%)			800
Subsidiary's Accounts (translated using current rate method):			
Accounts Payable	1,000	1.20	$1,200
Inventory	1,000	1.20	1,200

It is clear from the preceding schedule of account balances that the dollar values of the parent's accounts receivable and the subsidiary's accounts payable are equal and could be eliminated against each other. However, the problem arises with the elimination of the unrealized intercompany profit included in the ending inventory of the subsidiary. If the profit of 20% were eliminated using the translated value of the inventory, then $240 (20% × $1,200) of profit would be eliminated, which does not agree with the $200 of intercompany profit that actually existed at the date of the transaction. However, if the intercompany profit is eliminated using the rate of exchange that existed at the date of the transaction, no inconsistency exists. At the date of the transaction, the inventory had a dollar equivalent of $1,000 (1,000 FC × $1), and the 20% unrealized profit of $200 (20% × $1,000) would be the appropriate amount of profit to eliminate against the parent's gross profit of $200 (sales revenue of $1,000 versus the cost of sales of $800). Therefore, the exchange rate at the date of the original transaction must *always* be used to determine the amount of unrealized profit to be eliminated. Once again, this complication will be encountered only when translating from the functional currency into the parent's reporting currency.

Gains and Losses Excluded from Income

The other comprehensive income section of equity in which cumulative translation adjustments are reported also should include gains and losses attributable to:

1. Foreign currency transactions that are designated and effective as economic hedges of a net investment in a foreign entity, beginning with the designation date.
2. Intercompany foreign currency transactions that are long-term investments in nature (i.e., settlement is not planned or anticipated in the foreseeable future) when the entities involved in the transaction are consolidated, combined, or accounted for by the equity method in the reporting enterprise's financial statements.[4]

Foreign Currency Transactions as Hedges of a Net Investment in a Foreign Entity. When translating foreign financial statements from their functional currency into dollars, a translation adjustment is produced and classified as a component of other comprehensive income. Noting that OCI is a component of owners' equity, the translation adjustment has the effect of either increasing or decreasing the parent company's equity as a result of its net investment in the foreign subsidiary. A parent company would certainly want to minimize any adverse impact on equity and may decide to hedge against such impacts. This is referred to as a hedge of a net investment in a foreign entity. Not knowing whether the impact of translation on equity will be positive or negative, some companies hedge net investments as a matter of policy. Such hedges

---

4 FASB ASC 830-20-35-3, *Foreign Currency Matters—Foreign Currency Transactions—Subsequent Measurement.*

may be accomplished through the use of a nonderivative or derivative instrument. The purpose of the hedging strategy is to offset the negative (positive) effect of the translation adjustment on the net investment with the gain (loss) on the hedging instrument. The gain or loss on a designated and effective hedge of a net investment should be classified in the same manner as is the translation adjustment. Therefore, if the translation adjustment is classified as a component of other comprehensive income, the gain or loss on the accompanying hedge would also be classified as a component of other comprehensive income. As discussed in a subsequent section of this chapter, in some instances, the translation adjustment may be classified as a component of net income. In these instances, the gain or loss on a hedge of a net investment would also be similarly classified.

In order to demonstrate a hedge of a net investment in a foreign entity, recall the facts surrounding Illustration 11-4 and Worksheet 11-1. The facts supporting Illustration 11-4 were based on a parent company (Pome Corporation) acquiring a 90% interest in a subsidiary company (Sori Corporation) when the subsidiary's net equity was 100,000 FC. Initially not knowing whether the translation adjustment would have a positive or negative impact on equity, assume that the parent company, as a matter of policy, hedged its net investment in the foreign subsidiary. Assume that in order to hedge its investment on January 1, 2011, the parent company secured a foreign bank loan denominated in the foreign currency when the spot rate was 1 FC = $1.00. The bank loan has a principal amount of 90,000 FC (90% of the subsidiary's equity). Interest calculations are ignored for purposes of this example. The bank loan is designated as a hedge of the net investment and is considered to have satisfied all necessary criteria. Because the exchange rates have changed, the value of the hedging instrument has also changed as follows:

Value of loan payable at December 31, 2011 (90,000 FC × $1.050)...	$94,500
Value of loan payable at inception (90,000 FC × $1.000)	90,000
Change in value of loan payable	$ 4,500

The entry to record the change in value of the payable is as follows:

OCI—Translation Adjustment	4,500	
Loan Payable		4,500

Illustration 11-4 presented the translation of a foreign subsidiary's (Sori Corporation) financial statements into dollars. The translation resulted in a current-year translation adjustment of $5,780. The net amount of the translation adjustment that impacts the parent company's (Pome Corporation) OCI is determined as follows based on Worksheet 11-1:

Current-year translation adjustment (from Illustration 11-4).	$5,780
Portion allocated to noncontrolling interest (11-1).	(578)
Subtotal	$5,202
Increase due to distribution of excess and amortization	
[Worksheet 11-1 entry (D)]	675
Decrease due to amortization of excess	
[Worksheet 11-1 entry (A)]	(27)
Current-year translation adjustment allocated to parent company	$5,850

The above $5,850 translation adjustment would be shown as a component of the parent's OCI. Offset against this amount would be the $4,500 traceable to the hedge of the net investment. Therefore, the hedge was considered to be effective.

Note that the effectiveness of the hedging instrument (the FC denominated bank loan) against the net investment in the subsidiary is as follows:

Effect on parent's OCI of translation	$5,850	credit
Effect on OCI of hedge on net investment	4,500	debit
Net effect on OCI.	$1,350	credit

If the change in the value of the hedging instrument exceeds the related translation adjustment recognized during the period of the hedge, the excess is ineffective and recognized in earnings. In the above example, none of the hedge was ineffective. However, if the hedge had involved a loan for 130,000 FC, the change in the value of the loan payable would have been $6,500 [130,000 FC × ($1.05 − $1.00)], which would have exceeded the related translation adjustment. Therefore, the excess change in value that does not offset the translation adjustment would be recognized in current earnings.

The foreign currency strengthened against the dollar resulting in an increase in equity due to the translation adjustment. In retrospect, the parent should not have hedged its investment even though the hedge was effective in offsetting the effect on OCI of the translation. Once again, we are reminded that exchange rates may not actually change as one had hoped or anticipated.

The above example involved the hedge of a net investment with a nonderivative instrument. However, it is also possible to employ a derivative instrument such as a forward contract or foreign currency option and be accorded the same accounting treatment.

Intercompany Foreign Currency Transactions of a Long-Term Nature. The second example of an exchange gain or loss that may be excluded from income and be included as a component of equity relates to certain long-term investment transactions between a domestic company and its foreign subsidiary. For example, assume a U.S. parent borrows funds from a French subsidiary with the loan being denominated in euros. If the settlement of the loan is not planned or anticipated in the foreseeable future, the effect of rate changes on the loan also would not have a foreseeable effect on the income of the U.S. parent. Therefore, the effect of rate changes on long-term investment transactions, such as this loan example, should be reflected in owners' equity as other comprehensive income, not current net income.

Unconsolidated Investments: Translation for the Cost or Equity Method

Unconsolidated foreign investments are accounted for by either the cost method or the sophisticated equity method. Under the cost method, a complete translation of the foreign financial statements is not necessary. The parent company must record the cost basis of its investment in dollars. If the cost is incurred in foreign currency, the exchange rate at the date of acquisition should be used. Investment income is translated at the exchange rate at the date dividends are declared.

If the parent's interest in the foreign subsidiary is considered influential, the subsidiary will not be consolidated and the sophisticated equity method should be employed. This method requires the adjustment of subsidiary income or loss for the amortization of differences between book and market values of the investment and any intercompany profits or losses. Application of this method to an investment in a foreign entity will be demonstrated using the facts of Illustration 11-4.

Assume Pome Corporation paid 34,500 FC ($34,500) for a 30% interest in Sori Corporation on January 1, 2011. Furthermore, assuming that any excess is traceable to patents with a 10-year useful life, the excess of cost over book value is determined as follows:

Price paid		34,500 FC
Equity purchased:		
Common stock.	80,000 FC	
Retained earnings	20,000	
Total	100,000 FC	
30% Interest acquired		30,000
Excess cost traceable to patents.		4,500 FC

Pome's interest in the adjusted net income of Sori is calculated as follows:

Sori net income translated into dollars.	$40,170
Pome's share.	×30%
Pome's interest in Sori net income	$12,051
Amortization of excess related to the patents	
(4,500 FC ÷ 10 years × $1.03 average rate)	(464)
Pome's equity share of Sori net income adjusted for amortization of excess.	$11,587

The investor also must recognize its interest in the cumulative translation adjustment for 2011, calculated as follows:

Cumulative translation adjustment (from Illustration 11-4).	$5,780
Pome's share.	× 30%
Pome's interest in the cumulative translation adjustment	$1,734

The following entries are to record Pome's interest in the foreign entity under the sophisticated equity method:

```
2011
Jan. 1      Investment in Sori Corporation .......................   34,500
                Cash .........................................              34,500
                    To record the initial investment of 34,500 FC
                    when the spot rate was 1 FC = $ 1.00.

Dec. 31     Investment in Sori Corporation .......................   13,321
                Subsidiary Income...............................              11,587
                Cumulative Translation Adjustment ...................           1,734
                    To record share of net income adjusted for the
                    amortization of excess and share of cumulative
                    translation adjustment.
```

Notice that under the sophisticated equity method the investor recorded both the amortization of the excess of cost over book value and its share of the current year's translation adjustment.

REFLECTION

- If the foreign entity's currency is the functional currency, the current rate method is used and the translation process is as follows: all assets and liabilities are translated at current rates, net income at weighted-average rates, and equity accounts (excluding retained earnings) at historical rates.

- The translation is based on the premise that changes in exchange rates will have no immediate effect on the cash flows or economic well-being of the foreign entity or parent/investor. Therefore, the resulting translation adjustment is classified as a component of other comprehensive income and generally is not recognized in current earnings until there is a sale or liquidation of the foreign subsidiary.

- The net investment in a foreign entity may be hedged, and the change in value of the hedging instrument will be recognized as a component of other comprehensive income.

- The consolidation of a parent and a foreign subsidiary involves special adjustments involving the excess over cost and the elimination of intercompany profits. Under the sophisticated equity method, the parent must recognize its proportional interest in the translation adjustment.

REMEASURED FINANCIAL STATEMENTS: FOREIGN CURRENCY TO FUNCTIONAL CURRENCY

6

OBJECTIVE

Apply the remeasurement process to a trial balance, and explain how to account for the remeasurement gain or loss.

The previous illustrations of the translation process assumed that the currency of the foreign entity was the functional currency. However, there are certain instances when the functional currency is not the currency of the foreign entity. In these instances, the financial statements of the foreign entity must be remeasured into the functional currency before the financial statements can be translated into the parent's domestic currency. The remeasurement process is intended to produce financial statements that are the same as if the foreign entity's transactions had been originally recorded in the functional currency. In essence, *the historical exchange rates between the functional currency and the foreign currency are used to remeasure certain accounts.* The adjustment resulting from the remeasurement process is referred to as a *remeasurement gain or loss* and is included as a component of net income.

If the foreign entity's currency is not the functional currency, then the historical rate method is used for remeasurement/translation. The historical rate/temporal method requires that:

1. Monetary assets and all liabilities are translated at the current exchange rate at the date of translation. All other assets are translated at the historical exchange rate on the date the assets were acquired. (Use the historical rate on the date of the investment if assets were acquired before the investment was made in the foreign entity.)
2. Elements of income are translated at the weighted-average exchange rate for the period except for items that can be specifically identified with a date of acquisition. For example, use the historical rate on the date inventory and fixed assets were acquired for translating cost of goods sold and depreciation expense, respectively.
3. Equity accounts are translated as they were for the current method.

    a. Equity and retained earnings balances on the date of investment are translated at the historical exchange rate on that date.
    b. Income additions to retained earnings are included as translated in item (2).
    c. Dividend deductions to retained earnings are translated at the historical exchange rates at the date of declaration.

4. The remeasurement process will result in a remeasurement gain or loss that is classified as a component of net income expressed in the functional currency rather than as a component of other comprehensive income.

The remeasurement process is encountered in two situations. One situation arises when the entity's books of record (accounting records) and resulting financial statements are prepared in a currency that is not the functional currency. Another situation arises when the foreign entity is in a highly inflationary economy. In that case, the functional currency is the domestic entity's reporting currency (dollars for U.S. parent companies).

Books of Record Not Maintained in Functional Currency

Perhaps one of the most common situations in which the books of record are not maintained in the functional currency is when the functional currency is the parent/investor's currency. For example, assume that a U.S. company has a Mexican subsidiary. That parent invested dollars in that subsidiary, and dollar-denominated loans were arranged on behalf of the subsidiary. As shown in Illustration 11-5, the Mexican company acquires raw materials from Japanese suppliers that are paid in U.S. dollars and sells the manufactured products throughout Central and North America. The subsidiary's sales are denominated in dollars, and distributions of earnings are remitted to the parent in dollars. Based on the above information, it is clear that the Mexican company's functional currency is the U.S. dollar even though it maintains its books of record (BR) in Mexican pesos.

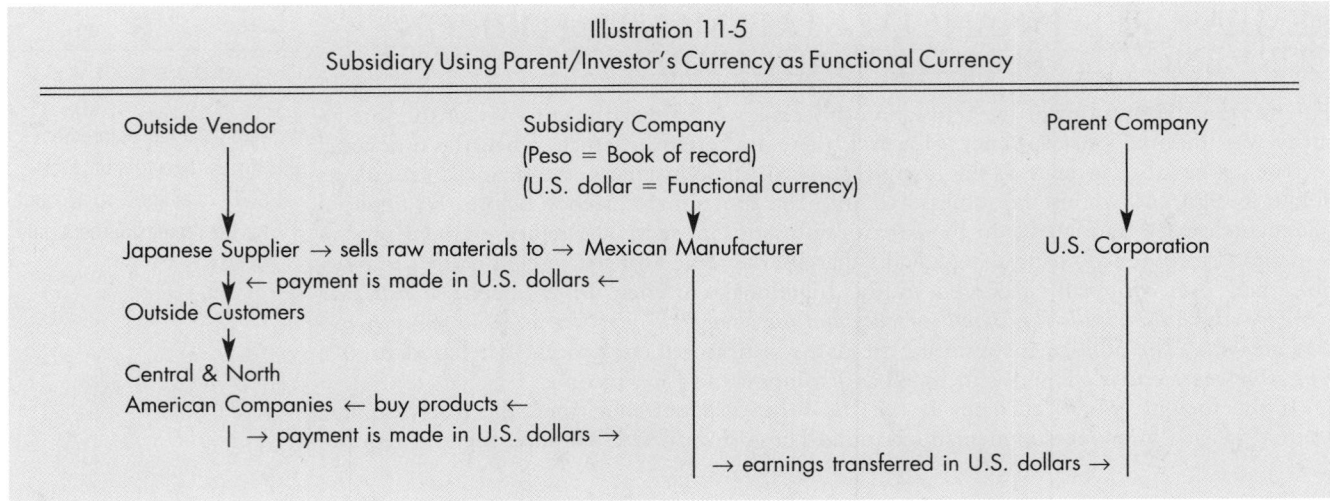

Illustration 11-5
Subsidiary Using Parent/Investor's Currency as Functional Currency

It is also possible that a foreign entity that maintains its books of record in its domestic currency may have a functional currency that is not the parent/investor's currency. For instance, as shown in Illustration 11-6, assume a Mexican subsidiary of an American company purchases materials from Belgian vendors with amounts due payable in euros. The materials are assembled in Mexico and then returned to Belgium for resale. Sales revenues are collected in euros. Considering the factors used to identify the functional currency, the euro would be the Mexican company's functional currency. However, the Mexican company maintains its books of record (accounting records) in pesos although its functional currency is the euro. In this example, a 2-step process is involved. First, the financial statements prepared in pesos would have to be remeasured into euros, the functional currency. Second, the remeasured financial statements would have to be translated from euros into dollars.

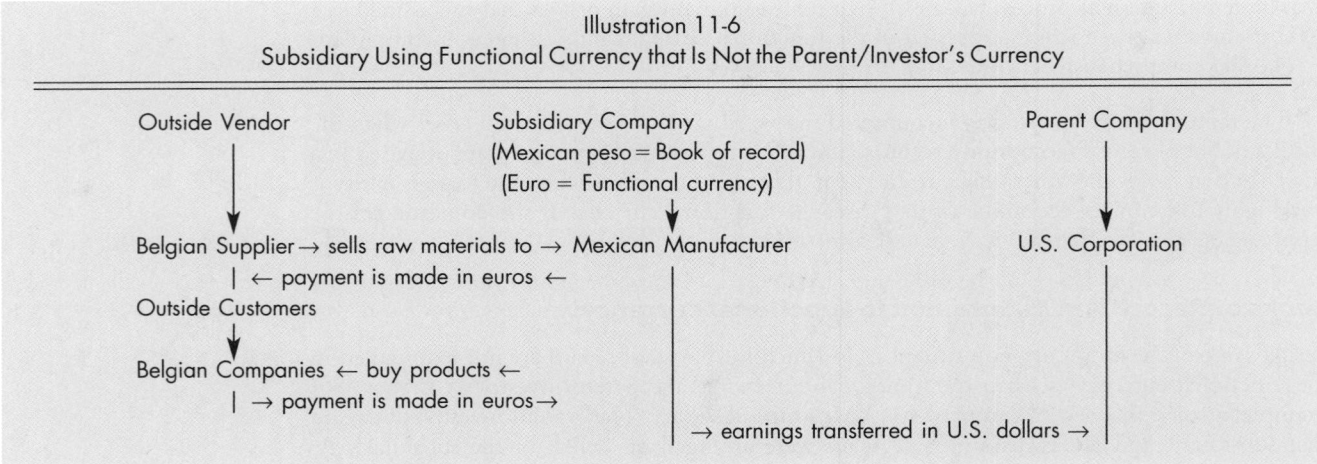

Illustration 11-6
Subsidiary Using Functional Currency that Is Not the Parent/Investor's Currency

If the books of record are not maintained in the functional currency, a remeasurement process, which differs significantly from the functional currency approach, is employed in order to express trial balance amounts in the functional currency.

Furthermore, *the adjustment resulting from the remeasurement is included as a component of net income rather than as a component of other comprehensive income.* It is important to remember that once the trial balance is remeasured into the functional currency, further translation may or may not be necessary. Possible scenarios are as follows:

1. Books of record currency (not U.S. dollars) remeasured to U.S. dollar functional currency. Therefore, no further translation is necessary. This is demonstrated in Illustration 11-7.

2. Books of record currency (not U.S. currency) remeasured into functional currency (not U.S. dollars). Therefore, further translation is necessary in order to translate the functional currency (not U.S. dollars) into U.S. dollars. This is demonstrated in Illustration 11-8.

Remeasurement when Functional Currency Is the Same as the Parent/Investor's Currency

Illustration 11-7 demonstrates the remeasurement process and is based on the same facts as Illustration 11-4 with the following additional information:

1. The U.S. dollar, rather than the books of record, is determined to be the functional currency.

2. Inventory is recorded at its market value of 30,000 FC even though its historical cost is 32,000 FC. The historical cost of sales is based on the FIFO method of costing. Ending inventory consists of the following:

> 10,000 FC acquired October 1, 2011
> 22,000 FC acquired November 1, 2011

3. The prepaid insurance represents amounts that were incurred on October 1, 2011.

4. The depreciable assets, with 10-year lives, were acquired as follows:

> 80,000 FC acquired on January 1, 2010*
> 60,000 FC acquired on July 1, 2011
>
> *20,000 FC of these assets were sold on July 1, 2011, for $19,760 U.S.

5. The cost of sales consists of the following purchases:

> 20,000 FC acquired December 1, 2010
> 60,000 FC acquired March 1, 2011
> 80,000 FC acquired July 1, 2011
> 20,000 FC acquired October 1, 2011

6. The other expenses include 3,000 FC of insurance expense that was originally prepaid on October 1, 2011. The balance of other expenses was incurred uniformly throughout the year.

7. The land and the related mortgage were acquired on March 1, 2011.

8. Selected exchange rates between the FC and the U.S. dollar functional currency are as follows:

Jan. 1, 2010	1 FC = $0.98	July 1, 2011	1 FC = $1.04
July 1, 2010	1 FC = 1.01	Oct. 1, 2011	1 FC = 1.045
Dec. 1, 2010	1 FC = 0.99	Nov. 1, 2011	1 FC = 1.043
Jan. 1, 2011	1 FC = 1.00	Dec. 31, 2011	1 FC = 1.05
Mar. 1, 2011	1 FC = 1.015	2011 average	1 FC = 1.03

A special remeasurement rule is necessary for inventory when the rule of cost or market value, whichever is lower, is applied. Before the rule is applied, the inventory cost and market values must be expressed in the functional currency. A possible result is for an inventory write-down to occur in the functional currency, even if no write-down is suggested in the books of record currency. It also is possible for a write-down in the books of record currency to no longer be appropriate in the functional currency. This special rule is demonstrated in Illustration 11-7.

In reviewing Illustration 11-7, it is important to note the following:

1. If amounts are to be remeasured at historical exchange rates that are traceable to transactions occurring prior to the parent's date of acquisition, they should be remeasured at the *historical exchange rate existing at the parent's date of acquisition.*

2. The remeasurement gain or loss is recognized as a component of income rather than as a component of other comprehensive income. Remeasurement gains or losses from prior years would be included in the remeasured amount of retained earnings at the beginning of the current year.

3. Because the functional currency is the U.S. dollar in this example, only the remeasurement process was necessary. If the functional currency had been in a different currency than that of the parent, it would have been necessary to first remeasure into the functional currency and then translate into the currency of the parent/investor. For example, if the book of record currency is the Japanese yen, the functional currency is the euro, and the currency of the parent/investor is the U.S. dollar, it would be necessary to remeasure the Japanese yen financial statements into euros and then translate the euros to U.S. dollars.

4. The remeasurement process resulted in a gain that favorably affects net income. This is because the FC strengthened against the dollar and made the parent's net investment in the subsidiary more valuable. If the FC had weakened, a remeasurement loss would have likely occurred. If the parent's management felt a remeasurement loss might occur, it might employ some type of financial instrument to hedge against the loss.

5. If the investor is using the equity method of accounting for its investment in the investee, income from the investment should include the investor's share of the remeasurement gain or loss. Therefore, the investment account must be adjusted to reflect the investor's interest in the remeasurement gain or loss. For example, if an investor has a 30% interest in an investee and there is a current remeasurement gain of $50,000, the following entry would be made under the equity method:

Investment in Investee	15,000	
Investment Income		15,000

Illustration 11-7
Sori Corporation
Trial Balance Remeasurement
December 31, 2011

Account	Balance in Books of Record (BR) Currency	Relevant Exchange Rate (Dollars/FC)	Balance in Functional Currency (Dollars)
Cash	10,000 BR	1.050	$ 10,500
Accounts Receivable	21,000	1.050	22,050
Allowance for Doubtful Accounts	(1,000)	1.050	(1,050)
Due from Pome	14,000	1.050	14,700
Inventory (at market, cost = 32,000)	30,000	Note A	31,500

Prepaid Insurance	3,000	1.045	3,135
Land.	18,000	1.015	18,270
Depreciable Assets	120,000	Note B	122,400
Accumulated Depreciation	(15,000)	Note C	(15,120)
Cost of Goods Sold	180,000	Note D	185,000
Depreciation Expense	10,000	Note E	10,120
Income Tax Expense	30,000	1.030	30,900
Other Expenses	23,000	Note F	23,735
Total.	443,000 BR		$456,140
Accounts Payable	20,000 BR	1.050	$ 21,000
Taxes Payable	30,000	1.050	31,500
Accrued Interest Payable.	1,000	1.050	1,050
Mortgage Payable—Land.	10,000	1.050	10,500
Common Stock	80,000	1.000	80,000
Retained Earnings	20,000	Note G	20,000
Sales—Pome	80,000	1.030	82,400
Sales—Other.	200,000	1.030	206,000
Gain on Sale of Depreciable Assets	2,000	Note H	2,760
Remeasurement Gain (to balance)			**930**
Total.	443,000 BR		$456,140

Note A—Inventory:

The historical cost and fair value of the ending inventory must be remeasured into the functional currency before the rule of cost or market, whichever is lower, may be applied.

	FC Exchange Rate		U.S. Dollars
Historical cost	(10,000 × $1.045)	. . . .	$10,450
	(22,000 × $1.043)	. . . .	22,946
		. . . .	$33,396
Fair value	(30,000 × $1.05)	. . . .	$31,500

Because the fair value in functional currency is still less than the historical cost in functional currency, fair value will be the carrying basis.

Note B—Depreciable Assets:

	Balance in BR	Exchange Rate (Dollars/FC)	Remeasured Functional Currency (Dollars)
January 1, 2010, acquisition	80,000 BR	1.00*	$ 80,000
July 1, 2011, acquisition.	60,000	1.04	62,400
July 1, 2011, disposition.	(20,000)	1.00	(20,000)
	120,000 BR		$122,400

*Note that the exchange rate on the parent's date of acquisition is used rather than any earlier historical exchange rates.

(continued)

Note C—Accumulated Depreciation:

	Balance in BR	Exchange Rate (Dollars/FC)	Remeasured Functional Currency (Dollars)
January 1, 2010, acquisition (60,000 BR ÷ 10 × 2)	12,000 BR	1.00	$12,000
July 1, 2011, acquisition (60,000 BR ÷ 10 × ½) . . .	3,000	1.04	3,120
	15,000 BR		$15,120

Note D—Cost of sales is remeasured as follows:

	Balance in BR	Exchange Rate (Dollars/FC)	Remeasured Functional Currency(Dollars)
December 1, 2011, acquisition	20,000 BR	1.000*	$ 20,000
March 1, 2011	60,000	1.015	60,900
July 1, 2011	80,000	1.040	83,200
October 1, 2011.	20,000	1.045	20,900
Total	180,000 BR		$185,000

*Note that the exchange rate on the parent's date of acquisition is used rather than any earlier historical exchange rates.

Note E—Depreciation Expense:

	Balance in BR	Exchange Rate (Dollars/FC)	Remeasured Functional Currency (Dollars)
January 1, 2010, acquisition (60,000 BR ÷ 10) .	6,000 BR	1.00	$ 6,000
July 1, 2011, disposal (20,000 BR ÷ 10 × ½) . .	1,000	1.00	1,000
July 1, 2011, acquisition (60,000 BR ÷ 10 × ½)	3,000	1.04	3,120
	10,000 BR		$10,120

Note F—Other expenses are remeasured as follows:

	Balance in BR	Exchange Rate (Dollars/FC)	Remeasured Functional Currency (Dollars)
Insurance expense.	3,000 BR	1.045	$ 3,135
Balance of expense	20,000	1.030	20,600
			$23,735

Note G—Retained Earnings:

	Balance in BR	Exchange Rate (Dollars/FC)	Remeasured Functional Currency (Dollars)
January 1, 2011, balance (date of investment).	20,000 BR	1.00	$20,000

The beginning balance of retained earnings normally is equal to the remeasured value of the previous period's ending retained earnings. However, since 2011 is the first year Pome has owned Sori, the beginning balance is set equal to the January 1, 2011 (acquisition date), balance of retained earnings in foreign currency remeasured at the January 1, 2011, spot rate. The balance sheet for 2011 would show a remeasured value for retained earnings equal to the remeasured beginning balance of retained earnings plus the remeasured value of net income less dividends remeasured at the rate existing on the declaration date.

Note H—Gain on Sale of Depreciable Assets:

	Balance in BR	Exchange Rate (Dollars/FC)	Remeasured Functional Currency (Dollars)
Cost	20,000 BR		
Accumulated depreciation	(3,000)		
Book value	17,000 BR	1.00	$ 17,000
Selling price in U.S. dollars			(19,760)
Gain			$ 2,760

Worksheet 11-2, pages 636 and 637, shows the consolidated financial statements of the Pome and Sori corporations. The trial balance for Sori has been remeasured into dollars based on Illustration 11-7 (see page 620). Note that the remeasurement gain is included in the subsidiary income distribution schedule.

Worksheet 11-2: page 636

Remeasurement and Subsequent Translation when Functional Currency Is Not the Same as the Parent/Investor's Currency

Illustration 11-8 demonstrates the remeasurement of a subsidiary's trial balance into the functional currency and the subsequent translation into the parent's reporting currency. This might be the case if, by way of example, the subsidiary records in Japanese yen, functions in euros, and has a U.S. parent. Illustration 11-8 is based on the following information:

1. Chen Corporation began operations on January 1, 2011, as a wholly owned foreign subsidiary of Drake Inc., a U.S. company. Chen maintains its financial statements in the books of record currency, and its functional currency is the FC.

2. Inventory in the books of record currency is carried at fair value even though its historical cost is 16,000 BR. Inventory was acquired uniformly throughout the year. The weighted-average cost method is used to determine the cost of sales.

3. Depreciable assets were acquired (sold) on the following dates:

Date	Cost
January 1, 2011	10,000 BR
	90,000
May 1, 2011	30,000
July 1, 2011	(10,000)

The asset sold was acquired on January 1, 2011. The selling price of this asset was 11,000 BR.

4. Depreciation is based on the straight-line method and a 10-year useful life.

5. Relevant direct exchange rates are as follows:

Date	FC/BR	Dollars/FC
January 1, 2011	1 BR = 2.0 FC	1 FC = $1.40
May 1, 2011	1 BR = 2.1 FC	1 FC = 1.30
July 1, 2011	1 BR = 2.4 FC	1 FC = 1.10
December 31, 2011	1 BR = 2.8 FC	1 FC = 1.00
2011 average	1 BR = 2.5 FC	1 FC = 1.25

Highly Inflationary Economies. When a foreign entity's financial statements are expressed in the functional currency, the statements are translated directly into the parent's reporting currency. However, this procedure is not followed for a foreign entity in a country that has a highly inflationary economy. The FASB defines such an economy as one that has a cumulative inflation rate of approximately 100% or more over a 3-year period. Other factors, such as the trend of inflation, also may suggest a highly inflationary economy.[5]

If a foreign entity's currency has lost its utility as a measure of value and lacks stability, its use as a functional currency is likely to produce misleading results. The translation of noncurrent assets of a foreign company in a highly inflationary economy at current rates of exchange produces curious results. The translated amounts may not represent reasonable dollar-equivalent measures of those assets' historical costs.

Suppose a foreign company acquires a fixed asset for a cost of 100,000 FC when the exchange rate is 1 FC = $1.00. Since that time, the foreign country has experienced a 3-year cumulative rate of inflation of 270%, and the current rate of exchange is 1 FC = $0.40. If the fixed asset was translated using the current-rate method, the translated value of the asset would be $40,000 versus its original translated cost of $100,000. One proposed solution to this curious result would be to adjust the foreign financial statements for inflation rates since acquisition and then apply the current-rate method. The inflation-adjusted value of the fixed asset would be 270,000 FC (100,000 FC × 270%), and its translated value at current rates would be $108,000 (270,000 FC × $0.40). This translated amount is more meaningful than the $40,000 value previously determined. The FASB decided against adjusting foreign amounts for inflationary effects and instead decided that the domestic currency (dollars) should serve as the foreign entity's functional currency. Thus, the foreign entity's statements should be remeasured into the functional currency (U.S. dollars). Applying this to the fixed asset example would require the use of the original historical rate of exchange and result in a remeasured value of $100,000 (100,000 FC × $1.00). This value is more meaningful than the $40,000 value previously determined, and it does not commingle historical and inflation-adjusted values into the same set of financial statements. It is important to note that (1) this will result in the remeasurement of the statements into dollars, making any further translation unnecessary, and (2) the remeasurement gain or loss should be included in the net income for the period.

IASB PERSPECTIVES

IAS 21, *The Effects of Changes in Foreign Currency Rates*, addresses the translation of foreign financial statements. The international standard addresses procedures to be employed when an entity's functional currency is the currency of a hyperinflationary economy. These procedures differ from the U.S. standard and require the application of International Accounting Standards 29 involving the restatement of financial statement amounts by applying changes in general price levels (i.e., the inflation-adjusted approach).

---

5 FASB ASC 830-10-45-11, *Foreign Currency Matters—Overall—Other Presentation Matters—The Functional Currency in Highly Inflationary Economies.*

Illustration 11-8
Chen Corporation
Trial Balance Translation
December 31, 2011

Account	Balance in BR	Relevant Exchange Rate (FC/BR)	Balance in FC	Relevant Exchange Rate (Dollars/FC)	Balance in Dollars
Cash	10,000 BR	2.80	28,000 FC	1.00	$ 28,000
Accounts Receivable	28,000	2.80	78,400	1.00	78,400
Inventory (at fair value)*	15,000	Note A	40,000	1.00	40,000
Prepaid Expenses	5,000	2.50	12,500	1.00	12,500
Depreciable Assets	120,000	Note B	243,000	1.00	243,000
Cost of Goods Sold	145,000	2.50	362,500	1.25	453,125
Depreciation Expense	11,500	Note C	23,200	1.25	29,000
Other Expenses	27,000	2.50	67,500	1.25	84,375
Income Tax Expense	16,500	2.50	41,250	1.25	51,562
Remeasurement Loss			**58,650**	**1.25**	**73,313**
Total Debits	378,000 BR		955,000 FC		$1,093,275
Accounts Payable	7,500 BR	2.80	21,000 FC	1.00	$ 21,000
Accrued Expenses	12,000	2.80	33,600	1.00	33,600
Notes Payable	84,000	2.80	235,200	1.00	235,200
Common Stock	40,000	2.00	80,000	1.40	112,000
Cumulative Transaction Adjustment	0		0		(33,075)
Retained Earnings	0	Note D	0		0
Sales	220,000	2.50	550,000	1.25	687,500
Gain on Sale of Depreciable Assets	1,500	Note E	7,400	1.25	9,250
Allowance for Doubtful Accounts	2,000	2.80	5,600	1.00	5,600
Accumulated Depreciation	11,000	Note F	22,200	1.00	22,200
Total Credits	378,000 BR		955,000 FC		$1,093,275

*In more complex instances, the remeasurement of ending inventory and cost of sales will depend on the inventory valuation method used. LIFO ending inventory will consist of the (1) beginning inventory multiplied by the applicable exchange rate(s) plus (2) unsold current purchases multiplied by the applicable exchange rate(s).

Note A—Inventory:

The historical cost and fair value of the ending inventory must be remeasured into the functional currency before the rule of cost or market, whichever is lower, may be applied.

BR × Exchange Rate	FC
Historical cost (16,000 BR × 2.50)	40,000
Fair value (15,000 BR × 2.80)	42,000

Because the historical cost in functional currency is less than the fair value in functional currency, historical cost will be the carrying basis.

(continued)

Note B—Depreciable Assets:

	Balance in BR	Exchange Rate (FC/BR)	Remeasured Functional Currency (FC)
January 1, 2011, acquisition	90,000 BR	2.00	180,000 FC
January 1, 2011, acquisition	10,000	2.00	20,000
May 1, 2011, acquisition	30,000	2.10	63,000
July 1, 2011, disposition	(10,000)	2.00	(20,000)
	120,000 BR		243,000 FC

Note C—Depreciation Expense:

	Balance in BR	Exchange Rate (FC/BR)	Remeasured Functional Currency (FC)
January 1, 2011, acquisition (90,000 BR ÷ 10)	9,000 BR	2.00	18,000 FC
May 1, 2011, acquisition (30,000 BR ÷ 10 × $^2/_3$) . .	2,000	2.10	4,200
July 1, 2011, disposal (10,000 BR ÷ 10 × ½)	500	2.00	1,000
	11,500 BR		23,200 FC

Note D—Retained Earnings:

The remeasured value of zero for retained earnings represents the beginning-of-period value. The balance sheet for 2011 would show a remeasured value for retained earnings equal to the remeasured value of undistributed net income. This value also would represent the remeasured value for beginning retained earnings in the 2012 trial balance.

Note E—Gain on Sale of Depreciable Assets:

The remeasured value of the gain must be inferred, based on the following entry to record the sale of the asset:

Cash (11,000 BR × 2.40)	26,400	
Accumulated Depreciation (500 BR × 2.00)	1,000	
Depreciable Assets (10,000 BR × 2.00)		20,000
Gain on Sale of Depreciable Assets		7,400

	Balance in BR	Exchange Rate (FC/BR)	Remeasured Functional Currency (FC)
Cost (see Note B)	10,000 BR	2.00	20,000 FC
Accumulated depreciation (see Note F)	(500)	2.00	(1,000)
Book value	9,500 BR		19,000 FC
Selling price	11,000 BR	2.40	(26,400)
Gain	1,500 BR		7,400 FC

Note F—Accumulated Depreciation:

	Balance in BR	Exchange Rate (FC/BR)	Remeasured Functional Currency (FC)
Annual expense	11,500 BR	see Note C	23,200 FC
Asset disposed	(500)	2.00	(1,000)
	11,000 BR		22,200 FC

Summary of Translation and Remeasurement Methodologies

This chapter has discussed the translation and/or remeasurement of foreign financial statements into the reporting currency (dollars) of the domestic parent/investor entity. The situations requiring the use of a particular translation and/or remeasurement methodology are summarized in Exhibit 11-2 and the flowchart in Exhibit 11-3.

Exhibit 11-2 compares the methodologies applicable to the remeasurement and translation processes. The following factors regarding Exhibit 11-2 should be noted:

1. When remeasuring, the exchange rates represent the relationship between the books of record currency and the functional currency. When translating, the exchange rates represent the relationship between the functional currency and the parent/investor currency.

2. Examples of accounts that should be remeasured (versus translated) at historical rates in order to measure them in terms of their functional currency include the following:

   ◆ Marketable securities carried at cost

   ◆ Inventories carried at cost

   ◆ Prepaid expenses such as insurance, advertising, and rent

   ◆ Property, plant, and equipment

   ◆ Accumulated depreciation on property, plant, and equipment

   ◆ Patents, trademarks, licenses, and formulas

   ◆ Goodwill

   ◆ Other intangible assets

   ◆ Deferred charges and credits except deferred income taxes and policy acquisition costs for life insurance companies

   ◆ Deferred income

   ◆ Common stock

   ◆ Preferred stock carried at issuance price

   ◆ Examples of revenues and expenses related to nonmonetary items:

     Cost of goods sold
     Depreciation of property, plant, and equipment
     Amortization of intangible items such as patents and licenses
     Amortization of deferred charges or credits except deferred income taxes and policy acquisition costs for life insurance companies[6]

3. If amounts to be remeasured at historical exchange rates are traceable to transactions occurring prior to the parent's date of acquisition, the historical exchange rate existing at the date of acquisition should be used.

4. The remeasurement gain or loss reflected in the remeasured functional currency trial balance is included as a component of net income. The translation adjustment only results from translating the remeasured trial balance into the parent/investor's (U.S. dollars) currency. The resulting translation adjustment reflected in the translated trial balance is not included as a component of net income but rather as a component of other comprehensive income.

7

OBJECTIVE

Differentiate between the two methods for converting functional currency to the parent/investor's currency, and explain the circumstances under which each should be used.

---

6 FASB ASC 830-10-45-18, *Foreign Currency Matters—Overall—Other Presentation Matters—Accounts to be Remeasured Using Historical Exchange Rates.*

Exhibit 11-2
Remeasurement and Translation Methodologies

	Remeasurement	**Translation**
	Investee's books of record remeasured into functional currency—**historical rate/temporal method**	Functional currency translated into parent/investor's reporting currency—**current rate/functional method**
When to use	When functional currency is not the books of record (local) currency or when the functional currency is highly inflationary	When functional currency is the books of record (local) currency or when the functional currency is not highly inflationary
Assets and Liabilities:		
Monetary items* or measured at current values	Remeasure using current exchange rate	Translate using current exchange rate
Not monetary items or not measured at current values	Remeasure using historical exchange rates	Translate using current exchange rate
Equity Accounts:		
Equity accounts (excluding retained earnings)	Remeasure using historical exchange rates**	Translate using historical exchange rates**
Retained earnings	Beginning remeasured balance plus (minus) remeasured net income (loss) less dividends (remeasured using historical exchange rates)	Beginning translated balance plus (minus) translated net income (loss) less dividends (translated using historical exchange rates)
Revenues and Expenses:		
Representing amortization of historical amounts	Remeasure using historical exchange rates	Translate using weighted-average exchange rate for the period
Other income and expense items	Remeasure using weighted-average exchange rate for the period	Translate using weighted-average exchange rate for the period
Accounting for remeasurement gain or loss and translation adjustment	Remeasurement gain or loss recorded as a component of current-period net income	Cumulative translation adjustment recorded as a component of other comprehensive income. The translation adjustment is recognized as a component of current-period net income when there is a partial or complete sale or complete or substantially complete liquidation of the investment in the foreign entity.

* Monetary items represent rights to receive or pay an amount of money which is (1) fixed in amount or (2) determinable without reference to future prices of specific goods/services; that is, its value does not change according to changes in price levels.
** If amounts are to be remeasured or translated at historical exchange rates which are traceable to transactions occurring prior to the parent's date of acquisition, they should be remeasured/translated at the historical exchange rate existing at the parent's date of acquisition.

Exhibit 11-3
Translation/Remeasurement Flowchart—The U.S. $ is the Reporting (Presentation) Currency

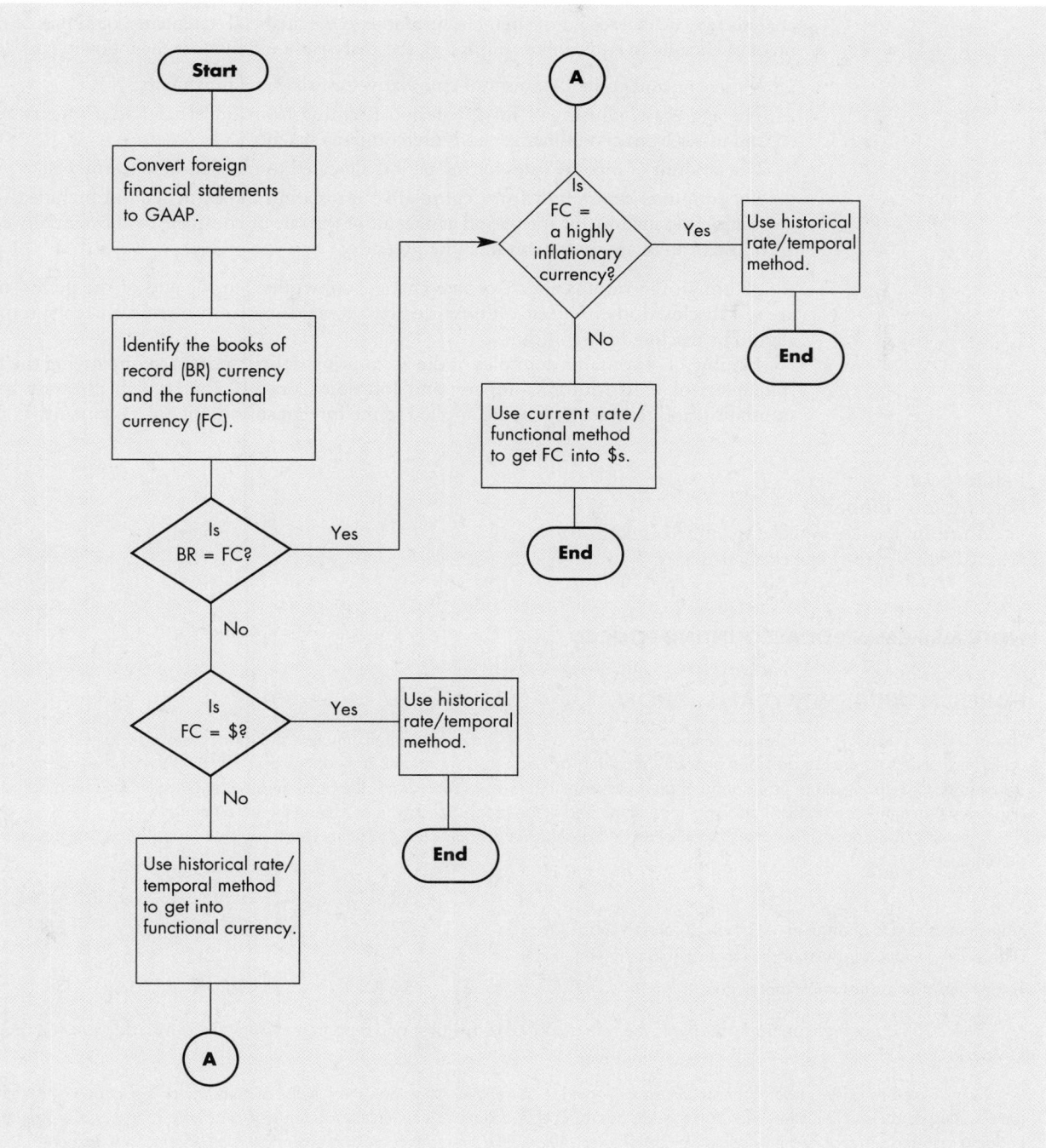

FASB standards require that foreign currency transaction and hedging gains or losses included in the determination of net income be disclosed in the financial statements or the accompanying notes. An analysis of the separate component of other comprehensive income affected by certain foreign currency transactions and hedges and translation adjustments should be presented. The analysis may be in a separate statement, in a note to the financial statements, or as part of the statement of changes in equity. At a minimum, the analysis should disclose the following:

1. Beginning and ending amount of cumulative translation adjustments.
2. The aggregate adjustment for the period resulting from translation adjustments and gains and losses from certain hedges and intercompany balances.
3. The amount of income taxes for the period allocated to translation adjustments.
4. The amounts transferred from cumulative translation adjustments and included in determining net income for the period as a result of the sale or complete or substantially complete liquidation of an investment in a foreign entity.[7]

Although the various effects of rate changes subsequent to the end of the period normally are not disclosed, their effects on unsettled balances arising from foreign currency transactions should be disclosed if significant.

Exhibit 11-4 contains examples of the accounting policies notes accompanying the financial statements of Ford Motor Company and Johnson Controls, Inc., which illustrate how both translation and remeasurement are applied to the foreign subsidiaries of a company.

Exhibit 11-4
Ford Motor Company
Fiscal Year Ending December 31, 2009 SEC Form 10-K
Selected Notes to the Financial Statements

NOTE 2. SUMMARY OF ACCOUNTING POLICIES

FOREIGN CURRENCY TRANSLATION

The assets and liabilities of foreign subsidiaries using the local currency as their functional currency are translated to U.S. dollars using end-of-period exchange rates and any resulting translation adjustments are reported in *Accumulated other comprehensive income/(loss)*. Upon sale or liquidation of an investment in a foreign subsidiary, the accumulated amount of translation adjustments related to that entity are reclassified to net income as part of the recognized gain or loss on the investment.

Increases/(decreases) in *Accumulated other comprehensive income/(loss)* resulting from translation adjustments were as follows (in billions):

	2009	2008	2007
Adjustments due to change in net assets of foreign subsidiaries	$2.0	$(3.8)	$1.8
Deferred translation (gains)/losses reclassified to net income*	0.3	(1.8)	—
Total translation adjustments (net of taxes)	$2.3	$(5.6)	$1.8

*   The 2008 adjustment primarily relates to the sale of Jaguar Land Rover and a portion of our stake in Mazda Motor Corporation ("Mazda")

Gains or losses arising from transactions denominated in currencies other than the functional currency of the locations, the effect of remeasuring assets and liabilities of foreign subsidiaries using U.S. dollars as their functional currency, and the results of our foreign currency hedging activities are reported in *Automotive cost of sales, Automotive interest income and other non-operating income/(expense), net,* and *Selling, administrative, and other* expenses. For additional discussion of hedging activities, see Note 26. The net after-tax gain/(loss) of this activity for 2009, 2008, and 2007 was $(757) million, $922 million, and $217 million, respectively.

NOTE 26. DERIVATIVE FINANCIAL INSTRUMENTS AND HEDGING ACTIVITIES

In the normal course of business, our operations are exposed to global market risks, including the effect of changes in foreign currency exchange rates, certain commodity prices, and interest rates. To manage these risks, we enter into various derivatives contracts. Foreign currency exchange contracts including forwards and options, are used to manage foreign exchange exposure. Commodity contracts including forwards and options are used to manage commodity price risk. Interest rate contracts including swaps, caps, and floors are used to manage the effects of interest rate fluctuations. Cross-currency interest rate swap contracts are used to manage foreign currency

---

7 FASB ASC 830-30-45-18, *Foreign Currency Matters—Translation of Financial Statements—Other Presentation Matters—Analysis of Changes in Cumulative Translation Adjustment.*

and interest rate exposures on foreign-denominated debt. The vast majority of our derivatives are over-the-counter customized derivative transactions and are not exchange-traded. Management reviews our hedging program, derivative positions, and overall risk management strategy on a regular basis. We only enter into transactions that we believe will be highly effective at offsetting the underlying risk.

Net Investment Hedges. We have used foreign currency exchange derivatives to hedge the net assets of certain foreign entities to offset the translation and economic exposures related to our investment in these entities. The effective portion of changes in the value of these derivative instruments is included in *Accumulated other comprehensive income/(loss)* as a foreign currency translation adjustment until the hedged investment is sold or liquidated. When the investment is sold or liquidated, the effective portion of the hedge is recognized in *Automotive interest income and other non-operating income/(expense), net* as part of the gain or loss on sale. We have had no active foreign currency derivatives classified as net investment hedges since the first quarter of 2007.

> Johnson Controls, Inc.
> Fiscal Year Ending September 30, 2009 SEC Form 10-K
> Selected Notes to the Financial Statements

11. DERIVATIVE INSTRUMENTS AND HEDGING ACTIVITIES

The Company selectively uses derivative instruments to reduce market risk associated with changes in foreign currency, commodities, stock-based compensation liabilities and interest rates. Under Company policy, the use of derivatives is restricted to those intended for hedging purposes; the use of any derivative instrument for speculative purposes is strictly prohibited. A description of each type of derivative utilized by the Company to manage risk is included in the following paragraphs.

The Company has entered into foreign currency denominated debt obligations to selectively hedge portions of its net investment in Japan. The currency effects of the debt obligations are reflected in the accumulated other comprehensive income (AOCI) account within shareholders' equity where they offset gains and losses recorded on the Company's net investment in Japan. As of September 30, 2009, the Company had 37 billion yen of foreign denominated debt outstanding designated as net investment hedges in the Company's net investment in Japan.

12. FAIR VALUE MEASUREMENTS

Foreign currency denominated debt—The Company has entered into certain foreign currency denominated debt obligations to selectively hedge portions of its net investment in Japan. As net investment hedges, the currency effects of the debt obligations are reflected in the foreign currency translation adjustments component of accumulated other comprehensive income where they offset gains and losses recorded on the Company's net investment in Japan. The Company's foreign denominated debt obligations are valued under a market approach using publicized spot prices. On January 15, 2008, the Company had entered into an 18 billion yen, three year, floating rate loan agreement. The Company did not elect to designate the debt as part of the hedge of the net investment in Japan and hedged the exposure of the change in value of the yen with an 18 billion yen cross-currency swap. The currency effect of the 18 billion yen loan was reflected in the consolidated statement of income. On January 17, 2009, the Company retired its 24 billion yen, three year, floating rate loan agreement that matured, leaving a significant portion of the net investment in Japan un-hedged. On that date, the Company unwound the cross-currency swap that hedged the 18 billion yen loan and elected to designate the latter as part of its net investment hedge in Japan.

Source: Ford Motor Company, 2003 Annual Report, Note 1. Accounting Policies.

REFLECTION

- If the foreign entity's functional currency is not its books of record (local) or reporting currency, the historical rate or temporal method is applied in order to remeasure the financial statements into the functional currency. This method is based on the premise that changes in the exchange rate between the books of record currency and the functional currency affect the cash flows and economic well-being of the foreign entity and parent/investor.

- The remeasurement process follows the historical rate/temporal method that remeasures foreign financial statements from their reporting currency into the functional currency. This method remeasures balances representing historical amounts using historical exchange rates.

- The remeasurement gain or loss is recognized as a component of current-period earnings.

- If the foreign entity's functional currency is not the parent/investor's currency, the remeasured functional currency financial statements must be translated into the parent/investor's currency. The current-rate or functional method is used to translate the remeasured functional currency financial statements into the parent/investor's currency.

Worksheet 11-1

Consolidating the Foreign Subsidiary
Pome Corporation and Subsidiary Sori Corporation
Worksheet for Consolidated Financial Statements (in dollars)
For Year Ended December 31, 2011

| | (Credit balance amounts are in parentheses.) | Trial Balance | |
	In U.S. dollars	Pome Corporation	Sori Corporation
1	Cash	58,300	10,500
2	Accounts Receivable	112,000	22,050
3	Allowance for Doubtful Accounts	(5,600)	(1,050)
4	Due from Pome		14,700
5	Inventory, December 31, 2011	154,700	31,500
6	Prepaid Insurance	9,050	3,150
7	Investment in Sori Corporation	139,653	
8			
9			
10	Land	125,000	18,900
11	Depreciable Assets and Patents	500,000	126,000
12	Accumulated Depreciation and Amortization	(100,000)	(15,750)
13	Accounts Payable	(112,000)	(21,000)
14	Taxes Payable	(150,000)	(31,500)
15	Accrued Interest Payable	(16,000)	(1,050)
16	Mortgage Payable—Land	(105,000)	(10,500)
17	Common Stock	(350,000)	(80,000)
18	Paid-In Capital in Excess of Par	(100,000)	
19	Retained Earnings, January 1, 2011	(116,000)	(20,000)
20	**Cumulative Translation Adjustment—Sori**		(5,780)
21			
22	**Cumulative Translation Adjustment—Pome**		
23			
24	Sales—Pome		(82,400)
25	Sales—Other	(908,600)	(206,000)
26	Gain on Sale of Depreciable Assets	(8,600)	(2,060)
27	Cost of Goods Sold	703,850	185,400
28	Depreciation and Amortization Expense	45,600	10,300
29	Income Tax Expense	108,000	30,900
30	Other Expenses (including interest)	51,800	23,690
31	Subsidiary Income	(36,153)	
32		0	0
33	Consolidated Net Income		
34	To Noncontrolling Interest		
35	Balance to Controlling Interest		
36	Total Noncontrolling Interest		
37	Retained Earnings, Controlling Interest, December 31, 2011		
38			

Worksheet 11-1 (see page 612)

Eliminations & Adjustments Dr.		Eliminations & Adjustments Cr.		Consolidated Income Statement	Noncontrolling Interest (NCI)	Controlling Retained Earnings	Consolidated Balance Sheet	
							68,800	1
							134,050	2
							(6,650)	3
		(IA)	14,700					4
							186,200	5
							12,200	6
		(CY1)	36,153					7
		(EL)	90,000					8
		(D)	13,500					9
							143,900	10
(D)	15,750						641,750	11
		(A)	1,575				(117,325)	12
(IA)	14,700						(118,300)	13
							(181,500)	14
							(17,050)	15
							(115,500)	16
(EL)	72,000				(8,000)		(350,000)	17
							(100,000)	18
(EL)	18,000	(NCI)	1,500		(3,500)	(116,000)		19
(A)	30	(D)	750		(650)			20
(CT)	5,850							21
		(CT)	5,850				(5,850)	22
								23
(IS)	82,400							24
				(1,114,600)				25
				(10,660)				26
		(IS)	82,400	806,850				27
(A)	1,545			57,445				28
				138,900				29
				75,490				30
(CY1)	36,153							31
	246,428		246,428					32
				(46,575)				33
				3,862	(3,862)			34
				42,713		(42,713)		35
					(16,012)		(16,012)	36
						(158,713)	(158,713)	37
							0	38

Eliminations and Adjustments:

(CY1)   Eliminate the entries in the subsidiary income account against the investment in Sori account to record the parent's 90% controlling interest in the subsidiary.

(EL)   Eliminate 90% of the subsidiary's January 1, 2011, equity balances against the balance of the investment account.

(CT)   Distribute the cumulative translation adjustment between controlling interest and NCI. ($6,500 × 90% = $5,850)

(D)/(NCI)   Distribute the excess of cost over book value of 13,500 FC to patent and NCI adjustment of 1,500 FC. Includes the exchange rate adjustment. (90% is allocated to the parent.)

(A)   Record appropriate patent amortization. Includes exchange rate adjustment. (90% is allocated to the parent.)

(IA)   Eliminate the intercompany trade balances.

(IS)   Eliminate the intercompany sales assuming that none of the goods purchased from Sori remain in Pome's ending inventory.

Subsidiary Sori Corporation Income Distribution		
	Internally generated net income	$40,170
Patent amortization ....(A) $1,545	Adjusted income	$38,625
	Noncontrolling share..............................	×10%
	NCI	$ 3,862

Parent Pome Corporation Income Distribution		
	Internally generated net income	$ 7,950
	Share of subsidiary income (90% × $38,625)..........	34,763
	Controlling interest	$42,713

Worksheet 11-2

Consolidating the Foreign Subsidiary
Pome Corporation and Subsidiary Sori Corporation
Worksheet for Consolidated Financial Statements (in dollars)
For Year Ended December 31, 2011

	(Credit balance amounts are in parentheses.) In U.S. dollars	Trial Balance	
		Pome Corporation	Sori Corporation
1	Cash	58,300	10,500
2	Accounts Receivable	112,000	22,050
3	Allowance for Doubtful Accounts	(5,600)	(1,050)
4	Due from Pome		14,700
5	Inventory, December 31, 2011	154,700	31,500
6	Prepaid Insurance	9,050	3,135
7	Investment in Sori Corporation	141,601	
8			
9			
10	Land	125,000	18,270
11	Depreciable Assets and Patents	500,000	122,400
12	Accumulated Depreciation and Amortization	(100,000)	(15,120)
13	Accounts Payable	(112,000)	(21,000)
14	Taxes Payable	(150,000)	(31,500)
15	Accrued Interest Payable	(16,000)	(1,050)
16	Mortgage Payable—Land	(105,000)	(10,500)
17	Common Stock	(350,000)	(80,000)
18	Paid-In Capital in Excess of Par	(100,000)	
19	Retained Earnings, January 1, 2011	(116,000)	(20,000)
20	**Remeasurement Gain**		(930)
21			
22			
23	Sales—Pome		(82,400)
24	Sales—Other	(908,600)	(206,000)
25	Gain on Sale of Depreciable Assets	(8,600)	(2,760)
26	Cost of Goods Sold	703,850	185,000
27	Depreciation and Amortization Expense	45,600	10,120
28	Income Tax Expense	108,000	30,900
29	Other Expenses (including interest)	51,800	23,735
30	Subsidiary Income	(38,101)	
31		0	0
32	Consolidated Net Income		
33	To Noncontrolling Interest		
34	Balance to Controlling Interest		
35	Total Noncontrolling Interest		
36	Retained Earnings, Controlling Interest, December 31, 2011		
37			

Worksheet 11-2 (see page 623)

Eliminations & Adjustments				Consolidated Income Statement	Noncontrolling Interest (NCI)	Controlling Retained Earnings	Consolidated Balance Sheet	
Dr.		Cr.						
							68,800	1
							134,050	2
							(6,650)	3
		(IA)	14,700					4
							186,200	5
							12,185	6
		(CY1)	38,101					7
		(EL)	90,000					8
		(D)	13,500					9
							143,270	10
(D)	15,000						637,400	11
		(A)	1,500				(116,620)	12
(IA)	14,700						(118,300)	13
							(181,500)	14
							(17,050)	15
							(115,500)	16
(EL)	72,000				(8,000)		(350,000)	17
							(100,000)	18
(EL)	18,000	(NCI)	1,500		(3,500)	(116,000)		19
				(930)				20
								21
								22
(IS)	82,400							23
				(1,114,600)				24
				(11,360)				25
		(IS)	82,400	806,450				26
(A)	1,500			57,220				27
				138,900				28
				75,535				29
(CY1)	38,101							30
	241,701		241,701					31
				(48,785)				32
				4,084	(4,084)			33
				44,701		(44,701)		34
					(15,584)		(15,584)	35
						(160,701)	(160,701)	36
							0	37

Eliminations and Adjustments:

(CY1)   Eliminate the entries in the subsidiary income account against the investment in the Sori account to record the parent's 90% controlling interest in the subsidiary.

(EL)   Eliminate 90% of the subsidiary's January 1, 2011, equity balances against the balance of the investment account.

(D)/(NCI)   Distribute the excess of cost over book value of 15,000 FC.

(A)   Record appropriate amortization of patent.

(IA)   Eliminate the intercompany trade balances.

(IS)   Eliminate the intercompany sales assuming that none of the goods purchased from Sori remain in Pome's ending inventory.

Subsidiary Sori Corporation Income Distribution

Patent amortization . . . .(A)$1,500	Internally generated net income	$42,335*
	Adjusted income	$40,835
	Noncontrolling share.	×10%
	NCI	$ 4,084

*This amount includes the remeasurement gain of $930.

Parent Pome Corporation Income Distribution

	Internally generated net income	$ 7,950
	Share of subsidiary income (90% × $40,835)	36,751
	Controlling interest	$44,701

UNDERSTANDING THE ISSUES

1. A foreign company maintains its books and records in its domestic currency. Identify several factors that might suggest that the domestic currency is not the entity's functional currency.

2. Assume that a U.S. company has a French subsidiary whose functional currency is the euro. Explain why the translation adjustment is not included as a component of net income on the consolidated income statement.

3. Explain how a German subsidiary's year-end balance in retained earnings is expressed in dollars assuming that the euro is the functional currency.

4. Assume that a U.S. company has a foreign subsidiary whose functional currency is the U.S. dollar. Explain how exchange rates between the foreign currency and the dollar would have to change in order to result in a current-year remeasurement loss and how the company could use a foreign currency loan receivable or payable to hedge against its net investment in the foreign subsidiary.

5. Explain why functional currency should be remeasured, rather than translated, when a foreign entity's functional currency is highly inflationary.

EXERCISES

Exercise 1 *(LO 2)* **The effect on a parent of alternative functional currencies.** Luxor Corporation has a 100% interest in a foreign subsidiary known as Luminaire. The foreign subsidiary was created for the primary purpose of distributing electronic components throughout a number of foreign countries. The parent initially invested 3,000,000 FC to finance equipment purchases, and it is anticipated that a dividend equivalent to $1,110,000 will be paid to the parent company at the end of each year. Luxor is trying to determine whether to structure the subsidiary with the foreign currency (FC) or the U.S. dollar ($) as Luminaire's functional currency. Projections for the subsidiary's first year of operations are as follows: sales of 10,000,000 FC; cost of sales (excluding depreciation) of 3,700,000 FC; and selling, general, and administrative expenses (excluding depreciation) of 1,200,000 FC. It is anticipated that the company will purchase 2,000,000 FC of equipment at the beginning of the year and another 1,000,000 FC of equipment at midyear. All equipment is depreciated over 10 years using the straight-line method.

It is anticipated that the exchange rate between the FC and the U.S. dollar are as follows:

Beginning of year	1 FC = $1.00
Average for year	1 FC = 1.06
Midyear.	1 FC = 1.05
End of year	1 FC = 1.11

For the first year, prepare a schedule to determine the effect on the parent company's translated net income, balance sheet, and cash flows assuming the functional currency is: (a) the dollar and (b) the FC. (*Hint:* Assume that all sales revenues increase cash and that all cost of sales and selling, general, and administrative expenses decrease cash.)

Exercise 2 *(LO 4)* **Hedging a net investment in a foreign subsidiary.** Crosswell, Inc., has a 100% interest in a foreign subsidiary whose functional currency is the FC. The interest is acquired when 1 FC = $1.45. As of September 30, 2014, the preclosing trial balance as of December 31, 2014, is forecasted to be as follows:

	Debit (Credit)
Cash	40,000 FC
Accounts Receivable	220,000
Inventory	320,000
Equipment (net of depreciation).	825,000
Accounts Payable	(360,000)
6% Note Payable	(400,000)
Accrued Interest Payable................	(4,000)
Common Stock	(200,000)
Contributed Capital in Excess of Par Value..	(200,000)
Beginning Retained Earnings	(140,000)
Sales	(600,000)
Cost of Sales	366,000
Selling Expenses	55,000
Administrative Expenses	48,000
Interest Expense......................	30,000
Total..............................	0 FC

Actual exchange rates between the FC and the dollar are 1 FC = $1.40 as of January 1, 2014, and $1.24 as of September 30, 2014. It is estimated that the year-end 2014 rate will be 1 FC = $1.20 and that the 2014 weighted-average rate will be 1 FC = $1.28.

Crosswell is considering hedging its investment in the foreign subsidiary by borrowing or lending FC as of September 30, 2014. The annual interest rate will be 6% with interest-only payments due at the end of each calendar quarter. At year-end 2013, the cumulative translation adjustment was a $120,000 debit balance. Determine the amount of the FC hedge that would be necessary to offset the 2014 change in the translation adjustment. Assume that the translated value of retained earnings at December 31, 2013, was $200,000.

Exercise 3 *(LO 5)* **Net investment under the sophisticated equity method.** On June 30, 2015, the shareholders' equity of Fabinet, a foreign corporation, was 10,500,000 FC. At that time, Newcore, a U.S. corporation, acquired 40% in Fabinet by paying $3,120,000 when 1 FC was equal to $0.60. Equipment, with a fair market value that exceeded cost by $240,000, accounted for a portion of the cost in excess of book value. The equipment was expected to have a remaining useful life of 10 years and be depreciated using the straight-line method. The balance of the cost in excess of book value was traceable to goodwill.

During the last six months of 2015, Fabinet reported net income of 1,260,000 FC of which 126,000 FC was declared and paid as a dividend. At the end of 2015, Newcore tested the goodwill for impairment and recognized an impairment loss of $100,000. Additional exchange rates are as follows:

Weighted average for last six months of 2015	1 FC = $0.64
Date of dividend declaration.............................	1 FC = 0.66
December 31, 2015	1 FC = 0.68

Prepare all relevant entries to record Newcore's interest in Fabinet under the sophisticated equity method.

Exercise 4 *(LO 6)* **Remeasurement of selected accounts.** Baxter Industries, Inc., is a U.S. company that has a wholly owned subsidiary. The subsidiary maintains its book and records in a foreign currency (FC) and the majority of its local expenses such as payroll, utilities, rent, etc., are paid in FC. However, the U.S. dollar is considered to be its functional currency. Selected exchange rates are as follows:

	1 FC =		1 FC =
March 1, 2009	$1.50	First quarter 2011	$1.50
November 1, 2009	$1.53	Second quarter 2011	$1.75
Third quarter 2010	$1.62	Third quarter 2011	$1.71
Fourth quarter 2010	$1.65	Fourth quarter 2011	$1.66
June 30, 2011	$1.70	December 31, 2011	$1.65

1. Identify several specific factors that would suggest that the U.S. dollar is the functional currency in spite of the fact regarding local expenses.
2. For each of the following compute the remeasured amount to be included as a component of the subsidiary's net income measured in its functional currency.
   a. Cost of sales for Product A is based on the FIFO method, and 6,200 units were sold during the current year 2011. The 2010 ending inventory consisted of 1,300 units purchased as follows: 400 units purchased at a cost of 53 FC per unit throughout the third quarter of 2010 and 900 units purchased at a cost of 55 FC per unit throughout the fourth quarter of 2010. Purchases during the year 2011 were as follows: 1,200 units at a cost of 58 FC per unit throughout the first quarter, 3,000 units at a cost of 59 FC per unit throughout the third quarter, and 1,700 units at a cost of 57 FC per unit throughout the fourth quarter. Determine the 2011 cost of sales for Product A.
   b. Equipment is depreciated over a 10-year life using the straight-line method of depreciation. Equipment was purchased at the beginning of March and November of 2009 in the amounts of 360,000 FC and 120,000 FC, respectively. Determine the 2011 depreciation expense.
   c. Also, on March 1, 2009, the subsidiary acquired a patent for $108,000. At that time, it was estimated that the patent would have a useful life of 12 years. At June 30, 2011, the value of the patent became impaired, and the subsidiary reclassified the assets as "held for resale" and carried the asset at its net realizable value of 32,000 FC. Determine the 2011 amortization expense and impairment loss associated with the patent.
   d. On June 30, 2011, the subsidiary borrowed 10,000 foreign currency A (FCA) from a foreign bank when 1 FCA was equal to 1.20 FC. Interest accrues semiannually at the annual rate of 6%, and the principal and accrued interest are due on June 30, 2012. At year-end 2011, 1 FCA was equal to 1.24 FC. Determine the effect on 2011 remeasured income as a result of this transaction.

Exercise 5 *(LO 3, 4)* **Measurement of the translation adjustment and hedging an investment.** Brico Enterprises, a U.S. corporation, acquired an 80% interest in Bandar Distributors in June 2008 when 1 FC equaled $1.62. Bandar is a foreign corporation whose functional currency is the FC. The condensed preclosing comparative trial balance for Bandar for the current year ended December 31, 2011, is as follows:

	Debit (Credit)	
	December 31, 2011	December 31, 2010
Current Assets	165,000 FC	185,000 FC
Long-Lived Assets (net)	420,000	400,000
Other Assets	170,000	165,000
Cost of Sales	525,000	425,000
Other Expenses	205,000	260,000
Current Liabilities	(175,000)	(135,000)
Other Liabilities	(125,000)	(225,000)
Net Sales	(820,000	(865,000)
Dividends Declared	25,000	30,000
Common Stock	(100,000	(100,000)
Retained Earnings (beginning)	(290,000)	(140,000)
Total	0	0

Dividends are declared on March 1 of each year and are paid on March 31 of that year. The translated balance in retained earnings at the beginning of 2010 was $227,300.

1. Determine the balance in the cumulative translation adjustment account as of December 31, 2011.
2. Determine how much of the cumulative translation adjustment balance as of December 31, 2011, is traceable to the years prior to 2011.
3. Given your answer to part (2), verify your answer by using an alternative approach to calculating the amount of the cumulative translation adjustment that is traceable to years prior to 2011.
4. Assume that Brico borrowed 100,000 FC on March 1, 2011, as a hedge against its investment in the subsidiary. Determine how much of the parent's interest in the current-year translation adjustment could have been offset by this hedge assuming that the loan remains unpaid as of year-end 2011.

Relevant exchange rates are as follows:

	Beginning of Year	March 1	1 FC equals March 31	Average	End of Year
2010	$1.75	$1.82	$1.85	$1.92	$1.95
2011	$1.95	$2.02	$2.00	$1.96	$1.92

Exercise 6 *(LO 3, 5)* **Translation of selected accounts and selected elimination entries.**

Techno Builders has acquired a 70% interest in the equity of a foreign company, Prefabco, whose functional currency is the FC. Although Prefabco began operations in June 2008 when 1 FC equaled $1.95, Techno did not acquire its interest until March 31, 2011, when 1 FC equaled $2.08. Techno paid 400,000 FC for its interest in Prefabco when the subsidiary's condensed preclosing trial balance was as follows:

Debit FC Balances		Debit FC Balances	
Current assets	250,000	Depreciable assets (net).	126,000
Depreciable assets (net).	350,000	Other liabilities	194,000
Other assets.	125,000	Capital stock	140,000
Cost of sales.	504,000	Retained earnings	134,000
Other expenses	125,000	Sales	720,000
Total.	1,354,000	Total.	1,314,000

Prefabco had net income and dividends, declared at year-end and paid in the first quarter of the next year, subsequent to Techno's acquisition as follows along with selected rates of exchange:

	Net Income	Dividends	Average Dollar/FC	Year-end Dollar/FC
Last 9 months of 2011	240,000	72,000	2.10	2.18
2012	305,000	91,500	2.25	2.21
2013	420,000	126,000	2.34	2.40

Prepare a schedule to determine the balance in Techno's account "Investment in Prefabco" as of year-end 2013 and also prepare all of the entries that would be necessary to eliminate the investment account in a worksheet to consolidate the parent company and its subsidiary for the year 2013. Techno uses the simple equity method to account for its interest in the subsidiary.

Exercise 7 *(LO 5, 6)* **Remeasured financial statements and sophisticated equity method.**

Champos Corporation is a foreign corporation that was formed on June 30, 2015. On July 1, 2016, Magnum Ventures, a U.S. venture capital firm, paid $700,000 to acquire a 30% interest in the equity of Champos. At the time of the acquisition, Champos had net assets as follows:

Monetary net assets.	200,000 FC
Inventory	150,000
Depreciable assets (net).	950,000
Land.	500,000
Total.	1,800,000

For the 6-month period ending December 31, 2016, Champos reported the following condensed income statement:

Condensed Income Statement		
Sales revenue		1,022,000 FC
Expenses:		
Cost of inventory sold (excluding depreciation)	480,000	
Depreciation expense	80,000	
Other operating expenses	60,000	620,000
Net income		402,000 FC

Selected exchange rates are as follows:

June 30, 2015	1 FC = $1.05
December 31, 2015	1 FC = 1.10
July 1, 2016	1 FC = 1.15
Second quarter 2016 average	1 FC = 1.14
Third quarter 2016 average	1 FC = 1.18
Fourth quarter 2016 average	1 FC = 1.20
Last six months of 2016 average	1 FC = 1.19
December 31, 2016	1 FC = 1.23

Campos employs the FIFO inventory method, and inventory layers during the second half of 2016 consisted of the following: 150,000 FC, 220,000 FC, and 210,000 FC, acquired during the second through fourth quarters of 2016, respectively. All depreciable assets were acquired on June 30, 2015. Of the excess over book value paid by Magnum Ventures, $54,000 is to be allocated to depreciable assets with a remaining useful life of nine years, and the balance is traceable to goodwill.

Determine the amount that Magnum Ventures should report for its investment in Champos Corporation as of December 31, 2016, under the sophisticated equity method.

PROBLEMS

Problem 11-1 *(LO 5)* **Elimination entries for a translated subsidiary.** Campione Manufacturing acquired an 80% interest in DaLuca Distributors, a foreign corporation established on November 1, 2006, for 650,000 foreign currency units (FC). Campione acquired its 80% interest on June 30, 2008, when DaLuca's shareholders' equity consisted of capital stock, paid-in capital in excess of par, and retained earnings in the amounts of 100,000 FC, 210,000 FC, and 300,000 FC, respectively. The excess of cost over book value was allocated to goodwill and depreciable assets in the amounts of 120,000 FC and 42,000 FC, respectively. The goodwill is annually tested for impairment, and no impairment in the value has been suggested. The depreciable assets are to be depreciated over 10 years assuming the straight-line method. DaLuca's income and dividends over the period from July 1, 2008, through the end of 2010 were as follows:

	FC Net Income	FC Dividends
Last half of 2008	75,000	—
2009	135,000	60,000
2010	160,000	80,000

The above dividends were declared at year-end.

DaLuca's condensed trial balance in FC as of December 31, 2011, is as follows:

	Balances		Balances
Cash	50,000	Accounts Payable	126,000
Receivables (net)	169,000	Dividends Payable	100,000
Prepaid Assets	24,000	Notes Payable	94,000
Invetory	304,000	Bonds Payable	274,000
Depreciable Assets (net)	780,000	Captial Stock	100,000
Other Assets	125,000	Paid-In Captial in Excess of par Value	210,000
Cost of Sales	315,000	Retained Earnings	530,000
Depreciation Expense	60,000	Sales	640,000
Other Expenses	147,000		
Dividends Declared	100,000		
Total	2,074,000	Total	2,074,000

The current-year dividend was declared on November 30, 2011. The FC is DaLuca's functional currency, and selected exchange rates between the FC and the dollar are as follows:

	1 FC =		1 FC =
November 1, 2006	1.80	December 31, 2009	$2.07
June 30, 2008	1.90	2010 Average	2.02
Last 6 months of 2008 average	0.92	December 31, 2010	2.00
December 31, 2008	1.94	2011 Average	1.95
2009 Average	2.05	November 30, 2011	1.94
		December 31, 2011	1.93

Required ▶ ▶ ▶ ▶ ▶   Prepare the translated trial balance for DaLuca and prepare all of the elimination and adjusting entries necessary to prepare consolidated financial statements. Assume that Campione uses the simple equity method.

Problem 11-2 *(LO 6)* **Prepare a remeasured trial balance and entries to eliminate excess of cost over book value.** On July 1, 2016, Spencer International acquired an 80% interest in the net assets of Quatro Corporation, which is a foreign company, for $6,260,000. At that time, the net assets of Quatro in foreign currency (FC) were as follows:

Common stock	8,000,000 FC
Paid-in capital in excess of par	1,000,000
Retained earnings	3,000,000

Any excess paid over book value was attributed to the fair value of certain licensing agreements that were held by Quatro. The agreements had an original useful life of 10 years, have a remaining life of five years, and are amortized using the straight-line method.

Spencer's investment in Quatro was designed to provide Spencer with additional manufacturing capacity for its product line and a distribution system that would allow for expanded sales in foreign markets. In order to implement these goals, Spencer loaned Quatro $5,940,000 in 2016 for the purpose of improving the manufacturing capacity. For the next five years, only interest payments at the rate of 8% would be made on a monthly basis. The loan originated on October 1, 2016, and the proceeds were disbursed at that time as follows:

Purchase of additional machinery	$3,410,000
Purchase of additional tooling	992,000
Purchase of additional inventory	1,538,000

On July 1, 2016, depreciable asset balances were as follows:

Machinery and Equipment	17,450,000 FC
Accumulated Depreciation—Machinery and Equipment	2,617,500
Tooling	4,400,000
Accumulated Depreciation—Tooling	660,000

All depreciable assets are depreciated using the straight-line method, and salvage values are ignored. Machinery is depreciated over a 10-year useful life, and tooling is depreciated over 10 years. No other additions or dispositions of depreciable assets have occurred since Spencer's acquisition of Quatro.

The manufacturing lead time for Quatro's products is such that the inventory typically turns over approximately four times a year; however, production costs are incurred fairly uniformly throughout the year. Virtually all material costs are denominated in U.S. dollars, although labor costs are denominated in FC. The company employs the FIFO inventory method, and 2017 ending inventory and cost of sales details are as follows:

Ending Inventory

2,200,000 FC acquired in the last quarter of 2017 when on average...............	1 FC = $0.55
1,500,000 FC acquired in the third quarter of 2017 when on average..............	1 FC = 0.56

Cost of Sales

800,000 FC acquired in the third quarter of 2016 when on average	1 FC = $0.61
1,200,000 FC acquired in the fourth quarter of 2016 when on average...............	1 FC = 0.62
3,200,000 FC acquired in the first quarter of 2017 when on average	1 FC = 0.60
4,100,000 FC acquired in the second quarter of 2017 when on average	1 FC = 0.57
3,400,000 FC acquired in the third quarter of 2017 when on average.................	1 FC = 0.56

	Debit	Credit
Cash and Receivables...............................	2,200,000 FC	
Inventory	3,700,000	
Machinery and Equipment	22,950,000	
Accumulated Depreciation—Machinery and Equipment		5,922,500 FC
Tooling	6,000,000	
Accumulated Depreciation—Tooling		1,520,000
Licensing Agreements	500,000	
Accumulated Amortization—Licensing Agreements		325,000
Accounts and Notes Payable		2,000,000
Due to Spencer		11,000,000
Common Stock		8,000,000
Paid-In Capital in Excess of Par		1,000,000
Retained Earnings		3,700,000
Sales Revenue		20,527,500
Cost of Sales (excluding depreciation)	12,700,000	
Depreciation Expense	2,895,000	
Amortization Expense	50,000	
Other Expenses	3,000,000	
Totals	53,995,000 FC	53,995,000 FC

The retained earnings balance as of December 31, 2017, reflects net income for the last half of 2016 of 1,300,000 FC (which had a translated value of $806,000) and dividend declarations in the amount of 300,000 FC each on both August 1, 2016, and August 1, 2017.

Additional exchange rates are as follows:

July 1, 2016	1 FC = $0.60	2017 Average..............	1 FC = $0.57
October 1, 2016.............	1 FC = 0.62	August 1, 2017.............	1 FC = 0.55
August 1, 2016..............	1 FC = 0.61	December 31, 2017	1 FC = 0.54
Last half of 2016 average	1 FC = 0.62		

Required ▶ ▶ ▶ ▶ ▶   1. Prepare a remeasured trial balance in dollars as of December 31, 2017, assuming that Quatro's functional currency is the dollar.
2. Prepare all of the necessary elimination entries to account for the acquisition price being in excess of the book value of net assets.

Problem 11-3 *(LO 6)* Remeasure equity accounts and determine noncontrolling interest values.
WTC Manufacturing, Inc., has an 80% interest in a foreign subsidiary, Mofoco Manufacturing. Relevant details regarding WTC's investment in Mofoco are as follows:

Date of acquisition. . . . . April 30, 2016	
Price paid for an 80% interest $3,600,000	
Mofoco credit balances as of June 30, 2016, in foreign currency (FC):	
Common stock.	1,200,000 FC
Contributed capital in excess of par value.	1,800,000 FC
Retained earnings	800,000 FC
Excess of cost over book value traceable to:	
Equipment with a remaining useful life of 8 1/3 years	100,000 FC
Goodwill . . . . The balance	

Although Mofoco maintains its books of record in the foreign currency (FC), its functional currency is the U.S. dollar. The partial preclosing trial balance for the year ended 2017 as it relates to shareholders' equity of Mofoco is as follows:

	Debit (Credit)
Common Stock	(1,200,000) FC
Contributed Capital in Excess of Par Value	(1,800,000)
Retained Earnings as of December 31, 2016.	(1,000,000)*
Sales	(3,100,000)
Cost of Inventory Sold (excluding depreciation)	2,200,000
Depreciation Expense	179,500
Patent Amortization	20,000
Other Operating Expenses	294,500
Loss on Disposal of Depreciable Assets	1,500

*The remeasured value of retained earnings on December 31, 2016, was $1,390,000.

Mofoco employs the FIFO inventory method, and inventory available for sale during 2017 consisted of a beginning balance of 300,000 FC, acquired in the fourth quarter of 2016, and purchases during quarters 1 through 4 of 2017 of 400,000 FC, 620,000 FC, 700,000 FC, and 380,000 FC, respectively. Depreciation expense is based on a 10-year useful life, no residual or salvage values, and the straight-line method. The 2017 depreciation expense is traceable to depreciable assets acquired as follows:

January 1, 2015, acquisition	1,060,000 FC
June 30, 2016, acquisition	450,000
March 31, 2017, acquisition	600,000

When the depreciable assets were acquired on March 31, 2017, Mofoco also disposed of depreciable assets with historical costs as follows: 160,000 FC acquired on January 1, 2015, and 60,000 FC acquired on June 30, 2016. The sales proceeds from the disposition of assets were 120,000 FC for the assets acquired on January 1, 2015 and 58,000 FC for the assets acquired on June 30, 2016. The patent amortization is traceable to a patent that was acquired on June 30, 2016, and is being amortized over 12 years by the straight-line method.

Relevant exchange rates are as follows:

January 1, 2015 . . . 1 FC = $1.40	December 31, 2017 . . . . 1 FC = $1.32	
April 30, 2016 . . . . 1 FC = 1.41	Fourth quarter 2016 average . . . . . 1 FC = 1.35	
June 30, 2016. . . . . 1 FC = 1.38	First quarter 2017 average . . . . 1 FC = 1.34	
March 31, 2017 . . . 1 FC = 1.36	Second quarter 2017 average . . . . 1 FC = 1.35	
2016 Average. . . . . 1 FC = 1.42	Third quarter 2017 average . . . . . . 1 FC = 1.32	
2017 Average. . . . . 1 FC = 1.35	Fourth quarter 2017 average . . . . . 1 FC = 1.31	

1. Given the preclosing trial balance for the year ended 2017 as it relates to shareholders' equity of Mofoco, calculate the remeasured U.S. dollar values. ◄ ◄ ◄ ◄ ◄ **Required**
2. Calculate the amount of 2017 consolidated net income that is traceable to the noncontrolling interest.

Problem 11-4 *(LO 6, 7)* **Remeasuring a trial balance and analyzing results.** In order to demonstrate the use of the remeasurement process, assume that at the beginning of the year a U.S. parent company invested 100,000 foreign currency B (FCB) to form a 100% owned subsidiary. The subsidiary immediately invested the foreign currency in land at a cost of 50,000 FCB and inventory with a cost of 50,000 FCB. At midyear, 50% of the inventory was sold for 40,000 FCB. At year-end, assume that the sale is still uncollected. Although FCB is the subsidiary's functional currency, the subsidiary maintains its books of record in foreign currency A (FCA). Assume the following exchange rates:

	Beginning of Year	Mid Year	End of Year
1 FCB equals	12.5 FCA	8 FCA	10 FCA
1 FCA equals.	0.08 FCB	0.125 FCB	0.10 FCB
1 FCA equals.	$0.20	$0.40	$0.30
1 FCB equals	$2.50	$3.20	$3.00

1. Prepare the entries to record the above transactions: (a) as they would have been recorded on the books of the subsidiary and (b) as they would have been recorded had they been recorded in terms of FCB. Also, prepare the trial balance that would have resulted under each of the recording models. ◄ ◄ ◄ ◄ ◄ **Required**
2. Prepare a schedule to remeasure the FCA trial balance into an FCB trial balance and then translate into U.S. dollars.
3. Prepare a schedule to directly calculate the translation adjustment to be reported in other comprehensive income.
4. Compare the remeasured FCB trial balance to the FCB trial balance in part (1) and comment regarding whether the objectives of translation have been achieved.

Problem 11-5 *(LO 3, 5)* **Translate a trial balance and prepare a consolidation worksheet with excess of cost over book value traceable to equipment.** Due to increasing pressures to expand globally, Pueblo Corporation acquired a 100% interest in Sorenson Company, a foreign company, on January 1, 2016. Pueblo paid 12,000,000 FC, and Sorenson's equity consisted of the following:

Common stock.	3,000,000 FC
Paid-in capital in excess of par	2,000,000
Retained earnings	4,200,000
Total.	9,200,000 FC

On the date of acquisition, equipment with a 10-year life was undervalued by 500,000 FC. Any remaining excess of cost over book value is attributable to additional equipment with a 20-year life. The trial balances for Pueblo and Sorenson as of December 31, 2018, are as follows:

	Pueblo Corporation	Sorenson Company
Cash	4,050,000	2,840,000 FC
Accounts Receivable	5,270,000	3,990,000
Inventory	5,540,000	5,800,000
Investment in Sorenson	20,969,000	
Fixed Assets.	21,000,000	15,000,000
Accumulated Depreciation	(12,560,000)	(6,800,000)
Accounts Payable	(3,450,000)	(1,580,000)
Long-Term Debt	(10,000,000)	(5,000,000)

Common Stock	(4,000,000)	(3,000,000)
Paid-In Capital in Excess of Par	(6,500,000)	(2,000,000)
Retained Earnings, January 1, 2018.	(12,180,000)	(7,950,000)
Sales	(26,000,000)	(10,000,000)
Cost of Goods Sold	16,380,000	7,500,000
Operating Expenses	3,210,000	1,200,000
Subsidiary Income.	(1,729,000)	
Totals	0	0 FC

The investment in Sorenson consists of the following:

Initial investment (12,000,000 FC × $1.20)	$14,400,000
2016 Income (1,750,000 FC × $1.28).	2,240,000
2017 Income (2,000,000 FC × $1.30).	2,600,000
2018 Income.	1,729,000
Total.	$20,969,000

Relevant exchange rates are as follows:

	1 FC =
January 1, 2016	$1.20
2016 Average.	1.28
January 1, 2017	1.25
2017 Average.	1.30
December 31, 2018	1.31
2018 Average.	1.33

Required ▶ ▶ ▶ ▶ ▶   Assuming the FC is Sorenson's functional currency, prepare a consolidated worksheet.

Problem 11-6 *(LO 3, 5)* **Translation and elimination entries.** On October 1, 2009, Kemper International acquired a 90% interest in the equity of Spruco Manufacturing when the subsidiary's equity was 8,000,000 foreign currency (FC), including retained earnings with a balance of 3,000,000 FC. Kemper paid 8,100,000 FC, when 1 FC = $1.18, for its 90% interest. The excess over book value was allocated to a patent in the amount of 360,000 FC with the balance being traceable to goodwill. It was estimated that the patent had a remaining useful life of 10 years and was to be amortized using the straight-line method.

Spruco's functional currency is the FC, and Kemper records its investment in the subsidiary under the simple equity method. Since its acquisition, relevant information regarding Spruco's net income and dividends is as follows:

	Remainder of 2009	2010	2011
Net income:			
Amount in FC.	350,000	920,000	740,000
Average exchange rate for period (1 FC =)	$1.20	$1.30	$1.25
Dividends declared:			
Amount in FC.	500,000	350,000	300,000
Exchange rate at date of declaration (1 FC =) . . .	$1.25	$1.32	$1.24

On December 31, 2011, when 1 FC = $1.22, Spruco reported total assets of 13,890,000 FC and liabilities of 5,030,000 FC.

Required ▶ ▶ ▶ ▶ ▶   Prepare the necessary entries to eliminate Kemper's investment in Spruco account at year-end 2011 and to record the depreciation/amortization on the relevant items of cost in excess of book value.

Problem 11-7 *(LO 3, 6, 7)* **Analyzing the effect of alternative functional currencies.** Patterson Distributors, Inc., purchases various electronic components from a variety of manufacturers and then distributes the products to end users. In the past, both domestic and foreign manufacturers of the components shipped the product to Patterson's two U.S.

distribution warehouses. In order to reduce costs and serve its customers on a timelier basis, Patterson is considering opening two international distribution centers. The company will form a 100%-owned foreign subsidiary to own the centers. The foreign subsidiary will need to secure financing and build and furnish a distribution warehouse in each location.

Projections, in the respective country's foreign currency (FCA), for the first 12 months of operations are as follows:

	Company A (FCA)
Investment of parent company	1,000,000 FCA
Debt financing:	
Principal balance at beginning of year	4,000,000 FCA
Interest rate	6%
Repayment frequency	quarterly
Amortization period	20 quarters
Periodic payment	232,983 FCA
Year-end principal balance	3,292,344 FCA
Sales revenue	2,200,000 FCA
Inventory:	
Purchases	1,460,000 FCA
Frequency of purchases	equal amounts at end of each quarter
Ending inventory per LIFO	140,000 FCA
Other expenses (excluding interest and depreciation)	158,068 FCA
Cost of distribution center:	
Land	1,600,000 FCA
Building	2,200,000 FCA
Furnishings	720,000 FCA
Useful life based on straight-line depreciation:	
Building	40 years
Furnishings	12 years
End of year:	
Accounts receivable	210,000 FCA
Accounts payable	130,000 FCA
Other current assets	50,000 FCA

Various projected exchange rates throughout the forecast period are as follows:

	1 FCA =
At beginning of year	$1.000
At end of first quarter	1.020
At end of second quarter	1.030
At end of third quarter	1.050
At end of fourth quarter	1.040
Average for the year	1.025

Although Patterson has prepared the projections in the respective foreign currencies, the company has the ability to structure transactions in such a way that either the foreign currency or the U.S. dollar is the functional currency.

Required ▶ ▶ ▶ ▶ ▶

1. Construct a year-end trial balance for the foreign subsidiary. Based on the information provided, calculate the translation adjustment and remeasurement gain or loss for the subsidiary assuming that the functional currency is the FCA and the dollar, respectively.

2. Discuss, in retrospect, whether the parent company would want to hedge its investment and, if so, how that might be accomplished.

3. Assume that the parent did hedge its investment in the subsidiary. This was accomplished by borrowing 600,000 FCA at the end of the first quarter. No principal payments were made during the year. How much of the gain or loss on this hedge would have been considered ineffective against the translation adjustment? The remeasurement gain?

Problem 11-8 *(LO 3, 5)* **Translate a trial balance and prepare a consolidation worksheet. Useful comparison with Problem 11-9.** Balfour Corporation acquired 100% of Tobac, Inc., a foreign corporation, for 33,000,000 FC. The acquisition, which was accounted for as a purchase, occurred on July 1, 2015, when Tobac's equity, in FC, was as follows:

Common stock..........................	19,000,000 FC
Paid-in capital in excess of par	8,480,000
Retained earnings	2,520,000

Any excess of cost over book value is traceable to equipment which is to be depreciated over 10 years. Balfour uses the simple equity method to account for its investment in Tobac.

On April 1, 2017, Tobac acquired additional equipment costing 4,000,000 FC. Equipment is depreciated by the straight-line method over 10 years. No other equipment had been acquired or disposed of since 2014. Tobac employs the LIFO inventory method. Ending inventory on December 31, 2017, consists of the following:

Acquired in the first quarter of 2014	1,000,000 FC
Acquired in the first quarter of 2015	500,000
Acquired in the first quarter of 2017	6,500,000

The cost of sales is traceable to goods purchased during 2017 as follows:

Acquired uniformly over the last 9 months.............	23,400,000 FC
Acquired in the first quarter	4,200,000

Other expenses were incurred evenly over the year.

On April 1, 2017, Tobac borrowed $1,280,000 from the parent company in order to help finance the purchase of equipment. The note is due in one year and bears interest at a rate of 8%. Principal and interest amounts are due to the parent in dollars.

Various spot rates are as follows:

	1 FC =		1 FC =
First quarter, 2014 average	$0.46	December 31, 2016...............	$0.60
2014 Average.................	0.49	First quarter, 2017 average	0.62
January 1, 2015	0.51	April 1, 2017	0.64
First quarter, 2015 average	0.53	2017 Average..................	0.67
July 1, 2015	0.55	Last 9 months, 2017 average	0.66
December 31, 2015.............	0.58	December 31, 2017..............	0.65
Last 6 months, 2015 average	0.57		
2016 Average.................	0.58		

The December 31, 2017, trial balances for Tobac and Balfour are as follows:

	Balfour Corporation	Tobac, Inc.
Cash	$ 4,463,200	3,087,385 FC
Net Accounts Receivable.	15,350,000	12,000,000
Inventory	16,300,000	8,000,000
Due from Tobac	1,356,800	
Investment in Tobac—See Note A	23,712,363	
Depreciable Assets	68,000,000	34,000,000
Accumulated Depreciation	(42,000,000)	(12,300,000)
Due to Balfour		(2,087,385)
Other Liabilities	(27,000,000)	(3,700,000)
Common Stock	(35,000,000)	(19,000,000)
Paid-In Capital in Excess of Par Value	(2,000,000)	(8,480,000)
Retained Earnings, January 1, 2017.	(4,500,000)	(7,520,000)
Sales	(98,000,000)	(40,000,000)
Cost of Sales	64,000,000	27,600,000
Depreciation Expense	8,076,800	3,300,000
Interest Expense on Balfour Loan (accrued on December 31, 2017)—See Note B		118,154
Exchange Gain on Balfour Loan—See Note B		(30,769)
Other Expenses	10,000,000	5,012,615
Interest Income.	(76,800)	
Subsidiary Income.	(2,682,363)	
Totals	$ 0	0 FC

Note A—Balfour's investment in Tobac consists of the following:

Initial investment (33,000,000 FC × $0.55)	$18,150,000
Last 6 months, 2015 income (2,000,000 FC × $0.57)	1,140,000
2016 Income (3,000,000 FC × $0.58)	1,740,000
2017 Income.	2,682,363
Balance	$23,712,363

Note B—The original loan from Balfour was 2,000,000 FC, or $1,280,000 (2,000,000 FC × $0.64). On December 31, 2017, it would require 1,969,231 FC ($1,280,000 ÷ $0.65) to settle the loan. This represents an exchange gain of 30,769 FC (2,000,000 FC – 1,969,231 FC).

The year-end balance due to Balfour is determined as follows:

Principal balance.	1,969,231 FC
Accrued interest ($1,280,000 × 8% × 9/12 ÷ $0.65)	118,154
Balance	2,087,385 FC

The interest is accrued at year-end; therefore, interest expense should be translated at the year-end rate.

Assuming the FC is Tobac's functional currency, translate Tobac's trial balance, and prepare a consolidating worksheet. ◄ ◄ ◄ ◄ ◄ **Required**

Problem 11-9 *(LO 5, 6)* **Same facts as Problem 11-8 except involve remeasurement. Useful comparison with Problem 11-8.** Assume the same facts as Problem 11-8 with the following exceptions:

a. Tobac's functional currency is the U.S. dollar.
b. Balfour's investment in Tobac consists of the following:

Initial investment (33,000,000 FC × $0.55)	$18,150,000
Last 6 months, 2015 income (including the remeasurement gain or loss) . . .	1,610,000
2016 income (including the remeasurement gain or loss)	1,860,000
2017 income (excluding the remeasurement gain or loss)	3,495,363
Balance	$25,115,363

Note that the balance has not yet been adjusted for the 2017 remeasurement gain or loss.

c. The trial balances for Tobac and Balfour are the same as in Problem 11-8 with the following exceptions:

Balfour

Investment in Tobac.	$25,115,363
Retained earnings, January 1, 2017	(5,090,000)
Subsidiary income	(3,495,363)

Required ▶ ▶ ▶ ▶ ▶   Remembering that Tobac's functional currency is the U.S. dollar, translate Tobac's trial balance and prepare a consolidating worksheet.

Remember that transactions traceable to pre-July 1, 2015, should be remeasured at the rate in effect on July 1, 2015. This is because on July 1, 2015, Balfour acquired its interest in Tobac and established the dollar basis of net assets existing at that time.

Interim Reporting and Disclosures about Segments of an Entity

CHAPTER

12

Learning Objectives

When you have completed this chapter, you should be able to

1. Explain the goal of interim reporting and how the interim period is viewed relative to an annual period.

2. Demonstrate how principles of revenue and expense recognition may be modified for interim reporting purposes.

3. Show how income tax expense or benefits tied to income from continuing operations are determined for an interim period.

4. Determine the income tax expense or benefit for nonordinary items of income and loss reported for interim periods.

5. Explain why segmental reporting is important, and define an operating segment.

6. Apply the criteria used to determine which segment is reportable.

7. Describe the information about a reportable segment that must be disclosed.

8. State which entity-wide disclosures must be provided.

This chapter focuses on two areas of significance to most large, publicly held entities: interim reporting and segmental disclosure. The relevance of financial information is enhanced if the information is provided on a timely basis. Interim financial reporting addresses the need for timely information and provides users with relevant data that may be used to evaluate the present and help to project future results. The division of an annual reporting period into shorter interim periods results in some unique accounting problems, which are addressed in this chapter. Disclosure about segments of an entity is designed to provide relevant information about the various business activities in which an entity is involved. Such disclosures also provide information about the economic environments in which entities operate. Many entities consist of operating segments that differ significantly from each other in terms of products, economic environments, markets served, and manufacturing methods. The disclosure of segmental information follows a management approach that emphasizes how management organizes the segments of the entity for decision-making purposes and evaluation of performance. This approach will allow users of such information to better understand the activities and environments that affect an entity's performance, cash flows, and business risks. The disclosures called for by this approach for both annual and interim reporting purposes are discussed in this chapter.

INTERIM REPORTING

To satisfy the need for timely financial information, many business entities have developed interim reporting models that provide financial information on a monthly or quarterly basis or at other defined intervals. These interim data may consist of statements of financial position

1

OBJECTIVE

Explain the goal of interim reporting and how the interim period is viewed relative to an annual period.

and retained earnings, income statements, and statements of cash flows. However, primary emphasis is placed on the public disclosure of interim income data.

A substantial amount of empirical research has been devoted to an examination of the utility of publicly disclosed interim financial reports. This research has identified significant stock market reaction to the issuance of interim reports and has noted the influence of interim reports on actual investment decisions. Interim reports provide such an important basis for the prediction of annual income that the demand for these reports nearly parallels the demand for annual reports.

The established utility of interim data emphasizes the importance of applying generally accepted accounting principles, including the principle of adequate disclosure, to interim reports. Therefore, the American Institute of Certified Public Accountants, the National Association of Accountants, the Financial Executives Institute, the Financial Analysts Federation, the Financial Accounting Standards Board, the Securities and Exchange Commission (SEC), and the principal stock exchanges have directed efforts toward the development and improvement of interim financial reporting.

Approaches to Reporting Interim Data

Earlier forms of interim reporting provided the user of such data with various disclosures other than the computation of net income. However, as the importance of interim income statements became more apparent, different views of the interim period developed. One view of the interim period is that it represents a distinct, independent accounting period, separate from the annual accounting period. Therefore, interim net income should be determined by using the same principles and estimations as would be used if the interim period were an annual accounting period. For example, annual research and development incurred during the interim period should be expensed in that period rather than deferred to future interim periods.

Another view of the interim period is that it is an integral part of the annual period and does not stand as a distinct, independent period. Therefore, interim data should include appropriate adjustments and estimates so that they can be used to predict annual amounts. For example, assume annual income normally includes a year-end accrual for executive bonuses in the amount of $120,000. If the interim statements are to serve as a predictor of annual values, it would seem appropriate that quarterly income statements should include a proportionate amount of this year-end adjustment. Including a $30,000 adjustment for bonuses in the quarterly income statement would allow one to predict annual bonuses in the amount of $120,000. If this interim adjustment were not made, bonuses would be reflected only in the fourth quarter, and previous quarters would not have provided the user with a basis for predicting this annual amount. From this example, one can see that an interim period is viewed as an integral part of a larger annual period. This view of the interim period has been adopted as the underlying theory used to formulate interim accounting principles and practices.

Accounting Principles Applicable to Interim Reporting

2
___

OBJECTIVE
___

Demonstrate how principles of revenue and expense recognition may be modified for interim reporting purposes.

The accounting principles relating to interim financial reporting are in response to a growing interest in the credibility of interim data and to the apparent need for an authoritative statement from the accounting profession regarding generally accepted accounting principles for such data. These principles are based on a fundamental conclusion that an interim period should be viewed as an *integral part of the annual period,* not as a distinct, independent period. Furthermore, the financial statements for each interim period should be based on the *same accounting principles and practices* that are used for the preparation of annual financial statements. However, certain modifications of these principles and practices that relate to costs and expenses may be necessary so that the reported results of an interim period are more indicative of anticipated annual income statement amounts. Modifications of accounting principles and practices also are necessary in order to provide timely information.

Modifications for Costs and Expenses. Those costs that are directly related or allocated to products sold or to services rendered for annual reporting purposes should be given similar treatment for interim reporting purposes. However, the following modifications are acceptable in the area of inventory costing:

1. The gross profit method or other estimation methods that are not acceptable for annual purposes may be used for interim purposes in those instances where taking an interim physical inventory would be too costly or where perpetual inventory records are lacking or unreliable. Furthermore, use of the gross profit method provides a timely measurement, which may not be the case if other methods of inventory accounting were employed. The inventory method used for interim purposes should be disclosed. Significant differences between estimates of the perpetual annual inventory and the annual physical inventory also should be recorded in interim statements on a proportionate basis.

2. Use of the LIFO method for interim purposes may result in inventory liquidations that will be replaced by year-end. To compensate for these interim liquidations, the interim cost of goods sold should include the *replacement cost* of temporarily liquidated inventory rather than its historical cost.

3. The use of lower of cost or market may suggest inventory losses for the interim period. Recoveries of these losses in subsequent periods should be recognized as gains to the extent of the losses previously recognized in interim periods within the same fiscal year. An exception to this rule is that temporary market declines that can reasonably be expected to be restored in the fiscal year need not be recognized for the interim period.

4. The use of standard costs for determining inventory generally should be applied on the same basis as is required for annual purposes. Price and volume variances that are planned and expected to be absorbed by year-end should be deferred at interim reporting dates.[1] However, unplanned or unanticipated variances should be reported at the end of an interim period.

Illustration of an Interim Liquidation of Inventory. In order to illustrate the special treatment given interim liquidations, assume a company's LIFO inventory available for sale during the third quarter consisted of beginning inventory of 1,200 units at a cost of $20 each and current purchases of 2,000 units at a cost of $30 each. Assume 2,500 units were sold during the quarter with the expectation that they would be replaced for $32 a unit. Management anticipates that the annual ending inventory will be 1,100 units. Therefore, although the beginning inventory has been liquidated by 500 units, management expects to replenish 400 of these units by year-end. Assuming the company anticipates paying $32 each to replenish the inventory, the third-quarter cost of sales would be calculated as follows:

Current purchases (2,000 units @ $30)	$60,000
Prior inventory (500 units @ $20 original cost)	10,000
Excess replacement cost (400 units @ $12)	4,800
	$74,800

The entry to record the third-quarter cost of sales would be as follows:

Cost of Sales	74,800	
Inventory		70,000
Excess of Replacement Cost for Temporary Liquidation		4,800
To record cost of sales with a historical cost of $70,000 and an excess of additional replacement cost equal to $4,800 ($12 × 400 units).		

The Excess of Replacement Cost for Temporary Liquidation is classified as a current liability on the interim financial statements. When the 400 units are replenished in the fourth quarter at an assumed cost of $32, the entry shown on page 656 is made.

---

[1] FASB ASC 270-10-45-6, *Interim Reporting—Overall—Other Presentation Matters—Costs Associated with Revenue.*

Inventory	8,000	
Excess of Replacement Cost for Temporary Liquidation	4,800	
Accounts Payable (cash)		12,800
To record replenishment of inventory previously liquidated.		

Notice that the 400 units replenish the inventory account at a cost of $20 each as though no liquidation had occurred. That is, the inventory now consists of 1,100 units (700 at the end of the third quarter plus the 400 replenished) at a cost of $20 each.

Illustration of Cost or Market for Interim Inventory. Assume at the end of the second quarter, ending inventory has a cost of $380,000 and a fair value of $350,000. The use of lower of cost or market would require a $30,000 loss due to market declines to be recognized in the second quarter. At the end of the third quarter, the company has ending inventory with a cost of $520,000 and a fair value of $560,000. Of the $40,000 excess of fair value over cost, the company can recognize $30,000 of this amount as a recovery of the second-quarter loss. Therefore, the third-quarter financial statements would include a $30,000 gain due to market recoveries.

Reporting of Costs Unrelated to Inventory. In reporting costs and expenses that are not allocated to products sold or to services rendered but are charged against income in the interim period, the following standards apply:

a. Costs and expenses other than product costs should be charged to income in interim periods as incurred or be allocated among interim periods based on an estimate of time expired, benefit received, or activity associated with the periods. Procedures adopted for assigning specific cost and expense items to an interim period should be consistent with the bases followed by the company in reporting results of operations at annual reporting dates. However, when a specific cost or expense item charged to expense for annual reporting purposes benefits more than one interim period, the cost or expense item may be allocated to those interim periods.
b. Some costs and expenses incurred in an interim period, however, cannot be readily identified with the activities or benefits of other interim periods and should be charged to the interim period in which they were incurred. Disclosure should be made as to the nature and amount of such costs unless items of a comparable nature are included in both the current interim period and in the corresponding interim period of the preceding year.
c. Arbitrary assignment of the amount of such costs to an interim period should not be made.
d. Gains and losses that arise in any interim period similar to those that would not be deferred at year-end should not be deferred to later interim periods within the same fiscal year.[2]

To illustrate the above concepts, assume the following expenditures have occurred at the beginning of the second quarter:

1. A 12-month insurance premium was paid in the amount of $1,200.
2. Research costs in the amount of $18,000 were paid and are expected to benefit the company over the next 18 months.
3. A contribution in the amount of $1,000 was made, although the benefits to subsequent quarters are uncertain.

The expenses to be recognized in the second quarter are as follows:

Insurance expense ($1,200 ÷ 12 × 3 months)	$ 300
Research costs ($18,000 ÷ 3 quarters—not to be deferred beyond year-end)	6,000
Contribution expense	1,000
	$ 7,300

Certain costs and expenses of an entity are subject to year-end adjustments, such as inventory shrinkage, allowance for uncollectible accounts, and year-end bonuses. These adjustments should not be recognized totally in the final interim period if they relate to activities of other

---

2 FASB ASC 270-10-45-8, *Interim Reporting—Overall—Other Presentation Matters—All Other Costs and Expenses.*

interim periods. Therefore, to generate interim financial reports that contain a reasonable portion of annual expenses, a portion of estimated year-end adjustments should be allocated to each interim period on the basis of a revenue or a cost relationship. For example, a company that estimates an expected material year-end adjustment to its perpetual inventory, based on a physical inventory, should allocate a portion of that estimated adjustment to each interim period. In this case, a portion of the annual estimated inventory shrinkage could be allocated to the quarter using a ratio of current quarter cost of sales to annual estimated cost of sales. Changes in earlier quarters' estimates should be accounted for in the current quarter.

The costs and expenses as well as revenues of some businesses are subject to seasonal variations. Since interim reports for such businesses must be considered as representative of the annual period, professional standards state that:

> . . . *such businesses should disclose the seasonal nature of their activities, and consider supplementing their interim reports with information for twelve-month periods ended at the interim date for the current and preceding years.*[3]

Adjustments Related to Prior Interim Periods. Normal recurring adjustments that result from the use of estimates should not be treated as adjustments to prior interim periods of the current fiscal year. For example, changes in the estimated provision for uncollectible accounts or the effective annual income tax rate should not be treated as a prior period adjustment. Instead, such adjustments or corrections should be accounted for in the current interim period and prospectively, as is the case with other changes in estimates. However, certain items are treated as adjustments related to prior interim periods of the current fiscal year. These items include an adjustment or settlement of litigation or similar claims, income taxes, renegotiation proceedings, or utility revenue under rate-making processes. Treating these items as prior-period adjustments is appropriate if all of the following criteria are met:

a. The effect of the adjustment or settlement is material in relation to income from continuing operations of the current fiscal year or in relation to the trend of income from continuing operations or is material by other appropriate criteria, and
b. All or part of the adjustment or settlement can be specifically identified with and is directly related to business activities of specific prior interim periods of the current fiscal year, and
c. The amount of the adjustment or settlement could not be reasonably estimated prior to the current interim period but becomes reasonably estimable in the current interim period.[4]

If such an item occurs in other than the first interim period of the current fiscal year and if all or part of the item is an adjustment related to prior interim periods of the current fiscal year, it should be reported as follows:

a. The portion of the item that is directly related to business activities of the entity during the current interim period, if any, shall be included in the determination of net income for that period.
b. Prior interim periods of the current fiscal year shall be restated to include the portion of the item that is directly related to business activities of the entity during each prior interim period in the determination of net income for that period.
c. The portion of the item that is directly related to business activities of the entity during the prior fiscal years, if any, shall be included in the determination of net income of the first interim period of the current fiscal year.[5]

Disclosure also is required regarding adjustments related to prior interim periods of the current year in the period in which the adjustment occurs. Disclosures should be made for each

---

3 FASB ASC 270-10-45-11, *Interim Reporting—Overall—Other Presentation Matters—Seasonal Revenue, Costs, or Expenses.*
4 FASB ASC 270-10-45-17, *Interim Reporting—Overall—Other Presentation Matters—Adjustments Related to Prior Interim Periods of the Current Fiscal Year.*
5 Ibid.

prior period of the current year setting forth both the effect on and actual adjusted amount of income from continuing operations, net income, and related per-share amounts.

Accounting for Income Taxes in Interim Statements

3

OBJECTIVE

Show how income tax expense or benefits tied to income from continuing operations are determined for an interim period.

Keeping in mind that the interim period is viewed as an integral part of a larger annual period, interim financial statements should reflect a proportionate amount of the estimated annual income taxes. Each interim period will not be viewed as a separate tax period; therefore, estimates of annual tax amounts and rates become critical. The basic objective of accounting for income taxes in interim periods is to estimate the annual effective tax rate and apply that rate to the interim periods' pretax net incomes.[6] The following general guidelines are applicable to the determination of an effective tax rate for interim purposes that are representative of the estimated annual effective tax rate:

1. The effective tax rate for the annual fiscal period must be estimated at the end of each interim period and applied to year-to-date interim income from ordinary continuing operations. The current interim period's tax expense or benefit is the difference between (a) the year-to-date tax expense or benefit and (b) the amounts of tax reported in previous interim periods of the current year.
2. The estimated effective tax rate should reflect tax planning alternatives, such as capital gains rates, permanent differences, and tax credits.
3. Nonordinary items of income or loss (unusual or infrequently occurring items, extraordinary items, and discontinued operations) are not included in the computation of the estimated annual effective tax rate, nor are these items prorated over the balance of the fiscal period. The tax effect on these items is determined incrementally.
4. Changes in tax legislation are to be accounted for in interim periods subsequent to the effective date of the legislation.

The first guideline is designed to ensure that the interim income tax rate is representative of the tax rate applicable to the entire fiscal period. For example, if income from continuing operations during the first interim period is $25,000, under a graduated taxing system the effective tax rate at this level of income might be 15%. However, if the annual ordinary income is expected to be $335,000, the effective annual tax rate might be approximately 34%. Therefore, the latter rate should be used as the interim tax rate. If this estimated annual effective tax rate were not used, a reader of the first interim period's financial statements might conclude that income is taxed at only 15%.

Mechanically speaking, the first guideline also provides a simple way of accounting for changes in the estimated annual effective tax rate. As mentioned earlier, normal recurring corrections and adjustments that result from the use of estimates are accounted for in the current interim period. Applying the estimated annual effective tax rate to the year-to-date income and then subtracting (adding) the tax expenses (benefits) traceable to prior interim periods of the current year results in a difference that represents:

1. The tax on the current interim period's pretax income at the present estimated annual effective tax rate, and
2. Corrections of previous interim periods' tax expenses or benefits resulting from a change in the estimated annual effective tax rate.

To illustrate, assume that the first quarter's pretax income of $40,000 was taxed at a 30% rate, resulting in a $12,000 tax expense. At the end of the second quarter, the estimated annual effective tax rate is 32%, and the second quarter's pretax income is $50,000. The tax on the year-to-date pretax income of $90,000 ($40,000 + $50,000) is $28,800 (32% × $90,000).

---

6 FASB ASC 740-270-30, *Income Taxes—Interim Reporting—Initial Measurement.*

Subtracting from this year-to-date amount the first-quarter tax expense of $12,000 results in a current second-quarter tax expense of $16,800. The $16,800 consists of:

1. The tax on the second quarter's pretax income at the present estimated annual effective tax rate ($50,000 × 32%) $16,000
2. Corrections of prior interim period's tax expense resulting from a change in the estimated annual effective tax rate [$40,000 × (32% − 30%)] 800

$16,800

If necessary, the estimated effective annual tax rate should be revised each interim period in order to reflect changed expectations. The guidelines indirectly emphasize that changes in the estimated annual effective tax rate should be accounted for as a change in estimate. Therefore, such changes in the tax rate from period to period should be reflected in the tax expense or benefit of the current period in which the change occurs. The second guideline emphasizes that tax planning alternatives should be reflected in the determination of the estimated effective annual tax rate. For example, if it is estimated that pretax operating income will include some tax-exempt income (a permanent difference), this should be reflected in a lower estimated tax rate. Tax credits and/or lower capital gains tax rates will also have the effect of lowering the estimated rate. Tax allocation principles resulting from the existence of timing differences would be factored into the calculation of the estimated effective annual tax rate as well.

The third guideline recognizes that nonordinary items of income or loss may have a distortive effect on estimated annual effective tax rates; therefore, they are excluded from such calculations. Furthermore, such items are required to be shown individually on a net of tax basis. Therefore, a separate incremental tax calculation, apart from the calculation of tax on ordinary continuing operations, must be made. The separate determination of the tax employs an incremental approach, which is demonstrated in a later section of this chapter.

The fourth guideline echoes the underlying theory of the first guideline in that changes in estimated tax rates are to be accounted for currently and prospectively. Changes in tax legislation are just one possible explanation for a change in estimated annual effective tax rates.

The computation of the estimated effective tax rate and the handling of a change in the estimated effective tax rate are demonstrated in Cases 1 through 3 on pages 660–661.

Year-to-Date Operating Losses. In some instances, an interim year-to-date (YTD) operating loss may be present. Given this loss, a question arises as to the potential tax benefit associated with the loss. The potential tax benefit is a function of several factors.

The YTD loss first must be combined with the projected income or loss for the remaining interim periods of the current fiscal year. If the YTD loss is offset by the projected income, a tax benefit traceable to the YTD loss may be recognized. However, if it is more likely than not that some portion of the projected income will not be recognized, then the recognized tax benefit traceable to the loss will be reduced accordingly. The concept of "more likely than not" means a level of likelihood at least more than 50% and requires the consideration of many sources of evidence, both positive and negative.[7] For example, a backlog of unfilled orders and/or a strong earnings history exclusive of the YTD loss would suggest that, more likely than not, losses may be offset by projected income. A history of operating losses or unsettled circumstances or economic conditions may suggest that, more likely than not, losses will not be offset totally by projected income.

---

7 Further discussion of the phrase "more likely than not" can be found in FASB ASC 740-10-30-7, *Income Taxes—Overall—Initial Measurement—Income Taxes Payable or Refundable.*

Case 1
Income in All Interim Periods—Tax Credit; No Permanent Differences

Year-to-date (YTD) pretax income is $170,000, and projected pretax income for the balance of the fiscal year is $30,000. No permanent differences exist, and it is anticipated that an annual tax credit of $13,250 will be available. Corporate income is taxed as follows: first $50,000 at 15%, next $25,000 at 25%, next $25,000 at 34%, amounts over $100,000 up to $335,000 at 39%. The effective tax rate is computed as follows:

	Pretax Income (Pretax Loss)
YTD income.	$ 170,000
Projected income	30,000
Estimated annual income	$ 200,000
Permanent differences	0
Estimated adjusted income	$ 200,000
Tax on estimated adjusted income	$ 61,250*
Tax credits.	(13,250)
Net tax	$ 48,000
Effective tax rate	(24%) ($48,000 ÷ $200,000)

*[($50,000 × 15%) + ($25,000 × 25%) + ($25,000 × 34%) + ($100,000 × 39%)]

Case 2
Income in All Interim Periods—Tax Credit; Permanent Difference; No Tax Credit

Year-to-date (YTD) pretax income is $30,000, and projected pretax income for the balance of the fiscal year is $90,000. Annual income includes $10,000 of expense, which is never deductible for tax purposes (i.e., a permanent difference). Assume that corporate income is taxed at the rates set forth in Case 1 above. The effective tax rate is computed as follows:

	Pretax Income (Pretax Loss)
YTD income.	$ 30,000
Projected income	90,000
Estimated annual income	$120,000
Permanent differences	10,000
Estimated adjusted income	$130,000
Tax on estimated adjusted income	$ 33,950*
Tax credits.	0
Net tax	$ 33,950
Effective tax rate	(28%) ($33,950 ÷ $120,000)**

* [($50,000 × 15%) + ($25,000 × 25%) + ($25,000 × 34%) + ($30,000 × 39%)]
** Note that the rate always is based on estimated annual pretax income versus adjusted income.

Case 3
Income in All Interim Periods—Change in Effective Tax Rate

In the third quarter, a change in the estimated annual income results in a change in the effective tax rate.

Interim Period (Quarter)	Ordinary Pretax Income (Loss)		Effective Tax Rate	Tax Expense (Benefit)		
	Current Period	Year-to-Date		Year-to-Date	Previously Reported	Current Period
First	$30,000	$ 30,000	28%	$ 8,400	—	$ 8,400
Second	40,000	70,000	28	19,600	$ 8,400	11,200
Third	20,000	90,000	32	28,800	19,600	9,200
Fourth	50,000	140,000	32	44,800	28,800	16,000

After considering the projected income or loss for the balance of the current year, an estimated annual operating loss may exist. The potential tax benefit traceable to this estimated annual operating loss is a function of the following factors:

1. The extent to which the operating loss may be offset by income of the prior two fiscal years included in the carryback period and/or
2. The extent to which the operating loss may be offset by subsequent years' annual income that is more likely than not to be recognized in the 20-year carryforward period.

The basic concern addressed by these factors is whether the operating loss is able to be offset against operating income and, therefore, result in a tax benefit. If the facts suggest that such a benefit is more likely than not, the benefit should be recognized in the calculation of the effective annual tax rate.[8]

Offsetting YTD Operating Losses against Subsequent Interim Income. The benefit associated with a YTD operating loss should be recognized if: (a) the benefit is expected to be realized during the year or (b) the benefit is recognizable as a deferred tax asset at the end of the year. If the benefit of the loss is recognized in case (a) above, the loss is expected to be offset against income in later interim periods of the current fiscal year. This offset against income may be recognized if it is more likely than not that such income will be recognized. Although "more likely than not" is a subjective concept, knowledge of a company's past performance, existing commitments relating to the future, and seasonal patterns must be considered.

The offset of an established seasonal loss by subsequent interim income is demonstrated in Case 4 that follows.[9] Case 5 demonstrates a YTD loss whose tax benefit is not initially certain but later becomes recognizable. It is important to note that, in both Cases 4 and 5, it is assumed that no pretax income is available in prior and/or subsequent years to absorb the current year's operating losses.

---

8 For additional examples involving the tax benefit of operating losses beyond those presented in the chapter, see FASB ASC 740-270-55, *Income Taxes—Interim Reporting—Implementation Guidance and Implementation.*
9 Note that throughout this chapter the effective tax rates used in the illustrative examples are not based on the actual corporate tax rates but, rather, are only for illustrative purposes.

Case 4
Seasonal YTD Loss Offset by Subsequent Interim Income
That Is "More Likely Than Not" and No Pretax Income Available in Other Years

Interim Period (Quarter)	Ordinary Pretax Income (Loss)		Effective Tax Rate	Tax Expense (Benefit)		
	Current Period	Year-to-Date		Year-to-Date	Previously Reported	Current Period
First	$(30,000)	$(30,000)	40%	$(12,000)		$(12,000)
Second	20,000	(10,000)	40	(4,000)	$(12,000)	8,000
Third	40,000	30,000	40	12,000	(4,000)	16,000
Fourth	40,000	70,000	40	28,000	12,000	16,000

Case 5
YTD Loss where Tax Benefit Is Initially Uncertain
and No Pretax Income Available in Other Years

Interim Period (Quarter)	Ordinary Pretax Income (Loss)		Effective Tax Rate	Tax Expense (Benefit)		
	Current Period	Year-to-Date		Year-to-Date	Previously Reported	Current Period
First	$(30,000)	$(30,000)	0%			
Second	20,000	(10,000)	0			
Third	40,000	30,000	40	$12,000		$12,000
Fourth	40,000	70,000	40	28,000	$12,000	16,000

Offsetting YTD or Annual Operating Losses against Income of Prior Fiscal Years. In certain instances, a current YTD interim loss may not be offset entirely by income in later interim periods of the current fiscal year. However, as suggested by the first factor discussed above, the tax benefit of the YTD loss should be recognized to the extent that the loss may be carried back against the prior two years of income. Loss carrybacks must begin with the earliest of the prior two years and then proceed to the next earlier year. The tax benefit traceable to the loss, therefore, is a function of the tax rate applied to a prior year's income. Case 6 involves the carryback of a YTD loss. Note that, in this case, the loss is not offset completely against prior income. However, the tax benefit is recognized to whatever extent possible.

The same carryback principles apply if an annual loss is anticipated. For example, if a company has a YTD loss of $40,000 and an anticipated annual loss of $100,000, the amount of tax benefit would be dependent upon the extent to which the $100,000 loss may be carried back. If a company has a year-to-date income of $60,000 and an anticipated annual loss of $20,000, the estimated annual effective tax rate would be dependent upon the tax benefit associated with the annual loss of $20,000. These principles are demonstrated in Case 7.

Case 6
YTD Loss with No Assurance of Subsequent Interim Income; $30,000 of Prior Two Years' Income Taxed at 50%

Interim	Ordinary Pretax Income (Loss)		Effective	Tax Expense (Benefit)		
Period (Quarter)	Current Period	Year-to-Date	Tax Rate	Year-to-Date	Previously Reported	Current Period
First	$(40,000)	$(40,000)	37.5%	$(15,000)*		$(15,000)
Second	10,000	(30,000)	50	(15,000)	$(15,000)	
Third	35,000	5,000	40**	2,000	(15,000)	17,000
Fourth	30,000	35,000	40	14,000	2,000	12,000

* Only $30,000 of the $40,000 loss can be offset against the prior years' income, resulting in a tax benefit of $15,000; $15,000 ÷ $40,000 = 37.5%.
** The current-year statutory tax rate is assumed to be 40%.

Case 7
YTD and Anticipated Annual Loss (of $100,000) with $60,000 of Prior Two Years' Income Taxed at 50%

Interim	Ordinary Pretax Income (Loss)		Effective	Tax Expense (Benefit)		
Period (Quarter)	Current Period	Year-to-Date	Tax Rate	Year-to-Date	Previously Reported	Current Period
First	$(40,000)	$ (40,000)	30%*	$(12,000)		$(12,000)
Second	(30,000)	(70,000)	30	(21,000)	$(12,000)	(9,000)
Third	5,000	(65,000)	30	(19,500)	(21,000)	1,500
Fourth	(35,000)	(100,000)	30	(30,000)	(19,500)	(10,500)

* The effective tax rate of 30% is based on a $30,000 tax benefit of ($60,000 × 50%) expressed as a percentage of the $100,000 anticipated annual loss.

Offsetting Annual Operating Losses against Future Annual Income. To the extent that losses are not absorbed by income in later interim periods of the current fiscal year and/or the prior two years of income, tax benefits still may be recognized currently as a deferred asset. In essence, future events are more likely than not such that the benefit of the current year's annual operating loss will be realized in a future year thus allowing for recognition in the current year of loss. Losses not already offset may be carried forward against future annual income that more likely than not will be recognized in the 20-year carryforward period. Estimating whether future annual income will more likely than not be recognized is one of the most difficult aspects of determining the estimated annual effective tax rate associated with operating losses. Certain amounts of future annual income may have a low level of likelihood that they will be recognized. For example, if an entity has a history of operating losses and is in an industry experiencing a significant number of bankruptcies, a low level of likelihood would seem reasonable. Alternatively, certain amounts of future annual income have a high level of likelihood. For example, the future taxable amounts represented by deferred tax liabilities are considered to have a very high level of likelihood. Therefore, such future taxable amounts will more likely than not be recognized and serve as a basis for offsetting a current annual operating loss. Another example might involve a company that has unfilled orders or contracts that will be realized in the near future such that it is more likely than not that there will be future income against which the current year operating loss can be offset. The principles of offsetting current annual operating losses against likely future annual income are demonstrated in Case 8.

Case 8
YTD and Anticipated Annual Loss (of $80,000) with Carrybacks and Carryforwards Available

Interim Period (Quarter)	Ordinary Pretax Income (Loss)		Effective Tax Rate	Tax Expense (Benefit)		
	Current Period	Year-to-Date		Year-to-Date	Previously Reported	Current Period
First	$(20,000)	$(20,000)	30%*	$ (6,000)		$ (6,000)
Second	15,000	(5,000)	30	(1,500)	$ (6,000)	4,500
Third	(35,000)	(40,000)	30	(12,000)	(1,500)	(10,500)
Fourth	(40,000)	(80,000)	30	(24,000)	(12,500)	(12,000)

*The calculation of the effective tax rate is based on the following:

Prior 2 years' total income of $10,000 taxed at a prior rate of 40%	$ 4,000
Deferred tax liability reversing within the next 20 years based on the current tax rate of 40% ($50,000 of temporary differences).	20,000
Total tax benefit.	$24,000

$24,000 ÷ $80,000 anticipated annual loss = 30%

Note: In Case 5, the likely future income for offsetting the loss is $50,000, resulting from temporary timing differences. However, if likely future income in the carryforward period had been at least $70,000, a tax benefit would have been recognized on the entire current operating loss of $80,000. The $80,000 of loss would have been carried back in the amount of $10,000 and carried forward in the amount of $70,000.

Operating Losses That Are Not Offset. If present net operating losses cannot be offset totally by any of the options discussed (subsequent interim income of the current fiscal year, income in the carryback or carryforward years), the potential tax benefit is reduced accordingly and no tax benefit is recognized currently on those losses that are not offset. However, the potential tax benefit associated with those losses that are not currently offset may be subsequently recognized by offsetting the losses against future years' recognized income or additional deferred tax liabilities that may arise in the carryforward period. When the tax benefit associated with these remaining losses is recognized, it is classified the same as the item against which the losses were offset. For example, if the remaining losses were offset against subsequent income from continuing operations, the benefit would become a component of income from continuing operations. However, if the remaining losses were offset against a subsequent extraordinary item, the tax benefit would be classified as extraordinary. To demonstrate these principles, consider the facts of Case 8. In this instance, the annual anticipated loss of $80,000 was used to offset $10,000 of prior years' income and $50,000 of likely future income in the carryforward period taxed at 40%. Therefore, the equivalent of $60,000 ($10,000 + $50,000) of the loss was offset in order to generate the $24,000 tax benefit. The remaining loss of $20,000 (original $80,000 − $60,000 offset) may offset future income or deferred tax liabilities arising in the 20-year carryforward period. Assuming the subsequent year has a recognized pretax income from continuing operations of $25,000 that would be taxed at 40%, a tax benefit of $8,000 ($20,000 × 40%), representing the offsetting of the remaining $20,000 loss against the income from continuing operations, would be recognized. The subsequent year's net tax expense on the continuing income would be $2,000 [($25,000 − $20,000) × 40%], for an effective tax rate of 8% ($2,000 ÷ $25,000). The net tax expense results from the tax expense of $10,000 on the $25,000 of income reduced by the $8,000 tax benefit.

Case 9 demonstrates a special limitation of the tax benefits associated with operating losses. This special limitation arises when a YTD operating loss exceeds the annual operating loss.

Case 9
YTD and Anticipated Annual Loss (of $48,000) with a $40,000 Carryback at 30% Available

Interim Period (Quarter)	Ordinary Pretax Income (Loss)		Effective Tax Rate	Tax Expense (Benefit)		
	Current Period	Year-to-Date		Year-to-Date	Previously Reported	Current Period
First	$(10,000)	$(10,000)	25%*	$ (2,500)		$(2,500)
Second	(20,000)	(30,000)	25	(7,500)	$ (2,500)	(5,000)
Third	(30,000)	(60,000)	Note	(12,000)	(7,500)	(4,500)
Fourth	12,000	(48,000)	25	(12,000)	(12,000)	

* The calculation of the effective tax rate is based on the following:

Prior 2 years' total income of $40,000 taxed at a prior rate of 30% $12,000

The effective tax rate of 25% is based on the $12,000 total tax benefit expressed as a percentage of the $48,000 anticipated annual pretax loss ($12,000 ÷ $48,000).

Note: If the rate of 25% were used, a YTD tax benefit of $15,000 would be suggested. However, a YTD loss of $60,000 could receive a benefit of only $12,000 (30% × $40,000 prior year's income). Therefore, the YTD benefit is limited to $12,000. This special rule arises **ONLY** when a YTD operating loss exceeds the annual anticipated operating loss. Notice that both YTD and annual amounts must be losses. In this case, the YTD tax benefit is limited to the amount ($12,000) that would be recognized if the YTD loss were the expected loss for the entire fiscal year ($48,000).

Nonordinary Items of Income or Loss. Certain elements making up an entity's net income are reported separately and/or shown net of tax. These elements may include unusual or infrequently occurring items, discontinued operations, and extraordinary items. For purposes of discussion, these items are referred to as nonordinary items. There also are interim gains or losses that are directly accounted for as a component of owners' equity. The tax impact on these items should be determined by the same methodology as is used for nonordinary items. As previously stated, these items are not included in the determination of the estimated effective tax rate applied to ordinary income. The estimated effective tax rate applied to ordinary income may not be appropriate for nonordinary items of income for a variety of reasons, including the following:

4

OBJECTIVE

Determine the income tax expense or benefit for nonordinary items of income and loss reported for interim periods.

1. Nonordinary items may be taxed at different statutory tax rates, such as capital gains tax rates, than ordinary items.
2. Nonordinary items, when combined with ordinary items, may cause the total income to increase (decrease), and a higher (lower) progressive tax rate will then become applicable.
3. Nonordinary items may, in total, represent a loss whose tax benefit is limited because there are not adequate sources of other income that can be offset by the loss.
4. Nonordinary items may, in total, represent income that provides a source against which ordinary losses may find tax benefit.

Therefore, the tax effect of these nonordinary items must be determined independently on an incremental basis.

If *one* nonordinary item exists, the incremental income tax is the *difference* between:

1. The income tax expense (benefit) traceable to the estimated annual pretax *ordinary* income (loss), and
2. The income tax expense (benefit) traceable to the *total pretax income* (loss) (the sum of the estimated annual pretax ordinary income or loss and the nonordinary income or loss).

For example, assume an estimated annual tax expense of $22,250 on estimated annual pretax ordinary income of $100,000. Also assume that total pretax income is $120,000 after including a nonordinary item of $20,000, with a resulting tax expense of $30,050. Therefore, the tax expense traceable to the nonordinary item is $7,800 ($30,050 − $22,250).

When several nonordinary items exist, the calculation of their individual tax impact becomes more complex. This complexity usually occurs because of differences in tax rates for nonordinary items, surtax charges, and tax credit limitations. If several nonordinary items exist, the incremental tax traceable to each nonordinary item or category is determined as follows:

1. The incremental income tax expense (benefit) traceable to *all* nonordinary categories (loss categories and gain categories) is the difference between:
   a. *The income tax expense (benefit) traceable to the estimated annual pretax ordinary income (loss) and*
   b. *The income tax expense (benefit) traceable to the total of all sources of pretax income (loss).*

2. The incremental income tax benefit traceable to *all* nonordinary *loss* categories is the difference between:
   a. *The income tax expense (benefit) traceable to the* total *of all sources of pretax income (loss) (step 1b) and*
   b. *The income tax expense (benefit) traceable to the* total *of all sources of pretax income (loss) excluding all nonordinary losses.*

3. The incremental income tax expense traceable to *all* nonordinary *gain* categories is the difference between:
   a. *The incremental income tax expense (benefit) traceable to all nonordinary items (step 1) and*
   b. *The incremental income tax benefit traceable to all nonordinary loss categories (step 2).*
   Note that the incremental tax expense or benefit traceable to all nonordinary items from step 1 has been allocated between nonordinary losses (step 2) and nonordinary gains (step 3).

4. Next, the incremental income tax benefit traceable to each *individual* nonordinary *loss* category is the difference between:
   a. *The income tax expense (benefit) traceable to the* total *of all sources of pretax income (loss) (step 1b) and*
   b. *The income tax expense (benefit) traceable to the total of all sources of pretax income (loss), excluding* the individual *nonordinary* loss *category.*
   Note that this step is repeated for each nonordinary loss category. Furthermore, it is likely that the sum of each of the incremental tax benefits will not equal the total tax benefit associated with all nonordinary losses, as calculated in step 2 above.

5. Then, the incremental income tax benefit traceable to *all* nonordinary *loss* categories (step 2) is *apportioned ratably* to each individual loss category based on the incremental income tax benefit of each *individual* nonordinary *loss* category (step 4).

6. The incremental income tax expense traceable to each *individual* nonordinary *gain* category is the difference between:
   a. *The income tax expense (benefit) traceable to the* total *of all sources of pretax income (loss) (step 1b) and*
   b. *The income tax expense (benefit) traceable to the total of all sources of pretax income (loss), excluding* the individual *nonordinary gain category.*
   Note that this step is repeated for each nonordinary gain category. Furthermore, it is likely that the sum of each of the incremental tax expenses will not equal the total tax expense associated with all nonordinary gains, as calculated in step 3 above.

7. Finally, the incremental income tax expense traceable to *all* nonordinary *gain* categories (step 3) is *apportioned ratably* to each individual gain category based on the incremental income tax expense traceable to each *individual* nonordinary *gain* category (step 6).

The tax impact of nonordinary gains and losses based on the above steps is demonstrated in Illustration 12-1. It is important to remember that the principles discussed earlier regarding offsetting YTD losses also are applicable to nonordinary loss categories. This particular illustration assumes the nonordinary gains and losses are separated into four categories.

Illustration 12-1
Tax Impact on Nonordinary Gains and Losses (Assuming Four Different Categories)

Facts:

Ordinary income of		$180,000
Nonordinary losses consist of:		
Loss (Category #1)	$(30,000)	
Loss (Category #2)	(20,000)	(50,000)
Nonordinary gains consist of:		
Gain (Category #3)	$ 20,000	
Gain (Category #4)	10,000	30,000
Total pretax income of		$160,000
Tax information:		
Tax rate on income	30%	
Surtax on income between $100,000 and $170,000[a]	5%	
Tax credit	$ 10,000	
Tax rate on gain (Category #3), which is also exempt		
from the surtax	20%	

[a] This surtax effectively means income between $100,000 and $170,000 is taxed at a 35% (30% + 5%) rate.

Calculation of Total Incremental Tax Impact (steps 1, 2, and 3):

	Ordinary Income	Total Income	Total Income Excluding Nonordinary Losses	Total Income Excluding Nonordinary Gains
Pretax income	$180,000	$160,000[b]	$210,000 ($160,000 + $50,000)	$130,000 ($160,000 − $30,000)
Tax expense (benefit)[c]	**A** 47,500 (step 1a)	**B** 38,000 (step 1b)	**C** 54,500 (step 2b)	

[b] Includes the $20,000 Category #3 gain.

[c]

Tax on income: $180,000 × 30% = $54,000	$160,000 {	$140,000 × 30% = $42,000	$210,000 {	$190,000 × 30% = $57,000	
		20,000 × 20% = 4,000		20,000 × 20% = 4,000	
		40,000 × 5% = 2,000		70,000 × 5% = 3,500	
Surtax: 70,000 × 5% = 3,500					
Tax credit: (10,000)		(10,000)		(10,000)	
Tax expense: **A** $47,500		**B** $38,000		**C** $54,500	

Incremental tax expense (benefit) traceable to:

D	All nonordinary items	($38,000 − $47,500)	$ (9,500)
		(step 1: **B** − **A**)	
E	All nonordinary losses	($38,000 − $54,500)	(16,500)
		(step 2: **B** − **C**)	
F	All nonordinary gains	[($9,500) − ($16,500)]	7,000[d]
		(step 3: **D** − **E**)	

[d] If the incremental tax associated with all nonordinary items is a $9,500 benefit and the incremental tax associated with all nonordinary losses is a benefit of $16,500, the incremental tax expense associated with all nonordinary gains must be $7,000 [($9,500) = ($16,500) + $7,000]. That is, the incremental tax associated with all nonordinary items must be allocated to either nonordinary losses or gains. Furthermore, the amounts allocated to nonordinary losses and gains must equal the amount traceable to all nonordinary items.

(continued)

Calculation of Incremental Tax Benefit Traceable to Each Individual Loss Category (step 4):

	Total Income	Total Income Excluding All Nonordinary Losses	Total Income Excluding Loss (Category #1)	Total Income Excluding Loss (Category #2)
Pretax income......................	$160,000	$210,000	$190,000	$180,000
Tax expense (benefit)[e]	**B** 38,000	**C** 54,500	**G** 48,500	**H** 45,000
			(step 4b)	(step 4b)

[e]Tax on income $190,000

$$\begin{cases} \$170,000 \times 30\% = \$51,000 \\ 20,000 \times 20\% = 4,000 \\ \text{Surtax:} \quad 70,000 \times 5\% = 3,500 \\ \text{Tax credit:} \quad (10,000) \\ \text{Tax expense:} \quad \textbf{G } \$48,500 \end{cases}$$

$180,000

$$\begin{cases} \$160,000 \times 30\% = \$48,000 \\ 20,000 \times 20\% = 4,000 \\ 60,000 \times 5\% = 3,000 \\ (10,000) \\ \textbf{H } \$45,000 \end{cases}$$

Incremental tax expense (benefit) traceable to:

E All nonordinary losses ($38,000 − $54,500)............................. $(16,500)
(step 2: **B** − **C**)

I Nonordinary loss (Category #1) ($38,000 − $48,500).............................. (10,500)
(step 4, first loss category: **B** − **G**)

J Nonordinary loss (Category #2) ($38,000 − $45,000)............................. (7,000)[f]
(step 4: second loss category: **B** − **H**)

[f]Notice that the sum of the incremental tax benefit on categories 1 and 2 of $17,500 [($10,500) + ($7,000)] does not equal the incremental tax benefit of $16,500 on all losses. It is for this very reason that an apportionment of the tax impact of individual categories is necessary.

Apportionment of Tax Benefit Traceable to Nonordinary Losses (step 5):

The $16,500 incremental tax benefit traceable to all nonordinary losses is ratably apportioned to each individual loss category as follows:

	Each Loss Category		Apportioned
	Incremental Benefit	Percent	Amount
Loss (Category #1)....................**I**	$(10,500)	60%	$ (9,900) = (60% × $16,500)
Loss (Category #2)....................**J**	(7,000)	40	(6,600) = (40% × $16,500)
	$(17,500)	100%	**E** $(16,500)

Calculation of Incremental Tax Expense Traceable to Each Individual Gain Category (step 6):

	Total Income	Total Income Excluding Gain (Category #3)	Total Income Excluding Gain (Category #4)
Pretax income.............................	$160,000	$140,000	$150,000
Tax expense (benefit)[g]	**B** 38,000	**K** 34,000	**L** 34,500
		(step 6b)	(step 6b)

[g]Tax on income

$$\begin{array}{l} \$140,000 \times 30\% = \$42,000 \\ \text{Surtax:} \quad 40,000 \times 5\% = 2,000 \\ \text{Tax credit:} \quad (10,000) \\ \text{Tax expense:} \quad \textbf{K } \$34,000 \end{array}$$

$150,000

$$\begin{cases} \$130,000 \times 30\% = \$39,000 \\ 20,000 \times 20\% = 4,000 \\ 30,000 \times 5\% = 1,500 \\ (10,000) \\ \textbf{L } \$34,500 \end{cases}$$

Incremental tax expense (benefit) traceable to:

F	All nonordinary gains	[($9,500) − ($16,500)]............................	$7,000
		(step 3: **D − E**)	
M	Nonordinary gain (Category #3)	($38,000 − $34,000).............................	4,000
		(step 6, first gain category: **B − K**)	
N	Nonordinary gain (Category #4)	($38,000 − $34,500).............................	3,500
		(step 6, second gain category: **B − L**)	

Apportionment of Tax Expense Traceable to Nonordinary Gains (step 7):

The $7,000 incremental tax expense traceable to all nonordinary gains is ratably apportioned to each individual gain category as follows:

		Each Gain Category		Apportioned
		Incremental Benefit	Percent	Amount
Gain (Category #3)	**M**	$4,000	53%	$3,710 = (53% × $7,000)
Gain (Category #4)	**N**	3,500	47	3,290 = (47% × $7,000)
		$7,500	100%	**F** $7,000

Summary of Tax Impact Associated with Ordinary and Nonordinary Items:

	Pretax Income (Loss)	Tax Expense (Benefit)
Ordinary Income	$180,000	**A** $47,500
Loss (Category #1)	(30,000)	(9,900)
Loss (Category #2)	(20,000)	(6,600)
Gain (Category #3)	20,000	3,710
Gain (Category #4)	10,000	3,290
Totals...............................	$160,000	**B** $38,000

If there is a nonordinary loss, the tax benefit of the loss should be recognized if it can be offset by other existing YTD elements of income and projected income for the balance of the year, which is likely. If the nonordinary loss category cannot be offset by elements of income in the current fiscal year, the principles discussed previously regarding carrybacks against prior years' income and carryforwards against likely future income would be applicable. Illustration 12-2 demonstrates the offsetting of a nonordinary (an extraordinary item) loss under various situations.

Illustration 12-2
Case A: Offsetting a Nonordinary Loss Against Sufficient Current-Year Ordinary Income

Interim Period (Quarter)	Type of Income	Pretax Income (Loss)		Effective Tax Rate	Tax Expense (Benefit)		
		Current Period	Year-to-Date		Year-to-Date	Previously Reported	Current Period
First	Continuing Op.	$ 40,000	$ 40,000	26%	$ 10,400		$ 10,400
Second	Continuing Op.	30,000	70,000	28	19,600	$ 10,400	9,200
Third	Continuing Op.	20,000	90,000	28	25,200	19,600	5,600
Third	Nonordinary	(50,000)	(50,000)	Note A	(14,000)		(14,000)
Fourth	Continuing Op.	40,000	130,000	30	39,000	25,200	13,800
Fourth	Nonordinary		(50,000)	Note B	(15,000)	(14,000)	(1,000)

Note A: The entire nonordinary loss can be offset against ordinary income, which has an effective tax rate of 28%.

Note B: Due to a change in the estimated effective tax rate from 28% to 30%, the benefit associated with the nonordinary loss has increased.

Case B: Offsetting a Nonordinary Loss—Assuming Future Interim Income Is *Not* "More Likely Than Not" and Carrybacks and Carryforwards Are *Not* Available

Interim Period (Quarter)	Type of Income	Pretax Income (Loss)		Effective Tax Rate	Tax Expense (Benefit)		
		Current Period	Year-to-Date		Year-to-Date	Previously Reported	Current Period
First	Continuing Op.	$ 40,000	$ 40,000	26%	$ 10,400		$ 10,400
Second	Continuing Op.	30,000	70,000	28	19,600	$ 10,400	9,200
Third	Continuing Op.	20,000	90,000	28	25,200	19,600	5,600
Third	Nonordinary	(110,000)	(110,000)	Note C	(25,200)		(25,200)
Fourth	Continuing Op.	40,000	130,000	30	39,000	25,200	13,800
Fourth	Nonordinary		(110,000)	Note D	(33,000)	(25,200)	(7,800)

Note C: Because future income is not "more likely than not," and carrybacks/carryforwards are not available, the nonordinary loss can be offset only against YTD income of $90,000.

Note D: Because additional income is available in the fourth quarter, an additional amount of tax benefit traceable to the nonordinary loss can be recognized. Additional benefit also is recognized because of the change in the effective tax rate from 28% to 30%.

Case C: Offsetting a Nonordinary Loss—Assuming Future Interim Income of $40,000 Is "More Likely Than Not" and a Carryback Is Available Against Prior Income of $30,000, Taxed at 30%

Interim Period (Quarter)	Type of Income	Pretax Income (Loss)		Effective Tax Rate	Tax Expense (Benefit)		
		Current Period	Year-to-Date		Year-to-Date	Previously Reported	Current Period
First	Continuing Op.	$ 40,000	$ 40,000	26%	$ 10,400		$ 10,400
Second	Continuing Op.	30,000	70,000	28	19,600	$ 10,400	9,200
Third	Continuing Op.	20,000	90,000	28	25,200	19,600	5,600
Third	Nonordinary	(180,000)	(180,000)	Note E	(45,400)		(45,400)
Fourth	Continuing Op.	40,000	130,000	28	36,400	25,200	11,200
Fourth	Nonordinary		(180,000)	Note F	(45,400)	(45,400)	

Note E: Because future income of $40,000 is assured, the nonordinary loss can be offset against $130,000 ($90,000 + $40,000) of current-year income at an estimated effective tax rate of 28%. This results in a tax benefit of $36,400. In addition, another $30,000 of the nonordinary loss can be offset against prior income of $30,000. This results in an additional tax benefit of $9,000 for a total benefit of $45,400 ($36,400 + $9,000). If future interim income had not been more likely than not, the total benefit would have consisted of $25,200 resulting from an offset of YTD income plus the $9,000 resulting from the carryback against prior years' income.

Note F: Of the $180,000 nonordinary loss, $160,000 has been offset ($130,000 against current income and $30,000 against prior years'). The tax benefit on the remaining $20,000 of loss not offset may be recognized in the future, as subsequent annual income becomes recognized. If $20,000 of future income was more likely than not to be recognized in the carryforward period, the tax benefit on the entire nonordinary loss could have been recognized in the current year.

Accounting for Discontinued Operations

Discontinued operations consist of the operating results of a component of an entity that either has been disposed of or is being held for sale. A component is defined by operations and cash flows that can be clearly distinguished from the rest of the entity both operationally and for financial reporting purposes. In order for the component to be reported as discontinued, both of the following conditions must be met:

1. The operations and cash flows of the component have been (or will be) eliminated from the ongoing operations of the entity as a result of the disposal transaction, and
2. The entity will not have any significant continuing involvement in the operations of the component after the disposal transaction.[10]

If a component qualifies as a discontinued operation, the income statement will report the results of the discontinued operations, less applicable taxes, as a separate component of income before extraordinary items and the cumulative effect of accounting changes. The reported results for a period will include the results of operations and disposals including any initial or subsequently recognized impairment losses (or revisions of earlier recognized impairment losses).

When interim statements are prepared, a problem arises in that income or losses traceable to the discontinued operation would have been classified in previous interim periods as part of continuing operations. Furthermore, these amounts would have influenced the determination of the estimated annual effective tax rate for those previous periods. Once a decision to dispose of a component has been made, known as the measurement date, the pretax measures of income (loss) and the related taxes for prior interim periods must be restated. The restatement involves allocating prior interim period amounts between income (loss) traceable to continuing operations and income (loss) traceable to the now-discontinued operations. This allocation of previously reported information is necessary in order to achieve comparability between prior and subsequent interim periods. Not only is this allocation applied to prior interim periods presented, but prior annual periods presented must also be restated to reflect the allocation between continuing and discontinued operations. In essence, the originally reported tax expense (benefit), which was at that time associated with continuing operations, is now being allocated between the restated continuing and discontinued operations. The originally reported tax expense (benefit) does not change in total but is merely reallocated to the continuing and discontinued components such that the tax expense (benefit) traceable to those components equals the originally reported total amount (the sum of the parts equals the original whole).

The restatement of pretax income (loss) and related taxes for each of the prior interim periods presented involves the following steps:

1. The original YTD and balance-of-the-year projections used to calculate the estimated effective tax rate are allocated between the now presently defined continuing and discontinued operations.
2. The original tax planning alternatives, permanent differences, and tax credits used to calculate the tax rate are allocated between the continuing and discontinued operations.
3. The projected items being allocated in (1) and (2) are the originally reported amounts. That is, the projections relating to the balance of the year are not changed or revised but remain the same as in the prior interim periods. To permit the revision of an earlier projection would have the effect of accounting for a change in estimate on a retroactive basis, which is not acceptable.
4. The amounts now allocated to continuing operations are used to calculate a new effective tax rate traceable to continuing operations. The tax on the continuing operations of the prior interim period(s) also is recalculated.
5. The new tax on the continuing operations of the prior interim period(s) is compared to the originally reported tax (which included both the continuing and discontinued operations), with the difference representing the tax traceable to the discontinued operations.

---

10 FASB ASC 205-20-45, *Presentation of Financial Statements—Discontinued Operations—Other Presentation Matters.*

From the measurement date forward, the discontinued operations will not be commingled with the continuing operations. Thus, the tax effect of the discontinued operations is calculated on an incremental basis, as is the case with other nonordinary items of income. The interim effect of a discontinued operation is demonstrated in Illustration 12-3.

Illustration 12-3
Discontinued Operation

Facts:

After issuing first-quarter interim data, the company adopted in the second quarter a formal plan calling for the disposal of one of its operations. Ordinary income reported in the first quarter included a $10,000 loss traceable to the operation being discontinued. It is assumed that any loss traceable to the discontinued operation will have tax benefits and that the estimated effective tax rate of 40% on income from continuing operations, used in the first quarter, is to be revised to 45% and applied to the remaining continuing operations.

Analysis:

The following schedule illustrates the retroactive restatement of previously issued interim data in order to disclose separately both continuing and discontinued operations:

Interim Period (Quarter)	Type of Income	Pretax Income (Loss)		Effective Tax Rate	Tax Expense (Benefit)		
		Current Period	Year-to-Date		Year-to-Date	Previously Reported	Current Period
First	Continuing Op.	$ 40,000	$ 40,000	40%	$ 16,000	$ —	$ 16,000
First—Restated	Continuing Op.	50,000	50,000	45	22,500	—	22,500
First—Restated	Discontinued Op. *	(10,000)	(10,000)	Note A	(6,500)	—	(6,500)
Second	Continuing Op.	30,000	80,000	45	36,000	22,500	13,500
Second	Discontinued Op.	(55,000)	(65,000)	Note B	(29,250)	(6,500)	(22,750)
Third	Continuing Op.	50,000	130,000	45	58,500	36,000	22,500
Third	Discontinued Op.	—	(65,000)	Note B	(29,250)	(29,250)	—
Fourth	Continuing Op.	55,000	185,000	45	85,250	58,500	24,750
Fourth	Discontinued Op.	(10,000)	(75,000)	Note C	(33,750)	(29,250)	(4,500)

* This amount is entirely traceable to premeasurement-date operations of the discontinued operation. None of this amount is traceable to the gain or loss on disposal of the discontinued operation.

Note A: The $6,500 tax benefit traceable to the discontinued operation is the result of comparing the tax of $22,500 traceable to continuing operations with the $16,000 of tax previously recognized on the continuing operations. Therefore, the difference between the two tax amounts relates to the exclusion and inclusion, respectively, of the results traceable to the discontinued operation. Notice that the total tax expense presented for the first period, restated, [$22,500 + ($6,500)] totals $16,000, which is the tax originally reported for the first quarter.

Note B: The YTD tax benefit of $29,250 traceable to the discontinued operation is the assumed incremental tax benefit associated with the component's YTD results of operations and disposals/impairments totaling a $65,000 pretax loss.

Note C: The fourth-quarter current-period loss of $10,000 is traceable to results of operations and disposals/impairments. The $33,750 YTD tax benefit is the assumed incremental tax benefit traceable to the discontinued operation.

Accounting for a Change in Accounting Principle

A change in accounting principle is a change from one generally accepted accounting principle to another and must be justified by management. Although it may be more convenient to change accounting principles at the beginning of a fiscal year, changes more often occur during a fiscal year. The implication for interim reporting is that such changes must be disclosed and their effect on previously reported interim periods must be presented. Currently, changes in accounting principle are accounted for on a retrospective basis. Retrospective application is defined by the FASB as:

> the application of a different accounting principle to one or more previous issued financial statements, or the statement of financial accounting position at the beginning of the current period, as if that principle had always been used, or a change to financial statements of prior accounting periods to present the financial statements of a new reporting entity as if it had existed in those prior years.[11]

In order to present the effect of a change in accounting principles on interim periods prior to the period of change, those prior interim periods must be retrospectively changed to reflect the newly adopted principle. Once the pretax income (loss) associated with the prior interim periods has been changed to reflect the newly adopted principle, the procedures previously discussed with respect to accounting for income taxes in interim periods would be applied. The end result is that the pretax, tax, and after-tax values after retrospective application will appear as though the new principle had always been used.

Retrospective application for a change in accounting principle impacting interim periods is demonstrated in Illustration 12-4.

Illustration 12-4
Change in Accounting Principle

Facts:

At the beginning of the third quarter, management decided to change inventory methods. The effect of the change is to decrease the pretax income of quarters 1 and 2 by $30,000 and $20,000, respectively.

Analysis:

The following schedule illustrates the restatement of previously issued interim data in order to reflect the retrospective effect of the change:

Interim Period (Quarter)	Type of Income	Pretax Income (Loss) Current Period	Pretax Income (Loss) Year-to-Date	Effective Tax Rate	Tax Expense (Benefit) Year-to-Date	Tax Expense (Benefit) Previously Reported	Tax Expense (Benefit) Current Period
First	Continuing Op.	$80,000	$ 80,000	40%	$32,000	—	$32,000
Second	Continuing Op.	50,000	130,000	40	52,000	$32,000	20,000
First—Restated	Continuing Op.	50,000	50,000	35*	17,500	—	17,500
Second—Restated	Continuing Op.	30,000	80,000	35	28,000	17,500	10,500
Third and Fourth	Continuing Op.	70,000	150,000	35	52,500	28,000	24,500

* Note that a new effective tax rate of 35% has been calculated as a result of modifications relating to only the change in accounting principle.

Disclosures of Summarized Interim Data

To maintain the timeliness of interim data, companies frequently report summarized interim data rather than complete financial statements. When publicly traded companies report summarized interim data, a number of minimum disclosures are required, some of which are:

1. Sales or gross revenues, provision for income taxes, extraordinary items (including related income tax effects), net income, and comprehensive income.

2. Basic and diluted earnings per share data for each period presented.

3. Seasonal revenue, costs, or expenses.

---

11 FASB ASC 250-10-20, *Accounting Changes and Error Corrections—Overall—Glossary.*

4. Significant changes in estimates or provisions for income taxes.

5. Disposal of a component of an entity and extraordinary, unusual, or infrequently occurring items.

6. Contingent items.

7. Changes in accounting principles or estimates.

8. Significant changes in financial position.

9. Information about reportable operating segments.[12]

The information in (9) above is more fully discussed in the following section of this chapter dealing with disclosures about segments of an entity.

In addition to providing these data for the current quarter, such data should be provided for the current year to date or the last 12 months to date, plus comparable data for the preceding year.

Frequently, companies do not issue separate fourth-quarter reports or provide fourth-quarter disclosure of summarized data because annual audited statements will be forthcoming. In such cases, a note to the annual financial statements should disclose the effect of the following items for the fourth quarter: disposals of a segment, extraordinary items, unusual or infrequently occurring items, and changes in accounting principles. Disclosure in the annual financial statements should also include the aggregate effect of year-end adjustments that are material to the fourth-quarter results.

IASB PERSPECTIVES

IAS 34, *Interim Financial Reporting*, establishes principles for reporting in interim periods. There are no major dissimilarities to U.S. generally accepting accounting principles (GAAP). The IASB recognizes an interim period as a part of a larger financial year as does U.S. GAAP. Acceptable modifications to costs as well as accounting for income taxes are also similar. There are some differences with respect to the content of interim disclosures, but they are not considered to be major differences.

IASB *standards*

REFLECTION

- Interim reporting generates timely and useful information that may provide insight into annual results.

- Since interim periods are treated as integral parts of a larger annual period, the results of one interim period can significantly affect other interim periods in the same fiscal year.

- While revenue recognition principles do not change, some expense recognition principles are modified for interim reporting purposes in order to provide more timely information.

- The income tax expense or benefits traceable to an interim period should reflect the estimated effective tax rate to be experienced for the entire annual period.

- The tax expense or benefit traceable to nonordinary items of income or loss is determined on an incremental basis.

5

OBJECTIVE

Explain why segmental reporting is important, and define an operating segment.

DISCLOSURES ABOUT SEGMENTS OF AN ENTITY

For various reasons, entities may develop a strategy that allows them to become involved in a variety of activities, some of which may be similar or related. For example, an entity in the entertainment/recreation industry may have business activities in film, theme parks, hotels, and restaurants.

---

12 For a complete list of required disclosures, see FASB ASC 270-10-50, *Interim Reporting—Overall—Disclosure*.

Entities with such activities are referred to as being *horizontally integrated*. In other instances, the activities may be *vertically integrated*, which suggests that they relate to the sales and distribution of a final good or service. For example, a manufacturer of modular housing may also be involved in activities such as the growing and harvesting of timber, the manufacture of windows, and the development of land for housing subdivisions. Entities may also become involved in activities that do not necessarily have a close relationship to their original core business but, rather, allow them to diversify their business. Such businesses are referred to as *conglomerates* or *diversified companies*. For example, a single entity may be involved in such diverse activities as radio and television broadcasting, managed care facilities, development of software for engineering applications, and the manufacture of fluid metering devices.

The traditional consolidated financial statements of a truly diversified entity would provide the user of these statements with limited information regarding the diversity of the entity's activities and the economic environments in which those activities function. For example, unless separate disclosures were present, it would not be possible to tell what portion of consolidated sales was traceable to various business activities. Certainly, the uncertainties affecting potential cash flows can be better understood if information related to an entity's products and services, as well as geographical areas of operation, is provided. Fortunately, special disclosures regarding the segments or activities of an entity are required and provide users with fundamental information through which they can better understand operating performance and prospects for future cash flows for both individual segments and the entity as a whole. Furthermore, such information will provide users with an improved basis for making comparisons between entities that are not diversified with those that are.

There is a strong body of empirical research that supports the position that segmental data have utility. This research and the prominence of diversified companies have effectively established the importance of segmental data for maintaining an efficient capital market. For example, studies have suggested that segmental data can lead to more accurate predictions of entity earnings and changes in earnings levels. In addition, surveys have shown that sophisticated users, such as financial analysts, find the use of segmental data to be a significant factor in the area of security valuation.

A number of professional groups, including the American Institute of Certified Public Accountants, the Financial Executives Institute, the Financial Analysts Federation, the International Accounting Standards Committee, the Association for Investment Management and Research, and the FASB, have consistently emphasized the importance of segmental disclosures. In 1976, the FASB issued Statement of Financial Accounting Standards No. 14, which also dealt with the topic of segmental disclosures. However, that statement came under criticism from both reporting entities and users of the information. A major criticism was that the definition of a segment resulted in the reporting of information that did not necessarily represent the information that the top management of an entity actually used for making internal operating decisions and assessing performance. It became obvious that an external reporting requirement that did not align with internal reporting, which was used for decision-making purposes, was not serving the needs of external users of segmental information. Why provide external users information that they will use to make assessments of an entity if the information is not what is being used by entity management to make decisions? Furthermore, the segmental disclosures called for were not consistent with how management discussed and analyzed segmental data in other sections of annual reports. Segmental reporting standards were also criticized for not requiring more information about a greater number of segments. **Aligning external reporting of segmental information with internal reporting helps users view an entity in a way that will allow them to better anticipate and understand the actions of management**.

Current Standards Regarding Segmental Reporting

The current standards regarding segmental reporting, which replaced the earlier Statement No. 14, are applicable to public business entities.[13] A company is considered to be a public entity if it (a) has issued debt or equity securities that are traded in a public market, (b) is required to file

---

13 FASB ASC 280, *Segment Reporting.*

financial statements with the Securities and Exchange Commission, or (c) provides financial statements for the purpose of issuing securities in a public market. Although the statement does not apply to nonpublic entities or not-for-profit organizations, such entities or organizations are encouraged to adopt the requirements of the standard.

Definition of an Operating Segment. The FASB chose to define operating segments by emphasizing a "management approach," which focuses on how management organizes information for purposes of making operating decisions and assessing performance. For example, assume that a public company, which manufactures circuit boards for a variety of applications, organizes information by sales-market area for decision-making purposes. Therefore, the segments of the company might logically be defined as sales-market areas such as North America, South America, etc. Also, consider a public company that is involved in a number of diverse industries such as banking, retail brokerage services, and real estate development. If this company organizes information for decision-making purposes according to the types of products or services it offers, such as life insurance, then its segments would be defined accordingly. The segments should be evident from the structure of the organization in terms of how information is organized for internal decision-making purposes. Furthermore, if this information is already being generated internally, then management should be able to disclose certain relevant portions of this information to external users without incurring significant incremental costs.

The segments that emerge from an analysis of how management organizes information for decision-making purposes are called *operating segments* and are defined as a component of a public entity:

1. That engages in business activities from which it may earn revenues and incur expenses (including revenues and expenses relating to transactions with other components of the same public entity),
2. Whose operating results are regularly reviewed by the public entity's chief operating decision maker to make decisions about resources to be allocated to the segment and assess its performance, and
3. For which discrete financial information is available.[14]

It is important to note that not all parts of an entity will necessarily qualify as an operating segment. For example, some parts may not earn revenues of an operating nature, such as is the case with corporate headquarters. The chief operating decision maker who reviews a segment is one who assesses performance and allocates resources. This is a function that could be held by one individual, such as a chief executive officer (CEO) or chief operating officer (COO), or a group of individuals. One or more individuals typically have responsibility to account and report to the chief operating decision maker. This function is carried out by segment managers whose identification may also help identify operating segments.

Once operating segments have been identified, it is possible that some of the segments will appear to be similar due to similar economic characteristics. These segments may have virtually the same future prospects, and separate reporting of them may provide users with additional data of limited utility. Therefore, it may be possible to combine two or more of these segments into a single segment, if they are similar in each of the following areas:

- The nature of the products or services.
- The nature of the production processes.
- The type or class of customer for their products and services.
- The methods used to distribute their products or provide their services.
- The nature of the regulatory environment (if applicable); for example, banking, insurance, or public utilities.[15]

---

14 FASB ASC, 280-10-50, *Segment Reporting—Overall—Disclosure.*
15 FASB ASC 280-10-50-11, *Segment Reporting—Overall—Disclosure—Aggregation Criteria.*

Once segments have been identified and aggregated, if necessary, information should be disclosed about those segments that are deemed to be reportable. That is, even though there may be an operating segment, it may not be significant enough to require disclosure. A *reportable segment* is one that is deemed to be significant because of any of the following:

6

OBJECTIVE

Apply the criteria used to determine which segment is reportable.

◆ Its reported revenue, including both sales to external customers and intersegment sales or transfers, is 10% or more of the combined revenue, internal and external, of all reported operating segments.

◆ The absolute amount of its reported profit or loss is 10% or more of the greater, in absolute amount, of (a) the combined profit of all operating segments that did not report a loss, or (b) the combined reported loss of all operating segments that did report a loss.

◆ Its assets are 10% or more of the combined assets of all operating segments.[16]

It is important to note that, even if a segment does not satisfy the above criteria, management may report information about that individual segment if they believe it to be useful to readers.

For those operating segments that do not meet the above criteria, they will constitute a separate "all other" category for reporting purposes. It is possible that those segments that qualify as reportable do not represent a significant enough portion of the entity's operating activities. The total of **external revenues** for reportable segments must constitute at least 75% of the total consolidated revenue. If this is not the case, then additional operating segments must be designated as reportable even though they did not initially qualify as such. The goal of these guidelines is to reach a balance between providing users with information about a reasonable number of segments and yet not be excessive. In the latter regard, if the number of reportable segments exceeds 10 in number, consideration should be given to whether this number should be reduced by aggregating certain segments. The above criteria used to identify reportable segments and analyze the appropriate number of reportable segments are shown in Illustration 12-5.

Illustration 12-5
Reportable Segments: Demonstration of Criteria

Facts:

Whalen Corporation has classified its operations into segments and has provided the following data for each segment:

	Revenues				
Segment	Unaffiliated Customers	Intersegment Sales	Total	Operating Profit (Loss)	Assets
A.............................	$100,000	$15,000	$115,000	$ 45,000	$ 280,000
B.............................	20,000		20,000	(10,000)	80,000
C.............................	230,000	40,000	270,000	130,000	1,100,000
D.............................	45,000	5,000	50,000	(60,000)	320,000
E.............................	37,000	8,000	45,000	25,000	295,000
F.............................	140,000	14,000	154,000	85,000	760,000
	$572,000	$82,000	$654,000	$215,000	$2,835,000
Corporate level..................	60,000		60,000	20,000	705,000
Total	$632,000	$82,000	$714,000	$235,000	$3,540,000

(continued)

16 FASB ASC, 280-10-50-12, *Segment Reporting—Overall—Disclosure—Quantitative Thresholds.*

Analysis:

The determination of which segments are reportable requires the following evaluation, in which only combined data relating to the segments (not including corporate-level activity) are employed:

1. Total sales to unaffiliated customers $572,000

   Total intersegment sales 82,000

   Combined revenue. $654,000

   Segment revenue required to satisfy criterion (a): $654,000 × 10% = $65,400

2.

Segment	Operating Profit	Operating Loss
A	$ 45,000	$ —
B	—	10,000
C	130,000	—
D	—	60,000
E	25,000	—
F	85,000	—
Total	$285,000	$70,000

   Portion of absolute amount of the greater of the operating profit or the operating loss to satisfy criterion (b): $285,000 × 10% = $28,500

3. Segment assets required to satisfy criterion (c): $2,835,000 × 10% = $283,500

   Whether the criteria are satisfied is summarized as follows:

Segment		Revenue		Criterion Satisfied Operating Profit (Loss)		Identifiable Assets	Segment Reportable
A	Yes	($115,000 > $65,400)	Yes	($45,000 > $28,500)	No	($280,000 < $283,500)	Yes
B	No	($20,000 < $65,400)	No	($10,000 < $28,500)	No	($80,000 < $283,500)	No
C	Yes	($270,000 > $65,400)	Yes	($130,000 > $28,500)	Yes	($1,100,000 > $283,500)	Yes
D	No	($50,000 < $65,400)	Yes	($60,000 > $28,500)	Yes	($320,000 > $283,500)	Yes
E	No	($45,000 < $65,400)	No	($25,000 < $28,500)	Yes	($295,000 > $283,500)	Yes
F	Yes	($154,000 > $65,400)	Yes	($85,000 > $28,500)	Yes	($760,000 > $283,500)	Yes

   All of the segments are reportable except for Segment B.

4. Significance of the reportable segments:

   Consolidated revenue $632,000

   Percentage requirement. . . . .   ×   75%

   Dollar requirement $474,000

   External revenue of reportable segments (all segments except Segment B) $552,000

   The reportable segments represent a significant portion of the entity.

5. Reasonableness of the number of reportable segments:

   The five reportable segments do not exceed the guideline number of 10.

Comparability of Segmental Information. Another issue regarding segments deals with comparability of segmental information over time. For example, it is possible for a segment to meet the criteria as being reportable in one fiscal period and not in another, resulting, therefore, in a lack of compatibility. In order to ensure comparability, the following guidelines are appropriate for both interim and annual periods:

1. If a segment is deemed to be reportable in the current period, prior-period segmental data should also include the segment for comparative purposes.
2. If a segment was deemed to be reportable in prior-period segmental data presented, the segment should continue to be deemed reportable if it is considered to be of continuing significance.
3. If an entity's structure changes such that the composition or makeup of segments changes, then prior-period segmental data presented should be restated, if practical, to reflect the new composition of segments. It should be disclosed as to whether or not prior-period information has been restated. If such information has not been restated, segment information for the current period should be presented on both the current and previous basis of segmentation. This dual presentation is appropriate only in the current period of change and if practical.

Content of Segmental Disclosures. Once the identification of reportable segments and the proper guidelines regarding the number of segments have been satisfied, various general and financial information regarding segments is required to be disclosed as part of a complete set of financial statements. The factors used to identify reportable segments must be disclosed along with a discussion of how the segments are organized. For example, segments could be organized around products or services, geographical areas, marketing areas, or products within geographical areas. For each reportable segment, the type of products and/or services from which they derive their revenues should be disclosed. Certain information about profit or loss and assets must also be disclosed for each reportable segment, and then these amounts must be reconciled to corresponding entity consolidated amounts.

Information about Profit or Loss and Assets. The measure of profit or loss, which is disclosed, is a function of what information is reviewed by the chief operating decision maker of the entity. For example, the measure could exclude items relating to the cost of capital, or the measure could include an allocation of general corporate overhead. It is important to note that the measure of profit or loss follows a management approach focusing on internal decision making rather than any strict definition of profit used by the entity for general purpose external reporting. Therefore, it is possible that segmental profit or loss may not necessarily incorporate the same generally accepted accounting principles as are employed at the consolidated level. For example, segment profit or loss may not include the effects of tax allocation or pension expense. The following items regarding profit or loss should be disclosed only if the items are included in the values reviewed by the chief operating decision maker: revenues from external customers, revenues from other operating segments, interest revenue, interest expense, depreciation, depletion, amortization expense, unusual items, equity in net income of investees accounted for under the equity method, income tax expense/benefit, extraordinary items, and other significant noncash items, other than depreciation, amortization or depletion, such as deferred tax expense. If a majority of a segment's revenues are from interest, such as those of a financial segment, and the decision-making process focuses on net interest (interest revenue less interest expense), then interest revenue may be reported net of interest expense.

In order to better evaluate a segment, it would be useful to disclose the assets that were employed to generate the profit or loss traceable to that segment. Therefore, those segment assets, which are evaluated by the chief operating decision maker, are also to be disclosed. The following items regarding assets should be disclosed only if the items are included in the values reviewed by the chief operating decision maker: the carrying basis of investments in investees measured under the equity method and total expenditures for additions to long-lived assets (other than financial instruments, long-term customer relationships of a financial institution, mortgage and other servicing rights, deferred policy acquisition costs, and deferred tax assets).

7

OBJECTIVE

Describe the information about a reportable segment that must be disclosed.

Because the measurement of segment profit or loss and assets follows a management approach, additional disclosures are necessary in order to assist users in understanding how these values are measured. For example, segment profit may not include the allocation of certain corporate-level expenses, or it may measure cost of sales using a method different from that used for consolidated purposes. Therefore, a public entity should disclose, at a minimum, the following:

1. The basis of accounting for any transactions between reportable segments.
2. The nature of any differences between the measurements of the reportable segments' profits or losses and the public entity's consolidated income before income taxes, extraordinary items, and discontinued operations (if not apparent from the reconciliations). Those differences could include accounting policies and policies for allocation of centrally incurred costs that are necessary for an understanding of the reported segment information.
3. The nature of any differences between the measurements of the reportable segments' assets and the public entity's consolidated assets (if not apparent from the reconciliations). Those differences could include accounting policies and policies for allocation of jointly used assets that are necessary for an understanding of the reported segment information.
4. The nature of any changes from prior periods in the measurement methods used to determine reported segment profit or loss and the effect, if any, of those changes on the measure of segment profit or loss.
5. The nature and effect of any asymmetrical allocations to segments. For example, a public utility might allocate depreciation expense to a segment without allocating the related depreciable assets to that segment.[17]

The various dollar amounts disclosed for reportable segments represent a significant portion of the respective consolidated dollar amounts. For example, the sum of profit or loss for all reportable segments will naturally represent a significant portion of consolidated profit or loss. However, all of the consolidated profit or loss will not be traceable to the reportable segments. The difference between the sum of the reportable segment values and the respective consolidated value is most often due to the following:

1. Not all segments are considered to be reportable. Therefore, some values are allocated to the category of segments known as "all other."
2. Segment revenues, profits, and assets include the effect of intersegment transactions that are eliminated from consolidated amounts. Note that intersegment transactions that have *not been realized* through an exchange with an outside entity must be eliminated from consolidated amounts.
3. Certain values are not allocated to segments because they are not part of the information that is used by the chief operating decision maker as a basis for evaluating performance and allocating resources.
4. Certain values cannot be allocated to segments on a reasonable basis.
5. The accounting methods used to determine values for a reportable segment may be different from those used to prepare consolidated values. This is due to the focus on the management approach and the information used for internal rather than external reporting purposes.

A requirement of segmental reporting is that the revenue, profit or loss, and asset amounts presented for reportable segments must be reconciled to the respective consolidated amounts for the entity as a whole. A reconciliation must also be made for other significant items presented by reportable segments such as liabilities. The reconciliation should be described in sufficient detail. Illustration 12-6 contains an example of the required segmental disclosures and the reconciliation to consolidated entity values.

---

17 FASB ASC, 280-10-50-29, *Segment Reporting—Overall—Disclosure—Measurement.*

Illustration 12-6
Presentation of Segmental Values

	Auto Parts	Motor Vessels	Software	Electronics	Finance	All Other	Totals
Revenues from external customers	$3,000	$5,000	$9,500	$12,000	$ 5,000	$1,000*	$35,500
Intersegment revenues	—	—	3,000	1,500	—	—	4,500
Interest revenue...............	450	800	1,000	1,500	—	—	3,750
Interest expense	350	600	700	1,100	—	—	2,750
Net interest revenue**	—	—	—	—	1,000	—	1,000
Depreciation and amortization...	200	100	50	1,500	1,100	—	2,950
Segment profit................	200	70	900	2,300	500	100	4,070
Other significant noncash items ..							
Cost in excess of billings on long-term contracts	—	200	—	—	—	—	200
Segment assets	2,000	5,000	3,000	12,000	57,000	2,000	81,000
Expenditures for segment assets ..	300	700	500	800	600	—	2,900

* Revenue from segments below the quantitative thresholds are attributable to four operating segments of Diversified Company. Those segments include a small real estate business, an electronics equipment rental business, a software consulting practice, and a warehouse leasing operation. None of those segments has ever met any of the quantitative thresholds for determining reportable segments.

** The finance segment derives a majority of its revenue from interest. In addition, management relies primarily on net interest revenue, not the gross revenue and expense amounts, in managing that segment. Therefore, only the net amount is disclosed.

Reconciliation of Segmental Values to Entity Consolidated Values

Revenues

Total revenues for reportable segments ($35,500 + $4,500 – $1,000).............................	$39,000
Other revenues	1,000
Elimination of intersegment revenues	(4,500)
Total consolidated revenues	$35,500

Profit or Loss

Total profit or loss for reportable segments ($4,070 – $100)	$ 3,970
Other profit or loss	100
Elimination of intersegment profits	(500)
Unallocated amounts:	
Litigation settlement received	500
Other corporate expenses...	(750)
Adjustment to pension expense in consolidation	(250)
Income before income taxes and extraordinary items...	$ 3,070

Assets

Total assets for reportable segments ($81,000 – $2,000).............................	$79,000
Other assets	2,000
Elimination of receivables from corporate headquarters	(1,000)
Goodwill not allocated to segments	4,000
Other unallocated amounts...	1,000
Consolidated total...	$85,000

(continued)

Other Significant Items

	Segment Totals	Adjustments	Consolidated Totals
Interest revenue........................	$3,750	$ 75	$3,825
Interest expense	2,750	(50)	2,700
Net interest revenue (finance segment only) ..	1,000	—	1,000
Expenditures for assets	2,900	1,000	3,900
Depreciation and amortization............	2,950	—	2,950
Cost in excess of billing on long-term contracts	200	—	200

The reconciling item to adjust expenditures for assets is the amount of expenses incurred for the corporate headquarters building, which is not included in segment information. None of the other adjustments are significant.

Source: FASB ASC 280-10-55–49, *Segment Reporting—Overall—Implementation Guidance and Illustrations—Case C.*

Interim Period Disclosures. When condensed financial statements of an interim period are presented, information regarding reportable operating segments must also be disclosed. For each reportable segment, the following must be disclosed: revenues from both external customers and intersegment sales, profit or loss, a reconciliation of reportable segments' profit or loss to the public entity's consolidated income before taxes, extraordinary items, discontinued operations, total assets that have materially changed from the values reported in the most recent annual report, and disclosure of any differences from the last annual report in terms of whether the basis for segmentation and/or measurement of segment profit or loss have changed. It is important to note that these disclosures are appropriate for only condensed financial statements of an interim period. If a complete set of financial statements is presented, then the more comprehensive disclosures discussed earlier would be appropriate.

8

OBJECTIVE

State which entity-wide disclosures must be provided.

Entity-Wide Disclosures. Because of the use of the management approach to defining segments, it is possible that segments may not necessarily be defined around product/service groups or geographical areas. For example, a segment may consist of several unrelated products because that is how information is structured for decision-making purposes. A company that produces beverages, produces snack foods, operates a chain of restaurants, and operates amusement parks may decide to include all but the amusement parks in a single segment. Segments may also be defined in such a way that a given segment includes activities that are occurring in more than one foreign geographical area. If information regarding product/service groups and/ or geographical areas is not provided as part of the segmental disclosures, such information must be provided as an additional disclosure. These additional disclosures must be presented if practical; if it is not practical, that fact must be disclosed. These additional disclosures are presented on an entity-wide basis, not on a segmental basis. Furthermore, the disclosures are required even if there is only one reportable segment. The entity is required to:[18]

1. Report revenues from **external** customers for each product or service or each group of related products or services. The revenues are based on the information used for general purpose financial statements.
2. Report revenues from **external** customers for the entity's country of domicile and all foreign countries in total. The revenues are based on the information used for general purpose financial statements. If material, revenues from separate foreign countries should be disclosed. Subtotals of revenue may also be disclosed by groups of foreign countries (e.g., South America). The basis used to allocate revenues to separate foreign countries must be disclosed. For example, revenues may be allocated based on where products are shipped or based on the location of customers.
3. Report **long-lived** assets (with certain exceptions) located in the entity's country of domicile and all foreign countries in total. The measurement of assets is based on the information used for general purpose financial statements. If material, assets traceable to separate foreign countries should be disclosed. Subtotals of assets may also be disclosed by groups of foreign countries (e.g., South America).

---

18 FASB ASC 280-10-50-38, *Segment Reporting—Overall—Disclosure—Entity-Wide Information.*

Disclosures Regarding Major Customers. Entities are also required to disclose information about major customers if revenues traceable to a single customer represent 10% or more of total entity revenues. For each such customer, the entity must disclose the total amount of revenues and identify the segment or segments to which the revenues are traceable. The specific identity by name of the major customer need not be disclosed. For purposes of this disclosure, a group of entities under common control is considered to be a single customer. Federal, state, local, and foreign governments or agencies should each be considered as a single customer.

IASB PERSPECTIVES

International Financial Reporting Standard (IFRS) 8, *Operating Segments*, establishes principles for reporting on operating segments. IFRS is very similar to U.S. GAAP and also uses a management approach to defining segments. Unlike U.S. GAAP, IFRS requires an entity to report a measure of a reportable segment's liabilities if such measures are regularly provided to the chief operating decision maker. The reported liabilities should be reconciled to total entity liabilities. The disclosure of IFRS recognizes that the characteristics of an operating segment may apply to two or more overlapping sets of components for which managers are held responsible. That structure is referred to as a "matrix form of organization." The reporting entity must decide which set of components constitutes the operating segment. U.S. GAAP does not use a matrix approach but rather generally identifies segments based on products and services.

REFLECTION

- A management approach is used to define what constitutes an operating segment.

- Operating segments are deemed to be reportable if a number of criteria involving segmental revenues, profits/losses, or assets are satisfied.

- A number of disclosures must be made for each reportable segment and the total of nonreportable segments. Furthermore, the financial disclosures are to be reconciled to the respective consolidated amounts.

- Given the management approach to defining an operating segment, information regarding product groups and/or foreign business activities may not otherwise be disclosed. Therefore, special entity-wide disclosures containing such information should be disclosed.

UNDERSTANDING THE ISSUES

1. What are the benefits of viewing an interim period as an integral part of a larger annual period rather than as a separate distinct period?

2. What factors are necessary for determining the estimated annual effective income tax rate?

3. Assume that a pretax operating loss was reported for the third quarter of the current year and that prior quarters reported pretax income that was taxed at an effective tax rate of 30%. What are the likely explanations as to why a tax benefit was not recognized on the entire third-quarter loss?

4. Why isn't the total operating profit of all reportable segments normally equal to the consolidated operating profit?

EXERCISES

Exercise 1 *(LO 1, 2)* **Accounting for R&D, tax rate differences.** Your client is seeking advice on each of the following interim reporting issues related to the current year:

1. In the first quarter of the current year, the client incurred $130,000 of research and development (R&D) costs that, hopefully, will generate additional revenues in the current and next four years. He is aware of the fact that the R&D will have to be expensed in its entirety in the current year. However, he is not sure how to report the item in the first-quarter financials. What advice would you give?
2. In the second quarter of the current year, your client revised his estimated effective annual tax rate on pretax income from continuing operations (PICO). The second-quarter tax expense expressed as a percentage of the second-quarter pretax PICO is greater than the statutory rate of tax. This confuses your client. What is the logical explanation for this?

Exercise 2 *(LO 2, 3)* **Cost of goods sold and tax expense in interim periods.** Granger Supply, Inc., has two main areas of inventory, industrial supplies and industrial cleaning equipment. The FIFO inventory method is used for industrial supplies, and the LIFO method is used for the cleaning equipment. Prior to considering special interim reporting modifications for LIFO liquidations and lower of cost or market, the company reported the following results for the first two quarters of the current year:

	Quarter 1	Quarter 2
Net sales	$12,000,000	$9,000,000
Cost of sales—industrial supplies	4,300,000	4,700,000
Cost of sales—cleaning equipment	3,000,000	3,200,000
Gross profit	$ 4,700,000	$1,100,000
Selling, general, and administrative	2,100,000	1,800,000
Income before taxes	$ 2,600,000	$ (700,000)

During the first quarter, the company experienced unprecedented demand for its cleaning equipment and as a result liquidated a significant portion of its beginning inventory of equipment. The cost of sales—cleaning equipment is based on the historical cost of the liquidated layers. Management anticipates that 400 units of beginning inventory that were included in cost of sales at $1,500 per unit will be replaced during the year and remain in ending inventory at a cost of $2,700 per unit. The cost of sales—industrial supplies does not reflect the fact that the ending inventory of supplies has a fair value of $120,000 less than FIFO cost.

During the second quarter, the market for industrial supplies strengthened and the inventory of industrial supplies at the end of the second quarter had a fair value of only $25,000 less than FIFO cost.

Interim income tax expense is based on the following estimates:

	At End of Quarter 1	At End of Quarter 2
Statutory tax rate	35%	35%
Projected income before taxes for the balance of the year	$5,100,000	$4,000,000
Annual deductions permanently disallowed for tax purposes	$ 60,000	$ 35,000
Estimated annual tax credits	$ 18,000	$ 30,000

Prepare an income statement for each of the first two quarters of the current year. All supporting schedules should be in good form.

Exercise 3 *(LO 2, 3)* **Explaining interim expenses and tax rates.** A colleague of yours has been reviewing the second-quarter income statements for a number of companies and is questioning a number of the expense items included in the statements. For each of the following independent questions, provide a written response to your colleague's questions.

1. A footnote accompanying Company A's second-quarter income statement states that $360,000 was expended on research and development during the quarter on activities that should benefit operations over the next 24 months. Why does the second quarter reflect an expense of $120,000 rather than $15,000?

2. Company B reported pretax income in both the first and second quarters, and the statutory tax rate during those periods and for the balance of the year is 30%. Assume that there were no net operating losses in prior years for tax purposes. However, both of the quarters reported an effective tax rate of less than 30%. What could possibly explain this?

3. Assume the same facts as in part (2) except that the company only began operations last year, and it reported a net operating loss for both accounting and tax purposes last year. How might this fact explain why the first two quarters of the current year reported an effective tax rate of less than 30%?

4. Company C is subject to a progressive tax rate schedule whereby additional amounts of income are taxed at increasing rates. The recognition of revenues and expenses for accounting purposes and tax purposes is exactly the same, and no tax credits are available. Why would the effective tax rate for the second quarter be lower than for the first quarter of the current year?

5. Company D reported taxable income in the prior two years but reported tax losses in the first two quarters of the current year. The recognition of revenues and expenses for accounting purposes and tax purposes is exactly the same, and no tax credits are available. A tax loss is predicted for the current year. The statutory rate was 25% in the prior two years, but it is 30% in the current year. The effective annual tax rates in the first and second quarters of the current year are 18% and 28%, respectively. What might explain why the second-quarter effective tax rate is greater than the first quarter and that of the prior two years but less than 30%?

6. Company E is a distributor that has experienced increasing costs for units of inventory due to a severe shortage of available goods. Furthermore, the shortage has resulted in the company selling more goods in the first six months of the current year than it had purchased. Given the use of LIFO, why wouldn't the current year-to-date cost of sales on a per-unit basis have decreased?

Exercise 4 *(LO 2, 3, 4)* **Tax benefits traceable to operating losses, change in accounting principles.** Logan Manufacturing has been challenged by increasing costs and pressures from competitors. Pretax income was $100,000 and $60,000 in 2015 and 2016, respectively. In 2017, the company reported first-quarter pretax income of $40,000 and forecasted pretax losses for the balance of the year of $210,000. The company reported pretax losses of $30,000 during the second quarter of 2017 and forecasted pretax losses of $150,000 for the balance of the year. During the third quarter of 2017, the company changed accounting principles with respect to inventory accounting. The result of retrospective application on pretax amounts was as follows:

a. Increase 2015 and 2016 pretax income by $20,000 and 25,000, respectively.

b. Increase first-quarter 2017 pretax income by $30,000 and decrease the forecasted pretax losses for the balance of the year (quarters 2, 3 and 4) by $55,000.

c. Decrease second-quarter 2017 pretax loss by $20,000 and decrease the forecasted pretax losses for the balance of the year (quarters 3 and 4) by $20,000.

Statutory tax rates for years 2015 through 2017 are as follows: 15% on the first $50,000, 25% on the next $25,000, 34% on the next $25,000, and 39% on remaining income up to $335,000.

Calculate the pretax income (loss) and related tax expense (benefit) for the first and second quarters of 2017 as reported before and after the change in accounting principle.

Exercise 5 *(LO 4)* **Ratable allocation for nonordinary items.** Baxter Corporation anticipated pretax values for the current year as shown on page 686:

Continuing operations.	$ 60,000
Nonordinary items:	
Item A.	(30,000)
Item B.	25,000
Item C.	5,000
Total	$ 60,000

The statutory tax rates are as follows: 15% on the first $50,000, 25% on the next $25,000, 34% on the next $25,000, and 39% on amounts in excess of $100,000.

Determine the tax expense traceable to nonordinary items B and C.

Exercise 6 *(LO 4)* **Tax on nonordinary items.** Richardson Company reported pretax income from continuing operations in the first six months of 2012 in the amount of $100,000. Projected pretax operating income for the balance of the year is $110,000. Estimates of annual income include income from municipal bonds in the amount of $5,000 that will never be subject to income tax. Furthermore, it is anticipated that $8,000 of tax credits will be available during the year.

During the third quarter of 2012, the company changed accounting principles that after retrospective application, resulted in pretax income for the first six months increasing by $20,000 and projections for the balance of the year increasing by $25,000. During the third quarter of 2012, the company experienced pretax operating income of $80,000 and projected a pretax operating income of $20,000 for the fourth quarter. At the end of the third quarter, the company estimated that annual income from municipal bonds would be $4,000 and the annual tax credit would only be $5,000. During the third quarter, the company also experienced a nonordinary loss of $40,000 and a nonordinary gain of $60,000.

Statutory income tax rates are 10% on the first $50,000 of income, 20% on the next $50,000 of income, 30% on the next $50,000 of income, 40% on the next $50,000 of income, and 35% on all remaining income.

1. Determine the impact on tax expense for the first six months of 2012 as a result of the change in accounting principle.
2. Determine the tax expense or benefit traceable to the two nonordinary items.

Exercise 7 *(LO 3, 4)* **Restating prior periods due to a discontinued operation.** Baxter Holdings reported pretax income from continuing operations of $800,000 in the first quarter of 2014. At that point, projected pretax income for the rest of the year was $1,000,000. At the end of that quarter, the company estimated an effective annual tax rate of 29.5% based on a statutory tax rate of 30% on the first $1,500,000 of pretax income and 35% thereafter, projected pretax income for the balance of the year of $1,100,000, and tax credits of $29,500.

During the second quarter of 2014, the company decided to discontinue a component of its business that manufactured custom cabinetry. At the end of the first quarter of 2014, the cabinetry component had reported pretax losses of $220,000, projected losses of $320,000 for the balance of the year, and no estimated tax credits for the year. During the second quarter of the year, the discontinued component reported pretax losses of $80,000 prior to being shut down. Pretax impairment losses of $400,000 were also reported for the component during the second quarter of 2014.

Excluding the discontinued component, the company reported pretax income in the second quarter of 2014 of $525,000 and projected pretax income for the balance of the year of $1,050,000. Annual tax credits of $15,000 traceable to the continuing operations are projected for the year.

For quarter 1 restated and quarter 2 of 2014, prepare a schedule that shows pretax income, tax expense or benefit, and net income for both continuing operations and the discontinued operation.

Exercise 8 *(LO 3, 4)* **Estimated effective annual tax rate for various fact situations.** The following data represent the accounting results for the year ended December 31, 2013, for four different manufacturing corporations. The effective tax rates were as follows: 30% for 2011, 32% for 2012, and 40% for 2013 and thereafter.

	Corporation A	Corporation B	Corporation C	Corporation D
YTD operating income (loss)	$95,000	$ 5,000	$ (80,000)	$ 20,000
Projected interim income (loss)	30,000	(70,000)	(50,000)	(35,000)
Tax exempt municipal income........................		15,000		
Deductions not allowed for tax purposes.................		8,000	2,000	
Annual tax credit available	2,000	3,500		1,000
Carryback income:				
For 2011		32,000	105,000	
For 2012		15,000	35,000	
Projected future income for carryforward period:				
More likely than not..............................				12,500
Not more likely than not...........................		40,000		

Calculate the estimated effective annual tax rate for each company.

Exercise 9 *(LO 6)* **Determination of reportable segments.** The chief operating decision maker of a publicly traded company has defined segments around four product/service groups. Various revenues, profits or losses, and assets associated with the segments are as follows:

	Film Studios	Software Development	Leisure Clothing	Office Design Group	Total Entity Values
Revenues:					
External	$82,000,000	$12,000,000	$45,000,000	$22,000,000	$177,000,000
Intersegment	0	3,400,000	0	2,700,000	0
Expenses	93,000,000	18,000,000	22,000,000	18,000,000	166,000,000
Assets...........................	38,000,000	5,400,000	13,000,000	5,000,000	70,000,000

Determine which segments are considered to be reportable and whether the reportable segments represent a significant portion of entity consolidated revenues.

Exercise 10 *(LO 6)* **Determination of reportable segments, reconciliation to consolidated totals.** A large diversified company divides its operations into several operating segments.

Determine which of the following segments are reportable, and reconcile the reportable segments to the consolidated revenue and profit.

	Publishing	Talent Agency	Cable Networks	Radio Stations	Film Production	Consolidated Totals
Revenues:						
External	$1,200,000	$ 850,000	$3,771,500	$ 810,700	$1,090,000	$9,074,000
Intersegment	110,000	0	672,000	0	57,800	0
Expenses	385,000	1,299,000	1,257,700	1,048,700	727,800	4,634,500
Assets....................	970,000	670,000	3,893,500	770,000	720,500	8,276,000

Assume that there is no intercompany profit included in ending inventory.

Exercise 11 *(LO 6, 7)* **Identifying reportable segments and reconciling to consolidated totals.** Murphy Oils, Inc., began as a distributor of oils and lubricants to auto and truck repair centers. Since that time, the company has expanded to include jet engine repairs, the wholesale distribution of specialized tools for the automotive repair industry, and truck leasing. Various annual revenues, pretax profits or losses, and assets for each of these areas are shown in page 688:

	Oils and Lubricants	Jet Engine Repair	Specialized Tools	Truck Leasing
Revenues: External	$2,750,00	$16,200,000	$7,640,000	$1,500,000
Intersegment	750,000	—	560,000	1,350,000
Pretax profits (losses)	605,000	2,916,000	993,200	(530,000)
Assets....................	1,650,000	24,300,000	1,910,000	4,800,000

1. If two of the above areas had to be combined into a separate segment, explain which two would be likely candidates.
2. If the chief operating decision maker had defined segments around the four separate areas, indicate which of the areas would qualify as a reportable segment.
3. If pretax profits for the entire company were approximately $4.9 million, identify four items that would likely comprise the reconciliation of total reportable segment amounts to companywide totals.

PROBLEMS

Problem 12-1 *(LO 2, 3)* **Interim cost of sale and tax expense.** Radix, Inc., operates primarily as a distributor of components for gasoline compressors. In the first quarter of 2011, the company reported a gross profit of $248,000 on net sales of $1,360,000. After considering selling, general, and administrative expenses, the company reported pretax income of $136,000 and a related tax expense of $40,800.

During the second quarter of 2011, the company reported net sales of $2,150,000 related to the compressor business, and it experienced a LIFO liquidation due to the sharp increase in sales. The LIFO cost of sales for the second quarter consisted of purchases from the current year totaling $1,564,000 and 2,100 units that were purchased in 2010 at a unit cost of $58. The current replacement cost for the 2010 units is $72 per unit, and it is expected that physical inventory levels at the end of 2011 will exceed those at the end of 2010. Unrelated to the distribution of components for compressors, the company also distributes oils and lubricants to automot·--- repair establishments. This operation reported sales of $540,000 and FIFO cost of sales ა $364,000 before consideration of lower-of-cost-or-market adjustments. Although the first quarter of 2011 included a market write-down of $18,000 in cost of sales, the second quarter experienced sharp increases in the market value of petroleum-based products which more than offset the declines in value experienced earlier in the year.

The company reported selling, general, and administrative expenses for the second quarter of 2011 in the amount of $210,000. Although management had strong pretax results in the second quarter, it is anticipating slightly lower pretax profits for the second half of 2011 in the amount of $438,000. The company is estimating annual tax credits of $17,000 and annual selling expenses of $32,000 which will never be deductible for tax purposes. The statutory tax rate is as follows: 15% on the first $50,000 of taxable income, 25% on the next $50,000 of taxable income, 30% on the next $150,000 of taxable income, and 35% on all remaining taxable income.

Required ▶ ▶ ▶ ▶ ▶   Prepare an income statement for the second quarter of 2011 and the 2011 year-to-date.

Problem 12-2 *(LO 3)* **Estimating the effective tax rate.** Roberts Corporation began operations in 2009 and finally began to report pretax profits in 2010. However, a major economic downturn in 2011 has negatively impacted the company's operations.

Required ▶ ▶ ▶ ▶ ▶   For each of the following quarters of 2011, determine the tax expense or benefit traceable to that quarter. Assume that the statutory tax rates for years 2009 through 2011 are 25%, 30%, and 35%, respectively.

	Quarter 1	Quarter 2	Quarter 3
Pretax income (loss) for the quarter	$(150,000)	$120,000	$ 97,000
Projected income (loss) for the balance of the year	(75,000)	(50,000)	33,000
Projected nondeductible expenses for the year	22,000	15,000	20,000

	Quarter 1	Quarter 2	Quarter 3
Projected nontaxable income for the year	$ —	$ 5,000	$ 7,000
Projected tax credits for the year	$ 6,000	6,000	8,000
Taxable income in 2010.......................	195,000	195,000	195,000
Taxable income in 2009.......................	(75,000)	(75,000)	(75,000)
Post-2011 income more likely than not	—	—	250,000

Assume that all current-year (2011) taxable losses and tax credits may be carried back against the prior two years to whatever extent possible. No tax credits were available in years 2009 and 2010.

Problem 12-3 *(LO 3, 4)* **Determining the tax expense traceable to various components of income.** McClure Manufacturing reported a pretax loss from operations of $45,000 for the first quarter of 2013. The estimated effective annual tax rate at that time was based on the following information:

1. A statutory tax rate of 32% and annual estimated tax credits of $7,000.
2. Projected annual pretax loss of $70,000.
3. Taxable income of $12,000 and $10,000, respectively, for 2011 and 2012.
4. Statutory tax rates in 2011 and 2012 of 30% and 28%, respectively.
5. No recognized tax benefit associated with net operating loss carryforwards.

During the second quarter of 2013, McClure decided to discontinue an operation that had reported pretax losses of $15,000 in the first quarter. At the end of the first quarter of 2013, the discontinued operation had accounted for $2,000 of the annual estimated tax credit and $55,000 of the annual pretax loss. In the second quarter, the discontinued operation reported pretax operating losses of $15,000 and pretax impairment losses of $42,000. Continuing operations reported second-quarter pretax income of $58,000, projected annual pretax income of $90,000, and annual estimated tax credits of $5,000.

During the third quarter of 2013, continuing operations reported pretax income of $40,000, projected annual pretax income of $110,000, and annual estimated tax credits of $8,000. Also during the third quarter, the discontinued operation reported operating losses of $30,000 and gains from the disposal of assets of $25,000, revised the earlier impairment losses from $42,000 to $34,000, and recorded additional impairment losses of $16,000.

Given the 2013 statutory tax rate of 32%, calculate the pretax income (loss) and related tax expense (benefit) for the first three quarters of 2013 for continuing and discontinued operations.   ◄ ◄ ◄ ◄ ◄ **Required**

Problem 12-4 *(LO 3, 4)* **Interim income statement, expense recognition, nonordinary income items.** Treetop Corporation is a manufacturer of specialty equipment used in the film editing industry. The company needs an income statement for the second quarter of its fiscal year and has requested that you prepare such a statement. Management of the company has provided you with the following information that may be relevant to your engagement:

1. Revenues for the quarter were $510,000. The revenues are traceable to the sale of 2,100 units.
2. The company employs the LIFO inventory method for the following items: beginning inventory of 900 units at a cost of $100 per unit and purchases of 1,500 units at a cost of $120 per unit. It is anticipated that ending inventory for the fiscal year will exceed the beginning levels of inventory. Furthermore, management anticipates that inventory acquired in the next quarter will cost approximately $124 per unit.
3. Selling, general, and administrative expenses, excluding the items in (4) through (5) below, totaled $110,000 for the quarter.
4. During the quarter, management expended $75,000 for research and development costs, which are expected to provide for new technologies in the coming fiscal year.
5. Management bonuses for the current fiscal year will be approximately $160,000.
6. Based on prior experiences, it is estimated that a year-end physical inventory will reveal that the perpetual inventory is overstated. The adjustment is estimated to be in the range of $30,000.
7. During the second quarter, the company experienced two unrelated extraordinary gains (A and B) in the amount of $20,000 and $15,000, respectively.

The company's income tax rates are as follows: 15% on the first $50,000 of taxable income, 25% on the next $25,000, 34% on the next $25,000, 39% on the next $230,000, and 34% thereafter. In the first quarter of the fiscal year, the company reported income before taxes of $20,000 and tax expense of $1,000. The company expects that for the last six months of the fiscal year there will be a pretax loss of $40,000 traceable to continuing operations. Annual tax credits will likely amount to $7,000.

Required ▶ ▶ ▶ ▶ ▶   Prepare an income statement for the second quarter of the current fiscal year. All supporting schedules should be presented in good form.

Problem 12-5 *(LO 3, 4)* **Effective tax rates and nonordinary items.** The following schedule was developed for Monroe Corporation to support interim reporting for the year 2014.

| | | Income (Loss) | | | |
Quarter	Type of Income (Loss)	Current Period	Year-to-Date	Effective Tax Rate	YTD Tax Expense (Benefit)
1	Continuing	$70,000	$ 70,000		$1,344
1 restated	Continuing		A		B
	Discontinued		(30,000)		C
2	Continuing	50,000			D
	Discontinued		E		F
	Extraordinary	20,000	20,000		

The following additional 2014 information is available:

1. The statutory tax rate is as follows:

   15% on the first $50,000 of taxable income
   20% on the next $50,000 of taxable income
   25% on the next $50,000 of taxable income
   30% on all additional taxable income

2. At the end of 2013, the first year of operations, the company reported a net operating loss of $80,000 and a tax credit of $5,000. At that time, the company did not recognize any of the tax benefit associated with the operating loss or tax credit. However, the company was hopeful that these benefits could be recognized in the future due to the ability to carry forward both items against future taxable income and taxes.
3. Originally, at the end of the first quarter, the company estimated pretax income for the balance of the year of $60,000.
4. During the second quarter, the company decided to discontinue an operation. Originally, in quarter 1, the operation had reported losses of $30,000 and projected losses for the balance of 2014 in the amount of $40,000. During quarter 2, the discontinued operation reported operating losses of $60,000 and realized losses on the disposal of assets of $25,000. Although not yet realized, the operation anticipated that assets to be sold in the future would net $30,000 less than their book value (carrying value) as reported at the end of quarter 2, 2014.
5. During the second quarter, the company reported pretax income from continuing operations of $50,000 and projected pretax income from continuing operations of $60,000 for the balance of the year. During the second quarter, the company also experienced an extraordinary pretax gain of $20,000.

Required ▶ ▶ ▶ ▶ ▶   Provide the value for the items A through F.

Problem 12-6 *(LO 6, 7, 8)* **Determination of reportable segments, disclosures, ratio analysis.** A U.S. multinational corporation has divided its operations into several operating segments and has provided the following data for each segment:

	Semiconductors	Control Devices	Educational and Productivity Solutions	Financing Activities	Corporate	Consolidated Totals
Revenues:						
External	$19,920,000	$61,700,000	$5,360,000	$3,300,000	$ 8,288,000	$ 98,568,000
Intersegment	3,970,000	11,411,000	0	964,000	0	0
Expenses	23,800,000	28,422,000	5,467,000	7,962,000	7,020,000	0
Total assets	28,220,000	36,320,000	6,750,000	6,015,000	23,000,000	100,305,000
Long-lived assets	18,230,000	24,000,000	5,540,000	3,760,000	15,434,000	66,964,000

It is important to note that all purchases of goods or services from other segments have been sold to outside parties except one. Control devices with a cost of $1,000,000 were sold to the Semiconductors segment for $1,700,000. These items remain in inventory at year-end.

	United States	Japan	Germany	Other International	Total of All Countries
Semiconductors:					
Revenues (excluding intersegment)	$12,967,000	$ 3,240,000	$1,880,000	$ 1,833,000	$19,920,000
Long-lived assets	13,440,000	2,100,000	1,200,000	1,490,000	18,230,000
Control devices:					
Revenues (excluding intersegment)	16,467,000	31,000,000	4,432,300	9,800,700	61,700,000
Long-lived assets	4,011,000	15,020,000	1,419,000	3,550,000	24,000,000
Educational and productivity solutions:					
Revenues (excluding intersegment)	3,007,000	807,000	526,000	1,020,000	5,360,000
Long-lived assets	2,900,000	1,020,000	550,000	1,070,000	5,540,000
Financing activities:					
Revenues (excluding intersegment)	1,902,000	303,300	770,900	323,800	3,300,000
Long-lived assets	2,000,000	192,900	893,000	674,100	3,760,000
Corporate:					
Revenues (excluding intersegment)	6,607,000	807,000	474,000	400,000	8,288,000
Long-lived assets	11,026,000	2,000,000	1,504,000	904,000	15,434,000
Total revenues	$40,950,000	$36,157,300	$8,083,200	$13,377,500	$98,568,000
Total long-lived assets	$33,377,000	$20,332,900	$5,566,000	$ 7,688,100	$66,964,000

1. Determine which segments are reportable. ◀ ◀ ◀ ◀ ◀ **Required**
2. Given the available information, prepare all of the necessary schedules and disclosures regarding the entity's segments, geographical areas, and reconciliations to consolidated amounts.
3. Identify and determine the value of several ratios that may be helpful in analyzing the above information.

Problem 12-7 *(LO 6, 7, 8)* **Determination of reportable segments, disclosures, reconciliation to consolidated amounts.** Autoplus International is a publicly traded company that manufactures and distributes a number of products for use within the automobile industry. Major products are categorized as follows:

    A. Automobile collision repair equipment
    B. Automobile battery and starter parts
    C. Automobile seating and safety belts
    D. Automobile paints and trim parts
    E. Automobile tire retreading equipment
    F. Miscellaneous automobile products

The chief operating decision maker for the entity uses information organized by product groups for purposes of evaluating performance and allocating resources. Current-year intersegment transactions can be summarized as follows:

Selling Segment	Buying Segment	Cost of Sales	Selling Price	Amount Included in Ending Inventory of Buying Segment
Miscellaneous Products	Battery and Starter Parts	$2,540,000	$3,556,000	$420,000
Paint and Trim Parts	Collision Repair Equipment	4,500,000	5,400,000	720,000
Seating and Safety	Collision Repair Equipment	1,650,000	2,200,000	440,000

For the current year ended December 31, amounts allocated to the segments are as follows:

Segment	Revenues (Including Intersegment Activity)	Cost of Sales	General and Administrative Expenses	Total Assets	Long-Lived Assets
A	$24,840,000	$17,560,000	$ 2,480,000	$ 45,720,000	$ 34,250,000
B	6,470,000	4,250,000	1,120,000	14,780,000	10,100,000
C	13,850,000	7,560,000	1,840,000	37,500,000	21,500,000
D	25,500,000	18,650,000	4,570,000	47,800,000	32,000,000
E	4,780,000	3,100,000	980,000	13,950,000	8,540,000
F	8,650,000	4,320,000	2,130,000	16,570,000	9,870,000
Corporate	6,750,000	0	4,730,000	29,860,000	15,500,000
	$90,840,000	$55,440,000	$17,850,000	$206,180,000	$131,760,000

The products of the entity are sold throughout the world. The percentage of revenues from external customers (excluding corporate revenues) and long-lived assets (including corporate assets) traceable to various geographic areas are as follows:

Percentage of	United States	United Kingdom	Italy	Germany	Mexico	All Other Foreign
External sales traceable to:	51%	20%	10%	5%	9%	5%
Long-lived assets traceable to:	54	21	8	4	10	3

Required ▶ ▶ ▶ ▶ ▶

1. Determine which of the segments are considered to be reportable and whether the guidelines regarding the number of reportable segments have been satisfied.
2. Given the available information, prepare all of the necessary schedules and disclosures regarding the entity's segments, geographical areas, and reconciliations to consolidated amounts.

Problem 12-8 *(LO 7, 8)* **Assorted questions regarding segmental reporting.** You are presenting segmental information regarding your company to the finance committee of the board of directors and have been asked the following questions.

Required ▶ ▶ ▶ ▶ ▶

Provide your response to each of the following questions:

1. How is it possible that the distribution of wine and spirits have been combined with the distribution of personal care products to constitute a single operating segment?
2. Why don't the third-quarter revenues traceable to reportable segments agree with the third-quarter revenues shown in the consolidated income statement?
3. From a competitive standpoint, would it be better to show more or fewer segments on our financial statements?

4. How is it possible that two of our segments, which have immaterial sales revenue compared to consolidated sales revenue, are being shown as reportable segments?
5. How is interest expense on the company's bonds payable allocated to the various segments?
6. How is it possible that the total of segmental net sales exceeds the net sales for the entire company?
7. Is it possible to roughly calculate a segment's annual cash flow?

Problem 12-9 *(LO 7, 8)* **Schedule of reportable segments and reconciliation to the consolidated company.** Tress Corporation is a rapidly growing company that has diversified into a number of different segments. The following partial trial balance, which includes the effect of intercompany transactions, is for the current year ended December 31:

Net Sales.	$(14,332,250)
Cost of Goods Sold	7,180,000
General and Administrative Expenses.	20,000
Gain on Sale of Fixed Asset.	(100,000)
Investment Income	(315,000)
Interest Income.	(162,000)

Tress Corporation has five distinct segments (A through E), in addition to corporate operations. Net sales are allocated to the segments as follows:

Segment	Net Sales
A.	$ 4,023,500
B.	2,749,000
C	574,500
D.	6,185,250
E.	800,000
Total	$14,332,250

Ten percent of D's sales are made to A, and 7% of B's sales are made to C. The cost of the goods sold to A by D is $200,000, and the cost of the goods sold to C by B is $144,000. The total cost of goods sold is allocated to the segments by the following percentages: A—30%, B—29%, C—6%, D—24%, and E—11%. Of the items C purchased from B, 25% are included in C's ending inventory.

Of general and administrative expenses, 20% are traceable to corporate operations. The balance is allocated in proportion to the segment revenues, including interest income and the gain on the sale of the fixed asset.

Investment income is traceable to corporate operations.

Interest income is traceable directly to the segments and the corporate level as follows:

Segment A.	$48,000
Segment B.	10,000
Segment C.	0
Segment D.	60,000
Segment E.	12,000
Corporate level	32,000

Unconsolidated assets are identifiable as follows:

	A	B	C	D	E	Corporate
Current assets	$ 912,000	$ 681,000	$ 305,000	$ 309,000	$ 389,000	$ 115,000
Property, plant, and equipment (net)	7,136,000	4,643,000	1,480,000	4,181,000	1,543,000	1,737,000

Included in B's property, plant, and equipment is a machine that B purchased at the beginning of the year from A for $300,000. Segment A originally purchased the machine for $250,000, two years prior to the sale. Accumulated depreciation (straight-line method) on the machine was $50,000 at the time of the sale. Segment B recorded $30,000 of depreciation on the machine for the year based on the straight-line method. The gain on the sale of equipment is traceable to Segment A.

Required ▶ ▶ ▶ ▶ ▶

1. Assuming that segments A, B, and D are reportable, prepare a schedule that discloses the revenues, operating profits or losses, and assets for each of the reportable segments and the "all other" segments.
2. Prepare a schedule that reconciles the above amounts to the respective entity consolidated amounts.

Chapter 13: *Partnerships: Characteristics, Formation, and Accounting for Activities*

Chapter 14: *Partnerships: Ownership Changes and Liquidations*

A business may be organized in a variety of ways: as a sole proprietorship, a commercial corporation, a limited liability company, a limited liability partnership, or a regular partnership. Partnerships continue to be a common form of organization, and even the recent limited liability entities have many of the characteristics of a partnership. Assisting business owners in the proper selection of an organizational form is a necessary, yet complex, part of serving the needs of a business. A partnership is governed by a partnership agreement or, in some instances, by the Uniform Partnership Act. The partnership agreement must be carefully drafted to cover a variety of topics, including the purpose of the partnership, the responsibilities of the partners, the allocation of profits and losses, the admission or withdrawal of a partner, and the valuation of the partnership given changes in the ownership structure. Changes in the ownership structure provide insight into some of the basic factors which must be considered in valuing a business, whether it be a partnership or not. If a decision is made to terminate a partnership, several legal doctrines and special accounting procedures must be applied in order to produce an equitable distribution of partnership assets.

Partnerships: Characteristics, Formation, and Accounting for Activities

Learning Objectives

When you have completed this chapter, you should be able to

1. **Explain the basic characteristics of a partnership.**

2. **Identify basic components that should be included in a partnership agreement.**

3. **Describe the relationship between a partner's drawing and capital accounts.**

4. **Demonstrate an understanding of the various bases that could be used to allocate profits or losses among partners.**

A partnership is an association of two or more people for the purpose of carrying on a trade or business as co-owners. Partnerships continue to be a popular form of organization for many smaller businesses as well as certain larger businesses. Common examples of partnerships include professional services, such as the practice of accounting or law, real estate investment/ development companies, and a variety of smaller manufacturing concerns. The magnitude of the partnership form of organization is suggested by the following statistics provided by the Internal Revenue Service:

- For 2008, there were 3,146,006 partnerships representing an increase of 1.6% over prior-year levels.
- For 2008, there were 19,300,250 partners representing an increase of 4.2% over prior-year levels.
- For 2008, the total net income (loss), or profit, was $458.2 billion representing a decrease of 33% from prior-year levels.

Information regarding domestic partnership levels for the year 2008 is as follows:

	Domestic General Partnerships	Domestic Limited Partnerships	Domestic Limited Liability Companies
Number of partnerships	669,601	411,698	1,898,178
Number of partners	2,623,041	7,054,319	7,524,172
Total net income	$80.4 billion	$178.3 billion	$54.7 billion

Source: Internal Revenue Service, Statistics of Income Division, Fall SOI Bulletin, August 2010.

In a majority of states, the legal nature and functioning of a partnership is governed by the *Uniform Partnership Act (1997)*, which has been revised and amended since 1997. The Uniform Partnership Act (1997), referred to as RUPA as in "revised UPA," deals with such topics as the rights of partners, relations with persons dealing with the partnership, and the dissolution and termination of a partnership.

CHARACTERISTICS OF A PARTNERSHIP

Practicing accountants are frequently asked to advise clients regarding the formation of a business and the accounting for the business activities. Often, a choice must be made between a partnership and a corporate form of organization. Therefore, it is important for accounting students to understand the basic characteristics of a partnership and the related accounting implications.

1

OBJECTIVE

Explain the basic characteristics of a partnership.

Relationship of Partners

A partnership represents a voluntary association of individuals carrying out a business purpose. In this association, a *fiduciary relationship* exists among the partners, requiring them to exercise good faith, loyalty to the partnership, and sound business judgment in conducting the partnership's business. An individual partner is viewed as a co-owner of partnership property, creating a *tenancy in partnership*. When specific assets are contributed by a partner, they lose their identity as to source and become the shared property of the partnership. Without the consent of all partners, such property cannot be utilized by any partner for personal purposes.

The relationship between partners also is characterized as one of *mutual agency*, which means that each partner is an agent for the other partners and the partnership when transacting partnership business. Therefore, in carrying on the business of the partnership, the acts of every partner bind the partnership itself, even when a partner commits a wrongful act or a breach of trust. However, if a partner has no authority to act for the partnership and the party with whom the partner is dealing knows this, the partnership is not bound by the partner's actions.

Legal Liability of a Partnership

Partnerships are classified as either general or limited regarding liability of the partners. In a *general partnership*, the partners act publicly on behalf of the partnership and are personally liable, jointly and severally, for the unsatisfied obligations of the partnership. This unlimited liability is in sharp contrast to the limited liability of a corporation and its shareholders. Thus, if a partnership were insolvent, the unsatisfied creditors could seek to recover against the net personal assets of individual partners. Newly admitted partners, who are personally liable for partnership debts incurred subsequent to this admission, are liable for debts of the previous partnership only to the extent of their capital interest in the partnership.

In contrast, a *limited partnership* consists of one or more general partners and one or more limited partners who contribute capital but do not participate in the management of the company. The one or more general partners have unlimited liability as in the case of a general partnership. However, the limited partners' liability for partnership obligations is restricted to a stated amount, usually equal to their capital interest in the partnership.

The legal liability of partners is obviously a serious factor to consider when assessing whether a partnership is the appropriate form of organization. One could argue that unlimited liability, as a matter of social policy, is a good thing. Society has a right to be protected from the consequences of serious errors in judgment whether they be unintentional or intentional. However, without proper limits, such exposure to liability may also impair an entity's ability to provide useful goods or services. Virtually every product or service industry, from cigarette manufacturers to the medical profession, has been affected by liability issues. For example, the public accounting profession has had to operate in such a litigious environment that major initiatives have been undertaken in response to the legal liability crisis.

In response to this growing concern, two new forms of organization have been created, a *limited liability company* (LLC) and a *limited liability partnership* (LLP). The LLC is a hybrid form of organization that has many of the advantages of both a partnership and a corporation but few of the disadvantages of either. Similar to a corporation, shareholders of an LLC do not have personal legal liability for actions undertaken by the entity. This limited liability does not necessarily protect an individual shareholder from personal liability for his/her own wrongs. This is consistent with common law doctrine which views each individual as being responsible for the consequences of his/her own negligence and the ability of courts to "pierce the corporate veil" in order to seek recovery for wrongdoings.

An LLP is a subcategory of general partnerships. The LLP compares favorably to limited or general partnerships with respect to liability. All partners in an LLP may participate in management (unlike limited partners) and still have limited liability. Partners in an LLP are not personally jointly and/or severally liable for obligations of the partnership arising from the omissions, negligence, wrongful acts, misconduct, or malpractice of other partners. However, a partner does remain personally responsible for liabilities arising from his/her own actions and the actions of those who are acting under the partner's actual supervision and control in the specific activity in which the action occurred.

Underlying Equity Theories

Equity theories relate to how an entity is viewed from an accounting and legal viewpoint. These theories deal with the question of who is the entity. For example, an entity may be viewed as being providers of capital, individual owners (partners/shareholders), management, or a separate, distinct legal entity. Partnerships have been primarily affected by the *proprietary theory*, which looks at the entity through the eyes of the owners. Characteristics of a partnership that emphasize that the entity is viewed as the individual owners include the following:

◆ Salaries to partners are viewed as distribution of income rather than a component of income.

◆ Unlimited liability of general partners extends beyond the entity to the individual partners.

◆ Income of the partnership is not taxed at the partnership level but, rather, is included as part of the partners' individual taxable income.

◆ An original partnership is dissolved upon the admission or withdrawal of a partner.

Partnerships also have been influenced by the *entity theory* which views the business unit as a separate and distinct entity possessing its own existence apart from the individual partners. This theory is characteristic of corporations; yet, it is the basis for certain partnership characteristics. For example, a partnership may enter into contracts in its own name. Also, property contributed to a partnership by individual partners becomes the property of the partnership, and the contributing partner no longer retains a claim to the specific assets contributed.

Formation and Agreements

A partnership may come into existence without having to receive formal, legal, or state approval and may result simply from the actions of the parties involved. This lack of formality may be viewed as an advantage of a partnership. However, it is still necessary to carefully plan and evaluate various factors affecting the partnership. Forward and formal thinking when organizing a partnership will benefit both the business and its partners.

In order to properly capture the intent of the partners involved, it is advisable to develop a written partnership agreement. Critical issues that must be addressed include admission of partners, withdrawal of partners, and the allocation of profits and losses. Such an agreement is referred to as the *articles of partnership* and, at minimum, should include the following provisions:

1. Partnership name and address
2. Partners' names and addresses
3. Effective date of partnership
4. A description of the general business purpose and the limited duration of such purpose, if applicable
5. Powers and duties of partners
6. Procedures governing the valuation of assets invested
7. Procedures governing the admission of a new partner(s)
8. Procedures governing the distribution of profits and losses
9. Procedures governing the payment of receipt of interest on loans (versus capital contributions) among partners
10. Salaries to be accrued to partners
11. Withdrawals of capital to be allowed each partner and the determination of what constitutes excess withdrawals
12. Procedures governing the voluntary withdrawal, disability, death, or divorce of a partner and the determination of the procedures for valuing the partner's interest in the partnership
13. Matters requiring the consent of all partners
14. The date when the profits and losses are divided and the partnership books are closed
15. The basis of accounting (e.g., accrual or cash)

As the accounting for a partnership is developed more fully in this text, it will become apparent that the articles of partnership provide crucial guidance. Even though the RUPA

2

OBJECTIVE

Identify basic components that should be included in a partnership agreement.

covers certain topics found in the articles of partnership, it is important to note that many sections of the RUPA are applicable only in the absence of a partnership agreement. In essence, the RUPA gives supremacy to the partnership agreement and is a series of "default rules" in those instances where the partnership agreement fails to clearly address a particular matter. The primary focus of the RUPA is the smaller, less formal, partnership. Legal and accounting issues affecting a partnership are often best resolved by evaluating the intent of the partners as set forth in a partnership agreement, rather than looking to the RUPA.

Acceptable Accounting Principles

There is a general presumption that an entity's financial position and results of operations should be accounted for in conformity with generally accepted accounting principles (GAAP). As GAAP has developed and become more complex, many have questioned the applicability of such principles to smaller business organizations, a large number of which are organized as partnerships. In response to this concern, it is recognized that, in some circumstances, a basis or method of accounting other than GAAP may be appropriate and may not adversely affect the fairness of the financial statements.

The Auditing Standards Board of the American Institute of Certified Public Accountants (AICPA) recognizes several *other comprehensive bases of accounting (OCBOA)* other than GAAP, including the following:

◆ The cash (receipts and disbursements) basis of accounting and modifications of the basis, such as a modified accrual basis.
◆ The tax basis of accounting based on taxation principles that are used to file an income tax return.

Tax-basis accounting generally consists of a cash-basis format or an accrual-basis format with certain exceptions primarily resulting from tax regulations differing from GAAP. The tax basis of accounting is a frequent choice of many partnerships. Depreciation accounting can be used to illustrate the focus of tax-basis accounting. Assume a depreciable asset has an economic useful life of six years and is consumed uniformly over its life. If accrual accounting were used, it would seem that the asset should be depreciated over six years using the straight-line method of depreciation. However, adoption of the tax basis of accounting could involve the use of a shorter life and an accelerated depreciation method. Furthermore, in some instances, tax-basis accounting would allow the immediate expensing of depreciable assets even though such treatment would not be justified by accrual accounting.

The recognition of these other comprehensive bases provides many smaller and more specialized entities, many of which may be partnerships, with an acceptable alternative to GAAP. The use of OCBOA will not impair the fairness of their financial statements as evaluated by outside independent accountants. In practice, it is very common to find partnerships using a comprehensive basis of accounting other than GAAP. Due to the special tax aspects of a partnership, many such entities use the tax basis of accounting rather than GAAP.

Partner Dissociation

Although a partnership is easily formed and does not need state approval, its life is limited and it may be dissolved much more easily than a corporation. A partner may be dissociated from a partnership upon the occurrence of a number of events. In some cases, the dissociation may be voluntary or involuntary. Some examples include a partner's desire to willingly dissociate, death, or becoming a debtor in bankruptcy. A partner's dissociation may or may not result in a *dissolution* and winding up of the partnership business. For example, a partner may sell their interest in a partnership and, therefore, become dissociated even though dissolution of the partnership does not occur. However, upon the occurrence of certain events, a partnership is dissolved and its business must be wound up. Some events that result in the winding up of the partnership include the express will of all of the partners, the occurrence of an event agreed to in the partnership agreement, or a judicial determination that it is not practical to carry on the partnership. A change in the ownership structure of a partnership, whether involving the withdrawal or admission of a partner, does not normally require that a partnership be dissolved and wound up. Accounting for the admission or withdrawal of a partner is more fully discussed in the next chapter of this text.

Tax Considerations

Unlike corporations, a partnership is not a separate taxable entity but a conduit through which taxable income or operating losses pass to the tax returns of the individual partners. The partnership must file an information return (Federal Form 1065) detailing the partnership revenues and expenses that pass through to the individual partners.

Even though a partnership is not a taxable entity, accounting for partnerships for tax reporting purposes can become extremely complex. The tax code does not view a partnership as a separate, distinct entity but focuses, rather, on the individual partners. Therefore, activities of the partnership must be evaluated from a tax standpoint based on their impact on individual partners. This viewpoint results in special rules that must be understood by practicing accountants. Furthermore, the unique tax-related aspects of a partnership must be understood in order to advise clients as to whether the partnership form of organization is appropriate.

REFLECTION

- Partnerships have a number of characteristics of a legal, tax, and accounting nature that distinguish them from other forms of organization.

- A number of factors must be considered before forming a partnership, and a partnership agreement is a critical document that will help guide and manage the partnership.

ACCOUNTING FOR PARTNERSHIP ACTIVITIES

The activities of a partnership consist of several phases, including the initial contribution of capital to the partnership. This initial phase provides the capital necessary to begin operating activities. The remainder of this chapter discusses accounting for the partners' capital investments and the allocation of operating profits and losses among the partners. Although partners' capital investments may be subsequently influenced by partners entering or exiting the partnership and the liquidation of a partnership, these topics are discussed in the next chapter.

Contributions and Distributions of Capital

The capital contributed by shareholders to a corporation is accounted for in several accounts, including Capital Stock, Paid-In Capital in Excess of Par, and Retained Earnings. Unlike a corporation, the capital investment in a partnership generally is accounted for through two accounts for each partner, a temporary account referred to as the *drawing account* and a permanent account referred to as the *capital account.*

It is not unusual for a partner to withdraw available assets (typically cash) from a partnership throughout the year. Preferably, the amount and timing of a partner's withdrawal of assets should be addressed in the articles of partnership. Practically speaking, however, withdrawals are often informal and are not easily projected due to cash flow constraints. In some instances, withdrawals in excess of some amount are considered to be direct reductions of a partner's capital account rather than a withdrawal. Some partnerships view any withdrawal as a direct reduction of a capital account. However, in some partnerships, a separate account referred to as a drawing account is used to record a partner's withdrawal of capital. Withdrawals of assets, regardless of how accounted for, reduce the overall net capital of individual partners and the partnership.

A partner's withdrawals also include payments that are made by the partnership on behalf of an individual partner. For example, if a partnership pays off an individual partner's automobile

3

OBJECTIVE

Describe the relationship between a partner's drawing and capital accounts.

loan, this is no different than if the partner had withdrawn the cash from the partnership and then paid off the loan personally.

The drawing account is a temporary account and is periodically closed to the partner's capital accounts. The balance sheet of a partnership, therefore, will present only the capital account balances of the partners. To summarize, the drawing account established for each partner is debited and credited for the following transactions:

Drawing Account

Debit	Credit
Periodic withdrawals of partnership assets up to a specified amount	Closing of balance to partner's capital account

Each partner's interest in the net assets of the partnership is measured at book value in the capital account established for that partner. This account indicates the destination of capital (claims to net assets) upon dissolution of the partnership. It is important to note that the capital balance does not normally reflect the fair value or tax basis of the partner's interest in the net assets of the partnership.

To summarize, the partner's capital account is debited and credited for the following transactions:

Capital Account

Debit	Credit
Withdrawals in excess of a specified amount	Initial and subsequent investments of capital
Closing of a net debit balance in the partner's drawing account	Partner's share of partnership profits
Partner's share of partnership losses	

As is the case with all entities, the investment of capital in a partnership should initially be measured at the fair value of all tangible and intangible assets contributed. An individual partner's liabilities that have been assumed by the partnership also should be recorded at fair value.

The exception to this would be in the case where a partnership has adopted the tax basis of accounting. The proper valuation of each partner's net investment of capital is extremely important. For example, if an asset invested by a partner is initially undervalued by the partnership and is sold immediately for a gain, all of the partners share in the realized gain, which properly should have accrued to the original investing partner.

The post-closing balances in the capital accounts of the various partners represent each partner's interest in the net assets of the partnership at a point in time. A partner's interest in the partnership is different from the partner's interest in the profits and losses of the partnership. To illustrate, assume Partners A and B have capital balances of $8,000 and $32,000, respectively. Also assume that profits and losses are allocated to Partners A and B in the amount of 40% and 60%, respectively. These profit and loss ratios should not be confused with the partners' capital ratios which are 20% ($8,000 divided by $40,000) and 80% ($32,000 divided by $40,000) for A and B, respectively.

Occasionally, partners will loan assets to the partnership, or the partnership will loan assets to partners. It is important from a legal standpoint to differentiate between a loan and an additional investment of capital, especially when the liquidation of a partnership occurs. The nature of such transactions should be made clear by examining the intent of the individual partner or the partnership. If the contribution by a partner is really an additional investment of capital, it should be accounted for in the partner's capital account. However, if the transaction is truly a loan, it should be accounted for in a separate loan account for the partner, and provision for the payment of interest on the loan should be made.

Illustration 13-1 demonstrates the use of various partnership accounts in order to record partnership activity.

Illustration 13-1
Examples of Accounting for Partnership Activity

Event	Entry		
Partner A contributes cash to the partnership. Partner B contributes inventory and office equipment, and the partnership assumes the liability associated with the equipment. The equipment was recorded by B at a book value of $6,000. However, the equipment's fair value is $4,000.	Cash .... Inventory .... Office Equipment....................... Note Payable......................... Partner A, Capital .... Partner B, Capital	10,000 5,000 4,000	2,000 10,000 7,000
Partner B loans the partnership $3,000 to be repaid in one year at a stated annual interest rate of 6%.	Cash .... Partner B, Loan........................	3,000	3,000
A personal debt owed by Partner A is paid by the partnership.	Partner A, Drawing .... Cash	500	500
Partners A and B withdraw cash of $500 and $1,200, respectively. Drawings in excess of $1,000 are viewed as excessive withdrawals and are charged against capital.	Partner A, Drawing .... Partner B, Drawing .... Partner B, Capital .... Cash	500 1,000 200	1,700
The net income of the partnership is divided equally between the partners.	Income Summary........................ Partner A, Capital .... Partner B, Capital	10,000	5,000 5,000
The partners' drawing accounts are closed to their respective capital accounts.	Partner A, Capital .... Partner B, Capital .... Partner A, Drawing .... Partner B, Drawing	1,000 1,000	1,000 1,000

The Allocation or Division of Profits and Losses

An important process to be outlined in the articles of partnership is the manner in which profits and losses are to be divided among the partners. There are several alternative methods of allocating profits and losses. However, if the articles of partnership are silent on this point, the RUPA states that profits and losses are to be divided equally among the partners. The division of partnership income should be based on an analysis of the correlation between the capital and labor committed to the firm by individual partners and the income that subsequently is generated. As a result, profits might be divided in one or more of the following ways:

1. According to a ratio.
2. According to the capital investments of the partners.
3. According to the labor (or service) rendered by the partners.

Profit and Loss Ratios. Partnership agreements frequently call for the allocation or division of profits and losses according to some ratio. Normally, the ratio set forth for the division of profits also is used for the division of losses, unless a specific provision to the contrary exists. This method obviously provides a simplified way of dividing profits and, if approached properly, may provide an equitable division as well. Theoretically, the ratio should attempt to combine into one base the capital and service contributions made by the respective partners. Again, it is important to note that a partner's interest in profits and losses is often different from the partner's interest in total partnership capital (net assets).

4

OBJECTIVE

Demonstrate an understanding of the various bases that could be used to allocate profits or losses among partners.

To illustrate this method, assume the articles of partnership state that partnership profits and losses should be divided between Partners A and B in the ratio of 60:40. Partnership income of $20,000 would be divided as follows:

	Partner A	Partner B
Income to partners:		
A: $20,000 × 60%............	$12,000	
B: $20,000 × 40%............		$8,000

Capital Investment of Partners. The capital investments of the partners, represented by the balances in their respective capital accounts, may be employed as a basis for dividing a portion of the profits. The division is accomplished by imputing interest on the invested capital at some specified rate. This interest is not viewed as a partnership expense but, rather, as a means of allocating profits and losses among the partners. Typically, the balance of profits not allocated on the basis of invested capital is allocated according to some profit and loss ratio.

When the partners' capital investments are to be used as the basis for allocating profits, the partnership agreement should specify the following:

1. Whether the respective partners' capital balances are to be determined before or after the partners' year-to-date withdrawals recorded in their drawing accounts are offset against their capital accounts.
2. Whether the amount of capital investment for allocation purposes is to be:

   a. Capital at the beginning of the accounting period,
   b. Capital at the end of the accounting period, or
   c. Weighted-average capital during the accounting period.

3. The rate of interest to be imputed on the invested capital.

With respect to the first point, it is important that the partnership agreement clearly establish how invested capital is to be determined. Since each partner's equity is really a combination of capital and drawing account balances, partners' drawings may be offset against the balances in their respective capital accounts for purposes of allocating income based on invested capital. However, a partnership agreement may state that only withdrawals above a certain limit are to be viewed as offsets against capital balances. It is possible for a partnership agreement to call for interest to be imputed only if the amount of invested capital exceeds some prescribed limit or average amount.

To illustrate the use of invested capital as a basis for allocating partnership profits, assume the following:

1. Partnership profit is $20,000.
2. Interest on invested capital is to be imputed at the rate of 10%. (Capital is determined before considering withdrawals.)
3. Profits not allocated on the basis of invested capital are to be allocated equally among the partners.
4. The capital accounts of Partners A and B, just prior to the closing of their drawing accounts, are as follows:

Partner A, Capital

Oct. 1, 2011...............	30,000	Jan. 1, 2011	100,000
		July 1, 2011	10,000

Partner B, Capital

Apr. 1, 2011...............	10,000	Jan. 1, 2011	60,000

If interest is to be imputed on the partners' invested capital at the beginning of the period (January 1, 2011), the partnership profit of $20,000 would be allocated as follows:

	Partner A	Partner B	Total
Interest on beginning capital:			
A: 10% × $100,000.	$10,000		$10,000
B: 10% × $60,000		$6,000	6,000
			$16,000
Balance per ratio (equally)	2,000	2,000	4,000
Allocation of profit.	$12,000	$8,000	$20,000

If interest is to be imputed on the partners' invested capital at the end of the period (December 31, 2011), the partnership profit of $20,000 would be allocated as follows:

	Partner A	Partner B	Total
Interest on beginning capital:			
A: 10% × $80,000.	$ 8,000		$ 8,000
B: 10% × $50,000		$5,000	5,000
			$13,000
Balance per ratio (equally)	3,500	3,500	7,000
Allocation of profit.	$11,500	$8,500	$20,000

If interest is to be imputed on the partners' weighted-average invested capital during the period, the partnership profit of $20,000 would be allocated as follows:

	Partner A	Partner B	Total
Interest on weighted-average capital:			
A: 10% × $97,500 (Schedule A)	$ 9,750		$ 9,750
B: 10% × $52,500 (Schedule B).		$5,250	5,250
			$15,000
Balance per ratio (equally)	2,500	2,500	5,000
Allocation of profit.	$12,250	$7,750	$20,000

Schedule A
Weighted-Average Capital of Partner A

(1) Amount Invested	(2) Number of Months Invested	(1 × 2) Weighted Dollars
$100,000	6	$ 600,000
110,000	3	330,000
80,000	3	240,000
	12	$1,170,000

Weighted-average capital: $1,170,000 ÷ 12 = $97,500

Schedule B
Weighted-Average Capital of Partner B

(1) Amount Invested	(2) Number of Months Invested	(1 × 2) Weighted Dollars
$60,000	3	$180,000
50,000	9	450,000
	12	$630,000

Weighted-average capital: $630,000 ÷ 12 = $52,500

Services Rendered by Partners. A partner's labor or service to the partnership may be a primary force in the generation of revenue. Normally, the profit and loss agreement recognizes variations in effort by calling for a portion of income to be allocated to partners as salary. Such salaries, like interest on capital investments, are viewed as a means of allocating income rather than as an expense. It is important to note that this treatment of partners' salaries differs from the treatment of employee/shareholder salaries in a corporation, and the difference should be considered when the performance of a partnership is compared with that of a competing corporation.

When dealing with a profit and loss agreement that employs salaries as a means of allocating income, it is important not to confuse such salaries with partners' drawings. For example, a partner's withdrawal of $1,000 a month from the partnership may suggest that $12,000 of partnership income is being distributed to the partner as an annual salary or that these withdrawals may be ignored for purposes of dividing profits. Generally, a partner's drawing is not viewed as a salary but as a withdrawal of assets that reduces the partner's equity. For clarification purposes, the partnership agreement should state whether regular withdrawals of specific amounts should be viewed as salary for purposes of allocating income among the partners.

Bonuses to partners also may be used as a means of recognizing a partner's service to the partnership. Such bonuses are most often stated as a percentage of partnership income either before or after certain other components of the allocation process. Bonuses may be stated in reference to a variety of variables such as sales, gross profit, or a particular component of net income. In its most simple form, the bonus is a percentage of net income. However, if the bonus is to reward service beyond that already recognized by salaries and/or interest, the bonus may be expressed as a percentage of partnership net income after salaries and interest. In some instances, the bonus may be expressed as a percentage of net income after the bonus. To illustrate the calculation of a bonus, assume a partnership has net income of $120,000 of which $60,000 and $5,000 have already been allocated as salaries and interest, respectively. The bonus is defined in the partnership agreement as 10% of partnership net income after salaries and interest. The bonus is calculated as follows:

$$\text{Bonus} = \text{X\% (Net Income} - \text{Salaries} - \text{Interest)}$$
$$\text{Bonus} = 10\% (\$120,000 - \$60,000 - \$5,000)$$
$$\text{Bonus} = 10\% (\$55,000)$$
$$\text{Bonus} = \$5,500$$

If the agreement had stated that the bonus would be calculated based on net income after salaries, interest, and bonus, the calculation would be as follows:

$$\text{Bonus} = \text{X\% (Net Income} - \text{Salaries} - \text{Interest} - \text{Bonus)}$$
$$\text{Bonus} = 10\% (\$120,000 - \$60,000 - \$5,000 - \text{Bonus)}$$
$$110\% \ \text{Bonus} = 10\% (\$120,000 - \$60,000 - \$5,000)$$
$$110\% \ \text{Bonus} = 10\% (\$55,000)$$
$$110\% \ \text{Bonus} = \$5,500$$
$$\text{Bonus} = \$5,000$$

Multiple Bases of Allocation. In many cases, income is allocated to the respective partners by combining several allocation techniques. To illustrate, assume a profit and loss agreement of ABC Partnership contains the following provisions:

1. Interest of 6% is to be allocated on that portion of a partner's ending capital balance in excess of $100,000.
2. Partner C is to be allocated a bonus equal to 10% of partnership income after the bonus.
3. Salaries of $13,000 and $12,000 are to be allocated to Partners A and C, respectively.
4. The balance of income is to be allocated in the ratio of 2:1:1 to A, B, and C, respectively.

Notice that these provisions govern the allocation of profit and not the actual distribution of assets.

Assuming a partnership income of $33,000 and ending capital balances of $80,000, $150,000, and $110,000 for Partners A, B, and C, respectively, income is allocated to the partners as shown in Illustration 13-2.

Illustration 13-2
Profit Allocation: Multiple Bases

	Partner A	Partner B	Partner C	Total
Interest on excess capital balance		$3,000	$ 600	$ 3,600
Bonus.			3,000*	3,000
Salaries	$13,000		12,000	25,000
Subtotal	$13,000	$3,000	$15,600	$31,600
Remaining profit	700	350	350	1,400
Income allocation	$13,700	$3,350	$15,950	$33,000

*Bonus = 10% (Net Income − Bonus)
Bonus = 10% ($33,000 − Bonus)
(110%) Bonus = $3,300
Bonus = $3,000

Allocation of Profit Deficiencies and Losses. In the previous examples of profit allocations, the partnership income was large enough to satisfy all of the provisions of the profit and loss agreement. However, if the income is not sufficient or an operating loss exists, one of the two following alternatives may be employed assuming that the agreement governs both the allocation of profits or losses:

1. Completely satisfy all provisions of the profit and loss agreement and use the profit and loss ratios to absorb any deficiency or additional loss caused by such action.
2. Satisfy each of the provisions to whatever extent is possible. For example, the allocation of salaries would be satisfied to whatever extent possible before the allocation of interest is begun.

To illustrate these alternatives, assume the same information used in Illustration 13-2 for ABC Partnership, except that the partnership income is $22,000. In Illustration 13-3, the income of $22,000 is divided by using the first alternative. When studying Illustration 13-3, it is important to note that the allocation of interest, bonus, and salaries results in an excessive allocation or deficiency of $8,600 (subtotal of $30,600 less the income of $22,000), which must be subtracted from the partners' previously allocated amounts. This deficiency is allocated among the partners according to their profit and loss ratios just like a remaining profit, except that the deficiency is subtracted rather than added.

Illustration 13-3
Profit Allocation: Deficiency Allocated in Profit and Loss Ratio

	Partner A	Partner B	Partner C	Total
Interest on excess capital balance		$ 3,000	$ 600	$ 3,600
Bonus.			2,000*	2,000
Salaries	$13,000		12,000	25,000
Subtotal	$13,000	$ 3,000	$14,600	$30,600
Deficiency	(4,300)	(2,150)	(2,150)	(8,600)
Income allocation	$ 8,700	$ 850	$12,450	$22,000

*Bonus = 10% (Net Income − Bonus)
Bonus = 10% ($22,000 − Bonus)
(110%) Bonus = $2,200
Bonus = $2,000

Normally, the first method also is used when the partnership has an overall loss. For example, given a partnership loss of $2,400, the methodology in Illustration 13-3 would be employed, except that a bonus would not be recognized.

However, it is possible that a separate provision governs those situations in which a net loss exists. The allocation of the assumed loss of $2,400 is shown in Illustration 13-4. In this case, the allocation of the interest and salaries results in allocating $28,600 of income even though there is a loss of $2,400. This results in a deficiency of $31,000 (subtotal of $28,600 plus the loss of $2,400) which must be allocated among the partners according to their profit and loss ratios.

Illustration 13-4
Loss Allocation: Deficiency Allocated in Profit and Loss Ratio

	Partner A	Partner B	Partner C	Total
Interest on excess capital balance		$ 3,000	$ 600	$ 3,600
Bonus (not applicable)				
Salaries	$ 13,000		12,000	25,000
Subtotal	$ 13,000	$ 3,000	$12,600	$ 28,600
Deficiency	(15,500)	(7,750)	(7,750)	(31,000)
Loss allocation	$ (2,500)	$(4,750)	$ 4,850	$ (2,400)

The second alternative, which is used less frequently, requires that the provisions of the profit and loss agreement be ranked by order of priority. Assuming the components listed in Illustration 13-3 are already in order of priority, a partnership income of $22,000 would be distributed as shown in Illustration 13-5.

Illustration 13-5
Profit Allocation: Deficiency Allocated by Order of Priority

	Partner A	Partner B	Partner C	Total
Interest on excess capital balance		$3,000	$ 600	$ 3,600
Bonus.			2,000*	2,000
Salaries	$8,528		7,872	16,400
Income allocation	$8,528	$3,000	$10,472	$22,000

*Bonus = 10% (Net Income − Bonus)
Bonus = 10% ($22,000 − Bonus)
(110%) Bonus = $2,200
Bonus = $2,000

The salaries of $16,400 would be allocated to Partners A and C according to the ratio suggested by their normal salaries of $13,000 and $12,000, respectively. Therefore, A would receive 13/25 of the $16,400, or $8,528, while C would receive 12/25, or $7,872.

Special Allocation Procedures. A partnership profit and loss agreement may include special provisions for handling items that represent (1) corrections of prior years' income or (2) current-period, nonoperating gains or losses. Even though a correction of prior years' income may not satisfy the criteria for a prior-period adjustment, as defined by the Financial Accounting Standards Board, it may be more equitable to allocate the item among the partners according to the profit and loss agreement for the relevant prior period rather than the current period. For example, assume that Partners A, B, and C, who previously shared profits equally, currently share profits in the ratio of 2:2:1. Also assume that, in the current year, the partnership incurs a loss of 10,000 due to the settlement of litigation involving a matter arising in a prior period. Rather than allocating the loss according to the current profit ratios, it may be more equitable to base the allocation on the prior ratios.

A similar procedure may be adopted for the current-period recognition of nonoperating gains or losses. Rather than allocating a gain on the sale of a plant asset according to the partners' current profit-sharing ratios, it may be more equitable to use the ratios that existed during the period when unrealized appreciation actually took place.

To illustrate, assume that land with a basis of $40,000 has been held for three years and is sold for $60,000 in the current period. Based on the assumed profit-sharing ratios of prior periods and amounts of annual appreciation, the $20,000 gain would be allocated to Partners A, B, and C as follows:

Year	Profit Ratio	Appreciation	Profit Allocation		
			A	B	C
1	1:1:2	$ 4,000	$1,000	$1,000	$2,000
2	2:1:2	10,000	4,000	2,000	4,000
3	2:2:2	6,000	2,000	2,000	2,000
		$20,000	$7,000	$5,000	$8,000

If the partnership had not established special provisions for handling such items, the gain of $20,000 would have been allocated equally among the partners according to their current profit ratio of 2:2:2.

REFLECTION

- The balance in a partner's drawing account, along with the share of profits or losses, is closed out to the partner's capital account.

- The nature of the business a partnership is engaged in should suggest the various bases that might be appropriate for an allocation of profits or losses.

- The allocation of profits or losses may be based on salaries, bonuses, interest on invested capital, and/or a profit/loss percentage.

UNDERSTANDING THE ISSUES

1. A major issue faced by people who are starting their own business is the form of organization they should select. What are some major characteristics of a partnership that might influence their decision?

2. Under what circumstances might a salary or bonus be more appropriate than interest on capital balances as a means of allocating profits?

3. If the income of a partnership is not sufficient enough to satisfy all of the provisions of the partnership's profit-sharing agreement, how should this deficiency be handled?

4. Generally speaking, what events or activities would normally result in a partner's capital account being debited?

EXERCISES

Exercise 1 *(LO 1)* **Characteristics of a partnership's financial statements.** A client of yours is considering investing in a partnership and has been analyzing the financial statements of the partnership. Their analysis has resulted in the following observations that that they are hoping you could address:

1. The balance sheet does not set forth the capital stock account at par value which would define some level of minimum legal liability.
2. The balance sheet does not include any accrual for either state or federal income taxes even though the partnership reported pretax income.
3. In analyzing the income statement, your client noted that no salaries to partners were listed as an expense even though they know that existing partners received a salary from the partnership.
4. Interest on a partner's capital balance is used as a means of allocating profits; however, no such interest appears on the income statement.

Provide a response to each of your client's observations regarding the partnership's financial statements.

(AICPA adapted)

Exercise 2 *(LO 2)* **Analyzing a Partnership Agreement.** A client of yours is forming a partnership and has asked you to review a draft of the partnership agreement. In particular, the client is interested in your thoughts regarding the section dealing with the withdrawal of a partner. Your client also anticipates that on an ongoing basis individual partners will draw significant funds out of the partnership after the fiscal year-end. These withdrawals will be based on a percentage of production fees generated by each of the partners. Selected excerpts from that section are as follows:

> *A withdrawing partner must notify the partnership of his/her intent to withdraw by registered mail. The partnership has the first right to acquire the withdrawing partner's interest in the partnership and must exercise its right within 60 days. If the partnership is not interested in*

acquiring the withdrawing partner's interest, then the interest may be sold to an individual partner or another individual. However, any sale to another individual requires the approval of the existing partners. If the partnership exercises its right to acquire the withdrawing partner's interest, consideration paid for the interest will be equal to 60% of the partner's interest in the capital of the partnership as of the end of the fiscal quarter preceding notification to withdraw. Capital balances will be measured in conformity with generally accepted accounting principles. The consideration due will be paid to the withdrawing partner as follows: one-third upon withdrawal and the balance to be paid in equal installments over the next 24 months.

Prepare a memo to your client that communicates your thoughts regarding the agreement.

Exercise 3 *(LO 3, 4)* **Profit allocation based on multiple factors.** Moore, Probst, and Tanski formed a partnership whose profit and loss agreement contained the following provisions:

Provision	Moore	Probst	Tanski
Interest on weighted-average capital after consideration of draws	10%	10%	10%
Annual salary	$20,000	$75,000	$65,000
Bonus as a percentage of income after the bonus		10%	10%
Profit and loss percentage	20%	40%	40%
Capital balance at beginning of 2011:			
March 31, 2011	$25,000	$40,000	$20,000
June 30, 2011	—	20,000	20,000
September 30, 2011	—	20,000	—

If the weighted-average capital is negative, interest at 10% will be charged against the partner's profit allocation. All provisions of the profit and loss agreement should be satisfied, and any resulting deficiency should be allocated based on the profit and loss percentages.

Assuming a 2011 income of $168,000, determine how the 2011 income should be allocated to the partners.

Exercise 4 *(LO 3, 4)* **Interest calculation; determination of capital account balances.** Xavier, Yates, and Zale are partners in a dry-cleaning business. Their partnership agreement provides that the partners shall receive interest on their respective average yearly capital balances at the rate of 8%. Any residual profits or losses shall be divided equally among the partners. The following information is available for the current calendar year:

a. Partners' capital balances as of the beginning of the current year:

Xavier	$24,000
Yates	17,500
Zale	13,000

b. Additional investments were made during the current year as follows:

Xavier	$4,500 on April 1
Zale	$2,000 on July 1
	$15,000 on September 1

c. The drawing accounts of the partners have the following debit balances at the end of the current year:

Xavier	$1,000
Yates	1,000
Zale	500

d. Partnership income for the year is $21,100.

1. Discuss the advantages and disadvantages of using the weighted-average capital balance as the base for determining interest on capital contributed.
2. Determine the interest on weighted-average capital balances that partners Xavier, Yates, and Zale should receive for the current year. Assume that the partners' withdrawals are not to influence the capital balances for purposes of computing interest.
3. Determine the capital account balances for Xavier, Yates, and Zale after all closing entries have been journalized and posted at the end of the current year. Supporting schedules should be in good form.

Exercise 5 *(LO 4)* **Evaluating alternative profit-sharing arrangements.** Patton is considering joining Microtech Enterprises as a partner. The company provides data imaging for a variety of end users. Patton will have to contribute $100,000 of capital upon admission as a partner and will need to decide on a profit-sharing arrangement. Three alternatives are being proposed as follows:

Alternative A—Patton will be allocated a salary of $120,000, 10% of average capital after considering withdrawals, and 10% of net income. At the end of each calendar quarter, $30,000 will be distributed to Patton. No additional profits will be allocated to Patton.

Alternative B—Patton will be allocated a salary of $96,000, 10% of average capital after considering withdrawals in excess of $60,000, and a bonus of 10% of net income. At the end of the second, third, and fourth calendar quarters, Patton will receive a distribution of $24,000. At the end of the first quarter of the following year, Patton will receive a distribution of $60,000. No additional profits will be allocated to Patton.

Alternative C—Patton will be allocated a salary of $80,000 and 20% of net income. Patton will receive a distribution of $20,000 at the end of calendar quarters 1 through 3 and $80,000 at the end of quarter 4.

Patton has retained you to assist in evaluating the above alternatives and has asked you to assume that cash distributions could be reinvested at 6%. Furthermore, Patton believes that the probability of various levels of partnership income are as follows: a 30% probability of $500,000 of income, a 50% probability of $560,000 of income, and a 20% probability of $600,000 of income.

1. Prepare a schedule that evaluates the alternatives in terms of profitability and the present value of cash flows for the first year of the partnership.
2. Discuss which alternative you consider to be the most attractive.

Exercise 6 *(LO 4)* **Allocating profits and losses.** Johnson, Larson, and Kragen own an advertising agency that they operate as a partnership. The partnership agreement includes the following:

a. Johnson receives a salary of $50,000.
b. Larson receives a salary of $60,000.
c. Kragen receives no salary but a bonus equal to 10% of income after the bonus.
d. All partners are to receive 10% interest on their average capital invested. The average capital balances are $40,000, $25,000, and $145,000, respectively, for Johnson, Larson, and Kragen.
e. Any residual amounts of profit are to be divided equally between the partners.

1. Determine how $220,000 of income would be allocated.
2. Determine how a loss of $34,000 would be allocated assuming a priority system for allocating losses is not followed.
3. Determine how $132,000 of income is allocated among the partners assuming the following priority system: income should be allocated by first giving priority to salary, then bonus, then interest on invested capital, and then according to the profit and loss percentages.

Exercise 7 *(LO 4)* **Approaches to the allocation of profits and losses.** Collins, Baker, and Lebo are partners in a business that distributes various electronic components used

to control machinery in the printing industry. The partners have a lucrative business and have allocated profits according to the following agreement:

1. Salaries of $50,000 to each of the partners.
2. A bonus to Baker of 5% of sales to International Printers, Inc., in excess of $1,000,000.
3. A bonus to Collins of 10% of net income after this bonus.
4. Interest of 10% on each partner's average annual invested capital in excess of $100,000.
5. Remaining profits to be allocated in the ratio of 5:3:2 for Collins, Baker, and Lebo, respectively.

In a typical year, the above agreement is applied under the following conditions: net income of $880,000; sales to International Printers, Inc., of $1,500,000; and average annual invested capital of $50,000, $120,000, and $250,000 for Collins, Baker, and Lebo, respectively.

Gordon, who is seeking to be admitted to the partnership, has approached the partners. Gordon has an exclusive licensing agreement with a manufacturer of control devices that can significantly reduce the amount of electricity used by machinery. Gordon is confident that these products will be extremely successful, but they lack an established customer base. Therefore, Gordon is most interested in pursuing discussions with the existing partnership. Gordon has proposed contributing $50,000 cash and the exclusive licensing agreement to the partnership in exchange for an interest in capital and profits. Furthermore, Gordon proposes that a new profit agreement be established with the following terms:

1. Salaries of $50,000 to each of the partners.
2. A bonus to Baker of 5% of sales to International Printers, Inc., in excess of $1,000,000 traceable to products not covered by the exclusive licensing agreement.
3. A bonus to Gordon of 15% of sales in excess of $2,000,000 traceable to those products covered by the exclusive licensing agreement. Gordon estimates that total sales associated with these products will be approximately $4,200,000.
4. Interest of 10% on each partner's average annual invested capital in excess of $100,000.
5. Remaining profits to be allocated in the ratio of 3:3:2:2 for Collins, Baker, Lebo, and Gordon, respectively.

Collins is your personal tax client and comes to you for advice. Baker and Lebo are very excited about the Gordon proposal. However, Collins feels that Gordon may be unrealistic regarding the success of this new product line. Collins is concerned about giving Gordon a voice in the management of the partnership; but more importantly, she feels that her interest in profits may be less under the Gordon proposal. You understand your client's concern and try to be positive by saying that the Gordon proposal may be worth it. Collins responds by saying, "Maybe it is worth it if I can make another $60,000 before taxes."

Prepare a quantitative analysis that your client Collins may use to better assess the implications associated with the Gordon proposal.

Exercise 8 *(LO 4)* **Evaluating alternative profit allocation formulas.** Banyan and Schultz operate a residential construction firm as a partnership and are considering admitting Witkowski as a partner. Witkowski has recently attended a seminar on the formation and management of partnerships and is proposing that the profit-sharing arrangement of the new partnership include a number of variables as follows:

a. Banyan, Schultz, and Witkowski receive salaries of $120,000, $80,000, and $40,000, respectively.
b. Witkowski receives a bonus of 5% on all income in excess of $200,000 and up to and including $260,000 and a bonus of 10% on income in excess of $260,000.
c. All partners are to maintain a minimum capital balance of $50,000 and will receive interest on this balance at the rate of 10% on the minimum balance.
d. Any residual amounts of profit are to be divided equally between the partners.
e. If profits are not adequate to complete the above provisions, no order of priority is to be followed.

Banyan and Schultz had been sharing profits per their profit and loss ratios of 60% and 40%, respectively, and had proposed to Witkowski that the new partnership allocate profits per the profit and loss ratios of 45%, 30%, and 25% for Banyan, Schultz, and Witkowski, respectively. The original partners are not convinced that Witkowski's proposal is worth the trouble.

Furthermore, they are concerned that they will not fare as well under Witkowski's proposal as compared to their proposal. Banyan and Schultz believe that the new partnership should generate income of $250,000 in its first year and grow by 20% in each of the two subsequent years in large part due to the admission of Witkowski as a partner.

Assuming that the new partnership were to adopt Witkowski's proposed agreement for a 3-year period, prepare a schedule to compare the Witkowski proposal against that being proposed by the original partners.

Exercise 9 *(LO 4)* Allocation strategies and the allocation of operating losses.

Three individuals are considering forming a partnership to operate a metal fabricating shop. It is anticipated that significant contributions of capital will be necessary during the first 18 months of operation and that operating losses will likely be incurred during the first 12 months of operation. The three individuals have asked you to respond to each of the following questions they have regarding a partnership agreement:

1. It is anticipated that one of the partners will not be active in the day-to-day conduct of the business but will be a major contributor of capital. Assuming that interest on invested capital will be one of the profit allocation provisions, what would be the best way to measure the capital upon which interest will be calculated?
2. What are some of the factors that should be considered in setting the interest rate to be used when interest on invested capital is involved?
3. The individuals are considering addressing the buyout of an existing partner by merely stating that the withdrawing partner would receive a payment from the partnership equal to 120% of their capital balance measured as of the end of the month preceding their withdrawal. What are some concerns with this proposal?
4. If salaries are used as a component of a profit- or loss-sharing agreement, when are the salaries paid? Monthly, weekly, or on what basis?
5. If a bonus is used as a component of a profit- or loss-sharing agreement, why is it recommended that a bonus be based on income after the bonus?
6. The individuals understand that operating losses can be allocated either by (a) satisfying each provision to whatever extent possible or by (b) satisfying all provisions and then using the profit and loss ratios to absorb any deficiency. Which approach would you consider to be more equitable?

Respond to each of the above questions, keeping in mind that the individuals want to emphasize fairness over ease of application.

PROBLEMS

Problem 13-1 *(LO 3, 4)* Allocation of profits and determination of withdrawals.

Sandburg and Williams are the owners of a partnership that manufactures commercial lighting fixtures. Profits are allocated among the partners as follows:

	Sandburg	Williams
Salaries	$100,000	$125,000
Bonus as a percentage of net income after the bonus	10%	0%
Interest on weighted-average capital including withdrawals and excluding current-year profits	5%	5%

Sandburg was divorced as of the beginning of 2015 and as part of the divorce stipulation agreed to the following:

1. The spouse is to receive annual distributions traceable to years 2015 and 2016. The annual distribution is to be the greater of $100,000 or 25% of base earnings.
2. Base earnings are defined as net income of the partnership less: (a) salaries traceable to Sandburg and Williams of $75,000 and $125,000, respectively, and (b) bonus to Sandburg as

stated subject to the limitation that it not exceed $50,000.

3. Sandburg's spouse would receive a distribution from the partnership on August 31 of each current year and on February 28 of each subsequent year. The August 31 target distribution is $50,000. If the August distribution is less than $50,000, Sandburg's spouse will receive one-half year's interest on the deficiency at the rate of 10% per year. The following distribution on February 28 must be of an amount such that the two distributions equal the required distribution traceable to the calendar year just ended plus any interest associated with the August distribution.

4. All distributions to Sandburg's spouse are to be considered as a withdrawal of capital by Sandburg.

5. Aside from distributions to Sandburg's spouse, Sandburg's annual withdrawals cannot exceed $125,000.

6. Upon sale or dissolution of the partnership prior to February 28, 2016, Sandburg's spouse would receive 50% of the net realizable value of Sandburg's partnership capital.

7. On February 28, 2017, Sandburg's spouse will receive an additional final distribution equal to 50% of the sum of Sandburg's capital balance as of December 31, 2016, less the amount of the February 2017 distribution as called for by item (3) above.

Capital balances at the beginning of 2015 were $180,000 and $125,000, respectively, for Sandburg and Williams. Activity related to the partnership during 2015 and 2016 is as follows:

	2015	2016
Partnership net income	$750,000	$700,000
Distribution to Sandburg's spouse:		
February 28	0	to be determined
August 31	40,000	50,000
Distributions to Sandburg:		
June 30	60,000	125,000
September 30	65,000	0
Distributions to Williams:		
June 30	30,000	300,000
September 30	90,000	20,000

Prepare a schedule to determine the total amount of the distributions due Sandburg's spouse ◀ ◀ ◀ ◀ ◀ **Required** as of February 28, 2017. Note that the solution requires one to determine the amount of the February 2016 distribution to Sandburg's wife.

Problem 13-2 *(LO 3, 4)* Evaluating whether or not to continue to share profits.

Raymond is a senior partner in a manufacturing firm and is approaching retirement age. In discussing succession planning with the company partners, two alternatives have been presented to Raymond. The first alternative would call for Raymond to receive a distribution of his share of current-year 2015 profits on March 31, 2016, along with a lump sum payment of $1,500,000 for his capital balance. The 2015 profit-sharing agreement is as follows:

Component	Raymond	Other Partners
Salaries	$125,000	$300,000
Bonus on income after the bonus	10%	0%
Percentage of remaining profits	40%	60%

The second alternative would consist of the following components:

1. A distribution of his share of current-year profits on March 31, 2016.
2. A distribution of his share of 2016–2017 profits on March 31 of each subsequent year. The profit-sharing agreement for 2016 and 2017 would be modified from the 2015 agreement as shown on page 716:

Component	Raymond	Other Partners
Salaries	$80,000	$350,000
Bonus on income after the bonus	0%	10%
Percentage of remaining profits.	20%	80%

3. On March 31, 2018, Raymond would receive a lump sum payment of $1,700,000 for his interest in capital.

In order for Raymond to make an informed decision he has come to you seeking your advice on which alternative to accept. Raymond believes that they can invest all cash proceeds at a rate of 8% compounded annually. It is anticipated that the partnership will have income for years 2015–2017 of $550,000, $605,000, and $682,000, respectively.

Required ▶ ▶ ▶ ▶ ▶   Prepare a schedule that compares the two alternatives and expresses the respective cash flows in terms of their present value as of March 31, 2016, assuming an 8% discount rate.

Problem 13-3 *(LO 3, 4)* **Investment decision, capital retention decision.** Rodriquez is one of your tax clients and has come to you seeking your input about a potential investment opportunity. Your client has the opportunity to acquire a 30% interest in the capital of a partnership. However, this would require him to give up his current job. The partnership will consist of Rodriquez, Monroe, and Zito, and the partners will allocate profits and losses as follows:

1. Salaries to Rodriquez and Monroe of $40,000 and $50,000, respectively.
2. Interest at the rate of 9% on weighted-average net capital in excess of $20,000. All partners are required to maintain $20,000 in their net capital accounts throughout the year. Net capital is defined in the partnership agreement as capital balances less drawing account balances. It is estimated that in all cases, Monroe and Zito will maintain weighted-average net capital balances of $40,000 and $150,000, respectively. Unless otherwise stated, it is assumed that Rodriquez will maintain the minimum balance of net capital.
3. Bonus to Monroe of 5% of sales in excess of $500,000. It is estimated that sales for the year will be $650,000.
4. Profit and loss percentages of 40%, 40%, and 20% for partners Rodriquez, Monroe, and Zito, respectively.

Rodriquez is very interested in the opportunities that the partnership presents. However, he is concerned that his allocation of profits may not justify changing jobs.

Required ▶ ▶ ▶ ▶ ▶
1. Determine how much partnership profit would have to be realized in order for Rodriquez's allocated portion to equal his current job salary of $60,000.
2. Determine whether Rodriquez is best advised to withdraw available capital in excess of the minimum balance or retain capital in the partnership.
3. Assume that annual sales were less than $500,000 and that Rodriquez maintained the minimum net capital balance during the year. The other partners are assumed to maintain capital balances as stated. Furthermore, assume that all allocated profits are withdrawn. What is the minimum amount of partnership income that would be necessary in order for Rodriquez not to have to make an additional investment of capital?

Problem 13-4 *(LO 3, 4)* **Correcting capital balances.** Rexcam is a partnership owned by Wilson, Watts, and Franklin that manufactures special machine tools used primarily in injection molding applications. The partnership had operated very profitably for the first five years of existence. However, in the last two years, 2009 and 2010, the company has been challenged by foreign competition and pricing pressures. During this time, Franklin, acting as the chief financial officer, began to have difficulty dealing with the financial pressures at work and issues in his personal life. Franklin had a fatal heart attack in early January of 2011, and the partnership agreement required the partnership to pay a deceased partner's estate: (a) five times the deceased partner's average annual share of profit based on the three years prior to death plus (b) 50% of their capital balance as of the year-end prior to date of death. The amount due to the deceased partner's estate was to be determined by an outside independent accountant.

Assuming you have been retained as the outside accountant, the following errors and/or irregularities associated with Franklin's accounting for the company have come to your attention:

1. During 2009 and 2010, sales of $25,000 and $75,000, respectively, were recorded as being made to Alcor Corporation. Alcor is a fictitious company that was set up by Mr. Franklin.
2. A physical inventory was taken at the end of both 2009 and 2010. Although the quantity of goods on hand was accurate, the physical quantities were incorrectly priced resulting in an overstatement of ending inventory in 2009 and 2010 of $35,000 and $75,000, respectively.
3. Annual casualty insurance premiums were $80,000 for 2010. However, the insurance carrier was only paid $20,000 even though it was recorded as though the entire premium had been paid. The difference of $60,000 that was not paid was then recorded as a payment toward the outstanding fictitious account receivable balance of Alcor Corporation [see item (1) above].
4. The coverage period for the liability insurance policy is from April 1 through March 31. A premium payment of $36,000 for the policy period beginning April 1, 2009, was made in March of 2009 and recorded as prepaid insurance. At the end of 2009, the recorded prepaid insurance balance was $15,000. The policy premium of $39,600 of the policy period beginning April 1, 2010 was paid in March of 2010. At the end of 2010, the recorded balance in the prepaid insurance account was $19,200.
5. At the end of each calendar quarter of 2009, every partner received a draw of $50,000. At the end of each calendar quarter of 2010, every partner received a draw of $10,000. However, at the end of the second and third quarters of 2010, Franklin paid himself an additional draw of $20,000 each quarter. The additional draws were recorded as equipment acquisitions that were depreciated by the straight-line method over a 5-year period.
6. In the last quarter of 2010, the company received a payment from a customer in the amount of $42,000. However, rather than correctly recording this as a payment on account, Franklin recorded it as a cash sale.

Profits and losses of the partnership are allocated according to the following:

1. Salaries to each of the partners of $150,000 per year.
2. Interest on weighted-average capital, after consideration of draws, at the rate of 10%. If the weighted-average capital is negative, interest at 10% will be charged against the partner's profit allocation.
3. A bonus to Wilson equal to 10% of sales over $1.5 million per year.
4. Remaining balance to be allocated 30%, 35%, and 35% to Wilson, Watts, and Franklin, respectively.
5. If profits are not adequate, all provisions of the agreement will be satisfied, and any deficiency is to be allocated to the partners according to their profit and loss percentages.

At the end of 2008, the company reported profit of $590,000 of which $190,000 was properly allocated to Franklin. After all closing entries, the year-end 2008 capital balances were $300,000, $250,000, and $200,000 for Wilson, Watts, and Franklin, respectively. As initially reported by Franklin, the income of the partnership was $500,000 and $480,000 for the years 2009 and 2010, respectively, on sales of $1.65 million and $1.58 million for the years 2009 and 2010, respectively.

Prepare a schedule to determine the correct amount the partnership should pay to the estate ◄ ◄ ◄ ◄ ◄ **Required** of Franklin.

Problem 13-5 *(LO 3, 4)* **Profit allocation involving interest on capital balances.** Rivera, Sampson, and Elliott are partners in a commercial plumbing business. Rivera and Sampson have also started another contracting company and have cash flow needs which require periodic distributions from the partnership. In order to deal fairly with the level of partnership withdrawals, the partnership agreement calls for profit sharing as follows:

Component	Rivera	Sampson	Elliott
Salaries	$80,000	$80,000	$100,000
Bonus on income after the bonus	0%	0%	10%
Interest on "average net capital"	10%	10%	10%
Percentage of remaining profits	30%	30%	40%

"Average net capital" is determined by netting the partners' drawing accounts against their capital accounts and weighting the net amounts for the appropriate portion of the year. On March 31 and September 30, $40,000 is allocated to each partner's capital account in anticipation of the annual actual amount of profit. Activity in the drawing and capital accounts is as follows for the current calendar year:

Drawing Account	Rivera	Sampson	Elliott
Beginning balance January 1	$ —	$ —	$ —
March 31 draws	30,000	40,000	—
June 30 draws	10,000	25,000	30,000
September 30 draws...............................	20,000	50,000	20,000
Capital Account			
Beginning balance January 1	40,000	50,000	70,000
March 31 anticpated profit allocation................	40,000	40,000	40,000
March 31 capital investment.......................	—	—	40,000
September 30 anticpated profit allocation	40,000	40,000	40,000
September 30 loan conversion	—	15,000	—

Sampson had loaned the partnership money in the past, and the transaction was properly classified as a loan payable on the statements of the partnership. On September 30, the loan and accrued interest totaling $15,000 were converted from a loan payable to a capital investment in the partnership.

Required ▶ ▶ ▶ ▶ ▶   Determine how the current year profit of $330,000 is to be allocated among the partners.

Problem 13-6 *(LO 4)* **Profit allocation based on various factors.** Rockford, Skeeba, and Tapinski are partners in a business which manufactures specialty railings. Their profit and loss agreement provides for the allocation of profits and losses as follows:

1. Salaries of $50,000, $40,000, and $55,000 for Rockford, Skeeba, and Tapinski, respectively.
2. Skeeba will receive a bonus equal to 5% of sales in excess of $1,000,000.
3. All partners will receive a bonus of 10% of net income in excess of $150,000 after their bonus.
4. Partners will be allocated interest on their weighted-average capital balance to the extent that it exceeds $50,000. Drawings in excess of annual salaries will be considered a reduction in capital. Interest is computed at the rate of 10%.
5. Remaining profits or losses will be allocated 35%, 25%, and 40% to Rockford, Skeeba, and Tapinski, respectively.
6. Gains or losses from the sale of depreciable assets will be excluded from the above provisions and will be equally allocated between Rockford and Tapinski.

Activity in the partners' capital and drawing accounts during the year was as follows:

	Rockford		Skeeba		Tapinski	
	Capital	Drawing	Capital	Drawing	Capital	Drawing
Beginning balance	$75,000	$ —	$125,000	$ —	$40,000	$ —
February 1..................		15,000		25,000		
March 31		10,000		5,000	10,000	15,000
June 1	10,000					
June 30		10,000		25,000		15,000
September 30		10,000				15,000
Ending balance	$85,000	$45,000	$125,000	$55,000	$50,000	$45,000

Required ▶ ▶ ▶ ▶ ▶   Determine how annual income of $280,000 (including a gain on the sale of equipment of $20,000) should be allocated among the partners. Annual sales revenue was $1,300,000.

Problem 13-7 *(LO 4)* **Expert witness, economic loss measurement.** A law firm that specializes in personal injury work has engaged you to assist in some litigation. The firm represents a Mr. Lawson, who was injured in an automobile accident and is alleging that he was totally disabled as a result of the accident. Lawson is seeking damages that in part reflect the loss of income from his interest in a partnership known as L & S Contractors (L & S). L & S is in the business of contracting to do residential remodeling jobs and has three partners: Lawson, Schmidt, and Jacobsen.

Sales and related income of the partnership have grown over the years although the residential construction industry is cyclical in nature. The law firm has provided you with copies of various partnership documents that may be relevant to this matter. A review of the partnership agreement reveals the following regarding the allocation of annual profits:

1. Salaries for Lawson, Schmidt, and Jacobsen of $60,000, $60,000, and $40,000, respectively.
2. Bonuses of 10% and 5% of net income after the bonuses for Lawson and Schmidt, respectively.
3. Profit and loss percentages of 30%, 30%, and 40% for Lawson, Schmidt, and Jacobsen, respectively.

Other relevant components of the partnership agreement are as follows:

1. Partners receive a draw on July 1 and December 1 of each year. Each partner's draw is equal to one-third of 40% of the net income from the preceding year. Partners will receive draws for all years in which they were active in the business.
2. Unless modified by a majority of the partners, no more than 80% of annual income may be distributed to the partners.
3. Upon total disability, death, or retirement of a partner (referred to as a triggering event), the partnership will acquire such partner's capital interest in the partnership. The amount paid will be equal to three times such partner's average share of annual partnership income for the two years prior to the year of the triggering event. The acquisition price will be paid out in four equal semiannual payments beginning six months after the triggering event.

The automobile accident involving Mr. Lawson occurred on December 31, 2013. At his deposition, Mr. Lawson indicated the following:

1. He anticipated retiring at the end of 2018.
2. Net income of the partnership for years 2011, 2012, and 2013 was $161,000, $207,000, and $210,000, respectively.
3. Based on past and projected factors, he anticipated net income for years 2014 through 2018 to be $230,000 per year.

Prepare a tentative measure of the economic loss suffered by Mr. Lawson as a result of the   ◄ ◄ ◄ ◄ ◄ **Required** alleged total disability. Your measure of loss should be expressed as of the date of the accident and include appropriate present value considerations.

Partnerships: Ownership Changes and Liquidations

Learning Objectives

When you have completed this chapter, you should be able to

1. Understand that changes in the ownership of a partnership do not necessarily result in the dissolution and winding up of a partnership.

2. Account for the partners' capital balances under the bonus method.

3. Account for the partners' capital balances under the goodwill method.

4. Describe the conceptual differences between the bonus and goodwill methods.

5. Account for the admission of a new partner through direct contribution to an existing partner.

6. Explain the impact of a partner's withdrawal from the partnership.

7. Describe the order in which assets must be distributed upon liquidation of a partnership, and explain the right-of-offset concept.

8. Understand the treatment for capital deficiencies and unsatisfied creditors.

9. Calculate the assets to be distributed to a given partner in a lump-sum or installment liquidation, and understand the concept of maximum loss absorbable.

10. Prepare an installment liquidation statement and a schedule of safe payments.

In theory, a partnership may be viewed as a conduit or entity through which individual partners carry on a common business purpose. It is natural that the circumstances surrounding the individual partners' lives may change and affect their involvement in the partnership. Individual partners may increase or decrease their interest in the partnership or withdraw entirely from the partnership. In turn, new partners may become involved in the partnership. Such ownership changes are common in a partnership just as they are in other forms of organizations, such as a corporation. The Uniform Partnership Act (1997) sets forth those circumstances under which the dissociation of a partner does and does not result in the dissolution and winding up of a partnership. The specifics of a particular situation must be evaluated, but generally speaking, a change in the ownership structure of a partnership does not necessarily require the dissolution and winding up of the partnership.

The previous chapter stressed the importance of a well-conceived partnership agreement. Changes in the ownership structure of a partnership are one of the most important areas that should be addressed. Often, the initial concerns of a new partnership are such that the partners overlook the certain reality that, someday, there will be a change in the ownership. Accountants can be of significant help to their clients in advising them in the structuring of buy/sell agreements for the partnership. Proper planning for such changes will help to ensure smooth and equitable transitions.

<table>
<tr><td>

1

O B J E C T I V E

Understand that changes in the ownership of a partnership do not necessarily result in the dissolution and winding up of a partnership.

</td></tr>
</table>

OWNERSHIP CHANGES

Changes in the ownership structure of a corporation are everyday occurrences, as evidenced by the activity of security exchanges. These changes typically involve transactions between existing and prospective shareholders and, therefore, create no special accounting problems for the corporate entity other than updating its listings of stockholders. In the case of a partnership, however, changes in ownership structure are events that require special accounting treatment.

A transfer, in whole or in part, of a partner's interest in a partnership is permissible and does not necessary result in the dissociation of the transferring partner of the dissolution and winding up of the partnership. The entity theory of partnership conceptually suggests that the partnership entity should continue if a partner is dissociated. However, changes in the ownership structure of a partnership are also influenced by the *propriety theory*, which views a partnership not as a distinct entity but, rather, as a group of individual investors. Measuring changes in the equity of the individual partners is a major aspect of partnership accounting. Ownership changes provide an excellent opportunity for accounting to measure the current wealth or equity of the partners. Changes in the ownership structure of the partnership are presumed to be arm's-length transactions which reflect the current value of the partnership. Therefore, such changes may indicate that:

1. Previously unrecorded intangible assets exist that are traceable to the original partnership; *and/or*
2. Intangible assets, such as goodwill, exist that are traceable to a new partner.

In practice, a change in ownership normally suggests the need to both revalue net assets and recognize intangible assets.

Admission of a New Partner

The admission of a new partner requires the approval of the existing partners, although a partner's interest may be assigned to someone outside the partnership without the consent of the other partners. However, assigning an interest does not dissolve the partnership, and it does not allow the assignee to participate in the management of the partnership or to review transactions and records of the partnership. The assignee receives only the agreed-upon portion of the assigning partner's profit or loss.

Assuming a new partner has been approved by the existing partners, the new partner, normally, will experience the same general risks and rights of ownership as do the other existing partners. A new partner is liable for all of the obligations of a partnership that arose before their admission except that such obligations can only be satisfied out of partnership assets and not the personal assets of the new partner.

<table>
<tr><td>

2

O B J E C T I V E

Account for the partners' capital balances under the bonus method.

</td></tr>
</table>

Contribution of Assets to Existing Partnership. One method of gaining admission to an existing partnership involves contributing assets directly to the partnership entity itself. In this case, the exchange represents an arm's-length transaction between the entity and the incoming partner. If the book value of the original partnership's net assets approximates fair value, the incoming partner's contribution would be expected to be equal to his/her percentage interest in the capital of the new partnership. For example, if an incoming partner is to acquire a one-fourth interest in a partnership that has a book value and a fair value of $60,000, the original $60,000 would now represent a three-fourths interest in the new partnership. Therefore, the total partnership capital must be $80,000, of which $60,000 is traceable to the original partners and $20,000 is traceable to the assets contributed by the new partner.

An incoming partner may acquire an interest in the partnership for a price in excess of that indicated by the book value of the original partnership's net assets. This situation would suggest the existence of:

1. Unrecognized appreciation on the recorded net assets of the original partnership, and/or
2. Unrecognized goodwill that also is traceable to the original partnership.

However, it is possible that an incoming partner may acquire an interest in the partnership at a price *less than* that indicated by the book value. This situation would suggest the existence of:

1. Unrecognized depreciation or write-downs on the recorded net assets of the original partnership, and/or
2. A contribution by the incoming partner of some intangible asset (goodwill) in addition to a measured contribution.

When an incoming partner's contribution is different from that indicated by the book values of the original partnership, the admission of the partner, typically, is recorded by either the *bonus method* or the *goodwill method*. These two methods are mutually exclusive of each other. Both methods comprehend the possibility of adjusting the value of existing assets and/or the existence of goodwill. However, they differ in how these conditions are recognized.

Bonus Method. The bonus method generally follows a *book-value approach*. That is, existing book values should not be adjusted to current values unless such adjustments would have otherwise been allowed by generally accepted accounting principles (GAAP). More specifically, increases in the value of assets as suggested by the admission of a new partner should not be recognized until they are realized through an actual subsequent exchange transaction. However, following the principle of conservatism, decreases or write-downs in the value of assets, which are suggested by the admission of a new partner, may be recognized even though they are not realized. Recognition of unrealized losses is not unique to partnership accounting and is not in conflict with GAAP. Even if no new partner were being admitted, unrealized losses suggested by economic events should be recognized. For example, if inventory has a cost in excess of market, or if long-lived assets are impaired, these losses should be recognized regardless of whether a new partner is being admitted. Therefore, use of the bonus method should not preclude a partnership from recognizing losses which would otherwise be recognized through the application of GAAP. However, the bonus method does preclude the recognition of asset appreciation, which would otherwise not be allowed per GAAP.

Therefore, when a new partner is admitted to an existing partnership, the total capital of the new partnership consists of the following:

1. The book value of the previous partnership *less*
2. Write-downs in the value of the previous partnership's assets as recognized by GAAP *plus*
3. The fair value of the consideration paid to the partnership by the incoming partner.

The book-value approach of the bonus method does not directly recognize increases in asset values suggested by the consideration that the incoming partner pays. However, the method does indirectly recognize such increases by reallocating or adjusting the capital balances of the partners. For example, if increases in net asset values are suggested as being traceable to the original partners, this suggests that their equity or capital has increased. This increase in capital, or *bonus*, is accomplished by increasing their capital balances. If increases in asset values are not directly recognized, the indirect recognition through the capital balances of original partners must be offset by decreasing the capital of the incoming partner. Therefore, **the incoming partner's new capital balance is equal to the value of the consideration paid by the incoming partner less the bonus or increase in capital recorded for the original partners**. These adjustments result in the new incoming partner's capital balance always being equal to:

1. The book value (BV) of the new partnership [book value of the previous partnership less asset write-downs plus the fair value (FV) of consideration received from the incoming partner] times
2. The interest in capital being acquired by the incoming partner.

$$\begin{bmatrix} BV \text{ of Original} \\ Partnership - Asset \\ Write\text{-}Downs \\ + \\ FV \text{ of New Partnership} \\ Contribution \end{bmatrix} \times \begin{matrix} New\ Partner's \\ Interest\ \% \end{matrix} = \begin{matrix} New\ Partner's \\ Capital\ Balance \end{matrix}$$

The difference between the value of the consideration received from the incoming partner and his/her capital balance represents the bonus traceable to the original partners. This bonus is allocated to the original partners according to their profit and loss ratios in existence prior to the new partner's admission.

It is important to note that the profit and loss ratios of the original partners are used for this allocation rather than their percentage interest in capital. If the increases in the value of assets, as suggested by the admission of a new partner(s), are traceable to the original partners, such increases could have been alternatively realized by a sale of appreciated assets to an outside party. If this were the case, the realized gains would have become a component of net income. This net income would have, in turn, been allocated to the original partners according to their profit and loss ratios.

If the gain on such appreciated assets were realized subsequent to the admission of a new partner(s), a portion of this gain would be allocated to the new partner based on his/her profit ratio. Keeping in mind that this original appreciation in value should not accrue to the benefit of the new partner, the reduction of his/her capital balance (equal to the bonus granted to the original partners) compensates for any subsequent allocation of gains resulting from the realization of such appreciated assets.

Bonus to the Original Partners. When an incoming partner's contribution indicates the existence of unrecorded asset appreciation and/or unrecorded goodwill, the bonus method does not record these previously unrecorded items but, rather, grants a "bonus" to the original partners. The bonus, which increases the capital accounts of the original partners and reduces the capital balance of the new partner(s), is made possible by recording in the new partner's capital account only a portion of the actual contribution to the partnership.

To illustrate this method, assume the following:

Existing Partners	Capital Balance	Percentage Interest in	
		Capital	Profit
Partner A	$30,000	40%	50%
Partner B	45,000	60	50

Then assume that C invests $27,000 in the partnership in exchange for a 20% interest in capital and a 20% interest in profits. The $27,000 of consideration invested by Partner C in exchange for a 20% interest in capital suggests that the total value of the new partnership is $135,000 ($27,000 ÷ 20%). The $135,000 of value is comprised of the following:

Book value of original partners	$ 75,000
Investment of new partner	27,000
	$102,000
Asset appreciation traceable to original partners	33,000
Total suggested value	$135,000

Partners A and B will each have a 40% interest in the profits of the new partnership. Since the total capital of the new partnership equals $102,000 ($30,000 + $45,000 + $27,000) and the new partner is acquiring a 20% interest in capital, it seems reasonable that the incoming partner's capital account initially should reflect 20% of the total capital, or $20,400. The

$6,600 difference between C's contribution and the interest recorded for C indicates the existence of unrecorded intangibles (goodwill) or unrecorded appreciation on existing assets. Regardless of the identity of the $6,600, the value must be allocated to the appropriate parties. If the unrecorded value had been realized through a sale, the resulting profit would have been divided between the original partners in accordance with their profit and loss agreement. Therefore, assuming the $6,600 is identified as a bonus to the original partners and is divided between them according to their profit and loss ratio prior to admission of the new partner, the entry to record C's investment is as follows:

Assets.	27,000	
A, Capital		3,300
B, Capital.		3,300
C, Capital		20,400

If the suggested appreciation in value of $33,000 were subsequently realized, it would be allocated among Partners A, B, and C according to their profit and loss percentages of 40%, 40%, and 20%, respectively. Therefore, Partner C will be allocated $6,600 (20% × $33,000) of the gain. The $6,600 reduction in Partner C's initial capital balance, represented by the bonus to the original partners, compensates for or negates the subsequent allocation of the realized gain to Partner C. In substance, none of the $33,000 gain should accrue to the benefit of the new partner. The bonus of $6,600 to the original partners is, in substance, the reallocation to them of the subsequently realized gain that would be allocated to Partner C.

Bonus to the New Partner. When the new partner invests some intangible asset, such as business acumen or an established clientele, it is possible to have a bonus credited to the new partner. For example, given the same basic facts as in the previous illustration, assume that C invests $10,000 for a 20% interest in capital and a 20% interest in profits. Total capital of the partnership would be $85,000 ($30,000 + $45,000 + $10,000), and C's share of the total capital would be 20%, or $17,000. Partner C is acquiring a $17,000 interest in capital in exchange for an investment of $10,000, and the original partners are transferring $7,000 of their capital to C in exchange for unrecorded intangible assets invested by C. Partner C's admission is recorded by the following entry:

Assets.	10,000	
A, Capital	3,500	
B, Capital	3,500	
C, Capital		17,000

Partner C's bonus may be viewed as a cost incurred to acquire C's goodwill. Since all costs to acquire assets eventually affect income and are allocated among the partners, C's bonus is allocated to A and B according to their profit and loss ratio.

Overvaluation of the Original Partnership. The recording of a bonus traceable to the incoming partner was based on the assumption that the new partner was contributing an intangible asset in addition to other assets valued at $10,000. However, the substance of the transaction may indicate that no intangibles are being contributed and the existing assets of the old partnership are overvalued. For example, in the previous illustration, C invested $10,000 in return for a 20% interest in the new partnership's total capital. Therefore, the total capital of the new partnership may be interpreted from C's investment to be equal to $50,000 ($10,000 ÷ 20%). Of this total, $10,000 is traceable to the new partner, and the balance of $40,000 represents the fair value of the original partners' capital. Assuming this is a proper interpretation of the substance of the transaction between the new partner and the partnership, it suggests that the assets of the original partnership are overvalued by $35,000 ($75,000 less $40,000). C's admission to the partnership is recorded as follows:

A, Capital	17,500	
B, Capital	17,500	
Assets.......................................		35,000

To record the write-down of the original partners' capital from a book value of $75,000 ($30,000 + $45,000) to its implied fair value of $40,000.

| Assets.. | 10,000 | |
| C, Capital .... | | 10,000 |

To record C's contribution of assets to the partnership.

After these entries are posted, the total capital of the new partnership is $50,000 ($30,000 + $45,000 − $35,000 + $10,000), of which C's share is $10,000 (20% × $50,000), as initially represented by the balance in C's capital account.

3

OBJECTIVE

Account for the partners' capital balances under the goodwill method.

Goodwill Method. Although the admission of new partner does not result in the dissolution and winding up of the previous partnership, the goodwill method views the admission of a new partner as an opportunity to revalue net assets as though a new entity had been created. Had a new entity been created, the assets transferred to this entity would have been recorded at their **current fair value**. After a complete analysis, both tangible and intangible assets acquired by the new entity, including goodwill created by the previous partnership, would be recorded. Therefore, the total capital of the new partnership will consist of the following values:

1. The book value of the net assets of the previous partnership plus
2. Unrecognized appreciation or less unrecognized depreciation on the recorded net assets of the previous partnership plus
3. Unrecognized goodwill (GW) traceable to the previous partnership plus
4. The fair value of the consideration, both tangible and intangible, received from the new incoming partner.

$$
\begin{array}{c}
\text{BV of} \\ \text{Original} \\ \text{Partnership}
\end{array}
+
\begin{array}{c}
\text{Unrecognized} \\ \text{Appreciation (or} \\ -\text{Unrecognized} \\ \text{Depreciation)}
\end{array}
+
\begin{array}{c}
\text{Unrecognized} \\ \text{GW of Original} \\ \text{Partnership}
\end{array}
+
\begin{array}{c}
\text{FV of New} \\ \text{Partner's} \\ \text{Contribution} \\ \text{Including GW}
\end{array}
=
\begin{array}{c}
\text{Total Capital} \\ \text{of New} \\ \text{Partnership}
\end{array}
$$

When the bonus method is used to account for the admission of a new partner, the total capital of the new entity equals the book value of the previous partners' capital adjusted for asset write-downs, if appropriate, plus the incoming partner's investment. When the goodwill method is employed, however, the total capital of the new partnership must approximate the fair value of the entity.

To illustrate the goodwill method, assume the following:

| | | Percentage Interest in | |
Existing Partners	Capital Balance	Capital	Profit
Partner A	$30,000	40%	50%
Partner B	45,000	60	50

If C invests $27,000 in the partnership in exchange for a 20% interest in capital and a 20% interest in profit, such an investment implies that the entity has a fair value of $135,000 ($27,000 ÷ 20%). However, the book value of the new partnership equals only $102,000 when the former partners' capital balances of $75,000 are added to C's $27,000 investment. Thus, $33,000 must be added to the existing book value.

Another interpretation of the transaction would be that, given the $102,000 book value of the new partnership, a 20% interest should have cost $20,400 ($102,000 × 20%). The new partner paid an extra $6,600 ($27,000 − $20,400) for a 20% interest in the difference between the implied fair value and the book value of the new entity. Therefore, the total difference must be $33,000 ($6,600 ÷ 20%).

Asset Appreciation. The difference between the higher fair value and the book value of the new entity, as previously discussed, may be traceable to unrecognized appreciation and/or unrecognized goodwill. Each of these possible explanations should be thoroughly analyzed to properly account for a change in the ownership structure of a partnership. If differences between the fair value and the book value of recorded assets are identifiable, appropriate adjustments to asset balances should be considered. Since a change in ownership structure creates a new, distinct legal entity, every attempt should be made to identify differences between fair and book values, whether such differences represent appreciation or write-downs in value. However, the absence of objective and independent valuations often prevents such an analysis. For example, fair values are not readily available for certain specialized assets, and the alternative of engaging an independent appraiser could become an expensive option. Furthermore, estimating fair values with the use of specific price-level indexes is often difficult because of the absence of relevant indexes. Another reason for not recording changes in fair values is that the resulting differences between the bases for tax purposes and the bases for book purposes would require more complex records.

Assuming objective measures of unrecorded appreciation are available, the appreciation would be recognized and allocated to the previous partners according to their old profit and loss ratios. To illustrate, assume that the $33,000 difference in values from our previous example is entirely traceable to the unrecognized net appreciation of the recorded net assets of the previous partnership as follows:

Land appreciation	$ 43,000
Inventory write-down	(10,000)
Net appreciation	$ 33,000

This appreciation and the investment by C would be recorded as follows:

Assets (from C)	27,000	
Land	43,000	
Inventory		10,000
A, Capital		16,500
B, Capital		16,500
C, Capital		27,000

Goodwill Traceable to the Original Partners. Unrecorded goodwill also may be identifiable. In the previous example, assuming there are no differences between the fair value and book value of recorded assets, the new partner's willingness to pay more than the proportionate book value of the new entity indicates that goodwill existed prior to the new partner's admission. If this intangible asset could have been sold prior to the admission of the partner, the realized profit would have been allocated to the original partners. Therefore, the goodwill is recorded and allocated to the original partners according to their profit and loss ratio. The investment by C is recorded under the goodwill method as follows:

Assets (from C)	27,000	
Goodwill	33,000	
A, Capital		16,500
B, Capital		16,500
C, Capital		27,000

It is important to note that the new partner's capital account balance represents a 20% interest in the total capital of the new partnership, as verified by the following computation:

Original capital	$ 75,000
C's investment	27,000
Goodwill	33,000
	$135,000
C's interest	20%
C's capital balance	$ 27,000

In comparing the assumption that the $33,000 difference was traceable to net appreciation of assets versus goodwill, it should be noted that:

1. In one case, the net appreciation is allocated to specific assets versus goodwill, yet the amount is the same.
2. Some combination of appreciated assets and goodwill could account for the $33,000 difference.
3. The adjusted capital balances of the partners are the same regardless of whether asset appreciation and/or goodwill is recognized.

The recognition of goodwill traceable to the previous partners is criticized by some accountants. If the concept of a new entity is cast aside, some would argue that the goodwill is self-created and, therefore, should not be recognized. Outside of partnership accounting, self-created goodwill is not recognized and only goodwill purchased from another entity may be recognized. To argue that the new partnership is, in substance, a continuation of the previous partnership would prevent the recognition of goodwill traceable to the original partnership. Furthermore, viewing the new partnership as a continuation of the previous partnership may prevent the recognition of appreciation on other assets as well.

It also may be argued that the difficulties associated with the measurement of the fair value of existing assets unjustifiably forces the recognition of goodwill for lack of a more precise analysis. However, the argument that the fair value of a new partnership, as indicated by the new partner's investment, is not objectively or independently determined overlooks the basic nature of the transaction. Negotiations between previous partners and a new partner would be described as arm's length, since both parties involved are independently seeking a fair price.

Asset Write-Downs. Given the same basic facts as in the previous illustrations, assume that C invests $10,000 to acquire a 20% interest in the partnership of A and B. C's investment implies a fair value of the new entity equal to $50,000 ($10,000 ÷ 20%). However, the book value of the new partnership equals $85,000, consisting of the original partners' capital balances of $75,000 plus C's investment of $10,000. This difference between the fair value and the higher book value indicates the existence of unrecorded net write-downs and/or goodwill contributed by the incoming partner.

If objective evidence supports the write-down of existing assets, the previous partners' capital balances would be reduced accordingly in proportion to their profit and loss ratios. The amount of the suggested write-down is calculated by comparing the implied fair value of $50,000 to the $85,000 representing the book value of the previous partnership plus the new partner's investment. Therefore, the difference of $35,000 is equal to the necessary net write-down. Assuming the net write-down is represented by land appreciation of $20,000 and a write-down of $55,000 to inventory, the net write-down would be recorded as follows:

A, Capital	17,500	
B, Capital	17,500	
Land.	20,000	
Inventory		55,000

This reduces the net assets of the previous partnership to $40,000, and the new partner's investment of $10,000 would then represent 20% of the new partnership's total capital of $50,000 ($40,000 + $10,000).

Goodwill Traceable to the New Partner. Assuming net assets of the original partnership are properly valued and should not be written down, it is possible that goodwill may be traceable to the incoming partner. The amount of this contributed goodwill may be computed as the difference between:

1. The amount that should have been paid by the new partner, as indicated by the book value of the previous partnership (calculated by dividing the original book value of the partnership by the total percentage interest of the original partners in the new partnership, and subtracting the original book value),

$$\left[\begin{array}{c} \text{Book Value of} \\ \text{Original} \\ \text{Partnership} \end{array} \div \begin{array}{c} \text{Original Partners'} \\ \text{Interest in \textbf{New}} \\ \text{Partnership} \end{array} \right] - \begin{array}{c} \text{Book Value} \\ \text{of Original} \\ \text{Partnership} \end{array} = \begin{array}{c} \text{New Partner's} \\ \text{Capital Balance} \end{array}$$

and

2. The amount of consideration, excluding any goodwill, contributed by the new partner.

Using the previous example, the $75,000 original book value would represent 80% of the new partnership capital, or $93,750 ($75,000 ÷ 80%). Therefore, it appears that the new partner should have paid $18,750 ($93,750 less the original $75,000 book value) for a 20% interest in the partnership; however, the partner actually paid only $10,000 cash. The difference between what should have been paid ($18,750) and the amount actually paid ($10,000) represents the goodwill traceable to the incoming partner. The investment by C would be recorded under the goodwill method as follows:

Assets.	10,000	
Goodwill	8,750	
C, Capital		18,750

Note that the new partner's capital account balance represents a 20% interest in the total capital of the new partnership, as shown by the following computation:

Original capital.	$75,000
C's investment of cash	10,000
Goodwill	8,750
	$93,750
C's interest.	× 20%
C's capital balance	$18,750

The fact that a new legal entity is created supports the recognition of goodwill and other contributed assets at their fair value. If the concept of a new entity is set aside, the goodwill may be viewed as being purchased by the previous partnership in exchange for partnership equity. Accounting theory and current practice support the recording of goodwill acquired or purchased from other entities.

Revaluation of Assets and Goodwill. The previous examples of accounting for a new partner's investment assumed that either asset revaluations or goodwill recognition were appropriate as mutually exclusive choices. In reality, some combination of the two may be appropriate. Continuing with the previous example, assume that the $75,000 book value of the previous partnership has a fair value of $64,000 and new partner C's investment remains at $10,000.

The first step to be taken is to recognize the write-down of the previous partnership's net assets as follows:

A, Capital	5,500	
B, Capital	5,500	
Assets.		11,000

The adjusted value of the previous partnership, then, is used to determine the goodwill traceable to the new partner. In this example, the $64,000 fair value of the previous partnership would represent 80% of the new partnership capital, or $80,000 ($64,000 ÷ 80%). Therefore, it appears that the new partner should have paid $16,000 ($80,000 less the fair value of the previous partnership) for a 20% interest in the partnership. The difference between what should have been paid ($16,000) and the amount actually paid ($10,000) represents the goodwill traceable to the incoming partner. The entry to record C's investment is as follows:

Assets.	10,000	
Goodwill	6,000	
C, Capital		16,000

Methodology for Determining Goodwill. An analysis of the previous examples reveals that goodwill may be traceable to either the original partners or the incoming partner. To properly apply the goodwill method, the following methodology may be helpful in identifying the origin of the goodwill and its amount:

1. Determine the entity's fair value, as indicated by the new partner's investment (new partner's investment divided by the percentage interest acquired in the partnership).
2. If the fair value determined is:
    a. Greater than the book value of the new partnership adjusted for net appreciation or net write-downs, implied goodwill is traceable to the original partners and is allocated among them according to their original profit ratios. The amount of goodwill is equal to the difference between (1) the fair value indicated by the new partner's investment and (2) the adjusted book value of the new partnership.
    b. Less than the adjusted book value of the new partnership, implied goodwill is traceable to the new partner. The amount of goodwill is equal to the difference between (1) the amount that should have been paid by the new partner to acquire an interest in the adjusted book value of the previous partnership and (2) the actual amount paid.
3. The initial capital balance of the new partner always is equal to the new partner's interest in the total capital of the new partnership after goodwill is recognized.

<table>
<tr><td>**4**</td></tr>
<tr><td>**OBJECTIVE**</td></tr>
<tr><td>Describe the conceptual differences between the bonus and goodwill methods.</td></tr>
</table>

Comparison of Bonus and Goodwill Methods. The bonus method adheres to the historical cost concept and is often used in accounting practice. It is objective in that it establishes total capital of the new partnership at an amount based on actual consideration received from the new partner. The bonus method indirectly acknowledges the existence of appreciation of assets and/or goodwill by giving a bonus to either original or new partners.

The goodwill method results in the recognition of an asset implied by a transaction rather than recognizing an asset actually purchased. Historically, goodwill has been recognized only when purchased so that a more objective measure of its value is established. Therefore, opponents of the goodwill method contend that goodwill is not determined objectively and other factors may have influenced the amount of investment required from the new partner. Also, certain recipients of partnership financial statements may question the valuation of goodwill, since increasing total assets may result in an understatement of the return on total assets or equity. However, in defense of the goodwill method, the current value of net assets, whether tangible or intangible, is reflected on the financial statements resulting in a more relevant measure of invested capital.

Use of the goodwill method could produce inequitable results if either of the following conditions exist:

1. The new partner's interest in profits does not equal the new partner's initial interest in capital.
2. After the formation of the new partnership, the former partners do not share profits and losses in the same relationship to each other as they did before the admission of a new partner.

The importance of these concepts can be illustrated using the following facts:

	Original Partners		New Partner
	A	B	C
Original capital	$30,000	$45,000	
Original profit and loss percentages	50%	50%	
New partner's capital			$27,000
New profit and loss percentages	33⅓%	33⅓%	33⅓%
New partner's interest in capital			20%

The new capital balances that result from using the goodwill method and the bonus method are as follows:

| | Original Partners | | New Partner |
	A	B	C
Goodwill method:			
Goodwill allocation.........................	$16,500	$16,500	
New capital balances	46,500	61,500	$27,000
Bonus method:			
Bonus allocation	3,300	3,300	
New capital balances	33,300	48,300	20,400

Assuming the recorded goodwill proves to be worthless (or experiences impairment of value), the decline in asset value would reduce the partners' capital balances according to their profit and loss ratio as follows:

| | Partners | | | |
	A	B	C	Total
Capital balances if goodwill method is used..........................	$ 46,500	$ 61,500	$ 27,000	$135,000
Goodwill impairment	(11,000)	(11,000)	(11,000)	(33,000)
Capital balances after impairment	$ 35,500	$ 50,500	$ 16,000·	$102,000
Capital balances if bonus method is used .	33,300	48,300	20,400	102,000
Differences.........................	$ 2,200	$ 2,200	$ (4,400)	$ 0

The capital balances that result from using the two methods are different because the new partner's interest in profits and interest in capital are not equal. In this illustration, C acquired a 20% capital interest and a 33⅓% interest in profits. Therefore, C paid for 20% of the implied goodwill but had to absorb 33⅓% of the goodwill impairment.

To further illustrate these concepts, assume the same facts, except that the new profit and loss percentages are 50%, 30%, and 20% for Partners A, B, and C, respectively. If the recorded goodwill proves to be worthless, the decline in asset value would affect the partners' capital balances as follows:

| | Partners | | | |
	A	B	C	Total
Capital balances if goodwill method is used..........................	$ 46,500	$61,500	$27,000	$135,000
Goodwill impairment	(16,500)	(9,900)	(6,600)	(33,000)
Capital balances after impairment	$ 30,000	$51,600	$20,400	$102,000
Capital balances if bonus method is used .	33,300	48,300	20,400	102,000
Differences.........................	$ (3,300)	$ 3,300	$ 0	$ 0

In this case, Partners A and B shared equally in the initial recording of goodwill but unequally in the subsequent impairment of goodwill.

Now, assume the same facts, except that the new profit and loss percentages are 40%, 40%, and 20% for Partners A, B, and C, respectively. After the impairment of goodwill, the capital balances would be identical to those achieved under the bonus method, as indicated in the table shown on page 732.

	Partners			
	A	B	C	Total
Capital balances if goodwill method is used....	$ 46,500	$ 61,500	$27,000	$135,000
Goodwill impairment	(13,200)	(13,200)	(6,600)	(33,000)
Capital balances after impairment	$ 33,300	$ 48,300	$20,400	$102,000
Capital balances if bonus method is used	33,300	48,300	20,400	102,000
Differences................................	$ 0	$ 0	$ 0	$ 0

The equality between the capital balances is achieved because neither of the two conditions that produce inequities exists. If these conditions do exist, preference is given, typically, to the bonus method because of the possible inequities that may result from the impairment of goodwill.

5

OBJECTIVE

Account for the admission of a new partner through direct contribution to an existing partner.

Contribution of Assets to Existing Partners. A new partner also may be admitted to the partnership by acquiring all or part of the capital interest of one or more existing partners in exchange for some consideration (assets). In this case, **the new partner deals directly with an existing partner or partners** rather than with the partnership entity. Therefore, the acquisition price is paid to the selling partner(s) and not to the partnership itself. The partnership records the redistribution of capital interests by transferring all or a portion of the seller's capital to the new partner's capital account but does not record the transfer of any assets.

To illustrate, assume the following facts:

		Percentage Interest in	
Existing Partners	Capital Balance	Capital	Profit
Partner A	$30,000	40%	50%
Partner B	45,000	60	50

Now, assume new Partner C purchased 50% of A's interest in capital and 50% of B's interest in capital in exchange for $50,000. This purchase resulted in C's having a 50% interest in the total partnership capital.

There are several alternative ways of recording the contribution of assets by C to the existing partners. If the consideration paid by the incoming partner is not used to impute the fair value of the partnership, the transaction would be recorded by the partnership entity as follows:

A, Capital (50% × $30,000)	15,000	
B, Capital (50% × $45,000)	22,500	
C, Capital		37,500

The $50,000 actually paid by C was not used as a basis for the entry because it represents consideration paid to the individual partners personally rather than to the partnership entity. This accounting treatment frequently is compared to that of a corporation when a stockholder sells shares or an interest in corporate capital to another investor in the corporation. The corporation does not record the transaction or use it as a basis for revaluing corporate assets but merely acknowledges the changing identity of its shareholders. The preceding entry would also be appropriate if the existing partners had sold their interests for less than book value. Even though depreciation of existing assets is suggested, such depreciation is not recorded because the transaction did not involve the partnership entity itself.

An alternative but less frequently used method of recording this transaction would be to impute the fair value of the partnership entity from the consideration paid by the new partner. For example, if C paid $50,000 to acquire a 50% interest in the capital of the partnership vis-à-vis the individual partners, the total implied current value of the original partnership would be $100,000 ($50,000 ÷ 50%). The difference between the imputed value of $100,000 and the partnership's previous book value of $75,000 ($30,000 + $45,000) is interpreted to represent undervalued existing assets and/or goodwill traceable to the original partnership. This alternative interpretation would result in recording the transaction as shown on page 733.

Assets and/or Goodwill	25,000	
A, Capital		12,500
B, Capital.		12,500
To record the previously unrecognized increase in value of the partnership		
A, Capital [50% × ($30,000 + $12,500)]	21,250	
B, Capital [50% × ($45,000 + $12,500)]	28,750	
C, Capital		50,000
To record the transfer of the original partners' adjusted capital to incoming Partner C.		

Normally, this alternative method is not employed because (a) the transaction was not between the partnership and the incoming partner but, rather, between individual partners and (b) the consideration paid by the incoming partner may not provide a reliable indicator of the partnership entity's current value. However, the method may provide useful information for deciding how to allocate the acquisition price between the selling partners. The selling partners' original capital plus their share of any imputed value increments may indicate the current values for which the incoming partner was paying. For example, the purchase price of $50,000 may be allocated to Partners A and B as follows:

	Partners		
	A	B	Total
Original capital	$30,000	$45,000	$ 75,000
Share of value increment	12,500	12,500	25,000
Total imputed value	$42,500	$57,500	$100,000
Percentage acquired by new partner	× 50%	× 50%	× 50%
Total purchase price	$21,250	$28,750	$ 50,000

Withdrawal of a Partner

When a partner withdraws, the partnership agreement should be consulted to determine whether any guidelines have been established that would influence the procedure. The withdrawal of a partner requires a determination of the fair value of the partnership entity and a measurement of partnership income to the date of withdrawal. Also, in many cases, the equity of the retiring partner may not be equal to the partner's capital balance as a result of (a) the existence of accounting errors, (b) differences between the fair value and the recorded book value of assets, and/or (c) unrecorded assets such as goodwill.

If accounting errors are discovered, they should be treated as prior-period adjustments and corrected by adjusting the capital balances of the partners. Theoretically, an error should be allocated to partners' capital balances according to the profit and loss ratio that existed when the error was committed. Therefore, it is necessary to identify the period to which the error is traceable. This practice can become complicated, and a well-designed partnership agreement should include procedures for dealing with the correction of errors.

Recognizing differences between book value and fair value may be as appropriate when an individual withdraws from the partnership as when an individual is admitted. If accounting recognition of such differences is not desired, however, these differences nevertheless should influence the amount to be paid to the withdrawing partner.

The Selling of an Interest to Existing Partners. As is the case with the admission of a partner, the withdrawal of a partner may involve (a) a transaction with existing partners or a new partner or (b) a transaction with the partnership entity itself. In the first case, the equity of the withdrawing partner will be purchased with the personal assets of existing or new partners rather than with the assets of the partnership.

6

OBJECTIVE

Explain the impact of a partner's withdrawal from the partnership.

To illustrate, assume the following:

	Partners		
	A	B	C
Capital balance.	$30,000	$50,000	$20,000
Profit and loss percentages	40%	40%	20%
Percentage interest in capital.	30%	50%	20%

Now assume Partner A withdraws from the partnership and C uses personal funds to purchase A's interest at its current value of $36,000. If the price paid by C is not used to impute the value of the entity, the transaction would be recorded as follows:

| A, Capital . . . . | 30,000 | |
| C, Capital . . . . | | 30,000 |

The above entry also may be appropriate if the existing partners sold their interests for less than book value. Even though depreciation of existing assets is suggested, such depreciation is not recorded because the transaction did not involve the partnership entity itself. As previously discussed, an alternative treatment would be to recognize any suggested appreciation or write-downs indicated by the transaction and then transfer the adjusted capital balances.

The Selling of an Interest to the Partnership. When a withdrawing partner sells an interest to the partnership rather than to an individual partner, the bonus or goodwill methods may be employed. The bonus method is used most frequently, but the choice between methods should be based on a thorough analysis of the transaction. Using the same facts as in the previous illustration and assuming the use of the bonus method, the purchase of A's equity by the partnership would be recorded as follows:

A, Capital	30,000	
B, Capital	4,000	
C, Capital	2,000	
Cash		36,000

The entry indicates that the remaining partners granted a bonus to A, measured by the difference between the recorded capital and the fair value of A's equity. The bonus is charged to the remaining partners according to their proportionate profit and loss ratio.

The goodwill method focuses on the payment to the withdrawing partner as an indication of the fair value of the partnership. If the imputed goodwill or undervalued assets were disposed of, the partners would divide the gain according to their profit and loss ratio. Assuming existing assets are properly valued, the $36,000 payment to A consists of A's capital balance of $30,000 plus a $6,000 share of the unrecorded goodwill. Therefore, the $6,000 represents A's 40% interest in total goodwill of $15,000 ($6,000 ÷ 40%). Notice that the $6,000 represents A's interest in the gain, which would be realized if the unrecorded goodwill were sold. Therefore, A's profit percentage is used to suggest the total value of the goodwill.

Two alternatives are now available: (a) recognize only the goodwill that is traceable to the retiring partner or (b) recognize the amount of goodwill traceable to the entire entity. The first alternative stresses the importance of recognizing only the amount of goodwill that actually is purchased from the withdrawing partner. Using this alternative, A's withdrawal would be recorded as follows:

Goodwill	6,000	
A, Capital		6,000
A, Capital	36,000	
Cash		36,000

If the amount of goodwill traceable to the entire entity is recognized, the goodwill would be allocated to the partners according to their profit and loss ratio, as reflected in the following entries to record A's withdrawal:

Goodwill	15,000	
A, Capital		6,000
B, Capital.		6,000
C, Capital		3,000
A, Capital	36,000	
Cash		36,000

Whether part or all of the goodwill is recognized, opponents of this procedure contend that transactions between partners should not be viewed as arm's length; therefore, the measure of goodwill may not be determined objectively. Also, inequitable results may be produced if the remaining partners subsequently change their profit and loss ratio.

It is important to note that a withdrawing partner could sell his/her interest in a partnership for less than book value. If that interest is sold to the partnership, the following recognition would take place depending on whether the bonus or goodwill method is employed:

1. Bonus method: A bonus traceable to the remaining partners would be recognized. The bonus would be measured as the difference between the withdrawing partner's capital balance and the consideration paid for the partner's interest.
2. Goodwill method: Paying less than the withholding partner's capital balance (book value) would suggest that existing assets are overvalued. A write-down of existing assets would be recognized as the difference between the withdrawing partner's capital balance and the consideration paid for the partner's interest. As an alternative, the asset write-down traceable to the entire entity could be recognized based on the amount suggested by the transaction with the withholding partner. The write-down traceable to the withdrawing partner represents his/her percentage interest (based on profit and loss ratios) in the asset write-down traceable to the entire entity.

Effects of a Partner's Withdrawal. When the interest of a withdrawing partner is acquired by the remaining partners or the partnership, serious demands upon the liquidity of the partners and the partnership may result. If withdrawal is due to the death of the partner, funds may be provided from the proceeds of life insurance policies taken out by the partnership itself or by individual partners. For example, if Partner A takes out a life insurance policy on Partner B, and B subsequently dies, the proceeds payable to A may be used to acquire B's interest.

The Uniform Partnership Act (RUPA), in Article 7, addresses the purchase of a dissociated partner's interest when the business is not wound up. Factors addressed include the "buyout" price, deferred payment, and the determination of interest on unpaid amounts. Once again, a partnership agreement that addresses the valuation of a withdrawing partner's interest and the means of payment is a valuable aid in properly accounting for the withdrawal of a partner.

REFLECTION

- A change in the ownership structure of a partnership provides an opportunity to recognize and value the net assets of the partnership.

- The bonus and goodwill methods are alternative methods of accounting for the change in ownership of a partnership when a new partner acquires an interest from the partnership entity itself.

- The more conservative bonus method only recognizes declines in the value of net assets suggested by a change in ownership.

- The goodwill method recognizes both increases and decreases in the value of net assets.

- If a new partner acquires an interest in the partnership directly from a partner(s) as compared to from the partnership entity itself, neither the bonus nor goodwill methods are employed.

- A partner may withdraw by selling his or her interest to individual partners or to the partnership itself. When a partner withdraws by selling an interest to the partnership, the bonus and goodwill methods are alternative methods of accounting for the change.

<table>
<tr><td>

7

OBJECTIVE

Describe the order in which assets must be distributed upon liquidation of a partnership, and explain the right-of-offset concept.

</td></tr>
</table>

PARTNERSHIP LIQUIDATION

The withdrawal or admission of a partner normally does not mean that the previous partnership is dissolved. However, the occurrence of certain events does result in the dissolution of the partnership and the winding up of its business. In essence, the partnership is liquidated resulting in the conversion of partnership assets into a distributable form and the distribution of these assets to creditors and owners. Examples of events that will result in the liquidation or winding up of a partnership may include, in part, the following:

1. In a partnership at will, notice from a partner of his or her express will to withdraw as a partner. A *partnership at will* is a partnership in which the partners have not agreed to remain as partners for a specified term or until a particular undertaking is completed. In essence, such a partner can force liquidation. However, this is a default rule, and a partnership agreement may allow other partners to continue the business. Furthermore, RUPA does provide for the ability of the remaining partners to waive the right to liquidate and terminate the partnership.

2. In a partnership with a definite term or specific undertaking, the death of a partner, the express will of all partners to liquidate the partnership, or the expiration of the term or the completion of the specific undertaking.

3. The occurrence of an event which, as agreed to in the partnership agreement, will result in liquidation.

4. An event that makes it unlawful to continue the partnership or upon the occurrence of a judicial determination that suggests it is not practical to continue the partnership.

Given an event that causes the winding up or liquidation of a partnership, fundamental guidelines must be adhered to in order to ensure an orderly and legally sound liquidation.

Liquidation Guidelines

The underlying theme in accounting for partnership liquidation is the equitable distribution of the assets. To be equitable, a distribution should recognize the legal rights of the partnership creditors and individual partners. All liquidation expenses and gains or losses from conversion of partnership assets also must be allocated to the partners before assets actually are distributed to the individual partners. Failure to consider these factors may result in the premature or incorrect distribution of assets to a partner. If a premature or incorrect distribution of assets cannot be recovered, the partnership fiduciary who authorized the distribution may be held liable.

The Settlement of Accounts and Contributions to Partners. The RUPA establishes rules governing the priority in which partnership assets are distributed to creditors and partners. Subject to any agreement to the contrary, the following sequence must be followed:

1. Assets of the partnership must first be used to discharge obligations to creditors. Creditors include partners who are creditors on parity with other creditors.

2. Profits and losses, including those resulting from the liquidation, must be allocated to the individual partner's accounts. Therefore, upon allocation, such profits or losses become part of a partner's capital balance.

3. A partner with a debit (deficit) capital balance shall make a contribution to the partnership of an amount equal to the debit balance. If the partner is not able to totally eliminate the debit balance, all other partners shall contribute the deficiency in proportion to the manner in which those partners share losses. If a partner contributes more than the proportionate share, he or she may recover the excess from the other partners.

4. Liquidating distributions should be made to partners to the extent that they have credit (surplus) capital balances.
5. After settlement of the partners' accounts, each partner shall contribute, in proportion to the manner in which they share losses, an amount necessary to settle partnership obligations that were not known at the time of the settlement.

Although amounts due partners that represent obligations on parity with other creditors (such as a loan from a partner) have a higher legal priority than amounts owed to partners as capital, the doctrine of *right of offset* sets aside this ranking in favor of procedural and economic considerations that facilitate the actual liquidation process. This doctrine is not addressed in the RUPA but may be incorporated in the partnership agreement. The effect of this doctrine is that amounts due to partners as creditors are combined with the respective partners' capital balances. Without the right of offset, it would be possible to distribute assets to a partner in payment of their creditor balance while at the same time the partner has a debit capital account balance. In order to eliminate the debit capital balance, the partnership would have to recover personal assets from the partner. Therefore, it is possible for the partnership to distribute assets to the partner and then try to recover assets from the partner, hoping that such assets are still available. The doctrine of right of offset eliminates this problem by combining the loan and capital balances. The right of offset doctrine should be applied when solving the end-of-chapter exercises and problems.

Liability for Debit Capital Balances. The RUPA states that partners should contribute assets to the partnership to the extent of their debit capital balances. However, if such a contribution is not possible, the RUPA states that the other partners should make additional capital contributions totaling the debit or deficit balance. As a practical matter, the remaining debit balance will typically be viewed as a realization loss and allocated according to the remaining partners' loss ratio rather than requiring an actual contribution of additional capital. It is possible for a partnership agreement to set forth separate loss ratios for operating losses as compared to capital losses. To illustrate, assume Partners A, B, and C share in profits and losses in the ratio of 1:2:1, respectively. If C is unable to contribute any asset needed to eliminate a debit capital balance, that balance would be allocated to A and B in the ratio of 1:2. Partners who absorb other partners' debit capital balances may maintain an action against the deficit partner for legal or equitable relief. However, the collectability of such a claim depends on the personal wealth of the deficient partners.

Under common law and federal bankruptcy law, amounts owed to partners by way of contribution are on an equal basis (*pari passu*) with personal creditors of the partner. For example, assume a partner has personal assets of $12,000, personal liabilities of $8,000, and a debit capital balance of $16,000. According to this rule, the $12,000 of personal assets would be distributed as follows:

Payable to personal liabilities [($8,000 ÷ $24,000) × $12,000]	$ 4,000
Payable to partnership for debit capital balance [($16,000 ÷ $24,000) × $12,000]	8,000
Total personal assets	$12,000

It is important to note that in the above example recovery for a debit (deficit) capital balance may be a time-consuming process. In practice, a deficit partner may not volunteer to contribute toward a deficit capital balance; in order to move the liquidation process forward, the remaining partners absorb all or part of the deficit balance. Although the absorbing partners have a claim against the deficit partner, such claims may be difficult to perfect.

Unsatisfied Partnership Creditors. In the winding up of a partnership, the first priority is to discharge the obligations of the partnership to creditors. However, if the partnership does not have adequate assets to fully dismiss these creditors, the unsatisfied creditors must look to the personal assets of the individual partners. This illustrates the fact that a partner is characterized by unlimited liability as discussed in the previous chapter. Prior to the RUPA, under what was referred to as *dual priority*, partnership creditors had first priority against the partnership assets and a partner's individual creditors had first priority against the partner's personal assets. However, under Section 807 of the current RUPA, unsatisfied partnership creditors share pro rata with the partners' personal or individual creditors in the assets of the partners' estate. Therefore, the priorities under the dual priority rule have been eliminated and are now in conformity with current bankruptcy law. For example, assume that a partnership has unsatisfied creditors in the amount of $16,000 and one or more partners, therefore, must have a debit (deficit) capital balance. If no additional contributions of capital are forthcoming, the unsatisfied creditors may seek recovery against any partner. Assume they seek

8

OBJECTIVE

Understand the treatment for capital deficiencies and unsatisfied creditors.

recovery from a partner with personal assets of $12,000 and personal liabilities of $8,000. The personal assets would be allocated between personal creditors and partnership creditors as follows:

Payable to personal liabilities [($8,000 ÷ $24,000) × $12,000]	$ 4,000
Payable to partnership for unsatisfied creditors [($16,000 ÷ $24,000) × $12,000]	8,000
Total personal assets	$12,000

The $8,000 contributed to the partnership by the partner would increase his or her capital balance, and the remaining $8,000 ($16,000 − $8,000) of partnership creditors would then attempt to seek recovery from the other partners. Although not specifically addressed by the RUPA, if an individual partner were personally insolvent, unsatisfied personal creditors could attach to a partner's capital balance in a solvent partnership but only to the extent of their capital balance.

The discharge of unsatisfied partnership creditors and personal creditors is demonstrated by the following cases:

Case 1
Insolvent Partnership

The partnership is insolvent, with unsatisfied liabilities of $2,000. Information relating to the individual partners is as follows:

	Partner A	Partner B
Total personal assets	$10,000	$ 6,000
Total personal liabilities.	6,000	6,000
Partnership capital balances	500	(2,500)

Analysis: The unsatisfied partnership creditors first move against Partner A and then Partner B as follows:

Because A's personal liabilities of $6,000 plus the $2,000 of partnership creditors are less than A's personal assets, A will be able to contribute $2,000 to the partnership.

	AB Partnership			
	Assets	Liabilities	A, Capital	B, Capital
Beginning balances.	$ —	$ 2,000	$ 500	$(2,500)
Capital contribution.	2,000		2,000	—
Payment of liabilities	(2,000)	(2,000)		
Balances	$ —	$ —	$2,500	$(2,500)

Because B has no net personal assets to contribute, Partner A will absorb B's capital deficit and seek to recover from B at a later time.

Case 2
Insolvent Partnership

The partnership is insolvent, with unsatisfied liabilities of $2,000. Information relating to the individual partners is as follows:

	Partner A	Partner B
Total personal assets	$10,000	$ 6,000
Total personal liabilities.	6,000	6,000
Partnership capital balances	500	(2,500)

Analysis: The unsatisfied partnership creditors first move against Partner B and then Partner A as follows:

Because B's personal liabilities of $6,000 plus the $2,000 of partnership creditors are greater than B's personal assets, the assets allocated to the partnership are 2/8ths of the assets. Therefore, 2/8 × $6,000 of personal assets, or $1,500, will be contributed to the partnership. Partner A has adequate personal assets to contribute another $500 to the partnership.

	AB Partnership			
	Assets	Liabilities	A, Capital	B, Capital
Beginning balances....	$ —	$ 2,000	$ 500	$(2,500)
Capital contribution....	1,500			1,500
Payment of liabilities ...	(1,500)	(1,500)		
Balances	—	500	500	(1,000)
Capital contribution....	500		500	
Payment of liabilities ...	(500)	(500)		
Balances	$ —	$ —	$1,000	$(1,000)

Because B has no more net personal assets to contribute, Partner A will absorb B's capital deficit and seek to recover from B at a later time.

Case 3
Insolvent Partner

The partnership is solvent, with total assets of $16,000 and total liabilities of $9,000. Information relating to the individual partners is as follows:

	Partner A	Partner B
Total personal assets	$10,000	$15,000
Total personal liabilities.................	13,000	18,000
Partnership capital balances	5,000	2,000

Analysis: Unsatisfied personal creditors may attach a partner's interest in the solvent partnership but only to the extent of the partner's capital balance. Thus, unsatisfied personal creditors seek recourse as follows:

	Partner A	Partner B
Unsatisfied personal creditors	$ 3,000	$ 3,000
Interest in partnership capital available to personal creditors	(3,000)	(2,000)
Personal liabilities not satisfied	$ 0	$ 1,000

Lump-Sum Liquidations

9

OBJECTIVE

Calculate the assets to be distributed to a given partner in a lump-sum or installment liquidation, and understand the concept of maximum loss absorbable.

The guidelines discussed in the preceding section are important factors influencing the procedural and legal aspects of a partnership liquidation. Upon liquidation of a partnership, the amount of assets ultimately to be distributed to the individual partners is determined through the use of either a lump-sum liquidation schedule or an installment liquidation schedule. A *lump-sum liquidation* requires that all assets be realized before a distribution is made to partners, thus avoiding the possibility of a premature distribution.

To illustrate a lump-sum liquidation, assume the following:

1. Asset, liability, loan, and capital balances are as shown in Illustration 14-1, after books for the final operational period are closed.

2. Profit and loss percentages for Partners A, B, and C are 40%, 40%, and 20%, respectively.
3. Personal assets and debts of the partners are as follows:

	A	B	C
Total personal assets	$30,000	$40,000	$20,000
Total personal liabilities..............................	10,000	37,200	24,000

Partners contribute to debit capital balances to the extent of their net personal assets.

4. Sales of assets are as follows:

Date	Book Value	Selling Price	Gain (Loss)
February 15	$50,000	$60,000	$ 10,000
March 2	30,000	10,000	(20,000)
March 7	40,000	20,000	(20,000)

5. Total liquidation expenses of $2,000 are paid on March 4.

Illustration 14-1
Lump-Sum Liquidation Statement

	Cash	Noncash Assets	Liabilities	Loan from A	Capital Balances A	B	C
Beginning balances.........	$ 10,000	$120,000	$ 80,000	$ 9,000	$ 25,000	$10,000	$ 6,000
February 15, sale of assets at a gain	60,000	(50,000)			4,000	4,000	2,000
March 2, sale of assets at a loss...............	10,000	(30,000)			(8,000)	(8,000)	(4,000)
Payment of liquidation expenses..............	(2,000)				(800)	(800)	(400)
March 7, sale of assets at a loss...............	20,000	(40,000)			(8,000)	(8,000)	(4,000)
Balances	$ 98,000	$ 0	$ 80,000	$ 9,000	$ 12,200	$ (2,800)	$ (400)
Payment of liabilities	(80,000)		(80,000)				
Balances	$ 18,000	$ 0	$ 0	$ 9,000	$ 12,200	$ (2,800)	$ (400)
B's contribution	2,800					2,800	
Balances	$ 20,800	$ 0	$ 0	$ 9,000	$ 12,200	$ 0	$ (400)
Absorption of C's balance....					(400)		400
Balances	$ 20,800	$ 0	$ 0	$ 9,000	$ 11,800	$ 0	$ 0
Payment to A	(20,800)			(9,000)	(11,800)		
Final balances	$ 0	$ 0	$ 0	$ 0	$ 0	$ 0	$ 0

Illustration 14-1 presents the lump-sum distribution and demonstrates the following concepts that were discussed previously:

1. Gains and losses on realization are allocated according to the partners' profit and loss ratio.
2. Claims against the partnership are paid in the proper order subject to the concept of the right of offset.
3. Partners with debit (deficit) capital balances should contribute personal assets to whatever extent possible in order to eliminate the deficit.

4. C's debit capital balance is charged against A, the only partner with a credit capital balance.

5. Partner A will have a claim against C's future personal assets for the debit balance that was absorbed.

Installment Liquidations

10

OBJECTIVE

Prepare an installment liquidation statement and a schedule of safe payments.

The complete liquidation process might extend over several months or longer, and it may not be possible to postpone payments to creditors and partners until all assets have been realized. Therefore, payments may be made on an installment basis to creditors and partners during the liquidation process. To avoid the problem associated with premature or incorrect distributions to partners, installment payments may be made to partners only after anticipating all liabilities, possible losses, and liquidation expenses. To provide a proper solution to installment liquidations, generally a *schedule of safe payments,* showing appropriate distributions to partners, is prepared as amounts become available for distribution.

Schedule of Safe Payments. The possibility of premature payments to partners is reduced by using a schedule of safe payments, which reflects a conservative approach to liquidation. The schedule indicates how available funds should be distributed to partners. It is based on the anticipation of all possible liabilities and expenses, including those expected to be incurred in the process of liquidation. The effect of these items on partnership capital is allocated among the partners according to their profit and loss agreement.

In keeping with the conservative approach, the schedule also is based on the assumption that all noncash assets will be worthless; therefore, the assumed loss is allocated among the partners according to their profit and loss ratio. The allocation of the assumed loss could produce debit balances in partners' capital accounts, and these balances are treated as being uncollectible. Therefore, the assumed debit capital balances are allocated to those partners with credit balances according to their proportionate profit and loss ratio. When the allocation of estimated liabilities, expenses, liquidation losses, and debit balances is completed, assets may be distributed safely to the partners in amounts equal to the resulting credit capital balances.

A new schedule of safe payments is prepared each time a distribution to partners is scheduled. These schedules support an installment liquidation statement, which summarizes changes in real account balances as the liquidation proceeds. When the partners' combined capital and loan balances are in the profit and loss ratio, all partners will share in a given distribution. All future distributions to partners will be allocated automatically according to their profit ratio, thus eliminating the need for another schedule of safe payments.

To illustrate the use of schedules of safe payments in conjunction with an installment liquidation, assume the following:

1. Asset, liability, loan, and capital balances are shown, in Illustration 14-2, after books for the final operational period are closed.

2. Profit and loss percentages for Partners A, B, and C are 40%, 40%, and 20%, respectively.

3. Sales of assets are as follows:

Date	Book Value	Selling Price	Gain (Loss)
February 15	$60,000	$40,000	$(20,000)
March 2	30,000	15,000	(15,000)
March 17	10,000	20,000	10,000
April 1	20,000	24,000	4,000

4. Liquidation expenses are estimated to be $10,000. Cash is to be restricted in that amount until expenses are paid.

5. Installment distributions of unrestricted cash are made on February 17, March 5, March 18, and April 2.

6. Total liquidation expenses of $8,000 are paid on March 4.

Illustration 14-2
Installment Liquidation Statement

| | | Noncash | | | Capital Balances | | |
	Cash	Assets	Liabilities	Loan from A	A	B	C
Beginning balances............	$ 10,000	$120,000	$ 30,000	$ 5,000	$25,000	$ 55,000	$15,000
February 15, sale of assets	40,000	(60,000)			(8,000)	(8,000)	(4,000)
Balances	$ 50,000	$ 60,000	$ 30,000	$ 5,000	$17,000	$ 47,000	$11,000
Payment of liabilities	(30,000)		(30,000)				
February 17, distribution							
(Schedule A)	(10,000)					(10,000)	
Balances	$ 10,000	$ 60,000	$ 0	$ 5,000	$17,000	$ 37,000	$11,000
March 2, sale of assets	15,000	(30,000)			(6,000)	(6,000)	(3,000)
Payment of liquidation							
expenses....................	(8,000)				(3,200)	(3,200)	(1,600)
Balances	$ 17,000	$ 30,000	$ 0	$ 5,000	$ 7,800	$ 27,800	$ 6,400
March 5, distribution							
(Schedule A)	(17,000)			(800)		(15,800)	(400)
Balances*	$ 0	$ 30,000	$ 0	$ 4,200	$ 7,800	$ 12,000	$ 6,000
March 17, sale of assets	20,000	(10,000)			4,000	4,000	2,000
Balances	$ 20,000	$ 20,000	$ 0	$ 4,200	$11,800	$ 16,000	$ 8,000
March 18, distribution							
(per P&L ratios)	(20,000)			(4,200)	(3,800)	(8,000)	(4,000)
Balances	$ 0	$ 20,000	$ 0	$ 0	$ 8,000	$ 8,000	$ 4,000
April 1, sale of assets...........	24,000	(20,000)	0	0	1,600	1,600	800
Balances	$ 24,000	$ 0	$ 0	$ 0	$ 9,600	$ 9,600	$ 4,800
Final distribution	(24,000)				(9,600)	(9,600)	(4,800)
Balances	$ 0	$ 0	$ 0	$ 0	$ 0	$ 0	$ 0

Schedule A—Schedule of Safe Payments

	A	B	C	Total
Profit and loss percentages	40%	40%	20%	100%
February 17 Distribution:				
Combined capital and loan balances before distribution	$ 22,000	$ 47,000	$ 11,000	$ 80,000
Estimated liquidation expenses	(4,000)	(4,000)	(2,000)	(10,000)
Balances	$ 18,000	$ 43,000	$ 9,000	$ 70,000
Maximum loss possible	(24,000)	(24,000)	(12,000)	(60,000)
Balances	$ (6,000)	$ 19,000	$ (3,000)	$ 10,000
Allocation of debit capital balances	6,000	(9,000)	3,000	0
Safe payment..	$ 0	$ 10,000	$ 0	$ 10,000
March 5 Distribution:				
Combined capital and loan balances before distribution	$ 12,800	$ 27,800	$ 6,400	$ 47,000
Maximum loss possible	(12,000)	(12,000)	(6,000)	(30,000)
Safe payments	$ 800	$ 15,800	$ 400	$ 17,000

* Note that the combined capital and loan balances for A, B, and C are $12,000, $12,000, and $6,000, respectively, and in total are $30,000. These balances are in the profit and loss ratios of 40%, 40%, and 20%, respectively. Therefore, subsequent to this point, all distributions will be allocated per the profit and loss ratio.

Illustration 14-2 is based on these facts and demonstrates the following concepts:

1. Gains and losses on realization are allocated according to the partners' profit and loss ratio.
2. Unsold noncash assets are assumed to be worthless for purposes of determining the safe payments to partners.
3. Loan balances are combined with capital balances according to the right of offset doctrine. This offset can result in partners receiving distributions of capital before other partners' loan accounts have been paid (as in the February 17 distribution in Illustration 14-2). However, such distributions may be placed in escrow until it is certain that debit balances will not develop in these partners' capital accounts.
4. Distributions are applied to a partner's loan balance before they are applied to the partner's capital balance.
5. Typically, debit capital balances are ignored until all assets have been realized, at which time debit balances in partners' capital accounts may be satisfied through contributions of personal assets.
6. A schedule of safe payments is an iterative process that will cease when the schedule indicates that a given distribution will be shared among all partners. Further distributions will be allocated among the partners according to their profit and loss ratio. For example, when the March 5 distribution in Schedule A indicates that all partners will receive a portion of the distribution, the distribution on March 18 would be made in the profit and loss ratio, with results identical to those that would have been indicated by continuing the schedule of safe payments.
7. The partner with the greatest ability to absorb anticipated losses (i.e., to preserve a credit capital balance after allocating anticipated losses) will be the first to receive a safe payment.

It is important to further understand the significance of item (7) above. In a worst-case scenario, during an installment liquidation, anticipated losses could arise from liquidation expenses, losses on the sale of assets, and the assumption of another partner's deficit balance. Obviously, the stronger a given partner is in terms of absorbing these losses, the more likely it is that the partner will receive a distribution during the course of the liquidation. The strength of the partner is measured by the maximum loss that they could absorb.

In order to calculate a partner's initial *maximum loss absorbable* (MLA), all anticipated but unrecorded liabilities and liquidation expenses are allocated to the various partners' capital balances according to their profit and loss ratio. The resulting capital balances then are evaluated to determine the maximum loss from realization that could be absorbed by the partners before a debit balance is created in each of their capital accounts. As suggested by the schedule of safe payments, the partner who maintains a credit capital balance after assuming that all noncash assets are worthless is the partner with the greatest ability to absorb realization losses. Therefore, that partner will be the first to receive an actual distribution of assets.

The maximum loss a partner could absorb, before a debit balance in the partner's capital account is created, is determined by the following calculation:

$$\text{Maximum Loss Absorbable (MLA)} = \frac{\text{Partner's Capital Balance}}{\text{Partner's Profit and Loss Percentage}}$$

Since the partner with the largest initial MLA will be the first to receive an actual distribution, the MLAs are used to indicate the order in which partners will receive distributions. However, it should be noted that the MLAs do not indicate the amounts of the distributions. To illustrate, assume a partnership consists of three partners (A, B, and C) who have capital balances, before the realization of noncash assets, of $70,000, $60,000, and $40,000, respectively, and profit and loss percentages of 35%, 25%, and 40%, respectively. The maximum losses absorbable by Partners A, B, and C are determined as follows:

Partner	(1) Capital Balance	(2) Profit and Loss Percentage	(1) ÷ (2) Maximum Loss Absorbable	Rank
A	$70,000	35%	$200,000	Second
B	60,000	25	240,000	First
C	40,000	40	100,000	Third

If all partners had identical MLAs, all partners would share in any given distribution. Therefore, the amount of any distribution to be paid to a particular partner can be determined by calculating the distributions needed ultimately to give all partners the same MLA. In the present example, Partner B should receive distributions first, until his/her MLA is equal to the next highest MLA of $200,000. If B's capital balance was reduced to $50,000 (next highest MLA multiplied by the partner's profit and loss percentage, $200,000 × 25%) as the result of an actual distribution of $10,000, B's new MLA would be equal to A's original MLA as follows:

Partner	(1) Capital Balance	(2) Profit and Loss Percentage	(1) ÷ (2) Maximum Loss Absorbable
A	$70,000	35%	$200,000
B	50,000	25	200,000
C	40,000	40	100,000

Therefore, the first $10,000, or any portion thereof, that is available for distribution to partners should be paid entirely to Partner B.

Partners A and B should now receive distributions until their MLAs of $200,000 are reduced to the next highest MLA of $100,000, traceable to Partner C. If A's capital balance was reduced to $35,000 ($100,000 × 35%) and B's capital balance was reduced to $25,000 ($100,000 × 25%) as the result of actual distributions of $35,000 and $25,000, respectively, to these partners, all partners would then have equivalent MLAs. This suggests that the next $60,000 ($35,000 + $25,000), or any portion thereof, that is available for distribution to partners should be paid to Partners A and B according to the profit ratio of 35:25 and all further distributions should be divided among all partners according to their respective profit ratio.

Knowledge of a partner's maximum loss absorbable is helpful in developing a general sense for which partners would be most likely to receive a distribution and to what extent during the course of an installment liquidation. Furthermore, this knowledge can also be used to develop a formal predistribution plan that would be followed during the course of the liquidation. However, if there should be any difference between the anticipated but unrecorded liabilities and liquidation expenses and the actual amounts, the predistribution plan would need to be revised. Therefore, a formal predistribution plan may have limited use in practice.

REFLECTION

- Upon liquidation of a partnership, the distribution of available assets must follow a prescribed order.

- The right-of-offset doctrine is important in a liquidation in order to make sure that partners with the potential for debit capital balances do not receive premature distributions of assets.

- When there are unsatisfied partnership creditors, such creditors may seek to recover against a partner's personal assets. The personal assets are allocated proportionately between the partner's personal creditors and the unsatisfied partnership creditors.

- The actual liquidation of a partnership may follow several approaches, including a lump-sum liquidation or an installment liquidation supported by a schedule of safe payments.

- In all cases, the goal is to convert assets into a distributable form, respect the rights of those with claims against the partnership, and not make premature distributions. The calculation of partners' maximum loss absorbable provides insight regarding the order in which partners are likely to receive distributions.

UNDERSTANDING THE ISSUES

1. A partnership is considering selling a 30% interest in the partnership to an incoming partner for 30% of the existing capital balances. What concerns might you have with this proposal?

2. If an individual were to acquire an interest in a partnership from the partnership entity itself, how would one calculate the suggested value of the acquired interest?

3. The liquidation of a partnership can be a complex and time-consuming process. What basic guidelines should be followed in order to ensure that the process is proper?

4. In the liquidation of a partnership, why might a partner be concerned that a fellow partner has a deficit net capital balance, and how might such a deficit be eliminated?

EXERCISES

Exercise 1 *(LO 1, 9)* **Admission of a new partner with determination of contribute vs. liquidation.** Arnold (A), Bower (B), and Chambers (C) are partners in a small manufacturing firm whose net assets are as follows:

	Book Value	Fair Value		Book Value	Fair Value
Current assets	$285,000	$210,000	Loan payable to Bower	$ 40,000	$ 40,000
Equipment (net of depreciation).	320,000	225,000	Other liabilities	430,000	434,000
			Arnold, capital.	50,000	
Vacant land	60,000	85,000	Bower, capital	100,000	
Other assets.	15,000	10,000	Chambers, capital	60,000	
Total assets.	$680,000	$530,000	Total liabilities	$680,000	$474,000

The partnership agreement calls for the allocation of profits and losses as follows:

a. Salaries to A, B, and C of $30,000, $30,000, and $40,000, respectively.
b. Bonus to A of 10% of net income after the bonus.
c. Remaining amounts are allocated according to profit and loss percentages of 50%, 20%, and 30% for A, B, and C, respectively.

Unfortunately, the business finds itself in difficult times: Annual profits remain flat at approximately $132,000, additional capital is needed to finance equipment which is necessary to stay competitive, and all of the partners realize that they could make more money working for someone else, with a lot fewer headaches.

Chambers has identified Dawson (D) as an individual who might be willing to acquire an interest in the partnership. Dawson is proposing to acquire a 30% interest in the capital of the partnership and a revised partnership agreement, which calls for the allocation of profits as follows:

a. Salaries to A, B, C, and D of $30,000, $30,000, $40,000, and $30,000, respectively.
b. Bonus to D of $20,000 if net income exceeds $250,000.
c. Remaining amounts are allocated according to profit and loss percentages of 30%, 10%, 30%, and 30% for A, B, C, and D, respectively.

An alternative to admitting a new partner is to liquidate the partnership. Net personal assets of the partners are as follows:

	Arnold	Bower	Chambers
Personal assets.	$240,000	$530,000	$300,000
Personal liabilities	228,000	150,000	200,000

Assuming that you are Bower's personal CPA, you have been asked to provide your client with your opinions regarding the alternatives facing the partnership.

1. Bower does not believe it would be worth it to him to admit a new partner unless his allocation of income increased by at least $10,000 over that which existed under the original partnership agreement. What would the average annual profit of the new partnership have to be in order for Bower to accept the idea of admitting a new partner?
2. Given the net assets of the original partnership, what is the suggested purchase price that Dawson should pay for a 30% interest in the partnership?
3. Assume that the original partnership was liquidated and Bower received a business vehicle, with a fair value of $15,000 and a net book value of $20,000, as part of his liquidation proceeds. Partners with a deficit capital balance will only contribute their net personal assets. How much additional cash would Bower receive if the partnership were liquidated?

Exercise 2 *(LO 2, 3)* **Determining the purchase price of a partnership interest.** Meyers is considering investing in one of several existing partnerships and is attempting to consider the price to be paid for a partnership interest. In addition to investing cash, Meyers would be contributing a piece of land that has a fair market value of $50,000. The existing partnerships are characterized as follows:

	Partnership		
	A	B	C
Total assets at:			
Book value	$ 500,000	$600,000	$800,000
Fair market value (excluding good will)	450, 000	725,000	850,000
Liabilities at book value and fair market value:			
Accounts payable	120,000	150,000	300,000
Bank loans	200,000	120,000	200,000
Notes payable to partners	—	100,000	—
Other	49,500	40,000	58,000
Interest to be acquired by new partner:			
In capital	30%	25%	20%
In profit and losses	25%	25%	20%

1. Determine the amount of consideration that Meyers should have to convey in order to acquire an interest in each of the partnerships.
2. Assume that in addition to the land Meyers was asked to convey cash of $4,000, $60,000, and $15,000 to partnerships A through C, respectively. Determine the amount of goodwill to be recorded assuming that all assets are adjusted to fair value. Indicate to whom the goodwill is traceable.

Exercise 3 *(LO 3, 4)* **Entry of a new partner under the goodwill method.** Pearson and Murphy have partner capital balances, at book value, of $45,000 and $65,000 as of December 31. Pearson is allocated 60% of profits or losses, and Murphy is allocated the balance. The partners believe that tangible net assets have a market value in excess of book value in the amount of $30,000 net. The $30,000 is allocated as follows:

	Book Value	Market Value
Accounts receivable	$120,000	$102,000
Inventory	200,000	258,000
Warranty obligations	20,000	30,000

They are considering admitting Warner to the partnership in exchange for total consideration of $84,000 cash. In exchange for the consideration, Warner will receive a 30% interest in capital and a 35% interest in profits.

1. Prepare the entries associated with the admission of Warner to the partnership under the goodwill method.
2. If the goodwill suggested by the admission of Warner proved to be worthless, determine by how much Warner would be harmed.

Exercise 4 *(LO 3, 4, 8)* **Issues involving goodwill and the liquidation of a partnership.** Your client has been asked to invest in a partnership which will develop a piece of real estate for commercial use. It is estimated that the development will occur over three years after which time the partnership will be liquidated. After reviewing selected historical and prospective financial information, your client has asked you to provide answers to the following questions:

1. I thought goodwill could only be recorded by a company if it purchased another company. Why does the historical balance sheet show goodwill as an asset even though the partnership has not acquired any other companies?
2. Apparently, a contribution of capital to a partnership can be recorded by either the bonus or goodwill method. For purposes of securing bank financing and reporting an attractive return on investment, which method would be most appropriate?
3. If the partnership secured a bank loan, upon liquidation of the partnership which would be paid back first, the bank loan or my invested capital balance?
4. If the partnership was liquidated and the partnership's liabilities exceeded the partners' capital balances, which partner would be responsible for the excess liabilities?
5. If I were to purchase a new office building for my existing company, would it be better to hold this office as a personal asset or set up a corporation that owns the office building given my possible investment in the partnership?
6. Would I be better off to loan the partnership a set amount of money as compared to contributing the money as a partner?
7. If during the course of the partnership I decided to sell my partnership interest, would I be better to sell it to the partnership itself or one of the existing partners?

Draft a memo to your client regarding the above questions.

Exercise 5 *(LO 4)* **Comparison of the bonus and goodwill methods.** Your client, Kennedy, is considering an investment in an existing partnership and is interested in knowing how her investment will be accounted for. You have explained to your client that an investment in a partnership may be accounted for by either the bonus method or the goodwill method. Your client has posed the following questions regarding these methods:

1. How do the methods differ with respect to how asset write-downs are accounted for?
2. How is goodwill traceable to the original partnership accounted for under the bonus method?
3. How is it possible that a new partner's initial capital balance may be more than the value of the net assets that the partner contributed to the partnership?
4. Which method would be most appropriate if the allocation of profits is based in part on interest on capital balances?
5. Assume that the goodwill method was used to recognize appreciated assets traceable to the original partners. If the value of these assets were erroneously overstated and subsequently restated, how would the end result differ from that which would have existed had the bonus method been used?

Provide a response to your client's questions.

Exercise 6 *(LO 6)* **Recording the withdrawal of a partner.** Petersen, one of your clients, has indicated that Jacobsen is interested in buying Petersen's interest in the partnership. Relevant information:

Information regarding partners:			
Partner	Jacobsen	Petersen	Olsen
Partner's capital balance	$150,000	$100,000	$50,000
Partner's profit and loss percent	30%	50%	20%

Information regarding net asset values:				
Account title	Note Payable	Net Receivables	Net Patents	Net Equipment
Book value	$130,000	$ 90,000	$50,000	$300,000
Market value	145,000	84,000	30,000	350,000

Petersen has asked you a number of questions regarding selling his interest in the partnership. It is important to note that the partners vote on partnership matters in the same proportion as their profit and loss percentages.

Prepare a response to each of the following questions:

1. Given the above information, what is the suggested value of Petersen's interest in the partnership?
2. Petersen believes that there is significant additional value traceable to the partnership that is not reflected in the above information. In particular, Petersen believes that the partnership has significant goodwill and feels that his interest in the partnership is worth $130,000. What amount of total entity goodwill is suggested by this value?
3. If Petersen were to sell half of his interest in the partnership to Jacobsen and half to Olsen, why might the value of the two halves not be the same?
4. If Petersen were to sell one-half of his interest to the partnership for $60,000, what would his new capital balance be after the sale? Assume that all previously recognized net assets are recorded at their market values but that only the goodwill traceable to Petersen's partial sale of an interest is recognized.
5. What might be some advantages to Petersen and Jacobsen of the partnership acquiring Petersen's interest rather than selling to an individual?

Exercise 7 *(LO 8, 9)* **Installment liquidation with insolvent partners, deficit capital balances.** Coleman, Moore, and Ramsey are partners in a business being liquidated. The partnership has cash of $8,000, noncash assets with a book value of $96,000, and liabilities of $63,000. The following information relates to the individual partners as of June 1, 2017:

	Coleman	Moore	Ramsey
Loan payable to partners		$ 5,000	
Capital balance (deficit)	$47,000	(14,000)	$ 3,000
Personal assets	10,000	15,000	25,000
Personal liabilities	5,000	6,000	15,000
Profit and loss percentages	60%	20%	20%

On June 15, 2017, assets with a book value of $30,000 were sold for $20,000 cash. The proceeds were used to pay off liabilities of the partnership. During the balance of June, no additional assets were liquidated, and outside creditors began to pressure the partnership for payment. On July 1, the partners agreed to contribute personal assets, to the extent of their net personal assets, in order to eliminate their respective capital deficits. Shortly thereafter, assets with a book value of $20,000 and a fair value of $23,000 were distributed to Coleman.

Assuming additional noncash assets with a book value of $40,000 are sold in July for $54,000, determine how available cash would be distributed.

Exercise 8 *(LO 9)* **Amounts to be received by a partner during liquidation.** A condensed balance sheet for a partnership to be liquidated is as follows:

Assets		Liabilities and Capital	
Cash	$ 20,000	Accounts payable	$ 92,000
Receivables (net)	88,000	Loan payable to Partner A . .	70,000

Assets		Liabilities and Capital	
Inventory	$ 70,000	A, capital...............	$ 46,000
Equipment (net)	145,000	B, capital...............	90,000
Other assets................	55,000	C, capital...............	80,000
Total assets	$378,000	Total liabilities	$378,000

The profit and loss percentages for Partners A, B, and C are 50%, 30%, and 20%, respectively. For each of the following independent scenarios, determine how much of the available cash, with the exception of $10,000, would be distributed to Partner B.

1. Assume that the receivables and the inventory were liquidated for $140,000 cash.
2. Assume that all noncash assets other than equipment were sold for $53,000 cash.
3. Assume that noncash assets with a book value of $300,000 were sold for $250,000 cash and that a distribution to Partner A was made in order to pay off the loan payable to them.

Exercise 9 *(LO 9)* **Adjustment of capital balances and lump-sum liquidation.** Palmyra Tooling is a partnership owned by Crawford, Meyer, and Jensen. Capital balances (deficits) and profit and loss percentages are as follows:

	Crawford	Meyer	Jensen
Capital balances at December 31, 2015	$55,000	$115,000	$60,000
Profit and loss percentages	50%	30%	20%

The partnership agreement grants each of the partners a single vote and requires a majority vote to approve certain partnership actions including the liquidation of the partnership. Crawford and Meyer, as founders of Palmyra Tooling, have seen the company experience significant growth and then lose significant market share in the past five years due to local and foreign competition. Given the near-term prospects of continuing difficulties and the further erosion of their capital balances, Crawford and Meyer have voted to liquidate the business. As of December 31, 2015, book values differ from net realizable values as follows (all other assets/ liabilities can be disposed of at book value):

	Book Value	Net Realizable Value
Accounts receivable	$130,000	$ 90,000
Inventory	35,000	15,000
Equipment (net)	725,000	645,000

Unlike his partners, Jensen feels that the company can restructure itself and that liquidation is not appropriate. Jensen is unable to persuade his partners and has offered to personally acquire Crawford's and Meyer's interests for $10,000 and $70,000, respectively. Unsure about the net personal assets of the individual partners, Meyer seeks your advice regarding whether it should accept Jensen's offer.

How would you advise Meyer?

Exercise 10 *(LO 9, 10)* **Installment liquidation, schedule of safe payments.** A real estate partnership had the following condensed balance sheet prior to liquidation:

Assets		Liabilities and Capital	
Cash	$ 12,000	Liabilities (to outsiders)........	$ 35,000
Noncash assets	180,000	Loan payable to A	15,000
		A, capital (50%)	45,000
		B, capital (30%).............	70,000
		C, capital (20%)	27,000
Total assets...............	$192,000	Total liabilities and capital...	$192,000

The percentages in parentheses after the partners' capital balances represent their respective interests in profits and losses. The following situations are independent of each other unless otherwise stated:

1. If assets with a book value of $30,000 were sold for $20,000, how much of the available cash could be distributed to Partner A?
2. If assets with a book value of $60,000 were sold for $70,000, how much of the available cash could be distributed to Partner A?
3. Assume assets with a book value of $70,000 were sold for $50,000 and that all available cash was distributed. For what amount would the remaining assets have to be sold in order for Partner B to receive a total of $79,000 cash from all liquidation activities?

PROBLEMS

Problem 14-1 *(LO 1, 2, 3, 5)* **New partner, asset and capital balance determination, bonus, goodwill.** Kravitz and Rowe are partners in an excavating business known as K & R Excavating. The partners are considering a number of options regarding the partnership, including the admission of a new partner and a potential sale of the partnership. The following information has been prepared as a basis for evaluating various alternatives:

Item	Book Value	Fair Value	Tax Basis
Cash and cash equivalents	$ 20,000	$ 20,000	$ 20,000
Accounts receivable	85,000	72,000	92,000
Inventory	42,000	30,000	50,000
Prepaid and other current assets	18,000	15,000	18,000
Property, plant, and equipment (net)	358,000	300,000	320,000
Total assets.	$523,000	$437,000	$500,000
Accounts payable	$ 54,000	$ 54,000	$ 54,000
Other current liabilities	29,000	35,000	29,000
Notes/loans payable	240,000	240,000	240,000
Kravitz, capital	120,000		
Rowe, capital.	80,000		
Total liabilities and capital.	$523,000		

The partners currently share profits and losses 60% and 40%, respectively, for Kravitz and Rowe.

Given the preceding information, respond to each of the following items:

Required ▶ ▶ ▶ ▶ ▶

1. Given the stated fair values, if Rowe were to sell one-half of her interest in capital to someone outside the partnership, what would be a suggested asking price?
2. Given the stated fair values, if a third party were to convey assets to the partnership in exchange for a 40% interest in the partnership, what would the value of those assets have to be?
3. Assume a new partner was admitted to the partnership with a 40% interest in capital in exchange for a cash contribution of $60,000. What would Rowe's capital balance be as a result of this transaction, assuming use of the bonus method?
4. Given the facts of (3) above, what would Rowe's capital balance be, assuming use of the goodwill method?
5. Assume a new partner was admitted to the partnership with a 30% interest in capital in exchange for a contribution of $55,000 of net tangible assets. What would the new partner's capital balance be as a result of this transaction, assuming use of the bonus method?

Problem 14-2 *(LO 2, 3, 5, 6)* **Admission and departure of partners under the good-will method.** Carlton, Weber, and Stansbury share profits equally and have capital balances of $120,000, $70,000, and $80,000, respectively, as of December 31, 2014. Effective January 1, 2015, Stansbury has transferred his interest in the partnership to Laidlaw for total consideration of $100,000. As part of agreeing to admit Laidlaw to the partnership, the profit- and loss-sharing agreement was modified as follows:

a. Carlton, Weber, and Laidlaw would receive annual salaries of $120,000, $90,000, and $90,000, respectively, to be withdrawn in equal amounts at the end of each calendar quarter.
b. A bonus of 20% of net income after the bonus will be allocated between Weber and Laidlaw in the ratio of 1 to 3. The bonus would be distributed at the end of the first quarter subsequent to year-end.
c. Profit and loss percentages are 40%, 30%, and 30%, respectively, for Carlton, Weber, and Laidlaw.
d. If income is not sufficient or an operating loss exists, all provisions of the profit-sharing agreement are to be satisfied, and the profit and loss percentages are used to absorb any deficiency or additional losses.

The original partners were excited about the new arrangement because Laidlaw had indicated that they would be able to attract a number of customers from his previous place of employment. Weber was willing to shift some salary to a bonus status in order to capture more of the upside potential being presented by Laidlaw. As expected, over the first six months of 2015, a number of Laidlaw's previous customers transferred their business to the partnership. However, the next 12 months were very disappointing. Not only did very few additional Laidlaw customers transfer their business, but it became clear that Laidlaw was not compatible with the other partners. Furthermore, a number of long-standing customers ceased doing business with the company due to issues with Laidlaw. Income for the year 2015 was $300,000, and income for the first six months of 2016 was only $120,000.

On July 1, 2016, Carlton and Weber agreed to acquire Laidlaw's interest in the partnership. The transaction would be recorded as a purchase of Laidlaw's interest by the partnership under the bonus method. Laidlaw was paid $79,000 for their capital balance as of June 30, 2016, and no other distributions were made to him.

After Laidlaw left the partnership, Carlton and Weber went back to sharing profits and losses equally with quarterly withdrawals of $10,000 per partner at the end of each calendar quarter. Weber agreed not to receive an additional distribution traceable to the bonus earned during the first six months of 2016. Income in the second half of 2016 was $73,000. However, the partners realized that they needed to expand operations if the company was to be saved. On January 1, 2017, the partnership admitted Wilson. Wilson contributed tangible assets of $70,000 and intangibles to the partnership in exchange for a 40% interest in capital and one-third interest in profits. The admission of Wilson was recorded using the goodwill method. Carlton, Weber, and Wilson continued to share profits equally, and the partnership experienced net income of $420,000 in 2017. Quarterly withdrawals of $30,000 were paid to each of the partners beginning in 2017.

During the first six months of 2018, the partnership had net income of $255,000 in spite of Carlton's reduced involvement due to health problems. On July 1, 2018, Carlton sold his interest to the partnership for $160,000. The sale was recorded by recognizing the goodwill traceable to the entire partnership.

Prepare a schedule analyzing the changes in partners' capital accounts since December 31, 2014. ◀ ◀ ◀ ◀ ◀ **Required** Supporting calculations should be in good form.

Problem 14-3 *(LO 2, 9)* **Exiting partners under the bonus method and liquidation.** Midway Construction was a partnership owned by Davis, Murray, and Clay with year-end 2013 capital balances of $50,000, 80,000, and $70,000, respectively. Davis and Murray each received an annual salary of $100,000. Clay was primarily involved in sales and received a salary of $70,000 and a bonus of 20% of net income after salaries. All remaining profits were allocated equally among the partners. In the event of insufficient income or operating losses, each provision of the agreement would be satisfied to whatever extent possible given the order of salaries, interest, bonus, and percentages. Salaries are distributed at the end of each calendar quarter, and Clay's bonus is distributed at the end of the first month subsequent to year-end.

Eighty percent of all other allocated income (income other than salary and bonus) is distributed to the partners at the end of the first quarter subsequent to year-end. During 2013, the partnership had net income of $450,000 and proceeded to construct a number of spec homes during 2014.

Unfortunately, during 2014, interest rates increased, and the economy experienced a significant slowdown, resulting in partnership income of only $300,000. In order to improve cash flows, on January 1, 2015, Rayburn made a capital contribution to the partnership of $59,000 cash and received a 50% interest in capital. Rayburn would receive a profit allocation equal to interest of $5,900 in 2015 and a 10% profit percentage. In 2016, Rayburn would receive interest of 10% on average capital, before allocation of 2016 profits, and a 10% profit allocation. The previous partners' profit and loss agreement was modified to provide for salaries at one-half of previous levels, none of which were to be distributed, and profit percentages of 30% each. All other aspects of the previous profit-sharing agreement remained in effect. During the year 2015, conditions worsened, and the partnership reported income of $142,000. At year-end 2015, Davis sold its capital interest to the partnership in exchange for $49,400 and received no further distributions. At the beginning of 2016, Murray loaned the partnership $50,000 with the necessary loan documents providing for interest at the rate of 6%. The profit-sharing agreement for 2013 was completely changed to simply provide for interest on capital to Rayburn as previously set forth and all remaining profits to be allocated 40%, 40%, and 20% for Murray, Clay, and Rayburn, respectively. The only withdrawal to take place during 2016 was the distribution of Clay's 2015 bonus.

The partnership could no longer sustain the economic downturn, and the decision was made to liquidate the partnership after having reported net income of $110,000 during the first six months of 2016. At the beginning of the liquidation process, the partnership had $15,000 in cash and liabilities, excluding loans from partners, of $84,000. Noncash assets of the partnership were liquidated as follows:

1. On August 1, 2016, assets with a book value of $220,000 were sold for $180,000.
2. On September 1, 2016, assets with a book value of $70,000 were sold for $82,000.

Prior to any further liquidation of assets, all available cash other than $10,000 held for future expenses was to be distributed to the partners on September 15, 2016.

Required ▶ ▶ ▶ ▶ ▶

1. Prepare a schedule analyzing the partners' capital prior to liquidation of the partnership. Assume use of the bonus method to record all changes in the ownership structure of the partnership.
2. Prepare a schedule of cash payments on September 15, 2016, of the liquidation, showing how the available cash was distributed. Supporting calculations should be in good form.

Problem 14-4 *(LO 3, 5, 6)* **Profit allocations, admission and withdrawal of partners under the goodwill method.** Murphy and Reinartz have been partners for several years and critical values related to their partnership are as follows:

	Murphy	Reinartz	Total
Profit allocation:			
Annual salaries	$80,000	$100,000	$180,000
Bonus on net income	20%	0%	
Profit and loss percentages	40%	60%	
Capital balances as of December 31, 2015.....	$54,000	$ 76,000	$130,000
Net assets as of December 31, 2015:			
At book value............................			$130,000
At market value			160,000
Loan due to partner as of December 31, 2015...	20,000	30,000	50,000

In 2016, the partnership reported net income of $230,000, and each partner received a $100,000 distribution at year-end. After much discussion, Hepburn was admitted as a partner on January 1, 2017. Hepburn paid $70,000 for a 25% interest in capital. The profit-sharing agreement was modified to also include a salary of $70,000 and a bonus of 5% of net income for Hepburn. The profit and loss percentages were also revised to 30%, 45%, and 25% for Murphy, Reinartz, and Hepburn, respectively. The partnership recognized income of $330,000 during 2017 and distributed $80,000 to each partner during the year. During 2017, Murphy became disappointed with the performance of the company and disagreed with Hepburn's management style. On January 1, 2018, Murphy sold its interest in the partnership to Reinartz for $200,000. The year 2018 was a transition year for the partnership, and Reinartz and Hepburn agreed to share annual profits of $200,000 equally between themselves. In 2018, Reinartz and Hepburn withdrew $60,000 and $80,000, respectively, from the partnership.

At the beginning of 2019, Reinartz decided to sell its interest in the partnership to the partnership for $350,000. It was agreed that net assets would be adjusted to reflect their fair value and that the sale would be recorded by the method whereby only goodwill traceable to Reinartz would be recognized. It was agreed that the following net asset adjustments should be made:

	Book Value	Market Value	Increase (Decrease) in Net Assets
Equipment (net of depreciation). . . .	$125,000	$150,000	$ 25,000
Land.	220,000	260,000	40,000
Patents (net of amortization)	60,000	20,000	(40,000)
Employee note receivable	10,000	—	(10,000)
Contingent liabilities	—	25,000	(25,000)
Total.			$(10,000)

Immediately after Reinartz sold its interest, Pioso purchased a 40% interest in the partnership by contributing to the partnership land and cash with a combined fair value of $75,000.

◀ ◀ ◀ ◀ ◀ **Required** Develop a worksheet that shows the various partners' capital balances from December 31, 2015, through the admission of Pioso. Note that if income is not sufficient to satisfy all provisions of the profit agreement, the profit and loss percentages are to be used to absorb any deficiencies.

Problem 14-5 *(LO 6)* **Impact on capital balances of a partner withdrawing.** After being a partner for over 10 years, Ziegler has decided to sell her interest in a partnership with Grossman and Casper. Prior to the date of the sale and subsequent to the allocation of profits and drawing balances, information concerning the partners was as follows:

	Grossman	Casper	Ziegler
Capital balance.	$125,000	$200,000	$150,000
Profit and loss percentage	40%	40%	20%

Not reflected in the above capital balances are market values of recorded net assets that differ from their book values as follows:

	Land	Net Receivables	Inventory	Net Equipment
Market value	$250,000	$125,000	$220,000	$340,000
Book value	225,000	135,000	245,000	310,000

◀ ◀ ◀ ◀ ◀ **Required** Determine the capital balances for Grossman and Casper assuming that Ziegler sells her interest in the partnership under the following independent scenarios.

1. Ziegler sells her interest to Grossman for $160,000, and the price paid is not used to recognize changes in value of recorded net assets of the entity.
2. Ziegler sells her interest to Grossman for $160,000, and the price paid is used to only recognize decreases in value of existing assets.
3. Ziegler sells her interest to the partnership for $160,000, and the bonus method is used to account for the transaction. Suggested decreases in the value of assets are recognized.

4. Ziegler sells her interest to the partnership for $160,000, and the goodwill traceable to the withdrawing partner is recognized. Suggested decreases in the value of assets are recognized.

5. Ziegler sells her interest to the partnership for $160,000, and the goodwill traceable to the entire partnership entity is recognized. Suggested decreases in the value of assets are recognized.

6. Ziegler sells her interest to the partnership for $160,000, and the goodwill traceable to the entire partnership entity is recognized. All changes in the value of existing assets are recognized.

Problem 14-6 *(LO 8, 9, 10)* **Installment liquidation and unsatisfied partnership creditors.** Prior to liquidation, the following information relates to the partnership:

Partnership trial balance:

			Partner Capital		
Cash	Other Assets	Liabilities	Adams	Beyer	Chenery
$25,000	$240,000	$200,000	$50,000	$(10,000)	$25,000
Profit and loss percentages	30%	30%	40%		

On June 30, other assets with a book value of $160,000 were sold for $120,000, and all available cash with the exception of $20,000 was used to reduce the partnership liabilities. At that time, partners with debit (deficit) capital balances were required to contribute additional capital to whatever extent possible. On July 28, the remaining assets of the partnership were sold for $10,000. Once again, partners with debit (deficit) capital balances were required to contribute additional capital to whatever extent possible. Net personal assets of the partners were as follows:

	Adams	Beyer	Chenery
June 30 balances:			
Partner personal assets	$44,000	$31,000	$52,000
Partner personal liabilities ...	36,000	25,000	30,000
July 28 balances:			
Partner personal assets	30,000	22,000	49,000
Partner personal liabilities ...	22,500	17,000	27,000

Required ▶ ▶ ▶ ▶ ▶ Assuming that the unsatisfied partnership creditors first look to Adams for satisfaction and then to Chenery, determine the amount to be contributed by each partner to satisfy the creditors.

Problem 14-7 *(LO 8, 9, 10)* **Installment liquidation, schedule of safe payments, capital contributions.** Ziegler, Nolan, and Petersen are partners in a residential construction business that has operated for the last 32 years in the Los Angeles area. The partners have decided to leave the business and focus on other pursuits. Initially, they had hoped to sell the business to an employee or other construction company. However, the weak housing market in the area has made liquidation of the company a more likely scenario.

You have been retained to account for the liquidation and to advise the partners as to how available assets of the company should be distributed. Events surrounding the liquidation during 2018 are as follows:

a. On June 1, the company's balance sheet reflected the following: cash—$12,000; noncash assets—$228,000; liabilities to nonpartners—$120,000; loan payable to Nolan—$15,000; Ziegler, capital—$20,000; Nolan, capital—$35,000; and Petersen, capital—$50,000. Ziegler, Nolan, and Petersen share profits and losses of 30%, 30%, and 40%, respectively.

b. A review of the financial statements reveals that additional adjustments may be in order. The company has a contingent liability associated with a previous building contract dispute. It is probable that the company will incur $13,000 of cost in connection with this matter. Final wages and related payroll tax liabilities totaling $4,400 have not been accrued.

c. On June 15, vehicles with a current value of $23,000 and a book value of $14,000 were conveyed to Ziegler. Other assets with a book value of $90,000 were sold for $70,000 to a competing contractor. All available cash was distributed.

d. On June 30, inventory, tools, and other equipment were sold to various employees for a total of $92,000. The items had a book value of $80,000.

e. On July 10, a subcontractor was paid $15,000 to complete work on a final construction project that had not been finished prior to the liquidation. The customer was billed $20,000 for the work performed, and final payment was expected by late July.

f. On July 15, available cash was distributed. However, in addition to the $13,000 of cash retained to satisfy the contingent liability, another $5,000 of cash was retained as a precaution.

g. On July 25, title to a vehicle with a fair value of $12,000 and a book value of $8,000 was transferred to Petersen.

h. At the end of July, the contingent liability was settled for $10,000, and $20,000 was received from the last customer in payment for services performed in July.

i. On August 1, all available cash was distributed.

j. At mid-August, all the remaining assets were disposed of for $24,000. Associated attorney and accounting fees of $6,000 were paid. All available cash was distributed.

After all of the above events, the personal financial statements of the partners reveal the following:

	Ziegler	Nolan	Petersen
Personal assets....................	$185,000	$187,000	$240,000
Personal creditors	165,000	140,000	120,000

Prepare an installment liquidation schedule with all necessary supporting schedules. ◀ ◀ ◀ ◀ ◀ **Required**

Problem 14-8 *(LO 9)* **Sell to a partner or liquidate partnership.** Jacobs, a client of yours, is a partner in a retail establishment that has been experiencing difficult times. Shortly after deciding to liquidate the partnership, partner Williams offers to buy out the interests of the other partners. Jacobs is trying to decide whether it would be best for her to liquidate the partnership or accept the offer to sell her interest.

Prior to liquidation, the partnership has the following condensed balance sheet:

Assets		Liabilities and Capital	
Cash	$ (15,000)	Liabilities	$160,000
Noncash assets	322,000	Loan payable, Williams	25,000
		Capital, Jacobs (30%)..........	52,000
		Capital, Williams (30%)	40,000
		Capital, Harrington (40%)	30,000
Total assets	$307,000	Total liabilities and capital.......	$307,000

The partners' profit and loss percentages are shown parenthetically after the above capital balances.

If the partnership is liquidated, the following information will be relevant:

1. Jacobs estimates that additional unrecorded liabilities of $12,000 will be discovered.
2. Noncash assets can be sold for approximately $232,000.
3. Liquidation expenses, including brokerage and professional fees, will be approximately $18,000.
4. Williams will require repayment of his loan to the partnership as soon as cash is available.
5. Harrington has a very weak financial situation with personal assets, excluding his interest in the partnership, of $145,000 and personal liabilities of $132,000. Harrington will agree to contribute his net personal assets to the partnership.
6. All remaining available cash will be distributed immediately upon conclusion of the liquidation process.

If the offer by Williams occurs, the following information will be relevant:

1. Total capital of the partnership will be reduced by $70,000 to reflect possible unrecorded liabilities and/or asset write-downs.
2. Jacobs and Harrington will be offered 60% of their capital balances after giving consideration to the above adjustments.

3. Williams will pay each of the partners 50% of the balance due as a down payment, and the balance due will be paid over 24 months in equal installments bearing a 0% interest. A reasonable market rate of interest will be 6%.

Required ▶ ▶ ▶ ▶ ▶ Prepare appropriate schedules that can be presented to Jacobs in order to assist her in her decision regarding which course of action to follow.

Problem 14-9 *(LO 9)* **Liquidate now or later.** At the end of 2015, Klaproth finds himself in a difficult situation. He is a partner in a residential construction company, and the housing market has been adversely impacted by interest rates, mortgage defaults, and a surplus of existing homes for sale. As a result, Klaproth and certain other partners are considering ceasing operations as of year-end 2015 and liquidating the partnership. Values of liquidated net assets are estimated to be as follows:

Item	Book Value	Market Value
Cash	$ 120,000	$ 120,000
Noncash assets	1,500,000	1,380,000
Liabilities	1,400,000	1,350,000
Klaproth, capital	110,000	
Stone, capital	20,000	
Jackson, capital.	90,000	
Unrecorded contingent liabilities. . .	—	60,000
Estimated liquidation expense.		25,000

As of March 31, 2016, the partners' personal net assets (deficit) were $220,000, $12,500, and $100,000 for Klaproth, Stone, and Jackson, respectively. If a partner develops a deficit capital balance, they would likely contribute an amount equal to their net personal assets.

Certain partners feel that things will improve over the next two years and have made an alternative proposal to Klaproth. Under this proposal, Klaproth would continue his involvement in the company and continue to share profits and losses as before. On March 31, 2018, the partnership would buy Klaproth's interest for 110% of his capital balance as of December 31, 2017, after adjusting receivables and inventory to their market values as of year-end 2017.

The partnership's profit-sharing agreement is as follows:

Component	Klaproth	Stone	Jackson
Salaries	$100,000	$130,000	$90,000
Bonus as a percent of traceable net sales . . .	5%	0%	10%
Profit and loss percentages	35%	30%	35%

If income is not sufficient to satisfy all provisions of the profit agreement, the profit and loss percentages are to be used to absorb any deficiencies. You are also to assume that all net income will be reinvested in noncash assets. It is anticipated that factors impacting the allocation of profits for the years 2016 and 2017 will be as follows:

2016 Factors	Klaproth	Stone	Jackson
Traceable net sales	$600,000	$800,000	$500,000
Annual draws	20,000	40,000	20,000
Investment of capital	50,000	30,000	—
Net income is $120,000			

2017 Factors	Klaproth	Stone	Jackson
Traceable net sales	$720,000	$1,000,000	$700,000
Annual draws	—	40,000	20,000
Net income is $200,000			

As of year-end 2017, receivables and inventory are forecasted to be as follows:

	Book Value	Market Value	Adjustment
Receivables	$ 350,000	$ 300,000	$ (50,000)
Inventory of raw materials	220,000	190,000	(30,000)
Work in process	610,000	500,000	(110,000)
Finished goods	600,000	440,000	(160,000)
Total.	$1,780,000	$1,430,000	$(350,000)

In anticipation of a meeting with Klaproth, prepare a schedule that will help him with ◄ ◄ ◄ ◄ ◄ **Required** respect to which course of action might be most appropriate.

Problem 14-10 *(LO 9)* **Installment liquidation, premature distributions, insolvent partners.** Green Acres Enterprises is a partnership that constructs and sells assisted living facilities for the elderly. The firm has been in existence for seven years, and the partners have decided that the market for such facilities has become saturated and that the partnership should be liquidated. The partners Dvorak, Kelsen, and Morgan share profits and losses 30%, 30%, and 40%, respectively. The following information, presented in chronological order, is relevant to the liquidation of the partnership.

a. The following balances existed prior to the commencement of the liquidation:

Assets		Liabilities and Capital	
Cash	$ 15,000	Accounts payable	$ 80,000
Accounts receivable	60,000	Note payable—mortgage.	450,000
Inventory	90,000	Note payable—Kelsen	40,000
Prepaid assets	12,000	Contingent liability	83,000
Furniture and fixtures (net)	150,000	Dvorak, capital	20,000
Office equipment (net)	30,000	Kelsen, capital.	47,000
Vehicles (net)	30,000	Morgan, capital	17,000
Assisted living home (net)	350,000		
Total assets.	$737,000	Total liabilities and capital. . .	$737,000

b. Accounts receivable with a book value of $40,000 were collected in the amount of $30,000. The inventory was sold for $60,000.
c. All the prepaid amounts were refunded to the company with the exception of $2,000 that was forfeited.
d. The partners agreed that any additional available cash should be used to pay off the accounts payable rather than the contingent liability.
e. Office equipment with a book value of $15,000 and a fair value of $12,000 was distributed to Morgan. A vehicle with a book value of $10,000 and a fair value of $8,000 was distributed to Dvorak.
f. The office equipment and vehicles were sold for 80% of their book value.
g. The contingent liability was settled for $43,000.
h. The partners agreed that 90% of any available cash should be distributed to the partners in as safe a manner as possible. At this time, it was assumed that the value of noncash assets would be at least adequate to pay off the remaining liabilities.
i. The furniture and fixtures were consigned to a broker who sold them for net proceeds of $120,000.
j. The balance of the accounts receivable had been turned over to a collection agency, and the partnership received $5,000 upon final settlement of all accounts.
k. The assisted living home proved difficult to dispose of and was finally sold for $400,000. Furthermore, legal fees and brokers' commissions totaling $25,000 were incurred in connection

with the sale. The note payable—mortgage was paid off in full in addition to previously unrecorded interest in the amount of $5,000.

l. Prior to distributing the remaining cash, partners with deficit balances were required to make the necessary contribution from net personal assets. At that time, the net assets (liabilities) of the partners were as follows: Dvorak, ($8,000); Kelsen, $140,000; and Morgan, $10,000.

m. All available cash was distributed to the partners.

Required ▶ ▶ ▶ ▶ ▶

1. Prepare a liquidation schedule for the above partnership.
2. Determine whether the distributions of office equipment and vehicles to the individual partners were, in fact, "safe" distributions.
3. What is the nature of the claim solvent partners have against a partner who is not able to satisfy a deficit capital balance?

Governmental and Not-for-Profit Accounting

G overnment and not-for-profit organizations are a major force in our society, comprising one-third of the United States expenditures and employing a substantial work force.

There are approximately 87,000 local governments in the United States. These include villages, towns, cities, counties, states, school districts, universities, public authorities, or special districts. There are over one million not-for-profits in the United States. These include schools; hospitals; social service, advocacy, cultural, and civic organizations; churches, synagogues, and mosques; and foundations.

The primary objective of external financial reporting for governmental units and not-for-profit organizations is accountability. However, there is no "bottom-line" amount or earnings per share figure to judge success. Instead, there is the elusive factor of service. To control activities and measure service, variations in the accounting and reporting process are introduced. Budgets have far greater power for control, particularly when they are entered formally into the accounting records in order to provide close comparisons with actual results. With financial resources being derived from many different sources, some with specific restrictions as to their consumption, fund accounting has traditionally been used to display proper use for intended purposes. More recently, standards setters have moved away from fund accounting for private not-for-profit organizations to an organization-wide reporting of unrestricted and donor-restricted assets and liabilities. Similarly, new government standards include entity-wide financial statements.

Governmental Accounting: The General Fund and the Account Groups

Learning Objectives

When you have completed this chapter, you should be able to

1. Differentiate between the financial reporting needs of governmental entities and those of profit-seeking business enterprises.

2. Identify the role of the various authoritative bodies for state and local government accounting and financial reporting.

3. State the difference between the financial resources measurement focus and the economic resources measurement focus, and indicate where each is reported under GASB Statement No. 34.

4. Identify the types of funds and account groups in state and local government.

5. Show how to account for transactions in governmental funds.

6. Explain the purpose of budgets and how governments account for appropriations.

7. Prepare journal entries for the general fund.

8. Demonstrate how to account for encumbrances.

9. Prepare fund financial statements for the general fund.

10. Complete schedules for general capital assets and long-term liabilities.

11. Demonstrate an understanding of the 13 basic governmental accounting principles. (Appendix)

This chapter, the first of two that address accounting procedures used by governmental bodies, deals with the general fund. This fund accounts for most of the ordinary transactions of a governmental body. Also explained are the unique methods used to record fixed assets and long-term debt in separate accounting records called *groups*. The presentation is applicable to state and local governments. The governmental accounting procedures used in Chapters 15–17 provide a general understanding of *fund* accounting and current governmental accounting standards issued by the Governmental Accounting Standards Board (GASB). Also included is a discussion of the significant recent changes to the existing government financial reporting model. The presentation in Chapters 18 and 19 incorporates Financial Accounting Standards Board (FASB) standards issued specifically for not-for-profits.

Accounting and financial reporting for governmental and not-for-profit (also called nonprofit) entities have become more important because an increasing portion of our national economy has been devoted to this sector. Decision makers, such as legislators, citizens, managers, and contributors, need better information about governmental and not-for-profit organizations if they are to make optimal resource allocations to those entities and manage them efficiently and effectively. In addition, many accounting students will hold governmental and not-for-profit accounting jobs, perform audits on such organizations, and take the CPA examination, which contains questions on governmental and not-for-profit accounting.

1

OBJECTIVE

Differentiate between the financial reporting needs of governmental entities and those of profit-seeking business enterprises.

COMMERCIAL AND GOVERNMENTAL ACCOUNTING: A COMPARISON

Exhibit 15-1A summarizes the flow of resources in a profit-seeking business entity. Demand for goods and services made by customers in the commercial sector of the economy is satisfied by business enterprises. Assets of a business enterprise are supplied voluntarily by proprietors, stockholders, bondholders, and other creditors. The assets are consumed during operating processes that produce goods and services sold to customers who choose to deal with the company. The sales generate revenue for the company. The objective of the entity is to generate net income. The income statement measures the attainment of this goal by matching revenues earned with expenses incurred using accrual accounting.

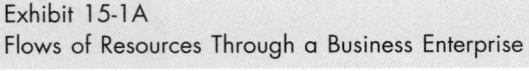

Exhibit 15-1A
Flows of Resources Through a Business Enterprise

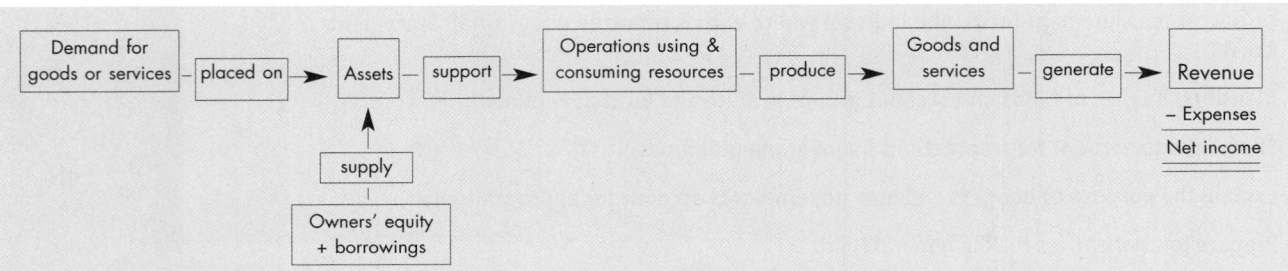

Expenses (outflows of economic resources) are incurred for the purpose of generating revenue. Owners share the resulting income or loss.

A separate cash flow statement is prepared to show the cash consequences of the period's operating, financing, and investing activities.

Exhibit 15-1B is a summary of the flow of resources for a governmental entity. Residents and businesses within a government's jurisdiction demand goods and services from that governmental unit. Assets of a government are supplied primarily through the involuntary payment of taxes by taxpayers. Typical taxes are those levied on property, income, and sales of goods and services. Creditors may also provide some financing. The assets are consumed during operating processes that produce goods and services dispensed to those who are legally entitled to receive them. The operations performed to provide services are not intended to generate a profit. Left-over resources at the end of a fiscal period merely lessen the need for revenue in the next period. The results of operations for an accounting period are summarized in a statement called the statement of revenues, expenditures, and changes in the fund balance.

To finance general governmental activities, revenues are raised according to laws and are increases in financial resources that flow from outside the governmental unit—for example, taxes based on incomes or property values. Expenditures, such as salary payments, debt principal and interest payments, and fixed assets purchases, follow from budget appropriations and are decreases in financial resources that flow to entities outside the governmental unit. The expenditures usually are not related to the amount of taxes people pay. For example, a 7-year-old child who pays no taxes may receive a public education. Other increases in financial resources for general governmental purposes are termed *other financing sources*. These include transfers from other funds within the same governmental unit and resources from several other

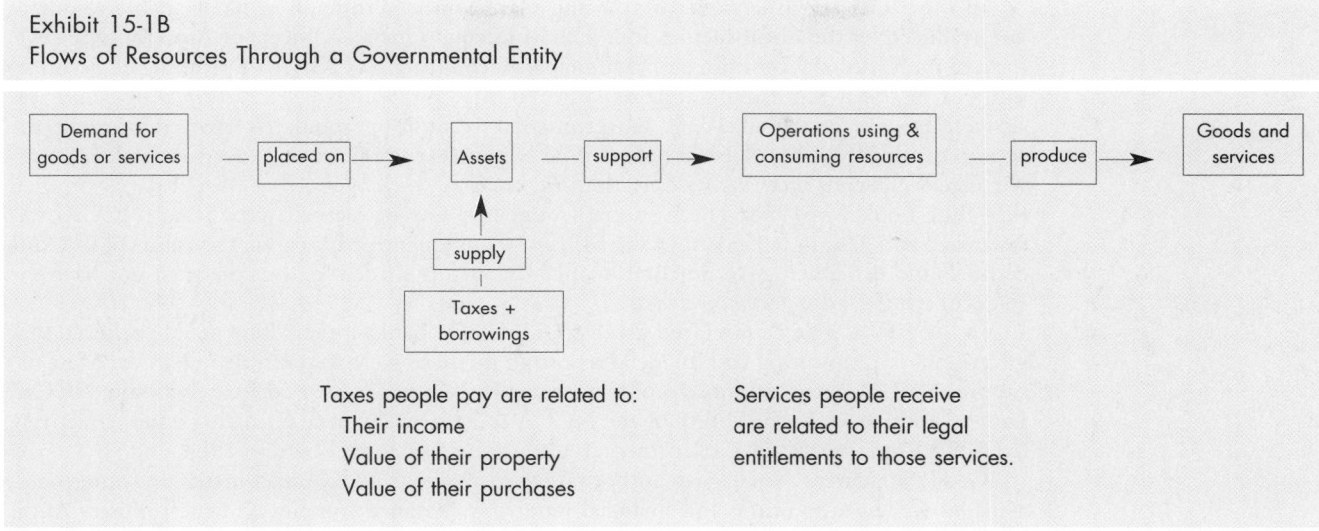

Exhibit 15-1B
Flows of Resources Through a Governmental Entity

sources including proceeds from bond issues and resources from the sale of fixed assets. Other decreases in financial resources for general governmental activities come from *other financing uses*, which are typified by a transfer of financial resources to another fund within the same governmental unit. In addition, many governments engage in business activities that provide goods or services to users and finance these activities through user charges.

An important focus of governmental financial reporting is demonstrating fiscal compliance. Operating statements report whether or not financial resources received during a period are sufficient to cover the expenditures of that period. Furthermore, in addition to total expenditures, whether or not spending in particular areas was in compliance with approved budgets is reported. Consequently, division of resources into funds, each of which is a self-balancing set of accounts, is used to keep track of the flows of financial resources dedicated to specific activities. Financial reporting on fund activities should reveal whether uses of financial resources were within restrictions imposed by law or by third parties.

A further environmental distinction between business enterprises and governmental units is ownership versus jurisdiction. The balance sheet residual of a business enterprise is owners' equity, denoting the ownership interest in the company. The balance sheet residual of a governmental unit, however, is fund balance, merely denoting the difference between assets and liabilities.

REFLECTION

- Because the decision-making environment for governments is not profit seeking, the accounting and financial reporting needs are different from those in the business environment.

HISTORY OF GOVERNMENTAL FINANCIAL REPORTING

Three prominent periods of development in modern governmental financial reporting followed crises. In the late 1800s, large cities were rocked by misuses of funds, and accounting and financial reporting recommendations developed by the National Municipal League were adopted by some cities. In 1904, the state of New York was first to require standardized financial reporting by cities.

2

OBJECTIVE

Identify the role of the various authoritative bodies for state and local government accounting and financial reporting.

In the 1930s, new demands were being placed on governments while available resources were reduced by the Great Depression. The Municipal Finance Officers of America (MFOA)[1] formed its National Committee on Municipal Accounting (NCMA)[2] to promulgate accounting and financial reporting standards. The NCMA Bulletin No. 1, *Principles of Municipal Accounting*, was issued in 1934. Governmental accounting standards evolved through the actions of the NCMA and its successors. The National Committee on Governmental Accounting issued *Governmental Accounting, Auditing, and Financial Reporting* (GAAFR), also called the "Blue Book," in 1968. The National Council on Governmental Accounting (NCGA) was organized in 1974, independent of the MFOA. Consequently, subsequent revisions of GAAFR codified and explained governmental financial reporting principles, but they did not have the status of *authoritative pronouncements*.

In the 1970s, many cities faced fiscal stress and near bankruptcy. Many people believed that governmental accounting and financial reporting methods were responsible in part for these fiscal problems and believed those problems were not being addressed adequately by the NCGA. Lack of confidence in the ability of the NCGA to address financial reporting issues effectively led to the formation of the Governmental Accounting Standards Board in 1984.

GASB Statement No. 1 gave authoritative status to all NCGA statements and interpretations, as well as accounting and financial reporting guidance contained in the Industry Audit Guide, *Audits of State and Local Governmental Units*, issued by the American Institute of Certified Public Accountants (AICPA) until superseded by subsequent GASB pronouncements.[3] A summary of the basic governmental accounting principles included in GASB Statement No. 1 is provided in the appendix to this chapter.

Financial reporting standard setting for governmental units has a long history and has been a focus of numerous standard-setting boards. Exhibit 15-2 presents an abridged history of financial reporting standards applicable to governments issued by major standard setters.

Organization and Processes of the FASB and the GASB

The GASB is a sister board to the Financial Accounting Standards Board. The Financial Accounting Foundation (FAF), which appoints both boards, is responsible for their funding and the determination of their respective jurisdictions, as well as the resolution of any disputes which may arise between the boards.

Both the FASB and the GASB subscribe to a due process of standard setting to ensure that preparers, attestors, and users of financial statements affected by standards have a voice in the establishment of those standards. Due process includes (a) issuing discussion memoranda setting forth financial reporting issues and arguments for and against possible alternative standards; (b) issuing exposure drafts proposing financial reporting standards regarding issues; and (c) issuing standards after considering written comments, testimony from public hearings, and research conducted by FASB and GASB staff and others throughout the due process period.

Jurisdictions of the FASB and the GASB

The authority to set external financial reporting standards for business and nonbusiness organizations rests with several standard-setting bodies. The identity of an entity's primary standard setter depends upon the nature of the operating activities of the entity issuing financial reports. Exhibit 15-3, on page 766, shows the primary standard setters for commercial, governmental, and not-for-profit entities.

Accountants and auditors often rely on financial reporting standards issued by bodies of expert accountants, such as AICPA committees, that are not the entity's primary financial reporting standard setter. In addition, accountants sometimes rely on widely recognized industry practices and other relevant accounting literature, such as accounting textbooks and AICPA issues papers, in preparing financial reports in accordance with generally accepted accounting

---

1 Now, the Government Finance Officers Association (GFOA).

2 Renamed National Committee on Governmental Accounting in 1951 and reorganized as the National Council on Governmental Accounting (NCGA) in 1974. The NCGA was superseded by the GASB in 1984.

3 GASB Statement No. 1, *Authoritative Status of NCGA Pronouncements and AICPA Industry Audit Guide* (Norwalk, CT: Governmental Accounting Standards Board, July 1984).

Exhibit 15-2
Major Contributions of Governmental Accounting Standard Setters

Year	MFOA/GFOA Committees	AICPA	GASB
1934 to 1941	NCMA—Principles of Municipal Accounting and 12 later standards		
1951 to 1968	NCGA—four publications including 1968 *Governmental Accounting, Auditing, and Financial Reporting* (GAAFR)		
1974		*Audits of State and Local Governmental Units*	
1979 to 1982	NCGA—four statements including the 1980 GAAFR, six interpretations and one Concepts Statement, *Objectives of Accounting and Financial Reporting for Governmental Units*		
1980		Statement of Position 80–2 declared that financial statements presented in accordance with NCGA Statement No. 1 are in conformity with generally accepted accounting principles.	
1984 to 2010			GASB, organized in 1984, has issued 51 standards and four concepts statements. A recent standard, GASB Statement No. 34, requires sweeping changes in the way financial reports are reported. *Codification of Governmental Accounting and Financial Reporting Standards* contains generally accepted accounting principles for governmental units and is issued annually.

principles (GAAP).[4] Generally, nongovernmental entities follow FASB pronouncements, APB Opinions, and AICPA Accounting Research Bulletins, while state and local governments follow GASB pronouncements and AICPA and FASB pronouncements if they are made applicable to state and local governments by GASB action.

---

4 Statement on Auditing Standards No. 69, *The Meaning of "Present Fairly in Conformity with Generally Accepted Accounting Principles" in the Independent Auditor's Report* (New York: American Institute of Certified Public Accountants, January 1992).

Exhibit 15-3
Authorities for Commercial, Governmental, and Not-for-Profit Accounting Reporting Standards

Type of Entity	Primary Financial Reporting Standard Setter(s)
Business enterprises	Financial Accounting Standards Board (FASB) and Securities and Exchange Commission (SEC)
Federal government	General Accounting Office (GAO), Comptroller General, Department of the Treasury, Office of Management and Budget (OMB), and Federal Accounting Standards Advisory Board (FASAB)
State/local governments	Governmental Accounting Standards Board (GASB)
Colleges and universities	Public—GASB Private—FASB
Heathcare organizations	Public—GASB Private—FASB
Voluntary health and welfare organizations	FASB
Other not-for-profit organizations	FASB

GASB Objectives of Financial Reporting

Differences in environments and purposes of financial reporting between business enterprises and governmental entities have led to the creation of separate financial reporting standard-setting boards for business enterprises and governments, and each board has examined and defined the objectives of financial reporting by its respective constituency. *Objectives of Financial Reporting by Business Enterprises*, Concept Statement No. 1, was issued by the FASB in 1978. *Objectives of Financial Reporting*, Concept Statement No. 1, was issued by the GASB in 1987.

In its Concept Statement No. 1, the GASB stated that "**accountability** is the cornerstone of all financial reporting in government."[5] A closely related concept referred to by the GASB in the concept statement is **interperiod equity**. Both concepts are described below.

The GASB believes that financial reporting helps a government fulfill its duty to be publicly accountable to its citizenry. They believe that taxpayers have a "right to know;" that is, a right to receive information about government activities that may lead to public debates. At a minimum, *accountability* through financial reporting means "providing information to assist in evaluating whether the government was operated within the legal constraints imposed by the citizenry."[6]

A significant part of accountability is *interperiod equity*, which may be demonstrated by showing "whether current-year revenues are sufficient to pay for current-year services or whether future taxpayers will be required to assume burdens for services previously provided."[7] As with business financial reports, state and local government financial reports should possess the characteristics of understandability, reliability, relevance, timeliness, consistency, and comparability.

---

5 GASB Concept Statement No. 1, *Objectives of Financial Reporting* (Norwalk, CT: Governmental Accounting Standards Board, 1987), par. 58.
6 Ibid.
7 Ibid., par. 61.

Measurement Focus and Basis of Accounting

Measurement focus refers to which resources are being measured. *Basis of accounting* refers to when the effects of transactions or events should be recognized for financial reporting purposes. The traditional measurement focus for state and local governments has been *financial resources*. In June 1999, the GASB issued Statement No. 34 after nearly 15 years of deliberation and dialogue with its constituents. Statement No. 34, *Basic Financial Statements—and Management's Discussion and Analysis—for State and Local Governments*, requires governments to prepare two separate, but related, sets of financial statements.[8] The first set, the fund financial statements, focuses on reporting activity as a collection of separate funds. Governmental and business-type funds are reported on separate statements. And, rather than follow the reporting of traditional fund-types (as described in the following section), these statements will report major funds and combine all the nonmajor funds into one column.

The second set of financial statements are government-wide statements that concentrate on the government as a whole. These statements adopt an *economic resources measurement focus* and consolidate all of a government's operations on *a full accrual basis* similar to that found in the business world.

The sections that follow present an overview of the main funds maintained by governments and describe the accounting for activities in the general fund. A discussion of accounting for long-term assets and liabilities also follows. Chapter 16 discusses accounting for activities in the remaining funds, while Chapter 17 describes the fund financial statements and the more recently required government-wide statements as well as the articulation from one to the other.

3

OBJECTIVE

State the difference between the financial resources measurement focus and the economic resources measurement focus, and indicate where each is reported under GASB Statement No. 34.

REFLECTION

- Governmental accounting and financial reporting standards for state and local governments are established by the GASB.

- GASB Statement No. 34 requires fund financial statements and government-wide statements.

GOVERNMENTAL ACCOUNTING STRUCTURE OF FUNDS

Governmental units create individual funds to account for financial resources used for specific purposes. Each fund is an accounting entity containing a self-balancing set of accounts for which financial statements can be prepared. Business enterprises, on the other hand, report all of their profit-making activity on a single income statement and summarize their financial position on a single balance sheet.

Historically, general purpose financial statements for governments aggregated financial information by fund type. The combined balance sheet is not subjected to the rules of consolidation for the purpose of eliminating the effects of interfund transactions and interfund balances. With the adoption of GASB Statement No. 34, governments are now required to prepare consolidated financial statements restricted to summarizing the effects of transactions between a governmental unit and external parties as presented in Chapter 17. Since many argue that governmental activity does not reduce well to a single statement about profit or loss, fund-based financial statements are also required under Statement No. 34, helping to demonstrate accountability (i.e., compliance with laws governing numerous activities).

4

OBJECTIVE

Identify the types of funds and account groups in state and local government.

---

8 GASB Statement No. 34, *Basic Financial Statements—and Management's Discussion and Analysis—for State and Local Governments* (Norwalk, CT: Governmental Accounting Standards Board, June 1999).

Three fund types and account groups are used in government financial reporting:

1. **Governmental funds** account for activities that provide citizens with services financed primarily by taxes and intergovernmental grants. These funds have a *working capital* focus and include only current assets and current liabilities.

2. **Proprietary funds** account for business-type activities that derive their revenue from charges to users for goods or services. They follow the commercial accounting model in measuring net income. An example would be a publicly owned utility.

3. **Fiduciary funds** account for resources for which the governmental unit acts as a trustee or an agent.

4. **Account groups** account for and serve as a record of general capital assets and general long-term liabilities. Account groups are not required under GASB Statement No. 34, but many governments continue to use them as a convenient means of keeping track of these items. Alternatively, some governments have changed their account systems to allow for the generation of lists of capital assets and long-term liabilities without using account groups.

The GASB specifies different methods of applying the accrual concept in accounting for governmental funds and proprietary funds. The *modified accrual basis*, a hybrid system that includes some aspects of both accrual- and cash-basis accounting, is used for recognition of revenues and expenditures of governmental funds. The accrual basis refers to recognition of revenues and expenses of proprietary funds and fiduciary funds as in business accounting.

Governmental Funds

All governments have a general fund and may have other governmental funds as well, depending on their types of activities. The five governmental funds are as follows:

1. The **general fund** accounts for resources that have no specific restrictions and are available for operational expenditures not relegated to one of the other governmental funds. Since it accounts for general operations, it is the most essential fund. Every governmental unit has a general fund.

2. **Special revenue funds** account for resources that legally are restricted to expenditure for specific operational purposes, such as a toll tax levied for road maintenance expenses.

3. **Capital projects funds** account for resources to be used for the construction or acquisition of major capital facilities.

4. **Debt service funds** account for resources to be used for payment of general long-term debt and interest.

5. **Permanent funds** account for resources that are legally restricted so that only their earnings, not the principal, may be used to finance operations.

5

OBJECTIVE

Show how to account for transactions in governmental funds.

Accounting for Transactions of Governmental Funds

The modified accrual method of accounting is used for governmental funds to measure the flow of working capital. Under modified accrual, revenue is recorded in the accounting period in which it is both measurable and available to finance expenditures made during the current fiscal period (this includes resources expected to be available shortly after year-end). Expenditures are recognized in the period in which the liabilities are both measurable and incurred.

Revenues. Increases in financial resources from transactions with external parties that do not have to be repaid are called revenues. Revenues may come from nonexchange or exchange transactions. Nonexchange transactions are those in which people and companies pay amounts to governments but governments give nothing directly to the payors in return. Exchange transactions are those in which the government provides goods or services for fees. Under modified accrual, some revenues are recognized on the accrual basis and some revenues are recognized on the cash basis. Revenue from property taxes, intergovernmental grants, entitlements, and shared revenues; interest on investments and delinquent taxes; and billed charges for services are normally recognized under the modified accrual basis if funds will be "collectible within the current period or soon enough thereafter to be used to pay liabilities of the current period."[9]

Property taxes, fines, and other *imposed* tax revenues are recorded as revenue at the time taxes are levied on property owners and others provided the taxes will be collected during the current period or soon enough after year-end to pay the liabilities of the current period. Taxes levied in one year but not available until the following year are recognized as deferred revenue. Governments are conservative in recognizing property tax revenue. Only the net amount estimated to be collected is recognized.

Resources to be received from federal, state, or local governmental units (intergovernmental grants, entitlements, and shared revenues for operational purposes) should be recognized as revenue in the year for which all eligibility requirements, including time restrictions, have been met and the resources are available to finance expenditures. If resources are received prior to the time period in which they may be used, or if the receivable is not expected to be collected soon enough to be used for the current fiscal period, Deferred Revenues is credited. Some grants to a governmental unit may carry strong restrictions on their use. For example, the federal government may be willing to give a locality a grant providing it builds a bridge over a river and connects its main road to the federal highway. In this case, the restricted grant should be recognized as revenue only to the extent that expenditures have been made, with the remainder of the grant recorded as deferred revenue. This type of restricted grant is sometimes called an *expenditure-driven* grant.

Revenues from voluntary nonexchange transactions, such as donations and certain grants, should be recognized in governmental funds when the assets are received. Donations of capital assets are not recognized in governmental funds. Rather, donated capital assets are recorded in the general fixed assets account group discussed later in this chapter.

Revenue for services charges should be recognized when billed if it is expected to be received within the current period or soon enough thereafter to be used to pay liabilities of the current period. Such revenues may be from goods or services provided for fees, such as golf course fees, garbage removal fees, inspection fees, and sales of maps and other publications.

Interest and dividend revenue from investments should be recognized when earned. Investment gains and losses should be recognized when an investment is sold.

Revenues normally recognized under the cash-basis method include fees for licenses and permits, fines and forfeits, and parking meter receipts. These resources are recognized when received in cash because the amount is usually not known prior to collection. In addition, these items are often not an important source of a governmental unit's income.

Taxes levied directly on taxpayers are accounted for in the same modified accrual basis of accounting that already applies to most other revenue sources.[10] Examples are taxes on income, inheritance, gasoline, general sales, and tobacco. Revenue from these taxpayer-assessed or *derived* taxes, net of estimated refunds, is recognized in the accounting period in which they become susceptible to accrual [e.g., when the underlying transaction (sale or earning of income) occurs and the amounts are measurable and will be collected within the current period or soon enough after year-end to finance expenditures for the period]. A lag often occurs from the time of the underlying transaction to the reporting of such events, so, in practice, revenue is recorded when either the merchant or the employer submits the required reports to the governmental unit.

Other Financing Sources. These inflows of financial resources arise from issuing general long-term debt, recording the present value of capital lease obligations, selling capital assets, and receiving of interfund operating transfers from other governmental funds. Use of the other

---

9 GASB Statement No. 33, *Accounting and Financial Reporting for Nonexchange Transactions* (Norwalk, CT: Governmental Accounting Standards Board, December 1998) identifies four classes of nonexchange transactions: *derived tax revenues,* such as income taxes and sales taxes; *imposed nonexchange revenues,* such as property taxes and fines; *government-mandated nonexchange transactions,* such as federal programs that state and local governments are required to perform; and *voluntary nonexchange transactions,* such as grants and private donations.

10 Ibid.

financing sources classification avoids multiple countings of inflows as revenues. Proceeds from issuing general long-term debt represent inflows of financial resources that must be repaid to lenders from later tax revenues. Tax revenue recorded in the general fund would be counted as revenue twice if amounts transferred to another governmental fund were recorded in the second fund as revenue rather than as other financing sources. The same is true for proceeds from the sale of a fixed asset. Financial resources raised by tax revenues are used to purchase fixed assets. Their later sale is a conversion of fixed assets into financial resources, not a raising of new financial resources from entities outside the governmental unit.

Expenditures. Most expenditures are decreases in financial resources as a result of transactions with external parties. Some expenditures, however, result from consumption of previously purchased financial resources, such as inventories and prepaid items. Expenditures are recognized in the period the fund liability is both measurable and incurred.[11] This usually means that an expenditure is recognized if the related liability is expected to be liquidated through the use of current-year expendable and available financial resources. Expenditures result from operating activities, acquiring capital assets, and payment of debt principal and interest. In many cases, expenditures will be recorded simultaneously with cash payments. Consider the following examples:

Expenditures	50,000	
Cash		50,000
To record the payment of current maintenance expenses.		
Expenditures	100,000	
Cash		100,000
To record the acquisition of a new capital asset for cash.		

Expenditures for interest and principal on general long-term debt are recorded on a cash basis when they are due to match them with the tax revenue raised for the interest and principal payment.

Expenditures	42,000	
Cash		42,000
To record the payment of $12,000 of interest and $30,000 principal on existing general obligation debt.		

Other expenditures will be recorded if the amount is to be paid with existing resources. Consider the following entries to record wages:

Expenditures	16,500	
Cash		10,500
Liability for State and Federal Withholdings		6,000

While the liability for withholdings is current, another common payroll liability for future payment of compensated absences (such as for vacations and holidays) is considered to be long term. Under the *modified accrual basis* of governmental accounting, such long-term liabilities would not be recorded in the general fund, but they would appear in the government-wide statements. The traditional means of keeping track of long-term obligations has been through the use of account groups. The concept of using accounts groups for internal control and support for financial reporting will be described in detail later in this chapter. Long-term vacation and sick leave liabilities are recorded in the general long-term debt account group as shown on page 771.

---

11 GASB Exposure Draft, *Recognition and Measurement of Certain Liabilities and Expenditures in Governmental Fund Financial Statements* (Norwalk, CT: Governmental Accounting Standards Board, June 1999).

| Amount to Be Provided in Future Periods............................. | 1,500 | |
| Liability for Compensated Absences .... | | 1,500 |

Only the expenditure and related current liability for compensated absences reasonably expected to be paid from the current governmental fund financial resources are included in the fund. All long-term liabilities are recorded separately.

GASB standards for recording pension expenditures require a calculation of the "actuarial required contribution" (ARC).[12] This calculation can be made using acceptable actuarial methods and assumptions. As in the preceding example for compensated absences, the portion of the ARC that will be paid from current resources will be recorded as an expenditure in the fund.

| Expenditures .... | 5,000 | |
| Current Pension Liability .... | | 5,000 |

The portion to be funded from future resources is recorded as general long-term debt in the account group as follows:

| Amount to Be Provided in Future Periods............................. | 2,000 | |
| Unfunded Pension Liability... | | 2,000 |

Governments are also required to measure and report on other postemployment benefits (OPEB) such as health care and life insurance in a manner similar to the illustration for pension benefits above.[13] This systematic, accrual-based, measurement and recognition of OPEB costs will provide information on the extent to which future cash flows will be affected.

The GASB requires a liability for claims and judgments outstanding to be recognized in the accounts if it is probable that the liability has been incurred and the amount can be reasonably estimated. During the year, the government will record the amounts paid or vouchered as payable as expenditures in the fund. The noncurrent liability for claims and judgments is recorded directly in the general long-term debt account group.

In many cases, cash will be paid or a liability recorded to purchase goods and services in advance of their use. These items are recorded in the fund as financial resources (assets) as follows:

Prepaid Rent	12,000	
Prepaid Insurance	18,000	
Supplies Inventory	40,000	
Cash		70,000
To record the acquisition of goods and services to be consumed in the future.		

Expenditures are recorded in the fund as follows when the financial resources are consumed:

Expenditures	45,000	
Prepaid Rent...		10,000
Prepaid Insurance		15,000
Supplies Inventory		20,000
To record the receipt of services and use of supplies acquired previously.		

Note that the expenditure examples in this section show the consumption of only those assets defined as financial resources. This is a narrower definition than expenses reported in the new government-wide statements where the measurement focus is flows of economic resources. Expenses are the expirations of economic resources that include not only the use of current

---

12 GASB Statement No. 27, *Accounting for Pensions by State and Local Governmental Employers* (Norwalk, CT: Governmental Accounting Standards Board, November 1994).
13 GASB Statement No. 45, *Accounting and Financial Reporting by Employers for Postemployment Benefits Other than Pensions* (Norwalk, CT: Governmental Accounting Standards Board, June 2004).

assets but also the amortization of long-term assets such as buildings and equipment. Examples of the differences between recording expenditures and expenses are as follows:

A Governmental Fund Using the Flows of Financial Resources Measurement Focus			Government-Wide Statements Using the Flows of Economic Resources Measurement Focus		
Expenditures	10,000		Salary Expense	10,000	
Cash		10,000	Cash		10,000
To record the payment of salaries; expiration of financial resource.			To record the payment of salaries; expiration of economic resource.		
Expenditures	90,000		Equipment	90,000	
Cash		90,000	Cash		90,000
To record the purchase of a truck; expiration of financial resource.			To record the purchase of a truck.		
			Depreciation Expense	15,000	
			Accumulated Depreciation		15,000
			To record the expiration of economic resource.		

Other Financing Uses. The greatest use of the other financing uses classification is for interfund operating transfers-out to other governmental funds. Using this classification for such fund outflows prevents double counting of expenditures. For example, if an amount transferred from the general fund to the debt service fund were debited to Expenditures and then debited to Expenditures again in the debt service fund when interest and long-term debt principal were liquidated, a double counting of expenditures would occur. Also classified as other financing uses are payments made from financial resources of refunding general long-term debt (using proceeds from issuing new debt to pay old debt).

The following summary shows the debit and credit effects of flows of financial resources through a governmental fund:

Governmental Fund Actual Transactions

Debits	Credits
Expenditures	Revenues
Other Financing Uses	Other Financing Sources

Operating Debt. Governments may issue short- and long-term debt to finance their operating activities. Such financing is treated as operating debt when the debt is not incurred to acquire capital assets or other long-term economic benefits for the government. Examples of short-term operating debt include accounts payable to vendors and tax anticipation notes. Examples of long-term operating debt include certain bonds or notes payable and long-term vendor financing. Also recognized as long-term operating debt are those obligations described above that a government incurs but does not pay for in a particular year (e.g., liabilities for compensated absences, claims and judgments, and unfunded pensions).

Short-term debt is recorded in the fund as a liability if it is "normally expected to be liquidated with expendable available financial resources." Hence, governmental fund liabilities (and a corresponding expenditure) are recorded if they are normally paid in a timely manner from current financial resources. Examples are salaries, professional services, supplies, utilities, and travel. Long-term operating debt is reported as a liability in the general long-term debt account group. As this debt matures and becomes due and payable, it will become a fund liability.

Tax anticipation notes are an example of short-term operating debt. Cash inflows from property tax or income tax collections peak near the due dates for payment. Prior to their receipt, a governmental unit may have obligations that must be paid. Local banks usually provide short-term financing, using as security the taxing power of the government, which is required to sign an instrument referred to as a tax anticipation note. Receipt of cash from such notes would be recorded in the general fund with the following entry:

Cash	150,000	
Tax Anticipation Notes Payable		150,000

Later, as cash inflows from taxes provide resources, the following entry would record the payment of the notes and the interest:

Tax Anticipation Notes Payable	150,000	
Expenditures (for interest)	1,875	
Cash		151,875

Interest associated with short-term operating debt is accrued. Interest associated with long-term operating debt is not accrued.

General Long-Term Capital Debt. Debt financing incurred to acquire capital assets or other long-term economic benefits through governmental funds is termed general long-term capital debt. The majority of the proceeds acquired from issuing this debt is accounted for in capital projects funds, as an other financing source. Capital project funds are discussed in Chapter 16. The face amount of capital debt is accounted for in the general long-term debt account group discussed later in this chapter. Debt service (principal and interest payments) expenditures on all general long-term debt are accounted for in the debt service funds discussed in Chapter 16.

Special and Extraordinary Items. Special items and extraordinary items are reported separately in both the governmental and proprietary fund financial statements. Extraordinary items are those that are both unusual in nature and infrequent in occurrence. Special items arise from significant transactions or other events that are (1) within the control of management and (2) either unusual in nature or infrequent in occurrence. Special items are to be reported separately in the financial statements below nonoperating revenue and before extraordinary items. The recognition of special items and extraordinary items follows the revenue, expenditure, other financing source, and use criteria described above. An example of an extraordinary item is a natural disaster. An example of a special item is the sale of a significant governmental asset or a loss incurred as a result of a civil riot. Separate reporting of such items serves to inform the citizens and other users of the financial statements when governments engage in unusual practices such as selling assets in order to balance the budget. Items that are either unusual or infrequent but not within the control of management should be disclosed in the notes to the financial statements.

REFLECTION

- Three fund types—governmental, proprietary, and fiduciary—are used to account for activities. Each fund type has a different measurement focus and basis of accounting.

- There are two types of account groups: general capital asset and general long-term liabilities.

- Governmental funds have a measurement focus of current financial resources and use a modified accrual basis of accounting.

- Revenues are recognized when they are measurable and available.

- Expenditures are recognized when current financial resources will be used.

6

OBJECTIVE

Explain the purpose of budgets and how governments account for appropriations.

USE OF BUDGETARY ACCOUNTING

Generally, finance personnel work with operating department personnel to develop a proposed expenditures budget for a fiscal year. The governmental unit's legislative body deliberates and acts on the budget, which authorizes a certain level of expenditures for operating activities, capital acquisitions, and debt service. Authorized expenditures are termed appropriations. An authorization to raise revenue and, perhaps, long-term debt is approved. Estimates for other financing sources and other financing uses are also budgeted. An executive head, such as a governor or mayor, may be responsible for approving the budget or sending it back to the legislative body for further action. The budget, as finally approved, is recorded in the general ledger in summarized control accounts and in the subsidiary ledgers in detail accounts.

General Ledger Entries

Budgetary totals for appropriations (which are authorized expenditures), estimated revenues, other financing sources, and other financing uses are recorded in the general ledger as control accounts over more detailed budgetary entries in subsidiary ledgers. The following summary shows the debit and credit effects of budgetary entries:

Governmental Fund Budgetary Entries

Debit	Credit
Estimated Revenues	Appropriations
Estimated Other Financing Sources	Estimated Other Financing Uses

If estimated inflows do not equal estimated outflows, the difference is either a debit or credit to Budgetary Fund Balance—Unassigned. A budgetary entry is made to the appropriate fund as follows:

Estimated Revenues	10,000,000	
Estimated Other Financing Sources	1,000,000	
Appropriations		9,300,000
Estimated Other Financing Uses		1,500,000
Budgetary Fund Balance—Unassigned		200,000
To record an approved annual budget.		

Actual transactions occurring during the budget year are recorded in separate general ledger accounts. This simplifies the closing process. To close the budgetary accounts, merely reverse the entry made to record the budget. Amounts may include amendments to the original budget recorded during the year. The closing entry must be entered in the same fund as follows:

Appropriations	9,300,000	
Estimated Other Financing Uses	1,500,000	
Budgetary Fund Balance—Unassigned	200,000	
Estimated Revenues		10,000,000
Estimated Other Financing Sources		1,000,000
To close an annual budget as amended.		

Subsidiary Ledger Entries

Illustration 15-1, on page 776, details the relationship between the general ledger control accounts and the subsidiary ledger detail accounts. Usually, budgets are prepared according to object of expenditure. These are, for example, salaries, employee benefits, utilities, and supplies. Each object of expenditure is a line item in the budget or a classification of authorized spending by a department or function of the government. The appropriation for each line item is recorded in an expenditures subsidiary ledger account as a credit. During the accounting period, such credits will be offset by debits recording actual expenditure transactions. The credit balance in the subsidiary ledger account tells managers how much money they have remaining to spend for that line item purpose. Budgetary amounts of estimated other financing uses and actual other financing uses are recorded in the same manner. The detailed information recorded in the subsidiary ledgers is a key mechanism of budgetary control. That is, the accounting records should show whether spending for a line item meets or exceeds the authorization.

A subsidiary ledger for revenues is also maintained. The budgetary amount of each revenue source is recorded in a revenues subsidiary ledger account as a debit. During the accounting period, such debits will be offset by credits recording actual revenue recognition. Budgetary amounts of estimated other financing sources and actual other financing sources are recorded in the same manner.

To emphasize accounting techniques and to conserve space, this text will use only general ledger control accounts in its examples for budgetary and actual accounts.

R E F L E C T I O N

- Governments use budgets and funds because of the need to demonstrate accountability.

OVERVIEW OF GENERAL FUND PROCEDURES

7

O B J E C T I V E

Prepare journal entries for the general fund.

Illustration 15-1 is designed to be a simple example of general fund procedures that is not burdened by the complexities that follow in this chapter. It is meant to acquaint you with the mechanics of governmental accounting. The accounting and financial reporting procedures shown for the general fund are similar to those used by the special revenue, capital projects, debt service, and permanent funds, which are illustrated in Chapter 16.

You should understand three important features of this example:

1. The general ledger includes three types of accounts. **Permanent balance sheet accounts** contain financial resources, liabilities, and fund balances. **Budgetary accounts** are used to record the budget. Budget amounts are entered at the start of the period, possibly amended during the period, and closed at the end of the period. There are no actual transactions recorded in these accounts during the period. **Operating accounts** contain the actual expenditures, other financing uses, revenues, and other financing sources that occur during the period.

2. Three types of journal entries are made during the accounting period. The **budgetary entry** enters the budget into the accounting records. The **operating entries** record actual events. The **closing entries** close the budgetary accounts in one entry and the actual accounts in a second closing entry.

3. For every entry in the general ledger, there are detailed entries in the subsidiary ledgers.

Each entry in Illustration 15-1 is explained as follows:

1. The budget is entered into the general ledger budgetary accounts. An excess of estimated revenues, estimated other financing sources over appropriations, and estimated other financing uses would create a credit to the budgetary fund balance. In this case, appropriations (there are no estimated other financing uses) exceed revenues and estimated other financing sources; thus, there is a debit to the budgetary fund balance. The debit entry to the budgetary fund balance anticipates a decrease in the fund balance during the period. Budgetary amounts may be amended during the year by legislative action but are otherwise left

Illustration 15-1
Simple Example of Governmental Accounts—General Ledger and Subsidiary Ledger Entries

GENERAL LEDGER ACCOUNTS:

Permanent Balance Sheet Accounts:

Cash

Jan. 1, 2018, Balance	8,000	(7) Pay vouchers	110,000
(5) Tax collection	90,500		
(3) Cash revenues	14,500		
(4) Asset sale	4,800		
Dec. 31, 2018, Balance	7,800		

Property Taxes Receivable

Jan. 1, 2018, Balance	12,000	(5) Tax collection	90,500
(2) Tax levy	85,000		
Dec. 31, 2018, Balance	6,500		

Vouchers Payable

(7) Pay vouchers	110,000	Jan. 1, 2018, Balance	13,000
		(6) Expenditures	106,800
		Dec. 31, 2018, Balance	9,800

Fund Balance

(9) Close 2018	2,500	Jan. 1, 2018, Balance	7,000
		Dec. 31, 2018	4,500

Budgetary Accounts:

Estimated Revenues

(1) Budget entry	97,000	(8) Close budget	97,000

Estimated Other Financing Sources

(1) Budget entry	5,000	(8) Close budget	5,000

Appropriations

(8) Close budget	105,000	(1) Budget entry	105,000

Budgetary Fund Balance

(1) Budget entry	3,000	(8) Close budget	3,000

Operating Accounts:

Revenues

(9) Close actual	99,500	(2) Tax levy	85,000
		(3) Cash revenues	14,500

Other Financing Sources

(9) Close actual	4,800	(4) Asset sale	4,800

Expenditures

(6) Expenditures	106,800	(9) Close actual	106,800

unchanged during the period and are reversed at the end of the period as part of the closing procedure, so they never actually impact the fund balance.[14] The budgetary entry is as follows:

Estimated Revenues	97,000	
Estimated Other Financing Sources	5,000	
Budgetary Fund Balance	3,000	
Appropriations		105,000

---

14 Some governments do not maintain separate budgetary accounts. These governments enter the budget into the actual accounts. Since the budget is reversed at year-end, the net effect is to increase or decrease the fund balance by the difference between actual revenues and expenditures—the same impact as would have been recorded had the budgetary entries not been made.

SUBSIDIARY LEDGER ACCOUNTS:

Expenditures—Salary

(6) Expenditures	57,000	(1) Enter budget	55,000
Balance	2,000		

Revenues—Property Tax

(1) Enter budget	82,000	(2) Tax levy	85,000
		Balance	3,000

Expenditures—Supplies

(6) Expenditures	22,000	(1) Enter budget	23,000
		Balance	1,000

Revenues—Fines

(1) Enter budget	12,000	(3) Cash collected	11,500
Balance	500		

Expenditures—Repairs

(6) Expenditures	9,600	(1) Enter budget	9,000
Balance	600		

Revenues—Licenses

(1) Enter budget	3,000	(3) Cash collected	3,000

Expenditures—Capital

(6) Expenditures	11,500	(1) Enter budget	11,000
Balance	500		

Other Financing Sources—Asset Sale

(1) Enter budget	5,000	(4) Cash collected	4,800
Balance	200		

Expenditures—Miscellaneous

(6) Expenditures	6,700	(1) Enter budget	7,000
Balance	300		

This entry is supported by detailed entries in subsidiary ledger revenue accounts, other financing sources accounts, and expenditure accounts. See entries marked "1" in the subsidiary ledger accounts. The real control feature of the budget entry is found in the subsidiary ledgers. Consider the subsidiary ledger revenue and other financing sources accounts. Budgeted amounts are entered in the accounts as debits so that they can be compared to the actual credits as they actually occur. At any time during the year, a fast comparison of budget versus year-to-date actual is possible. At the end of the year, actual amounts are compared to budgeted amounts to arrive at a variance. Appropriations (budgeted expenditures) are entered as credits so that they can be compared to actual debits as they occur. Again, there can be a comparison of budget versus year-to-date actual for variance analysis at the end of the period.

2. Property taxes are recorded as receivables at the time taxes are levied on property owners. Revenue is credited in the period for which the taxes are levied (that is, in the period the money will be spent) provided the taxes are due by the end of the period. Not shown are the individual receivables for each property recorded in a receivables subsidiary ledger.

Property Taxes Receivable.	85,000	
Revenues		85,000

3. Revenues from fines and licenses are recorded when cash is received because these amounts cannot be predicted accurately. The detailed source of each revenue is recorded in the subsidiary ledger.

Cash	14,500	
Revenues		14,500

4. Proceeds from the sale of used fixed assets are recorded in the general and subsidiary ledgers.

Cash	4,800	
Other Financing Sources		4,800

5. Property taxes are collected, including amounts from previous periods.

Cash	90,500	
Property Taxes Receivable		90,500

6. Expenditures are recorded when the liability is incurred and formal vouchers are prepared. Vouchers are documents attached to vendor invoices that contain information about the payables. They must be signed to authorize payments of the liabilities. Details of the expenditures are recorded in the subsidiary ledger.

Expenditures	106,800	
Vouchers Payable		106,800

7. Vouchers are paid.

Vouchers Payable	110,000	
Cash		110,000

8. The budgetary entry is closed by reversing the original budgetary entry. This "zeros out" the budgetary accounts.

Appropriations	105,000	
Estimated Revenues		97,000
Estimated Other Financing Sources		5,000
Budgetary Fund Balance		3,000

This entry is made only in the general ledger. The amounts in the subsidiary ledgers are not removed but remain so that the budget can be compared to actual amounts.

9. Actual revenues and actual other financing sources are closed against actual expenditures to arrive at the change in the actual fund balance for the year. Again, this entry is made only in the general ledger. Detailed amounts are left in the subsidiary ledger so that variance analysis may be performed.

Revenues	99,500	
Other Financing Sources	4,800	
Fund Balance	2,500	
Expenditures		106,800

Each subsidiary ledger revenue, other financing sources, and expenditures account now may be analyzed as to the cause of variances from budgeted amounts. Once the budgetary comparisons are done, the balances are closed to allow for the recording of the next period's activity.

Accounting for the General Fund—An Expanded Example

To visualize the accounting process of the general fund and the flow of information that produces the financial reports, the activities of the city of Middletown are examined for the fiscal year ended September 30, 2019. The general fund trial balance on September 30, 2018, appears in Illustration 15-2.

The city has $271,000 in financial resources (cash, net receivables, and inventory). The liability Vouchers Payable offsets $170,000 of the resources with the fund balances offsetting the remaining $101,000. There are five classifications of fund balances for the general fund: nonspendable fund balance, restricted fund balance, committed fund balance, assigned fund balance, and unassigned fund balance.[15] The nonspendable fund balance is determined first and consists

---

15 GASB Statement No. 54, *Fund Balance Reporting and Governmental Fund Type Definitions* (Norwalk, CT: Governmental Accounting Standards Board, February 2009).

Illustration 15-2
City of Middletown
General Fund Trial Balance
September 30, 2018

	Debit	Credit
Cash	82,000	
Investments	153,000	
Taxes Receivable—Delinquent	30,000	
Allowance for Uncollectible Delinquent Taxes		20,000
Tax Liens Receivable	24,000	
Allowance for Uncollectible Tax Liens		8,000
Supplies Inventory	10,000	
Vouchers Payable		170,000
Fund Balance—Nonspendable, Inventory		10,000
Fund Balance—Restricted for Social Services		16,000
Fund Balance—Committed to Education		2,000
Fund Balance—Assigned to Parks and Recreation		10,000
Fund Balance—Unassigned		63,000
Totals	299,000	299,000

of amounts that cannot be spent because they are either (a) not in spendable form or (b) legally or contractually required to be maintained intact. The inventory of $10,000 is not in spendable form and thus would be classified as nonspendable. The remaining fund balance that is determined to be spendable is then classified as restricted, committed, assigned, or unassigned.

A fund balance is considered to be restricted when constraints placed on the use of resources are either (a) externally imposed by creditors, grantors, contributors, or laws or regulations of other governments; or (b) imposed by law through constitutional provisions or enabling legislation. The $16,000 restricted for social services may reflect funds that by law must be used for welfare payments. Committed fund balances are amounts that can only be used for specific purposes pursuant to constraints imposed by formal action of the government's highest level of decision-making authority. The $2,000 committed to education could have come from the city council's intent to provide funds to hire additional teachers. Assigned fund balances are amounts constrained by the government's intent to be used for a specific purpose, but are neither restricted nor committed. Intent should be expressed by (a) the governing body itself or (b) a body or official to which the governing body has delegated the authority to assign amounts to be used for specific purposes. The $10,000 assigned to parks and recreation could have been authorized by the budget committee of the city council. Finally, all remaining fund balance amounts not previously accounted for are classified as unassigned. The $40,000 is unassigned and may be used for any purpose.

Uncollected property taxes may appear in three accounts. Taxes Receivable—Current is debited when property taxes are levied, and Revenue is credited. When uncollected property taxes are past due and interest revenue begins to accrue, the account balance is transferred to Taxes Receivable—Delinquent. When tax liens (a claim to take property for unpaid taxes) are placed on properties for uncollected taxes, the remaining amount of uncollected property taxes is transferred to Tax Liens Receivable. In the Middletown September 30, 2018, general fund trial balance, all property taxes receivable are past due. An allowance account for estimated uncollectibles is established for each receivable.

Recording the Budget. The city council and the mayor have approved the budget for the following fiscal year, with estimated revenues of $1,350,000, appropriations of $1,300,000, and an estimated transfer of $30,000 to be made during the year to the debt service fund. Again, transfers to other funds are not expenditures and are segregated in the budgetary entry into a budgetary account labeled Estimated Other Financing Uses. The October 1, 2018, entry to record Middletown's fiscal year 2019 budget for its general fund is as shown on page 780.

B1.   Estimated Revenues   1,350,000

Appropriations   1,300,000
Estimated Other Financing Uses   30,000
Budgetary Fund Balance—Unassigned.   20,000

To support total estimated revenues of $1,350,000, a breakdown of sources should be provided in the explanation of the budget entry or in a separate schedule. In practice, there could be as many as 100 or more revenue items. As an example, however, the number of revenue items is condensed, as shown in the schedule of estimated revenues (Illustration 15-3).

Illustration 15-3
City of Middletown
General Fund Estimated Revenues
For Year Ended September 30, 2019

General property taxes	$ 882,500
Fines	75,500
Licenses and permits	50,000
Revenue from federal grants	200,000
Other revenues	142,000
Total estimated revenues	$1,350,000

Just as the total projected income is debited to Estimated Revenues in the general ledger, so each of the detailed estimated sources is debited to its own account in the subsidiary revenue ledger. The following subsidiary account for general property taxes illustrates the procedure of posting to subsidiary records:

Revenue Ledger

ACCOUNT General Property Taxes					ACCOUNT NO.
DATE	ITEM	DEBIT (Estimate)	CREDIT (Actual)	BALANCE (DR.) CR.	
Oct. 1	Budget estimate	**882,500**		(882,500)	

Not only must the accounting system provide for control of revenues, but it also must accommodate expenditures. To provide a basis for comparison between expected and actual expenditures, budgetary as well as actual expenditures accounts are an integral part of the accounting system. In the entry to record Middletown's budget for its general fund, the credit to Appropriations represents the estimate of the expenditures of $1,300,000 for the coming year. In support of the appropriations total, a summary of approved estimated expenditures by departments or activities might appear as shown in Illustration 15-4.

Illustration 15-4
City of Middletown
Department or Activity Appropriations
For Year Ended September 30, 2019

General government: legislative, judicial, and executive	$ 129,000
Public safety	277,300
Education	591,450
Highways and streets	94,500
Sanitation and health	97,750
Welfare	51,000
Culture and recreation	59,000
Total appropriations	$1,300,000

Each of these departments or activities must submit detailed appropriation requests on the basis of subfunctions and object of expenditure. The Education Division, for example, might present the estimate of expenditures shown in Illustration 15-5.

Illustration 15-5
City of Middletown
Education Division
Request for Appropriation
For Year Ended September 30, 2019

Supplies.	$160,000
Salaries	350,000
Equipment	60,000
Professional fees	21,450
Total.	$591,450

A further modification to controlling expenditures is to establish subsidiary accounts by division or department. If this approach is followed by the city of Middletown, each of the expenditure items for the Education Division would have its own subsidiary account, such as the one that follows for supplies. Each expenditure account would be designed to show the original appropriation, the encumbrances (amounts committed), the expenditures (amounts spent), and the remaining unobligated (i.e., neither encumbered nor expended) balance.

Education Division Expenditure Ledger

ACCOUNT Supplies							ACCOUNT NO.
		ENCUMBRANCES			EXPENDITURES		UNOBLIGATED
DATE	ITEM	DEBIT	CREDIT	BALANCE	ITEM	TOTAL	BALANCE
Oct. 1	Budget appropriation						**160,000**

Recording Actual Revenues and Transfers. Property taxes are a major source of revenue for Middletown's general fund and should be recognized in the fiscal period for which the taxes are levied. The property tax roll provides information about property owners, legal descriptions, and amounts of gross tax levies. The following journal entry shows that the total tax levy against property owners is debited to Taxes Receivable—Current in a general ledger entry. The amount of allowance for uncollectible taxes is credited in the same journal entry, and the net amount (the amount the government expects to receive) is credited to Revenues:

1.	Taxes Receivable—Current.	919,000	
	Revenues		881,300
	Allowance for Uncollectible Current Taxes		37,700

Recording the revenue for the expected amount to be received is different from the accounting we would see for a business enterprise. A business enterprise would credit revenue for the entire amount of sales. In a separate entry, Bad Debt Expense would be debited for the amount of receivables expected to be uncollectible. In a business enterprise, bad debt expense is viewed as a cost of doing business. The costs of doing business for a period (expenses) are matched on the income statement with revenues for the same period to determine net income. In governmental funds, however, property tax revenues are generated by levying taxes rather than by earning them through the production and sale of goods and services. Consequently, uncollected taxes are viewed as reductions of revenue, not as costs of doing business. If allowance amounts eventually prove to be overstated, they are written down with an offsetting credit entry to Revenues. If understated, they are increased with an offsetting debit to Revenues.

The general property taxes account in the subsidiary revenue ledger is credited for the actual revenue. After the preceding entry is posted, General Property Taxes appears as follows:

Revenue Ledger

ACCOUNT General Property Taxes				ACCOUNT NO.
DATE	ITEM	DEBIT (Estimate)	CREDIT (Actual)	BALANCE (DR.) CR.
Oct. 1	Budget estimate	882,500		(882,500)
1	Tax levy		**881,300**	(1,200)

During the fiscal period, a debit balance in a subsidiary revenue account usually represents additional revenue expected in the future. At the end of the fiscal period, a debit balance indicates a deficiency of actual revenue as compared to estimated revenue, while a credit balance shows an excess of actual over estimated revenues.

During the year, the following additional events related to revenue are recorded in the general fund of Middletown, whose beginning trial balance is shown on page 779.

	Event	Entry in the General Fund		
2.	Of the total delinquent taxes of $30,000 carried over from the prior period, $14,000 is collected. The balance is uncollectible.	Cash . . . . Allowance for Uncollectible Delinquent Taxes . . . . . Taxes Receivable—Delinquent	14,000 16,000	30,000
3.	The excess allowance for uncollectible delinquent taxes is transferred to Revenues. This transaction is viewed as a change in an accounting estimate made in a prior period.	Allowance for Uncollectible Delinquent Taxes . . . . . Revenues	4,000	4,000
4.	Of $24,000 total tax liens carried over from the prior period, $11,000 is collected. The balance is uncollectible.	Cash . . . . Allowance for Uncollectible Tax Liens . . . . Tax Liens Receivable	11,000 8,000	19,000
5.	The remaining Tax Liens Receivable are charged against Revenues. This transaction is viewed as a change in an accounting estimate made in a prior period.	Revenues . . . . Tax Liens Receivable	5,000	5,000
6.	Of current taxes receivable (due on or before the end of the fiscal period), $850,000 is collected during the year and $12,700 is written off as uncollectible.	Cash . . . . Allowance for Uncollectible Current Taxes . . . . Taxes Receivable—Current	850,000 12,700	862,700
7.	A 1% sales tax on restaurant food and beverages beginning on the first day of the last quarter is adopted by Middletown. The annual budget is amended to reflect the impact of this new legislation.	Estimated Revenues . . . . Budgetary Fund Balance	9,000	9,000
8.	Restaurant food and beverage sales for the last quarter of the year are estimated at $950,000.	Sales Taxes Receivable . . . . Revenues	9,500	9,500

	Event	Entry in the General Fund		
9.	Police fines of $79,000 are imposed and collected during the year.	Cash .... Revenues	79,000	79,000
10.	Pet licenses are sold for 2-year periods. Half of the pet license fees collected during the current year apply to the current year. The other half apply to next year. None of the fees are refundable.	Cash .... Revenues .... Deferred Revenues..........................	12,000	6,000 6,000
11.	Revenues from other licenses and permits apply only to the current period and are not refundable.	Cash .... Revenues	35,000	35,000
12.	Interest revenue earned on investment of idle cash during the year.	Cash .... Revenues	17,000	17,000
13.	A contribution by a business to entice the city to extend a storm sewer to its property along a city street.	Cash .... Revenues	130,000	130,000
14.	City council decided that the city's Fund Balance—Unassigned was too lean and rescinded the assignment of the parks and recreation money	Fund Balance—Assigned .... Fund Balance—Unreserved, Undesignated....	10,000	10,000

15.	At year-end, property taxes not collected are classified as delinquent, as are the estimated uncollectible allowances.	Taxes Receivable—Delinquent ....
		   Taxes Receivable—Current
		   ($919,000 − $862,700) ....
			56,300	56,300

		Allowance for Uncollectible Current Taxes ....
		   Allowance for Uncollectible Delinquent Taxes
		   ($37,700 − $12,700) ....
			25,000	25,000

16.	Middletown receives a $150,000 check from the federal government for the current fiscal year to assist in the operation of its child-care program and documentation promising an additional $50,000, half of which is for the current fiscal year and half for the next fiscal year.	Cash ....
		Due from Federal Government ....
		   Revenues ....
		   Deferred Revenue ....
			150,000
			50,000
				175,000
				25,000

As indicated in the second and fourth entries, a revision of the estimated amount of uncollectible current and delinquent taxes and tax liens is treated as a change in accounting estimate through Revenues. Adjustments of confirmed errors of prior periods and adjustments from a change in accounting principle are recorded directly in the Fund Balance—Unassigned.

Recording Encumbrances and Actual Expenditures. To prevent overexpenditure, the Middletown general fund uses an encumbrance system. An encumbrance can be viewed as an *expected expenditure* and assists the administration to avoid overspending and to plan for payment of the *expected liability* on a timely basis. It can also be viewed as a contra account to the fund balance to reflect the ultimate decrease that will occur. Under this system, whenever a purchase order or other commitment is approved, an entry is made to record the estimated cost of the commitment. For example, an approved purchase order for school supplies, estimated to cost $10,000, is recorded as follows:

17.	Encumbrances..	10,000	
	Fund Balance—Assigned or Committed		10,000

The entry is posted to the general ledger, where Encumbrances is a quasi expenditure account and where Fund Balance—Assigned or Committed is a form of restriction of the fund

8

OBJECTIVE

Demonstrate how to account for encumbrances.

balance. The entry also is entered in the encumbrances section of the supplies account of the subsidiary expenditure ledger for the Education Division, reducing the unobligated balance, as follows:

Education Division Expenditure Ledger

ACCOUNT Supplies							ACCOUNT NO.
		ENCUMBRANCES			EXPENDITURES		UNOBLIGATED
DATE	ITEM	DEBIT	CREDIT	BALANCE	ITEM	TOTAL	BALANCE
Oct. 1	Budget appropriation						160,000
4	Purchase order	**10,000**		10,000			150,000

When the invoice is received for the purchase of items or services, the encumbrance entry is reversed. The contra account to the fund balance is no longer needed since the expenditure recorded will directly reduce the fund balance in the closing procedure. Note that it is always the amount of the original estimate and not the actual cost that is used in the reversing entry. Assuming that the invoice for supplies amounts to $10,200, the two entries to record the receipt of the supplies invoice are as follows:

18.	Fund Balance—Assigned or Committed	10,000	
	Encumbrances		10,000
	To reverse entry for encumbrance at estimated cost.		
19.	Expenditures	10,200	
	Vouchers Payable		10,200
	To record invoice at actual cost.		

The supplies account in the subsidiary expenditure ledger appears as follows:

Education Division Expenditure Ledger

ACCOUNT Supplies							ACCOUNT NO.
		ENCUMBRANCES			EXPENDITURES		UNOBLIGATED
DATE	ITEM	DEBIT	CREDIT	BALANCE	ITEM	TOTAL	BALANCE
Oct. 1	Budget appropriation						160,000
4	Purchase order	**10,000**		10,000			150,000
Nov. 7	Invoice received		**10,000**	0	**10,200**	10,200	149,800

When the encumbrance and the actual amount are identical, the unobligated balance is not changed. However, when the amounts are not identical, the net effect is an adjustment of the unobligated balance to reflect the amount of the actual expenditure. Thus, at any time, the subsidiary ledgers provide a continuing record of the unobligated balances and of how closely the actual expenditures match encumbrances. The following equation is derived from an examination of the supplies account:

Unobligated Balance = Appropriations − Expenditures Total − Encumbrances Balance

The encumbrances account can appear as a contra to the Fund Balance—Unassigned, at year-end as shown in the example on page 785.

Fund balances:

Assigned or Committed		XXX
Unassigned	XXX	
Less Encumbrances	XXX	XXX
Total Fund Balance.		XXX

It is, however, preferable to close it against the fund balance at year-end to clarify what amount of the fund balance is available for the future. At year-end, the remaining balance in the encumbrances account is closed against Fund Balance—Unassigned as follows:

Fund Balance—Unassigned	XXX	
Encumbrances		XXX

This will leave the amount of the outstanding encumbrances in Fund Balance—Assigned or Committed, which is reported in the fund balances section of the balance sheet. Such treatment demonstrates the commitment of the government to provide for outstanding purchase orders and serves to reduce the amount of expendable available financial resources for new expenditures indicated in Fund Balance—Unassigned. Encumbrances are not reported in the statement of revenues, expenditures, and changes in fund balances since the actual transaction with outside parties has not yet occurred. However, GASB Statement No. 54 requires significant encumbrances to be disclosed in the notes to the financial statements in conjunction with other commitments.

For expenditures such as salaries, which are subject to little variation and to additional internal controls, it is not customary to involve the encumbrance accounts. When salaries are paid, they are recorded directly as expenditures, and they reduce the unobligated balance of the salaries account in the subsidiary expenditure ledger.

Encumbrances of a Prior Period. When encumbrances are carried over from the prior year to the current year, the encumbrance closing entry of the prior year is reversed in order to reinstate the past commitments that will be honored in the current year.

Encumbrances	XXX	
Fund Balance—Unassigned		XXX

Included in the current-year budgetary entry for appropriations should be an amount equal to that prior year-end encumbrance. The encumbrances will be disposed of in the manner described earlier. The unassigned fund balance will ultimately be reduced by the current year's actual expenditures.

The following events relate to Middletown's expenditures and transfers during the year:

Event			Entry in the General Fund		
20.	Throughout the year, encumbrances totaling $738,000 were recorded; there were no prior-year encumbrances.		Encumbrances. . . . . Fund Balance—Assigned	738,000	738,000
21.	Vouchers were approved, liquidating $700,000 of encumbrances for:		Fund Balance—Assigned . . . . Encumbrances.	700,000	700,000
	Supplies.	$300,000			
	Building	200,000*	Inventory of Supplies	300,000	
	Other expenditures	272,000	Expenditures	472,000	
	Total	$772,000	Vouchers Payable		772,000

*This also requires an entry in the general fixed assets account group.

(continued)

Event		Entry in the General Fund		
22. Vouchers were approved for the following nonencumbered items:		Expenditures . . . . Vouchers Payable	518,000	518,000
Salaries	$490,000			
Other expenditures	28,000			
Total	$518,000			
23. Vouchers totaling $1,300,000 were paid.		Vouchers Payable . . . . Cash	1,300,000	1,300,000
24. Transfer of $30,000 is made to the debt service fund.		Other Financing Uses . . . . Cash	30,000	30,000
25. Supplies totaling $260,000 were consumed.		Expenditures . . . . Inventory of Supplies	260,000	260,000
26. Adjust Fund Balance—Nonspendable to equal inventory. (See following discussion.)		Fund Balance—Unassigned . . . . Fund Balance—Nonspendable	40,000	40,000

Fund Balance Nonspendable. The amount of unassigned fund balance represents expendable, available financial resources. Any resources not available to finance expenditures of the current or future years must be removed from the unassigned fund balance. The fund balance assigned or committed relating to encumbrances has already been discussed. An asset not available to finance expenditures for Middletown is the inventory of supplies, which will not be converted into cash and will not be available to meet future commitments. Therefore, the unassigned fund balance must be reclassified to nonspendable by an amount equal to the inventory on the financial statement date. In this case, the amount of the inventory at year-end is $50,000 ($10,000 + $300,000 − $260,000). The account Fund Balance—Nonspendable is kept equal to the inventory amount by periodic adjustment through the unassigned fund balance account.

Corrections of Prior Years' Errors. Corrections of previous years' errors are made directly through the account Fund Balance—Unassigned. For example, Middletown failed to record invoiced expenditures for last year of $30,600 that were not encumbered. Of this amount, $10,100 was paid this year and incorrectly debited to Expenditures. The unpaid portion of $20,500 is vouchered. The entry is as follows:

27.	Fund Balance—Unassigned	30,600	
	Expenditures		10,100
	Vouchers Payable		20,500
	To correct error for failure to record expenditures chargeable to last year.		

Reimbursement for Expenditure. When expenditures are made from the general fund on behalf of other funds, a transfer is made to reimburse the general fund. The reimbursement is recorded as an expenditure by the reimbursing fund and as a reduction in expenditures by the recipient (general) fund. For example, $3,000 is received from the special revenue fund to reimburse the general fund for payroll expenditures. The entry in the general fund is recorded as follows:

28.	Cash	3,000	
	Expenditures		3,000

Investments in Marketable Securities and Other Financial Instruments. Governmental entities frequently have cash available for short-, intermediate-, and long-term investment. For example, the general fund may have cash available for short periods of time pending disbursement for operating needs, the capital projects funds may have bond proceeds available for intermediate-term investment pending disbursement for construction costs, and fiduciary funds may have cash available for long-term investment. Investment pools used by several funds within a single government or by several governments may have cash available for investment for varying terms.

Governments usually make deposits with financial institutions (such as demand deposit accounts and certificates of deposit) and direct investments in U.S. government obligations. Governmental entities also invest in commercial paper, bankers' acceptances, mutual funds, pooled investment funds managed by a state treasurer, and repurchase agreements with broker-dealers. All investments, except for money market investments and participating interest-earning investment contracts with a remaining maturity of one year or less, are to be reported at *fair value* on the balance sheet. Fair value is defined as the amount at which an investment could be exchanged in a current transaction between willing parties, other than in a forced or liquidation sale.[16] The change in fair value of investments is reported as a *net increase (decrease) in the fair value of investments* and recognized as revenue in the operating statement. For example, if general fund investments increased in value during the period, the following entry would be made to reflect the change in fair value:

| 29. | Investments . . . . | 4,500 | |
| | Net Increase in the Fair Value of Investments . . . . | | 4,500 |

To meet cash flow requirements for operating or capital purposes, or to earn a higher return on investment, many governments enter into *reverse repurchase agreements* and/or *securities lending transactions*. In a reverse repurchase agreement, the government temporarily converts securities in their portfolios to cash by selling securities to a broker-dealer for cash, with a promise to repay cash plus interest in exchange for the return of the same securities.[17] In securities lending transactions, governments lend out their portfolio securities in return for collateral—which may be cash, securities, or letters of credit—and simultaneously agree to return the collateral for the same securities in the future.[18]

The investments must remain on the balance sheet of the government in both cases—whether selling securities with a promise to repurchase or lending them for a period of time. The agreements to repurchase (or return) are reported as fund liabilities. Any cash received (including cash received as collateral) is reported as an asset. Interest costs and broker fees are reported as expenditures and are not netted with any interest earned.

Extensive note disclosures on all investments and deposits with banks and other financial institutions are required. Governments must disclose their relevant accounting policies as to investments. They must also disclose credit risk, market risk, and legal risk for all investments, including derivatives.

Governments sometimes pledge or sell receivables and future revenue in exchange for immediate cash payments. As in business, the extent to which the government retains or gives up control over the receivables will determine if this exchange is recognized as revenue (sale) or liability (pledge).

Investments in Derivatives. Governmental entities have been investing in derivative instruments for years. Derivative instruments can be a useful tool for governmental entities hedging the interest rate risk associated with their issued bonds. However, speculative investments in derivatives can lead to large losses and have been a leading cause of fiscal distress for governmental entities. Two examples are Orange County, California, which filed for bankruptcy in 1994 due to losses incurred by its derivative investments, and more recently the case of Jefferson County, which lost millions in synthetic rate swaps and saw its debt balloon to $5 billion.[19]

GASB Statement No. 53, *Accounting and Financial Reporting for Derivative Instruments* (June 2008), requires derivatives to be reported at their fair market value. The changes in fair market value should be reported as gains or losses in the statement of changes in net assets. An exception is made for effective hedges. If the derivative is deemed to represent an effective hedge against other assets or liabilities, then gains and losses should be deferred and reported on balance sheets as deferred inflows or outflows. A derivative is determined to be an effective hedge if it significantly reduces financial risk by substantially offsetting the changes in cash flows or fair values of the item with which it is associated. Extensive details concerning how to determine if a derivative instrument is an effective hedge are provided in Statement No. 53.

---

16 GASB Statement No. 31, *Accounting and Financial Reporting for Certain Investments and for External Investment Pools* (Norwalk, CT: Governmental Accounting Standards Board, March 1997).

17 GASB Statement No. 3, *Deposits with Financial Institutions, Investments (including Repurchase Agreements, and Reverse Repurchase Agreements)* (Norwalk, CT: Governmental Accounting Standards Board, April 1986).

18 GASB Technical Bulletin No. 94-1, *Disclosure about Derivatives and Similar Debt and Investment Transactions* (Norwalk, CT: Governmental Accounting Standards Board, December 1994).

19 Matt Taibbi, "Looting Main Street," *RollingStone,* March 2010.

The preclosing year-end trial balance for Middletown is presented in Illustration 15-6.

Illustration 15-6
City of Middletown
General Fund Trial Balance
September 30, 2019

	Debit	Credit
Cash	50,000	
Investments	157,500	
Property Taxes Receivable—Delinquent	56,300	
Allowance for Uncollectible Delinquent Taxes		25,000
Deferred Revenue		31,000
Inventory of Supplies	50,000	
Vouchers Payable		190,700
Sales Taxes Receivable	9,500	
Due from Federal Government	50,000	
Fund Balance—Nonspendable		50,000
Fund Balance—Restricted		16,000
Fund Balance—Committed		2,000
Fund Balance—Assigned		38,000
Fund Balance—Unassigned		2,400
Revenues		1,336,300
Expenditures	1,250,100	
Other Financing Uses	30,000	
Encumbrances	38,000	
Estimated Revenues	1,359,000	
Appropriations		1,300,000
Estimated Other Financing Uses		30,000
Budgetary Fund Balance—Unassigned		29,000
Totals	3,050,400	3,050,400

Closing the General Fund

The simplest closing process is, first, to reverse the budgetary entries and then to close the actual revenue and expenditure accounts, including the other financing sources and uses accounts, into the fund balance—unassigned account. The outstanding balance in the encumbrances account is also temporarily closed. Budgetary closing entries for Middletown would appear as follows:

B2.	Appropriations	1,300,000	
	Estimated Other Financing Uses	30,000	
	Budgetary Fund Balance—Unassigned	29,000	
	Estimated Revenues		1,359,000
	To reverse entry recording budget (including amendment).		

The actual closing entries are as follows:

30.	Revenues	1,336,300	
	Expenditures		1,250,100
	Other Financing Uses		30,000
	Fund Balance—Unassigned		56,200
	To close the actual accounts.		

31.	Fund Balance—Unassigned	38,000	
	Encumbrances		38,000
	To close outstanding encumbrances.		

REFLECTION

- The general ledger contains permanent balance sheet, budgetary, and operating accounts.

- Budgetary, operating, and closing entries are used in accounting for the general ledger accounts.

- Understanding the accounting and reporting procedures of the general fund will help in understanding accounting for other funds.

FINANCIAL REPORTS OF THE GENERAL FUND

9

OBJECTIVE

Prepare fund financial statements for the general fund.

Financial statements covering all funds of state and local governments are presented in Chapter 17. The required financial statements include fund-based and consolidated government-wide statements. Greater detail, including comparative data, may be provided by supplemental reports for individual funds and account groups and will be illustrated when appropriate.

To illustrate the recommended form of the financial statements, the year-end reports of Middletown's general fund are developed from the year-end trial balance shown on page 800. These reports consist of a balance sheet and a statement of revenues, expenditures, and changes in fund balances.

Balance Sheet

The general fund year-end balance sheet for the city of Middletown, shown in Illustration 15-7 on page 790, differs substantially from its private business counterpart. First, it deals primarily with current assets and current liabilities, and the difference between these two amounts appears as the fund balance—nonspendable, restricted, committed, assigned, or unassigned. Second, the long-term classifications of assets and liabilities are excluded, since the general fixed assets are included in the general fixed assets account group, and the general long-term debt is carried in the general long-term debt account group.

Statement of Revenues, Expenditures, and Changes in Fund Balances

The statement of revenues, expenditures, and changes in fund balances is prepared on an all-inclusive basis, disclosing all elements that contribute to the change in fund balances. This operating statement contains details on the major revenue sources and on expenditures by function or program. Other financing sources or uses and any corrections that altered the fund balance are also presented. The detailed source of each revenue and purpose for each expenditure is obtained from the subsidiary ledger, not the control entries of the previous example.

For governmental funds for which an annual budget legally is adopted, a comparison of actual results to both the original and amended budget is required. The comparison can be accomplished either as a schedule provided as required supplementary information (RSI) immediately following the financial statements or as a separate statement. Both original and final budget amounts are compared with actual amounts, and a variance column showing the difference between budgeted and actual amounts is encouraged. In order for the comparisons to be meaningful, the actual amounts in the schedule are reported on the budgetary basis. Further,

Illustration 15-7
City of Middletown
General Fund Balance Sheet
September 30, 2019

Assets

Cash		$ 50,000
Investments		157,500
Property taxes receivable—delinquent	$ 56,300	
Less allowance for uncollectible delinquent taxes	25,000	31,300
Sales taxes receivable		9,500
Due from federal government		50,000
Inventory of supplies		50,000
Total assets		$348,300

Liabilities and Fund Equity

Liabilities:		
Vouchers payable	$190,700	
Deferred revenue	31,000	
Total liabilities		$221,700
Fund balances:		
Nonspendable	$ 50,000	
Restricted	16,000	
Committed	2,000	
Assigned	38,000	
Unassigned	20,600	
Total fund balance		126,600
Total liabilities and fund balance		$348,300

a reconciliation from the budgetary basis to GAAP is shown either on the face of the budgetary comparison statement or on a separate schedule.

The budgetary comparison schedule for the general fund of Middletown is shown in Illustration 15-8. Estimated and actual amounts of revenues, expenditures, and other changes are reported on a budgetary basis. The beginning and ending fund balances are reported. The final actual fund balances amount ($126,600) must agree with the total fund balance shown on the balance sheet.

REFLECTION

- The two year-end statements of the general fund are the balance sheet and the statement of revenues, expenditures, and changes in fund balances.

- Budgetary comparison schedules or statements are also required for the general fund and other funds for which a budget is adopted.

- Both annual statements differ significantly from those in the private sector.

Illustration 15-8
City of Middletown
Budgetary Comparison Schedule
General Fund
For Year Ended September 30, 2019
(budgetary basis)

	Original Budget	Amended Budget	Actual Results	Variance Favorable (Unfavorable)
Revenues:				
General property taxes	$ 881,000	$ 882,500	$ 880,300	$ (2,200)
Fines	75,000	75,500	79,000	3,500
Licenses and permits	50,000	50,000	41,000	(9,000)
Intergovernmental revenues	200,000	200,000	175,000	(25,000)
Sales taxes	10,000	9,000	9,500	500
Other revenues	145,000	142,000	151,500	9,500
Total revenues	$1,361,000	$1,359,000	$1,336,300	$(22,700)
Expenditures:				
General government	$ 130,000	$ 129,000	$ 120,305	$ 8,695
Public safety	275,000	277,300	252,795	24,505
Highways and streets	95,000	94,500	86,100	8,400
Sanitation and health	98,000	97,750	87,750	10,000
Welfare	50,000	51,000	46,000	5,000
Culture and recreation	60,000	59,000	53,400	5,600
Education	590,000	591,450	603,750	(12,300)
Total expenditures	$1,298,000	$1,300,000	$1,250,100	$ 49,900
Excess of revenues over expenditures	$ 63,000	$ 59,000	$ 86,200	$ 27,200
Other financing sources (uses)	(30,000)	(30,000)	(30,000)	0
Excess of revenues and other sources over expenditures and other uses	$ 33,000	$ 29,000	$ 56,200	$ 27,200
Fund balances, October 1, 2018	101,000	101,000	101,000	0
Correction of prior year's expenditures	0	0	(30,600)	(30,600)
Fund balances, September 30, 2019	$ 134,000	$ 130,000	$ 126,600	$ (3,400)

ACCOUNTING FOR GENERAL CAPITAL ASSETS AND GENERAL LONG-TERM OBLIGATIONS

10

OBJECTIVE

Complete schedules for general capital assets and long-term liabilities.

Accounting control over general capital assets and general long-term obligations (including capital debt) has traditionally been maintained in the general fixed assets account group (GFAAG) and the general long-term debt account group (GLTDAG). The account groups are used only to keep accounting control of general capital assets and general long-term debt of the governmental unit. Account groups are not reported on the fund financial statements, but detailed information about general capital assets and long-term obligations is required in the notes and in the government-wide statements. The presentation in this text assumes that governments maintain account groups as convenient means of keeping track of such long-term items and for internal control. Some governments use alternative types of records, including simple listings.

Accounting and Financial Reporting for General Capital Assets

Fixed assets of a proprietary fund or a fiduciary fund are accounted for within those funds and often are referred to as fund capital assets. All other fixed assets are considered general capital assets and are accounted for in the general fixed assets account group. This account group, which was created to report capital assets that are not resources of any specific fund, may be thought of as an inventory record of fixed assets for the purpose of assigning responsibility for custody and proper use. Typical capital asset categories include land, buildings, improvements other than buildings, machinery and equipment, and construction in progress. Each category should be substantiated by supporting detailed records. Major infrastructure assets, such as sidewalks, streets, curbs, and bridges acquired after 1980, must also be recorded. Major general infrastructure assets are networks or subsystems that comprise at least 10% of the total cost of all general capital assets. Intangible assets, such as easements (rights to use land for specific purposes such as building a highway), land use rights, computer software (purchased or developed internally) patents, and trademarks, are also treated as capital assets. Intangible assets are those that lack physical substance, are nonfinancial in nature, and have a useful life greater than one year.[20] Governments are encouraged, but not required, to capitalize their art and similar assets as long as they are (a) held for public exhibition, education, or research; (b) protected and cared for; and (c) subject to an organizational policy that requires proceeds from sales to be used for acquiring other items for the collection.

The general fixed assets account group is little more than a list of government-owned assets in double-entry form. The acquisition of a general capital asset is recorded in the general fixed assets account group by a debit to one of the six specific asset accounts. The offsetting credit indicates the original funding source of the asset, selected from the following recommended titles:

Investment in General Fixed Assets	
—Capital Projects Funds	—Special Revenue Funds
—General Fund Revenues	—Donations

To illustrate this procedure, a building acquired with general fund revenues would require the following entries:

Fund or Group in which Entry Is Recorded	Entry		
32. General fund	Expenditures	200,000	
	Vouchers Payable		200,000
	(This entry is part of the entry on page 785, which records vouchers of $772,000.)		
33. General fixed assets account group	Buildings	200,000	
	Investment in General Fixed Assets—		
	General Fund Revenues		200,000
	To record the fixed asset.		

General capital assets are recorded at cost or, if the assets are donated, estimated fair value at time of receipt. Subsequent to the acquisition of a capital asset, capital outlay and maintenance expenditures must be accounted for separately, as they are in commercial accounting, since maintenance expenditures should not increase the book values of fixed assets.

As will be explained in Chapter 17, depreciation expense is reported in the government-wide statements. Depreciation expense, however, is not reported in the governmental funds.

> *To record depreciation expense in governmental funds would inappropriately mix two fundamentally different measurements, expenses and expenditures. General fixed asset acquisitions require the use of governmental fund financial resources and are recorded as expenditures. General fixed asset sale proceeds provide governmental fund financial resources. Depreciation expense is neither a source nor a use of governmental fund financial resources, and thus is not properly recorded in the accounts of such funds.[21]*

---

20 GASB statement No. 51, *Accounting and Financial Reporting for Intangible Assets* (Norwalk, CT: Governmental Accounting Standards Board, May 2007).

21 Statement 1, *Government Accounting and Financial Reporting Principles* (Chicago: Municipal Finance Officers Association of the United States and Canada, March 1979), p. 10.

Governments must record accumulated depreciation of general capital assets in the government-wide statements. An entry is made in the general fixed assets account group by debiting the appropriate investment in the general fixed asset account and crediting the accumulated depreciation account.

When a governmental unit disposes of a general capital asset, the original cost (less accumulated depreciation) of the asset is removed from the general fixed assets account group. In the general fund, proceeds from the sale are recorded with a credit to Other Financing Sources. For example, if a governmental unit sells equipment for $90,000, carried in the general fixed assets account group at $100,000, the following entries would be made:

Fund or Group in which Entry Is Recorded	Entry		
34. General fund	Cash	90,000	
	Other Financing Sources		90,000
	To record the proceeds from the sale.		
35. General fixed assets account group	Investment in General Fixed Assets—		
	General Fund Revenues	100,000	
	Machinery and Equipment		100,000
	To remove the fixed asset.		

Instead of selling the equipment, assume the governmental unit traded it for a larger model costing $235,000, with an allowance of $90,000 for the smaller unit. The new asset is recorded at its total cost, with the trade-in value merely functioning as a reduction in the amount to be paid. The entries then would be as follows:

Fund or Group in which Entry Is Recorded	Entry		
36. General fund	Expenditures	145,000	
	Vouchers Payable		145,000
	To record the outflow of cash.		
37. General fixed assets account group	Investment in General Fixed Assets—		
	General Fund Revenues	100,000	
	Machinery and Equipment		100,000
	To remove the old asset.		
	Machinery and Equipment	235,000	
	Investment in General Fixed Assets—		
	General Fund Revenues		235,000
	To record the new fixed asset.		

Governments can avoid charging depreciation on infrastructure assets if they can demonstrate that they have incurred costs to preserve these assets at or above a conditional level established by the government. Under this *modified preservation approach*, all costs to maintain the assets are expensed, and no depreciation is recorded. If a government elects to follow the modified approach, it must assess periodically and disclose in the notes to the financial statements the condition of its infrastructure assets (usually an engineering report) and estimate the annual amount necessary to maintain and preserve the specified assets at or above the condition level. It must also disclose actual amounts spent compared to these estimates. A change from the depreciation method to the modified approach should be accounted for as a change in accounting estimate.

Governments are required to monitor and determine if impairment of a capital asset has occurred. A capital asset is considered impaired if *both* (a) the decline in service utility of the capital asset is large in magnitude *and* (b) the event or change in circumstance is outside the normal life cycle of the capital asset. Impaired capital assets that will no longer be used by the government should be reported at the lower of carrying value or fair value. Impairment losses on capital assets that will continue to be used by the government should be measured using a method that best reflects the diminished service utility of the capital asset, such as cost to restore, percentage of service units provided before and after the impairment, and deflated depreciated replacement cost.[22]

Disclosures about capital assets are required in the notes to the financial statements. Capital assets that are not being depreciated are disclosed separately from those assets that are being depreciated. In addition, beginning-of-year and end-of-year balances are shown along with capital acquisitions, sales, or other dispositions. A schedule of capital assets that will be included in the notes for Middletown is shown in Illustration 15-9.

Illustration 15-9
City of Middletown
Schedule of Capital Assets

	Beginning Balance	Additions	Retirements	Ending Balance
Governmental activities:				
Land	$ 8,595,000	$4,000,000		$ 12,595,000
Buildings	28,555,000		$ (200,000)	28,355,000
Improvements other than buildings	10,367,500			10,367,500
Machinery and equipment	4,390,000	135,000		4,525,000
Construction in progress	17,222,500			17,222,500
Infrastructure	120,000,000		(2,000,000)	118,000,000
Totals (at historical cost)	$189,130,000	$4,135,000	$(2,200,000)	$191,065,000
Less accumulated depreciation:				
Buildings	$ (850,000)	$ (85,000)	$ 40,000	$ (895,000)
Improvements other than buildings	(150,000)	(20,000)		(170,000)
Machinery and equipment	(215,000)	(50,000)		(265,000)
Infrastructure	(15,000,000)	(350,000)	1,000,000	(14,350,000)
Total depreciation	$ (16,215,000)	$ (505,000)	$ 1,040,000	$ (15,680,000)
Governmental activities capital assets (net)	$172,915,000	$3,630,000	$(1,160,000)	$175,385,000

Accounting and Financial Reporting for General Long-Term Debt

When long-term debt is related to and will be paid from proprietary or fiduciary funds, it is accounted for in those funds and is termed a specific fund liability. When long-term debt is related to and will be paid from governmental funds, the liability is recorded in the general long-term debt account group.

The general long-term debt account group, which was designed to monitor long-term debt that is not the responsibility of any particular fund, furnishes a record of the unmatured principal of all general long-term obligations of the governmental unit. Referring to a long-term obligation as *general* indicates that the community can use its taxing power to pay debt principal and interest. The general long-term debt account group is not limited to liabilities arising from debt issuance and may include numerous types of unmatured general government liabilities; for example, claims and judgments, accumulated sick leave and other compensated absences, underfunded pension contributions, unfunded postretirement benefits other than pensions, and capital lease obligations, as well as unmatured bonds and notes. Interest is not accounted for in the general long-term debt account group. To maintain the self-balancing nature of the account group, the incurrence of long-term obligations is recorded by debiting Amount to Be Provided for Payment of (properly identified) Debt and crediting a liability account. As emphasized in the previous section, the use of account groups is a convenient mechanism for keeping track of long-term liabilities that can also be achieved by other means, such as simple ledgers.

---

22 GASB Statement No. 42, *Accounting and Financial Reporting for Impairment of Capital Assets and for Insurance Recoveries* (Norwalk, CT: Governmental Accounting Standards Board, November 2003).

To illustrate the entries for the general long-term debt account group, assume that a unit incurs a general long-term obligation in the form of term bonds of $1,000,000 to acquire property.[23] Regardless of whether the bonds are issued at a premium or discount, the bond issue is recorded at its face amount in the general long-term debt account group. As shown in the following entry, the bonds are recorded in the general long-term debt account group at the face value to be redeemed at maturity:

38.	Amount to Be Provided for Payment of Term Bonds	1,000,000	
	Term Bonds Payable		1,000,000

Payment of both principal and interest is handled by the debt service fund, where *service* is synonymous with *payment*, but the general long-term debt account group records only amounts that become available in the debt service fund for retirement of general long-term debt principal. Assuming the debt service fund receives an annual appropriation of $80,000 to provide for the eventual retirement of the term bonds, the following entry is recorded in the general long-term debt account group:

39.	Amount Available in Debt Service Funds—Term Bonds	80,000	
	Amount to Be Provided for Payment of Term Bonds		80,000

If sound actuarial practices have been employed, the debt service fund will retire the obligation at the appropriate time and the general long-term debt account group will make the following entry:

40.	Term Bonds Payable	1,000,000	
	Amount Available in Debt Service Funds—Term Bonds		1,000,000

A schedule of general long-term liabilities for Middletown appears in Illustration 15-10. The schedule includes the example transactions in this section. Governments report long-term obligations on a full-accrued basis in the government-wide statements. A discussion of the adjusting entries needed to reflect amortization of premium or discount and interest accruals is found in Chapter 17.

Information about long-term debt, significant contingent liabilities, pension plan obligations, accumulated sick leave and other compensated absences, debt service requirements to maturity, commitments under noncapitalized leases, and changes in general long-term debt are required note disclosures.

Illustration 15-10
City of Middletown
Schedule of Long-Term Liabilities

	Beginning Balance	Additions	Retirements	Ending Balance
General long-term debt payable:				
General obligation debt	$21,962,000	$2,000,000	$999,950	$22,962,050
Special assessment debt	2,000,000			2,000,000
Unfunded pension costs.	139,000	2,123		141,123
Capital lease payable	99,950	35,944		135,894
Unfunded compensated absences.	160,325	3,433		163,758
Unfunded claims and judgment.	412,222	179,923		592,145
Total general long-term debt payable	$24,773,497	$2,221,423	$999,950	$25,994,970

23 A term bond is one in which the entire principal is due on one date; a serial bond issue is redeemed in periodic payments. Term bonds are rare, but they better illustrate entries in the general long-term debt account group.

Leasing of equipment has become common practice among governments. When leases qualify as operating, the rent expenditures are recorded in the fund, and no entry is made in the account group. However, if a lease qualifies as a capital lease (using the criteria of FASB No. 13), then the substance of the transaction is similar to the purchase of a fixed asset with long-term debt proceeds. Therefore, entries are as follows:

Event and Fund or Group in which Entry Is Recorded		Entry		
41.	At inception of the lease, the present value of the lease payments is recorded in the fund as expenditures and other financing sources.	General fund	Expenditures . . . . Other Financing Sources	50,000	50,000

42.	In the account group, the leased asset is recorded at its present value.	General fixed assets account group	Leased Asset . . . .
			    Investment in GFA—
			        General Funds . . . .
				50,000	50,000

43.	In the account group, the long-term lease obligation is recorded.	General long-term debt account group	Amount to Be Provided . . . . Lease Obligation	50,000	50,000

Subsequent lease payments are made from the Debt Service Fund as will be presented in Chapter 16.

REFLECTION

- Account groups have traditionally been used to keep track of capital assets and long-term debt and are a convenient means of recording additions and deductions from capital assets and long-term debt.

- Account groups are not reported on the financial statements. Rather, schedules of capital assets and long-term liabilities are presented in the notes to the financial statements. Capital assets and long-term debt are also reported in the government-wide statements.

- Governments are required to record infrastructure assets and depreciation.

REVIEW OF ENTRIES FOR THE GENERAL FUND AND ACCOUNT GROUPS

The following example will provide a comprehensive review of the general fund, the general fixed assets account group, and the general long-term debt account group. The general fund balance sheet for Junction City, as of December 31, 2018, is shown in Illustration 15-11.

Illustration 15-11
Junction City
General Fund Balance Sheet
December 31, 2018

Assets

Cash		$100,000
Taxes receivable, delinquent, 2018	$50,000	
Less allowance for uncollectible delinquent taxes, 2018	20,000	30,000
Tax liens receivable, 2017	$25,000	
Less allowance for uncollectible tax liens, 2017	5,000	20,000
Inventory of supplies		20,000
Total assets		$170,000

Liabilities and Fund Equity

Liabilities:		
Vouchers payable		$ 30,000
Fund balances:		
Nonspendable	$20,000	
Assigned	40,000	
Unassigned	80,000	
Total fund balance		140,000
Total liabilities and fund balance		$170,000

During 2019, the following entries are recorded in the general fund of Junction City. If an event also requires that an entry be made in one of the account groups, the necessary entry is indicated as part of the event.

Event		Entry in the General Fund		
The budget is approved.		Estimated Revenues	600,000	
Estimated inflows are from:		Estimated Other Financing Sources	284,000	
Revenues	$600,000	Budgetary Fund Balance—Unassigned	26,000	
General long-term debt issuance	200,000	Appropriations		860,000
Transfers from other funds	60,000	Estimated Other Financing Uses		50,000
Sales of fixed assets carried at				
$100,000	24,000			
Estimated outflows are for:				
Expenditures [Includes 2018 holdover encumbrances ($40,000) and use of supplies ($20,000)]	860,000			
Transfers to other funds	50,000			
The amount of the Fund Balance—Reserved for Encumbrances was reinstated in Encumbrances.		Encumbrances	40,000	
		Fund Balance—Unassigned		40,000
Property taxes of $500,000 are levied, of which $30,000 is estimated to be uncollectible.		Taxes Receivable—Current	500,000	
		Allowance for Uncollectible Current Taxes		30,000
		Revenues		470,000

(continued)

Event	Entry in the General Fund		
Cash obtained from local banks to finance government operations in advance of collection of first property tax installment.	Cash .... Tax Anticipation Note Payable	200,000	200,000

Collection of taxes and related interest for the year:

Current taxes	$450,000
Delinquent taxes, 2018	32,000
Interest on delinquent taxes	2,000
Tax liens, 2017	10,000
Interest on tax liens, 2017	1,000
Total	$495,000

Cash	495,000	
Taxes Receivable—Current		450,000
Taxes Receivable—Delinquent, 2018		32,000
Tax Liens Receivable, 2017		10,000
Revenues		3,000

Event	Entry in the General Fund		
Repayment of tax anticipation note payable plus interest upon collection of property taxes.	Tax Anticipation Notes Payable .... Expenditures .... Cash	200,000 3,000	203,000
Property against which there are unpaid tax liens for 2017 is sold for $7,000. (The loss is an adjustment of current revenue, since it represents a change in estimate.)	Cash .... Allowance for Uncollectible Tax Liens, 2017 .... Revenues .... Tax Liens Receivable, 2017	7,000 5,000 3,000	15,000
Tax liens totaling $18,000 are issued against 2018 delinquent taxpayers.	Tax Liens Receivable, 2018 .... Taxes Receivable—Delinquent, 2018	18,000	18,000

Allowance for Uncollectible Delinquent Taxes is reclassified and reduced, so as not to exceed the related receivable of $18,000. As a change in estimate, the credit is made to Revenues. Uncollected current taxes are declared delinquent, and the related allowance is reclassified.	Allowance for Uncollectible Delinquent Taxes,
	   2018 ....
	      Allowance for Uncollectible Tax Liens, 2018 ...
	      Revenues ....
	Taxes Receivable—Delinquent, 2019 ....
	   Taxes Receivable—Current ....
		20,000
		
		50,000
			
			18,000
			2,000
			50,000

	Allowance for Uncollectible Current Taxes ....
	   Allowance for Uncollectible Delinquent Taxes,
	      2019 ....
		30,000	
			
			30,000

Revenue for licenses, fees, and fines is recognized.	Fines Receivable .... Cash .... Revenues	3,000 67,000	70,000
To acquire land, a general long-term $200,000 serial bond issue is sold for 102.	Cash .... Other Financing Sources	204,000	204,000
The premium is transferred to the debt service fund.	Other Financing Uses .... Cash	4,000	4,000
This event requires an entry in the general long-term debt account group. Amount to Be Provided for Payment of Serial Bonds .... 200,000 Serial Bonds Payable .. 200,000			
Other funds transfer $60,000 to the general fund.	Cash .... Other Financing Sources	60,000	60,000
Additional amount encumbered for approved purchase orders was $600,000.	Encumbrances .... Fund Balance—Assigned	600,000	600,000

Event	Entry in the General Fund		
Compensated absences earned by employees amounted to $75,000.	No entry in the general fund		

This event requires an entry in the general long-term debt account group.

Amount to Be Provided for Payment of
Compensated Absences . . .   75,000
Unfunded Compensated Absences . . 75,000

Event	Entry in the General Fund		
The actuarial required contribution (ARC) of the government was calculated by the actuary to be $50,000. $20,000 was paid. The remaining $30,000 will not be funded this year.	Expenditures . . . . Cash	20,000	20,000

This event requires an entry in the general long-term debt account group.

Amount to Be Provided for Payment of
Pension Obligation   30,000
Unfunded Pension
Obligation   30,000

Event	Entry in the General Fund		
The following vouchers were approved: General expenditures . . . . $760,000 Purchase of equipment. . . . . 40,000 Purchase of supplies (a perpetual inventory system is used) . . . . 70,000 Total. $870,000	Expenditures . . . . Inventory of Supplies . . . . Vouchers Payable	800,000 70,000	870,000
Of this total, $630,000 was encumbered.	Fund Balance—Assigned . . . . Encumbrances	630,000	630,000

The following entry is required in the general fixed assets account group:

Machinery and
Equipment   40,000
Investment in General Fixed
Assets—General Fund   40,000

Event	Entry in the General Fund		
A lease agreement was signed for equipment. The present value of the lease payments is $30,000.	Expenditures . . . . Other Financing Sources	30,000	30,000

This event requires an entry in the general long-term debt account group.

Amount to Be Provided   30,000
Lease Payable   30,000

This event also requires an entry in the general fixed asset account group.

Leased Asset   30,000
Investment in General Fixed
Assets—Capital Lease   30,000

(continued)

Event	Entry in the General Fund		
$50,000 was transferred from the general fund to other funds.	Other Financing Uses .... Cash	50,000	50,000
Vouchers totaling $880,000 were paid.	Vouchers Payable .... Cash	880,000	880,000
The year-end supplies inventory amounted to $26,000.	Expenditures .... Inventory of Supplies ($20,000 + $70,000 − $26,000)	64,000	64,000
Fund Balance—Reserved for Inventory of Supplies is adjusted to agree with the inventory of supplies.	Fund Balance—Unassigned .... Fund Balance—Nonspendable ($26,000 − $20,000)	6,000	6,000
Equipment carried at $100,000 in the general fixed assets account group is sold for $24,000.			

The following entry is required in the general fixed assets account group:

Investment in General Fixed Assets—		
General Fund......	100,000	
Machinery and Equipment.....		100,000

	Cash .... Other Financing Sources	24,000	24,000
Closing entries.	Appropriations .... Estimated Other Financing Uses .... Estimated Revenues .... Estimated Other Financing Sources............. Budgetary Fund Balance—Unassigned...........	860,000 50,000	600,000 284,000 26,000
	Revenues .... Other Financing Sources...................... Fund Balance—Unassigned .... Expenditures .... Other Financing Uses	542,000 318,000 111,000	917,000 54,000
	Fund Balance—Unassigned .... Encumbrances	10,000	10,000

REFLECTION

- It is important to analyze each event to determine whether the entry is made to the general fund or to one of the account groups. Some events will require an entry in the fund and an entry in an account group.

11

OBJECTIVE

Demonstrate an understanding of the 13 basic governmental accounting principles.

APPENDIX: SUMMARY OF ACCOUNTING PRINCIPLES

There are 13 basic governmental accounting principles included in GASB Statement No. 1 and in *Codification of Governmental Accounting and Financial Reporting Standards*. These principles form a model of fund accounting theory and are summarized on the following pages.

Principle 1—Accounting and Reporting Capabilities

A governmental accounting system must make it possible both (a) to present fairly and with full disclosure the financial position and results of financial operation of the funds and account groups of the governmental unit in conformity with generally accepted accounting principles and (b) to determine and demonstrate compliance with finance-related legal and contractual provisions.

Principle 2—Fund Accounting System

Governmental accounting systems should be organized and operated on a fund basis. A fund is defined as a fiscal and accounting entity with a self-balancing set of accounts recording cash and other financial resources, together with all related liabilities and residual equities or balances, and changes therein, which are segregated for the purpose of carrying on specific activities or attaining certain objectives in accordance with special regulations, restrictions, or limitations. Fund financial statements should be used to report detailed information about the primary government, including its blended component units. The focus of governmental and proprietary fund financial statements is on major funds.

Principle 3—Types of Funds

The following types of funds should be used by state and local governments:

Governmental Funds:

1. The General Fund—to account for all financial resources except those required to be accounted for in another fund.
2. Special Revenue Funds—to account for the proceeds of specific revenue sources (other than expendable trusts or for major capital projects) that are legally restricted to expenditure for specified purposes.
3. Capital Projects Funds—to account for financial resources to be used for the acquisition or construction of major capital facilities (other than those financed by proprietary funds and trust funds).
4. Debt Service Funds—to account for the accumulation of resources for, and the payment of, general long-term debt principal and interest.
5. Permanent Funds—to account for legally restricted resources provided by trust in which the earnings, but not the principal, may be used for purposes that support the primary government's programs (those that benefit the government or its citizenry).

Proprietary Funds:

6. Enterprise Funds—to account for operations that are (a) financed and operated in a manner similar to private business enterprises where the intent of the governing body is that the costs (expenses, including depreciation) of providing goods or services to the general public on a continuing basis be financed or recovered primarily through user charges or (b) where the governing body has decided that periodic determination of revenues earned, expenses incurred, and/or net income is appropriate for capital maintenance, public policy, management control, accountability, or other purposes.
7. Internal Service Funds—to account for financing of goods or services provided by one department or agency to other departments or agencies of the governmental unit, or to other governmental units, on a cost-reimbursement basis.

Fiduciary Funds:
    These are trust and agency funds used to account for assets held by a governmental unit in a trustee capacity or as an agent for individuals, private organizations, other governmental units, and/or other funds. These include the following:

8. Private-Purpose Trust Funds.
9. Investment Trust Funds.
10. Pension (and other employee benefit) Trust Funds.
11. Agency Funds.

Principle 4—Number of Funds

Governmental units should establish and maintain those funds required by law and sound financial administration. Only the minimum number of funds consistent with legal and operating requirements should be established, however, because unnecessary funds result in inflexibility, undue complexity, and inefficient financial administration.

Principle 5—Reporting Capital Assets

A clear distinction should be made between general capital assets and capital assets of proprietary and fiduciary funds. Capital assets of proprietary funds should be reported in both government-wide and fund financial statements. Capital assets of fiduciary funds should be reported in only the statement of fiduciary net assets. All other capital assets of the governmental unit are general capital assets. They should not be reported as assets in governmental funds but rather in the governmental activities column in the governmental-wide statements of net assets.

Principle 6—Valuation of Capital Assets

Capital assets should be accounted for at historical cost. The cost of a capital asset should include ancillary charges necessary to place the asset into its intended location and condition for use. Donated capital assets should be recorded at their estimated fair value at the time of the acquisition plus ancillary charges, if any.

Principle 7—Depreciation of Capital Assets

Capital assets should be depreciated over their estimated useful lives unless they are either inexhaustible or are infrastructure assets using the modified approach as set forth in GASB Statement No. 34, pars. 23–26. A change from the depreciation method to the modified approach should be reported as a change in accounting estimate. Inexhaustible assets such as land and land improvements should not be depreciated. Depreciation expense should be reported in the government-wide statement of activities; the proprietary fund statement of revenues, expenses, and changes in fund net assets; and the statement of changes in fiduciary net assets.

Principle 8—Reporting Long-Term Liabilities

A clear distinction should be made between fund long-term liabilities and general long-term liabilities. Long-term liabilities directly related to and expected to be paid from proprietary funds should be reported in the proprietary fund statement of net assets and in the government-wide statement of net assets. Long-term liabilities directly related to and expected to be paid from fiduciary funds should be reported in the statement of fiduciary net assets. All other unmatured general long-term liabilities should be reported in the governmental activities column in the government-wide statement of net assets.

Principle 9—Measurement Focus and Basis of Accounting in the Basic Financial Statements

The government-wide financial statement of net assets and statement of activities should be prepared using the economic resources measurement focus and the accrual basis of accounting. Revenues, expenses, gains, losses, assets, and liabilities resulting from the exchange and exchange-like transactions should be recognized when the exchange takes place. Revenues, expenses, assets, and liabilities resulting from nonexchange transactions should be recognized in accordance with GASB Statement No. 33.

In fund financial statements, the modified accrual or accrual basis of accounting, as appropriate, should be used in measuring financial position and operating results.

1. Financial statements for governmental funds should be presented using the current financial resources measurement focus and the modified accrual basis of accounting. Revenues should be recognized in the accounting period in which they become available and measurable. Expenditures should be recognized in the accounting period in which the fund liability is incurred, if measurable, except for unmatured interest on general long-term liabilities, which should be recognized when due.

2. Proprietary fund statements of net assets and revenues, expenses, and changes in fund net assets should be presented using the economic resources measurement focus and the accrual basis of accounting.

3. Financial statements of fiduciary funds should be reported using the economic resources measurement focus and the accrual basis of accounting, except for the recognition of certain liabilities of defined benefit pension plans and certain postemployment healthcare plans.

4. Transfers between funds should be reported in the accounting period in which the interfund receivable and payable arise.

Principle 10—Budgeting, Budgetary Control, and Budgetary Reporting

An annual budget(s) should be adopted by every governmental unit. The accounting system should provide the basis for appropriate budgetary control. Budgetary comparison schedules should be presented as required supplementary information (RSI) for the general fund and each major special revenue fund that has a legally adopted annual budget. The budgetary comparison schedule should present both the original and the final appropriated budgets for the reporting period, as well as actual inflows, outflows, and balances, as stated on the government's budgetary basis.

Principle 11—Transfer, Revenue, Expenditure, and Expense Account Classification

Transfers and proceeds of general long-term debt issues should be classified separately from fund revenues and expenditures or expenses. Governmental fund revenues should be classified by fund and source. Expenditures should be classified by fund, function (or program), organization unit, activity, character, and principal classes of objects. Proprietary fund revenues and expenses should be classified in essentially the same manner as those of similar business organizations, functions, or activities. The statement of activities should present governmental activities at least at the level of detail required in the governmental fund statement of revenues, expenditures, and changes in fund balances—and, at a minimum, by function. Governments should present business-type activities at least by segment.

Principle 12—Common Terminology and Classification

A common terminology and classification should be used consistently throughout the budget, accounts, and financial reports of each fund.

Principle 13—Annual Financial Reports

A comprehensive annual financial report (CAFR) should be prepared and published, covering all funds and account groups of the primary government (including its blended component units) and providing an overview of all discreetly presented component units of the reporting entity—including the introductory section, management's discussion and analysis (MD&A), basic financial statements, required supplementary information other than MD&A, combining and individual fund statements, schedules, narrative explanation, and statistical section. The reporting entity is the primary government (including blended component units) and all discretely presented component units presented in accordance with GASB Statement No. 14.

The basic financial statements should include the following:

a. Government-wide financial statements.
b. Fund financial statements.
c. Notes to the financial statements.

The financial reporting entity consists of (a) the primary government, (b) organizations for which the primary government is financially accountable, and (c) other organizations for which the nature and significance of their relationship with the primary government are such that exclusion would cause the reporting entity's financial statements to be misleading or incomplete. The reporting entity's government-wide financial statements should display information about the reporting government as a whole, distinguishing between the total primary government and its discretely presented component units, as well as between the primary government's governmental and business-type activities. The reporting entity's fund financial statements should present the primary government's (including its blended component units, which are, in substance, part of the primary government) major funds individually and its nonmajor funds in the aggregate. Funds and components units that are fiduciary in nature should be reported only in the statements of fiduciary net assets and changes in fiduciary net assets.

The nucleus of a financial reporting entity usually is a primary government. However, a governmental organization other than a primary government (such as a component unit, joint venture, jointly governed organization, or other stand-alone government) serves as the nucleus for its own reporting entity when it issues separate financial statements. For all of these entities, the GASB financial reporting entity provisions should be applied in layers *from the bottom up*. At each layer, the definition and display provisions should be applied before the layer is included in the financial statements of the next level of the reporting government.

REFLECTION

- The 13 basic governmental accounting principles form a model of fund accounting theory.

UNDERSTANDING THE ISSUES

1. GASB Statement No. 34 requires reporting using both the financial resources measurement focus and the economic resources measurement focus. How do these two focuses differ, and what impact do they have on the presentation of financial information? Why would the addition of reporting under the economic resources focus provide added value to the understanding of the governmental operations? Identify two accounts that would be accounted for differently under the two focuses.

2. Name three advantages gained by government reporting through the use of the three different fund types and the account groups. Explain why this method of reporting is advantageous.

3. Why are budgets crucial in accounting for governmental entities? If appropriations were not included in fund accounting, what impact would this exclusion have on the financial statements?

4. What advantage is gained by categorizing fund balances first into nonspendable and then allocating the remaining fund balance into restricted, committed, assigned, and unassigned?

5. How does the use of an encumbrance system aid in accounting for governmental entities?

6. Why do some transactions require an entry in a fund and another in an account group? What impact would there be if a journal entry were made only in the fund or only in the account group?

7. (Appendix) What is the source of the 13 basic governmental accounting principles, and what benefit is there to studying these principles?

EXERCISES

Exercise 1 *(LO 1, 2, 3)* **Understanding state and local government financial statements.** Go to the GASB Web site at http://www.gasb.org. Write a brief description of the mission of the GASB, its relation to the FASB, and the current project agenda of the GASB board. Are there any exposure drafts, discussion memoranda, and/or invitations to comment documents outstanding to which you could respond? What is the purpose of the Governmental Accounting Standards Advisory Council?

Exercise 2 *(LO 3, 4, 5)* **Accounting for transactions.** Select the best answer for each of the following multiple-choice questions. (Nos. 4, 5, and 7–10 are AICPA adapted.)

1. In a governmental fund, which one of the following constitutes revenue?

   a. Cash received from another fund of the same unit
   b. Bond proceeds
   c. Property taxes
   d. Refund on an invoice for fuel

2. In a governmental fund, which of the following is considered an expenditure?

   a. The purchase of a capital asset
   b. The consumption of supplies
   c. Salaries earned by employees
   d. All of the above

3. In the recording of a city's budget, which one of the following accounts is debited?

   a. Appropriations
   b. Estimated Revenues
   c. Estimated Other Financing Uses
   d. Encumbrances

4. Which of the following accounts of a governmental unit is usually credited when taxpayers are billed for property taxes?

   a. Appropriations
   b. Taxes Receivable—Current
   c. Estimated Revenues
   d. Revenues

5. Fixed assets donated to a governmental unit should be recorded

   a. at estimated fair value when received.
   b. at the lower of donor's carrying amount or estimated fair value when received.
   c. at the donor's carrying amount.
   d. as a memorandum entry only.

6. The general long-term debt account group includes

   a. all long-term debt of a governmental unit.
   b. general long-term capital debt applicable to governmental funds.
   c. long-term capital debt and all long-term operating debt applicable to governmental funds.
   d. all general long-term capital debt plus accrued interest thereon.

7. When equipment was purchased with general fund resources, an appropriate entry was made in the general fixed assets account group. What account would have been debited in the general fund?

   a. Due from Other Funds
   b. Expenditures

   c. Appropriations

   d. No entry should be made in the general fund.

8. Which of the following accounts should Cook City close at the end of its fiscal year?

   a. Vouchers Payable

   b. Expenditures

   c. Fund Balance

   d. Fund Balance—Assigned

9. Which of the following accounts of a governmental unit is debited when a purchase order is approved?

   a. Appropriations

   b. Vouchers Payable

   c. Fund Balance—Assigned or Committed

   d. Encumbrances

10. Laster City recorded a 20-year building rental agreement as a capital lease. An asset for the building lease was recorded in the general fixed assets account group. Where should the lease liability be reported?

   a. In the general long-term debt account group

   b. In the debt service fund

   c. In the general fund

   d. A lease liability should not be reported.

Exercise 3 *(LO 3, 5, 7)* **Accounting for expenditures.** Prepare entries in the general fund for the following transactions that represent outflows of financial resources to the city of Cedar Creek in 2018:

1. Vouchers are prepared for the following items and amounts:

Salaries	$100,000
Repairs and maintenance	50,000
Inventory of supplies	45,000
Capital equipment.	125,000
Tax anticipation notes:	
Principal.	200,000
Interest	13,000

2. A transfer of $50,000 is made to the debt service fund.
3. There was no inventory of supplies at the start of the year. The inventory of supplies at year-end is $2,000.

Exercise 4 *(LO 3, 5, 7)* **Accounting for revenues and other inflows.** Prepare journal entries in the general fund for the following 2018 transactions that represent inflows of financial resources to Tyler City:

1. To pay the wages of part-time city maintenance employees, the Cemetery Expendable Trust Fund transfers $45,000 to the general fund.
2. A resident donates land worth $75,000 for a park.
3. The city is notified by the state that it will receive $30,000 in road assistance grants this year.
4. A fire truck with an original cost of $36,000 is sold for $9,000.
5. Sales of license stickers for park use total $5,000. The fees cover this year and next year. Security staff are paid from these fees to check for cars in the park without stickers.

Exercise 5 *(LO 3, 5, 7)* **Accounting for revenues.** The following information concerns tax revenues for the city of Fairfield. The balances concerning property taxes on January 1, 2018, were as follows:

Delinquent property taxes receivable	$105,000
Allowance for uncollectible delinquent taxes	(30,000)
Tax liens receivable	40,000
Allowance for uncollectible tax liens	(23,000)

Prepare entries in the general fund for the following 2018 events:

Jan.   Since current property taxes would not be collected for several months, $275,000 was borrowed using tax anticipation notes.

Feb.   Tax liens of $10,000 were collected; in addition, $2,000 of interest was collected that had not been accrued. The balance of tax liens was settled by receiving $13,000 for the property subject to the tax liens.

Apr.   Collections on delinquent property taxes were $100,000, and interest of $4,500 was collected. The interest had not been accrued. The balance of the account was converted into tax liens.

July   Current property taxes were levied for $422,000 with a 5% allowance for uncollectible amounts.

Sept.   Collection of current property taxes totaled $345,000. The tax anticipation notes were paid off with interest of $18,000.

Exercise 6 *(LO 3, 7, 8, 9)* **Accounting for expenditures and encumbrances.** Blushing City had the following balance sheet accounts and amounts as of January 1, 2018:

Inventory of supplies	$ 25,000
Fund balance, nonspendable	(25,000)
Fund balance, assigned	(18,000)
Fund balance, unassigned	(20,000)

Prepare general fund journal entries for the following 2018 transactions:

1. Prior-period supplies encumbrances are reinstated in 2018. These are included in the 2018 budget.
2. Orders are placed for supplies inventory at an estimated cost of $70,000.
3. All inventory ordered (including amounts encumbered last year) is received; actual invoices are for $82,000.
4. The physical inventory of supplies at year-end is $30,000.

Exercise 7 *(LO 4, 7)* **Journal entries, identify funds.** Belhurst purchased land costing $65,000 for park development. The amount had been encumbered at $70,000. Ten years later, because of a population shift, the park is no longer practical. The city sells the land for $105,000. Prepare journal entries to record the purchase and subsequent sale of the land, indicating in what fund or group each entry would be made. Use the following format:

Event	Fund or Group	Entry

Exercise 8 *(LO 4, 7)* **Journal entries, general long-term debt.** The following transactions directly affected Rose City's general fund and other governmental funds. Prepare journal entries to reflect their impact upon the general long-term debt account group.

1. Rose City employees earned $8.8 million in vacation pay during the year, of which they took only $6.6 million. They may take the balance in the following three years.
2. The employees took $0.4 million of vacation pay that they had earned in previous years.
3. Rose City settled a claim brought against it during the year by a building contractor. The city agreed to pay $7.5 million immediately and $11 million at the end of the following year.
4. Rose City issued $100 million in general obligation bonds at a price of $99.8 million—i.e., a discount of $0.2 million.
5. Rose City transferred $5 million from the general fund to the debt service fund. Of this, $4 million was for the first payment of interest; the balance was for repayment of principal.

6. Rose City earned $0.3 million in interest on investments held in the debt service fund. These investments have a fair value $4.5 million greater than at the end of last period. The funds are available for the repayment of debt principal.

Exercise 9 *(LO 4, 7)* **Journal entries, general long-term debt.** Prepare the entries that would be made in the general long-term debt account group for the following events:

a. To finance the construction of an art center, $13,000,000 of general obligation term bonds were sold for $12,500,000.
b. The general fund allocated $1,300,000 to a debt service fund to begin providing for retirement of the bonds in item (a) at maturity.
c. To help finance an addition to the community health center, $6,000,000 of 6%, 10-year serial bonds were sold at 101. $960,000 was transferred from the general fund to the debt service fund to cover the annual interest and the first serial redemption.
d. Serial bonds of $600,000 matured and were retired through the debt service fund.

Exercise 10 *(LO 4, 7, 10)* **Journal entries, capital assets.** For the following transactions, prepare the entries that would be recorded in the general fixed assets account group for the city of Evert.

a. The city purchased property costing $1,300,000, with three-fourths of the cost allocated to a building.
b. A mansion belonging to the great-granddaughter of the city's founder was donated to the city. The land cost the original owner $600, and the house was built for an additional $50,000. At the time of donation, the property had an estimated fair value of $550,000, of which $330,000 was allocable to the land. The property was accepted and is to be used as a park and a museum.
c. A central fire station, financed by general obligation bonds, was two-thirds complete at year-end with costs to date of $800,000 that were recorded in the capital project fund.
d. A new fire engine was purchased for $165,000. The city traded a used fire engine originally purchased for $100,000. The trade-in value was $25,000. Both engines were purchased from general property tax revenues.
e. A new street was completed at a cost of $250,000, which is to be charged, through the capital projects fund's special assessments, against property owners in the vicinity. The city follows GASB recommendations and records infrastructure assets.
f. Evert developed computer software valued at $70,000 with an estimated useful life of seven years.

Exercise 11 *(LO 5, 6)* **Budgetary accounting.** Given the following information, you have been asked to record the budget for the general fund of the city of Jackson.

1. Inflows for 2018 are expected to total $402,000 and include property tax revenue of $205,000, fines of $7,000, state grants of $90,000, and bond issue proceeds of $100,000.
2. Expenditures for general operations and equipment purchases for the year are estimated to be $500,000.
3. Authorized transfers include $20,000 to the debt service fund to pay interest on bond indebtedness and $10,000 to the capital projects fund to pay for cost overruns on construction of a new civic center.
4. Additional estimated receipts include a $15,000 operating transfer from the special revenue fund and a $50,000 payment from the Electric Utility Enterprise Fund for property taxes.

Exercise 12 *(LO 5, 7)* **Account for transactions.** Prepare the entries to record the following general fund transactions for the village of Del Valley for the year ended September 30, 2018:

a. Revenues are estimated at $520,000; expenditures are estimated at $515,000.
b. A tax levy is set at $378,788, of which 1% will likely be uncollectible.
c. Purchase orders amounting to $240,000 are authorized.

d. Tax receipts total $280,000.
e. Invoices totaling $225,000 are received and vouchered for orders originally estimated at $223,000.
f. Salaries amounting to $135,000 are approved for payment.
g. A state grant-in-aid of $100,000 is received.
h. Fines and penalties of $10,000 are collected.
i. Property for a village park is purchased, costing $120,000. No encumbrance had been made for this item.
j. Additional recreational property valued at $88,000 is donated.
k. Amounts of $12,000 due to other village funds are approved for payment. (*Note:* To establish the liability to other funds, credit Due to Other Funds.)
l. The village's share of sales tax due from the state is $30,000. Payment will be received in 30 days.
m. Vouchers totaling $175,000 are paid.
n. Accounts are closed at year-end.

Exercise 13 *(LO 5, 7, 9)* **Accounting and reporting.** Indicate the part [(a) through (e)] of the general fund statement of revenues, expenditures, and changes in fund balance affected by transactions (1) through (7).

a. Revenues
b. Expenditures
c. Other financing sources and uses
d. Residual equity transfers
e. Statement of revenues, expenditures, and changes in fund balance is not affected.

1. An unrestricted state grant is received.
2. The general fund paid pension fund contributions that were recoverable (reimbursed) from an internal service fund.
3. The general fund paid $60,000 for electricity supplied by the electric utility enterprise fund.
4. General fund resources were used to subsidize the swimming pool enterprise fund.
5. General fund resources of $90,000 were loaned to an internal service fund.
6. A motor pool internal service fund was established by a transfer of $80,000 from the general fund. This amount will not be repaid unless the motor pool is disbanded.
7. General fund resources were used to pay amounts due on an operating lease.

(AICPA adapted)

Exercise 14 *(LO 5, 7, 8, 9)* **Accounting for expenditures and encumbrances.** You are maintaining a subsidiary ledger account for Police-Training Expenditures for 2013. The following columns are used:

Date	Item	Encumbrances			Expenditures	Unobligated Balance
		Dr.	Cr.	Bal.		

Inventory purchases are initially recorded as expenditures.

Record the following 2013 transactions in the police-training expenditures subsidiary ledger account:

Jan.	1	The budget includes $23,000 for police-training expenditures.
	15	Equipment and supplies, estimated at $14,000 cost, are ordered.
Feb.	1	Vouchers for $5,000 are approved for items not encumbered.
	15	Items encumbered for $12,000 on January 15 are received with invoices totaling $12,300. Supplies are expended when purchased; however, an inventory is taken at year-end, and expenditures are adjusted at that time.
June	3	The remaining encumbered expenditures arrive. The invoice totals $4,300, including items not included in the encumbered amount.
Dec.	31	An inventory of training supplies is taken and recorded at $1,500.

Exercise 15 *(LO 9)* **Budgetary comparison schedule.** The preclosing trial balance of the general fund of Shorewood Village for fiscal year ended June 30, 2019, is as follows:

	Debit	Credit
Cash	190,000	
Receivables (net)	120,000	
Vouchers Payable		91,000
Fund Balance—Assigned		60,000
Fund Balance—Unassigned		92,000
Budgetary Fund Balance		50,000
Estimated Revenues	600,000	
Estimated Other Financing Sources..................	150,000	
Appropriations		650,000
Estimated Other Financing Uses		50,000
Expenditures	588,000	
Encumbrances......................................	60,000	
Revenues		595,000
Other Financing Sources...........................		166,500
Other Financing Uses	46,500	
Totals	1,754,500	1,754,500

1. Prepare closing entries.
2. Prepare a budget to actual comparison schedule. (Assume there are no differences between the original and final budgets.)
3. Prepare a balance sheet as of June 30, 2019.

PROBLEMS

Problem 15-1 *(LO 1, 2, 3)* **Measurement focus and basis of accounting.** Select the best answer for each of the following multiple-choice questions. (Nos. 1, 5, and 7–10 are AICPA adapted.)

1. The encumbrances control account of a governmental unit is increased when a voucher payable is

   a. not recorded and the budgetary accounts are not closed.
   b. not recorded but the budgetary accounts are closed.
   c. recorded and the budgetary accounts are closed.
   d. recorded but the budgetary accounts are not closed.

2. If not expenditure driven, a grant approved by the federal government to assist in a city's welfare program during the current year should be credited to

   a. Revenues.
   b. Fund Balance—Reserved for Welfare Programs.
   c. Fund Balance—Unassigned.
   d. Other Financing Sources.

3. Which one of the following equations will yield the available balance in an expenditure subsidiary ledger account?

   a. Appropriations − Expenditures Total
   b. Appropriations − Encumbrances Balance
   c. Appropriations − Expenditures Total − Encumbrances Balance
   d. Appropriations − Expenditures Total + Encumbrances Balance

4. Lacking sufficient cash for operations, a city borrows money from a bank, using as collateral the expected receipts from levied property taxes. Upon receipt of cash from the bank, the general fund would credit

   a. Revenues.
   b. Other Financing Sources.
   c. Tax Anticipation Notes Payable.
   d. Taxes Receivable—Delinquent.

5. Elm City issued a purchase order for supplies with an estimated cost of $5,000. When the supplies were received, the accompanying invoice indicated an actual price of $4,950. What amount should Elm debit (credit) to the reserve for encumbrances after the supplies and invoice were received?

   a. ($50)
   b. $50
   c. $4,950
   d. $5,000

6. The recorded amount for uncollectible taxes was overstated. To revise the estimate during the same fiscal period, the journal entry would credit

   a. Expenditures.
   b. Revenues.
   c. Allowance for Uncollectible Delinquent Taxes.
   d. Fund Balance—Unassigned.

7. Motor City's year-end is June 30. Motor levies property taxes in January of each year for the calendar year. One-half of the levy is due in May, and one-half is due in October. Property tax revenue is budgeted for the period in which payment is due. The following information pertains to Motor's property taxes for the period from July 1, 2010, to June 30, 2011:

	Calendar Year	
	2010	2011
Levy	$2,000,000	$2,400,000
Collected in:		
May	950,000	1,100,000
July	50,000	60,000
October	920,000	
December	80,000	

   The $40,000 balance due for the May 2011 installments was expected to be collected in August 2011. What amount should Motor recognize for property tax revenue for the year ended June 30, 2011?

   a. $2,160,000
   b. $2,200,000
   c. $2,360,000
   d. $2,400,000

8. Boa City had the following fixed assets:

Fixed assets used in proprietary fund activities	$1,000,000
Fixed assets used in general government activities	9,000,000

What aggregate amount should Boa account for in the general fixed assets account group?

 a. $9,000,000
 b. $10,000,000
 c. $10,800,000
 d. $11,800,000

9. The following information pertains to Cherry City's liability for claims and judgments:

Current liability at January 1, 2012 .... $100,000
Claims paid during 2012 800,000
Current liability at December 31, 2012 140,000
Noncurrent liability at December 31, 2012 200,000

What amount should Cherry report for 2012 claims and judgment expenditures?

 a. $1,040,000
 b. $940,000
 c. $840,000
 d. $800,000

10. Dodd Village received a gift of a new fire engine from a local civic group. The fair value of this fire engine was $400,000. Which of the following is the correct entry to be made in the general fixed assets account group for this gift?

		Debit	Credit
a.	Memorandum entry only		
b.	General Fund Assets	400,000	
	Private Gifts		400,000
c.	Investment in General Fixed Assets	400,000	
	Gift Revenue		400,000
d.	Machinery and Equipment	400,000	
	Investment in General Fixed Assets from Private Gifts		400,000

Problem 15-2 *(LO 1, 2, 3)* **Measurement focus and basis of accounting.** Select the best answer for each of the following multiple-choice questions. (Nos. 3 and 7 are AICPA adapted.)

1. What is the underlying reason a governmental unit uses separate funds to account for its transactions?

 a. Governmental units are so large that it would be unduly cumbersome to account for all transactions as a single unit.
 b. Because of the diverse nature of the services offered and legal provisions regarding activities of a governmental unit, it is necessary to segregate activities by functional nature.
 c. Generally accepted accounting principles require that not-for-profit entities report on a funds basis.
 d. Many activities carried on by governmental units are short lived, and their inclusion in a general set of accounts could cause undue probability of error and omission.

2. The primary authoritative body for determining the measurement focus and basis of accounting standards for governmental fund operating statements is the

 a. Governmental Accounting Standards Board (GASB).
 b. National Council on Governmental Accounting (NCGA).
 c. Government Accounting and Auditing Committee of the AICPA (GAAC).
 d. Financial Accounting Standards Board (FASB).

3. The measurement focus for governmental funds is the

   a. flow of cash.
   b. flow of financial resources.
   c. amount of gross revenue.
   d. matching of revenues and expenditures.

4. Interperiod equity measurement for governmental funds determines whether

   a. there is a positive cash flow.
   b. there is a profit.
   c. current-year revenues are sufficient to pay for current-year services.
   d. actual amounts exceed budgeted amounts.

5. The proceeds of a long-term bond issue were used by a county to acquire general fixed assets. The long-term liability is recorded

   a. only in the general long-term debt account group.
   b. only in the general fund.
   c. both in the general fund and in the general long-term debt account group.
   d. in the appropriate governmental fund, depending on the nature of the asset involved.

6. An expenditure for general obligation long-term debt is always recorded at year-end in the governmental funds for

   a. accrued interest and accrued principal.
   b. accrued principal but not accrued interest.
   c. accrued interest but not accrued principal.
   d. neither accrued interest nor accrued principal.

7. Encumbrances outstanding at year-end in a state's general fund should be reported as a

   a. liability in the general fund.
   b. fund balance reserve in the general fund.
   c. liability in the general long-term debt account group.
   d. fund balance designation in the general fund.

Problem 15-3 *(LO 3, 5, 7)* **Journal entries, pensions.** Hollander City maintains a defined benefit pension plan for its employees. In a recent year, the city contributed $12 million to its pension fund. However, its annual required contribution as calculated by its actuary was $22 million. The city accounts for the pension contributions in the general fund.

1. Record the pension expenditure and related liability in the general fund and account group. ◄ ◄ ◄ ◄ ◄ **Required**
2. Suppose that in the following year the city contributed $14 million to its pension fund, but its annual required contribution per its actuary was only $12 million. Prepare the appropriate journal entries.

Problem 15-4 *(LO 4, 7)* **Journal entries, identify funds.** Land City leases a fleet of garbage trucks. The term of the lease is 10 years, approximately the useful life of the equipment. Based on a sales price of $800,000 and an interest rate of 6%, the city agrees to make annual payments of $108,694. Upon the expiration of the lease, the trucks will revert to the city.

1. Prepare appropriate journal entries in the general fund, the general fixed assets account ◄ ◄ ◄ ◄ ◄ **Required** group, and the general long-term debt account group to record the signing of the lease.
2. Prepare appropriate journal entries in the same fund and account groups to record the first payment on the lease. The city records depreciation on garbage trucks using the straight-line method.

Problem 15-5 *(LO 4, 7, 9)* **Journal entries, statement of revenue expenditures, and change in fund balance.** On July 1, 2018, the beginning of its fiscal year, the trial balance of the general fund of the city of Wentworth was as follows:

	Debit	Credit
Cash	20,000	
Taxes Receivable—Delinquent	100,000	
Allowance for Uncollectible Delinquent Taxes		12,000
Interest and Penalties Receivable on Taxes	8,000	
Allowance for Uncollectible Interest and Penalties		800
Due from Other Funds	14,000	
Vouchers Payable		87,200
Fund Balance—Assigned		16,000
Fund Balance—Unassigned		26,000
Totals	142,000	142,000

The following events occurred:

a. The budget shows estimated general fund revenues of $400,000 and estimated expenditures (including $16,000 encumbered in the prior year) of $362,000.
b. In July, the item ordered in the previous year was received at an invoice cost of $16,400. A voucher is prepared.
c. Property taxes amounting to $300,000 were levied, with 4% estimated to be uncollectible.
d. Cash collections during the year were as follows:

Current taxes	$250,000
Delinquent taxes (in full settlement)	84,000
Interest and penalties on last year's taxes (in full settlement)	7,600
Due from other funds	14,000
Total	$355,600

The controller wishes variations in estimates to be recorded in the appropriate revenue or expenditure account.

e. Purchase orders totaling $276,000 were placed. Later, invoices for $260,000 were received and vouchered; supplies inventory purchases were $16,000 of the total. The purchase covered $254,000 of the encumbrances.
f. Payrolls of $50,000 were paid. (Ignore payroll taxes and other deductions.) In addition, vouchers totaling $280,000 were paid.
g. An automobile was purchased for the fire department. It cost $16,000 and was not previously encumbered. The invoice is vouchered.
h. At year-end, $6,000 in supplies was on hand. There were no supplies on hand a year ago. The city wishes to show the inventory and to establish a proper fund balance designation.

Required ▶ ▶ ▶ ▶ ▶
1. Prepare journal entries that would be made in the general fund for the above events.
2. Prepare closing entries.
3. Prepare a statement of revenues, expenditures, and changes in fund balance.

Required ▶ ▶ ▶ ▶ ▶

Problem 15-6 *(LO 4, 5, 7)* **Journal entries, general fund.** Prepare the necessary journal entries to record the following transaction for the city of Smallville during 2017 in the general fund and account groups, and specify the account group used. Entries in the debt service fund and capital projects fund should be ignored.

a. General obligation term bonds with a face value of $2,700,000 were sold for $2,705,000. The proceeds from the bond issue were to be used to construct a new library and were received by the capital projects fund.
b. $200,000 was transferred from the general fund to the debt service fund to begin saving for the retirement of the bonds in transaction (a) at maturity.
c. $135,000 was transferred from the general fund to the debt service fund to retire a portion of a serial bond due in 2019.

d. A police car was purchased for $22,000 plus the trade-in of an old police car with a fair value of $3,000, originally purchased for $15,000 from the general fund.

e. The serial bonds funded in transaction (c) were retired on their maturity date.

f. By year-end, $450,000 of the work had been completed on the new library.

Problem 15-7 *(LO 4, 7, 9)* **Journal entries, budgetary comparison schedule.** A summary of the general fund transactions for the city of Toma for the year ended December 31, 2019, is as follows:

a. A budget was approved, showing estimated revenues of $900,000, appropriations of $875,000, transfers-in of $27,000 from other funds, and required transfers of $20,000 to other funds.

b. The reserve for encumbrance at the end of 2018 was $15,000. Amounts encumbered in the prior period are included in appropriations for 2019.

c. Property taxes for $650,000 were levied. In past years, 1% of the property taxes levied proved uncollectible.

d. Encumbrances for $25,000 had not been liquidated by the end of 2018. Invoices for all these items were received in 2019 and totaled $24,000.

e. Collections from property taxes totaled $644,000, of which $20,000 represented collections on delinquent taxes. Delinquent taxes of $8,000 remain uncollected, on which a $3,000 allowance is carried. Remaining taxes receivable—current and taxes receivable—delinquent were converted into taxes receivable—delinquent and tax liens receivable, respectively.

f. Purchase orders totaling $700,000 were issued. Subsequently, invoices were received amounting to $685,000 for items estimated to cost $680,000. Included were supplies for $10,000.

g. An ending inventory of supplies amounted to $2,000, for which the fund balance should be reclassified. (There was no beginning inventory balance.)

h. A tract of land was purchased for $250,000. Payment was made from the general fund, in whose appropriations the item had been included. The amount had not been encumbered. The purchase was made with the intent of reselling the land to a suitable developer.

i. Toma received $300,000 as its part of federal revenue-sharing programs. Grants-in-aid of $60,000 due from the state government are recorded. None of the grants is expenditure driven.

j. Required transfers of $20,000 are made to other funds.

k. A $50,000 payment is made on a mortgage payable. The payment includes $21,000 of interest and a principal payment of $29,000.

l. An offer was received from a land developer who will pay $380,000 for the land acquired by the city in item (h). The sale is approved. The developer remits $100,000 with a note due in 90 days, bearing 8% interest. Any gain is to be considered revenue.

m. Transfers received from other funds amount to $23,000.

n. The developer in item (l) remits payment for the note plus interest.

1. Prepare journal entries to record the general fund transactions.   ◄ ◄ ◄ ◄ ◄ **Required**
2. Prepare closing entries for the general fund.
3. Prepare a budgetary comparison schedule. On January 1, 2019, the unassigned fund balance showed a debit balance (deficit) of $180,000.

Problem 15-8 *(LO 5, 7)* **Journal entries, general fund.** The general fund trial balance of the city of Oakpark at December 31, 2018, was as follows:

	Debit	Credit
Cash	62,000	
Taxes Receivable—Delinquent	46,000	
Allowance for Uncollectible Delinquent Taxes		8,000
Inventory	18,000	
Vouchers Payable		28,000
Fund Balance—Reserved for Inventory		18,000

Fund Balance—Assigned		12,000
Fund Balance—Unassigned		60,000
Totals	126,000	126,000

The following data pertain to 2019 general fund operations:

a. Budget adopted:

Revenues and other financing sources:

Taxes	$220,000
Fines, forfeits, and penalties	80,000
Miscellaneous revenues	100,000
Share of bond issue proceeds	200,000
	$600,000

Expenditures and other financing uses:

Program operations	$300,000
General administration	120,000
Supplies	60,000
Capital outlay	80,000
Transfer to debt service fund	20,000
	$580,000

Encumbrances from 2018 are included in the budget.

b. Taxes were assessed at an amount that would result in revenues of $220,800, after a deduction of 4% of the tax levy as uncollectible.

c. Orders placed for:

Program operations	$176,000
General administration	80,000
Capital outlay	60,000
	$316,000

d. The city council designated $20,000 of the unassigned fund balance for possible appropriation for capital outlay.

e. Cash collections and transfer:

Delinquent taxes (balance is uncollectible)	$ 38,000
Current taxes	226,000
Refund of overpayment on equipment invoice in 2018	4,000
Fines, forfeits, and penalties	88,000
Miscellaneous revenues	90,000
Share of bond issue proceeds	200,000
Operating transfer from capital projects fund	18,000
	$664,000

f. Vouchers approved for payment (all previously encumbered):

	Estimated	Actual
Applicable to prior year but rebudgeted	$ 12,000	$ 12,000
Program operations	144,000	154,000
General administration	84,000	80,000
Capital outlay	62,000	62,000
	$302,000	$308,000

g. Additional vouchers approved (not previously encumbered):

Program operations.	$148,000
Supplies.	40,000
General administration	38,000
Capital outlay	18,000
Transfer to debt service fund	20,000
	$264,000

h. A taxpayer overpaid 2019 taxes by $2,000. (The taxes were credited to miscellaneous reve-nue upon receipt.) The taxpayer applied for a $2,000 credit against 2020 taxes. The city council granted the request. The council instructed the city controller to adjust the esti-mated uncollectible current taxes to cover the remaining uncollected balance.
i. Vouchers paid amounted to $580,000.
j. Inventory on December 31, 2019, amounted to $12,000.

Using control accounts, prepare journal entries to record the foregoing data. Omit explanations. ◄ ◄ ◄ ◄ ◄ **Required**

(AICPA adapted)

Problem 15-9 *(LO 5, 7)* **Journal entries, leases.** Mack County has acquired equipment through a noncancelable lease-purchase agreement dated December 31, 2017. This agreement requires no down payment and the following minimum lease payments:

December	Principal	Interest	Total
2018	$40,000	$12,000	$52,000
2019	40,000	7,000	47,000
2020	40,000	2,000	42,000

1. What account should be debited for $120,000 in the general fund at inception of the lease if ◄ ◄ ◄ ◄ ◄ **Required** the equipment is a general fixed asset and Mack does not use a capital projects fund?
2. What account should be credited for $120,000 in the general fixed assets account group at inception of the lease if the equipment is a general fixed asset?
3. What journal entry is required for $120,000 in the general long-term debt account group at inception of the lease if the lease payments are to be financed with general government resources?

(AICPA adapted)

Problem 15-10 *(LO 5, 7)* **Journal entries, capital assets.** Prepare journal entries to ◄ ◄ ◄ ◄ ◄ **Required** record the following events using the general fund and the general fixed assets account group:

a. The general fund vouchered the purchase of trucks for $80,000. The purchase had been encumbered earlier in the year at $75,000.
b. Several years ago, equipment costing $15,000 was acquired with general fund revenues. It was sold for $6,000, with proceeds belonging to the general fund.
c. Early in the year, a citizen donated to the city land appraised at $100,000. She submitted plans for a new library and agreed to cover the total cost of construction, paying the com-pany directly as work proceeded. At year-end, the building was two-thirds finished, with costs to date of $300,000. The expenditures are recorded in a capital projects fund.
d. A snow plow was purchased with general fund cash for $92,000, which represented a cost of $110,000 less trade-in of $18,000 for an old snow plow originally purchased for $66,000 from special revenue funds. As an emergency purchase, the acquisition of the new snow plow had not been encumbered.

Problem 15-11 *(LO 5, 7, 9, 10)* **Journal entries, schedule of long-term debt.** The city of Clinton was incorporated on January 1, 2014. On December 31, 2019, a careful study of the city's records revealed the following information regarding long-term debt:

a. General obligation bonds in the amount of $1,500,000 were authorized and issued at face value on July 1, 2014, to finance the construction of a school. The 6% bonds pay interest semiannually on January 1 and July 1, and they mature 10 years from the issuance date.

b. Serial bonds of $1,000,000 were sold at 99 on January 1, 2016, to help finance a new city hall and cultural center. An additional $750,000 was received from an anonymous benefactor. The 5% serial bonds were to be redeemed in annual amounts of $100,000, beginning on January 1, 2019. A sinking fund was established on January 2, 2016, to provide for the retirement of the serial bonds. Deposits of $70,000 were to be made on January 2 of each year, beginning in 2016. All amounts deposited were invested immediately at a net yield of 8%.

c. Property owners were assessed $750,000, to be paid in five equal annual installments, to finance construction of a storm sewer system and repaving of the affected roadways. To have cash when needed to pay for the construction, $600,000 of 5%, 5-year bonds were issued at face value by the Storm Sewer Proprietary Fund.

d. Term bonds totaling $400,000 were sold at face value on January 1, 2017, to finance construction. The 5%, 10-year bonds pay interest semiannually on January 1 and July 1. Each year, starting with January 1, 2017, $40,000 was to be set aside in a sinking fund to provide for retirement of the bonds at maturity. Any income earned by the sinking fund was to be applied to the semiannual interest payments.

Required ▶ ▶ ▶ ▶ ▶

1. Prepare only the journal entries for the transactions that would be recorded in the general long-term debt account group through December 31, 2019.
2. Prepare a schedule of long-term liabilities for the city of Clinton as of December 31, 2019.

Problem 15-12 *(LO 5, 7, 9, 10)* **Journal entries, schedule of capital assets.** The following schedule of capital assets was obtained from the records of the city of Elmcreek:

City of Elmcreek
Schedule of General Fixed Assets
December 31, 2018

Governmental activities:	
Land	$1,000,000
Buildings	2,150,000
Machinery and equipment	800,000
Construction in progress	250,000
Infrastructure assets	1,400,000
Total general fixed assets	$5,600,000
Less accumulated depreciation:	
Buildings	$ 400,000
Construction in progress	0
Machinery and equipment	300,000
Infrastructure	500,000
Total investment in governmental capital assets	$4,400,000

A summary of fixed asset transactions for 2019 follows:

a. Construction on the new school, a capital project started during 2018, was completed at a total cost of $850,000, which was financed by a serial bond issue. No other construction was in progress at the beginning of 2019.

b. A citizen donated 400 acres of land to the city to be used as a park. The land had a fair value of $140,000 when donated.

c. The municipal waterworks constructed a new pumping plant at a cost of $120,000. The plant was financed from the water utility revenues. The water utility is accounted for in a proprietary fund.

d. The fire department traded in an old fire engine and $105,000 cash for a new model. The old equipment had originally cost $65,000, and $15,000 was allowed on the trade-in.

e. The city hall was refurbished at a cost of $40,000, which was paid from general fund revenues. The refurbishing constituted a capital improvement.

f. Road-use taxes of $30,000 were collected by a special revenue fund, of which $20,000 has been used for improvements other than buildings.

g. Depreciation of $100,000 on buildings, $50,000 on machinery and equipment, and $25,000 on infrastructure were recorded.

1. Prepare journal entries only for those transactions that are to be accounted for in the general ◄ ◄ ◄ ◄ ◄ **Required** fixed assets account group. Use the city's account titles.

2. Prepare a schedule of capital assets as of December 31, 2019.

Problem 15-13 *(LO 5, 8, 9)* **Financial statements.** The following selected information was taken from SunValley City's general fund statement of revenues, expenditures, and changes in fund balance for the year ended December 31, 2019:

Revenues:	
Property taxes—2019	$ 825,000
Expenditures:	
Current services:	
Public safety	350,000
Capital outlay (police vehicles)	100,000
Debt service	74,000
Expenditures—2019	$1,349,000
Expenditures—2018	56,000
Expenditures	$1,405,000
Excess of revenues over expenditures	$ 153,000
Other financing uses	(125,000)
Excess of revenues over expenditures and other financing uses	$ 28,000
Decrease in fund balance assigned (encumbrances) during 2019	15,000
Residual equity transfers-out	(190,000)
Decrease in unassigned fund balance during 2019	$ (147,000)
Unassigned fund balance, January 1, 2019	304,000
Unassigned fund balance, December 31, 2019	$ 157,000

The following information was taken from SunValley's December 31, 2019, general fund balance sheet:

Property taxes receivable—delinquent—2019	$ 34,000
Less: Allowances for estimated uncollectible taxes—delinquent	20,000
Vouchers payable	89,000
Fund balance:	
Nonspendable	38,000
Assigned—2019	43,000
Unassigned	157,000

Additional information is as follows:

a. Debt service was for bonds used to finance a library building and included interest of $22,000.

b. $8,000 of 2019 property taxes receivable was written off; otherwise, the allowance for uncollectible taxes balance is unchanged from the initial entry at the time of the original tax levy at the beginning of the year.

c. SunValley reported supplies inventory of $21,000 at December 31, 2018.

Required ▶ ▶ ▶ ▶ ▶ Provide the best answer to the following questions:

1. What recording method did SunValley use for its general fund supplies inventory?
2. What amount was collected from 2019 tax assessments?
3. What amount is SunValley's liability to general fund vendors and contractors at December 31, 2019?
4. What amount should be included in the general fixed assets account group for the cost of assets acquired in 2019 through the general fund?
5. What amount arising from 2019 transactions decreased liabilities reported in the general long-term debt account group?
6. What amount of total actual expenditures should SunValley report in its 2019 general fund statement of revenues, expenditures, and changes in fund balance—budget and actual?

(AICPA adapted)

Problem 15-14 *(LO 5, 9)* **Journal entries, balance sheet.** The January 2, 2018, trial balance of Oneida Township follows:

	Debit	Credit
Cash	45,000	
Taxes Receivable—Delinquent	20,000	
Allowance for Uncollectible Delinquent Taxes		2,000
Tax Liens Receivable	4,000	
Allowance for Uncollectible Tax Liens		1,000
Due from Parks Fund	12,000	
Inventory of Supplies	5,000	
Vouchers Payable		43,000
Due to Utility Fund		4,000
Fund Balance—Nonspendable		5,000
Fund Balance—Unassigned		31,000
Totals	86,000	86,000

The following events occurred during the first six months of 2018:

a. The adopted budget showed the following:

Estimated expenditures	$620,000
Transfers to other funds	27,000
Estimated revenues	655,000

b. Six-month tax anticipation notes were issued in the amount of $120,000.
c. Property taxes of $430,000 were levied, with 2% of the gross levy considered uncollectible.
d. Tax liens proved uncollectible. The property was foreclosed and sold for $4,000.
e. Amounts encumbered totaled $250,000.
f. Cash collected:

All delinquent property taxes	$ 20,000
Current taxes	290,000
Due from Parks Fund	11,000
Fines and penalties	23,000
	$344,000

g. Items vouchered totaled $186,000, representing $183,000 of encumbrances. Included in both were $26,000 for supplies, for which a perpetual inventory system is maintained.

h. Cash payments:

Vouchered items	$151,000
Nonvouchered items that were not encumbered	49,000
Due to Utility Fund	4,000
	$204,000

i. Supplies inventory on June 30 was $21,000.

1. Using the format below, complete the general fund worksheet for the six months ended June ◄ ◄ ◄ ◄ ◄ **Required** 30, 2018. Ignore entries for any other fund or group. Label entries on the worksheet according to their corresponding events. Formal journal entries are not required.
2. Prepare a balance sheet as of June 30, 2018.

	Trial Balance		Operating Entries		Revenues and Expenditures		Balance Sheet	
Accounts	Dr.	Cr.	Dr.	Cr.	Dr.	Cr.	Dr.	Cr.

Governmental Accounting: Other Governmental Funds, Proprietary Funds, and Fiduciary Funds

Learning Objectives

When you have completed this chapter, you should be able to

1. **Tell why governments use special revenue, permanent, capital projects, and debt service funds, and demonstrate how transactions are accounted for and reported using those funds.**

2. **Account for and prepare financial statements of proprietary funds.**

3. **Explain the usefulness of and the accounting process for fiduciary funds and how these funds are reported.**

4. **Identify and account for transactions that affect different funds and/or account groups.**

A variety of funds may be used to record events and to exhibit results for a specific area of responsibility. In a small town, there may not be enough activity to warrant more than a general fund, but the larger the governmental unit and the more diverse the activities with which it is involved, the greater the necessity to introduce special funds. While the Governmental Accounting Standards Board (GASB) recognizes the need for funds to manage and demonstrate accountability, it cautions against too many funds that unnecessarily fragment financial reporting. GASB Statement No. 1 suggests that a governmental unit establish only the *minimum* number of funds consistent with legal and operating requirements.

OTHER GOVERNMENTAL FUNDS

Typical funds used by state and local governments include special revenue funds, permanent funds, capital projects funds, and debt service funds. A special revenue fund would be used when revenues are collected for a specific purpose, such as road repair or education. Permanent funds are used to account for trusts that are set up to accomplish a specific, *public* purpose. The principal of a permanent fund must not be expended. When a major, general capital asset, such as a building, is being acquired, the governmental entity uses a capital projects fund to account for related transactions. Once the government has borrowed money for a capital project or for other reasons, the debt principal is recorded and tracked in the long-term debt account group (see Chapter 15), and the accounting for that debt is recorded in a debt service fund.

1

OBJECTIVE

Tell why governments use special revenue, permanent, capital projects, and debt service funds, and demonstrate how transactions are accounted for and reported using those funds.

Special Revenue Funds

When revenue obtained from specified sources is restricted by law or donor for a specified current operating purpose or to the acquisition of a relatively minor fixed asset, accounting is accomplished through a *special revenue fund*. Although the government will have only one general fund, it could have many special revenue funds, or none at all. Examples of activities that are accounted for in special revenue funds are nonexchange transactions, such as the hotel room taxes restricted for expenditures that promote tourism, federal and state grant proceeds restricted to financing community development expenditures, gasoline tax revenues for highway maintenance, specific federal and/or state funds for education, resources for food stamp programs administered by state governments, other pass-through grants and on-behalf payment programs for fringe benefits and salaries,[1] and exchange transactions such as golf fees charged at a city golf course to cover a portion of the cost of course maintenance.[2] Special revenue funds account for activities of an expendable public-purpose trust fund; that is, both the principal and earnings can be spent for the benefit of the government's programs. These revenues are recognized under the modified accrual method of accounting. The following are examples of revenues recorded in the special revenue funds.

Event	Entry in the Special Revenue Funds		
1. During the year, local hotels/motels paid to the city a room tax totaling $98,000. The remittance included $6,000 payable from last year and $92,000 expected to be available in the current year.	Cash .... Taxes Receivable................ Revenues	98,000	 6,000 92,000
2. In addition, the city estimates a $9,000 receivable from December rentals. In this city, the hotels/motels are allowed a 1-month administrative lead time and are not required to pay the December tax until January 31 of the following year.	Taxes Receivable.................. Revenues	9,000	 9,000
3. Federal food stamp coupons of $10,000 are received by the state government.	Food Stamp Coupons .... Deferred Revenues...............	10,000	 10,000
4. $9,000 of coupons are distributed.	Expenditures .... Food Stamp Coupons	9,000	 9,000
	Deferred Revenues................. Revenues	9,000	 9,000
5. Charges for services from exchange transactions for the year are as follows:	Cash .... Accounts Receivable .... Revenues .... Deferred Revenues...............	370,000 10,000	 360,000 20,000

	Earned	Collected
Golf fees (collected at time of use)	$ 35,000	$ 35,000
Garbage fees (collected in advance of providing service)	240,000	260,000
Snow removal fees (collected after service is provided).....	85,000	75,000
Total.................	$360,000	$370,000

Event	Entry in the Special Revenue Funds		
6. A $100,000 federal grant is received for economic development. An additional $50,000 is due prior to year-end. Revenue is recognized when expenditures are incurred for the grant program.	Cash .... Due from Federal Government .... Deferred Revenues...............	100,000 50,000	 150,000

1 GASB Statement No. 24, *Accounting and Financial Reporting for Certain Grants and Other Financial Assistance* (Norwalk, CT: Governmental Accounting Standards Board, June 1994). Pass-through grants are defined in GASB No. 24 as grants received by a government to transfer to or spend on behalf of a secondary recipient. Generally, these transactions are to be accounted for in a special revenue fund or a general fund if the government has discretion over the distribution of these funds.
2 When revenue raised for activities is on a fee basis for goods or services provided and the operations are intended to be self-supporting, the flows of resources are accounted for in proprietary funds discussed later in this chapter.

In a special revenue fund, the accounting must be designed to permit close scrutiny of activities. If resources are greater than anticipated, the project is not permitted to expand beyond the original authorization, nor is money permitted to accumulate beyond reasonable needs. However, sufficient resources should be generated to permit the activity. The desired control may be accomplished by using the same accounting procedures as those used by the general fund. Annual budgets are prepared for each special revenue fund and are required to be integrated into the accounting system by using the appropriate budgetary control accounts and their related subsidiary records. Commitments are recorded by using an encumbrance and expenditure system. Since both the accounting procedures and the financial statements for special revenue funds are so similar to those of the general fund, they will not be illustrated beyond the preceding revenue recognition examples.

When a governmental unit has more than one special revenue fund, major funds are identified (the criterion for determining major funds is described in Chapter 17) and nonmajor individual funds are presented in *combining* balance sheets and revenue and expenditure statements. Combining statements provide information on each special revenue fund plus a total column of all the nonmajor special revenue funds. Illustration 16-1 presents a combining balance sheet, and Illustration 16-2 presents a combining statement of revenues, expenditures, and changes in fund balances.

Illustration 16-1
City of Berryville—Nonmajor Special Revenue Funds
Combining Balance Sheet
December 31, 2019

Assets	Federal Food Stamp Program	Community Development Block Grant	Tourism Promotion Projects	Charges for City Golf Course	Total Nonmajor Special Revenue Funds
Cash		$100,000	$ 98,000	$370,000	$568,000
Taxes receivable			9,000	10,000	19,000
Due from other governmental agencies		50,000	40,000		90,000
Food stamp coupons	$1,000				1,000
Total assets	$1,000	$150,000	$147,000	$380,000	$678,000

Liabilities and Fund Balances					
Liabilities:					
Vouchers payable			$ 15,000	$105,000	$120,000
Due to other funds			10,000	55,000	65,000
Deferred revenues	$1,000	$150,000		20,000	171,000
Total liabilities	$1,000	$150,000	$ 25,000	$180,000	$356,000
Fund balances:					
Committed	$ 0	$ 0	$ 95,000	$175,000	$270,000
Assigned			27,000	25,000	52,000
Total fund balances	$ 0	$ 0	$122,000	$200,000	$322,000
Total liabilities and fund balances	$1,000	$150,000	$147,000	$380,000	$678,000

Illustration 16-2
City of Berryville
Nonmajor Special Revenue Funds
Combining Statement of Revenues, Expenditures, and Changes in Fund Balances
For Year Ended December 31, 2019

	Federal Food Stamp Program	Community Development Block Grant	Tourism Promotion Projects	Charges for City Golf Course	Total Nonmajor Special Revenue Funds
Revenues	$9,000	$40,000	$101,000	$360,000	$510,000
Expenditures	9,000	40,000	40,000	200,000	289,000
Excess of revenues over (under) expenditures	$ 0	$ 0	$ 61,000	$160,000	$221,000
Other financing sources (uses):					
Operating transfers-out	$ 0	$ 0	$ (10,000)	$ (55,000)	$ (65,000)
Total other financing sources (uses)	$ 0	$ 0	$ (10,000)	$ (55,000)	$ (65,000)
Excess of revenues and other financing sources over (under) expenditures and other financing uses	$ 0	$ 0	$ 51,000	$105,000	$156,000
Fund balances—January 1			71,000	95,000	166,000
Fund balances—December 31	$ 0	$ 0	$122,000	$200,000	$322,000

In addition, a government is required to present budgetary comparison information for any major special revenue fund that has a legally adopted budget. The purpose of the schedule is to compare the original and final amended budget information to actual amounts. A columnar format like the following is presented for these special revenue funds:

Special Revenue Fund A				Special Revenue Fund B			
Original	Final	Actual	Variance	Original	Final	Actual	Variance
Budget	Budget		Favorable (Unfavorable)	Budget	Budget		Favorable (Unfavorable)

Permanent Funds

Permanent funds are established to account for public-purpose trusts for which the earnings are expendable for a specified purpose, but the principal amount is not expendable. These funds are often referred to as endowments. As described in the previous section, public-purpose trusts for which both principal and earnings can be spent for a specified purpose are accounted for in special revenue funds. Further, private-purpose trusts are accounted for in fiduciary funds as will be described later in this chapter. Permanent funds will capture much of the current trust activity in local governments. These trusts have been established to benefit a government program or function, or the citizens, rather than an external individual, organization, or government. For example, resources received to be invested of which only the income, not the principal, is expended to support a park, cemetery, library, or some other government program, are now accounted for in permanent funds. All assets, including land and other real estate, are recorded at fair value. Changes in fair value are reported as investment income.

The following are examples of transactions recorded in permanent funds:

Event	Entry in the Permanent Fund		
7. During the year, securities were received to initiate a trust fund to support the operations of the town cemetery. The donors stipulated that the earnings, not the principal, be spent. The fair value of the securities at the date of donation is $750,000.	Investment in Stocks............... Revenues	750,000	750,000
8. Dividends are received on the investments, totaling $15,000.	Cash .... Revenues	15,000	15,000
9. The earnings are transferred out to the Cemetery Operating Fund. Cemetery operations are accounted for in a special revenue fund.	Other Financing Uses .... Cash	15,000	15,000

The entry in the special revenue fund to record the transfer-in is as follows:

Cash	15,000	
Other Financing Sources......		15,000

When a governmental unit has more than one permanent fund, major funds are identified and nonmajor individual funds are presented in *combining* balance sheets and revenue and expenditure statements. Combining statements provide information on each permanent fund plus a total column of all the permanent funds. These statements are similar in content and form to those presented in the previous section for special revenue funds and are not illustrated here.

Capital Projects Funds

Capital projects funds account for the purchase, construction, or capital lease of major, *general* capital assets, which excludes construction of capital facilities by proprietary funds that account for their own construction activities. Each project should be accounted for separately in subsidiary records to demonstrate compliance with legal and contractual provisions.

Resources for capital projects result from transfers received from the general fund or some other fund, proceeds of general obligation bonds, grants from another governmental unit, or special assessments levied against property owners who benefit from the project. Grants from another governmental unit and special assessments levied are recorded as revenues. Bond proceeds (because they must be repaid) and transfers from other funds (because they were previously recognized as revenue) are accounted for as other financing sources.

When the capital projects are expected to take several years to complete and will involve large amounts of money, budgetary control is advisable. The operating budget is prepared on an *annual* basis; therefore, it includes the expected revenues, estimated other financing sources, and estimated expenditures for only the current fiscal year. Adopting annual reporting permits the accounting for project events to be the same as for the general fund and the special revenue funds. The budget entry is as follows:

Estimated Other Financing Sources[a]	XXX	
Estimated Revenues[b]	XXX	
Appropriations[c]		XXX
Budgetary Fund Balance—Unassigned (either debited or credited)		XXX

[a]Resources from the general fund or other funds and the sale of general obligation bonds.
[b]Resources from county, state, or federal grants and interest income on temporary investments and from special assessments.
[c]Estimated expenditures for current year.

The full amount of the bond issue proceed is recorded as another financing source in the fund that will use the resources. Bond premiums and discounts are recorded separately as other financing sources or uses, respectively. Bond issuance costs are recorded as expenditures. Since bond premiums and discounts arise because of adjustments to the interest rate, the premium and any payment received for accrued interest are transferred to the debt service fund to cover future *interest* payments. If bonds are sold at a discount, a project authorization must be reduced by the bond discount amount and/or issuance costs unless additional resources are transferred from the general fund or other funds.

Governments sometimes issue short-term *bond anticipation* notes after obtaining necessary voter and legislative authorization to issue long-term bonds. Since these short-term notes are expected to be replaced by long-term bonds, they are, in essence, long term and are accounted for in the general long-term debt account group (GLTDAG), which was explained in Chapter 15. Proceeds of the bond anticipation notes are recorded in the governmental funds (often a capital projects fund) as other financing sources—proceeds from bond anticipation notes.[3]

Proceeds of bond issues not immediately needed for project expenditures are often temporarily invested to earn interest. These temporary investments are limited to securities whose yield does not exceed the interest rate of the tax-exempt borrowing. Interest earned on temporary investments is recognized as revenue in the capital projects fund. These earnings are often required to be transferred to the debt service fund to help finance bond interest expenditures.[4]

Capital projects funds have the authority through annually approved budgets to continue expenditures within prescribed limits until a project is completed. Although a project may not be completed at the end of a fiscal period, typical closing entries are recorded. Annual closing permits the actual activity to be compared with the legally adopted annual operating budget. Also, in the closing process, the credit to Expenditures provides the amount of capitalizable expenditures to be recorded in the general fixed assets account group as construction in progress.

The actual cost of a capital project probably will differ from its estimated cost. A deficiency usually is covered by a transfer from the general fund. If an excess of resources exists upon completion of the project, it generally is returned to the general fund or to the debt service fund. Such a transfer is reported as an other financing use on the statement of revenues, expenditures, and changes in fund balance. Upon completion of the project, it is customary to withhold part of the payment until final inspection and approval. The liability is recorded in contracts payable—retained percentage.

To illustrate accounting for capital projects funds, assume the city of Berryville plans to build a $300,000 addition to its municipal auditorium. The project will begin in 2018 and is to be completed in 2019. The following entries record the events that occur during construction:

Event	Entry in the Capital Projects Fund		

2018

10.	The project budget is $300,000, to be financed by a general bond issue. The bond proceeds are committed to the project. The 2018 operating budget is based on one-third of the work's being completed that year.	Estimated Other Financing Sources. . . . . . Appropriations . . . . Budgetary Fund Balance—Unassigned .	300,000	100,000 200,000
11.	A $300,000, 8% general obligation bond issue is floated at 101.	Cash . . . . Other Financing Sources . . . . Other Financing Sources—Premium . . .	303,000	300,000 3,000

An entry also is made in the general long-term debt account group as follows:

Amount to Be Provided	300,000	
Serial Bonds Payable.		300,000

---

3 The GASB states that a government may recognize bond anticipation notes as long-term obligations if, by the date the financial statements are issued, "all legal steps have been taken to refinance the bond anticipation notes and the intent is supported by an ability to consummate refinancing of the short-term note on a long-term basis." *Codification of Government Accounting and Reporting Standards* (Norwalk, CT: Governmental Accounting Standards Board, 1996, Section B50.101).

4 Governments are not required to capitalize construction-period interest for governmental activities.

Event	Entry in the Capital Projects Fund		
12. The bond premium is transferred to the debt service fund to be used for interest.	Other Financing Uses . . . . Cash	3,000	3,000

An entry also is made in the debt service fund as follows:

Cash 3,000
    Other Financing Sources 3,000
(*Note:* Since bond premium is assumed to be used for interest payments, no entry is made in the account group.)

Event	Entry in the Capital Projects Fund		
13. A contract is signed for the auditorium construction at an estimated cost of $270,000. The contract was approved by a city official.	Encumbrances . . . . Fund Balance—Assigned	270,000	270,000

14. The architect's bill for $10,650 is received, of which $7,650 is paid. Upon final building approval, the balance is due. The item was not encumbered.	Expenditures . . . .
	    Cash . . . .
	    Contracts Payable—Retained Percentage . .
		10,650	7,650
			3,000

15. A partial billing is received from the contractor for $60,000, equal to the amount encumbered for these items. The contracts payable account is credited for the liability to the principal contractor. (If the amount of equivalent encumbrance is not specified, the encumbrance entry is reversed for the amount of the billing.)	Fund Balance—Assigned . . . .
	    Encumbrances . . . .
	Expenditures . . . .
	    Contracts Payable . . . .
		60,000
		
		60,000
			60,000
			
			60,000

16. The contractor is paid $60,000.	Contracts Payable . . . . Cash	60,000	60,000
17. Books for 2018 are closed.	Budgetary Fund Balance—Unassigned . . . . . . Appropriations . . . . Estimated Other Financing Sources	200,000 100,000	300,000

18. The credit to Expenditures is the basis for the following entry in the general fixed assets account group:
 	
Construction in Progress 70,650
    Investment in General Fixed
    Assets—Capital Projects
    Funds 70,650
	Other Financing Sources . . . .
	    Expenditures . . . .
	    Other Financing Uses . . . .
	    Fund Balance—Committed . . . .
		303,000	70,650
			3,000
			229,350

19. Encumbrances are closed at year-end.	Fund Balance—Committed . . . . Encumbrances	210,000	210,000

2019

Event	Entry in the Capital Projects Fund		
20. The operating budget for 2019 is recorded; completion is estimated to cost an additional $215,000, including the amount encumbered in the previous year.	Budgetary Fund Balance—Unassigned . . . . . . Appropriations	215,000	215,000

21. The encumbrances are reinstated at the beginning of 2019.	Encumbrances . . . .
	    Fund Balance—Committed . . . .
	
	Fund Balance—Assigned . . . .
	    Encumbrances . . . .
		210,000
		
		210,000
			210,000
			
			210,000

22. The contract is completed in 2019. Additional cost is $227,000, of which $10,000 is withheld in a separate account until final inspection and approval.	Expenditures . . . .
	    Contracts Payable . . . .
	    Contracts Payable—Retained Percentage . .
		227,000	217,000
			10,000

(continued)

Event	Entry in the Capital Projects Fund		
23. The construction is accepted, and the contractor and architect are paid.	Contracts Payable . . . . Contracts Payable—Retained Percentage. . . . Cash	217,000 13,000	230,000
24. Books for 2019 are closed.	Appropriations . . . . Budgetary Fund Balance—Unassigned. . . .	215,000	215,000
25.	Fund Balance—Unassigned . . . . Expenditures	227,000	227,000

25.
> The credit to Expenditures is the basis for the following entry in the general fixed assets account group:
>
> Buildings 297,650
>   Construction in Progress   70,650
>   Investment in General Fixed
>   Assets—Capital Projects Funds .   227,000

Event	Entry in the Capital Projects Fund		
26. The residual balance is transferred to the debt service fund.	Other Financing Uses . . . . Cash	2,350	2,350

> An entry also is made in the debt service fund as follows:
>
> Cash   2,350
>   Other Financing Sources   2,350
> Other Financing Sources   2,350
>   Fund Balance—Reserved for
>   Debt Service.   2,350
> (*Note:* Since the project was financed with general obligation debt, an additional entry in the general long-term debt account group indicating availability of funds to repay the debt is required.)
>
> Amount Available in the Debt
>   Service Fund   2,350
>   Amount to Be Provided. . . .   2,350

Event	Entry in the Capital Projects Fund		
27. The Municipal Auditorium Capital Project Fund is closed.	Fund Balance—Committed . . . . Other Financing Uses	2,350	2,350

When a governmental unit has more than one capital project, major funds are identified and nonmajor funds are presented in combining financial statements. Illustration 16-3 presents a combining balance sheet for the city of Berryville's nonmajor capital projects funds. The 2018 year-end balance sheet for the auditorium project, for which the accounting entries are shown, and the 2018 year-end balance sheet for a bridge construction capital project, for which the accounting entries are *not* shown, are included in the combining balance sheet.

The combining statement of revenues, expenditures, and changes in fund balances (shown in Illustration 16-4) will show as revenues those resources obtained by special assessment, by grant, or from some other governmental unit. Transfers from other funds within the same governmental unit or proceeds of a bond issue are presented as other financing sources.

Debt Service Funds

As discussed in Chapter 15, the function of the general long-term debt account group is to provide a record of the unredeemed principal of long-term liabilities incurred to acquire general fixed assets. Closely related to this account group are *debt service funds*, whose primary function is to account for financial resources accumulated to cover the payment of principal and interest on general government obligations.

As in other governmental funds, the modified accrual basis is used for recognizing revenues, other financing sources, and expenditures in debt service funds. Interest and principal on

Illustration 16-3
City of Berryville
Nonmajor Capital Projects Funds
Combining Balance Sheet
December 31, 2018

Assets	Municipal Auditorium	Bridge Construction Project	Total Nonmajor Capital Project Funds
Cash	$232,350	$102,000	$334,350
Special assessments receivable		160,000	160,000
Investments		40,000	40,000
Total assets	$232,350	$302,000	$534,350

Liabilities and Fund Balance			
Vouchers payable		$157,000	$157,000
Contracts payable—retained percentage	$ 3,000	50,000	53,000
Total liabilities	$ 3,000	$207,000	$210,000
Fund balances:			
Restricted	$ 19,350	$ 5,000	$ 24,350
Assigned	210,000	90,000	300,000
Total fund balances	$229,350	$ 95,000	$324,350
Total liabilities and fund balances	$232,350	$302,000	$534,350

Illustration 16-4
City of Berryville
Nonmajor Capital Projects Funds
Combining Statement of Revenues, Expenditures, and Changes in Fund Balances
For Year Ended December 31, 2018

	Municipal Auditorium	Bridge Construction Project	Total Nonmajor Capital Projects Funds
Revenues		$118,000	$ 118,000
Expenditures	$ 70,650	157,000	227,650
Excess (deficiency) of revenues over expenditures	$ (70,650)	$ (39,000)	$(109,650)
Other financing sources (uses):			
Proceeds of bonds	$303,000	$196,000	$ 499,000
Payments to debt service	(3,000)	(62,000)	(65,000)
Total other financing sources (uses)	$300,000	$134,000	$ 434,000
Excess (deficiency) of revenues and other sources over expenditures and other uses	$229,350	$ 95,000	$ 324,350
Fund balances at beginning of year	0	0	0
Fund balances at end of year	$229,350	$ 95,000	$ 324,350

general long-term debt are items for which the accrual basis is modified. For example, assume a governmental unit has a fiscal year ending June 30, with interest and principal on long-term debt to be paid on July 31. Since expenditures are authorized by appropriations, it is essential that expenditures be recorded in the same period as the appropriations. Thus, the interest and principal will not be accrued on June 30, because the appropriation to cover the principal and interest will not be provided until the budget for the next period is recorded on July 1. This method recognizes expenditures for interest and principal when they are *due*.

The most popular method of raising long-term resources is by the issuance of serial bonds, which are redeemed in a series of installments. Term bonds, whose total face value becomes due at one time, are now extremely rare. When serial bonds are issued, there is no substantial accumulation of cash in a sinking fund. Instead, the budget for the year of payment provides for interest and principal redemption. In debt service funds, an entry to record the budget is seldom used because expenditures for principal and interest are known and there is no need to compare them with budgetary amounts.

Resources to cover expenditures may come from several sources. A portion of a property tax levy may be authorized to be recorded directly into a debt service fund. The entries would be similar to those made in the general fund to record a tax levy. The net amount of taxes estimated to be collected is credited to Revenues since the resources are received from outsiders. Transfers received by the debt service fund from funds that have already recorded the resources as revenues are credited to Other Financing Sources. As discussed in Chapter 15, this procedure prevents revenues from being credited in two funds for the same resources—once in the originating fund (in this case, the general fund) and again in the recipient fund (in this case, a debt service fund).

Prior to redemption, the bond liability for unmatured general obligation debt is not recorded in a debt service fund but is recorded in the general long-term debt account group or similar listing. However, when a serial bond matures and payment of interest is due, the following entry is recorded in a debt service fund:

Expenditures	XXX	
Matured Bonds Payable		XXX
Matured Interest Payable		XXX

The following entries would be made in a debt service fund for the indicated events that relate to a serial bond issue. As demonstrated by these entries, the interaction between funds and groups is especially prevalent in accounting for general obligation bond issues.

Event	Entry in the Debt Service Fund		
28. An 8%, $300,000 general obligation serial bond issue for bridge construction is sold at 101. The premium is transferred from the capital projects fund to the debt service fund.	Cash . . . . Other Financing Sources	3,000	3,000

Entries are also made in the capital projects fund as follows:

Cash	303,000	
Other Financing Sources		300,000
Other Financing Sources—Premium		3,000
Other Financing Uses	3,000	
Cash		3,000

Entries are also made in the general long-term debt account group:

Amount to Be Provided	300,000	
Serial Bonds Payable		300,000

Event	Entry in the Debt Service Fund		

29. Of the property taxes, $50,000 is levied specifically to cover debt service on these bonds; the levy, less 1% of the taxes estimated to be uncollectible, is recorded in the debt service fund.

Taxes Receivable—Current	50,000	
Allowance for Uncollectible Current Taxes .		500
Revenues		49,500

30. All property taxes are collected except for $400 that is written off. The difference between estimated and actual uncollectible taxes is recorded in Revenues.

Cash	49,600	
Allowance for Uncollectible Current Taxes . . .	400	
Taxes Receivable—Current		50,000
Allowance for Uncollectible Current Taxes . . .	100	
Revenues		100

31. Assuming $30,000 is to be used toward the first installment on the principal payment, an additional entry is made in the general long-term debt account group as follows:

Amount Available in the Debt		
Service Fund	30,000	
Amount to Be Provided		30,000

32. The fund receives $7,000 of its $9,000 share of state gasoline taxes. The city is not entitled to the balance until the next fiscal period.

Cash	7,000	
Due from State	2,000	
Revenues		7,000
Deferred Revenues		2,000

33. A transfer of $30,000 is received from the general fund.

Cash	30,000	
Other Financing Sources		30,000

Since the $30,000 is for payment of principal, an additional entry is made in the general long-term account group debt:

Amount Available in the Debt Service		
Fund	30,000	
Amount to Be Provided		30,000

34. Cash is transmitted to a fiscal agent for payment of the first $60,000 of maturing bonds and $24,000 of interest due on the last day of the fiscal period.

Cash with Fiscal Agent	84,000	
Cash		84,000

35. The matured bonds and interest are recorded.

Expenditures	84,000	
Matured Bonds Payable		60,000
Matured Interest Payable		24,000

Principal of $60,000 is matured and no longer long term. The entry to reclassify the debt in the general long-term account group debt is as follows:

Serial Bonds Payable	60,000	
Amount Available in the Debt		
Service Fund		60,000

36. The fiscal agent reports that all payments have been made except for $1,000 of interest.

Matured Bonds Payable	60,000	
Matured Interest Payable	23,000	
Cash with Fiscal Agent		83,000

37. Books are closed at year-end.

Revenues	56,600	
Other Financing Sources	33,000	
Expenditures		84,000
Fund Balance—Restricted		5,600

Assets transferred to a debt service fund must be used to redeem bonds or to pay interest. There are no unassigned assets. Any excess of assets over liabilities should be classified as either restricted, committed, or assigned for debt service. Therefore, at year-end, the accounts are closed to fund balance—restricted, committed, or assigned for debt service rather than to an unassigned fund balance.

In addition to term bonds and serial bonds, debt service funds may be used to service debt arising from notes or warrants having a maturity of more than one year after date of issue and to make periodic payments on capital leases. Although each issue of long-term debt is a separate obligation with unique legal restrictions and servicing requirements, GASB standards provide that, if legally permissible, a single debt service fund may be used to account for the service of all issues of tax-supported and special-assessment debt. If legal restrictions do not allow the servicing of all issues to be accounted for by a single debt service fund, the number of debt service funds should be held to a minimum.

Sometimes, governments will defease existing debt accounted for in the general long-term debt account group. Through advanced refunding, new debt is issued to provide resources to pay interest on old, outstanding debt as it becomes due and to pay the principal on the old debt either as it matures or for an earlier call date. As demonstrated by the following entries, when advanced refunding results in defeasance of debt (either legally or in substance), the proceeds of the new debt are reported as *other financing sources—proceeds of refunding bonds* in the debt service fund.[5] Subsequent payments from resources provided by the new debt to actually retire the old debt or to transfer funds to an escrow agent are other financing uses, not expenditures. In either case, the old debt is removed from the general long-term debt account group, and the new debt is reported as a long-term liability.

Event	Entry in the Debt Service Fund		

38. A $100,000 bond was issued, proceeds from which are restricted for the purpose of paying principal and interest of an $85,000 old bond issue. The criteria for in-substance defeasance is met.	Cash ....
	    Other Financing Sources—Proceeds
	      of Refunding Bonds ....
		100,000	100,000

39. Cash is transmitted to an escrow agent to administer the payment of principal and interest on the old debt. If the debt was actually retired, the debit would be to Other Financing Uses—Retirement of Old Bonds.	Other Financing Uses—Payment to
	    Escrow Agent ....
	      Cash ....
		100,000	100,000

The entries in the general long-term debt account group to record the new debt are as follows:

Bonds Payable	85,000	
Amount to Be Provided		85,000

The entries in the general long-term debt account group to record the new debt are as follows:

Amount to Be Provided	100,000	
Bonds Payable		100,000

---

5 GASB Statement No. 7, *Advanced Refunding Resulting in Defeasance of Debt* (Norwalk, CT: Governmental Accounting Standards Board, March 1987).

Debt service funds employ two financial statements for reporting purposes: a balance sheet and a statement of revenues, expenditures, and changes in fund balances. If two or more debt service funds are used, major funds are identified and nonmajor funds are presented in combining statements. Illustration 16-5 is a combining balance sheet for the nonmajor debt service funds of Vernon Town. This balance sheet has a column for general obligation debt, for which the entries were shown, and a column for special assessment debt explained later in this chapter, for which the entries were not shown.

Illustration 16-5
Vernon Town
Nonmajor Debt Service Funds
Combining Balance Sheet
December 31, 2018

Assets	General Obligation Debt	Special Assessment Debt	Total Nonmajor Debt Service Funds
Cash	$5,600	$ 20,000	$ 25,600
Cash with fiscal agents	1,000		1,000
Due from state	2,000		2,000
Special assessment receivable		20,000	20,000
Special assessment receivable—deferred..........		160,000	160,000
Total assets.................................	$8,600	$200,000	$208,600

Liabilities and Fund Balance			
Liabilities:			
Matured interest payable.....................	$1,000		$ 1,000
Deferred revenues	2,000	$160,000	162,000
Fund balance:			
Restricted for debt service	5,600	40,000	45,600
Total liabilities and fund balance...............	$8,600	$200,000	$208,600

The combining statement of revenues, expenditures, and changes in fund balances for Vernon Town's nonmajor debt service funds is shown in Illustration 16-6. This statement itemizes revenues by source and expenditures by function, and it summarizes the causes of changes in fund balances during the period.

Special Assessments. Local governments may provide capital improvements and services for the primary benefit of particular groups of property owners, which are paid partially or totally by the same property owners. Such arrangements are called *special assessment projects* and are accounted for through the local government.

Service-type special assessments cover operating activities, such as snow plowing, that do not result in increases in fixed assets. Payment for service special assessments seldom is arranged on an installment basis. A single charge is added to the property tax bill. Service assessments are accounted for in the fund type (usually the general fund, a special revenue fund, or an enterprise fund) that best reflects the nature of the transaction.

Capital-improvement special assessments result in additions or improvements to a government's fixed assets. If an improvement provides capital assets that become part of an enterprise activity, such as water main construction for a utility, accounting would be done in an enterprise fund. If the improvement results in a general fixed asset, such as streets, gutters, or sidewalks, the asset would be recorded in the general fixed assets account group (if the government records infrastructure assets), in which case the accounting is divided into two phases.

Illustration 16-6
Vernon Town
Nonmajor Debt Service Funds
Combining Statement of Revenues, Expenditures, and Changes in Fund Balances
For Year Ended December 31, 2018

	General Obligation Debt	Special Assessment Debt	Total Nonmajor Debt Service Funds
Revenues:			
Taxes	$ 49,600	$20,000	$ 69,600
Intergovernmental	7,000		7,000
Total revenues	$ 56,600	$20,000	$ 76,600
Expenditures:			
Principal retirement	$ 60,000		$ 60,000
Interest charges	24,000		24,000
Total expenditures	$ 84,000	$ 0	$ 84,000
Excess (deficiency) of revenues over expenditures	$ (27,400)	$20,000	$ (7,400)
Other financing sources (uses):			
Proceeds of refunding bonds	$ 100,000		$ 100,000
Operating transfers-in	33,000		33,000
Payment to escrow agent....................	(100,000)		(100,000)
Total other finance sources (uses)...........	$ 33,000	$ 0	$ 33,000
Excess (deficiency) of revenues and other financing sources over expenditures...........	$ 5,600	$20,000	$ 25,600
Fund balances at beginning of year	0	20,000	20,000
Fund balances at end of year	$ 5,600	$40,000	$ 45,600

The *first phase* consists of financing and constructing the project and usually is accounted for through a capital projects fund. The initiative for such projects is often taken by the property owners who request the improvement. However, authorization must be approved through appropriate channels. Special assessment projects typically are financed through issues of long-term debt but may be financed with existing government resources. Once the project is approved, the estimates for the budget period (not the total project budget) are recorded in a capital projects fund.

Proper recordings of inflows of financial resources into the capital projects fund depend upon the source of financing. Illustration 16-7 presents proper recording of inflows under three possible sources of financing. When the capital improvements are financed by special-assessment-related debt for which the government is obligated in some manner, such as accounting for resources raised and for the expenditure of funds during construction, accounting procedures are the same as for other capital projects, assuming secondary liability in the event of default by property owners.[6] When the capital improvements are financed by debt for which the government is not obligated in any manner, proceeds from issuing the debt are credited by the governmental unit to contributions from property owners, in the capital projects fund.

---

6 GASB Statement No. 6, *Accounting and Financial Reporting for Special Assessments* (Norwalk, CT: Governmental Accounting Standards Board, January 1987), states that a government is obligated in some manner if (a) it is legally obligated to assume all or part of the debt in the event of default or (b) the government may take certain actions to assume secondary liability for all or part of the debt—and the government takes, or has given indications that it will take, these actions.

When the capital improvements are financed by existing governmental resources and debt is not issued, transfers from other funds are credited as other financing sources, in the capital projects fund.

Expenditures are recorded in the capital projects fund as costs are incurred for the special assessment project. At year-end, the capitalizable costs of an unfinished special assessment project are entered in the general fixed assets account group.

40. Capital Projects Fund	Expenditures	80,000	
	Cash		80,000
41. General Fixed Assets Account Group	Construction in Progress	80,000	
	Investment in General Fixed Assets—		
	Capital Projects Funds		
	(special assessments)		80,000

Completion of the special assessment project in the second year is recorded with the following entries:

42. Capital Projects Fund	Expenditures	120,000	
	Cash		120,000
43. General Fixed Assets Account Group	Capital Asset Account	200,000	
(This entry is also shown in Illustration 16-7.)	Construction in Progress		80,000
	Investment in General Fixed Assets—		
	Capital Projects Funds		
	(special assessments)		120,000

The *second phase* of accounting for special assessment projects consists of collecting the special assessments on an installment basis from benefited property owners and repaying the cost of financing the project. When the project is financed with special assessment debt and the government is obligated in some manner for this debt, the liability should be recorded in the general long-term debt account group, as shown in this entry:

44. Amount to Be Provided for Payment of Special Assessment Debt	200,000	
Special Assessment Debt with Governmental Commitment		200,000

In some cases, the governmental unit has the primary responsibility for repayment of the bonds. In these situations, they are recorded, as follows, in the general long-term debt account group with the same type of entry used to record any other general obligation debt.

45. Amount to Be Provided for Payment of Special Assessment Debt	200,000	
Special Assessment Bonds Payable		200,000
(This entry is also used as an example in Illustration 16-7.)		

The special assessment receivable and special assessment revenue are divided between current and deferred portions in the debt service fund. Amounts levied and demanded to service-related debt in the current period are credited to Revenues as shown on the following page. The remainder to be collected and used for debt service in future periods is credited to Deferred Revenues.

Illustration 16-7
Accounting for Special Assessment Projects under Three Methods of Financing*

Debt Issued	Flows of Financial Resources through the Capital Projects Fund		
Government obligated in some manner	Cash	200,000	
	Other Financing Sources—Bond Proceeds		200,000
Government not obligated in any manner	Cash	200,000	
	Contributions from Property Owners		200,000
Debt not issued	Cash	200,000	
	Other Financing Sources—Transfers from Other Funds		200,000

Expenditures incurred during construction are recorded in the same manner as expenditures recorded for other capital projects.

*Note that budgetary entries have been omitted from this illustration.

46. Special Assessments Receivable—Current	20,000	
Special Assessments Receivable—Deferred	180,000	
Revenues		20,000
Deferred Revenues....................................		180,000

Through the term of the debt, the amount to be collected from property owners for a period is levied and demanded by the governmental unit; consequently, that portion of deferred revenue should be recognized as revenue in that period. Recognition of the receivable from the levy and the revenue are shown below. Details of the assessments are entered in a subsidiary ledger, where the levy against each property owner and collections from the owner are indicated.

47. Special Assessments Receivable—Current	20,000	
Special Assessments Receivable—Deferred		20,000
48. Deferred Revenues.....................................	20,000	
Revenues		20,000

The general long-term debt account group is updated to reflect the amount available in the debt service fund. The debt is liquidated in the same manner as other governmental-fund debt.

When the government is not obligated in any manner, collection of the special assessment and debt service payments should be accounted for through an agency fund (discussed on pages 853 through 855 in the Agency Funds section) since the government is acting merely as an agent for the property owners and bondholders. In that case, the debt is not shown in the general long-term debt account group; it should appear, however, in the notes to the financial statements.

When no debt is issued, Revenues is credited in the general fund for the current levy of the special assessment. Amounts to be levied and collected in future periods are credited to Deferred Revenues. These special tax assessments will serve as installments to pay back the original amount transferred from the general fund to the capital projects fund for the project costs.

Eventual Recording of Constructed Asset in the General Fixed Assets Account Group			Recording of Special Assessment Debt in the General Long-Term Debt Account Group		
Fixed Assets	200,000		Amount to Be Provided for Payment of Special Assessment Debt	200,000	
Construction in Progress		80,000			
Investment in General Fixed			Special Assessment Bonds		
Assets		120,000	Payable		200,000
Fixed Assets	200,000		Long-term debt is not recorded because the government is not obligated for the debt. Debt service is accounted for through an agency fund.		
Construction in Progress		80,000			
Investment in General Fixed					
Assets		120,000			
Fixed Assets	200,000		Long-term debt is not issued.		
Construction in Progress		80,000			
Investment in General Fixed					
Assets		120,000			

Liquidation of the special assessment debt is as described for all other general government debt.

REFLECTION

- Accounting and financial reporting for other governmental funds follow the modified accrual basis of accounting.

- Permanent funds account for nonexpendable trust funds established for the sole purpose of supporting governmental activities or programs.

- Also commonly used are special revenue funds, capital project funds, and debt service funds.

- When more than one fund of each type exists, major funds are identified and combining funds is necessary to total the amount of the nonmajor funds in each fund type. These totals are reported on the financial statements.

PROPRIETARY FUNDS

The funds discussed to this point have been governmental funds. The second category of funds—*proprietary funds*—will now be discussed. By definition, the term "proprietary" means pertaining to a proprietor and implies that users of goods or services will be charged on the basis of consumption, similar to the practice in private industries. Usually, charges are set to recover as much as possible of the total cost, including depreciation. Whatever is not recovered must be subsidized.

Governments account for their business-type activities in two types of proprietary funds. Enterprise funds account for operations in which goods or services are provided to the general public.

Internal service funds account for operations in which goods or services are provided by one government department to other departments within the same government or to other governments.

2

OBJECTIVE

Account for and prepare financial statements of proprietary funds.

Proprietary funds focus on capital maintenance to measure whether revenues are sufficient to cover expenses (including the amortization of noncurrent items) of the fiscal period. This is consistent with an economic resources measurement focus and the full accrual basis of accounting. Financial reporting for proprietary funds is similar to financial reporting for business enterprises in that income statements show revenues, expenses, and net income for a fiscal period, and balance sheets include both current and noncurrent assets and liabilities. The proprietary fund balance sheet residual is its net assets.

The GASB requires proprietary funds to follow all accounting standards set forth by the FASB prior to November 30, 1989, unless they have been specifically overridden by a GASB pronouncement. In addition, an enterprise fund (but not internal service funds) *may* apply all FASB pronouncements developed for business enterprises issued after that date unless they conflict with or contradict GASB standards.[7] Enterprise funds may also apply FASB standards and interpretations limited to not-for-profit organizations (such as ASC 958-205 and 958-605 described in Chapters 18 and 19). This option is designed to increase comparability between similar government enterprises and the private sector.

When proprietary funds furnish goods or services to other funds, for example, a computer center accounted for in an internal service fund provides service to departments accounted for in the general fund. This transaction is considered to be an "interfund service provided and used" and is *reported as if it were an external transaction.* Therefore, the billing represents revenue to the internal service fund and an expenditure to the general fund. Entries in each fund are as follows:

49. Internal Service Fund	Due from the General Fund	XXX	
	Revenues		XXX
50. General Fund	Expenditures	XXX	
	Due to the Internal Service Fund.		XXX

Conversely, if a proprietary fund pays the general fund for services, the proprietary fund records expenses, and the general fund records revenue. For example, the general government may bill an enterprise fund for payments in lieu of property taxes. Entries in each fund are as follows:

51. General Fund	Due from the Enterprise Fund.	XXX	
	Revenues		XXX
52. Enterprise Fund	Expenses	XXX	
	Due to the General Fund		XXX

Enterprise Funds

Enterprise funds account for goods or services provided by a governmental unit to the general public. The user is charged for these goods or services, based on consumption. For example, the operations of utilities, public housing, public parking, municipal solid waste landfills, economic development corporations, cultural activities, and airports would be covered by enterprise funds. These funds continue indefinitely and are self-supporting, depending upon the amounts charged to cover part or all of the costs of operation, debt service, and maintenance of capital facilities.

Governments *may* account for any activity in an enterprise fund as long as it charges a fee to external users. Government *must* use an enterprise fund if one of the following criteria is met: (1) the activity is financed solely with revenue debt secured merely by the revenues from a specific activity, (2) laws or regulations require that the activity's costs of providing services (including capital costs) be recovered by fees and charges rather than general taxes, or (3) the pricing policies of the activity establish fees and charges designed to recover its costs, including capital costs (such as depreciation or debt service).

---

7 GASB Statement No. 20, *Accounting and Financial Reporting for Proprietary Funds and Other Governmental Entities that Use Proprietary Fund Accounting* (Norwalk, CT: Governmental Accounting Standards Board, September 1993).

At the inception of an enterprise fund (or internal service fund), capital must be provided either by issuance of long-term debt or by transfer from some other source, such as a municipality's general fund. In the latter case, the contribution received is credited to an *interfund transfer-in* account from the general fund. These interfund transfers are reported below non-operating revenues as in Illustration 16-9. As a measure of original asset sources, the contribution remains in the fund indefinitely or until the fund is terminated. If operations are profitable and arrangements specify that profits shall be shared with the general fund, an amount is reported as an interfund transfer-out—classified with expenses. Financing may also be provided from loans or advances by the municipality. In such cases, the loans or advances are recorded as interfund payables in the proprietary funds and as interfund receivables in the general fund.

Enterprise funds, in particular, receive capital contributions both from internal (other funds) and external (customers, developers, other governments) sources. Whatever the source, these contributions are recognized as revenues on a line below income from operations.

An enterprise fund's operational efficiency may be monitored in part by the net income or net loss figure. As in commercial operations, budgets are prepared. However, budgets are not recorded formally in the accounts, perhaps because the fund's self-supporting nature requires a high degree of operational freedom, but more likely because fixed budgetary amounts would be of much less value when there is a variable demand by the public for goods and services.

Control accounts for revenues and expenses commonly are used, with details in supporting records. In accounting for revenues, two control accounts are used: operating revenues for charges for services and nonoperating revenues for grants and interfund transfers received, interest and rent earned, or other miscellaneous financial revenues. A similar breakdown is used to account for expenses: operating expenses for expenses directly related to goods or services produced, such as salaries, depreciation, heat, light, materials, and taxes and nonoperating expenses for financial expenses, such as bond interest. Recording of revenues and expenses, including adjustments, is much the same as in private enterprise accounting.

One of the unusual features of accounting for enterprise funds is the introduction of restricted assets and the current liabilities to be paid with restricted assets. *Restricted assets* are assets (cash and investments) upon which some limitation has been imposed that makes them available only for designated purposes. Examples of restricted assets are amounts of customer deposits subject to refund, proceeds from long-term debt for construction, and monies set aside for bond interest or principal redemption.

Restricted assets and their related current liabilities are recorded in specially designated accounts so that the segregation of these items is ensured. For example, if a water utility receives deposits covering meter installations for customers and these deposits are refundable, they would be recorded as follows:

53. Restricted Assets—Customers' Deposits Cash	XXX	
Customers' Deposits Payable from Restricted Assets		XXX

If the deposits are invested, the entry to record the investment would be as follows:

54. Restricted Assets—Customers' Deposits Investments	XXX	
Restricted Assets—Customers' Deposits Cash		XXX

The existence of restricted assets and their related current liabilities is especially common when an enterprise fund is used to account for a public utility. A major source of funding for utilities is the sale of revenue bonds, which are issued to permit the construction of, or an addition to, a facility. Since payments for these bonds depend on the existence of operating income, the bond indenture usually includes several restrictions. For example, it may require that the bond proceeds be expended only for construction, making the proceeds a restricted asset. The following entry would be required:

55. Restricted Assets—Revenue Bond Construction Cash	XXX	
Revenue Bonds Payable.		XXX

As amounts are committed, the liability would be identified as payable from a restricted asset.

56. Construction in Progress	XXX	
Construction Contracts Payable from Restricted Assets		XXX

Payment of the liability would be recorded with the following entry:

57. Construction Contracts Payable from Restricted Assets   XXX
            Restricted Assets—Revenue Bond Construction Cash   XXX

If a municipality received approval to expand its utility facilities by issuing a combination of special assessment bonds and revenue bonds, the following entry would be required in an enterprise fund:

58. Restricted Assets—Construction Cash   XXX
            Special Assessment Bonds Payable   XXX
            Revenue Bonds Payable   XXX

Note that the redemption and servicing of both the revenue bonds and the special assessment bonds are the financial responsibility of the utility enterprise fund. Therefore, the liability appears in the enterprise fund balance sheet rather than in the general long-term debt account group.[8] The balance sheet for the Clermont County Water and Sewer Fund, shown in Illustration 16-8, reports restricted assets following the regular current assets and preceding the capital assets. Note also that current liabilities are segregated to show amounts payable from regular current assets and amounts payable from restricted assets.

Per GASB Statement No. 34, the net assets of proprietary funds should be displayed in three broad components—invested in capital assets, net of related debt; restricted (distinguishing between major categories of restrictions); and unrestricted. Invested in capital assets, net of related debt consists of capital assets net of accumulated depreciation reduced by debt attributable to the capital assets. Restricted net assets are net assets restricted by external parties or enabling legislation. Note that the previously discussed fund balance classifications required by GASB Statement No. 54 (nonspendable, restricted, committed, assigned, and unassigned) pertain only to governmental funds.

Most revenue bonds for enterprise funds are serial bonds that require the earmarking of monies for the payment of interest and for the establishment of a fund for principal redemption. These resources are labeled restricted assets. The current interest and serial installment payables are recorded as current liabilities payable from restricted assets. To further protect the bondholder, at least psychologically, many serial revenue bonds require that unassigned retained earnings be restricted in an amount equal to the excess of restricted assets related to debt service of the bond issue over the current liability for interest and principal. If the amounts in the Water and Sewer Fund balance sheet are compared with assumed amounts at the end of the previous year, the additional amount to be reserved would be determined as follows:

	Dec. 31, 2018	Dec. 31, 2017 (assumed)
Restricted assets related to revenue bonds:		
Cash with fiscal agent for bond service	$ 80,444	$ 87,200
Revenue bond debt service cash	5,000	3,000
Revenue bond fund	124,155	93,975
Total	$209,599	$184,175
Current liabilities related to revenue bonds:		
Accrued revenue bond interest payable	$ 32,444	$ 37,200
Matured revenue bonds payable	48,000	50,000
Total	$ 80,444	$ 87,200
Excess of bond-related restricted assets over bond-related current liabilities	$129,155	$ 96,975

8 Governments are also required to capitalize construction-period interest for business-type activities.

Illustration 16-8
Clermont County
Water and Sewer Fund
Balance Sheet
December 31, 2018

Assets

Current assets:			
Cash		$ 257,036	
Receivables (net)		33,480	
Inventories and prepaid expenses		24,230	
Total current assets			$ 314,746
Restricted assets:			
Cash with fiscal agent for bond service		$ 80,444	
Revenue bond construction cash		17,760	
Revenue bond debt service cash		5,000	
Revenue bond fund:			
Cash	$ 10,355		
Investments	113,800	124,155	
Customers' deposits:			
Investments	$ 63,000		
Interest receivable on investments	650	63,650	
Total restricted assets			291,009
Property, plant, and equipment:			
Land		$ 211,100	
Buildings	$ 447,700		
Less accumulated depreciation	90,718	356,982	
Improvements other than buildings	$3,887,901		
Less accumulated depreciation	348,944	3,538,957	
Machinery and equipment	$1,841,145		
Less accumulated depreciation	201,138	1,640,007	
Construction in progress		22,713	
Total property, plant, and equipment			5,769,759
Total assets			$6,375,514

Liabilities and Fund Equity

Liabilities:			
Current liabilities (payable from current assets):			
Vouchers payable		$195,071	
Accrued wages and taxes payable		2,870	
Construction contracts payable		8,347	$ 206,288
Current liabilities (payable from restricted assets):			
Construction contracts payable		$ 17,760	
Accrued revenue bond interest payable		32,444	
Matured revenue bonds payable		48,000	
Customer deposits		63,000	161,204
Total current liabilities			$ 367,492
Long-term liabilities:			
Revenue bonds payable			2,448,000
Total liabilities			$2,815,492
Net assets:			
Invested in capital assets, net of related debt			$3,232,968
Restricted			3,961
Unrestricted			323,093
Total net assets			$3,560,022

If the bond indenture requires that the reserves be increased to equal the bond-related restricted assets that are not offset by bond-related current liabilities, the following entry becomes necessary:

59. Net Assets—Unrestricted ($129,155 − $96,975)................	32,180	
Net Assets—Restricted for Bond Debt Service		
($5,000 − $3,000).....................................		2,000
Net Assets—Restricted for Bond Retirement		
($124,155 − $93,975)		30,180

The statement of revenues, expenses (not expenditures), and changes in net assets for an enterprise fund, as shown in the GASB *Codification of Governmental Accounting and Financial Reporting,* focuses on total net assets, both restricted and unrestricted. Such a statement for the Clermont County Water and Sewer Fund is shown in Illustration 16-9.

Illustration 16-9
Enterprise Fund
Clermont County
Water and Sewer Fund
Statement of Revenues, Expenses, and Changes in Net Assets
For Year Ended December 31, 2018

Operating revenues:		
Charges for services		$ 727,150
Operating expenses:		
Personnel services (salaries and fees)	$306,100	
Materials and supplies................................	106,580	
Depreciation	103,600	
Heat, light, power, and taxes	47,900	
Total operating expenses...........................		564,180
Operating income......................................		$ 162,970
Nonoperating revenues (expenses):		
Operating grants.....................................	$ 5,000	
Interest revenue	2,830	
Rental income	1,000	
Interest expense.....................................	(92,988)	
Total nonoperating revenues (expenses)		(84,158)
Interfund transfers-in—Contributions from municipality..........		1,000,000
Change in net assets		$1,078,812
Total net assets at beginning of year		2,481,210
Total net assets at end of year		$3,560,022

GASB Statement No. 9, *Reporting Cash Flows of Proprietary and Nonexpendable Trust Funds and Governmental Entities that Use Proprietary Fund Accounting*, stipulates that a statement of cash flows for such funds shows movements of combined unrestricted and restricted cash and cash equivalents for the reported period, segregated into four categories:

1. Cash flows from *operating activities*, which would include cash received from sales of goods or services and cash paid to suppliers, employees, and providers of services.

2. Cash flows from *noncapital financing activities*, which would include proceeds from borrowings not related to capital asset acquisition and repayments thereon, as well as operating grants or transfers not related to capital asset acquisition.

3. Cash flows from *capital and related financing activities* to acquire or dispose of capital assets, which would include grants or transfers related to capital asset acquisition.

4. Cash flows from *investing activities*.

Government enterprises classify interest paid as financing activity and interest earned as investing activity rather than as operating activities. Whether interest paid is classified as capital or noncapital depends on the purpose of the underlying debt.

The statement of cash flows reports net cash provided or used for each of the four categories. Governments are required to use the direct method, as shown in Illustration 16-10A for a hypothetical electric utility. In addition, a reconciliation of net operating income to net cash flow from operating activities (Category 1) must be provided in a separate schedule to accompany the cash flows statement or in the notes to the financial statements. Such a reconciliation is presented in Illustration 16-10B on page 846.

Illustration 16-10A
Zenith City
Electric Utility Fund
Statement of Cash Flows
Increase (Decrease) in Cash and Cash Equivalents
For Year Ended June 30, 2018

Cash flows from operating activities:		
Cash received from customers	$ 456,000	
Cash paid to suppliers and employees	(400,300)	
Other operating revenues	7,500	
Net cash provided by operating activities		$ 63,200
Cash flows from noncapital financing activities:		
Net repayments under revolving loan arrangement	$ (10,700)	
Operating grants received	50,000	
Operating transfers-out to other funds	(37,500)	
Net cash provided by noncapital financing activities		1,800
Cash flows from capital and related financing activities:		
Proceeds from sale of capital bonds	$ 125,000	
Principal and interest paid on capital bonds	(100,000)	
Acquisition and construction of capital assets	(75,000)	
Proceeds from sale of equipment	70,000	
Net cash provided by capital and related financing activities		20,000
Cash flows from investing activities:		
Purchases of investment securities	$ (62,500)	
Proceeds from sale and maturities of securities	36,500	
Interest and dividends received on investments	3,000	
Net cash used in investing activities		(23,000)
Net increase in cash and cash equivalents		$ 62,000
Cash and cash equivalents at beginning of year		100,000
Cash and cash equivalents at end of year		$162,000

Illustration 16-10B
Zenith City
Electric Utility Fund
Reconciliation of Net Operating Income to
Net Cash Provided by Operating Activities
For Year Ended June 30, 2018

Net operating income (loss)		$ (49,800)
Adjustments to reconcile net operating income to net cash provided by operating activities:		
Depreciation	$122,000	
Provision for uncollectible accounts	1,000	
Changes in assets and liabilities:		
Increase in accounts receivable	(15,000)	
Decrease in inventory	2,000	
Decrease in prepaid expenses	500	
Increase in accounts payable	2,500	
Total adjustments		113,000
Net cash provided by operating activities		$ 63,200

Many governments account for landfill operations in enterprise funds. GASB standards require closure and post-closure costs to be recognized in the years in which the landfill is in operation rather than when they are to be paid.[9] Therefore, in each year of the landfill's useful life, the government recognizes, as both an expense and an increase in a liability, a portion of the estimated costs for closure and post-closure care. The estimated total cost of landfill closure and post-closure care includes:

1. The cost of equipment expected to be installed and facilities expected to be constructed (e.g., ground-water monitoring wells, storm-water management systems, gas monitoring systems, etc.) near or after the date that the landfill stops accepting waste.
2. The cost of final cover.
3. The cost of monitoring and maintaining the landfill during the post-closure period.

The current expense (and liability) is based on the percentage of the landfill actually used up during the current period multiplied by the total estimated cost of closure and post-closure care. For example, suppose a government uses 90,000 cubic feet of a landfill in one year. Total landfill capacity is estimated at 4.5 million cubic feet. If closure and post-closure care costs are estimated at $18,000,000, the entry to record the expense and liability for the year [based on $18,000,000 \times (90,000 \div 4,500,000)$] is as follows:

60. Landfill Expense	360,000	
Liability for Landfill Costs		360,000

In year 2, closure and post-closure cost estimates are adjusted to $18,500,000. Landfill used during the year totaled 210,000 cubic feet. Landfill capacity has decreased to 4,250,000. The entry to record the expense and liability for year 2 [$18,500,000 \times (300,000 \div 4,250,000)$], less $360,000 already recognized in year 1, is as shown on page 847.

---

9 GASB Statement No. 18, *Accounting for Municipal Solid Waste Landfill Closure and Post-Closure Care Costs* (Norwalk, CT: Governmental Accounting Standards Board, August 1993). Landfills accounted for in governmental funds will calculate the accrued liability the same as in the given example. These landfills will recognize expenditures and fund liabilities using the modified accrual basis of accounting. The long-term portion of the liability will be reported in the general long-term debt account group.

```
61.  Landfill Expense. . . . . . . . . . . . . . . . . . . . . . . . . . . . . . . . . . . . . . . . . .    945,882
         Liability for Landfill Costs . . . . . . . . . . . . . . . . . . . . . . . . . . . . . . .                945,882
```

These standards allow for all expenses to be recognized by the date of the landfill closing. Any landfill capital assets excluded from the calculation of the estimated total cost of landfill closure and post-closure care should be fully depreciated by the date that the landfill stops accepting solid waste.

If a municipality operates more than one enterprise fund, combining statements are required in order to disclose the details of each nonmajor fund. GASB standards also require that *different, identifiable activities* for major nonhomogeneous enterprise funds be presented to prevent misleading financial statements. Presentation of information about these activities in the notes to the financial statements is also required. An activity within an enterprise fund is *identifiable* if it has specific revenue stream and related expenses. An activity is *different* if the product, program, or services are generated from or provided by different activities. Examples of different, identifiable activities are natural gas, water, and electricity utility services that may be accounted for in one utility enterprise fund.

Internal Service Funds

Internal service funds are similar to enterprise funds in that they are self-sustaining, depend on amounts charged for services rendered, and receive start-up resources. The difference is that users of their services are other departments of the same governmental unit or other governmental units. A computer center, a printing department, a central purchasing department, a central garage, and risk financing and self-insurance activities are accounted for in internal service funds.

GASB Statement No. 34 permits governments to establish internal service funds "to report any activity that provides goods or services to other funds, departments, or agencies of the primary government and its component units, or to other governments, on a cost-reimbursement basis." Since internal service funds do not deal with the general public and usually do not issue bonds that result in restrictions, they do not have restricted assets. Their accounting procedures resemble those for a commercial business. Internal service funds must recover their costs, including depreciation, or be subsidized. Therefore, they maintain records of capital assets and use the accrual basis of accounting. Budgetary accounts are not used, although budget forecasts facilitate the calculation of overhead rates to be applied in determining charges. Billing rates of internal service funds have received much attention because of the impact on expenditures of other funds. Most experts agree that the amount of net income for any internal service fund should be sufficient to allow for replacement of capital assets or payment of risk-related losses but not so large as to accumulate large balances that could otherwise have stayed in the other funds.

As discussed for enterprise funds, the establishment of an internal service fund may be by a contribution or an advance from the municipality. Charges to customer departments are considered interfund services and appear as expenditures in the governmental funds, expenses in the other proprietary funds, and revenue to the internal service fund.[10] The financial statements of internal service funds consist of the balance sheet, the statement of revenues, expenses, and changes in retained earnings, and the statement of cash flows. When more than one internal service fund exists, combining statements are prepared. Major internal service funds are not highlighted. These statements closely resemble commercial financial statements and will not be illustrated.

---

10 GASB Statement No. 10, *Accounting and Financial Reporting for Risk Financing and Related Insurance Issues* (Norwalk, CT: Governmental Accounting Standards Board, November 1989), allows governments to use either the general fund or internal service fund for all risk financing and self-insurance activities. Many governments choose an internal service fund to charge other funds of the government entity for claims liabilities, including future catastrophe losses based on actuarial estimates.

REFLECTION

- Proprietary funds have a measurement focus of economic resources and use full accrual basis accounting.

- The two proprietary funds are enterprise funds and internal service funds.

- Interfund activities between the proprietary funds and governmental funds are either reciprocal transactions for the provision of goods or services (accounted for as revenue and expenditures) or nonreciprocal (accounted for as interfund transfers).

3

OBJECTIVE

Explain the usefulness of and the accounting process for fiduciary funds and how these funds are reported.

FIDUCIARY FUNDS: TRUST AND AGENCY FUNDS

As mentioned in Chapter 15, fiduciary funds account for resources for which a governmental unit is acting as a trustee or an agent for an external individual, organization, or government. This category of funds includes private-purpose trust funds, investment trust funds, pension trust funds, and agency funds.

Private-Purpose Trust Funds

This section will describe the accounting for private-purpose, investment, and pension trusts, whose primary beneficiaries are external individuals, organizations, or other governments. Examples of private-purpose funds are those established for holding performance deposits of licenses, the establishment of scholarship funds to benefit external individuals, endowments held to benefit needy employees or their families, Internal Revenue Code Section 457 deferred compensation plans,[11] and funds used to account for escheat property per GASB Statement No. 21. *Escheat property* is defined by the GASB as "the reversion of property to a government entity in the absence of legal claimants or heirs."[12] Since the rightful owner or heir can reclaim escheat property at any time, the receipt of escheat property is recorded in the governmental or proprietary fund in which the property ultimately will be used and is offset with a liability representing the best estimate of the amount ultimately expected to be reclaimed and paid. Revenue is recognized for the amount not expected to be reclaimed. Escheat property held for others is reported in a private-purpose trust or agency fund (depending on the length of time the assets are expected to be held). Agency funds are described later in this chapter.

Private-purpose trust funds are accounted for in much the same manner as proprietary funds. The establishment of these trusts results from the acceptance of assets that are invested to produce earnings for a designated external purpose. All assets, including land and other real estate, are recorded at fair value. Changes in fair value are reported as investment income.[13] It also would be essential to differentiate between principal items and revenue items. One common way to segregate the principal from revenues is to establish two funds—one to record principal items and another to account for the earnings. This procedure becomes especially useful if bonds are purchased at a premium as part of the trust fund. Cash flows and available revenue

---

11 GASB Statement No. 32, *Accounting and Financial Reporting Internal Revenue Code Section 457, Deferred Compensation Plans* (Norwalk, CT: Governmental Accounting Standards Board, October 1997).
12 GASB Statement No. 21, *Accounting for Escheat Property* (Norwalk, CT: Governmental Accounting Standards Board, October 1993) as amended by GASB Statement No. 37, *Basic Financial Statements—and Management's Discussion and Analysis—for State and Local Governments: Omnibus* (Norwalk, CT: Governmental Accounting Standards Board, June 2001).
13 GASB Statement No. 52, *Land and Other Real Estate Held or Investments by Endowments* (Norwalk, CT: Governmental Accounting Standards Board, November 2007).

are not identical because of the amortization of the premium. The segregation process protects the principal. When donors establish a private-purpose trust, the assets donated are credited to Additions-Contributions in the endowment principal fund. Later, revenues earned are credited to Additions-Revenues. A liability to the endowment earnings fund for the period's interest earnings is established, and a debit is made to recognize the interfund operating transfer.

The only source of assets for the endowment earnings fund is the net earnings transferred from the private-purpose principal fund. These earnings are credited to Additions-Interfund Operating Transfers. Distributions of such revenues are recorded as deductions. In the year-end closing process of the private-purpose earnings fund, any difference between the amounts received from the principal fund and total deductions is closed to Net Assets Held in Trust, which indicates that the undistributed assets are restricted.

The procedures for both the private-purpose endowment principal trust fund and the endowment earnings fund for Cedar City are shown by the events and entries in Illustration 16-12 on pages 850 and 851.

Two financial statements are required for private-purpose trust funds: a statement of fiduciary net assets and a statement of changes in fiduciary net assets. The statements of fiduciary net assets for Cedar City's Governmental Accounts Scholarship Fund are shown in Illustration 16-11.

Illustration 16-11
Cedar City
Governmental Accounts Scholarship Fund
Statement of Fiduciary Net Assets
For Period Ended December 31, 2018

Assets

Cash	$10,640
Investments	40,000
Unamortized premiums on investments	360
	$51,000

Liabilities

Due to governmental accounts scholarship earnings fund	1,000
Net assets held in trust for benefit of scholarship recipients	$50,000

Cedar City
Governmental Accounts Scholarship Fund
Statement of Fiduciary Net Assets
For Period Ended December 31, 2017

Assets

Cash	$ 560
Due from governmental accounting scholarship principal fund	1,000
	$1,560
Net assets held in trust for benefit of scholarship recipients	$1,560

Illustration 16-12

Event
Cedar City receives an endowment of $50,000 to establish a nonexpendable trust fund whose revenue is to be used to encourage students to study governmental accounting.
9% bonds with a face value of $40,000 are purchased at 101, maturing in 10 years. The premium will be amortized using the straight-line method.
Bond interest of $3,600 is received.
The liability to endowment revenues fund for net revenue is recorded.
Cash due is remitted.
A grant of $3,000 is given to a student.
Books are closed at year-end.

Investment Trust Funds

An *investment trust fund* is used to account for the assets, liabilities, net assets, and changes in net assets of external participants in an investment pool managed by the government for other governments and not-for-profit organizations. Because the accounting and financial reporting requirements are very similar to the private-purpose trust fund, already illustrated, no journal entries or financial statements are provided in this chapter. As in the examples of private-purpose trusts, proper accounting for gains and losses, whether realized through the sale of investments or unrealized through the appreciation or depreciation of fair value, is an important topic to the preservation of the trust. Thus, the economic measurement focus and full accrual basis of accounting are used in these funds.

Pension Trust Funds

Public employees retirement system funds are accounted for in *pension trust funds*. In no other area of accounting is actuarial assistance so vital. Abiding by the requirements of the retirement plan and considering the employee population as to age, gender, marital status, and the myriad of other variables that affect working lives and retirement, actuaries must estimate the amount of resources necessary as of a given date to meet retirement commitments. To protect the employees' interests, pension trust funds use a full accrual basis of accounting.

Contributions to a retirement plan may be from both the employer and employees (a contributory plan) or from the employer only (a noncontributory plan). Employees who resign usually have the option to withdraw their own contributions (but not the employer's

Entries in Endowment Principal Trust Fund (Nonexpendable Trust)			Entries in Endowment Earnings Trust Fund (Expendable Trust)		
Cash	50,000		No entry.		
Fund Balance		50,000			
Investments	40,000		No entry.		
Unamortized Premium	400				
Cash		40,400			
Cash	3,600		No entry.		
Unamortized Premium		40			
Revenues		3,560			
Operating Transfers-Out	3,560		Due from Endowment Principal Fund	3,560	
Due to Endowment Earning Fund		3,560	Other Financing Sources		3,560
Due to Endowment Revenues Fund	3,560		Cash	3,560	
Cash		3,560	Due from Endowment Principal Fund		3,560
No entry.			Expenditures	3,000	
			Cash		3,000
Revenues	3,560		Other Financing Sources	3,560	
Operating Transfers-Out		3,560	Expenditures		3,000
			Fund Balance—Reserved for Endowments		560

contributions) or to leave them in the plan as vested amounts, providing certain requirements are met. The amounts belong to the employee, who will have access to them upon meeting prescribed retirement conditions.

Increases in the resources of pension trust funds result from employee and employer contributions, investment earnings, and net appreciation (depreciation) in plan assets. Decreases in resources result from payments to retired employees, refunds to contributors, and administrative costs.

All assets of a pension trust belong to the employees, and claims against these assets are reflected in either the liabilities or the restricted net asset balance.

A statement of changes in plan net assets[14] is shown in Illustration 16-13 on page 852. The statement of changes in plan net assets reports *additions* to net assets rather than revenues, and *deductions* from net assets rather than expenses. The statement of plan net assets for Desert City's retirement plan as of June 30, 2018, is shown in Illustration 16-14 on page 853. The fund has been operating for several years and has significant investments.

The liability shown on the statement of plan net assets (see Illustration 16-14) is the current benefits payable. The long-term, actuarially determined, projected benefit obligation is disclosed in the footnotes.

---

14 GASB Statement No. 50, *Pension Disclosures: An Amendment to GASB Statements No. 25, Financial Reporting for Defined Benefit Pension Plans and Note Disclosures for Defined Contribution Plans,* and GASB statement No. 27, *Accounting for Pensions by State and Local Government Employees* (Norwalk, CT: Governmental Accounting Standards Board, May 2007 and November 1994).

Illustration 16-13
Desert City's Retirement Plan
Statement of Changes in Plan Net Assets
For Year Ended June 30, 2018

Additions:	
Contributions:	
Employer	$ 137,000
Plan member	90,000
Total contributions	$ 227,000
Investment income:	
Net appreciation (depreciation) in fair value	$ (241,400)
Interest	157,000
Dividends	123,900
Real estate operating income, net	10,700
Less investment expense	(54,000)
Net investment income	$ (3,800)
Total additions	$ 223,200
Deductions:	
Benefits	$ 170,434
Refunds of contributions	15,750
Administrative expense	5,000
Total deductions	$ 191,184
Net increase	$ 32,016
Net assets held in trust for pension benefits:	
Beginning of year	3,651,964
End of year	$3,683,980

The statement of plan net assets adheres to the all-inclusive approach, whereby the net increase (decrease) is added to the total of plan assets at the beginning of the period to yield their total at the end of the period. A statement of cash flows is not required. Governments must also include in the notes to the financial statements as Required Supplementary Information (1) a current funded status of plan, (2) a schedule of funding progress, (3) a schedule of employer contributions for at least six plan years, and (4) information on actuarial methods and assumptions.

Issued in 2004, GASB Statement No. 43 establishes accounting and financial reporting standards for plans that provide other postemployment benefits (OPEB), such as health care benefits and life insurance. The financial report of the participating employer plan sponsor, public employee retirement system, or other entity that administers the plan should include (1) a statement of postemployment plan net assets, (2) a statement of changes in postemployment plan net assets, and (3) notes to the financial statements, all prepared in accordance with the pension plan reporting standards.[15]

---

15 GASB Statement No. 43, *Financial Reporting for Postemployment Benefit Plans Other than Pension Plans* (Norwalk, CT: Governmental Accounting Standards Board, April 2004).

Illustration 16-14
Desert City's Retirement Plan
Statement of Plan Net Assets
As of June 30, 2018

Assets

Cash and short-term investments		$ 66,000
Receivables:		
Employer		$ 16,500
Interest and dividends		33,500
Total receivables		$ 50,000
Investments, at fair value:		
U.S. government obligations		$ 541,300
Municipal bonds		33,585
Domestic corporate bonds		892,300
Domestic stocks		1,276,500
International stocks		461,350
Mortgages		149,100
Real estate		184,900
Venture capital		26,795
Total investments		$3,565,830
Properties, at cost, net of accumulated depreciation		$ 6,350
Total assets		$3,688,180

Liabilities

Refunds payable		4,200
Net assets held in trust for pension benefits		$3,683,980

Agency Funds

An *agency fund* is required when money collected or withheld, such as deductions from government employees' salaries for social security or for hospitalization premiums, must be forwarded to the proper destination. Agency funds frequently have no end-of-period balances because money is transferred prior to the end of the period. When the money has not been forwarded, a liability to the ultimate recipient is shown. There is no fund equity, and the only financial statement would be a balance sheet listing the assets held and the related liabilities. If the agency fund is to receive a fee for its services, the amount usually is recorded as a liability to the general fund of the governmental unit. The general fund records a receivable and revenue if the amount is to be collected within the current period. For example, state law may give a county the responsibility for collecting property taxes levied within its boundaries, with the county receiving a fee to cover its administration of the plan. The county, as well as each political subdivision, would record its share of taxes receivable in its general fund. The tax agency fund of Zee County would make the following series of entries for the events described on page 854.

Event	Entry in Tax Agency Fund		
62. Gross taxes receivable to be collected for all units are as follows:	Taxes Receivable for All Units . . . . 　Due to Other Governmental Funds and 　　Units	1,000,000		1,000,000

Zee County . . . . $ 300,000
X City   600,000
T Town   100,000
　Total $1,000,000

Entry in Zee County general fund:

Taxes Receivable   300,000
　Revenues   300,000

Event	Entry in Tax Agency Fund		
63. Taxes are collected.	Cash . . . . 　Taxes Receivable for All Units	1,000,000		1,000,000
64. The liability to each unit is recorded, net of a 2% fee earned by the county for collection and processing for other units. (The county would not charge itself a fee.) The fee is to be remitted to the county general fund.	Due to Other Governmental Funds 　and Units . . . . 　　Due to Zee County General Fund. . 　　Due to X City . . . . 　　Due to T Town	1,000,000		314,000 588,000 98,000

Entry in Zee County general fund:
Due from Agency Fund   314,000
　Taxes Receivable   300,000
　Revenue   14,000

Event	Entry in Tax Agency Fund		
65. Cash is released to each governmental unit.	Due to Zee County General Fund . . . . . Due to X City . . . . Due to T Town . . . . 　Cash	314,000 588,000 98,000		1,000,000

Entry in Zee County general fund:

Cash   314,000
　Due from Agency Fund   314,000

The general fund of X City records the receipt of cash from the tax agency fund, net of the fee, as follows:

66. Cash (for net proceeds)   588,000
　　Expenditures (for fee charged)   12,000
　　　Taxes Receivable—Current   600,000

Agency funds also are used in the case of a capital project undertaken by a government in which special assessment bonds were issued but for which it has no financial responsibility in case of nonpayment. The government functions as an agent or a financial conduit between the bondholders and the owners of the assessed property. When property owners are assessed, an entry is recorded in the agency fund as follows:

67. Special Assessments Receivable—Current   XXX
　　Special Assessments Receivable—Deferred   XXX
　　　Due to Special Assessment Bond Creditors   XXX

When collections from assessed property owners are received by the agency fund, the entry shown on page 855 is made.

68. Cash . . . . 　XXX
　　　Special Assessments Receivable—Current . . . .　XXX
　　　　　Due to Special Assessment Bond Creditors (interest) . . . .　　　　XXX

Upon payment to the bondholders, the entry is as follows:

69. Due to Special Assessment Bond Creditors . . . .　XXX
　　　Due to Special Assessment Bond Creditors (interest) . . . .　XXX
　　　　　Cash . . . .　　　　XXX

Neither the liability for principal repayment nor the debt service expenditures are recorded in any other fund or group because the governmental unit was not obligated in any manner.

Finally, a government may account for the proceeds and disbursement of "pass-through" grants, entitlements, or shared revenues from federal or state governments in an agency fund only when it serves as a cash conduit, e.g., merely transmitting funds to the secondary recipient without having any administrative or direct financial involvement in the grant.[16]

R E F L E C T I O N

- Fiduciary funds include private-purpose trust funds, investment trust funds, pension trust funds, and agency funds.

- Fiduciary funds use full accrual-basis accounting.

- Financial statements of fiduciary funds include a statement of net assets and a statement of changes in net assets.

GOVERNMENTAL ACCOUNTING— INTERACTIONS AMONG FUNDS

4

OBJECTIVE

Identify and account for transactions that affect different funds and/or account groups.

In governmental accounting, each fund or group is a separate accounting entity, entrusted to record only a limited phase of an event. Complete recording, as shown in Chapters 15 and 16, often involves more than one fund or group. In addition, transactions among funds are frequent. Throughout this and the previous chapter, interfund transactions have been defined. They include:

1. Interfund operating transfers between governmental funds for services provided and used—recorded as other financing sources/uses;
2. Interfund operating transfers between governmental and proprietary funds for services provided and used—recorded as revenues and expenditures/expenses;
3. Interfund nonreciprocal transfers (where no expectation or requirement of repayment exists as in the case of contributions and payments in lieu of taxes)—recorded as other financing sources/uses if between governmental funds, and as interfund transfers that appear after nonoperating revenues if between governmental and proprietary funds; and
4. Interfund loans—classified into two categories—as either due to/from other funds for short-term amounts or advances to/from other funds for amounts that will be repaid over several years.

---

16 GASB Statement No. 24, *Accounting and Financial Reporting for Certain Grants and Other Financial Assistance* (Norwalk, CT: Governmental Accounting Standards Board, June 1994).

A final interfund transaction is a reimbursement where one fund may reimburse another for supplies or other items paid on its behalf. For example, the general fund might pay the entire rental of a facility even though the facility is to be used for both the general government and activities of a special revenue fund. When the expenditure is made by the general fund, the entry is as follows:

70. Expenditures	XXX	
Cash		XXX

When the reimbursement is received from the special revenue fund for its share of the rent, the entries in each fund are as follows:

Illustration 16-15
Matrix of Selected Events Requiring Entry in More than One Fund or Account Group

Events to Be Recorded

1. Purchase of equipment with general fund resources for $40,000.
2. Issuance of $500,000 of general obligation serial bonds at an $8,000 premium for city hall construction.
3. Transfer by general fund to meet $100,000 matured serial bonds and $50,000 interest payments.
4. Payment of $50,000 bond interest and $100,000 matured serial bonds. Fiscal agent is used for payment.
5. Completion of special assessment construction project. $150,000 paid to date; $50,000 final payment.
6. Levy of $5,000 property taxes by general fund against city's utility (quasi-external).
7. Billing of general and special revenue funds for central computer service ($12,000 and $20,000) (quasi-external).
8. Contribution made by city to establish a nonexpendable trust fund of $98,500. Income will be used for library operations.
9. Remittance of the city's $16,000 share of self-insurance costs for current period to an internal service fund.
10. Reimbursement of $15,000 by the special revenue fund to the general fund for general government supplies expenditures initially made in the general fund properly charged to a community development project.
11. Recording of depreciation, $6,000 enterprise fund, $13,000 internal service fund.
12. Redemption of final $100,000 serial of general obligation bonds, with $3,000 deficiency covered by general fund. Fiscal agent is used for payment.
13. Closing entry for capital projects fund involving a partially completed project. Cost to date is $130,000; revenues during the period are $300,000.
14. Payroll expenditures totaled $5,000 and included $1,000 payroll withholdings for taxes and insurance plus employer's share of these costs. $1,000 is transferred to an agency fund for remittance as follows: Private insurance company, $200; federal government, $600; and state government, $150. The agency fund makes the remittances.
15. A 5-year lease agreement was signed for equipment. The present value of the lease payments is $50,000.
16. The actuarial required contribution for pensions was $4,500. Of this amount, $3,000 was transferred to the pension trust and $1,500 will be transferred in the future.
17. Claims and judgments against the city were estimated at $15,000. The city attorney determined that it was probable that the claims would be settled against the city. Of the $15,000, $3,000 was estimated to be paid out this fiscal year.
18. Closure and post-closure costs of local landfill were estimated at $600,000. Landfill used this period was estimated at 1,000 cubic yards, and total landfill is 100,000 cubic yards. Landfill operations are accounted for in enterprise funds.
19. Debt was refunded. The refunding met the criteria for in-substance defeasance. Proceeds of the new debt issue were placed in trust with an escrow agent.
20. Investments carried at $5,500 have a fair value of $5,750 in the general fund. Pension investments carried at $102,000 have a fair value of $101,000.

71. General fund:

Cash	XXX	
Expenditures		XXX

Special revenue fund:

Expenditures	XXX	
Cash		XXX

To serve as a reference and to review governmental accounting, Illustration 16-15 provides a matrix of selected events that are recorded in more than one fund or group. Used in the matrix are the five governmental funds (general, special revenue, debt service, capital projects, and permanent funds), the two types of proprietary funds (enterprise and internal service), trust and agency funds, and the two account groups for general fixed assets and general long-term debt.[17]

The entries to record the events related to the 20 events in the matrix are as follows:

Governmental Funds					Proprietary Funds		Fiduciary Fund	Account Groups		
General	Special Revenue	Debt Service	Capital Projects	Permanent	Enterprise	Internal Service	Trust and Agency	General Fixed Assets	General Long-Term Debt	
X	—	—	—	—	—	—	—	X	—	1.
—	—	X	X	—	—	—	—	—	X	2.
X	—	X	—	—	—	—	—	—	X	3.
—	—	X	—	—	—	—	—	—	X	4.
—	—	—	X	—	—	—	—	X	—	5.
X	—	—	—	—	X	—	—	—	—	6.
X	X	—	—	—	—	X	—	—	—	7.
X	—	—	—	X	—	—	—	—	—	8.
X	—	—	—	—	—	X	—	—	—	9.
X	X	—	—	—	—	—	—	—	—	10.
—	—	—	—	—	X	X	—	—	—	11.
X	—	X	—	—	—	—	—	—	X	12.
—	—	—	X	—	—	—	—	X	—	13.
X	—	—	—	—	—	—	X	—	—	14.
X	—	—	—	—	—	—	—	X	X	15.
X	—	—	—	—	—	—	X	—	X	16.
X	—	—	—	—	—	—	—	—	X	17.
—	—	—	—	—	X	—	—	—	—	18.
—	—	X	—	—	—	—	—	—	X	19.
X	—	—	—	—	—	—	X	—	—	20.

---

17 GASB Statement No. 38, *Certain Financial Statement Note Disclosures* (Norwalk, CT: Governmental Accounting Standards Board, June 2001), requires that details about interfund transfers and balances are reported in the notes to the financial statements. These details should include the purpose of the transfer, the provider and recipient funds, and a description and amount of significant nonroutine transfers.

Journal Entries for Transactions Affecting More than One Fund

Event	Funds	Accounts		
1. Purchase of equipment with general fund resources for $40,000.	General Fund	Expenditures . . . . Vouchers Payable	40,000	40,000
	General Fixed Assets Account Group	Equipment . . . . Investment in General Fixed Assets— General Fund Revenues	40,000	40,000
2. Issuance of $500,000 of general obligation serial bonds at an $8,000 premium for city hall construction.	Capital Projects Fund	Cash . . . . Other Financing Sources . . . . Other Financing Sources—Premium . . . . . . Other Financing Uses . . . . Cash	508,000 8,000	500,000 8,000 8,000
	Debt Service Fund	Cash . . . . Other Financing Sources	8,000	8,000
	General Long-Term Debt Account Group	Amount to Be Provided for Payment of Serial Bonds. . . . . Serial Bonds Payable	500,000	500,000
3. Transfer by general fund to meet $100,000 matured serial bonds and $50,000 interest payment.	General Fund	Other Financing Uses . . . . Cash	150,000	150,000
	Debt Service Fund	Cash . . . . Other Financing Sources	150,000	150,000
	General Long-Term Debt Account Group	Amount Available in Debt Service Fund— Serial Bonds. . . . . Amount to Be Provided for Payment of Serial Bonds	100,000	100,000
4. Payment of $50,000 bond interest and $100,000 matured serial bonds. Fiscal agent is used for payment.	Debt Service Fund	Expenditures . . . . Matured Bonds Payable . . . . Matured Interest Payable	150,000	100,000 50,000
		Cash with Fiscal Agent . . . . Cash	150,000	150,000
	Debt Service Fund	Matured Bonds Payable . . . . Matured Interest Payable. . . . . Cash with Fiscal Agent	100,000 50,000	150,000
	General Long-Term Debt Account Group	Serial Bonds Payable. . . . . Amount Available in Debt Service Fund— Serial Bonds	100,000	100,000
5. Completion of special assessment construction project. $150,000 paid to date; $50,000 final payment.	Capital Projects Fund	Expenditures . . . . Cash	50,000	50,000
	General Fixed Assets Account Group	Improvements Other than Buildings. . . . . Construction in Progress . . . . Investment in General Fixed Assets— Capital Projects Funds (special assessments)	200,000	150,000 50,000
6. Levy of $5,000 property taxes by general fund against city's utility.	General Fund	Due from Enterprise Fund. . . . . Revenues	5,000	5,000
	Enterprise Fund	Property Tax Expense . . . . Due to General Fund	5,000	5,000

Event	Funds	Accounts		
7. Billing of general and special revenue funds for central computer service ($12,000 and $20,000, respectively).	Internal Service Fund	Due from General Fund	12,000	
		Due from Special Revenue Fund	20,000	
		Revenues		32,000
	General Fund	Expenditures	12,000	
		Due to Internal Service Fund		12,000
	Special Revenue Fund	Expenditures	20,000	
		Due to Internal Service Fund		20,000
8. Contribution made by city to establish a nonexpendable trust fund of $98,500. Income from this fund will be used for library operations.	General Fund	Other Financing Uses—Transfer to Trust Fund.	98,500	
		Cash.		98,500
	Permanent Fund	Cash	98,500	
		Other Financing Sources—Transfer from General Fund.		98,500
9. Remittance of the city's $16,000 share of self-insurance costs for current period to an internal service fund.	General Fund	Expenditures	16,000	
		Cash		16,000
	Internal Service Fund	Cash	16,000	
		Revenues		16,000
10. Reimbursement of $15,000 by the special revenue fund to the general fund for general government supplies expenditures initially made in the general fund and properly charged to a community development project.	Special Revenue Fund	Expenditures	15,000	
		Cash		15,000
	General Fund	Cash	15,000	
		Expenditures		15,000
11. Recording of depreciation, $6,000 enterprise fund, $13,000 internal service fund.	Enterprise Fund	Depreciation Expense	6,000	
		Accumulated Depreciation		6,000
	Internal Service Fund	Depreciation Expense	13,000	
		Accumulated Depreciation		13,000
12. Redemption of final $100,000 serial of general obligation bonds, with $3,000 deficiency covered by general fund. Fiscal agent is used for payment.	General Fund	Other Financing Uses	3,000	
		Cash		3,000
	Debt Service Fund	Cash	3,000	
		Other Financing Sources		3,000
		Cash with Fiscal Agent	100,000	
		Cash		100,000
		Expenditures	100,000	
		Matured Bonds Payable		100,000
		Matured Bonds Payable	100,000	
		Cash with Fiscal Agent		100,000
	General Long-Term Debt Account Group	Amounts Available in Debt Service Fund.	100,000	
		Amount to Be Provided for Payment of Serial Bonds.		100,000
		Serial Bonds Payable.	100,000	
		Amounts Available in Debt Service Fund. . .		100,000
13. Closing entry for capital projects fund involving a partially completed project. Cost to date is $130,000; revenues during the period are $300,000.	Capital Projects Fund	Revenues	300,000	
		Expenditures		130,000
		Fund Balance—Committed		170,000

(continued)

Event	Funds	Accounts		
13.	General Fixed Assets Account Group	Construction in Progress . . . . Investment in General Fixed Assets— Capital Projects Fund	130,000		130,000

14. Payroll expenditures totaled $5,000 and included $1,000 payroll withholdings for taxes and insurance plus employer's share of these costs. $1,000 is transferred to an agency fund for remittance as follows: private insurance company, $200; federal government, $650; and state government, $150. The agency fund makes the remittances.	General Fund	Expenditures . . . .
		    Due to Agency Fund. . . . .
		    Cash . . . .
			5,000		1,000
					 4,000

	Agency Fund	Due from General Fund . . . .
		    Due to Insurance Company . . . .
		    Due to Federal Government . . . .
		    Due to State . . . .
			1,000		200
					 650
					 150

	General Fund	Due to Agency Fund . . . . Cash	1,000		1,000
	Agency Fund	Cash . . . . Due from General Fund	1,000		1,000
		Due to Insurance Company . . . . Due to Federal Government. . . . . Due to State . . . . Cash		200 650 150	1,000
15. A 5-year lease agreement was signed for equipment. The present value of the lease payments is $50,000.	General Fund	Expenditures . . . . Other Financing Sources	50,000		50,000
	General Long-Term Debt Account Group	Amount to Be Provided . . . . Lease Payable	50,000		50,000

	General Fixed Assets Account Group	Leased Asset . . . .
		    Investment in General Fixed Assets—
		        Capital Lease . . . .
			50,000		50,000

16. The actuarial required contribution for pensions was $4,500. Of this amount, $3,000 was transferred to the pension trust. $1,500 will be transferred in the future.	General Fund	Expenditures . . . . Cash	3,000		3,000
	General Long-Term Debt Account Group	Amount to Be Provided . . . . Unfunded Pension Obligation	1,500		1,500
	Pension Trust Fund	Cash . . . . Receivable from Employer. . . . . Contributions—Employer	3,000 1,500		4,500
17. Claims and judgments against the city were estimated at $15,000. The city attorney determined that it was probable that the claims would be settled against the city. Of the $15,000, $3,000 was estimated to be paid out this fiscal year.	General Fund	Expenditures . . . . Claims and Judgments Payable	3,000		3,000
	General Long-Term Debt Account Group	Amount to Be Provided . . . . Claims and Judgments Payable	12,000		12,000
18. Closure and post-closure costs of local landfill were estimated at $600,000. Landfill used this period was estimated at 1,000 cubic yards, and total landfill is 100,000 cubic yards. Landfill operations are accounted for in enterprise funds.	Enterprise Fund	Landfill Expense. . . . . Liability for Landfill Costs	6,000		6,000

Event	Funds	Accounts		
19. Debt was refunded. The refunding met the criteria for in-substance defeasance. Proceeds of the new debt issue were placed in trust with an escrow agent.	Debt Service Fund	Cash	100,000	
		Other Financing Sources		100,000
		Other Financing Uses	100,000	
		Cash		100,000
	General Long-Term Debt Account Group	Bonds Payable........................	100,000	
		Amount to Be Provided................		100,000
		Amount to Be Provided	100,000	
		Bonds Payable.......................		100,000
20. Investments carried at $5,500 have a fair value of $5,750 in the general fund. Pension investments carried at $102,000 have a fair value of $101,000.	General Fund	Investments	250	
		Net Appreciation in Fair Value of Investments......................		250
	Pension Trust Fund	Net Depreciation in Fair Value of Investments.........................	1,000	
		Investments.........................		1,000

REFLECTION

- Each fund or account group is a separate accounting entity.
- One transaction often affects more than one fund or account group.

UNDERSTANDING THE ISSUES

1. Why are fixed assets, acquired with proceeds from general obligation bond issues, not permanently accounted for in a capital projects fund?

2. If a capital projects fund has authority to continue operations over several fiscal periods, why is it desirable to close its records at the end of each period?

3. Explain the necessity to introduce a deferred revenues account in the levy of capital special assessments.

4. The debt service fund does not use budgetary accounts. What is the logic for not doing so?

5. When a debt service fund receives resources, it might credit Revenues or Other Financing Sources. Under what circumstances would each of these credits be used?

6. What characteristic determines whether an activity should be accounted for in a special revenue fund or in a permanent fund?

7. Describe two major types of interfund transfers. Under what circumstances is each used?

8. What is the difference between an agency fund and a trust fund?

9. What is the difference between an enterprise fund and an internal service fund?

10. Explain the difference between expenses and expenditures in a state and a local government.

11. Describe the difference between accounting for governmental funds and proprietary funds.

12. What is the difference between a permanent fund and a private-purpose trust fund?

EXERCISES

Exercise 1 *(LO 1)* **Debt service fund, serial bonds.** Prepare journal entries required by a debt service fund to record the following transactions:

a. On January 2, a $5,000,000, 6%, 10-year general obligation serial bond issue is sold at 99. Interest is payable annually on December 31, along with one-tenth of the original principal.
b. At year-end, the first serial bond matures, along with interest on the bond issue.
c. The general fund transfers cash to meet the matured items.
d. A check for the matured items is sent to First Bank, the agent handling the payments.
e. Later, the bank reports that the first serial bond has been redeemed. One check for interest of $9,000 was returned by the post office because the bond owner had moved. The bank will search for the new address.

Exercise 2 *(LO 1, 3, 4)* **Endowment trust fund, special revenue fund.** On January 1, 2018, Jack Bauer donated $200,000 to the city of Alexander to be set aside as a trust fund for water quality improvements made by the city. The funds were fully invested in bonds purchased at a premium with a face value of $194,000. During the year, cash received on investments was $15,000. Premiums on the bonds purchased were amortized at $600 per year. A total of $12,000 was transferred to a special revenue fund to carry out the purpose of the trust. Prepare the journal entries to record these transactions in the permanent fund and closing entries. Prepare the balance sheet of the permanent fund as of December 31, 2018.

Exercise 3 *(LO 1)* **General obligation bonds, fixed asset construction.** Prepare journal entries to record the following events. Identify every fund(s) or group of accounts in which an entry is made.

a. The city authorized the construction of a city hall to be financed by a $6,000,000 contribution of the general fund and the proceeds of a $30,000,000 general obligation serial bond issue. Both amounts are budgeted to be received in the current year. Expenditures during the current year are estimated to be $14,000,000. Budgetary accounts are used.
b. The general fund remits the $6,000,000.
c. The bonds are sold for 99; issue costs totaled $50,000.
d. A contract is signed with Mader Construction Company for construction of the city hall for an estimated contract cost of $32,000,000. The contract was authorized by a city official delegated authority by the city council.
e. By year-end, $7,000,000 is paid against the contract with Mader Construction Company.

Exercise 4 *(LO 1)* **General obligation bonds, fixed asset construction.** Select the best response for each of the following multiple-choice questions that refer to the transactions of Beloit City. (No. 4 is AICPA adapted.)

   On March 2, 2018, Beloit City issued 10-year general obligation bonds at face amount, with interest payable on March 1 and September 1. The proceeds were to be used to finance the construction of a civic center over the period of April 1, 2018, to March 31, 2019. During the fiscal year ended June 30, 2018, no resources had been provided to the debt service fund for the payment of principal and interest.

1. On June 30, 2018, Beloit's debt service fund should include interest payable on the general obligation bonds for

   a. zero months.
   b. three months.
   c. four months.
   d. six months.

2. Proceeds from the general obligation bonds should be recorded in the

 a. general fund.
 b. capital projects fund.
 c. general long-term debt account group.
 d. debt service fund.

3. The liability for the general obligation bonds should be recorded in the

 a. general fund.
 b. capital projects fund.
 c. general long-term debt account group.
 d. debt service fund.

4. On June 30, 2018, the balance sheet part of Beloit's fund financial statements should report the construction in progress for the civic center in the

	Capital Projects Fund	General Fixed Assets Account Group
a.	Yes	Yes
b.	Yes	No
c.	No	No
d.	No	Yes

Exercise 5 *(LO 1, 2)* **Other governmental funds, proprietary funds.** Select the best answer for each of the following multiple-choice items. (Nos. 1, 2, 4, 6, 9, and 10 are AICPA adapted.)

1. Which of the following statements is *correct* concerning a governmental entity's statement of cash flows?

 a. Cash flows from capital financing activities and cash flows from noncapital financing activities are reported separately.
 b. The statement format is the same as that of a business enterprise's statement of cash flows.
 c. Cash flows from operating activities may not be reported using the indirect method.
 d. The statement format includes columns for the general, governmental, and proprietary fund types.

2. Which of the following funds of a governmental unit recognizes revenues in the accounting period in which they become available and measurable?

	General Fund	Enterprise Fund
a.	Yes	No
b.	No	Yes
c.	Yes	Yes
d.	No	No

3. If an internal service fund is intended to operate on a cost-reimbursement basis, then user charges should

 a. cover the full costs, both direct and indirect, of operating the fund.
 b. cover the full costs of operating the fund and provide for future expansion and replacement of capital assets.
 c. cover at a minimum the direct costs of operating the fund.
 d. do all of the above.

4. The billings for transportation services provided to other governmental units are recorded by the internal service fund as

   a. other financing sources.
   b. intergovernmental transfers.
   c. transportation appropriations.
   d. operating revenues.

5. Bonds are issued at a premium by a capital projects fund. The premium should be

   a. retained in the capital projects fund.
   b. credited directly to the restricted fund balance of the capital projects fund.
   c. transferred to the debt service funds.
   d. used to reduce the net cost of the project involved.

6. Revenues that are legally restricted to expenditures for specified purposes should be accounted for in special revenue funds, including

   a. accumulation of resources for payment of general long-term debt principal and interest.
   b. pension trust fund revenues.
   c. gasoline taxes to finance road repairs.
   d. proprietary fund revenues.

7. The police department of the city of Elizabeth acquires a new police car during the current year. In reporting the balance sheet for the governmental funds within the fund-based financial statements, what reporting is made of this police car?

   a. It is reported as a police car at its cost.
   b. It is reported as a police car at cost less accumulated depreciation.
   c. It is reported as equipment at fair value.
   d. It is not reported.

8. Resources for a capital improvement are provided by special assessments. At the start of the second year of the project, a reclassification entry in the debt service fund that debits Deferred Revenues would credit

   a. Special Assessments Receivable—Deferred.
   b. Revenues.
   c. Unassigned Fund Balance.
   d. Fund Balance Restricted for Special Assessments.

9. Eureka City should issue a statement of cash flows for which of the following funds?

	Eureka City Hall Capital Projects Fund	Eureka Water Enterprise Fund
a.	No	Yes
b.	No	No
c.	Yes	No
d.	Yes	Yes

10. Gaffney City's serial bonds are serviced through a debt service fund with cash provided by the general fund. In a debt service fund's statements, how are cash receipts and cash payments reported?

	Cash Receipts	Cash Payments
a.	Revenues	Expenditures
b.	Revenues	Operating transfers
c.	Operating transfers	Expenditures
d.	Operating transfers	Operating transfers

Exercise 6 *(LO 1)* **Special assessments levy, capital projects fund.** In 2018, the town of Bayview authorized the construction of two concrete roadways. The public works department estimates the project cost at $400,000, $20,000 of which is transferred from the general fund to the capital projects fund. The balance will be paid for through a special assessments levy on benefiting property owners. On January 1, 2018, $380,000, 4-year, 10% special assessment bonds are issued at face value to finance the property owners' portion. Payments of $47,500 plus interest are made each June 30 and December 31. The bonds were issued. The town guarantees payment of the debt.

Purchase orders totaling $80,000 are issued, and a contract is signed for the estimated $320,000 additional cost of the project. The purchase order was approved by a town official. The contract was approved by formal action of the town council, which is the highest level of authority within the town. Invoices for all purchase orders total $74,000. The actual contract cost is $375,000. Liabilities for these amounts are entered. Except for $30,000 withheld on the contract until final approval, all liabilities related to the completed construction are paid. Bayview does not use budgetary accounts for these projects. Prepare entries in the capital projects fund for these events.

Exercise 7 *(LO 1, 4)* **Special assessments levy, serial bonds, debt service fund, long-term debt account group.** This exercise is based on the facts of Exercise 6 for the town of Bayview's special assessment project. Assume special assessment property owners make the required payments to the debt service fund, and the debt service fund, in turn, makes the payments required by the serial bonds. Record all entries in the debt service fund and in the general long-term debt account group for 2018.

Exercise 8 *(LO 2)* **Enterprise fund.** Prepare journal entries to record the following events in the city of Rosewood's Water Commission enterprise fund:

a. From its general fund revenues, the city transferred $300,000, which is restricted for the drilling of additional wells.
b. Billings for water consumption for the month totaled $287,000, including $67,000 billed to other funds within the city.
c. The Water Commission collected $42,000 from other funds and $190,000 from other users on billings in item (b).
d. To raise additional funds, the utility issued $700,000 of 5%, 10-year revenue bonds at face value. Proceeds are restricted to the development of wells.
e. The contract with the well driller showed an estimated cost of $930,000.
f. The well driller bills $360,000 at year-end.
g. The utility pays a $300,000 bill from the well driller.

Exercise 9 *(LO 3, 4)* **Trust funds, various funds, and account groups.** Select the best answer for each of the following multiple-choice items. (Nos. 4, 7, and 10 are AICPA adapted.)

1. In which of the following fund types of a city government are revenues and expenditures recognized on the same basis of accounting as the general fund?

   a. Private-purpose trust funds
   b. Internal service
   c. Enterprise
   d. Debt service

2. Which of the following is *not* a fiduciary fund?

   a. Permanent fund
   b. Agency fund
   c. Investment trust fund
   d. Pension trust fund

3. Accounting for permanent funds closely resembles the accounting for

   a. general funds.
   b. capital projects funds.
   c. enterprise funds.
   d. agency funds.

4. In what fund type should the proceeds from special assessment bonds issued to finance construction of sidewalks in a new subdivision be reported?

   a. Agency fund
   b. Special revenue fund
   c. Enterprise fund
   d. Capital projects fund

5. When establishing an investment pool, Eureka City will account for all of the pooled investments in

   a. an investment trust fund at fair value at the date the pool is created.
   b. an agency fund at fair value as of the last balance sheet date.
   c. the general fund at fair value as of the last balance sheet date.
   d. the general fund at fair value at the date the pool is created.

6. A debt service fund should be used to account for the payment of interest and principal on

   a. debt recorded in the general long-term debt account group or similar list.
   b. debt secured by the revenues of an enterprise fund.
   c. debt recorded as a liability in the general fund.
   d. all of the above.

7. Taxes collected and held by Dunne County for a school district would be accounted for in which of the following funds?

   a. Trust
   b. Agency
   c. Special revenue
   d. Internal service

8. If a governmental unit makes no guarantees regarding repayment of a capital improvement special assessment bond issue, the liability for the bonds would

   a. not appear in the financial statements or in their notes.
   b. not appear in the financial statements but would appear in the notes to the financial statements.
   c. appear in the capital projects fund.
   d. appear in the general long-term debt account group.

9. The following is a correct entry:

Construction in Progress	XXX	
Investment in General Fixed Assets—Capital Projects Funds		XXX

   The entry would be found in the

   a. capital projects fund.
   b. enterprise fund.
   c. general fund.
   d. general fixed assets account group.

10. On June 28, 2019, Brock City's debt service fund received funds for the future repayment of bond principal. As a consequence, the general long-term debt account group reported

    a. an increase in the amount available in debt service funds and an increase in the fund balance.
    b. an increase in the amount available in debt service funds and an increase in the amount to be provided for bonds.
    c. an increase in the amount available in debt service funds and a decrease in the amount to be provided for bonds.
    d. no changes in any amount until the bond principal is actually paid.

Exercise 10 *(LO 4)* **Impact of transactions on different funds.** Indicate into which fund a city would record each of the following transactions. (You need not make any entries.)

a. Fixed assets are purchased with general fund cash.
b. Long-term serial bonds are issued to finance the construction of a new art museum. The bonds are sold at a premium.
c. The general fund transfers a sufficient amount of money to cover principal and interest requirements of a debt issue.
d. The fund receiving the payment in item (c) makes the scheduled payment of principal and interest.
e. A special assessment project is one-half completed at year-end.
f. Income is earned by an endowment fund and is transferred to a recipient fund, which is restricted as to its expenditures by the trust agreement specified for a government program.
g. Possible depreciation entries on assets are recorded.
h. The government-owned water utility issues debt to purchase new equipment.
i. The new city prison is completed, and leftover funds are transferred to the fund responsible for repaying the debt used to finance the project.

GF	General Fund	PF	Permanent Fund
SRF	Special Revenue Fund	PPT	Private-Purpose Trust Fund
DSF	Debt Service Fund	GFAAG	General Fixed Assets Account Group
CPF	Capital Projects Fund		
ENT	Enterprise Fund	GLTDAG	General Long-Term Debt Account Group
INT	Internal Service Fund		

Exercise 11 *(LO 4)* **Identification of fund type.** Identify the letter that *best* describes the accounting and reporting by the following funds and account groups:

1. Enterprise fund fixed assets.
2. Capital projects fund.
3. General fixed assets.
4. Infrastructure fixed assets.
5. Enterprise fund cash.
6. General fund.
7. Agency fund cash.
8. General long-term debt.
9. Special revenue fund.
10. Debt service fund.

a. Accounted for in a fiduciary fund.
b. Accounted for in a proprietary fund.
c. Accounted for in a quasi-endowment fund.
d. Accounted for in a self-balancing account group and included in financial statements.
e. Accounted for in a special assessment fund.
f. Accounts for major construction activities.
g. Accounts for property tax revenues.
h. Accounts for payment of interest and principal on tax-supported debt.
i. Accounts for revenues from earmarked sources to finance designated activities.
j. Reporting is optional.

(AICPA adapted)

Exercise 12 *(LO 4)* **Selection of appropriate debit or credit entry, various funds.**
Match the appropriate letter indicating the recording of the following transactions:

1. General obligation bonds were issued at par.
2. Approved purchase orders were issued for supplies.
3. The above-mentioned supplies were received, and the related invoices were approved.
4. General fund salaries and wages were incurred.
5. The internal service fund had interfund billings.
6. Revenues were earned from a previously awarded grant.

7. Property taxes were collected in advance.
8. Appropriations were recorded on adoption of the budget.
9. Short-term financing was received from a bank and secured by the city's taxing power.
10. There was an excess of estimated inflows over estimated outflows.

Recording of transactions:

a. Credit Appropriations.
b. Credit Budgetary Fund Balance—Unreserved.
c. Credit Expenditures.
d. Credit Deferred Revenues.
e. Credit Interfund Revenues.
f. Credit Tax Anticipation Notes Payable.
g. Credit Other Financing Sources.
h. Credit Other Financing Uses.
i. Debit Appropriations.
j. Debit Deferred Revenues.
k. Debit Encumbrances.
l. Debit Expenditures.

(AICPA adapted)

PROBLEMS

Problem 16-1 *(LO 1)* **Capital projects fund, financial statements.** The preclosing, year-end trial balance for a capital projects fund of the city of Clark as of December 31, 2019, follows:

	Debit	Credit
Cash	75,000	
Investments	200,000	
Contracts Payable—Retained Percentage		60,000
Revenues		16,600
Other Financing Sources		900,000
Expenditures	686,600	
Other Financing Uses	15,000	
Encumbrances	80,000	
Fund Balance—Assigned		80,000
Estimated Revenues	20,000	
Estimated Other Financing Sources	950,000	
Appropriations		640,000
Estimated Other Financing Uses		25,000
Budgetary Fund Balance—Unassigned		305,000
Totals	2,026,600	2,026,600

Required ▶ ▶ ▶ ▶ ▶

1. Prepare closing entries as of December 31, 2019, assuming that all inflows and outflows are designated assigned.
2. Prepare the year-end statement of revenues, expenditures, and changes in fund balance for this project that began on January 2, 2019.
3. Prepare the balance sheet for this project as of December 31, 2019.

Problem 16-2 *(LO 1, 4)* **Capital projects fund, special assessments, debt service fund, effect on other funds/groups.** In response to a petition signed by the property owners of Riverdale Subdivision, the city of Pewaukee will oversee the installation of sidewalks, curbs, and gutters in the subdivision, to be accounted for in the city's capital projects fund.

Pewaukee reports on a calendar-year basis. Construction is estimated to cost $900,000 and will be financed by a $100,000 county grant, a $50,000 transfer from the city's general fund, and special assessments of $750,000 to be levied against subdivision property owners. One-third of the levy is to be due on February 1 of each year, starting with 2018. The first $250,000 installment will be received by the capital projects fund directly. The remaining installments will be collected by the debt service fund and will be used to service the related bond debt. The project is to begin on January 15, 2018, and is to take 18 months to complete. It is estimated that 70% of the work will be completed during 2018.

To cover construction costs, a 6%, $500,000 special assessment serial bond issue will be floated on March 1, 2018. Interest is to be paid semiannually on September 1 and March 1 by the debt service fund. One-fifth of the principal will be redeemed on March 1 of each year, starting with 2019. Since interest earned on special assessments will offset bond interest cost, the city will not accrue interest.

Although the special assessments will provide cash to redeem the bond principal and pay the bond interest, Pewaukee has pledged its full faith and credit as security for the bond obligation. The following events happen during 2018:

January 2—	The city council adopted the annual budget for the Riverdale project in the capital projects fund.
January 2—	The receivables from the general fund and the county were recorded.
January 5—	Special assessments were levied in accordance with the plan, with one-third due on February 1.
January 9—	Amounts due from the general fund and the county were received.
January 10—	Encumbrances approved by a committee of the city council for the year were recorded at $675,000.
February 1—	The first special assessment installment was collected.
March 1—	Bonds with a $500,000 face value were sold at 101. Except for the price, other conditions remained in accordance with the bond plan. The premium was to be transferred to the debt service fund for interest payments.
March 1—	$600,000 was invested in a 5% money market account by the capital projects fund.
August 31—	$10,000 for interest payment was transferred by the capital projects fund to the debt service fund.
September 1—	The semiannual bond interest was paid by the debt service fund.
December 15—	The contractor submitted an invoice for $600,000 that was approved for payment, except for a 10% amount to be paid on completion and acceptance of the project. Related encumbrances totaled $595,000.
December 29—	$400,000 was withdrawn from the money market investment. Interest of $16,600 was received.
December 30—	The contractor was mailed a check for $540,000. In addition, vouchers for $76,600 were prepared and paid for items on the project that were not encumbered.
In addition—	The next assessment installment was reclassified upon special direction of the city council, and an amount equal to project expenditures-to-date was capitalized.

For each of the preceding events, prepare the journal entries for all of the funds and groups ◄ ◄ ◄ ◄ ◄ **Required** of accounts involved, using the following format:

Date	Fund or Account Group	Entry

Problem 16-3 *(LO 1, 4)* **Special assessments, capital projects fund, debt service fund, effect on other funds/groups.** You are given the following post-closing trial balance for the Special Assessment Capital Projects Fund of the city of StoneCreek Bank as of January 1, 2018. The project was started last year and should be completed in June of 2018.

	Debit	Credit
Cash	290,000	
Contracts Payable—Retained Percentage		60,000
Fund Balance—Restricted		150,000
Fund Balance—Assigned for Encumbrance		80,000
Totals	290,000	290,000

The special assessments are collected by the debt service fund, which also makes payments of principal and interest on special assessment bonds. The city has guaranteed payment of the debt in the event of nonpayment by the special assessment property owners. The debt service fund has the following balances, shown below, on January 1, 2018.

	Debit	Credit
Cash	20,000	
Special Assessments Receivable—Current	250,000	
Special Assessments Receivable—Deferred	250,000	
Revenues		250,000
Deferred Revenues		250,000
Fund Balance—Restricted for Debt Service		20,000
Totals	520,000	520,000

The following events occurred during 2018:

January 2—	The city adopted an operating budget for 2018 construction activities. Expenditures are estimated at $223,400, including amounts encumbered in the prior year. Budgetary accounts are used.
January 5—	Prior-year encumbrances are restored, and new encumbrances of $138,000 are recorded.
February 1—	$220,000 of current special assessments are collected, along with interest of $17,600. Interest of $2,400 was billed on the uncollected current assessments, which were classified as delinquent.
February 28—	$115,000 was paid on outstanding special assessment bonds, including interest of $15,000.
March 14—	Delinquent special assessments and interest thereon of $2,650 were collected.
May 1—	Expenditures of $220,000 were vouchered to Contracts Payable. The usual 5% retained percentage was entered. The project is now complete at a total cost of $896,000.
May 10—	A check for $100,000 was issued to the contractor.

Required ▶ ▶ ▶ ▶ ▶

Prepare journal entries to record each of the preceding events in the proper funds and groups of accounts using the following format:

Date	Fund or Account Group	Entry

Problem 16-4 *(LO 1, 4)* **Capital projects fund, effect on other funds/groups.** The following information pertains to Palmer Township's construction and financing of a new administration center:

Estimated total cost of project	$9,000,000
Project financing:	
State entitlement grant	$3,000,000
General obligation bonds assigned to the capital projects fund:	
Face amount	$6,000,000
Stated interest rate	6%
Issue date	December 1, 2018
Maturity date	November 30, 2028

Palmer's fiscal year ended on June 30, 2018. The following events occurred that affected the capital projects fund established to account for this project:

July 1, 2018—	The capital projects fund was assigned $250,000 from the general fund for preliminary expenses.
July 9, 2018—	Engineering and planning costs of $200,000, for which no encumbrance had been recorded, were paid to Krew Associates.
December 1, 2018—	The bonds were sold at 101. The premium is transferred to the debt service fund.
December 1, 2018—	The entitlement grant was formally approved by the state.

April 30, 2019—	A $7,000,000 contract was executed with Kimmel Construction Corporation, the general contractor for the major portion of the project. The contract was approved by a subcommittee of the township council. The contract provides that Palmer will withhold 4% of all billings pending satisfactory completion of the project.
May 9, 2019—	$1,000,000 of the state grant was received.
June 10, 2019—	The $250,000 transferred from the general fund was repaid back to the general fund.
June 30, 2019—	Progress billing of $1,200,000 was received from Kimmel.

Palmer uses encumbrance accounting for budgetary control. Unencumbered appropriations lapse at the end of the year.

1. Prepare journal entries in the administration center capital projects fund to record the fore- ◄ ◄ ◄ ◄ ◄ **Required**
going transactions.
2. Prepare the June 30, 2019, closing entries for the Administration Center Capital Projects fund.
3. Prepare the Administration Center Capital Projects Fund balance sheet at June 30, 2019.
4. Prepare entries needed in other funds and groups.

(AICPA adapted)

Problem 16-5 *(LO 2)* **Internal service fund, statement of cash flows.** Prepare a ◄ ◄ ◄ ◄ ◄ **Required**
statement of cash flows for the internal service fund of the city of Boniville from the following information:

Cash on hand at the beginning of the year	$ 122
Interest from investments	145
Wages and salaries paid	(3,100)
Purchases of supplies.	(1,650)
Collections (for services) from other funds	6,000
Interest paid on long-term debt	(150)
Repayment of loans from other funds.	(680)
Purchase of capital assets	(900)
Proceeds of revenue bonds	900
Purchase of investments.	(440)
Proceeds from sale of capital assets	23
Proceeds from sale of investments	33
Loans from other funds.	600

Problem 16-6 *(LO 2)* **Internal service fund.** The city of Cloverville operates a central computer center through an internal service fund. The Computer Internal Service Fund was established by a contribution of $1,000,000 from the general fund on July 1, 2017, at which time a building was acquired at a cost of $300,000 cash. A used computer was purchased for $600,000. The post-closing trial balance of the fund at June 30, 2018, was as follows:

	Debit	Credit
Cash	120,000	
Due from General Fund	140,000	
Inventory of Materials and Supplies	80,000	
Land.	60,000	
Building	300,000	
Allowance for Depreciation—Building		15,000
Computer Equipment.	660,000	
Allowance for Depreciation—Computer Equipment.		264,000
Vouchers Payable (to outsiders).		41,000
Contributions from General Fund		1,000,000
Net Assets—Unrestricted.		40,000
Totals	1,360,000	1,360,000

The following information applies to the year ended June 30, 2019:

a. Materials and supplies were purchased on account for $72,000.
b. The inventory of materials and supplies at June 30, 2019, was $65,000.
c. Salaries paid totaled $235,000, including related costs.
d. A billing from the Utility Enterprise Fund for $40,000 was received and paid.
e. Depreciation on the building and on the equipment was $6,500 and $133,000, respectively.
f. Billings to other departments for service were as follows:

General Fund.	$392,000
Water and Sewer Fund	84,000
Special Revenue Fund	42,000

g. Unpaid interfund receivable balances at June 30, 2019, were as follows:

General Fund.	$136,000
Special Revenue Fund	16,000

h. Vouchers payable at June 30, 2019, were $19,000.

Required ▶ ▶ ▶ ▶ ▶

1. For the period July 1, 2018, through June 30, 2019, prepare journal entries to record the transactions in the Computer Internal Service Fund. The city uses control accounts for revenues and expenses.
2. Prepare closing entries at June 30, 2019. *Note:* All net assets are designated unrestricted.

Problem 16-7 *(LO 2, 4)* **Internal service fund, effect on other funds/groups.**
Palto County elects not to purchase commercial insurance. Instead, it sets aside resources for potential claims in an internal service "self-insurance" fund. During the year, the fund recognized $4 million for claims filed during the year. Of this amount, it paid $2.3 million. Based on the calculations of an independent actuary, the insurance fund billed and collected $5.0 million in premiums from the other county departments insured by the fund. Of this amount, $3.2 million was billed to the funds accounted for in the general fund and $1.8 million to the county utility fund. The total charge for premiums was based on historical experience and included a reasonable provision for future catastrophe losses.

Required ▶ ▶ ▶ ▶ ▶

1. Prepare the journal entries in the internal service fund to record the claims recognized and paid and the premiums billed and collected.
2. Prepare the journal entries in the other funds affected by the above.
3. If the county accounted for its self-insurance within its general fund, how would the above entries differ?

Problem 16-8 *(LO 2, 4)* **Various funds and account groups, capital projects fund financial statement.** Mountain View's citizens authorized the construction of a new library. As a result of this project, the city had the following transactions during 2018:

a. On January 3, 2018, a $600,000 serial bond issue having a stated interest rate of 8% was authorized for the acquisition of land and the construction of a library building. The bonds are to be redeemed in 10 equal annual installments beginning February 1, 2019.
b. On January 10, 2018, the city made a $50,000 down payment deposit on the purchase of land, which is to be the site of the library. The contracted price for the land is $150,000, which is $40,000 below what the city estimated it would have to spend to acquire a site.
c. On March 1, 2018, the city issued serial bonds having a $450,000 face value at 102. The bond indenture requires any premium to be set aside for servicing bond interest.
d. On March 10, 2018, the city paid the remaining amount on the land contract and took title to the land.
e. On March 17, 2018, the city signed a $400,000 construction contract, approved by a city official, with Rower Construction Company.
f. On July 10, 2018, the contractor was paid $200,000 based on work completed to date.

g. On September 1, 2018, a semiannual interest payment was made on the outstanding bonds. [The general fund transferred funds to supplement the cash received from the premium in item (c).]

h. On December 1, 2018, the city issued serial bonds having a $100,000 face value at par.

i. On December 2, 2018, the contractor completed the library and submitted a final billing of $210,000, which includes $10,000 of additional work authorized by the city in October 2018 but not recorded as an encumbrance. The $210,000 was paid to the contractor on December 12, 2018.

j. Through December 10, 2018, the city had invested excess cash (from the bond offering) in short-term certificates of deposit. The amount collected on these investments totaled $12,000.

1. Prepare the journal entries in all fund/account groups. ◄ ◄ ◄ ◄ ◄ **Required**
2. Prepare any appropriate year-end adjusting and closing entries for the capital projects fund and the general fixed assets account group.
3. Prepare a statement of revenues, expenditures, and changes in fund balance for 2018 for the capital projects fund.

Problem 16-9 *(LO 2, 4)* **Enterprise fund, general fund.** In 2018, a city opens a municipal landfill, which it will account for in an enterprise fund. It estimates capacity to be 6 million cubic feet and usable life to be 20 years. To close the landfill, the municipality expects to incur labor, material, and equipment costs of $4 million. Thereafter, it expects to incur an additional $6 million of cost to monitor and maintain the site.

1. In 2018, the city uses 300,000 cubic feet of the landfill. Prepare the journal entry to record ◄ ◄ ◄ ◄ ◄ **Required**
   the expense for closure and post-closure care.
2. In 2019, it again uses 300,000 cubic feet of the landfill. It revises its estimate of available volume to 5.8 million cubic feet and closure and post-closure costs to $10.2 million. Prepare the journal entry to record the expense for closure and post-closure care.
3. Suppose the city accounts for the landfill in the general fund. How would the above entries for 2018 and 2019 differ?

Problem 16-10 *(LO 3)* **Trust fund, financial statements.** The following trial balance of the Employees' Retirement System Fund for Bedrock City was prepared by a clerk who used only balance sheet accounts in recording the events for the fiscal year ended June 30, 2018:

Cash	$ 38,000
Due from the city	4,000
Interest receivable	5,000
Investments, at fair value	497,000
Due to resigned employees	(1,000)
Annuities payable	(3,000)
Net plan assets	(540,000)
	$ 0
Balance on June 30, 2017	$ 464,000
Events during 2018:	
Amounts received from employees	32,000
Amounts received from employer	16,000
Amount due from city at year-end	4,000
Annuities paid during the year.	13,000
Refunds made during the year	2,500
Annuities payable at year-end	3,000
Due to resigned employees at year-end.	1,000
Investment earnings received.	30,000
Accrued earnings at year-end	5,000

(continued)

Difference between carrying value and fair value of the investments	13,500
Administrative expenses	5,000
Balance on June 30, 2018	$ 540,000

Required ▶ ▶ ▶ ▶ ▶   Prepare a statement of plan net assets and a statement of changes in plan net assets of the Employees' Retirement System Fund for the fiscal year ended June 30, 2018.

Problem 16-11 *(LO 3, 4)* **Agency fund, effect on various funds/groups.** In compliance with a newly enacted state law, Tilburg County assumed the responsibility of collecting all property taxes levied within its boundaries as of July 1, 2018. The following composite property tax rate per $100 of net assessed valuation was developed for the fiscal year ending June 30, 2019:

Tilburg County General Fund	$ 6.00
Reed City General Fund	3.00
Newport Township General Fund	1.00
	$10.00

All property taxes are due in quarterly installments and, after being collected, are distributed to the governmental units represented in the composite rate. To administer the collection and distribution of such taxes, Tilburg County has established a tax agency fund.

Additional information:

a. To reimburse itself for estimated administrative expenses of operating the tax agency fund, the county is to deduct 2% from the tax collections for Reed City and Newport Township. The total amount deducted is to be remitted to the Tilburg County General Fund.

b. Current-year tax levies to be collected by the tax agency fund are as follows:

	Gross Levy	Estimated Amount to Be Collected
Tilburg County	$3,600,000	$3,500,000
Reed City	1,800,000	1,740,000
Newport Township	600,000	560,000
Totals	$6,000,000	$5,800,000

c. In its original computation of the gross levy, Newport Township made an error that will reduce both the gross and estimated amounts to be collected by $10,000.

d. As of September 30, 2018, the tax agency fund has received $1,440,000 in first-quarter payments. On October 1, the agency fund made a distribution to the three governmental units on the basis of the composite property tax rate.

Required ▶ ▶ ▶ ▶ ▶   For the period July 1, 2018, through October 1, 2018, prepare journal entries to record the preceding transactions, using the following format:

	Tilburg County Tax Agency Fund		Tilburg County General Fund		Reed City General Fund		Newport Township General Fund	
Accounts	Debit	Credit	Debit	Credit	Debit	Credit	Debit	Credit

(AICPA adapted)

Problem 16-12 *(LO 4)* **Various funds and account groups.** The following information relates to Dell City, whose first fiscal year ended December 31, 2019. Assume Dell has only the long-term debt as specified below and only the funds necessitated by the following information.

1. General fund:

	Budget	Actual
Property taxes	$4,200,000	$4,500,000
Other revenues	2,000,000	1,500,000
Total revenues	$6,200,000	$6,000,000
Total expenditures	$5,600,000	$5,700,000
Property taxes receivable—delinquent		$ 520,000
Less allowance for estimated		
uncollectible taxes—delinquent		50,000
		$ 470,000

a. There were no amendments to the budget as originally adopted.
b. No property taxes receivable have been written off, and the allowance for uncollectibles balance is unchanged from the initial entry at the time of the original tax levy.
c. There were no encumbrances outstanding at December 31, 2019.

2. Capital projects fund:
a. Finances for Dell's new civic center were provided by a combination of general fund transfers, a state grant, and an issue of general obligation bonds. Any bond premium on issuance is to be used for the repayment of the bonds at their $1,000,000 par value. At December 31, 2019, the capital projects fund for the civic center had the following closing entries:

Revenues	800,000	
Other Financing Sources—Bond Proceeds	1,030,000	
Other Financing Sources—Operating Transfers-In	500,000	
Expenditures		1,080,000
Other Financing Uses—Operating Transfers-Out		30,000
Restricted Fund Balance.		1,220,000

b. Also, at December 31, 2019, capital projects fund entries reflected Dell's intention to honor the $900,000 purchase orders and commitments outstanding for the center.
c. During 2019, total capital projects fund encumbrances exceeded the corresponding expenditures by $52,000. All expenditures were previously encumbered.
d. During 2020, the capital projects fund received no revenues and no other financing sources. The civic center building was completed in early 2020, and the capital projects fund was closed by a transfer of $27,000 to the general fund.

3. Electric utility enterprise fund:
a. Dell issued $4,000,000 revenue bonds at par. These bonds, together with a $500,000 transfer from the general fund, were used to acquire an electric utility. Electric utility revenues are to be the sole source of funds to retire these bonds beginning in the year 2024.

Answer questions 1–15 with a yes (Y) or no (N) in the space provided. Answer questions ◄ ◄ ◄ ◄ ◄ **Required**
16–22 with the correct amount in the space provided.

1. Did recording budgetary accounts at the beginning of 2019 increase the fund balance by $300,000? _____
2. Should the budgetary accounts for 2019 include an entry for the expected transfer of funds from the general fund to the capital projects fund? _____
3. Should the $500,000 payment from the general fund, which was used to help establish the electric utility fund, be reported as "other financing uses—operating transfers-out"? _____

4. Did the general fund receive the $30,000 bond premium from the capital projects fund? _____

5. Should a payment from the general fund for electricity received for normal civic center operations be reported as "other financing uses—operating transfers-out"? _____

6. Does the net property taxes receivable of $470,000 include amounts expected to be collected after March 15, 2020? _____

7. Would closing budgetary accounts cause the fund balance to increase by $600,000? _____

8. After closing entries are made, do the budgetary accounts effect the fund balance on the balance sheet? _____

9. In the general fixed assets account group, should a credit amount be recorded for 2019 in "Investment in General Fixed Assets—Capital Projects Fund"? _____

10. In the general fixed assets account group, should Dell record depreciation on electric utility equipment? _____

11. Should the capital projects fund be included in Dell's combined statement of revenues, expenditures, and changes in fund balances? _____

12. Should the electric utility enterprise fund be included in Dell's combined governmental funds balance sheet? _____

13. Should Dell report capital and related financing activities in its statement of cash flows in its debt service fund? _____

14. Should Dell report capital and related financing activities in its statement of cash flows in its capital projects fund? _____

15. Should Dell report capital and related financing activities in its statement of cash flows in its electric utility enterprise fund? _____

16. What amount was recorded in the opening entry for appropriations? _____

17. What was the total amount debited to Property Taxes Receivable? _____

18. In the general long-term debt account group, what amount should be reported for bonds payable at December 31, 2019? _____

19. In the general fixed assets account group, what amount should be recorded for "Investment in General Fixed Assets—Capital Projects Fund" at December 31, 2019? _____

20. What was the completed cost of the civic center? _____

21. How much was the state capital grant for the civic center? _____

22. In the capital projects fund, what was the amount of the total encumbrances recorded during 2019? _____

(AICPA adapted)

Problem 16-13 *(LO 4)* **Various funds and account groups.** The following information relates to Carson City during its fiscal year ended December 31, 2019:

a. On October 31, 2019, to finance the construction of a city hall annex, Carson issued 8%, 10-year general obligation bonds at their face value of $600,000. Construction expenditures during the period equaled $364,000.

b. Carson reported $109,000 from hotel room taxes, restricted for tourist promotion, in a special revenue fund. The fund paid $81,000 for general promotions and $22,000 for a motor vehicle.

c. 2019 general fund revenues of $104,500 were transferred to a debt service fund and used to repay $100,000 of 9%, 15-year term bonds and $4,500 of interest. The bonds were used to acquire a citizens' center.

d. At December 31, 2019, as a consequence of past services, city firefighters had accumulated entitlements to compensated absences valued at $86,000. General fund resources available at December 31, 2019, are expected to be used to settle $17,000 of this amount, and $69,000 is expected to be paid out of future general fund resources.

e. At December 31, 2019, Carson was responsible for $83,000 of outstanding general fund encumbrances, including $8,000 for the following supplies.

f. Carson uses the purchases method to account for supplies. The following information relates to supplies:

Inventory:
        January 1, 2019 . . . . $ 39,000
        December 31, 2019   42,000
Encumbrances outstanding:
        January 1, 2019   6,000
        December 31, 2019   8,000
Purchase orders during 2019.   190,000
Amounts credited to vouchers payable during 2019   181,000

1. The amount of 2019 general fund operating transfers-out is _____ .   ◄ ◄ ◄ ◄ ◄ **Required**
2. The 2019 general fund liabilities from entitlements for compensated absences are _____ .
3. The 2019 reserved amount of the general fund balance is _____ .
4. The 2019 capital projects fund balance is _____ .
5. The 2019 fund balance on the special revenue fund for tourist promotion is _____ .
6. The amount of 2019 debt service fund expenditures is _____ .
7. The amount to be included in the general fixed assets account group for the cost of assets acquired in 2019 is _____ .
8. The amount by which 2019 transactions and events decreased the general long-term debt account group is _____ .
9. The amount of 2019 supplies expenditures using the purchases method is _____ .
10. The total amount of 2019 supplies encumbrances is _____ .

(AICPA adapted)

Problem 16-14 *(LO 4)* **Various funds and account groups.** The village of Fay was recently incorporated and began financial operations on July 1, 2018, the beginning of its fiscal year.

The following transactions occurred during this first fiscal year from July 1, 2018, to June 30, 2019:

1. The village council adopted a budget for general operations during the fiscal year ending June 30, 2019. Revenues were estimated at $400,000. Legal authorizations for expenditures were $394,000.
2. Property taxes were levied for $390,000. It was estimated that 2% of this amount would prove to be uncollectible. These taxes were available on the date of the levy to finance current expenditures.
3. During the year, a resident of the village donated marketable securities, valued at $50,000, to the village under the terms of a trust agreement. The agreement stipulated that the principal is to be kept intact. The use of revenue generated by the securities is to be restricted to financing college scholarships for needy students. Revenue earned and received on these marketable securities amounted to $5,500 through June 30, 2019.
4. A general fund transfer of $5,000 was made to establish an Intragovernmental Service Fund to provide for a permanent investment in inventory.
5. The village decided to install lighting in the village park. A special assessment project was authorized to install the lighting at a cost of $75,000. The appropriation was formally recorded. To finance the project, $3,000 is to be transferred from the general fund, and the balance is from special assessments.
6. Assessments were levied for $72,000, with the village contributing $3,000 from the general fund. All assessments and the village contributions were collected during the year.

7. A contract for $75,000 was signed and approved by a village official for the installation of lighting. At June 30, 2019, the contract was completed for $75,000. The contractor was paid all but 5%, which was retained to ensure compliance with the terms of the contract. Encumbrances and other budgetary accounts are maintained.

8. During the year, the internal service fund purchased various supplies at a cost of $1,900.

9. Cash collections recorded by the general fund during the year were as follows:

Property taxes	$386,000
Licenses and permits	7,000

10. The village council decided to build a village hall, at an estimated cost of $500,000, to replace space occupied in rented facilities. The village does not record project authorizations. It was decided that general obligation bonds bearing interest at 6% would be issued. On June 30, 2019, the bonds were issued at their face value of $500,000, payable in 20 years. No contracts have been signed for this project, and no expenditures have been made.

11. A fire truck, originally approved for purchase by the highest legislative body in the village, was purchased for $150,000, and the voucher was approved. Payment was made through the general fund. This expenditure was previously encumbered for $145,000.

Required ▶ ▶ ▶ ▶ ▶ Prepare journal entries to properly record each of the preceding transactions in the appropriate fund(s) or group of accounts of Fay for the fiscal year ended June 30, 2019. Use the following funds and groups of accounts:

a. General fund
b. Capital projects fund
c. Internal service fund
d. Private-purpose principal fund
e. Private-purpose earnings fund
f. General long-term debt account group
g. General fixed assets account group

Journal entries should be numbered to correspond with the appropriate transactions. Do not prepare closing entries for any fund.

Your answer sheet should be organized as follows:

Transaction No.	Fund or Account Group	Account Title and Explanation	Amount Debit	Credit

(AICPA adapted)

Problem 16-15 *(LO 4)* **Various funds and account groups.** A selected list of transactions for the city of Hope for the fiscal year ending June 30, 2018, follows:

1. The city government authorized a budget with estimated revenues of $4,500,000 and appropriations of $4,450,000.

2. The city's share of state gasoline taxes is estimated to be $264,500. These taxes are to be used only for highway maintenance. Appropriations are authorized in the amount of $250,000.

3. Property taxes of $3,000,000 are levied by the city. In the past, uncollectible taxes have averaged 2% of the gross levy.

4. A $1,000,000 term bond issue for construction of a school is authorized and sold at 99. Bond issue costs were $5,000.

5. Contracts approved by a city official are signed for the construction of the school at an estimated cost of $1,000,000.

6. The school is constructed at a cost of $1,250,000.

7. A transfer of $100,000 is made by the general fund to the debt service fund.

8. Land with a fair value of $500,000 is donated to the city.

9. The city received $205,000 in partial payment of its share of state gasoline taxes, with an additional $60,000 due from the state government in 60 days.

10. Vouchers totaling $410,000, which represent highway labor maintenance costs, are approved for payment by the special revenue fund.

For each event, prepare the journal entries for all of the funds and groups of accounts ◄ ◄ ◄ ◄ ◄ **Required** involved, using the following format:

Fund or Account Group   Journal Entry

Problem 16-16 *(LO 4)* **Various funds and account groups.** Which fund or account ◄ ◄ ◄ ◄ ◄ **Required** group should be used to record the following?

1. A primary government's general fund equity interest in a joint venture.
2. Fixed assets of a governmental unit, other than those accounted for in a proprietary fund.
3. A governmental unit's unmatured general obligation bonds payable.
4. Cost of maintenance for a municipal motor pool that maintains all city-owned vehicles and charges the various departments for the cost of rendering those services.
5. General long-term debt of a governmental unit.
6. Deferred compensation plans, for other than proprietary fund employees, adopted under IRC 457.
7. Debt service transactions of a special assessment issue for which the government is not obligated in any manner.
8. Taxes collected and held for a separate school district.
9. Investments donated to the city, income from which is to be used to acquire art for the city's museum.
10. Receipts from the federal government for the food stamp program.

Problem 16-17 *(LO 4)* **Bonds, various funds/groups.** During 2019, Kansas City issued bonds for financing the construction of a civic center and bonds for financing improvements in the environmental controls for its water and sewer enterprise. The latter bonds require a sinking fund for their retirement. Items (1) through (4) represent items Kansas City should report in its 2019 financial statements.

Determine in which of the following funds and account groups [(a) through (f)] each item ◄ ◄ ◄ ◄ ◄ **Required** [(1) through (4)] would be included:

a. General fund.
b. Enterprise funds.
c. Capital projects funds.
d. Debt service funds.
e. General fixed assets account group.
f. General long-term debt account group.

1. Bonds payable.
2. Accumulated depreciation.
3. Amounts identified for the repayment of the two bond issues.
4. Fund balance—assigned for encumbrances.

(AICPA adapted)

Problem 16-18 *(LO 4)* **Bonds, various funds/groups.** Rose City formally integrates budgetary accounts into its general fund. During the year ended December 31, 2019, Rose received a state grant to buy a bus and an additional grant for bus operation in 2019. In 2019, only 90% of the capital grant was used for the bus purchase, but 100% of the operating grant was disbursed. Rose has incurred the following long-term obligations:

a. General obligation bonds issued for the water and sewer fund which will service the debt.
b. Revenue bonds to be repaid from admission fees collected from users of the municipal recreation center.

These bonds are expected to be paid from enterprise funds and are secured by Rose's full faith, credit, and taxing power as further assurance that the obligations will be paid. Rose's 2019 expenditures from the general fund include payments for structural alterations to a firehouse and furniture for the mayor's office.

Required ▶ ▶ ▶ ▶ ▶

1. In reporting the state grants for the bus purchase and operation, what should Rose include as grant revenues for the year ended December 31, 2019?

	90% of the Capital Grant	100% of the Capital Grant	Operating Grant
a.	Yes	No	No
b.	No	Yes	No
c.	No	Yes	Yes
d.	Yes	No	Yes

2. Which of Rose's long-term obligations should be accounted for in the general long-term debt account group?

	General Obligation Bonds	Revenue Bonds
a.	Yes	Yes
b.	No	Yes
c.	Yes	No
d.	No	No

3. When Rose records its annual budget, which of the following accounts indicates the amount of authorized spending limitation for the year ending December 31, 2019?

    a. Restricted for Appropriations
    b. Appropriations
    c. Fund Balance—Assigned
    d. Encumbrances

4. In Rose's general fund balance sheet presentation at December 31, 2019, which of the following expenditures should be classified as capital assets?

	Purchase of Buses	Purchase of Municipal Park
a.	Yes	Yes
b.	No	Yes
c.	Yes	No
d.	No	No

(AICPA adapted)

Problem 16-19 *(LO 4)* **Various funds and account groups.** (Nos. 4, 5, and 8 are AICPA adapted.)

1. The following revenues were among those reported by Tosa Township in 2018:

Net rental revenue (after depreciation) from a parking garage owned by Tosa	$ 40,000
Interest earned on investments held for employees' retirement benefits.	100,000
Property taxes	6,000,000

What amount of the foregoing revenues should be accounted for in Tosa's governmental funds?

    a. $6,140,000
    b. $6,100,000
    c. $6,040,000
    d. $6,000,000

Items (2) and (3) are based on the following information:

The events relating to the city of Salbury's debt service funds that occurred during the year ended December 31, 2019, are as follows:

Debt principal matured	$2,000,000
Unmatured (accrued) interest on outstanding debt at January 1, 2019	50,000
Interest on matured debt	900,000
Unmatured (accrued) interest on outstanding debt at December 31, 2019	100,000
Interest revenue from investments	600,000
Cash transferred from the general fund for retirement of debt principal	1,000,000
Cash transferred from the general fund for payment of matured interest.	900,000

All principal and interest due in 2019 were paid on time.

2. What is the total amount of expenditures that Salbury's debt service funds should record for the year ended December 31, 2019?

   a. $940,000
   b. $950,000
   c. $2,900,000
   d. $2,500,000

3. How much revenue should Salbury's debt service funds record for the year ended December 31, 2019?

   a. $600,000
   b. $1,600,000
   c. $1,900,000
   d. $2,500,000

4. Financing for the renovation of Mink City's municipal park, begun and completed during 2019, came from the following sources:

Grant from state government.	$400,000
Proceeds from general obligation bond	500,000
Transfer from Mink's general fund.	100,000

What amounts should be recorded as revenue and other financing sources?

	Revenues	Other Financing Sources
a.	$1,000,000	$0
b.	$900,000	$100,000
c.	$400,000	$600,000
d.	$0	$1,000,000

5. On April 1, 2019, Rhine County incurred the following expenditures in issuing long-term bonds:

Issue costs	$400,000
Debt insurance.	90,000

When Rhine establishes the accounting for operating debt service, what amount should be deferred and amortized over the life of the bonds?

   a. $0
   b. $90,000
   c. $400,000
   d. $490,000

6. The initial contribution of cash from the general fund in order to establish an internal service fund would require the general fund to credit Cash and debit

   a. Accounts Receivable.
   b. Interfund Transfers-Out.

c. Interfund Loans Receivable.
d. Expenditures.
e. Residual Equity Transfers-Out.

7. The following assets are among those owned by the city of Forest Grove:

City hall	$ 800,000
Three fire stations.	1,000,000
City streets and sidewalks	5,000,000

What amount should be included in Forest Grove's general fixed assets account group?

a. Either $1,800,000 or $6,800,000
b. Either $1,000,000 or $6,000,000
c. Either $6,800,000 or $6,000,000
d. $6,800,000

8. Planter County received the following proceeds that are legally restricted to expenditure for specified purposes:

Levies on affected property owners to install sidewalks.	$500,000
Gasoline taxes to finance road repairs	900,000

What amount would be accounted for in Planter's special revenue funds?

a. $1,400,000
b. $900,000
c. $500,000
d. $0

Problem 16-20 *(LO 4)* **Various funds and account groups.** Select the *best* response for each of the following multiple-choice questions. (Nos. 1–8 are AICPA adapted.)

1. In 2019, a state government collected income taxes of $8,000,000 for the benefit of one of its cities that imposes an income tax on its residents. The state periodically remitted these collections to the city. The state should account for the $8,000,000 in the

a. general fund.
b. agency funds.
c. internal service funds.
d. special assessment funds.

2. Kew City received a $15,000,000 federal grant to finance the construction of a center for rehabilitation of drug addicts. The proceeds of this grant should be accounted for in the

a. special revenue funds.
b. general fund.
c. capital projects funds.
d. trust funds.

3. Lisa County issued $5,000,000 of general obligation bonds at 101 to finance a capital project. The $50,000 premium was to be used for payment of interest. The transactions involving the premium should be accounted for in the

a. capital projects funds, the debt service funds, and the general long-term debt account group.
b. capital projects funds and debt service funds only.
c. debt service funds and the general long-term debt account group only.
d. debt service funds only.

4. Oak Township issued the following bonds during the year ended June 30, 2011:

Bonds issued to help cover the general operating expenses of the township	$500,000
Revenue bonds to be repaid from admission fees collected by the	
Township Zoo Enterprise Fund.	350,000

What amount of these bonds should be accounted for in Oak's general long-term debt account group?

a. $0
b. $350,000
c. $500,000
d. $850,000

5. During 2019, Walnut City reported the following receipts from self-sustaining activities paid for by users of the services rendered:

Operation of water supply plant	$5,000,000
Operation of bus system	900,000

What amount should be accounted for in Walnut's enterprise funds?

a. $0
b. $900,000
c. $5,000,000
d. $5,900,000

6. Through an internal service fund, Maple County operates a centralized data-processing center to provide services to Maple's other governmental units. In 2019, this internal service fund billed Maple's Parks and Recreation Fund $25,000 for data-processing services. What account should Maple's internal service fund credit to record this $25,000 billing to the Parks and Recreation Fund?

a. Operating Revenues
b. Interfund Exchanges
c. Intergovernmental Transfers
d. Data-Processing Department Expenses

7. On December 31, 2019, Lilly Village paid a contractor $3,500,000 for the total cost of a new Village Hall built in 2019 on Lilly-owned land. Financing for the capital project was provided by a $2,000,000 general obligation bond issue sold at face amount on December 31, 2019, with the remaining $1,500,000 transferred from the general fund. What account and amount should be reported in Lilly's 2019 fund financial statements for the general fund?

a. Other Financing Sources.	$3,500,000
b. Expenditures	$3,500,000
c. Other Financing Sources.	$2,000,000
d. Other Financing Uses	$1,500,000

8. The following information pertains to Pinehurst City's special revenue fund in 2019:

Appropriations	$6,500,000
Expenditures	5,000,000
Other financing sources	1,500,000
Other financing uses	2,000,000
Revenues	8,000,000

After Pinehurst's general fund accounts were closed at the end of 2019, the fund balance increased by

a. $3,000,000.
b. $2,500,000.
c. $1,500,000.
d. $1,000,000.

Financial Reporting Issues

Learning Objectives

When you have completed this chapter, you should be able to

1. Identify the basic components of a comprehensive annual financial report (CAFR).

2. Explain which governmental entities are required to report financial information.

3. Demonstrate an understanding of the state and local government financial reporting model.

4. Tell when GASB Statement No. 34 took effect, list the requirements of the Single Audit Act, and describe what other reporting efforts the GASB has been encouraging.

As discussed in the previous chapters, in June 1999 the Governmental Accounting Standards Board (GASB) issued Statement No. 34, *Basic Financial Statements—and Management's Discussion and Analysis—for State and Local Governments*. Statement No. 34 significantly changed the financial reporting requirements for all state and local governments, including special purpose governments such as school districts, special taxing authorities, and districts. These requirements are the most significant change in the history of government financial reporting. This chapter highlights the financial reporting for state and local governments.

GASB Statement No. 34 requires several financial statements to include (1) government-wide financial statements, (2) funds-based financial statements, and (3) a management's discussion and analysis (MD&A) report. In addition, certain information must be presented in the footnotes or in separate statements or schedules. This information is considered required supplementary information (RSI). The reporting model builds from the accounting standards described in Chapters 15 and 16. The financial statements provide important information for decision makers. Information about the government as a whole is presented along with more detailed information about the funds.

ANNUAL FINANCIAL REPORTING

The principal role of financial reporting is to provide information. A *comprehensive annual financial report (CAFR)* should be prepared by every governmental unit in order to demonstrate that it has complied with the provisions of the law. The CAFR includes at least two sets of financial statements, along with their notes and any additional data that may be considered necessary. These two sets are (a) the general purpose financial statements (GPFS) and (b) combining statements for nonmajor funds by fund type.

A complete set of GPFS includes the following information:

1. Management's discussion and analysis statement.
2. Separate fund financial statements for governmental, proprietary, and fiduciary funds.
3. Government-wide financial statements presenting the entire government.

1

OBJECTIVE

Identify the basic components of a comprehensive annual financial report (CAFR).

4. Notes to the financial statements, including descriptions of the activities accounted for in the major funds, internal service fund type, and fiduciary fund types; length of time used to define "available" for purposes of revenue recognition in the governmental fund financial statements; actions taken to address significant violations of finance-related legal or contractual provisions; debt service requirements to maturity, separately identifying principal and interest for each of the subsequent five years and in 5-year increments thereafter; obligations under leases for each of the five subsequent years and in 5-year increments thereafter; a schedule of changes in short-term debt and the purpose for which short-term debt was issued; amounts due from other funds by individual major fund, nonmajor governmental funds in the aggregate, nonmajor enterprise funds in the aggregate, internal service funds in the aggregate, and fiduciary fund type, the purpose for those balances, and amounts that are not expected to be repaid within one year; interest requirements for variable-rate debt computed using the rate effective at year-end; terms of interest rate changes for variable-rate debt; details about major components of receivable and payable balances and identification of receivable balances not expected to be collected within one year; and amounts transferred from other funds by individual major fund, nonmajor governmental funds in the aggregate, nonmajor enterprise funds in the aggregate, internal service funds in the aggregate, and fiduciary fund type, a general description of the principal purposes of interfund transfers, and purposes for and amounts of certain transfers.

5. *Required supplementary information (RSI)* which includes a budgetary comparison statement or schedule, information about the condition of infrastructure assets, pension-related information, risk-financing and self-insurance activity. Although RSI contains information similar to the notes, it is not considered part of the basic financial statements and therefore may be subject to a lower level of audit scrutiny.

The general purpose financial statements as summarized in Illustration 17-1 provide the minimum financial reporting necessary for a fair presentation according to generally accepted accounting principles. The GPFS are part of the *financial section* of a comprehensive annual financial report along with the auditor's report and combining and individual funds statements that provide more detailed financial information than the combined statements. Chapter 16 illustrates several combining statements for nonmajor special revenue, permanent, capital project, and debt service funds. Combined statements are an aggregation of the individual fund financial statements. Combining statements are used to add together funds of the same type in order to present summary data in the combined statements as follows:

Combined Fund Statements

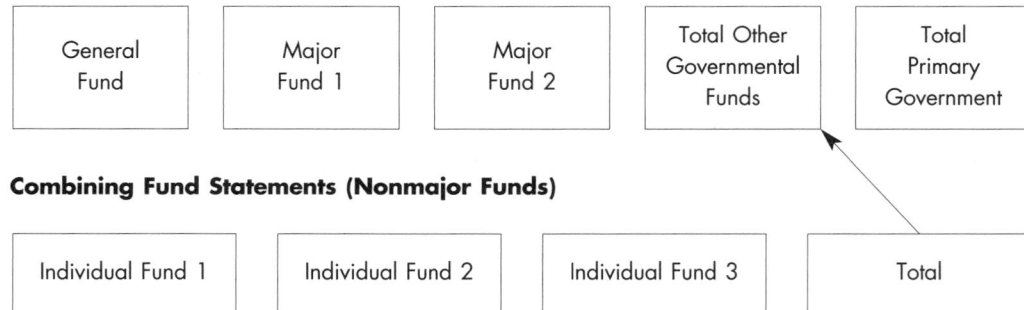

Combining Fund Statements (Nonmajor Funds)

Two additional sections of the CAFR, not part of the financial section, are the *introductory section* and the *statistical section*. The introductory section includes a table of contents, a letter of transmittal from the chief executive or finance officer to the mayor (or the mayor and legislative body), and other information. The letter of transmittal tells about the contents of the CAFR, management's view of the economic condition of the governmental unit, and the community and management's summary of governmental operating activity. The statistical section includes data, often in chart or graph form, about the governmental unit and the community such as general governmental expenditures by function and community demographic statistics.

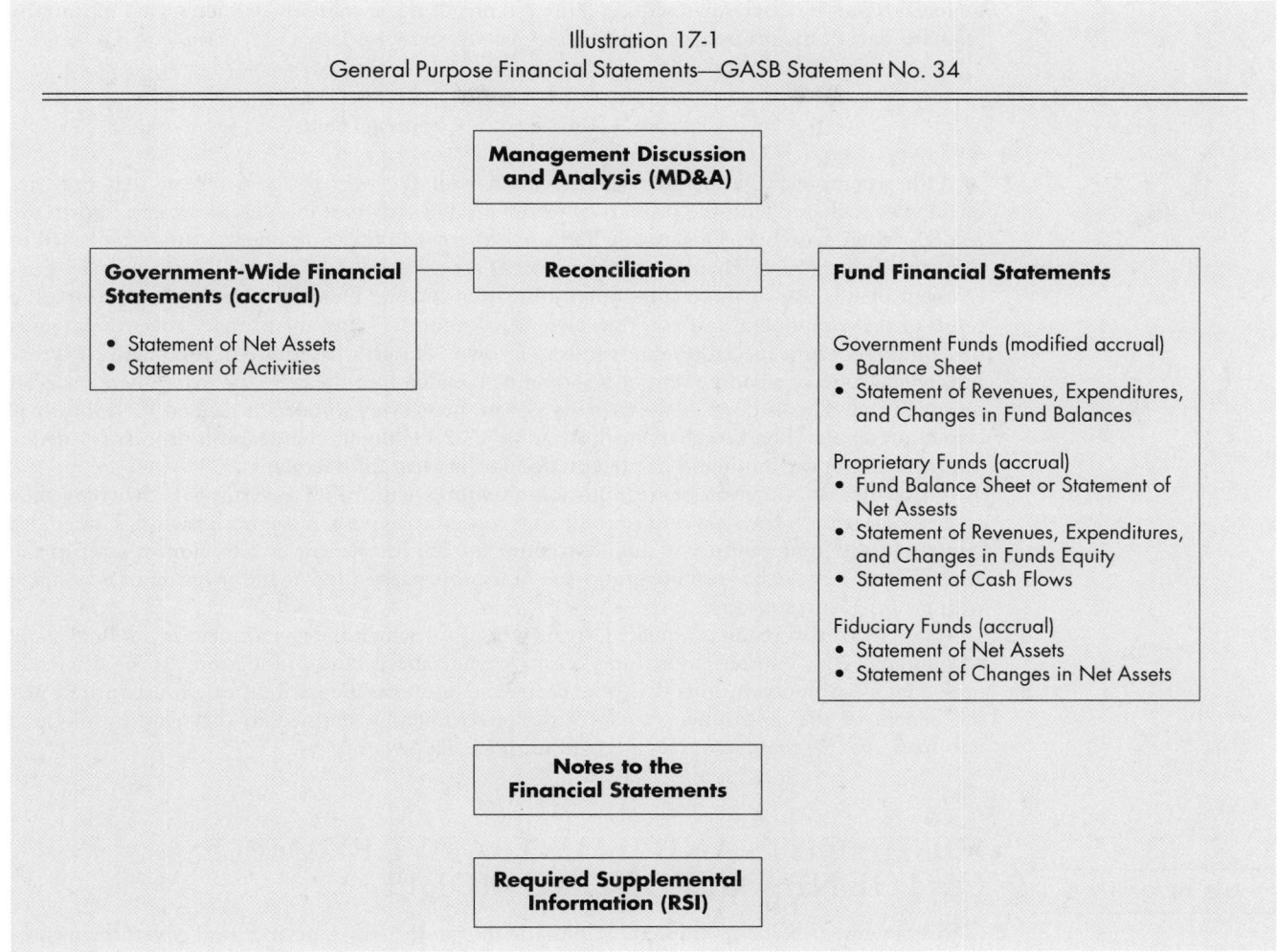

Illustration 17-1
General Purpose Financial Statements—GASB Statement No. 34

Management Discussion and Analysis (MD&A)

Government-Wide Financial Statements (accrual)

- Statement of Net Assets
- Statement of Activities

Reconciliation

Fund Financial Statements

Government Funds (modified accrual)
- Balance Sheet
- Statement of Revenues, Expenditures, and Changes in Fund Balances

Proprietary Funds (accrual)
- Fund Balance Sheet or Statement of Net Assets
- Statement of Revenues, Expenditures, and Changes in Funds Equity
- Statement of Cash Flows

Fiduciary Funds (accrual)
- Statement of Net Assets
- Statement of Changes in Net Assets

Notes to the Financial Statements

Required Supplemental Information (RSI)

REPORTING ENTITY

2

OBJECTIVE

Explain which governmental entities are required to report financial information.

GASB Statement No. 14, issued in June 1991, defines the criteria a government must use to determine whether its reporting entity should be limited to the primary government or whether one or more of the associated organizations (referred to as component units) are also part of the government's reporting entity. A primary government can be a state government, a general purpose local government such as a city or county, or a legally separate special purpose government that has a separately elected governing body and is fiscally independent of other state and local governments. A component unit is a legally separate organization for which the elected officials of the primary government are financially accountable or for which the nature and significance of the relationship with the primary government is such that exclusion would cause the financial statements of the primary government to be misleading or incomplete. Examples of component units are authorities, commissions, boards, pension plans, development corporations, hospitals, and school districts.

As indicated, the definition of the reporting entity is based primarily on the notion of *financial accountability*. Financial accountability is measured by (a) fiscal dependence or (b) the ability of a primary government to appoint a voting majority of an organization's governing body and either be able to impose its will on the potential component unit or have the potential to receive specific financial benefit or burden. Most component units should be included in the financial report by discrete presentation (i.e., in one or more columns that are separate from the financial data of the primary government) as shown below.

Total	Total
Primary Government	Component Units

Other component units are so intertwined with the primary government that they are blended or included with the primary government and only footnote disclosure can inform the reader of their existence. This usually happens either when the component unit is established to serve the primary government or the two boards are essentially the same. When a primary government blends one or more component units into its own financial statements, it reports the funds of the component unit as if they were its own funds. Thus, the primary government adds the component unit special revenue funds to its own. The only exception to this blending is that the general fund of a component unit should be blended into the primary government's special revenue fund. This is done so the primary government's very important general fund information is presented. The flowchart in Illustration 17-2 highlights the decision process for determining a component unit and its presentation in the financial statements.

Governments sometimes enter into joint ventures with other governments, whereby they agree to share both the risks and rewards of a common activity. If a government has an equity interest in the joint venture, it should account for the investment as a long-term asset in the general long-term debt account group (or in a proprietary fund if the investment was made with proprietary resources).

The GASB also requires affiliated organizations for which the government is not financially accountable, e.g., booster clubs, fund-raising organizations, and foundations, to be discretely presented as component units if (1) the economic resources are entirely, or almost entirely, for the benefit of the government, *and* (2) the government is entitled to the majority of these resources, *and* (3) these resources are significant to that government.[1]

<table>
<tr><td>

3

OBJECTIVE

Demonstrate an understanding of the state and local government financial reporting model.

</td></tr>
</table>

HIGHLIGHTS AND ILLUSTRATIVE EXAMPLES OF THE NEW REPORTING MODEL

GASB Statement No. 34 represents a dramatic shift in the way state and local governments present financial information to the public. The new statements will have more and easier-to-understand information about the government. The new reporting standard also reaffirms the importance of information that governments already include in their annual reports. Major innovations of GASB Statement No. 34 can be summarized as follows:

♦ An introductory narrative section highlighting and analyzing the governments' financial performance.

♦ A refinement of funds-based information.

♦ An overall view of the government in new government-wide statements.

♦ Comprehensive information about the cost of delivering services to citizens.

♦ Information about infrastructure assets—such as bridges, roads, and storm sewers.

Management's Discussion and Analysis

A management's discussion and analysis is provided as supplementary information before the basic financial statements. The purpose of the MD&A is to give a concise overview and analysis of the information in the government's financial statements. This analysis is focused on the

---

1 GASB Statement No. 39, *Determining Whether Certain Organizations Are Component Units—an amendment to GASB 14* (Norwalk, CT: Governmental Accounting Standards Board, May 2002).

Illustration 17-2
The Financial Reporting Entity

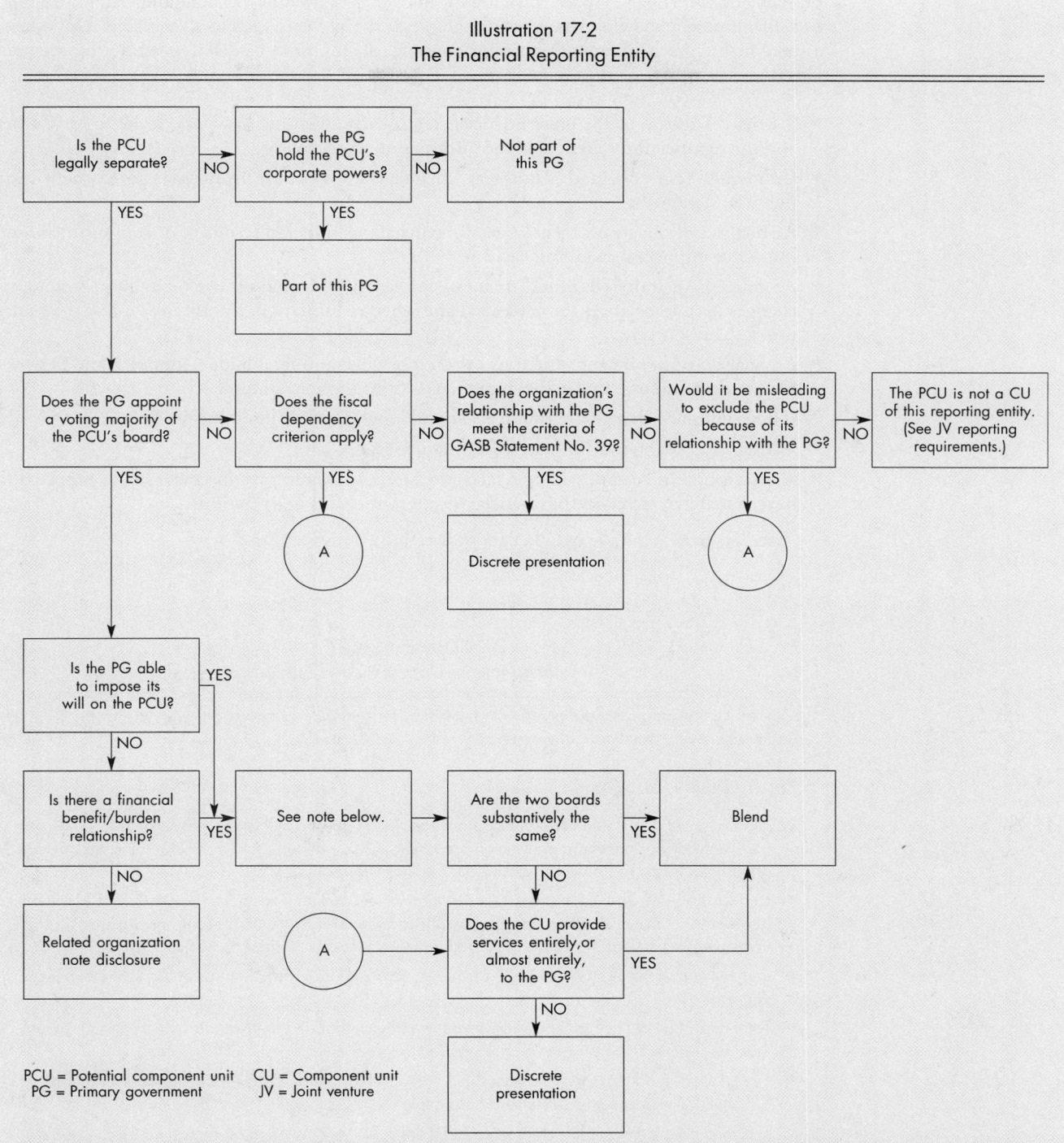

PCU = Potential component unit   CU = Component unit
 PG = Primary government   JV = Joint venture

Source: GASB Statement No. 39, *Determining Whether Certain Organizations Are Component Units—an amendment to GASB No.14, The Financial Reporting Entity,* May 2002.

primary government and is based on currently known facts, decisions, or conditions. It is not a forecast. Its purpose it to help users (citizens, the media, bond raters, creditors, legislators, and others) assess whether the government's financial position has improved or deteriorated during the year. Governments must limit the topics discussed in the MD&A to the following:[2]

◆ A brief discussion of the basic financial statements, including how they relate to each other and the significant differences in the information they provide.

◆ Condensed current- and prior-year financial information from the government-wide financial statement.

◆ An analysis of the government's overall financial position and results of operations including impact of important economic factors.

◆ An analysis of individual fund financial information, including the reasons for significant changes in fund balances (or net assets) and whether limitations significantly affect the future use of the resources.

◆ An analysis of significant variations between original and final budget amounts and between final budget amounts and actual budget results for the general fund.

◆ A description of changes in capital assets and long-term liabilities during the year.

◆ A discussion of the condition of infrastructure assets.

◆ A description of currently known facts, decisions, or conditions that have, or are expected to have, a material effect on the financial position or results of operations.

Excerpts from a sample MD&A are shown in Illustration 17-3.[3]

Illustration 17-3
Management's Discussion and Analysis

Our discussion and analysis of Dover's financial performance provides an overview of the City's financial activities for the fiscal year ended December 31, 2019.

Financial Highlights

◆ The City's net assets remained virtually unchanged as a result of this year's operations. While net assets of our business-type activities increased by $3.2 million, or nearly 4%, net assets of our governmental activities decreased by $3.1 million, or nearly 2.5%.

◆ During the year, the City had expenses that were $6.3 million more than the $99.5 million generated in tax and other revenues for governmental programs (before special items). This compares to last year, however, when expenses exceeded revenues by $8.9 million.

◆ In the City's business-type activities, revenues increased to $15 million (or 5.6%) while expenses decreased by 1.7%.

◆ Total cost of all of the City's programs was virtually unchanged (increasing by $800,000, or less than 1%) with no new programs being added this year.

◆ The general fund reported a deficit this year of $1.3 million despite the one-time proceeds of $3.5 million from the sale of some of our park land.

◆ The resources available for appropriation were $1.1 million less than budgeted for the general fund. However, we kept expenditures within spending limits primarily through a mid-year hiring and overtime freeze and our continuing staff restructuring efforts.

---

2 GASB Statement No. 37, *Basic Financial Statements—and Management's Discussion and Analysis—for State and Local Governments: Omnibus* (Norwalk, CT: Governmental Accounting Standards Board, June 2001) requires governments to confine topics in the MD&A.

3 Illustrations 17-3 through 17-13 are adapted from GASB Statement No. 34, *Basic Financial Statements—and Management's Discussion and Analysis—for State and Local Governments*, pp. 151, 201, 210–211, 220–224, 228–231, 235–236, 254–255, 258–261, and 269.

Using this Annual Report

This annual report consists of a series of financial statements. The statement of net assets and the statement of activities [on pages 904 (Illustration 17-12) pages 907 and 908 (Illustration 17-13)] provide information about the activities of the City as a whole and present a longer-term view of the City's finances. Fund financial statements start on page 894 (Illustration 17-4). For governmental activities, these statements tell how these services were financed in the short term as well as what remains for future spending. Fund financial statements also report the City's operations in more detail than the government-wide statements by providing information about the City's most significant funds. The remaining statements provide financial information about activities for which the City acts solely as a trustee or agent for the benefit of those outside the government.

Reporting the City as a Whole

The Statement of Net Assets and the Statement of Activities

Our analysis of the City as a whole begins on page 892 (Table 1). One of the most important questions asked about the City's finances would be, "Is the City as a whole better or worse off as a result of the year's activities?" The statement of net assets and the statement of activities report information about the City as a whole and about its activities in a way that helps answer this question. These statements include *all* assets and liabilities using *the accrual basis of accounting,* which is similar to the accounting used by most private-sector companies. All of the current year's revenues and expenses are taken into account regardless of when cash is received or paid.

These two statements report the City's net assets and changes in them. You can think of the City's net assets—the difference between assets and liabilities—as one way to measure the City's financial health, or *financial position.* Over time, *increases* or *decreases* in the City's net assets are one indicator of whether its *financial health* is improving or deteriorating. You will need to consider other nonfinancial factors, however, such as changes in the City's property tax base and the condition of the City's roads, to assess the *overall health* of the City.

In the statement of net assets and the statement of activities, we divide the City into three kinds of activities:

◆ Governmental activities—Most of the City's basic services are reported here, including the police, fire, public works, and parks departments, and general administration. Property taxes, franchise fees, and state and federal grants finance most of these activities.

◆ Business-type activities—The City charges a fee to customers to help it cover all or most of the cost of certain services it provides. The City's water and sewer system and parking facilities are reported here.

◆ Component units—The City includes two separate legal entities in its report: the City School District and the City Landfill Authority. Although legally separate, these "component units" are important because the City is financially accountable for them.

Reporting the City's Most Significant Funds

Fund Financial Statements

Our analysis of the City's major funds begins on page 893. The fund financial statements begin on page 894 (Illustration 17-4) and provide detailed information about the most significant funds—not the City as a whole. Some funds are required to be established by state law and by bond covenants. However, the city council establishes many other funds to help it control and manage money for particular purposes (like the Route 7 reconstruction project) or to show that it is meeting legal responsibilities for using certain taxes, grants, and other money (such as grants received from the U.S. Department of Housing and Urban Development). The City's two kinds of funds—*governmental and proprietary*—use different accounting approaches.

◆ Governmental funds—Most of the City's basic services are reported in governmental funds, which focus on how money flows into and out of those funds and the balances left at year-end that are available for spending. These funds are reported using an accounting method called

(continued)

modified accrual accounting, which measures cash and all other financial assets that can readily be converted to cash. The governmental fund statements provide a detailed short-term view of the City's general government operations and the basic services it provides. Governmental fund information helps you determine whether there are more or fewer financial resources that can be spent in the near future to finance the City's programs. We describe the relationship (or differences) between governmental activities (reported in the statement of net assets and the statement of activities) and governmental funds in a reconciliation at the bottom of the fund financial statements.

◆ Proprietary funds—When the City charges customers for the services it provides—whether to outside customers or to other units of the City—these services are generally reported in proprietary funds. Proprietary funds are reported in the same way that all activities are reported in the statement of net assets and the statement of activities. In fact, the City's enterprise funds (a component of proprietary funds) are the same as the business-type activities we report in the government-wide statements but provide more detail and additional information, such as cash flows, for proprietary funds. We use internal service funds (the other component of proprietary funds) to report activities that provide supplies and services for the City's other programs and activities—such as the City's Telecommunications Fund.

The City as Trustee

Reporting the City's Fiduciary Responsibilities

The City is the trustee, or fiduciary, for its employees' pension plans. It is also responsible for other assets that—because of a trust arrangement—can be used only for the trust beneficiaries. All of the City's fiduciary activities are reported in separate statements of fiduciary net assets and changes in fiduciary net assets on pages 901 and 902 (Illustration 17-9 and 17-10). We exclude these activities from the City's other financial statements because the City cannot use these assets to finance its operations. The City is responsible for ensuring that the assets reported in these funds are used for their intended purposes.

The City as a Whole

The City's combined net assets were virtually unchanged from a year ago—increasing from $209.0 million to $209.1 million. In contrast, last year net assets decreased by $6.2 million. Looking at the net assets and net expenses of governmental and business-type activities separately, however, reveals two very different stories. Our analysis below focuses on the net assets (Table 1) of the City's governmental and business-type activities.

Table 1
Net Assets
(in millions)

	Governmental Activities		Business-Type Activities		Total Primary Government	
	2019	2018	2019	2018	2019	2018
Current and other assets	$ 54.3	$ 49.0	$ 13.8	$ 15.7	$ 68.1	$ 64.7
Capital assets	170.0	162.1	151.4	147.6	321.4	309.7
Total assets.	$ 224.3	$211.1	$165.2	$163.3	$ 389.5	$ 374.4
Long-term debt outstanding	$ (79.3)	$ (61.8)	$ (78.3)	$ (77.3)	$(157.6)	$(139.1)
Other liabilities	(21.4)	(22.6)	(1.4)	(3.7)	(22.8)	(26.3)
Total liabilities	$(100.7)	$ (84.4)	$ (79.7)	$ (81.0)	$(180.4)	$(165.4)
Net assets:						
Invested in capital assets, net of debt	$ 103.7	$100.3	$ 73.1	$ 71.6	$ 176.8	$ 171.9
Restricted	22.8	27.1	1.4	2.8	24.2	29.9
Unrestricted (deficit).	(2.9)	(0.7)	11.0	7.9	8.1	7.2
Total net assets.	$ 123.6	$126.7	$ 85.5	$ 82.3	$ 209.1	$ 209.0

Source: Government Accounting Standards Board Statement No. 34, *Basic Financial Statements—and Management's Discussion and Analysis—for State and Local Government,* June 1999, Appendix C.

Net assets of the City's governmental activities decreased by 2.5% ($123.6 million compared to $126.7 million). Unrestricted net assets—the part of net assets that can be used to finance day-to-day operations without constraints established by debt covenants, enabling legislation, or other legal requirements—changed from a $700,000 deficit at December 31, 2018, to a $2.9 million deficit at the end of this year.

This deficit in unrestricted governmental net assets arose primarily because of three factors. First, the City did not include in past annual budgets the amounts needed to fully finance liabilities arising from property and casualty claims. The City does not purchase commercial insurance to cover these claims. The City also did not include in past budgets amounts needed to pay for unused employee vacation and sick days. The City will need to include these amounts in future years' budgets as they come due. Second, during the past two years, tax revenues and state grants have fallen short of amounts originally anticipated. Finally, the city council decided to draw down accumulated cash balances to delay the need to approve new tax increases.

The net assets of our business-type activities increased by 3.9% ($85.5 million compared to $82.3 million) in 2019. This increase, however, cannot be used to make up for the decrease reported in governmental activities. The City generally can only use these net assets to finance the continuing operations of the water and sewer and parking operations.

Source: Adapted from GASB Statement No. 34, *Basic Financial Statements—and Management's Discussion and Analysis—for State and Local Governments,* pp. 151, 201, 210–211, 220–224, 228–231, 235–236, 254–255, 258–261, and 269.

Funds-Based Statements

The focus in the funds-based statements is to provide detailed information about short-term spending and fiscal compliance by major funds. Separate funds-based statements for governmental, proprietary, and fiduciary funds are required. The statements highlight *major* funds in separate columns and aggregate nonmajor funds into one additional column. The general fund is always considered a major fund. Other major funds are defined as those in which assets, liabilities, revenues, or expenditures/expenses are at least 10% of all funds in that category or type (i.e., all governmental *or* all enterprise funds, respectively), *and* the same element is also at least 5% of all government and enterprise funds combined. In addition, a government may designate as major any other governmental or enterprise fund it believes is important to the users of its financial statements. This gives government officials great latitude in deciding how data are presented in the statements to promote better understanding of its activities and financial health.

Illustrations 17-4 and 17-5 (shown on pages 894 and 896) show examples of a governmental funds balance sheet and a governmental funds statement of revenues, expenditures, and changes in fund balances for the city of Dover. Following a separate column for the general fund and each major fund, the remaining nonmajor funds are added together into one column, and the final column presents a total of all governmental funds. Note that the nonmajor funds are included in the column titled *Total Nonmajor Funds* and that the fund balance includes special revenue, debt service, capital project, and permanent fund information, as described in Chapter 16 after adjusting out the major fund balances.

Proprietary funds statements will include enterprise funds and internal service funds. Enterprise funds that meet the percentage test described previously will be presented individually. A column that summarizes all nonmajor enterprise funds is included, and a total for all enterprise funds is provided. The enterprise funds are also called *business-type activities.* Internal service funds are classified as proprietary funds in the funds-based statements and reported as a separate column because their services usually are provided predominantly to general government activities. Internal service funds are *governmental activities.*

Illustrations 17-6 and 17-7 (shown on pages 896 to 898) present the proprietary funds balance sheet and the statement of revenues, expenses, and changes in fund net assets, respectively.

Illustration 17-4
City of Dover
Balance Sheet
Governmental Funds
December 31, 2019
(in thousands)

	General Fund	Housing Program	Community Block Grants	Parking and Recreation	Total Nonmajor Funds	Total Governmental Funds
Assets:						
Cash and cash equivalents	$3,418	$1,237			$ 5,607	$10,262
Investments	—	—	$13,263	$10,467	3,485	27,215
Receivables (net)	3,645	2,953	353	11	10	6,972
Due from other funds	1,371		—	—		1,371
Receivables from other governments		119	—	—	1,596	1,715
Liens receivable	792	3,196	—	—	—	3,988
Inventories	183	—	—	—	—	183
Total assets.	$9,409	$7,505	$13,616	$10,478	$10,698	$51,706
Liabilities and fund balances:						
Liabilities:						
Accounts payable	$3,409	$ 131	$ 191	$ 1,105	$ 1,075	$ 5,911
Due to other funds	—	25	—	—	—	25
Payable to other governments . . .	94	—	—	—	—	94
Deferred revenue	4,251	6,273	250	10	—	10,784
Total liabilities	$7,754	$6,429	$ 441	$ 1,115	$ 1,075	$16,814
Fund balances:						
Nonspendable						
Inventories	$ 183		$ —	$ —	$ —	$ 183
Restricted for:						
Debt services	—	—	—	—	3,832	3,832
Restricted for:						
Liens receivable	792		—	—	—	792
Assigned for:						
Encumbrances	40	$ 41	119	5,793	1,814	7,807
Other purposes			—	—	1,405	1,405
Special revenue funds		1,035	—	—	1,331	2,366
Capital projects funds	—	—	13,056	3,570	1,241	17,867
Unassigned in:			—	—	—	—
General fund	640		—	—	—	640
Total fund balances	$1,655	$1,076	$13,175	$ 9,363	$ 9,623	$34,892
Total liabilities and fund balances . .	$9,409	$7,505	$13,616	$10,478	$10,698	$51,706

Total fund balances—Governmental funds	$ 34,892
Amounts reported for governmental funds in statement of net assets are different because:	
Capital assets used in governmental activities are not financial resources and are not reported in the funds.	161,083
Other long-term assets not available to pay for current-period expenditures are deferred in the funds.	9,349
Internal service funds assets and liabilities are included in governmental activities in the statement of net assets.	2,995*
Long-term liabilities, including bonds payable, are not reported in the funds.	(84,760)
Net assets of governmental activities	$123,559

*See Illustration 17-7 (Internal service funds, Total net assets—ending)

Note: See Illustration 17-14 for a more detailed explanation.

Source: Adapted from GASB Statement No. 34, *Basic Financial Statements—and Management's Discussion and Analysis—for State and Local Governments*, pp. 151, 201, 210–211, 220–224, 228–231, 235–236, 254–255, 258–261, and 269.

Illustration 17-5
City of Dover
Statement of Revenues, Expenditures, and Changes in Fund Balances
Governmental Funds
For Year Ended December 31, 2019
(in thousands)

	General Fund	Housing Program	Community Block Grants	Parking and Recreation	Total Nonmajor Funds	Total Governmental Funds
Revenues:						
Property taxes	$51,173	$ —	$ —	$ —	$ 4,680	$ 55,853
Franchise taxes	4,056	—	—	—	—	4,056
Public service taxes	8,970	—	—	—	—	8,970
Fees and fines	607	—	—	—	—	607
Licenses and permits	2,288	—	—	—	—	2,288
Intergovernmental	6,120	2,578	—	—	2,831	11,529
Charges for services	11,374	—	—	—	31	11,405
Investment earnings	552	87	549	270	364	1,822
Miscellaneous	882	66	—	3		951
Total revenues	$86,022	$2,731	$ 549	$ 273	$ 7,906	$ 97,481
Expenditures:						
Current:						
General government	$ 8,631	$ —	$ 418	$ 17	$ 121	$ 9,187
Public safety	33,730	—	—			33,730
Public works	4,976	—	—		3,722	8,698
Engineering services	1,300	—	—	—	—	1,300
Health and sanitation	6,070	—	—	—	—	6,070
Cemetery	706	—	—	—	—	706
Culture and recreation	11,412	—	—	—	—	11,412
Community development	—	2,954	—	—	—	2,954
Education—payment to school district	21,893	—	—	—	—	21,893
Debt service				—		
Principal	—	—	—	—	3,450	3,450
Interest and other charges	—	—	—	—	5,215	5,215
Capital outlay	—	—	2,247	11,282	3,190	16,719
Total expenditures	$88,718	$2,954	$ 2,665	$ 11,299	$ 15,698	$121,334
Excess (deficiency) of revenues over expenditure	$ (2,696)	$ (223)	$ (2,116)	$(11,026)	$ (7,792)	$ (23,853)
Other financing sources (uses):						
Proceeds of refunding bonds	$ —	$ —	$ —	$ —	$ 38,045	$ 38,045
Proceeds of long-term capital-related debt	—	—	17,530	—	1,300	18,830
Payment to bond refunding escrow	—	—	—	—	(37,284)	(37,284)
Transfer-in	129	—	—	—	5,551	5,680
Transfer-out	(2,164)	(348)	(2,273)	—	(219)	(5,004)
Total other financing sources and uses	$ (2,035)	$ (348)	$15,257	$ —	$ 7,393	$ 20,267
Special item—proceeds from sales in park	$ 3,476	$ —	$ —	$ —	$ —	$ 3,476
Net change in fund balances	$ (1,255)	$ (571)	$13,141	$(11,026)	$ (399)	$ (110)
Fund balances—beginning	2,910	1,647	34	20,389	10,022	35,002
Fund balances—ending	$ 1,655	$1,076	$13,175	$ 9,363	$ 9,623	$ 34,892

(continued)

City of Dover
Reconciliation of the Statement of Revenues, Expenditures, and
Changes in Fund Balances of Governmental Funds to the Statement of Activities
For Year Ended December 31, 2019
(in thousands)

Net change in fund balances—total governmental funds	$ (110)
Amounts reported for governmental activities in the statement of activities are different because:	
Governmental funds report capital outlays as expenditures.	
However, in the statement of activities, depreciation expense is recorded. Necessary adjustment—the amount by which capital outlay exceeds depreciation.	14,040
In the statement of activities, only the gain on the sale of the park land is reported.	
Governmental funds report the proceeds from the sale as an increase in financial resources. Necessary adjustment—the cost of the land sold.	(823)
Revenues in the statement of activities that do not provide current financial resources are not reported as revenues in the funds.	1,921
Bond proceeds provide current financial resources to governmental funds, but issuing debt increases long-term liabilities in the statement of net assets. Repayment of bond principal is an expenditure in the governmental funds, but the repayment reduces long-term liabilities in the statement of net assets. Necessary adjustment—amount of proceeds less repayments.	(16,140)
Some expenses reported in the statement of activities do not require the use of current financial resources and therefore are not reported as expenditures in governmental funds.	(1,243)
The net revenue (expense) of internal service funds determined to be governmental type.	(759)
Total changes in net assets of governmental activities (see Illustration 17-13)	$ (3,114)

Source: Adapted from GASB Statement No. 34, *Basic Financial Statements—and Management's Discussion and Analysis—for State and Local Governments*, pp. 151, 201, 210–211, 220–224, 228–231, 235–236, 254–255, 258–261, and 269.

Illustration 17-6
City of Dover
Balance Sheet
Proprietary Funds
December 31, 2019
(in thousands)

	Major Enterprise Funds			Internal Service Funds
	Electric Utility	Water & Sewer	Totals	
Assets:				
Current assets:				
Cash	$ 8,417	$ 369	$ 8,786	$ 3,336
Investments	—	—	—	150
Receivables (net)	3,564	4	3,568	158
Due from other governments	41	—	41	—
Inventories	127	—	127	139
Total current assets	$ 12,149	$ 373	$ 12,522	$ 3,783

(continued)

| | Major Enterprise Funds | | | Internal Service |
	Electric Utility	Water & Sewer	Totals	Funds
Assets (continued):				
Noncurrent assets:				
Restricted cash and cash equivalents...............	$ —	$ 1,493	$ 1,493	$ —
Capital assets:			—	
Land..	814	3,022	3,835	—
Distribution and collection systems...............	39,504	—	39,504	—
Buildings and equipment.......................	106,136	23,029	129,165	14,722
Less accumulated depreciation	(15,329)	(5,787)	(21,115)	(5,782)
Total noncurrent assets....................	$131,125	$21,757	$152,882	$ 8,940
Total assets	$143,274	$22,130	$165,404	$12,723
Liabilities:				
Current liabilities:				
Accounts payable	$ 447	$ 304	$ 751	$ 781
Due to other funds	175	—	175	1,170
Compensated absences	113	9	122	237
Claims and judgments.........................	—	—	—	1,688
Bonds, notes, and loans payable.................	3,945	360	4,305	249
Total current liabilities	$ 4,680	$ 673	$ 5,353	$ 4,125
Noncurrent liabilities:				
Compensated absences	$ 451	$ 35	$ 486	$
Claims and judgments.........................	—	—	—	5,603
Bonds, notes, and loans payable.................	54,452	19,544	73,996	—
Total noncurrent liabilities	$ 54,903	$19,579	$ 74,482	$ 5,603
Total liabilities	$ 59,583	$20,252	$ 79,835	$ 9,728
Net assets:				
Invested in capital assets, net of related debt...........	$ 72,728	$ 361	$ 73,089	$ 8,690
Restricted for debt service	—	1,452	1,452	—
Unrestricted...................................	10,963	65	11,028	(5,695)
Total net assets................................	$ 83,691	$ 1,878	$ 85,569[a]	$ 2,995[b]
Total liabilities and net assets......................	$143,274	$22,130	$165,404	$12,723

[a]Although internal service funds are classified as proprietary funds, they account for governmental activities and are reported separately from the proprietary funds that account for business-type activities. Information in the Totals column on this statement flows directly to the Business-Type Activities column on the statement of net assets (see Illustration 17-12).

[b]Information in the Internal Service Funds column is combined with other governmental activities in Illustration 17-12.

Source: Adapted from GASB Statement No. 34, *Basic Financial Statements—and Management's Discussion and Analysis—for State and Local Governments,* pp. 151, 201, 210–211, 220–224, 228–231, 235–236, 254–255, 258–261, and 269.

Illustration 17-7
City of Dover
Statement of Revenues, Expenses, and Changes in Fund Net Assets
Proprietary Fund
For Year Ended December 31, 2019
(in thousands)

	Major Enterprise Funds			Internal Service Funds
	Electric Utility	Water & Sewer	Totals	
Operating revenues:				
Charges for services	$11,330	$ 1,340	$12,670	$15,255
Miscellaneous	—	4	4	1,067
Total operating revenues	$11,330	$ 1,344	$12,674	$16,322
Operating expenses:				
Personal services	$ 3,401	$ 762	$ 4,163	$ 4,157
Contractual services	345	96	441	584
Utilities	754	101	855	215
Repairs and maintenance	747	65	812	1,961
Other supplies and expenses	498	17	515	234
Insurance claims and expenses	—	—	—	8,004
Depreciation	1,163	542	1,705	1,708
Total operating expenses	$ 6,908	$ 1,583	$ 8,491	$16,863
Operating income (loss)	$ 4,422	$ (239)	$ 4,183	$ (541)
Nonoperating revenues (expenses):				
Interest and investment revenue	$ 455	$ 146	$ 601	$ 135
Miscellaneous revenue	—	105	105	21
Interest expense	(1,601)	(1,166)	(2,767)	(42)
Miscellaneous expense	—	(47)	(47)	(176)
Total nonoperating revenue (expenses)	$ (1,146)	$ (962)	$ (2,108)	$ (62)
Income (loss) before contributions and transfers	$ 3,276	$(1,201)	$ 2,075	$ (603)
Capital contributions	$ 1,646	$ —	$ 1,646	$ 19
Transfers-out	(290)	(211)	(501)	(175)
Change in net assets	$ 4,632	$(1,412)	$ 3,220	$ (759)
Total net assets—beginning	79,059	3,290	82,349	3,754
Total net assets—ending	$83,691	$ 1,878	$85,569	$ 2,995

Source: Adapted from GASB Statement No. 34, *Basic Financial Statements—and Management's Discussion and Analysis—for State and Local Governments,* pp. 151, 201, 210–211, 220–224, 228–231, 235–236, 254–255, 258–261, and 269.

In the net assets section of the balance sheet, equity (or net assets) of a proprietary fund is classified into three broad components:

1. *Invested in capital (fixed) assets, net of related debt*—This amount includes the fixed assets of the fund less all fixed asset-related debt (both current and long term).

2. *Restricted*—This amount includes the difference between assets externally restricted by creditors, grantors, donors, or laws and regulations of other governments or internally restricted by constitutional provisions or enabling legislation and any liabilities payable from these restricted assets.

3. *Unrestricted*—This amount includes the difference between the remaining assets and liabilities in the fund as well as reclassified restricted assets when the government has satisfied the restriction.

A statement of cash flows is also required for enterprise and internal service fund activities (see Illustration 17-8 on pages 899 and 900). All governments report their cash flows in four categories. *Operating cash flows* from basic operating purposes are reported first. Most of these cash flows are related to the provision of services and the production and sale of goods. *Cash flows from financing activities* are broken down into (a) *cash flows from noncapital financing* which relate to borrowing for purposes other than buying or constructing capital assets and to certain grants and subsidies to and from other governments and (b) *capital and related financing cash flows* from borrowing and repaying funds for the purposes of purchasing, building, or reconstructing capital assets and selling capital assets and aid received from other levels of government to finance capital. Finally, *investing cash flows* relate to the acquisition and sale of investments, loan of money, and collection on loans. Almost all of the receipts in this category are interest and dividends from investments. The *direct method* of presentation of cash flows from operations is *required*. In addition, major enterprise funds are reported in separate columns.

Fiduciary funds are presented using a format similar to the guidance in the pension standards (see Chapter 16, pages 852 and 853). Fiduciary funds are used to account for resources the government holds while acting as the trustee or agent for an outside individual or organization as defined in Chapter 16. The two required statements for the fiduciary funds, the statement of fiduciary net assets and the statement of changes in fiduciary net assets, are shown in Illustrations 17-9 and 17-10.

Illustration 17-8
City of Dover
Statement of Cash Flows
Proprietary Fund
For Year Ended December 31, 2019
(in thousands)

	Major Enterprise Funds			Internal Service Funds
	Electric Utility	Water & Sewer	Totals	
Cash flows from operating activities:				
Receipts from customers..........................	$11,400	$ 1,345	$ 12,745	$15,326
Payments to suppliers	(2,725)	(365)	(3,090)	(2,812)
Payments to employees	(3,360)	(751)	(4,111)	(4,210)
Internal activity—payments.......................	(1,297)	—	(1,297)	—
Claims paid.....................................	—	—	—	(8,482)
Other receipts (payments)	(2,325)	—	(2,325)	1,061
Net cash provided by operating activities..............	$ 1,693	$ 229	$ 1,922	$ 883
Cash flows from noncapital and related financing activities:				
Operating subsidies and transfers to other funds............	$ (290)	$ (211)	$ (501)	$ (175)
Cash flows from capital and related financing activities:				
Proceeds from capital debt	$ 4,041	$ 8,661	$ 12,702	$ —
Capital contributions.............................	1,646	—	1,646	—
Purchases of capital assets.........................	(4,194)	(145)	(4,339)	(400)
Principal paid on capital debt.......................	(2,178)	(8,895)	(11,073)	(954)
Interest paid on capital debt	(1,480)	(1,166)	(2,646)	(41)
Other receipts (payments)	—	19	19	131
Net cash (used) by capital and related financing activities.....................................	$ (2,165)	$(1,526)	$ (3,691)	$ (1,264)

(continued)

	Major Enterprise Funds			
	Electric Utility	Water & Sewer	Totals	Internal Service Funds
Cash flows from investing activities:				
Proceeds from sales and maturates of investments	$ 455	$ 144	$ 599	$ 145
Net cash provided by investing activities.	$ 455	$ 144	$ 599	$ 145
Net (decrease) in cash and cash equivalents.	$ (307)	$(1,364)	$ (1,671)	$ (411)
Balances—beginning of the year	8,724	1,733	10,457	3,747
Balances—end of the year	$ 8,417	$ 369	$ 8,786	$ 3,336
Reconciliation of operating income (loss) to net cash provided (used) by operating activities:				
Operating income (loss)	$ 4,422	$ (239)	$ 4,183	$ (541)
Adjustments to reconcile operating income to net cash provided (used) by operating activities:				
Depreciation expense	1,163	542	1,705	1,708
Change in assets and liabilities:				
Receivables (net)	653	1	654	32
Inventories	3	—	3	40
Accounts and other payables.	(297)	(87)	(384)	(475)
Accrued expenses	(4,251)	12	(4,239)	(831)
Net cash provided by operating activities.	$ 1,693	$ 229	$ 1,922	$ 883

Source: Adapted from GASB Statement No. 34, *Basic Financial Statements—and Management's Discussion and Analysis—for State and Local Governments*, pp. 151, 201, 210–211, 220–224, 228–231, 235–236, 254–255, 258–261, and 269.

Perhaps the most notable features of the funds statements are in the format (column titles) being given by major fund rather than by fund type; the use of separate statements for governmental, proprietary, and fiduciary funds; and the presentation of equity in the proprietary fund balance sheet. Other highlights include:

◆ Permanent funds account for assets legally restricted so that the earnings, but not the principal, may be used to finance governmental programs.

◆ General fixed assets, including infrastructure assets, and general long-term debt are included only in the government-wide financial statements. A schedule is required for general fixed assets detailing the beginning balances—followed by additions, deductions, and depreciation charged in the current period—to reconcile to the ending balance. A schedule is also required for general long-term debt to give information on beginning balances, new debt issued, debt principal retired, and ending balances.

◆ All interfund activity is classified as either reciprocal or nonreciprocal. Reciprocal interfund activities include (1) interfund loans, which are treated as due to/from (short-term) or advances to/from (long-term), and (2) interfund services between governmental and proprietary funds that are reported as revenue and expenditures/expenses. Nonreciprocal interfund activities include (1) interfund transfers and (2) interfund reimbursements. All transfers are reported in the government funds as "other financing sources or uses." And, in the proprietary funds, all transfers are reported simply as "transfers." Payments in lieu of taxes are classified as transfers. Extensive footnotes are required to provide users of the financial statements detailed information about the purpose and nature of these transfers and the funds affected.

Illustration 17-9
City of Dover
Statement of Fiduciary Net Assets
Fiduciary Funds
December 31, 2019

	Employee Retirement Plan	Private-Purpose Trust	Agency Funds
Assets:			
Cash and cash equivalents	$ 2,000	$ 1,250	$ 4,500
Receivables:			
Interest and dividends	$ 51,000	$ 700	$ —
Other receivables	7,000	—	18,000
Total receivables	$ 58,000	$ 700	$18,000
Investments, at fair value:			
U.S. government obligations	$ 13,000	$80,000	$ —
Municipal bonds	65,000	—	—
Corporate bonds	16,000	—	—
Corporate stocks	26,000	—	—
Other investments	32,000	—	—
Total investments	$152,000	$80,000	$ —
Total assets.	$212,000	$81,950	$22,500
Liabilities:			
Accounts payable	$ —	$ 1,950	$ —
Refunds payable and others	1,000	—	22,500
Total liabilities	$ 1,000	$ 1,950	$22,500
Net assets:			
Held in trust for pension benefits and			
other purposes	$211,000	$80,000	

Source: Adapted from GASB Statement No. 34, *Basic Financial Statements—and Management's Discussion and Analysis—for State and Local Governments*, pp. 151, 201, 210–211, 220–224, 228–231, 235–236, 254–255, 258–261, and 269.

◆ Special and extraordinary items are reported separately in both the governmental and proprietary fund financial statements. *Extraordinary items* are defined as in business accounting—both unusual in nature and infrequent in occurrence. *Special items* are defined as arising from significant transactions or other events that are (1) within the control of management and (2) either unusual in nature or infrequent in occurrence. Special items are reported separately and before extraordinary items. Footnote disclosure is required for any significant transactions or other events that are either unusual or infrequent but not within the control of management.

◆ Budgetary comparisons are required in either a separate statement or schedule as part of the integrated set of basic financial statements or as required supplementary information. Further, a column for the original budget as well as the final revised budget column must be included. The final budget is compared with actual amounts using the government's budgetary basis to determine compliance with the legally adopted budget. Budgetary comparisons are required for the general fund and for each annually budgeted major special revenue fund. Illustration 17-11 shows a budgetary comparison schedule for the city of Dover general fund. No budgetary comparisons are required in the basic financial statements or RSI for any capital project, debt service, or permanent funds.

Illustration 17-10
City of Dover
Statement of Changes in Fiduciary Net Assets
Fiduciary Funds
December 31, 2019

	Employee Retirement Plan	Private-Purpose Trust
Additions:		
Contributions:		
Employer	$ 47,000	$ —
Plan members	44,000	—
Total contributions	$ 91,000	$ —
Investment earnings:		
Net (decrease) in fair value of investments......	$ (11,500)	$ —
Interest	95,000	4,500
Dividends..	70,000	—
Total investment earnings........................	$153,500	$ 4,500
Less investment expense..........................	15,000	—
Net investment earnings.........................	$138,500	$ 4,500
Total additions	$229,500	$ 4,500
Deductions:		
Benefits	$ 24,500	$ 3,800
Refunds of contribution	46,000	—
Administrative expenses	9,000	700
Total deductions..................................	$ 79,500	$ 4,500
Change in net assets	$150,000	$ —
Net assets—beginning of the year	61,000	80,000
Net assets—end of the year........................	$211,000	$80,000

Source: Adapted from GASB Statement No. 34, *Basic Financial Statements—and Management's Discussion and Analysis—for State and Local Governments*, pp. 151, 201, 210–211, 220–224, 228–231, 235–236, 254–255, 258–261, and 269.

Illustration 17-11
City of Dover
Budgetary Comparison Schedule
General Fund
For Year Ended December 31, 2019

	Budgeted Amounts		Actual Amounts (Budgetary Basis)	Variance with Final Budget Positive (Negative)
	Original	Final		
Budgetary fund balance, January 1	$ 5,250	$ 5,250	$ 5,250	$ —
Resources (inflows):				
Property taxes	52,000	51,800	52,000	(200)
Franchise taxes	45,000	42,000	40,000	2,000
Public service taxes	90,000	90,000	90,000	—

(continued)

| | Budgeted Amounts | | Actual Amounts | Variance with Final Budget |
	Original	Final	(Budgetary Basis)	Positive (Negative)
Licenses and permits	$ 12,000	$ 12,300	$ 12,000	$ 300
Fines and forfeitures.........................	42,300	40,000	41,000	(1,000)
Charges for services	12,000	11,200	9,000	2,200
Grants	55,000	55,000	52,000	3,000
Sale of land	33,500	35,000	34,750	250
Miscellaneous	95,000	90,000	88,000	2,000
Interest received.............................	48,000	50,000	55,000	(5,000)
Transfers from other funds	50,000	50,000	53,000	(3,000)
Amounts available for appropriation...........	$540,050	$532,550	$532,000	$ 550
Charges to appropriations (outflows)				
General government:				
Legal	$ 26,000	$ 26,000	$ 25,500	$ 500
Mayor, legislative, city manager	25,000	25,000	24,000	1,000
Finance and accounting....................	9,000	9,500	8,000	1,500
City clerk and elections	5,000	3,500	3,000	500
Employee relations.........................	7,000	10,000	11,300	(1,300)
Planning and economic development	14,000	14,000	14,200	(200)
Public safety:				—
Police....................................	11,000	10,000	10,500	(500)
Fire department	17,000	16,000	15,500	500
Emergency medical services	12,000	12,000	12,000	—
Inspections...............................	5,000	5,000	5,000	—
Public works:				—
Public works administration	18,500	19,000	18,750	250
Street maintenance	11,500	11,000	11,250	(250)
Street lighting.............................	7,000	7,200	7,500	(300)
Traffic operations	8,000	8,000	8,000	—
Mechanical maintenance	5,000	5,000	4,500	500
Engineering services:				
Engineering administration	5,700	5,500	6,000	(500)
Geographical information system	7,500	7,500	7,100	400
Health and sanitation:				—
Garbage pickup	60,000	61,000	61,500	(500)
Cemetery:				—
Personal services	41,500	41,000	41,000	—
Purchase of goods and services..............	29,950	30,000	29,500	500
Culture and recreations:				—
Library	2,800	3,000	2,750	250
Parks and recreation	5,200	5,000	5,250	(250)
Community communications	3,000	3,000	3,000	—
Nondepartmental:				—
Transfers to other funds	71,000	71,000	71,000	—
Funding for school district	22,000	22,000	22,000	—
Total charges to appropriation..............	$429,650	$430,200	$428,100	$ 2,100
Budgetary fund balance, December 31	$110,400	$102,350	$103,900	$(1,550)

Source: Adapted from GASB Statement No. 34, *Basic Financial Statements—and Management's Discussion and Analysis—for State and Local Governments*, pp. 151, 201, 210–211, 220–224, 228–231, 235–236, 254–255, 258–261, and 269.

Government-Wide Financial Statements

The requirement for a government-wide set of financial statements prepared on an accrual basis has received much attention and resulted in a great deal of controversy. The required statements—a statement of net assets and a statement of activities—are shown in Illustrations 17-12 and 17-13. These statements have one column for governmental activities and one column for proprietary (business-type) activities. In addition, there is a total for the government as a whole. Discretely presented component units are also presented in a separate column.

The Statement of Net Assets

The statement of net assets for the city of Dover, shown in Illustration 17-12, includes all assets, such as infrastructure assets, and all liabilities of the government. The net assets (equity) are divided into three categories: unrestricted, restricted, and capital-related. The first column

Illustration 17-12
City of Dover
Statement of Net Assets
December 31, 2019
(in thousands)

	Primary Government			Component Units
	Governmental Activities	Business-Type Activities	Total	
Assets:				
Cash and cash equivalents	$ 13,598	$ 10,279	$ 23,877	$ 304
Investments	27,365	—	27,365	7,429
Receivable (net)	12,833	3,610	16,443	4,042
Internal balances	175	(175)	—	—
Inventories	322	127	449	84
Capital assets (net)	170,023	151,389	321,412	37,745
Total assets	$224,316	$165,230	$389,546	$49,604
Liabilities:				
Accounts payable	$ 6,783	$ 752	$ 7,535	$ 1,803
Deferred revenue	1,436	—	1,436	39
Noncurrent liabilities:				
Due within one year	9,236	4,426	13,662	1,427
Due in more than one year	83,302	74,482	157,784	27,106
Total liabilities	$100,757	$ 79,660	$180,417	$30,375
Net assets:				
Invested in capital assets (net of related debt)	$103,711	$ 73,089	$176,800	$15,906
Restricted for:				
Capital projects	11,706	—	11,706	492
Debt service	3,021	1,452	4,473	—
Community development projects	4,811	—	4,811	—
Other purposes	3,214	—	3,214	—
Unrestricted (deficit)	(2,904)	11,028	8,124	2,830
Total net assets	$123,559*	$ 85,569	$209,128	$19,228

*As reported in Illustration 17-4 (Net assets of governmental activities). This includes the internal service funds.

Source: Adapted from GASB Statement No. 34, *Basic Financial Statements—and Management's Discussion and Analysis—for State and Local Governments*, pp. 151, 201, 210–211, 220–224, 228–231, 235–236, 254–255, 258–261, and 269.

reports all assets and liabilities of general government activities, essentially on a consolidated basis and adjusted to reflect full accrual accounting.[4] The statement of net assets has several key characteristics, including the following:

◆ All capital assets are listed, including infrastructure assets.

◆ All capital assets are required to be depreciated. An exception for infrastructure assets is allowed if they are maintained in a condition that will result in an extended useful life. (See Chapter 16 for further discussion of the new requirements for infrastructure asset reporting.)

◆ General long-term liabilities are not recorded at face value but rather adjusted to reflect application of the effective interest method of accounting.

◆ Current and noncurrent liabilities are distinguished on the statement of net assets.

◆ Interfund payables and receivables between governmental funds are eliminated.

◆ Interfund payables and receivables between enterprise funds are eliminated.

◆ Net payables and receivables between governmental activities and business-type activities are shown separately as internal balances.

The Statement of Activities

The statement of activities for the city of Dover shown in Illustration 17-13, on pages 907 and 908, is a very unique statement that begins with a reporting of expenses by program. Direct expenses and allocated indirect expenses are reported in the first two columns. Then, revenue, generated from grants, fees, fines, forfeitures, and appropriations that are specifically connected to a program, is reported. The balance in each program after subtracting the program revenue is then the amount of expenses that must be paid for by general governmental revenues (e.g., from taxes, unrestricted grants and appropriations, and other financing sources).

In the statement of activities, program revenues are reported in three classifications: *charges for services, program-specific operating grants and contributions, and capital grants and contributions.* These revenues are deducted from the expenses of the related function or program. All revenues that are not program revenues are classified as general revenues.

Expenses, not expenditures, are reported for governmental activities in the government-wide statement of activities. Expenses include depreciation of general fixed assets, such as infrastructure assets, interest measured using the effective interest method, compensated absences, claims and judgments, pension accruals, and other changes in long-term liabilities. Expenses do not include capital outlay expenditures and debt principal retirement expenditures.

As discussed in Chapter 16 (page 847), internal service funds provide goods or services to other departments or agencies of the government. The charges to the user departments are set to reimburse for actual costs of running the internal service operation. Thus, internal service funds may be thought of as a cost allocation mechanism used by a government to allocate common costs to various activities or functions. Recognizing this relationship, the assets, liabilities, and net assets of an internal service fund are included in the Governmental Activities column in the government-wide statements. Further, in developing the government-wide financial statements, internal service fund revenues and expenses are eliminated (similar to a business parent company and subsidiary consolidation). Any differential between revenues and expenses (e.g., profit) is eliminated by reducing the expenses for internal service fund services that are charged to the various functions in the government-wide statements.

A controversial and challenging aspect of GASB Statement No. 34 for many governments is the requirement to report infrastructure assets. Most governments do not currently record or report their general infrastructure fixed assets. Most governments will also have difficulty implementing the necessary record-keeping involved in applying traditional fixed asset accounting and reporting of infrastructure assets such as streets, roads, sidewalks, curbs, storm

---

4 All FASB standards (and other business guidance) issued on or before November 30, 1989, that do not contradict GASB and predecessor body standards are to be applied to both governmental and business-type activities in the government-wide statements. FASB standards issued after 1989 are applied only to business-type activities if a government chooses the option to apply all subsequent FASB standards that do not conflict with GASB standards per GASB Statement No. 20.

sewers, and bridges. In recognition of this difficulty, the GASB included several special provisions in Statement No. 34 for infrastructure assets:

1. Delaying by four years the effective date for retroactive reporting (for years beginning after June 15, 2005 for large governments and later for medium-size governments) to allow governments time to inventory and assign costs to their infrastructure fixed assets.
2. Allowing various approaches to estimating infrastructure cost, including using price-level adjusted current replacement costs to estimate historical costs at implementation.
3. Allowing prospective-only application for small governments.
4. Limiting the requirement to major infrastructure fixed assets (defined as a network or subsystem) acquired after 1981 so that all larger governments have to include 25 years of data.
5. Permitting a *modified approach* to measuring the cost of using infrastructure assets that allows governments to avoid reporting depreciation expense. As indicated in Chapter 16, a government is permitted to use a modified approach if it can demonstrate that the eligible infrastructure assets are being preserved at or above a condition level established by the government. Under the modified "preservation" approach, all costs to maintain the assets are expensed and no depreciation is recorded. However, if a government stops maintaining the infrastructure at the target condition level, the government must depreciate those assets. A change from the depreciation method to the modified approach should be reported as a change in accounting estimate, i.e., similar to a change in service life from finite to infinite.

Converting Funds-Based Statements to Government-Wide Statements

Since the information necessary to prepare the fund financial statements and the government-wide statements is different, a reconciliation from the funds-based to the government-wide statements is required on the face of the funds-based statements. This reconciliation is necessary to convert from the modified accrual basis of accounting and the detail of fund accounting to the full accrual and summarized government-wide statements. It is quite easy to convert the business-type activities from the total enterprise funds column of the fund financial statements to the government-wide statements. The most common difference is that the government-wide statement of activities must present operating data by function (or program) and use a format that differs considerably from the proprietary funds statement of revenues, expenses, and changes in fund equity. Also, interfund payables and receivables must be eliminated, and internal balances from nonenterprise funds must be identified. In addition, the assets and liabilities of internal service funds whose primary customers are enterprise funds are aggregated with the enterprise fund data in the Business-Type Activity column. The expenses reported in the statement of activities for business-type activities must also be adjusted to eliminate the net increase or decrease in internal service net assets.

Conversion from the funds-based governmental funds statements to the aggregated governmental activities in the government-wide statements is much more complex. Steps in this conversion include the following:

1. To convert the governmental fund balance sheet to the government-wide statement of net assets:

   - Add general fixed assets, including infrastructure fixed assets, net of accumulated depreciation.
   - Add general long-term debt, measured at the appropriate carrying amount, using the effective interest method.
   - Add the assets and liabilities of most internal service funds (those whose primary customer is the general government).
   - Adjust assets and liabilities from the current financial resources measurement focus to an economic resources measurement focus.
   - Eliminate the fund balance and classify net assets as invested in capital assets, restricted net assets, and unrestricted net assets.

2. To convert the governmental fund statement of revenues, expenditures, and changes in fund balances to the government-wide statement of activities:

   - Eliminate other financing sources for general long-term debt proceeds.
   - Eliminate capital outlay expenditures.
   - Eliminate expenditures or other financing uses for debt principal retirement.
   - Record depreciation expense or maintenance/preservation costs and allocate the expenses to functions or programs.

Illustration 17-13
City of Dover
Statement of Activities
For Year Ended December 31, 2019
(in thousands)

Functions/programs	Expenses	Indirect Expenses Allocation	Program Revenues — Charges for Services	Program Revenues — Operating Grants and Contributions	Program Revenues — Capital Grants and Contributions	Net (Expense) Revenue Changes in Net Assets — Primary Government — Governmental Activities	Net (Expense) Revenue Changes in Net Assets — Primary Government — Business-Type Activities	Total	Component Units
Governmental activities:									
General government	$ 9,571	$(5,581)	$ 3,147	$ 843	$ —	$ —	$ —	$ —	$ —
Public safety	34,845	4,060	1,199	1,308	62	(36,336)	—	(36,336)	—
Public works	10,129	3,264	850	—	2,253	(10,290)	—	(10,290)	—
Engineering services	1,300	112	706	—	—	(706)	—	(706)	—
Health and sanitation	6,739	558	5,612	576	—	(1,109)	—	(1,109)	—
Cemetery	736	56	213	—	—	(579)	—	(579)	—
Culture and recreation	11,532	1,859	3,995	2,450	—	(6,946)	—	(6,946)	—
Community development	2,994	1,740	—	—	2,579	(2,155)	—	(2,155)	—
Education (payment to school district)	21,893	—	—	—	—	(21,893)	—	(21,893)	—
Interest on long-term debt	6,068	(6,068)	—	—	—	—	—	—	—
Total governmental activities	$105,807	$ 0	$15,722	$5,177	$4,894	$ (80,014)	$ —	$ (80,014)	$ —
Business-type activities:									
Electric utility	$ 8,509		$11,330	$ —	$1,646	$ —	$ 4,467	$ 4,467	$ —
Water & sewer	2,796		1,344	—	—	—	(1,452)	(1,452)	—
Total business-type activities	$ 11,305		$12,674	$ —	$1,646	$ —	$ 3,015	$ 3,015	$ —
Total primary government	$117,112		$28,396	$5,177	$6,541	$ (80,014)	$ 3,015	$ (76,999)	$ —
Component units:									
Landfill	$ 3,382		$ 3,858	$ —	$ 11	$ —	$ —	$ —	$ 487
Public school system	31,186		706	3,937	—	—	—	—	(26,543)
Total component	$ 34,568		$ 4,564	$3,937	$ 11	$ —	$ —	$ —	$(26,056)

(continued)

| | | Program Revenues | | | Net (Expense) Revenue Changes in Net Assets | | | |
| | | | | | Primary Government | | | |
Expenses	Indirect Expenses Allocation	Charges for Services	Operating Grants and Contributions	Capital Grants and Contributions	Governmental Activities	Business-Type Activities	Total	Component Units
General revenues:								
Taxes:								
Property taxes, levied for general purposes					$ 51,694	$ —	$ 51,694	$ —
Property taxes, levied for debt service					4,726	—	4,726	—
Franchise taxes					4,056	—	4,056	—
Public service taxes					8,970	—	8,970	—
Payment from city of Dover					—	—	—	21,893
Grant and contributions not restricted to specific programs					1,458	—	1,458	6,462
Investment earnings					1,957	601	2,558	882
Miscellaneous					885	105	990	22
Special item—gain on sale of park land					2,653	—	2,653	—
Transfers					501	(501)	—	—
Total general revenues, special items, and transfers					$ 76,900	$ 205	$ 77,105	$ 29,259
Change in net assets					$ (3,114)[a]	$ 3,220	$ 106	$ 3,203
Net assets—beginning					126,673	82,349	209,022	16,025
Net assets—ending					$123,559	$85,569[b]	$209,128	$ 19,228

[a] As reported in Illustration 17-5 reconciliation.
[b] As reported in Illustration 17-6 (Total major enterprise funds totals column, total net assets).

Source: Adapted from GASB Statement No. 34, *Basic Financial Statements—and Management's Discussion and Analysis—for State and Local Governments,* pp. 151, 201, 210–211, 220–224, 228–231, 235–236, 254–255, 258–261, and 269.

- ◆ Convert revenues from the flow of current financial resources modified accrual basis to the flow of economic resources accrual basis.

- ◆ Reclassify revenues as either program revenues or general revenues.

- ◆ Convert interest expenditures to interest expense by adjusting for interest accruals, amortization of premium/discount, bond issue costs, and deferred interest adjustments.

- ◆ Record bad debts expense.

- ◆ Convert other expenditures to expenses, i.e., compensated absences, pension, claims and judgments, landfill closure and postclosure care, and postretirement benefits other than pensions.

- ◆ Convert special items and extraordinary items to the economic resources measurement focus and accrual basis of accounting.

A comprehensive example of the conversion from fund financial statements to government-wide financial statements is provided in the next section.

PRACTICE CONVERTING FUNDS-BASED STATEMENTS TO GOVERNMENT-WIDE STATEMENTS

4

OBJECTIVE

Tell when GASB Statement No. 34 took effect, list the requirements of the Single Audit Act, and describe what other reporting efforts the GASB has been encouraging.

Based on the following trial balance for Lake Village, prepare a complete set of financial statements except for the budgetary comparison. To get to government-wide statements, assume the following:

- ◆ The village has no capital assets or long-term debt before the current year.

- ◆ The village follows straight-line depreciation. There is no residual. One full year of depreciation is taken in the year of acquisition. All equipment items and trucks have a 5-year life, and the modified preservation approach is applied.

- ◆ The book value of the truck sold was $21,000.

- ◆ The face value of the bonds issued is $182,000.

- ◆ The deferred tax revenue of $1,052,233 is deferred due to the tax revenue not being available.

Lake Village
Trial Balance

	Acct. No.	Debit	Credit
General Fund			
Cash	10100	212,133	
Cash—Tax Collection	10200	447,277	
Investments	10500	355,300	
Tax Receivable	10600	604,956	
Inventory of Supplies	10900	6,700	
Prepaid Expenses	10950	250	
Vouchers Payable	11100		6,812
Deferred Tax Revenue	11200		1,052,233
Unassigned Fund Balance	12100		281,620
Committed Fund Balance	12200		266,957
Nonspendable Inventory	12300		6,700
Revenues from Other Governments	41100		109,025
Village Property Tax	41200		1,032,761
Investment Revenue	41300		80,401
License Fees	41400		6,885
Building Permits	41500		25,289
Police Fines and Forfeitures	41600		36,984
Board of Appeals Fees	41800		750
General Government			
Administrative Salaries	51100	50,403	
Village Hall Maintenance	51105	5,829	
Professional Fees	51110	51,406	

(continued)

	Acct. No.	Debit	Credit
Casualty Insurance	51118	13,161	
Employee Benefits	51119	9,299	
Office Expenses	51131	29,548	
Fireworks	51152	5,225	
Building Inspector	51158	13,785	
Computer Capital	56001	1,491	
Public Safety			
Police Salaries	52001	413,737	
Uniforms	52010	3,437	
Squad Operations	52015	27,050	
Police Training	52035	3,699	
Safety Expenses	52040	12,440	
Lake Water Quality	52047	5,359	
Fire Protection (paid to Summit)	52055	134,981	
Legal Costs	52113	5,244	
Police Insurance	52118	5,853	
Police Benefits	52119	201,168	
Police Capital Equipment	57006	22,483	
Public Works			
Wages	55002	35,609	
Truck Operations	55005	6,851	
Road Repair and Forestry	55015	19,268	
Garbage Collection	55040	49,473	
Garage Operations	55052	4,140	
Benefits	55128	14,926	
Road and Bridges—Capital	58001	48,070	
Tools—Capital	58004	758	
Truck—Capital	58008	45,000	
Other Financing Sources, Asset Sale	60001		21,800
Transfers	60002	61,908	
Debt Service Fund			
Cash	11110	3,400	
Restricted Fund Balance	12330		2,100
Interest	53007	30,908	
Principal	53012	37,400	
Transfers	60002		69,608
Capital Projects Fund			
Cash	11120	45,500	
Due to Other Funds	12100		
Assigned for Encumbrances	12110		18,000
Committed Fund Balance	12120	20,500	
Revenue—Village Property Taxes	68000		18,000
Transfers	68050	1,200	
Construction Expenses	68100	150,000	
Special Assessment Bond Proceeds	61001		181,200
Permanent Fund			
Cash	11130	5,145	
Investments	11510	24,300	
Committed Fund Balance	12300		34,500
Transfers	12350	6,500	
Investment Revenue	12100		1,445
Boat Launch Enterprise Fund			
Cash	100	24,733	
Land	200	200,000	
Improvements	210	100,000	

	Acct. No.	Debit	Credit
Accumulated Depreciation	215		30,000
Prepaid Season Passes	310		3,100
Net Assets—Capital Assets	311		270,000
Net Assets—Unrestricted	312		5,600
Boat Launch Revenue	500		30,696
Wages	411	5,902	
Employee Benefits	412	86	
Sanitation Fees	413	1,150	
Sales Tax Paid	414	1,778	
Depreciation Expense	415	5,000	
Other Expenses	416	747	
Totals		3,592,466	3,592,466

From the trial balance, the governmental funds balance sheet and statement of revenues, expenditures, and changes in fund balances can be prepared as follows:

Government Funds Balance Sheet

	General Fund	Debt Service Fund	Capital Projects Fund	Permanent Fund	Total
Assets					
Cash	659,410	3,400	45,500	5,145	713,455
Investments	355,300			24,300	379,600
Tax receivable	604,956				604,956
Inventory of Supplies	6,700				6,700
Prepaid Expenses	250				250
Total Assets	1,626,616	3,400	45,500	29,445	1,704,961
Liabilities					
Vouchers Payable	6,812				6,812
Deferred Tax Revenue	1,052,233				1,052,233
Total Liabilities	1,059,045	0	0	0	1,059,045
Equity					
Unassigned Fund Balance	293,914				293,914
Committed Fund Balance	266,957		27,500	29,445	323,902
Restricted Debt Service Fund		3,400			3,400
Nonspendable Inventory	6,700				6,700
Assigned for Encumbrances			18,000		18,000
Total Equity	567,571	3,400	45,500	29,445	645,916
Total Liabilities and Equity	1,626,616	3,400	45,500	29,445	1,704,961

Government Fund Statement of Revenues, Expenditures, and Changes in Fund Balances

	General Fund	Debt Service Fund	Capital Projects Fund	Permanent Fund	Total
Revenues					
Village Property Tax	1,032,761		18,000		1,050,761
Revenues from Other Governments	109,025				109,025
Investment Revenue	80,401			1,445	81,846

(continued)

	General Fund	Debt Service Fund	Capital Projects Fund	Permanent Fund	Total
Police Fines and Forfeitures	36,984				36,984
Building Permits	25,289				25,289
License Fees	6,885				6,885
Board of Appeals Fees	750				750
Total Revenues	1,292,095	0	18,000	1,445	1,311,540
Expenditures					
General Government	180,147				180,147
Public Safety	835,451				835,451
Public Works	224,095				224,095
Interest		30,908			30,908
Principal		37,400			37,400
Construction Expenses			150,000		150,000
Total Expenditures	1,239,693	68,308	150,000	0	1,458,001
Net Profit (Loss)	52,402	(68,308)	(132,000)	1,445	(146,461)
Other Financing Sources, Asset Sale	21,800				21,800
Proceeds from Bond Issue			181,200		181,200
Transfers	(61,908)	69,608	(1,200)	(6,500)	0
	(40,108)	69,608	180,000	(6,500)	203,000
Net Change in Fund Balances	12,294	1,300	48,000	(5,055)	56,539
Beginning Fund Balance	281,620	2,100	(20,500)	34,500	297,720
Ending Fund Balance	293,914	3,400	27,500	29,445	354,259

The next step is to prepare the proprietary fund financial statements. Notice that there is only one proprietary fund, the Boat Launch Enterprise Fund.

Boat Launch Balance Sheet		**Boat Launch Income Statement**	
Total Assets		**Revenue**	
Current Assets		Boat Launch Revenue *(net of sales tax)*	28,918
Cash	24,733		
Capital Assets		**Expenses**	
		Wages	5,902
Land	200,000	Employee Benefits	86
Improvements	70,000	Depreciation Expense	5,000
(net of accumulated depreciation)		Sanitation Fees	1,150
Total Capital Assets	270,000	Other Expenses	747
Total Assets	294,733	Total Expenses	12,885

(continued)

Boat Launch		**Boat Launch**	
Balance Sheet		**Income Statement**	
Liabilities		Net Income	16,033
Prepaid Season Passes	3,100	Beginning Net Assets—Unrestricted	5,600
Net Assets		Ending Net Assets—Unrestricted	21,633
Invested in Capital Assets	270,000		
Unrestricted	21,633		
Total Net Assets	291,633		
Total Liabilities and Equity	294,733		

Once the fund financial statements are prepared, the governmental funds should be reconciled to convert them to the full accrual basis.

Reconciliation of Government Fund Balance Sheet and Government-Wide Net Assets

Note that the balances for the account groups are not available so it is difficult to prepare government-wide statements without access to further information:

◆ The village has no capital assets or long-term debt before the current year.

◆ The village follows straight-line depreciation and has no residual. One full year of depreciation is taken in the year of acquisition. All equipment items and trucks have a 5-year life, and the modified preservation approach is applied.

◆ The book value of the truck sold was $21,000.

◆ The face value of the bonds issued is $182,000. The deferred tax revenue of $1,052,233 is deferred due to the tax revenue not being available.

Fund Balance per Balance Sheet	645,916			
Capital Assets		Cash	21,800	
		Accumulated Depreciation	5,250	
Computers—General	1,491	Gain		800
Police Equipment—Public Safety	22,483	Truck		26,250
Roads and Bridges—Public Works	48,070	$21,000 \div 4/5 = 26,250$		
Trucks (45,000 − 26,250) —Public				
Works	18,750*			
Tools—Public Works	758			
Construction Work in Progress—				
General	150,000			
Accumulated Depreciation	(8,697)			
Total Capital Assets	232,855			
		Face Value of Bond	182,000	
Bonds Payable	143,800	Less Discount	(800)	
Deferred Revenue	1,052,233	Payment	(37,400)	
		Bonds Payable	$143,800**	
Net Assets per State of Net Assets	$1,787,204			

*Note:

Cash	21,800
Accumulated Depreciation	5,250
Gain	800
Truck	26,250
$21,000 / 4/5 = 26,250$	

**Note:

Face Value of Bond	182,000
Less Discount	(800)
Payment	(37,400)
Bond Payable	143,800

Notice that the gain from the sale of the truck, which was the difference between the book value of the truck ($21,000 given in the problem) and the cash received on the sale of the truck ($21,800), needed to be determined.

The bonds payable amount of $143,800 that will now need to be recorded on the government-wide financial statements is the face value of the bonds ($182,000 given in the problem), less the discount of $800 (the bond proceeds was $181,200), less the principal payment of $37,400.

To get the accumulated depreciation at the end of the year and depreciation expense, depreciation should be calculated as follows:

Computation of Depreciation	Total	General Government	Public Safety	Public Works	
Trucks (45,000 ÷ 5)	9,000			9,000	
	(5,250)				
Computers (1,491 ÷ 5)	298	298			
Police Equipment (22,483 ÷ 5)	4,497		4,497		
Tools (758 ÷ 5)	152			152	
	8,697	298	4,497	9,152	Totals
	Accumulated Depreciation			Depreciation Expense	
	d	a	b	c	

The reconciliation of the statement of revenues, expenditures, and changes in fund balances to the statement of activities is as follows:

Reconciliation of Government Statement of Revenues, Expenditures, and Changes in Fund Balances to the Statement of Activities

Profit (Loss) per Statement of Revenues, Expenditures, and Changes in Fund Balances	56,539
Deferred Tax Revenue	1,052,233
Depreciation Expense:	
General Government	(298) a
Public Safety	(4,497) b
Public Works	(9,152) c
Deduct Other Financing Sources not Revenue on the Statement of Activities:	
Proceeds from Capital Asset Sale	(21,800)
Proceeds from Bond Issue	(181,200)
Add Back Capital Asset Expenditures:	
Computers—General	1,491
Police Equipment—Public Safety	22,483
Roads and Bridges—Public Works	48,070
Trucks—Public Works	45,000
Tools—Public Works	758
Gain on Sale—Public Works	800
Principal—General	37,400
Construction Expenses—General	150,000
Net Income per State of Activities	1,197,827

Once the reconciliations have been prepared, the government-wide financial statements can be prepared. The statement of net assets is prepared on a full accrual basis with two main columns: Governmental Activities and Business Activities. Notice that the total net assets per the government activities equals the total net assets on the reconciliation.

Government-Wide Statement of Net Assets

	Government Activities	Business Activities	Total
Current assets:			
Cash	713,455	24,733	738,188
Investments	379,600		379,600
Tax receivable	604,956		604,956
Inventory of supplies	6,700		6,700
Prepaid expenses	250		250
Total current assets	1,704,961	24,733	1,729,694
Capital assets:			
Land		200,000	200,000
Improvements (net of accumulated depreciation)		70,000	70,000
Roads and bridges	48,070		48,070
Trucks (net of accumulated depreciation)	15,000		15,000
Computers (net of accumulated depreciation)	1,193		1,193
Police equipment (net of accumulated depreciation)	17,986		17,986
Tools (net of accumulated depreciation)	606		606
Construction Work in Progress	150,000		150,000
Total capital assets	232,855	270,000	502,855
Total assets	1,937,816	294,733	2,232,549
Current liabilities			
Vouchers payable	6,812		6,812
Deferred revenue		3,100	3,100
Total current liabilities	6,812	3,100	9,912
Long-term debt			
Bonds payable	143,800		143,800
Total liabilities	150,612	3,100	153,712
Net assets			
Unrestricted, undesignated	1,554,349	21,633	1,575,982
Invested in capital assets, net of related debt	232,855	270,000	502,855
Total	1,787,204	291,633	2,078,837
Total liabilities and net assets	1,937,816	294,733	2,232,549

To illustrate the government-wide statement of activities, for simplicity, only the government activities section is presented. Note that the net revenue over expenses of $1,197,827 agrees with the reconciliation.

Government-Wide Statement of Activities—Government Only

| | | | Revenues | | |
| | | | | Contribution and Grants | | |
	Expenses	Service Charges	Operations	Capital	Net
General government	178,954[a]	0	109,025	0	(69,929)
Public safety	817,465[b]	36,984			(780,481)
Public works	139,419[c]	32,924			(106,495)
Debt service	30,908				(30,908)
Net revenue (expenses) from government activities					$ (987,813)
General revenues					
Property taxes					2,102,994[d]
Investment revenue					81,846
Special item: Gain on sale of truck					800
Net revenue (expense)					1,197,827

[a]Fund-Based Expenditures + Depreciation − Capital Expenditures
[b]Fund-Based Expenditures + Depreciation − Capital Expenditures
[c]Fund-Based Expenditures + Depreciation − Capital Expenditures
[d]Fund-Based Property Tax Revenue + Deferred Revenue

REPORTING AND AUDITING IMPLEMENTATION AND ISSUES

GASB Statement No. 34 represents a dramatic shift in the way state and local governments present financial information to the public. In a June 10, 1999, news release, then GASB Chairman Tom L. Allen called GASB Statement No. 34 "the most significant change to occur in the history of governmental accounting."[5] Allen went on to state that "never before has the public been able to get a comprehensive overview of a state or local government's finances in one place. This new financial reporting system will give citizens a clearer picture of what a government is doing with the taxes it collects: Are current revenues paying for current services, or will the services be paid for by the next generations? How much is invested in roads and bridges? Are taxes subsidizing the local public pool, or are swimmers' fees covering operating costs? The new financial statements could help to answer those questions." This relatively new standard took effect for larger governments (those with $100 million or more in revenues) in fiscal years beginning after June 15, 2001, medium-sized governments (those with between $10 and $100 million in revenue) in fiscal years beginning after June 15, 2002, and smaller governments (those with $10 million or less in revenue) in fiscal years beginning after June 15, 2003. As previously indicated, prospective (forward-looking) recognition of infrastructure assets was required at the same time as the other provisions of GASB Statement No. 34. Large and medium-sized governments have three additional years to apply the 25-year retroactive implementation (back to 1981). Smaller governments are exempt from retroactive infrastructure reporting. Many governments continue to work on issues relating to reporting of their infrastructure assets.

Audits of State and Local Governments

In order for users of financial statements to have assurance that the statements are prepared in conformity with GASB accounting and reporting standards, the statements are accompanied by an audit report. Most governments are audited annually because of state or federal requirements or because long-term creditors demand audited statements as part of the debt

---

5 Governmental Accounting Standards Board, *Action Report* (Norwalk, CT: Governmental Accounting Standards Board, July 1999).

agreements. The audits of governmental units are broader than audits of a business and include both a financial audit and a performance audit. The *financial audit*, which is the primary audit, deals with compliance with fiscal requirements including applicable accounting standards and federal and state laws. As in business, the primary purpose of the financial audit is to render a report expressing an opinion about whether the financial statements present fairly the financial position, results of operation, and where appropriate, the cash flows of the government in accordance with generally accepted accounting principles (GAAP) or other financial related criteria. *Performance audits* emphasize economy, efficiency, program results, and managerial effectiveness. Performance audits are intended to provide an independent report, but not an opinion, about the extent to which government officials are carrying out their responsibilities in an efficient and economic way and also whether their programs are producing desired results.

Government auditing standards have been developed by the U.S. General Accounting Office (GAO) in its Yellow Book entitled *Government Auditing Standards*. The American Institute of Certified Public Accountants (AICPA) publishes the AICPA audit guide, *Audits of State and Local Governmental Units*, which incorporates the Yellow Book standards. In 1984, the federal government passed the *Single Audit Act* requiring audits of all entities receiving federal grants and contracts. The Single Audit Act, revised in 1996, requires state and local governments that receive $500,000 or more of federal financial assistance to have a single audit for that fiscal year. The act exempts governments receiving less than $500,000 of federal assistance. A single audit has two main components: an audit of the financial statements conducted under generally accepted government auditing standards and an audit of federal financial awards. Not all federal award programs are audited in a single audit. Larger programs (those with more than $300,000 or 3% of all federal assistance expenditures) must be audited unless they are considered low risk. In addition, certain high-risk smaller programs (less than $300,000 or 3% of federal assistance expenditures) are audited until at least 50% of the total federal awards expended are audited. A higher level of auditing is required of major federal award programs as defined by size and risk. This includes more testing and reporting on compliance with laws and regulations, internal control, and inherent risk. Audit reports prepared under the Single Audit Act include (a) an opinion on the fairness of financial statement presentation, (b) a report on the study and evaluation of internal control systems' ability to provide reasonable assurance that federal programs are being managed in compliance with laws and regulations, (c) a report on compliance with laws and regulations that may have a material effect on specific programs, and (d) a schedule of findings and questioned costs. Detailed guidance for administering and conducting single audits is provided in OMB Circular A-133, *Audits of State and Local Governments and Nonprofit Organizations*.

The Statistical Section

The statistical section information should focus on the primary government, rather than on the financial reporting entity, and include the following five categories:[6]

◆ *Financial trends information*—to help users understand and assess how a government's financial position has changed over time.

◆ *Revenue capacity information*—to help users understand and assess factors affecting a government's ability to generate its own source revenues.

◆ *Debt capacity information*—to help users understand and assess a government's debt burden and its ability to issue additional debt.

◆ *Demographic and economic information*—to help users understand the socioeconomic environment within which a government operates and compare financial statement information over time and among governments.

◆ *Operating information*—to provide contextual information about a government's operations and resources to help the user understand and assess a government's economic condition.

---

6 GASB Statement No. 44, *Economic Condition Reporting: The Statistical Section—an Amendment of NCGA Statement No. 1*, May 2004.

Ten-year trend information is required for government employment levels, operating statistics, capital assets, net assets, and changes in net assets. Trend information is also required for governmental fund balances and principal employers. All sources of information and assumptions used to produce information must be clearly identified and narrative explanations are to be used as appropriate.

Other Financial Reporting Issues

The GASB continues to encourage governments to experiment with developing and reporting *nonfinancial* measures of efficiency and effectiveness through its service efforts and accomplishments (SEA) projects. In 1994, the GASB issued Concepts Statement No. 2, *Service Efforts and Accomplishments Reporting*, which identified three broad categories of SEA measures to include service efforts and service accomplishments and measures that relate the two. Extensive research has been conducted on appropriate SEA measures for schools, hospitals, police and fire departments, mass transit, sanitation departments, and others. Many advocate the use of these nonfinancial measures in the financial statements or in separate performance reports in order to improve financial statement users' ability to assess the service efforts, costs, and accomplishments of a government.

Another effort by the GASB to encourage more effective communication of financial statement information is through the publication of popular reports. A growing number of governments prepare and distribute popular reports that provide condensed financial and budget information (and sometimes SEA measures). These reports often include graphs and charts to facilitate better understanding and decision making by those who use the financial statements. Popular reports do not replace the CAFR, but may serve to supplement it. Currently, this supplemental information is not audited.

Other organizations continue to participate in the efforts to improve financial reporting for governments. Two examples are the Government Finance Officers Association (GFOA) and Standard & Poor's (S&P) Corporation. The Government Finance Officers Association recognizes excellence in financial reporting through its Certificate of Achievement for Excellence in Financial Reporting award program. Certificates are awarded to governments that publish financial reports (CAFRs) demonstrating efficient, organized, full disclosure in accordance with GAAP. Standard & Poor's has also taken an active role in government financial reporting by requiring that governments follow GAAP. Because of the impact of the S&P bond rating on borrowing costs, the S&P requirement has significantly improved the quality of government financial reports. Other financial institutions and professional organizations continue to work with the GASB on issues of accounting and financial reporting in state and local governments.

UNDERSTANDING THE ISSUES

1. Compare the basis of accounting that is used to report governmental activities versus business-type activities.

2. Describe the purpose of each of the financial statements required under GASB Statement No. 34.

3. What are major funds? Describe major fund reporting.

4. What benefits are derived from including the management's discussion and analysis in state and local governmental financial reports? What information is required to be included in the MD&A?

5. Explain budgetary reporting requirements.

6. How are interfund transactions reported?

EXERCISES

Exercise 1 *(LO 2, 3)* **Reporting major funds.** Assume Round Rock City has the following fund structure:

General fund
Special revenue fund (3)
Capital projects fund (2)
Debt service fund (3)
Expendable trust funds (5)
Internal service funds (2)
Enterprise funds (8)
General fixed assets account group
General long-term debt account group

Round Rock City determined that Special Revenue Fund C, capital projects funds, Enterprise Fund D, and Enterprise Fund F are the only major funds.

1. Present the column headings that Round Rock City must use in its governmental fund statement of revenues, expenditures, and changes in fund balances.
2. Present the column headings that Round Rock City must use in its governmental fund statement of revenues, expenses, and changes in net assets.

Exercise 2 *(LO 2)* **Determining a major fund.** Based on the information presented in the 2009 city of Milwaukee, Wisconsin, financial statements, list the major funds disclosed by the city. How were these funds determined? Likewise, what minimum amounts of which statement items were used to determine whether a specific enterprise fund was a major fund?

Exercise 3 *(LO 1, 3)* **CAFR.** Select the best answer to the following multiple-choice questions:

1. Which of the following statements is correct concerning a governmental entity's combined statement of cash flows?

   a. Cash flows from capital financing activities are reported separately from cash flows from non-capital-related financing activities.
   b. The statement format is the same as that of a business enterprise's statement of cash flows.
   c. Cash flows from operating activities may be reported using the indirect method.
   d. The statement format includes columns for the general, governmental, and proprietary fund types.

2. In a government's comprehensive annual financial report, proprietary fund types are included in which of the following combined financial statements?

	Statement of Revenues, Expenditures, and Changes in Fund Balances	Statement of Net Assets
a.	Yes	Yes
b.	No	No
c.	No	Yes
d.	Yes	No

3. In a government's comprehensive annual financial report, account groups are included in which of the following combined financial statements?

	Net Assets	Statement of Activities
a.	Yes	No
b.	No	Yes
c.	Yes	Yes
d.	No	No

4. Clover City's comprehensive annual financial report contains both combining and combined financial statements. Total columns are

a. required for both combining and combined financial statements.
b. optional, but commonly shown, for combining financial statements and required for combined financial statements.
c. required for combining financial statements and optional, but commonly shown, for combined financial statements.
d. optional, but commonly shown, for both combining and combined financial statements.

5. Eureka City should issue a statement of cash flows for which of the following funds?

	Eureka City Hall Capital Projects Fund	Eureka Water Enterprise Fund
a.	No	Yes
b.	No	No
c.	Yes	No
d.	Yes	Yes

6. On March 2, 2011, Finch City issued 10-year general obligation bonds at face amount, with interest payable on March 1 and September 1. The proceeds were to be used to finance the construction of a civic center over the period from April 1, 2011, to March 31, 2012.

   During the fiscal year ended June 30, 2011, no resources had been provided to the debt service fund for the payment of principal and interest. On June 30, 2011, in which statements should Finch report the construction in progress for the civic center?

	Capital Projects Fund Balance Sheet	Government-Wide Statement of Net Assets
a.	Yes	Yes
b.	Yes	No
c.	No	No
d.	No	Yes

Exercise 4 *(LO 3)* **New standards.** Go to the GASB Web site, and review the list of current projects and recently released standards. What are the most pressing issues facing the Board? In your opinion, is the Board effectively communicating these issues to the public on its Web site?

Exercise 5 *(LO 3)* **Government-wide financial statements.** Select the best answer to the following multiple-choice questions:

1. Which of the following adjustments would likely be made when moving from governmental funds financial statements to government-wide financial statements?

a. Record an additional expense for compensated absences
b. Record an additional expense related to salaries earned at year-end
c. Both of the above
d. Neither of the above

2. Which of the following adjustments is necessary to move from governmental fund financial statements to government-wide financial statements?

   a. Eliminate expenditures for debt principal
   b. Eliminate expenditures for capital outlay and add depreciation expense
   c. Both of the above
   d. Neither of the above

3. Which of the following is *true* regarding government-wide financial statements?

   a. Internal service funds are normally included with governmental-type activities.
   b. Component units and fiduciary funds are not included.
   c. Both of the above
   d. Neither of the above

4. Which of the following is *true* regarding government-wide financial statements?

   a. All capital assets, including infrastructure, are required to be reported.
   b. Internal service funds are not included.
   c. Both of the above
   d. Neither of the above

5. Which of the following is *true* regarding government-wide financial statements?

   a. Internal service funds are not included with governmental-type activities.
   b. Component units and fiduciary funds are not included.
   c. Both of the above
   d. Neither of the above

6. Which of the following must exist in order for a government to use the modified approach for recording infrastructure?

   a. An up-to-date inventory of eligible infrastructure assets must be maintained.
   b. A condition assessment must be performed at least every three years.
   c. Both of the above
   d. Neither of the above

7. Which of the following would be considered a program revenue in the statement of activities for a governmental unit?

   a. A grant from the state restricted for an after-school child care program
   b. Hotel taxes restricted for tourist development
   c. Both of the above
   d. Neither of the above

8. Which of the following is *true* regarding the incorporation of internal service funds into government-wide financial statements?

   a. Internal service funds are not included in the government-wide financial statements.
   b. Internal service funds are incorporated into the business-type activities section of the government-wide financial statements.
   c. Both of the above
   d. Neither of the above

9. Which of the following is *true* about the reconciliation from governmental fund changes in fund balances to governmental activities changes in net assets?

   a. Reconciliation is required to be presented either on the face of the fund financial statement or as a separate statement.
   b. The reconciliation converts from modified accrual to full accrual.
   c. Both of the above
   d. Neither of the above

10. Which of the following is *true* regarding government-wide financial statements?

    a. The government-wide statements include a statement of net assets, a statement of activities, and a statement of cash flows.

    b. The government-wide statements include a statement of net assets and a statement of activities, but not a statement of cash flows.

    c. The government-wide statements include a balance sheet, an income statement, and a statement of cash flows.

    d. None of the above

Exercise 6 *(LO 3)* **Converting to government-wide statements.** List some of the major adjustments required when converting from fund financial statements to government-wide statements. Why are these adjustments necessary?

Exercise 7 *(LO 3)* **Infrastructure reporting.** What are the rules for recording infrastructure under the new GASB reporting model? When are these rules effective? What conditions must exist in order to use one method versus another? What are the advantages and disadvantages of each approach?

PROBLEMS

Required ▶ ▶ ▶ ▶ ▶   **Problem 17-1** *(LO 1, 2)* **Usefulness of reported information.** Search the Internet for a popular report of a state or city government. Evaluate the usefulness of the popular report from the perspective of the citizen. In particular, focus on financial accounting information provided in the report. Do you think this information is adequate? Does the state or city report nonfinancial measures of efficiency and effectiveness (service efforts and accomplishments) information? If so, evaluate its usefulness in determining the financial position and overall condition of the government.

Problem 17-2 *(LO 1, 3)* **Reporting under GASB Statement No. 34.** Select the best answer to the following multiple-choice questions:

1. In the statement of activities,

    a. all expenses are subtracted from all revenues to get net income.

    b. it is possible to determine the net program expense (revenue) for major functions and programs of the primary government and its component units.

    c. some tax revenues are considered program revenues, and others are considered general revenues.

    d. extraordinary items are those that are either unusual in nature or infrequent in occurrence.

2. Which of the following is *true* regarding financial reporting under GASB Statement No. 34?

    a. A comparison of budget and actual revenues and expenditures for the general fund is required as part of the basic financial statements.

    b. Infrastructure must be recorded and depreciated as part of the statement of activities in the basic financial statements.

    c. Public colleges and universities are to report in exactly the same manner as private colleges and universities.

    d. Special purpose governments that have only business-type activities are permitted to report only the financial statements required for enterprise funds.

3. Which of the following is *true* regarding the government-wide financial statements?

   a. The government-wide financial statements include the statement of net assets and the statement of activities.
   b. The government-wide financial statements are to be prepared using the economic resources measurement focus and the accrual basis of accounting.
   c. The government-wide financial statements include information for governmental activities, business-type activities, the total primary government, and its component units.
   d. All of the above are true.

4. Which of the following is *not* part of the basic financial statements?

   a. Governmental funds statement of revenues, expenditures, and changes in fund balances
   b. Budgetary comparison schedules—general and special revenue funds
   c. Government-wide statement of activities
   d. Notes to the financial statements

5. Which of the following is *not* part of the basic financial statements?

   a. Government-wide statement of net assets
   b. Proprietary funds statement of revenues, expenses, and changes in fund net assets
   c. Combining balance sheet—nonmajor governmental funds
   d. Notes to the financial statements

6. Which of the following is *true* regarding the organization of the comprehensive annual financial report?

   a. The three major sections are introductory, financial, and statistical.
   b. The management's discussion and analysis is considered to be part of the introductory section.
   c. The auditor's report is considered to be part of the statistical section.
   d. Basic financial statements include the government-wide statements, the budgetary statement, and the notes to the financial statements.

7. Which of the following is *true* regarding the government-wide financial statements?

   a. The government-wide financial statements include the statement of net assets and the statement of activities.
   b. The government-wide financial statements are prepared on the financial resources measurement focus for governmental activities and the economic resources measurement focus for business-type activities.
   c. Prior-year data must be presented.
   d. Works of art, historical treasures, and similar assets must be capitalized.

8. Under GASB Statement No. 34, which of the following is *true* of infrastructure?

   a. Infrastructure must be recorded and depreciated unless a modified approach is used, in which case, depreciation is not required.
   b. Infrastructure must be recorded and depreciated in all cases.
   c. Infrastructure is not to be recorded and depreciated.
   d. The state and local governments have the option, but are not required, to record and depreciate infrastructure.

9. Which statement is *true* regarding the "major" funds?

   a. The general fund is always considered major.
   b. Other funds are considered major if both of the following conditions exist: (1) total assets, liabilities, revenues, or expenditures/expenses of that individual governmental or enterprise fund constitute 10% of the governmental or enterprise categories, and (2) total assets, liabilities, revenues, or expenditures/expenses are 5% of the total of the governmental and enterprise categories.
   c. A government may choose to reflect a fund as major even if it does not meet the criteria for major funds.
   d. All of the above are true.

10. Which of the following groups sets *standards* for audits of federal financial assistance recipients?

    a. U.S. General Accounting Office
    b. U.S. Office of Management and Budget
    c. Governmental Accounting Standards Board
    d. Financial Accounting Standards Board

11. OMB Circular A-133 applies

    a. only to state and local governmental units.
    b. only to not-for-profit organizations.
    c. to both state and local governments and not-for-profit organizations.
    d. to neither state and local governments nor not-for-profit organizations.

12. The total amount of grant expenditures that must be covered in the audit of major programs is

    a. $500,000.
    b. 50% of federal expenditures.
    c. 25% of federal expenditures.
    d. 50% of federal expenditures generally but only 25% if the government is considered to be a low-risk auditee.

Required ▶ ▶ ▶ ▶ ▶   **Problem 17-3** *(LO 2)* **Reporting entity.** Define a financial reporting entity. Give an example of a primary government. Define and give an example of a component unit. Explain the two methods of reporting the primary government and component units in the financial reporting entity and when each is required.

Problem 17-4 *(LO 2)* **Reporting entity.** The Urban Development Authority (UDA) was created as a separate legal entity by an act of the state legislature and "activated" by action of the city council to plan and develop the downtown area of the city and to attract new businesses and residents. The governing board of the authority is appointed by the city council for fixed terms. The UDA has the complete authority to hire management and all other employees. There is no significant continuing relationship between the city and the authority for carrying out day-to-day functions.

The authority is a separate body and levies taxes against the property owners within the designated development district and may hold referendums of its constituents (for bond issues, tax increases, and so forth). The authority's levy and the levies of the city are independent of each other and are related only by the fact that they are levied against a common tax base within the authority's geographic boundaries. Property taxes from the authority's levy are its primary revenue source.

The city council receives the annual budget of the authority for informational purposes, but in the opinion of the city's legal counsel has no option except to "approve" the budget. Approval is considered to be a formality. The city is under no obligation to finance operating deficits of the authority and does not have claim to any surpluses. The authority has the power to issue bonds for its lawful purposes. The city has no responsibility for the debt of the authority.

Required ▶ ▶ ▶ ▶ ▶   Using the flowchart shown in Illustration 17-2, indicate whether or not the city should incorporate the Urban Development Authority into its own financial statements. If so, how would the city accomplish this?

Required ▶ ▶ ▶ ▶ ▶   **Problem 17-5** *(LO 2)* **Reporting entities.** Based on the following very limited information, indicate whether and how the city should report its related entity.

1. Its school district, although not a legally separate government, is managed by a school board elected by city residents. The system is financed with general tax revenues of the city, and its budget is incorporated into that of the city at large (and thereby is subject to the same approval and appropriation process as other city expenditures).

2. Its fixed asset financing authority is a legally separate government that leases equipment to the city. To finance the equipment, the authority issues bonds that are guaranteed by the city and expected to be paid from the rents received from the city. The authority leases equipment exclusively to the city.

3. Its housing authority, which provides loans to low-income families within the city, is governed by a 5-person board appointed by the city's mayor.

4. Its hospital is owned by the city but managed under contract by a private hospital management firm.

5. Its water purification plant is owned in equal shares by the city and two neighboring counties. The city's interest in the plant was acquired with resources from its water utility (enterprise) fund.

6. Its community college, a separate legal entity, is governed by a board of governors elected by city residents and has its own taxing and budgetary authority.

Problem 17-6 *(LO 3)* **Reporting under GASB Statement No. 34.** Go to the Web site featuring the financial statements of Minneapolis, Minnesota, at http://www.ci.minneapolis. mn.us/financial-reports/cafr-home.asp.

Provide brief answers to the following: ◄ ◄ ◄ ◄ ◄ **Required**

1. The financial section includes the basic financial statements, notes to the financial statements, required supplementary information, and supplementary information. Describe key features of each of these components of the financial statements. What key information do you see that was not included in the text? Compare the Minneapolis statements with those of the city of Milwaukee.

2. Compare the information found in the letter of transmittal (in the introductory section) with that found in the newly required management's discussion and analysis (in the financial section).

3. Where do you find budgetary comparison information?

4. List the major governmental funds. How does Minneapolis determine major funds? List the nonmajor governmental funds.

5. How is Minneapolis handling the requirements for reporting and depreciating infrastructure assets?

Problem 17-7 *(LO 3)* **Statement of activities.** From the following information, prepare ◄ ◄ ◄ ◄ ◄ **Required** a statement of activities for the city of Rose as of June 30, 2019.

Expenses:
General government	$1,300,000
Public safety	240,000
Public works	1,000,000
Health and sanitation	650,000
Culture and recreation	450,000
Interest on long-term debt, governmental type	60,000
Water and sewer system	1,500,000
Parking system	45,000

Revenues:
Charges for services, general government	100,000
Charges for services, public safety	25,000
Operating grant, public safety	70,000
Charges for services, health and sanitation	250,000
Operating grant, health and sanitation	150,000
Charges for services, culture and recreation	200,000
Charges for services, water and sewer	1,800,000
Charges for services, parking system	40,000
Property taxes	2,500,000
Sales taxes	2,000,000
Investment earnings, business-type	30,000
Special item—gain on sale of unused land, governmental type	140,000
Transfer from governmental activities to business-type activities	70,000

(continued)

Net assets, July 1, 2018, governmental activities 1,400,000
Net assets, July 1, 2018, business-type activities 2,500,000

Problem 17-8 *(LO 3)* **Fund-based statements.** The preclosing, year-end trial balance for a capital projects fund of the city of Rochester as of December 31, 2019, follows:

	Debit	Credit
Cash	110,000	
Investments	250,000	
Contracts Payable—Retained Percentage.		110,000
Revenues		41,600
Other Financing Sources		800,000
Expenditures	586,600	
Other Financing Uses	5,000	
Encumbrances	80,000	
Fund Balance—Reserved for Encumbrances		80,000
Estimated Revenues	10,000	
Estimated Other Financing Sources.	900,000	
Appropriations		600,000
Estimated Other Financing Uses		15,000
Budgetary Fund Balance—Unreserved		295,000
Totals	1,941,600	1,941,600

Required ▶ ▶ ▶ ▶ ▶
1. Prepare closing entries as of December 31, 2019.
2. Prepare the year-end statement of revenues, expenditures, and changes in fund balances for this project that began on January 2, 2019.
3. Prepare the fund balance sheet as of December 31, 2019.

Required ▶ ▶ ▶ ▶ ▶
Problem 17-9 *(LO 3)* **Converting to a government-wide statement of activities.** Using the information from Problem 17-8, illustrate and explain the adjustments necessary to convert to a government-wide statement of activities, assuming all expenditures are for capital assets and other finance sources are the result of issuance of general long-term obligations.

Required ▶ ▶ ▶ ▶ ▶
Problem 17-10 *(LO 3)* **Statement of net assets.** From the following information, prepare a statement of net assets for the city of Lucas as of June 30, 2019.

Cash and cash equivalents, governmental activities	$ 280,000
Cash and cash equivalents, business-type activities	75,000
Receivables, governmental activities.	36,000
Receivables, business-type activities	145,000
Inventories, business-type activities	56,000
Capital assets (net), governmental activities	1,500,000
Capital assets (net), business-type activities.	1,100,000
Accounts payable, governmental activities	65,000
Accounts payable, business-type activities	56,000
Noncurrent liabilities, governmental activities	500,000
Noncurrent liabilities, business-type activities	300,000
Net assets, invested in capital assets (net), governmental activities.	1,000,000
Net assets, invested in capital assets (net), business-type activities	800,000
Net assets, restricted for debt service, governmental activities	65,000
Net assets, restricted for debt service, business-type activities.	36,000

Problem 17-11 *(LO 4)* **Reconciliation schedule.** Packer City's balance sheet and statement of revenues, expenditures, and changes in fund balances are shown below for the governmental funds. Information on capital assets and long-term obligations are also provided from the notes to the financial statements.

Additional information:

a. Receivables include two items that were not available for current-period expenditures. These are $1,402,903 Advance to Water Utility and special assessments of $66,008.
b. Accrued interest payable was $114,765 on December 31, 2013, and it was $133,627 on December 31, 2014.
c. Funding of principal payments included in the tax levied, but to be used for future principal payments is $189,417.
d. Governmental activities deferred debits include unamortized debt expense of $104,357 (net of accumulated amortization of $12,777).
e. Special assessments receivable decreased $44,394.
f. Issue costs on the new debt issued were $6,389. They are expensed, but are capitalized in the statement of activities.
g. Of the noncapitalized capital outlays, $920,000 are for police equipment and the balance, $1,115,616, is attributed to highway maintenance.
h. Depreciation expense is charged to the functions as follows:

a. Highway	$563,326
b. Education and recreation	203,276
c. Unallocated depreciation	525,086

i. There is very limited information upon which to allocate revenues, fees, and grants against expenditures. Do your best and just try to reflect the spirit of the process.

◄ ◄ ◄ ◄ ◄ **Required**

1. Prepare a reconciliation schedule for balance sheet to statement of net assets.
2. Prepare a reconciliation for statement of revenues, expenditures, and changes in fund balances to the statement of activities.
3. Based on part (1), prepare the statement of net assets.
4. Based on part (2), prepare the statement of activities.

Balance Sheet
Governmental Funds
December 31, 2014

	General	Debt Service	Capital Budget	Nonmajor Governmental Funds	Total Governmental Funds
ASSETS					
Cash and cash equivalents	$ 3,871,433	$ 766,926	$3,521,364	$8,285,896	$ 16,445,619
Receivable (net)					
Accounts	73,059	—	—	531,344	604,403
Due from other governments	26,781	—	—	9,799	36,580
Taxes receivable	8,588,671	1,982,360	—	180,091	10,751,122
Special assessments receivable					
Due in installments	—	—	—	42,790	42,790
Deferred.	—	—	—	90,432	90,432
Due from other funds	1,900	—	—	—	1,900
Prepaid expenses.	8,689	—	—	—	8,689
Advance to Water Utility					
Current portion.	—	198,131	—	—	198,131
Due after 2015	—	1,204,773	—	—	1,204,773
Total assets	$12,570,533	$4,152,190	$3,521,364	$9,140,352	$ 29,384,439

(continued)

	General	Debt Service	Capital Budget	Nonmajor Governmental Funds	Total Governmental Funds
LIABILITIES AND FUND BALANCES					
Liabilities:					
Accounts payable	$ 409,125	$ —	$ 297,799	$ 336,620	$ 1,043,544
Accrued liabilities	142,235	—	—	—	142,235
Due to other funds	—	—	—	1,900	1,900
Due to other governments	—	—	—	320,000	320,000
Deferred revenue	8,697,725	3,385,263	—	331,392	12,414,380
Total liabilities	$ 9,249,085	$3,385,263	$ 297,799	$ 989,912	$ 13,922,059
Fund balances:					
Reserved for:					
Prepaids	$ 8,689	$ —	$ —	$ —	$ 8,689
Non-current receivables	—	—	—	91,618	91,618
Revolving loan purposes	—	—	—	228,359	228,359
Encumbrances	160,000	—	79,725	142,443	382,168
Debt service	—	766,927	—	2,899,974	3,666,901
Unreserved, reported in:					
General fund	3,152,759	—	—	—	3,152,759
Special revenue funds	—	—	—	4,233,295	4,233,295
Capital projects funds	—	—	3,143,840	554,751	3,698,591
Total fund balances	$ 3,321,448	$ 766,927	$3,223,565	$8,150,440	$ 15,462,380
Total liabilities and fund balances	$12,570,533	$4,152,190	$3,521,364	$9,140,352	

Amounts reported for governmental activities in the statement of net assets are different because:

Capital assets used in governmental funds are not financial resources and therefore are not reported in the funds.	26,870,578
Special assessments	66,008
Advance to Water Utility	1,402,904
Some liabilities, including long-term debt, are not due and payable in the current period and therefore are not reported in the funds.	(28,044,186)
NET ASSETS OF GOVERNMENTAL ACTIVITIES	$ 15,757,684

Statement of Revenues, Expenditures, and Changes in Fund Balances
Governmental Funds
For the Year Ended December 31, 2014

	General	Debt Service	Capital Budget	Nonmajor Governmental Funds	Total Governmental Funds
REVENUES					
Taxes	$ 8,466,838	$1,666,729	$ —	$ 10,465	$10,144,032
Intergovernmental	1,530,215	—	—	413,989	1,944,204
Licenses and permits	639,103	—	—	—	639,103
Fines, forfeitures, and penalties	154,270	—	—	—	154,270
Public charges for services	691,659	—	—	2,308,445	3,000,104
Public improvement revenues	—	—	—	159,636	159,636
Commercial revenues	232,598	6,745	51,217	360,725	651,285
Intergovernmental charges for services	102,637	—	—	—	102,637
Interdepartmental revenues	69,672	283,962	—	—	353,634
Total revenues	$11,886,992	$1,957,436	$ 51,217	$ 3,253,260	$17,148,905
EXPENDITURES					
Current:					
General government	$ 2,618,262	$ —	$ —	$ 143,768	$ 2,762,030
Protection of persons and property .	4,945,330	—	—	295,846	5,241,176

(continued)

	General	Debt Service	Capital Budget	Nonmajor Governmental Funds	Total Governmental Funds
Highway and transportation	1,423,885	—	—	—	1,423,885
Health and sanitation	—	—	—	863,461	863,461
Economic development	—	—	—	86,788	86,788
Education and recreation	1,768,889	—	—	130,257	1,899,146
Debt service:					
Principal	—	1,157,514	—	—	1,157,514
Interest	—	1,057,619	—	—	1,057,619
Bond issuance costs	—	—	57,496	—	57,496
Capital outlay	673,283	—	4,005,427	1,513,980	6,192,690
Total expenditures	$11,429,649	$2,215,133	$ 4,062,923	$ 3,034,100	$20,741,805
Excess (deficiency) of revenues over expenditures	$ 457,343	$ (257,697)	$(4,011,706)	$ 219,160	$ 3,592,900
OTHER FINANCING SOURCES (USES)					
Transfers-in	$ 647,067	$ 635,600	$ —	$ 1,330,686	$ 2,613,353
Transfers-out	(147,846)	—	(15,098)	(2,413,299)	(2,576,241)
Proceeds from the sale of capital assets	29,520	—	—	—	29,520
Debt refunded	—	(825,000)	—	—	(825,000)
Long-term debt issued	—	825,000	2,200,000	—	3,025,000
Total other financing sources and uses	$ 528,741	$ 635,600	$ 2,184,904	$(1,082,613)	$ 2,266,632
Net change in fund balances	$ 986,084	$ 377,903	$(1,826,802)	$ (863,453)	$ (1,326,268)
FUND BALANCES—BEGINNING OF YEAR	2,335,364	389,024	5,050,367	9,013,893	16,788,648
FUND BALANCES—END OF YEAR . .	$ 3,321,448	$ 766,927	$ 3,223,565	$ 8,150,440	$15,462,380

D. CAPITAL ASSETS

Capital asset activity for the year ended December 31, 2014 was as follows:

	Beginning Balance	Additions	Deletions	Ending Balance
Governmental Activities				
Capital assets not being depreciated				
Land	$ 2,991,833	$ 879,221	$ —	$ 3,871,054
Construction in progress	—	748,411	—	748,411
Total capital assets not being depreciated	$ 2,991,833	$1,627,632	—	$ 4,619,465
Capital assets being depreciated				
Land improvements	$ 1,880,024	$ —	$ —	$ 1,880,024
Buildings	10,844,461	—	—	10,844,461
Machinery and equipment	6,128,085	281,634	441,624	5,968,095
Library collection	1,694,087	98,349	211,913	1,580,523
Infrastructure	7,916,030	2,149,459	38,984	10,026,505
Total capital assets being depreciated	$28,462,687	$2,529,442	$692,521	$30,299,608
Less accumulated depreciation for land improvements	$ 1,059,680	$ 39,837	$ —	$ 1,099,517
Buildings	2,263,393	288,848	—	2,552,241
Machinery and equipment	2,977,625	563,326	403,019	3,137,932
Library collection	992,268	203,276	211,913	983,631
Infrastructure	79,853	196,404	1,083	275,174
Total accumulated depreciation	$ 7,372,819	$1,291,691	$616,015	$ 8,048,495
Capital assets being depreciated, net of depreciation	$21,089,868	$1,237,751	$ 76,506	$22,251,113

G. LONG-TERM OBLIGATIONS

Long-term obligations activity for the year ended December 31, 2014 was as follows:

	Beginning Balance	Increases	Decreases	Ending Balance	Amounts Due Within One Year
Governmental Activities					
Bonds and notes payable					
General obligation debt					
Promissory notes and bonds............	$22,360,692	$3,025,000	$1,982,514	$23,403,178	$1,468,727
Community development					
Lease revenue bonds	2,000,000	—	—	2,000,000	—
Total bonds and notes payable	$24,360,692	$3,025,000	$1,982,514	$25,403,178	$1,468,727
Other liabilities					
Accrued compensated absences—vacation					
and sick leave	2,124,462	582,066	94,790	2,611,738	100,000
Total governmental activities					
Long-term liabilities.................	$26,485,154	$3,607,066	$2,077,304	$28,014,916	$1,568,727
Business-Type Activities					
Bonds and notes payable					
Revenue bonds........................	$14,105,000	$ —	$ 755,000	$13,350,000	$ 795,000
Advances from municipality.............	1,592,321	—	189,417	1,402,904	198,131
Total business-type activities					
Long-term liabilities.................	$15,697,321	$ —	$ 944,417	$14,752,904	$ 993,131

Problem 17-12 *(LO 4)* **Measurement focus: comparing statements.** Under the reporting model required by GASB Statement No. 34, fund statements are required for governmental, proprietary, and fiduciary funds. Government-wide statements include the statement of net assets and the statement of activities.

Required ▶ ▶ ▶ ▶ ▶

1. Explain the measurement focus and basis of accounting for governmental fund statements, proprietary fund statements, fiduciary fund statements, and government-wide statements.
2. Explain some differences between fund financial statements and government-wide statements with regard to component units, fiduciary funds, and location of internal service funds.
3. What should be included in the statement of net assets categories invested in capital assets, net of related debt, restricted, and unrestricted?

Problem 17-13 *(LO 4)* **Audit concerns.** The city of Lydell expended federal awards from the following programs during 2019.

	Program	Amount Expended
1.	Lydell Community Block Grant.............	$ 450,000
2.	Hazardous Waste Management............	350,000
3.	Law Enforcement	200,000
4.	Energy Assistance	250,000
5.	Economic Development...................	100,000
6.	Clean Water Program....................	75,000
		$1,425,000

Assume the auditor has given an unqualified opinion on the financial statements and reports no material weaknesses or reportable conditions in internal control at the financial statement level. Also, assume the auditor has given an unqualified opinion on the schedule of expenditures of federal awards. Programs 2 and 4 are classified as low risk, and Program 6 was not assessed for risk due to its small size.

Required ▶ ▶ ▶ ▶ ▶

1. Which programs should the auditor audit as major programs for the purpose of internal control evaluation and compliance testing for the year 2019?
2. How would your answer differ if Program 2 was classified as high risk?

Accounting for Private Not-for-Profit Organizations

Learning Objectives

When you have completed this chapter, you should be able to

1. Distinguish not-for-profit organizations from other entities.

2. Explain the jurisdictions of the GASB and the FASB with regard to not-for-profit organizations.

3. Explain how financial accounting and reporting for private not-for-profit organizations differs from that of state and local governments.

4. Demonstrate an understanding of the accounting for unrestricted and restricted contributions.

5. Demonstrate an understanding of the accounting for expenses in a private not-for-profit organization.

6. Identify and describe the financial statements and notes disclosure required of not-for-profit organizations.

7. State the requirements an organization must meet to be classified as voluntary health and welfare, and describe the accounting for public support.

8. Explain how to account for revenues and costs in a VHWO.

9. Prepare financial statements for not-for-profit organizations.

10. Prepare journal entries related to typical events of a not-for-profit organization.

11. Describe the typical funds used to account for VHWO transactions, and prepare optional VHWO fund-based financial statements. (Appendix)

This chapter and the next detail accounting for the four major not-for-profit organizations. These organizations include: (1) colleges and universities, (2) hospitals, (3) voluntary health and welfare organizations, and (4) other organizations such as museums, country clubs, and religious organizations. Chapter 18 outlines the unique characteristics of not-for-profit organizations and the accounting and reporting standard-setting activities in this sector. The accounting and reporting guidance for all not-for-profits with specific illustration for voluntary health and welfare organizations is also described. Chapter 19 includes a discussion of the accounting and financial reporting for public (governmental) and private colleges and universities and health care organizations.

NOT-FOR-PROFIT ORGANIZATIONS

Not-for-profit activities make up a significant portion of the U.S. economy. All not-for-profit organizations provide services without the intention of realizing a profit. Such organizations are generally financed by contributions, earnings from endowments or other investments, charges for services, and government grants. The AICPA defines a **not-for-profit organization** as an entity that (1) has significant contributions from resource providers who do not expect to get anything in return, (2) has an operating purpose other than to make a profit, and (3) has no owners. Examples of not-for-profits include voluntary health and welfare organizations (VHWO) or human service organizations such as the American Cancer Society, American Red Cross, Girl Scouts, and Boy Scouts. Other not-for-profits have charitable, educational, or scientific purposes and can be classified as mutual not-for-profits. Examples are libraries and museums, performing arts and other cultural organizations, private elementary and secondary schools, private colleges and universities, not-for-profit health care organizations, public broadcasting stations, religious organizations, research and scientific organizations, cemetery organizations, civic and fraternal organizations, labor unions, political parties, private and community foundations, professional associations, social and country clubs, trade associations, and zoological and botanical societies. External users of a not-for-profit organization's financial statements have common interests in assessing (1) its services and ability to continue those services, and (2) how its managers discharge their stewardship responsibilities and perform in other aspects.[1]

Development of Accounting Principles

Accounting principles for not-for-profit organizations were originally developed by not-for-profit industry groups, such as the National Association of College and University Business Officers (NACUBO), the Health Care Financial Management Association (HFMA), and the National Health Council. These industry groups, representing colleges and universities, hospitals, voluntary health and welfare organizations, and other organizations such as museums, country clubs, and religious organizations, developed manuals with accounting guidance. In response to an increasing awareness of the not-for-profit sector, the American Institute of Certified Public Accountants (AICPA) worked in conjunction with these industry groups to develop and issue accounting and audit guides in the early 1970s. These guides have been updated and amended over the years. As a result of the separate evolution of standards by each not-for-profit industry group, significant differences have existed for the four types of not-for-profits in terms of fund classifications, measurement criteria, account classifications, and financial statement disclosures. Over the last decade, a considerable effort has been made by the AICPA, the Financial Accounting Standards Board (FASB), and the Government Accounting Standards Board (GASB) to standardize the accounting and financial reporting for the diverse set of not-for-profit organizations in this sector and to reduce the inconsistencies in and across organizations in the not-for-profit sector. Two current applicable AICPA accounting and audit guides also reflect standardization for private and governmental not-for-profit organizations: The Audit and Accounting Guide, *Not-for-Profit Organizations* (March 1, 2010), includes guidance for voluntary health and welfare organizations and other not-for-profits, and the Audit and Accounting Guide, *Health Care Organizations* (June 1, 2010), includes guidance for both private and governmental health care organizations.

Jurisdiction for accounting and financial reporting for not-for-profit organizations is shared by the FASB and the GASB. The GASB has jurisdiction over accounting and financial reporting of governmental not-for-profits (public colleges and universities and government hospitals). The FASB has jurisdiction over accounting and financial reporting of all private not-for-profit organizations including voluntary health and welfare organizations, private colleges and universities, private health care providers, and other private not-for-profits. The accounting and financial reporting for voluntary health and welfare organizations is described in this chapter. Chapter 19 will cover private and governmental health care organizations and colleges and universities.

---

1 FASB ASC 958-205-05-03.

REFLECTION

- The FASB sets standards for all private not-for-profit organizations.

ACCOUNTING FOR PRIVATE NOT-FOR-PROFIT ORGANIZATIONS

The full accrual basis of accounting is used in accounting and reporting for all not-for-profits. Financial reporting for private not-for-profits emphasizes the organization as a whole. FASB ASC 958-205 requires not-for-profit organizations to provide financial statements with organization-wide totals of assets, liabilities, and net assets as well as information concerning organization-wide changes in net assets and organization-wide cash flows. Fund accounting continues to be used under FASB ASC 958-205. *Three net asset classes—unrestricted, temporarily restricted, and permanently restricted—are used instead of fund balances.* These net asset classes provide a clear distinction between resources that are externally restricted and those that are internally designated by action of the governing board. Because of a shift away from a fund accounting focus toward an organization-wide focus, external financial statements are not required to include fund reporting. However, even though both the FASB and GASB have in recent years set standards that emphasize organization-wide financial reporting, not-for-profit organizations continue to use funds for *internal management*. To aid in understanding the relationship between traditional funds and the new reporting requirements, a discussion of the voluntary health and welfare fund structure and illustrative financial statements reporting fund detail are included in the chapter appendix.

Accounting for Revenues, Gains, and Contributions

Not-for-profit organizations record all events as either exchange transactions, contributions, agency transactions, capital acquisitions, or expenses. Contributions are distinguished from exchange transactions or agency relationships. Only contributions with donor-imposed restrictions affect the restricted assets. All other transactions, such as charges for services and government and other awards funding research or programs, are now considered exchange transactions, and they affect unrestricted net assets. Government or private-sponsored flow-through awards to individuals or other organizations are accounted for as agency transactions, rather than as restricted asset activities.

FASB ASC 958-605 requires private not-for-profits to recognize both contributions received and unconditional promises (pledges) to give as *revenues or gains* in the period the gift or promise is received. *Contributions* are defined as "unconditional transfers of cash or other assets to an entity or a settlement or cancellation of its liabilities in a voluntary nonreciprocal transfer."[2] These nonexchange transactions may include cash, securities, land, and buildings. They may also include noncash items or gifts in kind such as free or discounted use of facilities or utilities, donated materials and supplies, intangible assets, and services of unpaid workers. All of these items are recorded at the *fair value* at the date of the gift. In the case of noncash gifts, a corresponding asset or expense is recorded.

Exceptions to the general recognition provision are made for contributions of services and works of art. Donated services, typically relied on to supplement the efforts of paid employees, are recognized only if they (a) create or enhance nonfinancial assets or (b) require specialized skills, are provided by individuals possessing those abilities, and typically would have to be purchased if not provided by donation. Additionally, not-for-profit organizations need not recognize contributed works of art, historical treasures, and similar assets as contributions "if the donated

---

2 FASB ASC 958-605-20. The FASB defines a nonreciprocal transfer as a transaction in which an organization receives an asset or cancellation of a liability without directly gaining value in exchange.

3

OBJECTIVE

Explain how financial accounting and reporting for private not-for-profit organizations differs from that of state and local governments.

4

OBJECTIVE

Demonstrate an understanding of the accounting for unrestricted and restricted contributions.

items are added to collections that are (a) held for public exhibition, education, or research rather than financial gain, (b) protected and preserved, or (c) subject to an organization policy that requires the proceeds from sales of collection items to be used to acquire other items for collections."[3] Although organizations can choose whether or not to capitalize their collections, the choice must be applied to all collections. Capitalization may be done retroactively or prospectively.

Pledges (promises to give) are divided into unconditional pledges and conditional pledges. *Unconditional pledges* depend only on the passage of time or the demand by the not-for-profit to be collected and are recognized as a receivable and revenue or support in the year made. *Conditional pledges* depend on the occurrence of uncertain future events and should be recognized as revenue when the conditions are substantially met (i.e., the pledge becomes unconditional). An example of a conditional pledge might be a donation restricted for construction of a new building given only if the organization can raise the remaining funds through additional contributions. Pledges or other assets received subject to such conditions are recorded as refundable advances until the conditions have been substantially met, at which time revenue is recorded.

Unconditional pledges payable in the future, or multiyear pledges, are treated as temporarily restricted revenue or support and then reclassified to the unrestricted net asset class when the period of the donor stipulation is met. These pledges (or promises to give) are recorded at the present value of estimated future cash flows using a risk-adjusted discount rate. Promises receivable within one year need not be discounted. An allowance for doubtful contributions should be established based on historical experience and other factors to cover any uncertainties concerning collectibility. An unconditional pledge with no donor restriction is recognized as follows:

Contributions Receivable.	XXX	
Revenues—Unrestricted Contributions		XXX
Provision for Uncollectible Contributions.	XXX	
Allowance for Uncollectible Contributions		XXX

Donor-Imposed Restrictions and Reclassifications. All contributions received (or unconditional promises to give) are classified into one of three categories: unrestricted, temporarily restricted, or permanently restricted resources. *Donor-imposed restrictions* do not affect the timing of when contributions are recognized. Rather, these donor restrictions affect the manner of reporting contributions and related assets. If a donor does not stipulate how the asset should be used, then the gift is classified as unrestricted. If the donor does impose a restriction, such as identifying a particular program, capital asset, or time period that the donated asset may be used, the contribution is classified as temporarily restricted. Other assets may be donated as permanently restricted endowments.

A temporary restriction expires when (a) the stipulated time has elapsed, (b) the stipulated purpose has been fulfilled, or (c) the useful life of the donated asset has ended. Expenditure or time restrictions require a reclassification entry to release the restriction. Gifts of long-lived assets (or long-lived assets acquired with restricted gifts of cash) with donor stipulations specifying the use of the donated asset are initially reported as temporarily restricted. The expiration (or release) of the time restriction is recorded over the useful life of the asset. Organizations have an option to record long-lived assets acquired with donor-restricted cash as either temporarily restricted or unrestricted. If the asset is recorded as temporarily restricted, the organization reclassifies a portion of the temporarily restricted amount each year as depreciation is recorded. This *releasing of donor-imposed restrictions (reclassification)* simultaneously decreases temporarily restricted net assets and increases unrestricted net assets in order to *match* the expenses they support (operating expenses, depreciation, etc., which decrease unrestricted net assets).

Not-for-profits also have the option to record contributions whose restrictions are met in the same reporting period as increases in unrestricted net assets, instead of increases in temporarily restricted net assets with subsequent reclassifications from temporarily restricted net assets to unrestricted net assets.

---

3 FASB ASC 958-605.

Furthermore, if an expense is incurred for a purpose for which both unrestricted and temporarily restricted net assets are available, a donor-imposed restriction is fulfilled to the extent of the expense incurred, unless the expense is for a purpose that is directly attributable to another specific external source of revenue. This provision to use restricted resources first to fund expenses does not allow institutions to choose either restricted or unrestricted sources of funding.

A cash contribution restricted by the donor for a specific expenditure is recorded when received.	Cash XXX	
	Revenues—Temporarily Restricted Contributions ...	XXX
Expenses made in compliance with donor restrictions are funded by the restricted resources. Temporarily restricted net assets are released with a reclassification entry.	Expense.. XXX	
	Cash	XXX
	Reclassification Out—Temporarily Restricted—	
	Satisfaction of Donor Restrictions................ XXX	
	Reclassification In—Unrestricted—Satisfaction	
	of Donor Restrictions......................	XXX

Key to accurate accounting is the distinction between accounting for exchange transactions, agency transactions, and contributions. Exchange transactions, that is, reciprocal transfers in which each party receives and sacrifices approximately equal value, are not considered restricted. Many transactions that traditionally are thought of as contributions, for example, grants, awards, sponsorships, and appropriations, may be categorized as exchange transactions rather than contributions and accounted for as increases in unrestricted assets. Government grants that require performance by the not-for-profit organization are accounted for as refundable deposits (liabilities) until earned. Unrestricted revenue is earned when expenses are made in conjunction with the provisions of the grant. Other grants that just specify for support research or community work and do not have specific performance or rights to patents or products may be reported as contributions. And, government grants, which are essentially pass-through financial aid to students, are accounted for as agency transactions. Assets received on behalf of another individual or organization must be offset with a payable to the alternative beneficiary unless: (1) the donor has granted variance power to the not-for-profit organization (i.e., the right to redirect the use of the assets), or (2) the recipient organization and beneficiary are financially interrelated. In both cases, the not-for-profit organization recognizes the contribution as revenue.[4]

Grant monies received.	Cash XXX	
	U.S. Government Grants Refundable	XXX
Expenses incurred in conjunction with provisions of grant.	Expenses XXX	
	Cash	XXX
Revenue is recognized as the amount earned above expenses.	U.S. Government Grants Refundable XXX	
	Revenues—Unrestricted......................	XXX

Investments. Permanently restricted contributions are called *endowments*. Earnings on endowment investments are reported in the period earned as a credit to either unrestricted revenue or temporarily restricted revenue depending on donor specification as to the use of the earnings. Not-for-profit organizations must report all investments in equity securities that have readily determinable values and all debt securities at fair value. Reporting at original cost, amortized cost, or lower-of-cost-or-market is not allowed. Unlike businesses, there is no requirement for not-for-profits to classify their investments into trading, available-for-sale, and held-to-maturity categories. Realized and unrealized gains on endowment investments are reported as increases or decreases in unrestricted net assets unless their use is temporarily

---

4 FASB ASC 958-605.

or permanently restricted by explicit donor stipulations or by law. Losses on endowment investments reduce temporarily restricted net assets to the extent that donor-imposed restrictions on net appreciation have been met before the loss occurs. Any remaining loss would reduce unrestricted net assets.[5]

Most states have adopted the Uniform Prudent Management of Institutional Funds Act of 2006 (UPMIFA) to guide the treatment of endowments. In response to the UPMIFA, the FASB issued FASB ASC 958-205-45-28 to provide guidance to improve the quality of financial reporting of endowments. For not-for-profits in states where the UPMIFA is currently effective, FASB ASC 958-205-45-28 through FASB ASC 958-205-45-31 require the earnings on donor-restricted endowments not explicitly restricted by the donor to be classified as temporarily restricted net assets until appropriated for expenditure by the organization. This is a departure from FASB ASC 958-205-45-17 that considered these earnings to be unrestricted.

5
OBJECTIVE

Demonstrate an understanding of the accounting for expenses in a private not-for-profit organization.

Accounting for Expenses

Private not-for-profit organizations recognize expenses on an accrual basis rather than as expenditures. Furthermore, all expenses are reported as decreases in unrestricted net assets. Whereas expenditures denote outlays of resources, expenses denote *using up* of resources. Therefore, flows of resources involving outlays of cash to purchase other assets are not presented in the statement of activities but instead in the statement of cash flows. Depreciation of capital assets, including contributed capital assets, is also recorded as an expense per FASB ASC 958-360-35.[6] Land and individual works of art or historical treasures that have an extraordinarily long life are not depreciated.

Not-for-profit organizations segregate expenses between program functions and those functions supporting the programs. Program expenses include the direct and indirect cost of providing or conducting a particular mission or part of the organizational mission. Supporting expenses include management and general expenses and fund-raising activity. Natural or object classifications, e.g., supplies, salaries, and telephone, are allocated to the functions. Depreciation expenses are allocated to programs as well as to support function expenses.

Not-for-profits often conduct activities that combine program and fund raising. In the past, the cost of the joint activity often was reported entirely as a functional program expense with no allocation to the functional support expense of fund raising. In response to concerns about fund-raising costs being *hidden* within the program and management activities, the AICPA issued Statement of Position 98-2 making it more difficult to allocate *educating the public* or *advocacy* costs to programs. SOP 98-2, codified in FASB ASC 958-720-45, sets forth the following requirements:

1. Costs of all materials and activities that include a fund-raising appeal should be reported as fund-raising costs ... unless a bona fide program or management function has been conducted in conjunction with the appeal.
2. Criteria of purpose, audience, and content must be met in order to conclude that a bona fide program or management and general function has been conducted in conjunction with the appeal of funds.
3. If a bona fide program or management function has been conducted, the joint costs should be allocated using an equitable allocation base.
4. Certain information must be disclosed if joint costs are allocated.[7]

6
OBJECTIVE

Identify and describe the financial statements and notes disclosure required of not-for-profit organizations.

Financial Statements

Financial statements emphasize the organization as a whole. Classification of the organization's net assets is based on the existence or absence of donor-imposed restrictions. The financial statements must display three classes of net assets: unrestricted, temporarily restricted, and permanently restricted. Changes in each of these three classes of net assets must also be reported.

5 FASB ASC 958-205-45-22.
6 FASB ASC 958-360-35-1 through FASB ASC 958-360-35-7.
7 FASB ASC 958-720-45.

Reclassifications that simultaneously decrease temporarily restricted net assets and increase unrestricted net assets are reported separately.

Required external financial statements include the following:

1. *Statement of financial position* (balance sheet) which will report organization-wide totals for assets, liabilities, and net assets, and net assets identified as unrestricted, temporarily restricted, and permanently restricted.

2. *Statement of activities* which reports revenues, expenses, gains, losses, and reclassifications (between classes of net assets). Minimum requirements include organization-wide totals, changes in net assets for each class of assets, and all expenses recognized only in the unrestricted classification. A display of a measure of operations in the statement of activities is permitted.

3. *Statement of cash flows* with categories (operating, financing, investing, etc.) similar to business organizations.

4. *Statement of functional expenses* which reports detailed program, fund-raising, and management and general expenses (required only for voluntary health and welfare organizations).

In addition, information about liquidity must be provided. Liquidity is commonly reported through sequencing assets and liabilities according to nearness of conversion to or use of cash on the statement of financial position. Such sequencing requires cash and contributions receivable restricted by donors to investment in land, building, and equipment to be included in "assets restricted to investment in land, building, and equipment" rather than cash and contributions. Cash and equivalents of permanent endowment funds held temporarily until suitable long-term investment opportunities are identified must be included in the classification "long-term investments." Other organizations provide liquidity information in the notes to the financial statements.

Not-for-profit organizations are encouraged to develop the format for their financial statements that is most meaningful to their users. Models, suggested by the FASB and included in this chapter, are (1) a single-column, *corporate* format and (2) disaggregation by net asset class. Organizations appear to prefer the former model for the statement of financial position and the latter for the statement of activities. Illustration 18-2 (shown on page 949) presents the statement of activities. Illustration 18-4 (shown on page 950) presents the statement of financial position. A cash flow statement is included in Illustration 18-5 (shown on page 951).

Required note disclosures include a description of the fund accounting groups and their relationship to the classes of net assets, classification of revenues, expenses, gains, losses, classification and valuation of contributions, description of accounting policies for release of donor restrictions, anticipated collection period of contributions receivables, description of collections, and detail on contributed services not meeting the reporting criteria. Disclosure of expenses by natural classification is suggested but not required.

Proper recording of reciprocal exchange transactions, agency transactions, and nonreciprocal contributions is essential to providing organization-wide financial statements of assets, liabilities, net assets, changes in net assets, and cash flows. Managers of not-for-profit organizations will have to carefully analyze the nature of each transaction to properly identify contributions and exchange transactions.

The FASB recently revised the accounting standards for not-for-profit mergers and acquisitions, codified in FASB ASC 958-805. In the event a not-for-profit organization merges with another not-for-profit organization, the governing bodies of both entities cede control to create a new not-for profit entity. FASB ASC 958-805 requires the new entity to combine the assets and liabilities in its initial financial statement, called the *carryover method*, at amounts reported in the merging entities' separate financial statements at the merger date. The initial reporting period of the combined entity will be the date of the merger, and the merger itself will not be reported as an activity of the initial reporting period.

In the event a not-for-profit acquires another not-for-profit organization, the acquiring not-for-profit obtains control of the acquiree not-for-profit and follows the acquisition method of accounting. The acquisition method in FASB ASC 958-805 is similar to the method prescribed in FASB ASC 805 in that the acquirer recognizes and measures at fair value the identifiable net assets acquired from the acquiree along with any noncontrolling interest. The distinction lies in how goodwill is recognized. If the acquirer expects the acquiree to operate like a business (charging fees for service), then goodwill must be recognized as an asset at the acquisition date. If the acquirer expects the acquiree operations to be predominately supported by contributions and returns on investments, then a separate charge in the statement of activities in the amount that would have been recorded for goodwill should be recognized. When the acquirer receives net assets without transferring consideration, a contribution should be recognized as a separate credit in the statement of activities on the acquisition date.

REFLECTION

- Private not-for-profits use full accrual accounting.

- All transactions of a not-for-profit organization may be classified as exchange, nonexchange, or agency. Accounting for exchange transactions follows full accrual accounting. Agency transactions are accounted for in the same way as in governments.

- Nonexchange transactions, or contributions, are accounted for in the period received or made. Contributions may be classified as unrestricted, temporarily restricted, or permanently restricted by the donor.

- A reclassification (release of restriction) is made when the donor-imposed restriction is met. This may be a result of satisfying a program, equipment, or time restriction.

- The financial statements of all not-for-profits include a statement of financial position, statement of activities, and statement of cash flows. Each of the three net assets (unrestricted, temporarily restricted, and permanently restricted) and any changes to these asset categories are shown on the financial statements.

7

OBJECTIVE

State the requirements an organization must meet to be classified as voluntary health and welfare, and describe the accounting for public support.

ACCOUNTING FOR VOLUNTARY HEALTH AND WELFARE ORGANIZATIONS

To qualify as a *voluntary health and welfare organization* (VHWO), two criteria must be met. First, a primary source of revenue should be contributions from donors who do not themselves directly benefit from the organization's programs. Second, the program must be in the area of health, welfare, or community service, such as care for the elderly, the indigent, or the handicapped, or projects to protect the environment.

Accounting Principles and Procedures

The dependence upon public support for the majority of its resources influences the accounting for a VHWO. Two major categories are used to record and communicate inflows of resources: public support and revenues. Public support is the inflow of resources from voluntary donors who receive no direct, personal benefit from the organization's usual programs in exchange for their contributions. Revenues are inflows of resources resulting from a charge for service from financial activities or from other exchange transactions.

A significant aspect of accounting and reporting for VHWOs is that financial reports must show expenses on a program basis. As a result of this requirement, the costs of each program and supporting service are available, and the effectiveness with which the organization's resources have been managed can be measured.

Public Support

The following accounts are used to record receipts of assets in the public support category:

1. Contributions,
2. Special Events Support,
3. Legacies and Bequests, and
4. Received from Federated and Nonfederated Campaigns.

Contributions. Contributions are recognized as public support in the period received and as assets, decreases of liabilities, or expenses depending on the form of the benefits received.[8] Although most contributions to VHWOs are made with no restrictions attached, some donations specify the purpose for which they must be expended. Contributions also include unconditional promises to give (pledges). Therefore, unconditional promises to give must also be recognized as support in the period received. Contributions may be unrestricted or restricted for a specific purpose. Contributions that have no donor-imposed restrictions attached to them are reported as unrestricted. Contributions that have donor-imposed restrictions attached to them must be classified as temporarily or permanently restricted based on the nature of the restriction.

Cash collections that do not involve a previous promise to give are credited to the account Contributions. VHWOs also receive pledges for contributions, which are recorded at the gross amount as Contributions Receivable, with a credit to Contributions. A provision and an allowance for estimated uncollectible pledges are established, based on historical collection experience. The provision for uncollectible pledges is an expense account, while the allowance is a contra account to Pledges Receivable.

Expiration of donor restrictions must be recognized in the period in which the restriction expires. The expiration of a restriction may be based on the lapse of time, the fulfillment of a stipulated purpose, or both. Recognition of an expiration of donor restrictions is done with a reclassification entry. Reclassifications result in an increase in the unrestricted class of net assets and a decrease in temporarily restricted net assets class. Such a reclassification increases unrestricted net assets to *match* the decrease resulting from the stipulated expense.

Temporarily restricted unconditional promises to give (pledges) are reclassified to unrestricted in the period in which the unconditional promise is received or the restriction lapses. A gift or promise to give that involves a condition is not considered a contribution until the condition is met and is therefore not recognized as an increase in net assets in the period in which it is received but is disclosed in the footnotes.

Securities and other property received should be recorded at fair value at the time of receipt. These assets are most likely to be received as temporarily or permanently restricted contributions. The donor may restrict not only the purpose but also the timing of use. If the donation is not available for use until some future fiscal period, it is recorded as Contributions—Temporarily Restricted. The amount is released from restriction (unclassified) in the period when it becomes available.

Common to VHWOs is the donation of materials to be used in providing service or to be processed for subsequent sale. These materials should be recorded as inventory, with a credit to Unrestricted Contributions at their fair value when received, provided that they are substantial in amount and a measurable value for them can be established, either by sale shortly thereafter or by appraisal. An example would be the donation of clothing or household goods to Goodwill Industries.

Occasionally, a VHWO will be permitted to use building facilities rent free. In this situation, both the contribution and the rent expense should be recorded at fair rental value, usually equivalent to the amount that normally would be charged for rent. Donated fixed assets for which title is received, such as equipment, land, and buildings, should be entered as an unrestricted, temporarily restricted, or permanently restricted contribution at fair value depending upon the donor's stipulations. Expiration of donor restrictions will occur either at the time the asset is placed in service or over the asset's useful life. Permanent restrictions do not expire.

---

8 A contribution is defined as an "unconditional transfer of cash or other assets to an entity or a settlement or cancellation of its liabilities in a voluntary nonreciprocal transfer by another entity acting other than as an owner" (FASB ASC 958-605-20).

Although the range of personal services that volunteers donate varies between VHWOs, these services must be recorded if they are significant and if the following criteria are met:

1. The services received create or enhance nonfinancial assets, or
2. The services received require specialized skills, are provided by individuals possessing those skills, and would typically need to be purchased if not provided by donation. (Usually, the individuals performing such services are treated in a similar fashion to employees; they have schedules, perform assigned duties, are supervised, etc.)

Promises to give services are also included. Recognizing contributed services that are specialized and would need to be purchased indicates to readers of the financial statements the impact these contributions have on the organization. It also indicates the need for future cash outflows in the event these services are no longer contributed.

If the criteria are met, donated services are recorded with a debit to an expense account, such as Salary Expense, and a credit to Contributions. Contributed services received that are not required to be recognized as revenues are disclosed at their fair value in the footnotes to the financial statements.

Special Events Support. Another subdivision of the public support category covers an organization's special fund-raising events in which the participant has the opportunity to receive something of value in exchange for a contribution. Raffles, dinners, bingo games, and bake sales are examples of special events. The gross inflow of resources is credited to Special Events Support in the fund that it is to benefit. Direct costs of the event, excluding promotional costs, are charged to Cost of Special Events. Comparing these two balances permits one to judge the effectiveness of the event. It also determines that portion of the proceeds that is a contribution to the organization. If such *special events* are peripheral or incidental, they may be disclosed net of costs (which used to be the general practice), but if they are ongoing and major activities, then gross revenue is recorded and direct costs of those activities are considered fund-raising expenses. Promotional costs, such as advertising or the salaries of employees involved in the event, are charged against fund-raising expense. The portion of the budget consumed by fund-raising expenses must also be revealed.

Legacies and Bequests. Every VHWO hopes that its programs will be so deserving that they will encourage donors to make major contributions of personal property or real property through their wills. Since these items tend to be more substantial in amount, the audit guide recommends that such contributions be shown as a separate item of public support under Legacies and Bequests. They are entered as a credit to that account when the organization is reasonably certain of the amount to be received. Such contributions are classified as unrestricted, temporarily restricted, or permanently restricted based on donor stipulations.

Received from Federated and Nonfederated Campaigns. The final item considered as public support is the amount received from federated (associated) and nonfederated organizations. This amount is credited to Received from Federated and Nonfederated Campaigns. An amount allocated by United Way to a health and welfare organization would be an example of support received from a federated organization. An amount raised by independent, professional fund-raising groups would be an illustration of resources received from nonfederated campaigns. Usually, contributions received from federated and nonfederated campaigns are unrestricted.

Revenues

8

O B J E C T I V E

Explain how to account for revenues and costs in a VHWO.

In addition to public support, resources may be received from exchange transactions that are classified as unrestricted revenue. These resources would include the following accounts:

1. Membership Dues Revenue for dues charged members to join and use facilities or receive publications.
2. Program Services Fees for amounts charged clients for services of the organization, such as consulting, testing, or advising.
3. Sales of Publications and Supplies for proceeds from the sales of these items.

Investment transaction revenue, classified as unrestricted or restricted, could include the following accounts:

1. Investment Revenue for interest, dividends, and other earnings.
2. Realized Gain on Investment Transactions for gains from the sale or exchange of investments.
3. Net Increase (or Decrease) in Carrying Value of Investments for the unrealized appreciation (or depreciation) of investments if they are carried at fair value.

Each of the items of investment transactions revenue would be recorded as unrestricted or restricted depending on donor stipulations. Thus, the unrestricted revenue from an endowment would be recorded with a credit to Investment Revenue—Unrestricted. Restricted investment revenue is reported as temporarily or permanently restricted in compliance with the donor's wishes.

VHWOs are required to carry their investments at fair value.[9] When a relatively permanent reduction in fair value occurs, the impairment to cost must be recorded. The unrealized appreciation (or depreciation) is shown separately in Net Increase (or Decrease) in Carrying Value of Investments. Realized and unrealized gains and losses on all investments are considered increases or decreases in unrestricted net assets unless restricted by donor or law.

Program and Supporting Services Costs

VHWOs exist to render service or to conduct programs. Their operating statements will not show typical expenses, such as salaries or rent, but will show the cost of each program or service the organization provides—the costs in which the general public, the contributors, and the controlling agencies are primarily interested. For example, the operating statement of an environmental protection association might show the cost of conducting a program to reduce river pollution or to provide an animal and bird sanctuary. These projects fall in an expense grouping called Program Services. The other expense grouping shown on an operating statement is referred to as Supporting Services, which includes fund-raising costs, management and general costs, and membership development activities for the overall direction of the organization. Management and general activities include all management, financing, and administrative activities, except for direct activities of programs or fund raising. Fund-raising activities include publicizing and conducting fund-raising campaigns, maintaining donor mailing lists, conducting special fund-raising events, preparing and distributing fund-raising materials, and other activities involved with soliciting contributions. Membership development activities include soliciting for prospective members and membership dues, membership relations, and similar activities.

Individual expenses, such as salaries or rent, are recorded in the respective natural expense accounts in much the same way that they would be recorded in the accounts of profit entities. All expenses are considered reductions in unrestricted net assets. Therefore, when expenses are recorded for purposes stipulated by donors, a reclassification of temporarily restricted to unrestricted net assets is also recorded. At the end of the fiscal year, the expenses are allocated to the individual programs conducted and to the supporting services of management, fund raising, and membership development. Allocation of joint costs should be on some rational basis, such as assigning salaries on the basis of time expended, allotting rental charges on the basis of floor space, or apportioning supplies expense on the basis of consumption. However, it is not always simple to allocate costs.

For example, informational materials that attempt to educate the reader about proper health habits to avoid disease or infection, birth control and other family planning issues, and the need to protect endangered species or the environment are often distributed to the public by not-for-profit organizations. Included in much of this material is a fund-raising appeal. A question arises as to whether the total cost of sending such literature should be charged to the program publicized or to fund raising, or whether it should be allocated between them. Since board members, donors, and the general public pay particular attention to the percentages of revenue consumed by administrative and fund-raising purposes, the desire to keep those percentages at a minimum is understandable. AICPA guidance on joint-cost allocation described in the previous section must be followed by all VHWOs.

---

9 FASB ASC 958-320.

Closing Entries

After all expenses have been assigned, an entry is made to close the expense accounts and charge each of the expenses to the individual programs and supporting services. For the environmental protection association used earlier as an example, the following entry might be recorded:

River Pollution Program Expense	XXX	
Animal and Bird Sanctuary Program Expense	XXX	
Management and General Services Expense	XXX	
Fund-Raising Services Expense	XXX	
Salary Expense, Supplies Expense, etc.		XXX

The final closing entries close support and revenue accounts, as well as the program and services accounts, to the appropriate net asset classification. The closing entry for the Unrestricted Net Assets of the environmental protection association might be as follows:

Contributions—Unrestricted	XXX	
Legacies and Bequests—Unrestricted	XXX	
Membership Dues Revenue	XXX	
Investment Revenue—Unrestricted	XXX	
Reclassification In—Unrestricted—Satisfaction of Donor Restrictions	XXX	
River Pollution Program Expense		XXX
Animal and Bird Sanctuary Program Expense		XXX
Management and General Services Expense		XXX
Fund-Raising Services Expense		XXX
Unrestricted Net Assets		XXX

If the board of directors should decide to designate a specified sum of the Unrestricted Net Assets for a future program to reduce air pollution, the following entries are recorded:

Unrestricted Net Assets	XXX	
Unrestricted Net Assets—Designated for Air Pollution Program		XXX

Similar entries to close temporarily restricted and permanently restricted accounts include the following:

Contributions—Temporarily Restricted	XXX	
Legacies and Bequests—Temporarily Restricted	XXX	
Investment Revenue—Temporarily Restricted	XXX	
Reclassifications Out—Temporarily Restricted—Satisfaction of Donor Restrictions		XXX
Temporarily Restricted Net Assets		XXX

Contributions—Permanently Restricted	XXX	
Legacies and Bequests—Permanently Restricted	XXX	
Permanently Restricted Net Assets		XXX

9
OBJECTIVE

Prepare financial statements for not-for-profit organizations.

Financial Statements

Consistent with other not-for-profits, the financial statements for VHWOs are a statement of financial position, a statement of activities, and a statement of cash flows. In addition, VHWOs must provide a statement of functional expenses. A statement of financial position is prepared either in single-column form or with a column for each asset class. Organization-wide totals of assets, liabilities, and net assets are presented. An activities statement can be prepared after the expense allocation entry has been recorded. It is structured with a column for each asset class and shows how effectively the organization operated during the period. Since program costs and not the typical (natural) expenses, such as salaries, are shown in an operating statement, a summary of expenses by object-of-expense classification is provided in a separate statement. This statement of functional expenses supplements the operating statement. It presents the total of each functional expense to programs and supporting services.

Day Star Activity and Respite Center serves older adults afflicted with Alzheimer's disease or other memory impairment and their families. Day Star operates an adult day care center, which provides a respite from constant caregiving for primary caregivers. Day Star also provides limited home care for clients. The expenses that were incurred by Day Star are as follows:

Expense	Amount
Salaries and payroll taxes	$17,000
Crafts and activities	4,000
Meals on Wheels.	4,000
Office expenses.	2,000
Repairs and maintenance	1,500
Depreciation expense	5,000
Total expenses	$33,500

Day Star management has estimated the allocation of financial resources to organization activities and prepared the following allocation scheme:

	Day Care	Home Care	Management
Operating expenses	40%	35%	25%
Capital-related expenses.	90	10	0

Expenses are allocated to programs and supporting services in the following manner. Then, they are presented in the statement of activities.

	Total	Day Care	Home Care	Management and General
Operating expenses	$28,500	$11,400	$9,975	$7,125
Capital-related expenses.	5,000	4,500	500	0

Expenses also are allocated to programs and supporting services using the allocation matrix for presentation in the statement of functional expenses. The following example shows this procedure for three object-of-expense categories:

Object of Expense	Total	Day Care	Home Care	Management and General
Salaries and payroll taxes	$17,000	$ 6,800	$ 5,950	$4,250
Crafts and activities	4,000	1,600	1,400	1,000
Meals on Wheels.	4,000	1,600	1,400	1,000
Office expenses.	2,000	800	700	500
Repairs and maintenance	1,500	600	525	375
Depreciation	5,000	4,500	500	0
Total expenses	$33,500	$15,900	$10,475	$7,125

Illustrative Transactions for a Voluntary Health and Welfare Organization

To illustrate the recording of events and the preparation of financial reports for a VHWO, assume the People's Environmental Protection (PEP) Association, a voluntary community organization, has three programs: Valley Air Project, Fish in the Lakes, and Flood Control. The statement of financial position of PEP on December 31, 2018, is shown in Illustration 18-1.

10

OBJECTIVE

Prepare journal entries related to typical events of a not-for-profit organization.

Illustration 18-1
People's Environmental Protection (PEP) Association
Statement of Financial Position
As of December 31, 2018

Assets:

Cash and cash equivalents	$ 253,500
Contributions receivable (net of $3,100 allowance)	21,500
Inventories	10,000
Short-term investments	152,000
Property, plant, and equipment (net of $16,700 accumulated depreciation)	676,000
Long-term endowment investments	253,000
Total assets	**$1,366,000**

Liabilities and net assets:

Accounts payable	$ 37,000
Notes payable	100,000
Total liabilities	**$ 137,000**

Net assets:

Unrestricted	**$ 289,000**
Temporarily restricted	**687,000**
Permanently restricted	**253,000**
Total net assets	**$1,229,000**
Total liabilities and net assets	$ 1,366,000

The following events occur during the calendar year 2019. They are summarized to conserve space and minimize duplication. Entries are shown following each transaction. Although no fund designations are recorded, VHWOs may choose to use fund accounting for donor-restricted resources, plant, and permanently restricted endowments. Fund-based financial statements for VHWOs are illustrated in the appendix to this chapter.

Event	Entry		
1. As a result of its fund-raising program, cash contributions of $325,000 were received. $315,000 was unrestricted, and $10,000 was restricted for Valley Air Project operating costs. In addition, unconditional promises to give totaled $100,000, of which $80,000 was unrestricted and $20,000 restricted for acquisition of equipment.	Cash	325,000	
	Contributions—Unrestricted		315,000
	Contributions—Temporarily Restricted		10,000
	Contributions Receivable	100,000	
	Contributions—Unrestricted		80,000
	Contributions—Temporarily Restricted		20,000
2. Based on past experience, 5% of the promises to give was estimated to be uncollectible.	Provision for Uncollectible Contributions	5,000	
	Allowance for Uncollectible Contributions		5,000
3. During the year, cash was collected from some unconditional promises to give, while others were written off as uncollectible.	Cash	95,500	
	Allowance for Uncollectible Contributions	5,600	
	Contributions Receivable		101,100

Event	Entry		
4. A cash donation of $40,000 was received, with the donor stipulation that it be used to acquire equipment for water quality improvement.	Cash . . . . Contributions—Temporarily Restricted	40,000	40,000
5. With the donor's approval, the $40,000 served as a partial payment on the purchase of a filter system costing $50,000. A note was signed for the unpaid balance. PEP chooses to release the donor restriction over the life of the asset.	Land, Building, and Equipment . . . . Cash . . . . Notes Payable on Equipment.	50,000	40,000 10,000
6. PEP received $5,000 from an individual who restricted its use to a special project within the Fish in the Lakes program. If that special project is not accomplished within six months, the individual requested that the money be returned. PEP has not yet undertaken the project. Two months remain in the time period specified by the donor.	Cash . . . . Refundable Advances	5,000	5,000
7. The following bequests were received: $100,000 unrestricted and $20,000 to be invested in an endowment whose earnings are to be unrestricted.	Cash . . . . Legacies and Bequests—Unrestricted . . . . Legacies and Bequests—Permanently Restricted	120,000	100,000 20,000
8. PEP received donated goods with a fair value of $2,350. Of those donated goods, $750 is restricted by the donor for use in the Fish in the Lakes program; the remaining gifts can be used at management's discretion.	Inventories . . . . Contributions—Unrestricted . . . . Contributions—Temporarily Restricted	2,350	1,600 750
9. PEP held a special summer event to promote its activities, the net proceeds of which were unrestricted. Gross revenues totaled $9,000, with direct costs for the event amounting to $2,000.	Cash . . . . Special Events Support—Unrestricted . . . . Costs of Special Events . . . . Cash	9,000 2,000	9,000 2,000
10. PEP uses volunteers to distribute brochures about its operations, to assist the staff with routine office work, and to make phone calls during the annual fund-raising appeal. The volunteers provided 1,000 hours of service this year. If the volunteers were not available, the tasks would either be performed by staff at a later date or not done at all.			
11. Members were assessed, and all paid membership dues of $118,000.	Cash . . . . Membership Dues Revenues	118,000	118,000
12. The local PEP unit receives unrestricted cash of $16,000 as its share of a campaign run by its national affiliate.	Cash . . . . Received from Federated and Nonfederated Campaigns—Unrestricted	16,000	16,000
13. Earnings on endowment investments total $28,000, of which $21,000 is not restricted and $7,000 is restricted to investment in equipment for flood control.	Cash . . . . Investment Revenue—Unrestricted. . . . . Investment Revenue—Temporarily Restricted . .	28,000	21,000 7,000

(continued)

Event	Entry		

14. PEP carries its investments in all funds at fair value. Endowment investments are sold for $27,000. They had a cost of $20,000 and a carrying value of $25,000 in the investment account. All endowment gains are to be permanently restricted according to donor specifications.	Cash ....
	     Investment (at fair) ....
	     Gain on Sale of Investments—Permanently
	          Restricted ....
		27,000	25,000
			
			2,000

15. An additional $46,000 of investments are purchased from endowment funds.	Investments—Permanently Restricted........... Cash	46,000	46,000

16. Unrestricted investments have shown no material change in fair value over the year. At year-end, the fair value of permanently restricted endowment investments has increased from $265,000 to $294,000. All endowment gains are to be permanently restricted according to the donor specification.	Investments ....
	     Net Increase in Carrying Value of
	          Investments—Permanently Restricted ....
		29,000	29,000

17. A lawyer provided five hours of service to PEP to draw up an endowment agreement. She did not charge for her services. She normally would charge a client $500 for consultation on a similar type of agreement. In the absence of the donated professional services, PEP would have hired a lawyer to draft the agreement.	Professional Services....................... Contributions—Unrestricted	500	500
18. A special recreational building and dock costing $96,000 were purchased with unrestricted cash.	Land, Building, and Equipment .... Cash	96,000	96,000

19. Contributions received in the prior period with the stipulation that they be used for expenses of this period are now available.	Reclassification Out—Temporarily Restricted—
	     Satisfaction of Time Requirements ....
	          Reclassification In—Unrestricted—
	               Satisfaction of Time Requirements ....
		10,000	10,000

20. Accounts payable and expenses were paid or established. Operating expenses related to donor-specific programs totaled $103,000.	Accounts Payable (January 1) ....
	Salaries Expense ....
	Payroll Taxes ....
	Mailing and Postage Expense ....
	Rent Expense ....
	Telephone Expense ....
	Research Expense ....
	Professional Services: Legal and Audit ....
	Supplies Expense..........................
	Miscellaneous Expense ....
	     Accounts Payable ....
	     Cash ....
	Reclassification Out—Temporarily Restricted—
	     Satisfaction of Program Requirements ....
	          Reclassification In—Unrestricted—
	               Satisfaction of Program Requirements ....
		37,000
		200,000
		30,000
		50,000
		28,000
		6,000
		215,000
		34,000
		13,000
		5,000
		
		103,000
			
			32,000
			586,000
			
			103,000

Event	Entry		

21. Contributed goods of $1,450 were used during the year for the Fish in the Lakes program. This amount includes the $750 donor-restricted contribution in item (8).

Supplies Expense. 1,450
   Inventories   1,450
Reclassification Out—Temporarily Restricted—
   Satisfaction of Program Requirements 750
      Reclassification In—Unrestricted—
      Satisfaction of Program Requirements   750

22. Depreciation on equipment purchased with donor-restricted contributions amounted to $22,000 for the year. (Valley Air Project—$2,000; Fish in the Lakes program—$3,000; Flood Control program—$16,000; management and general services—$1,000). An equivalent amount of temporarily unspecified net assets is released from restrictions.

Depreciation Expense 22,000
   Accumulated Depreciation   22,000
Reclassification Out—Temporarily Restricted—
   Satisfaction of Equipment Acquisition
   Requirements 22,000
      Reclassification In—Unrestricted—
      Satisfaction of Equipment Acquisition
      Requirements   22,000

23. Early in the year, cash contributions for current operations were received, but they cannot be used until late in the following year.

Cash 2,000
   Contributions—Temporarily Restricted   2,000

24. At year-end, the expenses were allocated to the various programs and supporting services. The direct cost of a special event is not included in the allocation process because it is subtracted from the gross proceeds of that event. The special event is considered an incidental activity and reported "net" in the statement of activities.

Valley Air Project. 132,000
Fish in the Lakes Program. 184,450
Flood Control Program 251,000
Management and General Services 29,500
Fund-Raising Services 11,000
Membership Development 2,000
   Salaries Expense   200,000
   Payroll Taxes   30,000
   Mailing and Postage Expense   50,000
   Rent Expense   28,000
   Telephone Expense   6,000
   Research Expense   215,000
   Professional Services: Legal and Audit   34,500
   Supplies Expense.   14,450
   Miscellaneous Expense   5,000
   Provision for Uncollectible Contributions   5,000
   Depreciation Expense   22,000

(continued)

Event	Entry		
25. Closing entries. Each class of asset is closed separately.	Contributions—Unrestricted	397,100	
	Special Events Support	9,000	
	Legacies and Bequests—Unrestricted	100,000	
	Received from Federated and Nonfederated Campaigns	16,000	
	Membership Dues Revenue	118,000	
	Investment Revenue	21,000	
	Reclassifications In—Unrestricted—Satisfaction of Program Restrictions	103,750	
	Reclassifications In—Unrestricted—Satisfaction of Equipment Acquisition Restrictions	22,000	
	Reclassifications In—Unrestricted—Satisfaction of Time Restrictions	10,000	
	Valley Air Project		132,000
	Fish in the Lakes Program		184,450
	Flood Control Program.		251,000
	Management and General Services		29,500
	Fund-Raising Services		11,000
	Membership Development.		2,000
	Cost of Special Events		2,000
	Unrestricted Net Assets		**184,900**
	Contributions—Temporarily Restricted	72,750	
	Investment Revenue—Temporarily Restricted	7,000	
	Temporarily Restricted Net Assets	**56,000**	
	Reclassifications Out—Unrestricted— Satisfaction of Program Restrictions		103,750
	Reclassifications Out—Unrestricted— Satisfaction of Equipment Acquisition Restrictions		22,000
	Reclassifications Out—Unrestricted— Satisfaction of Time Restrictions		10,000
	Legacies and Bequests—Endowment— Permanently Restricted.	20,000	
	Net Increase in Carrying Value of Endowment Investments—Permanently Restricted.	29,000	
	Gain on Sale of Endowment Investments— Permanently Restricted.	2,000	
	Permanently Restricted Net Assets . . .		**51,000**

The final entry at year-end closes the support and revenue accounts, as well as the program and supporting services expenses, into the appropriate net asset accounts. With expenses allocated to programs and supporting services, it is now possible to prepare the statement of activities (see Illustration 18-2). The sequence of items is suggested by the title. Inflows of resources from public support, revenues, and reclassification are listed first, followed by the expense totals for each program and supporting service, taken directly from the closing and allocation entries. The beginning net asset balance for each class is added, resulting in the net asset balance at the end of the period.

Since the investments account is carried at fair value, it is entirely possible that the carrying value may decrease. If this situation occurs, the account Net Decrease in Carrying Value of Investments is debited, and the investments account is credited. The closing entry would credit Net Decrease in Carrying Value of Investments and debit unrestricted or permanently restricted net assets depending on donor specifications or law.

The statement of activities of a VHWO provides valuable data on the total cost per period of each program and of supporting services. To provide the reader of its financial statements with additional information, a statement of functional expenses is included in the reports. This statement shows the allocation of each expense (salaries, rent, etc.) and reveals the cost by function of carrying on the organization's activities. The statement of functional expenses for PEP is shown in Illustration 18-3 on page 950.

The statement of financial position for PEP on December 31, 2019, is given in Illustration 18-4 on page 950. The statement of cash flows shown in Illustration 18-5 (page 951) includes, under *financing activities*, all cash inflows from contributions and investment income restricted by donor for long-term investments (or endowments) or for acquisition of fixed assets.

As is true in reporting for-profit enterprises, financial statements of VHWOs would be prepared with comparative figures for the preceding year. The statements also should be accompanied by notes that would summarize significant accounting policies.

Illustration 18-2
People's Environmental Protection (PEP) Association
Statement of Activities
For Year Ended December 31, 2019

	Unrestricted	Temporarily Restricted	Permanently Restricted	Total
Public support:				
Contributions	$ 397,100	$ 72,750		$ 469,850
Special events (net of $2,000 direct costs)	7,000			7,000
Legacies and bequests.	100,000		$ 20,000	120,000
Received from federated and nonfederated campaigns . . .	16,000			16,000
Total public support	$ 520,100	$ 72,750	$ 20,000	$ 612,850
Revenue:				
Membership dues	$ 118,000			$ 118,000
Investment revenue	21,000	$ 7,000		28,000
Net increase in carrying value of investments			$ 29,000	29,000
Realized gain on investments.			2,000	2,000
Total revenue	$ 139,000	$ 7,000	$ 31,000	$ 177,000
Net assets released from restrictions:				
Satisfaction of program requirements	$ 103,750	$ (103,750)		
Satisfaction of equipment acquisition requirements.	22,000	(22,000)		
Expiration of time restrictions.	10,000	(10,000)		
Total net assets released from restrictions.	$ 135,750	$ (135,750)		
Total public support and revenue.	$ 794,850	$ (56,000)	$ 51,000	$ 789,850
Expenses:				
Valley Air Project	$ 132,000			$ 132,000
Fish in the Lakes program.	184,450			184,450
Flood Control program	251,000			251,000
Management and general.	29,500			29,500
Fund raising	11,000			11,000
Membership development.	2,000			2,000
Total expenses	$ 609,950			$ 609,950
Change in net assets	**$184,900**	**$ (56,000)**	**$ 51,000**	**$ 179,900**
Net assets beginning of year	**289,000**	**687,000**	**253,000**	**1,229,000**
Net assets end of year	**$473,900**	**$631,000**	**$304,000**	**$1,408,900**

Illustration 18-3
People's Environmental Protection (PEP) Association
Statement of Functional Expenses
For Year Ended December 31, 2019

	Total All Services	Program Services				Supporting Services			
		Valley Air Project	Fish in the Lakes	Flood Control	Total Programs	Management and General	Fund Raising	Membership Development	Total Supporting
Salaries	$200,000	$ 36,000	$ 60,000	$ 80,000	$176,000	$19,000	$ 4,500	$ 500	$24,000
Payroll taxes	30,000	5,400	9,000	12,000	26,400	3,000	500	100	3,600
Mailing and postage	50,000	10,000	20,000	19,700	49,700		200	100	300
Rent	28,000	8,000	5,000	11,600	24,600	2,000	400	1,000	3,400
Telephone	6,000	1,500	1,300	2,500	5,300		400	300	700
Research	215,000	35,000	80,000	100,000	215,000				
Professional: Legal and audit	34,500	24,000	2,000	4,000	30,000	4,500			4,500
Supplies	14,450	10,100	1,450	2,900	14,450				
Provision for uncollectible contributions	5,000						5,000		5,000
Miscellaneous	5,000		2,700	2,300	5,000				
Total expenses before depreciation	$587,950	$130,000	$181,450	$235,000	$546,450	$28,500	$11,000	$2,000	$41,500
Depreciation of building and equipment	22,000	2,000	3,000	16,000	21,000	1,000			1,000
Total expenses	$609,950	$132,000	$184,450	$251,000	$567,450	$29,500	$11,000	$2,000	$42,500

Illustration 18-4
People's Environmental Protection (PEP) Association
Statement of Financial Position
As of December 31, 2019

Assets:
Cash and cash equivalents . . . . $ 268,000
Contributions receivable (net of $2,500 allowance)   21,000
Inventories   10,900
Short-term investments   152,000
Property, plant, and equipment (net of $38,700 accumulated depreciation)   800,000
Long-term endowment investments   304,000

Total assets **$1,555,900**

Liabilities and net assets:
Accounts payable . . . . $ 32,000
Refundable advances   5,000
Notes payable   110,000

Total liabilities . . . . **$ 147,000**

Net assets:
Unrestricted . . . . **$ 473,900**
Temporarily restricted   631,000
Permanently restricted   304,000

Total net assets **$1,408,900**

Total liabilities and net assets . . . . $ 1,555,900

Illustration 18-5
People's Environmental Protection (PEP) Association
Statement of Cash Flows
For Year Ended December 31, 2019

Cash flows from operating activities:	
Cash received from members	$ 118,000
Cash received from contributions	402,500
Cash received from special events.	7,000
Cash received from federated and nonfederated campaigns	16,000
Cash received from legacies and bequests	100,000
Cash received on a refundable advance.	5,000
Interest and dividends received	21,000
Cash paid to employees and suppliers	(586,000)
Net cash provided by (used for) operating activities.	**$ 83,500**
Cash flows from investing activities:	
Proceeds from sales and maturities of investments.	$ 27,000
Purchases of investments	(46,000)
Purchase of land, building, and equipment.	(146,000)
Net cash provided by (used for) investing activities	**$(165,000)**
Cash flow from financing activities:	
Proceeds from issuance of notes payable	$ 10,000
Receipts of interest and dividends restricted for reinvestment	7,000*
Contributions received restricted for long-term investment.	20,000
Contributions received restricted for investment in plant	60,000
Net cash provided by (used for) financing activities	**$ 97,000**
Net increase (decrease) in cash and cash equivalents	**$ 15,500**
Cash and cash equivalents at beginning of year	**252,500**
Cash and cash equivalents at end of year	**$ 268,000**
Reconciliation of change in net assets to net cash provided by operating activities:	
Change in net assets	$ 179,900
Depreciation	22,000
Decrease in contributions receivable.	500
Increase in inventories	(900)
Increase in notes payable	10,000
Increase in refundable advances.	(5,000)
Decrease in accounts payable.	(5,000)
Increase in net carrying value of investments.	(29,000)
Gain on sale of investments	(2,000)
Interest restricted for long-term investment	(7,000)
Contributions restricted for long-term investment.	(20,000)
Contributions restricted for plant	(60,000)
Net cash provided by operating activities.	$ 83,500

*$4,000 of cash at beginning of year and $5,000 of cash at year-end are included in the classification "long-term endowment investments" on the statement of financial position.

REFLECTION

- Voluntary health and welfare organizations account for public support and revenues.

- Public support categories include contributions, special events, legacies and bequests, and federated and nonfederated campaigns.

- Expenditures are separated into program and supporting services. Joint cost allocation rules are followed for the allocation of fund-raising costs.

- A fourth financial statement is required of all VHWOs (but not of other not-for-profits)—the statement of functional expenses—which provides detailed information on the expenses for each program and support service.

The Budget

Budgets are also prepared in not-for-profit organizations. As in a commercial enterprise, the budgeting process involves the establishment of goals, the measurement of actual performance, and the comparison of actual with projected performance to evaluate results. This process requires the input of persons who can determine what resources will become available, what the organization desires to achieve with those resources, and how the resources should be applied to yield the greatest benefit. If the organization or program is well established, a useful starting point is the previous year's budget and its variances, adjusted for any changes in objectives. If the group or program is new, the preparation of an effective operating budget requires careful research to produce realistic estimates of both revenues and expenditures. Expenditures should be planned to maximize service output without producing either a surplus or a deficit. A sizable excess of revenues over expenditures implies that more or better service could be provided. A deficit may indicate the need to curtail future services, since future funds may have to be committed to cover past deficits.[10]

SUMMARY

FASB ASC 958 requires that information provided to readers of the financial statements include financial viability, financial flexibility, liquidity, cash flows, and service efforts. Use of financial statements based on net asset classifications is a much different concept from traditional fund group reporting. While the detailed examples in this chapter focused on a VHWO, these same standards apply to all not-for-profits, including those in the arts, health care, and education. An example of optional funds-based financial statements is presented in the appendix.

---

10 In accounting for not-for-profit organizations, it is not as common to find budgetary amounts formally entered into principal ledger accounts as it is in governmental accounting. If a budgetary entry is recorded, it would be similar to the one used in governmental accounting, and it would be reversed at year-end. Assuming estimated revenues exceed estimated expenditures and allocations, the budgetary journal entry for a governmental college or university would be as follows:

Estimated Revenues	XXX	
Estimated Expenditures (or Budget Allocations for Expenditures)		XXX
Unallocated Balance		XXX

APPENDIX: OPTIONAL FUND ACCOUNTING FOR VOLUNTARY HEALTH AND WELFARE ORGANIZATIONS

11

OBJECTIVE

Describe the typical funds used to account for VHWO transactions, and prepare optional VHWO fund-based financial statements.

To segregate resources and demonstrate compliance with restrictions, fund accounting is often used by voluntary health and welfare organizations for sound internal management. Voluntary health and welfare organizations have two current funds consisting primarily of current assets and current liabilities, a separate plant fund, and an endowment fund.

VHWO Funds

The following table lists the funds used by most VHWOs with the three *net asset* categories:

Funds	Unrestricted Net Assets	Temporarily Restricted Net Assets	Permanently Restricted Net Assets
Current Unrestricted	X		
Current Restricted	X	X	
Land, Building, and Equipment (Plant Fund)	X	X	X
Endowment Fund.		X	X
Agency (Custodial) Fund			

Current Unrestricted Fund. The current unrestricted fund accounts are for resources that have no external restrictions and are available for current operations at the discretion of the governing board. The board, however, may place its own limitations on the fund unrestricted net assets. In the same manner that industry appropriates retained earnings, the board of directors of a health and welfare organization may designate a portion of its unrestricted net assets for a special project. To reflect such an action, a subset of unrestricted net assets, Unrestricted Net Assets—Designated, may be displayed, provided the total amount of Unrestricted Net Assets is shown.

Current Restricted Fund. The current restricted fund accounts for assets received from outside sources for a current operating purpose specified by the donor. The distinguishing feature between unrestricted and restricted funds is whether or not an externally imposed restriction exists. A contribution received by a health agency to conduct nutrition classes is an example of a restricted resource. When donor-restricted contributions are expensed, the restriction is released or reclassified to offset the expense. Specifically excluded from this fund are contributions of endowments or contributions restricted to the acquisition of plant assets, which are recorded in other appropriate funds.

Some net assets of this fund may be unrestricted; for example, grants, awards, sponsorships, and appropriations have traditionally been recorded in the restricted current fund. These may now be defined as exchange transactions in which the grantor or sponsor expects to receive something of value in return for the grant.

Land, Building, and Equipment Fund (or Plant Fund). The plant fund accounts for the activity related to fixed assets, including the accumulation of resources to acquire or replace them and the liabilities related to them, as well as their acquisition, disposal, and depreciation. To determine the total cost of rendering service, depreciation of assets employed in providing that service must be recorded in the plant fund, with the typical depreciation entry debiting Depreciation Expense and crediting Accumulated Depreciation.

The plant fund of a VHWO may have all three net asset classes: unrestricted, temporarily restricted, and permanently restricted. Unrestricted net assets may be transfers from current funds at the discretion of the governing board. Assets acquired with unrestricted funds are unrestricted. Donor-restricted contributions specified for property and equipment are temporarily restricted. As with other not-for-profits, a VHWO may choose to release the restriction of these assets upon acquisition or over the useful life. Contributions of land are considered permanently restricted if the land cannot be sold. If no restriction exists, donated land is an unrestricted contribution.

Endowment Fund. The endowment fund accounts for gifts or bequests with the legal restriction that the principal be maintained in perpetuity (permanently restricted) or until the occurrence of a specified event (temporarily restricted). Various conditions are possible, depending upon the desires of the contributor. Unless otherwise specified, net gains or losses on the sale of endowment fund assets are increases or decreases of the fund principal.

Endowment fund investment revenue may be restricted or unrestricted. Income is recorded directly in the fund that is to receive it. Such income not subject to any restrictions by the principal donor may be recorded directly in the current unrestricted fund as unrestricted investment revenue. If the revenue is subject to a restriction, it would be recorded as temporarily or permanently restricted in the appropriate restricted fund.

Agency (Custodian) Fund. Agency funds of not-for-profit organizations account for assets that do not belong to the organization holding them. They are often established for payroll withholding. Custodian funds are established to account for assets received by an organization to be held or disbursed only on instructions of the person or organization from whom they were received. Flow-through government grants are examples of this latter use of agency funds. Assets are recorded when received, along with a related liability. Only when the assets are released by the contributor will they be recognized as revenue in the appropriate fund.

Pooling of Investments. If an organization accumulates substantial investments in its various funds, pooling may be advisable. Pooling of investments is the process of combining the investments of various funds into one group or pool to provide greater flexibility at lower cost and to provide diversification to spread the risk. Once pooled, individual investments lose their identity as to fund. Each contributing fund merely maintains in its investment account an amount representing its portion of the pool. Before any additions or withdrawals may be made, the fair value of the total portfolio must be determined. Realized gains and losses (and unrealized, if investments are carried at fair value rather than cost) are allocated to each participating fund on the basis of its share of the total fair value at the previous valuation date. The proportion of each fund's fair value may be expressed in terms of units or in terms of percentages of the total. The latter method is more flexible and is used in Illustration 18A-1, which shows changes in pooled investments over a period of time.

	(1) Cash and/or FV of Securities	(2) Original Equity Percent	(3) Total Pool December 31, 2010 Cost	(4) Total Pool December 31, 2010 Fair	(5) Fair Value Including $50,000	(6) Revised Equity Percent	(7) After Withdrawal of $25,000	(8) New Equity Percent
Illustration 18A-1 Pooling of Investments								
Fund								
Unrestricted . . .	$ 36,000	20%	$ 40,000	$ 50,000	$ 50,000	16.67%	$ 25,000	9.09%
Plant	54,000	30	60,000	75,000	75,000	25.00	75,000	27.27
Endowment . . .	90,000	50	100,000	125,000	175,000	58.33	175,000	63.64
Total	$180,000	100%	$200,000	$250,000	$300,000	100.00%	$275,000	100.00%

Illustrative Funds-Based Financial Statements for Voluntary Health and Welfare Organizations

Statements reflect information from the entries in the text for the People's Environmental Protection (PEP) Association within the existing funds structure for voluntary health and welfare organizations.

Note that in Illustration 18A-2, all the funds—total public support and revenue (A), total expenses (B), change in net assets (F = C + D + E), net assets beginning of year (G), and net assets end of year (H)—match up with the related disclosures in Illustration 18-2 (page 949). Similarly, the fund totals shown in Illustration 18A-3 present the same disclosures required in Illustration 18-4 (page 950). In addition, the net assets end of year (H) disclosure on both the statement of financial position and the statement of activities ties these two reports together.

Illustration 18A-2
People's Environmental Protection (PEP) Association
Statement of Activities
For Year Ended December 31, 2019

	Unrestricted Current Fund	Restricted Current Fund	Plant Fund	Endowment Fund	Total	
Public support:						
Contributions	$397,100				$ 397,100	
Special events (net of $2,000 direct costs)	7,000				7,000	
Legacies and bequests	100,000				100,000	
Received from federated and nonfederated						
campaigns	16,000				16,000	
Total public support	$520,100				$ 520,100	
Revenue:						
Membership dues	$118,000				$ 118,000	
Investment revenue	21,000				21,000	
Total revenue	$139,000				$ 139,000	
Net assets released from restrictions:						
Satisfaction of program restrictions		$ 103,750			$ 103,750	
Satisfaction of equipment acquisition						
restrictions			$ 22,000		22,000	
Expiration of time restrictions		10,000			10,000	
Total net assets released from restrictions		$ 113,750	$ 22,000		$ 135,750	
Total public support and revenue	$659,100	$ 113,750	$ 22,000		$ 794,850	A
Expenses:						
Valley Air Project	$117,000	$ 13,000	$ 2,000		$ 132,000	
Fish in the Lakes program	131,700	49,750	3,000		184,450	
Flood Control program	204,000	31,000	16,000		251,000	
Management and general	20,500	8,000	1,000		29,500	
Fund raising	8,000	2,000	1,000		11,000	
Membership development	2,000				2,000	
Total expenses	$483,200	$ 103,750	$ 23,000		$ 609,950	B
Increase (decrease) in unrestricted net assets	$175,900	$ 10,000	$ (1,000)		**$ 184,900**	C
Transfers among funds	$ (96,000)		$ (96,000)		—	

(continued)

	Unrestricted Current Fund	Restricted Current Fund	Plant Fund	Endowment Fund	Total	
Changes in temporarily restricted net assets:						
Contributions	$ 12,750	$ 60,000			$ 72,750	
Investment income on endowment.		7,000			7,000	
Net assets released from restrictions	(113,750)	(22,000)			(135,750)	
Increase (decrease) in temporarily restricted net assets.	$(101,000)	$ 45,000			$ (56,000)	D
Changes in permanently restricted net assets:						
Legacies and bequests.				$ 20,000	$ 20,000	
Net increase in carrying value of investments . .				29,000	29,000	
Gain on sale of investments				2,000	2,000	
Increase (decrease) in permanently restricted net assets.				$ 51,000	$ 51,000	E
Change in net assets	$ 79,900	$ (91,000)	$140,000	$ 51,000	$ 179,900	F
Net assets beginning of year	184,000	132,000	660,000	253,000	1,229,000	G
Net assets end of year	$263,900	$ 41,000	$800,000	$304,000	$1,408,900	H

Illustration 18A-3
People's Environmental Protection (PEP) Association
Statement of Financial Position
As of December 31, 2019

	Unrestricted Current Fund	Restricted Current Fund	Plant Fund	Endowment Fund	Total	
Assets:						
Cash and cash equivalents	$193,000	$40,000	$ 35,000		$ 268,000	
Contributions receivable (net of $2,500 allowance).	21,000				21,000	
Inventories	10,900				10,900	
Short-term investments	70,000	7,000	75,000		152,000	
Property, plant, and equipment (net of $38,700 accumulated depreciation)			800,000		800,000	
Long-term endowment investments.				$304,000	304,000	
Total assets.	$294,900	$47,000	$910,000	$304,000	$ 1,555,900	
Liabilities and net assets:						
Accounts payable	$ 31,000	$ 1,000			$ 32,000	
Refundable advances		5,000			5,000	
Notes payable.			$110,000		110,000	
Total liabilities.	$ 31,000	$ 6,000	$110,000		$ 147,000	
Net assets:						
Unrestricted.	$263,900	$10,000	$200,000		$ 473,900	
Temporarily restricted		31,000	600,000		631,000	
Permanently restricted.				$304,000	304,000	
Total net assets	$263,900	$41,000	$800,000	$304,000	$1,408,900	H
Total liabilities and net assets.	$294,900	$47,000	$910,000	$304,000	$ 1,555,900	

REFLECTION

- For external purposes, VHWOs may choose to prepare reports of the results of fund activities and the fund balances at period-end. These statements also reflect the organization-wide disclosures required.

- Most VHWOs use five different funds.

- Investments accounted for by different funds may be pooled together. Any net realized (or unrealized) gain or loss is allocated proportionately to the funds involved.

UNDERSTANDING THE ISSUES

1. How is it helpful for a private not-for-profit organization to account for current funds as restricted or unrestricted?

2. The FASB requires for-profit entities to classify their investments as trading, available-for-sale, or held-to-maturity. However, it does not require not-for-profit entities to do the same. What might be the reasoning for this difference in requirements? Which approach is more beneficial to the readers of the financial statements of a not-for-profit organization? Why?

3. Differentiate between public support and revenues as sources of assets for private not-for-profit organizations. What benefit is there in accounting for these differently?

4. Explain the accounting for funds received by an organization acting as an agent, a trustee, or an intermediary, rather than as a donor or donee. What might be the reasoning for the differences?

5. A voluntary health and welfare organization is required to present an additional financial statement that is not required of other private not-for-profit entities. Why is this an important statement?

6. (Appendix) Why would a VHWO wish to present its financial information on a fund basis rather than simply on an organization-wide basis? What benefits are there in fund-basis reporting?

EXERCISES

Exercise 1 *(LO 1, 2, 6)* **Understanding not-for-profit financial statements.** Go to the Web site of a not-for-profit organization. Are audited financial statements provided on the Web site? Is other financial information made available? Assuming you are a potential donor, evaluate its performance compared with similar organizations. What benchmarks (or industry averages) for this type of not-for-profit did you use in your evaluation? Were they financial or nonfinancial indicators of performance? [*Hint:* Goodwill Industries International, Inc., is a not-for-profit organization (http://www.goodwill.org). The BBB Wise Giving Alliance (http://www.give.org) and the Council of Better Business Bureau (CBBB) Philanthropic Advisory Service (http://www.bbb.org) have comparison data on not-for-profit organizations.]

Exercise 2 *(LO 1, 3, 8, 9)* **Comparison of accounting for VHWO and governmental organizations.** Distinguish between accounting and financial reporting for state and local governments and VHWOs for the following issues:

1. Measurement focus and basis of accounting
2. Revenue recognition

3. Depreciation expense
4. Capital assets

Exercise 3 *(LO 3, 4, 6)* **FASB ASC 958-605, contributions.** Select the best answer for each of the following multiple-choice items dealing with not-for-profit organizations:

1. Which of the following criteria would suggest that a not-for-profit capitalize its works of art, historical treasures, or similar assets?

   a. They are held for public inspection, education, or research in furtherance of public service rather than financial gain.
   b. They are protected, kept unencumbered, cared for, and preserved.
   c. They are subject to be used in the acquisition of other items for the collection.
   d. They are held primarily to be resold for financial gain.

2. Securities donated to voluntary health and welfare organizations should be recorded

   a. at the donor's recorded amount.
   b. at fair value at the date of the gift.
   c. at fair value at the date of the gift or the donor's recorded amount, whichever is lower.
   d. at fair value at the date of the gift or the donor's recorded amount, whichever is higher.

3. Which of the following is *not* a criterion that must be met under FASB ASC 958-605-25-16 for contributed services?

   a. They are provided by persons possessing required skills.
   b. They are provided by licensed professionals.
   c. They create or enhance nonfinancial assets.
   d. They would typically have to be purchased if not provided by the donors/volunteers.

4. Which of the following factors, if present, would indicate that a transaction is *not* a contribution?

   a. The resource provider entered into the transaction voluntarily.
   b. The resource provider received value in exchange.
   c. The transfer of assets was unconditional.
   d. The organization has discretion in the use of the assets received.

5. Which of the following statements is *true?*

   a. All not-for-profit organizations must include a statement of functional expenses.
   b. Donor-restricted contributions whose restrictions have been met in the reporting period may be reported as unrestricted support.
   c. Statements should focus on the individual unrestricted and restricted funds of the organization.
   d. FASB ASC 958-605 contains requirements that are generally more stringent than those relating to for-profit organizations.

Exercise 4 *(LO 4, 6)* **Contributions, statement of activities.** Early in 2018, a not-for-profit organization received a $2,000,000 gift from a wealthy benefactor. This benefactor specified that the gift be invested in perpetuity with income restricted to provide speaker fees for a lecture series named for the benefactor. The not-for-profit is permitted to choose suitable investments and is responsible for all other costs associated with initiating and administering this series. Neither the donor's stipulation nor the law addresses gains and losses on this permanent endowment. In 2018, the investments purchased with the gift earned $100,000 in dividend income. The fair value of the investments increased by $240,000.

Three presentations in the lecture series were held in 2018. The speaker fees for the three presentations amounted to $240,000. The not-for-profit organization used the $100,000 dividend income to cover part of the total fees. Because the board of directors did not wish to sell part of the investments, the organization used $140,000 in unrestricted resources to pay the remainder of the speaker fees.

For items (1) through (5), determine whether the transaction should be recorded in the 2018 statement of activities as an increase in:

A. Unrestricted net assets.
B. Temporarily restricted net assets.
C. Permanently restricted net assets.
D. Either unrestricted or temporarily restricted net assets.

1. The receipt of the $2,000,000 gift
2. The $100,000 in dividend income assuming the not-for-profit's accounting policy is to record increases in net assets, for which a donor-imposed restriction is met in the same accounting period as gains and investment income are recognized, as increases in unrestricted net assets
3. The $240,000 unrealized gain
4. The $100,000 in dividend income, assuming the lecture series is not to begin until 2019
5. The $240,000 unrealized gain, assuming the lecture series is not to begin until 2019

Exercise 5 *(LO 9)* **VHWO, statement of activities.** Whole Life Clinic is a VHWO that has three main programs:

> Drug rehabilitation
> Alcohol recovery
> Weight control

Unrestricted public support received during the period was $35,000; revenues from membership services were $12,000. The following expenses and allocations to program and supporting services are shown for 2019. Whole Life elects to release donor restrictions for property, plant, and equipment over the useful life of the asset.

		Distribution				
Item	Amount	Drug Rehabilitation	Alcohol Recovery	Weight Control	Fund Raising	General And Administrative
Secretarial salary...............	$ 2,000					100%
Office supplies.................	3,000	20%	10%	10%	10%	50
Printing	8,000	20	20	20	30	10
Depreciation (All depreciation is on assets acquired with donor-restricted contributions.) ...	4,000	20	20	20		40
Instruction	9,000	30	25	35	10	
Rent	20,000	30	20	30		20

Temporarily restricted net assets totaled $40,000 on January 1; the unrestricted net asset balance was $22,000. Prepare a statement of activities for the year.

Exercise 6 *(LO 10)* **VHWO, journal entries.** Record the following events of Mental Health Clinic, a VHWO:

1. A contribution of $20,000 was received and is to be used for the purchase of equipment, but not until an addition to the building is constructed. Construction has begun on the building.
2. Equipment costing $17,000, with a book value of $8,000, was sold for $10,000. The gain is unrestricted.
3. Depreciation of $9,000 is recorded on various plant items.
4. Equipment was purchased for $18,000, with payment due in 30 days from donor-restricted resources. Mental Health Clinic elects to release the donor restriction upon acquisition of the equipment.
5. The liability for the equipment purchased in item (4) was paid.

Exercise 7 *(LO 10)* **VHWO, journal entries.** Record the following events of Mayo Health Clinic, a VHWO:

1. In her will, a leading citizen left a bequest of $400,000 to the clinic. Stipulations were that the amount was to become the corpus of a permanent endowment. Any income received would be used first to cover any loss of principal, with the remaining revenue to be used for an educational program on mental problems. The total amount was received and invested in 10% municipal bonds purchased at face value on an interest date.
2. Three months later, half of the bond investment was sold at 101, plus $5,000 of accrued interest.
3. The remaining endowment bond investments earned $15,000.
4. At year-end, the remaining endowment bond investments have a fair value of $207,000.

Exercise 8 *(LO 10)* **VHWO, journal entries.** Record the following events of Chemical Dependency Clinic, a VHWO:

1. Membership dues of $9,000 were collected.
2. Cash contributions of $22,000 and pledges for $32,000 were received.
3. It is estimated that 10% of the above pledges will prove uncollectible.
4. A fund-raising dinner grossed $12,000 from the sale of 480 tickets. The catered dinner cost $15 each for the 420 people who attended, plus $200 for the rental of the dining room. Payment for these costs was made.
5. A classic car was donated to the organization. The car has an estimated fair value of $75,000. It will be the main attraction of an auction to be held in the next accounting period. The proceeds of the auction are part of the budget for activities in the next period.
6. To expand the services of the clinic, a professional fund-raising group was hired to undertake a 6-month campaign. At the end of the six months, the group submitted the report shown below.

Cash collected	$ 70,000
Pledges (estimated to be 95% collectible)	30,000
Total proceeds	$100,000
Less 20% fund-raising fee (regardless of collections)	20,000
Net proceeds from drive	$ 80,000

PROBLEMS

Problem 18-1 *(LO 3, 4, 7, 8, 9, 11)* **Assets.** Select the best answer for each of the following multiple-choice questions:

1. A VHWO receives a donation that is restricted to its endowment and another donation that is restricted to use in acquiring a child care center. How should these donations be reported in the year received, assuming neither donation is expended in that year?

	Donation for Endowment	Donation for Child Care Center
a.	Contributions—Temporarily Restricted	Contributions—Temporarily Restricted
b.	Deferred Capital Additions	Capital Additions
c.	Contributions—Unrestricted	Contributions—Unrestricted
d.	Capital Additions Deferred	Capital Additions
e.	Contributions—Permanently Restricted	Contributions—Temporarily Restricted

2. Donor-restricted contributions that have been given to a VHWO for the purpose of purchasing fixed assets should be recorded as increases to

   a. Unrestricted Net Assets.
   b. Temporarily Restricted Net Assets.

    c. Permanently Restricted Net Assets.

    d. Fund Balance—Restricted.

3. The following correct entry is found on the books of a VHWO:

Unrestricted Net Assets—Undesignated	XXX	
Unrestricted Net Assets—Designated for AIDS Research.		XXX

From the entry, one should conclude that the board of directors has

    a. designated a portion of the unrestricted net assets for a future AIDS research program.

    b. designated a portion of the restricted net assets for a future AIDS research program.

    c. transferred resources to an AIDS research program.

    d. directed that unused resources previously assigned to an AIDS research program be returned to the unrestricted net asset classification.

4. Friends of the Forest received a donation of marketable equity securities from a member. The securities had appreciated in value after they were purchased by the donor, and they continued to appreciate through the end of Friends of the Forest's fiscal year. At what amount should Friends of the Forest report its investment in marketable equity securities in its year-end balance sheet?

    a. Donor's cost

    b. Fair value at the date of receipt

    c. Fair value at the balance sheet date

    d. Fair value at either the date of receipt or the balance sheet date

5. The investments of a VHWO are carried at fair value. At the end of the period, there is a decrease in total fair value. The fair value decrease should

    a. not be recorded until the loss is realized.

    b. be debited to Realized Loss on Pooled Investments.

    c. be debited to Endowment Fund Balance.

    d. be debited to Net Decrease in Carrying Value of Investments.

(AICPA adapted)

Problem 18-2 *(LO 5, 7, 8, 9)* **Expenses.** Select the best answer for each of the following multiple-choice items. (No. 3 is AICPA adapted.)

1. Super Seniors is a not-for-profit organization that provides services to senior citizens. Super employs a full-time staff of 10 people at an annual cost of $150,000. In addition, two volunteers work as part-time secretaries replacing last year's full-time secretary who earned $10,000. Services performed by other volunteers for special events had an estimated value of $15,000. These volunteers were employees of local businesses, and they received small-value items for their participation. What amount should Super report for salary and wage expenses related to the above items?

    a. $150,000

    b. $160,000

    c. $165,000

    d. $175,000

2. EnvironRights, a community foundation, incurred $10,000 in management and general expenses during 2011. In EnvironRights' statement of activities for the year ended December 31, 2011, the $10,000 should be reported as

    a. a direct reduction of unrestricted net assets.

    b. part of supporting services expense.

    c. part of program services expense.

    d. a contra account to offset revenue and support.

3. In the statement of activities of a not-for-profit, depreciation expense should

   a. be included as an element of expense.
   b. be included as an element of other changes in fund balances.
   c. be included as an element of support.
   d. not be included.

4. When a not-for-profit organization combines fund-raising efforts with bona fide educational efforts or program services, the total combined costs incurred are

   a. reported as program services expenses.
   b. allocated between fund-raising and program services expenses using an appropriate allocation basis.
   c. reported as fund-raising costs.
   d. reported as management and general expenses.

5. The League, a not-for-profit organization, received the following pledges:

Unrestricted	$200,000
Restricted for capital additions	150,000

   All pledges are legally enforceable; however, the League's experience indicates that 10% of all pledges prove to be uncollectible. What amount should the League report as pledges receivable net of any required allowance account?

   a. $135,000
   b. $180,000
   c. $315,000
   d. $350,000

Problem 18-3 *(LO 8, 9)* **VHWO, accounting and reporting.** Select the best answer for each of the following multiple-choice items. Items (1) through (3) are based on the following:

The Bayview Humane Society, a VHWO caring for lost animals, had the following financial inflows and outflows for the year ended December 31, 2018:

Inflows:

Cash received from federated campaign	$880,000
Cash received that is designated for 2019 operations	20,000
Contributions pledged for 2018, not yet received.	100,000
Contributions pledged for 2019, not yet received.	35,000
Sales of pet supplies.	10,000
Pet adoption fees	50,000

Outflows:

Kennel operations	$450,000
Pet health care	200,000
Advertising pets for adoption.	50,000
Fund raising	70,000
Administrative and general	300,000

1. In the humane society's statement of activities for the year ended December 31, 2018, what amount should be reported under the classification of program services expense?

   a. $770,000
   b. $700,000
   c. $550,000
   d. $500,000

2. In the humane society's statement of activities for the year ended December 31, 2018, what amount should be reported under the classification of public support—unrestricted?

   a. $740,000
   b. $762,000
   c. $980,000
   d. $825,000

3. In the humane society's balance sheet as of December 31, 2018, what amount should be reported under the classification of public support—temporarily restricted?

   a. $55,000
   b. $30,000
   c. $25,000
   d. $0

4. Apex, Inc., donated a computer to Bird Shelter, a voluntary welfare organization. The computer cost Apex $40,000. On the date of donation, it had a book value of $25,000 and a fair value of $20,000. Bird Shelter's depreciation expense should be based on

   a. $40,000.
   b. $25,000.
   c. $20,000.
   d. $15,000.

5. Safe Haven, a voluntary welfare organization funded by contributions from the general public, received unrestricted pledges of $400,000 during 2018. It was estimated that 12% of these pledges would be uncollectible. By the end of 2018, $300,000 of the pledges had been collected, and it was expected that $40,000 more would be collected in 2019, with the balance of $60,000 to be written off as uncollectible. Donors did *not* specify any periods during which the donations were to be used. What amount should Safe Haven include under public support in 2018 for contributions?

   a. $400,000
   b. $352,000
   c. $340,000
   d. $300,000

6. The following expenditures were among those incurred by a voluntary welfare organization during 2019:

Printing of annual report	$10,000
Unsolicited merchandise sent to encourage contributions.	20,000

   What amount should be classified as fund-raising costs in the society's statement of activities?

   a. $0
   b. $10,000
   c. $20,000
   d. $30,000

Problem 18-4 *(LO 8, 9)* **Statement of activities, closing entries.** We Care, a VHWO, conducts two programs: Adult Services and Education. It has the typical supporting services of management and fund raising. The condensed trial balances after allocable expenses have been assigned are presented as follows:

We Care
Condensed Post-Allocation Trial Balances
December 31, 2019

Debits	
Assets.	716,000
Endowment Assets.	256,000
Adult Services Program	322,200
Education Program	184,100
Management and General Services	27,600
Fund-Raising Services	50,100
Cost of Special Events	18,000
Reclassification Out—Temporarily Restricted—	
Satisfaction of Program Restrictions.	143,000
Reclassification Out—Temporarily Restricted—	
Satisfaction of Equipment Acquisition Restrictions.	20,000
Total.	1,737,000

Credits	
Liabilities	179,000
Unrestricted Net Assets	202,000
Temporarily Restricted Net Assets	196,000
Permanently Restricted Net Assets.	201,000
Contributions—Unrestricted	407,000
Contributions—Temporarily Restricted	254,000
Special Events Support—Temporarily Restricted.	48,000
Legacies and Bequests—Permanently Restricted.	30,000
Investment Revenue—Unrestricted	13,000
Investment Revenue—Temporarily Restricted	11,000
Gain on Sale of Investments—Temporarily Restricted	8,000
Gain on Sale of Investments—Permanently Restricted.	25,000
Reclassification In—Unrestricted—	
Satisfaction of Program Restrictions.	143,000
Reclassification In—Unrestricted—	
Satisfaction of Equipment Acquisition Restrictions.	20,000
Total.	1,737,000

Required ▶ ▶ ▶ ▶ ▶

1. Prepare a statement of activities in the format shown in Illustration 18-2 on page 949.
2. Prepare closing entries for each net asset classification.

Problem 18-5 *(LO 8, 9, 10)* **Allocation of expenses, journal entries.** Outreach Clinic, a VHWO, conducts two programs: Alcohol and Drug Abuse and Outreach to Teens. It has the typical supporting services of management and fund raising. Expense accounts from the preallocation trial balances as of December 31, 2019, are as follows:

	Funded by Unrestricted Resources	Funded by Donor-Restricted Resources	Total
Salaries and Payroll Taxes.................	73,000	33,000	106,000
Telephone and Miscellaneous Expenses.......	20,000	2,000	22,000
Nursing and Medical Fees	70,000	70,000	140,000
Educational Seminars Expense	46,000	50,000	96,000
Research Expense	130,000	26,000	156,000
Medical Supplies Expense.................	65,000	22,000	87,000
Rent Expense		10,000	10,000
Interest Expense on Equipment Mortgage......	8,000		8,000
Depreciation Expense		40,000	40,000
Provision for Uncollectible Pledges	26,000		26,000
Totals	438,000	253,000	691,000

In preparation for the allocation of expenses to programs and supporting services, a study was conducted to determine an equitable manner for assigning each expense. The study resulted in the following table for percentage allocations:

Percentage of Allocations

Expenses to Be Allocated	Programs		Supporting Services	
	Alcohol and Drug Abuse	Outreach to Teens	Management	Fund Raising
All expenses (other than depreciation) financed by donor-restricted contributions	60%	40%		
Expenses financed by unrestricted resources:				
Salaries and payroll taxes	30	20	30%	20%
Telephone and miscellaneous	20	20	15	45
Nursing and medical fees	70	30		
Educational seminars.....................................	30	60		10
Research	60	40		
Medical supplies	90	10		
Equipment-related expenses:				
Interest...	50	10	30	10
Depreciation	50	10	30	10

1. Using a total of allocable expenses financed by donor-restricted resources, prepare a journal entry to assign those expenses to the programs.   ◀ ◀ ◀ ◀ ◀ **Required**

2. With the following format, prepare a schedule to show the assignment of the allocable expenses financed by unrestricted resources to the various programs and supporting services, using the percentages provided by the problem.

Outreach Clinic Allocation of Expenses
For Year Ended December 31, 2019

Expense Allocated	Total Amount	Programs		Supporting Services	
		Alcohol and Drug Abuse	Outreach to Teens	Management	Fund Raising

3. Using the schedule from part (2), prepare a journal entry to record the allocation and closing of expenses financed by unrestricted resources.
4. Prepare a journal entry to assign plant-related expenses to programs and support services.

Problem 18-6 *(LO 9)* **Statement of functional expenses.** From the expense accounts information and allocation schedule shown in Problem 18-5, prepare a statement of functional expenses for We Care for the year ended December 31, 2019.

Problem 18-7 *(LO 9, 10)* **Journal entries, statement of activities.** The following selected events relate to the 2019 activities of Fall Nursing Home, Inc., a not-for-profit agency:

a. Gross patient service revenue totaled $2,200,000. The provision for uncollectible accounts was estimated at $92,000. The allowance for contractual adjustments was increased by $120,000.
b. After a conference with representatives of Gold Star Insurance Company, differences between the amounts accrued and subsequent settlements reduced receivables by $60,000.
c. A grateful patient donated securities with a cost of $30,000 and a fair value at date of donation of $75,000. The donation was restricted to expenditure for modernization of equipment. The donation was accepted.
d. Cash of $45,000 that had been restricted by a donor for the purchase of furniture was used this year. Fall chose to release the donor restriction over the useful life of the asset.
e. The board voluntarily transferred $50,000 of cash to add to the resources held for capital improvements.
f. Pledges of $60,000 and cash of $20,000 were received to defer operating expenses. Of the pledges, 10% are considered uncollectible. Term endowments of $10,000 matured and were released to cover operations.
g. Equipment costing $250,000 was purchased on account. Restricted resources held for that purpose will be released from restriction over the useful life of the asset.
h. The nursing home uses functional operating expense control accounts. Expenses for the year were as follows:

Nursing services	$1,120,000
Dietary services	230,000
Maintenance services	115,000
Administrative services	285,000
Interest	160,000
Subtotal (of which $253,000 is unpaid)	$1,910,000
Depreciation [$20,000 from assets purchased with	
resources in items (d) and (g) above]	60,000
Total	$1,970,000

Required ▶ ▶ ▶ ▶ ▶

1. Omitting explanations, prepare journal entries for the foregoing events.
2. Prepare a statement of activities for the year ended December 31, 2019.

Problem 18-8 *(LO 9, 10)* **Journal entries, statement of activities.** Thirty years ago, a group of civic-minded merchants in Mayfair organized the "Committee of 100" for the purpose of establishing the Mayfair Sports Club, a not-for-profit sports organization for local youth. Each of the committee's 100 members contributed $1,000 toward the club's capital. In addition, each participant agreed to pay dues of $200 a year for the club's operations. All dues have been collected in full by the end of each fiscal year, which ends on March 31. Members who have discontinued their participation have been replaced by an equal number of new members by transferring the participation certificates from the former members to the new ones. Following are the Club's trial balances at April 1, 2018:

	Debit	Credit
Cash	29,000	
Investments (at market value, equal to cost)	88,000	
Inventories	5,000	
Land	10,000	

(continued)

	Debit	Credit
Building	164,000	
Accumulated Depreciation—Building		130,000
Furniture and Equipment	54,000	
Accumulated Depreciation—Furniture and Equipment		46,000
Endowment Investments.	400,000	
Accounts Payable		10,000
Participation Certificates (100 @ $1,000 each)		100,000
Unrestricted Net Assets		12,000
Temporarily Restricted Net Assets		52,000
Permanently Restricted Net Assets.		400,000
Totals	750,000	750,000

Transactions and adjustment data for the year ended March 31, 2019, are as follows:

a. Collections from participants for dues totaled $20,000.
b. Snack bar and soda fountain sales amounted to $31,000.
c. Interest and dividends totaling $6,000 were received. This investment income is unrestricted.
d. The following additions were made to the voucher register:

House expense	$17,000
Snack bar and soda fountain.	26,000
General and administrative.	11,000

e. Vouchers totaling $55,000 were paid.
f. Assessments for capital improvements not yet incurred totaled $10,000. The assessments were made on May 20, 2018, and were to be collected during the year ending March 31, 2019.
g. An unrestricted bequest of $5,000 was received.
h. Investments are valued at fair value, which amounted to $95,000 at March 31, 2019. There were no investment transactions during the year.
i. Depreciation for the year is as follows:

Building	$4,000
Furniture and equipment	8,000

Depreciation is allocated to

House expense	$9,000
Snack bar and soda fountain.	2,000
General and administrative.	1,000

j. The actual physical inventory, which was $1,000 at March 31, 2019, pertains to the snack bar and fountain.
k. A donor contributed $35,000 to be used to acquire land for expansion.
l. An unconditional pledge of $100,000 to be permanently restricted is received. Income is to be used to maintain the building.

1. Prepare entries for each of the above transactions. ◀ ◀ ◀ ◀ ◀ **Required**
2. Prepare the statement of activities for the year ended March 31, 2019.

(AICPA adapted)

Problem 18-9 *(LO 10)* **Journal entries.** Super Senior Agency is a VHWO. The following events occurred during the year. The agency uses one control account for its fixed assets, with supporting subsidiary records.

1. Property was purchased for $200,000. A down payment of $40,000 was made from unrestricted cash, and a 14% mortgage was signed for the remainder.

2. Office furniture was purchased for $9,000 on open account.

3. A local corporation donated and installed room partitions. The value of the donated items and services was $14,000. Super Senior's policy is to release donor restrictions over the useful life of the assets to match depreciation expense.

4. At year-end, a payment was made covering mortgage interest for one year, plus a $10,000 payment on the principal.

5. Office equipment costing $3,000, with a book value of $1,000, was sold for $1,800 cash. The gain is unrestricted.

6. Fully depreciated equipment costing $7,000 was written off. There was no scrap value.

7. A depreciation schedule was prepared, showing annual depreciation expense of $46,000, which was recorded. Depreciation of $20,000 was for equipment donated or purchased with donated cash.

8. Two years ago, the will of an agency volunteer granted $75,000 for the acquisition and installation of theater equipment, providing the organization acquired a new building. The amount now was expended in accordance with the stipulations of the will, and payment of $75,000 was made.

9. The account payable of $9,000 mentioned in item (2) was paid.

Required ▶ ▶ ▶ ▶ ▶   Prepare journal entries to record the preceding events.

Problem 18-10 *(LO 10)* **Journal entries.** Carleton Agency, a VHWO, conducts two programs: Medical Services and Community Information Services. It had the following transactions during the year ended June 30, 2019, shown below.

1. Received the following contributions:

Unrestricted pledges	$800,000
Restricted cash	95,000
Building fund pledges	50,000
Endowment fund cash	1,000

2. Collected the following pledges:

Unrestricted	$450,000
Building fund	20,000

3. Received the following unrestricted cash flows from:

Theater party (net of direct costs)	$ 12,000
Bequests	10,000
Membership dues	8,000
Interest and dividends	5,000

4. Program expenses incurred (processed through vouchers payable):

Medical services	$ 60,000
Community information services	15,000

5. Services expenses incurred (processed through vouchers payable):

General administration	$150,000
Fund raising	200,000

6. Purchased fixed assets:

Fixed assets purchased with donor-restricted cash	$ 18,000

Carleton's policy is to release donor restrictions when assets are placed in service.

7. Depreciation of all buildings and equipment in the land, buildings, and equipment fund was allocated as follows:

Medical services program.	$ 4,000
Community information services program.	3,000
General administration	6,000
Fund raising.	2,000

8. Vouchers paid:

Paid vouchers payable	$330,000

Record journal entries for the preceding transactions. Number your journal entries to coincide with the preceding transaction numbers.

◀ ◀ ◀ ◀ ◀ **Required**

(AICPA adapted)

Accounting for Not-for-Profit Colleges and Universities and Health Care Organizations

Learning Objectives

When you have completed this chapter, you should be able to

1. Explain how fund accounting is used by not-for-profit colleges and universities, and differentiate among those funds.

2. Demonstrate an understanding of the accounting for revenues and expenses for not-for-profit colleges and universities.

3. Demonstrate an understanding of the accounting for unrestricted and restricted contributions to not-for-profit colleges and universities.

4. Account for transactions of not-for-profit colleges or universities using funds.

5. Prepare financial statements for not-for-profit colleges and universities.

6. Explain GAAP and fund accounting as applied to governmental and private health care service providers.

7. Demonstrate an understanding of how revenues and expenses are calculated and accounted for by governmental and private health care service providers.

8. Demonstrate an understanding of the accounting for unrestricted and restricted contributions to governmental and private health care service providers.

9. Explain the financial impact of medical malpractice claims on governmental and private health care service providers.

10. Account for transactions of governmental and private health care service providers.

11. Prepare financial statements for governmental and private health care service providers.

Both colleges and universities and health care organizations are complex entities that cross public and private sectors. As a result, statements of the Financial Accounting Standards Board (FASB) and the Governmental Accounting Standards Board (GASB) directly impact accounting and financial reporting for these organizations. This chapter illustrates financial accounting and reporting for colleges and universities and not-for-profit health care organizations. Differences between generally accepted accounting principles for public and private institutions are noted where applicable.

ACCOUNTING FOR COLLEGES AND UNIVERSITIES (PUBLIC AND PRIVATE)

The responsibilities of a not-for-profit university may be classified as academic, financial, student services, and public relations. Academic functions include instruction, research, and public service. The financial sphere covers the management and reporting of business and financial affairs as well as auxiliary enterprises, such as housing, food service, and student union operation. Student services includes all student activities not directly classified as academic or financial, such as admissions, records, health, counseling, and publications. Public relations involves the communication and establishment of goodwill with academic and administrative staff, alumni, and the community.

The effectiveness with which a university accomplishes its objectives in these four areas depends in part upon the resources at its disposal. A university levies tuition fees, but these fees do not cover total operational costs. Therefore, other sources of revenue are essential. These sources include gifts, income from endowment funds, and grants from governmental units or foundations, and for public universities, appropriations from state legislatures.

Previous editions of this book have presented the accounting and financial statements for public colleges and universities following the guidance set forth in the AICPA *Audits of Colleges and Universities* (1994).[1] But, with the issuance of GASB Statement No. 35 in 1999, public colleges and universities are required to use the guidance for special-purpose governments engaged in business-type activities, engaged only in governmental activities, or engaged in both. Public colleges and universities are expected to follow the model for public institutions engaged only in business-type activities. Thus, the basic financial statements are those required of an enterprise fund (see Chapter 16). And, most probably, these institutions will be included as enterprise funds or component units of another government entity, e.g., state, city, or county. Private colleges and universities follow not-for-profit standards as outlined in Chapter 18. Today, several years after colleges and universities first implemented GASB Statement Nos. 34 and 35, the financial statements of both public and private colleges and universities emphasize the organization as a whole. The financial statements of both present organization-wide totals of assets, liabilities, and net assets as well as information concerning organization-wide changes in net assets and organization-wide cash flows. Because of a shift away from a fund group focus to an organization-wide focus, there is no requirement for external financial statements to include fund group reporting. But, most colleges and universities continue to use fund accounting for internal purposes. And, since both the FASB and GASB standards prescribe minimum reporting standards, many colleges and universities include additional fund information in the annual report. Because of the internal use of fund accounting, a presentation for colleges and universities following pronouncements set forth by the FASB and GASB using the fund structure in the 1994 Audit Guide is used in this chapter.[2]

Funds

College and university funds include three broad categories: current funds, plant funds, and trust and agency funds. The day-to-day activities of a university are recorded in its current funds, which consist of two self-balancing subfunds. The *unrestricted current fund* represents amounts that are available for any current activity commensurate with the university's

---

1 GASB Statement No. 15, Governmental College and University Accounting and Financial Reporting Models, requires public colleges and universities to use either the governmental model as outlined in Chapter 16 or the 1994 AICPA Audit Guide model which will be described in this chapter.

2 The divergence arising in financial accounting and reporting standards under the current 2-board structure is most pronounced in colleges and universities. Recent GASB statements suggest sharp differences of opinion between the two boards on many issues. For example, GASB Statement No. 8 (issued in 1988) does not require depreciation by governmental universities; Statement No. 15 (issued in 1991) allows governmental colleges and universities to follow either the governmental model or the AICPA Audit Guide (as amended in 1993); Statement No. 19 (issued in 1993) requires governmental colleges and universities to account for federally sponsored student financial aid in a current restricted fund; Statement No. 29 (issued in 1996) prohibits governmental colleges and universities from applying the provisions of FASB Statement Nos. 116 and 117; and GASB Statement No. 31 states that public colleges and universities that elect to follow the AICPA Audit Guide model should assign investment income, including changes in the fair value of investments, to funds.

objectives. The *restricted current fund* accounts for those resources available only for an externally specified purpose. The segregation of unrestricted current funds from restricted current funds substantiates that the limitations placed on restricted funds by outside sources have been observed. Plant funds account for capital assets and for resources to be used to acquire additional capital assets or to retire indebtedness related to capital assets. *Plant funds* consist of several subgroups, each of which is designed to record a certain phase of activity related to fixed assets. *Endowment and similar funds* account for endowments received. In addition, a university may employ *loan funds, annuity funds, life income funds, and agency funds.*

Accounting for Revenues

Colleges and universities recognize revenues in all funds on the accrual basis. A university might establish one master control account for unrestricted revenues, with details as to major sources recorded in subsidiary records. More commonly, separate revenue accounts are established, using the following three major groups of revenues:

> *Educational and general revenues group*, with accounts for:
> > Student tuition and fees (recognized when due or billed, net of an appropriate allowance for uncollectibles)
> > Governmental appropriations (detailed as to federal, state, and local)
> > Governmental grants and contracts (detailed as to federal, state, and local)
> > Gifts and private grants
> > Endowment income
> > Other sources
> *Auxiliary enterprises revenues*
> *Expired term endowment revenues*

Operating revenues and nonoperating revenues are recorded in these accounts. Student tuition and fees, federal appropriations, and governmental grants are classified as operating revenues. All appropriations from the state government, gifts, investment income, endowment income, and interest are recorded as nonoperating revenues. Auxiliary enterprises revenues are segregated to permit the evaluation of performance and the degree of self-support. Expired term endowment income represents dollar amounts of term endowments on which the restriction has lapsed, freeing them to become unrestricted resources.

Accounting for Expenses

Expenses are recognized in all funds on the accrual basis and may be classified on a natural basis or by function. The most common classification is by function for two major groupings, which are the same as the first two used to classify revenues.

> *Educational and general expenses group*, with accounts for:
> > Instruction (expenses for credit and noncredit courses)
> > Research (expenses to produce research results)
> > Public support (expenses for noninstructional services, including conferences, seminars, and consulting)
> > Academic support (expenses supporting instruction and public services, such as libraries, galleries, audiovisual services, and academic deans)
> > Student services (expenses for student admission and registration and cultural and athletic activities)
> > Institutional support (expenses for central administration)
> > Operation and maintenance of plant (expenses for capital repairs and depreciation)
> > Student aid (expenses for scholarships, fellowships, tuition remissions, and outright grants)
> *Auxiliary enterprises expenses*

2

OBJECTIVE

Demonstrate an understanding of the accounting for revenues and expenses for not-for-profit colleges and universities.

3

Demonstrate an understanding of the accounting for unrestricted and restricted contributions to not-for-profit colleges and universities.

Accounting for Contributions

Contributions are defined by FASB ASC 958-605, as noted in Chapter 18, as "unconditional transfers of cash or other assets to an entity or a settlement or cancellation of its liabilities in a voluntary nonreciprocal transfer ..."[3] and in GASB Statement No. 33 as voluntary non-exchange transactions with private parties. Other donated assets may include securities, land, buildings, use of facilities or utilities, materials and supplies, intangible assets, services, and unconditional promises to give those items in the future. Private colleges and universities recognize contributions and unconditional promises to give as revenues or gains in the period received. Public colleges and universities recognize contributions as revenue when any eligibility requirements and time requirements have been met. Exceptions to the general recognition provision are made for contributions of services and works of art. Contributions other than services in private universities are recognized in the period received and are measured at their fair value. Services would be recognized only if they (a) create or enhance nonfinancial assets or (b) require specialized skills, are provided by individuals possessing those abilities, and typically would have to be purchased if not provided by donation. Currently, GASB standards are silent on the issue of reporting revenue and expenses for services. Private and public colleges and universities are not required to recognize contributions of works of art, historical treasures, and similar assets if the donated items are added to collections, held for public exhibition, and preserved, cared for, and protected.

Conditional pledges depend on the occurrence of uncertain future events and are only recognized as revenue in both public and private colleges and universities when the conditions are substantially met (i.e., the pledge becomes unconditional). An example of a conditional pledge might be a donation restricted for construction of a new building given only if the organization can raise the remaining funds through additional contributions. Pledges or other assets received subject to such conditions are recorded as refundable advances until the conditions have been substantially met, at which time revenue is recorded.

When contributions extend over a long period of time, the college or university should report the "present value of estimated future cash flows using a discount rate commensurate with the risks involved." Promises receivable within one year need not be discounted. An allowance for doubtful contributions should be established based on historical experience and other factors to cover any uncertainties concerning collectibility. An unconditional pledge with no donor restriction is recognized as follows:

Contributions Receivable	XXX	
Revenues—Unrestricted Contributions		XXX
Provision for Uncollectible Contributions	XXX	
Allowance for Uncollectible Contributions		XXX

Donor-Imposed Restrictions and Reclassifications

Private universities following FASB ASC 958-605 are required to reclassify the net assets (a) when the donor's stipulated time has elapsed, (b) when the donor's stipulated purpose has been fulfilled, or (c) over the useful life of donated assets. Gifts of assets with no donor restrictions are classified as unrestricted. Public colleges and universities under GASB Statement No. 34 must maintain separate unrestricted and restricted net assets. Therefore, any expenses made in compliance with donor restrictions are funded directly out of restricted resources.

A cash contribution restricted by the donor for a specific expenditure is recorded when received.

Cash	XXX	
Revenues—Temporarily Restricted Contributions		XXX

---

3 FASB ASC 958-605-20. The FASB defines a nonreciprocal transfer as a transaction in which an organization receives an asset or cancellation of a liability without directly gaining value in exchange.

Expenses made in compliance with donor restrictions are funded by the restricted resources. Temporarily restricted net assets are released with a reclassification entry.	Expenses . . . . Cash	XXX	XXX
	Reclassification Out—Temporarily Restricted— Satisfaction of Donor Restrictions . . . . Reclassification In—Unrestricted—Satisfaction of Donor Restrictions	XXX	XXX

GASB Statement No. 33, FASB ASC 958-605, and the AICPA Audit and Accounting Guide Not-for-Profit Organizations distinguish between accounting for exchange transactions, agency transactions, and contributions. *Exchange transactions*, that is, reciprocal transfers in which each party receives and sacrifices approximately equal value, are not considered restricted. In private universities, grants, awards, sponsorships, and appropriations are now categorized as exchange transactions rather than contributions and accounted for as increases in unrestricted assets. Government grants that require performance by the not-for-profit organization are accounted for as refundable deposits (liabilities) until earned. Unrestricted revenue is earned when expenses are made in conjunction with the provisions of the grant. Other government grants, which are essentially pass-through financial aid to students, are accounted for as *agency transactions*.

In public universities, resources received that are externally restricted by creditors (such as through debt covenants), grantors, contributors, or laws and regulations of other governments and those that are imposed by law are recorded as restricted revenue.

Grant monies received.	Cash . . . . U.S. Government Grants Refundable	XXX	XXX
Expenses incurred in conjunction with provisions of grant.	Expenses . . . . Cash	XXX	XXX
Revenue is recognized up to the amount earned by incurring above expenses.	U.S. Government Grants Refundable . . . . Revenues—Unrestricted.	XXX	XXX

Permanently restricted contributions are called *endowments.* Earnings on endowment investments are reported in the period earned as a credit to Unrestricted Revenue or Temporarily Restricted Revenue depending on donor specification as to the use of the earnings. Realized and unrealized gains on endowment investments are reported as increases or decreases in unrestricted net assets unless their use is temporarily or permanently restricted by explicit donor stipulations or by law. Losses on endowment investments reduce temporarily restricted net assets to the extent that donor-imposed restrictions on net appreciation have been met before the loss occurs. Any remaining loss would reduce unrestricted net assets.[4]

University Accounting and Financial Reporting within Existing Fund Structure

4

OBJECTIVE

Account for transactions of not-for-profit colleges or universities using funds.

The following transactions are for private colleges and universities. Events are marked with an asterisk when public and private entries differ. The asterisk is followed by the appropriate *public college or university* entry.

Current Unrestricted Fund. The unrestricted current fund of a university is similar to the general fund of a state or local government in that it accounts for current assets available to cover current operational costs and resulting expenses for both private and public colleges and universities.

---

4 FASB ASC 958-205-45-22.

Event	Entry		

1. Educational and general revenue is earned or billed:

Student tuition and fees (of which $20,000		Accounts Receivable	2,750,000	
is considered uncollectible)	$1,700,000	Revenues—Student Tuition and Fees		1,700,000
Government appropriations	750,000	Revenues—Governmental Appropriations .		750,000
Endowment income	50,000	Revenues—Unrestricted Endowment		
Other investment income	250,000	Income		50,000
		Revenues—Unrestricted Other Investment		
		Income		250,000

The provision for uncollectible student accounts receivable is considered an expense and is allocated to institutional support.

Expenses—Institutional Support (provision for		
uncollectible student accounts receivable) . .	20,000	
Allowance for Uncollectible Student		
Accounts Receivable		20,000

Unrestricted contributions (the other investment income) are pledged in the amount of $250,000. Ten percent of these pledges is assumed uncollectible.

Contributions Receivable	250,000	
Revenues—Unrestricted Contributions		250,000
Expenses—Institutional Support (provision		
for uncollectible contributions)	25,000	
Allowance for Uncollectible		
Contributions		25,000

2. Of the total revenues, $2,800,000 is collected, including $200,000 of pledges.

Cash	2,800,000	
Accounts Receivable		2,600,000
Contributions Receivable		200,000

3. Revenue billed for dormitories (an auxiliary enterprise) is $400,000, of which $20,000 is not yet received.

Cash	380,000	
Accounts Receivable	20,000	
Revenues—Sales and Services of		
Auxiliary Enterprises		400,000

4. Purchase of materials and supplies totaling $400,000, of which $25,000 is not yet paid.

Inventory of Supplies	400,000	
Cash		375,000
Accounts Payable		25,000

5. Expenses are paid and assigned to:

Instruction	$1,050,000	Expenses—Instruction	1,050,000	
Research	100,000	Expenses—Research	100,000	
Academic support	150,000	Expenses—Academic Support	150,000	
Student services	200,000	Expenses—Student Services	200,000	
Institutional support	200,000	Expenses—Institutional Support	200,000	
Operation and maintenance of plant	400,000	Expenses—Operation and Maintenance		
Scholarships and fellowships	40,000	of Plant	400,000	
Sales and services of auxiliary enterprises	260,000	Expenses—Student Aid	40,000	
		Expenses—Sales and Services of Auxiliary		
		Enterprises	260,000	
		Cash		2,400,000

6. Materials and supplies used:

Instruction	$268,000	Expenses—Instruction	268,000	
Student services	22,000	Expenses—Student Services	22,000	
Auxiliary enterprises	90,000	Expenses—Sales and Services of Auxiliary		
		Enterprises	90,000	
		Inventory of Supplies		380,000

7. Aid is granted to students:

Remission of tuition	$140,000	Expenses—Student Aid	175,000	
Cash scholarships	35,000	Accounts Receivable		140,000
		Cash		35,000

Event	Entry		
8. *Services that meet the criteria of (1) creating or enhancing nonfinancial assets or (2) requiring specialized skills and are provided by individuals possessing those abilities are typically purchased if not donated. The fair value of the services is $35,000. Currently, GASB Statement No. 35 is silent on the reporting of services.	Expenses—Instruction . . . . Revenues—Unrestricted Contributions	35,000	35,000
9. Cash contributions are given without donor restriction.	Cash . . . . Revenues—Unrestricted Contributions	100,000	100,000

10. *Closing entries are prepared for the unrestricted net assets. Public universities will close to Net Assets—Unrestricted.	Revenues—Student Tuition and Fees . . . .
	 Revenues—Governmental Appropriations . . .
	 Revenues—Unrestricted Contributions . . . . . .
	 Revenues—Unrestricted Endowment
	    Income . . . .
	 Revenues—Unrestricted Other Investment
	    Income . . . .
	    Expenses—Instruction. . . . .
	    Expenses—Research . . . .
	    Expenses—Academic Support. . . . .
	    Expenses—Student Services . . . .
	    Expenses—Institutional Support. . . . .
	    Expenses—Operations and
	       Maintenance of Plant . . . .
	    Expenses—Student Aid . . . .
	    Unrestricted Net Assets . . . .
		1,700,000
		 750,000
		 385,000
		
		 50,000
		
		 250,000
			1,353,000
			 100,000
			 150,000
			 222,000
			 245,000
			
			 400,000
			 215,000
			 450,000

	Revenues—Sales and Services of Auxiliary
	    Enterprises . . . .
	    Expenses—Sales and Services of
	       Auxiliary Enterprises . . . .
	    Unrestricted Net Assets . . . .
		400,000	350,000
			 50,000

Current Restricted Fund. For an activity to enter the restricted current fund of a university, some limitation must exist on the resources received from an external entity. The same revenue and expense accounts used in the unrestricted current fund are available, but restricted current fund revenues arise primarily from governmental grants and contracts, private gifts, and endowment income. Expenses generally are relegated to instruction, research, and student aid.

Unless the restriction placed upon contributed resources or governmental grants is respected, these resources may have to be returned to the donor. Until they are expended properly, they should not be considered as revenue. As a consequence, expenditures govern the recognition of revenue. These resources are expenditure driven, similar to such items in governmental accounting. The current restricted fund will have both donor-restricted contributions and resources from exchange transactions, including government grants. A difficult decision for many universities will be to differentiate donor-restricted contributions from exchange transactions.

Event	Entry		
11. A donor-restricted cash contribution is received to assist in library operations.	Cash . . . . Revenues—Temporarily Restricted Contributions	70,000	70,000
12. Endowment income of $8,000 is restricted to student aid activities.	Cash . . . . Revenues—Temporarily Restricted Endowment Income	8,000	8,000

(continued)

Event	Entry		

13. Of the following expenses, all but $4,000 are paid.

For library operations $67,000	Expenses—Academic Support	67,000	
For student aid........................ 6,000	Expenses—Student Aid	6,000	
	Accounts Payable		4,000
	Cash		69,000

14. *Temporarily restricted revenues of $73,000 are reclassified as unrestricted when donor specifications are met. Public colleges and universities will not record the reclassification entry but will close expenses to Restricted Net Assets.

Reclassifications Out—Temporarily Restricted—Satisfaction of Program Restrictions	73,000	
Reclassifications In—Unrestricted—Satisfaction of Program Restrictions		73,000

15. Federal grants for student awards are through the Pell Grant. See Agency Fund events and entries. Program funds are received in the amount of $75,000. All $75,000 is distributed to qualified students.

16. A federal grant was awarded for research.

Cash	100,000	
U.S. Government Grants Refundable ..		100,000

17. Expenses for the research project totaled $45,000 to date. All expenses have been paid.
Revenue is recognized to the extent that resources have been properly spent.

Expenses—Research	45,000	
Cash		45,000
U.S. Government Grants Refundable.....	45,000	
Revenues—Government Grants and Contracts		45,000

18. *Closing entries are prepared for the unrestricted net assets. Public universities will close to Net Assets—Unrestricted.

Revenues—Unrestricted Government Grants and Contracts	45,000	
Reclassifications In—Unrestricted—Satisfaction of Program Restrictions ...	73,000	
Expenses—Academic Support......		67,000
Expenses—Student Aid		6,000
Expenses—Research		45,000
Unrestricted Net Assets		**0**

19. *Closing entries are prepared for the temporarily restricted net assets. Public universities will close to Net Assets—Restricted.

Revenues—Temporarily Restricted Contributions....................	70,000	
Revenues—Temporarily Restricted Endowment Income................	8,000	
Reclassifications Out—Temporarily Restricted—Satisfaction of Program Restrictions		73,000
Temporarily Restricted Net Assets.................		**5,000**

Loan Funds. Loan funds are established to account for resources that are available for loans primarily to students and possibly to faculty and staff. A separate fund is used because of the large amounts of federal and state resources made available to universities for student loans. In addition, donor-restricted contributions may also specify use of the contributed resources for student loan purposes. Loan funds are revolving (self-perpetuating), with repayments of principal and the excess of interest collected over costs incurred becoming the base for additional loans. Both principal and earnings must be available for loan purposes. If only the income from a gift or grant may be used for loan purposes, the principal should not be in the loan fund but in the endowment fund.

The resources of loan funds consist mainly of gifts restricted for loan purposes and unrestricted current fund resources transferred by authorization of the governing board. Although assets are not segregated by restriction, the net assets must reveal their restricted and unrestricted portions.

Event	Entry		
20. A contribution of $25,000 is received from an alumnus for student loan purposes.	Cash . . . . Revenues—Temporarily Restricted Contributions	25,000	25,000
21. Investments costing $5,000 are sold for $5,500. Gain is restricted.	Cash . . . . Investments. . . . . Revenues—Temporarily Restricted— Net Realized Gains on Investments . .	5,500	5,000 500
22. Loans totaling $24,000 are made to students. Collections from other loans made to students total $20,000 plus $1,000 of interest. (FASB ASC 958-605 assumes that restricted resources are used first.)	Loans Receivable . . . . Cash . . . . Reclassifications Out—Temporarily Restricted—Satisfaction of Program Restrictions . . . . Reclassifications In—Unrestricted— Satisfaction of Program Restrictions Cash . . . . Loans Receivable . . . . Revenues—Unrestricted Other Investment Income	24,000 24,000 21,000	24,000 24,000 20,000 1,000
23. Federal government monies of $30,000 restricted for student loans are received.	Cash . . . . U.S. Government Grants Refundable . .	30,000	30,000
24. A $500 student loan is uncollectible.	Expenses—Institutional Support (Loan Cancellations/Write-Offs) . . . . . . Loans Receivable	500	500
25. *Closing entries are prepared for the unrestricted net assets. Public universities will close to Net Assets—Unrestricted.	Revenues—Unrestricted Interest Income . . Reclassifications In—Unrestricted— Satisfaction of Program Restrictions . . . Expenses—Institutional Support . . . . . **Unrestricted Net Assets**	1,000 24,000	500 **24,500**
26. *Closing entries are prepared for the temporarily restricted net assets. Public universities will close to Net Assets—Restricted.	Revenues—Temporarily Restricted Contributions. . . . . Revenues—Temporarily Restricted Net Realized Gains on Investments . . . . Reclassifications Out—Temporarily Restricted—Satisfaction of Program Restrictions . . . . **Temporarily Restricted Net Assets**	25,000 500	24,000 **1,500**

Endowment and Similar Funds. Colleges and universities traditionally account for permanent endowments, term endowments, and board-designated (quasi-) endowment resources in separate funds. This practice is common because external users of financial data, such as the debt market, consider all three categories of endowments important in the lending decision. Each of these endowment funds has a unique purpose:

1. *Regular or pure endowments* are funds whose principal has been specified by the donor as nonexpendable. The resources are invested, and the earnings are available for expenditure, usually by the unrestricted current fund.

2. *Term endowments* are funds whose principal is expendable after a specified time period or after a designated event, at which point the resources are added to the unrestricted current fund, unless the original donor has specified some other application.

3. *Quasi-endowments* are funds set aside by the board or controlling body, usually from unrestricted current funds. Restricted current funds also may be set aside if the donor's limitations are not violated. Since these funds are discretionary, technically they do not belong to the endowment category; hence, the addition to the title of "and Similar Funds."

The resources for endowment funds often are pooled for investment purposes, with the various fund balances sharing proportionately in the outcome based on the fair values of investments at the time of pooling or at specified future dates. Procedures for investment pooling are discussed in Chapter 18. Income earned on restricted endowment resources is recorded directly in the restricted current fund, the loan fund, the endowment fund, or a plant fund, depending upon which fund the donor has specified should reap the benefits. Income on which there is no restriction is recorded directly in the unrestricted current fund, where it is credited to Endowment Income. The costs of managing endowment funds should be borne by the university's unrestricted current fund.

GASB Statement No. 31, *Accounting and Financial Reporting for Certain Investments and External Investment*, and FASB ASC 958-205-45-22 require all investments to be reported at fair value in the statement of net assets. All investment income, including changes in the fair value of investments, should be recognized as revenue in the operating statement. Realized gains are not displayed separately from unrealized gains and losses.[5]

Event	Entry		
27. Common stock with a fair value of $60,000 and $60,000 cash are received as pure endowment contributions.	Cash . . . . Endowment Investments. . . . . 　Revenues—Permanently Restricted 　　Contributions	60,000 60,000	 120,000
28. *Term endowments expire, making $20,000 cash available.	Reclassifications Out—Temporarily 　Restricted—Expiration of 　Time Restrictions . . . . 　　Reclassifications In—Unrestricted— 　　　Expiration of Time Restrictions	 20,000	 20,000
29. Endowment fund investments carried at $200,000 are sold for $260,000 and investment earnings are $40,000, of which $20,000 is temporarily restricted for research projects and $20,000 is unrestricted.	Cash . . . . 　Endowment Investments. . . . . 　Revenues—Unrestricted Net Realized 　　Gains on Endowment. . . . . 　Revenues—Temporarily Restricted 　　Endowment Income . . . . 　Revenues—Unrestricted Endowment 　　Income	300,000	 200,000 60,000 20,000 20,000
30. Investments are purchased with fund cash.	Endowment Investments. . . . . 　Cash	360,000	 360,000
31. *Closing entries are prepared for the unrestricted net assets. Public universities will close to Net Assets—Unrestricted.	Reclassifications In—Unrestricted— 　Expiration of Time Restrictions. . . . . Revenues—Unrestricted Income on 　Endowments . . . . Revenues—Unrestricted Net Realized 　Gains on Endowment . . . . 　　**Unrestricted Net Assets**	 20,000 20,000 60,000	 **100,000**

─────────────

5 GASB Statement No. 31, *Accounting and Financial Reporting for Certain Investments and External Investment* (1997), is effective for years beginning after June 15, 1997.

Event	Entry		
32. *Closing entries are prepared for the temporarily restricted net assets. Public universities will close to Net Assets—Restricted.	Revenues—Temporarily Restricted Endowment Income	20,000	
	Reclassifications Out—Temporarily Restricted—Expiration of Time Restriction		20,000
	Temporarily Restricted Net Assets		**0**
33. *Closing entries are prepared for the permanently restricted net assets. Public universities will close to Net Assets—Restricted.	Revenues—Permanently Restricted Endowment Contributions	120,000	
	Permanently Restricted Net Assets		**120,000**

Annuity and Life Income Funds. Resources may be accepted by a university under the stipulation that periodic payments are to continue as an annuity to the donor or other designated beneficiary for an indicated time period. Often referred to as *split interest trusts*, these resources should be accounted for in an annuity fund at their fair value on the date of receipt. A liability for the actuarially computed present value of expected total annuity payments is recorded, with the excess credited to Revenue from Contributions. As each payment is made, a debit is charged directly to Annuities Payable each period, and the liability is adjusted to bring it to an amount equal to the present value. For example, assume a retired administrator donated $50,000 to a university. The administrator is to receive annuity payments of $3,000 per year for life; thereafter, the principal is to be used for student aid. Assuming an estimated life of 15 years and an 8% interest rate, the present value of the annuity is actuarially computed to be $25,678. The entry to record receipt of the donation is as follows:

Cash—Annuity	50,000	
Annuities Payable		25,678
Revenues—Temporarily Restricted Contribution		24,322

During the year, interest earned on annuity investments is added to the fund balance. At the end of the first year, the present value of the liability is adjusted by adding interest of $2,054 (8% × $25,678). The administrator is mailed a check for $3,000. Entries to record the adjustment of the liability to present value and payment to the annuitant are as follows:

Annuity Interest Expense	2,054	
Annuities Payable		2,054
Annuities Payable	3,000	
Cash		3,000

A life income fund is used if all income received on contributed assets is to be paid to the donor or other specified recipient for life. When the original contributed assets are recorded at fair value, the corresponding credit is to Life Income revenues from contributions. As income is received, a liability for its payment is established immediately.

When the annuity payments or the life income payments cease, the principal is transferred to the donor-specified fund or to the unrestricted current fund if no donor restriction exists. Also, unless otherwise specified, gains or losses on the sale of investments are treated as changes in principal and are recorded directly in the appropriate fund net asset account.

Event	Entry		
34. Cash of $12,000 from life income fund investments and $18,000 from annuity fund investments are received.	Cash	12,000	
	Revenues—Temporarily Restricted Income on Investments		12,000
	Cash	18,000	
	Revenues—Temporarily Restricted Income on Investments		18,000

(continued)

Event	Entry		

35. A retired professor donated $100,000. The professor is to receive $6,000 per year for an estimated life of 10 years. Thereafter, the principal is to be used for student aid. The present value of the annuity at 8% is actuarially computed to be $40,260.	Cash . . . .
	  Annuities Payable . . . .
	  Revenues—Temporarily Restricted
	   Contributions . . . .
		100,000	40,260
			
			59,740

36. Interest on the annuity is recorded for the year (8% × $40,260 = $3,221).	Actuarial Adjustment of Annuities
	  Payable . . . .
	   Annuities Payable . . . .
		3,221	3,221

37. Payments are made to:
  Annuitant . . . . $ 6,000
  Life income beneficiaries 12,000
	Annuities Payable . . . .
	  Cash . . . .
	
	Life Income Beneficiaries . . . .
	  Cash . . . .
		6,000
		
		12,000
			6,000
			
			12,000

38. Annuity fund investments with a book value of $50,000 are sold for $59,500.	Cash . . . .
	  Annuity Investments . . . .
	  Revenues—Temporarily Restricted Net
	   Realized Gains on Investments . . . . .
		59,500	50,000
			
			9,500

39. *Closing entries are prepared for temporarily restricted net assets. Public universities will close to Net Assets—Restricted.	Revenues—Temporarily Restricted Contributions. Revenues—Temporarily Restricted Net Realized Gains on Investments . . . . Revenues—Temporarily Restricted Income on Annuity and Life Income Investments . . Payment to Life Income Beneficiaries . Loss on Actuarial Adjustment of Annuities—Payable . . . . **Temporarily Restricted Net Assets**	59,740 9,500 30,000	 12,000 3,221 **84,019**

Plant Funds. Private universities often account for properties in a separate fund. The plant funds of public universities are more complicated and include four separate, self-balancing subgroups:

1. *Unexpended plant fund* accounts for resources that are to be used to acquire properties.
2. *Plant fund for renewals and replacements* accounts for resources that are available to keep the physical plant in operating condition.
3. *Plant fund for retirement of indebtedness* accounts for the resources accumulated for the payment of interest and principal of plant fund indebtedness.
4. The *investment in plant* subgroup controls all plant assets and related long-term debt.

GASB Statement No. 35 requires public colleges and universities to record all capital assets, including infrastructure, and to include a *provision for depreciation* of all plant fund assets. The only exceptions are works of art and historical treasures that meet the provisions outlined in the standard.

Cost computations that include depreciation expenses are useful in establishing charges for auxiliary enterprise services, which include dormitories, bookstores, cafeterias and restaurants, medical service, and the student union. Especially for services provided to the general public, amounts charged should include depreciation considerations. Part of the amount that a university receives from grants reimburses it for overhead, which also should include depreciation.

FASB ASC 958-360-35 requires colleges and universities to disclose "depreciation expense for the period." Land and individual works of art or historical treasures that have an extraordinarily long life were excluded from these reporting requirements. The entries shown on page 983 assume one plant fund, although the subgroups described above could be retained.

Event	Entry		

40. Stock with a fair value of $90,000 is received from an art patron to finance an art gallery addition.	Investments ....
	    Revenues—Temporarily Restricted
	      Contributions ....
		90,000	90,000

41. A collection of first editions appraised at $30,000 is donated to the university. The university adopts a policy of recording contributed collections.	Library Books......................... Revenues—Unrestricted Contributions	30,000	30,000
42. An $800,000 bond issue is sold at face value to finance a business school wing.	Cash .... Bonds Payable.......................	800,000	800,000

43. Earnings received on investments are restricted for building acquisition.	Cash ....
	    Revenues—Temporarily Restricted Other
	      Investment Income ....
		45,000	45,000

44. Construction of the business school wing is one-fourth completed.	Construction in Progress .... Contracts Payable	200,000	200,000
45. Business school wing contract is completed at additional cost of $640,000 and is paid in full.	Construction in Progress .... Contracts Payable .... Cash	640,000 200,000	840,000
46. Completed building costs are transferred to the building account.	Building............................. Construction in Progress	840,000	840,000
47. Payment of $100,000 is made on mortgage related to the completed project.	Mortgage Payable.................... Cash	100,000	100,000

48. The cost of constructing an art gallery addition totals $250,000 and is financed with donor-restricted cash. University policy is to release restrictions when assets are placed in service.	Building.............................
	    Cash ....
	
	Reclassifications Out—Temporarily
	  Restricted—Satisfaction of Plant
	  Restrictions........................
	    Reclassifications In—Unrestricted—
	      Satisfaction of Plant Acquisition
	      Restrictions ....
		250,000
		
		250,000
			250,000
			
			250,000

49. Land valued at $160,000 is donated by an alumnus.	Land................................
	    Revenues—Unrestricted Property
	      Contribution......................
		160,000	160,000

50. Building repairs of $50,000 are paid, of which $5,000 is from restricted resources.	Expenses ....
	    Cash ....
	Reclassifications Out—Temporarily
	  Restricted—Satisfaction of Program
	  Restrictions........................
	    Reclassifications In—Unrestricted—
	      Satisfaction of Program Restrictions ...
		50,000
		
		5,000
			50,000
			
			5,000

51. *Depreciation expense for the current period is $150,000. Depreciation expenses are allocated to operation and maintenance of plant expenses. Public universities will have new depreciation expense.	Expenses—Operation and Maintenance of
	  Plant (provision for depreciation).........
	    Accumulated Depreciation ....
		150,000	150,000

52. *Closing entries are prepared for the unrestricted net assets. Public universities will close to Net Assets—Unrestricted.	Reclassifications In—Unrestricted—
	  Satisfaction of Plant Acquisition
	  Restrictions........................
	Reclassifications In—Unrestricted—
	  Satisfaction of Program Restrictions.......
	Revenues—Unrestricted Property
	  Contributions ....
	    Expenses—Operation and
	      Maintenance of Plant ....
	    Unrestricted Net Assets ....
		250,000
		
		5,000
		
		190,000
			200,000
			245,000

(continued)

Event	Entry		
53. *Closing entries are prepared for the temporarily restricted net assets. Public universities will close to Net Assets—Restricted.	**Temporarily Restricted Net Assets**	**120,000**	
	Revenues—Temporarily Restricted Contributions	90,000	
	Revenues—Temporarily Restricted Other Investment Income	45,000	
	Reclassifications Out—Temporarily Restricted—Satisfaction of Plant Acquisition		250,000
	Reclassifications Out—Temporarily Restricted—Satisfaction of Program Restrictions		5,000

Agency Funds. Agency funds account for resources that are not the property of the university but are held in the university's custody. An example of such resources is assets belonging to student organizations. The total amount of these resources represents a liability. As a result, there are no net assets. Federal monies that pass through the university to student recipients (Pell Grants) are accounted for as agency transactions. In public universities, the GASB requires that agency funds be used if there is no program administration responsibility or oversight.

Event	Entry		
54. Federal grants for student awards through the Pell Grant Program are received in the amount of $75,000. All $75,000 is distributed to qualified students.	Cash	75,000	
	Amounts Held on Behalf of Others		75,000
	Amounts Held on Behalf of Others	75,000	
	Cash		75,000

5
OBJECTIVE

Prepare financial statements for not-for-profit colleges and universities.

Financial Statements

The financial statements of public and private colleges and universities are very similar. Under the governmental standards, *public* colleges and universities are required to report the following financial statements:

1. *Statement of net assets* (balance sheet) which will report organization-wide totals for assets, liabilities, net assets, and net assets identified as invested in capital [net of related debt, restricted (nonexpendable and expendable), and unrestricted (see Illustration 19-1)].
2. *Statement of revenues, expenses, and changes in net assets* which reports operating revenues and expenses and nonoperating activities, including gifts, grants, and additions to endowments (see Illustration 19-2 on page 986).
3. *Statement of cash flows* with categories (operating, noncapital financing, capital and related financing, and investing activities) prescribed for all governments (see Illustration 19-3 on page 987).

Private colleges and universities have the following required financial statements:

1. *Statement of financial position* (balance sheet) which will report organization-wide totals for assets, liabilities, net assets, and net assets identified as unrestricted, temporarily restricted, and permanently restricted (see Illustration 19-4 on page 988).
2. *Statement of activities* which reports revenues, expenses, gains, losses, and reclassifications (between classes of net assets). Minimum requirements are organization-wide totals, changes in net assets for each class of assets, and all expenses recognized only in the unrestricted classification. A display of a measure of operations in the statement of activities is permitted (see Illustration 19-5 on page 989).
3. *Statement of cash flows* with categories (operating, financing, investing) similar to business organizations (see Illustration 19-6 on page 990).

Illustration 19-1
Public University
Statement of Net Assets
June 30, 2019

Assets:

Current assets:

Cash and cash equivalents	$ 1,470,100
Short-term investments	673,000
Accounts receivable (net)	130,000
Contributions receivable	335,481
Inventories of supplies	20,000
Prepaid expenses	28,000
Total current assets	$ 2,656,581

Noncurrent assets:

Restricted cash and cash equivalents	$ 24,200
Student loans receivable	55,500
Endowment investments	954,000
Other long-term investments	1,118,700
Assets restricted to investment in capital	1,350,000
Capital assets (net of accumulated depreciation of $150,000)	41,450,000
Total noncurrent assets	$44,952,400
Total assets	$47,608,981

Liabilities:

Current liabilities:

Accounts payable and accrued liabilities	$ 1,039,000
Deferred revenues	85,000
Other current liabilities	1,500
Total current liabilities	$ 1,125,500

Noncurrent liabilities:

Assets held on behalf of others	$ 110,000
Annuities payable	237,481
Long-term debt (capital related)	3,000,000
Total noncurrent liabilities	$ 3,347,481
Total liabilities	$ 4,472,981

Net assets:

Invested in capital assets, net of related debt	$38,450,000
Restricted for:	
Nonexpendable:	
Instruction	525,000
Research	429,000
Expendable:	
Scholarships and fellowships	45,000
Research	150,000
Instructional department uses	50,000
Loans	82,500
Capital projects	1,350,000
Other	336,000
Unrestricted	1,718,500
Total net assets	$43,136,000

Illustration 19-2
Public University
Statement of Revenues, Expenses, and Changes in Net Assets
For Year Ended June 30, 2019

Operating revenues:	
Student tuition and fees	$ 1,700,000
Contributions	575,000
Government appropriations, grants, and contracts	275,000
Sales and services of auxiliary enterprises	400,000
Total operating revenues	$ 2,950,000
Operating expenses:	
Salaries	$ 1,592,000
Benefits	582,500
Scholarships and fellowships	221,000
Utilities	50,000
Repairs and maintenance	400,000
Auxiliary enterprises expenses	350,000
Depreciation	150,000
Total operating expenses	$ 3,345,500
Operating income (loss)	$ (395,500)
Nonoperating revenues (expenses):	
Contributions	$ 164,740
Investment income	424,000
Interest on capital asset—related debt	(20,000)
Net nonoperating revenues	$ 568,740
Income before other revenues, expenses, gains, or losses	$ 173,240
Capital appropriations	520,000
Capital grants and gifts	200,000
Realized gains on investments	10,000
Adjustment on annuity obligations	(3,221)
Additions to permanent endowments	60,000
Increase in net assets	$ 960,019
Net assets—beginning of year	$42,175,981
Net assets—end of year	$43,136,000

Illustration 19-3
Public University
Statement of Cash Flows
For Year Ended June 30, 2019

Cash flows from operating activities:

Student tuition and auxiliary fees	$ 2,030,000
Governmental appropriations	275,000
Research activities receipts	100,000
Contributions received	150,000
Payments to vendors for goods and services	(958,000)
Salaries and wages paid to faculty and staff	(1,935,000)
Disbursements to students for financial aid	(105,000)
Repayments of loans from students and faculty	20,000
Payments to life income beneficiaries and annuitants	(18,000)
Other receipts (payments)	105,000
Net cash provided (used) by operating activities	$ (336,000)

Cash flows from noncapital financing activities:

Governmental appropriations	$ 180,000
Gifts and grants received for other than capital purposes:	
Private gifts for long-term investment	245,000
Net cash flows provided by noncapital financing activities	$ 425,000

Cash flows from capital and related financing activities:

Proceeds from capital debt	$ 800,000
Capital appropriations	195,000
Capital grants and gifts received	200,000
Purchases of capital assets	(840,000)
Principal and interest paid on capital debt and lease	(100,000)
Net cash used by capital and related financing activities	$ 255,000

Cash flows from investing activities:

Proceeds from sales and maturities of investments	$ 325,000
Interest and dividends received	383,000
Purchase of investments	(360,000)
Net cash provided (used) by investing activities	$ 348,000
Net increase in cash	$ 692,000
Cash—beginning of year	802,300
Cash—end of year	$ 1,494,300*

*Cash and cash equivalents ($1,470,100) + restricted cash and cash equivalents ($24,200) = $1,494,300.

Illustration 19-4
Private University
Statement of Financial Position
For Period Ended June 30, 2019

Assets:

Cash	$ 1,494,300
Short-term investments	673,000
Accounts receivable (net of $20,000 allowance)	130,000
Contributions receivable (net of $25,000 allowance)	335,481
Inventories of supplies	20,000
Prepaid expenses	28,000
Student loans receivable	55,500
Assets restricted to investment in land, buildings, and equipment	1,350,000
Land, buildings, and equipment (net of accumulated depreciation of $150,000)	41,450,000
Long-term investments	1,118,700
Endowment investments	954,000
Total assets	**$47,608,981**

Liabilities:

Accounts payable and accrued liabilities	$ 1,039,000
Other liabilities	1,500
Amounts held on behalf of others	110,000
U.S. government grants refundable	85,000
Annuities payable	237,481
Long-term debt	3,000,000
Total liabilities	$ 4,472,981

Net assets:

Unrestricted	**$40,168,500**
Temporarily restricted	**2,013,500**
Permanently restricted	**954,000**
Total net assets	**$43,136,000**
Total liabilities and net assets	**$47,608,981**

Illustration 19-5
Private University
Statement of Activities
For Year Ended June 30, 2019

	Unrestricted	Temporarily Restricted	Permanently Restricted	Total
Changes in net assets:				
Revenues and gains:				
Tuition and fees	$ 1,700,000			$ 1,700,000
Contributions	575,000	$ 244,740	$ 120,000	939,740
Governmental appropriations, grants, and				
contracts.	795,000			795,000
Investment income on endowment	70,000	28,000		98,000
Other investment income	251,000	45,000		296,000
Sales and services of auxiliary enterprises.	400,000			400,000
Investment income on life income and annuity				
agreements		30,000		30,000
Net realized gains on other investments.		10,000		10,000
Net realized gains on endowment.	60,000			60,000
Total revenues and gains	$ 3,851,000	$ 357,740	$ 120,000	$ 4,328,740
Net assets released from restrictions:				
Satisfaction of program restrictions	$ 102,000	$ (102,000)		$ 0
Satisfaction of plant acquisitions restrictions	250,000	(250,000)		0
Satisfaction of time restrictions	20,000	(20,000)		0
Total net assets released from restriction	$ 372,000	$ (372,000)		$ 0
Total revenues and gains and other support.	$ 4,223,000	$ (14,260)	$ 120,000	$ 4,328,740
Expenses and losses:				
Educational and general:				
Instruction.	$ 1,353,000			$ 1,353,000
Research	145,000			145,000
Academic support	217,000			217,000
Student services	222,000			222,000
Institutional support	245,500			245,500
Operation and maintenance of plant.	600,000			600,000
Student aid.	221,000			221,000
Total educational and general expenses	$ 3,003,500			$ 3,003,500
Auxiliary enterprises	350,000			350,000
Total expenses	$ 3,353,500	$ 0	$ 0	$ 3,353,500
Actuarial adjustment on annuity obligations		3,221		3,221
Payments to life income beneficiaries		12,000		12,000
Total expenses and losses	$ 3,353,500	$ 15,221	$ 0	$ 3,368,721
Increase (decrease) in net assets	**$ 869,500**	**$ (29,481)**	**$120,000**	**$ 960,019**
Net assets at beginning of year	**39,299,000**	**2,042,981**	**834,000**	**42,175,981**
Net assets at end of year	**$40,168,500**	**$2,013,500**	**$954,000**	**$43,136,000**

Illustration 19-6
Private University
Statement of Cash Flows
For Period Ended June 30, 2019

Cash flows from operating activities:

Student tuition and auxiliary fees	$ 2,030,000
Governmental appropriations	650,000
Research activities receipts	100,000
Interest and dividends received	308,000
Contributions received	395,000
Other receipts	75,000
Salaries and wages paid to faculty and staff	(1,935,000)
Payments to vendors for goods and services	(958,000)
Disbursements to students for financial aid	(81,000)
Payments to life income beneficiaries	(12,000)
Net cash provided by (used for) operating activities	$ 572,000

Cash flows from investing activities:

Proceeds from sales and maturities of investments	$ 325,000
Purchases of investments	(360,000)
Purchases of land, buildings, and equipment	(840,000)
Disbursements of loans to students and faculty	(24,000)
Repayments of loans from students and faculty	20,000
Net cash provided by (used for) investing activities	$ (879,000)

Cash flows from financing activities:

Proceeds from issuance of notes payable	$ 800,000
Payments on long-term debt	(100,000)
Receipts of interest and dividends restricted for reinvestment	75,000
Contributions received restricted for long-term investment	200,000
Payments to annuitants	(6,000)
Receipts of refundable government loans funds	30,000
Net cash provided by (used for) financing activities	$ 999,000
Net increase (decrease) in cash and cash equivalents	$ 692,000
Cash and cash equivalents at beginning of year	802,300
Cash and cash equivalents at end of year	$1,494,300

REFLECTION

- Private colleges and universities follow FASB standards.

- Public colleges and universities will report as special purpose governments engaged in business-type activities and, as such, follow FASB standards per GASB Statement No. 35.

- Student aid is considered an expense; Pell Grants are agency transactions.

- Universities use fund accounting for internal control and decision making, but funds are not required in the external financial reports.

ACCOUNTING FOR PROVIDERS OF HEALTH CARE SERVICES—GOVERNMENTAL AND PRIVATE

6

OBJECTIVE

Explain GAAP and fund accounting as applied to governmental and private health care service providers.

Advancement in medical practice and increased demand for access to health care services have led to significant growth in the health care industry. Expenditures for medical care now equal more than 17% of the gross national product. Health care entities include hospitals, clinics, continuing care retirement communities, health maintenance organizations, home health agencies, and nursing homes. Classified by sponsorship or equity structure, health care units fall into three categories:

1. Investor-owned health care entities (or proprietary entities), which are privately owned and operated for a profit.
2. Governmental health care entities (or public entities), which are operated by a governmental unit and accounted for as an enterprise fund, such as a veterans' hospital.
3. Voluntary not-for-profit health care entities, including those with a religious affiliation, which are organized and sustained by members of a community.

A modern health care provider may be a complex entity with medical, surgical, research, teaching, and public service aspects. One very unusual element about health care operations is the manner of payment for services. A significant portion of the fees for health care service is paid by a third party, such as Medicare, Medicaid, Blue Cross, or some other insurance provider. Health care entities are reimbursed not on the basis of listed prices but on the basis of the cost of providing services, as that cost is defined by the third-party payor. A cost determination must be made according to formulas agreed upon in the law (Medicare and Medicaid) or in the contract (other insurance providers). Cost determination requires allocation of overhead, including depreciation. Thus, not-for-profit health care organizations follow the accrual basis of accounting, permitting comparison of results with profit-oriented health care units.

Generally Accepted Accounting Principles

Generally accepted accounting principles (GAAP) for hospitals and other health care organizations have evolved through the efforts of two industry professional associations, the American Hospital Association (AHA) and the Health Care Financial Management Association (HFMA), and the American Institute of Certified Public Accountants (AICPA). The AICPA Accounting and Audit Guide, *Health Care Organizations*, updated in June 2010, incorporates FASB ASC 958-605 and FASB ASC 958-205 that were described in the previous chapter. Additionally, the guide incorporates FASB ASC 954, which is the codification of FASB standards applicable to health care entities. This guide is currently the principal source of accounting guidelines for private and governmental health care entities that choose to follow FASB standards.[6]

Governmental hospitals or health care providers are considered special purpose governments engaged in business-type activities for purposes of applying GASB Statement No. 34. As such, *health care entities will report as enterprise funds*. And, they may elect to apply all FASB statements and interpretations issued after November 30, 1989, except those that conflict with or contradict GASB pronouncements.

Funds

With the many restrictions resulting from donations, endowments, insurance company contracts, and government regulations for reimbursement, the activities of a health care provider have traditionally been accounted for using fund accounting.[7] Health care entities employ two classes of funds:

1. *General funds*, which account for resources available for general operations, with no restrictions placed upon those resources by an outsider, and other exchange transactions including

---

6 FASB ASC 958-605 and FASB ASC 958-205 are applicable to governmental health care organizations under GASB Statement No. 20, *Accounting and Financial Reporting for Proprietary Funds and Other Governmental Entities that Use Proprietary Fund Accounting* (Norwalk, CT: Governmental Accounting Standards Board, 1993), par. 7.

7 Most hospitals have traditionally used the fund structure described in this chapter. However, other health care entities, such as health maintenance organizations, nursing homes, and home health care agencies may find it unnecessary to use fund accounting.

resources from government grants and subsidies, tax support, and reimbursements from insurance contracts.

2. *Donor-restricted funds*, which account for temporarily and permanently restricted resources. This class is subdivided into:

   a. *Specific purpose funds*, which account for donor-restricted resources temporarily restricted for current but specified operations.
   b. *Plant replacement and expansion funds*, which account for resources temporarily restricted by the donor for the acquisition, construction, or improvement of property, plant, and equipment.
   c. *Endowment funds*, which account for resources that are received to create permanently restricted endowments (whose income only may be expended) and temporarily restricted term endowments (whose principal eventually will become available for expenditure).
   d. Other donor-restricted funds such as annuities, life income funds, or loan funds.

Each fund consists of a set of self-balancing accounts designed to reflect activities within its domain. Although the FASB guidance on accounting and financial reporting represents a shift away from fund accounting to an organization-wide perspective, health care organizations continue to use some form of fund accounting for internal management and reporting. Some may even choose to continue to include information on funds in the external financial reports. To demonstrate the organization-wide emphasis on accounting and financial reporting and to simplify the presentation, the following discussion assumes no fund structure.

Classification of Assets and Liabilities

Assets of a health care provider comprise three distinct segments: current assets, assets whose use is limited, and property and equipment. Assets and liabilities are sequenced by liquidity and are classified as current or noncurrent according to GAAP.

Assets whose use is limited include assets set aside by the governing board for a specific purpose, sometimes referred to as board-designated assets. For example, the board may authorize that $10,000 be set aside for capital improvements, which would be recorded as follows:

Cash—Limited in Use for Capital Expansion	10,000	
Cash		10,000

Since the limitation on these assets is internal, they remain unrestricted since "restrictions" can only be created by outside sources. This segment also includes assets resulting from an operational agreement entered into by the board, such as the proceeds of a bond issue limited in use as stipulated by the bond indenture. Assets set aside to provide for self-insurance or to meet depreciation fund requirements with third-party payors belong to this segment as well.

Property and equipment include the physical properties used in operations, along with their accumulated depreciation. Current liabilities may include accounts and notes payable, deposits from patients, and advances from and amounts payable to third-party payors. Long-term liabilities may include notes, mortgages, capital leases, bond payables, and estimated malpractice costs. The net assets of the entire health care organization (which represents the difference between assets and liabilities) are divided into three classes—permanently restricted net assets, temporarily restricted net assets, and unrestricted net assets—based on the existence or absence of donor-imposed restrictions.

Classification of Revenues, Expenses, Gains, and Losses

7

OBJECTIVE

Demonstrate an understanding of how revenues and expenses are calculated and accounted for by governmental and private health care service providers.

Revenues, expenses, gains, and losses increase or decrease the net assets of a health care entity. Other events, such as expirations of donor-imposed restrictions, that simultaneously increase one class of net assets and decrease another (reclassifications) are reported as separate items. Revenues and gains may increase unrestricted net assets, temporarily restricted net assets, or permanently restricted net assets. Expenses reduce unrestricted net assets.

Revenues and expenses are considered operating if they relate to the principal activity of providing health care services. Revenues, expenses, gains, or losses from activities that are incidental to the providing of health care services or from events beyond the entity's control are classified as nonoperating.

Hospital payment systems have changed significantly in recent years. The systems include fees based on *diagnosis-related groups (DRGs), capitation premiums* (paid per member, per month), *fees based on negotiated bids*, and *cost-reimbursement methods*. Some payments are established prospectively (in advance of service delivery) at fixed amounts. Other payment rates may be based on interim billing amounts, subject to retrospective (after the accounting period ends) adjustment. Medicare generally pays hospitals prospectively, based on DRGs. Under the DRG system, all potential diagnoses are classified into a number of medically meaningful groups, each of which has a different value. Each hospital in a specific geographical region receives the same amount for each DRG, depending on whether the hospital is classified as urban or rural, and teaching or nonteaching. The thinking behind the DRG system is that a hospital that is more efficient will benefit because it may keep any reimbursement in excess of cost.

Under capitation agreements with health management organizations (HMOs), hospitals generally receive agreed-upon monthly premiums based on the number of participants in the HMO. In exchange, the hospitals agree to provide all medical services to the HMO's subscribers. The hospitals will receive the capitation payment regardless of the actual services they perform. The hospitals may also receive fees from the HMO for certain services. Other payment methods include prospectively determined rates per discharge, prospectively determined daily rates, and discounts from established charges. When rates are determined retrospectively, the hospital is generally required to submit audited cost reports with detail on allowable costs. Retrospective adjustment can result in either an increase or a decrease to the rates allowed for interim billing purposes.

The following operating revenues classifications are used in health care:

1. *Patient Service Revenues*, the major revenue account for a hospital, in which the gross revenues earned are recorded on an accrual basis at established rates for:

   a. Routine services (room and board, general nursing, and home health care).
   b. Other nursing services (in operating, recovery, and delivery rooms).
   c. Professional services (physician's care, lab work, pharmacy, blood bank, radiology, dialysis, and physical therapy).

2. *Premium Revenues*, based on fees from agreements under which a hospital or HMO has agreed to provide any necessary patient services for a specific fee, e.g., a capitation agreement whereby the HMO receives an agreed-upon payment from another HMO for a specific number of members per month regardless of actual services.

3. *Resident Service Revenues*, the major revenue account for a nursing home or continuing care retirement community. It records rental fees earned from residents or amortization of their advance payment of fees.

4. *Other Operating Revenues*, which records revenue from services other than health care provided to patients and residents. Also recorded is revenue from sales or services to persons other than patients. Thus, Other Operating Revenues would include:

   a. Revenues from educational programs, such as nursing school tuition.
   b. Revenues from specific-purpose contributions.
   c. Revenues from government grants to the extent that the related expenditures are included in operations. Grants that may be refundable if provisions that are not met are recorded as a liability. As expenses are incurred, a matching portion of the grant is recorded from liabilities and recognized as current-period revenue.
   d. Revenues from sales of medical or pharmacy supplies to employees or physicians.
   e. Revenues from sale of cafeteria meals to employees, medical staff, and visitors.
   f. Revenues from snack bars, gift shops, parking lots, and other service facilities.

The control account *Nonoperating Revenues* records revenue not related directly to an entity's principal operations. These items are primarily financial in nature and include unrestricted and donor-restricted pledges, gifts, or grants, unrestricted income from endowment funds, maturing of term endowment funds, income and gains from investments, and gains on sales of hospital property. Investments are reported at fair value with both realized and unrealized gains included as part of nonoperating revenue.

Patient Service Revenues is initially recorded at the hospital's gross (established) rates. A third-party payor, such as Blue Cross, HMOs, Medicare, or Medicaid, may reimburse a hospital on the basis of predetermined amounts that are less than the original gross charges for described services. The difference between the gross revenue and the amount expected to be collected from the third-party payors is referred to as the *contractual adjustment*. It is deducted from the gross patient service revenue prior to preparing the financial statements. A credit is made to an allowance account in order to reduce the receivables to net expected. Also deducted from gross revenue are adjustments for services provided as courtesy allowances granted to hospital employees. Not-for-profit hospitals also provide care without charge (charitable services) to persons who have demonstrated an inability to pay. Each hospital is required to establish criteria for charity care consistent with its mission statement and financial ability. Charity services are not reported as revenues or as receivables in the financial statements. Hospitals may, however, initially record the patient services charges because of an initial lack of knowledge that an account qualifies as charity service and the need to disclose the level of charity service. Under these circumstances, the charity care amount is recorded as contra revenue with a credit to an allowance account to reduce the receivable similar to the contractual adjustment. Since charity care represents health care services that are provided but are never expected to result in cash flows, it is distinguished from bad debts. Other uncollectible amounts are reported as bad debt expense. The objective of grouping these items is to be able to show accurate net patient service revenue, an expense for uncollectibles, and net receivables on the financial statements. Illustrative entries are as follows:

Patient Accounts Receivable	XXX	
Patient Service Revenues		XXX
Contractual Adjustments	XXX	
Allowance for Uncollectible Third-Party Contracts and Charity		XXX
Provision for Bad Debts	XXX	
Allowance for Uncollectible Third-Party Contracts and Charity		XXX
Charity Services	XXX	
Accounts Receivable		XXX

Payments made to a health care unit by third parties include reimbursement for depreciation. Often, this portion of the payment is limited in use to replacing or adding to property, plant, or equipment. Total billings are included in revenue of the general funds to permit matching of total revenues and expenses. When collected, the specified portion is transferred to a special account with the following entry:

Cash—Assets Whose Use Is Limited by Agreement with		
Third-Party Payors for Funded Depreciation	XXX	
Cash		XXX

Titles given to operating expenses of a health care facility may differ, depending upon the nature of the facility's activities. Expenses may be reported on the face of the financial statements using either a natural classification or a functional presentation. Functional allocations are to be based on full cost allocations. The following functional expense categories are common to many health care organizations:

1. Nursing Services Expense, for the cost of nursing services directly related to the patient or resident.
2. Other Professional Services Expense, for professional services indirectly related to the patient or resident, such as lab fees or pharmacy costs. Note that some hospitals combine the two accounts Nursing Services Expense and Other Professional Services Expense into one account labeled Professional Care of Patients Expense.
3. General Services Expense, for costs of the cafeteria, food service, and housekeeping. Where food services constitute a major cost, some hospitals prefer to segregate them into the account Dietary Services Expense.
4. Fiscal Services Expense, for admitting, data processing, billing, and accounting costs.
5. Administrative Services Expense, for purchasing, public relations, insurance, taxes, and personnel costs.

6. Other Services.

7. Malpractice Insurance Expense, if not already allocated.

8. Depreciation Expense, if not already allocated.

9. Interest Expense, if not already allocated.

10. Provision for Bad Debts, if not already allocated.

For example, salaries expense is often recorded and allocated to the first six functional expense accounts at year-end. The statement of activities (operating statement) would show the total for each service, such as Nursing Services Expense, but not the nature of that total (salaries, supplies, etc.). The footnotes to the financial statements provide detail on the natural classifications of the expense, such as salaries, supplies, etc.

Accounting for Donations/Contributions Received

8

OBJECTIVE

Demonstrate an understanding of the accounting for unrestricted and restricted contributions to governmental and private health care service providers.

Health care entities may receive gifts or donations that meet the definition of an unconditional contribution. These contributions may be unrestricted as to use or may be limited to a specific use. Unrestricted contributions are recognized at fair value with a credit to Other Operating Revenues—Unrestricted, or Nonoperating Revenues—Unrestricted, depending on whether these contributions are deemed to be ongoing major or central activities, or peripheral or incidental transactions.

Bequests and gifts restricted by the donor to be used for (1) specific operating purposes, (2) additions to plant, (3) endowments, or (4) annuities or life incomes are recorded when received at their fair value with a credit to Revenues (other operating or nonoperating)—Temporarily Restricted or Revenues (other operating or nonoperating)—Permanently Restricted.[8] When expenditures are made consistent with the donor's stipulation, or when term endowments become available, a reclassification is made from the temporarily restricted net asset category to an unrestricted net asset category. Should resources from expired term endowments be restricted further, for example, to purchase equipment, they will remain in the temporarily restricted net asset category. Resources temporarily restricted for the purchase or construction of property, plant, and equipment may be released from restriction either in the period the asset is placed into service or over its useful life. Donor-restricted contributions in which the restriction will be met in the current period may be classified as unrestricted revenues. Some promises to give are conditional and will not be recognized until the condition is met.

Activities of health care providers are enhanced by volunteers who donate their time and abilities. Donated services must be recognized if the services received (1) create or enhance nonfinancial assets or (2) require specialized skills, are provided by individuals possessing those skills who are scheduled and supervised in much the same way as employees, and would typically need to be purchased if not contributed. Services provided by doctors, nurses, and other professionals in a health care entity may meet the above criteria. Incidental services provided by other volunteers for such things as fund raising or other activities that would not otherwise be staffed by employees would not meet the criteria. For example, most voluntary service by senior citizens, candy stripers, and others is not recorded. When an institution is operated by a religious group whose members receive token payment or no payment at all, the value of donated services should be charged to the proper expense account and credited to Other Operating Revenues or Nonoperating Revenues depending on the nature of the donated services.

Professional Care of Patients Expense	XXX	
Other Revenues—Donated Services		XXX

Donated items may also be unrestricted or restricted. Examples of donated items in a health care entity are laboratory and pharmaceutical supplies donated by drug companies or associa-

---

8 Prior to FASB ASC 958-605, health care organizations credited the appropriate temporarily restricted or permanently restricted fund balance account. When donor-restricted assets were used for their intended purpose, they were recorded as a transfer or, more commonly, as a direct debit to the appropriate fund balance. The transfer was recorded in the general fund as a credit to Other Operating Revenue or Nonoperating Revenue as appropriate. Revenue recognition was delayed until expenditures were incurred. Transfers for capital purchases were not recorded as revenue but as increases in the fund balance account of the general funds.

tions of doctors; donated property, plant, and equipment; and contributed use of facilities. Donated items are recognized at fair value with a credit to Other Operating Revenues—Unrestricted or Nonoperating Revenues—Unrestricted, depending on whether the donations constitute the entity's ongoing major or central operations or are peripheral or incidental transactions. If donated items have a donor-specified use, they may be temporarily restricted until they are used for their intended purpose. Unrestricted donations of property are recognized as Nonoperating Revenues—Unrestricted. If donations of property are donor restricted, the same entry is made but with a credit to temporarily or permanently restricted revenues.

Medical Malpractice Claims

9

OBJECTIVE

Explain the financial impact of medical malpractice claims on governmental and private health care service providers.

Settlements and judgments on medical malpractice claims constitute a potential major expense for hospitals. The current environment in relation to medical malpractice claims has caused insurance companies to raise premiums to health care providers dramatically or to limit the amount of risk they are willing to insure. To find a health care provider that is fully insured against medical malpractice losses is a rarity. Many have dropped their malpractice insurance or have adopted other approaches for protection. Some pay losses as they occur. Others establish trust funds with a trustee.

Whether expenses and liabilities need to be recognized on malpractice claims depends on whether risk has been transferred by the hospital to the third-party insurance company or to public entity risk pools. FASB ASC 954-450-25-2 stipulates that:

> *The ultimate costs of malpractice claims, which include costs associated with litigating or settling claims, should be accrued when the incidents that give rise to the claims occur. If the health care entity has not transferred risk to an external third party, it should evaluate its exposure to losses arising from malpractice claims and recognize a liability, if appropriate.*

The basic rule applies whether or not claims for incidents occurring before the balance sheet date [incurred but not reported (IBNR)] have been asserted. An estimate must be made for losses on IBNR claims if it is probable that incidents have occurred and that losses will result. Historical experience of both the hospital and the health care industry are often used in estimating the probability of IBNR claims. If the health care provider is covered by insurance, the premiums applicable to the reporting period are expensed. The entry to record payment of insurance premiums is as follows:

Medical Malpractice Costs (or administrative services expense)	XXX	
Cash		XXX

The entry to record an amount for estimated claim costs for the reporting period not covered by the insurance arrangement is as follows:

Medical Malpractice Costs (or administrative services expense)	XXX	
Estimated Additional Malpractice Liability		XXX

Although hospitals report expenses on a functional basis by major program area, the medical malpractice costs are sometimes segregated from the other administrative services costs to emphasize their critical nature.

As a result of the large settlements granted in malpractice cases, some health care organizations became self-insured, establishing a trust account with an outside trustee that determines funding requirements. Two entries are necessary. The first establishes the estimated claim costs and liability as follows:

Medical Malpractice Costs (or administrative services expense)	XXX	
Estimated Malpractice Liability		XXX

The second entry records the contribution to the trustee as follows:

Cash—Limited in Use Under Malpractice Funding Arrangement	XXX	
Cash		XXX

The amount in the trust account is reported in the balance sheet as an asset whose use is limited. Claims expected to be paid during the next operating cycle are classified as current liabilities, while the remainder of the liability balance is shown as noncurrent.

Whether the health care provider is covered by insurance, pays losses as they occur, or has a trust fund arrangement, the amount of the expense should reflect the best estimate of ultimate costs of malpractice claims related to incidents that occurred during the reporting period.

Illustrative Entries

To illustrate the recording of events for a hospital, the year's affairs of Columbia Hospital are summarized next. The illustrative entries employ broad categories of control accounts and natural expense classification that are allocated to the functional categories at year-end.

10

OBJECTIVE

Account for transactions of governmental and private health care service providers.

Event		Entry		
1. Gross charges to patients are for:		Accounts Receivable	5,200,000	
		Patient Service Revenues		5,000,000
Daily patient services.	$3,200,000	Other Operating Revenues—Unrestricted		200,000
Other nursing services.	500,000			
Professional services	1,300,000			
Other nonmedical services	200,000			
Total.	$5,200,000			
2. Estimates are made for:		Provision for Bad Debts	22,000	
		Contractual Adjustments	380,000	
Contractual adjustments	$ 380,000	Allowance for Uncollectible Receivables		
Uncollectibles	22,000	and Third-Party Contractual		
Total.	$ 402,000	Adjustments		402,000
3. An analysis of accounts receivable shows:		Cash	3,800,000	
		Allowance for Uncollectible		
Cash collected.	$3,800,000	Receivables and Third-Party		
Contractual adjustments with third-party		Contractual Adjustments	290,000	
payors.	200,000	Accounts Receivable		4,090,000
Uncollectibles	90,000			
Total.	$4,090,000			
4. The hospital determined that $200,000 of the services were to patients who met hospital criteria for charity care.		Charity Services	200,000	
		Accounts Receivable		200,000
5. Inventory purchases amounted to $700,000; payments totaled $690,000.		Inventories.	700,000	
		Cash		690,000
		Accounts Payable		10,000

(continued)

	Event		Entry		

6. Drugs and supplies costing $720,000 are requisitioned.

Drugs and Supplies Used	720,000	
Inventories		720,000

7. Salaries earned (ignore payroll deductions) amounted to $3,000,000, of which $2,950,000 is paid.

Wages, Salaries, and Benefits	3,000,000	
Cash		2,950,000
Accrued Expenses		50,000

8. Outside professional fees of $300,000 are paid.

Purchased Services	300,000	
Cash		300,000

9. Jacob Pharmaceutical Co. donated $2,000 of medicines to Columbia Hospital. Such contributions constitute a major ongoing activity of the hospital. If not donated, these medicines would have to be purchased.

Inventories	2,000	
Other Operating Revenues—Unrestricted		
(contributions)		2,000

10. Unrestricted earnings from long-term investments totaled $540,000.

Cash	540,000	
Nonoperating Revenues—Unrestricted		
(investment earnings)		540,000

11. Payments are made on:

Current installment of long-term debt	$ 80,000
Notes payable	200,000
Interest expense	66,000
Total	$346,000

Current Installment of Long-Term Debt	80,000	
Notes Payable	200,000	
Interest Expense	66,000	
Cash		346,000

12. A donor promised to give Columbia $50,000 annually for each of the next four years (recorded at present value).

Contributions Receivable	165,606	
Nonoperating Revenues—Unrestricted		
(contributions)		165,606

13. The hospital was recently served with a malpractice lawsuit. A prominent local trial attorney decided to assist in the defense of the hospital. Normal fees are $150 per hour. A total of 100 hours were devoted to the case.

Purchased Services	15,000	
Nonoperating Revenues—Unrestricted		
(contributions)		15,000

14. Equipment costing $110,000 is purchased for cash.

Property and Equipment	110,000	
Cash		110,000

15. Depreciation expense provision for the year is $400,000.

Depreciation Expense	400,000	
Accumulated Depreciation		400,000

16. The current portion of long-term debt is reclassified as current from:

Bonds payable	$50,000
Mortgage note payable	30,000
Total	$80,000

Bonds Payable	50,000	
Mortgage Note Payable	30,000	
Current Installment of Long-Term Debt		80,000

17. Professional services donated to the hospital were recognized:

Nursing services	$17,000
Other professional medical services	3,000

Wages, Salaries, and Benefits	20,000	
Other Operating Revenues—Unrestricted		
(contributions)		20,000

18. A provision for medical malpractice costs of $450,000 is recorded. The hospital is self-insured.

Medical Malpractice Costs	450,000	
Estimated Malpractice Liability		450,000

Event	Entry		
19. A malpractice self-insurance trust at Third Bank is increased by $230,000.	Cash—Limited in Use Under Malpractice Funding Arrangement . . . . Cash.	230,000	230,000
20. Third-party payor reimbursements of $250,000 are to be set aside for plant replacement.	Cash—Limited in Use by Agreement with Third-Party Payors for Plant . . . . Cash.	250,000	250,000
21. Columbia received $50,000 cash from a donor to cover operating costs of the student nursing unit.	Cash . . . . Other Operating Revenues—Temporarily Restricted (contributions)	50,000	50,000
22. Investment earnings are received in the amount of $75,000 restricted for cancer research.	Cash . . . . Nonoperating Revenues—Temporarily Restricted (investment earnings)	75,000	75,000
23. A $500,000 donation was made to Columbia Hospital for investments in long-term securities as a pure endowment.	Cash . . . . Nonoperating Revenues—Temporarily Restricted (endowment contributions) . . .	500,000	500,000
24. Securities were purchased.	Endowment Investments. . . . . Cash	500,000	500,000
25. A term endowment expired. The $150,000 principal is now available for use by the hospital administration.	Reclassifications Out—Temporarily Restricted— Satisfaction of Time Restriction. . . . . Reclassifications In—Unrestricted— Satisfaction of Time Restriction	150,000	150,000
26. Receipts of $200,000 and an unconditional promise to give $100,000 were recorded. Gifts were to be used for operating room equipment.	Contributions Receivable. . . . . Cash . . . . Other Operating Revenues—Temporarily Restricted (contributions)	100,000 200,000	300,000
27. Operating room equipment was purchased. The hospital elects to release the donor restriction over the useful life of the asset.	Equipment . . . . Cash	200,000	200,000
28. The first-year depreciation on the above operating equipment was recorded.	Depreciation Expense . . . . Accumulated Depreciation	40,000	40,000
29. The expiration of the donor restriction on the fixed asset is recognized by reclassifying from temporarily restricted to unrestricted. This reclassification "matches" the depreciation expense.	Reclassifications Out—Temporarily Restricted— Satisfaction of Plant Acquisition Restrictions. . . . . Reclassifications In—Unrestricted— Satisfaction of Plant Acquisition Restrictions	40,000	40,000
30. A $400,000 grant from a local manufacturer to be used for a patient nutritional study was received. Results of the study will be used to educate the public, not for the benefit of the donor.	Cash . . . . Other Operating Revenues—Temporarily Restricted (contributions)	400,000	400,000
31. Expenses were incurred for the patient nutritional study. Donor restrictions are expired to match specified expenses. A reclassification entry records the expiration of donor restrictions.	Wages, Salaries, and Benefits . . . . Drugs and Supplies Used. . . . . Purchased Services . . . . Cash . . . . Reclassifications Out—Temporarily Unrestricted— Satisfaction of Program Restrictions . . . . Reclassifications In—Unrestricted— Satisfaction of Program Restrictions . . .	25,000 10,000 15,000 50,000	50,000 50,000

(continued)

Event	Entry		
32. At year-end, Columbia allocates natural expenses to the functional areas based upon which program they benefited when incurred.	Nursing Services	1,774,000	
	Other Professional Services	1,240,000	
	General Services	995,000	
	Fiscal Services	283,000	
	Administrative Services	791,000	
	Wages, Salaries, and Benefits		3,045,000
	Drugs and Supplies Used		730,000
	Purchased Services		330,000
	Medical Malpractice Costs		450,000
	Depreciation Expense		440,000
	Interest		66,000
	Provision for Bad Debts		22,000
33. Closing entries. Each class of net assets is closed separately.	Patient Service Revenues—Unrestricted	5,000,000	
	Other Operating Revenues—Unrestricted	222,000	
	Nonoperating Revenues—Unrestricted	720,606	
	Reclassifications In—Unrestricted—Satisfaction of Equipment Acquisition Restrictions	40,000	
	Reclassifications In—Unrestricted—Satisfaction of Time Restrictions	150,000	
	Reclassifications In—Unrestricted—Satisfaction of Program Restrictions	50,000	
	Charity Care		200,000
	Contractual Adjustments		380,000
	Nursing Services		1,774,000
	Other Professional Services		1,240,000
	General Services		995,000
	Fiscal Services		283,000
	Administrative Services		791,000
	Unrestricted Net Assets		**519,606**
	Other Operating Revenues—Temporarily Restricted	750,000	
	Nonoperating Revenues—Temporarily Restricted	75,000	
	Reclassifications Out—Temporarily Restricted—Satisfaction of Equipment Acquisition Restrictions		40,000
	Reclassifications Out—Temporarily Restricted—Satisfaction of Time Restrictions		150,000
	Reclassifications Out—Temporarily Restricted—Satisfaction of Program Restrictions		50,000
	Temporarily Restricted Net Assets		**585,000**
	Nonoperating Revenues—Permanently Restricted Endowment Contributions	500,000	
	Permanently Restricted Net Assets		**500,000**

Financial Statements of a Private Health Care Provider

The financial statements of a private health care provider include a statement of activities, which presents organization-wide totals for changes in unrestricted net assets, temporarily restricted net assets, and permanently restricted net assets. The form is straightforward, showing operating revenues minus operating expenses as an increase (decrease) in net assets from operations. The nonoperating revenues are added to this amount. Expenses are reported using functional classifications. Further information on natural classifications of expenses is a suggested footnote disclosure. The results of only one year's activities are shown in Illustration 19-7.

11

OBJECTIVE

Prepare financial statements for governmental and private health care service providers.

Illustration 19-7
Columbia Hospital
Statement of Activities
For Year Ended December 31, 2019

	Unrestricted	Temporarily Restricted	Permanently Restricted	Total
Revenues, gains, and other support:				
Patient service revenues (net of adjustments)	$ 4,420,000			$ 4,420,000
Other operating revenues	222,000	$ 750,000		972,000
Net assets released from restrictions:				
Satisfaction of program restrictions	50,000	(50,000)		0
Satisfaction of equipment acquisitions restrictions . . .	200,000	(200,000)		0
Expiration of time restrictions	150,000	(150,000)		0
Total operating revenues and other support	$ 5,042,000	$ 350,000		$ 5,392,000
Expenses and losses:				
Nursing services	$ 1,774,000			$ 1,774,000
Other professional services	1,240,000			1,240,000
General services	995,000			995,000
Fiscal services	283,000			283,000
Administrative services	791,000			791,000
Total expenses and losses	$ 5,083,000			$ 5,083,000
Increase (decrease) in net assets from operations . . .	$ (41,000)	$ 350,000		$ 309,000
Nonoperating revenues.	$ 720,606	$ 75,000	$ 500,000	$ 1,295,606
Increase (decrease) in net assets	**$ 679,606**	**$ 425,000**	**$ 500,000**	**$ 1,604,606**
Net assets at beginning of year	**4,538,000**	**879,000**	**3,560,000**	**8,977,000**
Net assets at end of year	**$5,217,606**	**$1,304,000**	**$4,060,000**	**$10,581,606**

In addition to the statement of activities, a private health care organization provides a statement of financial position and a statement of cash flows. The statement of financial position, shown in Illustration 19-8, includes assets and liabilities of all funds. The sequence begins with current assets, assets whose use is limited, property and equipment, and possibly other assets. Also shown are the current and other liabilities of the organization and the three classes of net assets, which represent the equity of the hospital.

The statement of cash flows, shown in Illustration 19-9, follows FASB ASC 230 that encourages the use of the direct method to present cash flows, although it does accept the indirect method. FASB ASC 958-230-15 states that the provisions of FASB ASC 230 also should be applied to not-for-profit health care entities amended to include among the list of cash inflows from financing activities receipts from contributions and investment income that by donor stipulation are restricted for the purpose of acquisition, construction, improving property, plant, and equipment, or other long-lived assets, or establishing or increasing a permanent endowment or term endowment.

Illustration 19-8
Columbia Hospital
Statement of Financial Position
As of December 31, 2019

Assets:		
Cash and cash equivalents	$	735,000
Accounts and interest receivable		908,000
Inventories		81,000
Contributions receivable		265,606
Short-term investments		400,000
Assets restricted to investment in land, buildings, and equipment		445,000
Assets limited in use under malpractice funding agreement		440,000
Property, plant, and equipment (net of depreciation)		5,250,000
Long-term investments		540,000
Endowment investments		4,060,000
Total assets		**$13,124,606**
Liabilities and net assets:		
Accounts payable	$	53,000
Current installments of long-term debts		80,000
Accrued expenses		100,000
Notes payable		500,000
Estimated malpractice costs		640,000
Long-term debt		1,170,000
Total liabilities		**$ 2,543,000**
Net assets:		
Unrestricted		**$ 5,217,606**
Temporarily restricted		**1,304,000**
Permanently restricted		**4,060,000**
Total net assets		**$10,581,606**
Total liabilities and net assets		**$13,124,606**

Governmental Health Care Organizations

Governmental health care organizations are classified as special purpose governments engaged only in business-type activities. As such, they will present the financial statements required for organizations that use proprietary fund accounting. Many government health care organizations are also component units of another government, e.g., a university hospital, county health care organization or hospital, and state hospitals. If these organizations issue separate financial statements, the notes will identify the primary government and describe the nature of the relationship with the primary government. The financial statements required for government health care organizations include a statement of net assets (or balance sheet), a statement of revenues, expenses, and changes in net assets, and a statement of cash flows (direct method). These statements are similar to the balance sheet and operating statements illustrated for the private health care organizations and are not illustrated in this chapter. The statement of cash flows has four parts and follows governmental requirements for an additional section on cash flows from non-capital-related financing activities, such as unrestricted gifts, investment income, and gifts restricted for future periods.

Illustration 19-9
Columbia Hospital
Statement of Cash Flows
For Year Ended December 31, 2019

Cash flows from operating activities:	
Cash received from patients and third-party payors	$ 3,800,000
Cash received from contributions	450,000
Interest and dividends received	615,000
Cash paid to employees and suppliers	(3,990,000)
Interest paid	(66,000)
Net cash provided by (used for) operating activities	**$ 809,000**
Cash flows from investing activities:	
Purchases of investments	$ (500,000)
Purchases of land, buildings, and equipment	(310,000)
Net cash provided by (used for) investing activities	**$ (810,000)**
Cash flows from financing activities:	
Payments on notes payable	$ (200,000)
Payments on long-term debt	(80,000)
Contributions received restricted for endowment	500,000
Contributions received restricted for property, plant, and equipment	200,000
Net cash provided by (used for) financing activities	**$ 420,000**
Net increase (decrease) in cash and cash equivalents	**$ 419,000**
Cash and cash equivalents at beginning of year	**316,000**
Cash and cash equivalents at end of year	**$ 735,000**
Reconciliation of change in net assets to net cash provided by (used for) operating activities:	
Change in net assets	$ 1,604,606
Adjustments to reconcile change in net assets to net cash provided by (used for) operating activities:	
Depreciation	440,000
Increase in accounts receivable	(798,000)
Increase in contributions receivable	(265,606)
Decrease in inventories	18,000
Increase in accounts payable and accrued liabilities	60,000
Contributions received restricted for endowment	(500,000)
Contributions received restricted for property, plant, and equipment	(200,000)
Increase in liability for estimated malpractice costs	450,000
Net cash provided by (used for) operating activities	**$ 809,000**

REFLECTION

- Private health care organizations follow FASB standards.
- Governmental health care organizations will report as special purpose governments engaged in business-type activities and, as such, follow FASB standards.

- Contractual agreements, courtesy care, and charity care are reductions from patient services revenue. The provision for bad debts is recorded as an expense.

- Many health care organizations use fund accounting for internal control and decision making, but funds are not required in the external financial reports.

UNDERSTANDING THE ISSUES

1. What measurement focuses (identifying which resources are being measured) and bases of accounting (identifying when the effects of transactions or events should be recognized) are used by public and not-for-profit colleges and universities? How might the two measurement focuses benefit financial reporting for such entities?

2. Explain the accounting for contributions (of cash, pledges, or investments that may be converted into cash) for a private university. How does this accounting for contributions differ from that of a public university?

3. Explain how restricted gifts and grants are accounted for by public colleges and universities. Compare this with the accounting for restricted gifts and grants by private colleges and universities.

4. Distinguish assets limited as to use from restricted assets.

5. Explain a hospital's rigid adherence to gross revenue determination.

6. What is the special concern over accounting for medical malpractice claims? How does accounting for such claims compare to accounting for contingencies in a for-profit business environment?

EXERCISES

Exercise 1 *(LO 1, 2, 3, 4)* **Private universities, operating activities.** Record the following operating activities:

1. Student fees of $600,000 were assessed, of which $575,000 has been collected and $4,000 is estimated to be uncollectible.
2. The bookstore operates in rented space and is run on a break-even basis. Revenues totaled $100,000, of which 80% was collected to date. Salaries of $35,000 and rent of $10,000 are paid. Other operating expenses amount to $60,000, of which $15,000 has not been paid.
3. A mandatory transfer of $75,000 was made for a payment due on the gymnasium building mortgage.
4. The Student Aid Committee report showed the following:

   Cash scholarships issued $25,000
   Remission of tuition   10,000

5. A check for $10,000 and a pledge for $4,500 are received from the local medical society to cover part of the cost of research on drug effects, one of the university's educational programs. The educational programs will be conducted and paid for in the next fiscal period.
6. The endowment fund received a check for $12,000 of interest on investments. The premium amortization on the investment is $240. The unrestricted current fund is the recipient of the income.

Exercise 2 *(LO 1, 2, 3, 4)* **Private universities, loans.** Record the following events that affect the loan activities of Private University:

1. An alumnus donates $420,000 to establish the student loan fund. Students are charged a 5% annual interest rate.
2. Loans of $380,000 are made to students.
3. The remaining $40,000 is deposited in the university credit union, which pays a current interest rate of 7%.
4. Loans of $20,000 are repaid, plus $800 of interest.
5. Interest of $1,400 is received from the university credit union.
6. A student who had borrowed $1,000 was in a serious automobile accident and withdrew from school. The university wrote off the loan as uncollectible.

Exercise 3 *(LO 1, 2, 3, 4)* **Private universities, endowments.** Record the following endowment activity events of Private University:

1. An alumnus donates $250,000 to the endowment fund. The cash is fully invested in bonds with a face value of $242,000 that are purchased at an $8,000 premium. The income earned is to be available for the current restricted fund for curriculum improvement.
2. A check for $11,250 for interest is received. The premium amortization is $667.
3. The income is transferred to the restricted current fund.
4. The bonds are sold for $260,500.

Exercise 4 *(LO 1, 3, 4)* **Public and private universities, grants, contributions.** Record the following events that affect (1) Public University and (2) Private University:

a. A private grant of $200,000 was received to be used exclusively for defraying costs of holding conferences on the topic of genes.
b. By year-end, $110,000 of the grant mentioned in item (a) had been applied to the purpose stipulated.
c. The grant provided that amounts not awarded by year-end are to be transferred to the endowment fund. The liability to that fund is recorded.
d. An alumnus, who was a former athlete, contributed $15,000 to assist in the search for a basketball coach.

Exercise 5 *(LO 1, 4)* **Private universities, annuity and life income.** Record the following annuity and life income activities of Private University:

1. On July 1, 2010, R. W. Fields, emeritus professor of accounting, moved out of the state. Fields donated to the university common stock with a cost basis of $30,000 and a fair value of $90,000. Fields is to receive an annuity of $6,000 each year for life; at death, the securities are to be sold and the remaining cash balance is to be transferred to the student loan fund. At a 10% annual rate and a life expectancy of 12 years, the present value of the annuity payments is $34,068.
2. The stock paid $3,400 in dividends each 12-month period.
3. The annuities payable account is adjusted to present value. At year-end, a payment of $6,000 is made to Professor Fields.
4. The annuities payable account is adjusted to present value. A second payment was made a year later.
5. A month later, Professor Fields died, eliminating the liability for future annuity payments.
6. The common stock was sold for $97,000. The cash balance was transferred to the student loan fund.

Exercise 6 *(LO 1, 4)* **Private universities, plant fund transactions.** Record the following capital-related transactions for Private University plant funds:

1. Transfers of $250,000 are received from the current unrestricted fund for the purpose of funding the payment of existing debt principal ($50,000) and building an addition to the science building ($200,000).
2. Contributions of $30,000 restricted for major repairs of university buildings are received. $20,000 is spent for appropriate repairs.
3. A partial payment of $50,000 is made on the debt principal.
4. Work on the science building addition is completed with a total cost of $220,000. Unpaid contract costs total $35,000.
5. New gymnasium equipment costing $25,000 is purchased from funds previously donated by a former Olympic medalist for that purpose.
6. A building with a fair value of $300,000 was donated to the university by an alumnus.
7. Depreciation on all assets totaled $75,000.
8. During a celebration after a basketball victory, $2,000 of gym equipment disappeared.

Exercise 7 *(LO 3)* **Private university, contributions.** Indicate with choices (a) through (f) how the following events are recorded in a private university:

a. Credit Contributions—Unrestricted
b. Credit Contributions—Temporarily Restricted
c. Credit Contributions—Permanently Restricted
d. Credit Refundable Deposits
e. Credit Fund Balance
f. No entry

1. Receipt of an unconditional cash contribution. _____
2. Receipt of cash to be used for a specific purpose. _____
3. Receipt of an unconditional promise to give. _____
4. Receipt of an unconditional promise to give over a 5-year period. _____
5. Receipt of investments that are to be used to set up an endowment with earnings available for operations. _____
6. Receipt of a fixed asset with donor-specified use for an outreach program. _____
7. Receipt of a conditional promise to give. _____
8. Receipt of a fixed asset with no donor restriction. _____
9. Receipt of free accounting services. _____
10. Receipt of time of volunteers who helped with fund-raising mailings. _____
11. Receipt of a cash contribution to be used next year for general operations at the discretion of management. _____
12. Receipt of a cash contribution to be used next year for a research project. _____
13. Receipt of cash as part of a government grant funding a cancer research project. A report with research results will be prepared for the government funding agency. _____
14. Receipt of a cash contribution to be used for acquisition of fixed assets. _____
15. Receipt of a permanent collection of geography maps that will be displayed to the public. _____

Exercise 8 *(LO 6, 7)* **Health care, revenues.** A hospital has three revenue-controlling accounts: Patient Service Revenues, Other Operating Revenues, and Nonoperating Revenues.

1. State in general terms the type of revenues found in each controlling account.
2. Indicate into which of the three controlling accounts each of the following would be placed by using the symbols PS for Patient Service Revenues, OO for Other Operating Revenues, N for Nonoperating Revenues, and N/A if not a revenue item:

a. Tuition for entry to the nursing school. _____

b. An unrestricted gift of cash. _____

c. General nursing fees charged to patients. _____

d. Charges for physicians' care. _____

e. A restricted gift used for research on genes. _____

f. Dividends from the hospital's investments. _____

g. Revenues from gift shop sales. _____

h. Patient room and board charges. _____

i. Proceeds from sales of cafeteria meals. _____

j. Recovery room fees. _____

k. Contributions for plant replacement and expansion. _____

Exercise 9 *(LO 6, 7, 8, 10)* **Health care, financial statement impact of transactions.** Alpha Hospital, a nongovernmental not-for-profit organization, has adopted an accounting policy that does not imply a time restriction on gifts of long-lived assets. For items (1) through (6), indicate the manner in which the transaction affects Alpha's financial statements.

a. Increase in unrestricted revenues, gains, and other support.
b. Decrease in an expense.
c. Increase in temporarily restricted net assets.
d. Increase in permanently restricted net assets.
e. No required reportable event.

1. Alpha's board designates $1,000,000 to purchase investments whose income will be used for capital improvements.
2. Income from investments in item (1) above, which was not previously accrued, is received.
3. A benefactor provided funds for building expansion.
4. The funds in item (3) above are used to purchase a building in the fiscal period following the period the funds were received.
5. An accounting firm prepared Alpha's annual financial statements without charge to Alpha.
6. Alpha received investments subject to the donor's requirement that investment income be used to pay for outpatient services.

(AICPA adapted)

Exercise 10 *(LO 6, 7, 8, 10)* **Health care, revenues, expenses, contributions.** Record the following events of Elmwood Hospital:

1. Patients were billed for the following gross charges:

Room and board	$680,000
Physicians' care.	220,000
Laboratory and radiology	110,000

2. A donation of drugs with a fair value of $12,000 was received from a doctor. The drugs are normally purchased.

3. Revenues were reported from:

Newsstand and snack bar.....	$15,800
Parking lot charges	3,200
Vending machines...........	9,800

4. A charity allowance of $13,000 was granted to indigent patients.
5. Contractual adjustments granted to patients for Medicare charges totaled $68,000.
6. The hospital recorded an increase in the provision of $26,000 for uncollectible receivables.

Exercise 11 *(LO 7, 10)* **Private health care, journal entries, revenue and cash flow.** Transactions (a) through (e) took place in Stoney Heights Private Hospital during the year ending December 31, 2011.

a. Gross revenues of $5,000,000 were earned for service to Medicare patients.
b. Expected contractual adjustments with Medicare, a third-party payor, are $2,500,000; and an allowance for contractual adjustments account is used by Stoney Heights.
c. Medicare cleared charges of $5,000,000 with payments of $2,160,000 and total contractual allowances of $2,840,000 ($2,500,000 + $340,000).
d. Interim payments received from Medicare amounted to $250,000.
e. The hospital made a lump-sum payment back to Medicare of $100,000.

1. Record the transactions in the general journal.
2. Calculate the amount of net patient service revenues.
3. What is the net cash flow from transactions with Medicare?
4. What adjustments must be made at year-end to settle up with Medicare and properly report the net patient service revenues after this settlement?

Exercise 12 *(LO 11)* **Health care, statement of activities.** Recover Rehabilitation Hospital has the following balances that are extracted from its December 31, 2019, trial balance:

Account	Debit	Credit
Nursing Services Expense..	230,000	
Professional Fees Expense.......................................	140,000	
General and Administrative Expense	250,000	
Depreciation Expense	60,000	
Interest Expense...	13,000	
Asset Whose Use Is Limited	55,000	
Repairs and Maintenance Expense...............................	210,000	
Provision for Uncollectible Accounts	14,000	
Contractual Adjustments	16,000	
Patient Service Revenues..		840,000
Seminar Income..		23,000
Child Day Care Income..		15,000
Parking Fees		3,500
Endowment Income—Temporarily Restricted		220,000
Interest Income—Unrestricted		3,000
Donations—Temporarily Restricted...............................		38,000
Gains (Distributable) on Sale of Endowments—Temporarily Restricted		66,000
Net Assets—Unrestricted (January 1, 2019).........................		900,000
Net Assets—Temporarily Restricted (January 1, 2019)..................		855,000
Net Assets—Permanently Restricted (January 1, 2019)		850,000

From the above information, prepare a statement of activities for the year ended December 31, 2019.

PROBLEMS

Problem 19-1 *(LO 1, 2, 3, 4, 5)* **Public university, various transactions, statement of current funds revenues, expenses, and other changes.** A partial balance sheet of Tree State University, a public university, as of the end of its fiscal year, July 31, 2018, is as follows:

Tree State University
Current Funds Balance Sheet
July 31, 2018

Assets		Liabilities and Fund Balances	
Unrestricted:		Unrestricted:	
Cash	$200,000	Accounts payable	$100,000
Accounts receivable (net of $15,000		Due to other funds	40,000
allowance)	360,000	Deferred revenues—tuition and fees	25,000
Prepaid expenses.	40,000	Fund balance.	435,000
Total unrestricted	$600,000	Total unrestricted	$600,000
Restricted:		Restricted:	
Cash	$ 10,000	Accounts payable	$ 5,000
Investments.	210,000	Fund balance.	215,000
Total restricted	$220,000	Total restricted	$220,000
Total current funds	$820,000	Total current funds	$820,000

The following information pertains to the year ended July 31, 2019:

a. Cash collected from students' tuition totaled $3,000,000. Of this amount, $362,000 represented accounts receivable outstanding at July 31, 2018; $2,500,000 was for current-year tuition; and $138,000 was for tuition applicable to the semester beginning in August 2019.

b. Deferred revenues at July 31, 2018, were earned during the year ended July 31, 2019.

c. Accounts receivable at July 31, 2018, that were not collected during the year ended July 31, 2019, were determined to be uncollectible and were written off against the allowance account. At July 31, 2019, the allowance account was estimated at $10,000.

d. During the year, an unrestricted appropriation of $60,000 was made by the state, to be paid to Tree sometime in August 2019.

e. During the year, unrestricted cash gifts of $80,000 were received from alumni. Tree's board of trustees allocated $30,000 of these gifts to the student loan fund.

f. During the year, restricted fund investments costing $25,000 were sold for $31,000. Restricted fund investments were purchased at a cost of $40,000. Restricted fund investment income of $18,000 was earned and collected during the year. This income is restricted for an ongoing research project.

g. Unrestricted general expenses of $2,500,000 were recorded in the voucher system. At July 31, 2019, the unrestricted accounts payable balance was $75,000.

h. The restricted accounts payable balance at July 31, 2018, was paid. The restricted fund paid $10,000 from its investment income for costs of an ongoing research project.

i. The $40,000 due to other funds at July 31, 2018, was paid to the plant fund as required.

j. One-quarter of the prepaid expenses at July 31, 2018, expired during the current year and pertained to general education expense. There was no addition to prepaid expenses during the year.

1. Prepare journal entries in summary form to record the foregoing transactions for the year ◄ ◄ ◄ ◄ ◄ **Required** ended July 31, 2019. Letter each entry to correspond with the letter indicated in the description of its respective transaction, and omit explanations. Use the following format:

Entry		Current Funds			
		Unrestricted		Restricted	
Letter	Accounts	Debt	Credit	Debit	Credit

2. Prepare a statement of current funds revenues, expenditures, and other changes, including a total column, for the year ended July 31, 2019, and conclude with the fund balances at year-end.

(AICPA adapted)

Problem 19-2 *(LO 1, 2, 3, 4)* **Public university, various transactions.** The following events occurred as part of the operations of Craig State University, a public university:

1. To construct a new computer complex, the university floated at par a $22,000,000, 7% serial bond issue on October 1, paying interest on June 30 and December 31. Accrued interest is to be transferred to the retirement of indebtedness plant fund when construction begins. Construction costs are to be accumulated in the unexpended plant fund until the unit is completed.
2. Since construction has begun, the accrued interest, which must be used to assist in meeting bond interest payments, is transferred. Payments for construction to date total $5,000,000.
3. On December 31, a mandatory transfer of $385,000 is made from the unrestricted current fund to cover the remainder of the interest due on December 31 on the bond issue.
4. The bond interest due on December 31 is paid.
5. Construction of the complex is completed at an additional cost of $17,000,000. Payment is made for $16,000,000; the balance will be paid in one year under a retained percentage agreement.
6. The cost of the complex is transferred.
7. A required transfer of $2,770,000 is made from the unrestricted current fund to cover redemption of the first serial bond of $2,000,000 plus interest.
8. Payments are made for the bond principal and interest in item (7).
9. Gifts of land and a building were received, appraised at $200,000 and $350,000, respectively. The state's leading industrialist made the gift on condition that the university would assume a $90,000 mortgage on the property.
10. Pledges of $100,000 to be paid in one year were received with the understanding that the funds would be used to remodel the building received in item (9). It is estimated that $5,000 of the pledges will not be collected.
11. A donor contributed $100,000 in cash for the acquisition of rare first editions for the university library. The director of the library located a collection of the first editions that was available for $160,000. The university board transferred $60,000 from the unrestricted current fund to cover the difference.
12. The first edition collection is purchased, and payment is made.

Required ▶ ▶ ▶ ▶ ▶   Prepare journal entries to record the events, indicating in which funds the entries are made.

Problem 19-3 *(LO 1, 2, 3)* **Public and private schools, multiple-choice.** Select the best answer for each of the following multiple-choice items. (Nos. 2–10 are AICPA adapted.)

1. Which of the following is required as part of the complete set of financial statements for a private college or university?

   a. Statement of changes in financial position
   b. Statement of activities
   c. Statement of revenues, expenses, and changes in net assets
   d. None of the above

2. Financial resources of a college or university that are currently expendable at the discretion of the governing board and that have not been restricted externally and are nondesignated by the board for a specific purpose should be reported in the balance sheet as

   a. board-designated current funds.
   b. permanently restricted net assets.
   c. unrestricted net assets.
   d. temporarily restricted net assets.

3. Funds received by a private college from donors who have stipulated that the principal is nonexpendable but the income generated may be expended for current operating needs would be accounted for as

   a. contributions—permanently restricted.
   b. contributions—temporarily restricted.
   c. contributions—unrestricted.
   d. fund balance increases.

4. An alumnus donates securities to Rex Private College and stipulates that the principal be held in perpetuity and revenues be used for faculty travel. Dividends received from the securities should be recognized as revenues in

   a. endowment funds.
   b. quasi-endowment funds.
   c. restricted current funds.
   d. unrestricted current funds.

5. A private college's plant funds group includes which of the following subgroups?

   (1) Renewals and replacement funds
   (2) Retirement of indebtedness funds
   (3) Restricted current funds

   a. 1 and 2
   b. 1 and 3
   c. 2 and 3
   d. None of the above

6. The following funds were among those held by Olmstead College at December 31, 2019:

Principal specified by the donor as nonexpendable	$700,000
Principal expendable after the year 2025.	400,000
Principal designated from unrestricted net assets	300,000

What amount should Olmstead College classify as permanently restricted endowments?

   a. $1,400,000
   b. $300,000
   c. $400,000
   d. $700,000

7. At the end of the year, Cramer Private University's balance sheet comprised $15,000,000 of assets and $9,000,000 of liabilities (including deferred revenues of $300,000). What is the balance of Cramer's net assets?

   a. $5,700,000
   b. $6,000,000
   c. $6,300,000
   d. $15,000,000

8. In the loan fund of a private or public college, each of the following types of loans would be found *except*

   a. faculty loans.
   b. computer loans.
   c. staff loans.
   d. student loans.

9. In 2019, Public State University's board of trustees established a $300,000 fund to be retained and invested for scholarship grants. In 2019, the fund earned $10,000, which had *not* been disbursed at December 31, 2019. What amount should Public State report as unrestricted investment earnings at December 31, 2019?

   a. $0
   b. $300,000
   c. $10,000
   d. $310,000

10. On January 2, 2019, a graduate of Marimount Private College established a permanent trust fund and appointed Wells Bank as the trustee. The income from the trust fund is to be paid to Marimount and used only by the School of Business to support student scholarships. What entry is required on Marimount's books to record the receipt of cash from the interest on the trust fund?

   a. Debit Cash and credit Deferred Revenues
   b. Debit Cash and credit Temporarily Restricted Endowment Revenues
   c. Debit Cash and credit Unrestricted Endowment Revenues
   d. Debit Cash and credit Temporarily Restricted Contributions

Problem 19-4 *(LO 1, 2, 3)* **Public and private schools, multiple-choice.** Select the best answer for each of the following multiple-choice items dealing with universities:

1. Abbott Public University's unrestricted current fund comprised the following:

Assets..	$5,000,000
Liabilities (including deferred revenues of $100,000)	3,000,000

   The fund balance of Abbott's unrestricted current fund was

   a. $1,900,000.
   b. $2,000,000.
   c. $2,100,000.
   d. $5,000,000.

2. The following receipts are among those recorded by Middleton Private College during 2019:

Unrestricted gifts	$300,000
Restricted gifts (expended for current operating purposes)	100,000
Restricted gifts (not yet expended).	600,000

   The amount that should be included in revenues is

   a. $300,000.
   b. $700,000.
   c. $900,000.
   d. $1,000,000.

3. For the 2019 fall semester, Forest Public University assessed its students $6,000,000 (net of refunds), covering tuition and fees for educational and general purposes. However, only $5,700,000 was expected to be realized because tuition remissions of $80,000 were allowed to faculty members' children attending Forest, and scholarships totaling $220,000 were granted to students. What amount should Forest include in educational and general current funds revenues from student tuition and fees?

   a. $5,920,000
   b. $6,000,000
   c. $5,780,000
   d. $5,700,000

4. Leaf Private College is sponsored by a religious group. Volunteers from this religious group regularly contribute their skilled services to Leaf and are paid nominal amounts to cover

their commuting costs. If Leaf did *not* receive these volunteer services, it would have to purchase similar services. During 2019, the total amount paid to these volunteers was $10,000. The gross value of services performed by them, as determined by reference to lay-equivalent salaries, amounted to $400,000. What amount should Leaf record as expenses in 2019 for these volunteers' services?

a. $410,000
b. $400,000
c. $10,000
d. $0

5. The following expenditures were among those incurred by Cheviot Public University during 2019:

Administrative data processing	$ 50,000
Scholarships and fellowships	100,000
Operation and maintenance of physical plant	200,000

The amount to be included in the functional classification "Institutional Support" expenditures account is

a. $50,000.
b. $150,000.
c. $250,000.
d. $350,000.

6. On July 31, 2019, Sabio Public College showed the following amounts to be used for:

Renewal and replacement of college properties	$200,000
Retirement of indebtedness on college properties	300,000
Purchase of physical properties for college purposes, but unexpended at July 31, 2019	400,000

What total amount should be included in Sabio's plant funds at July 31, 2019?

a. $900,000
b. $600,000
c. $400,000
d. $200,000

7. The following information pertains to interest received by Beech Public University from endowment fund investments for the year ended June 30, 2018:

	Received	Expended for Current Operations
Unrestricted	$300,000	$100,000
Restricted	500,000	75,000

What amount should be credited to Endowment Income for the year ended June 30, 2018?

a. $800,000
b. $375,000
c. $175,000
d. $100,000

8. Assets that the governing board of a public university, rather than a donor or outside agency, has determined are to be retained and invested for purposes other than loan or plant would be accounted for as

a. an endowment.
b. unrestricted net assets.
c. deposits held in custody for others.
d. restricted net assets.

9. In 2017, the board of trustees of Bar Private University designated $300,000 from its current funds for college scholarships. Also in 2017, the university received a bequest of $500,000 from an estate of a benefactor who specified that the bequest was to be used for hiring teachers to tutor handicapped students. None of the bequest has been spent. What amount should be accounted for as restricted net assets?

   a. $0
   b. $300,000
   c. $500,000
   d. $800,000

10. Which of the following statements usually will *not* be included in the annual financial report of a public university engaged only in business-type activities?

   a. Statement of activities
   b. Statement of net assets
   c. Statement of cash flows
   d. Statement of revenues, expenses, and changes in net assets

(AICPA adapted)

Problem 19-5 *(LO 1, 2, 3, 4, 5)* **Private university, various transactions, statement of activities.** The statement of financial position of Washbud Private University as of the end of its fiscal year, June 30, 2018, is as follows:

Washbud Private University
Statement of Financial Position
For Year Ended June 30, 2018

Assets (in 000's)		Liabilities and Fund Balances (in 000's)	
Cash	$257,000	Accounts payable	$ 40,000
Accounts receivable student tuition and fees less allowance for doubtful accounts of $9,000	311,000	Deferred revenues	66,000
		Long-term debt	100,000
		Total liabilities	$206,000
		Net assets:	
		Unrestricted	$487,000
State appropriations receivable	75,000	Temporarily restricted	40,000
Endowment investments	50,000	Permanently restricted	50,000
Property, plant, and equipment (net)	90,000	Total net assets	$577,000
Total assets	$783,000	Total net assets and liabilities	$783,000

The following transactions occurred during the fiscal year ended June 30, 2019 (all numbers are in 000's):

a. On July 7, 2018, a gift of $90,000 was received from an alumnus. The alumnus requested that one-half of the gift be used for the purchase of equipment for the university athletic department and the remainder be used for the establishment of a permanently restricted endowment. The alumnus further requested that the income generated by the endowment be used annually to award a scholarship to a qualified disadvantaged student. On July 20, 2018, the board of trustees resolved that the funds of the newly established endowment would be invested in savings certificates. On July 21, 2018, the savings certificates were purchased.

b. Revenues from student tuition and fees applicable to the year ended June 30, 2019, amounted to $1,900,000. Of this amount, $66,000 was collected in the prior year, and $1,686,000 was collected during the year ended June 30, 2019. In addition, at June 30, 2019, the university had received cash of $158,000 representing fees for the session beginning July 1, 2019.

c. During the year ended June 30, 2019, the university had collected $308,000 of the outstanding accounts receivable at the beginning of the year. The remainder was determined to be uncollectible and was written off against the allowance account. At June 30, 2019, the allowance account was adjusted to $6,000.

d. During the year, interest charges of $6,000 were earned and collected on late student fee payments.
e. During the year, the state appropriation was received. An additional unrestricted appropriation of $40,000 was made by the state, but it had not been paid to the university as of June 30, 2019.
f. A gift of $30,000 cash restricted was received from alumni of the university for economic research expenses.
g. During the year, endowment investments that cost $21,000 were sold for $24,000. This includes accrued investment income amounting to $1,900. All income was restricted for programs to enhance teaching effectiveness.
h. During the year, unrestricted operating expenses of $1,800,000 were recorded. They include the following:

Instruction	$ 500,000
Research	400,000
Institutional support	100,000
Student aid	100,000
Student services	200,000
Operation and maintenance of plant	500,000
Total	$1,800,000

At June 30, 2019, $60,000 of these expenses remained unpaid.
i. Temporarily restricted funds of $13,000 were spent for specified economic research described in item (f).
j. The accounts payable at June 30, 2018, were paid during the year.
k. During the year, $7,000 interest was earned and received on the savings certificates purchased in item (a).
l. In honor of its 25th anniversary, Washbud Private University conducted a fund drive. Contributions of $16,000 were received. Additional unconditional pledges of $14,000 were promised for payment in December 2019. It is anticipated that $2,000 of the pledges will be uncollectible.

1. Prepare journal entries to record the transactions. Assume fund accounting is not used.  **◀ ◀ ◀ ◀ ◀ Required**
2. Prepare a statement of activities for the year ended June 30, 2019, using a column for each of the three net asset classifications and a total column.

Problem 19-6 *(LO 1, 2, 3, 4, 5)* **Private university, various transactions, statement of activities.** The following events occurred as part of the operations of Kronke Private University for the year 2018 (all amounts are in 000's):

a. To construct a new business building, the university floated at par a $20,000,000, 8% serial bond issued on July 1. Interest is to be paid on December 31 and June 30. In addition, contributions from the community specifically for the new building totaled $5,000,000.
b. Payments for construction to date total $7,000,000.
c. Interest payments are made on December 31.
d. Construction of the building is completed at an additional cost of $18,000,000. Payment is made for $16,000,000; the balance will be paid in one year under a retained percentage agreement. Institutional policy is to release donor restrictions when assets are placed in service.
e. The first bond serial payment of $2,000,000 plus interest is paid on December 31.
f. A gift of land and a building was received, appraised at $200,000 and $350,000, respectively. The gift was made on the condition that the university assume a $90,000 mortgage on the property. The university assumed the mortgage.
g. Pledges with a present value of $200,000 to be paid over the next five years were received. The funds will be restricted for remodeling the building received in item (f). It is estimated that $20,000 of the pledges will not be collected.
h. A donation of $500,000 of stock was made by a wealthy citizen. The stock cannot be sold for five years. After the 5-year period, the stock can be sold, and any proceeds are to be used to finance campus construction projects.

i. Dividends of $10,000 on the stock in item (h) were received and were also restricted for construction projects.

j. Depreciation on the building received in item (f) totaled $25,000.

Required ▶ ▶ ▶ ▶ ▶

1. Prepare journal entries to record these events for Kronke Private University. Assume that fund accounting is not used.
2. Prepare a statement of activities for the period ended June 30, 2018.

Required ▶ ▶ ▶ ▶ ▶ **Problem 19-7** *(LO 3,   4)* **Public and private schools, contributions versus exchange transactions.** Record the following transactions. Identify each as a contribution, agency, or an exchange transaction, and prepare any appropriate entries.

1. Private University coordinated its annual special event with the opening of the alumni weekend. Tickets to the special event were $200 and included a buffet (cost, $30), admission to the university symphony (cost, $30), and a reception (cost, $35). A total of 1,000 tickets was sold.
2. A local manufacturing company gave $2,000,000 to Private University to commission a study on the relationship of worker stress to chronic disease. The results of the study will be used to educate the general public.
3. Allen Corporation gave a contribution of $850,000 to Private University. Allen Corporation specifies that the gift is to be invested in perpetuity and that the income may be used by Private University to pay operating costs.
4. Local Corporation donated a building to Private College for use as new office space. The cost to Local was $750,000. The building was appraised by a professional real estate appraiser at $1,000,000, while another appraiser valued it at $1,100,000.
5. An alumna of XYZ Private College has notified the school that she will donate to the school any net proceeds in excess of $50,000 from her next novel. She stipulates that the college use her gift to buy new equipment for the writing lab.
6. Cheryl Debit, an accountant, spent Sunday afternoon at Private University sending out to alumni a mailing seeking more contributions for the building fund.
7. A very famous artist notified the local private university that she has included in her will her plans to donate all of her paintings for exhibit at the university art gallery. A copy of her will is included with her letter.
8. A grant in the amount of $400,000 from the U.S. Department of Labor and Economics was received by Private University to fund research on the impact of accounting standards. A report of research findings is to be submitted to the grantor.
9. U.S. government funds amounting to $50,000 flow to Private University to be held for students qualifying for financial aid.

Problem 19-8 *(LO 4, 5)* **Private college, closing entries, statement of activities.**
The preclosing trial balance of Excel Private College has the following balances:

	Debit	Credit
Expenses—Instruction	1,130,000	
Expenses—Research	840,000	
Expenses—Academic Support	200,000	
Expenses—Student Services	200,000	
Expenses—Institutional Support	325,000	
Expenses—Operation and Maintenance of Plant	300,000	
Expenses—Student Aid	350,000	
Expenses—Auxiliary Enterprises Expenses	575,000	
Reclassifications Out—Temporarily Restricted— Satisfaction of Program Restrictions	75,000	
Reclassifications Out—Temporarily Restricted— Satisfaction of Equipment Acquisition Restrictions	250,000	
Reclassifications Out—Temporarily Restricted— Expiration of Time Restrictions	50,000	
Tuition and Fees		2,500,000

Contributions—Unrestricted	365,000
Government Appropriations, Grants, and Contracts	700,000
Other Investment Income—Unrestricted	150,000
Sales and Services of Auxiliary Enterprises	300,000
Reclassifications In—Unrestricted—Satisfaction of	
Program Restrictions	75,000
Reclassifications In—Unrestricted—Satisfaction of	
Equipment Acquisition Restrictions	250,000
Reclassifications In—Unrestricted—Expiration of	
Time Restrictions	50,000
Contributions—Temporarily Restricted	100,000
Endowment Income—Temporarily Restricted	15,000
Contributions—Permanently Restricted	500,000
Net Realized Gains on Endowment—	
Temporarily Restricted	25,000
Unrestricted Net Assets, January 1, 2018	675,000
Temporarily Restricted Net Assets, January 1, 2018	975,000
Permanently Restricted Net Assets, January 1, 2018	2,500,000

◀ ◀ ◀ ◀ ◀ Required

1. Prepare closing entries for the three net asset classifications.
2. Prepare a statement of activities for the year ended December 31, 2018, using a column for each of the net asset classifications.

Problem 19-9 *(LO 5)* **Private college, statement of financial position.** Using the data in Problem 19-8 and the following additional information, prepare a statement of financial position for Excel Private College.

◀ ◀ ◀ ◀ ◀ Required

	Debit	Credit
Cash	255,000	
Accounts Receivable (net)	625,000	
Contributions Receivable	185,000	
Inventory of Supplies	175,000	
Student Loans Receivable	300,000	
Land, Buildings, and Equipment (net)	1,450,000	
Long-Term Investments	3,025,000	
Accounts Payable		120,000
Amounts Held on Behalf of Others		250,000
Long-Term Debt		660,000
U.S. Government Grants Refundable		100,000

Problem 19-10 *(LO 6, 7, 8, 10)* **Health care, multiple-choice.** Select the best answer for each of the following multiple-choice items dealing with hospitals:

1. In June 2018, Park Hospital purchased medicines from Jove Pharmaceutical Company at a cost of $2,000. However, Jove notified Park that the invoice was being canceled and the medicines were being donated to Park. Park should record this donation of medicines as

    a. a memorandum entry only.
    b. other operating revenues of $2,000.
    c. a $2,000 credit to Operating Expenses.
    d. a $2,000 credit to Nonoperating Expenses.

2. In 2018, Pyle Hospital received a $250,000 pure endowment grant. Also in 2018, Pyle's governing board designated, for special uses, $300,000 that had originated from unrestricted gifts. What amount of these resources should be accounted for as part of the unrestricted net asset class?

    a. $0
    b. $250,000
    c. $300,000
    d. $550,000

3. Cura Hospital's property, plant, and equipment, net of depreciation, amounted to $10,000,000, with related mortgage liabilities of $1,000,000. What amount should be included in the permanently restricted net asset class?

    a. $0
    b. $1,000,000
    c. $9,000,000
    d. $10,000,000

4. Palma Hospital's patient service revenues for services provided in 2018, at established rates, amounted to $8,000,000 on the accrual basis. For internal reporting, Palma uses the discharge method. Under this method, patient service revenues are recognized only when patients are discharged, with no recognition given to revenues accruing for services to patients not yet discharged. Patient service revenues at established rates using the discharge method amounted to $7,000,000 for 2018. According to GAAP, Palma should report patient service revenues for 2018 of

    a. either $8,000,000 or $7,000,000, at the option of the hospital.
    b. $8,000,000.
    c. $7,500,000.
    d. $7,000,000.

5. Ross Hospital's accounting records disclosed the following information:

Net resources invested in plant assets (hospital policy is to release donor restrictions when assets are placed in service)	$10,000,000
Board-designated funds.	2,000,000

What amount should be included as unrestricted net assets?

    a. $12,000,000
    b. $10,000,000
    c. $2,000,000
    d. $0

6. In 2018, Wells Hospital received an unrestricted bequest of common stock with a fair value of $50,000 on the date of receipt of the stock. The testator had paid $20,000 for this stock in 2018. Wells should record this bequest as

    a. nonoperating revenues of $50,000.
    b. nonoperating revenues of $30,000.
    c. nonoperating revenues of $20,000.
    d. a memorandum entry only.

7. On March 1, 2018, A. C. Rowe established a $100,000 endowment fund, the income from which is to be paid to Elm Hospital for general operating purposes. Elm does not control the fund's principal. Rowe appointed West National Bank as trustee of this fund. What journal entry is required by Elm to record the establishment of the endowment?

a.	Cash	100,000	
	Nonexpendable Endowment Fund		100,000
b.	Cash	100,000	
	Nonoperating Revenues		100,000
c.	Nonexpendable Endowment Fund	100,000	
	Endowment Fund Balance		100,000

    d. A memorandum entry only.

8. Under Cura Hospital's established rate structure, patient service revenues of $9,000,000 would have been earned for the year ended December 31, 2019. However, only $6,750,000 was collected because of charity allowances of $1,500,000 and discounts of $750,000 to third-party payors. For the year ended December 31, 2019, what amount should Cura record as net patient service revenues?

   a. $6,750,000
   b. $7,500,000
   c. $8,250,000
   d. $9,000,000

9. An organization of high school seniors performs services for patients at Leer Hospital. These students are volunteers and perform services that the hospital would not otherwise provide, such as wheeling patients in the park and reading to patients. These volunteers donated 5,000 hours of service to Leer in 2017. At the minimum wage rate, these services would amount to $22,500, while it is estimated that the fair value of these services was $27,000. In Leer's 2017 statement of revenues and expenses, what amount should be reported as nonoperating revenues?

   a. $27,000
   b. $22,500
   c. $6,250
   d. $0

10. Cedar Hospital has a marketable equity securities portfolio that is included appropriately in noncurrent assets in unrestricted funds. The portfolio has an aggregate cost of $300,000. It had an aggregate fair value of $250,000 at the end of 2019 and $290,000 at the end of 2020. If the portfolio was reported properly in the balance sheet at the end of 2020, the change in the valuation allowance at the end of 2020 should be

   a. $0.
   b. a decrease of $40,000.
   c. an increase of $40,000.
   d. an increase of $50,000.

(AICPA adapted)

Problem 19-11 *(LO 6, 7, 8, 10, 11)* **Health care, various transactions, statement of activities.** The June 30, 2018, adjusted trial balances of Bayshore Community Health Care Association follow:

Bayshore Community Health Care Association
Adjusted Current Funds Trial Balances
June 30, 2018

	Unrestricted	Restricted
Cash	11,000	29,000
Bequest Receivable		5,000
Pledges Receivable	12,000	
Accrued Interest Receivable	1,000	
Investments (at cost, which approximates market)	140,000	
Endowment Investments		250,000
Accounts Payable and Accrued Expenses	50,000	1,000
Refundable Deposits	2,000	
Allowance for Uncollectible Pledges	3,000	
Net Assets, July 1, 2017:		
Designated, Unrestricted	12,000	
Undesignated, Unrestricted	26,000	

Temporarily Restricted.			3,000
Permanently Restricted.			250,000
Endowment Revenues—Temporarily Restricted. . .			20,000
Contributions.		300,000	15,000
Membership Dues		25,000	
Program Service Fees		30,000	
Investment Income		10,000	
Auction Proceeds.		42,000	
Auction Expenses	11,000		
Deaf Children's Program.	120,000		
Blind Children's Program.	150,000		
Management and General Services	49,000		
Fund-Raising Services	9,000		
Provision for Uncollectible Pledges	2,000		
Reclassifications In—Satisfaction of			
Program Restrictions.		5,000	
Reclassifications Out—Satisfaction of			
Program Restrictions			5,000
Totals.	505,000	505,000	289,000	289,000

Required ▶ ▶ ▶ ▶ ▶   1. Prepare a statement of activities for the year ended June 30, 2018.
2. Prepare a statement of financial position as of June 30, 2018.

(AICPA adapted)

Problem 19-12 *(LO 7, 8)* **Health care, multiple-choice.** Select the best answer for each of the following multiple-choice items dealing with health care organizations.

1. Hospital financial resources are required by a bond indenture to be set aside to finance construction of a new pediatrics facility. In which of the following hospital net asset classes should these resources be reported?

   a. Permanently restricted
   b. Temporarily restricted
   c. Unrestricted
   d. Refundable deposits

2. During 2018, Trained Hospital received $90,000 in third-party reimbursements for depreciation. These reimbursements were restricted as follows:

For replacement of fully depreciated equipment	$25,000
For additions to property	65,000

   What amount of these reimbursements should Trained include in revenues for the year ended December 31, 2018?

   a. $0
   b. $25,000
   c. $65,000
   d. $90,000

3. A hospital should report earnings from endowment funds that are restricted to a specific operating purpose as

   a. temporarily restricted revenues.
   b. permanently restricted revenues.
   c. unrestricted revenues.
   d. unrestricted revenues when expended.

4. Inventory donated for use in a hospital should be reported as
   a. other operating revenues.
   b. nonoperating revenues.
   c. an addition to the unrestricted net assets.
   d. an addition to the restricted net assets.

5. Dee City's community hospital, which uses enterprise fund reporting and chooses to follow FASB guidelines, normally includes proceeds from sale of cafeteria meals in
   a. patient service revenues.
   b. other operating revenues.
   c. ancillary service revenues.
   d. deductions from dietary service expenses.

6. Land valued at $400,000 and subject to a $150,000 mortgage was donated to Beaty Hospital without restriction as to use. Which of the following entries should Beaty make to record this donation?

   a. Land.. 400,000
       Mortgage Payable.................................... 150,000
       Endowment Fund Balance............................ 250,000

   b. Land.. 400,000
       Mortgage Payable.................................... 150,000
       Contributions—Unrestricted 250,000

   c. Land.. 400,000
       Debt Fund Balance.................................. 150,000
       Endowment Fund Balance............................ 250,000

   d. Land.. 400,000
       Mortgage Payable.................................... 150,000
       Unrestricted Fund Balance........................... 250,000

7. In hospital accounting, restricted net assets are
   a. not available unless the board of directors removes the restrictions.
   b. restricted as to use only for board-designated purposes.
   c. not available for current operating use; however, the income generated by the funds is available for current operating use.
   d. restricted as to use by the donor, grantor, or other source of the resources.

8. Not-for-profit health care organizations are typically sponsored by
   a. community organizations.
   b. religious organizations.
   c. universities.
   d. any of the above.

9. A not-for-profit hospital that follows FASB standards should report investment income from an endowment that is restricted to a specific operating purpose as
   a. general fund revenues.
   b. endowment fund revenues.
   c. unrestricted revenues.
   d. temporarily restricted revenues.

10. Board-designated funds are
    a. not available unless the board of directors removes the restrictions.
    b. unrestricted net assets.
    c. not available for current operating use; however, the income earned on the funds is available.
    d. restricted as to use only for board-designated purposes.

(AICPA adapted)

Problem 19-13 *(LO 11)* **Health care, statement of cash flows.** You are provided with a summarized version of the cash account of Lakeside Hospital, a not-for-profit organization for 2018.

Cash Account	Debit	Credit
Cash balance, January 1, 2018	275,900	
Cash received from: Patients	2,061,900	
Third-party payors	6,500,000	
Operation of gift shop	517,700	
Unrestricted gifts.	323,500	
Contributions restricted for endowment	500,000	
Donor-restricted contributions for purchase of property		
and equipment.	183,000	
Early repayment of long-term debt.		242,300
Cash paid to: Employees		1,151,000
Suppliers.		6,200,000
Providers of consultation services		800,000
Bank for interest		147,000
Contractor for purchase of property		
and equipment.		501,200
Cash balance, December 31, 2018	1,320,500	

Required ▶ ▶ ▶ ▶ ▶ Prepare a statement of cash flows, using the direct method, for the year ended December 31, 2018.

Required ▶ ▶ ▶ ▶ ▶ **Problem 19-14** *(LO 11)* **Health care, reconciliation of change in net assets to net cash provided by operating activities.** Using data from Problem 19-13 and the following additional information, prepare a reconciliation of change in net assets to net cash provided by operating activities that would accompany Lakeside Hospital's statement of cash flows for the year ended December 31, 2018.

The following condensed statement of activities for the year ended December 31, 2018, shows the following:

Total operating revenues	$9,312,400
Total operating expenses.	8,780,100
Income from operations.	$ 532,300
Nonoperating revenues.	1,102,900
Excess of revenues over expenses	$1,635,200

Included in the condensed statement of activities were as follows:

Depreciation and amortization	$422,500
Noncash gifts and bequests	37,500
Increase in expense and liability for estimated	
malpractice costs	12,300

An analysis of comparative balance sheet items showed the following changes in balances during 2018:

Increase in patient accounts receivable.	$266,300
Decrease in supplies inventory	11,800
Increase in accounts payable	10,100

Problem 19-15 *(LO 11)* Health care, various transactions, statement of activities.

The following nominal accounts were extracted from the December 31, 2018, adjusted trial balance of Landmark Private Hospital:

	Debit	Credit
Gross Patient Service Revenues..................................		10,049,200
Research Grant Revenue to the Extent Expended		361,000
Revenues from Sale of Cafeteria Meals to Guests and Employees		108,000
Donated Services of Nurses and Physicians (skilled services		
otherwise purchased)		145,000
Unrestricted Gifts and Grants		100,200
Unrestricted Endowment Income..............................		12,000
Gifts Restricted for Equipment Purchase.......................		440,000
Donor-Restricted Investments for Permanent Endowment............		150,000
Temporarily Restricted Endowment Income......................		25,000
Revenues from Parking Lot...................................		31,000
Revenues from Vending Machines		68,000
Income on Investments Whose Use Is Limited by the Board for		
Capital Improvements		107,000
Contributions Restricted by Donor for Pediatric Unit Operations.......		225,000
Reclassifications In—Unrestricted—Satisfaction of Program Restrictions		125,000
Reclassifications In—Unrestricted—Satisfaction of Plant Acquisition		
Restrictions...		220,000
Unrestricted Net Assets, January 1, 2018.......................		625,000
Temporarily Restricted Net Assets, January 1, 2018...............		825,000
Permanently Restricted Net Assets, January 1, 2018		2,350,000
Reclassifications Out—Temporarily Restricted—Satisfaction of		
Program Restrictions	125,000	
Reclassifications Out—Temporarily Restricted—Satisfaction of		
Plant Acquisition Restrictions	220,000	
Administrative Services (including $30,000 malpractice cost)........	112,500	
Contractual Adjustments under Third-Party Reimbursement Programs ..	1,328,500	
Charity Care	215,000	
Provision for Uncollectibles	241,600	
Nursing Services (including $125,000 in pediatric unit)	6,589,100	
Dietary Services...	511,200	
Maintenance Services......................................	838,300	
Depreciation and Amortization...............................	378,200	
Interest Expense..	142,200	
Loss on Sale of Endowment Investments........................	5,300	

Prepare a statement of activities for the year ended December 31, 2018.

◀ ◀ ◀ ◀ ◀ **Required**

Fiduciary Accounting

Chapter 20: *Estates and Trusts: Their Nature and the Accountant's Role*

Chapter 21: *Debt Restructuring, Corporate Reorganizations, and Liquidations*

Effective estate planning continues to be an ever-increasing service provided by practicing accountants. As the value of capital markets continues to grow, more and more individuals find that their estate has increased in value. The desires of those owning an estate may be communicated through a variety of trusts or a will. It is important to properly account for the activity of an estate so that these desires are properly carried out. Furthermore, many estates are subject to an estate tax, and it is important to have a basic knowledge as to how estate taxes may be minimized through gifting and the use of trusts.

Unfortunately, for a variety of reasons, a company may find that it is insolvent and unable to continue its business operations unless certain changes occur. A variety of options is available to such troubled companies. In many instances, it is possible for the company to continue operations by use of a quasi-reorganization, a debt restructuring, or a corporate reorganization. In other instances, it is apparent that the company must declare bankruptcy and liquidate its net assets. Corporate reorganizations and liquidations are subject to a number of legal requirements set forth in the Bankruptcy Code. All these corrective actions must be accounted for according to special principles that have an effect on both the debt and equity interests in a company.

Estates and Trusts: Their Nature and the Accountant's Role

Learning Objectives

When you have completed this chapter, you should be able to

1. Describe the goals of estate planning.

2. Account for the various factors that affect estate principal and income.

3. Describe various forms in which an estate may be distributed.

4. Explain how one's estate is taxed and how such taxes may be minimized.

5. Explain what a trust is and what the basic accounting issues are.

This chapter examines the basic nature of estates and trusts and how the practicing accountant may be involved with them. A tremendous amount of complexity surrounds the legal and tax aspects of estates and trusts; therefore, this chapter provides only a broad overview.

An estate consists of the net assets of an individual at the time of his or her death. Until these net assets are completely distributed or consumed, the estate also exists as a separate, distinct entity that is governed, managed, and accounted for. Often, the net assets of an estate are distributed to a trust, which is also a separate, distinct entity. The trust is an arrangement whereby assets are protected, conserved, and/or distributed by a trustee according to the terms of the trust agreement. Persons who are responsible for the management of the net assets of an estate or trust have a fiduciary responsibility. These persons, called *fiduciaries*, are held accountable by law and are required to prepare specialized reports that account for their actions. The role of the accountant in the preparation of these reports is discussed in this chapter.

THE ROLE OF ESTATE PLANNING

Estate planning has a primary goal of reflecting the desires of the deceased individual, referred to as the *decedent*. Proper estate planning for individuals with sizeable asset values involves estate tax and gift-giving strategies. As the net assets of an estate increase in value and nature, so does the complexity of the necessary estate planning. Many attorneys and accountants specialize in estate planning, which requires special knowledge of law, taxation, and accounting.

As the complexity of an estate increases, so do the goals of estate planning, which should include the following:

1. Discover and clearly communicate the desires and wishes of the decedent.
2. Ensure that the estate is administered or managed properly in order to satisfy the desires and wishes of the decedent.
3. Maximize the economic value of the estate's net assets through proper planning before death.
4. Minimize the taxes that may be assessed against the assets and income of the estate.

5. Define the necessary liquidity of the estate's assets so that desired conveyances and distributions may be achieved.

6. Provide a proper and timely accounting of the activities of the estate and its fiduciary.

Communicating through a Will

Obviously, a deceased individual is not available to directly communicate his or her intentions regarding the estate. Therefore, it is critical that prior to death the person communicate through the creation of a valid *will*, a legal declaration containing directions as to the disposition of property. When an individual dies having left a will, the decedent is said to have died *testate*. The will is presented to a *probate* court, which determines the validity of the will and identifies the fiduciary responsible for administering the will. The probate process also involves identifying the decedent's assets and liabilities, determining asset values, disbursing assets to pay debts and taxes, and distributing the net assets of the estate per the instructions in the will. Although probate law is developed by each state, the Uniform Probate Code was designed, in part, to encourage uniformity of probate law among states and simplify the probate process. Adoption of the Uniform Probate Code has been resisted by certain parties and as a result has not been adopted by a majority of states.

A fiduciary responsible for the administration of a will may be named or nominated in the will. This person is referred to as a *personal representative* or an *executor* and, assuming he or she is able and has the desire to serve, normally will be confirmed by the probate court. If the will does not name a personal representative or the representative is unable to serve, the court will appoint a party referred to as an *administrator*. Once the will has been probated, the decedent's assets are managed by the fiduciary subject to the oversight or control of the court.

If a decedent has no will or an invalid will, the person is said to have died *intestate*. In this situation, the probate court appoints an administrator and distributes the net assets of the estate according to state inheritance laws. Usually, the order of distribution is to spouse, children, grandchildren, parents, grandparents, and then collateral relations such as siblings, aunts, and uncles. In many states, if there is a spouse and children, the estate is split: one-half to the spouse and one-half to the children.

Many individuals prefer to avoid the probate process for a number of reasons. The process takes time and money and probate documents are public. An *inter vivos* or "living" trust is a popular way of passing property to one's heirs and avoiding the probate process by transferring property to the trust. The individual(s) making the transfer becomes a trustee of the trust. Upon his or her death, a successor trustee is appointed and will have the ability to distribute the assets of the trust according to the terms of the trust.

<table>
<tr><td>**2**</td></tr>
<tr><td>**OBJECTIVE**</td></tr>
</table>

Account for the various factors that affect estate principal and income.

SETTLING A PROBATE ESTATE

Once the validity of a decedent's will has been determined and the personal representative has been appointed, the fiduciary must focus on carrying out the provisions of the decedent's will. This requires a careful accounting of the transactions affecting the principal or corpus of the estate as well as the income of the estate. If the decedent dies intestate, distribution of estate assets is governed by applicable state law but nevertheless requires a careful accounting of activity.

Identifying the Probate Principal or Corpus of an Estate

One of the first responsibilities of the fiduciary of an estate is to identify the assets of the estate. A decedent may have two types of estates. One, the *probate estate*, is described in this section and includes all of the decedent's assets passing to others by means of the will. The other estate, the *gross estate*, is the one that is used to determine the federal and state estate tax liability and is discussed in a subsequent section of this chapter.

The assets of the estate are referred to as the principal or *corpus* of the estate. These assets vary in nature and must be measured at their fair market value. The value of certain assets, such as publicly traded securities, is determined with relative ease, while other assets, such as an interest in a closely held business or art, may require independent valuations or appraisals. In identifying the principal, the fiduciary must identify, or inventory, those assets that were the legal property of the decedent at the time of death. Therefore, the assets will include accrued items such as interest and rents. Items frequently comprising the estate principal include the following:

1. Cash on hand and in bank accounts.
2. Investments such as stocks, bonds, mutual funds, retirement accounts, money market funds, and survivorship annuities.
3. Accrued interest and declared dividends on the above investments as of the decedent's death.
4. Capital interests in businesses, such as closely held corporations, partnerships, and/or sole proprietorships.
5. Life insurance proceeds that are receivable by the estate or the result of the decedent having an ownership interest in the insurance policy. Therefore, if the decedent or the estate has an "incident of ownership," the proceeds are included in the estate.
6. Investments in real estate, including accrued rents at the date of the decedent's death.
7. Intangible assets, such as patents and royalties, including related accrued income at the date of the decedent's death.
8. Loans or notes receivable, including accrued interest at the date of the decedent's death.
9. Unpaid wages and other forms of earned income accruing to the decedent at the date of the decedent's death.
10. Personal valuables, including furniture, fixtures, jewelry, vehicles, boats, and collectible items such as coins, stamps, and artwork.

It is important to note that the preceding inventory of the principal is not reduced by the liabilities of the decedent. These obligations are recognized when they are paid or satisfied through the distribution of estate principal rather than being immediately recognized on an accrual basis. Often, it is not possible for the fiduciary to identify all of the assets of an estate initially. Those assets that are discovered subsequently must be included ultimately in the estate principal.

Exempt Property and Special Allowances. Certain types of assets generally pass outside of the probate process. For example, real estate, investments, and bank accounts that are owned jointly pass to the surviving joint owner. This requires that the ownership in such assets is titled as joint tenants. Although exempt from probate, the interest owned by the decedent is included in their estate for tax purposes. A surviving spouse's interest in community property (held as tenants in common) or marital property (in a marital property state) is not included in the decedent's estate. However, the decedent's interest in such property is included in the estate. Although part of the probate estate, other assets of the decedent may be removed from the estate principal by way of a *homestead allowance* and a *family allowance*. Such assets are intended to support the family homestead and its members. Certain items of personal property (clothing, furniture, automobiles, etc.) are also exempt. However, such allowances differ significantly from state to state.

Accounting for the Inventory of a Probate Estate. After the special exemptions and allowances for estate assets have been provided for, the fiduciary must file a report with the probate court identifying the estate principal, which consists of the initial assets transferred to the estate as well as those assets subsequently discovered stated at their fair value. An initial accounting of the estate principal requires an entry debiting the various assets at fair value and crediting an estate principal account.

In order to demonstrate the initial accounting for estate principal, assume Jane Jacoby died on June 1 of the current year. Jane's will names her attorney, Howard Wells, as personal representative of the estate. Through special exemptions and allowances, Jane's residence, $2,000 cash, clothing, and furniture passed to her husband, Walter Jacoby. Life insurance proceeds of $50,000 also were paid to the beneficiary, Robert Williams, Jane's son from a prior marriage.

The remaining assets of the estate are subject to probate and are recorded at their fair value as follows:

Principal Cash	81,000	
Investment in XYZ Stock and Mutual Funds	1,144,000	
Declared Dividend on XYZ Stock.	3,000	
Investment in J&D Partnership	155,000	
Automobile	15,000	
Wages Receivable	2,000	
Estate Principal		1,400,000

An investment in Apex bonds valued at $20,000, along with accrued interest of $1,000, was discovered subsequently and is recorded as follows:

Investment in Apex Bonds	20,000	
Accrued Interest.	1,000	
Estate Principal: Assets Subsequently Discovered		21,000

After recording the inventory of the estate principal, the fiduciary would submit a listing of the inventory to the probate court.

Subsequent to the initial recording of the inventory, sales or other dispositions of the assets may occur. Gains on such transactions increase the estate principal, while losses reduce principal. Continuing the above examples for the estate of Jane Jacoby, the following entries account for the sale of estate assets:

Principal Cash	165,000	
Investment in J&D Partnership		155,000
Gain on Realization of Principal Asset.		10,000
Principal Cash	19,500	
Loss on Realization of Principal Asset	1,500	
Investment in Apex Bonds		20,000
Accrued Interest.		1,000
Principal Cash	5,000	
Wages Receivable		2,000
Declared Dividend on XYZ Stock.		3,000

Identifying Claims against the Probate Estate

The discovery and identification of claims against the decedent's estate are of equal importance to the discovery and identification of estate principal. Notification of the decedent's death to creditors is required by law, and valid claims must be identified within a prescribed period of time. The fiduciary must evaluate the validity of claims and place them in an order of priority for payment purposes. The order of priority varies from state to state. The following order of priority is one example:

1. Claims having a special lien against property, but not to exceed the value of the property.
2. Funeral and administrative expenses.
3. Taxes: income, estate, and inheritance.
4. Debts due the United States and various states.
5. Judgments of any court of competent jurisdiction.
6. Wages due domestic servants for a period of not more than one year prior to date of death and medical claims for the same period.
7. All other claims.

Within a class, each claim is satisfied on a pro rata basis if funds are inadequate to accomplish total payment for that class.

The following claims against the estate of Jane Jacoby are accounted for as follows:

Funeral Expenses	5,000	
Administrative Expenses	3,000	
Debts of Decedent Paid	23,000	
Medical Expenses	7,000	
Principal Cash		38,000

Measurement of Estate Income

For a number of reasons, including tax implications, it is necessary for the fiduciary to carefully analyze activities and determine whether they affect estate corpus and/or estate income. Income is the return derived from the use of estate principal assets after the date of death. Furthermore, a decedent's will may stipulate certain provisions regarding estate income that differ from those regarding principal. For example, a will might stipulate that the interest income earned on bonds subsequent to the decedent's death is to accrue to a particular beneficiary for a period of time. The recipient of the income is referred to as an *income beneficiary*, and the party ultimately receiving the principal is referred to as the *remainderman*.

It is not always clear as to whether or not a transaction impacts estate corpus and if so to what extent. For example, if a stock held at death is subsequently sold, should the appreciation subsequent to death be considered part of the original corpus? Generally accepted accounting principles (GAAP) do not control in such cases, and the correct answer may in fact appear illogical given GAAP. Answers to such specific questions may be found in the decedent's will or applicable state law.

When defining estate income, careful attention must be paid to the provisions of the will and/or state statute. Many states have adopted the *Revised Uniform Principal and Income Act*, which provides guidance as to the measurement of estate principal and income. Generally speaking, one would expect income to include the following:

- Rents collected or accrued on principal assets.
- Interest on monies lent.
- Interest and dividends received on principal assets which were not accrued or declared as of date of death.
- Business profits including farming and extractive (mining, timbering) endeavors.

Note that income does not include the gain or loss on the disposition or transfer of estate principal nor does it include changes in the form of principal. Income also does not typically include the cost of investing or reinvesting principal assets or the payments on indebtedness associated with the principal assets.

Generally speaking, one would expect charges against income to include the following:

- Ordinary expenses incurred in connection with the principal assets after the date of death such as ordinary repairs, taxes, and utilities.
- Professional fees associated with income issues and the management of income. For example, a portion of the trustee's compensation associated with income.
- Taxes imposed on income.
- A reasonable allowance for depreciation on property typically subject to depreciation per generally accepted accounting principles as well as an allowance for depletion.

When bonds are a part of the estate at the time of death, the premium or discount on the bonds is not amortized. However, if bonds are purchased subsequently by the fiduciary, a premium is generally amortized, whereas a discount is not amortized. If the decedent wishes to protect principal for the depreciation factor, the will should state that depreciation should be charged against income, and an amount equal to the depreciation should be transferred from income to principal. For the depletion on wasting assets, the general rule is that income should be charged for the depletion because of the possibility of total consumption of principal.

Summary of Items Affecting Estate Principal and Income

A variety of items can affect the estate of a decedent, and the presence of a valid will certainly provides direction in this regard. Today's professional accountant can support the estate's fiduciary and ensure that a proper accounting of both principal and income has occurred. A review of the items affecting estate principal and income will help to ensure a proper accounting.

The items that are usually chargeable against principal and the account debited when each item is recorded are as follows:

Item	Account Debited
Debts of the decedent incurred prior to death	Debts of Decedent Paid
Funeral and administrative expenses	Funeral and Administrative Expenses
Medical expenses	Medical Expenses
Costs incurred in probating the will	Funeral and Administrative Expenses
Final income taxes of decedent	Debts of Decedent Paid
Federal estate tax* and any state inheritance tax	Funeral and Administrative Expenses
Legal and other professional fees to preserve estate principal	Funeral and Administrative Expenses
Charges applicable to personal property that produces no income	Expenses Chargeable against Principal
Distributions of assets to heirs in a testate distribution	Legacies Distributed or Devises Distributed (often combined with legacies)
Distributions to trusts	Principal Assets Transferred to Trust
Disposition of estate assets at a loss	Loss on Realization of Principal Assets (a gain would be credited to Gain on Realization of Principal Assets, with total proceeds on any sale of a principal asset debited to Cash—Principal)

*The Uniform Probate Code provides that where the will does not stipulate treatment of estate taxes, they are to be prorated to the recipients of estate assets on the basis of the value of the asset received relative to the aggregate value of all assets subject to tax.

When income cash is received, Estate Income is credited, and if the estate is large, a subsidiary ledger is maintained that details the types of income. The items for which income cash usually is disbursed and the account debited when each item is recorded are as follows:

Item	Account Debited
Expenses incurred after the date of death to protect income flow (such as insurance, property taxes, utilities, ordinary repairs)	Expenses Chargeable against Income
Distributions of income cash to beneficiaries	Distributions to Income Beneficiaries
Distributions of income cash to trusts	Income Assets Transferred to Trust

<table>
<tr><td>**3**</td></tr>
<tr><td>OBJECTIVE</td></tr>
</table>

Describe various forms in which an estate maybe distributed.

Distributions of Property

After the debts of an estate and the applicable estate taxes have been determined and paid, the fiduciary must focus on carrying out the remaining provisions of the decedent's will as they relate to principal and income. In a testate situation, a distribution of real property is a *devise*, and the recipient of the property is the *devisee*. Distributions of personal property are called bequests or *legacies*, and the recipient of personal property is called the *legatee*.

A devise is usually a distribution of a specific piece of real property. In contrast, legacies may include one or more of the following types:

1. A *specific legacy* is a gift of a particular, specified thing, distinguishable from others. Example: My 3-carat diamond ring to my son Ryan, the painting "Light of the Day" by Peter Ray

James on the north wall of my study to my daughter Rebecca, and all of my remaining wine will go to my Uncle Harold.

2. A *demonstrative legacy* is a gift of an amount from a specific source, with the will stipulating that if the amount cannot be satisfied from that source, it shall be satisfied from the general estate. If proceeds are inadequate to meet the amount, the difference shall constitute a general legacy. Example: $50,000 from several identified insurance policies to be divided equally between my two grandchildren.

3. A *general legacy* is a gift of an indicated amount or quantity of something: Example: $5,000 to each of my two sisters, $10,000 to my only brother. However, the specific source of the payment is not designated.

4. A *residuary legacy* is composed of all estate property remaining after assigning the specific, demonstrative, and general legacies. Example: The balance of my estate to be divided equally between my two children, Ryan and Rebecca.

If the remaining estate principal, after paying debts and expenses, is not adequate to satisfy the various legacies, a process called *abatement* is followed. Abatement requires that the legacies be satisfied to whatever extent possible in the order in which they are presented above [items (1) through (4)]. If the amount of assets designated as a general legacy is not available, the available amount is abated proportionately among the recipients. For example, if the entire $20,000 called for by the above general legacy were available, it would be allocated 5/20, 5/20, and 10/20 among the two sisters and one brother, respectively. However, if only $12,000 were available, this amount would be allocated among the legatees based on the original proportions with the two sisters each receiving $3,000 and the brother receiving $6,000.

In order to more fully demonstrate the process of abatement, assume the above legacies and the following alternative scenarios:

	Scenario		
Estate Assets	A	B	C
Diamond ring	available	does not exist	does not exist
"Light of the Day" painting	available	available	does not exist
Insurance policy proceeds.............	$40,000	$60,000	$30,000
20 Bottles of wine	available	does not exist	available
Other available cash................	$150,000	$20,000	$30,000

In Scenario A, the demonstrative legacy is not satisfied in its entirety and, therefore, the deficiency of $10,000 due the two grandchildren becomes a general legacy. Given the amount of other available cash, the above deficiency ($10,000) along with the general legacies ($20,000) will be distributed with the remaining $120,000 of cash being divided equally between the two children, Ryan and Rebecca. In Scenario B, Ryan does not receive the diamond ring because it does not exist at the time of the decedent's death although it may have existed at the time the will was drafted. The daughter, Rebecca, receives the painting, and the excess insurance proceeds become available to satisfy general legacies. The uncle does not receive any wine and of the now available cash of $30,000 (other of $20,000 plus the $10,000 of extra insurance proceeds), $20,000 goes to satisfy the general legacies and the balance is a residual legacy to be divided equally between the two children, Ryan and Rebecca. In Scenario C, no specific legacies can be satisfied except for the wine and the $20,000 deficiency traceable to the insurance proceeds becomes a general legacy. The other available cash of $30,000 is allocated proportionately between the $20,000 traceable to the original general legacy and the $20,000 deficiency in insurance proceeds. Therefore, the $30,000 of available cash is allocated as follows: $3,750 to each of the two sisters, $7,500 to the one brother, and $7,500 to each of the two grandchildren. There is no residual legacy.

If a decedent dies intestate, real property is distributed according to the laws of descent of the state in which the real property is located. Personal property is distributed according to the laws of distribution of the state in which the decedent is a resident, called the *state of domicile*. In general, only a spouse or blood relative may receive an intestate distribution.

In order to illustrate the accounting for principal or corpus and income, we continue the earlier example regarding Jane Jacoby's estate. Events (1) through (6) of Illustration 20-1 relate to Jane's estate. Events (7) through (14) relate to the accounting for estate income and property distributions. Events (15) and (16) reflect the closing of estate principal and income.

Illustration 20-1
Accounting for the Estate of Jane Jacoby

Event	Entry		
1. Recording of the initial estate inventory after special exemptions and allowances.	Principal Cash	81,000	
	Investment in XYZ Stock and Mutual Funds	1,144,000	
	Declared Dividend on XYZ Stock	3,000	
	Investment in J&D Partnership	155,000	
	Automobile	15,000	
	Wages Receivable	2,000	
	Estate Principal		1,400,000
2. Subsequent discovery of estate assets.	Investment in Apex Bonds	20,000	
	Accrued Interest	1,000	
	Estate Principal: Assets Subsequently Discovered		21,000
3. Sale of estate assets: J&D Partnership for $165,000 cash.	Principal Cash	165,000	
	Investment in J&D Partnership		155,000
	Gain on Realization of Principal Asset		10,000
4. Sale of estate assets: Apex bonds plus accrued interest for $19,500.	Principal Cash	19,500	
	Loss on Realization of Principal Asset	1,500	
	Investment in Apex Bonds		20,000
	Accrued Interest		1,000
5. Receipt of accrued wages and dividends receivable.	Principal Cash	5,000	
	Wages Receivable		2,000
	Declared Dividend on XYZ Stock		3,000
6. Payment of claims against the estate.	Funeral Expenses	5,000	
	Administrative Expenses	3,000	
	Debts of Decedent Paid	23,000	
	Medical Expenses	7,000	
	Principal Cash		38,000
7. Receipt of interest on cash accounts.	Income Cash	1,000	
	Estate Income		1,000
8. Receipt of dividend declared on XYZ stock subsequent to decedent's death.	Income Cash	3,000	
	Estate Income		3,000
9. Distribution of specific legacy of automobile to Jane's nephew.	Legacies Distributed	15,000	
	Automobile		15,000
10. Distribution of general legacy of $25,000 to Jane's sister.	Legacies Distributed	25,000	
	Principal Cash		25,000
11. Distribution of specific legacy of 5,000 shares of XYZ stock to Riveredge Nature Center.	Legacies Distributed	186,000	
	Investment in XYZ Stock		186,000
12. Payment of administrative expenses of which $100 is traceable to income.	Administrative Expenses	300	
	Expenses Chargeable against Income	100	
	Principal Cash		300
	Income Cash		100

Event	Entry		
13. Distribution of income cash traceable to dividends received to Jane's brother.	Distribution to Income Beneficiary . . . . Income Cash	3,000	3,000

14. Distribution of all estate assets to the Jacoby children's trust administered by First National Trust Company.	Principal Assets Transferred to Trust . . . .
	Income Assets Transferred to Trust . . . .
	  Principal Cash . . . .
	  Investment in XYZ Stock and Mutual Funds . . . .
	  Income Cash . . . .
		1,165,200
		900
			207,200
			958,000
			900

15. Closing of estate principal.	Estate Principal . . . .
	Estate Principal: Assets Subsequently Discovered . . . . .
	Gain on Realization of Principal Asset . . . .
	  Loss on Realization of Principal Asset . . . .
	  Funeral Expenses . . . .
	  Administrative Expenses . . . .
	  Debts of Decedent Paid . . . .
	  Medical Expenses . . . .
	  Legacies Distributed . . . .
	  Principal Assets Transferred to Trust . . . .
		1,400,000
		21,000
		10,000
			1,500
			5,000
			3,300
			23,000
			7,000
			226,000
			1,165,200

16. Closing of estate income.	Estate Income . . . .
	  Expenses Chargeable against Income . . . .
	  Distributions to Income Beneficiary . . . .
	  Income Assets Transferred to Trust . . . .
		4,000	100
			3,000
			900

The Charge and Discharge Statement

Periodically, the fiduciary will prepare a report to the court summarizing the results during the period of stewardship. This report is called a *charge and discharge statement* or a final account. The preparation of the report is simplified if a double trial balance has been prepared, since the charge and discharge statement is divided into two parts—one as to principal and one as to income. The statement for the estate of Jane Jacoby on December 31 of the year of death, appears as Illustration 20-2.

Illustration 20-2
Charge and Discharge Statement
Estate of Jane Jacoby
Howard Wells, Executor
Charge and Discharge Statement
For Period June 1 to December 31 of the Year of Death

As to Principal		
I charge myself with:		
Assets per original inventory	$1,400,000	
Assets subsequently discovered	21,000	
Net gain on realization of principal assets	8,500	
Total charges		$1,429,500

(continued)

As to Principal		
I credit myself with:		
Funeral and administrative expenses......................	$ 8,300	
Medical expenses	7,000	
Debts of decedent paid	23,000	
Legacies distributed...................................	226,000	
Total credits		264,300
Balances as to estate principal, consisting of:		
Cash—principal	$ 207,200	
XYZ stock and mutual funds	958,000	
		$1,165,200

As to Income		
I charge myself with:		
Estate income..		$ 4,000
I credit myself with:		
Expenses chargeable against income	$ 100	
Distributions to income beneficiaries	3,000	
Total credits		3,100
Balances as to estate income, consisting of:		
Cash—income.......................................		$ 900

In a more complex estate, each of the items in the charge and discharge statement would be supported by a schedule providing detail. For example, a supporting schedule for gains and losses on realization of principal assets might appear as follows:

Schedule of Gains and Losses on Realization of Principal Assets

	Inventory Value	Proceeds on Realization	Loss	Gain
J&D Partnership........................	$155,000	$165,000		$10,000
Apex bonds and accrued interest	21,000	19,500	$(1,500)	
Totals	$176,000	$184,500	$(1,500)	$10,000

If the fiduciary had completed his or her responsibilities to the estate, all assets comprising estate principal and income would have been distributed. In this case, the charge and discharge statement would reflect zero balances as to estate principal and income. Final distributions of estate principal often are made in the form of a residual legacy and/or a trust for the benefit of designated parties. After all final distributions, the estate records are closed with the estate principal and estate income accounts serving as clearing accounts. The final distributions of the estate of Jane Jacoby, along with necessary closing entries, are recorded as events (14) through (16) of Illustration 20-1.

R E F L E C T I O N

- Estate principal or corpus consists of a variety of assets that are to be measured at fair value; claims normally exist against such assets.

- It is important to properly analyze activities of the estate in order to properly determine the impact on estate principal and estate income.

- The assets of an estate may be distributed in a number of ways, including charitable transfers, devises, and legacies.

- A charge and discharge statement is used to summarize the disposition of estate principal and income.

TAX IMPLICATIONS OF AN ESTATE

4

OBJECTIVE

Explain how one's estate is taxed and how such taxes may be minimized.

During one's lifetime certain transfers of property may be subject to gift tax, and certain transfers upon death may be subject to estate tax. The federal gift and estate tax rates are the same and are referred to as the unified transfer tax rate. There is also a unified credit amount that may be used to reduce the tax associated with gifts and estates. Although most estates are not subject to estate tax, for those that are, a major claim against the assets of an estate may result from the imposition of a federal estate tax, a state estate tax, or a state inheritance tax. An estate is considered to be a separate, distinct taxable entity during the period of administration or settlement although this period of time may not be unduly prolonged. The estate will be considered terminated after a reasonable period of time is allowed for administration and settlement. For the most recent year available (2009), the Internal Revenue Service reported that:

- Over 33,000 federal estate tax returns were filed of which over 14,000 were taxable returns.

- The gross estate (monetary value used to determine estate tax liability) for all returns filed was approximately $194 billion. Of which $102 billion was traceable to taxable returns.

- Approximately $21 billion of net estate tax (after considering all applicable credits) was traceable to the over 14,000 taxable returns.[1]

Minimizing the taxes imposed on an estate is a very complex topic, and prudent estate tax planning is critical. During one's lifetime, serious consideration should be given to how various divestitures and trusts could be used to manage one's taxable estate. In addition, proper planning should address the following considerations:

1. Maximizing benefits of the marital deduction.
2. Making gifts during one's lifetime.
3. Taking actions to accomplish a step-up in property basis.
4. Taking actions to benefit from a loss in property values.
5. Utilization of charitable deductions.
6. Planning estate liquidity.

Recipients of gifts or estate assets do not pay the gift or estate tax nor do they pay income taxes on amounts received. The gift tax is paid by the party making the gift. The estate tax must be paid by the estate within nine months from the date of death. The estate must have a certain amount of liquid assets to pay taxes and the probate/administrative costs associated with carrying out the provisions of a will. If the estate lacks adequate liquidity, a forced sale of estate assets might result. It is not uncommon that some form of life insurance is recommended to provide liquidity and flexibility in meeting the estate tax liability, as well as additional value for the estate.

As previously stated, taxable gifts and taxable estates are taxed at the same rate schedule which is referred to as the *unified transfer tax rate*. The tax rates are progressive in nature and have changed over time. The *Economic Growth and Tax Relief Reconciliation Act of 2001* resulted in scheduled reductions in transfer tax rates and increases in the unified credit through the year 2009. For the year 2010, the estate tax was repealed. In 2011, if Congress does not take further action, estate and gift regulations will revert to what they were prior to passage of the act of 2001.

---

1 Internal Revenue Service, Statistics of Income Division, Estate and Gift Tax Statistics for 2009; http://www.irs.gov/taxstats/indtaxstats.

CURRENT STATUS OF THE ESTATE TAX

As of November 2010, Congress had not taken any further action to change the status of the Economic Growth and Tax Relief Reconciliation Act of 2001. However, based on current professional opinions, it seems unlikely that Congress will allow estate and gift tax regulations to revert to what they were prior to passage of the act of 2001. Congress will likely take action to establish regulations that are more consistent with current economic times and wealth levels. As a result, rather than basing the text examples on the pre-2001-act rates, which are highly likely to change in the near future, it has been determined that the regulations applicable to the year 2009 will be used for purposes of this text. Furthermore, discussions with estate tax planners in late 2010 suggested that current estate planning is being done on the assumption that 2009 regulations are closer to what is likely to occur in the near future. At the time of publication (for 2011 and 2012), up to $5,000,000 can be passed from an individual upon his or her death without incurring estate tax. For married couples, the applicable amount is $10,000,000. The tax rate on a taxable estate is 35 percent.

All examples and end-of-chapter materials will be based on rates and amounts applicable for the year 2009. In 2009, rates ranged from 18% to 45%. Taxable estates up to $10,000 were taxed at 18%, while taxable amounts exceeding $2,000,000 were taxed at 45%. The Unified Transfer Tax Rate Schedule is presented in Exhibit 20-1.

Exhibit 20-1
Unified Transfer Tax Rate Schedule for the Year 2009

Taxable Amount over	Taxable Amount Not over	Tax on Amount in Column A	Rate of Tax on Excess over Amount in Column A
$ 0	$ 10,000	$ 0	18%
10,000	20,000	1,800	20
20,000	40,000	3,800	22
40,000	60,000	8,200	24
60,000	80,000	13,000	26
80,000	100,000	18,200	28
100,000	150,000	23,800	30
150,000	250,000	38,800	32
250,000	500,000	70,800	34
500,000	750,000	155,800	37
750,000	1,000,000	248,300	39
1,000,000	1,250,000	345,800	41
1,250,000	1,500,000	448,300	43
1,500,000	2,000,000	555,800	45
2,000,000	Not applicable	780,800	45

Estate Reduction with Gifts

The taxation of an estate can be a complex process and is dependent on the proper assessment of a number of factors. One of those factors relates to gifts that have been made during one's lifetime. Proper estate planning is essential in order to achieve the maximum benefit of strategies designed to reduce estate tax. Obviously, as estates grow in size through inflation, investments, and capital appreciation, the importance of minimizing estate taxes also increases. One simple way to reduce a taxable estate is to annually make nontaxable gifts. Currently, the first $13,000 ($26,000 with a consent from spouse) gifted to any one person during any calendar year is excluded in determining taxable gifts. This is an annual exclusion and is scheduled to change due to inflation indexing.[2]

---

2 Although the annual exclusion amount is increased for inflation, it is not adjusted every year and when adjusted it has tended to increase by an even $1,000. Future exclusion amounts are not currently known; therefore, all examples and end-of-chapter materials will be based on the assumption that the annual exclusion is $13,000.

Based on current annual exclusion amounts, consenting spouses who participate for 10 years in an annual gift program involving six recipients would be able to transfer $1,560,000 [($13,000 × 2 spouses) × 6 recipients × 10 years] without incurring any gift tax. Spouses also can make gifts to each other. No matter what the amount, such gifts between spouses are not subject to gift tax. Furthermore, charitable gifts, tuition payments made directly to an educational organization, and/or medical payments made on another's behalf are not considered taxable gifts. However, if the payment was made to the individual and used for educational or medical expenses, it would be considered a taxable gift if it exceeds certain defined amounts.

Transfers that do not qualify as nontaxable gifts are therefore deemed to be taxable gifts and are subject to tax based on the unified transfer tax rates as set forth in Exhibit 20-1. For example, if consenting spouses each gave $20,000 to 6 recipients for 10 years, then $420,000 of gifts by each spouse would be taxable [($19,000 × 2 spouses) versus ($13,000 × 2 spouses) × 6 recipients × 10 years allocated to 2 spouses]. Based on the rates in Exhibit 20-1, the tax on the cumulative taxable gift of $360,000 would be $108,200 [($360,000 − $250,000) × 34% = $37,400 + $70,800 for a total of $108,200]. There is a unified credit that accompanies the unified transfer tax. Currently, a lifetime credit of $345,800 may be credited against the gross tax on taxable gifts. The benefit of this exclusion amount is that taxes on $1,000,000 of gifts, which would otherwise be $345,800 (based on unified transfer tax rates for the year 2009), are not imposed. Therefore, in the above example, the tax of $108,200 on the cumulative taxable gifts would have been offset by the credit. It is important to remember that this credit is a lifetime credit. Given the above example, after the consenting spouses made gifts for the 10 years, of which $360,000 was taxable, the tax on only another $640,000 of taxable gifts could be offset by the remaining credit associated with $1,000,000 of gifts. For example, assuming that one of the spouses subsequently made a $890,000 taxable gift, the tax on that gift would be determined as follows:

Current taxable gift		$ 890,000
Previous taxable gifts		360,000
Total lifetime taxable gifts		$1,250,000
Tax on lifetime taxable gifts (see Exhibit 20-1)		$ 448,300
Less: Tax on previous taxable gifts (based on current rates)		(108,200)
Tax on current-period gift		$ 340,100
Less: Unified credit	$ 345,800	
Previously used credit	(108,200)	(237,600)
Net tax due on current-period gift		$ 102,500

In the above example, the entire available unified credit against gift tax of $345,800 has been used and the tax on any further taxable gifts will not be reduced by the unified credit. It is also important to note that the unified transfer tax system has one unified credit of which the gift tax credit is a part. Therefore, if a portion of the credit is used to offset gift tax, there is less remaining available credit to reduce potential estate tax. This concept will be discussed shortly.

One might ask, "Assuming there have been no previous gifts, what is the maximum total gift a husband and wife may give to one individual at one time in 2014 without incurring any tax?" For gift tax purposes, a gift made by one person to someone other than his or her spouse may be considered as having been made one-half by each spouse under the *gift splitting* provisions provided that both spouses agree to splitting. Each spouse is entitled to a unified credit of $345,800 (in 2014), or an exemption equivalent gift of $1,000,000, plus the annual $13,000 exclusion. Therefore, a husband and wife together could give $2,026,000 (2 spouses × $1,013,000) to one person (assuming none of the lifetime exclusion amount had been previously used) without incurring any gift tax. The unified gift tax credit is not an annual credit but rather a lifetime credit. Therefore, once used, a unified transfer (gift) tax would be due on taxable gifts without the benefit of a reduction due to the unified credit.

Federal Estate Taxation

Significant changes regarding gratuitous transfers of property resulted from the *Tax Reform Act of 1976*. Prior to its enactment, transfers of property during the owner's lifetime were subject to the federal gift tax, while property passing as a result of death was subject to the federal estate tax. As previously stated, as a result of the Tax Reform Act, the separate gift tax and estate tax were combined into a unified transfer tax, which addresses both life (gift) and death transfers made after 1976. Therefore, taxable gifts and taxable estates are both taxed at the same rates (the unified transfer tax rate).[3] However, the tax associated with gifts and the tax associated with an estate must be separately determined.

The computation of the federal estate tax may be summarized as follows:

Gross estate.	XX
Less deductions allowed	−XX
Taxable estate	XX
Add post-1976 taxable gifts	+XX
Unified tax base.	XX
Tentative tax on total transfers	XX
Less tax credits.	−XX
Estate tax due.	XX

The starting point for the computation of the federal estate tax is the determination of the gross estate, which includes the fair market value of all property in which the decedent had an interest at the date of death, regardless of the nature of the property or to whom it passes. Whether it is real or personal, tangible or intangible, business or nonbusiness, the property is includable. The gross estate, for tax purposes, is often greater than the estate for probate purposes due to special tax rules (for example, special rules regarding joint tenancy). The gross estate also includes life insurance proceeds payable to the estate, or if the decedent owned the insurance policy, the proceeds payable to their heirs. The gross estate also includes transfers by the deceased during his or her lifetime in which certain rights are retained by the decedent (such as the right to enjoyment, or possession, the right to designate persons who will possess or enjoy, and of transfers which at the date of the decedent's death were subject to the decedent's power to alter, revoke, terminate, or amend the transfer). In order to prevent significant reductions in one's gross estate, certain property that the decedent transferred within three years prior to death may be included in the gross estate.

The taxable estate is determined by subtracting the total of the following allowable deductions:

1. Allowable expenses, such as funeral expenses and costs of administrating the estate;
2. Indebtedness against property included in the gross estate, such as a mortgage and other debts of the decedent;
3. Unpaid property and income taxes of the decedent to date of death;
4. Uninsured losses from casualty or theft of estate assets during the period of settlement;
5. Transfers to the United States, any state, political divisions of a state, or charitable organizations (for use in charitable purposes) specified by the will;
6. State inheritance taxes; and
7. Marital deduction, which is unlimited in amount, for estate property that passes to the surviving spouse if he or she is a U.S. citizen.

The unified transfer tax approach requires that the taxable estate be increased by any taxable gifts made after 1976 by the decedent prior to death. Gifts during one's lifetime may be subject to the unified transfer tax. It is important to remember that a unified credit may be taken against the tax imposed on taxable gifts. Currently, this credit is $345,800 traceable to a lifetime applicable exclusion amount of $1,000,000 of taxable gifts. However, any unified credit that is applied against

---

3 The unified transfer tax has a graduated tax rate that begins at 18% on the first $10,000 of taxable amount. The rate increased to a top marginal tax rate of 45% for years 2008 through 2009. The estate tax (but not the gift tax) was repealed for 2010; however, the top marginal gift tax rate was 35% for 2010 on taxable transfers over $500,000.

gift tax reduces the unified credit that may be applied against estate tax. Therefore, in order to make sure that the unified credit used to reduce gift tax reduces the unified credit on estate tax, the post-1976 taxable gifts are added to the taxable estate in order to arrive at a unified tax base. Adding taxable gifts to the taxable estate results in a unified tax base to which the unified transfer tax rates are applied which in turn results in a total unified tax on total transfers (during life and upon death).

Application of the tax rates to the unified tax base results in a tentative estate tax which is then reduced by certain credits and the net tax is due nine months from the date of death. The two most common credits relate to taxes paid on post-1976 taxable gifts and the unified credit. Recalling that post-1976 taxable gifts are added to the taxable estate to produce a unified tax base, it is apparent that the taxable gifts are again being taxed at the applicable rates. If there were no further adjustment, this would result in double taxation on taxable gifts, once at the time of the gift and again as part of the estate tax calculation. Therefore, a credit for taxes associated with post-1976 gifts is calculated. The credit is equal to the tax that would be imposed on the taxable gift based on unified transfer tax rates that are in effect at the time of the decedent's death (even though the gift tax at the time of the gift may have been calculated using different rates). If the credit were merely the amount of tax originally paid on the gift, it is possible that the gift could be currently taxed, as part of the unified tax base, at rates that were different than at the time of the gift. In that case, the credit would not offset the current tax associated with the gift. Therefore, the credit associated with gifts is based on current rates in effect.

The *unified credit* is a significant factor for most estates and in substance results from excluding a portion of taxable estate from taxation. The maximum amount of the credit and excluded amounts are as follows:

For Decedents Dying and Gifts During	Applicable Credit Amount	Applicable Exclusion Amount
2009	$1,455,800	$3,500,000

The applicable credit amount corresponds with the unified transfer tax, which would be due on the applicable exclusion amount. For example, if one had a taxable estate of $3,500,000 in the year 2009, the unified transfer tax would be $1,455,800, which corresponds with the applicable credit. Additional credits against the tax due are based on state death or inheritance taxes paid and foreign death taxes. After recognizing applicable credits, the net tax due is paid out of the principal of the estate. If the estate principal does not have adequate cash to pay the taxes, other principal assets must be liquidated in order to generate the necessary cash.

In order to demonstrate the application of the unified transfer tax to an estate, assume that a single person died in 2009 with a gross estate of $5,240,000 after having made $2,000,000 of taxable gifts during their lifetime. The calculation of the estate tax is as follows:

Gross estate.		$ 5,240,000
Less deductions allowed:		
Funeral expenses.	$ 15,000	
Administrative expenses	25,000	
Charitable transfers in will	100,000	
Mortgage payable.	100,000	(240,000)
Taxable estate.		$ 5,000,000
Post-1976 taxable gifts		2,000,000
Unified tax base.		$ 7,000,000
Tentative tax on total transfers (see Exhibit 20-1).		$ 3,030,800
Less credits:		
Tax on taxable gifts at current rates*		(435,000)
Unified credit		(1,455,800)
Net estate tax due**		$ 1,140,000

*This is the tax of $780,800 on a $2,000,000 gift less the lifetime exclusion amount of $345,800.

**The tax on all of the transfers of $7,000,000 is $3,030,800 less the unified credit of $1,455,800 resulting in a net tax on all transfers of $1,575,000. Of this net tax, $435,000 was paid as a gift tax, and $1,140,000 was paid as an estate tax.

Marital Deduction

In the computation of the taxable estate, recall that a marital deduction is allowed for the value of qualifying property passing to a surviving spouse. The amount of the deduction is unlimited. No matter how large the estate, a bequest of all property to one's surviving spouse will completely eliminate federal estate taxes for the decedent's estate. That statement is technically correct but incomplete. It should also state that the deduction may defer estate taxes only until the death of the surviving spouse. Upon the death of the surviving spouse, their estate (which includes the remains of their previously deceased spouse's estate) may become subject to tax. At that point, it may be discovered that use of the unlimited marital deduction actually increased the overall estate tax. This can result because the tax rates are progressive (the higher the tax base, the higher the rates), and the effect of the unlimited marital deduction is to channel all assets into the estate of the surviving spouse.

To illustrate, assume Ruth Marshall's will stipulated that her husband William was to receive all of her gross estate valued at $7,300,000. Outstanding debts of $150,000 and funeral and administrative expenses totaling $50,000 are paid out of the estate. Also, assume that later in the same year William dies with Ruth's estate assets of $7,100,000 still intact plus other assets of $1,100,000 for a total of $8,200,000. At the time of William's death, debts of his estate total $80,000, and $20,000 of funeral and administrative costs have been incurred. With an unlimited marital deduction, their estate tax computations are as follows:

	Ruth		William	
Gross estate		$ 7,300,000		$ 8,200,000*
Less deductions:				
Debts	$ 150,000		$80,000	
Funeral and administrative costs	50,000		20,000	
Marital deduction	7,100,000	(7,300,000)	0	(100,000)
Taxable estate		$ 0		$ 8,100,000
Estate tax before credits				$ 3,525,800
Less unified credit (available in 2009)				(1,455,800)
Estate tax due				$ 2,070,000

*This represents the $7,100,000 transferred per the marital deduction plus William's separate assets of $1,100,000.

As an alternative strategy, Ruth's will or trust document could have stipulated that an amount equal to the applicable exclusion amount ($3,500,000) be placed in a trust for the benefit of William. William will be the income beneficiary and will have access to the principal amount with few restrictions (for example, assets may be used for William's medical and educational expenses as well as for his general maintenance and support). At the time of William's death, the remaining assets of the trust would transfer to their children free of tax, even if they have greatly appreciated. The objective of using a trust in this instance is to maximize the use of the unified credit by not just one of the spouses but by both spouses. A common form of trust used for this purpose is a *credit shelter trust,* as it "shelters" a portion of the total estate from estate tax by using the unified credit available to each spouse. Sometimes, these trusts are also referred to as marital deduction trusts, family trusts, bypass trusts, or "A-B" trusts. In any case, if these trusts meet IRS guidelines, they are not subject to estate tax when the surviving spouse (William) dies. Therefore, if properly designed, the trust amount would be included in the decedent's (Ruth) taxable estate and incur tax but be offset by the unified credit. The balance of the decedent's (Ruth) net estate would be offset by the marital deduction and avoid estate tax. The balance of the decedent's net estate would pass to the surviving spouse. In our example, Ruth's taxable estate would consist of the amount of the credit shelter trust ($3,500,000), the tax on which would be offset by the unified credit. The balance of Ruth's net estate of $3,600,000 ($7,300,000 − $150,000 debts − $50,000 costs − $3,500,000 placed in trust) would go directly to William and qualify for the marital deduction. Now, their estate computations would be as follows, once again assuming that William has additional other assets of $1,100,000:

	Ruth		William	
Gross estate.		$ 7,300,000		$ 4,700,000*
Less deductions:				
Debts	$ 150,000		$80,000	
Funeral and administrative costs . . .	50,000		20,000	
Marital deduction	3,600,000	3,800,000	0	100,000
Taxable estate		$ 3,500,000		$ 4,600,000
Estate tax before credits**		$ 1,455,800		$ 1,950,800
Less unified credit (available in 2009).		(1,455,800)		(1,455,800)
Estate tax due.		$ 0		$ 495,000

*This represents the $3,600,000 transferred per the marital deduction (outside of the trust) plus William's separate assets of $1,100,000.
**This amount of tax is based on the rates in Exhibit 20-1.

Without the use of a credit shelter trust, Ruth and William paid a total of $2,070,000 in estate taxes as compared to paying $495,000 if a credit shelter trust had been used. The use of the trust saved over $1,500,000 in estate taxes (compare this to the cost of setting up a trust). Not knowing which spouse would be the first to die, both spouses usually create a revocable trust during their lifetime. Upon death, their trust becomes irrevocable and the surviving spouse terminates their revocable trust. Consideration should also be given to how the couple's assets are held. For example, if assets are held as joint tenants, then the property passes automatically to the surviving spouse and cannot be placed in a trust. If the assets had been held as tenants in common, then the decedent's share of such assets could become part of their estate and could be used as the basis for a trust.

Valuation of Assets Included in the Gross Estate

For estate tax purposes, the assets included in a decedent's gross estate must be measured at fair value. Assets are included in the estate at their fair value on the date of death or on an alternate valuation date, if the personal representative so elects. If the alternate valuation date is elected, all estate property must be valued as of six months after the decedent's death, except for property sold, distributed, or otherwise disposed of during the 6-month period. Such property is valued as of the date of disposition. The alternate valuation date may be used only if it would reduce the total gross estate and decrease the estate tax liability. The alternate valuation date protects estates if there should be a significant decrease in property values during the 6-month interval.

Formerly, it would have been possible for a fiduciary, knowing that there would be no estate tax to pay, to select the alternate valuation date if assets increased in value, thereby giving the heirs a higher basis for their inherited property, at no cost to the estate. To prevent this windfall, Congress took an action that permitted election of the alternate valuation date only if it would reduce the total gross estate and decrease the estate tax liability.

The recipient of assets from the gross estate must establish their inherited basis of the assets for purposes of their own personal tax situation. The basis of property acquired from a decedent is the fair value on the date of death or alternate valuation date, and this may result in a stepped-up basis. For example, assume Jane Jacoby held stock with a cost of $100,000. At the date of her death, it was worth $500,000 and was willed to her nephew, whose basis now becomes the stepped-up amount of $500,000. A subsequent sale of the stock by the nephew would measure the gain or loss on the sale for income tax purposes against this basis of $500,000. Although the value of the stock must be included in the inventory of the estate, which would be subject to the unified transfer tax only if the estate is large enough, the $400,000 gain would escape taxation on the decedent's personal income tax return filed for his or her year of death. The provision allowing for the step-up of basis can result in significant tax savings if a decedent does not have estate tax. However, if a decedent does have estate tax, in essence, the gain from stepping up the basis is subject to tax in the form of an estate tax rather than an income tax. In the above example, if Jane had sold the stock before her death, the gain would have been subject to personal income tax. Tax planning would suggest that, if possible, property that has appreciated substantially in value should be held as part of an estate because of the advantage of the step-up in basis. The opposite is true if there is a substantial decline in value. If Jane's stock had a value of $5,000 on the valuation date, that would become the basis to her nephew. Neither he nor the estate would derive any income tax benefit from the $95,000 loss in value. If Jane had sold the stock prior to her death, benefits resulting from the deductibility of the loss for her personal income tax purposes would have materialized.

Other Taxes Affecting an Estate

In addition to federal estate taxes, about half of the states assess an estate or inheritance tax on the value of estate assets conveyed to heirs. Regarding inheritance tax, certain transfers of assets are exempt, while other transfers are partially exempt, depending on the amount of the transfer and the relationship of the heir. The taxable amount of nonexempt transfers is reduced further by certain deductions such as funeral and administrative expenses, debts of the decedent, and mortgages on real property. As previously stated, state inheritance taxes are an allowable deduction against the gross estate in order to arrive at the taxable estate.

Depending on the complexity of an estate, it is possible that a significant period of time will be needed to settle an estate. Upon his or her death, the decedent's estate becomes a separate distinct taxable entity that may continue to exist for some time until all estate assets are distributed. In certain instances, an estate subsequently will generate income that is not included in the initial estate principal. Estate income that is distributed currently and properly to a beneficiary generally is excluded from the taxable income of the estate. Therefore, the estate functions as a conduit through which the income passes to the recipient. Income passing in this manner retains the same character it had in the hands of the estate. For example, if the estate receives and distributes nontaxable income such as interest on municipal bonds, the interest remains tax free in the hands of the recipient. Normally, the beneficiary is taxed on any taxable income that he or she receives, and the estate, as a separate entity, is taxed on any income that it accumulates. Income taxes on the estate entity are assessed at rates similar to those used for individual taxpayers except that the levels of income at which rates become effective are much lower for estates than they are for individuals. Obviously, these highly progressive rates are designed to encourage estates to distribute income to the intended parties on a timely basis.

REFLECTION

- One's taxable estate may be reduced in a number of ways, including annual gifting, the creation of trusts, and the marital deduction.
- The taxable estate consists of the gross estate less allowable deductions. The amount of estate tax is also reduced by a unified credit.

TRUST ACCOUNTING ISSUES

5

OBJECTIVE

Explain what a trust is and what the basic accounting issues are.

A trust is a separate, distinct entity that receives assets from an individual for the purpose of managing and distributing them over a period of time. A trust is also recognized as a taxable entity until trust assets have been distributed and the administration of the trust is completed. Trusts may be created for a wide variety of reasons. It is possible that heirs to an estate currently lack the maturity, sophistication, or prudence necessary to receive substantial assets directly. Therefore, a trust is established to manage the asset for the intended heir(s). Trusts also provide opportunities for assets to be exempt from the probate process and, more important, taxes imposed on an estate. Finally, trusts are used as a means to convey assets to special organizations or causes, such as charities, universities, and other not-for-profit organizations. Rather than conveying estate assets directly to these organizations, a trust presents an opportunity to recognize the needs of individual heirs prior to such distributions.

Trusts may take a variety of forms, and various strategies can be used to create a trust. A *charitable remainder trust* distributes the income from trust assets to individual beneficiaries over a period of time (often for the rest of their lives), at which time the assets go to the remainderman which must be a charitable organization. Under such an arrangement, a charitable deduction is available to the grantor when the trust is created. Upon death of the grantor, the property is excluded from the estate, thereby avoiding estate taxes. A *bypass or credit shelter trust* is designed to split assets between a surviving spouse and a trust so that the value of the marital deduction and unified credit are maximized. Generally, the surviving spouse receives income during his or her lifetime after which the trust assets are distributed to surviving children or heirs. A *qualified terminable interest property trust* (QTIP trust) is similar to a bypass or credit shelter trust.

Noting that trusts may be designed to accomplish a variety of purposes, they may become operative while the grantor is alive or they may be created through a will to become effective upon the grantor's death. The former type of trust is an *inter vivos*, or *living, trust*, while the latter is referred to as a *testamentary trust*. For example, an individual grantor may establish an *irrevocable life insurance trust* to become operative during his or her lifetime. This trust owns a life insurance policy on the grantor and typically receives contributions from the grantor which are used to pay the insurance premiums. Upon death of the grantor, the insurance proceeds are excluded from the gross estate, and policy proceeds pass to the designated beneficiaries. An example of a testamentary trust would be when a decedent's will, upon his or her death, calls for the creation of a trust for the benefit of his or her minor children. Typically, after attaining some age set forth in the trust, the trust assets will be distributed to the children and the trust terminated. In order to carry out the provisions of a trust, a *trustee* must be appointed. The trustee may be an individual; however, banks frequently serve as trustees. Most major banks have a trust department whose services are available for a fee.

Financial Accounting for Trusts

The accounting for a trust is very similar to the accounting for an estate. The distinction between principal and income must be maintained through the use of *trust principal* and *trust income accounts*. The trust agreement should provide direction regarding how income is to be determined. A charge and discharge statement is required periodically for both trust principal and income.

Illustration 20-3 demonstrates the accounting for various events affecting the trust established by Jane Jacoby's will.

Illustration 20-3
Accounting for the Jacoby Children's Trust

Event	Entry		
1. Receipt of distribution from the estate of Jane Jacoby.	Principal Cash	207,200	
	Investment in XYZ Stock and Mutual Funds	958,000	
	Trust Principal		1,165,200
	Income Cash	900	
	Trust Income		900

(continued)

Event	Entry		
2. Sale of mutual funds.	Principal Cash	200,000	
	Income Cash	5,000	
	Investment in Mutual Funds		200,000
	Trust Income		5,000
3. Receipt of dividend and interest income.	Income Cash	5,300	
	Trust Income		5,300
4. Payment of trustee's fees and allocation to principal and income.	Administrative Expenses: Principal	400	
	Administrative Expenses: Income	200	
	Principal Cash		400
	Income Cash		200
5. Distribution of income cash to beneficiaries.	Distribution to Income Beneficiary	11,000	
	Income Cash		11,000

To demonstrate adherence to the terms of the trust, the trustee must provide annual, confidential reports to income beneficiaries and remaindermen. For a testamentary trust, a report must also be rendered to the probate court of the county in which the will was admitted to probate. The nature of the report is dependent upon the statutory requirement of the relevant state. Generally, within 30 days after the end of each year, a report must be filed that shows:

1. The trust principal on hand at the beginning of the period.
2. Changes in the trust principal during the period, such as asset acquisitions or dispositions.
3. The trust principal on hand at the end of the period, its composition, and the estimated fair values of all investments.

As to trust income, the report shows:

1. The trust income on hand at the beginning of the period.
2. Trust income received during the period, including its sources and amounts.
3. Distributions of trust income made during the period to income beneficiaries.
4. The trust income on hand at the end of the period and how it is invested.

These requirements may be met by the periodic filing of a charge and discharge statement, provided that sufficient detail as to principal and income is incorporated into the report. At the time the statement is submitted to the court, many trustees prefer to close trust books to have them correspond to the annual time frame used in filing reports. Trust Principal and Trust Income are the clearing accounts used in the closing process, paralleling the procedures for closing an estate.

The trust will terminate when all trust property is distributed in accordance with the trust arrangement. For example, a trust may have been created to provide a beneficiary with income until this beneficiary reaches a specified age, at which time trust principal is released. The trustee's final report will take the same form as the periodic reports but, in addition, will itemize total distribution of trust principal and income to indicate termination of stewardship.

REFLECTION

- A trust is a separate, distinct entity, and its principal and income must be separately accounted for.

UNDERSTANDING THE ISSUES

1. Estate planning is becoming more important to many individuals. Identify several goals of estate planning.

2. Explain why it may be wise for a wealthy spouse to use the unified credit rather than to transfer all of his or her estate to the surviving spouse in the form of the marital exclusion.

3. Explain why it is important to separately account for the principal and income of an estate and what happens if such assets are not adequate to satisfy demonstrative or general legacies.

EXERCISES

Exercise 1 *(LO 2)* **Distinguishing between principal and income.** Roger Kramer's wife Sarah passed away five years ago, and she made Roger promise to continue to provide care for Sarah's sister Margaret Smith and let her live in their residence for a period of time. Roger and Sarah had no children, and Margaret Smith was like a daughter to them. Roger passed away, and his will contained the following provisions:

a. $200,000 of estate principal should be donated to the Sierra Club and the balance, less appropriate expenses, should be placed in the Margaret Smith trust.
b. The Margaret Smith trust calls for 80% of periodic net income to be paid out to Margaret Smith with the balance to be considered trust corpus.
c. The trust is to be terminated two years after Roger's death at which time 60% of the corpus will be given to Margaret Smith and the balance to the Milwaukee Foundation to be placed in a fund to support environmental issues dealing with alternative energy sources.

The following events occurred within one year of Roger's death:

1. In addition to the personal residence (valued at $350,000), the inventory at fair value of Roger's estate consisted of $230,000 cash, securities worth $210,000, personal effects worth $12,000, and a sailboat worth $8,000.
2. Mortgage payments on the residence were paid in the amount of $24,000, of which $8,000 was interest ($2,000 of which had accrued as of Roger's date of death).
3. Funeral and attorney fees to administer the estate were $27,000. Medical expenses incurred up to Roger's death were $21,000. Income taxes of $13,000 were due on Roger's final personal tax return.
4. Securities existing at the date of death with a cost of $130,000 and a market value of $178,000 were subsequently sold for $164,000. The proceeds upon sale were reinvested into bonds. Interest of $4,000 was received on the bonds.
5. A delinquency notice was received indicating that real estate taxes on the residence from last year remained unpaid in the amount of $12,000 plus interest and penalties of $2,000.
6. Dividends on the securities were received in the amount of $27,000, of which $7,000 were declared as of Roger's death.
7. Utilities and normal repairs and maintenance on the residence were $7,200, of which $1,200 had remained unpaid as of the date of death.
8. Out of estate assets, $15,000 was spent to replace the roof on the residence and $3,000 was paid for lawn care.
9. A bill was received from the Yacht Club indicating that Roger had unpaid dues and charges of $1,400. Margaret decided to continue membership in the club and paid additional dues and charges of $2,800.

Assuming that the trustee of the trust has approved all of the above, prepare a schedule to determine the principal and income balances after periodic distributions have been made to Margaret.

Exercise 2 *(LO 2)* **Accounting for estate principal and income.** Jason Jackson was killed in a mountain-climbing accident in British Columbia. As Jason's trusted friend and CPA, you have been named executor of his estate and guardian to his minor child, Cody Jackson. Jason's estate consists of the following assets subject to probate:

Cash	$ 15,000
Vacant land in Colorado	130,000
Investment in Merkt stock	54,000
Investment in GTE stock	13,000
Dividends declared on GTE stock	1,000
Investment in Trident bond fund	40,000
Accrued interest on Trident bond fund	2,000
Royalties receivable	17,000

Prepare journal entries to record the above inventory and the following events related to the estate principal and income:

1. Final medical and funeral expenses of $22,000 are paid.
2. An individual retirement account (IRA) naming Jackson's estate as beneficiary and having a value of $37,000 subsequently is discovered.
3. Cash dividends of $1,000 on the GTE stock and $2,700 on the Merkt stock are received.
4. The vacant land in Colorado is sold for $150,000 less accrued property taxes of $2,000 and a broker's commission of $8,000.
5. Interest of $2,400 is received on the Trident bond fund, and the royalty receivable is also collected.
6. Income taxes of $4,000 on the decedent's final tax return are paid, along with $24,000 of other claims against the estate.
7. A legacy of $15,000 is paid to the High Adventure Climbing School.
8. Administrative expenses of $3,200 are paid, of which $100 is traceable to income.

Exercise 3 *(LO 2)* **Charge and discharge statement.** Given the facts of Exercise 2, (1) prepare the charge and discharge statement that would have resulted from the above events and (2) prepare the entries to transfer all estate principal and income amounts to a trust for the benefit of Cody Jackson.

Exercise 4 *(LO 3)* **Allocating legacies.** Calvin Hughes's will provided for the following distributions:

a. The 40-acre parcel in Leona, Wisconsin, is to be given to The Nature Conservancy along with $50,000.
b. My 1970 GTO Pontiac convertible along with my 1937 Chevrolet pickup truck are to be given to the "Piston Auto Club" located in Slinger, Wisconsin.
c. The collection of Zuni Kachina dolls is to be given to my nephew William Hughes.
d. My Northwestern Mutual insurance policy number 14378 has named my son Calvin, Jr., as beneficiary. Policy number 48002 has named the estate as beneficiary. However, I want my sister Roberta and my brother Roger to each receive $30,000 from the policy proceeds.
e. My residence at 110 Hillcrest Road is to be given to the Riveredge Nature Center located in Newburg, Wisconsin, provided that the center has not already grown to include more than 500 acres.
f. My grandchildren, Riley, Corey and Toby, are to receive $50,000 each for the purpose of hopefully funding their college education. This bequest is not contingent upon their going to college or having already finished college.
g. The balance of my estate is to be divided equally between my son Calvin, Jr., and my daughter, Susan.

Determine the amount of cash to be received by the decedent's grandchild Riley and his son Calvin Hughes, Jr., under each of the following scenarios:

Scenario A: The following additional information is available at the date of death: the estate only consisted of $40,000 cash, William Hughes was deceased, the Kachina collection was sold for $45,000, insurance policy number 14378 had a death benefit of $50,000, insurance policy number 48002 had a death benefit of $40,000, Riveredge Nature Center consisted of 560 acres, and the residence at 110 Hillcrest Road was sold for $220,000.

Scenario B: The following additional information is available at the date of death: the estate only consisted of $15,000 cash, William Hughes was thrilled to receive the Kachina collection which was valued at $45,000, insurance policy number 14378 had a death benefit of $50,000, insurance policy number 48002 had a death benefit of $40,000, Riveredge Nature Center consisted of 160 acres, and the residence at 110 Hillcrest Road was sold for $220,000.

Exercise 5 *(LO 3, 4)* **Distribution of estate, taxable estate, and the resulting tax.**
Determine the correct value for each of the following questions:

1. Assuming that a single person has made taxable lifetime gifts of $1.2 million, what is the largest taxable estate that could exist and still not incur any estate tax?
2. Helen made separate lifetime taxable gifts of $1.5 million and died leaving her entire $5 million estate to her husband George. George had made taxable gifts of $500,000 prior to Helen's death. In the year following her death, George made gifts of $50,000 to each of their four children. George died shortly after making the gifts leaving a taxable estate of $7 million, including the intact $5 million inherited from Helen. What is the net estate tax due on George's estate?
3. Given the facts in item (2) above, now assume that Helen had established a credit shelter trust in the amount of $3.5 million for the benefit of her husband George. What is the net estate tax due on George's estate?
4. Roger Pillsbury died leaving an estate consisting of the following: a 1984 Ford Mustang, a savings account of $40,000 at LaSalle Bank, and a parcel of land in Oklahoma that was subsequently sold for $195,000. His will stipulated that the Ford Mustang go to his brother Robert and that his sister Ann receive $60,000 from his savings account at LaSalle Bank. Per his will, each of his six children were to receive $40,000, and the balance of his estate was to be given to the University of Oklahoma. What amount would Roger's sister receive from his estate?
5. Given the facts of item (4) above, assume that Roger had hoped that the University of Oklahoma would receive $100,000 from his estate. What would the land in Oklahoma have had to sell for in order for this to have been possible?

Exercise 6 *(LO 4)* **Taxation of gifts.** Determine the correct value for each of the following questions:

1. Assume that an individual gives cash to the following parties: $25,000 to a charitable organization, $15,000 to her grandson for his college tuition, $8,000 to her granddaughter to buy a car, and $14,000 to her spouse for a trip to France. What amount of gifts is considered taxable?
2. Assume that an individual has given $25,000 to each of his four grandchildren for each of the past three years and $50,000 to a charitable organization. If he wants to make a single gift to each of his four grandchildren, what would the maximum gift per grandchild be in order to avoid all gift tax?
3. Your client made the following gifts last year: $200,000 to each of her three children, $50,000 to her brother, and $10,000 to each of her eight grandchildren. Prior to that, your client made a single gift of $50,000 to each of her two nieces. If she made a gift of $500,000 to her sister in the current year, what amount of gift tax would be due?
4. Assume the same facts as in item (3) above except that your client married during the current year prior to making the gift to her sister. Furthermore, assume that her spouse is a consenting spouse for purposes of gifting to the sister and they both gave the gift to the sister. The new spouse had prior taxable gifts of $100,000. What amount of gift tax would be due?
5. Assume that an individual and his consenting spouse had made no gifts prior to last year. However, last year, they gave $50,000, $32,000, and $72,000, to their daughter, son, and neighbor, respectively. This year, they want to do significant gifting to the same three individuals but do not want the cumulative net tax on gifts to exceed $61,500 per spouse. Assuming a minimum gift of $30,000 to each party, what is the sum of all gifts that could be made this year?

Exercise 7 *(LO 4)* **Determination of estate tax.** Charles Kamp, a divorced person, died in February of the current year with an estate consisting of assets valued at $7,008,000 and liabilities of $380,000. Charles's will contained the following provisions:

a. Robert Sullivan would serve as executor of the estate and trustee for the Kamp Children Trust.
b. Timberland with a market value of $560,000 would be placed in a charitable remainder trust. The income from the trust would accrue to the benefit of his sister Marsha Kamp Rodriquez. Income would be reduced by the depletion charge associated with the number of board feet of lumber harvested.
c. Securities with a value of $25,000 would be given to the Milwaukee Art Museum, recognized as a charitable organization.
d. Securities with a value of $600,000 would be given to his married daughter, Maria Kamp Wilson.
e. Each of his three best hunting friends would be paid $180,000 from the proceeds of the sale of Charles's investment in hunting land in Alaska. The hunting land was valued at $475,000 and subsequently sold for $480,000.
f. His long-time friend Ernest Kampmeyer would be given $3,940,000.
g. Proceeds from the life insurance policy with a death benefit of $1,200,000 would be placed in a trust for the benefit of Charles's two minor children.

Administrative and funeral expenses associated with Charles's estate totaled $30,000. Charles's income tax returns for the year of death reported unpaid federal and state income taxes of $13,000.

1. Assuming the unified transfer tax rates and unified credit as set forth in the text, determine the amount of estate tax due on Charles Kamp's estate.
2. Prepare a schedule showing the amounts and recipients of general legacies.

Exercise 8 *(LO 4)* **Strategies to minimize estate taxes.** Edith Leppert and her husband, Gerald Leppert, have net assets with market values of $4,300,000 and $2,400,000, respectively. The Lepperts have begun to do some estate tax planning and are developing various strategies based on the following assumptions:

a. Due to preexisting health conditions, it is assumed that Edith will precede her husband in death and Gerald will survive Edith by three years.
b. Gerald's net assets, including those assets received upon Edith's death, are expected to appreciate at an annual compound rate of 5% per year.
c. Administrative and funeral expenses are estimated to be $25,000 per person.
d. Both Edith and Gerald have each earmarked $150,000 of their net assets to be donated to charitable organizations.

Based on the above information, determine the amount of estate tax that both Edith and Gerald Leppert would be exposed to given: (1) that no trusts were established and (2) that a credit shelter trust is created by each person for the benefit of their children in the amount of $3,500,000. Unified transfer tax rates and the unified credit as set forth in the text should be used.

Exercise 9 *(LO 5)* **Analysis of trust activity.** Jack Mason is a single parent with three minor children. His will provides for the creation of a trust for the benefit of his three children. His entire net estate is to be placed into the trust, and the trustee is authorized to approve disbursements to the children until they reach the age of 25. Upon reaching the age of 25, each child is to receive their proportionate share of the trust principal and income. For example, the first child to reach age 25 will receive one-third of the trust principal and income. The next child to reach age 25 will receive one-half of the trust principal and income at that time.

The following facts relate to the trust between the time of Mason's death and the first child's 25th birthday.

a. The following assets were transferred to the trust after the settlement of Jack Mason's estate: Cash, $100,000; stock in IBM, $150,000; investment in real estate partnership, $400,000; and forest land, $200,000.
b. Subsequent to Mason's death, an investment in a limited partnership was discovered. The investment was valued at $40,000.
c. One-half of the investment in the real estate partnership was sold for $220,000.

d. Dividends on the IBM stock were received in the amount of $20,000. The dividend was declared prior to Mason's death.

e. All cash balances were invested in a short-term interest-bearing account, and the trust received $5,000 in interest.

f. The trustee for the benefit of the children approved disbursements in the amount of $32,000. Disbursements are first considered to be a distribution of available trust income and then as a distribution of trust principal.

g. Trustee's fees in the amount of $10,000 were paid. All such fees are to be allocated equally between principal and income.

h. Eight percent bonds with a face value of $80,000 were purchased for $84,000. The bonds have a remaining life of five years, and any premium is to be amortized.

i. Income from the harvest of timber in the amount of $22,000 was received. The trust document calls for a charge against income for depletion. Depletion is calculated based on a units-of-output method that is based on board feet of timber harvested. Approximately 11% of the total board feet is represented by this harvest. The land is expected to have a residual value of $60,000 after removal of the timber.

j. Real estate taxes on the land in the amount of $6,000 were paid. Such taxes are considered a component of trust income.

k. The real estate partnership made a distribution of income in the amount of $22,000 to the trust.

l. A semiannual interest payment on the bonds was received by the trust.

m. The trustee paid $6,000 of taxes on trust income.

n. IBM stock with a basis of $60,000 was sold for $80,100.

Prepare a schedule to determine the amount of trust principal to be received by the first child to reach the age of 25. The schedule should show the cash balance available at any point in time.

PROBLEMS

Problem 20-1 *(LO 2)* **Recording activities for an estate and a trust.** At the time of Robert Granger's death, his estate consisted of the following assets and liabilities measured at fair market value:

Assets	
Cash	$ 50,000
Personal residence	450,000
Automobile and sailboat	65,000
Investment in mutual funds	3,280,000
Collection of antique duck decoys	85,000
Death benefit of life insurance policy	500,000
Farmland in Ozaukee County	800,000
Total assets	$5,230,000

Liabilities	
Mortgage on personal residence	$ 150,000
Life insurance policy loan	50,000
Credit card balances	5,000
Total liabilities	$ 205,000

The following information is relevant to the administration of Robert's estate:

a. Robert is a single person and has two minor children from a previous marriage. After satisfying the other provisions of his will, the balance of Robert's estate is to be transferred to a trust for the benefit of his minor children. Annual trust income in the amount of $15,000 is to be transferred to the children. Upon attaining the age of 21, each child would receive corpus of $25,000. The remaining corpus of the trust and any undistributed income is to be paid out to the children when they both have attained the age of 25.

b. Title to the personal residence, subject to the mortgage, will be transferred to Robert's sister who is to serve as the guardian for his minor children.

c. The collection of antique duck decoys is to be given to Ducks Unlimited which is a qualifying charitable organization.

d. Robert's sailboat, valued at $35,000, is to be given as a charitable contribution to the Milwaukee Community Sailing Center. The automobile will be given to his nephew Roger Stevens.

e. Funeral and administrative expenses of the estate are $25,000.

f. Investments in mutual funds with an estate value of $170,000 were sold for $180,000 to provide necessary liquidity.

Subsequent to the settlement of Robert's estate, the following activity occurred in the children's trust during the first month:

a. The farmland was rented for $25,000. Property taxes and other operating expenses associated with the farmland were incurred in the amount of $8,000.

b. Mutual funds with an estate value of $120,000 were sold for $132,000. Mutual funds with an estate value of $50,000 were sold for $45,000.

c. Income on the mutual fund investments was $22,000.

d. The trustee made a payment of corpus to Robert's daughter upon her turning 21 years of age.

e. After distributing the required amount of trust income, all available cash with the exception of $5,000 of income cash was invested in mutual funds.

Required ▶ ▶ ▶ ▶ ▶ Prepare all necessary entries to record the activities of the estate and the trust. Unified transfer tax rates and the exclusion amount as set forth in the text should be used.

Problem 20-2 *(LO 2)* **Recording estate principal and income.** Laurel Rose has been the personal representative of her brother's estate since his death on February 1, 2016. The following events occurred during her administration:

1. Included in the principal assets were 40, $1,000, 8% city of Pittsburgh bonds paying interest on January 1 and July 1. The bonds had a fair value of 101 on February 1, 2016. Laurel sold the bonds at 103, plus accrued interest, on March 1, 2016.

2. On March 1, 2016, Laurel purchased 50, $1,000, 5% city of Detroit bonds at 98, plus accrued interest. The bonds pay interest on April 1 and October 1. The bonds mature on April 1, 2018.

3. On March 1, 2016, she also purchased $10,000 (face value), 7% city of Newark bonds at 102 plus accrued interest. The bonds pay interest on June 1 and December 1. The bonds mature on December 1, 2017.

4. On April 1, 2016, she received a check for the interest on the Detroit bonds.

5. On June 1, 2016, she received a check for the interest on the Newark bonds.

6. On September 1, 2016, she sold the Detroit bonds at 101, plus accrued interest.

Required ▶ ▶ ▶ ▶ ▶ Prepare journal entries to record each of these events. Use the straight-line method of amortization where applicable.

Problem 20-3 *(LO 3, 4)* **Determining estate tax and general legacies.** Walter Campbell was a very giving person all of his life. His surviving children speak frequently of his generosity not only toward his deceased wife but also to many beyond his immediate family. Unfortunately, Walter's will proved to be more generous than his estate was able to support. Provisions of Walter's will included the following:

a. My entire collection of Navajo rugs and Acoma pottery (fair value at date of death is $120,000) is to be given to the Museum of Northern New Mexico, a charitable organization.

b. My residence (fair value at date of death is $550,000) is to be given to my younger brother Thomas along with $2,500,000 from my brokerage account at Wachovia Securities (fair value at date of death is $2,200,000).

c. My brokerage account at Schmidt Investment Services (fair value at date of death is $900,000) is to be liquidated with $500,000 going to each of my two sisters.

d. My collection of antique pistols (fair value at date of death is $85,000) is to be given to my son-in-law Eric Jacobsen.

e. My hunting land in Buffalo County, Wisconsin (fair value at date of death is $750,000), is to be sold and my uncle is to receive $700,000 of the proceeds.

f. Of the proceeds from my life insurance policies (fair value at date of death is $250,000), $200,000 is to be given to First Church of Brookfield, a charitable organization.

g. Each of my eight grandchildren is to receive $50,000, and each of my three children is to receive $400,000.

h. The balance of my assets is to be divided equally between the Kohler Arts Center in Kohler, Wisconsin, and the Wisconsin Maritime Museum in Manitowoc, Wisconsin.

In addition to the above listed items, all other assets of Walter's estate were liquidated for a total amount of $1,500,000 cash. Allowable deductions, excluding charitable donations, against his gross estate amounted to $235,000. All calculations of estate tax should use the rates and unified credit set forth in the text.

Prepare a schedule to determine who will receive a general legacy from Walter's estate and the amount of each legacy.   ◄ ◄ ◄ ◄ ◄ **Required**

Problem 20-4 *(LO 4)* **Strategies to minimize estate tax.** James and Susan Wagner have assets with fair market values of $5,700,000 and $1,800,000, respectively. James has been diagnosed with a terminal illness and is expected to pass away within the current year 2015. James wants to minimize his estate taxes, and any appropriate planning should consider the following factors:

a. James Wagner has debts of $210,000 against the assets in his estate.

b. It is estimated that administrative and funeral expenses will be $25,000 each for James and Susan.

c. It is estimated that Susan would be able to live comfortably for the balance of her life if she had an estate of $3,000,000 at the time of her husband's death. Susan will make charitable contributions to the extent that her estate exceeds $3,000,000 as a result of her husband's death.

d. Assume that Susan will live for three years after the death of her husband.

e. It is anticipated that at the time of Susan's death her estate would have appreciated by $150,000 per year for years 2015 through 2017.

f. Neither James nor Susan has made any gifts during the current year 2015.

g. The couple has two children and three grandchildren. One of the grandchildren is attending the University of Wisconsin and is expected to graduate in 2017. Annual tuition costs are $10,000 per year.

h. James has agreed to make a $200,000 charitable contribution to the Sierra Club out of his estate.

i. If any trusts are created, the income from the trust will benefit the surviving spouse, and any corpus will ultimately pass to the children.

Develop an estate plan for the Wagners that would minimize estate taxes and incorporate the above factors. The unified transfer tax rates and exclusion amounts set forth in the text should be used. Assume that annual nontaxable gifts up to $13,000 per donor will be made to all children and grandchildren to whatever extent possible.   ◄ ◄ ◄ ◄ ◄ **Required**

Problem 20-5 *(LO 4)* **Determining and minimizing estate tax.** Spencer Cook died on July 18 of the current year, leaving a gross estate of $4,600,000. Claims to be settled against that estate included funeral, administrative, and medical expenses of $180,000 and other debts of $210,000. Spencer's wife Sara has a considerable estate of her own, and she and Spencer have each agreed to leave $500,000 of their personal estate to charity. One year after Spencer's death, Sara passed away. Allowable expenses against Sara's estate totaled $420,000 excluding charitable bequests.

Required ▶ ▶ ▶ ▶ ▶   Using the estate tax rates and unified credit in the text:

1. Determine the estate tax to be paid by both Spencer and Sara assuming that no credit shelter trusts are employed and that Sara's gross estate is $7,300,000 including the assets inherited from Spencer.
2. Assume that prior to death Spencer and Sara both created a credit shelter trust calling for the surviving spouse to be the income beneficiary and their children to be the recipient of the principal. The principal of the trust is equal to the applicable exclusion amount. Determine the estate tax to be paid by both Spencer and Sara assuming that Sara's gross estate at the date of her death was $5,400,000 including the assets inherited from Spencer.

Problem 20-6 *(LO 4)* **Calculation of gift and estate tax.** Early in 2011, Nancy Fable was diagnosed with a terminal illness, and doctors gave her one more year to live. Aside from a 2010 $1,000,000 gift to the University of Georgia, she had not done any other gifting prior to 2011. She made the following gifts during 2011:

Gift to the First Baptist Church	$ 50,000
Gift to the Red Cross	25,000
Gift to Medcap Manufacturing Co. for a new fitness center	100,000
Payment to Princeton University for her only newphew's tuition	30,000
Gift to her only sister	70,000
Gifts to each of her three nieces.	45,000
	$320,000

Early in 2012, she made gifts of $25,000 each to her sister, three nieces, and a nephew. In the spring of 2012, Nancy passed away, leaving an estate consisting of the following at her date of death:

a. One thousand shares of Google stock valued at $900 per share.
b. Real estate in Macon County, Georgia, valued at $3,250,000.
c. Household effects valued at $21,000.
d. Bank accounts totaling $780,000 and gold coins valued at $310,000.
e. Loan against the Macon County real estate consisting of $300,000 plus accrued interest of $7,200.

Funeral and other estate administrative expenses totaled $45,000. Property taxes of $4,000 on the real estate and income taxes of $27,000 were paid by the personal representative. In addition to the above insurance policy, Medcap Manufacturing owned an insurance policy on Nancy's life that had a death benefit of $150,000.

Subsequent to Nancy's death, but within the 6-month alternative valuation date, the following occurred:

a. Two months after Nancy's death, the Macon County land was sold for $3,050,000, and the principal amount of the real estate loan was paid off along with revised accrued interest of $8,300.
b. Three months after Nancy's death, the gold market began to collapse, and the coins were sold for $250,000.
c. ExxonMobil stock was discovered. The stock had a value of $22,000 at Nancy's date of death and was subsequently sold for $23,000.
d. The bubble burst and four months after Nancy's death, the Google stock was sold for $780 per share.
e. The household effects were distributed to family and friends and are excluded from estate assets.
f. All remaining cash, including $21,000 of interest since Nancy's date of death, was distributed as follows: one-third to immediate family and the balance to the University of Georgia to endow a chaired professorship in the Theatre Department.

Required ▶ ▶ ▶ ▶ ▶   Determine the total amount to be paid for both estate and gift taxes over the 3-year period of 2010 through 2012 by year.

Problem 20-7 *(LO 4)* **Preparation of a charge and discharge statement.** Eleanor Matsun died on June 1 of the current year, leaving a valid will with James Madison being named as her personal representative. All of the following occurred in the year of her death:

a. The personal representative prepared the following inventory of assets at fair market value as of the date of death:

Cash	$ 31,000
1,000 Shares of Pal Corporation common stock at $60 per share	60,000
2,000 Shares of BVD Corporation common stock	40,000
Rapid Transit Corporation (RTC) 8% bonds, interest payable April 1 and October 1, $30,000 face value	30,300
Time share condominium unit at Lake Tahoe	25,000
50% Interest in Matsun Limo Service, a partnership	70,000
Personal residence	185,000

b. Subsequent to filing the above inventory with the court, the personal representative discovered the decedent's gold coin collection valued at $18,000.

c. On June 20, $2,500 was received from Pal Corporation for dividends declared on May 10 to shareholders of record on May 31.

d. On July 7, the time share condominium was sold for $30,000.

e. The following items were paid during the period from June 2 through July 31:

The decedent's charge card balances	$ 2,900
Funeral expenses	16,000
Legal fees to probate the will	2,500
Cost to remodel the personal residence prior to sale	13,000
Payment to the personal representative as approved by the court	4,000

f. On July 5, a check for $15,000 was received for the decedent's portion of Matsun Limo Service income earned during the quarter ended June 30. Income is assumed to be earned evenly over the quarter.

g. The decedent's partner in the limo service offered the personal representative $65,000 for the decedent's interest in the partnership. After much negotiation, the interest was sold for $80,000.

h. In mid-September, the decedent's personal residence was sold for $162,000, net of brokerage and closing costs totaling $15,000. The outstanding mortgage and accrued interest were promptly paid in the amount of $82,800. At the date of death, the mortgage balance along with accrued interest was $81,100.

i. On October 1, a check was received for interest on the RTC bonds.

j. On November 5, the decedent's income tax return for the year of death was filed and $6,400 of additional taxes was sent in with the return.

Prepare a charge and discharge statement as of December 31 of the current year. ◄ ◄ ◄ ◄ ◄ **Required**

Debt Restructuring, Corporate Reorganizations, and Liquidations

Learning Objectives

When you have completed this chapter, you should be able to

1. **Describe various ways in which debt may be restructured and how it impacts the debtor's financial records.**

2. **Explain why a company may decide to engage in a quasi-reorganization and how it impacts the company and its shareholders.**

3. **Explain various remedies available to a troubled enterprise under bankruptcy law and the steps followed in seeking a remedy.**

4. **Apply the principles of bankruptcy to the preparation of the statement of affairs.**

5. **Apply the principles of bankruptcy to the preparation of the statement of realization and liquidation.**

The principles of accounting are based on several important underlying assumptions, one of which is the going concern assumption. Since this assumption assumes that a business entity will have a long, extended life as a separate, distinct entity, valuation and classification of account balances are significantly influenced by it. For example, both the valuation of a building at depreciated historical cost, rather than net realizable value, and the classification of a building as a noncurrent asset, rather than a current asset, are in recognition of the going concern assumption. Certainly, without this assumption, all assets and liabilities would be classified as current in nature.

However, over time, the going concern assumption may not hold true for all business entities. An entity may voluntarily decide to cease its business purpose. For example, a research and development (R&D) venture may cease operations at the completion of a successful or unsuccessful R&D effort. Unfortunately, a business entity also may face difficulties that cause the going concern assumption to be challenged. A business may suffer from several factors, including poor management, poor accounting controls, uncontrolled growth, loss of market share, resistance to change, government intervention, and/or a declining profit margin. Although many businesses may be able to respond to these factors in a positive manner, other businesses may become troubled or insolvent and seek corrective action. A business is considered to be insolvent if it is unable to service its liabilities, or if it technically has liabilities in excess of assets. Businesses experiencing such difficulties often are viewed as bankrupt, which is a state of lacking all or part of the means to service debts. This chapter focuses on several corrective actions available to a troubled or insolvent business, including troubled debt restructurings, reorganizations, and liquidations.

No business is immune from the factors that may result in financial difficulty. Large, small, young, and mature companies alike may find themselves having to cope with such difficulties. Along with the expansion of business comes the inevitable fact that some businesses may become troubled and/or fail. These difficulties are an everyday occurrence affecting both young and mature companies. Exhibit 21-1 contains information suggesting the magnitude of business failures.

Exhibit 21-1
The Magnitude of Business Failures

A total of 43,546 and 60,837 businesses filed for bankruptcy in 2008 and 2009, respectively. Nonbusiness filings were 1,074,225 and 1,412,838 for 2008 and 2009, respectively.

The largest public company bankruptcy filings from the beginning of 2010 through November 8, 2010, include Ambac Financial Group with assets of almost $19 billion; Blockbuster, Inc., with assets of $1.523 billion; and any number of bank holding companies. The 20 largest bankruptcies from 1980 to the present include some familiar names with huge pre-bankruptcy assets. Consider the following examples:

Company	Pre-Bankruptcy Assets (in billions)
Lehman Brothers Holdings, Inc.	$691
Washington Mutual, Inc.	328
General Motors Corporation	91
Chrysler LLC	39
Texaco, Inc.	35

Source: http://www.bankruptcydata.com.

   The accounting profession is involved with troubled businesses in a variety of ways. Providing consulting services and sound financial planning and reporting, accountants may be of invaluable service in thwarting or managing the forces leading to financial difficulty. Accountants also provide an important discovery and reporting function for those businesses seeking relief from their financial difficulties.

RELIEF PROCEDURES NOT REQUIRING COURT ACTION

1

OBJECTIVE

Describe various ways in which debt may be restructured and how it impacts the debtor's financial records.

When a business becomes insolvent or is not able to service its debts on a timely basis, several remedies are available that do not require court approval. Since several of these remedies are discussed in intermediate textbooks, they will only be highlighted in this section. Seeking relief to financial problems outside of bankruptcy court offers several advantages. The time required to implement relief procedures is significantly less than the time required to seek relief through bankruptcy proceedings. Not requiring court action also allows the debtor's financial problems to be less public and more discreet. Knowledge of a company's financial troubles can adversely affect its ability to generate new business and acquire goods and services from vendors.

Troubled Debt Restructurings

A basic approach to resolving an inability to service debt is to seek some concessions or compromises from major creditors. A *troubled debt restructuring* is a process whereby creditors grant concessions to the debtor that they would not consider otherwise. However, both the debtor and creditor are faced with a difficult situation, and a restructuring offers the creditor the best opportunity to recover the debt, as compared to nonrestructuring alternatives.

   In a debt restructuring, it is not uncommon for the debtor to recognize a gain on the restructuring activity. Companies often engage in debt restructurings as part of their routine capital risk management; therefore, such restructurings are not unusual and/or nonrecurring. Furthermore, restructuring gains would not normally be recognized as an extraordinary item unless the criteria for recognition, unusual and nonrecurring in nature, as an extraordinary item are met.[1]

---

1 FASB ASC 470-50-45-45-1, *Debt—Modifications and Extinguishments—Other Presentation Matters—General.*

Although not all debt restructurings qualify as troubled debt restructurings, those that do generally take several forms. The most common forms of restructuring, along with the appropriate debtor accounting, are summarized in the sections that follow.

Transfer of Assets in Full Settlement

◆ Form: The debtor transfers assets, such as third-party receivables, real estate, and other assets, to the creditors in order to satisfy the debt either totally or partially.

◆ Accounting by Debtor: The debtor records a gain on restructuring measured by the excess of the carrying basis of the debt, including related accrued interest, premiums, etc., and the fair value of the transferred assets. The difference between the book value of assets transferred to the debtor and their fair value results in a gain or loss, which is not part of the gain on restructuring.

◆ Example: Assets with a book value of $100,000 and a fair value of $120,000 are transferred to a creditor in full settlement of a loan of $130,000 plus accrued interest of $2,000.

Loan Payable...	130,000	
Accrued Interest Payable...................................	2,000	
Gain on Assets..		20,000
Assets..		100,000
Gain on Restructuring		12,000

Granting an Equity Interest

◆ Form: Excluding existing terms for converting debt into equity (e.g., convertible debt), an equity interest in the company is granted to the creditor in order to satisfy the debt either totally or partially.

◆ Accounting by Debtor: The debtor records a gain on restructuring measured by the excess of the carrying basis of the debt and the fair value of the equity interest.

◆ Example: Preferred stock with a par value of $20,000 and a fair value of $120,000 is granted to a creditor in full settlement of a loan of $130,000 plus accrued interest of $2,000.

Loan Payable...	130,000	
Accrued Interest Payable...................................	2,000	
Preferred Stock (at par)		20,000
Paid-In Capital in Excess of Par		100,000
Gain on Restructuring		12,000

Modification of Terms

◆ Form: The terms of the debt are modified in several possible ways involving interest and/or principal. Interest rates may be reduced, and/or accrued interest may be reduced. The principal amount of the debt may be reduced and/or the maturity date of the loan may be extended.

◆ Accounting by Debtor: If the total future cash payments (both principal and interest) specified by the restructuring are less than the carrying basis of the debt, a gain on restructuring is recognized. After recognizing the gain, all subsequent cash payments made per the terms of the restructuring should be accounted for as a reduction of the debt payable. Therefore, no interest expense shall be recognized on the restructured debt. If the total future cash payments (both principal and interest) specified by the restructuring are more than the carrying basis of the debt, no gain on restructuring is recognized. However, interest expense is recognized between restructuring and maturity. The interest recognized should be based on an effective interest rate that equates the present value of restructured future cash payments to the carrying value of the debt.

- Example A: The terms of an outstanding debt of $130,000 plus accrued interest of $2,000 have been modified as follows: payments of $60,000 per year will be made over the next two years in full satisfaction of the debt.

Loan Payable.	130,000	
Accrued Interest Payable.	2,000	
Restructured Loan Payable.		120,000
Gain on Restructuring		12,000
Restructured Loan Payable.	60,000	
Cash		60,000
Restructured Loan Payable.	60,000	
Cash		60,000

- Example B: Same situation as Example A except that the payments are $76,057 each year, which results in an effective interest rate of 10%.

Loan Payable.	130,000	
Accrued Interest Payable.	2,000	
Restructured Loan Payable.		132,000
Restructured Loan Payable.	62,857	
Interest Expense (10% × $132,000)	13,200	
Cash		76,057
Restructured Loan Payable.	69,143	
Interest Expense (10% × $69,143).	6,914	
Cash		76,057

Combination Restructurings

- Form: A restructuring may involve some combination of the above restructuring features.
- Accounting by Debtor: The accounting for a combination restructuring is the same as discussed above except that first, the carrying basis of the debt should be reduced by the fair market value of assets transferred and/or equity interests granted. This step does not result in the recognition of a gain on restructuring. Second, the remaining carrying basis of the debt is compared against the "modification of terms" portion of the restructuring and accounted for accordingly.
- Example: Land with a fair value of $52,000 and a cost basis of $45,000 is transferred to a creditor in partial settlement of a debt of $130,000 plus accrued interest of $2,000. The balance of the debt is satisfied by the payment of $35,000 per year for each of the next two years.

Loan Payable.	50,000	
Accrued Interest Payable.	2,000	
Gain on Transfer of Land.		7,000
Land.		45,000
Loan Payable.	80,000	
Restructured Debt.		70,000
Gain on Restructuring		10,000
Restructured Debt.	35,000	
Cash		35,000
Restructured Debt.	35,000	
Cash		35,000

As seen from the previous examples, a troubled debt restructuring may be accomplished in a variety of ways. Regardless of the method used, a formal agreement must be reached between the debtor and individual creditors. Generally, such agreements take the form of a creditor agreement or a composition agreement. A creditor agreement is used to extend the terms of a debt or make other concessions regarding future interest rates. A composition agreement is used to scale down a creditor's claims against the debtor. For example, creditors might agree to accept $0.70 per dollar of debt owed to them.

Although the above discussion of troubled debt restructuring has focused on the necessary accounting by the debtor, special principles relate to the necessary accounting by the creditor. A creditor in a troubled debt restructuring, involving only a modification of terms of a receivable, should measure the loan receivable based on the present value of the expected future cash flows discounted at the loan's effective interest rate. The effective interest rate is based on the original contractual rate, not the rate in the restructuring agreement. The logic is that the restructured loan is not a new loan but rather the original loan that the creditor is attempting to recover. As a practical matter, the creditor may measure the loan receivable at the loan's observable market price or the fair value of the collateral, assuming the loan is collateral dependent. If the measure of the impaired loan receivable is less than the recorded investment in the loan, the difference is charged to bad debt expense and a valuation allowance is established.[2]

IASB PERSPECTIVES

International Accounting Standard 39 deals briefly with the topic of extinguishment of debt. If there is an exchange between an existing lender and a borrower of debt instruments with substantially different terms, the original debt should be extinguished and a new liability should be recognized. The substantial modification of terms on existing debt should also be given the same recognition. If the net present value of the cash flows on the new debt, using the original effective interest, is at least 10% different than the net present value of the original debt's remaining cash flows, the debt instruments are considered to have substantially different terms. The accounting for third-party costs or fees such as legal fees differs between the international standard and U.S. GAAP.

IASB *standards*

Quasi-Reorganizations

A corporation may not be insolvent and yet may have accumulated a relatively large deficit as a result of such problems as an excessive investment in plant assets or inventory, or management's inability to recognize and influence market demands. If management is replaced and if profits result from new policies, most state laws still will not permit declaration of dividends until the deficit is eliminated. The turnabout period and deficit elimination may take so long that the investors' interest in the company vanishes, and capital acquisition becomes difficult. To overcome such a handicap, the corporation might seek a *quasi-reorganization*.

Quasi-reorganization does not require court action, nor does it require the consent of creditors since creditor interests are not altered. However, the procedure is described in state laws, many of which require a quasi-reorganization to be approved by two-thirds of the stockholders. The accounting literature is not specific regarding the conditions under which a quasi-reorganization can occur. However, it was most frequently viewed as an approach that would allow for net assets to be reduced to lower fair values and a deficit in retained earnings to be eliminated. The Securities and Exchange Commission has set forth specific criteria which must be satisfied before a quasi-reorganization is accepted. Furthermore, SEC Staff Accounting Bulletin (SAB) No. 78 does not allow registrants to use this procedure just to eliminate a deficit in retained earnings. Net assets must also be restated, and the net result must be a write-down in value versus a write-up.

The primary purpose of a quasi-reorganization is to eliminate a large deficit and take such action as will permit successful operations in the future. Excessive plant capacity and equipment may be sold, and remaining assets and liabilities will be revalued to reflect their fair values. For example, long-lived assets will be written down to reflect an impairment in their value.[3] Such

2
OBJECTIVE

Explain why a company may decide to engage in a quasi-reorganization and how it impacts the company and its shareholders.

---

2 FASB ASC 310-40-35, *Receivables—Troubled Debt Restructurings by Creditors—Subsequent Measurement.*
3 FASB ASC 360-10-35, *Property, Plant and Equipment—Overall—Subsequent Measurement.*

revaluations most often increase the deficit in retained earnings. The deficit remaining after these revaluations must be reduced to zero.

It should be noted that the write-down of the assets increases the deficit, which then will be eliminated by subsequent changes in the capital structure.

The deficit is eliminated by charges against the existing paid-in capital in excess of par or stated values. If no such paid-in capital exists, it may be created by altering the capital structure and substituting stock with lower par value or lower stated value for existing shares. To illustrate the manner in which the owners' equity section in the balance sheet is revised by a quasi-reorganization, assume the following stockholders' equity:

Common stock ($10 par, 12,000 shares outstanding)	$120,000
Retained earnings (deficit)	(45,000)
Total stockholders' equity	$ 75,000

On March 1, 2010, the stockholders approve a reduction in par value to $1. Note that such a maneuver has absolutely no effect on the proportionate interests of each stockholder. The entries to record the quasi-reorganization are as follows:

Common Stock ($10 par)	120,000	
Common Stock ($1 par)		12,000
Paid-In Capital from Reduction in Stock Par Value		
(or Reorganization Capital)		108,000
To record the reduction in par value.		
Paid-In Capital from Reduction in Stock Par Value	45,000	
Retained Earnings		45,000
To eliminate the deficit.		

Immediately following the quasi-reorganization, the owners' equity section would show the following:

Common stock ($1 par, 12,000 shares outstanding)	$12,000
Paid-in capital from reduction in stock par value	63,000
Retained earnings (subsequent to March 1, 2010)	0
Total stockholders' equity	$75,000

In future financial statements, retained earnings must be dated to indicate the starting point of new accumulations. The process of dating retained earnings should be continued for as long a period of time as is deemed advisable, but rarely does it exceed 10 years.

Corporate Liquidations

A corporation may decide to liquidate its assets, distribute available amounts to creditors, and terminate the business. Such a liquidation may be accomplished without a formal bankruptcy proceeding through the use of a general assignment for the benefit of creditors, which generally must be agreed to by all creditors. Shareholders of the corporation receive any net assets remaining after fully satisfying the claims of creditors. Usually, assets are not adequate to fully satisfy creditor claims. In this case, creditors share according to the terms of the general assignment.

REFLECTION

- Troubled debt may be restructured in a number of ways, including forgiveness of debt, transfer of assets, granting an equity interest, and/or a modification of terms.

- If a company has a deficit in retained earnings and yet has opportunities for future profits, the deficit may prevent the timely distribution of such profits in the form of dividends. A quasi-reorganization is designed to eliminate the deficit in retained earnings and provide the company with a fresh start.

SOLUTIONS AVAILABLE THROUGH THE BANKRUPTCY CODE

3

OBJECTIVE

Explain various remedies available to a troubled enterprise under bankruptcy law and the steps followed in seeking a remedy.

If a satisfactory solution cannot be reached out of court or through applicable state laws, perhaps under the procedures described in the previous paragraphs, the legal proceedings for a federal bankruptcy case may be initiated. Modern bankruptcy procedures attempt to give a debtor a fresh start, unburdened by former obligations, while simultaneously accomplishing an equitable distribution of the debtor's property among creditors.

In an attempt to modernize an antiquated system existing under the Bankruptcy Act of 1898, as amended by the Chandler Act of 1938, Congress passed the Bankruptcy Reform Act of 1978 (Title 11 of the U.S. Code), which became effective on October 1, 1979. The 1978 Act has been amended on multiple occasions (in 1988, 1990, and 1994) and most recently by the Bankruptcy Abuse Prevention and Consumer Protection Act of 2005. A bankruptcy case may be filed under one of the operative chapters of the Code. Although certain provisions of the bankruptcy law deal with issues involving individuals seeking protection under the law, only issues involving larger businesses will be discussed in this section of the text. Chapters of the Code that are most applicable to businesses are as follows:

Chapter 7: Liquidation. A nonbusiness debtor or any business not wishing to remain in operation, except a railroad, governmental unit, bank, insurance company, or savings and loan association, may file a petition under this chapter.

Chapter 11: Reorganization. The purpose of Chapter 11 is to allow a company (or an individual) to pay a portion of its debts, discharge remaining debts, and continue in business. This chapter is used primarily by corporate or partnership debtors. Although the chapter may be used by an individual proprietor, the procedures are more cumbersome and more expensive than those of Chapter 13. Only individuals with substantial assets and liabilities resort to Chapter 11 proceedings.

Chapter 13: Adjustment of Debts of an Individual with Regular Income. This chapter is limited exclusively to individuals, including sole proprietors, and allows the debtor to retain assets and propose a plan by which creditors can be repaid.

There are provisions for the movement or conversion of a case from one chapter to another, such as converting an unsuccessful reorganization (Chapter 11) to a liquidation (Chapter 7). This section of the text will focus on reorganizations (Chapter 11) and liquidations (Chapter 7).

Commencement of a Bankruptcy Case

The Act states that a debtor either must be a person (individual, partnership, or corporation) residing in or having a domicile, business, or property in the United States. If a debtor initiates the action of filing a petition with the court of bankruptcy under the appropriate chapter of the Act, it is *a voluntary case.* Filing constitutes an *order for relief,* which represents a stay of action known as an *automatic stay.* The filing will stay or prohibit the following proceedings against the debtor: commencement or continuation of legal actions, repossession, foreclosure, and creditor harassment. In essence, the debtor is given time during which negotiations can occur to resolve the debtor's financial situation.

If the petition is filed by someone other than the debtor, an involuntary proceeding results. Even if a debtor is not insolvent, a petition may be filed against them if they are not typically paying their debts as they become due. Certain parties (such as farmers or a corporation that is not a moneyed, business, or commercial corporation) may not have an involuntary petition filed against them. An involuntary petition may be filed under *Chapter 7 (Liquidation)* or *Chapter 11 (Reorganization),* but not under *Chapter 13,* where the individual debtor is willing to make payments to creditors. Certain small businesses are allowed to use streamlined ("fast track") procedures in order to facilitate a solution to bankruptcy issues. Under Chapters 7 and 11, three or more of them may file an involuntary petition, providing the total of their noncontingent, unsecured claims is over a proscribed dollar amount.[4] If there are less than 12 creditors, one or more of them may initiate an involuntary case, but the same dollar limit applies. In an

---

4 Currently, per Section 303 of the Bankruptcy Code, the undisputed claims must aggregate at least $10,000 more than the value of a lien on the debtor's assets that serve as collateral on the debt held by such creditors.

involuntary case, the claims must have arisen before the order for relief was issued. The court will issue such an order if the debtor files no answer to the involuntary petition. If an answer is filed by the debtor, the court will hold a hearing, following which it will either dismiss the case, issue an order for relief, or postpone the decision pending receipt of additional information.

Corporate Reorganizations—Chapter 11

The ultimate goal of a reorganization is to restructure the debt and/or equity of a company so that the company may continue to carry on its business purpose and become a financially sound business. Unfortunately, the vast majority of reorganizations never achieve this goal. Such a reorganization often is more attractive than a debt restructuring not involving a bankruptcy proceeding because the reorganization may be more generous toward the debtor company. Generally, a reorganization reduces debt through forgiveness to a greater extent than a conventional debt restructuring. Furthermore, interest on unsecured debt is not accrued during the period of reorganization. The period of reorganization provides a company with an opportunity to delay creditors from bringing suit for delinquent debts as well as to seek protection from a variety of business risks, which may affect a company's ability to continue as a going concern. Companies have used Chapter 11 procedures to gain court protection for a broad spectrum of purposes.

Developing a Plan of Reorganization. A petition seeking a corporate reorganization may be filed voluntarily or involuntarily to seek an order for relief. Normally, the debtor remains in charge of the business, although in unusual instances, a trustee (receiver) may be appointed to take control of the company. Those unusual instances include management fraud, deceit, and/or gross mismanagement.

After the filing of the petition, the law provides that the debtor shall not be harassed by creditors or stockholders so that the debtor can devote full energy to the reorganization. For the first 120 days, the debtor has the exclusive right to file a plan of reorganization. Thereafter, a plan may be filed by any party of interest. However, if the debtor's plan has not been accepted within 180 days, then any party of interest may file a plan. The court appoints a committee of the unsecured creditors typically consisting of the creditors holding the seven largest claims against the debtor. A committee of equity security holders or other specialized classes of creditors also may be appointed. Their primary functions are to consult with the debtor in possession (or the trustee) about the administration of the case and to assist in the formulation of a plan of reorganization.

The plan of reorganization must detail the methods and means by which it will achieve its objectives. Possible arrangements will involve eliminating some debt, reducing debt principal and/or interest, reducing interest rates, postponing payment, and exchanging an equity interest for creditor claims or exchanging a lower ranking for a higher equity interest, such as substitution of common stock for preferred stock. The plan identifies the various classes of claims (secured versus unsecured) and classes of interests (stockholders or limited partners). It indicates the claims of interests (stockholders or limited partners), as well as the claims or interests that are not impaired, as well as the treatment to be accorded those that are impaired. A class is impaired if the plan alters its legal or contractual rights, it does not cure the debtor's default, or the class has not already been paid.

If a class is not impaired, it is considered to have accepted the plan. The holder of a claim or interest impaired by the plan may accept or reject it. Parties impaired are provided a description of the reorganization plan along with a court-approved disclosure statement regarding the plan. After evaluating the plan, the affected parties must vote to approve or reject it; it is important to note that the voting is done by classes of claim holders. A plan affecting impaired creditors is accepted if a favorable vote is received from creditors representing at least two-thirds of the dollar amount of the class's claims and more than 50% of those voting have voted in favor of the plan. A plan affecting shareholders or equity interests is accepted if a favorable vote is received by those holding at least two-thirds in amount of the outstanding securities held by the class.

Upon approval by the impaired parties, confirmation by the bankruptcy court is sought. Before confirmation, the court verifies that under the plan each holder of a claim or interest will receive or retain property of a value that is not less than the amount such a holder would receive under a Chapter 7 liquidation. In certain instances, courts have the authority to approve the plan even though the creditors have not approved it (the cram-down provision).

Once a plan is confirmed by the court, its provisions are binding on the debtor, known as a "debtor in possession," and on all creditors and equity security holders, whether or not they accepted the plan. Confirmation vests property in the debtor company or trustee. Such property is free of all claims of creditors and interests of equity holders, except as stipulated in the provisions of the plan. Under Chapter 11, once a plan is confirmed, the payment obligation on the debtor is fixed, regardless of any subsequent increase in the debtor's net cash inflow. If the reorganization is not accomplishing its intended objectives during the period outlined in the plan, a request for modification may be submitted to the court for approval, or a request may be filed to convert to a Chapter 7 liquidation.

Accounting for the Reorganization. The accounting professional is involved significantly in providing expertise regarding corporate reorganizations. Accountants may help in the discovery of assets and liabilities or in the determination of the impact of a reorganization. Prospective information also must be generated in order to determine the effect of a reorganization plan on future operations of the company. A plan of reorganization includes debt and/or equity restructuring similar to that discussed in the earlier section of this text involving troubled debt restructurings and quasi-reorganizations.

Restructuring of Debt. With respect to the restructuring of debt in a bankruptcy reorganization, the principles set forth in FASB ASC 470 do not apply to a bankruptcy reorganization; therefore, a different approach is used to measure the gain or loss on restructuring involving a modification of terms. In a bankruptcy reorganization, the gain on restructuring is measured as the difference between the fair value of the restructured consideration received (its discounted present value) and the carrying basis of the debt being restructured. In FASB ASC 470, the gain on restructuring is measured as the difference between the total future cash payments (both principal and interest) to be received and the carrying basis of the debt being restructured. The gain on restructuring in a bankruptcy reorganization is recorded separately as a reorganization item on the income statement.

The recognition of subsequent interest on the restructured debt also differs for a bankruptcy reorganization. In this case, the total interest recognized on the restructured debt is imputed at market rates and represents the difference between the fair value of the new debt (its discounted present value using market rates) and the total of all principal and interest payments. The FASB accounting for the restructuring measures the total interest as the difference between the carrying basis of the debt being restructured and the total of all principal and interest payments. Therefore, under FASB principles, no interest is recognized if the total of all principal and interest payments made under the restructuring agreement do not exceed the carrying basis of the original debt being restructured.

Generally, the books of record used to account for the company prior to reorganization also are employed during the reorganization. However, if a trustee is appointed, the trustee may elect to establish a new set of books. While the trustee is in control, the corporation's financial story is contained partly in the records of the trustee and partly in those of the corporation. The two records, after all necessary adjusting entries, must be combined in order to produce a trial balance for the entity being reorganized.

Statement of Position (SOP) 90-7. Statement of Position (SOP) 90-7, *Financial Reporting by Entities in Reorganization Under the Bankruptcy Code*, was issued by the American Institute of Certified Public Accountants (AICPA) to provide specific guidance regarding generally accepted accounting principles to be followed by entities that have filed and expect to reorganize under Chapter 11 of the Bankruptcy Code or have emerged from Chapter 11 under a confirmed plan of reorganization.[5] The Statement only applies to reorganizations under the Bankruptcy Code and therefore does not apply to liquidations under the Code or other forms of restructurings/reorganizations outside of Chapter 11. Several technical topics are addressed by the Statement including deferred taxes, interest income/expense, net operating loss carryforwards, goodwill, professional fees, and reporting/disclosure requirements.

Modifications to normal financial statement presentation are required by this SOP. For example, balance sheets must distinguish between prepetition liabilities subject to compromise and those that are not compromised and postpetition liabilities. Prepetition liabilities should be reported at the amounts allowed by the court. The income statement should disclose revenues, expenses, gains, and losses traceable to the reorganization separately as reorganization items. Even the statement of cash flows should separately disclose the impact of reorganization items.

---

5 Statement of Position 90-7, *Financial Reporting by Entities in Reorganization Under the Bankruptcy Code* (New York: American Institute of Certified Public Accountants, 1990).

This SOP also addresses fresh-start accounting which must be adopted by certain debtors emerging from Chapter 11. Fresh-start accounting involves reporting balance sheet items at current values and eliminating all prior retained earnings or deficits. In order to determine if fresh-start accounting is required, an entity must determine its "reorganized value." This value is the fair value of the assets of the reorganized entity plus the net realizable value of assets to be disposed of before the reorganization and focuses on the asset side of the balance sheet, rather than the liability and equity side, to determine value. The reorganization value approximates the amount that a willing buyer would pay for the entity's assets immediately after restructuring. The value is generally based on discounted future cash flows for the reorganized entity and from the expected cash proceeds traceable to assets not required in the reorganized entity. Fresh-start accounting will be required if (a) the reorganized value, immediately before the date the reorganization plan is confirmed, is less than the value of the liability claims against the entity (postpetition and prepetition allowed claims) and (b) original voting shareholders retain less than 50% of the voting shares of the reorganized entity.

As a result of fresh-start accounting, the following should occur:

◆ The reorganization value should be allocated to the entity's tangible and intangible assets including goodwill.

◆ Liabilities other than deferred taxes should be reported at their present values based on appropriate current interest rates.

◆ Benefits realized from the application of prepetition net operating losses should be given special accounting treatment, possibly impacting goodwill and paid-in capital in excess of par.

◆ The new reorganized fresh-start entity should have no beginning retained earnings or deficit.

◆ Notes to the financial statements should disclose various information regarding the fresh-start including but not limited to debt forgiveness, asset value adjustments, methods of measurement, and significant assumptions.

Corporate Liquidations—Chapter 7

The only solution for certain insolvent companies is to liquidate the assets of the company, service its debts, distribute any remaining funds to shareholders, and terminate the business. Unfortunately, corporate reorganizations frequently are not successful and ultimately result in liquidation. Commencement of a plan to liquidate may be voluntary or involuntary. Approval of the plan is subject to the same requirements as a reorganization. The commencement of a voluntary or involuntary case under Chapter 7 (Liquidation) creates an estate that consists of the assets of the debtor. Periodic filings containing an inventory of property and debts/claims must be filed with the bankruptcy court.

Appointment of a Trustee in Liquidation. As soon as possible after issuing the order for relief, the court appoints an interim trustee to take charge until a permanent trustee is selected, and then a meeting of creditors is called. Creditors either may elect a permanent trustee or have the interim trustee serve in that capacity. Proofs of claim are examined by the trustee, who may accept them or, if they are improper, disallow them. To be considered in the settlement, a claim normally must be filed within 90 days after the date set for the first meeting of creditors.

The debtor is required to be present at the meeting of creditors in order to be subject to examination by the creditors or the trustee and must cooperate with the trustee in the preparation of an inventory of property, the examination of proofs of claim, and the general administration of the estate. To assist the trustee, a debtor files a *statement of affairs*, consisting of answers to a series of stated questions about the identity of the debtor's records and books, transactions, and events affecting the financial condition of the debtor, including any prior bankruptcy proceedings. This legal statement of affairs is not to be confused with the accounting statement of affairs discussed later in the chapter.

Duties of Trustee. The trustee shall:

1. Collect and reduce to money the nonexempt property of the estate.
2. Account for all money and property received, maintaining a record of cash receipts and disbursements.

3. Investigate the financial affairs of the debtor, including a review of the forms filed by the debtor.

4. Examine proofs of claim and disallow any improper claim.

5. Furnish information reasonably requested by a party of interest.

6. Operate the business of the debtor, if any, when so authorized by the court if such operation is in the best interest of the estate and consistent with its orderly liquidation.

7. Pay dividends to creditors as promptly as practicable, with regard for priorities. (The law applies the term "dividend" to any payment made to a creditor.)

8. File reports of progress, with the final report accompanied by a detailed statement of receipts and disbursements.

Disposition of Property. One duty of the trustee is to dispose of property, even if another entity has an allowed claim secured by a lien on the property. The claim is secured to the amount of the value of the property. For example, if a creditor has an allowed claim of $20,000, with a sole lien against real property whose fair value is $30,000, the claim is fully secured. Upon realization of the property, the excess of $10,000 would be available to meet unsecured claims in the order of priority. If the creditor in the example has an allowed claim of $35,000, there is a secured claim of $30,000 and an unsecured claim of $5,000.

Priorities for Unsecured Claims. An order of priority to receive distributions from amounts available to meet unsecured claims has been established by the Act and the priority is relevant to both reorganizations and liquidations. Each class must be paid in full or provided for before any amount is paid to the next lower class. When the amount is inadequate to pay all claims of a given class, the amount is distributed on a pro rata basis within that class. When the amount is sufficient to pay the claims of all classes, which is highly unlikely, the excess amount is returned to the debtor. Although not inclusive, major categories of unsecured claims having priority against a business (presented in order of priority) are as follows:[6]

♦ Expenses to administer the estate. Those who administer the estate should be assured of payment; otherwise, competent attorneys and accountants would not be willing to participate.

♦ Debts incurred after the commencement of a case of involuntary bankruptcy but before the order for relief or appointment of a trustee. These items, referred to as "gap" creditors, are granted priority in order to permit the business to carry on its operations during the period of legal proceedings.

♦ Wages, salaries, or commissions (including vacation, severance, and sick leave pay) up to $10,000 per individual or corporation, earned within 180 days before the filing of the petition or the cessation of the debtor's business, whichever occurs first.

♦ Unpaid contributions to employee benefit plans, arising from services performed up to 180 days prior to filing the petition or the cessation of business, to the extent of $10,000 per employee times the number of employees covered by such a plan less the aggregate amount paid to such employees per the above bullet point.

♦ Claims of grain producers and fishermen against storage and/or processing facilities.

♦ Deposits up to $1,800 each for goods or services never received from the debtor.

♦ Certain tax claims of a governmental unit. These taxes are nondischargeable (i.e., they still must be met by the debtor after the termination of the case).

♦ Claims based on any commitment of the debtor to a federal depository institution regulatory agency to maintain the capital of an insured depository institution.

♦ Claims of general creditors not granted priority. All remaining unsecured claims fall into this category.

It is important to note that although the goal of liquidation is to discharge debts, certain debts are not dischargeable. For example, certain taxes, fines, and/or penalties are nondischargeable.

---

6 For additional details, see U.S. Code, Title 11, Chapter 5, Subchapter I, Section 507 "Priorities."

REFLECTION

- Bankruptcy law provides for various remedies: liquidation and reorganization are the most frequently used solutions. A company must carry out, voluntarily or involuntarily, a number of steps when seeking a remedy. The claims of various parties must be identified and prioritized.

<table>
<tr><td>**4**</td></tr>
<tr><td>**OBJECTIVE**</td></tr>
</table>

Apply the principles of bankruptcy to the preparation of the statement of affairs.

PREPARATION OF THE STATEMENT OF AFFAIRS

Earlier in this chapter, a reference was made to the legal statement of affairs, which consists of responses to questions regarding a debtor's financial condition. The other report with the same name is the accounting statement of affairs, which is discussed in this section of the chapter. The primary purpose of the *accounting statement of affairs* is to approximate the estimated amounts available to each class of claims. It thereby assists all concerned parties in reaching a decision as to what insolvency action is preferable. It is a balance sheet of a potentially liquidating concern rather than of a going concern. Thus, it shifts the emphasis for assets to estimated realizable values and the allocation of proceeds to creditors and stockholders. It is important to note that the statement of affairs is based on estimated values available to creditors, and the actual values realized from the liquidation of assets may differ. Although the statement assumes a liquidation of the insolvent company, the statement also is used to evaluate the reasonableness of a corporate reorganization. Plans for a corporate reorganization will not be confirmed by the court unless creditors will receive at least as much as they would under liquidation.

The statement of affairs is split into two sections, one dealing with assets and the other with liabilities and owners' equity. Before the statement of affairs is prepared, however, the account balances should be adjusted fully, an income statement should be prepared, and owners' equity should be adjusted to include the net profit or net loss to date.

The asset portion of the statement of affairs identifies the assets of the liquidating entity and their book value, estimated net realizable value, and estimated gain or loss upon liquidation. Available assets are identified as follows:

1. Assets pledged with fully secured creditors.
2. Assets pledged with partially secured creditors.
3. Free assets available to unsecured creditors.

For each asset, the net realizable value must be estimated, using whatever information is available. For example, receivables would exclude unrealizable amounts; marketable securities would be based on current market reports; and real estate would reflect current market appraisals. Some assets, such as goodwill, may have no realizable value. For each asset, the difference between realizable value and book value is entered as a gain or loss upon liquidation. The assets available to unsecured creditors also are identified on the asset section of the statement of affairs.

The liability and owners' equity section on the statement of affairs identifies the following components:

1. Fully secured creditors.
2. Partially secured creditors.
3. Unsecured creditors with priority.
4. Unsecured creditors without priority.
5. Owners' equity deficiency or surplus.

In order to illustrate the statement of affairs, assume Insolve Corporation's adjusted balance sheet as of February 28, is as appears in Illustration 21-1.

Prior to liquidation, management has decided to complete the work in process by incurring $12,000 of additional labor costs and $4,000 of additional overhead. It is expected that, upon completion, the additional finished goods can be sold for $94,000. The mortgage payable is secured by the land and building, and the bank loan is secured by the equipment. Accounts payable totaling $180,000 are secured by inventory with a book value of $180,000 and an estimated net realizable value of $160,000.

Illustration 21-1
Insolve Corporation
Balance Sheet
February 28

Assets

Current assets:			
Cash		$ 4,000	
Accounts receivable	$ 84,000		
Less allowance for uncollectible accounts	(14,000)	70,000	
Marketable securities		20,000	
Inventories:			
Raw materials	$ 35,000		
Work in process	63,000		
Finished goods	124,000	222,000	$316,000
Property, plant, and equipment:			
Land		$ 110,000	
Building		340,000	
Less accumulated depreciation—building		(158,000)	
		290,000	
Equipment		290,000	
Less accumulated depreciation—equipment		(140,000)	442,000
Goodwill (net of amortization)			48,000
Total assets			$806,000

Liabilities and Owners' Equity

Current liabilities:		
Accounts payable	$240,000	
Accrued liabilities—other	12,000	
Accrued income taxes	6,000	
Accrued mortgage interest	24,000	
Accrued liquidation expenses	13,000	
Accrued payroll taxes	14,000	
Accrued payroll (not exceeding $4,000 per person)	33,000	$342,000
Long-term liabilities:		
Mortgage payable	$280,000	
Bank loan payable	200,000	480,000
Total liabilities		$822,000
Owners' equity:		
Common stock	$ 10,000	
Paid-in capital in excess of par	40,000	
Deficit	(66,000)	(16,000)
Total liabilities and owners' equity		$806,000

The statement of affairs for Insolve Corporation is based on assumed net realizable amounts and appears as Illustration 21-2.

There are several important things to note about the mechanics of the statement of affairs. First, the two major sections of the statement (Assets and Liabilities and Owners' Equity) should be completed in conjunction with each other. For example, when identifying assets pledged with partially secured creditors, the secured and unsecured amounts of liabilities to such creditors should be identified. Second, the statement is constructed to provide crossfootings as a check

Illustration 21-2
Insolve Corporation
Statement of Affairs
February 28

Book Value	Assets	Estimated Net Realizable Value	Estimated Amount Available for Unsecured Creditors	Estimated Gain or (Loss) on Liquidation
	Assets pledged with fully secured creditors:			
$110,000	Land.	$130,000		$ 20,000
182,000	Building (net)	210,000		28,000
	Total.	$340,000	$ 36,000	
	Assets pledged with partially secured creditors:			
150,000	Equipment (net)	$118,000		(32,000)
	Inventory			
35,000	Raw materials	18,000		(17,000)
63,000	Work in process (less estimated completion costs of $16,000)	78,000		15,000
124,000	Finished goods	112,000		(12,000)
	Total.	$326,000	48,000	
	Free assets:			
4,000	Cash	$ 4,000	4,000	
70,000	Accounts receivable (net)	70,000	70,000	
20,000	Marketable securities	14,000	14,000	(6,000)
48,000	Goodwill			(48,000)
	Estimated amount available for unsecured creditors with and without priority.		$172,000	
	Less unsecured creditors with priority		(66,000)	
	Estimated amounts for unsecured creditors without priority:			
	Net realizable amount available.		$106,000	
	Deficiency (to agree with total unsecured amount without priority) . . .		68,000	
$806,000	Totals	$754,000	$174,000	$ (52,000)
	Fully secured creditors:			
$ 24,000	Accrued mortgage interest.	$ 24,000		
280,000	Mortgage payable	280,000		
	Total.	$304,000		
	Partially secured creditors:			
200,000	Bank loan payable.	$118,000		$ 82,000
180,000	Accounts payable	160,000		20,000
	Total.	$278,000		
	Unsecured creditors with priority:			
6,000	Accrued income taxes		$ 6,000	
13,000	Accrued liquidation expenses		13,000	
14,000	Accrued payroll taxes		14,000	
33,000	Accrued payroll		33,000	
	Unsecured creditors without priority:			
12,000	Accrued liabilities—other			12,000
60,000	Accounts payable			60,000
$822,000	Totals	$582,000	$ 66,000	$174,000
(16,000)	Owners' deficiency			
$806,000				

on the mathematical accuracy and completeness of the schedule. For example, in the asset section the book value of the assets should equal the assets' estimated net realizable value plus (minus) the estimated loss (gain) on liquidation ($806,000 = $754,000 + $52,000). In the liabilities and owners' equity section, the book value total before the owners' deficiency should equal the total of estimated secured and unsecured liabilities ($822,000 = $582,000 + $66,000 + $174,000). Finally, the deficiency traceable to unsecured creditors without priority ($68,000) should equal the difference between the estimated net realizable value of the assets and the total of estimated secured and unsecured amounts due creditors ($68,000) = $754,000 − ($582,000 + $66,000 + $174,000). This deficiency represents the extent to which the net realizable value of assets is inadequate to meet the claims of creditors. Certainly, if the net realizable value of such assets exceeded the creditors' claims, the excess would be available to satisfy the claims of owners/shareholders.

Of interest to the unsecured creditors without priority and the bankruptcy court is a ratio that is referred to as the dividend to general unsecured creditors. This ratio is computed as follows:

$$\text{Dividend} = \frac{\text{Net Proceeds Available to Unsecured Creditors Without Priority}}{\text{Total Claims of Unsecured Creditors Without Priority}}$$

The dividend is an estimate of how much will be received by unsecured creditors without priority for each dollar owed to them, and it is expressed either in absolute amount or in percentage form.

The approximate dividend to unsecured creditors without priority of Insolve Corporation will be computed as follows:

$$\frac{\$106,000}{\$174,000} = \$0.61 \text{ on one dollar, or } 61\%$$

REFLECTION

- The statement of affairs identifies the various assets of a troubled enterprise and their net realizable values. These values are then applied toward the claims of various secured and unsecured creditors.

PREPARATION OF OTHER ACCOUNTING REPORTS

5

OBJECTIVE

Apply the principles of bankruptcy to the preparation of the statement of realization and liquidation.

The trustee appointed to a company in liquidation is expected to make periodic reports to the bankruptcy court regarding the activities of the trustee. In the absence of specific reporting requirements imposed by the Act, each bankruptcy court identifies the type of accounting reports to be submitted by the trustee.

Generally speaking, a court will require the trustee to provide an accounting regarding the following items pertaining to the insolvent company:

1. Unrealized assets assigned to the trustee including those subsequently discovered.
2. Assets that have been realized or liquidated.
3. Liabilities to be liquidated that have been assigned to the trustee.
4. Liabilities that have been liquidated.

The preceding information may be presented in a worksheet format that identifies critical balances and relevant cash receipts and disbursements. We will refer to this worksheet as the *statement of realization and liquidation.*

The statement of realization and liquidation differs from the statement of affairs in the following respects:

1. The statement of realization and liquidation reports the actual liquidation results. In contrast, the statement of affairs is of a pro forma nature and is based on estimated rather than actual results.

2. The statement of realization and liquidation provides an ongoing reporting of the trustee's activities and is updated throughout the liquidation process. The statement of affairs is a summary of the estimated results of a completed liquidation.

In order to illustrate the preparation of a statement of realization and liquidation, the balance sheet of Insolve Corporation, which was presented in Illustration 21-1, will be used as a starting point. Assuming the assets and liabilities contained in Insolve's balance sheet were assigned to the trustee, a statement of realization and liquidation for the period March 1 to March 31, is presented in Illustration 21-3. In reviewing this illustration, note that it reports actual results rather than estimated amounts, as contained in the statement of affairs. Also note that the statement reports liquidation activity to date and may be updated to reflect subsequent activity.

Illustration 21-3
Insolve Corporation
Statement of Realization and Liquidation
For Period March 1 to March 31

| | Assets | | Liabilities | | | | |
| | | | | | Unsecured | | |
	Cash	Noncash	Fully Secured	Partially Secured	With Priority	Without Priority	Owners' Equity
Beginning balances, assigned March 1	$ 4,000	$ 802,000	$304,000	$ 380,000	$66,000	$ 72,000	$(16,000)
Subsequently discovered and other items:							
Assets		15,000*					15,000
Loans from officers						20,000*	(20,000)
Additional liquidation expenses[a]					2,000		(2,000)
Cash receipts:							
Sale of marketable securities	16,000*	(20,000)					(4,000)
Partial collection of accounts receivable	52,000	(52,000)					
Sale of equipment	124,000*	(150,000)					(26,000)
Sale of inventory[b]	134,000*	(148,000)					(14,000)
Cash disbursements:							
Partial payment of bank loan[c]	(124,000)			(200,000)		76,000	
Partial payment of accounts payable[d]	(98,000)			(135,000)		37,000	
Ending balances	$ 108,000	$ 447,000	$304,000	$ 45,000	$68,000	$205,000	$(67,000)

*These amounts differ from the estimated amounts included in the statement of affairs.
[a]Liquidation expenses were originally estimated to be $13,000. However, actual liquidation expenses to date total $15,000.
[b]The sale of inventory consists of the following:

	Book Value	Amount Realized
Raw materials	$ 35,000	$ 18,000
Work in process (less completion costs of $18,000)	63,000	76,000
Finished goods	50,000	40,000
	$148,000	$134,000

[c]The bank loan of $200,000 is secured by the equipment, which was disposed of for $124,000, net of expenses. Therefore, $76,000 of the loan is reclassified as an unsecured liability.
[d]The sale of inventory described in footnote b included inventory securing the accounts payable. This inventory had a book value of $135,000 and was sold for $98,000. Therefore, accounts payable with a value of $135,000 were secured only to the extent of $98,000. The unsecured portion of $37,000 ($135,000 − $98,000) is reclassified as such.

The statement also may be used to reassess the effect of liquidation on various claims of liabilities. For example, as of March 31, Insolve Corporation still has $447,000 of noncash assets to be realized. A statement of these assets and their newly revised estimated net realizable values follows:

Noncash Assets	Book Value	Estimated Net Realizable Value
Accounts receivable (net)	$ 18,000	$ 18,000
Inventories	74,000	70,000*
Land	110,000	130,000
Building (net)	182,000	210,000
Goodwill	48,000	0
Assets subsequently discovered	15,000	17,000
Total assets	$447,000	$445,000

*$44,000 of this amount is traceable to partially secured accounts payable.

The estimated net realizable value of noncash assets of $445,000 plus the available existing cash of $108,000 represents a total of $553,000, which would be available to satisfy liabilities and owners' equity. A tentative distribution of this total follows:

Liabilities and Owners' Equity	Book Value	Estimated Distribution	Dividend (Payout) Percentage
Fully secured liabilities	$304,000	$304,000	100%
Partially secured liabilities:			
Book value of $45,000 less unsecured portion of $1,000 .	44,000	44,000	100
Unsecured liabilities:			
With priority	68,000	68,000	100
Without priority:			
Book value of $205,000 plus unsecured portion of			
partially secured liabilities	206,000	137,000	67
Owners' equity (deficit)	(67,000)		
Total liabilities and owners' equity	$555,000	$553,000	

Although corporate reorganizations and liquidations are significantly influenced by law, the accounting profession also may be significantly involved in the entire process. Accountants assist in the identification and valuation of assets and liabilities traceable to the insolvent company. The activities of a company involved in a Chapter 11 reorganization or a Chapter 7 liquidation must be periodically reported to the bankruptcy courts. This periodic reporting function is a major area involving the expertise of the accounting profession.

REFLECTION

- The statement of realization and liquidation accounts for various events undertaken to liquidate an enterprise. The statement reports the disposition of assets and the application of proceeds to the settlement of various creditor claims.

UNDERSTANDING THE ISSUES

1. If a debt is restructured through a modification of terms, explain how the gain on restructuring is determined when the restructuring is not under bankruptcy law versus one that is.

2. Distinguish between a corporate reorganization and a liquidation as provided for under bankruptcy law.

3. Explain how the claims of fully secured and partially secured creditors affect the dividend that may be received by unsecured creditors.

4. Explain what purpose the statement of realization and liquidation serves.

EXERCISES

Exercise 1 *(LO 1)* **Troubled debt restructurings, impact on earnings.** Ridgeway Builders, Inc., is in the residential construction industry and has been experiencing a business downturn. As a result of these economic conditions, the company is having difficulty serving its outstanding debt and is seeking relief outside of the bankruptcy courts. The following summarizes outstanding debt and management's proposed restructuring:

| | Outstanding Debt | | | |
	A	B	C	D
Stated interest rate.	6%	8%	10%	6%
Unpaid principal	$80,000	$500,000	$320,000	$340,000
Accrued interest.	4,000	20,000	8,000	10,000
Total amount due	$84,000	$520,000	$328,000	$350,000
Components of restructuring				
Transfer of assets:				
Book value of assets	60,000	100,000		40,000
Market value of assets	80,000	120,000		48,339
Issuance of common stock:				
At par value.		240,000		
At market value		380,000		
Revised semiannual payments:				
Amount of payment	—	—	75,000	64,000
Number of payments	—	—	4	5

For each of the above debts, determine the gain or loss on restructuring and the interest expense to be recognized for the 6-month period after the restructuring.

Exercise 2 *(LO 1)* **Impact of restructuring on the income statement.** Cutler Manufacturing manufactures and distributes specialty piping used in the construction industry. Due to the recent contraction in the commercial construction market, Cutler has had difficulty servicing its outstanding debt. In particular, debt bearing interest at a stated rate of 6.00% with 42 remaining payments of $15,000 per month is being considered for restructuring. The creditor and Cutler have identified the following two alternatives:

a. Alternative A: Convey vacant land with a fair market value of $380,000 and a book value of $260,000 to the creditor along with a commitment to make 40 monthly payments of $5,067.60 each. The market rate of interest for a loan with similar characteristics is 6.24%.

b. Alternative B: Convey vacant land with a fair market value of $380,000 and a book value of $260,000 to the creditor along with a commitment to make 60 monthly payments of $3,000 each. The market rate of interest for a loan with similar characteristics is 6.60%.

For each of the above restructuring alternatives, determine the impact on Cutler's income statement for the first two months of the restructuring period.

Exercise 3 *(LO 1, 2)* **Effect of a quasi-reorganization.** For the last several years, Manion Corporation has encountered a declining market for its major product line. Attempts to diversify have led to additional disappointments. This unfortunate set of circumstances has left the company with significant debt and an inability to service its debt. The existing debt consists of $20,000,000 of principal and $875,000 of accrued interest. Discussions with the creditors have resulted in a proposed restructuring of debt. The restructuring would consist of the following actions:

a. Exchanging preferred stock with a fair value of $5,100,000 and a par value of $5,000,000 in exchange for full settlement of $5,500,000 of principal debt.
b. Exchanging land with a value of $4,000,000 and a book value of $3,000,000 in exchange for $4,500,000 of principal debt.
c. The remaining debt and accrued interest would be repaid over the next 10 years with semi-annual payments due every six months. The annual stated rate would be 8.5%.

Past operating losses have resulted in a deficit in retained earnings of $3,400,000. In addition to the deficit, the company's equity includes common stock at par value of $6,000,000 and contributed capital in excess of par value in the amount of $1,000,000.

Prepare a schedule that determines the effect on current income of the debt restructuring and the reduction in par value of the common stock necessary to eliminate any deficit in retained earnings. Assume that the restructuring is not part of a formal bankruptcy filing.

Exercise 4 *(LO 1, 3)* **Cash flows, debt restructuring, effect on income under bankruptcy and nonbankruptcy law.** In an attempt to avoid liquidating the company, the management of Carter, Inc., is considering a reorganization that calls for the restructuring of $2,100,000 of debt maturing in three years and related accrued interest payable of $72,737. The restructuring agreement calls for monthly payments over the next 60 months, a reduction in the interest rate to 8%, and the cancellation of $200,000 of debt. The market rate of interest for such a refinancing would be 13%. In addition to the debt restructuring, management is proposing to reduce the par value of its common stock in order to generate enough paid-in capital in excess of par value to absorb a $500,000 deficit in retained earnings. The present balance of paid-in capital in excess of par value is $80,000.

1. Prepare a schedule to determine the total gain resulting from the forgiveness and restructuring of debt and the amount of future interest expense assuming (a) a nonbankruptcy approach and (b) a bankruptcy approach to the reorganization.
2. Determine by how much the par value of common stock would have to be reduced in order to absorb the deficit in retained earnings assuming (a) a nonbankruptcy approach and (b) a bankruptcy approach.

Exercise 5 *(LO 1, 3)* **Cash flows, debt restructuring, effect on income under bankruptcy and nonbankruptcy law.** Rather than entering into a lengthy bankruptcy proceeding, Peltzer Manufacturing has reached agreement with its long-term creditors to restructure various loans. The restructured loans are described below.

Loan A—This debt has a principal balance of $4,000,000 and accrued interest of $80,000. Under the restructuring agreement, $500,000 of debt would be forgiven, and the balance of the amounts due would be refinanced at a rate of 10% with monthly installment payments of $50,000 and a term of eight years. Assets with a net realizable value of $2,500,000 would also be pledged as additional security against the restructured loan.

Loan B—This debt has a principal balance of $1,000,000 and accrued interest of $25,000. Under the restructuring agreement, the accrued interest would be forgiven, and the principal amount would be exchanged for preferred stock with a par value of $500,000 and a fair value of $900,000.

Loan C—This debt has a principal balance of $2,000,000 and accrued interest of $37,500. Under the restructuring agreement, the creditor would receive a parcel of land with a book value of $200,000 and a net realizable value of $250,000. The remaining unpaid balance would be refinanced over five years at a 9% interest rate. Installment payments would be on a quarterly basis.

1. Determine the total quarterly cash outflows that will be required by Peltzer's debt restructuring.
2. Covering the first quarter subsequent to restructuring, prepare a schedule that compares the effect on Peltzer's net income of accounting for the restructuring as part of a formal bankruptcy filing versus it not being part of such a filing.

Exercise 6 *(LO 1, 3)* **Evaluation of restructuring alternatives.** Baxter Manufacturing, Inc., has an outstanding note payable with a balance of $2,000,000. The note calls for 14 semiannual payments of $183,141 based on a 7% interest rate. The company has experienced declining markets and serious cash flow problems. In an attempt to improve cash flows, the company is negotiating a restructuring of the above note. The following alternatives are being considered:

a. Dispose of a parcel of land that the company had purchased as a future plant site. However, given current conditions, the likelihood of a relocation seems remote. The site has a book value of $400,000 and a current market value of $550,000. Transaction costs to dispose of the land are estimated to be $35,000. The net proceeds from the sale of the land would be used to reduce the note payable. The balance of the note would be restructured with 14 semiannual payments of $100,000 each.
b. Dispose of the parcel of land as set forth above and apply $300,000 of the net proceeds to reduce the note. The balance of the note would be restructured with 20 semiannual payments of $90,000 each.

1. Assuming that current borrowing rates are 6%, compare the income statement and balance sheet effect of the two alternatives assuming (a) a nonbankruptcy approach and (b) a bankruptcy approach.
2. Given a nonbankruptcy approach and ignoring the effect on the financial statements, discuss which alternative would be preferred.

Exercise 7 *(LO 2)* **Benefits of a quasi-reorganization.** Barber Technologies designs and develops software to be used for the management of inventory by both retailers and manufacturing firms. Over the past three years, the company has experienced significant competition and a declining market resulting in a significant deficit in retained earnings. In response to this condition, you have suggested that management consider the following:

a. Recognize all asset impairments.
b. Restructure the long-term debt by committing to make future payments that are less than the basis of the original debt.
c. Adjust the par value of common stock to eliminate the deficit in retained earnings.

   Discuss how the above actions will likely affect:

1. The current ratio, debt-to-equity ratio, and return on equity.
2. The determination of net income in subsequent periods.

Exercise 8 *(LO 4)* **Determining proceeds to various classes of claims.** Tebon Manufacturing is considering seeking relief under Chapter 7 of the Bankruptcy Code. However, the company would prefer to engage in out-of-court activities that would allow for a restructuring of debts in an orderly manner. Before approaching its creditors, the company is attempting to estimate the amount of consideration that would be received by various

classes of creditors if the company did liquidate. The company's assets and liabilities are as follows:

Assets	Book Value	Realizable Value	Liabilities	Book Value
Cash	$ 60,000	$ 60,000	Accounts payable	$ 280,000
Receivables	420,000	360,000	Note payable—A	600,000
Inventory	400,000	350,000	Note payable—B	500,000
Equipment	380,000	360,000	Mortgage payable	180,000
Land..............	200,000	260,000	Accrued interest...........	12,000
Other.............	60,000	45,000	Other..................	24,000
Total..............	$1,520,000	$1,435,000	Total....................	$1,596,000

Of the accounts payable, $130,000 is secured by inventory which has a net realizable value of $150,000. Note A is secured by the balance of the inventory and receivables. Note B is secured by equipment with a net realizable value of $300,000, and the mortgage payable and accrued interest are secured by the land. All of the other liabilities are unsecured, although $10,000 is unsecured with priority over the balance.

Prepare a schedule that sets forth the classes of claims (fully secured, partially secured, unsecured) and the assets that satisfy each class. For each class, compute the dividend and determine the total amount of consideration to be received in satisfaction of Note Payable—B.

Exercise 9 *(LO 5)* **Statement of realization and liquidation, dividend to unsecured creditors without priority.** A partially completed statement of realization and liquidation is as follows:

The Rodak Corporation
Statement of Realization and Liquidation
For Period July 1, to August 12, 2019

	Assets		Liabilities				
					Unsecured		
	Cash	Noncash	Fully Secured	Partially Secured	With Priority	Without Priority	Owners' Equity
Beginning balances, assigned July 1, 2019......	$12,000	$590,000	$200,000	$175,000	$54,000	$150,000	$23,000
Cash receipts: Sale of inventory	30,000	(25,000)					5,000

The following additional transactions have occurred through August 12, 2019:

a. Receivables collected amounted to $39,000. Receivables with a book value of $15,000 that were not allowed for were written off.
b. A $12,000 loan that was fully secured was paid off.
c. A valid claim was received from a leasing company seeking payment of $15,000 for equipment rentals.
d. Securities costing $18,000 were sold for $23,000, minus a brokerage fee of $500.
e. Depreciation on machinery was $3,200.
f. Payments on accounts payable totaled $25,000, of which the entire amount was secured by the inventory sold.
g. Machinery that originally cost $85,000 and had a book value of $45,000 sold for $36,000.
h. Proceeds from the sale of machinery in (g) were remitted to the bank, which holds a $50,000 loan on the machinery.

1. Update the statement of realization and liquidation to properly reflect transactions (a) through (h).

2. Assuming the remaining noncash assets can be realized for $410,000, determine the estimated dividend to be received by unsecured creditors without priority.

Exercise 10 *(LO 5)* **Amounts to be received by creditors under Chapter 7.** Casper Blueprinting, Inc., has filed under Chapter 7 of the Bankruptcy Code. The estimated net realizable value of its assets is as follows:

Cash and cash equivalents	$ 23,000
Accounts receivable	42,000
Inventory and supplies	15,000
Blueprinting equipment	114,000
Furniture and fixtures	12,000
Computer hardware and software	21,000
Deliver vehicle	14,000
Total	$241,000

Creditors' claims are summarized as follows:

a. Bank loan balance of $82,000 plus accrued interest of $3,000 with a first lien against blueprinting equipment.
b. Dealer-financed vehicle loan with an outstanding balance of $18,000, which is secured by the delivery vehicle.
c. Accounts payable due vendors in the amount of $21,000 and secured by the inventory and supplies.
d. A line of credit balance due of $30,000 secured by the accounts receivable.
e. Unpaid payroll and income taxes of $23,000.
f. Accounting and legal fees due in the amount of $12,000 in connection with the administration of the bankrupt estate.
g. Unpaid wages to employees totaling $4,200 ($700 represents the largest amount due any one employee).
h. Loans due shareholders of the corporation totaling $80,000.
i. Other unsecured creditors without priority in the amount of $31,000.

Prepare a schedule to show the estimated amount to be received by each major category of creditor.

PROBLEMS

Problem 21-1 *(LO 1)* **Entries to record restructuring of debt.** Rose Corporation was unable to service its outstanding debt. In an attempt to avoid filing for bankruptcy, it took the following measures:

a. Patents with book value of $140,000 and accumulated amortization of $115,000 were sold for $20,000.
b. Goodwill with a book value of $150,000 resulted from the acquisition of a small manufacturing firm in Indiana. The goodwill was tested for impairment, and it was concluded that $100,000 of the goodwill was impaired.
c. A mortgage on a parcel of vacant land had a book value of $230,000. The land with a book value of $210,000 was sold for net proceeds of $185,000 after payment of $10,000 of transaction costs. The mortgage holder accepted the proceeds in full settlement of the mortgage and related accrued interest of $15,000.
d. A loan from a major shareholder/employee had a remaining principal amount of $150,000 plus accrued interest of $4,500 based on the stated rate of 12% payable quarterly. Given significantly lower current market rates, the shareholder agreed to restructure the debt as follows: 6% interest, 16 quarterly payments of principal and interest in the amount of $8,810.25, and receipt of a cash bonus of $30,000 in satisfaction of any remaining debt.

e. A major vendor had a payable balance of $85,000, which had remained unpaid for over five months. In satisfaction of the payable, the vendor agreed to receive an immediate cash payment of $15,000 plus six monthly payments of $10,000 each.

f. Bank debt with an outstanding balance of $532,000 including accrued interest of $22,000 was reduced by $80,000 in exchange for investment securities that were recorded at their market value of $62,000. Another $200,000 of debt was exchanged for treasury stock of the company that had a par value of $50,000 and an original cost of $150,000. The balance of the debt was restructured calling for 10 quarterly payments of $27,470.38.

g. A bank note payable with a balance of $60,000 was restructured by making three quarterly payments of $17,000.

h. A partially secured creditor with a debt balance of $120,000 repossessed equipment that served as collateral. The equipment had a book value of $220,000 and accumulated depreciation of $150,000. The remaining $40,000 of debt was to be paid over the next six quarters in equal payments bearing interest at 5.6%.

Prepare all of the necessary entries to record the above events (a) through (h). Determine the total amount of interest expense to be recognized in connection with the first quarterly payment associated with the restructured debts. ◄ ◄ ◄ ◄ ◄ **Required**

Problem 21-2 *(LO 1)* **Restructuring versus liquidation.** Atoyo Fabricating, Inc., has not been able to service its debts adequately. The company is a family business that has been in existence for 35 years. The shareholders want to avoid liquidating the business and are seeking your help in formulating a plan of reorganization which:

a. Provides creditors with at least as much consideration as, if not more than, they would receive if the company were liquidated.

b. Does not require monthly debt service in excess of $75,000.

Information regarding the various creditor claims and possible restructuring parameters is as follows:

a. Accounts payable due vendors total $134,000. Terms are generally 2/10 net 30, and virtually all accounts are past due. Vendors with balances of $40,000 due have indicated that in satisfaction of the amount due, they would accept equal monthly installment payments bearing no less than 12% and not exceeding three months in duration. These vendors have secured their claims with inventory that has a book value and net realizable value of $55,000 and $42,000, respectively. Vendors with a balance due of $74,000 have a secured interest in inventory with a book value of $60,000 and a net realizable value of $46,000. These vendors would accept three monthly installment payments of $20,000 including interest at the rate of 12% in satisfaction of the amount due. The remaining payables represent unsecured amounts that would be paid $3,000 per month for the next five months including interest at 12%.

b. The equipment note has a balance due of $320,000 plus accrued interest of $18,000. Equipment with a book value of $280,000 and a net realizable value of $325,000 serves as collateral for this loan. The original loan had an interest rate of 11% and a remaining term of 30 months. The creditor will not agree to a change in the interest rate but will accept a revised term of 36 to 42 months in exchange for a personal guarantee of the amount due by each of the shareholders of record.

c. The note due a shareholder in the amount of $20,000 is secured by the cash surrender value of an insurance policy in the amount of $15,000 and is payable on demand. The shareholder would accept four semiannual payments, including interest at 12%, if the present value of these payments is equal to 120% of what would have been received if the company had been liquidated.

d. The mortgage payable of $420,000 plus accrued interest of $28,000 is fully secured by real estate with a book value of $310,000 and a net realizable value of $460,000. The original mortgage has a remaining term of 334 months and an interest rate of 9%. The mortgage company would agree to a restructuring of 360 months and an interest rate of 11%.

e. All other creditors totaling $160,000 are unsecured without priority. Management would like to propose that these creditors receive monthly payments over the next eight months with interest at 12%. The net present value of these payments should equal 110% of what would have been received had the company been liquidated.

The book values and net realizable values of the company's assets are as follows:

	Book Value	Net Realizable Value
Cash and cash equivalents	$ 5,000	$ 5,000
Accounts receivable (net)	120,000	85,000
Inventory	145,000	100,000
Equipment (net)	330,000	345,000
Real property (net)	310,000	460,000
Cash surrender values	25,000	25,000
Licensing agreement	30,000	10,000
Furniture and fixtures	25,000	12,000
	$990,000	$1,042,000

Required ▶ ▶ ▶ ▶ ▶

Prepare a schedule that analyzes the proposed restructuring against the goals set by management.

Problem 21-3 *(LO 1)* **Recording restructuring transactions.** St. John Corporation is barely solvent and has been seeking an equity investor that would be interested in making a capital contribution so that the company would hopefully return to performance levels it had experienced in the past. The company's year-end 2015 balance sheet is presented below.

Assets		Liabilities and Equity	
Cash	$ 42,000	Accounts payable	$ 812,000
Accounts receivable (net)	380,000	Note payable—officer	400,000
Inventory	680,000	Bank A note payable	2,100,000
Other current assets	240,000	Bank B note payable	820,000
Equipment (net)	1,300,000	Mortgage payable	1,500,000
Manufacturing plant	2,100,000	Other liabilities	220,000
Development land	700,000	Common stock	200,000
Patents (net)	210,000	Paid-in capital in excess of par	100,000
Investment in Sky Industries	300,000	Retained earnings	(200,000)
Total	$5,952,000	Total	$5,952,000

Selected transactions occurring during the first six months of 2016 were as follows:

a. Patents with a fair value of $230,000 were transferred to the officer in partial satisfaction of their note. The remaining balance on the note would be paid over five quarters with the first payment of $35,026.77 due on June 30, 2016.

b. The mortgage payable was restructured with 40 quarterly payments of $51,178.05, beginning on June 30, 2016, in addition to an immediate lump sum payment of $100,000.

c. The bank A note payable was restructured as follows: the development land with a net realizable value of $980,000 was conveyed along with marketable securities having a book value of $80,000 and a market value of $95,000. The balance of the note was to be over 10 quarters with payments of $111,145.03 beginning on June 30, 2016.

d. The bank B note payable was partially secured by equipment which had a book value of $240,000 and a net realizable value of $220,000. The equipment was seized by the bank and the company agreed to settle the balance of the note by making 10 quarterly payments of $55,000 beginning on June 30, 2016.

e. On June 30, 2016 all payments required by item (a) through (d) above were paid.

f. Common shareholders approved a reduction in par value from $10 per share to $5 per share and the deficit was eliminated.

Required ▶ ▶ ▶ ▶ ▶

Prepare all necessary entries to record the above transactions (a) through (f).

Problem 21-4 *(LO 5)* **Preparation of a statement of realization and liquidation.**

Problem 21-3 presents the balance sheet of St. John Corporation as of year-end 2015. Assume that the company is not able to service its debts and is unable to secure any significant restructuring arrangements from its primary lenders. As a result, St. John has decided to liquidate the corporation and has submitted a plan for liquidation. The plan has received all necessary approvals, and the liabilities affected by the plan are described as follows:

Accounts payable: Of these accounts, $400,000 is fully secured by claims against inventory with a book value of $430,000. The inventory was completed at an additional cost of $25,000, it was sold for $480,000, and the secured payables were paid. Another $320,000 of the payables is secured by the remaining inventory which is estimated to have a net realizable value of $200,000. The balance of the payables is unsecured.

Note payable—officer: This note is secured by the investment in Sky Industries which has a net realizable value of $320,000.

Bank A note payable: This note is secured by all of the equipment and the patent. Equipment with a book value of $800,000 has been sold for $700,000 by a broker who was paid a fee of $10,000. It is estimated that the balance of the equipment will have a net realizable value of $400,000. The patent was sold to an officer of the corporation for $250,000. Net proceeds from the collateral were paid to Bank A.

Bank B note payable: This note is secured by the development land. The land consists of two separate parcels with book values of $400,000 and $300,000. The $300,000 parcel was sold for $360,000 and it is estimated that the remaining parcel will have a net realizable value of $500,000.

Mortgage payable: This mortgage is secured by the manufacturing plant and other current assets with a book value of $130,000. The plant is currently listed for sale with an asking price of $1,800,000. Realistically, it is estimated that the plant could sell for $1,500,000 before commissions of $90,000. The other current assets securing the mortgage were sold for $100,000.

Other liabilities: $90,000 of these liabilities is secured by all receivables of the company. Receivables with a book value of $150,000 have been collected, and an additional $40,000 of allowance for uncollectible accounts has been established on the balance of the accounts. The $90,000 of other liabilities was paid. Of the remaining other liabilities, $95,000 is unsecured without priority, and the balance is unsecured with priority. Since year-end, $20,000 of the unsecured liabilities with priority has been paid out of available assets.

Since year-end 2016, additional assets with a net realizable value of $15,000 have been discovered, and administrative/legal expenses of $20,000 in connection with the liquidation have been incurred of which half have been paid.

Assuming that all of the above activity occurred within the first six months of 2016, prepare a statement of realization and liquidation to reflect the above activity and information.   ◄ ◄ ◄ ◄ ◄ **Required**

Problem 21-5 *(LO 1, 2)* **Effect of a quasi-reorganization.** Marshall Tool and Die Company has been experiencing significant foreign competition and a declining market. Annual net losses from operations have averaged $250,000 over the last three years. The company's balance sheet as of December 31, 2017, is as follows:

Assets		Liabilities and Equity	
Cash	$ (15,000)	Accounts receivable (net)	$ 320,000
Accounts payable	500,000	7% Note payable	1,500,000
Inventory	150,000	Common stock at par.........	550,000
Plant and equipment (net)	1,560,000	Contributed capital in	
		excess of par	550,000
Goodwill	150,000	Retained earnings	(300,000)
Other assets.....................	35,000	2017 Net income	(240,000)
Total assets	$2,380,000	Total liabilities and equity	$2,380,000

After analyzing accounts receivable and inventory, it has been determined that the allowance for uncollectibles should be increased by $75,000 and the inventory should be written down by $20,000. Based on recent appraisals, it is estimated that the plant and equipment have a market value of $1,285,000. The goodwill is traceable to the purchase of a small tooling company in 2013. Based on an analysis of cash flows associated with that acquisition, it is estimated that the goodwill has an impaired value of $0. Other assets represent a note receivable from officers of the corporation. The note calls for five annual payments of $8,309 including interest at the rate of 6%.

In response to the current situation, the company has decided to take the following actions:

a. Record the suggested impairment in all assets.
b. Restructure the note receivable from the officers to reflect four annual payments and an interest rate of 7.5%.
c. Restructure the note payable, which was due in 2019, to provide for 12 semiannual payments of $120,000 including interest at the annual rate of 6%.
d. Engage in a quasi-reorganization to eliminate the deficit in retained earnings.

Required ▶ ▶ ▶ ▶ ▶   1. Prepare a revised classified balance sheet to reflect the effect of management's actions.
2. Compute the following ratios before and after management's actions: current ratio and debt-to-equity ratio.
3. Given the above ratio analysis, if the ratios do not suggest an improvement, discuss the benefits of management's actions.

Problem 21-6 *(LO 4)* **Statement of affairs.** A creditor's committee of Carlton Company has obtained the March 31, 2015, balance sheet shown below.

Carlton Company
Balance Sheet
March 31, 2015

Assets			
Current assets:			
Cash		$ 11,250	
Marketable securities		28,750	
Notes receivable	$ 10,000		
Less notes receivable discounted	10,000	0	
Accounts receivable	$ 15,000		
Less allowance for doubtful accounts	1,000	14,000	
Subscriptions receivable		20,000	
Inventories:			
Finished goods	$ 27,500		
Work in process	11,250		
Materials	15,000	53,750	
Total current assets			$127,750
Property, plant, and equipment:			
Land and building	$112,500		
Equipment	60,000	$172,500	
Less accumulated depreciation		50,000	
Total property, plant, and equipment			122,500
Total assets			$250,250

Liabilities and Stockholders' Equity			
Current liabilities:			
Notes payable..................................		$ 87,500	
Accounts payable		60,000	
Salaries payable		2,650	
Property tax payable		1,150	
Total current liabilities		$151,300	
Long-term liabilities:			
First mortgage payable	$37,500		
Second mortgage payable	50,000	87,500	
Total liabilities			$238,800
Stockholders' equity:			
Common stock, $100 par (1,000 shares authorized):			
750 shares issued		$ 75,000	
250 shares subscribed........................		25,000	
Total......................................		$100,000	
Retained earnings (deficit).......................		(88,550)	
Total stockholders' equity			11,450
Total liabilities and stockholders' equity			$250,250

An analysis of the company's accounts disclosed the following activities through April 30, 2015:

a. Carlton Company started business on April 1, 2010, with authorized stock of $100 par. Of the 1,000 authorized shares, 750 were paid for in full at par, and 250 were subscribed at par, with a required 20% down payment and the balance payable upon call. All the subscriptions receivable are due from W. Krueger, president of the company, and are fully collectible.

b. Marketable securities include the $25,000 cost of U.S. Treasury bonds valued at $23,200 and 25 shares of Groves Company common stock, costing $3,750, with a fair value of $3,300.

c. The land originally cost $10,000, and the building was erected at a cost of $102,500. Of the accumulated depreciation, $30,000 is applicable to the building. The realizable value of the real estate is $75,000.

d. Notes receivable were endorsed with recourse when discounted and are expected to be dishonored. Of the accounts receivable, $3,000 are considered collectible.

e. Inventories are shown at cost. Any finished goods are expected to yield 110% of cost. If scrapped, goods in process have a realizable value of only $2,200. It is estimated, however, that the work in process can be completed by the addition of $3,000 of present materials and an expenditure of $3,500 for labor. The materials deteriorate rapidly and will realize only 20% of cost. (Use the cost completion method illustrated in the text.)

f. Equipment is estimated to have a realizable value of $12,000.

g. Notes payable include a $25,000 note to Aerotex Company and a $62,500 note to B. Williams. Aerotex holds the U.S. Treasury bonds as security for its loans. It also holds the first mortgage of $37,500 on the company's real estate, interest on which is paid through March 31, 2015. The note payable to Williams is secured by a chattel mortgage on factory equipment. Interest on the note has been paid through March 31, 2015. Williams also holds the second mortgage on the real estate.

h. Any expenses not specifically mentioned need not be considered. All salaries qualify for priority, including labor to complete the work in process.

Prepare a statement of affairs for Carlton Company.   ◀ ◀ ◀ ◀ ◀ **Required**

Problem 21-7 *(LO 1)* **Financial statements after a reorganization.** Crawford Distributors, Inc., is a distributor of industrial cleaning supplies throughout the Midwest. Unfortunately, the company has experienced a downturn in sales due to plant closings and relocations throughout its Midwest market. The company is seeking protection under Chapter 11 of the

Bankruptcy Code. Condensed financial statements for the year-to-date period ending March 31 of the current year are as follows:

Balance Sheet
As of March 31

Assets:

Cash and cash equivalents	$ (46,000)
Accounts receivable	847,000
Inventory	1,100,000
Equipment (net of depreciation)	325,000
Other assets	110,000
Total	$2,336,000

Liabilities and equity:

Accounts payable	$1,530,000
Note payable A	600,000
Note payable B	550,000
Other liabilities	125,000
Shareholders' equity	(469,000)
Total	$2,336,000

Income Statement
For Year Ended March 31

Net sales	$ 853,000
Cost of sales	700,000
Gross profit	$ 153,000
Selling, General, and Administrative Expenses	385,000
Operating income	$(232,000)
Interest expense	17,250
Net income before tax	$(249,250)

During the next three months, the company engaged in the following activities regarding its reorganization:

a. Net sales of $600,000 have occurred with a gross profit margin of 15.00%. Eighty percent of these sales has been collected in full, and 5.00% of the remaining balance is deemed to be uncollectible.

b. Of the receivables existing at March 31, 90.00% has been collected. Of the remaining balance, 5.00% is deemed to be uncollectible.

c. In an attempt to reduce inventory levels, only $230,000 of inventory was purchased on account. Payments against accounts payable were $800,000.

d. Accounts payable of $135,000 were satisfied by returning the inventory that was purchased. The inventory was carried at its market value of $120,000. Based on current interest rates, another $360,000 of accounts payable was restructured as a note beginning on May 1 calling for 15 monthly payments of $24,971.17.

e. Note A was restructured by a conveyance of assets and a modification of terms. A vacant lot with a book value of $60,000 and a market value of $116,000 was conveyed to the creditor. As of May 1, the remaining balance of the note, along with accrued interest of $6,000 as of April 30, is to be satisfied by making 30 payments of $16,000 bearing a market interest rate of 6.12%.

f. Note B was restructured on June 30 by forgiving $50,000 of debt and making 48 equal monthly payments of $11,000 based on a market interest rate of 6.30%.

g. Included in other liabilities is a short-term note with a book value of $15,000. Based on current interest rates, the note has a present value of $14,704. Common stock of the company has been issued to the creditor in full satisfaction of the note.

Required ▶ ▶ ▶ ▶ ▶ Given the above information, prepare the company's trial balance for the 6-month period ending June 30 of the current year. It may be helpful to prepare a worksheet with the following column headings: Account, Trial Balance as of March 31 (Debit and Credit columns), Second Quarter Activities/Adjustments (Debit and Credit columns), and Trial Balance as of June 30 (Debit and Credit columns). The use of Excel or some other computer spreadsheet is highly recommended.

CASES

Structured Example of Goodwill Impairment   *Case 1-1*

(Note: The use of a financial calculator or Excel is suggested for this case.)

Modern Company acquires the net assets of Frontier Company for $ 1,300,000 on January 1, 2011. A business valuation consultant arrives at the price and deems it to be a good value.

Part A. The following list of fair values is provided to you by the consultant:

Assets and Liabilities	Comments	Valuation Method	Fair Value
Cash equivalents	Seller's values are accepted.	Existing book value.	$ 80,000
Inventory	Replacement cost is available.	Market replacement cost for similar items is used.	150,000
Accounts receivable	Asset is adjusted for estimated bad debts.	Aging schedule is used for valuation.	180,000
Land	Per-acre value is well established.	Calculation is based on 20 acres at $10,000 per acre.	200,000
Building	Most reliable measure is rent potential.	Rent is estimated at $80,000 per year for 20 years, discounted at 14% return for similar properties. Present value is reduced for land value.	329,850
Equipment	Cost of replacement capacity can be estimated.	Estimated purchase cost of equipment with similar capacity is used.	220,000
Patent	Recorded by seller at only legal cost; has significant future value.	Added profit made possible by patent is $40,000 per year for four years. Discounted at risk-adjusted rate for similar investments of 20% per year.	103,550
Current liabilities	Recorded amounts are accurate.	Recorded value is used.	(120,000)
Mortgage payable	Specified interest rate is below market rate.	Discount the $50,000 annual payments for five years at annual market rate of 7%.	(205,010)
Net identifiable assets at fair value			$ 938,390
Price paid for reporting unit			1,300,000
Goodwill	Believed to exist based on reputation and customer list.	Implied by price paid.	$ 361,610

► ► ► ► ► **Required**   Using the information in the preceding table, confirm the accuracy of the present value calculations made for the building, patent, and mortgage payable.

Part B. Frontier does not have publicly traded stock. You make an estimate of the value of the company based on the following assumptions that will later be included in the reporting unit valuation procedure:

a. Frontier will provide operating cash flows, net of tax, of $150,000 during the next fiscal year.

b. Operating cash flows will increase at the rate of 10% per year for the next four fiscal years and then will remain steady for 15 more years.

c. Cash flows, defined as net of cash from operations less capital expenditures, will be discounted at an after-tax discount rate of 12%. An annual rate of 12% is a reasonable risk-adjusted rate of return for investments of this type.

d. Added capital expenditures will be $100,000 in year 5, $120,000 in year 10, and $130,000 in year 15.

e. An estimate of salvage value (net of the tax effect of gains or losses) of the assets after 20 years is estimated to be $300,000. This is a conservative assumption since the unit may be operated after that period.

Required ▶ ▶ ▶ ▶ ▶

1. Prepare a schedule of net-of-tax cash flows for Frontier and discount them to present value.

2. Compare the estimated fair value of the reporting unit with amounts assigned to identifiable assets plus goodwill less liabilities.

3. Record the acquisition.

Part C. Revisit the information in Part A that illustrates the reporting unit valuation procedure.

Assume that by fiscal year-end, December 31, 2011, events occur that suggest goodwill could be impaired. You have the following information. These new estimates are made at the end of the first year:

Net book value of Frontier Company including goodwill	$1,300,000
Estimated implied fair value of the reporting unit, based on cash flow analysis discounted at a 12% annual rate.	1,200,000
Estimated fair value of identifiable net assets using methods excluding goodwill	1,020,000

Required ▶ ▶ ▶ ▶ ▶

Has goodwill been impaired? Perform the impairment testing procedure. If goodwill has been impaired, calculate the adjustment to goodwill and make the needed entry.

Case 1-2

What Will Schering-Plough Do to Merck's EPS?

One of the biggest acquisitions of 2009 was the merger of Schering-Plough into Merck & Co., Inc. Both are major drug producers. The acquisition occurred on November 3, 2009. Merck's financial year ended on December 31, 2009. The issue to study is the impact on EPS of the acquisition. The following information is available for your analysis by looking up Merck's 2009 Form 10K:

◆ The consolidated income statement for Merck for the year ended December 31, 2009 which is included in Item 8 of the 2009 Form 10K which includes the financial statements (see **http://www.merck.com/investors/financials/annual-reports/home.html** for information).

◆ The "Preliminary Allocation of Consideration Transferred to Net Assets Acquired" taken from the note 3 of the 2009 Merck Financial Statements

◆ Supplemental pro forma data from the note 3 to the 2009 Merck Financial Statements (see **http://www.merck.com/investors/financials/annual-reports/home.html** for information).

Required ▶ ▶ ▶ ▶ ▶

Prepare your response to the following questions:

1. What part of Schering-Plough's 2009 income statement is included in Merck's 2009 statement of consolidated income? What are Merck's 2009 and 2008 EPS amounts?

2. What would have been Merck's EPS amounts if Schering-Plough's results were added to Merck's results for 2008 and 2009?

3. What portion of the total assets acquired in the acquisition will create amortization charges to future periods?

4. What hope for the future of the merger did Merck offer to shareholders in its 2009 Annual Report? Check Item 7, Part II on page 63 of Merck's 2009 Annual Report. (See **http://www.merck.com/investors/financials/annual-reports/home.html** for information.)

Disney Acquires Marvel Entertainment

Case 1-3

On December 31, 2009, The Walt Disney Company acquired all the capital stock of Marvel Entertainment Company. Marvel has created heroes such as Spiderman, the Hulk, and Iron Man.

Disney acquired 79.2 million shares of Marvel Entertainment's shares. Disney issued 59 million shares of Disney stock plus $30 for each share of Marvel Entertainment stock. Disney stock, which has a par value of $0.01 per share, had a market value of $32.25 per share. The estimated fair value of Marvel Entertainment accounts were as follows:

Cash and cash eqivalents	$ 105,000,000
Receivables	141,000,000
Capitalized film costs	269,000,000
Intangible assets	3,140,000,000
Accounts payable	(325,000,000)
Other liabilities*	(83,000,000)
Deferred income tax liability	(1,121,000,000)

*Other liabilities was actually a noncontrolling interest which is actually an equity interest that is discussed in Chapter 2.

1. Using the Federal Trade Commission's classification of merger types, how would you classify the acquisition?

◄ ◄ ◄ ◄ ◄ **Required**

2. Calculate the total price paid for Marvel Entertainment. Is there goodwill or a gain?

3. Record the acquisition.

Case 2-1
Consolidating a Bargain Purchase

Your client, Great Value Hardware Stores, has come to you for assistance in evaluating an opportunity to purchase a controlling interest in a hardware store in a neighboring city. The store under consideration is a closely held family corporation. Owners of 60% of the shares are willing to sell you the 60% interest, 30,000 common stock shares in exchange for 7,500 of Great Value shares, which have a fair value of $40 each and a par value of $10 each.

Your client sees this as a good opportunity to enter a new market. The controller of Great Value knows, however, that all is not well with the store being considered. The store, Al's Hardware, has not kept pace with the market and has been losing money. It also has a major lawsuit against it stemming from alleged faulty electrical components it supplied that caused a fire. The store is not insured for the loss. Legal counsel advises that the store will likely pay $300,000 in damages.

The following balance sheet was provided by Al's Hardware as of December 31, 2011:

Assets		Liabilities and Equity	
Cash	$ 180,000	Current liabilities	$ 425,000
Accounts receivable	460,000	8% Mortgage payable	600,000
Inventory	730,000	Common stock ($5 par)......	250,000
Land.........................	120,000	Paid-in capital in excess of par	750,000
Building	630,000	Retained earnings	(80,000)
Accumulated depreciation—building ..	(400,000)		
Equipment	135,000		
Accumulated depreciation—equipment	(85,000)		
Goodwill	175,000		
Total assets....................	$1,945,000	Total liabilities and equity ..	$1,945,000

Your analysis raises substantial concerns about the values shown. You have gathered the following information:

1. Aging of the accounts receivable reveals a net realizable value of $350,000.
2. The inventory has many obsolete items; the fair value is $600,000.
3. Appraisals for long-lived assets are as follows:

Land............................	$100,000
Building	300,000
Equipment	100,000

4. The goodwill resulted from the purchase of another hardware store that has since been consolidated into the existing location. The goodwill was attributed to customer loyalty.
5. Liabilities are fairly stated except that there should be a provision for the estimated loss on the lawsuit.

On the basis of your research, you are convinced that the statements of Al's Hardware are not representative and need major restatement. Your client is not interested in being associated with statements that are not accurate.

Your client asks you to make recommendations on two concerns:

1. Does the price asked seem to be a real bargain? Consider the fair value of the entire equity of Al's Hardware; then decide if the price is reasonable for a 60% interest.
2. If the deal were completed, what accounting methods would you recommend either on the books of Al's Hardware or in the consolidation process? Al's Hardware would remain a separate legal entity with a substantial noncontrolling interest.

The Noncontrolling Interest's Concern
with Intercompany Transactions

Henderson Window Company was a privately held corporation until January 1, 2011. On January 1, 2011, Cool Glass Company acquired a 70% interest in Henderson at a price well in excess of book value. There were some minor differences between book and fair values, but the bulk of the excess was attributed to goodwill.

Harvey Henderson did not sell his shares to Cool Glass as a part of the January 1, 2011, Cool Glass purchase. He wanted to remain a Henderson shareholder since he felt Henderson was a more profitable and stable company than was Cool Glass. Harvey remains an employee of Henderson Window, working in an accounting capacity.

Harvey is concerned about some accounting issues that he feels are detrimental to his ownership interest. Harvey told you that Henderson always bought most of its glass from Cool Glass. He never felt the prices charged for the glass were unreasonable. Since the purchase of Henderson by Cool Glass, he feels the price charged to Henderson by Cool Glass has risen dramatically and that it is out of step with what would be paid to other glass suppliers.

The second concern is the sale of a large Henderson warehouse to Cool Glass for less than what Harvey would consider to be the market value. Harvey agrees that the sale is reasonable since the new just-in-time order system has made the space unnecessary. He just feels the sale price is below market.

Harvey did make his concerns known to the president of Cool Glass. The president made several points. First, she said that the price charged for the glass was a little high, but Harvey should consider its high quality. She went on to say that the transfer price washes out in the annual report, and it has no impact on reported net income of the corporation. She also stated that the warehouse sale was at a low price, but there was a reason. It was a good year, and a large gain wasn't needed. She would rather have lower depreciation in future years. Her last point was: "We paid a big price for Henderson. We are stuck with a big investment in goodwill, and our stockholders expect a return on that investment. We should get some benefits from it!"

Write a memo to Harvey Henderson suggesting how he might respond to the president's comments.

◀ ◀ ◀ ◀ ◀ **Required**

Case 5-1

Methods of Eliminating Subsidiary Debt

Power Pro, Inc., is a large manufacturer of marine engines. In recent years, Power Pro, like other engine manufacturers, has purchased a controlling interest in independent boat builders. The intent of the acquisitions is to control the engine choice of the boat builder. By including the outboard engine in the boat package, it is not necessary to sell to and finance many small dealers.

Power Pro purchased an 80% interest in Swift-Craft during the last year. Swift-Crafts are built in California and are sold only in western states. Power Pro wants to build the boats in the Midwest as well, so as to expand sales without paying major shipping costs from the West. A new plant will cost $1,000,000 to build and another $1,500,000 to equip for production.

Currently, Swift-Craft has $800,000 in long-term debt. It has 11% annual interest bonds outstanding in the hands of local investors. Current investors have no interest in lending any more funds. The interest rate Swift-Craft pays is high due to its size and credit rating.

Power Pro has ready access to the bond market and borrows at 7.5% annual interest. Power Pro also has expertise in constructing and equipping new facilities since it has built many new plants. Power Pro also has a sophisticated fixed asset accounting system. Power Pro would prefer to build the new plant and turn it over to Swift-Craft when it is complete. It is considering either selling the building to Swift-Craft and taking back the mortgage or leasing the asset to Swift-Craft under a long-term capital lease.

Power Pro would like you to cover the options it has in using its borrowing ability and asset management experience in assisting Swift-Craft. There is a concern as to existing debt and with respect to funds needed to finance the new plant. Your discussion should consider the impact of alternatives on the consolidation process and on NCI shareholders.

Case 5-2

Impact of Alternative Methods to Retire Subsidiary Debt

Magna Company is the parent company that owns an 80% interest in Metros Company. The interest was purchased at book value, and the simple equity method is used to record the ownership interest. The trial balances of the two companies on December 31, 2016, were as follows:

	Magna Company	Metros Company
Cash	258,000	100,000
Other Current Assets	50,000	200,000
Investment in Metros	316,000	
Plant and Equipment	800,000	500,000
Accumulated Depreciation	(300,000)	(200,000)
Current Liabilities	(40,000)	(5,000)
Bonds Payable		(200,000)
Common Stock (par)	(300,000)	(100,000)
Retained Earnings	(746,000)	(285,000)
Sales	(150,000)	(170,000)
Cost of Goods Sold	90,000	130,000
Expenses	30,000	10,000
Interest Expense		20,000
Subsidiary Income	(8,000)	
Totals	0	0

As of December 31, 2016, Magna Company was considering acquiring the $200,000 of Metros's 10% bonds from the current owner. Based on a 12% current interest rate for bonds of this risk, the purchase price of the bonds would be $185,000. There are two possible options as follows:

a. Magna could lend $185,000 to Metros at 8% annual interest. Metros would then use the funds to retire the bonds.
b. Magna could buy the bonds and hold them as an investment and enjoy the high interest rate.

◄ ◄ ◄ ◄ ◄ Required

1. Prepare a pro forma consolidated income statement and balance sheet for 2016 assuming option (a) is used.
2. Indicate how your solution to part (1) would change if the second option were used.

Alternative Ways to Transfer Asset to Subsidiary

Case 5-3

Pannier Company is the parent company that owns an 80% interest in Jodestar Company. The interest was acquired at book value, and the simple equity method is used to record the ownership interest. The trial balances of the two companies on December 31, 2016, were as follows:

	Pannier Company	Jodestar Company
Cash	258,000	100,000
Inventory	150,000	40,000
Other Current Assets	50,000	160,000
Investment in Jodestar	316,000	
Plant and Equipment	650,000	500,000
Accumulated Depreciation	(300,000)	(200,000)
Current Liabilities	(40,000)	(5,000)
Long-Term Debt		(200,000)
Common Stock (par)	(300,000)	(100,000)
Retained Earnings	(746,000)	(285,000)
Sales	(150,000)	(170,000)
Cost of Goods Sold	90,000	130,000
Expenses	30,000	10,000
Interest Expense		20,000
Subsidiary Income	(8,000)	
Totals	0	0

As the year ended, Pannier was planning to transfer a major piece of equipment to Jodestar. The equipment was just purchased by Pannier and is included in its inventory account. The equipment cost Pannier $100,000 and would be transferred to Jodestar for $125,000. There are two options as follows:

a. Sell the equipment to Jodestar for $125,000 and finance it with a 5-year, 10% interest installment note.
b. Lease the equipment to Jodestar on a 5-year lease requiring payments of $29,977 in advance.

◄ ◄ ◄ ◄ ◄ Required

1. Make the journal entries for both companies if the intercompany sale was consummated on December 31.
2. Prepare a consolidated income statement and balance sheet for the company for 2016. (*Note:* The effect of the equipment sale is not included in the trial balance.)
3. Make the journal entries for both companies if the intercompany lease was executed on December 31.
4. If the lease were used, how would the consolidated statements differ from those in part (2)?

CITY OF MILWAUKEE, WISCONSIN
BASIC FINANCIAL STATEMENTS: GOVERNMENT-WIDE FINANCIAL STATEMENTS
FOR THE YEAR ENDED DECEMBER 31, 2009

Source: City of Milwaukee Web site. For the full report, go to http://city.milwaukee.gov/ ImageLibrary/User/pmensa/2009_Financial_ReportWeb.pdf.

CITY OF MILWAUKEE
STATEMENT OF NET ASSETS
December 31, 2009
(Thousands of Dollars)

Exhibit 1

| | Primary Government | | | Component Units |
	Governmental Activities	Business-type Activities	Total	
Assets				
Cash and cash equivalents	$ 238,763	$ 38,743	$ 277,506	$ 55,778
Investments	2,855	-	2,855	10,347
Receivables (net):				
Taxes	214,885	-	214,885	2,837
Accounts	27,981	42,774	70,755	-
Unbilled accounts	1,225	15,060	16,285	-
Special assessments	12,889	-	12,889	-
Notes and loans	65,554	-	65,554	89,124
Accrued interest	215	113	328	4,443
Due from component units	18,295	-	18,295	-
Due from primary government	-	-	-	410
Due from other governmental agencies	247,078	-	247,078	19,412
Inventory of materials and supplies	7,075	2,616	9,691	-
Inventory of property for resale	26	-	26	8,225
Prepaid items	254	40	294	926
Deferred charges	2,043	370	2,413	1,056
Other assets	-	254	254	451
Total Noncapital Assets	839,138	99,970	939,108	193,009
Capital assets:				
Capital assets not being depreciated:				
Land	164,250	18,167	182,417	56,526
Construction in progress	40,839	18,095	58,934	3,179
Capital assets being depreciated:				
Buildings	257,076	89,407	346,483	488,043
Infrastructure	1,377,383	802,717	2,180,100	789
Improvements other than buildings	11,687	7,717	19,404	1,725
Machinery and equipment	164,265	215,306	379,571	3,509
Nonutility property	-	5,509	5,509	-
Accumulated depreciation	(1,085,505)	(361,726)	(1,447,231)	(244,430)
Total Capital Assets	929,995	795,192	1,725,187	309,341
Total Assets	1,769,133	895,162	2,664,295	502,350

CITY OF MILWAUKEE
STATEMENT OF NET ASSETS
December 31, 2009
(Thousands of Dollars)

Exhibit 1 (Continued)

| | Primary Government | | | Component Units |
	Governmental Activities	Business-type Activities	Total	
LIABILITIES				
Accounts payable	$ 34,965	$ 17,246	$ 52,211	$ 11,099
Accrued expenses	32,764	2,767	35,531	13,103
Accrued interest payable	10,064	960	11,024	-
Internal balances	(43,490)	43,490	-	-
Due to component units	410	-	410	-
Due to other governmental agencies	355	-	355	2,442
Deferred revenue	309,784	25	309,809	4,074
Revenue anticipation notes payable	228,000	-	228,000	-
Other payables	-	-	-	-
Other liabilities	-	-	-	7,300
Due to primary government:				
Due within one year	-	-	-	1,408
Due in more than one year	-	-	-	16,887
Long-term obligations:				-
Due within one year	108,973	11,787	120,760	4,494
Due in more than one year	839,185	137,858	977,043	133,613
Total Liabilities	1,521,010	214,133	1,735,143	194,420
NET ASSETS				
Invested in capital assets, net of related debt	367,061	650,478	1,017,539	187,782
Restricted for:				
Debt Service	163,870	11,159	175,029	10,546
Other purposes	141	-	141	8,095
Unrestricted	(282,949)	19,392	(263,557)	101,507
Total Net Assets	$ 248,123	$ 681,029	$ 929,152	$ 307,930

The notes to the financial statements are an integral part of this statement.

CITY OF MILWAUKEE
STATEMENT OF ACTIVITIES
FOR THE YEAR ENDED DECEMBER 31, 2009
(Thousands of Dollars)

Exhibit 2

Functions/Programs	Expenses	Charges for Services	Operating Grants and Contributions	Capital Grants and Contributions
Primary government:				
Governmental Activities:				
General government	$ 207,504	$ 9,011	$ 2,825	$ -
Public safety	331,409	16,649	14,475	-
Public works	167,983	62,553	4,025	-
Health	22,995	1,078	11,421	-
Culture and recreation	22,901	1,482	2,325	-
Conservation and development	50,683	284	17,323	-
Capital contribution to Milwaukee Public Schools	5,153	-	-	-
Contributions	21,026	-	21,300	-
Interest on long-term debt	23,985	-	-	-
Total Governmental Activities	853,639	91,057	73,694	-
Business-type Activities:				
Water	67,946	73,132	-	3,353
Sewer Maintenance	34,847	48,199	-	14,975
Parking	24,659	42,245	-	-
Port of Milwaukee	3,811	5,212	-	346
Metropolitan Sewerage District User Charges	44,545	44,244	-	-
Total Business-type Activities	175,808	213,032	-	18,674
Total Primary Government	$ 1,029,447	$ 304,089	$ 73,694	$ 18,674
Component units:				
Housing Authority	$ 92,230	$ 20,366	$ 50,727	$ 13,677
Redevelopment Authority	18,131	5,497	5,543	4,140
Milwaukee Economic Development Authority	3,601	3,340	906	-
Neighborhood Improvement Development Corporation	1,783	888	372	-
Total Component Units	$ 115,745	$ 30,091	$ 57,548	$ 17,817

General revenues:
  Property taxes and other taxes ....
  State aids for General Fund ....
  Miscellaneous ....
Transfers ....
  Total General Revenues and Transfers ....

Change in Net Assets ....

Net Assets - Beginning ....

Net Assets - Ending ....

The notes to the financial statements are an integral part of this statement.

Exhibit 2 (Continued)

| | Net (Expenses) Revenue and Changes in Net Assets | | | |
| | Primary Government | | | |
Governmental Activities	Business-type Activities	Total	Component Units
$ (195,668)		$ (195,668)	
(300,285)		(300,285)	
(101,405)		(101,405)	
(10,496)		(10,496)	
(19,094)		(19,094)	
(33,076)		(33,076)	
(5,153)		(5,153)	
274		274	
(23,985)		(23,985)	
(688,888)		(688,888)	
-	$ 8,539	8,539	
-	28,327	28,327	
-	17,586	17,586	
-	1,747	1,747	
-	(301)	(301)	
-	55,898	55,898	
(688,888)	55,898	(632,990)	
			$ (7,460)
			(2,951)
			645
			(523)
			(10,289)
270,191	-	270,191	-
272,337	-	272,337	-
47,217	120	47,337	4,371
40,111	(40,111)	-	-
629,856	(39,991)	589,865	4,371
(59,032)	15,907	(43,125)	(5,918)
307,155	665,122	972,277	313,848
$ 248,123	$ 681,029	$ 929,152	$ 307,930

This page left blank intentionally.

**FUND
FINANCIAL
STATEMENTS**

CITY OF MILWAUKEE
BALANCE SHEET
GOVERNMENTAL FUNDS
DECEMBER 31, 2009
(Thousands of Dollars)

Exhibit A-1

	General
ASSETS	
Assets:	
Cash and cash equivalents	$ 46,884
Investments	141
Receivables (net):	
Taxes	141,577
Accounts	25,712
Unbilled accounts	1,225
Special assessments	-
Notes and loans	37
Accrued interest	145
Due from other funds	76,750
Due from component units	1,538
Due from other governmental agencies	441
Advances to other funds	12,036
Inventory of materials and supplies	6,801
Inventory of property for resale	26
Prepaid items	254
Total Assets	**$ 313,567**
LIABILITIES AND FUND BALANCES	
Liabilities:	
Accounts payable	$ 21,345
Accrued expenses	32,183
Due to other funds	1,891
Due to component units	1
Due to other governmental agencies	-
Deferred revenue	186,791
Revenue anticipation notes payable	-
Advances from other funds	-
Total Liabilities	242,211
Fund Balances:	
Reserved for debt service	-
Reserved for delinquent taxes receivable	-
Reserved for economic development	-
Reserved for encumbrances, prepaids, and carryovers	21,919
Reserved for inventory	6,827
Reserved for mortgage trust	141
Reserved for environmental remediation	303
Reserved for tax stabilization - 2010	13,070
Reserved for tax stabilization - 2011 and subsequent years' budgets and advances to other funds	29,096
Unreserved:	
Undesignated	-
Special assessment (deficit)	-
Total Fund Balances	71,356
Total Liabilities and Fund Balances	**$ 313,567**

The notes to the financial statements are an integral part of this statement.

Exhibit A-1 (Continued)

	General Obligation Debt Service	Public Debt Amortization	Capital Projects	Nonmajor Governmental Funds	Total
	$ 124,411	$ 44,229	$ 4,361	$ 18,878	$ 238,763
	-	2,714	-	-	2,855
	57,126	-	2,795	13,387	214,885
	-	-	2,054	215	27,981
	-	-	-	-	1,225
	-	-	12,889	-	12,889
	24,752	21,245	-	19,520	65,554
	17	53	-	-	215
	-	-	-	714	77,464
	16,562	-	138	57	18,295
	228,000	-	6,042	12,595	247,078
	-	-	-	-	12,036
	-	-	274	-	7,075
	-	-	-	-	26
	-	-	-	-	254
	$ 450,868	$ 68,241	$ 28,553	$ 65,366	$ 926,595
	$ 8	$ -	$ 8,366	$ 5,246	$ 34,965
	6	-	295	280	32,764
	3,269	-	21,509	7,305	33,974
	-	-	262	147	410
	-	-	-	355	355
	138,805	-	22,570	9,749	357,915
	228,000	-	-	-	228,000
	-	-	12,036	-	12,036
	370,088	-	65,038	23,082	700,419
	80,780	68,241	-	14,849	163,870
	-	-	-	10,830	10,830
	-	-	-	829	829
	-	-	2,017	-	23,936
	-	-	274	-	7,101
	-	-	-	-	141
	-	-	-	-	303
	-	-	-	-	13,070
	-	-	-	-	29,096
	-	-	(27,929)	15,776	(12,153)
	-	-	(10,847)	-	(10,847)
	80,780	68,241	(36,485)	42,284	226,176
	$ 450,868	$ 68,241	$ 28,553	$ 65,366	$ 926,595

This page left blank intentionally.

CITY OF MILWAUKEE
**RECONCILIATION OF THE GOVERNMENTAL FUNDS BALANCE SHEET
TO THE STATEMENT OF NET ASSETS**
DECEMBER 31, 2009
(Thousands of Dollars)

Exhibit A-2

Fund balances - total governmental funds		$ 226,176
Amounts reported for governmental activities in the statement of net assets (Exhibit A-1) are different because:		
Capital assets used in governmental activities are not financial resources and therefore are not reported in the funds. Those assets consist of:		
Land	$ 164,250	
Buildings, net of $72,025 accumulated depreciation	185,051	
Infrastructure, net of $911,616 accumulated depreciation	465,767	
Improvements other than buildings, net of $7,731 accumulated depreciation	3,956	
Machinery and equipment, net of $94,133 accumulated depreciation	70,132	
Construction in progress	40,839	
		929,995
Deferred charges for debt issuance costs are not available to pay for current-period expenditures and therefore are deferred in the funds.		2,043
Some revenues are deferred in the funds because they are not available to pay current period's expenditures.		
Taxes to be collected after year-end	10,539	
Special assessments to be collected after year-end	11,627	
Other revenues to be collected after year-end	1,213	
Notes and loans receivable to repay long-term bonds and notes	24,752	
		48,131
Long-term liabilities are not due and payable in the current period and therefore are not reported in the funds. Interest on long-term debt is not accrued in governmental funds, but rather is recognized as an expenditure when due. All liabilities - both current and long-term - are reported in the statement of net assets.		
Accrued interest payable	(10,064)	
Bonds and notes payable	(742,752)	
Deferred amount on refunding	4,000	
Unamortized premiums	(23,839)	
Compensated absences	(38,904)	
Net other postemployment benefits obligation	(122,944)	
Claims and judgments	(23,719)	
		(958,222)
Total net assets of governmental activities (Exhibit 1)		$ 248,123

CITY OF MILWAUKEE   Exhibit A-3
STATEMENT OF REVENUES, EXPENDITURES AND CHANGES IN FUND BALANCES
GOVERNMENTAL FUNDS
FOR THE YEAR ENDED DECEMBER 31, 2009
(Thousands of Dollars)

	General
Revenues:	
Property taxes	$ 156,410
Other taxes	3,504
Special assessments	-
Licenses and permits	12,186
Intergovernmental	272,337
Charges for services	91,057
Fines and forfeits	4,802
Contributions received	21,300
Other	19,967
Total Revenues	581,563
Expenditures:	
Current:	
General government	222,809
Public safety	276,060
Public works	97,093
Health	10,446
Culture and recreation	17,329
Conservation and development	4,230
Capital outlay	-
Debt Service:	
Principal retirement	-
Interest	-
Bond issuance costs	-
Total Expenditures	627,967
Excess (Deficiency) of Revenues over Expenditures	(46,404)
Other Financing Sources (Uses):	
General obligation bonds and notes issued	119,000
Proceeds current refunding	-
Payment current refunding	
Loans receivable activities	-
Issuance premium	-
Transfers in	43,834
Transfers out	(118,081)
Total Other Financing Sources and Uses	44,753
Net Change in Fund Balances	(1,651)
Fund Balances - Beginning	73,007
Fund Balances - Ending	**$ 71,356**

The notes to the financial statements are an integral part of this statement.

Exhibit A-3 (Continued)

	General Obligation Debt Service	Public Debt Amortization	Capital Projects	Nonmajor Governmental Funds	Total
	$ 70,606	$ -	$ 6,506	$ 5,310	$ 238,832
	23,879	2,908	-	-	30,291
	-	-	2,418	-	2,418
	-	-	-	-	12,186
	1,202	-	4,641	53,958	332,138
	2,441	-	-	-	93,498
	-	-	-	-	4,802
	-	-	-	-	21,300
	4,938	1,992	3,667	10,118	40,682
	103,066	4,900	17,232	69,386	776,147
	315	3	-	4,198	227,325
	-	-	-	14,475	290,535
	-	-	-	4,025	101,118
	-	-	-	11,421	21,867
	-	-	-	2,325	19,654
	-	-	-	24,068	28,298
	-	-	98,003	-	98,003
	205,228	-	-	-	205,228
	31,941	-	-	-	31,941
	463	-	-	-	463
	237,947	3	98,003	60,512	1,024,432
	(134,881)	4,897	(80,771)	8,874	(248,285)
	-	-	83,845	24,680	227,525
	66,585	-	-	-	66,585
	(71,800)	-	-	-	(71,800)
	-	-	-	(250)	(250)
	9,437	-	-	-	9,437
	149,201	3,695	200	-	196,930
	(9,002)	(200)	(2,408)	(27,128)	(156,819)
	144,421	3,495	81,637	(2,698)	271,608
	9,540	8,392	866	6,176	23,323
	71,240	59,849	(37,351)	36,108	202,853
	$ 80,780	$ 68,241	$ (36,485)	$ 42,284	$ 226,176

This page left blank intentionally.

CITY OF MILWAUKEE
RECONCILIATION OF THE STATEMENT OF REVENUES,
EXPENDITURES, AND CHANGES IN FUND BALANCES OF GOVERNMENTAL FUNDS
TO THE STATEMENT OF ACTIVITIES
FOR THE YEAR ENDED DECEMBER 31, 2009
(Thousands of Dollars)

Exhibit A-4

Net change in fund balances - total governmental funds (Exhibit A-3)		$ 23,323
Amounts reported for governmental activities in the statement of activities are different because:		
Governmental funds report capital outlays as expenditures. However, in the statement of activities the cost of those assets is allocated over their estimated useful lives and reported as depreciation expense. This is the amount by which capital outlay ($33,775) exceeded depreciation expense ($47,702) in the current period less loss on disposals ($11,553)		(25,480)
Notes and loans receivable to repay long-term bonds and notes		10,897
Revenues in the statement of activities that do not provide current financial resources are reported as deferred revenue in the funds.		
Taxes accrued in prior years	$ 1,068	
Special assessments deferred revenue beginning of the year $12,922 less deferred at end of the year $11,627	(1,295)	
Other revenues deferred at year end	1,213	
		986
The issuance of long-term debt (bonds, leases) provides current financial resources to governmental funds, while the repayment of the principal of long-term debt consumes the current financial resources of governmental funds. Neither transaction, however, has any effect on net assets. Also, governmental funds report the effect of issuance costs, premiums and similar items when debt is first issued, whereas these amounts are deferred and amortized in the statement of activities. This amount is the net effect of these differences in the treatment of long-term debt and related items.		
Debt issued:		
Bonds and notes issued	(294,110)	
Issuance premiums	(9,437)	
Issuance costs	463	
Repayments:		
Principal retirement	277,028	
Amortization:		
Premiums	8,480	
Issuance costs	(470)	
Deferred amount on refunding	(1,197)	
		(19,243)
Under the modified accrual basis of accounting used in the governmental funds, expenditures are not recognized for transactions that are not normally paid with expendable available financial resources. In the statement of activities, however, which is presented on the accrual basis, expenses and liabilities are reported regardless of when financial resources are available. In addition, interest on long-term debt is not recognized under the modified accrual basis of accounting until due, rather as it accrues. The adjustment combines the net changes of the following balances.		
Compensated absences	(7,696)	
Net other postemployment benefits obligation	(47,239)	
Claims and judgments	4,747	
Accrued interest on bonds and notes	673	
		(49,515)
Changes in net assets of governmental activities (Exhibit 2)		$ (59,032)

The notes to the financial statements are an integral part of this reconciliation.

		CITY OF MILWAUKEE **STATEMENT OF NET ASSETS** **ENTERPRISE FUNDS** DECEMBER 31, 2009 *(Thousands of Dollars)*		Exhibit B-1

	Water Works	Sewer Maintenance	Parking	Nonmajor Enterprise Funds	Total
ASSETS					
Current Assets:					
Cash and cash equivalents	$ 6,565	$ -	$ 21,019	$ -	$ 27,584
Restricted cash and cash equivalents	667	1,823	-	-	2,490
Receivables (net):					
Accounts	14,092	14,675	718	13,289	42,774
Unbilled accounts	9,882	2,283	-	2,895	15,060
Accrued interest	4	109	-	-	113
Due from other funds	4,446	719	-	1,074	6,239
Due from other governmental agencies	-	-	-	-	-
Inventory of materials and supplies	2,616	-	-	-	2,616
Prepaid items	40	-	-	-	40
Deferred charges	-	370	-	-	370
Other assets	254	-	-	-	254
Total Current Assets	38,566	19,979	21,737	17,258	97,540
Noncurrent assets:					
Restricted cash and cash equivalents	-	8,669	-	-	8,669
Capital assets:					
Capital assets not being depreciated:					
Land	1,936	-	8,440	7,791	18,167
Construction in progress	15,635	16	2,435	9	18,095
Capital assets being depreciated:					
Buildings	24,135	-	51,788	13,484	89,407
Infrastructure	338,510	448,298	-	15,909	802,717
Improvements other than buildings	-	-	5,429	2,288	7,717
Machinery and equipment	202,027	4,419	4,068	4,792	215,306
Nonutility property	5,509	-	-	-	5,509
Accumulated depreciation	(193,770)	(111,415)	(34,793)	(21,748)	(361,726)
Net Capital Assets	393,982	341,318	37,367	22,525	795,192
Total Noncurrent Assets	393,982	349,987	37,367	22,525	803,861
Total Assets	432,548	369,966	59,104	39,783	901,401

	CITY OF MILWAUKEE STATEMENT OF NET ASSETS ENTERPRISE FUNDS DECEMBER 31, 2009 (Thousands of Dollars)				Exhibit B-1 (Continued)

	Water Works	Sewer Maintenance	Parking	Nonmajor Enterprise Funds	Total
LIABILITIES					
Current Liabilities:					
Accounts payable	$ 3,849	$ 2,788	$ 1,121	$ 9,488	$ 17,246
Accrued expenses	1,242	772	573	180	2,767
Accrued interest payable	280	-	188	44	512
Compensated absences	1,248	-	-	-	1,248
Due to other funds	9,492	27,958	-	12,279	49,729
Deferred revenue	-	-	25	-	25
General obligation debt payable - current	2,507	270	1,492	430	4,699
Revenue bonds payable - current	939	-	-	-	939
Total Current Liabilities	19,557	31,788	3,399	22,421	77,165
Current Liabilities Payable from Restricted Assets:					
Revenue bonds payable	-	4,901	-	-	4,901
Accrued interest payable	-	448	-	-	448
Total Current Liabilities Payable from Restricted Assets	-	5,349	-	-	5,349
Noncurrent Liabilities:					
General obligation debt	13,131	6,897	10,164	2,317	32,509
Revenue bonds payable	8,461	92,758	-	-	101,219
Other post employment benefits obligation	2,400	904	673	153	4,130
Total Noncurrent Liabilities	23,992	100,559	10,837	2,470	137,858
Total Liabilities	43,549	137,696	14,236	24,891	220,372
Net Assets:					
Invested in capital assets, net of related debt	368,944	236,492	25,711	19,778	650,925
Restricted for Debt Service	667	10,492	-	-	11,159
Unrestricted	19,388	(14,714)	19,157	(4,886)	18,945
Total Net Assets	$ 388,999	$ 232,270	$ 44,868	$ 14,892	$ 681,029

The notes to the financial statements are an integral part of this statement.

This page left blank intentionally.

CITY OF MILWAUKEE
STATEMENT OF REVENUES, EXPENSES AND CHANGES IN FUND NET ASSETS
ENTERPRISE FUNDS
FOR THE YEAR ENDED DECEMBER 31, 2009
(Thousands of Dollars)

Exhibit B-2

	Water Works	Sewer Maintenance	Parking	Nonmajor Enterprise Funds	Total
Operating Revenues:					
Charges for Services:					
Water sales	$ 59,051	$ -	$ -	$ -	$ 59,051
Statutory sewer user fee	-	-	-	42,878	42,878
Sewer maintenance fee	-	48,199	-	-	48,199
Rent	-	-	7,574	5,106	12,680
Fire protection service	6,421	-	-	-	6,421
Parking meters	-	-	4,653	-	4,653
Parking permits	-	-	3,165	-	3,165
Vehicle towing	-	-	5,471	-	5,471
Parking forfeitures	-	-	20,879	-	20,879
Other	7,597	-	3	1,366	8,966
Total Operating Revenues	73,069	48,199	41,745	49,350	212,363
Operating Expenses:					
Milwaukee Metropolitan Sewerage District charges	-	-	-	39,666	39,666
Employee services	-	8,522	7,857	1,901	18,280
Administrative and general	6,054	-	-	55	6,109
Depreciation	13,328	4,759	2,533	936	21,556
Transmission and distribution	22,483	-	-	3,450	25,933
Services, supplies, and materials	-	7,916	13,713	928	22,557
Water treatment	14,339	-	-	-	14,339
Water pumping	7,884	-	-	-	7,884
Billing and collection	2,819	-	-	1,274	4,093
Total Operating Expenses	66,907	21,197	24,103	48,210	160,417
Operating Income	6,162	27,002	17,642	1,140	51,946
Nonoperating Revenues (Expenses):					
Investment income	88	32	-	-	120
Grant Revenue	-	14,632	-	-	14,632
Interest expense	(1,039)	(3,552)	(556)	(146)	(5,293)
Gain (Loss) on disposal of fixed assets	-	-	-	-	-
Other	63	(10,098)	500	106	(9,429)
Total Nonoperating Revenues (Expenses)	(888)	1,014	(56)	(40)	30
Income before Contributions and Transfers	5,274	28,016	17,586	1,100	51,976
Capital contributions	3,353	343	-	346	4,042
Transfers in	-	-	-	670	670
Transfers out	(9,440)	(9,300)	(19,940)	(2,101)	(40,781)
Change in Net Assets	(813)	19,059	(2,354)	15	15,907
Total Net Assets - Beginning	389,812	213,211	47,222	14,877	665,122
Total Net Assets - Ending	**$ 388,999**	**$ 232,270**	**$ 44,868**	**$ 14,892**	**$ 681,029**

The notes to the financial statements are an integral part of this statement.

CITY OF MILWAUKEE
STATEMENT OF CASH FLOWS
ENTERPRISE FUNDS
FOR THE YEAR ENDED DECEMBER 31, 2009
(Thousands of Dollars)

Exhibit B-3

	Water Works	Sewer Maintenance	Parking	Nonmajor Enterprise Funds	Total
CASH FLOWS FROM OPERATING ACTIVITIES:					
Receipts from customers and users	$ 67,381	$ 45,406	$ 41,005	$ 48,808	$ 202,600
Receipts from interfund services provided	5,408	-	-	-	5,408
Payments to suppliers	(22,063)	(7,244)	(13,902)	(45,001)	(88,210)
Payments to employees	(24,860)	(8,102)	(7,623)	(1,844)	(42,429)
Payments from other funds	-	15,078	-	1,714	16,792
Payments to other funds	(4,604)	-	-	(2,285)	(6,889)
Net Cash Provided by Operating Activities	21,262	45,138	19,480	1,392	87,272
CASH FLOWS FROM NONCAPITAL FINANCING ACTIVITIES:					
Miscellaneous nonoperating revenue	63	14,632	-	-	14,695
Other nonoperating expenses	-	(10,098)	-	-	(10,098)
Transfers from other funds	-	-	-	670	670
Transfers to other funds	(9,440)	(9,300)	(19,940)	(2,101)	(40,781)
Net Cash Used for Noncapital Financing Activities	(9,377)	(4,766)	(19,940)	(1,431)	(35,514)
CASH FLOWS FROM CAPITAL AND RELATED FINANCING ACTIVITIES:					
Capital contributions	-	-	-	1,346	1,346
Proceeds from sale of bonds and notes	225	3,863	2,595	-	6,683
Acquisition of property, plant, and equipment	(20,530)	(35,196)	(1,314)	(642)	(57,682)
Retirement of bonds, notes, and revenue bonds	(2,905)	(5,020)	(1,722)	(508)	(10,155)
Interest paid	(1,114)	(3,734)	(571)	(157)	(5,576)
Other	-	-	500	-	500
Net Cash Used for Capital and Related Financing Activities	(24,324)	(40,087)	(512)	39	(64,884)
CASH FLOWS FROM INVESTING ACTIVITIES:					
Investment income	119	(73)	-	-	46
Net Increase (Decrease) in Cash and Cash Equivalents	(12,320)	212	(972)	-	(13,080)
Cash and Cash Equivalents - Beginning	19,552	10,280	21,991	-	51,823
Cash and Cash Equivalents - Ending	$ 7,232	$ 10,492	$ 21,019	$ -	$ 38,743

CITY OF MILWAUKEE
STATEMENT OF CASH FLOWS
ENTERPRISE FUNDS
FOR THE YEAR ENDED DECEMBER 31, 2009
(Thousands of Dollars)

Exhibit B-3 (Continued)

	Water Works	Sewer Maintenance	Parking	Nonmajor Enterprise Funds	Total
Cash and Cash Equivalents at Year-End Consist of:					
Unrestricted Cash	$ 6,565	$ -	$ 21,019	$ -	$ 27,584
Restricted Cash	667	10,492	-	-	11,159
	$ 7,232	$ 10,492	$ 21,019	$ -	$ 38,743
RECONCILIATION OF OPERATING INCOME (LOSS) TO NET CASH PROVIDED BY OPERATING ACTIVITIES:					
Operating income	$ 6,162	$ 27,002	$ 17,642	$ 1,140	$ 51,946
Adjustments to reconcile operating income (loss) to net cash provided by (used for) operating activities:					
Depreciation	13,328	4,759	2,533	936	21,556
Changes in assets and liabilities:					
Receivables	(703)	(2,611)	(714)	(615)	(4,643)
Due from other funds	1,370	(182)	-	(540)	648
Due from other governmental agencies	-	-	-	73	73
Inventories	(285)	-	-	-	(285)
Prepaid items	408	-	-	-	408
Other assets	31	-	-	-	31
Accounts payable	519	672	(188)	371	1,374
Accrued liabilities	(387)	96	(3)	2	(292)
Net other postemployment benefits obligation	819	324	236	56	1,435
Due to other funds	-	15,078	-	(31)	15,047
Deferred revenue	-	-	(26)	-	(26)
Net Cash Provided by Operating Activities	$ 21,262	$ 45,138	$ 19,480	$ 1,392	$ 87,272

Non-cash Activities:

During the year, water mains and related property, installed by others were deeded to the Water Works in the amount of $3.4 million.

During the year, the Sewer Maintenance Fund removed infrastructure assets costing $64,608 with a net value of $0, and, received donated assets in the amount of $342,482.

The notes to the financial statements are an integral part of this statement.

CITY OF MILWAUKEE
STATEMENT OF FIDUCIARY NET ASSETS
FIDUCIARY FUNDS
DECEMBER 31, 2009
(Thousands of Dollars)

Exhibit C-1

	Pension and Other Employee Benefit Trusts	Private-Purpose Trusts	Agency Funds
ASSETS			
Cash and cash equivalents	$ 402	$ 2,158	$ 336,934
Investments	-	2,887	-
Total Assets	402	5,045	$ 336,934
LIABILITIES			
Liabilities:			
Accounts payable	-	10	1,511
Due to other governmental agencies	-	-	335,423
Total Liabilities	-	10	$ 336,934
Net Assets			
Employees' pension benefits and other purposes	$ 402	$ 5,035	

The notes to the financial statements are an integral part of this statement.

CITY OF MILWAUKEE

STATEMENT OF CHANGES IN FIDUCIARY NET ASSETS

FIDUCIARY FUNDS

FOR THE YEAR ENDED DECEMBER 31, 2009

(Thousands of Dollars)

Exhibit C-2

	Pension and Other Employee Benefit Trusts	Private-Purpose Trusts
Additions		
Contributions:		
Plan members	$ 1,331	$ -
Private donations	-	2,564
Total Contributions	1,331	2,564
Investment earnings:		
Net appreciation in fair value of investments, dividends and interest	-	6
Total Additions	1,331	2,570
Deductions		
Benefits	1,280	-
Fees remitted from Trust	-	2,084
Other	-	1,401
Total Deductions	1,280	3,485
Change in Net Assets	51	(915)
Net Assets - Beginning	351	5,950
Net Assets - Ending	$ 402	$ 5,035

The notes to the financial statements are an integral part of this statement.

Key for Worksheet Elimination and Adjusting Entries

Code	Chapter (Worksheet or Page) First Used	Usage
EL	2 (2-1)	Eliminate investment against subsidiary equity
D	2 (2-2)	Distribute excess, Key items D1 – Dn; Dt1 – Dtn is related deferred tax liability
NCI	2 (2-5)	Adjust noncontrolling interest to fair value
A	3 (3-1)	Amortize excess, Key A1 – An to match D series (except for inventory and goodwill); At1 – Atn is realization of the deferred tax liability applicable to A series
CY1 (or CY)	3 (3-1)	Eliminate current year equity income (CY used when there are no intercompany dividends)
CY2	3 (3-1)	Eliminate current year intercompany dividends
CV	3 (3-4)	Convert to simple equity
Dnt	3 (3-9)	Deferred tax liability attaching to distribution of excess numbered to match distribution number
Ant	3 (3-9)	Tax adjustment related to amortization of above deferred tax liability number to match Dnt item
IS	4 (4-1)	Eliminate intercompany merchandise sales
IA	4 (4-1)	Eliminate intercompany trade accounts
BI	4 (4-3)	Eliminate beginning inventory profit
EI	4 (4-2)	Eliminate ending inventory profit
LA	4 (p. 215)	Eliminate intercompany profit on land
F1	4 (4-5)	Eliminate fixed asset profit at start of year (or time of sale)
F2	4 (4-5)	Adjust depreciation for current year
F3	4 (4-7)	Adjust for later sale of intercompany asset to outside interest
LT	4 (p. 221)	Adjust long-term construction contracts LT1 – LTn as needed
LN1	4 (4-8)	Eliminate intercompany loan and accrued interest
LN2	4 (4-8)	Eliminate intercompany interest expense/revenue on intercompany loans
B (or B1)	5 (5-1)	Eliminate intercompany bonds and interest expense/revenue; B1 is used if there is accrued interest
B2	5 (5-1)	Eliminated any accrued interest receivable/payable related to intercompany bonds
OL1	5 (p. 275)	Eliminate rent on operating lease
OL2	5 (p. 275)	Reclassify asset under operating lease
CL1	5 (5-5)	Eliminate intercompany interest expense/revenue (first year of lease); in later years, CL1a adjusts interest for current year and CL1b adjusts interest for prior years
CL2	5 (5-5)	Eliminate intercompany debt balances
CL3	5 (5-5)	Reclassify asset depreciation under capital lease
T	6 (6-1)	Adjust for provision for income tax for consolidated taxation
T1	6 (6-2)	Allocate tax, beginning retained earnings, separate tax
T2	6 (6-2)	Allocate tax, current year, separate tax
PS	7 (7-3)	Allocate retained earnings to preferred stock
CYP	7 (7-4)	Eliminate income on intercompany preferred stock ownership
ELP	7 (7-4)	Eliminate investment in preferred stock against subsidiary preferred stockholder equity
TS	8 (8-2)	Reclassify subsidiary owned parent shares as treasury stock at cost
TR	8 (8-3)	Transfer investment in parent owned by subsidiary to the investment in subsidiary account
adj	8 (8-3)	Amortization adjustment caused by change in ownership percentage
CT	11 (11-1)	Distribute the parent's share of the subsidiary's cumulative translation adjustment

Index

A

D